OLD TESTAMENT PSEUDEPIGRAPHA

Old Testament Pseudepigrapha
More Noncanonical Scriptures

VOLUME 2

Edited by
James R. Davila
Richard Bauckham

WILLIAM B. EERDMANS PUBLISHING COMPANY
GRAND RAPIDS, MICHIGAN

Wm. B. Eerdmans Publishing Co.
2006 44th Street SE, Grand Rapids, MI 49508
www.eerdmans.com

© 2025 James R. Davila and Richard Bauckham
All rights reserved
Published 2025
Printed in the United States of America

31 30 29 28 27 26 25   1 2 3 4 5 6 7

ISBN 978-0-8028-8441-1

Library of Congress Cataloging-in-Publication Data

A catalog record for this book is available from the Library of Congress.

Contents

List of Abbreviations ... ix

Introduction ... 1
James R. Davila

I. TEXTS ORDERED ACCORDING TO BIBLICAL CHRONOLOGY

Alleged Jewish Pseudepigrapha Cited in the Cologne Mani Codex ... 9
John C. Reeves

No Longer "Slavonic" Only: 2 Enoch Attested in Coptic from Nubia ... 18
Joost L. Hagen

The Book of Giants: General Introduction ... 39
James R. Davila

The Aramaic Book of Giants ... 59
Loren T. Stuckenbruck

The Book of Giants: Iranian Manichean Version ... 90
Prods Oktor Skjærvø

The Manichean Book of Giants: Old Turkic Version ... 170
Peter Zieme

The Book of the Mysteries (Sefer Ha-Razim) ... 184
James R. Davila

The Prophecy of the Witch Sibyl (Prophetia Sibyllae magae) or
"The Earth Was My Origin" (Mundus origo) ... 244
Johannes Magliano-Tromp

The Narration of Joseph ... 257
Anders Klostergaard Petersen

An Apocryphon about Aseneth ... 273
Richard Bauckham

Contents

The Hebrew Testament of Naphtali *Vered Hillel*	280
Fragments of the Assumption of Moses and the Testament of Moses *Richard Bauckham*	299
The Sword of Moses (Ḥarba de-Moshe) *Yuval Harari*	322
The Phylactery of Moses *Roy D. Kotansky*	356
Jannes and Jambres *W. B. Henry and T. M. Erho*	372
A Coptic Exodus Apocryphon *Frederic Krueger*	386
Fragments of Elijah Apocrypha *Richard Bauckham*	401
The Somniale Danielis and the Lunationes Danielis *Lorenzo DiTommaso*	433
The Syriac Apocalypse of Daniel *Matthias Henze*	459
Armenian 4 Ezra *Introduction by Vered Hillel* *Translation by Michael E. Stone*	496
Two Pseudo-Philonic Works *Sze-kar Wan*	536

II. THEMATIC TEXTS

Justinus's *Book of Baruch* *Todd E. Klutz*	583
The Fifteen Signs before Judgment *Brandon W. Hawk*	609
Old Testament Pseudepigrapha Known Only by Title *Liv Ingeborg Lied and Matthew P. Monger*	635

Appendix: Summary of the Complete Ethiopic Version of Jannes and Jambres	651
T. M. Erho	
Index of Modern Authors	655
Index of Scripture and Other Ancient Texts	663

Abbreviations

Unless listed below, all abbreviations used in this volume are found in *The SBL Handbook of Style*, 2nd ed. (Atlanta: SBL Press, 2014).

APAW	*Abhandlungen der Preussischen Akademie der Wissenschaften, Philosophisch-Historische Klasse*
AR	The unknown author of the Refutation of All Heresies
BR	Midrash Bereshit Rabbati
CJ	Chronicles of Jerahmeel
CMC	Cologne Mani Codex
Evv	English versions
GMPT	Betz, Hans Dieter, ed. *The Greek Magical Papyri in Translation: Including the Demotic Spells*. Chicago: University of Chicago Press, 1986. 2nd ed. 1992.
Heb. T. Naph.	Hebrew Testament of Naphtali
JBB	Justinus's *Book of Baruch*
MOTP 1	Bauckham, Richard, James R. Davila, and Alexander Panayotov, eds. *The Old Testament Pseudepigrapha: More Noncanonical Scriptures*. Grand Rapids: Eerdmans, 2013.
PGM	Preisendanz, Karl, ed. and trans. *Papyri Graecae Magicae: Die griechischen Zauberpapyri*. 2nd ed. 3 vols. Leipzig: Teubner, 1973–1974.
Sh-R	Sefer ha-Razim (The Book of the Mysteries)

Sigla

[text]	Square brackets indicate damaged, illegible, or missing text, whether restorable or unrecoverable.
(text)	Parentheses or round brackets indicate words added by the translator for clarity.
\<text\>	Pointed brackets indicate a correction or emendation made to a text by the *MOTP* translator.
{text}	Braces enclose dittographies or other erroneous readings in a manuscript or text.
{. . .}	Braces containing three ellipsis points indicate that a textual tradition (i.e., involving more than one manuscript) has lost one or more words in transmission and that the original reading cannot be reconstructed with any confidence.

Introduction

by James R. Davila

The More Old Testament Pseudepigrapha Project was initiated by Richard Bauckham and myself more than twenty years ago. The first-fruits of the project was *Old Testament Pseudepigrapha: More Noncanonical Scriptures*, volume 1 (*MOTP* 1), which was published by Eerdmans in 2013. We are pleased to present you with the second outcome of the project with this volume.

The expression "Old Testament pseudepigrapha" is a modern coinage, referring to a grab bag of ancient texts that purport to be written by figures known from the Hebrew Bible (and in a few cases from additional books in some major Christian Old Testament canons) or to recount events that supposedly occurred in the same times and places as the events related in the Hebrew Bible/Old Testament. The term *pseudepigraphon* is a Greek word meaning "false title." It has been traditionally applied to these books, since their author ascriptions and contents are fictional, generally from a much later time than they claim. This is not a particularly helpful characterization, since some books of the Hebrew Bible are similarly ascribed fictionally to supposed earlier authors (e.g., Daniel) or relate likely fictional stories from an earlier period (e.g., the book of Job). Nevertheless, the term has stuck, and so far no one has come up with a better one.

The introduction to volume 1 has more on the issue of terminology, as well as a brief history of the composition of the pseudepigrapha, a survey of modern scholarship on it, and a discussion of the methodological issues faced by the project. We refer the reader there for those matters. The current volume is arranged like the first, with the texts presented in the traditional biblical chronological order as determined by the reputed author or main characters in each text. We again also include a final section of thematic texts that survey a long period of biblical history or authorship, or are set primarily in an eschatological framework. Again, like the first volume, this one contains both complete and fragmentary texts in a wide variety of genres, including apocalypses, prose narratives, magical and divinatory tractates, prophecies, and synagogue sermons. A more detailed survey of its contents follows.

From Adam to the Flood

The volume opens with a chapter by John Reeves featuring a group of alleged quotations of ancient apocalypses attributed to the antediluvian patriarchs Adam, Seth(el), Enosh, Shem, and Enoch. The quotations are found in the Cologne Mani Codex, a Greek manuscript containing a biography of the third-century CE Babylonian prophet Mani. Mani was the founder of Manicheism, an eclectic dualistic religion influenced by, inter alia, Judaism, Christianity, and Zoroastrianism. These quotations are our first introduction in this volume to "quotation fragments," excerpts or summaries of ancient works that are

Introduction

either now lost or that only existed in the imagination of the quoting authority. These five apocalypses, whether they circulated as independent works or are the creation of Mani's biographer, appear to have originated within early Manichean tradition.

We include a translation of the recently discovered fragments of Coptic 2 Enoch. The book of 2 Enoch is a long apocalypse attributed to the patriarch Enoch, who "walked with God and God took him," according to Gen 5:24. Early on, interpreters understood Enoch to have been made immortal and translated to heaven. The book of 2 Enoch is one of the ancient works that describes his adventures in the heavenly realm after his ascent. Its date and provenance are much debated. It survives complete only in an Old Church Slavonic version, apparently translated from Greek. But in 2006 a postgraduate student named Joost Hagen discovered fragments of a Coptic version (a language descended from ancient Egyptian and written in a variant of the Greek alphabet) among manuscripts excavated in the 1960s and 1970s at the site of Qasr Ibrim in Egypt. Presumably they too are translated from Greek. The fragments themselves have not yet been located, but photographs of them survive. The Coptic text is not yet fully published, but we reprint Hagen's article here, which translates the fragments into English. Second Enoch survived in two recensions of considerably different length. The new Coptic material comes from the "short recension" and provides new evidence for it being more original than the "long recension."

Alongside the better-known books of 1–3 Enoch, the Book of Giants circulated in the same ancient circles and dealt with many of the same stories, characters, and themes. Genesis 6:1–4 tells the story of the mating of the "sons of God" with mortal women before the Flood and the mighty offspring that followed. In the Enochic tradition, as arguably in the Bible, these offspring were giants. Their tragic story, which ended in destruction with the Flood, is told in the Book of Giants. Apart from occasional references by much later writers, the book was lost entirely for many centuries.

The original Aramaic text of this work was composed in Palestinian Jewish circles in the Second Temple period. In time it was discarded by Jews, but the prophet Mani, mentioned above, adopted and adapted a version of it as one of his scriptures. It circulated among the Manicheans for some centuries and it was translated by them into many languages. In the early twentieth century German and Japanese expeditions excavating the site of Turfan in Central Asia recovered highly fragmentary manuscripts of the Book of Giants translated into three Middle Iranian languages and Old Turkic (Uyghur). Some decades later, fragmentary manuscripts of the original Aramaic text were recovered among the Dead Sea Scrolls.

All the manuscripts of the Book of Giants in any language are very poorly preserved. But by pooling the information in them we can reconstruct a substantial part of the story. In this volume James R. Davila provides a general introduction to the book. Loren T. Stuckenbruck translates the Aramaic manuscripts, Prods Oktor Skjærvø translates the Iranian Manichean material, and Peter Zieme translates the Old Turkic fragments. Our volume presents English translations of all surviving fragments of the Book of Giants for the first time ever.

The Book of the Mysteries (Sefer ha-Razim), is a substantial magical handbook written in Hebrew. It was composed roughly in the talmudic era, while drawing on many ideas known from the somewhat earlier Greco-Egyptian magical traditions. Its prologue tells us that the angel Raziel first revealed it to Noah. Noah passed it on to his descendants until eventually it reached Solomon, who became the master magician in Jewish tradition. Sefer ha-Razim contains a collection of spells and rituals, some with very dark content, which claim to allow the magician to compel the angels of the various levels of heaven to harm enemies, to give success in love, to dominate others, to see the future, interpret dreams, heal afflictions, and even to speak with the dead.

The Sibyl was a legendary Roman prophetess who appears in many guises (or perhaps as many sibyls) and who was adopted into the biblical prophetic tradition by Second Temple–era Jews and early Christians. Previous volumes of pseudepigrapha have translated many ancient books of Sibylline oracles. This volume includes yet another, the Prophecy of *Sibylla Maga*, or the Witch Sibyl. This Latin late-antique Christian work is translated by Johannes Magliano-Tromp. It contains a prayer of the Sibyl and her warnings about the Day of Judgment.

In the Roman tradition the Sibyl was a figure of remote antiquity. A few references in the Jewish and Christian Sibylline oracles place her in the time of Noah, either as his daughter or daughter-in-law.[1] Without assuming that all these Sibylline traditions accepted or even knew this dating, we place the Prophecy of the Witch Sibyl at this point in our volume for convenience.

The Time of the Patriarchs

The Coptic Narration of Joseph is a late-antique retelling of the Joseph story that survives in a single, somewhat damaged manuscript. The surviving text deals with the selling of Joseph to the Ishmaelites by his brothers (cf. Gen 37:15–35). It diverges in some respects from the biblical story, notably by introducing the devil as a character, disguised as an old man, and by having Joseph apologize to his brothers for his grandiose dreams. This work is translated by Anders Klostergaard Petersen.

A Greek quotation, from a lost work of the heterodox third-century theologian Origen, cites a lost apocryphon that retold the story of Aseneth the wife of Joseph. This Apocryphon of Aseneth reportedly identified her father Potiphara with Potiphar, Joseph's original Egyptian patron. Potiphar's wife tried to seduce Joseph, which led to him being thrown into prison. In this account, Aseneth convinced her father of Joseph's innocence and the father in turn married her to Joseph. This intriguing citation of a lost book within a quotation of a lost book leaves it clear that Origen believed the story to come from a lost Jewish apocryphon, although we do not know whether he read it himself. Long and abridged versions of the quotation survive. Richard Bauckham translates both.

The Hebrew Testament of Naphtali is a medieval text that has considerable overlap with the Greco-Roman-era Greek Testament of Naphtali and some connection with a Qumran fragment and another medieval text called *Bereshit Rabbati*. A lost Second Temple–era Hebrew work ("Original Naphtali") seems to lie behind them. The Hebrew Testament of Naphtali tells the story of the patriarch Naphtali's two prophetic dreams and his warning to his sons of the disasters that will come from their following the sons of Joseph rather than the sons of Judah and Levi. Vered Hillel translates the Hebrew Testament of Naphtali and reconstructs what we can know about the content of Original Naphtali.

The Time of Moses

There is good evidence that two apocrypal works attributed to Moses circulated in antiquity, only fragments of which survive today. Both recounted a dispute between Satan and

---

1. See Sib. Or. Prologue 22, 1:289; 3:827; and J. J. Collins, "Sibylline Oracles," *OTP* 1:317 and n. 9.

Introduction

the archangel Michael over the dead body of Moses. Richard Bauckham collects what we can recover of the fragments of the Assumption of Moses and the Testament of Moses. Bauckham argues that the earlier work was the Testament of Moses, in which Satan asserted that Moses murdered an Egyptian (Exod 2:11–12) and therefore did not deserve an honorable burial. Michael rebuked him and buried Moses's body nonetheless. Arguably, Jude 9 refers to this work and a large section of it (lacking the dispute scene) survives in a Latin translation. The Assumption of Moses was a somewhat later anti-Gnostic work, perhaps based on the Testament. In it, Satan, as the "master of matter," claimed Moses's body, but Michael refuted his claim on the basis that God was Creator of the world.

We also include two magical works attributed to Moses. The first, the Sword of Moses (Ḥarba de-Moshe) presents the verbal "sword" that Moses supposedly brought down from heaven (a panoply of divine and angelic names) and instructs the magician on how to deploy it to control a heavenly hierarchy of angels in order to use the large collection of magical rituals in the work. These rites involve many matters, including healing, harm to others, self-protection, augmenting the user's powers, finding love, controlling spirits, and financial prosperity. Yuval Harari translates the Sword of Moses from Hebrew and Aramaic. His translation was originally commissioned for *MOTP*, but it was first published in the journal *Magic, Ritual, and Witchcraft*. We reprint it with some updates here.

The Phylactery of Moses is an imperfectly preserved *historiola*, a story with magical power, which claims to present the contents of the magical amulet that Moses used to protect himself during his ascent on Mt. Sinai. It promises the user protection from evil and sorcery, and claims to have powers of healing. The Phylactery of Moses survived only in a lacunose but repetitive inscription on a metal amulet discovered in Sicily in the nineteenth century and now lost. The object was inscribed sometime between the late second and early fourth century CE. Roy Kotansky translates its Greek text.

Jannes and Jambres is a narrative work about the Egyptian magicians said to have opposed Moses in the story of the exodus. These magicians are unnamed in the book of Exodus, but Jannes is mentioned in the Dead Sea Scrolls and by the first-century Roman natural philosopher Pliny the Elder, and both are named in the New Testament. The surviving text tells of the preparations of Jannes for his own foretold death, his failed opposition to Moses and Aaron before Pharaoh, his death, and his posthumous necromantic conversation with his brother Jambres. Jannes and Jambres was composed in Greek in the Greco-Roman era and survives in Greek manuscripts, a Latin excerpt, and a recently discovered fragment of an Ethiopic translation. Benjamin Henry translates the Greek and Latin material and Ted Erho translates the Ethiopic.

The Coptic Exodus Apocryphon recounts a military confrontation between the Pharaoh of the exodus and the martially impressive departing Israelites, who are led by Moses. This episode has no counterpart in the book of Jannes and Jambres, but these two magician brothers appear again here, deploying magical forces against the Israelites. The Coptic Exodus Apocryphon survives in a single, badly damaged papyrus manuscript copied in roughly the fourth century CE. The presumed Greek original from which the Coptic was translated must have been composed sometime before this. Frederic Krueger translates the surviving Coptic text.

The Time of the Monarchy

In "Fragments of Elijah Apocrypha," Bauckham collects seven quotation fragments and summaries from one or more ancient Greek works attributed to the prophet Elijah. These are to be distinguished from the Coptic Apocalypse of Elijah and the Hebrew Apocalypse of Elijah, both of which we have essentially complete. Bauckham argues that probably at least two, perhaps more, of these fragments preserve material from a Greek Apocalypse of Elijah in which Elijah was taken on a tour of the realm of the dead and saw a place of rest, presumably for the righteous, and a place where the wicked are tormented. The words of two of the other fragments are also quoted in the New Testament, although not specifically from any work attributed to Elijah.

The Babylonian Exile and Afterward

We include three works attributed to the mantic sage and dream interpreter Daniel of the biblical book of Daniel. Lorenzo DiTommaso translates two divinatory texts that circulated in Daniel's name in late antiquity and the Middle Ages. The Somniale Danielis is a work of dream interpretation (oneiromancy). It lists hundreds of dreams grouped by subject matter and listed in multiple alphabetic sequences, each dream followed by a brief interpretation. The Lunationes Danielis is a "lunary," a genre that enumerates the thirty days of the lunar month, for each day listing events and actions that are either fortunate and successful or unlucky and unsuccessful. Both books were composed in Greek, but circulated mostly in Latin translations whose individual manuscripts exhibit a great deal of textual variation. DiTommaso's translation is based on Latin versions of both works found in an important medieval manuscript.

The Syriac Apocalypse of Daniel is a first-person narrative that, like its biblical counterpart, opens with a narrative section recounting Daniel's experiences in the Babylonian royal court, including episodes not found in the biblical book. The bulk of the apocalypse then continues, again like the biblical book, with eschatological visionary material. The vision culminates in the coming of the Messiah (Jesus), the building of the New Jerusalem, and the resurrection of the dead. This translation, by Matthias Henze, is of the only complete manuscript, which dates to the fifteenth century. The apocalypse itself was probably composed in Syriac in the seventh century.

We reprint here a translation of Armenian 4 Ezra by Michael Stone. The apocalypse of 4 Ezra, translated in earlier pseudepigrapha collections, is a first-century CE Jewish work written in the name of the postexilic biblical sage Ezra. It questions and ultimately defends the justice of God in condemning the vast majority of the human race to eternal damnation. The Greek (original?) form circulated extensively among Christians in late antiquity and they translated it into many other languages. The Armenian translation, made in the fifth century, is of special interest because it translates a Greek text that had been extensively revised, reordered, and rewritten, often with a theological agenda. Vered Hillel provides a new introduction to Stone's translation.

We include two ancient homilies that seem to have been intended for presentation as sermons in synagogue worship. They were composed in Greek, but survive only in Armenian translation. They are found in an Armenian collection of the works of the first-century CE Jewish philosopher Philo of Alexandria. They are not by him, but they too were likely composed in first-century Alexandria. De Sampsone deals with three episodes in Samson's life, exploring the question of why God made the immoral and impulsive figure of Samson a judge. De Jona retells the story of Jonah, with special attention to the sin of the Ninevites in failing to worship God and the theme of God's universal love for the human race. These works are not, strictly speaking, Old Testament pseudepigrapha. But they retell biblical stories in an ancient Jewish setting and they are arguably

Introduction

the only surviving sermons from the ancient Greek-speaking synagogue. We judged them worthy of wider circulation in this volume. They are translated by Sze-kar Wan.

Thematic Texts

The Refutation of All Heresies, a third-century CE work of uncertain authorship, contains a summary of a lost book by a second-century writer known as Justinus (or Justin) the Gnostic. Justinus's *Book of Baruch* presented a gnostic retelling of biblical history from the creation to Jesus and included an oath of initiation into the mysteries of Justinus's movement. The book tells us that the mating and estrangement of primordial, "unreproduced" beings led to angelically initiated conflict between the sexes on earth. The angel Baruch was sent successively to Adam, Moses, unnamed prophets, and the pagan "prophet" Herakles, with good teachings, but each time he was thwarted by the angel Naas, whose evil teachings proved more persuasive. Only Jesus of Nazareth followed Baruch's teaching and resisted those of Naas. As a result Jesus was crucified, but nonetheless he ascended on high. Todd E. Klutz translates the Greek text of the Refutation's summary of Justin's *Book of Baruch*.

The Fifteen Signs before Judgment Day is an eschatological work that survives in a great many manuscripts and a number of different-language versions. The earliest of these is the Latin version, which may or may not be the original language. The basic text advances fifteen traditional signs that will lead up to the Final Judgment: rising and burning seas, falling stars, resurrection of the dead, and so on. The wording and order of the signs vary substantially among the versions and even from manuscript to manuscript. The earliest Latin manuscripts date to the eleventh century, but copy a text that originated centuries earlier. How much earlier is unclear. Brandon Hawk translates the three earliest recensions of the Latin version. We also reprint translations by Michael Stone of several recensions of the Armenian version and of one Hebrew version.

Our volume closes, as it opened, with attention to lost pseudepigrapha known only by tenuous references in later literature. Liv Ingeborg Lied and Matthew P. Monger catalog references to pseudepigrapha known only by title in ancient lists of scriptures and references in patristic literature, other Old Testament pseudepigrapha, and elsewhere. They also address the difficult methodological question of how to assess these references. Are they titles of actual books that are now lost or did they exist only in the minds of authors of other works who imagined them as a literary convenience? Or is the problem still more complicated?

* * *

Much has happened in the years since the publication of *MOTP* 1. For various reasons we were not able to include a number of the texts we had hoped to publish in this volume. Perhaps that was serendipitous. We could scarcely have fitted more texts into it than we have. Be that as it may, the very substantial volume now in your hands should provide you with some fascinating reading material. We hope you enjoy it!

I. Texts Ordered according to Biblical Chronology

Alleged Jewish Pseudepigrapha Cited in the Cologne Mani Codex
A new translation and introduction

by John C. Reeves

Modern study of Manicheism, a dualist religion founded by the third-century Babylonian prophet Mani that achieved a remarkable notoriety in the Roman, Sasanian, and Islamicate cultural spheres, was transformed by the late twentieth-century discovery and publication of a tiny Greek codex bearing the running title "On the Genesis of His Body" and now known among scholars as the Cologne Mani Codex (henceforth CMC).[1] Of uncertain archaeological provenance, it is thought to originate from Lycopolis in Upper Egypt,[2] and it was paleographically dated by its initial editors to the fourth or fifth centuries CE. Inscribed with a majuscule Greek lettering whose wording displays signs of its possible derivation from a Semitic language predecessor,[3] it consists of 192 extremely lacunose pages that provide a biographical summary of the early life, visionary experiences, and initial travels of the religion's founder. The book is structured as a series of testimonia attached to a small group of named figures who were active in the propagation of Mani's teachings during the first few generations of the religion's spread. Arranged in a roughly chronological order, most of the traditions that they convey portray Mani speaking authoritatively in an autobiographical, first-person style.

Its chief import for modern scholars lies in the light it sheds upon the religious and cultural background of Mani. According to the CMC, Mani spent his formative years sequestered among the members of a socially isolated sectarian community in southern Mesopotamia termed "baptists" (CMC 11.1–4 and passim) whose founding leader was the late first-century Jewish Christian visionary known as Elchasai (CMC 94.10–12).[4] Its

---

1. For the publication details, see the bibliography below.
2. Ludwig Koenen, "Zur Herkunft des Kölner Mani-Codex," *ZPE* 11 (1973): 240–41; Albert Henrichs, "The Cologne Mani Codex Reconsidered," *HSCP* 83 (1979): 349; Iain Gardner and Samuel N. C. Lieu, *Manichaean Texts from the Roman Empire* (Cambridge: Cambridge University Press, 2004), 41; Michel Tardieu, *Manicheism*, trans. M. B. DeBevoise (Urbana: University of Illinois Press, 2008), 50.
3. Raimund Köbert, "Orientalistische Bemerkungen zum Kölner Mani-Codex," *ZPE* 8 (1971): 243–47; Albert Henrichs, "Mani and the Babylonian Baptists: A Historical Confrontation," *HSCP* 77 (1973): 35–39, doi:10.2307/311059; Henrichs, "Cologne Mani Codex Reconsidered," 352–53; Alexander Böhlig, "Der Synkretismus des Mani," in *Synkretismus im syrisch-persischen Kulturgebiet: Bericht über ein Symposion in Reinhausen bei Göttingen in der Zeit vom 4. bis 8. Oktober 1971*, ed. Albert Dietrich (Göttingen: Vandenhoeck & Ruprecht, 1975), 149–50; Böhlig, "Die Bedeutung des CMC für den Manichäismus," in *Codex Manichaicus Coloniensis: Atti del Secondo Simposio Internazionale (Cosenza 27–28 maggio 1988)*, ed. Luigi Cirillo, Studi e ricerche 5 (Cosenza: Marra Editore, 1990), 38–41; Riccardo Contini, "Hypothèses sur l'araméen manichéen," *Annali di Ca' Foscari* 34 (1995): 65–107, esp. pp. 83–85; Gardner and Lieu, *Manichaean Texts*, 42.
4. Wilhelm Brandt, *Elchasai, ein Religionsstifter und sein Werk: Beiträge zur jüdischen, christlichen und allgemeinen Religionsgeschichte* (Leipzig: Hinrichs, 1912); Joseph Thomas, *Le mouvement baptiste en Palestine et Syrie (150 av. J.-C.–300 ap. J.-C.)* (Gembloux: Duculot, 1935), 140–56, 242–52; A. F. J. Klijn

account of Mani's life within this sect converges remarkably with the much later testimonies about this heresiarch's background independently supplied by the eighth-century Christian bishop Theodore bar Konai and the tenth-century Muslim bibliophile Ibn al-Nadīm, the former of whom situates Mani as a young "slave" among a sectarian group called the "Pure Ones" who dressed in white garments,[5] and the latter of whom depicts Mani growing up among a sect known as the *Mughtasila* ("those who wash themselves," i.e., baptists).[6] Ibn al-Nadīm's separate discussion of the *Mughtasila*, there qualified as "the marshland Ṣābians," or "baptists," names al-Ḥasa(y)ḥ, that is, Elchasai, as the original "leader" of that religious sect.[7] All three biographical narratives report on Mani's separation from the baptist community before engaging in his own religious ministry, and two of them (CMC, Theodore bar Konai) represent his departure from his erstwhile coreligionists as one marked by acrimony and based upon a widening fissure between the beliefs and practices endorsed by the sect and those being espoused by their young acolyte, the latter of which are grounded in revelatory visions supposedly experienced by Mani while living among them.

Nascent Manicheism thus appears to spring out of a separatist movement focused upon ritual washings whose roots extend backward and westward to first-century Palestine, the Transjordan, and Arabia, and that exhibits important links with nativist, Jewish, and Christian currents of thought.[8] Significant connections between the Elchasaites and certain ideas or practices found in a wide variety of Jewish texts have been signaled by Ithamar Gruenwald, Burton Visotzky, and Joseph Baumgarten.[9] The CMC account of Mani's expulsion from the Elchasaite sect also exhibits some intriguing correspondences with the organizational nomenclature and prescribed judicial procedures attested among

---

and G. J. Reinink, *Patristic Evidence for Jewish-Christian Sects*, NovTSup 36 (Leiden: Brill, 1973), 54–67; Gerard P. Luttikhuizen, *The Revelation of Elchasai: Investigations into the Evidence for a Mesopotamian Jewish Apocalypse of the Second Century and Its Reception by Judeo-Christian Propagandists*, TSAJ 8 (Tübingen: Mohr, 1985); Luttikhuizen, "Elchasaites and Their Book," in *A Companion to Second-Century Christian "Heretics,"* ed. Antti Marjanen and Petri Luomanen, Supplements to Vigiliae Christianae 74 (Leiden: Brill, 2008), 335–64; F. Stanley Jones, *Pseudoclementina Elchasaiticaque inter Judaeochristiana: Collected Studies*, OLA 203 (Leuven: Peeters, 2012), esp. 359–449; Simon Claude Mimouni, *Early Judaeo-Christianity: Historical Essays*, trans. Robyn Fréchet, Interdisciplinary Studies in Ancient Culture and Religion 13 (Leuven: Peeters, 2012), 248–76; Nils Arne Pedersen and John Møller Larsen, *Manichaean Texts in Syriac: First Editions, New Editions, and Studies*, Corpus Fontium Manichaeorum, Series Syriaca 1 (Turnhout: Brepols, 2013), 187–93.

5. John C. Reeves, *Prolegomena to a History of Islamicate Manichaeism*, Comparative Islamic Studies (Sheffield: Equinox, 2011), 29–30.

6. Reeves, *Prolegomena*, 36–38.

7. Ibn al-Nadīm, *Kitāb al-Fihrist*, ed. Riḍa Tajaddud (Tehran: Maktabat al-Assadī, 1971), 403.28–404.3.

8. Thomas, *Le mouvement baptiste*; Kurt Rudolph, *Antike Baptisten: Zu den Überlieferungen über frühjüdische und frühchristliche Taufsekten* (Berlin: Akademie, 1981); repr., *Gnosis und spätantike Religionsgeschichte: Gesammelte Aufsätze*, Nag Hammadi and Manichaean Studies 42 (Leiden: Brill, 1996), 569–606. See also Rudolph, "The Baptist Sects," in *The Early Roman Period*, ed. William Horbury, W. D. Davies, and John Sturdy, CHJ 3 (Cambridge: Cambridge University Press, 1999), 471–500; Christelle Jullien and Florence Jullien, "Le mouvement baptiste en Orient, un phénomène marginal pour la christianisation?," in *Apôtres des confins: Processus missionnaires chrétiens dans l'empire iranien*, Res Orientales 15 (Bures-sur-Yvette: Groupe pour l'Étude de la Civilisation du Moyen-Orient, 2002), 137–51.

9. Ithamar Gruenwald, "Manichaeism and Judaism in Light of the Cologne Mani Codex," ZPE 50 (1983): 29–45; Burton Visotzky, "Rabbinic Randglossen to the Cologne Mani Codex," ZPE 52 (1983): 295–300; Joseph M. Baumgarten, "The Book of Elkesai and Merkabah Mysticism," JSJ 17 (1986): 212–23.

certain Qumran texts.[10] The fact that the later Manichean church lists a so-called Book of Giants among the roster of books comprising its canonical scriptures reputedly authored by Mani himself—a work that is actually based upon an older apocryphal text recovered from among the Dead Sea Scrolls—serves to confirm that Mani and his early followers must have had access to biblically affiliated literature emanating from Jewish, Christian, and other allied groups.[11] How did he or his closest disciples acquire this knowledge?

Unfortunately, the precise means facilitating his or their exposure to these noncanonical materials remains frustratingly opaque. The Syro-Mesopotamian culture sphere harbored a handful of religious communities who possessed ethnic, historical, commercial, scholastic, or ideological linkages with Palestine and its immediate environs. Groups self-identifying as Jews and Christians constituted significant population blocs in Syria and Mesopotamia by the middle of the third century CE. The earlier Assyrian and Babylonian incursions into West Asia during the mid-first millennium BCE forcibly relocated select biblically attached population groups to Mesopotamia and the Iranian highlands. It seems possible that some precanonical texts or traditions may have traveled alongside or were freshly regenerated among them in their new surroundings, particularly if they belonged to the priestly or scribal classes. The later Mandean foundation legend recounts the voluntary eastward migration of a sectarian group from Palestine to Mesopotamia in the late first century CE,[12] an account that finds thematic echoes in the report supplied by Theodore bar Konai about the proto-Mandean sect of the Kanteans and their alleged Palestinian roots.[13] Certainly the so-called real Ṣābians, who are situated by the eleventh-century Muslim polymath Bīrūnī in the swamps of southern Iraq and southwestern Iran, is a collective label encoding marginal Mesopotamian baptist movements like Mani's Elchasaites, Ibn al-Nadīm's *Mughtasila*, or even the Mandeans themselves. Bīrūnī portrays them as the lineal descendants of those Israelite captives whom Nebuchadnezzar once removed from Jerusalem and settled in Babylonia, and who then declined to return to their homeland after the advent of the Achaemenid rulers. Their religious doctrines, he says, are a mixture of Magian and Jewish teachings, and they allegedly view themselves as the progeny of the biblical forefather Enosh ben Seth ben Adam.[14] Bīrūnī's ethnographic analysis of this particular "Jewish" group effectively shrinks what may have been an ongoing series of eastward population shifts to one particularly memorable moment of

---

10. John C. Reeves, "The 'Elchasaite' Sanhedrin of the Cologne Mani Codex in Light of Second Temple Jewish Sectarian Sources," *JJS* 42 (1991): 68–91.

11. J. T. Milik, ed., *The Books of Enoch: Aramaic Fragments of Qumrân Cave 4* (Oxford: Clarendon, 1976), 298–339. See also the chapters on the Book of Giants in this volume. Manichean exploitation of both Jewish and Christian apocryphal traditions for the formulation of its own doctrines has been widely recognized by scholars since the first "modern" study of Manicheism, the two-volume *Histoire critique du Manichée et du Manichéisme* of Isaac de Beausobre (Amsterdam: Bernard, 1734–1739). Regarding the importance of this latter work, see esp. Guy G. Stroumsa, *A New Science: The Discovery of Religion in the Age of Reason* (Cambridge: Harvard University Press, 2010), 113–23.

12. E. S. Drower, *The Haran Gawaita and The Baptism of Hibil-Ziwa*, Studi e testi 176 (Vatican City: Biblioteca Apostolica Vaticana, 1953).

13. Henri Pognon, *Inscriptions mandaites des coupes de Khouabir* (Paris, 1898; repr., Amsterdam: Philo, 1979), 151.9–152.12; Theodore bar Konai, *Liber Scholiorum*, ed. Addai Scher, 2 vols., CSCO 65–66 (Paris: Poussielgue, 1910–1912), 2:342.6–343.11.

14. Bīrūnī, *Kitāb al-āthār al-bāqiya 'ani'l-qurūn al-khāliya: Chronologie orientalischer Völker von Albêrûnî*, ed. C. Eduard Sachau (Leipzig: Brockhaus, 1878; repr., Leipzig: Harrassowitz, 1923), 206.9–15; 318.4–14.

national trauma; nevertheless, it opens conceptually a possible conduit for the delivery, conservation, and retooling of Canaanite/Israelite cultural traditions in the East, a process exemplified in bar Konai's report about "the stupid Kanteans" and their earnest attempts to adapt their ritual commemoration of the death of a biblical "giant" (Goliath) from a Palestinian to a Babylonian setting. Moreover, to judge from the breadth of the manuscript evidence that has been recovered from Qumran, later biblically affiliated interstitial groups such as the Elchasaites or the Syrian communities responsible for the Pseudo-Clementine corpus of Christian writings could conceivably have been the custodial heirs to a dense penumbra of oral and literary traditions surrounding various scriptural texts, characters, events, and teachings, a heritage to which Mani may have been exposed during his years of tutelage within his baptist sect.

Among the new data contributed by the CMC for the elucidation of the religiohistorical background of Mani and his dualist religion are five alleged citations from pseudepigraphic "apocalypses" attributed to the biblical forefathers Adam, Seth(el),[15] Enosh, Shem, and Enoch. We do not know whether these are citations from actual lost books or passages composed as part of the CMC to look as though they are citations of lost books. These quotations occur within a longer integral section of the CMC (45.1–72.7) that was editorially structured by one "[Ba]rai[es the teacher],"[16] an early figure of some importance in the initial development and expansion of the Manichean religion after the death of its founder in a Sasanian jail. To judge from the redactional statements that open and close this particular section, its primary purpose was to convince readers (and hearers) of the veracity of Mani's claim to being the final link in a chain of prophetic emissaries who were recognized by certain biblically affiliated groups as authentic messengers bearing revelatory truths to humanity on earth. In addition to the five biblical characters mentioned above, Baraies also incorporated analogous "testimonies" culled from the writings of the Christian apostle Paul (CMC 60.13–62.9) and from texts authored by Mani himself (CMC 63.16–70.9). Crucial for the argument being constructed by Baraies are the common threads that unite the reported visionary adventures of these seven "apostles" from the heavenly Realm of Light. In each case, an autobiographically couched ascent experience to a higher plane of existence is described. The visionary interacts with one or more supernal entities, secrets about the cosmos and human existence are revealed, and the seer is encouraged to impart these mysteries to his contemporaries. But perhaps most importantly, each apostle records a written account of their otherworldly experiences for the benefit of future generations: "for when each one of them had ascended, [all those things which he sa]w and heard he recorded and revealed, and he himself bore witness to his revelation" (CMC 71.20–72.4). This observable emphasis upon the textualization of religious authority, or the phenomenon of scripturalism, becomes one of the hallmarks of prophetic authenticity among a number of religious communities

---

15. The use of the name "Sethel" in place of the name "Seth" for the third biblical son of Adam is a peculiar feature of both Manichean and Mandean literature. For a discussion of its possible significance, see John C. Reeves, *Heralds of That Good Realm: Syro-Mesopotamian Gnosis and Jewish Traditions*, Nag Hammadi and Manichaean Studies 41 (Leiden: Brill, 1996), 112–17.

16. Redactional subheadings inserted at CMC 14.3; 72.8; 79.13 have undamaged occurrences of this name and title. Its likely reconstruction at 45.1 is convincingly established by Henrichs, "Cologne Mani Codex Reconsidered," 354–56. The name of Baraies figures among those of Mani's disciples who are listed in the so-called long Greek abjuration formula; see Alfred Adam, *Texte zum Manichäismus*, 2nd ed., KlT 175 (Berlin: de Gruyter, 1969), 101.

in the Near East during late antiquity and the early medieval era, and it has particular importance within Manicheism.[17]

It is interesting to observe that the five quotations that are cited from "apocalypses" of Adam, Seth(el), Enosh, Shem, and Enoch are not copied from any known Jewish or Christian pseudepigraphic works. While they exhibit remarkable affinities with a number of the traditions that crystallized around the name of each forefather in the Roman and Sasanian East during late antiquity, they are almost certainly not authentic relics of pre-Christian scribal activity, but instead clever adaptations fashioned by authors who were steeped in the growing esoteric lore surrounding these figures among biblically affiliated circles and sects. It of course remains possible that Mani or his early disciples encountered actual textual compilations of this kind during their sojourn among or interactions with groups like the Elchasaites or kindred organizations. A close scrutiny however of the themes and vocabulary found in these five apocalypses complicates such a supposition, for it shows that they are each carefully constructed to propound a revelatory message that is consonant with the teachings and ideological structure of Mani's own prophetic revelation. This state of affairs suggests that these five apocalypses—although rooted in authentic pseudepigraphic formulations associated with scriptural characters like Adam, Seth, and Enoch—actually originate within nascent Manicheism and were designed to advance the latter religion's vigorous missionary enterprise.[18]

The following translations are based on the critical edition of the CMC published in 1988 by Koenen and Römer,[19] and represent a revision of the renderings previously published by the present author.[20] For more extensive annotations and a line-by-line commentary keyed to each "apocalypse," readers should consult that latter volume.

Bibliography

Attridge, Harold W. "Valentinian and Sethian Apocalyptic Traditions." *JECS* 8 (2000): 173–211, esp. pp. 199–202.

Cameron, Ron, and Arthur J. Dewey, eds. *The Cologne Mani Codex (P. Colon. inv. nr. 4780): "Concerning the Origin of His Body."* SBLTT 15. ECL 3. Missoula, MT: Scholars Press, 1979.

Cirillo, Luigi. "From the Elchasaite Christology to the Manichaean Apostle of Light: Some Remarks about the Manichaean Doctrine of the Revelation." Pages 47–54 in *Il Manicheismo: Nuove prospettive della richerca, Dipartimento di Studi Asiatici, Università degli*

---

17. John C. Reeves, "Manichaeans as *Ahl al-Kitāb*: A Study in Manichaean Scripturalism," in *Light against Darkness: Dualism in Ancient Mediterranean Religion and the Contemporary World*, ed. Armin Lange, JAJSup 2 (Göttingen: Vandenhoeck & Ruprecht, 2011), 249–65.

18. Reeves, *Heralds*, 15–17, 209–11; David Frankfurter, "Apocalypses Real and Alleged in the Mani Codex," *Numen* 44 (1997): 60–73, doi:10.1163/1568527972629876; Dylan M. Burns, *Apocalypse of the Alien God: Platonism and the Exile of Sethian Gnosticism*, Divinations (Philadelphia: University of Pennsylvania Press, 2014), 201 n.85.

19. Ludwig Koenen and Cornelia Römer, eds., *Der Kölner Mani-Kodex: Über das Werden seines Leibes; Kritische Edition*, Papyrologica Coloniensia 14, Abhandlungen der Rheinisch-Westfälischen Akademie der Wissenschaften (Opladen: Westdeutscher Verlag, 1988), 30–40.

20. John C. Reeves, *Heralds of That Good Realm: Syro-Mesopotamian Gnosis and Jewish Traditions*, Nag Hammadi and Manichaean Studies 41 (Leiden: Brill, 1996), 67, 111–12, 141–42, 163–64, 183–84. We are grateful to Brill Publishers for permission to republish this material with revisions. Permission conveyed through Copyright Clearance Center, Inc.

studi di Napoli "L'Orientale," Napoli, 2-8 Settembre 2001. Edited by Aloïs van Tongerloo and Luigi Cirillo. Manichaean Studies 5. Turnhout: Brepols, 2005.

Fonkic, B. L., and F. B. Poljakov. "Paläographische Grundlagen der Datierung des Kölner Mani-Kodex." *ByzZ* 83 (1990): 22–30. doi:10.1515/byzs.1990.83.1.22.

Frankfurter, David. "Apocalypses Real and Alleged in the Mani Codex." *Numen* 44 (1997): 60–73. doi:10.1163/1568527972629876.

Gardner, Iain, and Samuel N. C. Lieu, eds. *Manichaean Texts from the Roman Empire.* Cambridge: Cambridge University Press, 2004.

Henrichs, Albert, and Ludwig Koenen. "Ein griechischer Mani-Codex (P. Colon. inv. nr. 4780)." *ZPE* 5 (1970): 97–216; 19 (1975): 1–85; 32 (1978): 87–199; 44 (1981): 201–318; 48 (1982): 1–59.

Himmelfarb, Martha. "Revelation and Rapture: The Transformation of the Visionary in the Ascent Apocalypses." Pages 79–90 in *Mysteries and Revelations: Apocalyptic Studies Since the Uppsala Colloquium.* Edited by John J. Collins and James H. Charlesworth. JSPSup 9. Sheffield: Sheffield Academic, 1991.

Koenen, Ludwig, and Cornelia Römer, eds. *Der Kölner Mani-Kodex: Abbildungen und diplomatischer Text.* Papyrologische Texte und Abhandlungen 35. Bonn: Habelt, 1985. Photographs available online at http://www.uni-koeln.de/phil-fak/ifa/NRWakademie/papyrologie/Manikodex/bildermani.html.

———, eds. *Der Kölner Mani-Kodex: Über das Werden seines Leibes; Kritische Edition.* Papyrologica Coloniensia 14. Abhandlungen der Rheinisch-Westfälischen Akademie der Wissenschaften. Opladen: Westdeutscher Verlag, 1988.

Philonenko, Marc. "Une citation manichéenne du Livre d'Hénoch." *RHPR* 52 (1972): 337–40.

Reeves, John C. *Heralds of That Good Realm: Syro-Mesopotamian Gnosis and Jewish Traditions.* Nag Hammadi and Manichaean Studies 41. Leiden: Brill, 1996.

———. "Jewish Pseudepigrapha in Manichaean Literature: The Influence of the Enochic Library." Pages 173–203 in *Tracing the Threads: Studies in the Vitality of Jewish Pseudepigrapha.* EJL 6. Edited by John C. Reeves. Atlanta: Scholars Press, 1994.

Tigchelaar, Eibert. "Baraies on Mani's Rapture, Paul, and the Antediluvian Apostles." Pages 429–41 in *The Wisdom of Egypt: Jewish, Early Christian, and Gnostic Essays in Honour of Gerard P. Luttikhuizen.* Edited by Anthony Hilhorst and George H. van Kooten. AGJU 59. Leiden: Brill, 2005.

Alleged Jewish Pseudepigrapha Cited in the Cologne Mani Codex

From an alleged Apocalypse of Adam[a]
[Thu]s has Adam first[b] [clearl]y said [in] his [apocalypse: "I saw an a]ngel [... rev]ealed ... [before] your ra[diant] face that I do not recognize." Then he said to him: "I am Balsamos, the greatest angel of light.[c] Therefore receive (and) write these things just as I reveal them to you on exceedingly clean papyrus that is unspoiled and that has not harbored worms."

Moreover there were many other things that he revealed to him in the vision. Very great was the glory that surrounded him. He beheld [. . .] angels an[d high offic]ials [and] mig[hty powers] . . . (five lines lost) . . . Adam and was made superior to all the powers and angels of creation. Many other similar things to these are in his writings.[d]

From an alleged Apocalypse of Sethel[e]
Also Sethel[f] his son has similarly written in his apocalypse, saying that "I opened my eyes and beheld before me an [ang]el whose [radiance] I am unable to (adequately) represent . . . . [lig]htning . . . . to me . . . (three lines lost) . . . [Wh]en I heard these things, my heart rejoiced and my mind changed and I became like one of the greatest angels. That angel placed his hand upon my right (hand) and took me out of the world wherein I was born and brought me to another place (that was) exceedingly great. Behind me I heard a loud uproar from those angels whom [I l]eft behind [in] the world that the[y pos]sessed . . . (at least two lines missing) . . . ."

---

a. CMC 48.16–50.7. In what follows, [ ] signifies textual restorations of Koenen and Römer, *Der Kölner Mani-Kodex: Kritische Edition*; ( ) signifies translator's additions for clarity. Short forms used in this chapter are Koenen and Römer for Koenen and Römer, *Der Kölner Mani-Kodex: Kritische Edition*.

b. Gardner and Samuel N. C. Lieu, *Manichaean Texts*, 54; Luigi Cirillo, "From the Elchasaite Christology to the Manichaean Apostle of Light: Some Remarks about the Manichaean Doctrine of the Revelation," in *Il Manicheismo: Nuove prospettive della richerca, Dipartimento di Studi Asiatici, Università degli studi di Napoli "L'Orientale," Napoli, 2–8 Settembre 2001*, ed. Aloïs van Tongerloo and Luigi Cirillo, Manichaean Studies 5 (Turnhout: Brepols, 2005), 53. Correct accordingly Reeves, *Heralds*, 67–69.

c. Unattested elsewhere as an angelic name. For a survey of the correlations and explanations that have been offered, see Reeves, *Heralds*, 70–74.

d. For Adam as author, see Reeves, *Heralds*, 33–35.

e. CMC 50.8–52.7.

f. With regard to this name, see the introduction.

M[any things simil]ar to these are described in his writings,[a] and as he was transported by that angel from world to world, he revealed to him the awesome secrets of (divine) majesty.

From an alleged Apocalypse of Enosh[b]

Moreover it says thusly in the Apocalypse of Enosh: "In the tenth month of the third year I went out to walk in the region of the wilderness, considering mentally [he]aven and earth and [al]l works [and deed]s (wondering) b[y whose will] they exist. [Then there appeared to me an angel. He taught me about the world of de]ath.[c] He took me up with great silence. My heart became heavy, all my limbs trembled, and the vertebrae of my back shook violently, and my feet could not stand upon their joints. I came to numerous plains[d] and I saw lofty mountains there. The Spirit[e] seized me and brought me with silent power to a mountain.[f] There num[erous awes]ome [visions were rev]ealed to me."

Moreover [he says that "the an]gel . . . [and brought me to the] nort[hern region] where I beheld immense mountains and angels and many places. He spoke to me and said: 'The Preeminent Almighty One has sent me to you so that I might reveal to you the secret things that you contemplated, since indeed you were chosen for the truth. Write down all these hidden things upon bronze tablets and deposit (them) in the region of the wilderness. Everything that you write recor[d most p]lainly (carefully?). For [my] revela[tion, which shall not] pass away, is ready [to be] reve[aled to] al[l the breth]ren . . .'"

[Many other] things similar to these are in his writings[g] (that) set forth his ascension and revelation, for everything that he heard and saw he recorded (and) left behind for the subsequent generations, all those belonging to the Spirit of Truth.[h]

From an alleged Apocalypse of Shem[i]

Similarly also Shem spoke this way in his apocalypse: "I was thinking about the way that all things came to be. While I pondered (these things), the Living S[pirit] suddenly to[ok] me and [lift]ed me with great f[orce, and se]t (me) on [the summit] of a lof[ty] mountain, [and] spoke [to me thusly, say]ing: ['Do not be afraid; rather,] give praise to the Great King of Honor.'"

Moreover he says that "silently doors were opened and clouds were parted by the wind. I beheld a glorious throne-room[j] descending from the highest

a. For Seth as author, see Reeves, *Heralds*, 36–37.
b. CMC 52.8–55.9.
c. Koenen-Römer propose this restoration on the basis of a passage from the "Apocalypse of Enoch" below (CMC 59.22–23).
d. Correct accordingly Reeves, *Heralds*, 142, 148.
e. Scribal use of the *nominum sacrum* suggests "Spirit" instead of "wind."
f. Cf. the Apocalypse of Shem below (CMC 55.15–56.3) where it is the "Living S[pirit]" that provides transport to a mountain peak.
g. For Enoch as author, see Reeves, *Heralds*, 37–38.
h. A reference to the Johannine Paraclete (John 14:16–17; 15:26; 16:13), with whom Mani was equated by the Manichean community.
i. CMC 55.10–58.5.
j. The rare Greek word used here connotes a small "sitting-room" (*PGL*, s.v. "*kathestērion*," 688).

height and a mighty angel standing by it. The image of the form of his face was very beautiful and lovely, more so than the brig[ht rad]iance [of the su]n, even more than [lightning]. Similarly [he radiated light like] sunlight, [and his robe . . .] of diverse hues (?) like a crown plaited with May[a] blossoms. Then the feature(s) of my face changed so that I collapsed upon the ground. The vertebrae of my back shook, and my feet could not stand upon their joints. A voice bent over me, calling from the throne-room, and having approached me took my right hand and raised (me and) blew a breath of life into my nostrils, increas[ing my] power [and] glory." Gen 2:7

Numer[ous] other [simil]ar things are in his writings,[b] including that which the angels revealed to him saying: "Write these things for a memoir!"

From an alleged Apocalypse of Enoch[c]

Moreover Enoch also speaks in a similar manner in his apocalypse: "I am Enoch the righteous.[d] My sorrow was great, and a torrent of tears (streamed) from my eyes because I heard the insult that the wicked ones uttered."

He says: "While the tears were still in my eyes and the prayer was yet on my lips, I beheld approaching me s[even] angels descending from heaven. [Upon seeing] them I was so moved by fear that my knees began knocking."

He says moreover: "One of the angels, whose name was Michael, said to me: 'I was sent to you for this purpose—in order that we might show you all the deeds and reveal to you the place (appointed) for the pious, and to show you the place (appointed) for the impious, and what sort of place of punishment the lawless are experiencing.'"[e]

He says also: "They seated me upon a chariot of wind[f] and brought me to the ends of the heavens.[g] We traversed worlds—the world of [dea]th, the world of [dar]kness, and the world of fire. And after these (worlds) they brought me into a world of extraordinary richness that was resplendently luminous, even more beautiful than the heavenly luminaries that I (also) beheld."[h]

All these things he saw, and he questioned the angels, and that which they told him he recorded in his writings.[i]

---

a. Literally "Pharmouthi blossoms," where Pharmouthi refers to an Egyptian month coinciding with the Roman calendar's seasons of late spring/early summer.

b. For Shem as author, see Reeves, *Heralds*, 38, 164–67.

c. CMC 58.6–60.12. See also Jonas C. Greenfield and Michael E. Stone, "The Enochic Pentateuch and the Date of the Similitudes," *HTR* 70 (1977): 62–63, doi:10.1017/S0017816000017624; John C. Reeves, "Jewish Pseudepigrapha in Manichaean Literature: The Influence of the Enochic Library," in John C. Reeves, ed., *Tracing the Threads: Studies in the Vitality of Jewish Pseudepigrapha*, ed. John C. Reeves, EJL 6 (Atlanta: Scholars Press, 1994), 181–84.

d. This is a standard epithet for Enoch in Enochic and dependent literature. See 1 En. 1:2 (cf. 12:4); the prologue to 2 Enoch; T. Levi 10:5; T. Judah 18:1; T. Dan 5:6; and the discussion in Reeves, *Heralds*, 184–85.

e. Cf. 1 En. 39:3–5; 41:2.

f. The same conveyance figures in 1 En. 70:2 (*pace* Greenfield and Stone, "Enochic Pentateuch," 62).

g. Cf. 1 En. 71:3–4.

h. Cf. the Greek version of 1 En. 22:2.

i. For Enoch as author, see Reeves, *Heralds*, 39–41.

No Longer "Slavonic" Only: 2 Enoch Attested in Coptic from Nubia

by Joost L. Hagen

This article contains the first translation of the recently identified Coptic fragments of the short recension of 2 Enoch, together with an introduction describing their discovery and an elaborate commentary comparing the text with the evidence of the Slavonic versions based on their translations. The author is presently preparing the publication of these fragments as part of the ongoing research for his doctoral dissertation about the Coptic manuscript texts from Qasr Ibrim.

Rediscovery and Identification of the Coptic Fragments of "Slavonic Enoch"
During the last fifty years or so, the Egypt Exploration Society excavations at the cathedral-fortress site of Qasr Ibrim in Egyptian Nubia, once elevated high above the Nile, but since the building of the Aswan High Dam in the 1960s reduced to a small island in Lake Nasser, have brought to light, among many other things, a rich variety of textual sources, including papyrus, parchment, paper, and leather manuscripts in the four languages of the late-antique and medieval Christian kingdom of Makuria and Nobadia, Greek, Coptic, Old Nubian, and Arabic. Regrettably, many of these finds still remain unpublished, among them many texts in the Sahidic dialect of Coptic, the language of Christian Egypt, also widely used in Nubia. One example of how important these Qasr Ibrim manuscripts are shall appear in the following pages.[1]

Probably in April 2006, during one of my working visits to Cambridge in order to prepare my doctoral dissertation on the Coptic manuscripts from Qasr Ibrim, using the EES excavation archive (at that time still kept in the faculty of Oriental Studies basement, but since then moved to the British Museum in London), I opened one of the notebooks of Coptologist Professor J. M. Plumley (director of the Qasr Ibrim excavations from 1963 to 1976) and came across a transcription of a fragmentary Coptic text on parchment which was identified by the number 72.3.3 (Plumley Notebook 3, 11–17).

---

1. A general introduction to Christian-period Qasr Ibrim and its texts can be found in J. L. Hagen, "A Pleasant Sense of Mild Bewilderment: Re-excavating the Coptic Texts from Qasr Ibrim," *Ancient Egypt* 10, no. 2 (October/November 2009): 46–54. A more detailed account is given in J. L. Hagen, "'A City That Is Set on an Hill Cannot Be Hid': Progress Report on the Coptic Manuscripts from Qasr Ibrim," in *Between the Cataracts, Part Two: Session Papers (fasc. 2)*, ed. W. Godlewski and A. Łajtar, PAM Supplement 2.2.2 (Warsaw: Warsaw University Press, 2010), 719–26.

This article was originally published on pp. 7–34 of *New Perspectives on 2 Enoch: No Longer Slavonic Only*, ed. Andrei A. Orlov and Gabriele Boccaccini, Studia JudaeoSlavica 4 (Leiden: Brill, 2012). We are grateful to the author and to Brill Publishers for permission to reprint it here. The original article included three photographic figures at the end. These are omitted in this reprint. Please consult the original publication for them. A bibliography has been added.

When I first saw Prof. Plumley's notes concerning these fragments, excavated in 1972, and later also the photos made at the time of their discovery, I immediately realized these were the remnants of a very interesting text, but I also knew it would be very difficult, maybe even impossible, to make full sense of them. First of all, the fragments were only four in number, with two of them being very small at that. The complete height of the pages had not been preserved, and about half of the width of the lines seemed to be lost, making it very difficult to assess what the text was all about. The content which I could glimpse, however, was intriguing enough (quoted here in the order of Plumley's notes): "The circle of the moon I have measured [. . .] and the . . . (?) of its light," "great heat," "one of the angels," "and the appearance [. . .] was like snow, and [. . .] were like ice," "[. . .] spoke to me all these words," "I have come to know everything," "and their chambers," "my descendants . . ."

First I thought all this might have something to do with the book of Job, but he, of course, in the end had to admit he did not know everything, or anything much, about creation and its secrets. I then concluded that the fragments might belong to a work supposedly written by Cyprian the magician, who also claimed to have much arcane knowledge; I could find some near-parallels in Coptic texts, but did not manage to identify the fragments as belonging to a copy of a known work. I did not then expect I would ever be able to find a match; too much of the text was lost, and not all of what Plumley had copied in his notes was visible in the photos, making it difficult to establish definitive readings. I have tried to locate the original fragments in the Egyptian and Coptic museums in Cairo and the Nubia Museum in Aswan, but in vain. Plumley's notebook and the excavators' photos remained and still are my only sources.

As a result of these disappointments, I all but forgot about these fragments and went on to study better preserved Coptic manuscripts from Qasr Ibrim, both literary and documentary in content, of which there are quite a few. But when in March 2009 I tried to make a final version of the list of texts to be included in, and excluded from, my dissertation, I decided that it would not do to leave these "Cyprian" fragments out. I felt I simply had to make whatever sense of them I could and publish them.

At the time, I was rereading a book I had studied several years before for my MA thesis about the Coptic encomium on the four Creatures of the book of Revelation and the visions of Ezekiel, attributed to John Chrysostom, and had just been reminded of the important role of the antediluvian patriarch Enoch in texts concerning the interpretation of Ezekiel and Revelation, like the encomium.[2] Just theoretically at first, I tried reading my four long-abandoned pieces of parchment as if they were, not about Cyprian the magician, but about Enoch, who, I knew, had been told about the secrets of creation before being made, according to the Coptic tradition, "the scribe of righteousness" in heaven.[3] And suddenly, things started to fall into place, and I recognized things like "I wrote," "in the books," and "of righteousness." The text already seemed to make somewhat more sense. But all the missing parts of the lines and the pages were still there, or

---

2. MA thesis: J. L. Hagen, "'Mens en dier verlost Gij, HERE': De Lofrede voor de feestdag van de Vier Wezens, toegeschreven aan Johannes Chrysostomos" (Leiden, 2003; in Dutch; unpublished). The book I reread was D. J. Halperin, *The Faces of the Chariot: Early Jewish Responses to Ezekiel's Vision*, TSAJ 16 (Tübingen: Mohr Siebeck, 1988).

3. For Enoch in the Coptic tradition, see B. A. Pearson, "Enoch in Egypt," in *For a Later Generation: The Transformation of Tradition in Israel, Early Judaism and Early Christianity*, ed. R. A. Argall et al., Festschrift for G. W. E. Nickelsburg (Harrisburg, PA: Trinity Press International, 2000), 216–31.

rather, not there, and I did not seriously intend to read through all ancient texts about Enoch until I found a parallel to the text preserved in these Qasr Ibrim fragments. Moreover, knowing something about Coptic literature, I realized this could very well be an otherwise unattested, late work originating in Christian Egypt, or something only having to do with Enoch in a marginal way, like John Chrysostom's encomium on the four Creatures, fragments of which have also been wrongly interpreted as remains of an Enoch apocryphon.[4] But I decided to try my hand at an identification all the same.

I looked again at the "unfinished sentences, amputated stumps of words" (Umberto Eco, *The Name of the Rose*) and tried to use my experience, and my imagination, to reconstruct enough text to be able to understand what was happening in this work. Enoch the Scribe already seemed to make more sense than Cyprian the magician. I took several of the phrases quoted above, and others, and typed them (the truth will out!) into Google's Advanced Search, with no very clear results, but what results came up had, indeed, to do with Enoch. Then, I tried the "appearance" that was said to be "like snow." What, or whose, appearance? Before the "was," there was the Coptic equivalent of "that": "And the appearance [of] that [. . .] was like snow." In the line above, mention was made of "one of the angels," so I guessed: "[of] that [angel]." I typed this sentence into the computer, and one second later, thanks to Google books, I was in the middle of an English translation of the work known as 2 Enoch, Slavonic Enoch, and "The Book of the Secrets of Enoch."[5]

Not only did I find this particular sentence, but I also recognized the narrator's claim to "know everything," including "the circle of the moon." It clearly was the same text. (When reading the phrases quoted above, it might have been immediately obvious to some experts!) I could use the English translation of the Slavonic text (I do not read Slavonic) to reconstruct the reading order of the Coptic fragments and the sequences of recto and verso, and I could even start, using again my experience and my imagination, to restore the missing parts of every line. (I have not yet been able to identify the contents of Plumley's fourth fragment; see below.) Translating the English into Coptic, I could fill one gap, and another, sometimes with certainty, sometimes hesitating about a synonym or a grammatical construction; but the mutilated scraps of parchment began to make more and more sense, and my preliminary filling of the lacunae succeeded line after line after line, until there could no longer be any doubt: This was a Coptic version of 2 Enoch.

At the moment of this discovery, I did not yet realize that 2 Enoch was not called "Slavonic" for nothing, or that there were a long and a short recension of the work, or, indeed, that my discovery might be worth more than a short remark in a footnote. But this soon changed. I started looking things up, and within days of my discovery, I sent an email to Professor Christfried Böttrich from Greifswald, of whom I had once attended a lecture about apocrypha in the Slavonic tradition, thinking he might be interested to hear about my identification of the first non-Slavonic version of 2 Enoch. Little did I know he was one of the world's leading 2 Enoch experts. However, I soon found out. To

---

4. B. A. Pearson, "The Munier Enoch Fragments, Revisited," in *For the Children, Perfect Instruction: Studies in Honor of Hans-Martin Schenke on the Occasion of the Berliner Arbeitskreis für koptisch-gnostische Schriften's Thirtieth Year*, ed. H. G. Bethge et al. (Leiden: Brill, 2002), 375–83.

5. A. Pennington's translation in *The Apocryphal Old Testament*, ed. H. F. D. Sparks (Oxford: Clarendon, 1984), 321–62, referred to below as Pennington/Sparks.

make a long story short, he kindly recommended me for an invitation to the Fifth Enoch Seminar which was to be held in Naples three months later, in June 2009, specifically devoted to . . . 2 Enoch. The organizers, Professor Gabriele Boccaccini and Professor Andrei Orlov, most kindly saw to it that I could give a lecture there in order to present the preliminary results of my work on the Coptic fragments. During the preparations for this, and while participating in the discussions in Naples, I learned just how important my chance find might be . . .

The Four Fragments and Their Contents

As stated above, two of the four Coptic parchment fragments that presently seem to be the only pieces to survive from this first non-Slavonic version of 2 Enoch discovered so far are quite small, and the contents of only one of them (frag. 1, Prof. Plumley's no. 3; see below) could be identified so far; the other (Plumley's and my frag. 4) has been left out of the translation presented in this article. There might be just enough text preserved to identify this piece too, but one of Plumley's readings looks suspect, and I have not yet been able to find a photo of the fragment. The other three fragments can be numbered, and their recto and verso sides identified, according to the sequence of the parts of the text they are bearing (see below).

Two sets of photographs are available for the three fragments translated below: 72v11/16–19 and 72v22/22–25, 30, 31. Three of them are reproduced as figures 1, 2, and 3 at the end of this article (in the original publication). As far as can be judged from these photos, the dimensions of the fragments are the following (excluding the folded parts, which cannot be measured in this way): Fragment 1 ca. 5 × 5 cm (with about half of it empty margins), fragment 2 ca. 8 × 7 cm, and fragment 3 ca. 6 × 6 cm. Fragment 1 preserves the end (recto) and the beginning (verso) of the first five lines of two sides of a leaf, with part of the upper and the outer margins. Fragment 2 contains seventeen (recto) and sixteen (verso) lines, with most of the ends of the lines preserved on the recto and on the verso most of the beginnings; between one-fourth and one-half of the width of the lines is lost. On fragment 3, each side contains the remains of eleven lines of text; reconstruction of the lost parts is more difficult here because both the beginnings and ends of the lines are lost. According to Plumley's notes, fragment 4, otherwise not treated here, has four ("recto") and three ("verso") lines of between two and eight letters each, with their beginnings and ends lost.

To judge from the best preserved leaf, fragment 2, and the part of its text lost between recto and verso, compared to the Slavonic version of 2 Enoch in the translation of Pennington/Sparks, this fragment probably represents about two-thirds of the original height of the leaf (some sixteen lines are preserved and probably about eight lines are lost; so the original number of lines was probably ca. 24). Whether or not the first line of preserved text also was the first line of the page, as in the case of fragment 1, is uncertain, as with fragment 3, but both fragments probably represent the upper part of the original leaves. If the number of lines on a complete page was indeed twenty-four or thereabout, fragment 1 would be the upper fourth or fifth part of a leaf. Because of the folded state of the fragments at the time when the available photos were made, I do not attempt to reconstruct the original dimensions of the leaves in centimeters. The average number of letters on a line is thirty.

As can be seen from their contents (see below), fragments 1, 2, and 3 must be remnants of three consecutive leaves of the original codex presumably containing all of

No Longer "Slavonic" Only: 2 Enoch Attested in Coptic from Nubia

2 Enoch in Coptic translation. Whether Plumley's fragment 4 represents a fourth leaf or a piece of the lower part of one of the other three remains unclear. Unfortunately, no page numbers seem to be preserved in the upper margins of fragment 1 (see fig. 1 [in the original publication]).

The content of the three fragments translated below is as follows:[6]

Fragment 1r (pl. 3v):	36:3 (end); 36:4 = 39:1; [39:2, 3 (beg.)]
Fragment 1v (pl. 3r):	39:3 (cont.)–5; [39:6, 7 (beg.)]
Fragment 2r (pl. 1v):	[39:7 (cont.)]; 39:8; 37:1, 2; 40:1, 2; [40:3, 4 (beg.)]
Fragment 2v (pl. 1r):	40:4 (cont.), 5, 8–10 (beg.)
Fragment 3r (pl. 2v):	[40:10 (cont.)]; 40:11–13; [41:1, 2; 42:1 (beg.)]
Fragment 3v (pl. 2r):	[42:1 (cont.)]; 42:2, 3 (beg.)

From this overview, the importance of these Coptic fragments is immediately apparent. Fragments 1 and 2 show that the sequence of the disputed chapters 36–40 in this version of 2 Enoch is 36–39–37–40, without chapter 38, exactly as in the Slavonic manuscripts of the short recension. (Incidentally, the English translation of the short recension by Pennington/Sparks is the only one actually giving them in this order, and not adapting them to the "standard" of the long recension.) The transition from chapter 36 to 39 on fragment 1r is damaged but certain, as are those from 39 to 37 and 37 to 40 on fragment 2r. Luckily our copy of Coptic 2 Enoch contains these transitions on the middle of its pages; had the chapter transition happened to coincide with a transition between two sides of a leaf or from one leaf to another, there could have been some doubt about the identification of recto and verso and the reading order of the leaves.

Furthermore, fragmentt 2v shows that the verses 40:6, 7 are absent in this version: The transition from v. 5 to v. 8 is clearly preserved. As far as the other "additions" of the Slavonic long recension are concerned, which occur in places where the Coptic version is damaged by lacunae: for the extra part of 37:2 (an explanation of what is described in the preceding verse) there clearly is no place, just as for the extras in 40:12a (creation measured) and 40:12b–42:2 (judgment).

Finally, fragment 1r demonstrates that the Coptic version included the "peculiar material" at the end of chapter 36 (vv. 3 and 4) that is present only in the oldest Slavonic manuscript of 2 Enoch, U (fifteenth century), and in manuscript A (sixteenth century), which is closely related to U; the "disarray of the text at this point" has been called "a patch job which makes U inferior."[7]

The above facts are sufficient to prove that the Coptic version of 2 Enoch preserved in these fragments was a representative of the short recension. The fact that this, the first non-Slavonic copy of the work, which antedates the oldest surviving Slavonic manuscript by several centuries and might very well be earlier than the time at which 2 Enoch was translated into Slavonic in the first place (on the dating of the Coptic fragments, see the next paragraph), so clearly is a text of the short recension (even sharing "peculiar"

---

6. Round brackets: Prof. Plumley's order of the pieces, according to size, and his recto and verso sides; chapter and verse division after Andersen/Charlesworth, on which see the introduction to the translation; square brackets: text lost in lacuna.

7. F. I. Andersen referring to Vaillant. Andersen, "2 (Slavonic Apocalypse of) Enoch," in *The Old Testament Pseudepigrapha*, ed. J. H. Charlesworth, 2 vols. (New York: Doubleday, 1983, 1985), referred to here as Andersen/Charlesworth, 1:160, n. 36a.

readings with the oldest Slavonic manuscript U), seems to call into question the way in which the evidence of the manuscripts of that recension has, by some, been interpreted as secondary, even "inferior" to that of the texts of the long recension (for a preliminary evaluation, see the conclusion of this article).

The Archaeological Context; Palaeographical Evidence for Dating the Fragments

In Prof. Plumley's notebook, where I first came across these Coptic fragments of 2 Enoch, they are given the number 72.3.3, which is also written on the pieces themselves (visible on frag. 2r, fig. 2 [in the original publication]). This number, which does not look like one of the excavation or registration numbers usually given to the Qasr Ibrim finds (but see below), links it to several other Coptic parchment fragments bearing 72.3 numbers, which contain Old Testament and hagiographical texts: 72.3.1, a bifolium and some fragments with parts of Isaiah 16–17, 22–23, and 28–29; 72.3.2, fragments of Jeremiah, including 40:1, 2; 72.3.4, probably also biblical, but not yet identified; and 72.3.7, several fragmentary pages of what must be the best preserved copy of the Coptic version of the Martyrdom of Saint Mark the Evangelist known so far. I have not yet been able to find the pieces to which the numbers 72.3.5 and 72.3.6 refer, and it is also unclear to me whether or not there were more than seven numbers in this series; however, one of these two or more numbers (72.3.9?) should refer to the piece containing the end of Haggai and the beginning of Zechariah transcribed in Plumley's notes as "fragment 9" (Notebook 3, pp. 29, 31).

The Isaiah and Jeremiah fragments are said to have been found in association with four fragmentary leaves of a parchment codex with the Gospel of Mark in Greek, which were given the number 72.4, and this must be true in the case of the other 72.3 texts, including the 2 Enoch fragments, as well. Whether the finds called 72.1 and 72.2 (and possibly 72.5 and more) also came from the same spot is not yet clear to me, but I expect so. As far as the numbers are concerned, if they are not simply a subdivision of the usual registration numbers (72.3 etc.), 72 surely indicates the year of excavation, the second part might indicate the language (3 for Coptic, 4 for Greek) and the third individual texts, if necessary (this would mean the Gospel of Mark was the only Greek to have been found then and there). The Greek fragments with the number 72.4 and the Coptic fragments of the 72.3 series, at least, were "found in a pit in front of and a little to the south of the altar" of the small church "built alongside the south wall of the great cathedral" of Qasr Ibrim. According to Prof. Plumley, this church "can be dated to the ninth century, but the pit and its contents clearly antedate its building."[8] This suggests that the textual material found in this pit is older than the first of the two known phases in the existence of this so-called South Church, whereas more recent references to this building suggest the finds antedate its second phase and stem from the first: The earlier incarnation of the church, built with red brick, was probably destroyed during Saladin's brother Shams ed-Dawla's famous raid on Qasr Ibrim in 1172–1173, after which "a dense rubble of broken brick, painted and inscribed plaster, and hundreds of burned and torn fragments of religious manuscripts," here taken to be remains of the earlier phase of the church and its library (or maybe rather that of the cathedral just next door, also damaged in the raid), were

---

8. This and the preceding quotation in J. Martin Plumley and C. H. Roberts, "An Uncial Text of St. Mark in Greek from Nubia," *JTS*, New Series 27 (1976): 34–45 (34).

buried under the floor of its mud-brick successor, built soon afterwards.[9] This would mean the texts antedate the destruction of the first church in the second half of the twelfth century, rather than its building in the ninth; of course, both would be true at the same time in case they really were older than the ninth century, but that should be proven on other grounds.

The fragments of the Greek copy of the Gospel of Mark have been palaeographically dated to the fifth century and might "have been brought to Nubia in the middle of the sixth century when Nubia became officially Christian."[10] The Coptic finds from the South Church most probably are of a less impressive age, but my first attempt to date them by palaeographical means (always difficult and rather imprecise in the case of Coptic manuscripts) suggests an eighth- to ninth-, maybe tenth-century dating for both the 2 Enoch fragments and the martyrdom of Saint Mark (on their relation, see below). This would be compatible with both the ninth- and the twelfth-century *ante quem* dating described above. Hopefully, future study of published and unpublished records of the "South Church" and its excavation, or a more precise judgment on the palaeography of its textual finds, can shed more light on the problem of the age of the Coptic fragments of 2 Enoch.

However important a possible archaeologically based dating prior to the building of the South Church in the ninth century rather than merely prior to its destruction and rebuilding in the twelfth would be, already the general dating, on palaeographical grounds, of the manuscript to the eighth to tenth centuries (that is, without the possibility to further limit this period of time to its first half), is significant: This means that the fragments antedate the accepted date of the translation of 2 Enoch into Slavonic (tenth or eleventh century) and that they are some several hundred years older than the earliest Slavonic witness of Merilo Pravednoe ("The Just Balance"), a work with extracts of the ethical passages in 2 Enoch (fourteenth century). These Coptic fragments represent the oldest version of "Slavonic Enoch" known so far.

Concerning the Possible Present Location and Condition of the Fragments

In the preliminary report on the finds of the 1972 excavation season at Qasr Ibrim, published in 1974, among the Coptic finds reference is made to "smaller parchment pieces" with "part of what appears to be a homily."[11] This probably refers to the Martyrdom of Saint Mark the Evangelist, but might also include or refer to the fragments of 2 Enoch; even though they were given different numbers (72.3.7 and 72.3.3, respectively) their handwriting and state of preservation look remarkably similar (compare figs. 1–3 of the present article [in the original publication with plates i–v of the article by Abdul Moeiz Shaheen mentioned in note 12 below).

Of the texts of the 72.3 and 72.4 series, probably found in October or November 1972, at least the Greek Gospel and the Coptic Martyrdom of Saint Mark and the Coptic Isaiah (I do not remember having recognized the Coptic Jeremiah and Haggai/Zechariah, but these are small, unremarkable fragments) are now kept in the manuscript library of the

---

9. W. Y. Adams, *Qasr Ibrim: The Late Mediaeval Period* (London: Egyptian Exploration Society, 1996), 78–79; referred to in W. Y. Adams, *Qasr Ibrim: The Earlier Medieval Period* (London: Egyptian Exploration Society, 2010), 9.

10. Plumley and Roberts, "An Uncial Text of Saint Mark," 35.

11. J. Martin Plumley and W. Y. Adams, "Qasr Ibrim, 1972," *Journal of Egyptian Archaeology* 60 (1974): 212–38 (214).

Coptic Museum in Cairo, and I have not found Coptic material from 1972 elsewhere, that is to say, in the Egyptian Museum or in the Nubia Museum at Aswan. I would therefore expect the 2 Enoch fragments to be in the Coptic Museum too, but I have not been able to find them there (yet). Maybe also they are stored in one of the other museums or magazines of the Antiquities Organization in Egypt.

So at present, as stated before, the photos and, for the parts of the text not visible on the photos, Plumley's transcription are the only sources for the text of the fragments (to get an impression of what this means in practice, see the text accompanying frag. 3). Like the uncertainty about the interpretation of the archaeological record referred to above, this is not uncommon for textual finds from the Qasr Ibrim excavations. Also in the case of another Coptic manuscript from the 1972 season, a documentary text (contrary to the 2 Enoch fragments not small, but said to be 95 cm long and 48/49 cm wide, with another 3/4 cm of its width lost), the other texts belonging to the same group all are in the Coptic Museum and the piece itself cannot (or hopefully, could not yet) be found, there or elsewhere. Also for this text (a very interesting letter written in the summer of 760 CE) access to the original would be needed in order to supplement the photos and check the readings from Prof. Plumley's transcriptions.

Whether the 2 Enoch fragments, in case they are eventually found, will still look like they do on the photos is doubtful and can in fact only be hoped. When I first saw the original pages from the Martyrdom of Mark mentioned above, I did not recognize them. In contrast to the state in which they had been excavated and photographed, they are no longer folded but flat, kept between glass. However, what had been merely invisible on the photos is now ugly or even unreadable on the original, making the excavator's transcriptions the only source for those parts of the text; that is to say, provided they could be included in the transcription at the time, before the actual flattening of the parchment. But in the case of the Martyrdom, as in that of 2 Enoch, this apparently was the case (a partly folded manuscript can be turned around in order to try to look into its hidden corners, which unfortunately cannot be done with a photograph of the same). The fragments from the Martyrdom of Saint Mark the Evangelist have, frankly speaking, been ruined; their original beauty has been destroyed and the text has not gained much in legibility. In a 1981 article, Abdul Moeiz Shaheen of the Coptic Museum describes how the pieces of the Martyrdom, and related finds, were experimented upon in order to find the best way to treat them.[12] It probably is too far-fetched to imagine that some pieces might have fallen victim to this process altogether, being destroyed and thrown away, but reading the article and seeing the difference between "before" and "after treatment" make one pray the Enoch fragments escaped a similar fate and can be properly treated in the future.

Be that as it may, for the time being we must make do with what is available, and that already is a lot, as we shall see. Although it would be quite useful to be able to check some of Plumley's readings with the original, his transcriptions combined with the available photos contain enough material to surprise the world of Enochic scholarship.

---

12. A. Moeiz Shaheen, "Treatment of Some Pieces of Parchment and Papyrus Found in the Excavations of the Society of Egyptian Archaeology, London, in Kasr Ibrim, Nubia, 1972," *Annales du Service des Antiquités de l'Égypte* 64 (1981): 137–48, with plates I–XXI. For the experimental phase of the project, the worst to be mentioned is of "the writings" being "slightly damaged" and a "very slight change" in the color of the parchment (138), but this is not how I would describe what happened to the fragments of the Martyrdom of Saint Mark.

Introduction to the Translation

The following translation of the text of the three identified Coptic fragments of 2 Enoch from Qasr Ibrim is adapted from, in the sense that it is as far as possible identical to, the English translation of the Slavonic short recension (based on the oldest manuscript, U, of the fifteenth century) by Pennington published in Sparks's *Apocryphal Old Testament*, pp. 342–345 (chaps. 11:37, 38; and 13:1–27), but with the more generally accepted chapter and verse numbers from the translation of the short recension by Andersen in Charlesworth's *Old Testament Pseudepigrapha*, 1:161–69 (chaps. 36:3–42:3). The translation of Pennington/Sparks is the only one I have seen giving the chapters in their manuscript order, without adapting them to the allegedly superior sequence in the long recension. As the text of the Coptic fragments seems to be very close to that of the short recension as trustworthily presented by Pennington/Sparks, including the same order of chapters (36–39–37–40–41–42), readers interested to see what a complete Coptic 2 Enoch might have looked like, without the gaps and with all its pages preserved, can get their best first impression of this most curious text by reading the translation used here as my point of departure. The (main) differences between the text of the Coptic fragments and that of the Slavonic manuscripts are referred to in the commentary following my translation, where also the reconstructions of text lost in the lacunae in the manuscript are explained. Other translations than Pennington/Sparks have been used by me as well, first of all the above-mentioned Andersen/Charlesworth (from which I took the idea of indicating the "I, I have . . ." when it appears in the Coptic text of chaps. 39 and 40), but also those by Böttrich, Forbes and Charles, Riessler, Vaillant, and Vaillant-Philonenko, and I have a long list of all observed "translational (if not textual) variants," only a part of which is given below. Sometimes an indicated uncertainty in my translation is based on their differences from Pennington/Sparks; relevant details are referred to in the commentary. Next to the line numbers of the Coptic fragments in italics, chapter and verse numbers (see above) are added in bold script. In the case of reconstructions in lacunae, their correct place often cannot be exactly determined, especially on fragment 3, where both the beginning and the end of the lines are lost. I make use of the following brackets and signs:

[text]: text lost but reconstructed using Slavonic parallel(s) or Coptic context
[ ]: text lost and reconstruction too uncertain to be attempted
<text>: text (probably) forgotten by copyist and added by editor
(text): text not in the Coptic but added to make the translation clearer
(and): in the Coptic perfect tense, "and" is sometimes not written but implied
/ separates translation alternatives (?) and refers to preceding word
(??) refers to more than the preceding word, sometimes to the complete filling of a gap

The translation presented here is as true to the Coptic, as closely based on Pennington/Sparks, as readable and as reliable, that is, next to the above, avoiding speculation (much more could have been taken from the Slavonic and put within the square brackets of the translation that has no basis in the surviving fragments and could therefore never securely be filled in in the text), as possible, and being the first published translation of the Coptic 2 Enoch fragments it is of course preliminary and subject to change following possible further progress in my work on the text.

Bibliography

Adams, W. Y. *Qasr Ibrim: The Earlier Medieval Period*. Excavation Memoir 89. London: Egyptian Exploration Society, 2010.

———. *Qasr Ibrim: The Late Mediaeval Period*. Excavation Memoir 59. London: Egyptian Exploration Society, 1996.

Andersen, F. I. "2 (Slavonic Apocalypse of) Enoch." OTP 1:91–222.

Hagen, Joost L. "'A City That Is Set on an Hill Cannot Be Hid': Progress Report on the Coptic Manuscripts from Qasr Ibrim." Pages 719–26 in *Between the Cataracts: Proceedings of the 11th Conference for Nubian Studies, Warsaw University, 27 August–2 September 2006, Part Two; Session Papers*. Edited by Włodzimierz Godlewski and Adam Łajtar. PAM Supplement 2.2.2. Warsaw: Warsaw University Press, 2010.

———. "'Mens en dier verlost Gij, HERE': De Lofrede voor de feestdag van de Vier Wezens, toegeschreven aan Johannes Chrysostomos." MA Thesis, University of Leiden, 2003.

———. "A Pleasant Sense of Mild Bewilderment: Re-excavating the Coptic Texts from Qasr Ibrim." *Ancient Egypt* 10, no. 2 (October/November 2009): 46–54.

Halperin, David J. *The Faces of the Chariot: Early Jewish Responses to Ezekiel's Vision*. TSAJ 16. Tübingen: Mohr, 1988.

Pearson, Birger A. "Enoch in Egypt." Pages 216–31 in *For a Later Generation: The Transformation of Tradition in Israel, Early Judaism and Early Christianity*. Edited by Randal A. Argall, Beverly Bow, and Rodney Alan Werline. Harrisburg, PA: Trinity Press International, 20.

———. "The Munier Enoch Fragments, Revisited." Pages 375–83 in *For the Children, Perfect Instructio: Studies in Honor of Hans-Martin Schenke on the Occasion of the Berliner Arbeitskreis für koptisch-gnostische Schriften's Thirtieth Year*. Edited by Hans-Gebhard Bethge, Stephen Emmel, Karen King, and Imke Schletterer. Nag Hammadi and Manichaean Studies 54. Leiden: Brill, 2002. doi:10.1163/9789004439924_024.

Pennington, A. "2 Enoch." *AOT*, 321–62.

Plumley, J. Martin, and W. Y. Adams. "Qasr Ibrim, 1972." *Journal of Egyptian Archaeology* 60 (1974): 212–38.

Plumley, J. Martin, and C. H. Roberts. "An Uncial Text of St. Mark in Greek from Nubia." *JTS* NS 27 (1976): 34–45.

Shaheen, A. Moeiz. "Treatment of Some Pieces of Parchment and Papyrus Found in the Excavations of the Society of Egyptian Archaeology, London, in Kasr Ibrim, Nubia, 1972." *Annales du Service des Antiquités de l'Égypte* 64 (1981): 137–48.

Translation of the Coptic Fragments of 2 Enoch 36:3–42:3

(1r) **(36:3)** [. and you shall] be for me [a witness of/in (?) the judgment of the] last [age (?). All this the Lord said to] me as [a man speaks with his friend].

(36:4=39:1) Now then, *(5)* [O my children, listen to the voice of your father, and every]thing [I command to you today. . . . **(39:2)**. . . . **(39:3)** I, I have seen the face] *(1v)* of the Lord, [like iron heated] in the furnace [and scattering sparks (??)] and (?) [.   **(39:4)** I, I have seen the] eyes of the [Lord, like the rays of the shining sun]. *(5)* **(39:5)** I, [I have seen the right hand of the Lord,. . . . **(39:6)**. . . . **(39:7)** . . . *(2r)*. . . . **(39:8)**. . . .] Who shall be able to endure (??) [the infinite fear and] the heat, which is great?

(37:1) [but the Lord] called (?) one of the angels of Tarta[rus (and)] set] him by me; and the appearance *(5)* [of] that [angel] was like snow, and [his hands] were like ice; and he [cooled] my face with/between (?) them, for I was unable to endure [(that) terror] and that heat. **(37:2)** And [so the] Lord spoke to me all these words.

(10) **(40:1)** [Now then, O my children,] I, I have learned everything, <some things> (??) from [the mouth of the Lord], and some others I have seen [with my eyes], from the beginning to the end, from [the end to the resur]rection (?).

(40:2) I, I know [every]thing, [and I, I have written] in the books the [extent *(15)* of the heavens, and their] contents I, I have measured, [and I, I have come to know] all their hosts [. . .] . . . [. . . . **(40:3)** . . . . **(40:4)** The circle of the sun I, I have measured, . . . *(2v)* . . . and its] goings in and its [goings out and its] entire movement, and also its names [I, I have written]. **(40:5)** The circle of the moon I, I have measured, and [its movements] and the waning of its light, [every day] *(5)* and every hour, and its alte[rations] I, I have written.

(40:8) The dwelling-place of [the clouds and] their mouth and their wings and their [rains and their] drops I, I have explored. **(40:9)** I have [written the sounds (?)] of the thunderbolts and the wonders [of the lightnings. They] *(10)* showed them to me, (they), that is, their (?) [custodians (?), and] their place of going up <and> the<ir> place (??) [of going down (??)] with measure; they bring them [up by means of a chain/bound (??)] and they lead them [down by means of a chain/bound (??)], lest they turn themselves aside [and (?) . . .] *(15)* rough (?) [. . .]. **(40:10)** And the [treasuries of the snow and the storehouses of the i]c[e . . . *(3r)*. . . . **(40:11)** The dwelling place of the winds I, I have written. I looked and saw their custodians bringing balances and measures: (??)]first they put [them on the balance], and [then] in the measure, and by [measure they bring them down] over the whole world, [lest *(5)* they shake] the earth with a rough breath.

(40:12) [And then (?) I was taken] down from [that] place [(and) I came to] the dwelling place of the judgment, [and I saw hell] open, **(40:13)** and I saw [a certain plain (??)], as if it were a prison, *(10)* [a judgment place (?) without measure]. And I went [down . . .] . . . [. . . . **(41:1)**. . . . **(41:2)**. . . . **(42:1)** And I saw the keepers of the keys of hell, (??) . . . **(3v)**] **(42:2)** And I spoke [to them, saying: it would] be well if I had not seen [you, and if I had not] seen your chambers; [. . . (?) may none] among my descendants come to you, [or] *(5)* see your chambers!

(42:3) And (?) [I was taken from] that place, (and) I went [up into the paradi]se of righteousness, [and in that place I] saw a [blessed] dwelling place, [and] every [creature] that was in [that] place [is blessed . . .] *(10)*

[. . .] . . . [. . .] . . . [. . .]

Commentary

It does not seem useful or indeed proper to list and justify all variants between these Coptic fragments and the Slavonic manuscripts on the basis of the above translation and of my other work so far, without giving a Coptic text (a first edition of which would involve too many notes and comments to be feasible in the present contribution) and only based on (English, German, and French) translations of the Slavonic texts. Many of the differences I noted down in the long list of "variants" referred to above, from which for the remarks presented below I took only the ones I thought the most important, probably are mere nuances in translation, and therefore not the object of textual criticism proper.

What should at some point be checked in the case of these differences is whether the Slavonic can be translated or interpreted according to the reading of the Coptic. Despite all of the variants listed below, the two versions (Coptic and the earliest short recension Slavonic) are quite close to each other, and they might be even closer than their translations now seem to imply. What this means for their common *Vorlage* remains to be seen (see my conclusion, below); it would be very instructive to attempt a Greek reconstruction of those parts of chapters 36–42 that are now available in both Slavonic and Coptic.

In the following commentary I first and foremost list the real and supposed differences between the text of the Coptic fragments and the Slavonic manuscripts of the short recension available to me in translation. Readings of the Slavonic long recension (mostly its "additions") are mainly mentioned in those places (essentially all) where it can be clearly shown that these extras are absent from the Coptic version. Readings of the Slavonic very short recension as given in Forbes's and Charles's translation of the sixteenth-century manuscript N ("minuses") are not referred to, in order not to burden this commentary and confuse the reader, but it is equally clear that the Coptic fragments do not represent a text of that type either. The early Slavonic extracts from 2 Enoch in the fourteenth-century copy of the Merilo Pravednoe are mentioned only once. Lastly, references to authors are references to their translation of and notes concerning the passage being commented upon.

Fragment 1, Recto

36:3 The first of the three Coptic fragments translated here only preserves the very last words of the Lord's long speech to Enoch before the latter temporarily returns to earth. The translations from the Slavonic manuscripts seem to be divided between "testimony" and "witness" (in the sense of someone bearing testimony), and between "witness of " (someone present at) and "witness in" (implying closer involvement). The Slavonic reads "great age" (in the sense of "era"), for which the Coptic might have had something like "last [day]" or "last [judgment]," although I tentatively reconstructed "last [age]." There seems to be a variant reading here.

36:4=39:1 Even though the verse is damaged, it is clear that what we have here, after the end of chapter 36, is the beginning of Enoch's long speech to his children (or sons; the Coptic word probably used can mean both, and I noticed both occur in the translations from the Slavonic), without any indication of a transition from heaven back to earth as present in the Slavonic long recension in the form of chapter 38. This does not seem to me as much of a problem as it apparently is for some; it implies that the preceding part of the text, in which Enoch tells about his heavenly journey, was also told to his children (When and where exactly is Enoch supposed to relate or write the present work, and to whom?), and no mention of his return was necessary, especially as the topic continues to be Enoch's vision of the Lord and his words. The same argument can be used to explain the absence of the transition chapter after chapter 37, which in these Coptic fragments, as in the Slavonic short recension, follows chapter 39 (see below).

Fragment 1, Verso

39:2–7 Unfortunately, most of this much-debated passage, in which the situation of Enoch speaking to his children is compared to the situation of the Lord speaking to Enoch, is lost in the Coptic fragments, but it is clear that mention is indeed made of various body parts of the Lord: "[the face] of the Lord" in v. 3, "[the] eyes of the [Lord]" in v. 4, and therefore surely also "[the right hand of the Lord]" in v. 5, with the Lord's "mouth" (or "lips," earlier in v. 3), "body" (by implication, v. 6), and "words" (v. 7) entirely lost in lacunae. What is unclear, however, is whether the Coptic actually mentioned the corresponding body parts of Enoch, with which in the Slavonic text those of the Lord are compared. In fact, in the one instance where this can be judged, between "[I have seen the] eyes of the [Lord]" and "I [have seen the right hand of the Lord]," there is just enough space in the gap to fill in (about the Lord's eyes) "like the rays of the shining sun" or something similar, but not for another whole clause: "you see my right hand . . . , but." It must be admitted that this is based on a reading in Prof. Plumley's notes that cannot be checked from the photos and must remain authoritative until it can (if ever) be verified using the original fragments. But also just before that, between "[the face] of the Lord, [like iron heated] in the furnace" and our "[I have seen the] eyes of the [Lord]," there is room for something like "[and scattering sparks] and [being incandescent]" (about the Lord's face), but not for "you see my eyes . . . , but." (I tentatively took "being incandescent" from the Slavonic long recension, but did not dare to use it in the translation proper. The lacunae in lines 2 and 3 seem somewhat long for "scattering sparks" only; the interpretation of the beginning of line 3 as "and" is uncertain.) It should therefore be tentatively concluded that, for whatever reason, (this copy of) the Coptic 2 Enoch did not contain references to Enoch's face, eyes, etc., but only to those of the Lord. This almost seems like an ironic answer to those who thought a text like this could (or should) not refer to the Lord's body, and that the "I have seen the Lord's . . ." sentences are secondary; but without them, there would be no need for the "you see my . . ." sentences either, which is not true the other way round.

Fragment 2, Recto

39:8 How the Coptic version treated the comparison between earthly king and heavenly king in this verse remains unknown because of another lacuna. The translations from the Slavonic in their description of the heavenly king agree on "fear" (or "terror") and "heat" (or "burning"), but not on how these two are combined: fear "of" heat, fear "or" heat? (in 37:1, below, the Coptic connects "[terror]" and "heat" with "and," but in the Slavonic, "of" seems to be dominant). A difference between Coptic and Slavonic appears to be the tense of the verb: "who shall be able to" vs. "who can" endure.

37:1-2 Here, the Coptic version clearly shows that the disputed interpretation "angel of Tartarus" (Forbes and Charles, for which Andersen, according to a footnote accompanying his translation, was "not able to find any basis;" by others translated as "the horror," "the cold" or "terrible, terrifying") is correct. Although I think the idea that this could not be the case, and the angel in question should be an archangel (he is called "elder" or "senior" in the Slavonic texts), being in attendance on the Lord, is somewhat far-fetched, it seems to me it is only logical it should be "one of the angels of Tartarus," with his "appearance like snow," who is given the task to cool down Enoch in the fiery presence of the Lord (39:8, in this version immediately preceding, unlike in the long recension) with "[his hands] like ice." (Literally, the Coptic reads "like a snow" and "like the ice.") The Coptic text, unlike the Slavonic ones, also expressively shows how the angel did this: "he [cooled]" Enoch's "face with" (or: "between") his icy hands, but whether this was added in the Coptic or left out of the Slavonic remains unclear. What is being described here need not have happened at the very end of Enoch's presence with the Lord, where it is located in the text; it could have happened earlier (or even have been going on all the time, as the Coptic imperfect tense suggests) and be told only now in order not to interfere with the description of the more important part of what happened. The Coptic for "that" referring to "heat" can refer back to the preceding "terror" as well, which for reasons of grammar and space could only have had the definite article, "the." Being protected from both terror and heat (see also the comment on 39:8 above) like this, Enoch was able to listen to the words of the Lord, which in the previous chapters he reported to his children (?). In the fragments, there is no place for the Slavonic longer recension's added comparisons after its variant "the fear of the Lord" at the end of v. 1, nor for its extra sentence in v. 2, which interprets what happened in v. 1 as necessary preparation for Enoch's temporary return to humanity, let alone for a parallel of the transition chapter 38, placed between chapters 37 and 39 in the long recension.

40:1 With this verse begins the main part of Enoch's long speech, in which he informs his children about the knowledge he has gained in heaven, partly by hearing about it from the Lord and partly by seeing it for himself. (I tentatively emended "<some things>," based on the Slavonic reading, but this might not be necessary.) Whereas the Slavonic has "my eyes have seen," after "I have seen" in the Coptic, the following lacuna can only be restored "[with my eyes]." Enoch now knows "everything," "from the beginning to the end" as well as "from the end to" what the Slavonic versions apparently call "the renewal" or "the return" (but hardly Enoch's return to earth, as Vaillant/Philonenko interprets it!) and the Coptic seems to call "the rising" or "the resurrection."

40:2-3 At the beginning of his list of the heavenly objects and phenomena he described in his "books," Enoch mentions "all hosts" of heaven, the stars (in the Coptic fragments, lost in the lacuna with the second half of v. 2 and all of v. 3). It is a pity these lists are so poorly preserved, because in combination with the way in which the Coptic here and elsewhere focuses on the nominal object by putting it before the verb, after which it is again expressed in its proper place by means of a resumptive pronoun, this makes it difficult to see whether or not the text is the same as in the Slavonic versions. The present verse, for example, which I reconstructed as closely as possible (see below!) to the Slavonic ("I know [every]thing, [and I have written] in the books the [extent of the heavens, and their] contents I have measured, [and I have come to know] all their hosts"), might also have been interpreted as: "I know [every] thing, [and I have written it (!)] in the books; the [extent of the heavens and their] contents I have measured, [and I have come to know] all their hosts," with "the [extent of the heavens]" as object of "I have measured" rather than of "[I have written] in the books." The Slavonic longer recension is different again: "I know everything, and everything I have written down in books, the heavens and their boundaries and their contents. And all the armies and their movements I have measured" (Andersen/Charlesworth). Actually, the Slavonic short recension is somewhat longer here than the Coptic: in the center of the parallel to "I have written down in the books the extent of the heavens and all that is in them: I have measured their movements and I know their hosts" (Pennington/Sparks), the Coptic has: "[their] contents (cf. Slavonic "all that is in them") I have measured," which looks like a shortened version of "I have written down ... their contents and their movements I have measured," combining the object of the first with the verb of the second part of the sentence, while leaving out the Slavonic "their movements" (as well as "their boundaries" of the longer recension, which should go without saying). I am not sure how to account for this building-block "and their movements" in the Slavonic texts, which in the short recension seems to be used with the heavens or their "contents" and in the long one with their "armies," and is absent from the Coptic. Finally, the "all" in "[and I have come to know] all their hosts" might be a rare or even unique example of the Coptic version providing us with a reading of the Slavonic long recension ("and all the armies and their movements," also with "measured"). As seen above, the short recension simply has "their hosts."

Translation of the Coptic Fragments of 2 Enoch 36:3–42:3

Fragment 2, Verso

40:4 In the lost first part of Enoch's description of the sun, I do not dare to reconstruct the part referring to "its" (or "their"!) "rays" or "faces" (or "face"!) of the Slavonic versions. In the preserved part, the Coptic reads "[its] entire movement" for Slavonic "all its movements" (that is, singular rather than plural) and "and also its names" for "and their names," where it has been suggested (by Vaillant) "its" should be read; in this last instance, the Coptic version confirms an emendation of Slavonic textual criticism.

40:5 The description of the moon is better, but not completely preserved; there does not seem to be enough room in the lacuna in which I restored "[its movements]" to include the Slavonic adjective "daily" as well. The Greek word used for the "waning" of the moon's light seems to be rare (see fig. 3 [in the original publication]). For the Coptic "its alte[rations] I have written," the Slavonic reads "its names I have written," and adds "in the books," but whether this was left out in the Coptic or added in the Slavonic is unclear.

The extra verses 40:6, 7 of the long recension, which appear to be somewhat out of place here, and therefore probably are secondary (v. 6 about measuring time from seasons and years to days, and especially v. 7 about the fruits of the earth), are clearly absent from the Coptic version.

40:8 In the description of the clouds, the Coptic refers to their "dwelling place" and their "mouth," in the singular, whereas the Slavonic uses the plural and seems to take "mouths" sometimes not literally, but as "organization" or "ruler." In my translation I have given a clear-cut transition to the next verse, but the two sentences could also be connected by the unexpressed "(and)."

40:9 Also in the case of the sound(s) (proof of work in progress: I have not yet been able to find a Coptic equivalent to "rumblings") and wonder(s) of thunder(bolts) and lightning(s), Coptic and Slavonic go their separate ways, this time Coptic using the plural and Slavonic the singular, but as in the previous verse, this might very well be a matter of idiom and need not reflect any real differences in the underlying text. A very interesting case is the second sentence of the present verse. Here, the translations from the Slavonic, "And they showed me their custodians" (Pennington/Sparks) and "And I have been shown their keepers" (Andersen/Charlesworth) suggest to me a passive construction also possible in Coptic. But in the Coptic version, beginning "[They] showed them to me" ("them" referring back to the thunderbolts and lightnings), the pronominal subject "[they]" of the verb is identified with the help of a focus particle following it, which I translated "that is." Although damaged, probably "their" can be read, and the word following it in the lacuna can only have been "custodians" or "keepers." So, instead of "they" (who? guiding and interpreting angels?) showing to Enoch the custodians of thunderbolts and lightnings after having shown him thunder and lightning itself, "their [custodians]" themselves showed him the above-mentioned sounds and wonders of what they are guarding. Which seems to make sense (too). It would be interesting to find out whether the Slavonic can also be read in this way or whether an intermediate Greek *Vorlage* could explain both readings. According to the Slavonic versions, thunder and lightning are going, or being brought, first up then down (but see below), where maybe the opposite might be expected, from the perspective of their heavenly storehouse(s). Unfortunately, the Coptic cannot help us here. It clearly reads "their place of going up" first, but of the supposedly following "and their place of going down," the "and" and the possessive part of the article "their" seem to be left out (forgotten?) by the copyist, and the word for "place" is damaged (but the only source for this passage is Plumley's transcription, so maybe it was he who made a mistake here). And in the more detailed description of the process immediately afterwards, the words for "up" and "down" and their order are lost in another lacuna, which also prevents us from learning how the Coptic version expressed the Slavonic "by means of a chain" or (according to Pennington/Sparks) "bound." The Slavonic short recension does not include "and their place of going down" (the long has "going in" and "going out," again maybe not the order one might expect—also in 40:4, about the sun). Although the preserved Coptic text appears to be somewhat strange here, the length of the following lacuna would suggest that something like it was there. In this case, the evidence of these fragments cannot do more than show that there might be something wrong in both the Coptic and the Slavonic versions. In the damaged last part of the verse, "lest they turn themselves aside" does not look like an exact parallel to "lest they tear down the clouds," and the last surviving word, "rough," rather reminds one of v. 11 later on, "lest they shake the earth with a rough breath," unless this be the adjective describing the violence with which escaped thunder and lightning might break through the clouds and destroy everything on earth.

40:10 The next verse, describing Enoch's visit to the treasuries of snow, ice, and cold airs, is almost completely lost in the Coptic fragments, and only its beginning could be reconstructed, thanks to two surviving letters of the word for "ice," transcribed by Plumley.

Fragment 3, Recto

40:11 The entire first part of the following verse is also lost, but can be reconstructed with some confidence at least in the translation, in order to indicate that it is the winds being carefully checked with balances and measures before their custodians release them over the world. The words "and measures ... on the balance," present in other manuscripts, are said to be absent from the oldest Slavonic manuscript U; that this is indeed a (*homoioteleuton*) mistake is shown by the presence of this phrase in Coptic. Apparently manuscripts A and U read "he" (who?) "puts" rather than "they put" (in A: the winds on the balance and in the measure); that this is an inferior reading is confirmed by the Coptic version. For the winds' "rough breath," see the comment on v. 9 above.

40:12 This verse is again very damaged, but the gaps can be more or less easily filled with Coptic equivalents to the elements of the Slavonic short recension; there clearly is no place for Enoch's measuring of all the earth, and of all creation from the seventh heaven to the lowermost hell, the detour used by the long recension to arrive at the beginning of the following verse. Although there seems to be too much room in the lacuna to fit in the exact equivalent of the Slavonic "And I was taken" (in my reconstruction, I therefore tentatively add "then"), the presence of the word "down" in the preserved part of the verse proves that there was no need for Vaillant to suspect that "they made me descend" is a mistake for "they conducted me," unless indeed both the Coptic and the Slavonic manuscripts stem from a common mistaken *Vorlage*.

40:13 One of the greatest disappointments of these Coptic fragments must be that, because of yet another lacuna, they do not solve the riddle of the present verse, in which Enoch, next to "hell open" also sees either "something more" (Merilo Pravednoe) or "a certain plain" or the like (Slavonic 2 Enoch proper). However, the gap seems to be too large for just the equivalent of "something more" and I tentatively reconstructed "a certain plain." Also in the case of the choice between "judgment place" (Pennington/Sparks) and mere "judgment" (all other translators), I chose the former as the longer option.

41:1, 2 This short chapter, in which Enoch wept over the perdition of the impious, is completely lost in the Coptic fragments, but it probably did not contain the mention of Enoch seeing all of his ancestors, including Adam and Eve, which is present in the Slavonic long recension.

42:1 Also the beginning of the next chapter, introducing "the keepers of the keys of hell" with their frightening looks, to whom Enoch addresses himself in the next verse, is lost.

Fragment 3, Verso

42:2 In the Slavonic versions (by means of equivalents of "it would be well" suspected to be corrupt by Pennington/Sparks), Enoch "openly" (for which there is no place in the Coptic lacuna) says he would have preferred never to have seen (or heard of?) hell's doorkeepers and their "activities," and expresses the wish that none of his kinsmen (or: members of his tribe) need ever meet them. It is unclear whether in the Coptic there was something more (unparalleled in Slavonic) in between the two parts of the sentence or not; there might just have been room for one or two words in the lacuna. Parallel to the "activities" in the first part and unparalleled in the second (with Enoch's "descendants" rather than people of the same or earlier generations) are the Coptic references to seeing the doorkeepers' apparently frightening "chambers" (or "storehouses"). Once again, it hardly needs to be said, the additions of the long recension (eternal punishment for even small sins) are absent also here.

42:3 There seems to be too much room in the lacuna at the beginning of this verse for merely accommodating "And [from]"; maybe we could read "And [I was taken away from] that place (and) went . . . ," which however does not have a parallel in the Slavonic manuscripts. The letters here interpreted as part of "And" could also be the perfect tense and subject part of the passive construction "They took me" (meaning: "I was taken") which otherwise would be all lost. Before the text of our three Coptic fragments finally breaks off, we get a glimpse of the happier part following in the rest of this chapter, in which Enoch visits "[the paradi]se of righteousness," which in Slavonic is called "the paradise of the righteous." The description of what Enoch saw here is much damaged, but again, the text lost in the lacunae can be restored using the parallel text of the Slavonic short recension.

Conclusion

Although the three fragments of the Qasr Ibrim manuscript containing a copy of a Coptic translation of "Slavonic Enoch" introduced, translated, and commented upon above represent only a small portion of the original codex, they contain one of the most interesting parts of 2 Enoch one could have wished for, the chapters 36–42, with the transition between two of the three main parts of the work: Enoch's heavenly tour with its revelations of the secrets of creation and his brief return to earth before finally assuming his task back in heaven. Because they are witnesses of precisely these chapters, in which the short and the long recensions of the Slavonic manuscript tradition show so many major differences, there can be no doubt that the Coptic version represents a text of the standard short recension, without chapter 38 and the other "additions" of the long recension, with chapters 37 and 39 in the order 39 then 37 between chapters 36 and 40, and including the "minuses" absent in the Slavonic very short recension. The Coptic fragments also contain the allegedly "extra" material at the end of chapter 36 which the oldest Slavonic manuscript U contains and the great majority of the later manuscripts do not. In fact, the Coptic version seems to be very close to the text of MS U as translated by Pennington/Sparks; the variants observed do not seem to be larger in number or more serious in nature than the inner-Slavonic ones. The only exception to this, a major difference remarkable indeed, is the apparent absence of the "you see my . . ." clauses in the "you see my . . . , but I have seen the Lord's . . ." ("face," etc.) part of chapter 39. In general, the Coptic text is quite fragmentarily preserved, but it proved to be possible to reconstruct part of its missing contents using (translations of) the Slavonic versions, and several theories about 2 Enoch formulated by Slavists and theologians have already been confirmed or proven wrong.

Recently, the priority of the longer recension has been advocated (again). But the discovery of this first non-Slavonic witness, at the same time the oldest manuscript of the work known so far, calls for renewed discussion of this matter. Although I sympathize with Andersen's remark "the long recension is more logical whether original or not" (in his comments on chaps. 37–39), the evidence of the short recension, especially that of the oldest Slavonic manuscript U, has to be taken more seriously (again) from now on. No final conclusions, however, can be based on the new evidence provided by the Coptic fragments. The facts now available can still be interpreted in more than one way and need not indicate the priority of the short recension, even though that might now seem more likely than before. Whatever was the original version of the text could already have split up into the two main recensions in the original Greek (on which, see below); if the long one was the first, whatever happened to it to make it short could have happened already before this secondary, short recension was translated into Coptic; and maybe also the long recension was translated into Coptic, but does not survive . . .

The Coptic fragments of 2 Enoch from Qasr Ibrim have been preliminarily dated, on palaeographical grounds, to the eighth–tenth centuries; archaeological evidence might be able to limit this period to about its first half. This would mean that the fragments antedate the accepted moment of the translation of 2 Enoch into Slavonic (tenth, eleventh century) and that they are about half a millennium older than the earliest Slavonic witness, a copy of the work Merilo Pravednoe (fourteenth century) and the earliest surviving manuscript of "Slavonic Enoch" proper (fifteenth century).

The Coptic 2 Enoch manuscript presented here appears to be part of the remains of a church library, found among fragments from copies of biblical books and hagiographical texts like the Martyrdom of Saint Mark the Evangelist, legendary founder of the Patriarchate of Alexandria. We can now read anew the late-antique and medieval texts mentioning Enoch from the Christian continuum of northeast Africa (Egypt, Nubia, and Ethiopia), with the knowledge that at least some of their authors, copyists, and readers also had 2 Enoch available to them, a work certainly tying in well with the fervent interest in angelology and popular theological speculation of the region.

How, when, and where the Coptic version of 2 Enoch came into being must remain unknown. For most Coptic texts, a translation from a Greek original is taken for granted, as it is for 2 Enoch in its Slavonic versions. The existence of a Coptic incarnation of the work might well confirm the assumption of a Greek original of 2 Enoch, from Egypt, probably Alexandria; in fact it is only the discovery of these Coptic fragments which finally proves that the other theory, long abandoned by most scholars, according to which 2 Enoch might be of medieval date and Slavonic, maybe even Bogomile, origin, cannot be valid. Translations from Greek into both Coptic and Slavonic, and a distribution from Alexandria both southwards to Coptic-speaking Egypt and Nubia and northwards to the Slavonic-speaking world seem very likely. As for the attribution of such an original to Alexandrian Jews in the first century, I am in no position to give an opinion here and can only say that experience has taught me to be wary when people try to postulate early originals for texts in late manuscripts. From fourteenth-century "Slavonia" to first-century Alexandria seems a long distance, and the newly discovered milestone from eighth–tenth-century Qasr Ibrim is not yet even halfway. For the time being it seems to me very important to study 2 Enoch from scratch, as it were, both in its already well-known Slavonic context and in its newly discovered context of the Coptic from Egypt and Nubia. Only when all the evidence, old and new, of the available manuscripts (which essentially is all there is after all) has been sufficiently investigated is it time to look at the (thus also better-established) contents of the work again, and see how far it can be connected to first-century, Second Temple Judaism.

One of the results of the presentation of my discovery at the 2009 Enoch Seminar in Naples was the kind and almost immediate acceptance by those present of the statement in my title, "No Longer 'Slavonic' Only." Now that we also have this work "attested in Coptic from Nubia," it is more appropriate to refer to it only by its other name of "2 Enoch," locating it between "Ethiopic" 1 Enoch and Hebrew 3 Enoch. If my position as the one who rediscovered, that is, identified, the Coptic fragments of 2 Enoch entitles me to make a few recommendations more, I would suggest to look again at the inner-Slavonic textual variants in light of the readings on the Coptic fragments, and plead for further publication and translation of actual Slavonic manuscripts, not yet postulated recensions, faithfully reproducing their evidence, not adapting them to the standard of others, and translating as literally as possible. Especially a new English translation of and a list of inner-Slavonic variant readings in chapters 36–42 would be very helpful for a more detailed comparison with the Coptic text, as well as for the eventual reconstruction of the Greek *Vorlage* of (this part of) the work. My own commitment is first of all to publish the Coptic text of the Qasr Ibrim fragments as part of my doctoral dissertation, sometime before the end of 2013, but I would be very willing also before that to work with Slavists and other scholars to further explore "the secrets of Enoch."

The Book of Giants: General Introduction

by James R. Davila

The text commonly referred to today as the Book of Giants is found in two versions: one known from Qumran manuscript fragments and written in Aramaic and one known from fragments found in northeastern Xinjiang, formerly known as Chinese Turkestan, and written in three old Iranian languages and in Old Turkic (Uyghur). The Iranian Book of Giants was one of the canonical books of Mani (ca. 216–276 or 277 CE), who founded his own religion, Manicheism.

The storyline of the Book of Giants is closely related to that of the Book of the Watchers (1 En. 1–36) and harkens back to Gen 6, with its story of the "sons of God" who noticed human females and took their wives from among them and sired on them the *gibborim*. This was also, we are told, the time when the *nephilim* appeared on earth. We are further told that, after this, human wickedness was great on the earth and the earth was filled with violence (Gen 6:5, 11).

This is the basis for the Book of the Watchers, as well as the Aramaic and Manichean Book of Giants, which contain many of the same themes. Here, too, we are told of the descent of heavenly beings to earth, the Nephilim in the Aramaic book, "the aborted ones" in the Manichean book, and, in the Book of Enoch, "watchers," attracted by the beauty of the women. Their offspring were the Aramaic *gabbarim* and the Iranian *kay*s (Old Turkic *alp*), commonly understood since antiquity as "giants," but more probably "heroes (of war)." The Book of Giants then gives us fragments of the story of these two classes of divine and half-divine beings and their troubles and infighting until the four archangels were sent down to earth to incite them to destroy each other in a great war. Like the Book of the Watchers, the Book of Giants contains several descriptions of heavenly journeys, but they are undertaken by one or more of the giants, rather than by Enoch, in both the Aramaic and the Manichean versions.

Since both versions of the Book of Giants are extremely fragmentary and overlap each other to a small degree only, the book can only be reconstructed in part, and many large gaps in both the texts and our understanding of the surviving fragments remain. Fortunately, however, the Coptic Manichean sources frequently refer to the story in some detail, and later Christian and Arabic authors mention the book by its title and refer to and sometimes summarize the contents. These provide some background and allow us to fill in some of the gaps.

Due to its fragmentary nature, identifying and reading the extant material can be quite difficult, and determining the order of the fragments without knowing more of the storyline, is a daunting task, although physical clues, such as the shape of the fragments or the remains of two columns of a scroll on a single fragment, can help. Many scholars have labored to produce what is presented here. In the end, we must try to infer the order of events based on clues in the incomplete and disconnected narratives of the surviving bits, a precarious process at best, but cautious evaluation of all the evidence gives us some idea of the storyline of the Book of Giants.

Very few fragments of the Aramaic Book of Giants manuscripts contain even relatively complete blocks of text, while there are also a few complete, or almost complete, folios of the Manichean book.

At the end of this introduction is an attempt at a more detailed reconstruction of the story, based on all the evidence and giving specific references to the relevant fragments in all surviving versions of the story. In their chapters Loren Stuckenbruck also offers a detailed reconstruction of the Aramaic original and Prods Oktor Skjærvø of the Manichean version.

For details of all of the above, see the introductions to the Aramaic, Iranian, and Old Turkic texts in the chapters that follow.

Contents

The Book of Giants was written in the late Second Temple period in Aramaic. The book was entirely lost in all its versions for some centuries. This summary draws on all versions and sources to reconstruct a coherent narrative. For details of what is found in each version, see the final section of this introduction.

The original Aramaic book seems to have opened with an account of the descent of the Watchers from heaven and their interbreeding with mortal women, resulting in the birth of the giants. (The Manichean version probably prefaced this with a prologue that recounted the latter part of Mani's cosmology and the story of Adam and Eve.) The Watcher Shemihazah then fathered two giant sons, Ohyah and Ahyah, while the Watcher Baraq'el fathered the giant Māhaway. The race of giants enslaved and slaughtered human beings and inflicted ruin on the natural order. Human beings then called on God and the archangels for help. Ohyah and Ahyah seem each to have had a dream. Māhaway traveled to the distant realm where Enoch lived in order to consult with him. In the Turkic version, Enoch seems to have warned him to descend from the air before his wings caught fire. Enoch interpreted the dreams. There is mention of two stone tablets, the second of which bore a message from Enoch. It foretold the defeat of the Watchers and the destructions of the giants. The giants were demoralized by this message, but then a message from the giants Hobabish and Gilgamesh somehow cheered them up.[1] According to the Manichean version, Māhaway went to Atanbish (Utnapishtim?) and told him everything.

Ohyah and Ahyah had another pair of dreams, which they described in the assembly of the giants. Once again, Māhaway flew to Enoch to ask for his interpretation. The Watchers promised to repent and asked Enoch for mercy. But once again, Enoch warned them that they faced imminent ruin. He also referred to a time of blessing coming after the Flood. The placeable fragments of the Aramaic Book of Giants end here. It is uncertain how much of the narrative that follows in the Manichean version was also in the original Aramaic.

---

1. See Prods Oktor Skjaervø's discussion of the nuances of the relevant terms in the Manichean tradition in his introduction to the Manichean book in this volume, section "The Title of the Manichean Book of Giants." In that tradition these figures may be "valorous warriors of renown" rather than giants. I retain the term "giants" here for simplicity's sake.

The Manichean Book of Giants tells of a final conflict between the Watchers and the angels. The Watchers took the form of human beings and hid among them. Nevertheless, they were detected and separated from real humans and from the giants. Some of the giants or their children seem to have been led to safety in towns prepared for them. A battle between the four archangels and the Watchers followed. Atanbish was involved and there were casualties on both sides. The archangels bound the Watchers in a dark prison. Ohyah did battle with the primordial monster Leviathan and then with the archangel Raphael. This version probably closed with an epilogue that taught Manichean doctrine and gave instruction to lay followers of the religion.

The Two Versions of the Book of Giants

Fragments of the Aramaic original of the Book of Giants were first identified among the Dead Sea Scrolls and published in the 1970s by J. T. Milik.[2] The book was evidently popular among the Qumran sectarians: nine or ten manuscripts of it survive from the Qumran library, more copies than of any of the books that make up 1 Enoch and more copies even than most of the books of the Hebrew Bible. Loren Stuckenbruck describes the manuscripts in more detail in his introduction to the Aramaic version of the book in this volume.

Fragments of the Manichean Book of Giants in three Iranian languages (Middle Persian, Parthian, Sogdian), as well as in Old Turkic (Uyghur) were discovered by German Expeditions to Turfan (located in the northeastern corner of Xinjiang, formerly Chinese Turkistan) in the early twentieth century. Here Buddhism, Manicheism, and Christianity flourished at various times during the first millennium CE and many hundreds of complete and fragmentary Buddhist, Manichean, and Christian manuscripts were recovered from ruins and cave temples.[3]

---

2. Milik, *The Books of Enoch: Aramaic Fragments of Qumrân Cave 4* (Oxford: Clarendon, 1976), 298-339 and pls. XIX, XXX-XXXII. As Milik (298) notes, he first announced the discovery in 1971. Aside from Milik's preliminary publication, the major editions of the Aramaic Book of Giants are: John C. Reeves, *Jewish Lore in Manichaean Cosmogony: Studies in the* Book of Giants *Traditions*, HUCM 14 (Cincinnati: Hebrew Union College Press, 1992) (ch. 2 transcribes and translates the Aramaic fragments published up to 1992 in the context of the relevant Manichean fragments); Klaus Beyer, *Die aramäschen Texte vom Toten Meer: Aramaistische Einleitung, Text, Übersetzung, Deutung, Grammatik* (Göttingen: Vandenhoeck & Ruprecht, 1984), 258-68; and Beyer, *Die aramäschen Texte vom Toten Meer: Ergänzungsband* (Göttingen: Vandenhoeck & Ruprecht, 1994), 119-24 (all of the Aramic fragments); Loren T. Stuckenbruck, *The Book of Giants from Qumran: Texts, Translation and Commentary*, TSAJ 63 (Tübingen: Mohr Siebeck, 1997) (all of the Aramaic fragments); Stephen J. Pfann et al., *Qumran Cave 4.XXVI: Cryptic Texts and Miscellanea, Part 1*, DJD XXXVI (Oxford: Clarendon, 2000), 8-94 (the official edition, by Stuckenbruck, of some of the Aramaic manuscripts); Émile Puech, *Qumrân grotte 4.XXII: Textes Araméens première partie 4Q529-549*, DJD XXXI (Oxford: Clarendon, 2001), 9-115 (the official edition of the rest of the Aramaic manuscripts).

3. The major editions and previous translations of the Manichean fragments are: W. B. Henning, "The Book of the Giants," *BSOAS* 11 (1943-1946): 52-74 (the Manichean fragments in their various original languages and in English translation); Prods Oktor Skjaervø, "Iranian Epic and the Manichean *Book of Giants*: Irano-Manichaica III," *Acta Orientalia Academiae Scientiarum Hungaricae* 48 (1995): 187-223 (includes translations of most of the Manichean fragments); Werner Sundermann, "Ein weiteres Fragment aus Manis Gigantenbuch," in *Orientalia J. Duchesne-Guillemin emerito oblata*, Acta Iranica 23, Hommages et Opera Minora 9 (Leiden: Brill, 1984), 491-505 (an additional fragment in Middle Persian); Enrico Morano, "Il '*Libro dei Giganti*' di Mani," in *Il mito e la dottrina: Testi manichei dell'Asia centrale e della Cina*, vol. 3 of *Il Manicheismo*, ed. Gherardo Gnoli (Milan: Mondadori, 2008), 71-107, 367-73 (an Italian translation of all the Manichean fragments as of 2008); Morano, "Some New Sogdian Fragments Related to Mani's *Book of Giants* and the Problem of the Influence of Jewish Enochic Literature," in *Ancient Tales*

The Book of Giants: General Introduction

Literary Context
Literary Background
Mesopotamian traditions about Gilgamesh are the earliest known influences on the Book of Giants.[4] Gilgamesh was a legendary figure in Sumerian and Akkadian literature, best known from the Epic of Gilgamesh, a work whose importance in ancient Mesopotamia was comparable to that of the Homeric epics in ancient Greece. It told the story of Gilgamesh, the ancient king of the Mesopotamian city-state Uruk. Gilgamesh befriended the wildman Enkidu. They had adventures, notably the defeat of the monster Humbaba of the Cedar Forest, until Enkidu's untimely death at the hands of the goddess Ishtar. Distraught by the loss of his friend, Gilgamesh set out to find the secret of eternal life. He went on a quest to consult with Utnapishtim, the Babylonian Noah figure and the only man to survive the great flood. The gods gave Utnapishtim and his wife eternal life. But Gilgamesh was unable to achieve immortality for himself. He had to be content with his own great reputation for his vast accomplishments.[5]

Gilgamesh, Humbaba, and perhaps Utnapishtim appear as characters in the Book of Giants. Gilgamesh and Humbaba (Hobabish) seem to be giants in the Aramaic version, and Utnapishtim (Atanbish) may be a giant or Enoch himself in the Manichean version. The Book of Giants has no direct references to the events in the Epic of Gilgamesh, but there are hints that the author was familiar with elements of it. In both the Aramaic Book of Giants and the epic, Gilgamesh was a semidivine being associated with dreams that foretold disaster. Both present Gilgamesh and Humbaba/Hobabish as giant warriors. In the Epic of Gilgamesh, Humbaba is associated with Mount Hermon in Lebanon. The site is important also in the Enochic version of the story of the Watchers and the giants (cf. 1 En. 6:6; 13:7–9). It very likely figured in the Book of Giants as well.[6] In Mesopotamian tradition Gilgamesh became a judge in the underworld, and in the giants traditions in the Book of Giants and the Enochic literature the giants became disembodied demonic forces after their deaths who afflict human beings with illness and suffering (1 En. 15:8–16:1; Jub. 10:1–14). It is possible that the author of the Book of Giants knew the Epic of Gilgamesh in a late Aramaic translation, but it is no less likely that the author was working with oral traditions about Gilgamesh.[7]

The most important influence on the Book of Giants was the legend of the Watchers and their offspring preserved mainly in the Enochic literature, especially the Book of the Watchers (1 En. 1–36) and the Similitudes of Enoch (1 En. 37–71). There are also references to the story in the Book of Dream Visions (1 En. 83–90). Outside the Enochic

---

of Giants from Qumran and Turfan: Contexts, Traditions, and Influences, ed. Matthew Goff, Loren T. Stuckenbruck, and Enrico Morano, WUNT 360 (Tübingen: Mohr Siebeck, 2016), 187–98. For additional small Manichean fragments see the complete list in Morano, "New Research on Mani's Book of Giants," in *Der östliche Manichäismus Gattungs- und Werksgeschichte; Vorträge des Göttinger Symposiums vom 4.–5. März 2010*, ed. Zekine Özerturla and Jens Wilkens, Abhandlungen der Akademie der Wissenschaften zu Göttingen NS 17 (Berlin: de Gruyter, 2011), 101–111, esp. 106–8.

4. For discussions of the manuscripts, date, provenance, genre, and structure of the Aramaic and Manichean versions of the Book of Giants, see the introductions to the chapters by Loren Stuckenbruck, Prods Oktor Skjærvø, and Peter Zieme, which follow.

5. For an English translation, see Andrew George, *The Epic of Gilgamesh: The Babylonian Epic Poem and Other Texts in Akkadian and Sumerian* (London: Penguin, 1999).

6. See the discussion of Turkic fragment A by Zieme below in his translation.

7. Matthew Goff, "Gilgamesh the Giant: The Qumran *Book of Giants*' Appropriation of *Gilgamesh* Motifs," *DSD* 16 (2009): 221–53, doi:10.1163/156851709X395740.

literature the story is mentioned in the Book of Jubilees and occasionally in the Dead Sea Scrolls.[8]

The versions of the Enochic legend of the Watchers vary slightly among themselves, but the basic narrative is something like the following: The Watchers were a group of angels whose job was to worship God unsleepingly and to guard his throne (1 En. 14:23; 39:12–13; 71:7). A group of Watchers descended to earth, either with good intention to teach humankind righteously (Jub. 4:15) or because from heaven they saw mortal women and desired to mate with them (1 En. 6:1–2; 39:1; 86:1–3). The chief of the fallen Watchers was Shemihazah (1 En. 6:3; 69:2) or Azazel (1 En. 54:5; 55:4; or Asa'el; cf. 1 En. 9:6) and some of their other leaders are named (1 En. 6:7–8; 8:3; 69:2–13). Once on earth they taught mortals how to make weaponry, jewelry, and makeup, as well as secrets of metallurgy, sorcery, and astrology (1 En. 7:1; 8:1–4; 9:6–8; 64:2; 65:6–7). The unions of the angels with mortal women resulted in the birth of monstrous cannibalistic giants who brought ruin to the earth (1 En. 7:2–6; 9:9; 86:4–6).

The four archangels brought the situation to the attention of God, who ordered them to intervene (1 En. 9:1–10:3). They subdued the fallen Watchers and banished them to a deep abyss where they lie chained, awaiting their fiery judgment at the eschaton (1 En. 10:4–8, 11–14; 54:1–6; 67:4–11; 69:28; 88:1–3; 90:21, 23–24). The archangels also incited the giants to take up a war against one another until all (or nearly all?) of them were dead (1 En. 10:9–10, 12, 15; 56:2–4?; 87:1, 4; 88:2). Some of them also seem to have died in the great flood (1 En. 89:6), which took place after these events. Perhaps some even survived beyond the Flood (see below). In any case the disembodied spirits of the dead giants, or some of them at any rate (Jub. 10:1–14), survived as demonic forces that afflict human beings with illness and suffering (1 En. 15:8–16:1). This story is assumed as the background of the narrative in the Book of Giants.

Some of the traditions in the Bible also provide background to the Book of Giants, although it is unclear whether any of these traditions actually influenced it directly. The enigmatic episode in Gen 6:1–4 almost certainly has some connection with the story of the Watchers and the giants. This passage tells us that before the Flood "the sons of God" (i.e., the angels; cf. Job 1:6; 2:1) saw the beauty of human women and took some of them as wives. This seems to have displeased YHWH, who in turn placed a time limit of one hundred twenty years on the spirit dwelling in human beings. We are also told that the "Nephilim" lived at the time (and also "afterward") when the sons of God were mating with the mortal women who bore children to them. And we are told that these Nephilim were famous warriors.

What does all this mean? Why did angels behave in this way, unparalleled elsewhere in the Hebrew Bible? On what is the one hundred twenty years a time limit? Who are the Nephilim? The word comes from a root meaning to fall ("fallen ones?") and in later Hebrew it means "abortions." Were the Nephilim the same creatures as the offspring of the mortal women by the angels? The text may imply they were, but it does not say so explicitly.

One possibility is that the writer of Genesis knew some version of the story of the Watchers and the giants, whether the one now found in the Book of the Watchers or a

---

8. The best English translation of 1 Enoch is George W. E. Nickelsburg and James C. VanderKam, *1 Enoch: A New Translation Based on the Hermeneia Commentary* (Minneapolis: Fortress, 2012). For a convenient translation of Jubilees, see O. S. Wintermute, "Jubilees," *OTP* 2:35–142. For the relevant passages in the Dead Sea Scrolls, see the chapter on the Aramaic Book of Giants by Stuckenbruck in this volume.

common tradition shared by it. The mythological notion of gods mating with human beings may not have appealed to the writer of Genesis, but the story was too well known to ignore. So the writer gave just a brief and allusive account before moving on to the Flood narrative. Another possibility is that Gen 6:1–4 was the inspiration for the story of the Watchers and the giants. Subsequent exegetes pondered the puzzling details of these four verses and filled in the blanks to produce something like the story we now find in 1 Enoch. Different specialists have argued for each of these possibilities and we need not try to decide between them here.[9]

In the Book of Giants (4Q530 2 ii 16b–20a) one of the giants has what seems to be a predictive dream in which he sees God descend from heaven to earth and occupy a throne, while other thrones are also set up. Books are opened, judgment declared, and God's judgment written down. This passage has close similarities in thought and wording to the throne theophany scene in Dan 7:9–10. It also has notable similarities to the throne theophany in 1 En. 14:18–23, a passage that also shares wording and ideas with Dan 7:9–10. The relationship between the theophanies in Dan 7 and 1 En. 14 has been debated for some time. Milik concluded that the Book of Giants was dependent on Daniel. Some scholars have subsequently challenged his view while others have supported it. There is no consensus on which of the three came first and influenced the others or whether they all drew on an independent written or oral tradition. Again, it suffices for our purposes to note the problem without attempting to solve it.[10]

In addition, there are a number of stories in the Bible about giants.[11] These provide some context for our understanding of the Book of Giants. Although Genesis places the Nephilim in the time before the Flood, it hints that they had a further history. And indeed they appear again in the context of the survey of Canaan by the Israelite spies in Num 13. In 13:32–33 the spies report that the people of the land were of great size and that there the spies saw the Nephilim, whose stature made them feel like grasshoppers. This is the only indication in the Bible that the Nephilim were giants, although this point is also specified in 1 En. 7:2.[12] The passage also mentions in passing that the "Anakim" were descended from the Nephilim. This leads us to another group of biblical giants.[13]

---

9. For the ancient Near Eastern and related background to Gen 6:1–4, see Ronald Hendel, "The Nephilim Were on the Earth: Genesis 6:1–4 and Its Ancient Near Eastern Context," in *The Fall of the Angels*, ed. Christoph Auffarth and Loren T. Stuckenbruck, TBN 6 (Leiden: Brill, 2004), 11–34. For a discussion of Gen 6:1–4 and its relation to the Watchers tradition, see Chris Seeman, "The Watchers Traditions and Gen 6:1–4 (MT and LXX)," in *The Watchers in Jewish and Christian Traditions*, ed. Angela Kim Harkins, Kelley Coblentz Bautch, and John C. Endress (Minneapolis: Fortress, 2014), 25–38, doi:10.2307/j.ctt22nmb25.6.

10. For a discussion with bibliography, see Amanda M. Davis Bledsoe, "Throne Theophanies, Dream Visions, and Righteous(?) Seers: Daniel, the *Book of Giants*, and *1 Enoch* Reconsidered," in Goff, Stuckenbruck, and Morano, *Ancient Tales of Giants*, 81–96.

11. The biblical references to giants are covered in detail in Brian R. Doak, *The Last of the Rephaim: Conquest and Cataclysm in the Heroic Ages of Ancient Israel*, Ilex Foundation Series 7 (Boston: Ilex Foundation; Washington, DC: Center for Hellenic Studies, 2012). For a summary see Doak, "The Giants in a Thousand Years: Tracing Narratives of Gigantism in the Hebrew Bible and Beyond," in Goff, Stuckenbruck, and Morano, *Ancient Tales of Giants*, 13–32.

12. In Ezek 32:27 there is a reference to "fallen warriors of old" in the underworld (Sheol). The phrase could also be read as "warrior Nephilim of old" and this may have been its original meaning. The dual sense of Nephilim as ancient warriors and as ghosts coheres well with the biblical sense of Rephaim with whom they are associated (see below).

13. Deuteronomy 1:28 also refers to the report by the spies that the people of the land were

The first mention of the Anakim in the Bible is also in the story of the Israelite spies. Numbers 13:22 reports that the spies also encountered the children of Anak in Hebron and it mentions three of them by name. Then, in his account of the invasion of the land by the Israelites, Moses comments in an aside that the "Emim" had once inhabited Moab and that they were as tall as the Anakim and, like the Anakim, were reckoned as "Rephaim." Likewise, he says that the land of the Ammonites was reckoned as a land of the Rephaim (whom the Ammonites called "Zamzumim"), because formerly the Rephaim inhabited it (Deut 2:10–11, 19–21). Deuteronomy 9:2 also reinforces the strength and stature of the Anakim.

The name Rephaim leads us still further. It can mean something more or less equivalent to "ghost" (e.g., Prov 21:16; Isa 14:9), but it usually refers to a group of people who inhabited Canaan before the Israelites did. Notably, one of the few named giants in the Bible—Og King of Bashan—is called the last of the Rephaim in Deut 3:11. The description of Og's enormous bed makes it clear that he too was a giant.[14]

By far the most famous biblical giant is, of course, Goliath of Gath, whose downfall at the hands of David is familiar from 1 Sam 17. Goliath was a Philistine, but he too is connected with the primordial Rephaim. In 2 Sam 21:15–22 we find a collection of brief stories about four Philistine warriors who were descended of Rapha, that is, were among the Rephaim. One named Ishbi-benob carried an enormous spear and so presumably was a giant. He nearly killed David in battle, but another Israelite intervened and killed the Philistine.[15] Another named Saph was slain by an Israelite in a battle at Gob. Then there is an alternate account of the killing of Goliath the Gittite by one Elhanan son of Jaare-oregim the Bethlehemite.[16] The fourth was an unnamed man of great stature who had six fingers on his hands and six toes on his feet. He was slain by a nephew of David. Three of these four are presented as large men, confirming the identification of the Rephaim with giants.[17]

---

powerful and tall and that they saw the children of the Anakim there. It does not, however, mention the Nephilim.

14. It was argued by Wolfgang Rölling that an ancient Phoenician grave inscription from Byblos (Byblos 13) also mentions Og. Rölling, "Eine neue phoenizische Inscrift aus Byblos," *Neue Ephemeris für Semitische Epigraphik* 2 (1974): 1–15 and pl. 1. The inscription dates to about 500 BCE and invokes a curse on anyone who disturbs the bones of the occupant of the grave. The suggestion is interesting, but it involves a number of philological difficulties. Subsequent analysis of the inscription, including by Röllig, has not found this interpretation to be credible. For a review of the scholarship see Laura Quick, "Laying Og to Rest: Deuteronomy 3 and the Making of a Myth," *Bib* 98 (2017): 161–72, esp. 170–71. The legend of Og the giant continued to develop in the postbiblical period through late antiquity, the Middle Ages, and even into the modern period. For a survey of the Og legend see Admiel Kosman, "The Story of a Giant Story: The Winding Way of Og King of Bashan in the Jewish Haggadic Tradition," *HUCA* 73 (2002): 157–90.

15. This episode is omitted in the parallel passage in 1 Chr 20:4–8, but cf. n. 21 below.

16. The parallel passage in 1 Chr 20:5 says that Elhanan slew *Lahmi the brother* of Goliath. The difference between the Hebrew texts of the two passages is slight and it is difficult to tell which is original. The passage in 1 Samuel may have accidently been miscopied so that it refers to Goliath rather than his brother. Or the Chronicler may have accidentally or deliberately miscopied the text so that it now refers to Goliath's brother, not Goliath himself, thus resolving the contradiction with 1 Sam 17. In any case, both versions imply Goliath's descent from the Rephaim.

17. The alphabetic cuneiform texts from Ugarit, a city in Syria in the late second millennium BCE, provide some background information on the Rephaim. The Ugaritic language is closely related to Hebrew and the Ugaritic texts refer from time to time to the *rāpi'ūma*. These appear to be the deceased spirits of ancestral kings. This meaning has similarities to the biblical usage of Rephaim, which can mean either the ancient inhabitants of Palestine or the ghosts of the dead. In both usages they are sometimes

Finally, in 1 Chr 11:22–23, we read of an Egyptian giant who also carried a huge spear. He was killed with his own weapon by one of David's chief warriors.

The Greek Bible also has a number of references to "giants" (Greek *gigas*).[18] Some of the uses of the words in the Septuagint (LXX) translation are helpful for understanding how some of the passages in the Hebrew Bible discussed above were understood in the late Second Temple period.[19] The term Nephilim is translated as "giants" in its occurrences in Gen 6:4 and Num 13:33 (LXX 13:34). The Hebrew word *gibbor* normally means "warrior," but sometimes its use in context led the translators to translate it as "giant" (Gen 6:4; 10:8–9, cf. 1 Chr 1:10 [of Nimrod]; Gen 14:5; Ps 19:5 [LXX 18:6]; 33:16 [LXX 32:16]; Isa 3:2; 13:3; 49:24–25; Ezek 32:12, 21, 27;[20] 39:18, 20).

The term Rephaim is frequently, although not always, translated as "giants." Og is called one of the giants in Josh 12:4 and 13:12, although Rephaim is transliterated as *Raphain* in Deut 3:11. Likewise, the word Rapha is transliterated into Greek letters all four times in 2 Sam 21:15–22, but 21:22 does specify that they were all giants.[21] The geographical name "the valley of Rephaim" is translated as "the valley of giants" in 1 Chr 11:15 and 14:9, 13. In Prov 21:16; Isa 14:9; and Job 26:5 the meaning of Rephaim in its original context in Hebrew is "ghost," but it is translated as "giants." In Deut 1:28 the term Anakim is translated as "giants." The Greek of Sir 16:7 refers to a revolt of ancient giants but the Hebrew text uses another word that does not normally mean giant. The Greek of Sir 47:4 refers to Goliath (who is named) as a giant. The Hebrew of this verse does not survive.

There are a few other references to giants in books of the Greek Bible that were composed in Greek or whose Hebrew originals are entirely lost. There is mention of the doom of the ancient giants before the Flood in Wis 14:6 and 3 Mac 2:4. Baruch 3:26 echoes the language of Gen 6:4 when referring to the giants. In her hymn of victory, Judith gloats over the fact that a woman, rather than Titans or giants, vanquished her enemy (Jdt 16:5–6).[22] In 1 Maccabees the poem in praise of Judah the Maccabee says that he "put on a breastplate like a giant" (1 Mac 3:3).

Thus we see that there was a rich mythology of giants in the Hebrew Bible and it continued to develop in the Second Temple period. Space does not permit further discussion of traditions about giants in the Classical world or the ancient Near East, but a few more references to giants in Second Temple Jewish literature should be noted. Sibylline oracles were originally pithy oracles attributed to the Sibyl, a pagan

---

specified as kings. For a detailed review of the Ugaritic evidence and its implications for the biblical word, see Hedwige Rouillard-Bonraisin, "Rephaim," *DDD*, 692–700.

18. For a more detailed discussion of giants traditions in Jewish Greek literature see Michael Tuval, "'Συγωγὴ γιγάντων' (Prov 21:26): The Giants in the Jewish Literature in Greek," in Goff, Stuckenbruck, and Morano, *Ancient Tales of Giants*, 41–57.

19. For an English translation of the Septuagint, see Albert Pietersma and Benjamin G. Wright, eds., *A New English Translation of the Septuagint* (Oxford: Oxford University Press, 2007).

20. The Hebrew word *gibbor*, "warrior," in Ezek 32:21, 27 refers to the dead in the underworld (cf. n. 12 above).

21. The parallel passage in 1 Chr 20:4–8 translates Rapha as "giants" twice and transliterates it once. In 20:8 it too specifies that all "four" were giants, even though only three are mentioned (cf. n. 15 above). The reference to "Dan son of Ioa, from the descendants of the giants [= Rephaim?]" in the Greek text of 2 Sam 21:11 is missing in the Hebrew.

22. For the Titans see Samantha Newington, "Greek Titans and Biblical Giants," in Goff, Stuckenbruck, and Morano, *Ancient Tales of Giants*, 33–40.

prophetess. Some collections of her oracles were known in ancient Rome. They are now almost entirely lost. But Jews and Christians composed many books in the name of the Sibyl in antiquity. The first three books of Sibylline Oracles, of Jewish origin but with some Christian editing and interpolation, provide some passages of interest. Sibylline Oracle 1:87–103 retells the story of the Watchers briefly, but treats them as its third generation of human beings. It mentions giants in 1:123, but it is unclear that they are the giants of the Watchers myth. The seventh generation is identified as Titans, but these are also the human beings who built the Tower of Babel (Sib. Or. 1:307–23). The latter story is much expanded in Sib. Or. 3:97–161. This passage tells a version of the traditional story of the conflict between the Titans and Cronus that led to the birth of Zeus.[23]

The first-century BCE chronographer Alexander Polyhistor refers twice to earlier traditions about Abraham that mention giants. The work of Alexander is lost, but the fourth-century CE historian Eusebius of Caesarea quotes the relevant passages in his *Praep. ev.* 9.17.2–9 and 9.18.2.[24] Alexander attributes the first passage to the Jewish writer Eupolemos, although some think that he was mistaken and that it was written by someone else, possibly a Samaritan. In any case, the passage creatively retells the story of Abraham, prefacing it with an account of the founding of the city Babylon and the building of the Tower of Babel by giants after the Flood. These giants spread over the earth after God destroyed the tower. It also identifies Enoch with Atlas, a Titan. In the second passage Alexander relates that certain anonymous works say that Abraham claimed to be descended from the giants.

The first-century CE Jewish philosopher Philo of Alexandria wrote an entire treatise on Gen 6:1–4 called *On the Giants*.[25] As is his usual practice, he allegorizes the story, making it about the temptation of the soul by worldly pleasures. He cautions his readers that the story is not a myth, hinting that he perhaps knew and disapproved of the story of the Watchers and the giants. But he does not directly refer or allude to that story. The first-century Jewish historian Josephus mentions giants a number of times in his works, mostly following the Greek narrative of the Septuagint. In his treatment of Gen 6:1–4 in *A. J.* 1.72–73 he interprets the passage to say that angels mated with mortal women and that the unions produced offspring. He does not call the latter giants directly, but he hints that he knows of a tradition in which they committed outrages similar to those committed by the giants of Greek mythology. Otherwise, he does not refer directly to the story of the Watchers and the giants, although he does say that the bones of some of the giants mentioned in Num 13:33 were on display in his day (*Ant.* 5.125).

Nothing in the Hebrew Bible, the Greek Bible, or the Jewish traditions in Greek from the Second Temple period surveyed above show any knowledge of the narrative in the Book of Giants. But their wide-ranging interest in the mythology of giants gives us a sense of the broader cultural matrix in which the Book of Giants was composed. On the different, Iranian, context of the Manichean characters, see Skjærvø's introduction to the Manichean book in this volume.

---

23. For an English translation see John J. Collins, "Sibylline Oracles," *OTP* 1:317–472.
24. For an English translation see R. Doran, "Pseudo-Eupolemos," *OTP* 2:873–82.
25. See also Loren T. Stuckenbruck, *The Myth of Rebellious Angels: Studies in Second Temple Judaism and New Testament Texts*, WUNT 335 (Tübingen: Mohr Siebeck, 2014), 131–41.

The Book of Giants: General Introduction

The Transmission of the Book of Giants

We have little knowledge of the transmission of the book in the early centuries CE. If Mani's Book of Giants was written in Syriac (a dialect of Aramaic), it seems likely that he still had access to the original Aramaic Book of Giants in the third century CE.

There is a possible reference to the Book of Giants in the fifth-century Gelasian Decree, a Latin listing of canonical and apocryphal scriptural books. One of the apocryphal works listed is "the Book of the Giant named Ogias, who, it is asserted by heretics, after the Flood fought with a dragon." One might think at first that this Ogias is the biblical Og, but there is no report of Og fighting with a dragon. The Manichean fragments of the Book of Giants, however, do allude to an episode in which the giant Ohyah was in a battle with the biblical dragon Leviathan and the archangel Raphael. It thus seems that Ohyah has been confused with Og and this book must be the Book of Giants, quite possibly the Manichean version. The implication is that it existed in a Latin translation. This may also imply the existence of a Greek translation that was the source of the Latin. Various other references to the book and its contents survive from late antiquity and the early Middle Ages in Greek, Latin, Coptic, and Arabic sources.[26]

The Manichean book was one of Mani's canonical books, which were written by himself and repeatedly copied for the current and new Manichean communities, as the faith expanded. In fact, at various times Manicheism was practiced virtually from the Atlantic to the Pacific Oceans. The extant manuscripts from Turfan may have been copied before and during the rule of the Uyghur Bögü-qaghan, who converted to Manicheism and made it the state religion of the Uyghur Empire from 763 to 840. For details, see Skjærvø's introduction to the Manichean book in this volume.

The latest evidence for the transmission of the Book of Giants is found in a brief Hebrew work known as the Midrash of Shemhazai and Aza'el (cf. Shemihazah and Asa'el in the Watchers story). This midrash is known from several medieval European Jewish sources, the earliest of which is a commentary on Genesis by R. Moses ha-Darshan of Narbonne in the eleventh century.[27]

The collection of traditions in this work has so many parallels to the Book of Giants that it can scarcely be doubted that the authors had access to the Book of Giants in some form, whether it be the Aramaic original, the Manichean version, or oral traditions deriving from one or the other.

Influence of the Book of Giants

It is difficult to trace the influence of the Book of Giants outside the Manichean traditions surveyed by Skjærvø. There are references to the story of the fall of the Watchers and the begetting of the giants in various late-antique and Byzantine works.[28] But these mostly refer to traditions that are found in the Book of the Watchers, although this work has some overlap with the Book of Giants. It is possible that some of these traditions refer to the latter, but in most cases we cannot tell. The following references seem worth mentioning.

---

26. Reeves, *Jewish Lore*, 20–32.

27. Milik edited four manuscripts of this work and translated it into English. See Milik, *Books of Enoch*, 321–29.

28. Annette Yoshiko Reed, *Fallen Angels and the History of Judaism and Christianity: The Reception of Enochic Literature* (Cambridge: Cambridge University Press, 2005).

In the New Testament the Synoptic Gospels show a great deal of interest in the class of evil spirits known as "demons" or "unclean spirits." These creatures possess and afflict human beings. A prominent feature of Jesus's ministry was the exorcism of such spirits from their human hosts. Perhaps surprisingly, there is no reference in the New Testament to the origin of these spirits, but their behavior corresponds to what we would expect from the traditions about them in the Enochic literature and the Book of Giants. According to the latter accounts, the spirits of some or all of the giants survived after their deaths. They retained enough of a connection to the material world for them to be able to afflict human beings. The Synoptics do not offer an etiology of demons and unclean spirits, but they may assume their origin from the giants.[29]

We find a few hints of awareness of the story of the Watchers and the giants in the Synoptics. The insistence of Jesus that the angels in heaven do not marry (Mark 12:25// Matt 22:30//Luke 20:36) may imply his knowledge of a tradition that some angels descended from heaven and did marry mortal women—with disastrous results. In Luke's version of the exorcism of the Gerasene demoniac the demons beg Jesus not to banish them to the abyss (Luke 8:31). In the Enochic literature just such an abyss was prepared for the eschatological punishment of the Watchers and their minions (1 En. 10:11–14; 18:6–19:1; 21:7–10; 54:3–6; 56:1–4). And in Jesus's description of the possession process (Matt 12:43–45), there is an odd aside to the effect that between victims the possessing unclean spirit wanders in "waterless places." It is possible that he alludes to the tradition reflected in 1 En. 15:11 that the damned disembodied spirits of the giants are thirsty. This evidence does not imply that any of the New Testament writers were acquainted with the Book of Giants itself, but it does point to the possibility that their demonology was consistent with the demonology of the story of the Watchers and the giants.

This understanding of the references to demons in the Synoptics is to some degree supported by the demonology of the Testament of Solomon.[30] This is a late-antique Christian exorcism manual written pseudepigraphically in the name of King Solomon. It tells us in 5:3 that the demon Asmodeus had a human mother but was the son of an angel. Another demon presents itself as the spirit of a lustful giant who died in the carnage of the time of giants (17:1).[31] These passages are at least compatible with the myth that the children of the Watchers were giants, but after their deaths they became afflicting demons. That said, the demon Beelzeboul claims to be a fallen angel who evaded imprisonment (6:1–3), so the work's demonology is multifaceted.

The Byzantine chronographer George Syncellus preserved some quotations of the Book of the Watchers in Greek translation. One such passage is of interest here because, although Syncellus attributes it to the Book of the Watchers, the passage that he quotes and paraphrases does not quite correspond to anything found in the Book of the Watchers as we have it now. It says that the mountain on which the Watchers descended is accursed and it will be melted down at the eschaton. It then warns human beings (perhaps to be emended to the Watchers) that their beloved sons (the giants?) are doomed and will die within one hundred twenty years. Milik suggests that Syncellus was

---

29. The reference to the fiery punishment of "the devil and his angels" in the parable of the sheep and the goats in Matt 25:41 sounds more like a reference to the punishment of the Watchers (cf. 1 En. 54:3–6; 55:4; 56:1–4) than to the demons or unclean spirits.

30. For an English translation see D. C. Duling, "Testament of Solomon," *OTP* 1:935–87.

31. Cf. also the huge dog-shaped demon that claims to have once been a very strong man who did much evil in the world (10:1–2).

mistaken and the passage is actually from the Book of Giants.[32] Milik advances some parallels with a Manichean fragment and an Aramaic fragment of the Book of Giants. His suggestion is possible, but it rests on limited evidence and cannot be verified with any confidence at present.

Finally there is one passage in the Babylonian Talmud that shows knowledge of a tradition found in the Book of Giants, but not anywhere in the Enochic literature.[33] In b. Nid. 61a we read that "Sihon and Og were brothers . . . Sihon and Og were the sons of Ahiyah son of Shemihazai." A little later it adds, "This is Og who escaped out of the generation of the Flood." There is a certain amount of confusion here, but "Ahiyah son of Shemihazai" is surely the same as Ahyah, the giant in the Book of Giants who is called the son of Shemhazai (Shemihazah) in the Midrash of Shemhazai and Aza'el. We have seen above that Ahyah's brother Ohyah became confused over time with the better-known biblical giant Og. Such assimilation of a lesser-known figure to a better known one is common in folklore. It is tempting to infer that the filial association of Og with Ahiyah in this passage is a garbled memory of Ohyah and his fraternal relationship with Ahyah. This possibility finds support in the descent of both from the angel Shemihazai and in Og's origin before the Flood.

A Tentative Reconstruction of the Book of Giants

What follows is a provisional attempt to reconstruct the original narrative of the Book of Giants. This is a speculative enterprise at best and some of the ordering is certainly debatable. The siglum "M" refers to the Manichean Book of Giants, with all its forms consolidated. The siglum "A" refers to the Aramaic Book of Giants, with all its manuscripts consolidated. Abbreviations for specific passages are those of Skjærvø in this volume.[34] Entries within square brackets [] are reconstructed on the basis of references to the events elsewhere in the book. The placement of entries within wavy brackets {} is based in general on their content and is more or less speculative.

Mo. The Manichean version probably opened with a prologue that described the begetting of the spiritual "abortions" in Mani's cosmology, followed by their fall to earth and transformation into various kinds of spiritual beings. There followed a version of the story of Adam and Eve. This material was not in the original Aramaic Book of Giants. (0:KawJ Middle Persian; 4:KawX Parthian, 1; 3:KawZs1; 2:KawZs3 Sogdian)

M1. The two hundred demons (Egregoroi—Watchers) descend to earth (5:KawK Sogdian; KawL; KawM; KawP Coptic).

M2. Their descent from heaven stirs up the human beings (5:KawK).

M3 (from an instructional text). On the paths that lead to death: The two paths of the two hundred demons are those of "speech of harm" and "harsh torment" (0:KawJ Middle Persian).

---

32. Milik, *Books of Enoch*, 317–20. For an evaluation of this proposal, see Florentino García Martínez, "The Book of Giants," in *Qumran and Apocalyptic: Studies on the Aramaic Texts from Qumran*, STDJ 9 (Leiden: Brill, 1992), 97–115, esp. 109–10, doi:10.1163/9789004350106.

33. Noted by Milik in *Books of Enoch*, 320–21.

34. Skjærvø's abbreviations are based on those of Morano in "New Research," 105–8. "Zieme D" is not on Morano's list. Zs3 is forthcoming. Morano attempts to reconstruct the Manichean Book of Giants (with some reference to the Aramaic version) on pp. 102–5. My reconstruction of the middle of the work takes more account of the Aramaic evidence and is somewhat different from his and from Skjærvø's.

M4. They descend because of the beauty of earthly women (4:KawX Parthian; cf. Gen 6:2; 1 En. 6:1–2; Jub. 5:1).

M5. They reveal forbidden arts and heavenly mysteries and they bring about ruin on the earth (KawM Coptic; cf. 7:KawH Sogdian; Gen 6:5, 11–12; 1 En. 7–8; 9:8; Jub. 5:2–3).[35]

{M6. They subjugate the human race, killing hundreds of thousands of the righteous in fiery battle. The angels hid Enoch (cf. Gen 5:24; 1 En. 70:1–3; 87:3–4; Jub. 4:21, 23). The Watchers forcibly marry beautiful women, both women elect and women hearers. The nations are set to work.[36] (6:KawAi Middle Persian).}

M7. Shahmīzād (Shemihazah, cf. 1 En. 6:3; 9:7) begets two giant sons, Sāhm (= Sām, Ohyah) and Pād-Sāhm (= Narīmān, Ahyah/Hahyah).[37] The other demons and Yakshas beget the rest of the giants (7:KawH Sogdian; KawO Arabic).

A1. The angelic Watchers beget the rapacious Nephilim and the giants through miscegenation with mortal women. Bloodshed ensues. (4Q531 1; cf. Gen 6:1–4; 1 En. 6:1–7:6; Jub. 5:1).

{M8. Many thousands of the righteous endure burning and Enoch the sage is mentioned (KawQ; KawR Coptic).}[38]

M9. The giants grow up and wreak ruin upon the earth and the human race. The lamentation of humanity reaches up to heaven (cf. A3 [4Q530 1 i 4] and possibly Narīman's dream in 15:KawAg).[39]

A2. The rapacious giants and Nephilim inflict bloodshed and corruption upon the earth and treat sea animals, birds, plants, cattle, and humanity harshly (4Q531 2 + 3; 1Q23 9 + 14 + 15; 4Q532 2?; cf. Gen 6:5, 11–12; 1 En. 7–8; 9:8; Jub. 5:2).

[A3. The spirits of the murdered humans bring a complaint against their killers (inferred from 4Q530 1 i 4—see A15 below; cf. 1 En. 8:4–9:11)].

{M10. Mass suicides occur and the King of Honor sends the four angels down to stop the carnage at the end. (Zieme F; Wilkens Zu3 Uyghur; cf. 1 En. 10:9, 13; 31a:KawZmp1).}[40]

M11. Someone boasts that Sāhm (Ohyah) and his brother will live and rule forever in their unequaled power and strength (KawI Sogdian).[41]

{A4. This bloodshed is reported to Enoch, the scribe (4Q206a 2–3).}[42]

{A5. Enoch (?) addresses God, praising him for his glory, knowledge, strength, and creative acts. (4Q203 9–10).}[43]

---

35. M1–5 belong at the beginning of the narrative.

36. The reference in M6 to the forcible marriage of beautiful women points to 6:KawAi belonging to the early part of the story, as placed here (cf. Henning, "Book of Giants," 63 n. 4).

37. On the names, see Skjærvø's introduction to the Manichean book in this volume, section "Manuscripts and Versions."

38. M8 fits well in the same vicinity as M6–M7, or perhaps after M25.

39. M9 must come after the arrival of the Watchers and the seduction of mortal women. Henning Ag seems to refer to this lamentation (as described retrospectively by Narīmān in his dream). If this interpretation is correct, M9 belongs after M7 and at the same time as M12. M8 fits here plausibly, but could belong elsewhere, e.g., before M7 or at the end of M25.

40. M10 fits this context if the mass suicides are of human beings in despair over their oppression by the giants. But its placement is speculative.

41. M11 fits well somewhere in this vicinity, although its placement is speculative.

42. A4 fits in this context, although it could also go after M25.

43. The wording of A5 is similar to that of 1 En. 84:2–5, where Enoch prays a similar prayer in response to the depredations of the Watchers before the Flood.

The Book of Giants: General Introduction

M12. Yam accepts the homage of humankind as they plead for help (10:KawV Sogdian; cf. 1 En. 9:2–4).[44]

{A6. A number of giants, including Māhaway (who may be the speaker), Hobabish (Humbaba), and ADK[(name damaged), and the Watcher Baraq'el (cf. 1 En. 6:7), have a conversation in which they may discuss killing (4Q203 1–2–3). This could be the same episode as the first part of M15.}

{A7. The giant Aḥiram, several Watchers, the Nephilim, and giants are addressed in an obscure context that involves sinful killing by the sword of one of them, which was like rivers, presumably of blood (4Q531 7). This may refer to the fighting by the giants among themselves mentioned in 1 En. 7:5; 10:9; Jub. 5:7, 9. This too could be the same episode as M15 or it could go with A11–A13.}

{M13. Sām (= Sāhm, Ohyah), Shahmīzād (Shemihazah), and Māhaway have a conversation. There are obscure references to an arrow and bow and a blessing on someone who saw something and did not die.[45] Māhaway mentions his father, Wirōgdād (Baraq'el). Shahmīzād affirms what someone has said. Sām and Māhaway do something that involves a chariot (18:KawAc Middle Persian).}

{M14. Someone gives satisfactory assurance to Māhaway that he will be protected from Sāhm but nevertheless Sāhm and Māhaway fall out and begin to fight (19:KawC Sogdian)}[46]

M15. Wirōgdād (Baraq'el) is mentioned. Hōbābīsh[47] addresses someone (the giant Ahir[am]?) about the abduction of someone's wife. The giants fall out among themselves and begin killing one another (cf. 1 En. 7:5; 10:9). Other creatures do likewise.[48] Sām (Ohyah) and his brother are mentioned and someone or something is bound. It appears that Sām has a dream in which a tablet was thrown in the water. It seems to have borne three signs, portending woe, flight, and destruction. Narīmān (Ahyah) has a dream about a garden full of trees in rows, from which (?) two hundred shoots come out (11:KawAj/R/; 14:KawAj/V/ Middle Persian; cf. 6Q8 frags. 2–3).

{A8. The Midrash of Shemhazai and Aza'el tells a story in which the two sons of Shemhazai (Shemihazah), Heyya (Ohyah), and Aheyya (Hahyah/Ahyah) had dreams. It is possible that this passage preserves some memory of the two dreams in M15. If so, the Aramaic manuscripts of the Book of Giants may preserve a fragment of each dream. The first dream seems to have involved the effacing of a writing-tablet by submerging it in water (2Q26). The first dream may have told of an angel doing the effacing as a symbol of the destruction wrought by the Flood. The second may have told of an angel descending and cutting down all but three shoots (representing the sons of Noah) in the garden.}

M16. Ohyah and Ahyah agree to honor a pledge to their father involving battle and doing something together. The text seems to go on to describe things that are useful in battle and those that are not. Narīmān (Ohyah) tells how he saw (in the dream?) some

---

44. I follow Skjaervø in taking Yam (the Avestan Yima, see Skjærvø's introduction in this volume, n. 90) as representing the King of Honor in Mani's system and God in 1 Enoch ("Iranian Epic," 203–4). If this is correct, M12 corresponds to the praise of God by humans in 1 En. 9:2–4.

45. Or who would not have died if he had seen something.

46. M13 and M14 seem to follow a natural progression and to go well with the conflict of the giants early in M15, but other placements are possible for both.

47. There is also a reference to Hōbābīsh in a fragmentary context in Zs2.

48. 20–21:KawZs4–5 may belong with M15 if they pertain to the falling out of the giants among themselves.

who were weeping and lamenting and many others who were sinful rulers (29:KawAk; 15:KawAg Middle Persian).[49]

[A9. Māhaway is sent to Enoch to consult him for the first time. The episode is entirely lost in Aramaic, but we may infer it was there from the back reference to Māhaway's *first* trip to Enoch in 4Q530 2 ii + 6 + 7 i + 8–11 + 12 lines 22–23, as well as to the reference to his current *second* trip in 7 ii 7. The beginning of the episode is lost in the Manichean versions.]

M17. The giant Māhaway, son of Wirōgdād (Baraq'el), hears a cautioning voice as he flies along at sunrise over Mount Hermon and he is guided to safety by Enoch "the apostle" and the heavenly voice, which warn him to descend before the sun sets his wings on fire (reminiscent of Icarus). He lands and the voice leads him to Enoch (KawB Uyghur).

M18. Enoch interprets a dream, indicating that the trees represent the Watchers and also mentioning the giants who were born of women. Water is drawn (from a well?) (12:KawD Middle Persian).[50]

M19. Sām reports that someone ordered him to bring two stone tablets to his father, but first to send a message to Narīmān (Ahyah), who, it seems, is running intently. The bearer of the tablets has come to read out to the giants something pertaining to them. Shahmīzād (Shemihazah) says to read the document of Enoch the interpreter. (16:KawW).

[A10. The two tablets were also introduced at around this point in the Aramaic version. We infer this from the mention of them in 4Q203 7b ii 2 and 8 3. The revelation of the content of the first tablet is lost in the Aramaic version, but based on the conversations in A14 and A15, Enoch's message may have said that the Watchers and giants would not be forgiven for their sins, but rather would be punished (cf. 1 En. 12:3–13:3).]

{A11. The giants Ohyah and Māhaway have a conversation in which Māhaway tells Ohyah something he heard while in the presence of his (Māhaway's) father, the Watcher Baraq'el. Ohyah responds that he too has heard marvels and he begins to make a comparison involving a sterile woman giving birth (6Q8 1).}[51]

A12. The giants have a conversation in which one of them admits that, despite his own might, he had been unable to prevail in a war against "[a]ll flesh" and some other holy beings who may have been the archangels. Ohyah mentions an oppressive dream that disturbed him. (4Q531 22 1–11).

A13 The giant Gilgamesh says something about "your dream," presumably Ohyah's (4Q531 22 12).[52]

A14. Ohyah tells Hahyah that someone (an archangel?) has punished the Watcher Azazel rather than them. He refers to Watchers and giants and to others who will not be forgiven. Perhaps this idea comes from Enoch's interpretation of the first set of dreams in the lost passage about the first tablet (see A10). Ohyah adds that this person has imprisoned "us" and defeated Hahyah (4Q203 7a–b i; cf. Lev 16:7–10; 1 En. 8:1; 9:6; 10:4–8; 54:5; 55:4).

---

49. M16 is either a continuation of Narīmān's dream in M15, in which case it belongs here, or part of Enoch's interpretation of it. If the latter, it should be placed after M18.
50. M17 and M18 must come after the account of the dreams and in this order.
51. A11 fits in with the content of A12–A14, but its placement is uncertain.
52. A12–A13 are on a single fragment and must take place after Ohyah's dream.

{A15. Another fragment may continue this speech. The speaker refers to the slain who protest against their killers and he says that "we" (the giants?) shall die together. There is further reference to the speaker sleeping, to bread, and to a vision. Someone then enters the assembly of the giants (4Q530 1 i).[53] Perhaps a conversation continues in which the giants anticipate with dread their coming destruction in the Flood for their sins, in which they will be stripped of their form and reduced to being evil spirits (4Q531 19; cf. 1 En. 15:8–12). Again, this conversation may be about elements of Enoch's interpretation of the dreams in the lost passage about the first tablet (see A10; cf. 16:KawW).}

A16. A person is addressed in a conversation, perhaps the same one as in A15. The speaker mentions the two tablets and says that the second has not yet been read (4Q203 7b ii).[54]

A17. Someone reads the second tablet, which is a letter from Enoch the scribe to the Watcher Shemihazah and his companions. There is reference to their action, their wives, and their sexual activity and corruption on the earth, which have come to the attention of the archangel Raphael. Ruin is coming upon the world. Enoch's interpretation (of their dreams or perhaps of the second dream?) is bad for the listeners (the giants?) and he warns them to free their prisoners (cf. the opening of M25) and pray (4Q203 8; cf. 1 En. 9:1).[55]

M20. Sāhm exhorts the other giants to cheer up and eat, but they are too sorrowful to eat and instead fall asleep. Māhaway goes to Atanbīsh (Utnapistim—either one of the giants or another name for Enoch) and tells him all. When Māhaway returns, Sāhm has a dream in which he ascends above heaven. He sees the water of the earth consumed with heat and the demon (?). Wrath comes out of the water. Some radiant beings become invisible. He sees the heavenly rulers (16:KawW Middle Persian).[56]

A18. Ohyah informs the giants of a message from Gilgamesh. Hobabis (the spelling is different in this fragment) is judged, and he (or some guilty person) curses some rulers. This cheers the giants up, but someone curses someone else. (4Q530 2 ii + 6 + 7 col. 1 + 8–11 + 12 (?) lines 1–3a).

A19. Then the two giants Hahyah and Ohyah again have dreams. Hahyah describes his in the assembly of the Nephilim. He dreamed of gardeners watering a garden that produced great shoots. But a fire destroyed the garden. The other giants cannot interpret his dream. It is proposed that they consult Enoch for an interpretation. Then Hahyah's brother, Ohyah, reports that he too had a dream, in which God descended to the earth, thrones were set up, and God sat amid a multitude of angels and presided over a judgment based on the opening of certain books (cf. Dan 7:9–10). The giants, presumably unable to interpret this dream either, summon Māhaway and send him to Enoch, whom he has encountered before, to ask him to interpret the dreams (4Q530 2 ii + 6 + 7 i + 8–11 + 12 (?) lines 3b–24).[57]

---

53. Col. ii has only one readable Aramaic word: "to the mouth." Stuckenbruck places 4Q530 1 i after A17. This is also possible.

54. A14 and A16 are contiguous columns on the same fragment and must come in this order. The events in them must take place after the introduction of the two tablets as reconstructed in A10. The placement of the fragments in A15 is speculative but their content fits the context.

55. A17 must come after A16, in which the second tablet has not yet been read.

56. M19 and M20 are at the bottom of opposite sides of the same page with some lost material between them. A11–A17 fit best between M19/A10 and M20: they seem to cover the giants' discussion of the content of the first tablet, along with the revelation of the content of the second tablet. But if this is correct, the narrative may have been condensed in the Manichean (or at least the Sogdian) version.

57. A18–A19 seem to overlap with the events in M20: both involve Ohyah addressing the giants to cheer them up (unsuccessfully in M20 and successfully in A18) and a dream of Ohyah that involved heat consuming the water of the earth.

The Book of Giants: General Introduction

A20. Māhaway flies with his hands across a desolate vast desert until Enoch sees him and calls to him. Māhaway refers to this as his second visit and requests the interpretation (4Q530 7 ii 3–10a).

A21. There is reference, perhaps beginning Enoch's interpretation, to gardeners who descended from heaven (4Q530 7 ii 10b–11).[58]

{A22. Someone (Māhaway, having returned to the giants?) describes how he fell on his face before an exalted person (Enoch?) who did not dwell among or learn from mortals (4Q531 14).}[59]

M21. The spirits are glad to see the "apostle" (Enoch) and assemble in fear of malefactors. Apparently they promise to sin no more (22:KawE Sogdian; cf. 1 En. 13:4–6, 9).[60]

M22. The giant Saxm prays for forgiveness and falls to his knees. Then he rises and confesses abjectly to the light Sun-God regarding his murderous sins (Zieme D; Wilkens Zu1, Zu6 Uyghur).[61]

M23. Enoch the apostle gives a message of judgment to the demons and their children, telling them that they will have no peace (cf. 1 En. 12:5; 13:1; 16:4)[62] and that they will see the destruction of their children (the giants; cf. 1 En. 14:6; Jub. 4:22). He refers to someone ruling for one hundred twenty years (cf. Gen 6:3; Jub. 5:8). Then he predicts either an era of earthly fecundity, presumably after the Flood (cf. 1 En. 10:16–22), or else the Flood itself (cf. Gen 7:8–9) (17:KawAl Middle Persian; cf. A24).

{A23. A group (of Watchers?) prostrate themselves before someone (Enoch?). He tells one of them that he will have no peace (4Q203 13).}[63]

{A24. Enoch pronounces an eschatological or postdiluvian blessing of earthly prosperity (1Q23 1+6+22; cf. Gen 7:8–9; 1 En. 10:17–11:2; M23).}[64]

---

58. A18–A21 are pieced together from fragments that come on three contiguous columns. They must come in this order. On the basis of codicological reconstruction of 4Q203, Stuckenbruck infers that, after the rest of the column containing A21, this scroll contained at least two, but no more than three additional columns. Assuming that the content was relatively stable among the Aramaic Qumran manuscripts the remaining columns would have included A22, A23, and A24. It would be speculative to assume that the content of the book remained relatively stable through its editing by Mani and transmission and translations into other languages among the Manicheans. But it is possible that some, or even much, of the subsequent material that survives in the Manichean fragments was also found in the last two or three columns of the original Aramaic version.

59. This interpretation and placement of A22 is plausible but speculative.

60. M21 appears to describe a meeting between Enoch and the Watchers. Their repentant demeanor implies that this took place after they had already received one of his messages of doom. I infer that Enoch sent the two tablets with his message in response to the first set of dreams, but that he returned with Māhaway to meet with the giants after the second set of dreams (cf. 1 En. 12:1–4; 13:8–10). According to M27, he is returned to occultation after the imprisonment of the Watchers and the destruction of the giants. If this is correct, perhaps Enoch is speaking to Sāhm/Ohyah as per M22.

61. M22 is placed here because its content is similar to that of M21.

62. In the Aramaic version, 1Q24 8 preserves the single phrase "no peace for you (pl.)." Cf. also A23.

63. Milik has proposed that the small bit of text in A23 refers to the same event as in M23. In both someone tells his listener(s) that he or they will have no peace (cf. 1Q24 8, cited in n. 62). Moreover, Milik suggested that a Greek passage that Syncellus preserves and attributes to the Book of the Watchers is actually from this episode in the Book of Giants and addresses the Watchers rather than human beings. It describes the melting down of Mount Hermon at the eschaton, along with the annihilation of the sons of the Watchers, who will live no more than one-hundred-twenty years. See Milik, *Books of Enoch*, 317-20. But M23 could also go after M19.

64. A24 is placed here because of its similarity to the end of M23.

The Book of Giants: General Introduction

M24. Someone (Enoch?) warns a group (the demons?) that they will be consigned to a fire to face eternal damnation, despite their belief that they were safe forever. He also addresses their "wicked brats" (the giants?; cf. Gen 6:2) and describes how the righteous will fly over the fire of damnation and gloat over the souls inside it (23:KawF cols. CDEFA Middle Persian).[65]

M25. "They," presumably the angels, imprison the companions (cf. the end of A17). The angels then descend from heaven, terrifying the two hundred demons, who take human form and hide among human beings (cf. 1 En. 17:1; 19:1). The angels separate out the human beings and set a watch over them, seize the giants from the demons, and lead a group to safety in thirty-two distant towns prepared for them by the "Living Spirit" in Aryān Wēzhan, where Yam was king, in the vicinity of the sacred Mount Sumeru.[66] These people were skilled in the arts and crafts. The two hundred demons fight a massive battle with the four fire-wielding angels (28:KawG Sogdian).[67]

M26. Atanbish does battle, accompanied by Watchers and giants. Someone kills three of those giants. An angel, perhaps a Watcher, is killed. Others are also dead (31:KawY Middle Persian).[68]

M27. The four angels, by divine command, bind the Egregoroi (Watchers) with an everlasting chain in "the prison of the blackened ones," according to the Coptic, and bound to the planets and the constellations of the Zodiac, according to the Parthian (cf. 1 En. 10:11–14; 54:1–5; 56:1–3; Jub. 5:6, 10). The angels annihilate their children (cf. 1 En. 10:15; 15:8–12; Jub. 5:7–9, 11). Someone hides Enoch (KawP Coptic; 32:KawT Parthian recto; cf. KawZ6).

M28. Even before the rebellion of the Egregoroi (Watchers), this prison had been built for them under the mountains. In addition, thirty-six towns had been prepared for the habitation of the wicked and long-lived sons of the giants before they were even born (KawS Coptic).[69]

M29. Ohyah (or Ahyah), the primordial monster Leviathan (cf. Job 41; Ps 74:14; Isa 27:1), and the archangel Raphael engage in a great battle. They perished or vanished, or both (30:KawN Parthian; 31a:KawZmp1 Middle Persian).[70]

M30. Three thousand two hundred eighty years passed between the time of Enoch and the time of the peaceful reign of King Wishtāsp in [Aryān] Wēzhan (32:KawT verso Parthian; cf. KawR Coptic?).[71]

M31? A doctrinal epilogue about the five elements and the duties of the Manichean hearers probably ended the Manichean version of the Book of Giants. It would not

---

65. M24 fits as Enoch's response to the appeal of the demons for mercy, although it could also go after M19. Cf. the eschatological gloating of the righteous over the wicked kings and the mighty in 1 En. 62:9–12 (cf. 27:3; 48:8–9) and the fiery judgment on Mount Hermon cited in n. 63.

66. Cf. Colditz Zp1 and Morano Zp2 and see Skjærvø's introduction in this volume, section "Elements from Iranian Epic in Mani's Writings."

67. M25 fits here as an account of the final battle of the Watchers and giants vs. the angels.

68. M26 fits plausibly in the same context as M24, but it could conceivably also go with M12–M15.

69. M27 comes after the battle in M25. M28 assumes the events in M25 while referring to still earlier events whose exact placement is uncertain.

70. M29 could also go with M25–M26. I place it here because the Latin tradition about Ogias's battle with the dragon places the event after the Flood.

71. M30 Manichean concludes the story by bringing it from the time of the defeat of the Watchers and giants to the reign of King Wishtāsp (see above). Henning included KawU Parthian at this point, but Skjaervø thinks that it is not part of the Book of Giants.

have been in the original Aramaic version (33:KawAe; 34:KawAb; 35:KawAh. 36:KawAf. 37:KawAa; 38:KawAd; 39:KawAm; 40:KawA; 41:KawAn; Zieme I).

Bibliography

Baker-Brian, Nicholas J. *Manichaeism: An Ancient Faith Rediscovered*. London: T&T Clark, 2011.

Doak, Brian R. *The Last of the Rephaim: Conquest and Cataclysm in the Heroic Ages of Ancient Israel*. Ilex Foundation Series 7. Boston: Ilex Foundation; Washington, DC: Center for Hellenic Studies, 2012.

Goff, Matthew. "Gilgamesh the Giant: The Qumran *Book of Giants*' Appropriation of *Gilgamesh* Motifs." *DSD* 16 (2009): 221–53. doi:10.1163/156851709X395740.

Goff, Matthew, Loren T. Stuckenbruck, and Enrico Morano, eds. *Ancient Tales of Giants from Qumran and Turfan: Contexts, Traditions, and Influences*. WUNT 360. Tübingen: Mohr Siebeck, 2016.

Henning, W. B. "The Book of the Giants." *BSOAS* 11 (1943–1946): 52–74. (The original English publication of most of the Manichean fragments.)

Kosman, Admiel. "The Story of a Giant Story: The Winding Way of Og King of Bashan in the Jewish Haggadic Tradition." *HUCA* 73 (2002): 157–90.

Milik, J. T., ed. *The Books of Enoch: Aramaic Fragments of Qumrân Cave 4*. Oxford: Clarendon, 1976. (The Book of Giants is covered on pp. 298–339 and pls. XIX, XXX–XXXII.)

Morano, Enrico. "Il '*Libro dei Giganti*' di Mani." Pages 71–107, 367–73 in *Il mito e la dottrina: Testi manichei dell'Asia centrale e della Cina*. Vol. 3 of *Il Manicheismo*. Edited by Gherardo Gnoli. Milan: Fondazione Lorenzo Valla Arnoldo Mondadori Editore, 2008. (An Italian translation of all of the known Manichean fragments as of 2008.)

———. "New Research on Mani's Book of Giants." Pages 101–11 in *Der östliche Manichäismus Gattungs- und Werksgeschichte; Vorträge des Göttinger Symposiums vom 4.–5. März 2010*. Edited by Zekine Özerturla and Jens Wilkens. Abhandlungen der Akademie der Wissenschaften zu Göttingen NS 17. Berlin: de Gruyter, 2011.

Nickelsburg, George W. E., and James C. VanderKam. *1 Enoch: A New Translation Based on the Hermeneia Commentary*. Minneapolis: Fortress, 2012.

Pfann, Stephen J., Philip S. Alexander, Monica Brady, and James C. VanderKam. *Qumran Cave 4.XXVI: Cryptic Texts and Miscellanea, Part 1*. DJD XXXVI. Oxford: Clarendon, 2000. (The official edition, by Loren Stuckenbruck, of some of the Qumran Aramaic manuscripts is on pp. 8–94.)

Puech, Émile. *Qumrân grotte 4.XXII: Textes Araméens première partie 4Q529–549*. DJD XXXI. Oxford: Clarendon, 2001. (The official edition of some of the Aramaic manuscripts from Cave 4 is on pp. 9–115.)

Reed, Annette Yoshiko. *Fallen Angels and the History of Judaism and Christianity: The Reception of Enochic Literature*. Cambridge: Cambridge University Press, 2005.

Reeves, John C. *Jewish Lore in Manichaean Cosmogony: Studies in the* Book of Giants *Traditions*. HUCM 14. Cincinnati: Hebrew Union College Press, 1992. (Chapter 2 covers the Aramaic fragments published up to 1992 in the context of the relevant Manichean fragments.)

Seeman, Chris. "The Watchers Traditions and Gen 6:1–4 (MT and LXX)." Pages 25–38 in *The Watchers in Jewish and Christian Traditions*. Edited by Angela Kim Harkins, Kelley Coblentz Bautch, and John C. Endress. Minneapolis: Fortress, 2014. doi:10.2307/j.ctt22nmb25.6.

Skjaervø, Prods Oktor. "Iranian Epic and the Manichean *Book of Giants*: Irano-Manichaica III." *Acta Orientalia Academiae Scientiarum Hungaricae* 48 (1995): 187–223.

Stuckenbruck, Loren T. *The Book of Giants from Qumran: Texts, Translation and Commentary*. TSAJ 63. Tübingen: Mohr Siebeck, 1997.

———. *The Myth of Rebellious Angels: Studies in Second Temple Judaism and New Testament Texts*. WUNT 335. Tübingen: Mohr Siebeck, 2014.

The Aramaic Book of Giants
A new translation and introduction

by Loren T. Stuckenbruck

The title "Book of Giants" was given by Jósef T. Milik to fragments from a number of manuscripts recovered among the Dead Sea Scrolls[1] on the basis of apparent textual overlaps with later fragments that Walter B. Henning had identified as the "The Book of the Giants" in the Manichaean tradition.[2] While the title itself does not occur in any of the Dead Sea fragments and although the textual overlaps are not extensive, they leave little doubt for maintaining continuity in the transmission of the work between Second Temple times and materials that emerged in various languages in use along the Silk Road during the first millennium CE (in particular, Middle Persian, Parthian, Sogdian, Old Turkic). The Aramaic fragments from Qumran thus provide valuable evidence for the existence and scribal transmission of the Book of Giants during the last two centuries BCE, not least because copies were recovered from four of the eleven caves.

Manuscripts

The Book of Giants survives in the original Aramaic in a number of very fragmentary manuscripts from Qumran.[3] Five of the manuscripts (1Q23, 4Q203, 4Q530, 4Q531, 6Q8)

---

1. Jósef T. Milik, "Turfan et Qumran: Livre des Géants juif et manichéen," in *Tradition und Glaube: Das frühe Christentum in seiner Umwelt* (ed. Gerd Jeremias, Heinz-Wolfgang Kuhn, and Hartmut Stegemann; Göttingen: Vandenhoeck & Ruprecht, 1971), 117–27; and Milik, *The Books of Enoch: Aramaic Fragments from Qumrân Cave 4* (Oxford: Clarendon, 1976), 298–339.

2. Cf. Walter B. Henning, "The Book of the Giants," *BSOAS* 11 (1943–1946): 52–74.

3. Aside from Milik's preliminary publications in *Books of Enoch* ([[n. 1 above]]), the major editions of the Aramaic Book of Giants are: Milik, "Deux apocryphes en Araméen," in *Qumran Cave 1*, ed. Dominique Barthélemy and J. T. Milik, DJD I (Oxford: Clarendon, 1955), 97–99 (1Q23 and 1Q24); Maurice Baillet, "Fragment de Rituel?," in *Les "petit grottes" de Qumran*, ed. Maurice Baillet, J. T. Milik, and Roland de Vaux, DJD III (Oxford: Clarendon, 1962), 90–91 (2Q26); Baillet, "Une apocryphe de la Genèse," in Baillet, Milik, and de Vaux, *Les "petit grottes" de Qumrân*, 116–19 (6Q8); John C. Reeves, *Jewish Lore in Manichaean Cosmogony: Studies in the Book of Giants Traditions*, HUCM 14 (Cincinnati: Hebrew Union College Press, 1992) (ch. 2 transcribes and translates the Aramaic fragments published up to 1992 in the context of the relevant Manichean fragments); Klaus Beyer, *Die aramäischen Texte vom Toten Meer: Aramaistische Einleitung, Text, Übersetzung, Deutung, Grammatik* (Göttingen: Vandenhoeck & Ruprecht, 1984), 258–68; and Beyer, *Die aramäischen Texte vom Toten Meer: Ergänzungband* (Göttingen: Vandenhoeck & Ruprecht, 1994), 119–24 (all of the Aramaic fragments); Loren T. Stuckenbruck, *The Book of Giants from Qumran: Texts, Translation and Commentary*, TSAJ 63 (Tübingen: Mohr Siebeck, 1997) (all of the Aramaic fragments); Stephen J. Pfann et al., *Qumran Cave 4.XXVI: Cryptic Texts and Miscellanea, Part 1*, DJD XXXVI (Oxford: Clarendon, 2000), 8–94 (the official edition, by Stuckenbruck, of 4Q203 and 4Q206, with republications of 1Q23; 1Q24; 2Q26; and 6Q8); Émile Puech, *Qumrân grotte 4.XXII: Textes Araméens première partie 4Q529-549*, DJD XXXI (Oxford: Clarendon, 2001), 9–115 (the official edition of 4Q530–533, plus 4Q203 1).

The Aramaic Book of Giants

can be confidently identified with the Book of Giants. There is a good case that two other manuscripts (2Q26, 4Q532) also belong to the book and it is plausible that two other very fragmentary ones (1Q24, 4Q206) also do. Fragments of 4Q533 (formerly 4Q556) have also been identified with the Book of Giants, but this is speculative and 4Q533 is not translated here.

1Q23 (1QEnGiants[a] ar) consists mostly of small fragments, but the text of one overlaps strikingly with the wording of a passage in one of the Iranian Manichean manuscripts of the Book of Giants. This and the content of some of the other fragments make its identification with the Book of Giants secure.

1Q24 (1QEnochGiants[b]? ar) is written in an early to mid-Herodian hand and can be dated to roughly the last third of the first century BCE. It is very poorly preserved. What survives is consistent with themes in the Book of Giants, but the case that 1Q24 is a manuscript of the latter work is inconclusive.

2Q26 (2QEnGiants ar) survives only in a single fragment written in a semicursive early Herodian hand that can be dated to roughly the final third of the first century BCE. The content of the fragment has parallels to an episode that seems to be shared by the Midrash of Shemhazai and Aza'el and one of the Iranian Manichean manuscripts of the Book of Giants. This makes it likely that 2Q26 was also a manuscript of the latter work.

4Q203 (4QEnGiants[a] ar) is written in an early Herodian hand and in the same handwriting as 4Q204 (4QEn[c] ar). It is possible that the two formed one manuscript on which was written not only the Book of Giants, but also the Book of the Watchers (1 En. 1–36), the Book of Dreams (83–90), and the Epistle of Enoch (91–107). This led Milik to conclude that there was an Aramaic "Enochic Pentateuch" in the Second Temple period, analogous to the five Enochic books in the Ethiopic book of 1 Enoch. The Aramaic collection would have included the Book of Giants but not the Parables of Enoch (1 En. 37–71). But it is debatable whether 4Q203 and 4Q204 actually composed a single manuscript, so Milik's suggestion should be received with caution.[4]

4Q530 (4QEnGiants[b] ar) is written in a semicursive Hasmonean hand that Émile Puech dates to the end of the second century or the first quarter of the first century BCE. It contains some relatively well-preserved passages and its identification with the Book of Giants is secure.

4Q531 (4QEnGiants[c] ar) is written in a formal late-Hasmonean hand that Puech dates to the second third of the first century BCE. It too contains some relatively well-preserved passages and its identification with the Book of Giants is secure.

4Q532 (4QEnGiants[d] ar) is written in what Puech calls an elegant formal Hasmonean hand that he dates to the first half or quarter of the first century BCE. It is poorly preserved, but what survives is consistent with the content of the Book of Giants and it is likely that it belongs to that book.

4Q206 (4QEn[e] ar and 4QEnGiants[f]? ar) fragments 2 and 3. Milik argued that these fragments belong to the Enochic manuscript 4Q206, but his case is inconclusive. The little surviving content of these fragments is not found in any of the works that compose 1 Enoch but it is consistent with themes in the Book of Giants. It is plausible that they come from the Book of Giants, but its poor state of preservation leaves this uncertain.

---

4. Milik, *Books of Enoch*, 181–84, 310. For a critical evaluation, see Loren T. Stuckenbruck, "201–206, Appendixes 1–4," in Pfann et al., *Qumran Cave 4.XXVI*, 8–10.

6Q8 (6QpapGiants ar) is written on papyrus in a semicursive hand that has been dated either to the second half of the first century BCE or to the middle of the first century CE. Most of its fragments are tiny, but enough survives to make its identification with the Book of Giants secure.

Content, Structure, and Interpretive Issues

The highly fragmentary state of the remains among manuscripts assigned to the Book of Giants has made it difficult to reconstruct the work as it existed in Aramaic. Indeed, it is not certain, given very few overlaps among the fragments themselves, how fixed the tradition itself was. Nevertheless, it is possible, on the basis of internal codicological clues, textual content, and parallels with closely related literature (including a few Manichaean materials), to suggest an outline for the Book of Giants about which there is broad agreement.[5] As it is important to distinguish between a more and less likely placement of content within the narrative sequence of the book, the outline uses double squared brackets "[[. . .]]" to indicate less certain locations. In any case, it should be noted that the precise narrative context for sections that are designated C, E, F, H, L, and P should, for all their plausibility, be considered speculative.[6] This outline is followed by a narrative summary of the book's storyline.

(A) Account about the angelic rebellion, their siring of a gigantic offspring through women of the earth (4Q531 1; cf. 1 En. 6–7; Jub. 5)
(B) The giants' violent activities on the earth against the natural order and against humanity (4Q531 2 + 3; 1Q23 9 + 14 + 15; cf. 4Q532 1 ii + 2; cf. 1 En. 7:3–5)
(C) Complaint to God by the souls of humans killed by the giants (cf. 4Q530 1; 1 En. 8:4–9:11)
(D) [[A report about the giants' terrible deeds, that is brought to Enoch's attention (4Q206a 2?)]]
(E) Enoch's petition to God about the situation, appealing to God's royal rule (4Q203 9–10; cf. 1 En. 84:2, 5)
(F) [[Conversations among the giants about their activities (4Q203 1?)]]

---

5. Whereas the translation below follows a numerical sequence assigned to the fragments of the individual manuscripts when they were published, the outline here offers a synthetic reconstruction that takes all the Qumran cave materials into consideration.

6. The outline is adapted from Loren T. Stuckenbruck, "The *Book of Giants* among the Dead Sea Scrolls: Considerations of Method and a New Proposal on the Reconstruction of 4Q530," in *Ancient Tales of Giants from Qumran and Turfan: Contexts, Traditions, and Influences*, ed. Matthew Goff, Loren T. Stuckenbruck, and Enrico Morano, WUNT 360 (Tübingen: Mohr Siebeck, 2016), 129–41, esp. 136–37. The references to the Manichaean texts are based on Henning, "Book of the Giants"; and that of Werner Sundermann, "Ein weiteres Fragment aus Manis Gigantenbuch," in *Orientalia J. Duchesne Guillemin Emerito Oblata*, Acta Iranica 23, Hommages et Opera Minora 9 (Leiden: Brill, 1984), 491–505. These and further Manichaean materials have been taken into account in the contributions by Gábor Kósa, "The *Book of Giants* Tradition in the Chinese Manichaica," in Goff, Stuckenbruck, and Morano, *Ancient Tales of Giants from Qumran and Turfan*, 145–86; Enrico Morano, "Some New Sogdian Fragments Related to Mani's *Book of Giants* and the Problem of the Influence of Jewish Enochic Literature," in Goff, Stuckenbruck, and Morano, *Ancient Tales of Giants from Qumran and Turfan*, 187–98; and Jens Wilkens, "Remarks on the Manichaean *Book of Giants*: Once Again on Mahaway's Mission to Enoch," in Goff, Stuckenbruck, and Morano, *Ancient Tales of Giants from Qumran and Turfan*, 213–29.

(G) A first pair of dreams given to the giants (2Q26?; cf. Midrash of Shemhazai and Azaʾel; Manichaean Book of Giants [M101j])
(H) First journey to Enoch by the giant Mahaway (cf. 4Q530 7 ii 7—"a second time")
(I) First tablet written by Enoch; denouncing the angels and giants, it is delivered (by Mahaway?) and read before the giants (cf. 4Q203 7b ii; and 4Q203 8; cf. Sundermann's fragment L recto, lines 6–8 and 9–11)
(J) Discussion between the giants Ohyah and Hahyah about their dreams (6Q8 1)
(K) A rebellious angel's account of his powerlessness before God's angels (4Q531 22, esp. lines 4–5)
(L) Ohyah tells Gilgamesh(?) about his dream (4Q531 22.9–12)
(M) Intramural conflict among the giants (4Q531 7; cf. 1 En. 7:5; 10:9; Jub. 5:7, 9)
(N) Punishment of Azazel and the giants by imprisonment (4Q203 7a + 7b i; cf. 1 En. 10:4–8)
(O) Reading of the second tablet written by Enoch that pronounces punishment on the angels and giants, who are told to pray (4Q203 8; 4Q530 1; cf. 4Q203 7b ii)[7]
(P) [[(Second?) complaint by the souls of humans who have been killed; cf. 4Q530 1]]
(Q) Some giants rejoice (because they hope not to be punished?) (4Q530 2 ii 1–3)
(R) The giants Hahyah and Ohyah are given a second pair of dreams (4Q530 2 ii 4–20)
(S) The giant Mahaway is sent by the giants a second time to Enoch for an interpretation of the dreams (4Q530 2 ii 20–24; 7 ii 3–10)
(T) Enoch interprets the second pair of dreams (4Q530 7 ii 10–11)
(U) [[Mahaway reports his second encounter with Enoch to the giants (4Q531 14?)]]
(V) A prophecy or vision of eschatological, reproductive bliss (by Enoch?; cf. 1Q23 1 + 6 + 22; cf. 1 En. 10:17–11:2)

This outline, supplemented in part by the parallel and more skeletal account in the Book of the Watchers (1 En. 6–11), allows contours for a storyline to emerge: Angelic beings in heaven, drawn by the beauty of human women on earth, reach an irrevocable decision to mate with them, from which a gigantic offspring results. The giants, due to their size, engage in violent activities on the earth to assuage their insatiable appetites; they not only begin to destroy the natural order but also consume human flesh, generating a crisis of survival for the creation. The souls of humans who have been killed raise a complaint about this disastrous situation. Following on this, the giants' terrible deeds are reported to Enoch who, in turn, petitions God to intervene with God's royal power. In the meantime, as the giants boast about their exploits with one another, two of them (Ohyah and Hahyah), who are brothers, are each given an ominous dream. Needing help to understand the meaning of both dreams, they send Mahaway to Enoch for an interpretation. Mahaway returns from Enoch with a written message that denounces both the angels and giants for their misdeeds. Upon hearing the message, Ohyah and Hahyah have further discussions about their dreams (perhaps not fully convinced by the message

---

7. For the text immediately following this section, Milik suggests the addition of content from a Greek passage cited by Georgius Syncellus (and attributed to "the first book of Enoch concerning the Watchers"), in which Mount Hermon (a "passive accomplice") and the giants ("active accomplices") are cursed, supposing that the judgment pronounced in 4Q203 8 is singly focused on the Watchers; see Milik, *Books of Enoch*, 317–20. It is not clear, however, that the curses pronounced in the text follow on from the exhortation to "pray" in 4Q203 8 rather than being an extension and resumé of content from 1 En. 6 and 12–16.

from Enoch), while one of the rebellious angels underscores the coming punishment by recounting his own powerlessness in the face of the might of God's angels. Ohyah decides to tell another giant, Gilgamesh, about his dream, and an intramural conflict among the giants breaks out about its meaning. An initial punishment by imprisonment of one of the angels, Azazel, and of some giants ensues, followed by the reading of a second written message from Enoch that pronounces punishment on the angels and giants, who are told to pray. For a second time, the souls of humans killed by the giants raise a complaint about the lack of justice. As some giants remain hopeful that they will not be punished for their deeds, Ohyah and Hahyah are given a second pair of ominous dreams with judgment scenes, respectively, one by water and fire and another of judgment in a divine court descended to earth. Again the giants send Mahaway to Enoch in order to secure an interpretation. Mahaway returns from his second encounter with Enoch with the same message of punishment. It is possible, though not certain, that Enoch's second message was followed by a brief narrative regarding events of the great flood. The book may have closed with a vision (by Enoch?) of eschatological blessing to come upon the created order that includes a reproductive bliss as God intended it to be. Thus the tale, which begins with creation being threatened with destruction, closes with a vision of hope.

Regarding the structure and content, two features of the work can be readily observed. The first is the attention it gives to the number 2. The story seems to have devoted some attention to the experiences of the two giant brothers Ohyah and Hahyah. Moreover, they are each given a pair of dream-visions. Though not certain, it is possible that the text recounts the complaints of murdered humans' souls twice. Finally, Mahaway has two encounters with Enoch that, each time, results in announcements of judgment.

The second feature to mention is the book's interest in providing proper names for individual giants, something not given in any other related literature from the Second Temple period. These names, insofar as they are preserved among the fragments, include the following: (1) 'Aḥiram; (2) 'Adk; (3) Ḥobabis(h) (reminiscent of Humbaba in the Gilgamesh Epic [Neo-Assyrian; Huwawa in Old Babylonian]); (4) Gilgames(h) (who battles Humbaba in the Gilgamesh Epic); (5) Mahaway (who acts as an intermediary between the giants and Enoch to secure dream interpretations); (6) Ohyah and (7) Hahyah (the sibling offspring of the rebellious angel-leader Shemihazah).[8] The conspicuous use of proper names indicates the extent to which, unlike other literature, the narrative of the book focuses on the story of antediluvian evil, the flood, and its aftermath from the giants' point of view.

Considerations of the overriding message of the Book of Giants have entertained several emphases. The most common way of interpreting the work, with its focus on the giants, has focused on its treatment of evil. On the one hand, the narrative might be read against the background of an Enochic demonology (cf. 1 En. 15–16). The giants, whose bodies are destroyed in the deluge, exist thereafter as disembodied spirits that forthwith cause suffering among humans and lead them astray (4Q531 19.3–4; 1 En. 15:8–16:2; Jub. 10). The Book of Giants, set in antediluvian times, could be seen to recount how those powers deemed to be behind suffering, wrongdoing, and oppression have already, in principle, been defeated. In this state, their future destruction is assured, despite all

---

8. Loren T. Stuckenbruck, *The Myth of the Rebellious Angels: Studies in Second Temple Judaism and New Testament Texts*, WUNT 335 (Tübingen: Mohr Siebeck, 2014), 41–54.

experience to the contrary.[9] The effect of a story that presents perpetrators of evil as cognizant of their own demise is the assurance that it will altogether disappear and that the world at present remains under divine rule.

A different way of reading the text has been proposed by Matthew Goff.[10] Told from the giants' point of view, the story evokes a certain empathy with the plight they find themselves in as they realize the wrong they have done and hope to avoid destruction. A plural imperative, "pray!," in Enoch's message directed at the giants (4Q203 8.15), might not be so much an ironic request (as if the giants have no chance to be saved) but can be taken as genuine: it is an opportunity for the giants, upon realizing that they have sinned (cf. 4Q531 18.3), to repent and acknowledge "the power and superiority of God" (4Q203 9.4; 7b i 5).[11]

Goff argues that a similar picture emerges from the later rabbinic story Midrash of Shemhazai and Aza'el, which focuses on two (giant) brothers Heyya and Aheyya. When one of the siblings has a vision of a garden of trees that is destroyed except for a tree that has three branches (cf. 6Q8 2.1), one is not automatically to think of the survival of Noah, but of the possibility that, as in the midrash, they do not die in the deluge. Since in variant forms of the midrash, found in Bereshit Rabbati (at 10.10–31.2)[12] and Pugeo Fidei,[13] the brothers actually live on to sire the Canaanite giants Sihon and Og, known in rabbinic tradition,[14] the story functions "not as a paradigm of God's punishment of iniquity through the Flood, but as an etiology for the early inhabitants of Canaan."[15]

A third approach, taken by Joseph Angel, has been to read the storyline against the backdrop of the military conflicts among the Ptolemies and the Seleucids during the third and second centuries BCE, perhaps even the Hellenistic crisis associated with the Maccabean revolt in 167-164 BCE. In this vein, the motif of the giants' punishment functions "to portray symbolically the humbling of real imperial oppressors."[16]

While Goff's interpretation would mark a reversal of the storyline in the Book of the Watchers, according to which the rebellious angels' pleas for mercy go unheeded (cf. 1 En. 12–16), an understanding that aligns the giants with demonic evil draws on texts among the Dead Sea Scrolls in which the disembodied spirits of the giants are referred to as "bastard spirits" (4Q444 1–4 i 5.8; 4Q510 1.5; 4Q511 2 ii 3; 10.1; 35.7; 48–49+51.3; 182.1;

---

9. Cf. Stuckenbruck, *Myth of the Rebellious Angels*, 12–21; Archie T. Wright, *The Origin of Evil Spirits: The Reception of Genesis 6:1–4 in Early Jewish Literature*, rev. ed. (Minneapolis: Fortress, 2015).

10. Goff, "The Sons of the Watchers in the *Book of Watchers* and the Qumran *Book of Giants*: Contexts and Prospects," in Goff, Stuckenbruck, and Morano, *Ancient Tales of Giants from Qumran and Turfan*, 115–27.

11. Goff, "Sons of the Watchers," 124–27.

12. Following the edition of Hanoch Albeck, *Midrash Bereshit Rabbati* (Jerusalem: Maize Nirdamim, 1940).

13. Raymundus Martini (thirteenth cent.), in *Pugio Fidei adversus Mauros et Judaeos cum observationibus Josephi de Voisin et introductione Jo. Benedicti Carpzovi* (Leipzig and Frankfurt, 1687).

14. Cf. Brian Doak, "The Giant in a Thousand Years: Tracing Narratives of Gigantism in the Hebrew Bible and Beyond," in *Ancient Tales of Giants in Qumran and Turfan* (ed. Goff, Stuckenbruck, and Morano), 1–32, esp. pp. 19–21 and 29–31.

15. Goff, "Sons of the Watchers," 126.

16. Angel, "The Humbling of the Arrogant and the 'Wild Man' and 'Tree Stump' Traditions," in Goff, Stuckenbruck, and Morano, *Ancient Tales of Giants in Qumran and Turfan*, 61–80, esp. 78. Angel, careful not to look for a one-to-one correspondence between protagonists in the Book of Giants and events and powers in the third and second centuries BCE, concludes that the fragmentary remains preserve "a complex allegory, whose original references cannot be recovered" (80).

cf. 1 En. 10:9). Whether or not the Book of Giants refers in any way to sociopolitically oppressive powers, as Angel proposes, it is certainly correct to caution against any interpretation that is overly reductionistic. Indeed, with theological or etiological possibilities in the background, the work may also have been told and retold or rewritten as a form of serious entertainment.

Literary Context and Reception

The Book of Giants expands significantly on a storyline that is told much more briefly or hinted at in a number of Second Temple texts. The most significant parallels to the narrative, all of which also reflect various degrees of engagement with tradition found in Genesis chapters 5 to 10, are found in 1 En. 6–11 and 12–16 (Book of the Watchers); 1 En. 85–90 (Animal Apocalypse); 1 En. 106–107 (Birth of Noah); Genesis Apocryphon (1Q20) cols. ii–v; Jub. 5–10; the so-called Pseudo-Eupolemos fragments 1 and 2 (preserved by Eusebius, *Praep. ev.* 9.17.1–9 and 9.18.2). Nevertheless, aside from the Book of the Watchers, the importance of these texts for establishing the structure of the Book of Giants is negligible. Further sources, which mention or allude to the antediluvian giants or the fallen-angels tradition in which they play a part, include the Damascus Document (cf. CD A col ii); 4Q180 1.7–10 (par. 4Q181 2); 4Q370 1 i 1–10; 4Q510–511 (par. 4Q444); Sir 16:7; Wis 14:6; 3 Macc 2:4; 3 Bar. 4:10; and Philo in *De gigantibus*—an extended metaphorical treatment, though less concerned with the storyline itself.

The clear association between the Book of Giants and traditions of 1 Enoch is supported by a consideration of the manuscripts in Qumran Cave 4. The scribal hand of 4Q203, which contains the Book of Giants, and of 4Q204, which contains several parts of 1 Enoch, appears to be the same, though it is debated whether these numerically distinct designations actually belonged to the same manuscript, as Milik argued.[17] Thus at the very least the Book of Giants formed part of the Enochic scribal tradition. Given the prominence of Enoch in the work as a dream interpreter and pronouncer of judgment, this link with the 1 Enoch traditions reflects a degree of socioscribal continuity.

There is little question about the book's reception in the Manichaean tradition (see the related versions in this volume). In addition, giants traditions found in the Book of Giants appear to have been received in the above-mentioned Midrash of Shemhazai and Azaʾel of rabbinic tradition[18] and the related works mentioned above ([[n. 12]]). Although the text of 1 Enoch is most fully preserved in the Geʿez manuscript tradition, there is no direct textual evidence in it for the Book of Giants. Possible allusions to giants traditions found in some texts such as Jannes and Jambres, of which fragments are preserved in Greek and Geʿez (see the contribution by Ted Erho and Ben Henry in this volume), and a late fourteenth-century compilation of homilies known as Rətuʿa Haymanot ("Orthodox Faith"),[19] have yet to be fully explored.

---

17. Milik, *Books of Enoch*, 178–79 and 310. For a different view, see Stuckenbruck, "203. 4QEnochGiantsᵃ ar," in Pfann et al., *Qumran Cave 4.XXVI*, 8–41, esp. 8–10.

18. Milik, *The Books of Enoch*, 321–35.

19. For an initial study, see Ralph Lee, "Little Known Giants Traditions in Ethiopian Literature," in Loren T. Stuckenbruck and Amsalu Tefera, *Representations of Angelic Beings in Early Jewish and in Christian Traditions*, ed. Amsalu Tefera and Loren T. Stuckenbruck, WUNT 2/544 (Tübingen: Mohr Siebeck, 2019), 205–20.

Genre

Some discussion has been devoted to the kind of literature the Book of Giants represents. Its close relation to 1 Enoch, especially the Book of the Watchers, suggests that it may be thought of as an apocalyptic work. As such, it includes mediator figures (Enoch, and even the giant Mahaway) who convey revelatory knowledge that is ultimately eschatological within a framework of recounting divine activity in the sacred past. By associating the book codicologically among and in content with the other parts of 1 Enoch, Milik, however, casually regarded it as "pseudepigraphal."[20] Whether or not the Book of Giants is to be linked to other parts of 1 Enoch in this way, it bears a different narrative character. Whereas the other Enochic works largely claim to be written by Enoch himself (with 1 En. 6–11 being a notable exception), Enoch is never clearly presented as a first-person narrator in the Book of Giants, in which, indeed, a third-person narrative predominates.[21] If an apocalypse, it is a mythical legend composed by a formally anonymous author that reconfigures the rebellious angels tradition known in the Book of the Watchers by zooming in on the giants' point of view. Whereas the Book of the Watchers narrates how the culpable angels learn that their judgment is inescapable, the writer emphasizes how it is that the giants learn that they will be held to account and punished for their oppressive activities against humanity and the created order.

Date

On balance, comparison with the Book of the Watchers suggests that the Book of Giants is derivative in character in its supply of elaborating (the giants' activities and conversations) and specifying details (e.g., the giants' proper names). If composed under the influence of the Book of the Watchers, then its *terminus a quo* would be the late third century BCE, or perhaps earlier, if the Book of Giants only shows an awareness of its earliest sections (chs. 6–16). It is more difficult to determine its latest possible date of composition. The close parallels between details in the vision of judgment in 4Q530 2 ii + 6–7 i + 8–12, lines 16b–20 and those of Dan 7:9–10 leave little doubt that the Danielic version preserves a more developed form.[22] This, in turn, suggests that at least the form of the tradition in the Book of Giants predates Dan 7. A date for that tradition, and perhaps with it the Book of Giants itself, points to a time of composition during the first third of the second century BCE.

Bibliography

Angel, Joseph L. "The Humbling of the Arrogant and the 'Wild Man' and 'Tree Stump' Traditions in the *Book of Giants* and Daniel 4." Pages 61–80 in *Ancient Tales of Giants from Qumran and Turfan: Contexts, Traditions, and Influences*. Edited by Matthew Goff, Loren T. Stuckenbruck, and Enrico Morano. WUNT 360. Tübingen: Mohr Siebeck, 2016.

---

20. Milik, *Books of Enoch*, 183.

21. Although Enoch functions as the fictive author of a message in 4Q203 8, he is not presented as an ideal figure speaking or writing in the first person. Cf. Devorah Dimant, "The Biography and the Books of Enoch," *VT* 33 (1983): 14–29, esp. 16, doi:10.2307/1517991. In addition, Milik's reading of 4Q206 2–3 (now designated 4Q206a 1–2) as words in the first person attributed to Enoch is questionable. Cf. Émile Puech, "Livre des Géants," in *Qumran Cave 4.XXII: Textes araméens, première partie: 4Q529–549*, ed. Émile Puech, DJD XXXI (Oxford: Clarendon, 2001), 9–115, esp. 111–13.

22. For a full comparison and discussion of its implications, see Stuckenbruck, *Myth of the Rebellious Angels*, 112–18.

Bledsoe, Amanda M. Davis. "Throne Theophanies, Dream Visions, and Righteous(?) Seers." Pages 81–96 in *Ancient Tales of Giants from Qumran and Turfan: Contexts, Traditions, and Influences*. Edited by Matthew Goff, Loren T. Stuckenbruck, and Enrico Morano. WUNT 360. Tübingen: Mohr Siebeck, 2016.

Goff, Matthew. "The Sons of the Watchers in the *Book of Watchers* and the Qumran *Book of Giants*: Contexts and Prospects." Pages 115–28 in *Ancient Tales of Giants from Qumran and Turfan: Contexts, Traditions, and Influences*. Edited by Matthew Goff, Loren T. Stuckenbruck, and Enrico Morano. WUNT 360. Tübingen: Mohr Siebeck, 2016.

Puech, Émile. "Les fragments 1 à 3 du *Livre des Géants* de la grotte 6 (*pap6Q8*)." *RevQ* 19.74 (1999): 227–38.

———. "Les songes des fils de Šemiḥazah dans le *Livre des Géants* de Qumrân." *CRAI* 144 (2000): 7–26.

———. "Livre des Géants." Pages 9–116 in *Qumrân Grotte 4.XXII: Textes araméens, première partie: 4Q529–549*. DJD XXXI. Oxford: Clarendon, 2001.

———. *Qumrân grotte 4.XXII: Textes Araméens première partie 4Q529–549*. DJD XXXI. Oxford: Clarendon, 2001.

Reeves, John C. *Jewish Lore in Manichaean Cosmogony: Studies in the* Book of Giants *Traditions*. HUCM 14. Cincinnati: Hebrew Union College Press, 1992.

Stuckenbruck, Loren T. "201–206, Appendixes 1–4." Pages 3–94 in *Qumran Cave 4.XXVI: Cryptic Texts and Miscellanea, Part 1*. Edited by Stephen J. Pfann, Philip S. Alexander, Monica Brady, and James C. VanderKam. DJD XXXVI. Oxford: Clarendon, 2000.

———. "The *Book of Giants* among the Dead Sea Scrolls: Considerations of Method and a New Proposal on the Reconstruction of 4Q530." Pages 129–41 in *Ancient Tales of Giants from Qumran and Turfan: Contexts, Traditions, and Influences*. Edited by Matthew Goff, Loren T. Stuckenbruck, and Enrico Morano. WUNT 360. Tübingen: Mohr Siebeck, 2016.

———. *The Book of Giants from Qumran: Texts, Translation, and Commentary*. TSAJ 63. Tübingen: Mohr Siebeck, 1997.

———. *The Myth of the Rebellious Angels: Studies in Second Temple Judaism and New Testament Texts*. WUNT 335. Tübingen: Mohr Siebeck, 2014.

The Aramaic Book of Giants

The materials related to the Book of Giants among the Dead Sea Scrolls are presented here in translation as follows. First, for the sake of completeness all the fragments are included.[a] Second, they appear in numerical sequence: according to the common numeration of the Qumran caves (1Q, 2Q, 4Q, 6Q); according to the numerical designation of the manuscripts within each of the caves (1Q23, 1Q24, etc.); and according to the numerical sequence of fragments assigned by the editors in the official publications. These numerical sequences are broken in instances of overlap within a manuscript and of overlaps based on reconstructions from different manuscripts (underlined), to which cross-references are made at the appropriate points. Third, for a sense of the possible overall narrative structure, see the outline reconstruction of the Book of Giants from the Dead Sea Scrolls in the introduction above. Next to each fragment number of combination of fragments, cross-references to the section of the outline indicate a possible placement of the content within the book.

1Q23 (1QEnGiants[a] ar)

Fragments 1 + 6 + 22 (cf. outline V)

1 En. 10:18–20;
KawAl 21

1.] . [   ] . . [
2. two hundred donkeys, [two] hundred wild asses[
3. two hundred sheep, [tw]o hundred rams[
4. field from every kind of living being, and thousands from a gr[apevine
5. upon . . *g vacat* [   ]then [

Fragment 2
1.   ]. they[
2.]'*yn* .[

Fragment 3
1.   ].*l* from it[
2.] and I was [
3.]' and [the] corrupt one[

---

a. For the base text underlying the translation, see Stuckenbruck, "201-206, Appendixes 1–4" (for 1Q23-24; 2Q26; 4Q203; 6Q8); and Émile Puech, "Livre des Géants" (for 4Q530-533). The translation only follows more certain reconstructions.

Fragment 4
1.] . . [
2.] . draw near[
3.]*l*[

Fragment 5
1.]*b* . . [
2.]*tb*[

Fragment 7
1.] . [
2.] and behol[d
3.   ]*l* . . [

Fragments 9 + 14 + 15 (cf. outline B)   1 En. 7:2–5; Jub. 5:2
1.   ]*n*[
2.   ]and they knew *r*[
3.   ].*h* great upon the earth[
4.   ].*h* and they killed man[y
5.]a hundred giants, [a]ll who[
6.   ] . . *l*[   ]*l*[

Fragment 10
1.]*rb*.[
2.]*ltyw* .[

Fragment 11
1.]he/it arose be[fore(?)
2.] . . gia[nts(?)

Fragment 12
1.   ]*n*
2.]which
3.] .

Fragment 13
1.   ] . fou[r
2. the Eu]phrates(?) river[
3.   ] . he went[

Fragment 16
1. [the] tablet
2. and th[en(?)
3.   ]*l*[

Fragment 17
1. and they went in[
2. with their hands . [
3. and they began to[

Fragment 18
1.] . . . . . [
2.]you wish . [
3.].*l*[

Fragment 19
1.] on [the] ear[th
2.].*b* '[

Fragment 20
1.   ]*n* [
2.]their father. The[n
3.   ] . ages . [
4.   ]all the sons of[
5.   ] . . . [

Fragment 21
1.   ] . [ ]*m* [
2.]you(?) will subdue everything that[
3.   ]*l*. . . . .[

Fragment 23
1.].*n* '.[
2.   ]*l.* .[

Fragment 24
1. not[
2. agai[n
3. waters[
4. . . [

Fragment 25
1.   ]*n*[
2.]. L. . .[
3.].*y.* vacat [
4.].*bw* vacat [
5.   ]to the earth[

Fragment 26
1.   ] . . . [
2.]. . *m. k.r* [
3.   ] . . . . [

Fragment 27
1.]. these '[
2.]Mahaway   [
3.].b. . [
4.] until [
5.] k. [

Fragment 28
1.]h his son[

Fragment 29—parallel to 6Q8 frag. 1
(overlap with 6Q8 1 4–5, underlined)
1.   ]to ']Ohyah, "Ba[raq'el my father . . . ."
2. Mahaway]had not finished[

Fragment 30
1.   ]he began
2.] . . [

Fragment 31
1.   ] . [
2.] . . t h[
3.] the tablet .[

1Q24 (1QEnGiants[b]? ar)
Fragment 1
1.] . [ ]hi[s
2.   ] . . *vacat* and . . .[ ]n and *hy*[
3.   ]l[ ]y' and the river [
4.   ]the(?) and the donkeys and l[
5.   ] . *vacat* and every
6.   ].py' and m.[
7.   ]the[ ] and the lightning bolts[
8.   ]l.[ ] . [

Fragment 2
1.   ] . [
2.]upon [the] ear[th
3.   ]l[

Fragment 3
1.   ] . [
2.]t' *vacat* [
3.]for every . . [

Fragment 4
1.]water(?) h.[

The Aramaic Book of Giants

Fragment 5
1.]*m*[ ] . [
2.]*rwš* and *yṣ*.[
3.]their [ ].*r* and every [
4.]and the rain and [the] dew[
5.   ]*l*[ ]*l*[

Fragment 6
1.]for all [
2.]*l* . . *y py*[

Fragment 7
1.] . day of the end[
2.] everything is finished[
3. u]pon those who[

Fragment 8
1.] . . *n*[   ] . [
2. there will be]no peace for you[

1 En. 12:5; 13:1; 16:4; 4Q203 frag. 13 3; KawAl

KawAj KawAj; Midrash of Shemhazai and Aza'el 9

2Q26 (2QEnGiants ar)
(cf. outline G)
1.]"Wash the tablet in order to sm[ooth out its surface!"
2.]and the waters went up over the [tab]let[
3.] . . and they lifted the tablet from the waters, the tablet that[
4.   ].*hr*.[   ]for them every[

4Q203 (4QEnGiants^a ar)

Fragment 1
1. And]when I conse[crate
2. Baraq'el [
3. my face/anger still[
4. I am standing[

Fragment 2
1. . [ ] '.[
2. concerning them[
3. *vacat*   [
4.   and] Mahawa[y answer]ed

Fragment 3
1.   ] . [
2. his companions [
3. Ḥobabish and *'dk*.[
4. And what will you give me for k[illing(?)
          bottom margin

4Q530 frags. 2 ii +6+7 i 8–11+12 2; KawZs2; KawAj

72

Fragment 4
1.]their [
2.   *vacat*
3.]. 'Ohyah said to Ha[hyah
4.]. from above the earth and š.[
5.]the[ear]th *vacat* W[hen
6.   ]they bowed and wept bef[ore
7.   ]*l*[

Fragment 5
1.] . . [
2.]he harmed the[m
3.]they were killed .[

Fragment 6
1.   ] . [
2.]he was to us [
3.]*l*. . [

Fragment 7a i (cf. outline N)
1.]   ] *n*. . [
2.   ] . . . [
3. and [you]r streng[th
4.   *vacat*
5. The[n] 'Ohyah [said] to Hahya[h
6. us [   ] . to 'Aza[ze]l, and he made for [him   Lev 16:7–10; 1 En. 8:1;
7. the giants and the W[atchers]. All [their] com[panions] will lift themselves   9:6; 10:4–8; 54:5; 55:4
   up [against
      bottom margin

Fragment 7b col. I (cf. outline N)
1.   ] n [
2.   ] *vacat*
3.   ]Then they answered, "They have given birth   1 En. 6:1; 7:2
4.   from]Watchers
5.].*lh* he imprisoned us and overpowered yo[u(?)   Cf. 1 En. 10:4–8; 54?
      bottom margin

Fragment 7b col. ii (cf. outline O)
1.   to you *b*.[
2. the two   tablets[4Q203 frag. 8 3;
3. and the second has not been rea[d] until now[KawW

Fragment 8 (cf. outline O)
    top margin
1. [The] bo[ok of

The Aramaic Book of Giants

	2.　　　　*vacat*
4Q203 frag. 7b 2	3. A copy of the s[eco]nd tablet of the le[tter
	4. In a [doc]ument (written) by Enoch, the eminent scribe[. . .　　Thus says the Watcher]
Dan 4:10, 20 (Evv 4:13, 23)	5. and holy one to Shemihazah and to all [his] com[panions
	6. "Let it be known to you (pl.) th[at]*l*[
	7. your deeds and those of [your] wi[ves
	8. they [and their] sons(?) [and] the[wi]ves o[f
	9. through your fornication on the earth, and it (the earth) has [risen up
Gen 6:11–12	ag]ainst y[ou and is crying out]
	10. and raising a complaint against you [and ag]ainst the deeds of your sons[
	11. the corruption that you have committed on it (the earth).　　*vacat* [
1 En. 9:1	12. has reached Raphael. Behold, destruct[ion will come upon all who are in the heavens and who are on the earth,]
	13. and who are in the deserts, and wh[o] are in the seas. And the meaning of [this] matter[. . . will come to pass]
	14. on you as evil. So now, loosen your bonds *mh*[
	15. and pray."　　　　*vacat*　　　　[

1 En. 84:2–5

Fragment 9 (cf. outline E)
1. 　　　　　　　　] . . . and every [
2. 　　　　](they) [sh]ake before [your] glo[rious splendor[
3. be bl]essed because [you] kno[w] all mysteries [
4. 　　　　] and nothing is too strong for you [
5. 　　　　　　　　be]fore you. And now *q*[
6. 　　　　　　　　]your great rule *lš*[
7. 　　　　　　　　].*wm vacat* [
8. 　　　　　　　　]*yn* . . [

Fragment 10 (cf. outline E)
1. and]now, my Lord[
2. 　　　　]. you have increased. And if .[
3. 　　　　　　　　]you wish and *k*[

Fragment 11 col. ii
1. [. . .]
2. the dew and [the]rai[n
　　　　bottom margin

Fragment 12
1. and until [
2. 　　　*vacat*　　[
3. Th[e]n[

Fragment 13
1. and]they [bowe]d from . . [
2. Th]en he said to him,[". . .

3. There is no pea[ce] for you[
4.   ]*l.* was [

1 En. 12:5; 13:1; 16:4;
1Q24 frag. 8; KawAl

Fragment 14
1. those, he brought a giant who '[
2. bright, Shemi[hazah] prevailed[
3. behold, he did [his/the] deed[
4. And if .

4Q530 (4QEnGiants^b ar)
Fragment 1 col. i
1.   ] . [   ] . [   ] . . [
2.   for] a curse and sorrow. I am the one who confessed
3.   ]. and the whole house of refuge that I go to him
4. the souls of] ones[ki]lled complaining against their killers and crying out

1 En. 9:10

5.   ] .*t'* that we shall die together and be put to an end
6.   ]*sp* much, and I will sleep, and bread

Cf. KawW?

7.   ]ways to my dwelling. The vision and also
8.   ]he entered the assembly of the giants

Fragments 2 col. i + 3
              top margin
1.   ]he will place it
2.] . [the hea]vens together with
3.   ] they will be numbered with all
4.]. they will be reckoned with the reckoning of years, from
5. these [se]ven (or: fo]ur) days in their wa[tch
6. you will [n]ot rejoice, and you shall not[

Fragment 4
1.   ]*n ṭ*[ ]*n*[
2. they [will] be reckon[ed] with[

Fragment 5
1.] his brother [r]uled ov[er
2. he [c]an[not] seek ou[t
3.].*yn* may he/they not kno[w
4.   ]and not[

Fragments 2 col. ii + 6 + 7 col. i 8–11+12 (cf. outline Q, R)
(plus reconstruction with 6Q8 3 3 + 2, underlined)
              top margin
1. concerning the death of our souls. [And] all his companions [ca]me in [and 'O]hyah informed them about that which Gilgames^a had said to him.

---

a. "Gilgames" is a variant spelling of the name "Gilgamesh." Likewise, "Ḥobabis" in line 2 is a variant spelling of "Ḥobabish."

The Aramaic Book of Giants

<small>4Q203 frag. 3 3;
KawZs2; KawAj</small>

2. And Ḥ[o]babis roared, and [ju]dgment was announced against his soul, and the guilty one cursed the magnates,
3. and the giants rejoiced concerning him. And he returned and was cur[s]ed(?) [and complai]ned against him. Then the two of them dreamed dreams,
4. and the sleep of their eyes fled from them and [they] aro[se {[sleep of]their eyes from them and they arose}[a] and] they [op]ened their eyes
5. and came to [... And then] they recounted their dreams in the assembly of [their] com[panions]

<small>KawAj; Midrash
of Shemhazai and
Aza'el 10</small>

6. the Nephilim. [And Hahyah the giant said, ["In] my dream [I] was seeing during this night, and behold,
7. [there was a big garden ... and it] had gardeners, and they were watering
8. [every tree in the garden ... and] huge [shoo]ts sprang forth from their root,
9. [and from one tree there sprang forth three roots.] I was [looking] until tongues of fire [came down] from [heaven]
10. I continued looking until]the [dus]t [was covered] with all the waters, and the fire was burning all
11. [the trees of this entire paradise, but it did not burn the tree and its shoots on]the earth as [...]
12. [...]'. Here is the end of the dream." *vacat*
13. [Then Hahyah asked for an interpretation of the dream and]the giants were [un]able to tell him
14. [the dream.... And he said,] "This [drea]m you shall give [to Eno]ch, the eminent scribe, so that he will interpret for us
15. the dream. *vacat* Then his brother 'Ohyah [answ]ered and said before the giants, "I have also
16. seen in my dream during this night, O giants, [and]behold, the Sovereign of heaven descended to the earth,

<small>Dan 7:9–10</small>

17. and thrones were set up. And the Great Holy One sa[t down. A hundred hu]ndreds were serving him, a thousand thousands [were bowing to] him.
18. [Al]l were standing [be]fore him. And behold, [boo]ks were opened, and judgment was spoken, and the judgment of
19. [the Great One]was [wr]itten [in a book], and (it was) signed with a signature .[...] over every living being and flesh and over
20. [all those with autho]rity. Here is the end of the dream"[...] All the giants became afraid
21. [... and]they called Mahaway, and he came to the as[sem]bly of[the ...] giants. And they sent him to Enoch,
22. ...]*bw* and said to him, "Go [to him ...] . [...] the place is familiar to you because
23. you heard his voice the first time." And he said to him, "He will tell [y]ou the in[ter]pretation of the dreams and so that everything will be put to rest
24. [togeth]er with (those who) hungrily[b] desire (it). If there is deception[

---

a. A copyist error results here in reduplication of text.
b. The term *knp* ("to hunger") is applied metaphorically.

The Aramaic Book of Giants

Fragment 7 col. ii (cf. outline S) KawB
top margin
1. if . [
2. still[ ] . [
3. I wanted (to know) the longevity[a] of the giants [
4. like whirlwinds, and he flew with his wings[b] {like whirl-}[c] like an eag[le . . . he flew over]
5. the inhabited world and passed over (the place of) seclusion, the great desert [
6. and Enoch saw hi[m] and called out to him and said to him, "Mahaway, what[. . . I have been sent]
7. here, and to you a second time to tell [you two dreams, . . . so that we may hear
8. your words, and all the Nephilim of the earth. If he brings [
9. who have sw[orn with]their [oath], and it will be add[ed t]o[
10. that we] may know from you the[i]r interpretation *vacat* [Then Enoch answered Mahaway and said
11. to him the interpretation: "Concerning the gard]eners that ca[me down] from heaven, [they are the Watchers who descended

Fragment 13
1. concerning/upon[
2. gardeners [
3.] . . [

Fragment 14
1.   ] . [
2.] . the giants [

Fragment 15
1.] . [
2.]'Ohyah [

Fragment 16
1.].*yn* to them[
2.]bread . . [

Fragment 17
1.] in them[ ]'.[
2.]he has walked with t[hem(?)

a. I.e., the remaining duration of the giants' lives.
b. Literally "his hands."
c. Copyist error through homoioarcton results in reduplication of several letters from the beginning of the line.

Fragment 18
1.]ma[ny(?) *or* they/he]bow[ed(?)
2.]he/they will bea[r
3.]he *or* he/it was [

Fragment 19
1.]*n*[
2.]their .[

Fragment 20
1.]deception[

4Q531 (4QEnGiants^c ar)
Fragment 1 (cf. outline A))
       top margin(?)
1.   Watcher]s defiled [
2.   ]giants and Nephilim .[
3.   Watchers] begot, and behold, as g[iants(?) they came forth
4.   ]by his blood and upon the hand of *mh*[
5. giant]s that was not enough for them and for [their]chi[ldren
6.   ] and (they) were seeking to devour many *ml*[
7.   vacat
8.   ]the Nephilim [op]ened it [

1 En. 7–8; Jub. 5:2

Fragments 2 + 3 (cf. outline B)
1.   ]the moon[
2.   all that]the earth produced[
3. the hea]ve[ns and all]the grea[t] fish . . . [
4.   ]and all the birds of heaven along with every kind of fruit[
5. and with] herbs seeding the earth, and every kind of grain, and all the trees[
6.   and with]sheep, small cattle, along with[
7.   and ever]ything that creeps on the earth, and after everything[
8.   ever]y cruel deed and utterance from[
9.   ]male and female and among humankind to[
10.   ]knowledge[ ]. wisdom and *r*.[

Fragment 4 (cf. outline E?)
1.]fountains of[
2.]and everything that creeps on the ea[rth
3.]you have made all t[hese
4. the]great [ ]. . ' [

Fragment 5
1.] . [
2.]   vacat   [
3.]he [s]aid to him, "I know tha[t

4 .].h and all that is upon you t[
  bottom margin or vacat

Fragment 6
1.   ] . . [
2.   ] . (they were) taking .[ ] . [ ] . [ ] . . [
3.]you gave him this reminder . . [
4.] they committed a [grea]t [defilement] against you (plur.) . . [

Fragment 7
Cf. 1 En. 7:5; 10:9; Jub. 5:7, 9?

1.   ]and to Aḥiram and[
2.   and to] 'Ana'el and to Baraq'e[l and to the Ne]philim [
3.   ]l and to Na'am'el and to Ra[zi'el] and to 'Ami'el[
4. and to]all these giants. What sins were yours that [you] killed
5.   ] . Did not all these go by your sword[
6.   blood] like great rivers upon [the]ea[rth
7.   ]against you 'A[sa'el

Fragment 8
1.]'el and to '[
2.   ]lš[

Fragment 9
1. to]do evil[(?)
2.   ]'l [
3.   ]l[

Fragment 10
1.] vacat [
2. ki]lled ones[

Fragment 11 (cf. outline G)
1.   ].r from .[
2. I] saw(?) his throne and .[
3.   f]ive before him[
  bottom margin or vacat

Fragment 12
1.   ]there is every[
2. he [th]rew down his garment[
3.]. and as sparks o[f fire

Fragment 13
1.]I have bound him and I will loosen[
2.].' before ḥd[
3.].y glorious[
4.] from the splendor r[

5.] in his likeness [
6.]of(?) light .[

Fragment 14 (cf. outline G, H)
      top margin or *vacat*

Dan 7:10   1.].*th* a thousand thousands [were bowing]to him
2.]his[   ]is not afraid of any king and '*l*[
3. fear]seized (me), and I fell on my face. [I] hear[d] his voice[
4.]he does [no]t dwell among human beings and he has not learned from
Cf. Gen 5:24?   them[
5.   *vacat*
6.   ]which *m*[   ] . . . [   ]a vessel, two[
7.   ] . . . [ ] ∴[

Fragment 15
1.].*š*.[
2.] . is not[. . . ?
3.]and I was late [
4.   ].*h*[

Fragment 16
1.] .[
2.] and (he/they/I) said[
3.] I smell(?)[
4.] your[

Fragment 17 (cf. outline E)
      top margin or *vacat*
1. righ]teous ones, and you have set apart[
2.   ] eternal. You have made for me[
3.   ]to mourn all the times of[
4.   ] you have sent [ ]*l*.[
5.   ]flesh and *l*.[

Fragment 18
      top margin
1.]holy, exalted place[
2.]a luminary, ruin[a] of destruction [
3.].' we who have sinn[ed
4.] and I am ruined and [they/he] shall per[ish
5.   human]kind . . [

Fragment 19
1.   ] . [   ] . [
2.]many [dee]ds of violence on the dry land

    a. "ruin" or "swords."

3.]n[ot] bones we are, and not flesh   Cf. 1 En. 15:8–12
4. f]lesh, and we shall be wiped out from our form
5.]. . your holy ones to us[
6.   ]   *vacat*   [

Fragment 20
1.].*p* the neck[
2.]   *vacat*   [
3.]who sin and *l*[
4.   ] . [

Fragment 21
1.] and you
2. the ord]er of ages
3.   bottom margin or *vacat*

Fragment 22 (cf. outline K, L)
1. [to t]he[left] and the right[   ]every house[and a righ]teous man was not [found]
2. [   ]their [see]d(?)   *vacat*
3. [. . .]powerful [and I], and by the mighty strength of my arm and by my powerful force
4. [. . . a]ll flesh, and I made war against them, but [I was] not
5. [strong enough, and] I was [not] able to prevail against them, because my adversaries
6. [are angels who] dwell [in heave]n, and they reside in holy places. *vacat* And [they have] not
7. [been defeated because the]y are stronger than I.   *vacat*   1 En. 9–10
8. [. . .]*rh* of the wild creature has come, and a wild man (they) call (me).
9. [. . .]and thus 'Ohyah said to him: *vacat*   "My dream was inflicted on m[e]
10. [and] the [sl]eep of my eyes [fled from me] to see a [vis]ion. Behold, I know that concerning
11. [the vision I]will [not] sleep, and I will not seek for t[hem . . .]*t*'[
12. [. . .   Gi]lgamesh said, "Your [d]ream [   ] pea[ce(?)."
       bottom margin or *vacat*

Fragment 23
1. to live for a period of days[
2. all the wicked ones *m*[
3. I will be killed, and I will die .[
4.   ]everything he will de[stroy(?)
5.   ] . [   ] . [

Fragment 24
1.   ] . . [
2.]he bound and *ntl*[

3.]the hand of great ones is changed[
    bottom margin or *vacat*

Fragment 25
1.   ]n[
2.] . which is done in .[
3.] . . my traveler/my transgressor and *lm*[
4.]no [   ] will come to an end[
5.] . they are dying[a] . [

Fragment 26
1. he]speaks about you, a king, .[
2.]the downfall of your sons and[
3.] . [   ]*l*[

Fragment 27
1.] . . . [
2.].*m* for you
3.]the dust in this
4.]   *vacat*
5.] . '*l*[
6.] . [

Fragment 28
1.   ]n[
2.] by th[eir] blood[
3.]they [sai]d(?) thus [
4.]now to you[
5.]I/you said[
6.] for *m*.[

Fragment 29
1.] . [   ] . [
2.]my voice(?)[
3.]to see [
4. ho]ly .[

Fragment 30
1.   ] . . [
2.   ] . and not *t*.[
3. from(?)]which we shall be loosed [
4.   ] *vacat*   [

Fragment 31
1.]   *vacat*   [

---

a. "they are dying" or "they are two hundred."

2.]his [ ]. and as the one who is like[
3.].*yh* changed *b*.[

Fragment 32
1.]...*h* '[
2.]and now by the blood[
3.   ]. *vacat* [

Fragment 33
1.]they will become angry[
2.]*n* upon[

Fragment 34
1.   ].' *q*.[
2. you] have [d]one and upon[
3.   ]*ryh* '[

Fragment 35
1.]until *t*[
2.]sins .[

Fragment 36
1.] . to [the] wat[chers
2. a]ngel[

Fragment 37
1. wr]ote(?) it[
2.] around[

Fragment 38
1.   ]dead[
2.]. around[

Fragment 39
1. to]meditate[
2.]to the mountain of [

Fragment 40
1.]of the bo[dy
2.]his [wo]rd(?)[

Fragment 41
1.   ]rather (or: except)[
2.]the sea[
3.]' [

Fragment 42
1. y]ou
2.]they

Fragment 43
1.] not [
2.]*dly* [
3.].*h*[

Fragment 44
1.   ]. . ' *l*.[
2.   ]' to Enoch, to[the eminent scribe(?)
3.]beaten[a] and [the] tru[th(?)
4.   ] . [

Fragment 45
1.   ]I was freed (or: distanced myself) [
2.]   vacat [
3.]*yn* they went forth terrified .[
4.]' unto heaven[
5.]. *mq*[

Fragment 46
1.]and I Oh[yah(?)
2.]I ascended and entered hea[ven

Fragment 47 (cf. outline R)
1. books]were [op]ened in .[
2.   ]holy '[
3.   ] . . [

Fragment 48
1.]and to the gia[nts(?)

Fragment 49
1.]in goodness[
2.]' in '.[
3.]*l*[ ]*l*[ ] . [

Fragment 50
1.]this[
2.]*ll*[

Fragment 51
1.]š[

a. "beaten" or "living."

4Q532 (4QEnGiants[d] ar)
Fragment 1 cols. i–ii

	col. i	col. ii
1.		l[
2.		great[
3.		as d[(or: wh[en)
4.		ʿ.[
5.	]they [he]ard	to the one rai[sing
6.	]judgment	by h[
7.	they are s]ent to you	and for .[
8.	]her diviners, he went forth	and h[
9.	]female he made	.[
10.	al]l flesh	which[
11.	]' he gave	they will be [
12.	].y eternal	and the peace of[
13.	]n and he knew	
14.	]l[	

Fragment 2　　　　　　　　　　　　　　　　　　　　　　　Gen 6:5, 11–12; Jub. 5:2

1.]the[ear]th
2.]in [the]fles[h
3.]and [the] Nephili[m
4.]' they were stand[ing
5.]the earth tr[
6.]they were contemplating to[
7.]which is/was from the Watchers upon[
8. at the]end he will perish and die   [
9.]a great corruption he has caused on [the] ea[rth
10. not] enough for them to ea[t
11.].y the earth and until l.[
12.]on the earth in every b[
13.]great. And now not š[
14.]they [pu]t a stron[g] bond[
    bottom margin or *vacat*

4Q533 (4QEnGiants[e] ar)
Fragment 1 cols. i–ii

	col. i	col. ii
1.	]..	
2.	].t	lm.[
3.	]	which .[
4.	]when	affliction[

Fragment 2

1.].k.[
2. and]now b[
3.]h whs[

4.   ]we[

Fragment 3
1.   ] children prayed before him [
2.   ]' «written» and everyone will seek you concerning[
3. there is]written conc[er]ning you a decree [saying

Fragment 4
1.   to de]ceive[upon]the earth all w[ho
2. blood]was being poured out and lies were being [told
3.   G]o[d], a flood upon the earth[

Fragment 5
1.] upon[
2. he] told[(or: I]will tell[)
3.] . [ ] . [

Fragment 6
1.]*yn t*[
2.]*l*[

Fragment 7
1.]he said[(or: they]said[)

Fragment 8
1.   ]*n*[
2.].' and he went[
3.].*m* over all[

4Q206 (4QEn^e ar) 2 and 3 (4QEnGiants^f? ar)
Fragment 2 (cf. outline D)
1.   ]*yn* and all[
2. it was to]ld to Enoch [the eminent]sc[ribe
3.   ] . [ ]*r* Behold, the Great One[

Fragment 3 (cf. outline C)—parallel to 4Q533 frag. 4?
1.]the[earth] all[   ]*m* (they were) planning
2.] . in it blood was being poured out
3.]they were *m*[ ] . [ ].*yn* in it[ev]ery
        bottom margin

6Q8 (6QpapGiants ar)
Fragment 1
1. [ ] . [
2. [ ]'Ohyah [answer]ed and said to Mahaway .[
3. [ ]and does not shudder? Who has shown you everything? '[Mahaway answered]

4. [and said to 'Ohya]h, "Baraq'el my father was with me."   vacat [
5. [and]Mahaway [had]not [fi]nished [t]elling him what [Baraq'el had showed him]
6. [when 'Ohyah answered and said to]him, "Behold, I have heard wonders! If a barre[n (woman)] were to give birth[
   bottom margin

Fragment 2
(cf. 4Q530, frags. 2 col. ii + 6 + 7 col. i 8–11+112, lines 9–11)   KawAj; Midrash
1. three of its roots [. . .]   of Shemhazai and
2. I was [looking] until they came[Aza'el 10
3. this entire paradise *m*[

Fragment 3
(cf. 4Q530, frags. 2 col. ii + 6 + 7 col. i 8–11+112, lines 7–8)
1.] great [
2.] for its trees(?) [

Fragment 4
1.] . [
2. .*bh* and *y.*[
3. you will draw[
4. . . . and not .[

Fragment 5
   top margin
1.]*n* all the gardeners
2.   ].*l*[

Fragment 6
1.]to them sufficiently[
   bottom margin

Fragment 7
1.] in *yr.*[
2.]. . *d.*[

Fragment 8
1.] they will say .[
2.]. . . .[

Fragment 9
1.]*n* and .[
2.]he will cut[

Fragment 10
1.] . . [   ] . [

2.].wn to ky.[

Fragment 11
1.] . . [
2.]l. . [

Fragment 12
1.]. . .[
2.]mu[ch bl]ood

Fragment 13
1.] .r [

Fragment 14
1.]and he (or: they/you) ope[ned

Fragment 15
1.]h every[

Fragment 16
1.].l[
2.]w.[

Fragment 17
1.]rather (or: except)[
2.] . . t[

Fragment 18
1.]to Yared .[

Fragment 19
1.] . . [

Fragment 20
1.]m [
2.] . [
3.]ḥ[

Fragment 21
1.] belonging to[

Fragment 22
1.]. lr. .[
2.] to db[

Fragment 23
1. a]ges[

Fragment 24
1.]*h* .[
2.] . [

Fragment 25
1.]*rb*.[

Fragment 26
1. Lubar ʿ[
2. in the direction .[
3. and he chose *š*[
4. and]my sons . . [

Fragment 27
1.]and(?) he trembled *m*[
2.] . . .*mr*. . [

Fragment 28
1.] . . . Raphae[l(?)

Fragment 29
1.]*k* this[
2.]*l*[

Fragment 30
1.]   ]*n*[
2.]. which *m*.[
3.]. *h*.[

Fragment 31
1.]. .*g*[
2.].ʿ*l* .[

Fragment 32
1.] . [
2.]*t š*.[

Fragment 33
1.   ]ʾ
2.]*l*.ʾ[

The Book of Giants: Iranian Manichean Version
A new translation and introduction

by Prods Oktor Skjærvø

The Manichean Book of Giants was one of the canonical books of Mani, founder of Manicheism in the third century CE. Fragments of the book from numerous manuscripts written in three Iranian languages—Middle Persian (ancestor of modern Persian), Parthian, spoken in Northeastern Iran, and Sogdian, spoken in the area of modern Uzbekistan—as well as in Uyghur (Old Turkic)[1] were discovered in the early twentieth century by German, Russian, and Japanese archaeologist-explorers in the area of Turfan.[2] Today this is a town located in a low-lying oasis (down to 154 m below sea level) in the northeastern corner of the Tarim Basin, part of Xinjiang Autonomous Region of China (formerly called Chinese Turkestan) and inhabited by Muslim Uyghurs (not descendants of the ancient Uyghurs). Turfan and its surroundings were once a center for Western religions proselytizing in the east and close to the capital of the Uyghur Empire, Khocho (Qocho) or Karakhoja (Chinese Gaochang). Quotations from and references to the book are also found in Manichean Coptic texts discovered in Egypt in the 1930s, as well as in references to Manicheism in the works of Christian and Muslim authors.

Contents
The narrative of the Manichean Book of Giants begins with the conclusion of Mani's cosmogony[3] and the making of the first two humans, then segues into what was Mani's take on the biblical story in Gen 6:1–4 of the *nephilim* who were on earth before the Flood and the descent to the earth of the "sons of god," who copulated with the women, after which the women gave birth to the *gibborim*, at least according to the Aramaic and Mani's Book of Giants.[4] Mani interpreted *nephilim* as "the fallen ones" and identified them with the abortions that *fell* from heaven and from whom the first two humans were made according to his own cosmogony and anthropogony.[5]

The Manichean Book of Giants tells the story of the creation of mankind (the Prologue) and the two hundred heavenly demons (the Watchers) who, lusting after earthly women, came down to the earth and sired bastard progeny, which in the Coptic and Greek texts were identified as giants. As in the Aramaic Book of Giants, this story was connected with the narrative we see in 1 Enoch, but also included a cast of characters

---

1. See Zieme's chapter in this volume.
2. Uyghur Turpan, Chinese Tulufan.
3. See the section below on "Mani's Cosmongony."
4. See Fröhlich 2016. On the *nephilim* see also Stroumsa 1984, 158–67; Reeves 1992, 70–72, 135; Stuckenbruck 1997, 111–12.
5. See Henning (1943: 53) and the section below, "The Prologue of the Book of Giants." On the titles of the book, see the section below, "The Title of the Manichean Book of Giants."

taken from ancient Mesopotamian traditions, to which Mani and his followers added elements from Iranian and Indic traditions.

Central to the story is the giant Māhaway, who travels to find Enoch and ask him about the meaning of his fellow giants' dreams. Enoch's interpretations are written on tablets that Māhaway brings back. Enoch warns the giants that they will be punished for their sins, but they do not listen. He then promises them eternal damnation in the fiery pits of hell, where they are observed by the righteous.

Four angels are sent down to take care of the problems. They round up and relocate the two hundred demon Watchers and then fight a fierce battle with the giants and their offspring, with losses on both sides.

The Manichean book ends with an instructional text (the Epilogue) about how to avoid harming the Light imprisoned in Matter[6] and how to be a good hearer (Manichean layman).

The Manuscript Discoveries[7]

The Turfan area is rich in archeological sites, with remnants of ancient monasteries and grottos (Manichean, Christian, Buddhist), the largest site being Khocho, which lies in the plain. Others lie in a river valley going up into the Flaming Mountains (e.g., Toyoq, where they have been seriously damaged by earthquakes and floods), still others along other rivers in the area (e.g., Bezeklik and Sängim), which early on attracted the attention of visitors (see Sundermann 2004 for further details). Manichean fragments were discovered mainly during four German expeditions (1902–1914) led by Albert Grünwedel (1856–1935), director of the Indian Department of the Museum für Völkerkunde, and Albert von Le Coq (1860–1930), a German brewery owner and wine merchant turned archaeologist. The Japanese mounted three expeditions (1902–1914), the first led by Count Kozui Ōtani. The Russian Sergei Fedorovich Ol'denburg, director of the Asiatic Museum in St. Petersburg, led two expeditions to Turfan (1909–1915). From 1928, the Chinese also excavated in the area.[8]

Publication of the material began in 1904, when Friedrich W. K. Müller published two articles containing manuscript remains from the Berlin Turfan collection (Middle Persian and Sogdian).[9] It continued quickly with publications of manuscripts and studies on Manicheism by Carl Salemann (1904, 1908: Middle Persian, recovered mainly during the German expeditions), Albert von Le Coq (1911, 1912: "Türkische Manichaica aus Chotscho"); Édouard Chavannes and Paul Pelliot published Manichean Chinese texts from Dunhuang (1911, 1913: the Chinese "Traité manichéen"),[10] and A. V. William Jackson (1932: study of cosmogonic texts). The Preussische Akademie der Wissenschaften had entrusted the publication of the Iranian Turfan material to the German Iranologist

---

6. See the sections below, on "Mani's Cosmogony" and "The Epilogue."

7. The manuscripts are cited here according to the practice in Durkin-Meisterernst 2004 (see the section "Manuscripts and Versions" below). Thus, M101h/R/1/ = MS M101h in the Turfan collection, recto line 1. The fragments are identified as follows: 4:KawX = no. 4 in the sequence of fragments in the translation section, siglum KawX. Occasionally, recto and verso are added, e.g., 1:KawZs1/R/ = no. 1 in the sequence, siglum KawZs1, recto.

8. On the expeditions, see http://idp.bl.uk/pages/collections.a4d; Sundermann 2004.

9. At the end of his first article (1904, 352), Müller, as the first, stated that the manuscripts must be remnants of the Manichean literature.

10. See Schmidt-Glintzer (1987, 5–8) on the Chinese texts.

Friedrich Carl Andreas (1846–1930), and, at the death of Andreas, Walter B. Henning (1908–1967), Andreas's student, was entrusted with the publication of the texts Andreas had prepared.[11] Henning quickly published the material, as well as a series of articles, including an edition (1934) of a text (MS M299) in which Enoch (*hwnwkh*) is listed in the Manichean chain of apostles.[12] His remarks on the new sources for the study of Manicheism (1933) and on central Asian Manicheism (1934) were fundamental.

During and after World War II, publication of the Iranian texts proceeded slowly at first, mainly in articles by Henning (among them "The Book of Giants," 1943). In 1960, Mary Boyce published a catalog of the Manichean manuscripts in Berlin, and, in 1975, she published a large number of the then-known Manichean Persian and Parthian texts in transliteration (including fragments of the Book of Giants) accompanied by a glossary.

By then, the East-German scholar Werner Sundermann had begun producing major editions of Manichean texts in the Turfan collection (1973: cosmological texts and parable texts; 1981: texts relating to the history of the Manichean church; etc.). In between, he published numerous fragments of considerable interest, including several dealing with the Book of Giants. Christiane Reck published a catalog of Manichean fragments in Sogdian script[13] in the Turfan collection in 2006, listing several fragments of the Book of Giants. The Manichean manuscripts found by the German expeditions are now at the section Turfanforschung of the Berlin-Brandenburgische Akademie der Wissenschaften and in the Museum für Indische Kunst in Berlin. All the manuscripts at the Turfanforschung are available online at the Digitales Turfan-Archiv (http://turfan.bbaw.de/dta/m/dta_m_index.htm).

Manichean Paintings

Several Chinese Manichean texts and paintings were discovered in Xiapu county, present-day Fujian province in southeastern China, and published by Chen Jinguo and Lin Yun in 2010.[14] In the same year, Yutaka Yoshida published an article on the cosmogony depicted in a number of Manichean paintings discovered in Japan, which are currently thought to have been parts of Mani's *Picture Book*, the Ārdahang.[15] Here, Yoshida noticed that several of the events pictured in the paintings illustrated the Book of Giants, which he elaborated on in 2015.

---

11. See Henning 1933.

12. The apostles who appeared at intervals in the history of the world to bring Knowledge (*gnosis*) to mankind (see n. 116 below), the last of whom was Mani himself. See Henning 1934b, and the section below on "Mani and His *Dēn*." On Enoch in the Manichean texts, see also Asmussen, 1984. Note that the apostles, "messengers" (the word also means "angels") in general and Mani in particular, are not called "prophets" in the Iranian and Coptic texts. In the Iranian texts, the rare word "bringer of the word," is used for "prophet" in "[. . .], the prophets and the Scriptures," apparently followed by "the Buddha," and so may refer to the biblical prophets (Sundermann 1981, 33 line 303). In MS M83/I/V/7/ = M496a/V/12/ = M759/II/R/11/ we read "the apostle, Lord Marī-Mānī." Mani is also commonly called the Apostle of Light and, according to his letter to Marcellus (*Acta Archelai* 5), he referred to himself as "Manichæus apostle of Jesus Christ," quoted by Augustine (*Epistula Fundamenti*, frag. 1; Gardner and Lieu 2004, 168).

13. On the scripts, see the section below, on "Languages and Scripts."

14. See Kósa 2016, part 1.

15. See Yoshida 2015. For further bibliography and descriptions, see also Kósa 2016, part 2, and Kósa 2017.

Coptic Texts and the Cologne Mani Codex

The first half of the twentieth century had more surprises in store. In 1930, the German Coptologist Carl Schmidt (1868–1938), during one of his travels to Egypt, discovered a batch of Coptic papyri in an antique shop in Cairo, which turned out to be from an ancient Manichean library. The running head of the papyri contained the word *kephalaion*, which Schmidt (p. 5 [6]) connected with the remark by Epiphanius (bishop of Constantia in Cyprus, ca. 310–403) in his *Panarion* (374–377) that the name of one of the books of the Manicheans was Kephalaia.[16] He therefore concluded that the whole batch must contain Manichean writings.

Meanwhile, Alfred Chester Beatty (1875–1968), American mining magnate and philanthropist, as well as collector of Oriental antiquities, had also come across the Coptic papyri and bought a considerable part of them, which were subsequently housed in the Chester Beatty Library, Dublin.

In 1931–1932, Schmidt made another trip to Egypt and found further parts of the same collection, which he also bought. This time he was also able to identify the place where the finds had been made: the basement of a house in Medinat Mādi in Fayyum, a military colony founded in the Ptolemaic period, southwest of Cairo. An extensive report on the finds was published by Schmidt in 1933, in which he described the circumstances surrounding the acquisition of the papyri, as well as the contents of the two collections. The Kephalaia, in particular, contains important texts describing the events narrated in the Book of Giants.[17]

Another important find from Egypt became known much later. In the late 1960s a minuscule Greek codex in the papyrus collection of the University of Cologne was noticed (the Cologne Mani Codex).[18] The codex was successfully opened and conserved in 1969 and the contents made known to an astounded world of Manichean scholars in 1970 by Albert Henrichs and Ludwig Koenen. Here, Mani tells in detail about his life in an Elchasaite (baptist) community, founded by a certain Alkhasaios (Latin Elchasai). A preliminary edition and translation was published in two articles (1975–1978) by Henrichs, Albert, and Ludwig Koenen, "Ein griechischer Mani-Codex (P. Colon. inv. nr. 4780)" in *ZPE* 5 (1970): 97–216,[19] and a partial translation by Ron Cameron and Arthur J. Dewey in 1979. A complete edition containing text and facsimiles was published by Koenen and Cornelia Roemer in 1985. The date of the codex is somewhat debated. While the original editors thought it might be from as early as the fourth century, paleographic analyses have led others to suggest fifth- or even seventh/eighth-century dates.[20]

More recently the remains from another Egyptian Manichean community of the fourth century were discovered at Kellis (Ismant el-Kharab), also in Upper Egypt.[21]

---

16. Williams 2009, 213, 229.
17. On these discoveries, see Gardner 1995, xv–xxi; Gardner and Lieu 2004, 35–39.
18. See Sundermann 1992.
19. According to Koenen and Römer 1985, p. vii n. 2, it was published in four parts in *ZPE* (*Zeitschrift für Papyrologie und Epigraphik*): *ZPE* 19, 1975, pp. 1–85 (text and comm.); *ZPE* 32, 1978, pp. 87–199 (text and comm.); *ZPE* 44, 1981, pp. 121–92; *ZPE* 48 (1982), pp. 1–59 (text).
20. See Gardner and Lieu 1996, 39–43.
21. See Gardner and Lieu 1996, 43–45; Lieu 1994, 87–89.

The Book of Giants: Iranian Manichean Version

Qumran

Barely two years after the Nag Hammadi discovery, in 1947, another sensational find was made, this time in Judea, where Bedouin boys discovered a cache of manuscripts in caves on the shore of the Dead Sea. Publication of these texts proceeded slowly, but today, all, or almost all, the material has been published in facsimile and translation. On the basis of a Sogdian fragment edited by Henning, the Polish biblical scholar Józef Tadeusz Milik (1922–2006) was able to identify some Book of Giants fragments among the Qumran fragments (1971, 1976). Since then, comparison with the Manichean texts has been included in studies of the Qumranic material, notably Reeves 1992 and 1996 and Stuckenbruck 1997 and 2016.[22]

Work on the Iranian Manichean Book of Giants

It was early noticed that Enoch was mentioned in Manichean texts also outside the chain of apostles, but, while 1 Enoch, with its story of the Watchers and giants,[23] was well edited by the beginning of the twentieth century, not much was known about the Book of Giants until the Turfan discoveries. The first Enoch fragments to be published were some Uyghur ones published by von Le Coq in 1922.[24]

The Iranian fragments gradually yielded up further references to Enoch and the giants. In his 1934 article, Henning also published a fragment (12:KawD) in which he identified the terms for giant (*kaw*, pl. *kawān*) and Watcher (*ʿīr*) and the interpretation of a dream. He compared this with a fragment in which *Kawān* was listed among works by Mani,[25] which he compared with references to Mani's Book of Giants, and concluded that this must be it. References to the contents of the book he found in Edouard Sachau's (1845–1930) translation of al-Biruni's (973–1048) *Chronology* and Isaac de Beausobre's (1659–1738) history of Manicheism (1734, 1739), where Beausobre (1734, 429)—correctly as it turned out—suggested the Book of Giants drew upon the fables found in 1 Enoch. Finally, Henning announced that he had, in fact, identified numerous fragments from the Book of Giants among the Turfan fragments. He provided further details in an article on the new Manichean materials (1936, 3–6) and then published the fragmentary manuscripts he had identified in 1943 with copious notes and references.[26]

Several additional fragments of the Iranian Manichean Book of Giants have been identified since Henning's groundbreaking edition, to which only minor corrections have been made since. Sundermann published 31:KawY (1973, 77–78) and 1/3:KawZs1 (1994), of which Henning had published only one folio, as well as 16:KawW in the Oriental Institute in St. Petersburg.

A translation of all the fragments by Enrico Morano (based on Henning), also the Coptic and Uyghur ones, was included in volume 3 of *Il Manicheismo* edited by Gherardo Gnoli (2008). Here, Morano maintained Henning's alphabetic number-

---

22. *Nag Hammadi and Manichaean Studies* 41. For all references to the Aramaic Book of Giants, see Stuckenbruck's chapter in this volume.
23. The Book of the Watchers = 1 En. 1–36.
24. See Zieme's chapter in this volume.
25. MS M5815/II/; see the section below, "The Title of the Manichean Book of Giants."
26. It must be kept in mind that Henning's edition of the manuscripts M101 and M911 was based on a copy he had made almost ten years earlier and that he was unable to recollate the manuscripts "under the present circumstances" (Henning 1943, 56).

ing, adding 16:KawW, 4:KawX, 31:KawY, 1/3:KawZs1, and 13:KawZs2, all published by Sundermann.

To accommodate the additional texts beyond Text Z, Morano adopted the sigla Zp = Parthian text, Zs = Sogdian text, and Zu = Uyghur text, and then used consecutive numbering for each category: Zp1–2, Zs1–2, Zu1–6 (complete list in Morano 2011).

In his 2011 article (basically an English translation of Morano 2008, but without the texts), Morano added 27:KawZp1, published by Iris Colditz, and 8:KawZp2, published by him. Here, he also described the contents of the text fragments, gave references to 1 Enoch, the Qumran fragments, the biblical narrative, etc.

In her catalog of Manichean texts in Sogdian script in the Turfan collection also from 2011, Reck pointed out a number of fragments that belonged or might belong to the Book of Giants. Morano did not assign sigla to these, but they are found here as KawZs3–6. Of these, he published 20–21:KawZs4–5 and 26:KawZs6 in Morano 2016, while 2:KawZs3 will be published in Morano forthcoming. 13:KawZs2, a fragment in the Ōtani collection, was published by Kudara *et al.* (1977). Ōtani 6207 (ibid.) is included among the Book of Giants fragments for the first time here as 31a:KawZmp1.[27]

Jes P. Asmussen wrote an article on the Book of Giants for the *Encyclopædia Iranica*, which was published in 1984, and Sundermann an updated article published in 2001.

Manuscripts and Versions[28]

Most of the surviving manuscripts of the Manichean Book of Giants are single fragments from different manuscripts, of varying size and state of preservation. The exceptions are: M7800: a complete folio in double columns; M813 fragments of two folios; So 14255 + 14256 and So 14638: both damaged complete folios; and So 10700a + So 20193a and So 10701a + So 20193b: two damaged folios of the same manuscript.

Overlapping manuscripts: M35 and M740a; So 14255+56 and M7800.

The Middle Persian and Parthian manuscripts are written in the Manichean script, the Sogdian ones in the Manichean and Sogdian scripts.[29]

> M and So = Manuscripts in the Berlin-Brandenburgische Akademie der Wissenschaften.[30] All those from the Book of Giants were found at Khocho.
> SIO = manuscript in the Ol'denburg collection at the Oriental Institute of the Russian Academy of Sciences, St. Petersburg.
> Ōtani = manuscript fragments in the Ōtani collection kept in the Ryūkoku University Library, Kyoto.

Middle Persian
- M101 (KawAa–n: 29:KawAk, 33:KawAe, 34:KawAb, 35:KawAh, 36:KawAf, 37:KawAa, 38:KawAd, 39:KawAm, 41:KawAn): 14 pieces, all of the same size and roundish shape, about 10 lines, with first and last lines more fragmentary.

---

27. This fragment was noticed only after this text was finalized and was given the sequential number 31a. It did not seem practical to renumber the manuscript sequence.
28. Since the manuscripts can be seen at the Turfan Project website and complete descriptions are found in Boyce 1960 and Reck 2004 and, for those published later, in the respective publications, the descriptions here are cursory.
29. See the section below, "Languages and Scripts."
30. See Boyce 1960 and Reck 2006.

- M625c (12:KawD): small fragment with 5 lines written in two columns, with one and a half columns and one margin preserved.
- M911 (40:KawA): small piece from the same MS as M101, 6 lines.
- M5900 (31:KawY): top of folio; 16 lines; margins on both sides. Header: "Sp[eech about the] Mā[zendarān]."
- M5750 (0:KawJ): one folio written in two columns delineated by red lines, 24 and 21 lines, wide margins; top and bottom of one column and top of the other missing.
- M6120 (23/25:KawF): one folio of a manuscript, three columns preserved, tops and bottoms missing, 20, 16, and 15 lines; on one side, a part of the upper layer of the paper has come off. According to Henning (1943, 66 n. 4), there are other fragments of the same manuscript, which shows that there were 3 columns per page.
- SIO/120 (16:KawW): top of one folio, 13 lines of text + header; of the last lines only traces of a couple of letters; photo in Sundermann 1984 (Russian transl.). Headers: "Concerning the Māzendars" and "Sām of the Giants."
- Ōtani 6207 (31a:KawZmp1): small fragment, 7 lines; of the first and last lines only traces of a couple of letters.

Parthian
- M35 (30:KawN): slightly damaged folio with bottom missing, 18 lines, bottom lines fragmentary (overlaps with M740): the obverse contains a different text. Header: "Discourse on the Ārdahang."
- M291a (32:KawT): fragment from top/bottom of folio, 7 lines. To write the obverse, the scribe turned the paper upside down rather than right to left.
- M413 + M2086 (27:KawZp1): two pieces from top of a folio; 7, 3 lines + header, the last line only fragment of a letter; the smaller piece separated from the larger by a space of 3–5 letters.
- M740 (30:KawN): small fragment from top of folio, 8 lines, one margin preserved (overlaps with M35).
- M813 (8:KawZp2): fragments of two folios still attached to each other, 13 lines, only 2 complete; Parthian citation in a Manichean Sogdian text on M813/i/ lines 9–13.[31]
- M2086, see M413.
- M4990 (42:KawU): fragment of one column, 8 lines, no margins; obverse blank.
- M8280 (4:KawX): fragment of two columns, 7 lines + header, with header and last lines mostly lost.

Manichean Sogdian
- M363 (5:KawK): fragment of folio, 11 lines, one margin; end of section and beginning of next in red.
- M500n (9:KawI): bottom of column, 7 lines, top line fragmentary.
- M648b (19:KawC): fragment from middle of folio with one margin; 9 lines, top and bottom lines fragmentary.
- M692 (10:KawV): fragment from middle of folio with one margin; 13 lines, top and bottom lines fragmentary.
- M813/i/ (8:KawZp2): see Parthian above.

---

31. Manuscript M813/ii/ is in Uigur, published in Zieme 1975, 56–57 (no. 25).

- M7800 (1:KawZs1): complete folio with double columns; original now missing, photo extant.
- M7800/I/A/ (28:KawG): Header: "Explanation of the battle (?) of the four angels with the 200 [demons]." Same MS as 1/3:KawZs1, from which it is separated by an unknown number of leaves.
- M7800/ii/R/ (1/3:KawZs1): Header: "Discourse / on the demon abortions."
- M8005 (22/24:KawE): 12 lines, top and bottom mostly lost.

Sogdian Sogdian
- So 10700a + So 20193a (20:KawZs4): same MS as 21:KawZs5; a strip from the left/right edge of a folio with margin, now in two parts that fit together, 18 lines; a few lines missing at the top.
- So 10701a + So 20193b (21:KawZs5): same MS as So 10700a + So 20193a, 9 lines, a narrow strip in two parts from the left/right edge of a folio, 17 lines, more damaged than 20:KawZs4; the line at the break has fragments of letters on both parts.
- So 14255 + 14256 (2:KawZs3): damaged complete folio (28 cm × ca. 10 cm), one column broken in the middle, but continuous, fragments of margin; 28 lines. Header: "[Explanat]ion of / the fall[ing of the 200 demons]."
- So 14638 (7:KawH): slightly damaged complete folio (ca. 25 cm × ca. 14 cm), with the Book of Giants on the one side, 20 lines, Book of Giants lines 1–16; end of one section and beginning of the next in red. Header: "The coming of the two hundred demons" (cited at the end of the text).
- So 20193b, see So 10701a.
- So 20220/ii/ (26:KawZs6): one complete column of slightly damaged folio, one margin; 24 lines + header, 24 lines. Header: "Exposition of / autumn."
- Ōtani 7447/R + 7468/R (13:KawZs2): two small fragments, four and three fragmentary lines, separated by a short space, as shown by the Chinese sutra text written on the obverse.

Henning classified the manuscript fragments into three groups:

Those belonging to the Book of Giants itself: 6:KawAi, 11/14:KawAj, 15:KawAg, 17:KawAl, 18:KawAc, 29:KawAk, 33:KawAe, 34:KawAb, 35:KawAh, 36:KawAf, 37:KawAa, 38:KawAd, 39:KawAm, 40:KawA, 41:KawAn (all from manuscript M101/ M911) and 28:KawG.
Excerpts, that is, parts of the *Book of Giants* cited in other works (7:KawH, 9:KawI).
Quotations and allusions: 0:KawJ, 5:KawK, 12:KawD, 19:KawC, 22/24:KawE, 23/25:KawF, 30:KawN, including Coptic (KawL, KawM, KawP, KawQ, KawR, KawS) and Uyghur (KawB) fragments, as well as one Arabic (KawO).

Two "epic" fragments were added in an appendix (42:KawU, 10:KawV), but he was not sure they were part of the book.[32]

That the fragments actually belong to the Book of Giants is assumed mainly on the basis of the contents, but is sometimes confirmed by headers and chapter titles.

---

32. Henning 1943, 55 n. 5.

Other clues are found, first of all, in the mention of giants and their names. Those mentioned in the Iranian texts are the following, all in Middle Persian:[33]

Ahiram, a Watcher (11/14:KawAj);
Shahmīzād[34] (1 En. 6:7: Shemihazah), leader of the Watchers and his two giant sons:
Ohyā, Sāhm; Sogd. Sāhm (Uyghur Sāxm), a giant;
Ahyā, Narīmān; Sogd. Pāt-sāhm, a giant.[35]
Wirōgdād[36] (1 En. 6:7), one of the Watchers and his giant son:
Māhaway, a giant, son of Wirōgdād.[37]
Hōbābīsh[38] and Atanbīsh,[39] two giants.

In addition, the angel Raphael (Rufāēl) and the Leviathan (Lewyātān) are mentioned in a reference to the Book of Giants narrative (30:KawN).

Note that the presence of the names does not guarantee that we are dealing with texts from the Book of Giants; several fragments contain only *references* to the narrative, not the narrative itself.

Style

The texts refer to themselves by various terms, which are rendered in the various languages as "speech (about)" (Middle Persian), "discussion, sermon" (Parthian), and "discourse," "explanation" (Sogdian), and "question."[40] On the whole, they contain straightforward and terse narratives characterized by short sentences interspersed with direct speech. In particular, many of the direct speeches attributed to Enoch in the Book of Giants stem from speeches by the Most High, as in the case of 1 En. 10–11, which provides material for Enoch's speeches in 17:KawAl.

Events briefly mentioned in 1 Enoch are elaborated on, for example, in 6:KawAi, where the "cleansing of the earth" is described in detail (1 En. 10:20), while the paradisiac conditions of the righteous who escaped the butchery (1 En. 10:18–19) described in 17:KawAl were already in the Aramaic Book of Giants (1Q23 frags. 1+6+22).[41]

---

33. Morano 2011, 101: "Dramatis Personae." On the individual names, see also Stuckenbruck (2014, 41–57).

34. The name has been Iranicized by the suffix -*zād* "born of."

35. On the name, see also Skjærvø 1995a, 199 n. 32, where (Middle-Persian) Pād-husraw, brother of Zarēr and King Wishtāsp (see the comments on 42:KawU below), are compared.

36. Lit. "given by lightning," translation of Baraq'el.

37. Henning (1943, 55 n. 3) already argued that this name was from the Aramaic *Book of Giants*, rather than being the Iranian name Māhōy.

38. Milik (1976, 311–13) identified him with Humbāba, a terrifying giant, guardian of the abode of the gods, in the *Epic of Gilgamesh*. See also Reeves 1993, 114. Asmussen (1984, 728a) equated him with Kokabiel (1 En. 6:7, in Syncellus's Greek version: Khōbābēl), but see Stuckenbruck 1997, 72. See also Davila's general introduction to the Book of Giants in this volume.

39. See Reeves 1992, 84 and 1993, for the possibility that the name represents Utnapishtim, who played the same role in the Flood narrative of the *Epic of Gilgamesh* as Noah in the Biblical one. Further discussion in Stuckenbruck 1997, 73 n. 43.

40. Some of this modern terminology only tentatively renders the meaning of the Iranian words.

41. Thus Henning, "Book of the Giants," n. 7; see also Stuckenbruck, *Book of Giants from Qumran*, 57.

Mani and Manicheism

Mani may have been born in 216 CE in Babylon/Ctesiphon, when the Parthians (247 BCE–224 CE) still ruled greater Iran.[42] The last Parthian king, Ardawān (Artabanus) V, was overthrown by Ardashīr, founder of the Sasanian dynasty (224–651), which ruled the Near East until the Arab conquest of Iran. Having passed his youth in a baptist community, the Elchasaites, Mani came out publicly as an apostle at the age of twenty-four, as described in the Cologne Mani Codex (18.11). After several years spent traveling throughout Iran, he returned to Ctesiphon and approached King Shapur (Shābuhr) I (r. 239/240?–272?), son of Ardashīr, who permitted him to travel throughout his domains.[43]

The need for sending missions to disseminate Mani's teachings is set forth in his Ten Points (see the section below, "Mani and His *Dēn*"), and, according to the hagiographical texts published by Sundermann, Mani sent missionaries to the west and east, who became the founders of the western and eastern Manichean communities.[44] He sent Mar Adda west into eastern Roman territories, while others traveled west into northern Egypt, where they founded the communities that yielded up the Manichean Coptic scriptures. From there they continued into the Roman provinces of North Africa. Their presence was so noticeable that the emperor Diocletian (244–311) was disturbed by reports that a new Persian religion was spreading throughout the empire and wrote (in 302?) to his proconsul in Africa, Julianus, demanding that "the authors and leaders of these sects be subjected to severe punishment and, together with their abominable scriptures, be burnt by fire."[45] This did not stop them, however, and the young Augustine (354–430) also joined them, but converted to Christianity in 386.

Moving eastward, Manichean missionaries traveled through the Kushan Empire and Sogdiana (the area of modern Uzbekistan).[46] The Muslim conquest of Sogdiana (705–715) probably exerted strong pressure on the Manicheans to leave and travel eastward into the Tarim Basin and along the northern Silk Road to Turfan and, finally, to China.[47]

In 719, a Manichean teacher from Tokharistan came to the Chinese court, and, in 731/732, the emperor commissioned a summary of Manichean doctrines in Chinese, perhaps the so-called Compendium of the Teachings and Rules of Mani, the Buddha of Light, part of which was taken away by Aurel Stein and the concluding part by Paul

---

42. See Werner Sundermann, "Mani," *EIr*, http://www.iranicaonline.org/articles/mani-founder-manicheism; Sundermann, "Manicheism v: Missionary Activity and Technique," *EIr*, http://www.iranicaonline.org/articles/manicheism-iv-missionary-activity-and-technique-.

43. The text beginning at the end of 7:KawH may contain a description of a meeting between the king and Mani. Cf. Sundermann, *Mitteliranische manichäische Texte*, 105–7; Gardner and Lieu, *Manichaean Texts*, 73–74.

44. Sundermann, *Mitteliranische manichäische Texte*. See also Samuel N. C. Lieu, *Manichaeism in the Later Roman Empire and Medieval China: A Historical Survey* (Manchester: Manchester University Press, 1985), ch. 3; Gardner and Lieu, *Manichaean Texts*, ch. 3.

45. Gardner and Lieu, *Manichaean Texts*, 118.

46. The Kushan Empire (second century BCE–third century CE) replaced the Greco-Bactrian kingdom founded by Alexander the Great's soldiers in northern Afghanistan and also covered areas in modern Pakistan and western India.

47. The northern Silk Road went along the Heavenly Mountains north of the Taklamakan Desert, the southern along the Kun Lun and Pamir Mountains south of the desert. On Manicheism on the Silk Road, see Sundermann, "Der Manichäismus an der Seidenstrasse," 153–69.

Pelliot from the Mogao caves at Dunhuang in northwestern China.[48] Already in 732, however, an imperial edict against Manicheism was issued, whereby Manicheism was ousted from the capital Chang'an. The religion received its strongest support along the Silk Road in 762/763, when the Uyghur ruler Bögü-qaghan converted to Manicheism, which became the state religion of the Uyghur Empire from 763 to 840.[49]

At that time, the copying of Manichean manuscripts flourished and translations into Uyghur were made. It must be noted that Middle Persian and Parthian manuscripts by themselves do not prove the presence of native Persians or Parthians at Turfan at the time. There is some evidence, however, that there were Persians along the Silk Road and at Turfan, and Parthians had already long been working as translators of Buddhist texts into Chinese, so they may well have been settled in the area.[50]

Languages and Scripts

The known Manichean fragments of the Book of Giants, as well as quotations and references to it, are written in five languages: three Iranian languages (Middle Persian, Parthian, and Sogdian), Old Turkic (see Zieme's chapter in this volume), and Coptic.[51] Parthian had been the official language under the Parthians, and the third-century Sasanian kings had their inscriptions written in both Middle Persian and Parthian, some also in Greek. Both Parthian and Middle Persian were written using local Iranian scripts based on Aramaic and were difficult both to read and to write.[52] The Manichean script is based on Syriac scripts, but is not identical with any of the three common ones (Jacobite, Nestorian, and Estrangelo), so today it is usually just called the Manichean script. This script was used to write Middle Persian, Parthian, and Sogdian, as well as Bactrian (one Manichean fragment survives) and some other languages in Xinjiang.[53]

The earliest Manichean texts are probably those in Middle Persian, and it was only as the missionaries moved eastward that it became important to know Parthian, as we learn from the Middle Persian text describing how Mani sent Mar Ammō, who "knew the Parthian script and language," to northeastern Iran.

In Sogdiana, another script based on Aramaic was also being used. This script, too, gradually became rather difficult to read, and the missionaries adopted the Manichean script to write Sogdian, adding a few letters and using diacritics to distinguish others.

---

48. Tokharistan is a region in the upper Oxus Valley. For the Manichean teacher before the Chinese emperor, see Lieu, *Manichaeism in the Later Roman Empire*, 189–90. Helwig Schmidt-Glintzer, "Dunhuang i: The Cave Sites; Manichean Texts," *EIr*, 6, http://www.iranicaonline.org/articles/dunhuang-1.

49. On the Turfan manuscript M1, dated in 763, see Müller 1912; Boyce, *Catalogue of the Iranian Manuscripts*, 1.

50. See Edwin Pulleyblank, "An Shih-Kao," *EIr* 1:1000–1001, https://www.iranicaonline.org/articles/an-shih-kao.

51. Middle Persian is the descendant of the Old Persian of the Achaemenid inscriptions and the ancestor of Modern Persian (Farsi).

52. Notably because of historical spellings (as in English and French) and the use of arameograms (also called heterograms), i.e., Aramaic words to be read in Iranian (e.g., *YDḤ* spelling *dast* "hand"). A later version of this script is used in a fragment of the Psalms of David, also found at Turfan, and a still later version is found in the Zoroastrian literature from the ninth century and later, commonly called Pahlavi.

53. For script tables, see, e.g., Prods Oktor Skjærvø, "Iranian Alphabets Derived from Aramaic," in *The World's Writing Systems*, ed. Peter T. Daniels and William Bright (Oxford: Oxford University Press, 1996), 515–35.

The local Manicheans used the old Sogdian script as well, which then traveled along with the Sogdian merchants and missionaries to eastern Xinjiang, where the Uyghurs and later also the Mongols adopted and adapted it for their own use.

The Sogdian versions of the Book of Giants are clearly later than the Middle Persian and Parthian ones. Many of them were probably translations of Parthian texts, although often embroidered upon.

The Title of the Manichean Book of Giants
The title of the book is attested to by numerous sources.

Manichean sources:
The title of the book is Kawān/Qāwān "giants" in Middle Persian and Parthian.

M5815/II/R/i/16–25/ Parthian (Andreas, ed. Henning 1934, 13 [858], text b, lines 127–36), Mani writing in Marv:
Now I have dispatched (Brother Zurwāndād) to Zamb,[54] and sent the dear Mārī Ammō with him to Khorasan. He brought with him a Kawān and an Ārdahang, and made another Kawān in Marv.

Chinese sources:
The Chinese Compendium (Haloun and Henning 1953, 195, 207–8; Schmidt-Glintzer 1987, 73, 123b):
Sixth: section on Kawān, interpreted as "warriors of great strength."

The term *kaw* (Avestan *kawi*, Pahlavi *kay*) is taken from the Iranian epic tradition, where it is the epithet of a sequence of mythological heroes who lived in the Kayanian era (which preceded the rule of King Wishtāsp).[55] In Manichean texts, the term is also applied to entities other than the giants, such as the apostles, the last of whom was Mani.[56] Apparently, the meaning "giant" is never required in either Iranian Manichean or the much later Pahlavi texts; rather, it may be closer to the meaning usually ascribed to the biblical *gibborim*, who are also not described as giants, but rather as military men "of renown."[57] This description, in fact, fits perfectly the Avestan *kawi*s and Pahlavi *kay*s, who are engaged in a long war against the Turanians, which is only won under the last of them, Avestan Kawi Haosrawah, Pahlavi Kay Husraw, whose name means "he of good renown." Uyghur has *alp* "hero,"[58] and, finally, the Chinese Compendium says that *kawān* means "warriors of great strength." Thus, the Kawān was more likely to have been (the narrative) of the valorous men of renown rather than giants, as 1 Enoch has it (7:2).[59]

---

54. Unidentified.
55. See Skjærvø, 2013 sec. i. On King Wishtāsp see below in the sections "Elements from Iranian Epic in Mani's Writings," 32:KawT, and 42:KawU.
56. Waldschmidt and Lentz 1933, 553–54; Durkin-Meisterernst and Morano 2010, 155, sec. 497. Interestingly, in Christian Sogdian, *par kawyāq* "by (their) being *kaw*s, like *kaw*s" renders Syriac *ganbārā'īṯ* "like *gabbār*s, like heroes."
57. Fröhlich 2016, 106–14.
58. In Zieme B, *alp Saxm* corresponds to Sogdian *Sāxm kawi* in 20:KawZs4.
59. Fröhlich (2016, 107) suggested it was the Greek translation that introduced the term "giant." The

The Book of Giants: Iranian Manichean Version

The Iranian word for "giants" is likely to be *māzendarān* in 16:KawW and, possibly, in 31:KawY.[60]

Coptic sources:
Homilies 25.1–6 (Polotsky 1934; Pedersen 2006):
They will get into the hands of the Just and the devoted: the Gospel and the Treasure of Life, the Pragmateia, and the Book of Mysteries, the Book of Giants, and the Letters, the Psalms and the Prayers of my Lord; his Image (the Picture Book) and his revelations, his parables and mysteries.

Christian sources:
Decretum Gelasianum: De Libris Recipiendis et Non Recipiendis (sixth century?):
The book with the name of Ogia the giant, who is imagined to have fought with a dragon after the Flood: apocryphal.[61]

Timothy Presbyter: "the deeds [*pragmata*] of the giants." Cited in Joannis Meursii (John Meursius) *Variorum divinorum* (p. 117).[62]

Heraclian, bishop of Chalcedon (early sixth century) in Photius's ninth-century *Bibliotheca* (85, 65a/b):[63]
Read the twenty books of Heraclian, bishop of Chalcedon, *Against the Manichaeans*. . . . He refutes the Gospel, Book of the Giants, and the Treasures of the Manichaeans.

Arabic sources:
Authors writing about Manicheism list the Book of Giants as one of Mani's canonical books.[64]

Ibn al-Nadim, *Fihrist*, trans. Dodge 1970, vol. 2, 798:
The Book of Giants, which includes ——— [unfortunately left unwritten].

Muhammad al-Ghadanfar al-Tabrīzī cited in Sachau 1878, XIV (Henning 1943, 72):

---

term *Book of Giants* was also used by Milik (see Goff in Goff et al. 2016, 119 with nn. 15–16). Goff stresses (ibid., 127) that violence is not the main characteristic of the giants in the Qumran book.

60. Sundermann's (1994, 42) statement based on his reading of M2157 that the Manichaean term *māzendar* could designate the demons imprisoned in the skies seems doubtful to me, as what he read as *nryshyzd*, the Third Messenger, is not visible on the online photo. See also Sundermann 2018 and Kósa's summary (2016, 150–51).

61. *Patrologia Latina*. Edited by J.-P. Migne, vol. 59.1, 57–64; Henning 1943, 53.

62. *Variorum divinorum liber unus: In quo auctores theologi Graeci varii, antehac nunquam vulgati* (Lyon: Isaacum Elzevirium, 1579–1639, 117) in Johannes Albertus Fabricius, *Bibliothecæ Græcæ liber de scriptoribus Græcis Christianis aliisque qui vixere a Constantini M. ætate ad captam S. C. MCCCCLIII a Turcis Constantinopolin* (Hamburg: Liebezeit, 1712), 5:282; and in Fabricius, *Codex Apocryphus Novi Testamenti, Collectus, Castigatus Testimoniisque, Censuris & Animadversionibus illustratus*, 2nd ed., 3 vols. (Hamburg: Schilleri & Kisneri, 1719), 139. My thanks to Rea Matsangou, Leiden University, for identifying the title for me, abbreviated as *Var. Divin.* by Beausobre (1734, 428 n. 2).

63. Patriarch of Constantinople (858–867); Gardner and Lieu 2004, 129–30.

64. Gardner and Lieu 2004, 153–56.

The Book of Giants: Iranian Manichean Version

And the Book of the Giants by Mani the Babylonian is filled with stories of those giants, among them Sām and Narīmān. He had probably taken these two names from the book Afdistāk (= Avesta) by Zardusht the Azerbaijanian.

Versions

As a general rule, the texts became more detailed as the missionaries traveled eastward. Thus, the Middle Persian versions are usually short and terse, while the Sogdian versions are more expansive.

From Sogdian So14255/V/ (2:KawZs3) and M7800/ii/V/ (1/3:KawZs1), we see that there must have been at least two fairly different Sogdian translations in circulation (see table), which probably means they must have been translated by two different translators and, perhaps, even from two Parthian manuscripts that already contained somewhat different versions. Here, So 14255+56/R/ lower half continues directly in So 14255+56/V/1–12/ upper half, which excludes the possibility that So 14255+56 should have had their recto and verso switched.

So 14255+56/R/ upper half:	M7800/ii/R/1–19/, V/1–2/:
Description of the activities of the fallen abortions	Description of the activities of the fallen abortions
So 14255+56/R/ lower half	
The giants (?) fear the "companions" (Watchers?)	
Those who fell into the northern and eastern worlds	
So 14255+56/V/1–12/ upper half:	
Those who fell in the western and southern worlds	
So 14255+56 lower:	M7800/ii/V/2–19/:
Āz dons Shaklūn and Pēsūs and commands them	Āz dons Shaklūn and Pēsūs and commands them
	M7800/ii/V/2–19/
	Description of Shaklūn and Pēsūs devouring the brood of the abortions, from which they fashion man in the image of the Third Messenger

The only non-Sogdian fragment of a manuscript that may have contained a significantly different version of the narrative is the Parthian 4:KawX. This fragment is shown to be from the Book of Giants by the reference to those who came to earth because of the beauty of the females. Where it differs from the Middle Persian versions is in the names of the two demons who fashioned Adam and Eve: [*Daw]īt and Halā'īt, which are found nowhere else in the Iranian Manichean texts, but show up in the Apocryphon of

103

John as Daveithai and Eleleth, two of the four Illuminators, in whose realms are placed Adam, Seth, seed of Seth, and Penitens.[65]

Literary Context
The Manichean and Aramaic Book of Giants
Because of the fragmentary nature of the two texts, comparison between them is problematic. That they are both based on the Enochic Book of the Watchers seems certain, but it cannot be verified whether this is the direct source. The relationship between the two is also uncertain, but there are elements that suggest that the Manichean version may be based on the Aramaic one, but was further iranicized. Elements not in 1 Enoch, but already in the Aramaic Book of Giants, include the Watchers' and giants' names (also in the Midrash of Shemhazai and Aza'el) and their dreams and journeys into the beyond; the list of animals in 1Q23 frags. 1+6+22 and 17:KawAl; and the borrowing of names of giants from the Gilgamesh tradition. The cleansing of the earth in 1 En. 10:20 is described in detail in 6:KawAi, listing the various *Iranian* provinces and so goes beyond the Aramaic book.

Mani and His Dēn
Manicheism unites ideas from a variety of intellectual currents in the Near East in the first centuries of our era and hence is often called a syncretistic religion. The same goes for Mani's writings. In the baptist milieu where he grew up, Mani would have become acquainted with the books of the Old and New Testament, in particular the four gospels in the harmonized form of the *Diatesseron* of Tatian,[66] and the writings of Paul. He also read the Revelations of the founder of the sect, Elchasai, as well as the various revelations current in Mesopotamia of Judeo-Christianity at the time: the apocalypses of Adam, Seth, Enoch, and Noah,[67] as well as the Gospel and Acts of Thomas, brother of Jesus, whom Jesus was said to have sent to the far east to preach the gospel. The texts, including the Book of Giants, bear abundant witness to these principles, with their borrowings from Mesopotamian, Jewish, Christian, Zoroastrian, and Buddhist literature.[68] There are also indications that he may have been familiar with Sethian doctrines (see on 4:KawX). On elements shared with the Midrash of Shemhazai and Aza'el, see Reeves 1992, 84–88.

It is commonly assumed that Mani wrote only in Aramaic (Syriac) and that everything else must either be translations of Mani's Aramaic works or compositions by his Persian followers.[69] The premise is not obvious, however. According to the Manichean texts, Mani was supposed to have been born in Babylonia, although we have no information of where exactly the baptist sect to which his father belonged may have been located. According to Ibn

---

65. On Daveithai and Eleleth in the Sethian myth, see King 2006, 87. Note that, to Mani, here as elsewhere, the benevolent entities have become characters belonging to the Darkness.

66. See Tardieu 1981, 41–42.

67. See Reeves 1996 and his contribution to this volume, and Sundermann's (1994, 48) discussion of the relationship between the Manichean *Book of Giants* and the Jewish Books of Enoch, in which he concluded that it "was Mani's own gnostic or gnosticized reading of some Jewish legends which Mani came to learn in his paternal Elchasaite community."

68. See, e.g., Skjærvø 1995a, passim.

69. See Henning's (1943, 55) discussion of the descent of the book in various languages from Syriac (now partly outdated).

al-Nadim, Mani's Twin,[70] who told him to leave the baptist community and revealed to him the mysteries, first visited Mani in Babylonia while he was still only twelve.[71] If so, he must have reached manhood in a very multicultural society. The Sasanian kings had their capital built at Weh-Ardashīr, in the area of ancient Babylon, where there were communities of Jews and various denominations of Christians, and where Buddhists passed through.[72]

Thus, Mani grew up in a multilingual environment. It is therefore not completely unlikely that Mani, probably an exceptionally intelligent person, may have been bilingual (or multilingual) and perhaps fluent in Middle Persian. Seeing that, to Mani, writing was of paramount importance, he may even have invented the script used to write these texts, which served his purpose of propagating his teachings better. He may himself have composed and written the book containing an exposition of the Manichean doctrine that he, possibly, presented to King Shapur: the Middle Persian Shābuhragān named after the king.

The fact that Mani gave Shapur a book (if that is what he did), is quite remarkable, as Iranian religious literary traditions were fundamentally oral. Although we do have royal inscriptions in Middle Persian and Parthian from the third century, there is no evidence that any of the religious or, indeed, epic traditions were committed to writing before the early Islamic period, when the Zoroastrian tradition probably began being written down (the earliest known dates are in the ninth century).[73] What Mani and his followers acquired of Iranian lore is therefore likely to have been oral.

To understand why Mani emphasized writing and drew on so many disparate elements in his writings, not only terminology, but also narrative elements, we need to understand how he conceived of his *dēn*, a concept Mani borrowed from Zoroastrianism, where it referred to the totality of the time-honored and sacred oral traditions about the world: how it came into being and how it will be in the end, and about the creation of living beings and their role in history past, present, and future. This *dēn* was, at least originally, all oral, and information from it is referred to in the Pahlavi texts, "as the *dēn* says, as it is manifest from the *dēn*," etc. An important part of the *dēn* was the Avesta,[74] transmitted to Zarathustra[75] by his god, Ohrmazd,[76] and its commentary, the *zand*.

---

70. An evocation of the Great Nous; see the section below on "Mani's Cosmogony."
71. Dodge 1970, 2:774.
72. Cf. the inscriptions of the high priest Kartīr (spelled *krtyr*, also transcribed as Kerdīr, Kirdēr, etc.); see Skjærvø 2011.
73. That the magi wrote pamphlets (*biblidion*) against Mani to show to the king (*Homilies* 81; Polotsky 1934; Pedersen 2006) does of course not say anything about whether they wrote books. The Avesta, the sacred book of the Zoroastrians (see n. 74), itself composed in an archaic language no one understood any more, was probably not written down, but the secondary literature around it, the so-called *zand*, i.e., the local translation of the Avestan with commentaries, may have been. For one thing, the orthography in the royal inscriptions and, especially, those of Kartīr give the impression of having long been used for narrative texts, rather than only for written official documents. See also Dilley's discussion of the "Law of Zarades" in Gardner et al. 2015, chap. 5.
74. The Zoroastrian sacred book, a collection of texts recited at a large variety of rituals. It is known from manuscripts written between the thirteenth and nineteenth centuries, but may have been committed to writing already in the early Muslim period. It contains the Gathas, five poems commonly ascribed to the historical Zarathustra in the West, but not in the Avesta itself. On the problem with the assumption of historical Zarathustra and his authorship of the Gathas, see Skjærvø 2015.
75. The (mythical) prophet of Zoroastrianism, Avestan Zarathushtra, Middle Persian Zardusht. The Greeks transformed the name into Zoroaster (often used in English) and the Coptic Manicheans into Zarades.
76. In the oldest texts, Avestan Ahura Mazdā, "the omniscient lord," is still a noun plus adjective,

The Book of Giants: Iranian Manichean Version

Mani's *dēn* contained much the same, but with crucial differences. Mani thought of himself as the last in a long chain of apostles beginning with Adam and including numerous Old Testament characters, notably Seth (Shitil) and Enoch, as well as the Messiah/Jesus (34:KawAb), all of whom received parts of the *dēn*:[77]

M22 (not on the Turfan website), Henning (1934, 28 [342] n.7):
. . . Shitil, [Enō]sh, Sēm, and Shēm . . . [An]d you, Enoch [. . .].

Psalm Book 142.7–11 (Henning's KawQ; Allberry 1938):
   About the toil and endurance of the fighters of evil, among them Adam, Sethel, Enosh, Noah, Shem, Enoch, Jesus.

Manuscript M299a/R/ (Henning 1934, 27–28 [341–42]):
   . . . and thereafter, in era after era, the Pure Word[78] also proclaimed his own greatness through the mouth of the primeval Pillars, who are none other than:
   Shem, Sem, Enosh, Nikotheos (*nkty'wys*), D[anie]l, and Enoch, until the [coming of the M]āzendars.[79]

Homilies 68.12–17 (Henning's KawR; Polotsky 1934; Pedersen 2006; cf. 4:KawX, 6:KawAi)
   [. . .] of the first [. . .] of the fleshes [. . .] from Eve, his true sister [. . .] for [. . .]
   . . . fell three t[imes. . . .] Adam.
   He was three hundred seventy-three [years?]
   [. . .] from Cain and all his kin [. . . E]nosh, Sem Shem, and Nikotheo[s . . .]
   [. . .] evil . . .]
   Four hundred thousand righteous [perished. . . .] Enoch's years.

As Manicheism spread eastward, other apostles were added, among them Buddhist ones. Some of the most comprehensive lists are found in the Coptic texts:

Kephalaia, ch. 1 (Berlin copy; Gardner 1995, 18)
   The advent of the Apostle has occurred at the occasion . . . as I have told you:
   From Sethel, the first-born of Adam up to Enosh, together with Enoch.
   From Enoch up to Sem, the son of Noah. [. . .
   . . .] Buddha to the East, and the Aurentes,[80] and the other [. . .] who were sent to the East.

---

but later only a name: Old Persian Ahuramazdā, Middle Persian Ohrmazd (Ohrmezd), modern Persian Hormozd.

77. See also Reeves 1996. For similar lists in Zoroastrian texts, see Skjærvø 1995a, 192–94.
78. Here the Great Nous is probably meant, the cosmic intelligence who sends the apostles and bestows gnosis (see n. 116).
79. See above on the title of the book, with n. 60.
80. Probably Buddhist Sanskrit *arhat* (also in 9:KawI), which denotes somebody in an advanced stage on the road to enlightenment (details differ in the various variants of Buddhism). Here it may refer to the Manichean elect, who have obtained gnosis and are at the top of the religious hierarchy, although their function here is unclear. On *aurentēs*, see Tardieu 1989; Skjærvø 1997, 332–33 n. 79.

From the advent of the Buddha and the Aurentes up to the advent of Zarathustra[81] to Persia, the occasion that he came to King Hystaspes [i.e., Wishtāsp].[82]

From the advent of Zarathustra up to the advent of Jesus Christ, the son of greatness [...] who came to the Jews.

Kephalaia (Dublin copy, codex 2 K; BeDuhn in Gardner *et al.* 2015, 267)

From the advent of Zarathustra up to the advent of Jesus Christ, the son of greatness [...] who came to the Jews.

The Lord Zarathustra came to Persia, to King Hystaspes; he revealed the law that is still really established in Persia.

The Lord Buddha, the wise, the fortunate: he came to the land of India and to the Kushans; he revealed the law that is still really established in all of India and among the Kushans.

After him came the Aurentes and *Kebellos[83] to the East; they revealed the law that is still really established in the East: the Middle of the world, and in Parthia. He revealed the law of truth among all these.

Afterward, Jesus Christ in the West of the Romans came to all the land of the West.

Shahristani (Gimaret and Monnot 1986, 661–62)

As for the laws and the prophets his belief was as follows. The first whom God (may he be exalted!) sent with knowledge and wisdom was Adam, father of humanity. Then Seth, then Noah, then Abraham. Then he sent the Buddha to the land of India, Zarathustra to the land of Persia, the Christ (the Word of God and his Spirit) to the land of Byzantium and the West, and Paul (after Christ) to the same ones. Then the Seal of the Prophets will come to the land of the Arabs.

Mani claimed that his predecessors did not write their books, but that their followers remembered and wrote them down (cf. above on Iranian religious literary traditions), which might be taken to mean that he had at least been told about them, perhaps even been shown them. This insistence on books was in accordance with his main tenet, namely, that he was the last in a chain of apostles and that all the former *dēn*s contained some truth, but that they deteriorated for various reasons, stated in his Ten Points. These crucial elements of Mani's philosophy regarding writing are presented in Ten Points in which his *dēn* is superior to others. In the incomplete Middle Persian version,[84] the first point states that the previous religions were only in one land and in one language, but Mani's was taught in all lands and in all languages. In the fourth point, Mani states that the earlier apostles did not write down their teachings as Mani did. Other points explain how, in contrast to his predecessors, Mani himself organized his church, and so his *dēn* was truly a religion in the modern sense.[85] Finally, in the fragmentary fifth point, Mani

---

81. The (mythical) prophet of Zoroastrianism, Avestan Zarathushtra, Middle Persian Zardusht. The Greeks transformed the name into Zoroaster and the Coptic Manicheans into Zarades.

82. See below on 42:KawU.

83. A Jain? See references in Skjærvø 1997.

84. Andreas, ed. Henning, 1933, 295–96 (M5794/I/); Sundermann 1981, text 24.1 lines 2208–13.

85. See BeDuhn in Gardner et al. 2005, chap. 9.

The Book of Giants: Iranian Manichean Version

says: "all the writings and the wisdom and parables of the former *dēn*s, when [they come] to this [*dēn* of mine . . .]."

A more complete statement is preserved in the Kephalaia:

Kephalaia 151 (Gardner and Lieu 2004, 266)
The writings and the wisdom and the apocalypses[86] and the parables and the psalms of all the first churches have been collected in every place. They have come down to my church. They have been added to the wisdom that I have revealed the way water might add to water and become many waters.

Again, this is also the way that the ancient books have added to my writings and have become great wisdom; its like was not uttered in all the ancient generations. They did not write, nor did they unveil the books the way that I, I have written it.

The simile of the *dēn* as water is elaborated on in a Sogdian text (Sundermann 1985, texts a–b), where Mani compares his own *dēn* to the World Ocean, which can be seen in the whole world and in every place, while the former *dēn*s are like small bodies of water which appeared in one place only.

The implication of the above texts is obviously not only that Mani's teachings were in all languages, but also that they were *written down* in all languages.

Elements from Iranian Epic in Mani's Writings

The main characteristics of Mani's version of the *Book of Giants* are those he took from "Zarathustra," that is, from the Zoroastrian tradition.[87]

Several names of characters in the Book of Giants come from the Iranian epic tradition as we know it from the Avesta, via the Pahlavi literature, to Ferdowsi's *Book of Kings* and the Islamic historians. Numerous parallels between the Book of Giants and the Iranian epic characters were explored in Skjærvø 1995a, and additional material has now been found in the Coptic 2 Ke Codex, which contains the famous story of King Kay Khosrow and his occultation,[88] whose son Siyāvash is mentioned in 8:KawZp2.

The identification of the Sogdian Yam[89] with the King of Honor[90] and the Most High in 1 Enoch is based on several parallels between them, among them: the Most High's throne is described in 1 En. 14:18 as looking "like crystal and its wheels like the shining sun," while Jamshid's throne was a glass chariot. The King of Honor is in charge of a wheel that is like a big mirror or lens that allows him to see everything (Kephalaia

---

86. In the *Cologne Mani Codex*, apocalypses (i.e., revelations) are ascribed to several of Mani's predecessors: Adam (48–50), Sethel (50–55), Shem (55–57), Enoch (58–60), and Paul (60). Of them, Shem is said to have been taken to the throne of the King of Honor (on whom see also the sections below, "Mani's Cosmongony" and "Mani's Version of the Book of the Watchers Narrative"). See also the contribution by Reeves in this volume.

87. Henning (1943, 53–54) denied that the epic names were used by Mani himself and ascribed them to his disciples as translations of the original Syriac names. See also BeDuhn in Gardner et al. 2015, 152–58.

88. "Khasrō the blessed" in the Dublin *Kephalaia* (BeDuhn in Gardner *et al.* 2015, chap. 6). See also Skjærvø: 1998a.

89. Avestan Yima, Middle Persian Jamshēd, modern Persian Jamshid. He was the mythical first king of the Iranians and lived in Avestan Airyana Vaejah, Sogdian Aryān Wēzhan, Middle Persian Ērān-wēz. See Skjærvø 1995a.

90. See below in this section and on 10:KawV below. See also the depiction of the King of Honor in the Manichean painting in Kósa 2016, 2017.

88:3–33),[91] while Jamshid has a famous cup that allows him to see everything that goes on in the world.

It is also tempting to compare the Avestan Yima's *vara*, a kind of bunker in which pairs of all living beings take refuge from a flood[92] and from which they will only come out in the future to replenish the decimated population. Mani may have given these events his typical negative slant, associating the enclosure designed to save mankind with the prison of the King of Honor in which the archons were kept as well as the Watchers who appeared on earth and ravished(?)[93] the women and wreaked havoc.

The Sogdian Yam's abode is in Aryān Wēzhan, which, in the Zoroastrian cosmology, is the original homeland of the Iranians. In the Avesta, the Peak of Haraitī is in the middle of Aryāna Vaejō, with stars, moon, and sun turning around, and, in the Sogdian Book of Giants, the mountain in the middle of the earth is called by its Indic name, Sogdian Sumēr = Indic Sumeru (28:KawG). Compare, perhaps, 1 En. 26, where Enoch is transported to the middle of the earth, where he sees a sacred tree.[94]

As for the names of the giants, Sām (= Ohyā), who fought with the Leviathan (30:KawN), recalls Middle Persian Kersāsp, also a dragon-slayer and son of Sāma (Pahlavi Sām). His Avestan epithet was *naire.manah*, approximately "of manly spirit," Pahlavi Narīmān, which in Mani's version became the name of Sām's brother. Another aspect of Sām has come to light in the Uyghur fragments, which mention his confession to the sun god and repentance. This recalls the story about the soul of Kersāsp told in the Pahlavi literature,[95] where Ohrmazd blames Kersāsp for having extinguished his Fire[96] and refuses to admit him to paradise. In the end, Kersāsp confesses his sins to the Fire and is forgiven.

In 42:KawU, we have references to King Wishtāsp,[97] his queen Hudōs, and various heroes associated with Wishtāsp. According to the epic legend, Zarathustra sought out Wishtāsp, who refused to accept the *dēn*, but after his soul was transported to paradise and he was shown its benefits, he told Hudōs to fetch Zarathustra and became his first convert to the *dēn*.[98]

Finally, the Coptic Kephalaia in Dublin has yielded up a chapter on the writings of Zarades, in which there are several references to Iranian epic narratives, including some details also found in the Book of Giants.[99]

Mani's Cosmogony

The Manichean Book of Giants starts with the end of Mani's cosmogony and the making of the first two humans, so, to understand the plot of the book and the references to divine entities, a brief summary of the Manichean cosmology may be useful.[100]

---

91. Gardner 1995, 92. See Henning 1948, 315–16, on the lens, which matches the wheel/mirror in the Xiapu document; see Kósa 2017, 262, 266.

92. According to the Pahlavi texts, caused by the Malkūsān rain or snow-melt after the three Malkūsān winters.

93. The crucial verb is missing in 6:KawAi.

94. In the Manichean painting, the mountain is depicted as a tree (see Kósa 2016, 182).

95. See Williams 1990, 39–43.

96. Note that Ohrmazd's Fire can also be interpreted as the sun, although this is not the obvious interpretation in the Pahlavi story.

97. Avestan Vishtāspa, modern Persian Goshtāsp, Greek Hystaspes (also the name of Darius's father).

98. See Williams 1990, 76–79. Cf. *Kephalaia*, ch. 1.

99. See on 42:KawU below.

100. Beside the Iranian texts, Theodore bar Konai gives the clearest exposition of the cosmology. See Jackson's (1932) translation and commentary.

The Book of Giants: Iranian Manichean Version

Mani found the solution to the "problem of evil" (given a good god, how to explain the existence of evil?) in the dualist religion of Iran.[101] In Zoroastrianism, the problem had been solved by postulating two separate principles, both existing *from* eternity, although not *for* eternity. Evil came into the world when the forces of evil or darkness (down below) perceived the realm of goodness and light (up above) and wanted to possess and destroy it. Ohrmazd, the lord of the realm of light, was aware that the power of darkness could only be overcome in battle and allowed it to break through the border separating the two realms and then created the invisible and visible worlds as battlefields. At the end of a given period the forces of evil would be overcome and the world return to its original state.

Similarly, according to Mani, in the beginning there were two principles, one luminous and good up above and the other dark and evil down below, and between them there was the Border. The realm of light was ruled by the Father of Greatness[102] and populated by various Light entities, and the realm of darkness was ruled by the King of Darkness along with various dark entities. During its chaotic movement, the Darkness made it up to the Border, saw the Light and wanted to possess it.

In order to avoid this the Father devised a plan to get rid of the Darkness once and for all. Ruling out the possibility of using his companions, who were not intended for war, he decided to go himself (Syriac: by his self).[103] For this purpose he began a series of evocations[104] from himself. First the Mother of Life, who in turn evoked First Man,[105] who evoked his five sons (= the five elements: ether, wind, light, water, and fire; cf. 33:KawAe).[106] First Man donned his sons as armor and was sent down to do battle with the Darkness. He was attacked, overcome, and rendered unconscious, and his sons were devoured by the sons of Darkness. Since all the evocations were part of the Father, "of one and the same substance," as Augustine put it,[107] a part of the (Light of the) Father, the Living Soul, became imprisoned in Matter.[108] This was the Father's plan, however, who was using the sons as bait.

The rest of prehuman and human history was devoted to the rescue of the Living Soul and returning it to its origin, its *family* or *homeland* (cf. 7:KawH).

First, a rescuing action was set in motion, and, having rescued First Man, a scheme had to be invented to extract his five sons, who were now in the bowels of the Sons of Darkness.[109] The plan consisted in creating the world to serve as a mechanism of salvation, which would gradually extract all the Light (= the Living Soul) from Matter and return it to and reunite it with its Origin.

---

101. In 1 Enoch, the answer lies in the descent of the Watchers, who transgressed against the cosmic order (Fröhlich 2016, 102–3).
102. Called *Zruwān*, borrowed from the Zoroastrian god of time. His adversary is Ahrimen, who has the same function in Manicheism and Zoroastrianism.
103. Allusion to what later became the Living Soul, Parthian the living self.
104. The Parthian expression is "called (forth) and set in place." Bar Konai has *qʾrā* "called" (Jackson 1932, 224–25).
105. Called Lord Ohrmazd, name borrowed from the Zoroastrian highest god.
106. Called *mahrāspand*s after the *six* entities begotten by the Zoroastrian highest god, which represent living beings, fire and the sun, metals, earth, water, and plants (cf. 34:KawAb).
107. *Contra Faustum* 15.6, *Contra Fortunatum* 14, cf. Gardner and Lieu, nos. 49, 69.
108. See on Āz in n. 121.
109. Called archons, "rulers" (i.e., of the heavens) in Bar Konai's Syriac description of the Manichean cosmogony (Jackson, *Researches on Manichaeism*, 227), as well as in the Acta Archelai (Gardner and Lieu, *Manichaean Texts*, 182–83).

The Book of Giants: Iranian Manichean Version

When the First Man came to, he called up to the Father of Greatness, and the Father evoked the Friend of the Lights, who evoked the Great Builder, who evoked the Living Spirit,[110] who evoked *his* five sons: (1) the Keeper of Splendor, (2) the King of Honor, (3) the Light Adamas (the warrior god), (4) the Glorious King, and (5) the Carrier God (Atlas).[111]

The Living Spirit ordered three of his five sons to kill and flay the sons and daughters of Darkness and took their hides to the Mother of Life, who made ten heavens out of them. In this way, some of the Light was also imprisoned in the heavens.

The three sons next threw the carcasses of the archons down onto the original dark earth, making eight Earths on top of it. The bones of the Sons became the mountains and their flesh and excrements became the earth. This means that the entire world, including living beings, is nothing but the archons, inside whom the original Light is in captivity and only waits to be liberated so it can return to its homeland. In particular, in the Book of Giants, the Light mingled with darkness in the heavens are the stars imprisoned in the zodiac (26:KawZs6).

Prominent among the sons of the Living Spirit is the King of Honor, who is seated on a throne in the seventh firmament,[112] from where he watches over the earths and heavens, in which the archons are imprisoned, guarded by Watchers, and thus corresponds to the Most High in 1 Enoch. In the Middle Persian texts, the King of Honor is appropriately called "master of the watch-posts."[113]

The Living Spirit then revealed his forms to the Sons of Darkness, making them vomit part of the Light they had swallowed. This Light the Living Spirit distilled once to make the sun, moon, and stars. The Mother, First Man, and the Living Spirit next went before the Father and asked him to provide a Savior, and the Father evoked the Third Creation: the Third Messenger (Coptic: the Ambassador),[114] Jesus the Splendor[115] (who in due course would awaken Adam), the Great Nous,[116] and other divine beings. Finally the Great Nous evoked The Apostle of Light (= Mani) and (Mani's) Twin.

The androgynous Third Messenger, appearing radiant on top of heaven, then revealed his male and female forms to the female and male archons, respectively, who were caught up in a burning desire for him/her (cf. 1:KawZs1/R/). The male archons released the

---

110. Manichean Middle Persian Lord Mihr, from Avestan Mithra, deity associated with the sun.

111. See the Kephalaia texts cited in the section below, "The Coptic Kephalaia on the Descent of the Watchers."

112. On "in the third firmament" in *Kephalaia* 92:24–25 (Gardner 1995, 97), see Kósa 2017, 264.

113. See Skjærvø 1995a, 203–7, 213.

114. Parthian Mihr and Sogdian Mish, both from Avestan Mithra. In Middle Persian called God Narisah, from the name of the Avestan messenger deity of the gods.

115. Middle Persian God Khradīshahr, presumably a construct from *khrad* = wisdom and *shahr* = realm (see Skjærvø 1995b, 281a). He is also called Yishō Aryāman, which echoes the name of one of the central Avestan prayers, the Aryaman Ishiyō, named after the deity Aryaman, the embodiment of peace and harmony.

116. The Great Nous is the cosmic intelligence who sends the apostles and, through Jesus the Splendor, bestows Knowledge (*gnosis*) about the origins of the world and, in particular, where the Living Soul comes from. In Sogdian he is called the Mazdayasnian Dēn after the common Zoroastrian name of the *dēn*. He is also called the Great Wahman after the first of (the Zoroastrian) Ohrmazd's offspring, Avestan Vohu Manah "Good Thought," Middle Persian Wahman. This aspect of the Manichean teaching, which is similar to what we see in the so-called gnostic movements, has sometimes caused scholars to refer to Manicheism as an Iranian gnostic religion. It has little resemblance to the various gnostic movements, however, and lacks several of the characteristics of Gnosticism, a term that is itself problematic (King 2003).

The Book of Giants: Iranian Manichean Version

Light they contained through their sperm. The Third Messenger then hid his forms and filtered out the Light from the sperm, which fell down on the earth, half of it on the wet part, the other half on the dry part of the earth (cf. 2:KawZs3).[117] That which fell on the wet part became a giant female sea monster, Leviathan.[118] Light Adamas, the fifth of the sons of the Living Spirit, was sent to battle it, overcame it, and stretched it out in the north, from east to west.

The Prologue of the Book of Giants

That the Manichean Book of Giants contained "a kind of cosmogonic prologue to the book,"[119] as suggested by Morano (2011, 108), is most strongly supported by 4:KawX, which, on the recto, contains a reference to Adam and Eve and their creators, here called [Daw?]īt and Halaʾīt, and on the verso a reference to the descent of the demons on account of the beautiful women. The reason why Mani started the narrative at this point is quite likely his interpretation of *nephilim* as the "fallen ones," that is, the demon abortions, which links it with that of the *gibborim*, the story of the giants.[120]

In the Shābuhragān the story goes as follows:

The daughters of Darkness, because of the unbridled intercourse in the realm of Darkness from eternity, were already pregnant, and after seeing the male form of the Third Messenger they *aborted their fetuses*, which *fell* down upon the earth and started eating the shoots of the trees (cf. 1:KawZs1/R/). After seeing the Third Messenger, Āz[121] worried that the Light might escape her and made a plan for retaining it more securely. In the voice of Shaklūn, the son of the King of Darkness, she instructed the abortions, called monsters and leaders,[122] to bring him their sons and daughters so he could make a figure of the *same form* (as they had seen in the sky) (3:KawZs1/V/). So they did, and he ate the males and gave the females to his female companion, Pēsūs (Syriac Nebrōēl), thus gathering all the Light from the abortions in the two of them.

As for the first two humans, Gēhmurd and Murdiyānag,[123] it is not clear who gave birth to them. According to the Shābuhragān, their creation was the result of a chain of

---

117. Cf. Kephalaia 92, quoted below.
118. Cf. 30:KawN and 31a:KawZmpi.
119. Similarly, the Book of Noah may have begun with the descent of the Watchers (García Martínez 1992, 43).
120. In 1 En. 15:11 and 16:1, the *nephilim* are evil spirits, offspring of the giants.
121. Greek Hulē, Matter. In Zoroastrianism, Āz, Lust, is the female companion of Ahrimen. In 3:KawZs1/V/ she is called the Thought of Death, matching Coptic the Enthymesis of Death beside Hulē (Kephalaia 26, Gardner 1995, 30; see also Schmidt and Polotsky 1933, 77–78). She also matches the Yetzer in the Midrash of Shemhazai and Azaʾel. See the relevant note to 7:KawH in the translation.
122. The meanings of Middle Persian *mazan* and *āsarēshtār* are uncertain, but probably the Great Ones and the Leaders, where "Great" applied to the female demon would match Bar Konai's *rūḥā saggīthā* "great spirit" (Jackson 1932, 250) and *āsarēshtār* might mean literally "standing at the head/beginning." The translation of *mazan* as "monster" follows Henning (1943, 54).
123. Middle Persian Gēhmurd and Murdiyānag after the Zoroastrian Middle Persian names of First Man (Gayōmard) and the first woman, replacing the element *mard* "man" by *murd* "dead." Note that, in Zoroastrianism, First Man is not the first male human (called *Martīy), but a spherical creature killed by the Evil One during the first attack and whose semen went into the earth, from which the first two humans grew up in the shape of a plant (rhubarb?). He must therefore be distinguished from the Manichean First Man (see Skjærvø 1995b, 274). The standard names will be used here, as they are also used in the Parthian 4:KawX, but it is important to remember that the Hebrew names do not have the connotation of *death* of the Middle Persian names.

events (1/3:KawZs1): when the female archons saw the Third Messenger, they aborted their offspring, which fell down on the earth, where they grew and became female and male monsters and leaders. Āz entered them through their food[124] and donned them as her garment. She then began teaching lust and coition to all the abortions that fell from heaven. The resulting misbirths were given to Shaklūn and Pēsūs, who devoured them.[125]

Āz used the two, who "mingled together," to fashion the Manichean Adam and Eve, Gēhmurd first: "a body in male shape with bones, tendons, flesh, veins, and skin" (cf. 34:KawAb); Murdiyānag next in the same way. Gēhmurd's body was shaped after the form of the Third Messenger, but Āz connected it to the evil archons and the star signs and planets in the heavens (cf. 4:KawX, 5:KawK), so that he would partake of their evil nature and be "filled with concupiscence and lust."[126]

Adam lay in a torpor, having forgotten where he came from and his own divine origin. Since a large part of the Light was by now gathered in Adam, he became the first target of the second rescue mission. Jesus the Splendor came down and awakened Adam (cf. 0:KawJ), bringing him the *dēn* (cf. 5:KawK) and showing him the Fathers in the height and how his Soul was imprisoned.[127] Thus Adam was not only the first human, but also the first human to be apprised of his true condition, receiving Knowledge, that is, of his true origin.

There follow the stories of the creation of Eve and the birth of their son Shitil (Seth),[128] who became one of the first in the chain of apostles.

Mani's Version of the Book of the Watchers Narrative[129]

Adam and Eve initiated humanity, including the beautiful women, who caused the demons (Watchers) to descend to earth and upon whom the demons sired the giants.

Several fragments deal with the descent of the Watchers, but the larger background for their descent is told only in the Coptic Kephalaia.

The Coptic Kephalaia On the Descent of the Watchers

The background of the story is told succinctly in several places in the Manichean Coptic literature. Kephalaia chapters 38 and 70 contain descriptions of how the five sons of the Living Spirit each had their appointed watch-districts. In each of them there were rebellions at some time, which were dealt with by the gods. In the watch-district of the Keeper of Splendor, the abortions came down and made trees and the great monster of the sea. Next came the watch-district of the King of Honor in the seventh heaven, followed by the descriptions of what happened in the watch-district of Adamas.

The descent of the Watchers was caused by treachery and anger occurring in the camp of the King of Honor, where the demons were imprisoned, instigated by their guardians, the Watchers. On earth, they then taught humans all kinds of crafts, as well

---

124. Hutter 1992, 42–44, lines 283–316.
125. Hutter 1992, 83–86, lines 924–58.
126. Hutter 1992, 88–89.
127. Jackson 1932, 249–54.
128. Sundermann 1973, 72–73, 77.
129. The narrative of the Watchers descending to the earth, set after humanity began flourishing, does not seem to have been found in the Manichean cosmogonic texts so far, perhaps because it was reserved for the Book of Giants.

as the mysteries of heaven, but, in the end, four angels captured and bound the Watchers in a prison and "obliterated their children from upon the earth."

Psalms 219.12 (Wurst 1996, 22–23)
[The King] of Honor, the strong god, who is [in] the seventh heaven,
who judges the demons, the ab[ortions of the aby]ss, we sing to him and praise him.

Kephalaia 117.1–9 (cf. 28:KawG; Gardner 1995, 123)
Again, before the Watchers rebelled and came down from heaven, a prison was fashioned and constructed for them in the depths of the earth, below the mountains.
Before the children of the giants were born, they who had [no] knowledge of righteousness in them nor divinity, thirty-six cities were assigned and co[nstructed] for them wherein the children of t[he giants would] live; they who would come to beget from each othe[r, they w]ho shall spend ten hundred years alive.

Kephalaia 171 (Henning's KawL; Gardner 1995, 181)
An earthquake and treachery occurred in the watch of the great King of Honor, which the Watchers, who had arisen at the time and had [...] they who were sent came down until they were humbled.
Also, in the watch of the Adamant, the abortions came to the earth and fashioned [the] figure of flesh.

Kephalaia 92 (Henning's KawM, cf. 2:KawZs3; Gardner 1995, 97)
The Keeper of Splendor is set firm in the Great Mind, in the camp above the prison of the bound ones, for he brings to nothing [a]ll the gloo[m] of de[ath].
An[d a] treachery came about and an uprising. The sin abor[te]d. It tangled in with the Soul...
It was detached and came down to that which is dry and that which is moist.
It [fashio]ned the trees [upon] the dry (land), but in the sea it immediat[ely] took form and made a great uprising in the sea.
The great King of Honor, who is the thought (*ennoia*), he is in the thi[rd] firmament. He is made [...] with wrath.
And an uprising [came about]! A treachery and a[n] anger happened in his camp. The Watchers of heaven, who came down to the earth in his watch-district, they did all the deeds of treachery. They have revealed crafts in the world and have unveiled to people the mysteries [of] heaven. An uprising came about, and a destruction, on the earth [...] to it.
The Adamant... a treachery came about in his camp; the occasion when the abortions fell to the earth. They formed Adam and Eve. They begat them so as to reign through them in the world....

Kephalaia 93 (KawP; Gardner 1995, 98)
Conversely, because of the treachery and the uprising that happened in the watch of the great King of Honor, which is the Watchers who came down to earth from the heavens; four angels were called upon about them. They bound the Watchers with an eternal chain, in the prison of the blackened ones. They obliterated their children from upon the earth.

Then again, the abortions descended in the watch of the Adamant and begat Adam and Eve; because of that great treachery which happened, and the mystery of wickedness, he sent Jesus [to answer?] the prayer of the five sons. He assumed them [...] the abortions. He fastened them beneath the [... the] mind of Adam.

Also because of the earthquake that happened in these three earths, and in that the paths were hindered and the springs of wind and water and fire were impeded, Jesus cast himself down. He assumed Eve; and he straightened the tracks of the wind, the water, and the fire.

He opened the springs for them, and he set in order the path of their ascent.

The Narrative of the Giants

This narrative begins with the birth of the giants and is followed by journeys into the beyond undertaken by several of them, notably Māhaway, who hears or meets Enoch.[130] Two other giants, Ohyā/Sām and Ahyā/Narīmān play important roles and their discussions are featured prominently.[131] There follows discord among them and several periods of internecine killings and exchanges between the giants.

Enoch enters the narrative when the giants find several inscribed tablets, apparently sent by Enoch, which they want to have interpreted. Enoch reveals to the giants what their fates will be. Finally, four angels are sent down to do battle with the two hundred demons (Watchers), a battle joined by the giants against the demons.

The Epilogue

After the end of the narrative, Mani added a section probably intended to illustrate some fundamental aspects of correct living, notably how not to harm the Living Soul, which is in all things, and the value of the hearers, contrasting with the bloody chaos that concludes the narrative itself. This epilogue is vaguely comparable with the parables concluding 1 Enoch, notably with its emphasis on the righteous and the elect.[132]

Analysis of the Contents of the Manichean Book of Giants

The Prologue is followed by the narrative of the descent of the Watchers and their siring giants on the daughters of men based on 1 En. 6–8.

The outline of the following narrative can be said to be provided by the speech of the Most High in 1 En. 10–13, with further details in the following chapters. A brief version is found in the Parables (1 En. 39:1–3).

About the Fall of the Abortions and the Creation of Adam and Eve
0:KawJ

"Ten paths" are listed, including those caused by Āz, the Third Messenger (who caused the female demons to abort), the abortions, Jesus (who brought Knowledge to Adam), and the two hundred demons (Watchers).

---

130. See Goff 2014, 79–80.
131. On the names see the section "The Narrative of the Giants," above.
132. The elect were at the top of the Manichean hierarchy, lived in monasteries, and were financed by gifts and foundations. The hearers were the common people, who procreated, worked the earth, picked fruits, etc., and so were more easily exposed to harming the Living Soul. See on the epilogue below.

The Book of Giants: Iranian Manichean Version

1:KawZs1/R/
Mani's narrative begins with the story of the fall of the abortions, the aborted offspring of the archons imprisoned in the zodiac.[133]

They begin to eat and drink and look upward for the beautiful Third Messenger.

2:KawZs3
Description of the abortions and where they fall and how they settled in mountains, plains, etc., hiding from the "companions." Descriptions of those who fell in the four quarters of the world.

Āz tells them to stop looking upward, as she will make something else for them to look at.

> In Christian Sogdian, the word here rendered as "companion" is applied to the women who were with Mary Magdalene when Jesus appeared to her according to the Gospels, where it has no correspondent.[134] In a parable published by Sundermann it is applied to two snakes, inseparable because of their fondness for each other.[135] It therefore seems that the most likely meaning is, in fact, "companion" in the sense of someone who one is closely connected to, that is, here, the other giants. This still leaves unexplained, however, who the "companions in the heavens" are (28:KawG).

3:KawZs1/V/
Āz dons the two chief abortions, Shaklūn and Pēsūs, and tells the other abortions not to look up, but to go and copulate, then bring their brood to her. The abortions bring their brood to Shaklūn and Pēsūs, which they eat. Recalling the beauty of the Third Messenger, they decide to make something in the image of the gods.[136]

About Adam and Eve and Humanity and the Descent of the Two Hundred Demons[137]

4:KawX
There follows the creation of the bodies of Adam and Eve. Eve makes Adam turn away from the *dēn* three times. The demon Watchers come down because of the women's beauty.[138]

5:KawK
Meanwhile, humans are probably just going about their work peacefully, when the descent of the demons causes turmoil among them.

The narrative returns to Adam, who now needs saving, and the next chapter deals with the coming of Jesus the Splendor, who will bring the *dēn* to Adam and his son Shitil.[139]

---

133. Cf. below on 26:KawZs6.
134. Sims-Williams 1985, 115–17.
135. Sundermann 1985, 30 line 166.
136. See also the section "About the Fall of the Abortions and the Creation of Adam and Eve," above.
137. Morano's seq. 1: "Rebellion of the Demons and Their Falling to Earth."
138. Morano places Zieme G after 4:KawX here at the end of his seq. 1.
139. See above in the section "Mani and His *Dēn*."

The Demons Wreak Destruction on Earth and Ravish the Women
6:KawAi/R/

The demons and giants subjugate the human race, apparently killing off the competition (1 En. 7:1, 4). Four hundred thousand righteous perish in the mountains (where they had presumably fled).[140] At this point Enoch is "hidden" by the angels. The demons then seize the women and copulate with them.

> Compare the Coptic Manichean Psalm Book (Allberry 1938, 142.7–9): "The Righteous who were burnt in the fire, they endured. This multitude that were wiped out, four thousand [. . .]."
>
> The puzzling mention of the angels hiding Enoch between the killing of the righteous and the rape of the women can possibly be explained as reflecting 1 En. 12:1, where Enoch had been taken up into the heavens "before these things," after which the story about the women and demons are then told for the fourth time, by the "Lord of majesty" himself.

The women, identified here as "the female elect and the female hearers"[141] are subjected to work and service, cleaning up in the various provinces of Iran.

> Compare 1 En. 10:20 (cf. 10:7), where the Most High commands his archangels to clean the earth and heal it.

The Demons (Watchers) Teach Human Beings: Birth of the Giants[142]
7:KawH

The demons teach humans what they had learned in heaven (cf. 1 En. 7–8). There follows the birth of Ohyā/Sāhm and Ahyā/Pāt-sāhm sired by Shahmīzād and the other giants from the other demons.

> Compare 1 En. 7:2, where no names are mentioned; Midrash of Shemhazai and Azaèl 7: "Shemhazai sired two sons called Heyyā and Aheyyā."
>
> KawH probably features a meeting between Mani and the King of kings, in which the king asks Mani questions about the world and Mani answers. The current question, which is not finished, was about "the coming of the two hundred demons," and the next question is about "Āz's world of death," which is Mani's take on what the Zoroastrians (and we) would call "the world of the living."

8:KawZp2

Both sections 8 and 9 refer to the life span of the giants. The Parthian quotations in this Sogdian text, which are explicitly said to be from Mani's own writings, contain a series of examples of renowned characters who would not have died had something been dif-

---

140. This is remedied by the Most High in 1 En. 10:17, when "the righteous shall escape and shall live till they beget thousands."
141. The apparent anachronism of the (Manichean) female elect and hearers agrees with Mani's views of the sequence of apostles: according to him, Enoch was supposed to have done what Mani did later, and had presumably also established the religious hierarchy.
142. Morano's seq. 2: "The Demons Sire Giants."

ferent. The case of Sām and Narīmān is unclear: if they had [not][143] lived like giants and men, they would, presumably, had long or eternal life "at the feet of the dearest [. . .]," where "the dearest" contains no clue to the identity. Shahmīzād seems unlikely.

> Compare 1 En. 10:10, where the Most High decrees that the giants shall not live forever, but expect to live only five hundred years.
> The phrase "like giants and men" literally means "in gianthood and manhood." Morano translated "gianthood" as "nobility," and Durkin-Meisterernst (2004, 230b) has "manliness" for "manhood," both of which make little sense here. Rather, the point seems to be that, if they had been born in heaven sired by the Watchers (?), rather than being born on earth among men, they would have had a place at the feet of the Most High.[144] Similarly, in 9:KawI, "like men" is for "[in] manhood" and "like tyrants" for "tyranthood."

9:KawI

This Sogdian fragment contains on one side a reference to Sāhm and his brother as examples of beings who, by reason of their great strength, would live forever (in men's memory?), with which cf. Kephalaia 117.1–9,[145] according to which they would live ten hundred years. On the obverse, there is a reference to the giants, apparently as examples of powerful or righteous men, who will not know complete salvation.

Complaint of the Earth and Its Human Inhabitants[146]
10:KawV

In the narrative of 1 Enoch (8:4; 9:10) and, presumably, in the Qumran version (4Q203 frag. 8), there follows the complaint of the earth[147] and its inhabitants to the Most High, who then comes down to earth.

This event may be reflected in the fragment about Yam,[148] who, apparently, had come down from his heavenly residence ("Yam was in the world") and receives the kings of the earth on New Year's day.[149] On this day they might be given an opportunity to voice both praise for and complaints about what was happening in the world, as suggested by Ferdowsi's description: "The temporal world was relieved through (his) passing of judgments."[150]

If at all from the Book of Giants, the story may have been inserted by Mani into Sām/Ohyā's dream, as told in 4Q530 frag. 2 col. ii + 6 + 7 col. i 8–11+12 ll. 16–17, where Ohyah sees the Sovereign of Heaven descend to the earth and thrones being set up, books being opened, and judgments being spoken.

143. Broken out in the manuscript.
144. See also n. 90.
145. Gardner 1995, 123.
146. Morano's seq. 5: "[The Four Archangels (?) Bring the Laments of the Earth to the Rex Honoris = Yima(?)] and Adore Him.] Enoch Appears to the Demons."
147. Cf. Skjærvø 1995a, 218–19 for Greek and Indic parallels.
148. Henning (1943, 55 n. 5): "It is not clear whether Yima . . . had been given a place in the Sogdian Kawān." For Iranian parallels with the description of the Most High in 1 Enoch 9, see Skjærvø 1995a, 203–7. It seems unlikely that the "flood" mentioned in 4Q533 frag. 4 has any possible connection with the Avestan story about Yima and the flood (Skjærvø 2008, 505). See above in the section "Elements from Iranian Epic in Mani's Writings."
149. See Skjærvø 2008, 504.
150. Skjærvø 1995a, 205–6.

The Giants' Dream

The narrative then focuses on a few specific first-generation giants born from two of the demons: Māhaway son of Wirōgdād (Baraq'el in 1 En. 6:7) and Ohyā (Middle Persian Sām, Sogdian Sāhm) and Ahyā (Middle Persian Narīmān, Sogdian Pāt-sāhm) sons of Shahmīzād (Shemihazah in 1 En. 6:7).[151]

11:KawAj/R/

Sām and Narīmān have dreams, conceivably sent by the Most High or one of his angels as a response to the earth's complaint, expecting Enoch to interpret them.

Sām's dream features a tablet that he throws into water and another with three signs on it foreboding bad things, while Narīmān sees a garden with trees, from which two hundred shoots(?) come out. According to 12:KawD/V/ii/, the dream may have contained water drawn from a well.

> With the "water," cf. 2Q26. With the "three signs," cf. Midrash of Shemhazai and Aza'el 9. With Narīmān's dream, cf. 4Q530 frag. 7b col. ii, frag. 2 col. ii + 6 + 7 col. i 8–11+12 l. 8. According to Midrash 9, the two dreams foreboded the Flood and the survival of only one man and his two sons: Heyyā (Ohyā) saw a large stone covering the earth like a carpet and covered with writing with a knife. An angel came down and erased the writing with a knife except a line with four words. Ahyā (Narīmān) saw a garden full of various trees and various precious things. An angel came down and cut all the trees with an axe, except one tree with three branches.

12:KawD

The two remaining words "outside" and "Māhaway" on the recto may refer to Māhaway's dream trip.

On the verso, Māhaway (?) tells Enoch (?) to interpret the dreams the two giants dreamed. The direct speech may be that of Sām telling Māhaway what to say to Enoch.

Enoch then interprets the dream as referring to the Watchers ('īr) and the giants who came out of the women. He also interprets the water drawn from a well, but the interpretation is missing.

> In Zieme A (Henning's KawB), Māhaway, son of Wirōgdād, flies up to heaven just before sunrise. A voice from above tells him he has seen too much and to turn back. Then he hears Enoch's voice coming from the south, warning him that he is too close to the sun and that his wings will catch fire so that he will burn and die. Māhaway quickly flies down, just as the sun rises above the mountain. The voice of Enoch calls out to him again.

13:KawZs2

Enoch (?) tells Māhawāy (?) that the gods are angry, presumably about what is going on down below. He gives him a tablet (on which the giants may have been asked to mend their ways?) and tells him to show it to the giant Hōbābīsh and the other giants.

---

151. There is no trace in the Iranian manuscripts of the remaining Watchers mentioned in 1 En. 6:7.

The Book of Giants: Iranian Manichean Version

14:KawAj/V/
There appears to be a mention of Wirōgdād, Māhaway's father.

Hōbābīsh tells the giant Ahiram that someone abducted his wife (whose name looks like no Iranian name), which causes the giants, as well as the animals, to start slaughtering one another. (Rather than mending their ways, the giants are behaving worse than ever?)

Then Sām rises up in front of the sun, telling "everything" to his brother (Narīmān; cf. 16:KawW), perhaps about someone *bound* as punishment.

> Seeing the seven stars "*bound* together" in the pits, Enoch asks: "For what iniquity have they been *bound*?" (1 En. 21: 3–4). See also 1 En. 10:12: "*bind* them for seventy generations in valleys of the earth."

15:KawAg
Sām recounts how he saw place-to-place filled with the souls of the damned lamenting, followed by series of aphorisms. Because of the gap in the manuscript, it is unclear who is speaking (Sām? Enoch?) and to whom (Sām? Narīmān?). Narīmān then starts talking.

> Cf. 1 En. 22: 5: "There I saw a spirit of a dead man making complaint; and his lamenting reached up to heaven as he cried and complained."[152] See also 4Q530 frags. 2 2 col. ii + 6 + 7 col. i 8–11+12, where Ohyā says he too saw . . .
>
> In 4Q530 frag. 2 col. ii + 6 + 7 col. i 8–11+12 ll. 20–24, after Ohyah recounts his dream, the giants are frightened and call Māhaway and ask him to go to [Enoch] because he will interpret the dreams. In frag. 7 col. ii, Māhaway's (second) flight is then described, and Enoch interprets the dreams.

16:KawW[153]
Māhaway presumably brings back two tablets with Enoch's interpretation apparently written on them and gives them to Sām. Sām tells Māhaway (?) to take the tablets to "[. . .] father," presumably to Sām's father Shahmīzād (rather than Māhaway's father Wirōgdād; the possessive pronoun is missing), since Shahmīzād then tells (him?) to read "the manuscript of Enoch the interpreter."

> There perhaps follows Sām's Book of Confession, which we learn about in the Uyghur fragments Zieme B-C-D.[154] Here, Sām says he confessed to having been a brutal killer, but no longer is one. Sām's good spirits in 16:KawW/V/ may then be caused by his confession before the "sun god," which may have "released" him from his sins.

Happy because of having been released from his sins(?), Sām tries to cheer up the giants with food and merrymaking, but they are not in the mood, perhaps with their promised punishments in mind, and go to sleep.

Māhaway goes to another giant, Atanbīsh, and tells him "everything," then comes "a second time," which recalls 4Q530 frag. 7 "a second time."

---

152. Translation from Black 1985.
153. Morano's seq. 8: "Message from Enoch (Tablets) to the Demons and the Giants. Sām's Dream."
154. Morano's seq. 9.3–5.

Zieme J, with its "eating and drinking" and someone being "sinless," can conceivably be related to the previous text.

Sām then has a dream about flying up above heaven, where he has an apocalyptic vision of the earth and the heavens. Wrath comes out of the water. The archangels become invisible, and Sām sees the rulers of heaven (i.e., the archons imprisoned in the heavens?).

> Wrath may here refer to the dragon of the sea, which was made from the abortions that fell on wet land: "And that one part that fell on the ocean—an ugly, ravenous, and fearful monster came of it, and it crawled out of the ocean and began to do harm in the world."[155] Note also that the heavenly demons (or a special group of them) are also called the wrathful ones. In the Zoroastrian myth, Wrath is the demon of the night sky, who, at nightfall, strikes the creation with his bloody club (image of the sunset).

17:KawAl[156]

Enoch tells Sām what to tell the giants: to greet them with an "antigreeting" and to promise punishment for their sins: they will be overcome and ruled over for one hundred and twenty years.

> The "antigreeting" corresponds to 1 En. 16:3: "Say to them therefore, 'You shall have no peace'";[157] cf. also 1Q24 l. 8. Sām's dream and Enoch's prophecy may be based on the Most High's prophecy in 1 En. 10:11–16.

> The verso of this fragment contains a list of animals (perfect parallel in 1Q23 1+6+22), quite likely referring to the paradisiac conditions after the demons have been taken to hell, while the righteous have escaped in 1 En. 10:18–19, when "the earth shall be tilled in righteousness . . . and filled with blessing"[158] (cf. 4Q531 frag. 2+3?). Rather than confining himself to tilling, planting, and harvesting, Mani has described all the activities of husbandry hyperbolically, similar to the Most High's promise that they shall "beget thousands," conceivably borrowing the description of the animals from the preparations for the flood.

18:KawAc/R/[159]

Māhaway recalls seeing a giant (?) draw a bow to shoot him, but Shahmīzād says to Sām it may not all be true. Sām asks his father a question.

---

155. Shābuhragān M 7981/I/R/i/7–15; Hutter 1992, 39–40 243–51.
156. Morano's seq. 7: "Message from Enoch to the Giants."
157. Interestingly, the king of Sakas, i.e., the (vice) king of Sagestān, modern Sīstān, greets Mani in the same way: "You are not welcome!" See Gardner and Lieu 2004, 84–85 (on the identity of the king, see Gardner in Gardner et al. 2015, 177–79).
158. Thus Henning 1943, n. 7. Stuckenbruck (1997, 56–58) also doubted these are fragments of the actual Flood story (against Reeves 1992, 122) and instead suggested the fragments contain text spoken by Enoch and refer to a postdiluvian period.
159. Morano's seq. 3 begins with 18:KawAc and includes 19:KawC and Zieme A: "Deeds of the Giants and the First Heavenly Messages."

Cf. 1 En. 17:3: "where (I saw) a bow of fire, arrows, and their quivers, and a fiery sword and all the lightning-flashes." 6Q8 frag. 1: "Behold, I have heard wonders!" may be an indication of Ohyah's disbelief in Māhaway's story.[160]

Māhaway then apparently tells of a (dream?) trip he and his father made in a chariot (?), during which they saw the hells in which the Watchers and giants (?) were confined. Shahmīzād confirms the story. Sām and Māhaway begin searching for the chariot(?).

Cf. 6Q8 frag. 1, where Māhaway says to Ohyah: "Baraq'el my father was with me" in different context.

Infighting among the Giants
19:KawC
The following fragments feature events that took place among the giants, but they contain no clues to what events.

Somebody warns Māhaway (?) that Sām may want to kill him, but that he will fight him himself, which allays Māhaway's worries.

Sām, in fact, does get angry and tries to kill Māhaway.

20:KawZs4
There follows a conversation between two giants, one of whom is Sāhm and the other, presumably, Māhaway, mentioning [2]00 giants. Sām gets angry. A great (water?) and a cloud are mentioned, as well as the Great Ocean, presumably in a simile, and mountains, possibly also a great distance to go, 100 (farsangs?).[161]

An angel appears before the giants (Sām and Māhaway?), blaming somebody for having unjustly killed somebody else. Sām answers the angel. The water's shore is mentioned.

Cf. 1 En. 17:4–8, where Enoch is taken to "subterranean waters," "great rivers," the "Great Ocean," and "storm clouds."

21:KawZs5
Criminals and an army, the color red, and the Great Ocean are mentioned. Somebody orders somebody else to sit down and be quiet. Sām and the companions are mentioned.

For the color "red" and "the Great Ocean," see again 1 En. 17:4–5: "the fire of the West" and "the Great Ocean."

22:KawE/R/
The spirits happily gather to hear the apostle (= Enoch), hoping he will help them against tyrants and criminals of whom they were afraid.

---

160. Goff 2016, 125.
161. From Greek *parasang*, unit of distance originally ca. 5.5 km/3.5 miles. See 27:KawZp1.

Note that what Henning translates as "demon" in this fragment is not the common word δēw, but čētē "spirit," possibly another term for the Watchers *or* the giants *or* the offspring of the giants.[162] Cf. 1 En. 15:8–12: "And now the giants, who have been produced from spirits and flesh,[163] shall be called spirits upon the earth. . . . Evil spirits shall come forth from their bodies, for from men they have come, and from the holy Watchers is the beginning of their creation."

23:KawF/ColB (15–24) + KawE/V/[164]
Enoch rebukes them for not having improved.

> Cf. 1 En. 17–19: punishments; 1 En. 20: the angels who keep watch.

24:KawE/V/
The spirits (Watchers?) promise they will no longer commit crimes, so Enoch should be lenient toward them and lift (?) the "heavy command."

> The "heavy command" may be the command by the Most High (1 En. 10) that they shall all be destroyed[165] or what is described in 1 En. 15:8–12, but, perhaps, more likely that described in 1 En. 13, when the fallen angels were afraid, after which Enoch wrote down their petition. Thus, when they see him again, they are "happy" because they expect the outcome to be good for them, but instead they are presented with another "heavy command" (1 En. 15–16; cf. also Q530 frags. 2 col. ii + 6 + 7 col. i 8–11+12 l. 21: "the giants rejoiced concerning him," on which see Stuckenbruck 1997, 106–7.

About the Fire in Hell
25:KawF Columns CDEFA
The giants continue their apology/defense (lines 25–35). There follows a description of the fiery pits of hell and those punished in them, while the righteous watch them. Possibly an elaboration on 1 En. 18:6–12; 54:1–6.

Enoch, apparently, is unconvinced and promises eternal damnation in the fiery pits of hell (lines 36–53).

The righteous stand outside or fly over them, while going after those trying to escape (lines 54–72, 75–88). The ones who persecuted[166] the happiness (*farroxīy*) of the righteous will be annihilated, falling into the "mother of all burnings" (lines 1–14).

> Zieme F may describe how the demons and giants reacted to (Enoch's threat?), jumping from mountains, into the ocean, or killing themselves in various ways. Those remaining (?) "fell into an everlasting sleep."[167]
>
> This is followed by the Lord of Heaven addressing the four angels, presumably telling them to go down and put an end to the rule of the demons/giants(?).

162. Cf. Fröhlich 2016, 107.
163. I.e., from the Watchers and the human women.
164. Morano's seq. 6 begins here: "Enoch (?) Speaks to the Demons (?) Predicting Their Final Ruin."
165. Cf. Goff's reflections (2016, 126).
166. In the concrete sense. Henning (1943, 67 n. 1) has *murzīdan* "persecute, harass."
167. Morano has this as seq. 4.2, following 11:KawAj.

The Book of Giants: Iranian Manichean Version

26:KawZs6

As in 1 En. 18, this is followed by the story of the fallen stars imprisoned in the zodiac, that is, among the archons: because "they transgressed the commandment of the Lord at the beginning of their rising" (1 En.18:15–16).

When the material world was built, the stars thought it would be a place for them to be the rulers, but instead it became a prison for them.[168] There follows the lament over the stars, which ruined the world by their own ignorance (spoken by whom?).

27:KawZp1

This contains a description of the earth (?) similar to what the angels show Enoch in 1 En. 26–32 and is perhaps the answer to Enoch's question in 1 En. 27. The mention of Mount Sumēr, which is probably the mountain in the middle of the earth (as in Indian mythology), suggests that this is a description of Aryān Wēzhan.[169]

The verso contains a mention of the angels who ruled there who were disciples.

Descent of the Angels and the Battle between the Angels and the Demons[170]
28:KawG

The four angels[171] bind all the companions (of the giants) in the heavens, then descend, obeying the command of the Most High in 1 En. 10. They scare the two hundred demons, who hide in human form. The angels, however, separate the (real) humans from the demons and set Watchers over them. They remove their offspring and settle them in Aryān Wēzhan in thirty-two towns,[172] which the Living Spirit had prepared for them, and there they practice the skills and customs they have learned. Then the angels return and fight the demons in a fierce battle that is not over until the angels engulf them with fire, naphtha, and sulfur.

29:KawAk[173]

Ohyā and Ahyā join the battle. The mention of the battle apparently provided Mani with an opportunity to describe what is useful in battle and what is not. Direct martial action is said to be superior to threats, etc.

30:KawN

The Parthian fragments M35/V/ and M740/V/, contain a series of similes describing the effects of the great fire, among them a reference to how "Ohyā, Leviathan, and Raphael cut each other apart and died and disappeared."

There is also a reference to the elect's ability to filter out by their internal fire and wind (burping) the Light = Living Soul in food they eat (cf. 36:KawAf).[174]

---

168. See above on 1:KawZs1/R/.
169. See also the next section on 28:KawG and above in the section "Elements from Iranian Epic in Mani's Writings."
170. Morano seq. 10.
171. Michael, Sariel, Raphael, and Gabriel.
172. See Kósa 2016, 171–72, on the representation in the Picture Book of the thirty-two "palaces."
173. Morano's seq. 9 begins here: "Sāhm and Narīmān Prepare for Combat. The Giants Regret (?)."
174. See, e.g., Augustine, *Haer.* 1, 3; Augustine, *Faust.* 20, 11; Kephalaion 104 in Gardner 1995, 263; and BeDuhn 2000, 163–79.

31:KawY

Atanbīsh, too, has joined (started?) the battle. He seizes the two hundred demons and brings them before somebody. This somebody (?) kills the two hundred demons (?) and throws them down upon the earth. Thus the battle is presumably fought in the air. The somebody kills the three giants who were with Atanbīsh (= ?).

After the battle someone sings (apparently) an elegy or a victory paean.

In Zieme F, there is a description of how the demons and giants reacted to the appearance of the four angels, jumping from mountains, into the ocean, or killing themselves in various ways. Those remaining (?) "fell into an everlasting sleep." The Lord of Heaven addresses the four angels.

In Zieme H2, the battle may be described, followed by somebody praising the victory(?).

31a:KawZmp1

If this fragment belongs to the Book of Giants, it may reflect the battle between the angels and the giants and their offspring and their punishment in "the fiery abyss" as ordered by the Most High in 1 En. 10:9, 13. Note also Enoch's apocalyptic vision in 1 En. 17:3, with its "fiery sword and all the lightning-flashes"; "others fell by knife" in Zieme F, and "did not all these go by your sword" (4Q531 frag. 7 5).

The identity of the weapon in question (čēlān) is not quite certain. Henning (1940, 35) suggested "dagger," seeing that it appears to correspond to two different Sogdian words for sword-like weapons in a Middle Persian–Sogdian glossary. In any case, the appearance of the weapon would exclude the possibility that the fragment belongs to the cosmogony or, indeed, the eschatology (cf. Hutter 1992, 121).

32:KawT

The vanquished giants are all alike, like mirror images of one another (?). Enoch is "hidden" (for the last time?). The vanquished enemies are rounded up like cattle and returned to the prison of heaven, among the planets and the constellations.

Cf. 5:KawK/V/ and Sundermann 1973, 45 text no. 3.2, on the making of the heavens in which the "demons" were chained.

When 328[-] years have passed, Wishtāsp is crowned king, and, presumably, organizes his realm.

He has all his subjects come to the gate of his palace, which had apparently been broken during the battles. They stand "unhappy," presumably not knowing what will happen, when he comes out in full armor (and tells them all is going to be all right?).

Wishtāsp may have been presented as upholding the *dēn* of Zardusht,[175] which may have been a lead-in to the epilogue, which contains important parts of Mani's own *dēn*.

---

175. As he does in the Pahlavi text Memorial of Zarēr, the Zoroastrian version of the battle over the *dēn*, where Zarēr commands the Iranian army, which victoriously fights the enemies of the Iranians.

The Book of Giants: Iranian Manichean Version

Epilogue

The question whether the two doctrinal texts, the one about the five Mahrāspands—the five Elements (sons of First Man)—and the one about the duties of the hearers, which follow the Book of Giants in Henning's MS A, belong to the book is still open, but the Uyghur fragment U 269, part of the manuscript containing the fragments of the Manichean Book of Giants, also contains a piece of a text on the duties of the hearers (header preserved), notably not to harm the Living Soul (the "elements" *mahrāspand*s), and Morano suggested that these texts were part of the conclusion of the Manichean Book of Giants (Wilkens 2000, 144).

The book may then have been concluded by a section rehearsing what a good Manichean should do to combat the evil that entered the world from the beginning to the arrival of Mani.

Epilogue 1: On the Living Soul[176]

That the last fragments of M101 belonged to the Manichean Book of Giants is strongly suggested by Zieme I, which has as header "The book [of the rules] of the hearers," which agrees with the header of 35:KawAh, "[. . .] concerning the hearers."

33:KawAe

Although the *mahrāspand*s are mentioned in this fragment, it is not certain it belongs in the section on the Living Soul. Rather, it looks like a list of disparate exhortations and may have been part of the section on the hearers.

34:KawAb

One side of this fragment is more clearly about not harming the Living Soul that is in everything, notably water and all that grows. There are some puzzling elements as well, however, for instance, "they will fill (themselves?) with victuals." Since the elect are the only ones who can filter out the Living Soul by digesting food, the "they" may be people who in their arrogance and self-confidence, in which "they clothe themselves," believe they can do the same.

The obverse contains a recapitulation of the creation of Adam, in whom much of the Living Soul is contained, and of how the Light Nous sent the apostles to educate people.

35:KawAh/R/1–4/

This fragment may continue the previous one directly, as it describes those deluded, who, instead of true Knowledge, have received a distorted one regarding their true nature and origin.[177]

Epilogue 2: On the Elect and the Hearers[178]

35:KawAh

The five commandments of the elect are (1) truth, (2) nonviolence, (3) purity of behavior, (4) purity of mouth (not eating meat), (5) blessed poverty. The three seals are (1) seal of the mouth (cf. fourth commandment), (2) seal of the hands (cf. second commandment), (3) seal of the heart (Coptic "purity of virginity," cf. third commandment).

---

176. Morano seq. 11: "Doctrinal Text on the Five Elements."
177. See also the section "About the Fall of the Abortions and the Creation of Adam and Eve,'" above.
178. Morano seq. 12: "Exegetical Text on the Hearers." See Gardner 2004, 231–37.

The Book of Giants: Iranian Manichean Version

The ten commandments of the hearers included rejection of false gods ("declaration of faith") and purity of speech ("truthfulness"). Others were purity in culinary habits, marital fidelity, sexual abstention on days of fasting, helping those who suffer and abstaining from greed, guarding against hurting unnecessarily all beings, etc.

They should pray four times a day, turned toward the sun at day, at night toward the moon.

They should also give alms, including bread, fruits, vegetables, clothes, and sandals (all products of the earth) to the elect, who could not themselves provide themselves with the foodstuffs. This in turn forced the hearers to sin by harming the Living Soul in matter, but by presenting the produce to the elect, their sins could be confessed and be forgiven.

36:KawAf
Similes describing the uneducated and educated hearer and the value of alms-giving.

About the ability of the elect to filter out the Living Soul from food digested in their bodies (see on 30:KawN, above).

37:KawAa
More similes describing the good hearer, followed by a simile describing the elect, hearers, and Wahman = the leader of the congregation.

38–41:KawAd, KawAm, KawA, KawAn
More similes describing the good hearer.

42:KawU
This fragment (one side only) is probably not from the Book of Giants, but the conclusion of a story related to Wishtāsp told in alphabetic hymnic form. The story referred to here is obviously Mani's take on the story told in the Memorial of Zarēr, in which Wishtāsp was the peaceful king forced to fight a battle against the Chionians and Zarēl was the general of Wishtāsp's army. Wēzhan, however, the famous Bizhan of the Persian epic tradition, son of Giv (Pahlavi Gēw), was a great warrior under Kay Khosrow (son of Siyāwash, see 8:KawZp2), under whom the great war with the Turanians, which had lasted for generations, was finally concluded.

After he went into occultation, Kay Khosrow was followed by Luhrāsp and then by his son Wishtāsp. The story of Khosrow and his warriors Tēo and Iuzan (= Gēw and Wēzhan) has now been found in the Dublin Kephalaia.[179] Wahman (modern Persian Bahman) was king after Wishtāsp and ancestor of Darius I according to the epic tradition.[180]

The reference to Wishtāsp's queen Hudōs and the verb *received* may be taken from the story that she received the *dēn* before her husband, which has some support in the Pahlavi texts.[181]

The reference to a *palace* is also in 8:32:KawT.

---

179. See BeDuhn in Gardner *et al.* 2015, 146.
180. See Skjærvø 1998a, 2013.
181. See the section above, "Elements from Iranian Epic in Mani's Writings." Boyce (1975a, 187), who assumed that these stories represented historical truth, suggested Hudōs was instrumental in Wishtāsp's conversion to Zarathustra's religion.

The Translation

This translation is based on those of the first editors, Henning, Sundermann, and Morano, but all the manuscripts have been checked and rechecked.[182]

Given the fragmentary nature of the Manichean text, much escapes us, but much can also, to a certain extent, be guessed by comparison with 1 Enoch and the Aramaic Book of Giants.[183] One major problem with recovering the structure of the text is the frequency of repeated events, such as the recurrent dreams and dream journeys, tablets, and mentions of Enoch. The descriptions in 1 Enoch of the corruption of the beautiful women, for instance, is first told, then told *to* the Most High, then told *by* the Most High, and then once more by Enoch. The determining of recto and verso is mostly based on contents.

The reordering of the fragments here is often based on personal preferences and is not to be taken as the last word on the matter. In particular, the assumption that some fragments overlap without there being any identical texts, that is, in sequences such as A recto, B recto, A verso, B verso *or* A recto, B recto, B verso, A verso, is hard to prove, but, in view of the fact that the complete folios are written in twenty to thirty lines per page and the fragments contain only half this many lines and sometimes much less, it seems at least possible.

A technical problem has been to what extent source language should be quoted, since, sometimes, explanations cannot be made without citing the Iranian words. In particular, it seemed impossible to avoid quoting the originals in cases where the present trans-

---

182. We are grateful to Desmond Durkin-Meisterernst for permission to translate the Book of Giants fragments found in the database of transcriptions of all published Middle Persian and Parthian texts at https://turfan.bbaw.de/texte-en/mirtext.html. Likewise to Cambridge University Press for permission to translate W. B. Henning's edition of the following Sogdian fragments published in "The Book of the Giants," *BSOAS* 11 (1943–1946): 52–74: texts C (pp. 65–66); E (p. 66); G (pp. 68–69), H (pp. 69–70), I (p. 70), K (pp. 70–71), and V (p. 74). Likewise to Enrico Morano and Harrassowitz Press for permission to translate the Sogdian-Parthian fragment M813/I published in his article "'If They Had Lived . . .': A Sogdian-Parthian Fragment of Mani's *Book of Giants*," pp. 325–30 in *Exegisti Monumenta: Festschrift in Honour of Nicholas Sims-Williams*, ed. Werner Sundermann, Almut Hintze, and François de Blois, Iranica 17 (Wiesbaden: Harrassowitz, 2009); to Morano and De Gruyter Press for permission to translate the Sogdian fragment M500n/B/1–7/ published in his article "New Research on Mani's Book of Giants," pp. 101–11 in *Der östliche Manichäismus Gattungs- und Werksgeschichte: Vorträge des Göttinger Symposiums vom 4.–5. März 2010*, ed. Zekine Özertural and Jens Wilkens, Abhandlungen der Akademie der Wissenschaften zu Göttingen NS 17 (Berlin: de Gruyter, 2011); to Morano and Mohr Siebeck Press for permission to translate the Sogdian fragments So 10700a + So 20193a–b and So 20220/ii published in his article "Some New Sogdian Fragments Related to Mani's *Book of Giants* and the Problem of the Influence of Jewish Enochic Literature," pp. 187–98 in *Ancient Tales of Giants from Qumran and Turfan: Contexts, Traditions, and Influences*, ed. Matthew Goff, Loren Stuckenbruck, and Enrico Morano, WUNT 360 (Tübingen: Mohr Siebeck, 2016); to Morano and the *Journal of Iranian Linguistics* for permission to translate the Sogdian text of fragment So 14255+56, published in his article "Where the Demons Fell: A Manichaean Sogdian Folio on the Myth of the Fallen Abortions." Likewise to the Yad Ben Zvi Institute in Jerusalem for permission to translate the Sogdian fragment M 7800 published by Werner Sundermann in "Mani's 'Book of the Giants' and the Jewish Books of Enoch: A Case of Terminological Difference and What It Implies," pages 40–48 in *Irano-Judaica III: Studies Relating to Jewish Contacts with Persian Culture throughout the Ages*, ed. Shaul Shaked and Amnon Netzer (Jerusalem: Ben-Zvi Institute for the Study of Jewish Communities in the East, 1994).

183. See also Sundermann's (1994, 48) discussion of the relationship between the Manichean Book of Giants and "the Jewish Books of Enoch," in which he concluded that the Manichean Book of Giants "was Mani's own gnostic or gnosticized reading of some Jewish legends which Mani came to learn in his paternal Elchasaite community."

lations differ significantly from earlier ones, as in 35:KawAh, where Henning's *pdm'd* "measured" should be read as *pd m'd* "as mother."

Where alternative translations are equally possible, they are in the notes, not in the text.

In the case of a few words not found elsewhere or incomplete words, the assumed meaning is marked by an asterisk (*).

Bibliography

Adam, Alfred. 1969. *Texte zum Manichäismus*. Ausgewählt und herausgegeben. 2. verbesserte u. vermehrte Auflage. Berlin: de Gruyter.

Adhami, Siamak. 2011. "Two Pahlavi Chapters on Medicine." *Early Science and Medicine* 16: 331–51. doi:10.1163/157338211X587379.

Alberry, M. A. 1938. *A Manichean Psalm-Book*. Part II, with a contribution by Hugo Ibscher: Stuttgart: W. Kohlhammer.

Andreas, F. C. 1932–1934. *Mitteliranische Manichaica aus Chinesisch-Turkestan*. Edited by W. B. Henning. 3 vols. SPAW 7, 10, 27. Berlin: de Gruyter. Repr., pages 1–48, 191–260, 275–339 in vol. 1 of *Selected Papers*. Edited by W. B. Henning. Acta Iranica 14. Hommages et Opera Minora 5. Leiden: Brill, 1977. (Often referred to as Mir. Man. i–iii.)

Asmussen, Jes P. n.d. "Aknūk, Enoch, in Manichean Texts." *EIr* 1:727–28. http://www.iranica online.org/articles/aknuk-enoch-in-manichean-texts.

———. 1965. *X^uāstvānīft: Studies in Manichaeism*. ATDAn 7. Copenhagen: Munksgaard.

Baur, Ferdinand Christian. 1831. *Das manichäische Religionssystem nach den Quellen neu untersucht und entwickelt*. Göttingen: Vandenhoeck & Ruprecht (repr. 1928).

Beausobre, Isaac de. 1734–1739. *Histoire critique de Manichée et du Manichéisme*. 2 vols. Amsterdam: Bernard.

BeDuhn, Jason D. 2000. *The Manichaean Body in Discipline and Ritual*. Baltimore: Johns Hopkins University Press.

Black, Matthew, ed. 1985. *The Book of Enoch or I Enoch: A New English Edition with Commentary and Textual Notes*. SVPT 7. Leiden: Brill.

Boyce, Mary. 1960. *A Catalogue of the Iranian Manuscripts in Manichean Script in the German Turfan Collection*. Veröffentlichung 45. Berlin: Akademie.

———. 1975a. *A History of Zoroastrianism*. HdO 8.1, 2, 2A. Leiden: Brill.

———. 1975b. *A Reader in Manichaean Middle Persian and Parthian*. Acta Iranica 9. Leiden: Brill.

Bryder, Peter. 1988. *Manichean Studies: Proceedings of the First International Conference on Manichaeism, August 5–9, 1987*. Manichaean Studies 1. Lund: Plus Ultra.

Cameron, Ron, and Arthur J. Dewey, eds. 1979. *The Cologne Mani Codex (P. Colon. inv. nr. 4780): "Concerning the Origin of His Body."* SBLTT 15. ECL 3. Missoula, MT: Scholars Press.

Chavannes, Édouard, and Paul Pelliot. 1911, 1913. "Un traité manichéen retrouvé en Chine: Traduit et annoté." *Journal Asiatique*, 10th ser., no. 18: 499–617; 11th ser. no. 1: 99–199, 261–392.

Chen, Jinguo 陈进国, and Yun Lin 林鋆. 2010. "明教的新发现—福建霞浦县摩尼教史迹辨析 (Mingjiao de xin faxian—Fujian Xiapu xian Monijiao shiji bianxi) [New Manichaean Discoveries: An Analysis of the Relics of Manichaeism in Xiapu County, Fujian]." Pages 343–89 in 不止于艺—中央美院"艺文课堂"名家讲演录 (*Bu zhi yu yi—Zhongyang meiyuan "yiwen ketang" mingjia jiangyan lu*). Edited by Li Shaowen 李少文. Beijing: Beijing Daxue Chubanshe.

Cirillo, Luigi, and Alois van Tongerloo. 1997. *Atti del terzo congresso internazionale di studi "Manicheismo e Oriente Christiano Antico." Arcavacata di Rende—Amantea 31 agosto–5 settembre 1993.* Manichean Studies III. Brepols: Lovanii.

Colditz, Iris. 1987. "Bruchstücke manichäisch-parthischer Parabelsammlungen." *AoF* 14: 274–313. doi:10.1524/aofo.1987.14.12.274.

Dodge, Bayard, ed. and trans. 1970. *The Fihrist of al-Nadīm: A Tenth-Century Survey of Muslim Culture.* 2 vols. Records of Civilization: Sources and Studies 83. New York: Columbia University Press.

Durkin-Meisterernst, Desmond. 2004. *Dictionary of Manichaean Middle Persian and Parthian.* Corpus Fontium Manichaeorum. Dictionary of Manichaean Texts 3. Texts from Central Asia and China, Part 1. Turnhout: Brepols.

Durkin-Meisterernst, Desmond, and Enrico Morano, eds. 2010. *Mani's Psalms: Middle Persian, Parthian and Sogdian Texts in the Turfan Collection.* Berliner Turfantexte 27. Turnhout: Brepols.

Feldmann, Erich. 1987. *Die Epistula Fundamenti der nordafrikanischen Manichäer: Versuch einer Rekonstruktion.* Altenberg: Akademische Bibliothek.

Flügel, Gustav. 1862. *Mani, seine Lehre und seine Schriften: Ein Beitrag zur Geschichte des Manichäismus; Aus dem Fihrist des Abû-lfaradsch Muḥammad ben Isḥak al Warrâk, bekannt unter dem Namen Ibn Abî Jaʻkûb an-Nadîm im Text nebst Uebersetzung, Commentar und Index zum ersten mal harausgegeben.* Leipzig: Brockhaus.

Frölich, Ida. 2016. "Giants and Demons." Pages 97–114 in *Ancient Tales of Giants from Qumran and Turfan: Contexts, Traditions, and Influences.* Edited by Matthew Goff, Loren T. Stuckenbruck, and Enrico Morano. WUNT 360. Tübingen: Mohr Siebeck.

Gardner, Iain. 1995. *The Kephalaia of the Teacher: The Edited Coptic Manichaean Texts in Translation with Commentary.* Nag Hammadi and Manichaean Studies 37. Leiden: Brill.

Gardner, Iain, and Samuel N. C. Lieu. 2004. *Manichaean Texts from the Roman Empire.* Cambridge: Cambridge University Press.

Gardner, Iain, Jason BeDuhn, and Paul Dilley. 2014. *Mani at the Court of the Persian Kings: Studies on the Chester Beatty* Kephalaia *Codex.* Nag Hammadi and Manichaean Studies 87. Leiden: Brill.

———. 2020. *The Founder of Manichaism. Rethinking the Life of Mani.* Cambridge University Press.

Gignoux, Philippe. 1995a. "Dinar. i. In Pre-Islamic Iran." Pages 412–13 in *Encyclopaedia Iranica* 7/4. Online: http://www.iranicaonline.org/articles/dinar#pt1.

———. 1995b. "Dirham. i. In Pre-Islamic Iran." Pages 424–26 in *Encyclopaedia Iranica* 7/4. Online: http://www.iranicaonline.org/articles/dirham.

Gimaret, Daniel, and Guy Monnot, trans. 1986. *Livre des religions et des sectes.* By Muḥammad ibn-ʻAbd-al-Kārim al-Shahrastani. Collection UNESCO d'œuvres representatives, Série arabe 1. Leuven: Peeters.

Gnoli, Gherardo, ed. 2008. *Il mito e la dottrina: Testi Manichei dell'Asia Centrale e della Cina.* Vol. 3 of *Il manicheismo.* Milan: Mondadori.

Goff, Matthew. 2014. "When Giants Dreamed about the Flood: The Book of Giants and Its Relationship to the Book of Watchers." Pages 61–88 in *Old Testament Pseudepigrapha and the Scriptures.* Edited by Eibert J. C. Tigchelaar. BETL 270. Leuven: Peeters.

———. 2016. "The Sons of the Watchers in the *Book of Watchers* and the Qumran *Book of Giants*: Contexts and Prospects." Pages 115–27 in *Ancient Tales of Giants from Qumran and Turfan*. Edited by Matthew Goff, Loren T. Stuckenbruck, and Enrico Morano. WUNT 360. Tübingen: Mohr Siebeck.

Goff, Matthew, Loren Stuckenbruck, and Enrico Morano, eds. 2016. *Ancient Tales of Giants from Qumran and Turfan: Contexts, Traditions, and Influences*. WUNT 360. Tübingen: Mohr Siebeck.

Haloun, Gustav, and W. B. Henning. 1953. "The Compendium of the Doctrines and Styles of the Teaching of Mani, the Buddha of Light." *Asia Major* NS 3: 184–212.

Henning, W. B. 1933. "Neue Quellen zum Studium des Manichäismus." *Forschungen und Vortschritte* 9: 250–51.

———. 1934a. "Zum Zentralasiatischen Manichäismus." *OLZ* 37: 1–11. doi:10.1524/olzg.1934.37.16.1. (Review of *Manichäische Dogmatik aus chinesischen und iranischen Texten*, by Ernst Waldschmidt and Wolfgang Lentz.)

———. 1934b. *Ein manichäisches Henochbuch*. SPAW 11. Berlin: Akademie. Repr., pages 341–49 in *Selected Papers*. Vol. 1. Edited by W. B. Henning. Acta Iranica 14. Hommages et Opera Minora 5. Leiden: Brill, 1977.

———. 1936. "*Neue Materialien zur Geschichte des Manichaismus*." ZDMG 90: 1–18. Repr. pages 379–96 in *Selected Papers*. Vol. 1. Edited by W. B. Henning. Acta Iranica 14. Hommages et Opera Minora 5. Leiden: Brill, 1977.

———. 1940. *Sogdica*. James G. Forlong Fund 21. London: The Royal Asiatic Society.

———. 1943. "The Book of the Giants." *BSOAS* 11: 52–74. Repr., pages 115–37 in *Selected Papers*. Vol. 2. Edited by W. B. Henning. Acta Iranica 15. Hommages et Opera Minora 6. Leiden: Brill, 1977.

———. 1944. "The Murder of the Magi." *JRAS*: 133–44. Repr. pages 139–50 in *Selected Papers*. Vol. 2. Edited by W. B. Henning. Acta Iranica 15. Hommages et Opera Minora 6. Leiden: Brill, 1977.

———. 1948. "A Sogdian Fragment of the Manichaean Cosmogony." *BSOAS* 12: 306–18. doi:10.1017/S0041977X0008023X. Repr., pages 301–13 in *Selected Papers*. Vol. 2. Edited by W. B. Henning. Acta Iranica 15. Hommages et Opera Minora 6. Leiden: Brill, 1977.

———. 1977. *Selected Papers*. Edited by Mary Boyce and Ilya Gershevitch. 2 vols. Acta Iranica 5–6. Tehran: Brill.

Henrichs, Albert, and Ludwig Koenen. 1970. "Ein griechischer Mani-Codex (P. Colon, inv. nr. 4780; vgl. Tafeln IV–VI)." *ZPE* 5: 97–216.

Hutter, Manfred. 1988. *Mani und die Sasaniden: Der iranisch-gnostische Synkretismus einer Weltreligion*. Scientia 12. Innsbruck: Institut für Sprachwissenschaft der Universität Innsbruck.

———. 1992. *Manis kosmogonische Šābuhragān-Texte*. StOR 21. Wiesbaden: Harrassowitz.

Jackson, Abraham Valentine Williams. 1932. *Researches on Manichaeism, with Special Reference to the Turfan Fragments*. Columbia University Indo-Iranian series 13. New York: Columbia University Press.

Kiel, Yishai. 2016. *Sexuality in the Babylonian Talmud: Christian and Sasanian Contexts in Late Antiquity*. Cambridge: Cambridge University Press.

King, Karen L. 2003. *What Is Gnosticism?* Cambridge: Harvard University Press.

———. 2006. *The Secret Revelation of John*. Cambridge: Harvard University Press.

Koenen, L., and C. Römer, eds. 1985. *Der Kölner Mani-Kodex: Abbildungen und Diplomatischer Text*. Bonn: R. Habelt.

Koenen, Ludwig, and Cornelia Römer, eds. 1985. *Der Kölner Mani-Kodex: Über das*

Werden seines Leibes; Kritische Edition. Papyrologica Coloniensia 14. Abhandlungen der Rheinisch-Westfälischen Akademie der Wissenschaften. Opladen: Westdeutscher Verlag.

Kósa, Gábor. 2016. "The *Book of Giants* Tradition in the Chinese Manichaica." Pages 145–86 in *Ancient Tales of Giants from Qumran and Turfan: Contexts, Traditions, and Influences*. Edited by Matthew Goff, Loren T. Stuckenbruck, and Enrico Morano. WUNT 360. Tübingen: Mohr Siebeck.

———. 2017. "Who Is the King of Honour and What Does He Do? Gleanings from the New Chinese Manichaean Sources." Pages 259–72 in *Zur lichten Heimat: Studien zu Manichäismus, Iranistik und Zentralasienkunde im Gedenken an Werner Sundermann*. Iranica 25. Wiesbaden: Harrassowitz.

Kudara, Kōgi, Werner Sundermann, and Yutaka Yoshida. 1977. イラン語断片集成：大谷探検隊収集・龍谷大学所蔵中央アジア出土イラン語資料 (*Iranian Fragments from the Ōtani Collection: Iranian Fragments Unearthed in Central Asia by the Ōtani Mission and Kept at the Library of Ryūkoku University*). Vol. 1: *Text and Translation*. Vol. 2: *Facsimiles*. Kyoto: Hōzōkan.

Le Coq, Albert von. 1911. *Türkische Manichaica aus Chotscho*. Vol. 1. APAW 6. Berlin: Akademie.

———. 1922. *Türkische Manichaica aus Chotscho*. Vol. 3: *Nebst einem christlichen Bruchstück aus Bulayïq*. APAW 3. Berlin: Akademie.

Lieu, Samuel N. C. 1985. *Manichaeism in the Later Roman Empire and Medieval China: A Historical Survey*. Manchester: Manchester University Press.

———. 1994. *Manichaeism in Mesopotamia and the Roman East*. RGRW 118. Leiden: Brill.

Midrash of Shemhazai and Azaʾel. n.d. https://pages.charlotte.edu/john-reeves/course-materials/rels-2104-hebrew-scripturesold-testament/bereshit-rabbati-on-shemhazai-azael/.

Milik, J. T. 1971. "Turfan et Qumran: Livre des Géants juif et manichéen." Pages 117–27 in *Tradition und Glaube: Das frühe Christentum in seiner Umwelt; Festgabe für Karl Georg Kuhn zum 65. Geburtstag*. Edited by Gert Jeremias, Hartmut Stegemann, and Heinz-Wolfgang Kuhn. Göttingen: Vandenhoeck & Ruprecht.

———. 1976. *The Books of Enoch: Aramaic Fragments of Qumrân Cave 4*. Oxford: Clarendon.

Morano, Enrico. 2008. "Il '*Libro dei Giganti*' di Mani." Pages 71–107, 367–73 in *Il mito e la dottrina: Testi manichei dell'Asia centrale e della Cina*. Vol. 3 of *Il Manicheismo*. Edited by Gherardo Gnoli. Milan: Mondadori.

———. 2009. "'If They Had Lived …': A Sogdian-Parthian Fragment of Mani's *Book of Giants*." Pages 325–30 in *Exegisti Monumenta: Festschrift in Honour of Nicholas Sims-Williams*. Edited by Werner Sundermann, Almut Hintze, and François de Blois. Iranica 17. Wiesbaden: Harrassowitz.

———. 2011. "New Research on Mani's Book of Giants." Pages 101–11 in *Der östliche Manichäismus Gattungs- und Werksgeschichte: Vorträge des Göttinger Symposiums vom 4.–5. März 2010*. Edited by Zekine Özertural and Jens Wilkens. Abhandlungen der Akademie der Wissenschaften zu Göttingen NS 17. Berlin: de Gruyter.

———. 2016. "Some New Sogdian Fragments Related to Mani's *Book of Giants* and the Problem of the Influence of Jewish Enochic Literature." Pages 187–98 in *Ancient Tales of Giants from Qumran and Turfan: Contexts, Traditions, and Influences*. Edited by Matthew Goff, Loren T. Stuckenbruck, and Enrico Morano. WUNT 360. Tübingen: Mohr Siebeck.

———. 2024. "Where the Demons Fell: A Manichaean Sogdian Folio on the Myth of the Fallen Abortions." *Journal of Iranian Linguistics* 1: 4–16.

Müller, Friedrich W. K. 1904. *Handschriften-Reste in Estrangelo-Schrift aus Turfan, Chinesisch-Turkestan*. 2 vols. SPAW 9. Berlin: Akademie.

———. 1913. *Ein Doppelblatt aus einem manichäischen Hymnenbuch (Maḥrnāmag)*. Abhandlungen der Königlisch Preussischen Akademie der Wissenschaften 5. Berlin: Reimer.

Panaino, Antonio. 1998. *Tessere il Cielo: Considerazioni sulle Tavole astronomiche, gli Oroscopi e la Dottrina dei Legamenti tra Induismo, Zoroastrismo, Manicheismo e Mandeismo*. Serie Orientale Roma 79. Rome: Istituto italiano per l'Africa e l'Oriente.

Pedersen, Nils A., ed. 2006. *Manichaean Homilies: With a Number of Hitherto Unpublished Fragments*. Corpus Fontium Manichaeorum 2. Turnhout: Brepols.

Polotsky, Hans J. 1934. *Manichäische Handschriften der Sammlung A. Chester Beatty*. Vol. 1: *Manichäische Homilien. Mit einem Beitrag von Hugo Ibscher*. Stuttgart: Kohlhammer.

Pulleyblank, Edwin G. 1989. "An Shih-Kao." *Encyclopaedia Iranica* 1, no. 9: 1000–1001. Online: https://www.iranicaonline.org/articles/an-shih-kao.

Reck, Christiane. 2004. *Gesegnet sei dieser Tag: Manichäische Festtagshymnen; Edition der mittelpersischen und parthischen Sonntags-, Montags- und Bemahymnen*. Berliner Turfantexte 22. Turnhout: Brepols.

———. 2006. *Mitteliranische Handschriften, Teil 1: Berliner Turfanfragmente manichäischen Inhalts in soghdischer Schrift*. Verzeichnis der Orientalischen Handschriften in Deutschland 18.1. Stuttgart: Steiner.

Reck, Christiane, Dieter Weber, Claudia Leurini, and Antonio Panaino. 2001. *Manichaica Iranica. Ausgewählte Schriften von Werner Sundermann*. Vols. 1–2. Serie Orientale Roma, 89.1. Rome: Istituto Italiano per l'Africa e l'Oriente.

Reeves, John C. 1992. *Jewish Lore in Manichaean Cosmogony: Studies in the* Book of Giants *Traditions*. HUCM 14. Cincinnati: Hebrew Union College Press.

———. 1993. "Utnapishtim in the Book of Giants?" *JBL* 112: 110–15. doi:10.2307/3267870.

———. 1996. *Heralds of That Good Realm: Syro-Mesopotamian Gnosis and Jewish Traditions*. Nag Hammadi and Manichaean Studies 41. Leiden: Brill.

Sachau, Eduard, ed. 1878. *Chronologie orientalischer Völker von Albêrûni*. Leipzig: Brockhaus.

Salemann, Carl. 1904. *Ein bruchstük manichaeischen schrifttums im Asiatischen Museum (mit einem facsimile)*. Mémoires de l'Académie Impériale des Sciences de St. Pétersbourg, classe historico-philologique VIIIe Série 6. St. Petersburg: Prodaetsia u komissionerov Imperatorskoi Akademii nauk.

———. 1907, 1911. *Manichaica*. Bulletin de l'Académie Impériale des Sciences de St. Pétersbourg. Vols. 1–2, 3–4.

———. 1908. *Manichäische Studien I: Die mittelpersischen Texte in revidierter transcription, mit glossar und grammatischen bemerkungen*. Mémoires de l'Académie Impériale des Sciences de St. Pétersbourg, classe historico-philologique VIIIe Série10. St. Petersburg: Prodaetsia u komissionerov Imperatorskoi Akademii nauk.

Schmidt, Carl, and Hans Jakob Polotsky. 1933. *Ein Mani-Fund in Ägypten: Originalschriften des Mani und seiner Schüler*. Berlin: de Gruyter.

Schmidt-Glintzer, Helwig. 1987. *Chinesische Manichaica: Mit textkritischen Anmerkungen und einem Glossar*. StOR 14. Wiesbaden: Harrassowitz.

Sims-Williams, Nicholas. 1985. *The Christian Sogdian Manuscript C2*. Berliner Turfantexte 12. Berlin: Akademie.

Sims-Williams, Nicholas, and Desmond Durkin-Meisterernst. 2012. *Dictionary of Manichaean Sogdian and Bactrian: Dictionary of Manichaean Texts 3; Texts from Central Asia and China Part 2*. Corpus Fontium Manichaeorum. Turnhout, Belgium: Brepols.

Skjærvø, Prods Oktor. 1995a. "Iranian Epic and the Manichean *Book of Giants*: Irano-Manichaica III." *Acta Orientalia Academiae Scientiarum Hungaricae* 48: 187–223.

———. 1995b. "Iranian Elements in Manicheism: A Comparative Contrastive Approach; Irano-Manichaica I." Pages 263–84 in *Au carrefour des religions: Mélanges offerts à Philippe Gignoux*. Edited by Rika Gyselen. Res Orientales 7. Paris: Groupe pour l'étude de la Manicheism du Moyen-Orient.

———. 1996a. "Zarathustra in the Avesta and in Manicheism: Irano-Manichaica IV." Pages 597–628 in *Convegno internazionale sul tema La Persia e l'Asia centrale da Alessandro al X secolo: Accademia nazionale dei Lincei, in collaborazione con l'Istituto Italiano per il Medio ed Estremo Oriente (Roma, 9–12 novembre 1994)*. Rome: Academia Nazionale dei Lincei.

———. 1996b. "Iranian Alphabets Derived from Aramaic." Pages 515–35 in *The World's Writing Systems*. Edited by Peter T. Daniels and William Bright. Oxford: Oxford University Press.

———. 1997. "Counter-Manichean Elements in Kerdīr's Inscriptions: Irano-Manichaica II." Pages 313–42 in *Atti del terzo Congresso internazionale di studi "Manicheismo e oriente cristiano antico," Arcavacata di Rende, Amantea 31 agosto–5 settembre 1993*. Edited by Luigi Cirillo and Alois van Tongerloo. Manichean Studies 3. Leuven: Brepol.

———. 1998a. "Eastern Iranian Epic Traditions I: Siyāvaš and Kunāla." Pages 645–58 in *Mír Curad: Studies in Honor of Calvert Watkins*. Edited by Jay Jasanoff, H. Craig Melchert, and Lisi Oliver. Innsbruck: Institut für Sprachwissenschaft.

———. 1998b. "Eastern Iranian Epic Traditions II: Rostam and Bhīṣma," *Acta Orientalia Hungarica* 51: 159–70.

———. 2008. "Jamšīd." *Encyclopaedia Iranica* 14, no. 5: 501–22. Online: http://www.iranica online.org/articles/jamsid-i.

———. 2011. "Kartīr." *Encyclopaedia Iranica* 15, no. 6: 608–28. Online: http://www.iranica online.org/articles/kartir.

———. 2013. "Kayāniān I–XIV." *Encyclopaedia Iranica* 16/2: 148–74. Online: http://www .iranicaonline.org/articles/kayanian-parent.

———. 2015. "The *Gāthās* as Myth and Ritual." Pages 59–68 in *The Wiley-Blackwell Companion to Zoroastrianism*. Edited by Michael Stausberg and Yuhan S.-D. Vevaina. Chichester, West Sussex: Wiley Blackwell.

Stroumsa, Guy. 1984. *Another Seed: Studies in Gnostic Mythology*. NHS 24. Leiden: Brill.

Stuckenbruck, Loren T. 1997. *The Book of Giants from Qumran: Texts, Translation and Commentary*. TSAJ 63. Tübingen: Mohr Siebeck.

———. 2016. "The *Book of Giants* among the Dead Sea Scrolls: Considerations of Method and a New Proposal on the Reconstruction of 4Q530." Pages 129–41 in *Ancient Tales of Giants from Qumran and Turfan: Contexts, Traditions, and Influences*. Edited by Matthew Goff, Loren T. Stuckenbruck, and Enrico Morano. WUNT 360. Tübingen: Mohr Siebeck.

Sundermann, Werner. 1973. *Mittelpersische und parthische kosmogonische und Parabeltexte der Manichäer*. Berliner Turfantexte 4. Berlin: Akademie. Repr., pages 615–29 in vol. 2 of *Manichaica Iranica: Ausgewählte Schriften von Werner Sundermann*. Edited by Christiane Reck. 2 vols. Rome: Herder, 2001.

———. 1981. *Mitteliranische manichäische Texte kirchengeschichtlichen Inhalts*. Berliner Turfantexte 11. Berlin: Akademie.

———. 1984. "Ein weiteres Fragment aus Manis Gigantenbuch." Pages 491–504 in *Orientalia J. Duchesne-Guillemin Emerito Oblata*. Acta Iranica 23. Leiden: Brill.

———. 1985. "Die vierzehn Wunden der lebendigen Seele." *AoF* 12: 288–95. doi:10.1524/aofo.1985.12.12.288. Repr., pages 633–45 in vol. 2 of *Manichaica Iranica: Ausgewählte Schriften von Werner Sundermann*. Edited by Chistiane Reck et al. Rome: Herder, 2001.

———. 1992. "Cologne Mani Codex." *Encyclopædia Iranica* 6/1: 43–46. Online: http://www.iranicaonline.org/articles/cologne-mani-codex-parchment.

———. 1997. *Der Sermon von der Seele: Eine Lehrschrift des östlichen Manichäismus; Edition der parthischen und soghdischen Version*. Berliner Turfantexte 19. Turnhout: Brepols.

———. 2001a. "Der Manichäismus an der Seidenstrasse: Aufstieg, Blüte und Verfall." Pages 153–69 in *Die Seidenstraße: Handel und Kulturaustausch in einem eurasiatischen Wegenetz*. Edited by Ulrich Hübner, Jens Kamlah, and Lucian Reinfandt. Asien und Afrika 3. Hamburg: EB-Verlag.

———. 2001b. "Giants, the Book of." *Encyclopædia Iranica* 10/6: 592–94. Online (2018): https://www.iranicaonline.org/articles/giants-the-book-of.

———. 2001c. *Manichaica Iranica: Ausgewählte Schriften von Werner Sundermann*. Edited by Christiane Reck. 2 vols. Rome: Herder.

———. 2001d. "Mani's 'Book of the Giants' and the Jewish Books of Enoch: A Case of Terminological Difference and What It Implies." Pages 40–48 in *Irano-Judaica III: Studies Relating to Jewish Contacts with Persian Culture throughout the Ages*. Edited by Shaul Shaked and Amnon Netzer. Jerusalem: Ben-Zvi Institute for the Study of Jewish Communities in the East, 1994. Repr., pages 697–706 in vol. 2 of *Manichaica Iranica: Ausgewählte Schriften von Werner Sundermann*. Edited by Chistiane Reck. Rome: Herder.

———. 2004. "Turfan Expeditions." *Encyclopaedia Iranica*. Online: http://www.iranicaonline.org/articles/turfan-expeditions-2.

———. 2007. "God and His Adversary in Manichaeism—the Case of the 'Enthymesis of Death' and the 'Enthymesis of Life.'" Pages 137–49 in *Religious Texts in Iranian Languages: Symposium Held in Copenhagen May 2002*. Edited by Fereydun Vahman and Claus V. Pedersen. Copenhagen: Det Kongelige Danske Videnskabernes Selskab.

———. 2009a. "Mani." *Encyclopaedia Iranica*. Online: http://www.iranicaonline.org/articles/mani-founder-manicheism.

———. 2009b. "Manicheism v: Missionary Activity and Technique." *Encyclopædia Iranica*. Online: http://www.iranicaonline.org/articles/manicheism-iv-missionary-activity-and-technique-.

———. 2018. "Manicheism iii: The Manichean Pandaemonium." *Encyclopædia Iranica*. Online: http://www.iranicaonline.org/articles/manicheism-pandaemonium.

Tardieu, Michel. 1981. *Le manichéisme. Que sais-je?* 1940. Paris: Presses universitaires de France. 2nd rev. ed., 1997.

———. 1989. "La diffusion du bouddhisme dans l'Empire kouchan, l'Iran et la Chine, d'après un kephalaion manichéen inédit." *SIr* 17: 153–82. doi:10.2143/SI.17.2.2014582.

Thomassen, Einar. 2011. *Manikeiske skrifter, utvalgt og innledende essay av*. Oversatt av Prods Oktor Skjærvø og Einar Thomassen. Verdens hellige skrifter. Bokklubben.

Waldschmidt, Ernst, and Wolfgang Lentz. 1933. *Manichäische Dogmatik aus chinesischen und iranischen Texten*. SPAW 13. Berlin: Akademie.

Wilken, Jens. 2000. "Neue Fragmente aus Mani's Gigantenbuch." *ZDMG* 150: 133–76.

Williams, Alan V. 1990. *The Pahlavi Rivāyats Accompanying the Dādestān ī Dēnīg*. Part 1, *Transliteration, Transcription and Glossary*. Part 2, *Translation, Commentary and Pahlavi Text*. Copenhagen: Munksgaard.

Williams, Frank, trans. 2009. *The Panarion of Epiphanius of Salamis, Books 2 and 3: De fide*. 2nd rev. ed. Nag Hammadi and Manichaean Studies 79. Leiden: Brill.

Wurst, Gregor. 1996. *The Manichaean Coptic Papyri in the Chester Beatty Library, Psalm Book, Part II, 1: Die Bema-Psalmen*. Corpus Fontium Manichaeorum 2. Turnhout: Brepols.

Yoshida, Yutaka. 2015. "絵画の内容の解釈をめぐって：絵 画に表現されたマニ教の教義と教会の歴史 (*Kaiga no naiyō no kaishaku wo megutte: kaiga ni hyōgen sareta Manikyō no kyōgi to kyōkai no rekishi*) [On the Contents and Details of the Paintings: The Manichaean Teachings and Church History as Depicted in the Paintings. First Part: Interpretations of the Paintings and Their Details]." Pages 77–147 in 中国江南マニ教絵画研究 = *Studies of the Chinese Manichaean Paintings of South Chinese Origin Preserved in Japan*. Kyoto: Rinsenshoten.

———. 2019. *Three Manichaean Sogdian Letters Unearthed in Bäzäklik, Turfan*. Kyoto: Rinsen Book Co.

Zieme, Peter. 1975. *Manichäisch-türkische Texte: Texte, Übersetzung, Anmerkungen*. Berliner Turfantexte 5. Berlin: Akademie.

The Book of Giants (Iranian Manichean Version)[a]

Prologue: About the Fall of the Abortions and the Creation of Adam and Eve

0:KawJ. Reference. M5750/V/i–ii/, Middle Persian (Henning 1943, 70; Morano 2008, 82).[b]

End of a section on "the ten paths," which lists the coming of Narīsahyazd (the Third Messenger), Āz and the abortions (*abgānagān*), Jesus, [. . .], and the two hundred demons (two paths). The section that follows in the manuscript is "About the paths of the body."

M5750/V/i/4–24/ (right column)

And at the coming of Āz, three paths of death become manifest: (that of) the hidden fire and the visible fire (leading to) the "turning" (in the cycle of rebirths) and the fragrance and flowers of paradise.

And at the coming of the abortions four paths: *thorny (*nīš*...) sleep, the breath of corpses (leading) to the turning, and copulation (leading) to hell.

And at the coming of Jesus two paths: speech devoid of harm and the wealth of being righteous [. . . (leading)] to parad[ise], and [the . . .] speech [. . .]

M5750/V/ii/1–5 (left column; Henning 1943, 70)

[And at the com]ing of the two hundred demons two paths: speech of harm and harsh torment. These [lead] to hell. The evil ones [. . .].[c]

1:KawZs1/R/. Text. M7800/ii/R/, Sogdian (Sundermann 1994, 45–46; Morano 2008, 105–6).

The text partly overlaps with 2:KawZs3. Contents: Fall of the abortions, begotten when the Third Messenger showed his form to the female archons.[d]

---

a. See also the introduction to the Manichean Book of Giants for additional information on the individual fragments translated below.

b. Henning cites only /V/ii/1–5 from this fragment. The rest is from Durkin-Meisternst's transcription of all the published manuscripts and including some unpublished parts, available at the Turfan webpage, https://turfan.bbaw.de/texte/mirtext.html.

c. Manuscript punctuation in red (which Henning omitted) separates "hell" and "the evil ones."

d. See the introduction on 2:KawZs3.

The Book of Giants (Iranian Manichean Version)

V–R/Header: Discourse / on the demon abortions.
M7800/ii/R/1–7/
[. . .] they ate the fruits of the forest.[a]

And when the abortions fell down, then they began to drink from the water of the wells and the fruit of the trees.

And they remembered the beauty of Mih[r-b]ag (the Third Messenger) (and) began to look (upward).

2:KawZs3. Text. So 14255+56, Sogdian (Morano 2024, 4–8, 15–16).

So 14255+56/R/ overlaps with the end of 1:KawZs1 recto. Contents: (1) About the abortions. (2) Āz and the two demons (Shaklūn and Pēsūs) prepare to fashion the first two humans.

So 14255+56/R/upper part of column
Header: of the fall[ing . . .]
[. . .] and they began [to . . .]. And one by one [. . .] separated[b] [. . .]. And there were some who began living in a mountain cracked open,[c] some who (stayed) in luxuriant meadows, some who [. . .] the [. . .], some [who . . .] in the plain, [some] who [. . .] in darkness. [. . .] uncovered [. . .] and, at night, they would go out

So 14255+56/R/lower part of column
for] fear of the companions.[d] [. . .].
And whoever was weak [. . .] he would make [. . .] of the strongest and take him from [. . .] and [. . .] (him)self [. . .].

And the entire world became [dry and] wet[e] from those [. . .] and they were [. . .] from one another, if[f]
[. . .].
[And] those who fell into the n[orthern] world, were called "gods."
And [those] who fell [into] the eastern direction, they were called "angels."

So 14255+56/V/1–12/ upper part of column (Morano, forthcoming)
[And those who] fell [in] the western [world] and were called [. . .]s.
And those who fell into the southern world, [they were] all . . .-er and foul[er? . . .] and were called [. . . .].
[Those] who . . .-ed with this [. . . wo]rld and from him[g]

---

a. In this Sogdian text, a Sanskrit word for "forest" is used.
b. Alternatively: "divided."
c. Cf. 4Q531 frag. 1 8 "the Nephilim [op]ened it"?
d. On this term, see the introduction on 2:KawZs3. Cf. "all his companions" in Q530 frags. 2 col. ii + 6 + 7 col. i 8–11+12 1 and "his companions" in 4Q203 frag. 3 2; frags. 2 col. ii + 6 + 7 col. i 8–11+12 1.
e. Cf. Kephalaia 92, translated in the introduction.
f. "if" or "that"
g. "him" or "her"

So 14255+56/R/1-12/ lower part of column.
[. . .-]ed (pl.). And (he/she) wished [to . . .] the other. Thereby, Āz [. . . -]ed [. . .] Shaklūn and Pēsūs, who had a [. . .] .?. [. . .] the other demons [. . .] and most .?. [. . .]. And to/in the [. . .] lust, [. . . like?] a craftsman.[a]

And to the demons she said that: "Do not look toward the enemy, [but] copulate in lust with each other! [Bear children] and [bring them] to me!"

3:KawZs1/V/. Text. M7800/ii/R–V/, Sogdian (Sundermann 1994, 45–46; Morano 2008, 105–6).

Contents: Āz and the two demons prepare to fashion the first two humans.

M7800/ii/R/7-19/ + /V/1-19

At that time, the Thought of Death, (that is) Āz, cl[oth]ed (herself) in the two demon abortions Shaklūn and Pēsūs and in the voice of Shaklūn com[man]ded the other abortions thus: "You! Do not look upward! For it is your e[nemy]! But now, go, you, and copulate, male with female, and pursue lust and desire with each other! Bear children, and bring individually(?) your brats[b] to me!

And I shall make such a something (because of) which there will be no need to look up."

Then those abortions accepted th[is] command and did so. They brought 80,000 brats before Shaklūn and Pēsūs, and they accepted them. Then one [by one] they entered [a pla]ce(?). And [40],000 brats Shaklūn ate, and 40,000 Pēsūs.

Then they copulated with each other and spoke thus: "We have our *heartfelt thought[c] toward Mi[hr-bag] so that [. . .] who is born from us [will resemble] the gods [. . .]."

About Adam and Eve and Humanity and the Descent of the Two Hundred Demons

4:KawX. Text/excerpt? M8280/V/ii–R/ii/, Parthian (Sundermann 1973, 76–77, ll. 1523–42; Morano 2008, 83).

Contents: (1) Creation of the human body. (2) The two demons (here called [*Dāw]īt and Hala'īt) make Eve turn (?) Adam away from the *dēn*[d] three times.[e] (3) Descent of the demons (Watchers) because of their desire for the women.   See Gen 6:2; 1 En. 6:1–2; Jub. 5:1

a. Cf. Āz's activities compared with those of a builder, a tailor, or a painter in the Shābuhragān (Hutter 1992, 111–12).

b. This word, which denotes the offspring of the "abortions," is probably a pejorative term for offspring, not another word for "abortion."

c. The meaning of the Sogdian word translated as "*heartfelt," assuming it as an adjective of *mān*, "heart," is uncertain. Sundermann (1994, 46) has "intentional thought," but without comment. Elsewhere, in one text, the partly reconstructed phrase is in a context with "indifference, forgetfulness, malice, weakness" and, in another, it qualifies "desire" (see references in Sims-Williams and Durkin-Meistererernst 2012, 108b).

d. For this term, see the introduction, the section "Mani and His *Dēn*."

e. Cf. Homilies 68.7–30 and M18248/i/17–18 (Sogdian; Henning 1944, 138 [16], 140): "The first calumniator and sinner was Martēn (Eve), who three times led Adam astray from the *dēn*."

The Book of Giants (Iranian Manichean Version)

M8280/V/ii/1-4/ left column
[...] made of flesh and [...] blood ...[a] and [...] hair,[b] costume[c] [...] ... narrow [...].

M8280/R/i/1-6/ right column
[...] those two, [*Dāw]īt and Hala'īt,[d] (made) Ahwāy (= Eve) sinful [and turned] Adam [away] from the *dēn* a third time.
And [...] that purity [...]

M8280/R/ii/1-2 left column
[...] humans, animals ... [...] like the seed [...]

M8280/V/i/1-7 right column
[...] they *came [down] to earth because of the beauty of the females, [li]ke when attackers [...] by/with [...] have leapt from [their horses[e] ...]

5:KawK. Text. M363, Sogdian (Henning 1943, 70–71; Morano 2008, 82–83).
Contents: (1) Humanity is thrown into turmoil because of the descending demons. This concludes: "The exposition of the three worlds." (2) Beginning of the chapter on Adam and Eve and their son Shitil and Adam's enlightenment through Jesus (the Splendor).

M363/R/1-10/
[... who] were [...] before. And they all[f] pursued their own work according to the law. They were therefore now thrown into great turmoil because the two hundred demons had descended from high heaven [...] below to the zodiac and [had ...] the [...].

M363/V/1-10/
[... humans?] in the world were thrown into great turmoil, for the lines of their life and the lines of their[g] pneumatic veins are tied to the zodiac.[h]
Completed: "The exposition of the three worlds."

Begun: "The coming of Jesus and his [bringing] of the *dēn* to Adam (and) Shitil."

a. MS clear *langārīft* only here and of unknown meaning.
b. Cf. M101b/V/.
c. Sunderman took "hair, costume" together as "hairstyle" with query. Cf. Midrash of Shemhazai and Aza'el 7, where 'Aza'el is put in charge of cosmetics and jewelry.
d. Reading [...]*yt hl'yt*, rather than Sundermann's [...](š)t hl(c)yt. See the introduction, the section "About the Fall of the Abortions and the Creation of Adam and Eve."
e. "horses" or "chariots"?
f. Henning (1943, 71 n. 2) suggested these may be the stellar demons, which seems less likely in the context.
g. Adam and Eve and the rest of mankind?
h. Described in the Shābuhragān (Hutter 1992, 89).

The Book of Giants (Iranian Manichean Version)

[. . . do (pl.) not] tremble! And [. . .]

The Demons Wreak Destruction on Earth and Ravish the Women

6:KawAi. Text. M101i/R–V/, Middle Persian (Henning 1943, 58, 62; Morano 2008, 97).

Contents: (1) the demons and giants subjugate the human race and forcibly marry beautiful women. (2) Humans set to work cleaning.

M101i/R/2–9/

[. . .] many [. . .] were killed. Four hundred thousand righteous [perished in] the mountains from fire, naphtha, and sulphur.[a]

And the angels hid Enoch.[b]

And (they = the demons?) [seized?] the female elect and the female hearers and copulated with (them). (They) selected beautiful [women] and [made] them (their) wives. As (they) wished (they) *defil[ed] (them).

M101i/V/1–8/

[. . .] all [. . . were] carried off. Each and every one was subjected to work and service. And they [brought] them from town (to) town and ordered them to perform servant duties to the [. . .]. Those from Mesene [were ordered] to *tidy up,[c] those from Khuzistan to sweep [and] [p]our [water? = irrigate?], those from Fars [to . . .].[d]

See Gen 5:24; 1 En. 12:1; 70:1–3; Jub. 4:21, 23(?)

See 1 En. 7:1, 4

See 1 En. 7:1; 4Q531 frag. 2 [. . .]

See 1 En. 10:20

The Demons (Watchers) Teach Human Beings. Birth of the Giants

7:KawH. Excerpt. So 14638/i/R/1–17/, Sogdian (Henning 1943, 69–70; Reck 2006, 153; Morano 2008, 84–85).

Contents: (1) The demons (Watchers) teach mankind the mysteries. (2) They sire children, the giants. From a narrative in which the King of Kings interviews Mani about the origin of the world of men. Mani answers by recounting, briefly, first the story of the Watchers, then the origin of the world of men.

Begun is the question concerning Āz's world of death.[e]

And whatever they had seen in the heavens among the gods and whatever they had seen in the darkness of their own family into which they were born and whatever they had seen in the world, good and evil, they began to teach mankind and train them in.

And now two sons were born to Shahmīzād. And he named [one] of them [Oh]yā, who in Sogdian is called Sāhm the giant. And furthermore a second son was born to him, and he named him Ahyā, and, furthermore, in Sogdian his (name) is Pād-sāhm.

See Midrash of Shemhazai and Azaël 7

a. Cf. 28:KawG; Homilies 68.12–17.
b. Cf. 32:KawT/R/.
c. Henning has "prepare."
d. Provinces of the Sasanian Empire: Mesene, Khuzistan, and Fārs.
e. Note Midrash of Shemhazai and Azaël 3: "As long as you live in this world the evil 'inclination' (*yetzer*) would rule over you"; and see Kiel 2016.

The Book of Giants (Iranian Manichean Version)

See 1 En. 7:2   And the other giants were born from the remaining demons and yakshas.[a]

Completed: The coming of the two hundred demons.

Begun: The King of King's [que]stioning regarding the world.
And again the King of Kings asked the Light Apost[le] (= Mani) [thus]:
This world where people are, why do they call it "Āz's death?"

8:KawZp2. Quote. M813/i/, Parthian (Morano 2009, 326–28).

Contents: Sogdian with Parthian quotations dealing with the giants' lifespan.

M813/i/R/8–12/

[Sogd.] *The way it says in the Lord's* (= Mani's)[b] *writ[ing]*:
"If they had [not] lived like giants and men,[c] then Ohyā [and his] b[roth]er Narīmān [would] not [have d]ied. [A]t the feet of the dearest [they would have . . .]."[d]

This is, apparently, followed by similar examples, only one of which is preserved:

M813/i/V/9–12/

And if he had lived among the beautiful, then King Siyāwash [would not have d]ied, in/for whose beauty [. . .].[e]

9:KawI. Reference. M500n, Sogdian (Henning 1943, 70 [only side A]; Morano 2008, 104).[f]

Contents: The giants as examples of eternal life, but also as beings that cannot be completely saved.

M500n/A/1–7/

[It is said that? . . . he who lived?] like men like mighty tyrants would not die, and (that) Sāhm the giant, together with his brother will live forever. For in the whole world [they had no equals] in power and strength and in [. . .].

---

a. In Sanskrit a kind of demon.
b. The use of the word *bagh* "god, lord" to refer to Mani has apparently not so far been found elsewhere.
c. See the introduction on 8:KawZp2.
d. Morano tentatively suggests "at the feet of his dearest (father?)."
e. On the story of Siyāwash, son of Kay Kawād, who was desired by his stepmother, who then maligned him to the king, see Skjærvø 1998a and 2013, sec. 3. He became the father of Kay Khosrow (see the introduction on 42:KawU).
f. Apparently Henning had a poor photo at his disposal. Except for the first line and the beginning of the second, the fragment is perfectly legible. The obverse, originally covered by a piece of paper, was recovered when the paper was removed (Morano 2011, 104–5).

M500n/B/1–7/

[...] will bring release.
Neither from a pardon, nor from a pious death (?) can there be complete salvation. Neither the giants, nor the arhats,[a] nor the rulers, nor the kings, nor [...].

Complaint of the Earth and Its Human Inhabitants
10:KawV. Excerpt? M692, Sogdian (Henning 1943, 74; Morano 2008, 889).
Contents: The complaint of the earth and its human inhabitants brought before Yam = the King of Honor (see Introduction nn. 89 and 90).

M692/R/1–12

[...] on account of [...] and to abandon[b] the house of the gods and the eternal happiness and goodness.
For thus it is said[c] that, at that time, Yam was in the world. And, on New D[ay],[d] all the glor[ious][e] (ones) in the world assembled, [and] (they) all [...]

M692/V/1–11   See 1 En. 9:2–4?

[...] and they brought five garlands in homage. And Yam accepted all their garlands. And he [...] those [garlan]ds which [...]. And (Yam) was a great [...] king. And he -ed upon them [...] and fame.[f] And out of his goodness he placed [the gar]land on his head. [And all the kings?] of the world [...]

The Giants' Dream[g]
11:KawAj/R/. Text. M101j/R/, Middle Persian (Henning 1943, 57, 60; Morano 2008, 87–88).
Contents: Sām and Narīmān see tablets in their dreams.

M101j/R/1–9

   [...] plac[ed ...]
   [...] on a tablet.
   [He -ed] to the angels [...] from heaven.
   He threw a tablet in [the fire? and] a tablet into the water.   See 2Q26.

---

a. See n. 80.
b. Sims-Williams and Durkin-Meisterernst (2012, 37a) have *'wxryy* "abandon." Henning 1943, 72 n. 4: "'to abandon' ... appears to be of no use here."
c. Sims-Williams and Durkin-Meisterernst 2012, 206b (s.v. *wxs-*).
d. Reading *nwy m[yδ]*, i.e., New Year, Persian *now-ruz* (Skjærvø 1995a, 204), rather than Henning's *nwy m[ʾh]* "new moon." Cf. Reck 2006, 41.
e. Henning has "blessed," Morano *felici*.
f. Henning argues for "acclamations, cheering."
g. Morano's seq. 4: "Contests between the Giants [14:KawAj/V/]. Warning Dreams [11:KawAj/R/]."

The Book of Giants (Iranian Manichean Version)

<small>See Midrash of Shemhazai and Aza'el 9</small>

At the en[d], he saw [in] a dream a tablet (with) three signs (on it) [one ...], one (portending)[a] woe and flight, and one [death?] and annihilation.

<small>See 6Q8 frags. 2–3</small>

Narīmān saw a ga[rden[b] of] trees in rows.
[T]wo h[undred[c] shoots?] came out.
The trees [...]

12:KawD. Text. M625c, Middle Persian (Henning 1943, 66; Morano 2008, 88).

Contents: (1) Māhaway asks Enoch to interpret the dreams. (2) Enoch interprets the dreams.

M625c/R/i/1–3/
   [... o]utside [...]
   [... Mā]haway[d] [...]

M625c/R/ii/1–5/
   [Tell him? :] "*Interpret[e] (sg.) that dream we dreamed!"
   (Two lines free)
   Then Enoch [interpreted the dreams] as follows: [...]

M625c/V/i/
   [... who] came out [from the ...] and the [shoots of the?] trees, are those Watchers ('īr)[f] and giants who came out of the women.
   And [...]

M625c/V/ii/
   [That] water [which] had been drawn [from the well? ...] onto[g] [...]

13:KawZs2. Text. Ōtani 7447/R + 7468/R, Sogdian (Kudara et al., 1977, vol. 1, 139 [text and Japanese trans.], vol. 2, 67 [photo]; Morano 2008, 106).

Contents: Enoch interprets the dream and tells Māhaway what to do next.

[...] *them [...] the gods got angry.
Now [...] we have placed [...] you [...].
And now (you) must [...] them[h] [and show?] this [tablet? to Hōb]ābīsh

<small>4Q203 frag. 3</small>

together with the giants [...].

---

a. Thus Henning.
b. There does not appear to be enough space for [full of].
c. Thus Henning, reading [d]wys[d]; wys[t] "20" is also possible, conceivably referring to the twenty leaders of the Watchers, although the following text makes this less likely.
d. Henning (1943, 66), although he knew the name Māhaway, took hwy to be the Middle Persian word for "left (side)," which Morano erroneously took to be from "to leave" (lasciato).
e. The word translated as "interpret" (pāčīg) is not found elsewhere.
f. This and 31:KawY are the only fragments to mention the "Watchers" by their Aramaic/Syriac term 'īr.
g. Prep. abar "on(to)" or word beginning with abr-/abar-.
h. Or "and now they must [...]."

The Book of Giants (Iranian Manichean Version)

14:KawAj/V/. Text. M101j/V/, Middle Persian (Henning 1943, 57, 60).
Contents: (1) The giants begin to kill one another. (2) Sām rises up before the sun.

M101j/V/1–9/
[... Wir]ōgdā[d] ...[a] (?) [..].
Hōbābīsh [said?] to Ahiram:[b] "[...] carried off his wife [...]naxtag."[c]   4Q203 frag. 3
Then the giants [began] to kill one another and to [car]ry off (the others') [wives?...].   1 En. 10:9
And the animals, too, began to kill [one anoth]er.
Sām [ro]se[d] up before the sun, one hand in the ether and one [on the earth],[e] and [he told?] everything he had found to (his) br[other].
[...] bound[f] [...].   1 En. 10:12; 18:10–19:1?

15:KawAg. Text. M101g, Middle Persian (Henning 1943, 57–58, 61–62; Morano 2008, 94).
Contents: (1) Sām tells what he saw in the pits of hell. (2) A series of aphorisms (addressed to Narīmān?). (3) Narīmān then starts talking.

M101g/A/1–9/
[...] And I (= Sām?) saw (in?) yet another place [....-]s, who were lamenting for the annihilation that had come [upon] them. And their cries and howls went all the way up to heaven.   1 En. 22:5; 4Q530 frag. 1 i 4
And I saw yet another place, [where] (there were) many tyrants and kings who had lived in sin and evil-[...], when [...].[g]

M101g/B/1–9/
[...] not (he) who stands by the law,[h] but who is truthful in speech;
not the *[frui]t of evil deeds, but the poison that is in it;
[not (those) who] are given a place [in] heaven, but the god [of all] the lands;[i]
not does a servant boast, but the [rule]r who (is) above him;
not the envoy [...], but that man who sent (him).[j]
Then, Narīm[ān ... and s]aid: [...].

---

a. Henning restored the damaged word as *(k)[wš]t* "killed." Other possible reconstructions are *(k)[yš]t* "sowed" and, perhaps, *(x)[w's]t* "sought, requested."
b. One of the Watchers, also in 4Q531 frag. 7.
c. The name is incomplete.
d. Cf. "rise up before the Father!" in Sundermann 1981, 74, line 1057 in a different context. Same formula in Uyghur frag. 1, but also in a different context; 1Q23 frag. 11 "arose be[fore]."
e. Reminiscent of Midrash of Shemhazai and Aza'el 12: "Shemhazai hovering between heaven and earth, feet up, head down." There is only room for a short word.
f. Henning (1943, 60) has "imprisoned," which is too specific for the fragmentary context.
g. See also Stuckenbruck 1997, 24–25 with n. 94.
h. Henning had "engages in quarrels," which is an unlikely meaning of the phrase.
i. "[in] the lands"?
j. Henning (p. 61 n. 1) compared to John 13:16.

The Book of Giants (Iranian Manichean Version)

16:KawW. Text. SIO/120/i/V/, Middle Persian (Sundermann 1984; Morano 2008, 92–93).

Contents: (1) Shahmīzād, his two sons Sām and Narīmān, and the two tablets. (2) Sām tries to cheer up the giants, but they are too sad. (3) Sām has a second dream.

Header: "Concerning the Māzendars (= giants)."[a]

4Q203 frag. 7b ii, frag. 8 3

SIO/120/i/R/0–13/

[...] would not last. (?)[b]

Again he (= Sām) said, "Take these two stone tablets to (our/your?) father,[c] since (it is?) written.[d] First bring the message to that Narīman: "Why are you (pl.) running so fiercely?"[e]

Now I (= Sām) have come and I have brought these two tablets so that [you] may read[f] to the giants the one to the Māzendars."

Shahmīzād said, "Read the manuscript of Enoch the interpreter,[g] [...] from "The speech [...]"!"

Header: "Sām of the giants."

SIO/120/i/V/0–13/

Then Sām said to the giants, "Come let us eat and be happy!"

Because of (their) sorrow they did not eat anything.[h] They went to sleep.

4Q530 frag. 1 i 5–6?

Māhaway went to Atanbīsh (and) told (him) everything. Māhaway came a second time.

Sām had a dream: He came up above heaven. Heat reached (up) from the earth.[i] All the water was swallowed up. Wrath came out from the water. The Radiances[j] became invisible.[k] He saw before him the rulers of heaven. [...]

---

a. Cf. Stuckenbruck 1997, 83–87.

b. Also possible, with Sundermann: "nicht bleibst" ("you do not stay/remain"). The form can be 2nd-person sg. indicative or 3rd-person sg. optative.

c. Assuming the word spelled *pd* is for common *pyd* "father" (like *pdr* for *pydr* "father"); Sundermann (1984, 496) read it as *pr* (*r* = *d* with superscript point, here very vague) based on a doubtful etymology.

d. Unclear; it could also be read as "where (they were) written."

e. Sundermann (2001, [630]) suggests as alternative: "the message ... on account of which."

f. The ending of the verb is lost. It can also be restored as "you read, he reads" or imperative "you read!"

g. Morano (2008, 369 n. 33) discusses the meaning of the word translated here as "interpreter" and suggested comparison with 4Q203, frag. 8 4, where Enoch is called "eminent scribe."

h. Lit. "eat bread," the common idiom for "eat, eat dinner" as in the famous M3/R/4–5/ "and the king was at dinner." Cf. "I shall sleep and [eat] bread" (different context) in 4Q530 frag. 1 i, 6.

i. Rather than "fever reached (him) from the earth" (Sundermann 1984, 497).

j. The Radiances (*farrahān*) include the archangels, first of them Jacob (M43/R/6–7/ in Reck 2004, 159 lines 942–956). In early Zoroastrian mythology, "Radiance" (*xwarrah* = *farrah*) is a luminosity distributed over the earth by the sun and the moon.

k. The Radiances may have just hidden themselves, but, in Zoroastrian mythology, Wrath represents the darkness of the night sky. Mani may have combined and adjusted the myths and suggested that the Wrath/darkness covered the Radiances. On Jacob as Frēdōn, another Iranian dragon slayer, see also Skjærvø 1995a, 210–12.

SIO/120/ii/V/0-6
/II/R/Ü/ Explanation.
[He removed] the pure splendor from hatred(?),
from sorrow, evil, envy,
*brutishness. He bound them in the bones.
He set up splendor in it. He created from his own creation love,
happiness, gratitude,
spaciousness, and *silence,
in such a way that love itself should be
a wakeful guardian between those pure and those mixed.
Love is comparable to the sun, son of rulers.

SIO/120/ii/V/7-13
/II/V/Ü/ Explanation.
Dung [...]
and his powers. And belief is like a well-prepared
banquet, like a *sealed letter, like a *covered virgin
from the family of kings.

Again he purified and took understanding from the understanding
of the Soul. And he took off him greed, *conflict
... (?) transmigration, and ...(?) (and) bound them in the flesh.
[And he created] from his] own [creation . . .].

17:KawAl. Text. M101/R–V/, Middle Persian (Henning 1943, 57, 61; Morano 2008, 91–92).
Contents: (1) Enoch tells Sām what to tell the giants(?). (2) The paradisaic conditions of the righteous who escaped the butchery(?).

M101/R/1/2-8
[... Eno]ch the apostle [said: Bring to the demons and?] to the children the message:
"To you (pl.) [greetings?] not of well-being! [The judgment is]ᵃ for you to to be bound for the sin you have committed. For [that ... sin?], you (pl.) shall see the victory over your children [and a r]uler [shall be (appointed?) over you]ᵇ for one hundred and twenty [years. ...]

1 En. 12:5; 13:1; 16:4; 1Q24 frag. 8; 4Q203 frag. 13 3

1 En. 13:1

1 En. 10:12; 13:2; 14:6; Jub. 5:7

Gen 6:3; Jub. 5:8

M101/V/1/1-7
[...] wild asses, ibexes, rams, goats, gazelles, [...], oryxes, two hundred each in pairs [and] f[ull] of the other wild beasts, birds, and animals.<

1Q23 frag. 1+6+22

a. Henning's restoration.
b. Cf. 25:KawF lines 67–69 "and they shall be rulers over all who are in it."

147

The Book of Giants (Iranian Manichean Version)

1 En. 10:18–19

And they shall have wine—six thousand jugs—and . . .ᵃ of [wa]ter [. . .] and for them *twoᵇ [. . .].

18:KawAc. Text. M101c/R/, Middle Persian (Henning 1943, 56–57, 60; Morano 2008, 85–86).

Contents: (1) Māhaway tells Shahmīzād and Sām/Ohyā what he saw. (2) Māhaway recounts incidents he witnessed on a (dream?) trip together with his father in a chariot.

M101c/R/1–11

[. . . a] firm [. . . he thre]w an arrow [from his fie]ry bow,ᶜ the one the g[iants?] had *drawn *against [me?]."

Sam said, "Blessed be [you, who] saw this (and) did not die!"ᵈ

6Q8 frag. 1?

Then [Shahm]īzād said to Sām, his [son]: "All that Māhaway [says? is not? the *tr]uth."

Next, his [son Sām] said [thus]: "Until [when?] were we [. . .], and [for what reason? did we co]me [to . . .]?"

M101c/V/1–10

[Māhaway said: ". . . are now in the fire of? the *h]ells,ᵉ [in] whose blaze they stand, when my father, Wirōgdād, was w[ith] me.

Shahmīzād s[aid], "He speaks the truth. He says one of thousands.ᶠ Because (it is) one of thousands of *h[ells]."ᵍ

Sām then began [to . . . and] Māhaway, too, [looked in?] many pl[aces], until [he came] to the pla[ce where] the chariotʰ [was].

And o[n that chariot they drove . . . ?].

Infighting among the Giants

19:KawC. Text. M648b, Sogdian (Henning 1943, 65–66; Morano 2008, 86–87).

Contents: Māhaway and Sām become enemies.

M648b/R/1–8/

[. . . beg]an [to . . .] and [said . . . : ". . .do n]ot fear! For [. . . Sā]hm, the giant, will want [to hurt/kill] you, but I shall not let him. [And] I shall hurt [him] myself!"

a. The word (s'ryšn) is hardly the same as the Pahlavi word meaning "provoke" (Henning 1943, 61 with n. 8: "irritation").

b. Henning in his handcopy must have had rw[yn], comparing "wine and oil (rwyyn)" in another text (ibid, 58 n. to line 56) and 1 En. 10:19, but there is no dot on the d, which would make it r.

c. Cf. 1 En. 17:3: a bow of fire, arrows and their quiver (different context).

d. Thus Henning. Morano translates this as "[. . .] had [he?] seen this, he would not have died." Either translation is possible.

e. The damaged word here may be restored as *[na]ragān* "hells," a loan from Sanskrit *naraka*.

f. Henning (p. 1, n. 1) explains this as "far less than he could say."

g. Restore *n[aragān]*? "Thousands" is also in 4Q531 l. 17, where "a thousand thousands" is the number of those bowing to the "Sovereign of Heaven" as he descended to earth.

h. MS *rhyy*. Henning (and Morano) took it to be a form of a verb meaning "to escape."

The Book of Giants (Iranian Manichean Version)

[And the]n Māhaway, the giant, was [quite?] satisfied [. . .].
[. . .]

M648b/V/1–7/
[. . .] I may see.
And now, at that time, S[āhm, the giant] became [very] angry, and reached for M[āhaway, the giant?] (thinking): "I shall kill [yo]u!"
And [now] the other g[iants . . .].

20:KawZs4. Text. So 10700a + So 20193a, Sogdian (Morano 2016).
Contents: (1) Conversation between two giants, one of whom is Sāhm and the other, presumably, Māhaway. (2) An angel comes down and accuses them of evil deeds.

So 10700a/R/1–7/
[. .]
[. . .] they . . .-ed[a] [. . .]
[. . . thus/when] the [. . .] own [. . .],
[. . . -]oo[b] giants [. . .] and from [. . . the -]oo *complete [. . .] was [. . .]
And [. . .] they

So 20193a/R/1–10/ (8–17)
brought [. . .].
And [. . . S]āhm the giant [got on his?] feet [. . .].
[. . .] anger [. .] hands
[. . .] split the [. . . and] broke (it).
And [. . .] so great a [water?? . . .] and the cloud [. . .the] Great Ocean[c]   1 En. 17:5
[. . .] and mountains.
[. . .] you (plur.) might go [. . .] from that [. . .] 100 [. . .]

So 10700a/V/1–7/
[. . .] the giant answ[ered . . .].
[. . .] Sāhm the g[iant . . . Māhaway?] the giant [. . .].
[. . .] an angel from [heaven came down/appeared and stood?] be[fore] the giants.

So 20193a/V/1–10/ (= 8–17)
[. . .] the giants [. . .].
A[nd], against the law, [you have?] kil[l(ed?) . . .].
And Sāhm the gia[nt answered?] the angel.
[. . .] tearing [. . .].

a. The verb [. . .]t'βt- can mean "sealed" (thus Morano) or "heated, lit (up)" (reading [. . . p]t'βt-; see Sims-Williams and Durkin-Meisterernst 2012, 151a).
b. Morano (2016, 190), in the translation, has [. . .1]oo and [. . .]100 without commentary.
c. Sogdian *samutr* from Sanskrit *samudra*.

The Book of Giants (Iranian Manichean Version)

[And?] Sāhm the g[iant's] leading (?) [of . . .].
[. . .] went [. . .].
And [. . .] the water's shore [. . .].

21:KawZs5. Text. So 10701a + So 20193b, Sogdian (Morano 2016, 189; Reck 2006, nos. 61, 319).
Contents: Uncertain.

So 10701a/R/1–7/
Heading: [. . .] ex]position [. . .]
[. . .] took away [. . .].
[. . .] to that/those [. . .] criminals [. . . the]re where [. . .] red [. . .] Great Ocean [. . .]
When they approached [. . .]

1 En. 17:4–5

So 20193b/R/1–10/ (8–17)
[. . .]
[. . .] they . . .-ed as much as [. . .] they looked. Thus [. . .]
[. . .]
[. . .] for that [. . .]
And [. . .] that [. . .]
[. . .] the giant after [. . .]
[. . .] army and *there [. . . went?] after [. . .]

So 10701a/V/1–8/
[. . .] are coming [. . .] again.
And [. . .] the giant [. . .]
[. . .] said (or: so much) yo[u? (plur.) . . .] did not order [. . .] self [. . .] from [. . .]

So 20193b/1–9/ (9–17)
"[. . .s]it down there (where you are and be) quiet!
Do not [look?] at me! [. . .].
For [. . .]."
[. . .] you hear [. . . and] listen [to . . .]"
[And] Sāhm the gi[ant . . .] words . . .].
[. . .] to(gether} with . . . and] the companions [. . .].

22:KawE/R/. Text. M8005/R/, Sogdian (Henning 1943, 66; Morano 2008, 89).
Contents: The spirits go to see Enoch.

M8005/R/1–10/
[. . .] they saw the apostle [. . .] (they went) to meet the apostle, (and) those spirits [. . .] to [. . .] had been [. . .] became very happy to see the apostle, and they all gathered before his face.

1 En. 13

The Book of Giants (Iranian Manichean Version)

And they were also very [worried?] and fearful[a] of those who were tyrants and criminals.[b]

And agai[n . . .].

23:KawF ColB. Text. M6120/I/, Middle Persian (Henning 1943, 66–67; Morano 2008, 90).

Contents: (1) Enoch repeats the words of the Most High. (2) Enoch addresses the giants directly.

M6120/ColB = KawF lines 15–24

[. . .] you (pl.) have not become better, and in your delusion you thought you are (safe) in that deceptive command forever. You [have committed?] all this injustice [. . .] he/him [. . .].

1 En. 10:10

24:KawE/V/. Text. M8005/V/, Sogdian (Henning 1943, 66; Morano 2008, 89).

Contents: (1) Enoch continues addressing the spirits (= Watchers)? (2) The spirits begin their apology/defense.

M8005/V/1–10/

[. . . ". . .] and in [. . .] you (pl.) bear[c] [. . .]! [. . . you have] d[one] of old [. . .]."

[. . .] they did not [. . .] toward the [*col]umn.

And then, those powerful spirits spoke thus to the beneficent apostle thus:

"Since, O lord, no further [will] any sin [be committed] by us, so why, O lord, do you (pl.) [. . .] and [. . .] a heavy command [. . .]?"

About the Fire in Hell

25:KawF. Text. M6120 cols. CDEFA, Middle Persian (Henning 1943, 66–68; Morano 2008, 90–91).

Contents: The giants continue their apology/defense.

M6120/ColC = KawF lines 25–35

"[. . . he] who, with the voice of deception scorns[d] us.

And neither did we thus become visible for your sake, so that you should see us, nor [did we] thus [. . .] to you our own selves by the praise and greatness that was [. . .] *given to us, but rather [. . .] came [. . .]."

---

a. Henning cited the similar phrases in 1 En. 13:3, 9.

b. Morano took "tyrants and criminals" to be the subject of "were . . . fearful," but the syntax is clear, Sogdian lit. "fear[ed] *from* those . . ."

c. "bear" or "carry."

d. Alternately 2nd-person pl.: "[you] who . . . scorn us," literally "howl at us" (cf. 15:KawAg/A/). The expression "howl at" in the sense of "boo, scorn" is found already in the oldest Avestan texts, the Gathas (Yasna 5:8), where it is also used of the "evil gods," the *daēuua*s, Middle Persian *dēw*, the word for "demon" (although not explicitly mentioned).

The Book of Giants (Iranian Manichean Version)

Enoch continues addressing the Watchers and giants.[a]

M6120/ColD = KawF lines 36–53

1 En. 10:9 […of you?] the wicked ones stands manifest where, from this fire, your soul/self is prepared for eternal annihilation.

1 En. 10:9 And you, wicked brats of the wrathful soul/self, who sully the true sayings of that pure one, and disturb the actions of doing good deeds, who attack piety, who […] the living […] who […] destroy…-ness […] their own […] … […].[b]

The righteous will be watching them.

M6120/ColE = KawF lines 54–72

They will [… and] on bright wings they will fly and soar outside and above that fire and will look into its depth and height.

And those righteous ones themselves, who will stand around it, outside and above, they themselves will have command over that great fire and over everything in it. The blaze [will become] *known […], and the […] souls who […] it […].

M6120/ColF = KawF lines 75–88

[…] they are purer and stronger [than] the great fire of annihilation, which makes the worlds burn. And they themselves will stand outside and all around above it. And brightness will shine above them. And they will soar outside and above it, (going) after the souls who shall wish to escape from that fire, and that […].

M6120/ColA = KawF lines 1–14

[…] …[c] […] persecuted the happiness[d] of the Righteous. For this reason they will fall into that annihilation and eternal ruin and that fire, the mother of all burnings, and the foundation of all harsh annihilations. And when the brats of the annihilation of the wicked ones […] into those

1 En. 18:6–12; 54:1–6 *crevices and […]

26:KawZs6. Text. So 20220/ii/, Sogdian (Morano 2016, 191–93). Contents: Elegy for the stars imprisoned in the zodiac.

Headers: Exposition of / autumn.

a. Cf. the Cologne Mani Codex (58–60, translated by Reeves in this volume). Enoch is taken into the heavens and is shown by Michael "the place of punishment" of "the lawless" and "the world of [dea]th, the world of [dar]kness, and the world of fire."

b. Henning (1943, 68 n. 1) identified the two groups of sinners addressed here as the Watchers, who will be "transferred to the permanent hell at the end of the world," and the giants.

c. This word, which Henning restored as "poverty," is uncertain.

d. The exact meaning of the word (*farroxīh*) is hard to pin down, and "fortune, bliss" are other approximations.

The Book of Giants (Iranian Manichean Version)

So 20220/ii/V/1–24/

...[when] this world was built, you all became happy. And you thought thus:

They will build a hostel and palace for our sake. And there we shall [be] lords [and] rulers [of . .], and we are not letting any [. . .]. But (it is) built just like a *house and dwelling [inside which?] we are bound and [im]prisoned, and we cannot escape from this, and we are not released outside. For that reason the gods will take from us the power to move about, and they have also taken from us the rulership.

(empty line)

And now this is a [d]eep and great secret and [. . .].

So 20220/ii/R/1–23/

[. . .] they had removed them to [. . .] and bound and imprisoned them in the zodiac.

(empty line)

And woe, woe, alas, alas you stars! who have left it, your own place and native (land)!

1 En. 18:15–16, 21:3

And you have [. . .-]ed (come) hither to this [. . .].

De[ception and] deceit because of this [. . .] upon your [. . .]

[. . .] powerful ruler has bound and imprisoned [you].

And moreover you were made [. . .] from the battle.

And you burnt your own (. . .?) and your own dwelling place and your own world and have turned it into something *ruined and destroyed by your own ignorance.

And at that time when [. . .]

27:KawZp1. M413 + M2086, Parthian (Colditz 1987, 297–99; Morano 2008, 98 [Zp]).

Contents: Description of some land at the center of earth and its angel rulers.

Header: [Spee]ch [about] / the g[iants].

M413+M2086/R/1–6/

[. . .] there is at the bottom.

For Mount [Samēr]u g[oes] to the east [t]o the town.

And [. . .] also go[es . . .]

From the second [. . . go(es)] to the wes[t . . .].

From [. . .].[a]

M413+M2086/V/1–6/

[. . .] the greatest. And the [ang]els who rule there were (his) [di]sciples, because [. . .] (two-thirds lines empty)

[. . . he/it] will be [. . .].

a. *až h*[. . .] "from [. . .]," apparently not *h[rdyg]* "third," as the dot above the *r* would have been preserved.

153

The Book of Giants (Iranian Manichean Version)

In the heights [...].
And at/by/in [...] farsangs[a] [...].

Descent of the Angels and the Battle between the Angels and the Demons

28:KawG. Text. M7800/I/A, Sogdian (Henning 1943, 68–69; Morano 2008, 96–97).

Contents: (1) Battle between angels and Watchers. (2) Relocation of the humans.

Headers: "Explanation of the *battle[b] / of the four angels with the two hundred [demons]."

M7800/I/A/R/

[...] they took all the companions who were in the heavens and bound them.

Then those angels themselves descended from heaven to the earth. And the two hundred demons saw those angels and were (very) afraid and concerned. And they took the shape of humans and hid.

Then those angels seized the humans from the demons and set them to one side. And [they set] Watchers over them, [those who] were the sons of the giants [and? . . .], and [were in the same?] form with [one anoth]er,[c] (and) themselves [. . .] with one another, and those [. . .] who had been born from them, (those) they seized from the demons and led one half of them.

1 En. 17:1

M7800/I/A/V/

In the eastern direction and one half in the western direction, on the skirts of four great mountains, toward the foot of Mount Sumeru, into thirty-two towns, which the Living Spirit had prepared from the beginning for their sake. And they call it Aryān Wēzhan.[d]

And those men were [skilled] in the fir[st] usages and custo[ms]. They made [...]

[And the] angels [. . .] and departed toward the demons [to fight(?). And tho]se two hundred demons fought a hard battle with the f[our angel]s, until the [ange]ls [poured?] fire, naphtha a[nd . . . and] sulphur [over them].[e]

a. See introduction n. 161.
b. Sogdian *pašān* is not otherwise known. The resemblance to Avestan *peshana* "battle" is probably deceptive, since that is from *pertana*.
c. Cf. 32:KawT "[. . .] many forms [in] a mirror."
d. Cf. the "thirty-six cities" in Kephalaia 117.1–9 (translated in the introduction, the section "The Coptic *Kephalaia* on the Descent of the Watchers") that were prepared for the children of the giants. Henning (1943, 55–56) suggested the change of the number was connected with the Indic narrative related to Mount Sumeru, that "the heaven of Indra . . . is situated between the four peaks of the Meru, and consists of *thirty-two* cities of devas" (citing Eitel's *Handbook of Chinese Buddhism*). On Aryān Wēzhan, see introduction, the section "Elements from Iranian Epic in Mani's Writings" and n. 169.
e. Similar phrase in 6:KawAi.

29:KawAk. Text. M101k, Middle Persian (Henning 1943, 57, 61; Morano 2008, 93–94).

Contents: (1) Ohyā and Ahyā join the battle. (2) Description of what is useful in battle and what is not(?).

M101k/R/1-9/
[. . .] comf[ort[a] your] father!" [And] until the completion of his [labors?] they will bring [. . .] to you (pl.): in battle and in (its) . . .,[b] [in . . .]. And in . . .[c] Ohyā and Ahyā [each . . .] said to his brother: "Get up and let us take the [. . .] which our father commanded [us]! The pledge we gave [to do ba]ttle and [. . .] the giants! [Let us?] together [. . .]!"

M101k/V/1-9/
[. . . not] the lion's [roar?], but [the swiftness] of its f[eet(?);
not the . . .] of the rainbow, but a firm bow;
not the sharpness of the bl[ade, but] the strength of the *jackal;
not the [. . .] eagle. but the wings it (comes) with;
not the [. . .] gold, but the brass (hammer) that strikes it;
not the proud r[uler], but the diadem on his [head];
not the resplendent cypress, but the [. . .] of the mountain [. . .].

30:KawN. Reference M35 and M740, Parthian (Henning 1943, 71–72; Morano 2008, 99).[d]

Contents: Reference to the Great Fire[e] in a series of similes. The recto contains a different text.

Header: "Discourse on the Ārdahang"
M35/V
And the parable about the great fire, how it devours in terrible rage the fire in this world[f] and it seems delightful to it.
Just as this fire in the bodies devours the external fire that comes in fruits and foods, and is pleased.

---

a. Reading *wyw(')[synd]* (Durkin-Meisterernst 2004, 360a). Henning restored *wywd[g'n]* "nuptials" with query.

b. Either "fruit, *outcome" or "share (of booty?)."

c. The word (*āhānag*) is apparently only here (it is missing in Durkin-Meisterernst 2004, 34). Henning has "in the nest" (see Henning 1943, 57 n. 60) presumably assuming misspelling of Parthian *āhiyānag* (Persian *āshiyāna*) "nest."

d. Henning included only the first sentence of M740. He also suggested the text might have been an explanatory text accompanying the Picture Book.

e. At the end of the world, the Living Soul still remaining in matter will be extracted in a great fire burning for 1468 years. Kephalaia 75.22, 104.4 (Gardner 1995, 76, 107–8).

f. Henning assumed it is the fire that swallows the world, but "the fire in this world" is marked as direct object (Henning's "like *unto*"). The fire in the bodies probably refers to digestion in the bodies of the elect, by which the Living Soul is released, cf. 23:KawAf.

The Book of Giants (Iranian Manichean Version)

Next, just as the two brothers who found a treasure and a . . .[a] man. [They] cut [each other] apart and died.

Just as Ohyā, Leviathan, and Raphael cut each other apart and disappeared.

Just as a lion cub and a calf in a meadow (?) and a fox cut each other apart [and died].

In that way [the great fire swallows][b] both fires [. . .].

M740/V/

[Just as] Ahyā, Leviathan [and Raphael] cut [each] other apart and disappeared.

Just as a lion cub, [a calf in a *meadow, and] a fox [cut] [each other] apart and disappeared,

[in that way] that [Great] Fire *swallows both fires [. . .].

And *opp[ression . . .] *share [. . .].

31:KawY. Text. M5900, Middle Persian (Sundermann 1973, 77–78;[c] Morano 2008, 99).

Contents: The battle between the Watchers and giants continues.

"[Spee]ch [about] the Mā[zendars]"

M5900/R/1–16/

[. . .] Then, Atanbīsh seized the two hundred [demons] and split the[ir? . . .], and he [brought them?] before [. . .].

[. . .] you (sg.) are filled and [. . .]

[. . .] *broken[d] And he threw (them) [down into] the four borders of the e[arth].

And he took[e] his own w[eapon] and killed also those three giants who were with Atanbīsh. And he threw them before those W[atcher]s[f] and giants who were with him.

And when those [. . . to] Atanbīsh [. . .].

---

a. The meaning of the adjective (*pashag*) describing the man is uncertain. It also characterizes a man whose shape the Evil One assumes to discredit a female hearer (Sundermann 1981, 59 lines 723–28), but also characterizes a troublesome "teaching" someone hears (ibid., 73 lines 1017–1018) and the hardship suffered by the apostles in various lands, who were chased from land to land and were just like "exiles and *pashags* in the whole land" (ibid., 77 lines 57–59). Thus, Henning's "pursuer" seems unlikely.

b. Thus Henning (1943, 72).

c. Sundermann's copy was apparently less clear than what can be seen on the website. Durkin-Meisterernst gives a few additional readings and a few more are proposed here.

d. The meaning of the verb (*prsys(t)*) is uncertain. It is elsewhere only found in Andreas, ed. Henning, 1934, 36 [881] text k, beginning: "(Jesus) chose to *break the fiery waves, so that all would burn in fire."

e. The subject of "he took" is uncertain.

f. Sundermann's restoration is not in doubt, the 'ayn of '[yr']n being quite clear.

The Book of Giants (Iranian Manichean Version)

M5900/V/1–16/
> [...] and [t]ake (them?) for teaching[a] and dry (them?)!"
> [And] *he who [was tallest?] in height, [put on (his)?] helmet [and] came [to the . -]s.
> Killed (was) he who [. .] the mountains, and [he who . . .] (them) a hundredfold (was) killed.
> Killed (was) that great angel, who was their envoy!
> Slaughtered were those [ch]ewers of flesh!
> And overcome were the victorious *crushers!
> Killed (was) the one who [. . .] with one [two?] steps!

31a:KawZmp1. Text. Ōtani 6207, Middle Persian (Kudara *et al.* vol. 1, 208; vol. 2, 114).

Contents: On the battle between the angels and the giants and their offspring and their punishment (?).

Ōtani 6207/A/3–6
> [. . .] . . . firm[b] [. . .]
> [. . .] . . . and strong [. . .]
> [. . .] of gather[ing?]
> [. . .] . . .[c] two [. . .]

Ōtani 6207/B/2–7
> [. . .] and [. . .]
> [. . .] with dagger[s . . .]
> [. . .] the great [. . .]
> [. . . was?] stretched out[d] and [. . .]
> [. . . in?] a fiery circular wall[e] [. . .]
> [. . .] . . .[f] and [. . .]

32:KawT. Text. M291a, Parthian (Henning 1943, 73; Morano 2008, 98).

Contents: (1) Enoch is hidden again. (2) The giants (?) and demons are chained to the planets and stars, which happened during the creation and is now repeated (?). (3) King Wištāsp is crowned.

---

a. Sundermann read the word as *hmwc*, which is normally "teach!" Durkin-Meisterernst leaves the final consonant untranscribed, but the word is most probably to be read as *hamwq* (more commonly *hmwg*) "teaching."
b. The word can also mean "harsh."
c. The incomplete word [. . .](s)nyl is reminiscent of the names of the four angels ending in -ēl, as well as the disobedient angels (?) listed in 4Q531 frag. 7 3: Naʿamʾel, Razi'el, ʿAmi'el (Stuckenbruck 2014, 40 n. 13).
d. In the *Shāhbuhragān*, the sea monster is fought by Adamas and "stretched out" from east to west (Hutter 1992, 41–42).
e. Fiery circular walls were also built in hell to contain the demons (cf. Hutter 1992, 13–14).
f. The incomplete word [. . .]g'n could be "angels."

The Book of Giants (Iranian Manichean Version)

M291a/R/1–7/

[... as one sees?] many forms [in] a mirror.[a] [...] distributed [...] people [...].

And he hid Enoch.[b]

And they received [...-]s.

Then [they were driven?] with donkey-goads [like?] slaves and endured[c] without water.

Th[en they] bound [the giants? and] the demons, and they a[ttached their ... to?] the Seven (planets) and the Twelve (constellations of the zodiac).[d] [...].

M291a/V/1–7/

[When there had passed in? the] land three thousand two hundred and eighty-[... years, the diadem was placed on?] King Wishtāsp's[e] head,[f] a[nd his brilliance?] shone forth[g] in the palace. At night, too, [it was light as day?].

Next, [...] men [were led?] to the broken gate: physicians, merchants, farmers [...] with armor.

*Unhappy [...].

Armed he went out [from ...].

Epilogue 1: On the Living Soul

33:KawAe. M101e/R/, Middle Persian (Henning 1943, 58, 62–63; Morano 2008, 100).

Contents: (1) About not harming the Living Soul by killing living things (?). (2) Various similes. (3) About various religious beliefs (?).

M101e/R/

[... and] he/his [...]

[... k]illing [of the ...].

[...] the righteous [... the Apo]stle.

Good deeds.

[... the Mahr]āspands.[h]

Crown, diadem. [...] garment.[i]

a. Cf. "[were in the same?] form with [one anoth]er" in 28:KawG/R/.

b. Cf. 6:KawAi/R/.

c. The word is a homonym of "tree" (*draxt*), but is here probably the past of *draxs-* "endure" (not found elsewhere). Henning (1943, 73) has "waterless trees" with a query.

d. Cf. Sundermann 1973, 45 lines 39–42. See also 5:KawK/V/, 26:KawZs6, and the comments on all three passages in the introduction.

e. On Wishtāsp, see introduction n. 55 and 42:KawU below.

f. Henning (1943, 73) has "the beginning of King Vištāsp," but *sar* "head" is most often "end."

g. Like the dawn of a new day (New Year)? Cf. Andreas, ed. Henning, 1932, 192 n. 6 (M5260/V/3–4/) "dawn and sunrise has come, light has shone (forth) from the east."

h. I.e., the five sons of the First Man (the five elements) = the Living Soul.

i. Henning (1943, 62) explains this as a garment of light. The objects are also presented to

The seven demons.[a]
Like a blacksmith [who himself?] ties and himself loosens.[b]
[Like a . . .] who [. . .] from the seed of [. . .].
And serve (pl.)[c] the king!
[Do not] hurt [. . .]!

When [. . . lodges?] complaint [. . .] with mercy.
[. . .] hand [. . .]

M101e/V
[. . .] before [. . .]
Qryst'[.] op[ened] (his) purse [to the well-d]oers. Qxs'n gave a gift.[d]
There was someone who buried the idol[s].
The Jews [did] good deeds and ev[il] deeds.
There are some who make their own god half d[emon] half god.
The . . . (is not) to be slain.
*Opp[ression is not to be . . .?]
The seven demons [are to be] how[led at? like a *w]olf at [the moon?
. . .].[e]
[. . .] ey[e? . . .].

34:KawAb. M101b, Middle Persian (Henning 1943, 58, 63; Morano 2008, 100–1).

Contents: (1) About not harming the Living Soul that is in everything, notably water and all that grows. (2) About the fashioning of Adam and the Light Nous sending the apostles.

M101b/R/1/–10/
[. . . which is lay]ered(?)[f] [with] variegated color, which (is) in [. . . wa]ter, and poison.[g]
If [one] s[trives to stay away? as much as one c]an from (harming?) the five Mahrāspands,[h] [h]ow (would there be) a way that one would not die.[i]

---

the souls of the elect when they die (see Skjærvø 1995b, 276a, 277a).

a. The seven planets? Cf. 32:KawT.
b. Alternatively: "closes and himself unties/opens." Cf. Q4Q531 frag. 13 1 "I have bound him and I will loosen."
c. 2nd-person pl. "serve!" Henning (1943, 62) has 3rd sg. "serves."
d. These proper names (?) have not been explained.
e. See the relevant note on 25:KawF above.
f. The manuscript has [. . .]cyd, which Henning (1943, 63) does not comment on. The verb ncyd is used to build by layering on top of one another, e.g., in the Shābuhragān (Hutter 1992, 12–13, lines 33–37).
g. Henning has "bile," but the context is too fragmentary to exclude the primary meaning of wiš, which is "poison."
h. See introduction n. 106.
i. Henning (ibid.): "as if (it were) a means not to die," the (unclear) syntax does not permit this analysis. The verb is 3rd-person sg. optative (as translated here), but 2nd-person sg. indicative is equally possible.

The Book of Giants (Iranian Manichean Version)

They will fill (themselves?]) with victuals, and (they) will clothe[a] themselves in *their [...].

This corpse[b] is [transient?] and not stable. [It is ... and] its foundation is not stable.

[...] goes out [...] there is [...].

M101b/V/2–11/

[...] bound [in this corp]se, in bones, ten[dons, flesh, ve]ins, and skin,[c] (and Āz her)self entered in[to (it)]. Then (she?) shrieked[d] (falsehoods) about the Just Go[d],[e] the sun and moon. Two ...[f] she gave[g] (to use?) on the Mahrāspands, the trees, and the creatures.

Then God (*bay*) [Wahman?][h] in age after a[ge] sent Shit[il, Zardusht, the [B]uddha, Mashī[hā ... and the other] apostle[s ...].[i]

35:KawAh. M101h, Middle Persian (Henning 1943, 58–59, 63; Morano 2008, 101–2).

Contents: (1) About not knowing one's origin. (2) About not knowing about the Living Soul.

M101h/R/1–4/

[...] having bad awareness[j] [about? things such as this] that: from where [... and from which ...-]s he came.

Those deluded do not know the five elements, [the five] (kinds of?) trees, the five (kinds of?) living beings.[k]

---

a. 3rd-person sg. indicative or 2nd-person pl. imperative.
b. "This corpse" is the human body, while "the great corpse" is the cosmos.
c. Cf. 4:KawX/V/ii/.
d. Henning (ibid.) has "he (= Man) cries out," but the verb *drāy*- is a Zoroastrian term denoting demonic speech manner.
e. The Third Messenger (Henning, ibid.).
f. Henning (1943, 61) assumed this word (*ty*) to be short form for *tyy* "sharp edge; sun ray" and rendered it as "flame," presumably from M12 (at his time unpublished), where *ty* concludes a list of sharp things and *tyy* is in a list of hot or burning things. Sundermann, in his edition of M12 (1985, 293 [618]), rendered "all other *ty*" as "all other things" and *tyy* as "flames," with reference to Henning. (Henning's suggestion that *ty* might be for *ty[gr]* "sharp" is a lapse, since the manuscript is not damaged in this place.)
g. Lit. "gave into the hands," cf. M470/V/1 cited by Henning 1943, 64 n. 3: "give a rope (= lifeline) into (our) hands."
h. Henning suggested [*Zruwān*] with query, but one expects the Great Nous, Wahman. *Wahman bay* does not seem to be otherwise attested, however.
i. Zruwān, commonly Zruwān-bay "god Zruwān," is the Middle Persian name of the Father of Greatness. On the sequence of apostles, see introduction, the section "Mani and His *Dēn*."
j. Henning has "evil-intentioned" instead of the literal "having bad awareness." Sundermann (1981, 173) has "ignorant, having wrong knowledge."
k. Cf. "the roots and the fleshes" in Kephalaia 123 (Gardner 1995, 130). The five fleshes are mankind, quadrupeds, birds, fish, reptiles (Kephalaia 91; Gardner 1995, 96). The five trees are probably different kinds of vegetation, which also contain the Living Soul.

The Book of Giants (Iranian Manichean Version)

Epilogue 2: *On the Elect and the Hearers*
This new chapter follows after an empty line. Contents: (1) About the five commandments and three seals established by Mani himself to govern the behavior of the elect. (2) The ten commandments and other duties of the hearers.[a]

> Chapter title: [...] concerning the hearers.
> M101h/R/5–8/
> [That which] we [re]ceive from Lord Mani [are ...] the five commandments to [...] and the three seals.
>
> M101h/V/2–11/
> [...] living/alive [...] adherence to the *dēn* (of Mani),[b] tr[uthfulness, ..., an]d wisdom.
> [Do] hom[age to?] the moon![c] [Give?] respite from the power of its/his/your [...]!
> And regard the earth as a mother,[d] [who produces?] trees and springs with/by two [...]; water and fruit, milk [and ... as ...]!
> Do not harm (your) brother an[d] the clever [hearer] who, like [the leaves] of juniper [is ...].[e]

36:KawAf. M101f, Middle Persian (Henning 1943, 59, 63–64; Morano 2008, 102).
Contents: On various kinds of hearers told in similes.

> M101f/R/2–12/
> [...] first [...]
> [... mu]ch benefit, like a farm[er who] sows [se]ed in man[y ...].[f]
> hearers [who ha]ve [no] knowledge (are) like a man who threw rennet[g] [into the m]ilk: it became solid, not [...].
> (One's?) share of annihilation [...] first heavy, like [a ... jud]gment. At first [..., like a man who] com[es to ho]nor [...] might [sh]ine.
>
> M101f/V/1–11/
> [...] al[l ...]
> [...] six days.

a. See introduction n. 132 and on 35:KawAh.
b. A Zoroastrian term (*āstawānīh*) that expresses a person's adherence to the Mazdayasnian *dēn*.
c. The moon contains the thrones of Jesus the Splendor, the First Man, and others.
d. Henning's handcopy had *wmyg* "mixture," which he suggested (1943, 59 n. 168, 63) might be an error for *zmyg* "earth" (which is clear), and (Parthian) *pdm'd* "measured" (also Morano) for *pd m'd* "(regard) as mother." The earth as mother is also a common Zoroastrian concept.
e. Henning (n. 6) cited M171/I/V/9–17/ "some hearers are like unto the juniper which is ever green, and whose leaves are shed neither in summer nor in winter. So also the pious hearer ... is constant in his charity and faith." Enoch sees juniper trees in the desert in 1 En. 30.
f. Henning (1943, 63 n. 7) compared Mark 4:3–8.
g. On *frušag* "rennet" (rather than "bee stings" as earlier assumed), see Adhami 2011, 349–50.

The Book of Giants (Iranian Manichean Version)

The hearer [who] gives [al]ms (is) like a p[oor] man who presents his daughter to the king and comes to great honor.[a]

(Food as) alms, in the body of the Righ[teous] (= elect), becomes clean[b] like [...] which [is...] by fire and wind.

[...] a beautiful garment[c] [...] on a cl[eansed] body [...].

37:KawAa. M101a, Middle Persian (Henning 1943, 59, 64; Morano 2008, 102).

Contents: On the hearers and the alms told in similes.

M101a/R/1–15/

[... w]itness [...].

[...] swallowed.[d]

[... t]ree(s) [...] ...[e] [...].

[...] for the sake of [...] ...[f]

Like [... who seeks?] firewood [for the fire?].

[...] draw (pl.) [furrows?], like [gr]ain a[nd] sprouting (?).[g]

And the hearer in [the world?] (and) the alms in the *dēn* (are) like a ship [in the middle of the se]a, the towing-line[h] (being) in the hand of the [tower o]n the shore, the sailor [on board the ship. The s]ea is the world, the ship is [... the al]ms, the one who tows is [..., the towing-li]ne is Wisdom.

[...]

M101a/V/1–15/

[...] is similar [...]. The hearer is [... li]ke a young branch that [grew from a tree?] without fr[uit?...]

[... wi]thout fruit, wh[ich ... -]s and hearer[s...], fruit which [...] good deeds.

[Thus] the E[lect], hearer, and Wahman[i] are just l[ike] three brothers to whom there remained [various] things from (their) father's [estate]: ground, w[ater?,...], and grain. [They] became partners [and] reap and ... [...].

The [h]earer's b[ody? is thus just] li[ke...].

38:KawAd. M101d, Middle Persian (Henning 1943, 59, 64; Morano 2008, 103).

---

a. See Henning (p. 64 n. 1) for an "elaborate version of this parable" (M221/R/9–23), also in Sundermann 1973, 103–4.

b. See introduction on 30:KawN.

c. Possibly like the white garment of the elect.

d. Henning "fruit," dividing the letters differently.

e. Unknown word (*wyrdyd*). Henning (p. 59 n. on 201) wondered if it might be an error for *wydryd* "passes (on), crosses."

f. The fragmentary word can most probably be restored as "[hea]ling" or "[goo]dness."

g. Henning (ibid.) has "radiance" from a homophonous verb.

h. On "towing-line" (*zyyg*), see Panaino 1998, 124.

i. Wahman here denotes the leader of the congregation (Asmussen 1965, 230–31).

The Book of Giants (Iranian Manichean Version)

Contents: (1) About the benefits of alms-giving. (2) Various similes to explain the duties hearers.

M101d/R/1–11/

[... like] a paint[er who made? a like]ness of the king, cast in gold: the king gave (him) a gift.

[The hear]er who writes a book is j[ust lik]e the sick person who gave go[ld^a ... to a ... m]an.

The hearer who gives [his own] daughter to the *dēn*, is just like [the father] (held as) security, who gave (his) son to [...] to be educated: to [...] the father (held as) security [...]

[...] to [...]

[...]

M101d/V/1–11/

[...] ...^b [... he]arer.

Next, a hear[er, how]ever [he] stumbl[es], (his) soul is [p]urified by (his) [being] a devotee.

[L]ike the Roman woman who [gave] a certain [foo]tsoldier (inner) shoes and (outer) sh[oes], and that some that were [(only) to be bought?] for a dinar!^c The wind had torn one off, [the other] was ....^d

[...] from the beginning^e wa[s ...].

39:KawAm. M101m, Middle Persian (Henning 1943, 59–60, 64–65; Morano 2008, 103).

Contents: Unclear similes explaining the duties of hearers.

M101m/R/1–7/

[... w]ere sent [...].

The hearer who makes one [... and one understa]nding is just like [a *compassion]ate *m[other]^f who received seven sons: the enemy kil[led them] all.

[The hea]rer is [just like] (one) who ...... *good] *deeds [...].

[...]

M101m/V/1–8/

[... one i]n a well, one o[n the ocean shore(?), one] in the sea, one on a sh[ip. The one who is on] the shore [pu]lls the one o[n the ship]. The one on the ship [pulls the one in] the sea up on[to the ship].

a. Uncertain. Henning also suggested words for "armor" and "ornament, jewelry" (all of them beginning with *zy*-).
b. The incomplete word could be "wicked," which does not fit the context, however.
c. In third-century Iran, the dinar was "a gold coin, struck mainly for purposes of prestige" and valued by its weight (7–7.4 g). See Gignoux 1995a.
d. Henning (ibid.): "abashed" (discussion in n. 6).
e. Or "from the bottom," Henning (ibid.): "from the ground."
f. Thus Henning without comment, but with query; cf. M90/V/4a/ "the Virgin of Light is a compassionate mother."

[... l]ike a righteous person .... l]ike pearls [......] a diade[m ...].
[...]

40:KawA. M911, Middle Persian (Henning 1943, 60, 65; Morano 2008, 103–4).

Contents: About the hearers' honesty.

M911/R/2–5/
[...] the *dēn*, like the man who [bought?] fruits and flowers [and] then they (= someone) [would?] steal(?)[a] (them).
[...] a tree with [f]ruit.
[...] gr[een ...].

M911/V/2–6/
[... like] a man who bought a plot of land. The land [contained?] a spring, full of drachmas.[b] [He brought (them) to the court?]. The king was amazed [and] shared [the drachmas with the man?].
[...](held as) [s]ecurity [...].
[...]

41:KawAn. M101n, Middle Persian (Henning 1943, 60, 65; Morano 2008, 104).

Contents: Similes describing the hearers.

M101n/R/3–6/
[...] many...-s[c] [...]
[...] a hearer, on [...].
[The ...] (is) like a garment [...].
[The ...] (is) like [...].
[...]

M101n/V/1–6/
[The ... is just like] the lord [...].
[The ...] is just [like a goldsmith] and a blacksmith, [...]. The goldsmith [came] to honor [..., but] the blacksmith to sc[orn[d] ...]. One [came] to [...].
[...]

42:KawU. M4990 (one side only), Parthian (Henning 1943, 73–74; Morano 2008, 104–5).

a. Henning has "praise." The verbs for "bless" and "steal" are homonyms.
b. The available space does not have room for Henning's "[On that] piece of land [there was] a well, [and in that well a bag] full of drachmas," and there is no preposition before "the land." The restored "contained" is unlikely, but shows what the syntax is likely to have been. In third-century Iran, the drachma was a silver coin (ca. 4 g). See Gignoux 1995b.
c. Or: "...-s that (were) very..."
d. See the relevant note on 25:KawF above.

The Book of Giants (Iranian Manichean Version)

From an alphabetical hymn (R-Š-T). Probably an epimythion, in which the characters of a story are identified with known (mythological) persons (cf. 32:KawT). Probably not from the Book of Giants.

M4990

[. . .] gif[t]s.

The peaceful (*Rāmgar*) ruler [. . .] (was?) King Wishtāsp [. . .], Wēzhan,[a] Wahman, and Zarēl [were . . .].

[The ru]ler's (*[Šah]rδār*) queen (was?) Khudōs [. . .] received the [*dēn*?].[b]

The prince[c] (was?) [. . .].

The palace (*Talwār*) and rest [. . . they] found forever.

---

a. Henning's restoration of [Ary]ān before Wēzhan is doubtful (rather than Wēzhan, who "in connection with Vištāspa is incomprehensible"). The letter before the final -*n* is definitely not *aleph*, but looks more like š.

b. Henning's restoration of "[*bel]ief" is based on the legend that Wishtāsp's Queen Hudōs received the *dēn* before her husband; see introduction on 42KawU.

c. *kumār*, "prince" or "young boy."

165

The Book of Giants (Iranian Manichean Version)

		Morano 2008		Morano 2011
	KawL	1	Coptic	1.1
	KawM	2	Coptic	1.2
	KawP	3	Coptic	1.3
0	KawJ	4		1.4
5	KawK	5		1.5
4	KawX	6		1.6
	KawZu4	7	Uyghur	1.7
7	KawH	8		2.1
	KawO	9	Arabic	2.2
18	KawAc	10		3.1
	KawB	11	Uyghur	3.2
19	KawC	12		3.3
11	KawAj/R	13		4.1
13	KawAj/V	13		4.1
	KawZu3	14	Uyghur	4.2
12	KawD	15		4.3
10	KawV	16		5.1
22	KawE/R	17		5.2
24	KawE/V	17		5.2
25	KawF	18		6
23	KawF(15–24)	18		6
17	KawAl	19		7
16	KawW	20		8
29	KawAk	21		9.1
15	KawAg	22		9.2
	KawZu1	23	Uyghur	9.3
	KawZu6	24	Uyghur	9.4
28	KawG	25		10.1
6	KawAi	26		10.2
	KawQ	28	Coptic	10.5
	KawR	27	Coptic	10.4
32	KawT	29		10.3
27	KawZp1	30		10.6
8	KawZp2	30		unc.
31	KawY	31		10.7
30	KawN	32		10.8
	KawS	33	Coptic	10.9
33	KawAe	34		11.1
34	KawAb	35		11.2
35	KawAh	36		11.3
35	KawAh	36		12.1
36	KawAf	37		12.2
37	KawAa	38		12.3
38	KawAd	39		12.4
39	KawAm	40		12.5

The Book of Giants (Iranian Manichean Version)

		Morano 2008		Morano 2011
40	KawA	41		12.6
41	KawAn	42		12.7
9	KawI	43		unc.
42	KawU	44		unc.
1	KawZs1/R	45		unc.
3	KawZs1/V	45		unc.
14	KawZs2	46		unc.
	KawZu2	47	Uyghur	unc.
	KawZu5	48	Uyghur	unc.
2	KawZs3			
20	KawZs4			
21	KawZs5			
26	KawZs6			

		Morano 2008	Morano 2011
0	KawJ	4	1.4
1	KawZs1/R	45	unc.
2	KawZs3		
3	KawZs1/V	unc.	unc.
4	KawX	6	1.6
5	KawK	5	1.5
6	KawAi	26	10.2
7	KawH	8	2.1
8	KawZp2	30	10.6
9	KawI	unc.	unc.
10	KawV	16	5.1
11	KawAj/R	13	4.1
12	KawD	15	4.3
13	KawAj/V	13	4.1
14	KawZs2	unc.	unc.
15	KawAg	22	9.2
16	KawW	20	8
17	KawAl	19	7
18	KawAc	10	3.1
19	KawC	12	3.3
20	KawZs4		
21	KawZs5		
22	KawE/R	17	5.2
23	KawF(15–24)	18	6
24	KawE/V	17	5.2
25	KawF	18	6
26	KawZs6		
27	KawZp1	30	10.6
28	KawG	25	10.1

The Book of Giants (Iranian Manichean Version)

		Morano 2008		Morano 2011
29	KawAk	21		9.1
30	KawN	32		10.8
31	KawY	31		10.7
32	KawT	29		10.3
33	KawAe	34		11.1
34	KawAb	35		11.2
35	KawAh	36		11.3
35	KawAh	36		12.1
36	KawAf	37		12.2
37	KawAa	38		12.3
38	KawAd	39		12.4
39	KawAm	40		12.5
40	KawA	41		12.6
41	KawAn	42		12.7
42	KawU	44		unc.
	KawL	1	Coptic	1.1
	KawM	2	Coptic	1.2
	KawP	3	Coptic	1.3
	KawZu4	7	Uyghur	1.7
	KawO	9	Arabic	2.2
	KawB	11	Uyghur	3.2
	KawZu3	14	Uyghur	4.2
	KawZu1	23	Uyghur	9.3
	KawZu6	24	Uyghur	9.4
	KawQ	28	Coptic	10.5
	KawR	27	Coptic	10.4
	KawS	33	Coptic	10.9
	KawZu2	unc.	Uyghur	unc.
	KawZu5	unc.	Uyghur	unc.

		Morano 2008	Morano 2011
40	KawA	41	12.6
37	KawAa	38	12.3
34	KawAb	35	11.2
18	KawAc	10	3.1
38	KawAd	39	12.4
33	KawAe	34	11.1
36	KawAf	37	12.2
15	KawAg	22	9.2
35	KawAh	36	11.3
35	KawAh	36	12.1
6	KawAi	26	10.2
11	KawAj/R	13	4.1
13	KawAj/V	13	4.1

The Book of Giants (Iranian Manichean Version)

		Morano 2008		Morano 2011
29	KawAk	21		9.1
17	KawAl	19		7
39	KawAm	40		12.5
41	KawAn	42		12.7
	KawB	11	Uyghur	3.2
19	KawC	12		3.3
12	KawD	15		4.3
22	KawE/R	17		5.2
24	KawE/V	17		5.2
25	KawF	18		6
23	KawF(15–24)	18		6
28	KawG	25		10.1
7	KawH	8		2.1
9	KawI	43		unc.
0	KawJ	4		1.4
5	KawK	5		1.5
	KawL	1	Coptic	1.1
	KawM	2	Coptic	1.2
30	KawN	32		10.8
	KawO	9	Arabic	2.2
	KawP	3	Coptic	1.3
	KawQ	28	Coptic	10.5
	KawR	27	Coptic	10.4
	KawS	33	Coptic	10.9
32	KawT	29		10.3
42	KawU	44		unc.
10	KawV	16		5.1
16	KawW	20		8
4	KawX	6		1.6
31	KawY	31		10.7
27	KawZp1	30		10.6
8	KawZp2	30		unc.
1	KawZs1/R	45		unc.
3	KawZs1/V	45		unc.
14	KawZs2	46		unc.
2	KawZs3			
20	KawZs4			
21	KawZs5			
26	KawZs6			
	KawZu1	23	Uyghur	9.3
	KawZu2	47	Uyghur	unc.
	KawZu3	14	Uyghur	4.2
	KawZu4	7	Uyghur	1.7
	KawZu5	48	Uyghur	unc.
	KawZu6	24	Uyghur	9.4

The Manichean Book of Giants (Old Turkic Version)
A new translation and introduction

by Peter Zieme

Here I bring together all fragments that might belong to a Turkic version of the Book of Giants including some new ones whose allocation is uncertain or remains doubtful. Although only a few remnants of the Turkic version of the Book of Giants are left, it is clear that the book was popular with the Manicheans.

In 1922 Albert von Le Coq published the third and last part of his *Türkische Manichaica*. The author edited there, inter alia, the fragment Mainz 317 (TM 423d) as No. 8,VIII: "Fragment einer iranischen Legende; Erwähnung des Chorugh Burchan, des Sohnes des Farruch-dād, und des Gebirges Kögmän."[1] Not able to give the correct identification, the editor recognized the main elements, but the correct reading of the name Enoch was still undetected. Willy Bang reedited the text in 1931, but only in 1943 finally W. B. Henning found out that a hitherto incorrectly transcribed word had to be the name of Enoch, and gave a new translation of this leaf (his text B) as a part of a Central Asian version of the Book of Giants in Sogdian and Old Turkic.[2]

Although I published in 1975 the greater part of the hitherto unedited Manichean-Turkic fragments, it was only in 2000 that Jens Wilkens was able to identify a considerable number of further fragments edited in Berliner Turfantexte 5 or not yet edited ones as parts of a Turkic version of the Manichean Book of Giants.[3] As a result of great detective work he identified six fragments of different manuscripts.[4] In the same year Wilkens also published the catalog of the Manichean-Turkic texts of the Berlin Collections, where by far the majority of the Manichaica is preserved.[5] Concerning full descriptions of the fragments in the following I refer to this catalog and do not repeat the details here. Wilkens continued the work on the Turkic version of the Book of Giants with valuable contributions.[6]

---

1. Le Coq, *Türkische Manichaica aus Chotscho*, III: *Nebst einem christlichen Bruchstück aus Bulayïq*, APAW 2 (Berlin: Akademie, 1922), 4.
2. Bang, "Manichäische Erzähler," *Mus* 44 (1931): 1–36; Henning, "The Book of the Giants," *BSOAS* 11 (1943–1946): 52–74.
3. Peter Zieme, *Manichäisch-türkische Texte: Texte, Übersetzung, Anmerkungen*, Berliner Turfantexte 5 (Berlin: Akademie, 1975).
4. Wilkens, "Neue Fragmente aus Manis Gigantenbuch," *ZDMG* 150 (2000): 133–76.
5. Jens Wilkens, *Manichäisch-türkische Texte der Berliner Turfansammlung*, Verzeichnis der Orientalischen Handschriften Deutschlands 13, Alttürkische Handschriften 8 (Stuttgart: Steiner, 2000).
6. Jens Wilkens, "Funktion und gattungsgeschichtliche Bedeutung des manichäischen Gigantenbuchs," in *Der östliche Manichäismus: Gattungs- und Werksgeschichte; Vorträge des Göttinger Symposiums vom 4./5. März 2010*, ed. Zekine Özertural and Jens Wilkens, Abhandlungen der Akademie der Wissenschaften zu Göttingen NS 17 (Berlin: de Gruyter, 2011), 63–85, doi:10.1515/9783110262391.63; Wilkens, "Remarks on the Manichaean *Book of Giants*: Once Again on Mahaway's Mission to Enoch," in *Ancient*

Detailed descriptions of the state of the fragments are given in the respective articles and in Wilkens's catalog. As most of the texts were edited before, here I give the text only in transliteration when discussing problematic words or word remnants. The originals are available in photographs on the internet sites of the Berlin-Brandenburgische Akademie der Wissenschaften (BBAW: http://www.bbaw.de/) and the International Dunhuang Project (IDP: http://idp.bl.uk/).

I tried to translate from the very fragmentary texts as much as possible, but in case of words not fully preserved I did not give all possibilities of emendations. Hopefully new fragments will appear helping us to a better understanding. The reader might find some parts of the translation disappointing, but disregarding the Sino-Manichaica and some well-preserved texts from Egypt or Central Asia, the major part of the Manichean literature has come to us only in such a desperate state, just as fragments. The reader may regard this article as a further step to the reconstruction of a Manichean book that attracted readers and writers of the past. Generally speaking, the Turkic fragments cannot provide us with new important insights into the multifaceted literature of the Central Asian Manicheans. Rather they offer us the chance to compare them with their Middle Iranian counterparts, as they were more or less dependent on them, either because of their use of Middle Iranian terminology or because they were translated from Middle Iranian. But they do give us some illuminating variants or even some points not known from the Iranian material that is the nearest to the Turkic.

Looking at the contents, the best we can obtain through the study of the Turkic fragments are some additional moments that lead to a better understanding of the story. Recapitulating some major results of Wilkens's study, I would like to mention his identification of *Saxm toŋa* as one of the two sons of Šāhmīzād known from Sogdian *[s']xm qwyy* (M 648) "the giant Saxm."[7] In connection with this equation and with the header of Mainz 344a ("[The book] of the confession of the [strong] giant [Saxm]"), he concluded that it must be Sāhm himself who confesses his sins. Wilkens refers to the book of John Reeves, who cites from the Midrash of Shemhazai and Aza'el that God sends an envoy to Shemhazai about the coming flood.[8] Therefore Shemhazai repents of his sins. God sends to his sons threatening dreams. But Wilkens excludes the possibility that the Turkic fragment refers to the first return of Māhaway. Rather he thinks, as already Werner Sundermann did, of several missions, and of Saxm's confession as the final result of several dreadful visions.[9] He refers to the Qumran fragment in which according to J. T. Milik's translation the brothers 'Ōhyah and Ha[hyah] "began to weep before [Enoch(?) . . .]."[10]

Tales of Giants from Qumran and Turfan, ed. Matthew Goff, Loren T. Stuckenbruck, and Enrico Morano, WUNT 360 (Tübingen: Mohr Siebeck, 2016), 213–29; Wilkens, "The Old Uygur Version of the Manichaean Book of the Giants and Its Context," in *Language, Society, and Religion in the World of the Turks: Festschrift for Larry Clark at Seventy-Five*, ed. Zsuzsanna Gulácsi, Silk Road Studies 19 (Turnhout: Brepols, 2018), 281–99.

7. Wilkens, "Neue Fragmente aus Manis Gigantenbuch," 136, 137. He mentions Henning's text H in which *s'xm* (Sāhm, Sāxm) is identified as 'wxy' (= Aram. 'Ōhyah). This figure also appears in some of the Qumran fragments.

8. Wilkens, "Neue Fragmente aus Manis Gigantenbuch," 138; Reeves, *Jewish Lore in Manichaean Cosmogony: Studies in the* Book of Giants *Traditions*, HUCM 14 (Cincinnati: Hebrew Union College Press, 1992).

9. Wilkens, " Neue Fragmente aus Manis Gigantenbuch," 140–41.

10. Wilkens, "Neue Fragmente aus Manis Gigantenbuch," 140. This is 4Q203 frag. 4, translated similarly by Stuckenbruck in this volume.

A relation between the Qumran passage and the Old Turkic version is only possible, as Wilkens correctly says,[11] if one assumes that the brothers did not weep in front of Enoch, but of God. But this is difficult to decide, as there are no traces of letters left.

The Manuscripts and the Grouping of the Fragments

Nearly all fragments are written in the so-called Uyghur script, which is a variety of the Sogdian script that goes back to some kind of Aramaic script. Old Turkic Manichean texts were written in two other scripts: in the runic or runiform script known from the Old Turkic and Uyghur inscriptions of Mongolia and elsewhere, but also in the Manichean script that was created for the codification of the Manichean scriptures. If my suggestion is correct, the Berlin fragment U 349 (K) which is written in Manichean script, would be a testimony for a variant in Manichean script. All fragments were found in the Turfan oasis; according to the finding signatures that are preserved, some of them stem from D = Dakianusšahri (= Qočo), others from the ruin α in that city. Exact dates of the manuscripts are not available, but they were probably written at the time when Manicheism was still the leading religion in the West Uyghur kingdom, that is, around the turn of the tenth century till the early years of the eleventh century.

Before presenting the texts, I would like to give some general information on the manuscripts. It is obvious that fragments of several manuscripts have survived, but it is impossible to elaborate the exact manuscript affiliation of each piece. Therefore I can give here only a general outline. Some fragments are remnants from one and the same manuscript, as already observed by Wilkens. In his description he regarded Mainz 344a (here = C) and U 222 (= B) as parts of one manuscript that have common traits, such as the special form of some final letters.[12] These two fragments cannot be joined: they are remnants of two leaves. Under catalog no. 122 Wilkens treats Mainz 372 + U 200 as belonging to the same manuscript, but the content is different. It apparently contains a parable.[13] The fragment U 288 (= E) was added by Wilkens to this same manuscript, too, but in this case it is not sure (unfortunately no final -*m,* one of the signaling letter shapes, is preserved). Wilkens made no statements on the other fragments. One has to admit that, especially in the case of very small fragments, an exact allocation is highly speculative. For this reason I also treat here the other fragments without further definite statements about their possible allocations within the book.

1. Mainz 317 (A) is the earliest published and best-preserved leaf of a composite book that also contained the fragments of the Sermon of the Light Nous.
2. The fragments Mainz 344a (B), U 222 (C), U 216 (D) are surely remnants of one and the same manuscript, but that is different from manuscript A. On the one hand, U 288 (E) was considered by Wilkens as a further candidate for belonging to this second manuscript, but in my view this is not sure. On the other hand, U 204 and

---

11. Wilkens, "Neue Fragmente aus Manis Gigantenbuch," 140.
12. Wilkens, "Neue Fragmente aus Manis Gigantenbuch," 141, calls these graphemes "Signalgrapheme."
13. Wilkens, "Neue Fragmente aus Manis Gigantenbuch," 143–44. Following statements by Henning and Iris Colditz he argues that fragments of the Book of Giants and parable texts can belong to one and the same manuscript. Colditz, "Bruchstücke manichäisch-parthischer Parabelsammlungen," *AoF* 14 (1987): 274–313. doi:10.1524/aofo.1987.14.12.274.

Mainz 372 + U 200 contain parables and are parts of the same manuscript, although they are not translated here.[14]

3. The grouping of the fragments U 217 (F), Mainz 347 (G), U 269 (I) is still an open question.
4. The Kyoto fragment Ot.Ry. 2271 (J) seems to be from the same manuscript as Ot.Ry. 2266, which contains a passage of the Sermon of the Light Nous. This demonstrates that several composite books existed that contained both scriptures.
5. While all so-far mentioned fragments are written in Uyghur script, the Berlin fragment U 349 (K) is written in Manichean script. If it really belongs to the Book of Giants, it shows once more that the text was widely known among the Uyghurs.[15]

Bibliography

Arnold-Döben, Victoria. *Die Bildersprache des Manichäismus.* Arbeitsmaterialien zur Religionsgeschichte 3. Cologne: Brill, 1978.

Asmussen, Jes P. *Die Gnosis, Dritter Band: Der Manichäismus.* Bibliothek der alten Welt. Zurich: Artemis, 1980.

Bang, Willy. "Manichäische Erzähler." *Mus* 44 (1931): 1–36.

Bang, Willy, and Annemarie von Gabain. *Türkische Turfan-Texte 2: Manichaica.* Berlin: Akademie, 1929.

Baur, Ferdinand Christan. *Das manichäische Religionssystem nach den Quellen neu untersucht und entwickelt.* Tübingen: Osiander, 1831.

Clark, Larry V. "The Turkic Manichaean Literature." Pages 89–141 in *Emerging from Darkness: Studies in the Recovery of Manichaean Sources.* Edited by Paul Mirecki and Jason BeDuhn. Nag Hammadi and Manichaean Studies 43. Leiden: Brill, 1997. doi:10.1163/9789004439726_005.

———. *Uygur Manichaean Texts.* Vol. 3: *Ecclesiastic Texts.* Corpus Fontium Manichaeorum, Series Turcica 3. Turnhout: Brepols, 2017.

Colditz, Iris. "Bruchstücke manichäisch-parthischer Parabelsammlungen." *AoF* 14 (1987): 274–313. doi:10.1524/aofo.1987.14.12.274.

Erdal, Marcel. *Old Turkic Word Formation: A Functional Approach to the Lexicon.* Vols. 1–2. Turcologica 7. Wiesbaden: Harrassowitz, 1991.

Hamilton, James R. *Manuscrits ouïgours du IXe–Xe siècle de Touen-Houang.* 2 vols. Paris: Peeters, 1986.

Henning, W. B. "The Book of the Giants." *BSOAS* 11 (1943–46): 52–74. Repr., pages 115–37 in *Selected Papers 2.* Edited by W. B. Henning. Acta Iranica 15. Hommages et Opera Minora 6. Leiden: Brill, 1977.

———. *Ein manichäisches Henochbuch.* SPAW 11. Berlin: Akademie, 1934. Repr., pages 341–49 in *Selected Papers 1* . Edited by W. B. Henning. Acta Iranica 14. Hommages et Opera Minora 5. Leiden: Brill, 1977.

Kara, György. "Late Mediaeval Turkic Elements in Mongolian." Pages 73–119 in *De Dunhuang à Istanbul: Hommage à James Russell Hamilton.* Edited by Louis Bazin and Peter Zieme. Silk Road Studies 5. Turnhout: Brepols, 2001.

---

14. U 204 = Wilkens text no. 121; Mainz 372 + U 200 = Wilkens text no. 122 (Wilkens, *Manichäisch-türkische Texte*).

15. For fragments that are now lost, see the introduction to section H in the translation.

Klimkeit, Hans-Joachim. "Der Buddha Henoch: Qumran und Turfan." *ZRGG* 32 (1980): 367–77. doi:10.1163/157007380X00324.

———. *Hymnen und Gebete der Religion des Lichts: Iranische und türkische liturgische Texte der Manichäer Zentralasiens*. Abhandlungen der Rheinisch-Westfälischen Akademie der Wissenschaften 79. Opladen: Westdeutscher Verlag, 1989.

Le Coq, Albert von. *Türkische Manichaica aus Chotscho*. Vol. I. APAW 6. Berlin: Akademie, 1911.

———. *Türkische Manichaica aus Chotscho*. III: *Nebst einem christlichen Bruchstück aus Bulayïq*. APAW 2. Berlin: Akademie, 1922.

Lindt, Paul van. *The Names of Manichaean Mythological Figures: A Comparative Study on Terminology in the Coptic Sources*. StOR 26. Wiesbaden: Harrassowitz, 1992.

Milik, J. T. *The Books of Enoch. Aramaic Fragments of Qumrān Cave 4*. Oxford: Oxford University Press, 1976.

———. "Turfan et Qumran: Livre des Géants juif et manichéen." Pages 117–27 in *Tradition und Glaube: Das frühe Christentum in seiner Umwelt; Festgabe für Karl Georg Kuhn zum 65. Geburtstag*. Edited by Gert Jeremias, Hartmut Stegemann, and Heinz-Wolfgang Kuhn. Göttingen: Vandenhoeck & Ruprecht, 1971.

Özertural, Z. "Sogdisch-uigurische Beziehungen: Das alttürkische Verb *kädilmäk*." *Ural-Altaische Jahrbücher* NS 19 (2005): 65–71.

Puech, Henri-Charles. *Le manichéisme: Son fondateur, sa doctrine*. Musée Guimet 56. Paris: Civilisations du Sud, S. A. E. P., 1949.

Reeves, John C. *Jewish Lore in Manichaean Cosmogony: Studies in the* Book of Giants *Traditions*. HUCM 14. Cincinnati: Hebrew Union College Press, 1992.

Röhrborn, Klaus. *Uigurisches Wörterbuch: Sprachmaterial der vorislamischen türkischen Texte aus Zentralasien*. Vol. 1, fascs. 1–6. Wiesbaden: Steiner, 1977–1998.

Schmidt-Glintzer, Hedwig. *Chinesische Manichaica: Mit textkritischen Anmerkungen und einem Glossar*. StOr 14. Wiesbaden: Harrassowitz, 1987.

Skjærvø, Prods Oktor. "Counter-Manichean Elements in Kerdīr's Inscriptions: Irano-Manichaica II." Pages 313–42 in *Atti del terzo Congresso internazionale di studi "Manicheismo e oriente cristiano antico," Arcavacata di Rende, Amantea 31 agosto–5 settembre 1993*. Edited by Luigi Cirillo and Alois van Tongerloo. Manichean Studies 3. Leuven: Brepols, 1997.

———. "Iranian Elements in Manicheism: A Comparative Contrastive Approach; Irano-Manichaica I." Pages 263–84 in *Au carrefour des religions: Hommages à Philippe Gignoux*. Edited by Rika Gyselen. Res Orientales 7. Paris: Groupe pour l'étude de la Manicheism du Moyen-Orient, 1995.

———. "Iranian Epic and the Manichean Book of Giants: Irano-Manichaica III. *Acta Orientalia Academiae Scientiarum Hungaricae* 48 (1995): 187–223.

———. "Zarathustra in the Avesta and in Manicheism: Irano-Manichaica IV." Pages 597–628 in *La Persia e l'Asia centrale da Alessandro al X secolo: Atti del Convegno internazionale (Roma, 9–12 novembre 1994)*. Rome: Academia Nazionale dei Lincei, 1996.

Stuckenbruck, Loren T. *The Book of Giants from Qumran: Texts, Translation, and Commentary*. TSAJ 63. Tübingen: Mohr Siebeck, 1997.

Sundermann, Werner. "Iranische Personennamen der Manichäer." *Die Sprache* 36 (1994): 244–70.

———. *Mittelpersische und parthische kosmogonische Texte der Manichäer*. Berliner Turfantexte 4. Berlin: Akademie, 1973.

———. "Namen von Göttern, Dämonen und Menschen in iranischen Versionen des manichäischen Mythos." *AoF* 6 (1979): 95–133. doi:10.1524/aofo.1979.6.jg.95.

Widengren, Geo. "Iran and Israel in Parthian Times with Special Regard to the Ethiopic Book of Enoch." *Temenos* 2 (1966): 139–77. doi:10.33356/temenos.6469.

Wilkens, Jens. "Funktion und gattungsgeschichtliche Bedeutung des manichäischen Gigantenbuchs." Pages 63–85 in *Der östliche Manichäismus: Gattungs- und Werksgeschichte; Vorträge des Göttinger Symposiums vom 4./5. März 2010*. Edited by Zekine Özertural and Jens Wilkens. Abhandlungen der Akademie der Wissenschaften zu Göttingen NS 17. Berlin: de Gruyter, 2011. doi:10.1515/9783110262391.63.

———. *Manichäisch-türkische Texte der Berliner Turfansammlung*. Verzeichnis der Orientalischen Handschriften Deutschlands 13. Alttürkische Handschriften 8. Stuttgart: Steiner, 2000.

———. "Neue Fragmente aus Manis Gigantenbuch." *ZDMG* 150 (2000): 133–76.

———. "The Old Uygur Version of the Manichaean Book of the Giants and Its Context." Pages 281–99 in *Language, Society, and Religion in the World of the Turks: Festschrift for Larry Clark at Seventy-Five*. Edited by Zsuzsanna Gulácsi. Silk Road Studies 19. Turnhout: Brepols, 2018.

Zieme, Peter. "Alttürkisch, Amboß.'" *Türk Dilleri Araştırmaları* 18 (2008): 429–36.

———. *Buddhistische Stabreimdichtungen der Uiguren*. Berliner Turfantexte 13. Berlin: Akademie, 1985.

———. *Manichäisch-türkische Texte: Texte, Übersetzung, Anmerkungen*. Berliner Turfantexte 5. Berlin: Akademie, 1975.

———. "A Turkish Text on Manichaean Cosmogony." Pages 395–409 in *Atti del Terzo Congresso Internazionale di Studi, "Manicheismo e Oriente Christiano Antico."* Edited by Luigi Cirillo and Alois van Tongerloo. Manichaean Studies 3. Turnhout: Brepols, 1997.

The Manichaean Book of Giants (Turkic Fragments)

A. A leaf of a codex book: Mainz 317 (T I / TM 423d).[a]
Description: This leaf belongs to a composite manuscript whose other parts represent the translation of the Sermon of the Light Nous. As Wilkens underlined, the special worth of this Turkic fragment lies in the fact that it is the only one that describes the journey of the giant Māhaway[b] in this way.[c] For some places I was able to give new readings that make the text clearer. The translation is based on that of Henning, but also contains some new interpretations.[d]

Translation
(recto) [...] fire was going to come out. And [...][e] the sun was at the point of rising. (He) rose and above without being hung[f] was going to start rolling. Then when from the air above a voice came, (it) called me, it spoke thus: "Oh son of W(i)rogdad, your destiny[g] is thus.[h] Here you have seen too much. Do

---

a. Wilkens, *Manichäisch-türkische Texte*, no. 164 = Henning B.

b. Called "son of W(i)rogdad"; cf. Wilkens, "Neue Fragmente aus Manis Gigantenbuch," 136 n. 18.

c. Wilkens, "Neue Fragmente aus Manis Gigantenbuch," 134.

d. W. B. Henning, "The Book of the Giants," *BSOAS* 11 (1943–1946): 52–74. We are grateful to Cambridge University Press for permission to reprint Henning's translation of Mainz 317 (T I / TM 423d) on p. 60, with minor revisions. Likewise to Dr. Jens Wilkins and Harrassowitz Publishers for permission to translate the following fragments published in his article "Neue Fragmente aus Manis Gigantenbuch," *ZDMG* 150 (2000): 133–76; Mainz 344a (pp. 156–58), U 288 (p.159), U 217 (pp. 160–63), Mainz 347 (pp. 165–67), U 269 (pp. 168–69), and U 222 (pp. 170–74). Likewise to the Berlin-Brandenburg Academy of Sciences and Humanities to publish translations of two hitherto unpublished fragments held in the Berlin Turfan-Collection in the Depositum of the Berlin-Brandenburg Academy of Sciences and Humanities in the State Library of Berlin–Prussian Cultural Heritage Oriental Department: U 216 (T I α x 4) (https://turfan.bbaw.de/dta/u/images/u0216recto.jpg and https://turfan.bbaw.de/dta/u/images/u0216verso.jpg) and U 349 (T I x 3) [1053] (https://turfan.bbaw.de/dta/u/images/u0349seite1.jpg and https://turfan.bbaw.de/dta/u/images/u0349seite2.jpg). And likewise to Ryukoku University to publish a translation of the hitherto unpublished fragment MA02271 (Ot.Ry. 2271) (https://idp.bl.uk/collection/F142618C9E5C40B29801A50F9781EBDE/?return=%2Fcollection%2F%3Fterm%3DMS02271) in the Omiya Library collection.

e. Henning inserted "[I saw]," but this is difficult from the point of view of the grammar.

f. So far everyone wanted to see the verb "to increase." But the fourth letter is -r-, which lets one suppose a derivation from "to hang." Now cf. Wilkens, "Remarks," 215.

g. Klaus Röhrborn translates "der Befehl für dich lautet folgendermaßen: . . ." ("the command for you is as follows"). Röhrborn, *Uigurisches Wörterbuch: Sprachmaterial der vorislamischen türkischen Texte aus Zentralasien* (Wiesbaden: Steiner, 1977–1998), 2:71. But Willy Bang and Annemarie von Gabain had already argued to understand here "'Dein Wort' (oder "Schicksal??," "your word" [or "destiny??"]). Bang and von Gabain, *Türkische Turfan-Texte 2: Manichaica* (Berlin: Sitzungsberichte der Preussischen Akademie der Wissenschaften. Philosophisch-historische Klasse, 1929), 420.

h. Henning translated the word by "lamentable."

not die now prematurely, but turn quickly back from here and go." (Thus it) spoke. And again, besides this (voice), I heard the voice of Enoch, the apostle, from the south,[a] without, however, seeing him at all. Speaking my name very lovingly, he called (me). And downward from [...] then [...]

(verso) [...] Why? Because the closed door of the sun will open, the sun's light and heat will descend and set your wings alight. You will burn and die," said he. Having heard these words, I beat my wings and quickly flew down from the heaven. I looked back. Dawn was dawning.[b] With its light the sun had come to rise over the Kögmän Mountains. And again a voice came from above. Bringing the command of Enoch, the apostle, it said: "I call you, I know (you) the son of W(i)rogdad, you are the one on the side (?) [...] Now quickly [...] with the people [...] you [...]"[c]

Commentary

As Loren Stuckenbruck noted, Milik held the opinion that the Uyghur text is a description of Māhaway's first journey to Enoch, while Reeves related it directly to 4Q530.[d] Stuckenbruck concludes:

> If Reeves' correlation is correct, then the Manichaean fragment contains an elaborated account of the 4Q530 journey and encounter. If Milik is correct that the fragment refers to Mahaway's first encounter with Enoch and if the numerous details in the Manichaean source may be thought to have derived from the first journey as described in a (now lost) portion of the Qumran BG, then the more cursory description in col. iii is explicable. In any case, common to Milik and Reeves' respective interpretations is the view that the Manichaean fragment is concerned with an initial encounter between Mahaway and Enoch. If the arguments advanced above about 4Q530 col. iii describing a second encounter are correct, then the context assigned by Milik to the Uyghur fragment appears to be valid.[e]

Stuckenbruck mentions further three elements that align the Uyghur text closely with the cited Qumran text: "(1) the initiation of the encounter through Enoch's calling Mahaway; (2) the attribution to Mahaway of an ability to fly with wings; and (3) hints that Mahaway is or has been the recipient of special treatment from Enoch."[f]

Thanks to Henning's identification the following facts are now clarified: *xwnwq* is Enoch; "son of W(i)rogdad" is Māhaway; and the Kögmän

---

a. The phrase translated "from the south" could also be translated "at one side."
b. Marcel Erdal translates "dawn had broken." Erdal, *Old Turkic Word Formation: A Functional Approach to the Lexicon*, vols. 1–2, Turcologica 7 (Wiesbaden: Harrassowitz, 1991), 73.
c. The new translation by Wilkens should be taken into account ("Remarks," 213–29). Here it cannot be discussed in detail.
d. Milik, *The Books of Enoch*, 300; Reeves, *Jewish Lore*, 93.
e. Stuckenbruck, *The Book of Giants from Qumran: Texts, Translation, and Commentary*, TSAJ 63 (Tübingen: Mohr Siebeck, 1997), 133.
f. Stuckenbruck, *Book of Giants from Qumran*, 133.

mountain is the Hermon.[a] Hans-Joachim Klimkeit commented on Enoch, the apostle.[b]

The name *kögmän* is a substitute for Mount Hermon. Marcel Erdal explains the sentence in the following way: "Dawn had broken, it was rising and coming together with the light of the sun over the bluish mountain."[c] He holds the opinion that this place name cannot be the same as the famous Kögmän mountain of the Turks in Mongolia. His argument that there is a difference between kökmän in Uyghur script and Kögmän in the runiform script of the Old Turkic inscriptions is not valid; in Uyghur script there is no distinction between *k* and *g* in writing, as opposed to their being two distinct letters in the runiform script.[d] In my opinion this famous place name could serve as a substitute, especially as the second syllable resembles the second syllable of its paragon Hermon.[e]

B. Mainz 344a (T I α-x 9).[f]

Description: A small fragment of a codex book with preserved right margin. The headline is written in red color and starts and ends in flower decoration.

Translation

(*header*) [The book] of the confession of the [strong] giant [Saxm].

(*recto*) The strong [giant] Saxm, after having bowed on his knees, stood up and made a confession against the light sun god whose peak is mercy.[g] He said: "Merci[ful . . .]

(*verso*) Whoever [. . .] truly[h] reaches (there), [. . .] at one time, they do not [. . .] The light sun god whose peak is mercy, releasing [from sins . . .(?)]

Commentary

Wilkens compared the hero Saxm of this fragment to the Sogdian *[Sa]xm qwyy* of M 648. Following his comment the repenting and confessing person should be this Saxm.[i] This can be concluded from the reconstruction of the headline as well as from the text B (U 222), where Saxm says that he himself became a murderer of living beings and of the giants.

---

a. For the name Māhaway, see Henning, "Book of Giants," 55.

b. Klimkeit, "Der Buddha Henoch: Qumran und Turfan," *ZRGG* 32 (1980): 368, doi:10.1163/157007380X00324.

c. Erdal, *Old Turkic Word Formation*, 73.

d. Erdal, *Old Turkic Word Formation*, 74.

e. Wilkens, "Remarks," 228: "bluish mountain."

f. Wilkens, *Manichäisch-türkische Texte*, no. 165; Wilkens, "Neue Fragmente aus Manis Gigantenbuch," 156–58. For the sequence B and C I follow Wilkens, "Neue Fragmente aus Manis Gigantenbuch," 141.

g. This means "with utmost mercy." It is a special expression not known from other texts.

h. One can also read the word translated as "truly" to mean "the day of."

i. Wilkens, "Neue Fragmente aus Manis Gigantenbuch," 137.

C. U 222 (T I D).[a]

Description: A fragment of a codex leaf, heavily destroyed in its upper part. The Uyghur script is one of the oldest types. The punctuation marks are encircled in red.

Translation

(recto) The light [sun]-g[od with utmost mercy] [. . .] through ([. . .] may forgive!). Now, (as) I [bec]ame [. . .], (as) I became wrong through sinful sins, as I became a murderer of all l[iving beings and as I have [separated] many [. . .] from their lives, thus now I [thought:] [. . .] from now on it shall not be! I will not kill a single living being!

> Further there is no son of a creature who [will not be judged] on the day of counting [. . .]

(verso) [. . .] Now [. . .] [se]ven (?) day[s] [. . .] have passed (?), he said (:) "[I repent] for my sin, my wrongdoing [. . .] my sin [. . .] and [. . .] my soul [. . .] shall not be for the dark demons food and drink! In front of the sun-[god] of utmost light I bow down on my two knees and praise your [name]. Oh you Light (?), for what avail has the hero Saxm such a big body?" That now [. . .]

Commentary

The question to whom Saxm repents has been solved by Wilkens by assuming that it is the "merciful sun-god."[b] He refers to James Hamilton's identification of the "dieu Soleil Eclatant" with the "Envoy of the Lights of the third creation" (Third Envoy).[c] In the texts of eastern Manichaeism it came to a nearly complete equation of the sun god and the Third Envoy.

D. U 216 (T I α x 4).[d]

Description: As this fragment apparently belongs to the same manuscript as B and C, it might also be a part of the Book of Giants. Unfortunately, the verso (?) side is greatly rubbed off. As the preserved parts let us assume a confession text, this remnant may be seen in a strong relationship to Mainz 344a, but it cannot directly be joined. It might be assumed that U 216 preceded Mainz 344a.

Translation

(recto?) [. . .] in order to [. . .], [. . .] in order to become released from sins, I could [. . .], my God! In order to call [your [. . .] name while praising your [. . .], my God, I bring my head to earth and respectfully bow down in front of your special, choosen [. . .] voice [. . .] service [. . .] your sense [. . .]

---

a. Cf. Wilkens, *Manichäisch-türkische Texte*, no. 166; Wilkens, "Neue Fragmente aus Manis Gigantenbuch,"170–74.

b. Wilkens, "Neue Fragmente aus Manis Gigantenbuch," 142–43.

c. Hamilton, *Manuscrits ouïgours du IXe–Xe siècle de Touen-Houang*, 2 vols. (Paris: Peeters, 1986), no. 5.

d. Cf. Wilkens, *Manichäisch-türkische Texte*, no. 326.

(verso?) [. . .] fruit-garden [. . .] insight und understanding [. . .] ög[a] [. . .] soul of [. . .]

E. U 288: (T I α x 24).[b]
Description: According to Wilkens's observations some slight variations of the distances between the lines are no obstacle for assuming that this fragment too belongs to the same manuscript.[c] The distinctive marks as mentioned above are missing here, and therefore I treat this piece as a separate one, as it is not certain that it belongs to the manuscript Mainz 344a + U 222 etc.

Translation
(recto) [. . .] all [. . .] of oneself, [. . .] if one thinks [. . .] son[s] of [. . .]
(verso) [. . .] will be[d] [. . .] forever [. . .][e] may disappear.

Commentary
Wilkens interprets these broken lines as an exegesis of Enoch's dreams announcing the extinction of the giants.[f]

F. U 217 (T I α).[g]
Description: It is a piece from the middle of the leaf, no margins are preserved. The paper is light brown.[h]

Translation[i]
(recto) [They (?)] died because of [. . .], they heard of [. . .]. Some [threw] themselves from the mountain, and some of them became moistened[j] by the ocean and died. Others strangled themselves, others fell through knife, [others killed] each other and die[d [. . .]

(verso) [Al]l bodies (?) slackened (?) and fell into an everlasting sleep. And at that time the Lord of the heaven ventured to speak to the four angels. [. . .] "[Oh], angel [. . .]el, [. . .]"

---

a. It is not clear which *ög* is meant here, "mother" or "thought, reflection."
b. Cf. Wilkens, *Manichäisch-türkische Texte*, no. 166; Wilkens, "Neue Fragmente aus Manis Gigantenbuch," 159.
c. Wilkens, "Neue Fragmente aus Manis Gigantenbuch," 141–42.
d. "will be" or "will find."
e. Wilkens thinks of the "tribe of the giants" ("Neue Fragmente aus Manis Gigantenbuch," 159).
f. Wilkens, "Neue Fragmente aus Manis Gigantenbuch," 142.
g. Cf. Wilkens, *Manichäisch-türkische Texte*, no. 168; Wilkens, "Neue Fragmente aus Manis Gigantenbuch," 160–63.
h. For further features see Wilkens, "Neue Fragmente aus Manis Gigantenbuch," 142.
i. Wilkens, "Neue Fragmente aus Manis Gigantenbuch," no. 3. The order of recto and verso is opposite to that of the editor, because if *iki* "two" is, as I assume, part of a header, this side can be the verso side.
j. Wilkens read *[tü]šip*, but the regular form should be *tüš-üp* ("Neue Fragmente aus Manis Gigantenbuch," 163. As the *y* is rather clear, I propose the verb *öli-*, "to be moist," or "to become moistened."

Commentary

Unfortunately the names of the "four angels" are not preserved, but they may be, as Wilkens already suggested, Raphael, Michael, Gabriel, and Sariel, who are mentioned in Middle Iranian prayers.[a]

G. Mainz 347.[b]

Description: It is a fragment of the left upper corner of a large leaf of which the lower part was cut for some reason. A part of the upper and of the left margins are preserved. The punctuation dots are encircled in red, the floral ornaments are likewise in red, the center in black.[c]

Translation

(*header*) The good book of the degression of the [shamel]ess demons.

(*recto*) If it happened that they flew, [. . .] till the ceremony (?), they [. . .] as long as there was not, they (?)[. . .] if not [. . .], they [were] killing (them).

Then as that *tav*[. . .][d] becomes [. . .][e], thus [. . .] it becomes (?), demons[f] [. . .]

(*verso*) [. . .] they tantalized and punished. [. . .] downward the earths [. . .] if they did not stand, [. . .] the [demons] in the heavens will do [. . . sin]s [. . .] [they did] heavy sins, that [. . .]

H. Lost fragments

Wilkens connected Mainz 347 with a lost fragment known only by a transcription made by Annemarie von Gabain.[g] Under the header "T III M 200" she transcribed thirty-two Manichaean fragments that were supposed to belong to the same manuscript.[h] Judging by those that survived, one can state that not all belong to one and the same manuscript. As "XXXII" she transcribed a small fragment that also contains the expression "shameless demon." I follow here Wilkens's idea that this fragment, too, was part of the Book of the Giants.

H1 "XXXII"

Translation

(*recto*) [. . .] if one does not hold, they are [. . .]. And him (?) [. . .] if they. . . . . .][. . .] they dark [. . .] having thrown on [earth?].

    a. Wilkens, "Neue Fragmente aus Manis Gigantenbuch," 144–45.

    b. Cf. Wilkins, *Manichäisch-türkische Texte*, no. 235; Wilkins, "Neue Fragmente aus Manis Gigantenbuch," 164–67.

    c. For further details see Wilkens, "Neue Fragmente aus Manis Gigantenbuch," 153.

    d. Wilkens, "Neue Fragmente aus Manis Gigantenbuch," 165: *tavar* "goods."

    e. Wilkens reads the word as "like a prisoner" ("Neue Fragmente aus Manis Gigantenbuch," 165).

    f. With Wilkens but other readings are also possible ("Neue Fragmente aus Manis Gigantenbuch," 165).

    g. Wilkens, "Neue Fragmente aus Manis Gigantenbuch," 165, following an Old transcript of A. von Gabain. A selection (III, X, XXI, XXV, XXX, XXIII, XII, XXXII) of this folder was presented in Peter Zieme, "A Turkish Text on Manichaean Cosmogony," in *Atti del Terzo Congresso Internazionale di Studi, "Manicheismo e Oriente Christiano Antico,"* ed. Luigi Cirillo and Alois van Tongerloo, Manichaean Studies 3 (Turnhout: Brepols, 1997), 395–409. For further information see Wilkens, *Manichäisch-türkische Texte*, no. *215–*232, *239–249.

    h. Cf. the entries in Wilkens, *Manichäisch-türkische Texte*, nos. 215–249.

(*verso*) male [. . .] the numerous light [. . .] the tastes of [. . . . . .] from the shameless demon [. . .]. And [. . .]

H2 "XII"

I put here also the lost fragment "XII" of von Gabain's transcript, because Wilkens already suggested that it might belong to the Book of the Giants.[a]

Translation

(*recto*) [. . .] their anger [. . .] they became [. . .] to the fight, [. . .] with both [. . .] they fought [. . .] they struggled [. . .] their feet [. . .] earths, mountains [. . .]? ? [. . .bec]ame. And

(*verso*) the guardian (acc.) [. . .] like them [. . . . . .] they may keep [. . .] they ? [. . . . . .] that ? [. . .] were. Th[ey . . .] And [. . .] ? [. . .] they praised [. . .] that ? [. . .]

I. U 269.[b]

Description: Fragment of the left lower corner of a leaf. The left and the lower margins are partly preserved. Like Mainz 347, the leaf was cut. The punctuation marks are encircled in red. The header on the recto side is written in black with a floral ornament in red, while on the verso side this is vice versa.[c]

Translation

(*header*) The book [of the rules] of the hearers.
(*recto*) . . . because of . . . that truly [. . .] from his wisdom . . .
(*verso*) those who will be, not good . . . they will [. . .]

J. Ot.Ry. 2271

Description: The fragment Ot.Ry. 2271 is the upper right corner of a codex leaf.[d] The script very much resembles that of U 269. Especially noteworthy is the fact that the flower decoration at the beginning and the end of the header is just the same. The outer circle on the line has a slight stroke to the right.

There is no direct proof for demonstrating that this new fragment belongs to the Book of Giants, but the terminology gives some hints; see below.

Translation

(*header*) M[. . .][. . .] through . . .
(*recto*) [. . .] having killed [al]l [. . .], [. . .] eating, drinking [. . .] seeing [. . .] knowing [. . .] downward [. . .] the good [. . .]
(*verso*) [. . .] is necessary. If no *vidang* know[ledge . . .] is, it is [. . .] necessary to [. . .]. Sinless [. . .], and no [. . .]

---

a. Wilkens, "Neue Fragmente aus Manis Gigantenbuch," 149–50.
b. Cf. Wilkens, *Manichäisch-türkische Texte*, no. 234; Wilkens, "Neue Fragmente aus Manis Gigantenbuch," 168–69.
c. Further details in Wilkens, "Neue Fragmente aus Manis Gigantenbuch," 153.
d. A photograph of it is available at the International Dunhuang Project (IDP: http://idp.bl.uk).

Commentary

Recto 01 The word "to kill" is not an exact key word to understand the fragment, but if we think of the killing of the giants, we can compare several parts of parallel fragments.

Recto 05 Compare "sinless" in M I 10,7.

Verso 02 The word *vidang* seems to be the same as the *vidang* in M I edited by Le Coq.[a] Recently, Larry Clark suggested a new interpretation of this word. He translates it as "your aroma," but in the context it still remains doubtful, as in this new text, too.[b]

K. U 349 (T I x 3) [1053].[c]

Description: This number is a small fragment in Manichaean script of the middle part of a codex leaf. The punctuation dots are encircled in red.

Translation

(*recto?*) [. . .] he speaks [. . .] more [. . .] virtuous [. . .] the mi[ght (?)] of the hero [Saxm (?)] [. . .] [Bud]dha Go[d] [. . .]

(*verso?*) [. . .] king Go[d] [. . .] [div]ine good [. . .] that we [. . .] your [. . .]

---

a. Le Coq, *Türkische Manichaica aus Chotscho* I, 39.

b. Clark, *Uygur Manichaean Texts*, vol. 3: *Ecclesiastic Texts*, Corpus Fontium Manichaeorum, Series Turcica 3 (Turnhout: Brepols, 2017), 82, 84, 85.

c. Wilkens, *Manichäisch-türkische Texte*, no. 571.

The Book of the Mysteries (Sefer Ha-Razim)
A new translation and introduction

by James R. Davila

Sefer ha-Razim (The Book of the Mysteries) is a magical handbook from late antiquity. Written in Hebrew, it claims to have been revealed by the angel Razi'el to Noah. It describes the angels in the seven heavens ("firmaments") and provides numerous magical spells to make these angels do the will of the magician. The text is poorly preserved, but the overall structure and contents are not in doubt. Sefer ha-Razim was remarkably influenced by pagan Greek magic and in turn had a tremendous influence on Jewish magic and esotericism from the early Middle Ages on, as well as on later Christian magicians and kabbalists.

Contents

Sefer ha-Razim can be divided conveniently into two uneven parts. The prologue introduces the book and presents it as a divine revelation delivered by the angel Razi'el ("Mystery of God" or "God is my mystery") to the antediluvian patriarch Noah. Noah passed the book down to his descendants until it reached King Solomon, and its powers gave him his proverbial mastery over demons. The prologue extravagantly extols the powers that the book grants to the practitioner who makes proper use of it.

The second and much larger part, the Seven Firmaments, is divided into seven sections. The first six describe the angelic inhabitants of each of the seven celestial firmaments and present the practitioner with magical rites and adjurations to compel these angels to perform specified tasks. These rites have many parallels with late antique Greco-Egyptian magic and contain surprising pagan customs such as prayer and sacrifice to Greek gods. The work includes some rites for malefic practices such as necromancy and the sending of angels to harm or even destroy the enemies of the magician.

The section on the first firmament describes seven "camps" of angels and reveals one rite to be used on the angels of each camp. The section on the second firmament describes twelve "stages" or "steps" on which groups of angels stand, with a rite to go with each stage. The section on the third firmament lists three angelic princes in charge of it and gives a rite to go with each prince. The section on the fourth firmament lists the angels that lead the bridal chamber of the sun during the day and those that lead the bridal chamber of the sun during the night, along with a rite to go with each group. The section on the fifth firmament lists the twelve angelic princes who are over the twelve months of the year and gives a single rite to go with them all. The section on the sixth firmament lists the chief angels of the western and eastern camps of that firmament and provides one rite for them all. The final section, on the seventh firmament, consists of a hymn praising God and a series of closing benedictions. It contains no rites or adjurations.

The Book of the Mysteries (Sefer Ha-Razim)

Manuscripts and Versions

An eclectic critical edition of Sefer ha-Razim was published by Mordecai Margalioth in 1966.[1] On the one hand, specialists were excited and intrigued to gain access to a clearly Jewish text from late antiquity that contained beliefs and ideas so different from and indeed incompatible with contemporary rabbinic Judaism. Margalioth himself found the document distasteful. But on the other hand, some scholars expressed skepticism whether the text as reconstructed by Margalioth on the basis of highly fragmentary and eclectic sources ever existed in the form he reconstructed.[2] To complicate matters further, the manuscript variants to his eclectic text were placed in small print in the pages following the eclectic text, so that they were very difficult to consult. At times he also emended the text without any basis in the manuscripts.

These difficulties in using his edition and the fact that his introduction, commentary, and notes were published in Modern Hebrew led to this important document receiving less attention in the subsequent half-century than it deserved. But a more comprehensive collection of manuscript evidence for Sefer ha-Razim was published by Bill Rebiger and Peter Schäfer in 2006. It is a diplomatic edition, with German translation and commentary, which presents the main manuscripts in synoptic columns.[3] Their work leaves no doubt that Margalioth reconstructed a real ancient text, whose structure and general contents are assured. I summarize their text-critical conclusions here, with some observations of my own.

Sefer ha-Razim survives in two main versions. Version I, which has a clear redactional integrity, is the one translated here. Version II, arguably adapted from version I and so dependent upon it, is also known as the Book of Adam (Sefer Adam). Like version I, it begins with a haggadic introduction, but in it the angel Raz'iel reveals the book to Adam rather than to Noah. Raz'iel gives instructions for the use of the book, then there follows a list of angels arranged according to "watches," one for each month of the year. The book concludes with some final admonitions concerning its use.[4] From here on, I will treat version I as Sefer ha-Razim and ignore version II.

The most important textual source for Sefer ha-Razim consists of forty-three manuscript fragments from the Cairo Geniza (a repository of discarded medieval Jewish manuscripts associated with the Ben Ezra Synagogue in the old city of Cairo). Some fragments belong to the same manuscript, so the total number of manuscripts represented is fewer. Twenty-two are fragments of Hebrew manuscripts of the work and six contain excerpts of the Hebrew text used in other contexts. These date from the tenth to the fourteenth century and frequently preserve a good text. Unfortunately they are badly damaged and when taken in total they represent only about three-quarters of the work. Twelve frag-

---

1. Margalioth, *Sepher ha-Razim: A Newly Recovered Book of Magic from the Talmudic Period Collected from Geniza Fragments and Other Sources* (Jerusalem: Yediot Achronot, 1966) [Heb.]. I am grateful to Emanuel Margalioth, Dr. Margalioth's son, for permission to use his father's edition for my translation.

2. For overviews of the discussion, see Rebecca Macy Lesses, *Ritual Practices to Gain Power: Angels, Incantations, and Revelation in Early Jewish Mysticism*, HTS 44 (Harrisburg, PA: Trinity Press International, 1998), 422–25; and Bill Rebiger and Peter Schäfer, *Sefer ha-Razim I und II: Das Buch der Geheimnisse I und II*, vol. 2: *Einleitung, Übersetzung und Kommentar*, TSAJ 132 (Tübingen: Mohr Siebeck, 2009), 2:32–35 (see next note).

3. Rebiger and Schäfer, *Sefer ha-Razim*. I am grateful to the authors and to Mohr Siebeck for permission to use this edition for my translation and to the authors for providing me with material from it in advance of its publication.

4. See Rebiger and Schäfer, *Sefer ha-Razim* 1:106*–117* (§§361–99); 2:68–81, 179–91, 272–83.

ments of two Arabic translations written in Hebrew letters (Judeo-Arabic) also survive from the Cairo Geniza and also preserve a good text. These cover most of firmament 1 and parts of firmaments 2–4. Three fragments preserve a little of a *Namenversion* that pares down the text of the work to its lists of angels, with minimal transitional material. These are also in Judeo-Arabic, but one contains material in Hebrew as well.

The fourteen complete Hebrew manuscripts bound in codices are comparatively late (from the fifteenth to the nineteenth centuries) and the text they preserve is often very poor, with numerous omissions and corruptions. Latin translations also survive, of which the earliest goes back to two manuscripts from the thirteenth century. Two late manuscripts of an Arabic translation are also known, but only excerpts from them have been published.[5]

Margalioth had access to only fourteen of the Hebrew Geniza fragments and ten of the Judeo-Arabic ones, and to only seven complete Hebrew manuscripts, two of which were of little text-critical interest and which he did not use. He was also aware of four others but they were unavailable to him. The Latin translation came to his attention only near the end of his work and he made little use of it. He also made no effort to construct a stemma to work out the interrelationships of the manuscripts with one another.

All these textual sources have been divided by Rebiger and Schäfer into three recensions, the most important of which is recension A. Almost all of the Hebrew Geniza fragments and all of the Judeo-Arabic ones belong to this recension, as does the Latin translation. It is found in three complete Hebrew manuscripts (and a fourth unpublished one) and is excerpted in another. The manuscripts of recension A can be traced back to a single lost archetype and they represent the best text that can be reconstructed of the putative original work from late antiquity. The best text of the complete manuscripts is found in M738, an Italian manuscript of the fifteenth century. Although it is the best complete surviving text of this recension, it has many corruptions and some missing passages. This manuscript, along with the late (eighteenth/nineteenth century) Yemenite manuscript TA42 and the Geniza fragments in Hebrew and Judeo Arabic, represent recension A in the main text of the synoptic edition of Schäfer and Rebiger. The Hebrew Geniza fragments are cited in my translation according to their sigla, which contain the capital letter "G" followed by a number. M738 is cited as "M7" and TA42 as "TA."[6]

The best preserved Judeo-Arabic version is overall a literal translation, but on a thought-for-thought basis rather than a word-for-word one. It freely changes the wording, grammar, and word order, but is generally faithful to the sense of the Hebrew. A characteristic feature is its use of double translation: words and phrases are often given in two alternative translations. It is unclear to me whether this is the work of a single translator or whether copyists incorporated variants from one or more different Arabic translations. Occasionally it also appears to translate two variant Hebrew readings of a given word or phrase. The manuscripts have numerous corruptions, but where they overlap, one manuscript sometimes preserves the correct reading.[7] It is often difficult to

---

5. See Alexander Fodor, "An Arabic Version of *Sefer Ha-Razim*," *JSQ* 13 (2006): 412–27, doi:10.1628/094457006780130411; Dóra Zsom, "Another Arabic Version of *Sefer Ha-Razim* and *Ḥarba de-Moše*: A New *Sifr Ādam* Manuscript," *The Arabist* 37 (2016): 179–201; and Rebiger and Schäfer, *Sefer ha-Razim* 2:20–21.

6. Rebiger and Schäfer, *Sefer ha-Razim* 2:42–52.

7. Most of the Judeo-Arabic manuscripts preserve a single translation, but the small fragments G29–G30, which are probably from the same codex, preserve a different one. See the relevant note to §106.

reconstruct the Hebrew original behind the Judeo-Arabic version, which complicates its use for text-critical purposes. But it sometimes does preserve or confirm useful variants. Two Judeo-Arabic manuscripts omit the fourth firmament entirely (§§201–16), although a third one includes it.[8] The Judeo-Arabic evidence is cited as "JA."[9]

The Latin translation takes the Hebrew text of recension A as its basis, but it often expands on it, giving multiple translations of the same word(s), filling in details freely, and expanding on the basic ideas. It adds a section from version II (§§362–67) between §3 and §10. Occasionally it adds material from Jewish traditions, such as the description of the shamir-worm in §13b. It uses some neologisms and appears to transcribe some Arabic words for flora. It often adds instructions for the timing of the rituals and for the details of self-purification and self-fumigation. It adds chapter numbers and descriptive headers to each unit. Occasionally the text refers to variants that the translator or scribe found in other manuscripts. It can sometimes be useful for confirming variant readings found in the other witnesses, but it paraphrases too much to provide credible variants on its own. The evidence of the Latin translation is cited as "L."[10]

Recension B is secondary to recension A and derives from it. It contains a poorer text overall, but nevertheless it must not be ignored, because at times it preserves better individual readings. One Geniza fragment is from recension B, but otherwise it is known from nine complete Hebrew manuscripts and two that contain only extracts. Two of the complete ones belong to the base recension B. The sixteenth-century Sephardic-Oriental manuscript M248 preserves both the complete text and an abbreviated subrecension. This complete text is the best representative of recension B, although it does not reproduce it perfectly. Manuscript P849 is an autograph copy by Yohanan Alemanno (1435– early 1500s), a Jewish teacher of Christian kabbalist Pico della Mirandola. Alemanno gave the document a literary reworking, but it is based on a good text of the recension. These two manuscripts represent base recension B in the main text of the edition of Schäfer and Rebiger, cited, respectively, as M2 and P in my translation.[11]

Most of the manuscripts of recension B preserve a subrecension in which the text is significantly rearranged.[12] This *Umstellungtyp* (rearrangement-type) is found in six complete manuscripts and one extract. It is represented by the fourteenth-century manuscript F44 (Margalioth's manuscript *Pe*) in the main text of the edition of Schäfer and Rebiger, cited as F in my translation.[13] I have cited the evidence of F and of N (see below) according to the original ordering of Sefer ha-Razim.[14]

---

8. Rebiger and Schäfer suggest that the passage may have been omitted deliberately, because it contained an objectionable prayer to the Greek god Helios (*Sefer ha-Razim* 2:93–94).

9. See also Rebiger and Schäfer, *Sefer ha-Razim* 2:20, 45–46.

10. See also Rebiger and Schäfer, *Sefer ha-Razim* 2:21, 81–85.

11. Rebiger and Schäfer, *Sefer ha-Razim* 2:52–59, 111–14.

12. In F the following material is placed after the end of the seventh firmament in a slightly mixed order: §§186–200 (the three princes in charge of the third firmament and their rites; as §§300–314); §§204–5 (the angels of the fourth firmament who lead the bridal chamber of the sun during the day and night; as §§319–20); §§212–16 (the adjuration to see the sun going by the north wind during the night; as §§327–31); §§232–38 (the chiefs of the eastern and western camps of the sixth firmament and their bodyguard illusion rite; as §§332–38); §§220, 222–28 (the twelve princes of the fifth firmament and their foreknowledge rite; as §§341, 344–49). N (which constitutes its own unique recension, see below) expands these passages with other additions from the body of the work. Details are given in the notes to the translation.

13. Rebiger and Schäfer, *Sefer ha-Razim* 2:59–62.

14. Margalioth took a seventh manuscript, B244 (his *Qof*), to contain the best-preserved text of Sefer

Recension C is a curious combination found only in manuscript N8117 (Margalioth's manuscript *Samekh*). The scribe had a Hebrew text based on the *Umstellungtyp* and a Latin translation of uncertain origin based on recension A. The scribe combined them, retranslating the Latin back into Hebrew to fill in missing material in the Hebrew source and otherwise to supplement it. This manuscript is also included in the main text of the edition of Schäfer and Rebiger, although its text-critical usefulness is limited. It is cited as N in my translation.[15]

In addition, Sefer ha-Razim had a great influence on later magical and esoteric Jewish literature and many later texts excerpted and incorporated large portions of it. Margalioth drew on the texts of a number of these magical handbooks, amulet collections, and the like to reconstruct the text of Sefer ha-Razim. These include Sefer Razi'el ha-Mal'akh (Margalioth's *Dalet* and *Dalet*1); various amulet collections (his *He* and *He*1); Mafteaḥ Shlomo (his *Ḥet*); Sefer Ha-Malbush (his *Lamed*); Sefer Sha'arei Siyyon LeR. Natan Neta' Hanover (his *Ṣade*); Sefer Soddei Razayya (his *Resh* and *Resh*1); and a manuscript of the Shi'ur Qomah, along with the highly problematical edition of that text found in Musajaoff's *Merkava Shelemah*, folios 1a–6a (Margalioth's *Mem* and *Mem*1).

Only three of these sources were available to me. Rebiger and Schäfer include the relevant material from Sefer Razi'el ha-Mal'akh and Mafteaḥ Shlomo in their edition and I have made full use of them, citing the works by name.[16] Reliable editions of the passage on the seventh firmament in Shi'ur Qomah have been published by Martin Cohen and by Peter Schäfer.[17] I have consulted both, but I cite variants from the passage according to Schäfer's edition. All three of these sources are based on recension A.

Genre, Structure, Prosody

The basic genre of Sefer ha-Razim is that of the magical handbook, a collection of magical recipes and spells, presented in a more or less elaborate narrative framework. Jewish examples include Ḥavdalah di R. Akiva (a handbook structured around the weekly Sabbath-closing ceremony) and Ḥarba di-Moshe (the Sword of Moses, translated in this volume).[18] An important Christian example is the Testament of Solomon, a collection of exorcism rites presented in a pseudepigraphic narrative by Solomon about his life.[19] Sefer ha-Razim is the most elaborately structured magical handbook

---

ha-Razim among the complete manuscripts, but Schäfer and Rebiger have shown that it is actually a derivative version of the *Umstellungstyp* in which the editor has secondarily reconstructed the original order of the text on the basis of internal hints in the context. See *Sefer ha-Razim* 2:62–65.

15. Rebiger and Schäfer, *Sefer ha-Razim* 2:65–67.
16. Rebiger and Schäfer, *Sefer ha-Razim* 1:*205–*9; 2:15–20, 42, 94–95, 114–17.
17. Cohen, *The Shi'ur Qomah: Texts and Recensions*, TSAJ 9 (Tübingen: Mohr Siebeck, 1985), 112–17, 169–82. Schäfer, Margarete Schlüter, and Hans Georg von Mutius, *Synopse zur Hekhalot-Literatur*, TSAJ 2 (Tübingen: Mohr Siebeck, 1981), §§966–67, 969.
18. Yuval Harari, "The Sword of Moses (Ḥarba di-Moshe)."
19. For a discussion of Jewish magical handbooks, see Philip S. Alexander, "Incantations and Books of Magic," in *The History of the Jewish People in the Age of Jesus Christ (175 B. C.–A. D. 135)*, by Emil Schürer, ed. Geza Vermes, Fergus Millar, and Martin Goodman, rev. ed., 3 vols. (Edinburgh: T&T Clark, 1973–1987), 3:342–79; and Alexander, "Contextualizing the Demonology of the Testament of Solomon," in *Die Dämonen: Die Dämonologie der israelitisch-jüdischen und frühchristlichen Literatur im Kontext ihrer Umwelt*, ed. Armin Lange, Hermann Lichtenberger, and Diethard Römheld (Tübingen: Mohr Siebeck, 2003), 613–35. For an English translation of the Testament of Solomon, see D. C. Duling, "Testament of Solomon," *OTP* 1:934–87. Pablo A. Torijano Morales compares the prologue of Sefer ha-Razim to the roughly contemporary Greek magical handbook the Hygromanteia of Solomon. See Torijano, *Solo-*

that survives from antiquity. It begins with a prologue that traces its origin to an angelic revelation to Noah, thus giving the text features of an apocalypse. It is then divided into seven sections, each devoted to one of the celestial firmaments and how to recruit the angels dwelling therein to provide services for the practitioner. Each section begins with a list of the angels and their overseers, with rites to control them following for firmaments one to six. No rites are assigned to the seventh firmament; instead this section contains a hymn praising God on his throne and concluding the document with a series of benedictions to God.

Each rite has its own specific purpose. The range of purposes includes to harm enemies; to give the practitioner foreknowledge or influence over others; to practice divination, necromancy, or dream interpretation; to cause someone to fall in love; to protect groups or individuals from harm; to provide practical benefits such as lighting a cold stove or giving racehorses stamina; to heal afflictions such as migraine headaches and paralysis from stroke; and to create useful illusions of things such as fire and bodyguards.

The rites may well have been adapted from numerous sources, but they are generally structured similarly. They begin with an *introduction*: a conditional clause explaining what the rite does. There follow *instructions for a ritual* that often makes use of specific materials and that may be set in a specific location or time and may involve measures to attain a state of ritual purity. Then there is almost always an *invocation* of the relevant angels of that firmament, either in writing or verbally. Most of the rites then include a *verbal adjuration* to be recited to the angels, which tells them what to do. Additional *concluding ritual instructions* follow, sometimes including a *release formula* that may involve an additional adjuration, further ritual actions, or both.[20]

A convenient example is found in the rite for the angels of the fourth stage of the second firmament (§§137–40). The opening conditional clause gives its function as causing an enemy to have insomnia. The rest of the sentence prescribes a ritual involving the severed head of a black dog and a cold-water pipe, and the names of the angels of the fourth stage are written on the latter. The adjuration instructs these angels in flowery poetic language to afflict the named enemy with lack of sleep. There follow further instructions on putting a written copy of the adjuration in the dog's mouth, sealing it, and concealing it in a place associated with the victim. The rite concludes with a final, optional, ritual to release the victim from the magical affliction.

Date and Provenance

None of the surviving manuscripts of Sefer ha-Razim is older than the tenth century, but there is good reason to conclude that it was composed some centuries before this time.

---

mon the Esoteric King: From King to Magus, Development of a Tradition, JSJSup 73 (Leiden: Brill, 2002), 200–208. Torijano translates the Greek work as "The Hygromancy of Solomon" in *MOTP* 1:305–25.

20. Jens-Heinrich Niggemeyer provides a detailed analysis of the adjurations. See Niggemeyer, *Beschwörungsformeln aus dem "Buch der Geheimnisse,"* Judaistische Texte und Studien 3 (Hildesheim: Olm, 1975). Lesses analyzes the rituals and adjurations in the mystical *hekhalot* literature (see below) from the perspective of speech-act theory and, in the context of related material in the Greek Magical Papyri, Sefer ha-Razim, and similar texts. See Lesses, *Ritual Practices to Gain Power*; Sefer ha-Razim is covered especially in ch. 5. Naomi Janowitz discusses the relationship of words to ritual acts in the recipes of Sefer ha-Razim. See Janowitz, *Icons of Power: Ritual Practices in Late Antiquity*, Magic in History (University Park: Pennsylvania State University Press, 2002), ch. 6.

The Book of the Mysteries (Sefer Ha-Razim)

The external evidence is inconclusive. The first reasonably clear mention of the work is by the ninth-century Karaite writer Daniel al-Qumisi who wrote,[21]

> And who today commits sorceries in Israel? Is it not the rabbis, who recite the pure name and the impure name, who write amulets, who play tricks, and who call the name of their writings [*Sefer*] *Yashar, Sefer ha-Razim, Sefer Adam, Raza Rabba*, and suchlike books of sorceries? If you seek to draw a man near to a woman for love, if you seek to make them hate one another, if you seek to shorten the journey—many such abominations, may the Lord keep us far from them![22]

Although we are given only the title of the work, the context supports the conclusion that it is our Sefer ha-Razim. As we have seen above, Sefer Adam may well be a reference to version II. These are evidently magical handbooks and al-Qumisi quotes the introductory conditional clauses of a number of rites therein. The first one, a love spell, has thematic parallels to Sefer ha-Razim §§65, 74–75, and 93.

But the internal evidence is more important for establishing the composition date of Sefer ha-Razim. The manuscripts come from a wide range of dates and locations and many of them are quite corrupt, so reconstructing the original grammar and orthography of the Hebrew of the work is no simple task. Overall this Hebrew shows features of the Mishnaic dialect, but is not entirely Mishnaic, so no conclusions can be drawn with confidence about its date (although the Greek loanwords it contains, discussed below, are another factor to take into account).[23] Margalioth noted a chronological hint in the mention of "the enumeration of fifteen years of the reckoning of the kings of Greece" in §37. This is clearly a reference to the "indiction," a Roman agricultural tax that came in a fifteen-year cycle and became used as a dating system from the mid-fourth century—originally in Egypt, but spreading throughout Europe into the Middle Ages. This gives us a lower limit of the mid-fourth century for the composition of this passage.[24] That said, Sefer ha-Razim gives many indications of being composed from disparate materials that may come from different times. We should not rule out the possibility that some of its contents were composed earlier or later than this passage.

An upper limit is equally difficult to establish. But some important evidence is found in the connections between Sefer ha-Razim and the Greco-Egyptian magical literature of late antiquity, known from the so-called Greek Magical Papyri (*PGM*). These collections of magical rites and spells date from the second century BCE to the fifth century CE, with the largest surviving collections coming from the latter part of this period.[25] Numerous Greek words have been transliterated into Hebrew letters in Sefer ha-Razim and many of these words are also found in the *PGM* with the same meaning and in similar

---

21. The Karaites are a Jewish group that has existed since the early Middle Ages. They reject the innovations of rabbinic Judaism and they practice what they believe to be the original, biblical form of Judaism.

22. This is from his commentary on Malachi. Al-Qumisi also mentions Sefer ha-Razim in his commentary on Joshua, where he condemns it along with Sefer Bilaam, Sefer Adam, Sefer ha-Yashar, and Raza Rabba. For both quotations, see Margalioth, *Sepher ha-Razim*, 36; and Rebiger and Schäfer, *Sefer ha-Razim*, 2:90–93.

23. For a discussion of the linguistic features of the Hebrew of the work, see Rebiger and Schäfer, *Sefer ha-Razim*, 2:4–5.

24. Margalioth, *Sepher ha-Razim*, 24–26. See note to §37 in the translation below.

25. For an English translation of the *PGM* see Betz, *GMPT*. See also Todd E. Klutz, "The Eighth Book of Moses," *MOTP* 1:189–235.

contexts.[26] Likewise, the Hebrew handbook and the Greek papyri prescribe similar actions in their magical rites, and many of these rites share similar objectives.[27] A prayer to the Greek god Helios is transcribed in Greek transliterated into Hebrew letters (§213) and the goddess Aphrodite is invoked as well (§66). The pervasive pattern of linguistic and thematic parallels can hardly be coincidental, and it is safe to conclude that the thought-world that produced Sefer ha-Razim owed much to something closely related to the thought-world that produced the Greco-Egyptian magical texts. The bulk of the *PGM* manuscripts were produced in the fourth and fifth centuries CE and it seems reasonable to place the origin of Sefer ha-Razim in something like the same chronological horizon or at latest (granting the conservative nature of magical traditions) within no more than a century or two thereafter, narrowing its date of composition to the fourth to the seventh centuries CE.

We can only conjecture about the place of composition. The parallels with the Greco-Egyptian magical texts and the mention of hieratic script (§58) support an origin in Egypt, but there is little evidence that there were Jews in Egypt in this period who were composing works in Hebrew, so a Palestinian origin remains plausible as well.[28]

Literary Context

Although the content of Sefer ha-Razim is highly idiosyncratic for a Jewish work of late antiquity, the Hebrew Bible still forms an important backdrop to it. The prologue sets the

---

26. These include references to "saucers" (*PGM* IV. 224, 3210; cf. Sh-R §43); a "hieratic document" written with "myrrh ink" (*PGM* II. 60–61, 233; cf. Sh-R §58); "spikenard oil" (*PGM* I. 278; cf. Sh-R §59); "storax" and "myrrh" (*PGM* IV. 2460–2461; cf. Sh-R §66); the goddess "Aphrodite" (*PGM* IV. 2891; cf. Sh-R §66); a "tin *lamella*" (*PGM* IV. 1255; cf. Sh-R §74); an angel named "Bouel/BW'L" (*PGM* IV. 972; cf. Sh-R §107); magical "characters" (*PGM* I. 266; II. 60; VII. 195; cf. Sh-R §130); and a "cold-water pipe" (*PGM* VII. 397; cf. Sh-R §137).

27. Similar ritual actions include making use of water from seven springs (*PGM* I. 234–236; cf. Sh-R §43); tearing out the heart of an animal or bird (*PGM* III 425 [a hoopoe]; cf. Sh-R §65 [a lion cub]); sacrificing a rooster in running water (*PGM* IV. 35–45; cf. Sh-R §91); keeping the sun from seeing an object (*PGM* VII. 915; cf. Sh-R §§94, 173, 226); making use of a place of the dead (*PGM* IV. 2207–2208; V. 332–333 [the grave of someone untimely dead]; cf. Sh-R §102 [the place of the "killed"]); carrying out a rite in the third hour of the night (*PGM* XXXVI. 136; cf. Sh-R §§110, 210); refraining from eating fish (*PGM* I. 290; cf. Sh-R §119) and from meat (*PGM* IV. 735; cf. Sh-R §176); refraining from sex for three days (*PGM* IV. 897–898; cf. Sh-R §§120, 167) or for seven days (*PGM* I. 41–42; cf. Sh-R §171); putting *materia* in the mouth of a dead dog (*PGM* XXXVI. 370; cf. Sh-R §139); being naked in the sun (*PGM* IV. 173–175; cf. Sh-R §148); making a statue that is standing in a certain pose (*PGM* IV. 2379–2382; cf. Sh-R §156); writing on seven laurel leaves (*PGM* I. 263–268; cf. Sh-R §164); and using a thread or cloth of seven colors on a metal object (*PGM* VII. 271; cf. Sh-R §176). The shared objectives include giving someone insomnia (*PGM* IV. 2943–2966, 3255–3274; VII. 374–376; cf. Sh-R §137); curing a migraine headache (*PGM* VII. 199–201, 201–202; XCIV. 39–60; cf. Sh-R §176); determining the date when someone will die (*PGM* I. 188–189; cf. Sh-R §224); gaining foreknowledge (*PGM* III. 263–275; cf. Sh-R §§109); making someone fall in love (*PGM* IV. 94–153, 1390–1495, 1496–1595; cf. Sh-R §§127–29); protection from wild animals (*PGM* VII. 370–373; cf. Sh-R §155); winning the horse races (*PGM* VII. 390–393; cf. Sh-R §§193–94); and necromancy (consulting the dead) (*PGM* IV. 2140–2144; cf. Sh-R §§98–102).

28. Margalioth dates the composition of Sefer ha-Razim to the third or fourth centuries CE (*Sepher ha-Razim*, 26–28). Ithamar Gruenwald dates it somewhat later, to the sixth or seventh century, as does Gideon Bohak. See Gruenwald, *Apocalyptic and Merkavah Mysticism*, AGJU 14 (Leiden: Brill, 1980), 226; Bohak, *Ancient Jewish Magic: A History* (Cambridge: Cambridge University Press, 2008), 170–75. Rebiger and Schäfer are inclined to date the composition of the final form of the work to the seventh or eighth century CE (*Sefer ha-Razim*, 2:3–9, 87–90). I agree with Bohak that the complete lack of Islamic or Arabic influence in Sefer ha-Razim makes it difficult to date later than the seventh century.

book in a fictional biblical historical context in which it was revealed by an angel to Noah, who then passed it down through the generations to King Solomon. It mentions Adam and Eve as well. In addition, the work quotes or alludes to the Bible fairly frequently. These biblical quotations and allusions can be divided into several categories. Most common are those found in hymnic sections that praise God using biblical passages. Good examples are found in the adjuration in §111, which uses Isa 40:12; Nah 1:4; and Ps 107:33, and in §§239–43, a concluding hymn that draws on Dan 2:22; 7:10; Isa 6:2–4; Exod 33:20; Job 12:22; 23:13; 26:11; 41:17; Ps 104:2; and Ezek 1:5, 15–21. It is also common for the work to absorb scriptural phrases into the wording of passages. In some cases the use fits the original context of the scriptural verse, such as the use of Qoh 3:2–3 in §10. More often a passage borrows a scriptural phrase with no connection between its original meaning and its new context. See, for example, the use of Prov 25:13 in §187 or of Dan 8:4 in §194. Some of these recontextualizations are very striking indeed, such as the reuse of the divine "pillar of fire and cloud" (Exod 13:21; 14:24) to describe the appearance of a divinatory apparition in §§110–11, or the reuse of the condemnation of sorceries in Isa 47:13 in a positive context to describe the angelic princes of the fifth firmament in §219.

The work draws upon the language of biblical passages dealing with angels to describe the angels (e.g., §121 [Ezek 1:14]; §§230, 237, 251 [Ps 68:18]; §242 [Ezek 1:5, 15–21; Isa 6:2]). It also reapplies passages on other subjects to angels: in §142 we find 2 Chr 25:5 and 1 Sam 17:5, which originally applied to human warriors, used this way, and in §183 the description of the third firmament applies the appearance of the earthly chariots of Nah 2:4 to angels. There are a few allusions to biblical episodes that function as abbreviated *historiolae* (stories with magical power), notably the destruction of Sodom and Gomorrah (Deut 29:23; Jer 48:19) in §49 and the destruction of the Assyrian king Sennacherib's army (2 Kgs 19:35//Isa 37:36//2 Chr 32:21) in §237. Very occasionally the text draws on biblical purity regulations to formulate its own rules for magical ritual purity, for example, in avoiding menstrual impurity and touching the dead (e.g., §119; cf. Ezek 18:6; Lev 21:11).

Sefer ha-Razim also has notable parallels with the older nonbiblical apocalypses, especially those with tours of multiple heavens. In each of the six heavens below the seventh, the Ascension of Isaiah has an enthroned angel who oversees the other angels in that heaven. We find a similar organization in 2 En. 19 and Greek fragment A of the Apocalypse of Zephaniah.[29] We find angels standing on steps in 2 En. 20:3. The idea of angels standing on steps perhaps reflects elements of the temple cult involving the Levites standing on steps while singing (m. Sukkah 5:4; m. Mid. 2:5). Like Sefer ha-Razim, the apocalypses see the heavens as the sources of meteorological phenomena, such as rain, snow, and dew, and as the spheres in which the sun and moon move (cf., e.g., 1 En. 69:22–24, 72–82).[30]

Remarkably, a very significant influence on Sefer ha-Razim was the fund of Greek-language magical traditions that also produced the Greco-Egyptian Greek Magical Papyri.[31] The writer of Sefer ha-Razim was clearly very familiar with similar Greek-language rites and spells and drew on them extensively for inspiration, as was demonstrated in the previous section. But the influence went well beyond individual words or elements

---

29. For the latter see O. S. Wintermute, "Apocalypse of Zephaniah," *OTP* 1:497–516, esp. 508.
30. The information in this paragraph is based on a private communication from Richard Bauckham.
31. These parallels are discussed in detail by Margalioth in *Sepher ha-Razim*, 1–16. Cf. Rebiger and Schäfer, *Sefer ha-Razim*, 2:5, 87.

of rites and extended to religious practices that would have been anathema to contemporary rabbininc Judaism. The work prescribes the offering of libations and incense to angels (§§3, 28, 38). It takes pagan astrology for granted as a reality (§§93, 128). It associates a sacrifice and adjuration with the planet Venus, identified with the love goddess Aphrodite (§§65–67); it prescribes an offering to Hermes, the god who leads the dead to the underworld (§§98–99); and offers a Greek prayer to the sun god Helios (§213).[32] We have no way of knowing the reasoning of the writer so as to permit these practices, but the Judaism of these practitioners apparently took a very broad view of such matters and found no conflict between them and monotheism.[33]

Margalioth was at pains to distance Sefer ha-Razim from rabbinic tradition, but he did have to note the respect this work showed to the rabbis in the offhand comment that the angels of the sixth stage of the second firmament are "fearsome as sages of the academy" (§147).[34] It is true that Sefer ha-Razim shows little interest in rabbinic traditions, but it does not ignore them entirely. Most notably, the chain of tradition from Noah to Solomon in §13 is clearly modeled after and verbally echoes the late Mishnaic passage m. 'Abot 1:1. And in the same paragraph the description of Solomon's relations with the demons may show some knowledge of rabbinic stories about Solomon as magician (cf. b. Giṭ. 68a–b).

Merkavah mysticism is another fund of traditions that overlaps with and may have exerted some influence on Sefer ha-Razim. Merkavah mysticism is described in a corpus of texts known as the *hekhalot* literature, the literature of the (heavenly) "palaces" where God is enthroned. These texts draw heavily on biblical accounts of the divine throne room (esp. Ezek 1), describing the mystical adventures of second-century rabbis such as Ishmael, Akiva, and Nehuniah ben HaQanah, and giving detailed instructions for rituals and spells that allow the practitioner, the "descender to the chariot," to travel to God's throne-chariot in heaven or to call down angels and compel them to teach the practitioner the secrets of Torah.[35]

The complete manuscripts of Sefer ha-Razim are consistently bound together with *hekhalot* literature (and sometimes related texts such as Massekhet Hekhalot, Shiur Qomah, and Ma'aseh Bereshit). One of the Geniza fragments is also bound together with a copy of the Hekhalot Rabbati. This demonstrates that somewhat later copyists thought these works belonged together. In addition Sefer ha-Razim has a number of parallels with the *hekhalot* texts. In the prologue we are told that Noah learned from the book how "to take up the searching out of the stages of the heights and to rove everywhere in the seven

---

32. Sefer ha-Razim is not unique in its use of pagan imagery and theology. Mosaics in a number of late antique Galilean synagogues depict the twelve signs of the zodiac and the god Helios in his sun chariot. See Rebiger and Schäfer, *Sefer ha-Razim*, 2:5; Lee Levine, "Jewish Archaeology in Late Antiquity: Art, Architecture, and Inscriptions," in *The Late Roman-Rabbinic Period*, ed. Steven T. Katz, CHJ 4 (Cambridge: Cambridge University Press, 2006), 542–47.

33. Rebiger and Schäfer have also noted some intriguing parallels to Sefer ha-Razim in the angelic hierarchy and use of Scripture of the late-antique Syriac Christian work the Testament of Adam (*Sefer ha-Razim*, 2:6–7, 265–66; cf. §237 below). The Syriac Testament of Adam is available in an English translation by S. E. Robinson, "Testament of Adam," *OTP* 1:989–95.

34. Margalioth, *Sepher ha-Razim*, 22.

35. See Peter Schäfer, *The Hidden and Manifest God: Some Major Themes in Early Jewish Mysticism*, SUNY Series in Judaica (Albany: State University of New York Press, 1992); and James R. Davila, *Hekhalot Literature in Translation: Major Texts of Merkavah Mysticism*, Supplements to the Journal of Jewish Thought and Philosophy 20 (Leiden: Brill, 2013), ch. 1.

The Book of the Mysteries (Sefer Ha-Razim)

habitations" (§3). But perhaps not too much should be made of this apparent claim to teach how to ascend to heaven, given that none of the rites in the book are devoted to this ability. Sefer ha-Razim also makes similar claims to those of the *hekhalot* literature about the powers of the practitioner, as is illustrated by this passage from the Hekhalot Zutarti about the powers of the descenders to the chariot:

> And what mortal man is it who is able
> to ascend on high,
> to ride on wheels,
> to descend below,
> to search out the inhabited world,
> to walk on the dry land,
> to gaze at his splendor,
> to unbind by means of his crown,
> to be transformed by his glory,
> to recite his praise,
> to combine letters,
> to recite their names,
> to have a vision of what is above,
> to have a vision of what is below,
> to know the explanation of the living,
> and to see the vision of the dead,
> to walk in rivers of fire,
> and to know the lightning?[36]

If we set aside the question of heavenly ascents, there are still intriguing connections. Like the practitioner in this passage, the user of Sefer ha-Razim has supernatural knowledge of the world (§§57–62, 223); sees God's splendor (§§239–43); is able to unbind spells (§§112–13, 140, 189–90, 199); uses divine power to transform himself (§164); offers praise to God in the adjurations (§§111, 207, 225, 237), and in the concluding benedictions (§§244–59) manipulates letters and names in the procedures (§§28, 44, 65, 111, 152, 197, 212, 237); knows the organization of the heavenly realm in each firmament (passim); has a vision of what is above (§§3, 206–16); has special knowledge about living people (§§10, 109–11); calls up visions of the dead (§§98–101); and has power over fire (§§143–45, 184, 186–88, 197–99) and knowledge of lightning (§§10, 121, 212, 219).

Sefer ha-Razim and the *hekhalot* literature share a similar cosmology, containing a multitiered universe of seven firmaments with the throne of God placed at the top level. The firmaments are filled with angels, and the holy living creatures and the *ophannim* ("wheels") dwell with God's throne. These texts also draw on some of the same scriptural passages to construct their descriptions of the heavenly realm, notably Ezek 1 and 10; Isa 6; and Ps 104. Both Sefer ha-Razim and the *hekhalot* texts make use of ritual purifications in preparation for their rites and adjurations, they both use the names of angels in these rites and adjurations, and both seek to compel angels to do the bidding of the practitioner.

All that said, there are also crucial differences. There are no explicit ascents to heaven in Sefer ha-Razim, nor are there rites for accomplishing such an ascent. Its rites and

---

36. Hekhalot Zutarti §349. The translation is from Davila, *Hekhalot Literature in Translation*, 205–6.

adjurations provide power over angels, but this is to bring about mundane goals such as making someone fall in love, gaining political power, or even lighting a cold oven. There are no rites for giving the practitioner supernatural knowledge of Torah-learning (Sar Torah adjurations), and such a goal seems far from the interests of the writer. Although the names of angels form an important component of the spells, there is no use of the nonsense-word *nomina barbara* found frequently in *hekhalot* adjurations. In short, there is some overlap between the thought worlds of the *hekhalot* literature and Sefer ha-Razim, but the writer and practitioners of the latter were not descenders to the chariot.[37]

Sefer ha-Razim had an extraordinary influence on medieval Jewish magic, as well as on the later medieval Christian magic that drew on this Jewish magic.[38] Its popularity in the Geonic era (late sixth to early eleventh centuries) in the Middle East is established by the numerous fragmentary manuscripts of it and its Arabic translation recovered from the Cairo Geniza, and the Karaite criticisms of it, although there is no corresponding evidence for its dissemination in Babylonia. The use of Sefer ha-Razim by other, not easily dated, Jewish works such as Maphteaḥ Sholomo and Sefer Malbush has already been noted. Maimonides (1135–1204) quoted the book without mentioning it by name and condemned its contents in his *Mishneh Torah*. In European circles the earliest certain use of it is found in the esoteric compendium *Sode Razayya* (*The Counsels of the Secrets*) by the Ashkenazic sage El'azar of Worms (ca. 1165–1230). Without citing his source by name, he incorporated considerable cosmological and angelogical material from Sefer ha-Razim into this work. An important and influential early modern compilation of old material, Sefer Razi'el ha-Mal'akh (the Book of Razi'el the Angel), included some of the material from Sefer ha-Razim found in *Sode Razayya*, as well as material from the short version of Sefer ha-Razim and version II of this work. Sefer ha-Razim and its descendants were also known to later kabbalistic writers.

In the Christian West, we find esoteric material about the angel Razi'el being cited as early as the twelfth century and some of this material may go back to one recension or another of Sefer ha-Razim. It was translated more than once into Latin and the earliest translation whose origin we can trace goes back to the second half of the thirteenth century in the court of Alfonso X in Castille as part of his project of translating Jewish and Arabic esoteric texts into Latin and Spanish. This translation survives in two manuscripts as the sixth of seven books of the Latin work Liber Razielis. This Liber Razielis was widely disseminated in Europe, was translated into many European languages, and had considerable influence on the Christian kabbalists of the early Renaissance.

---

37. Cf. James R. Davila, *Descenders to the Chariot: The People behind the Hekhalot Literature*, JSJSup 70 (Leiden: Brill, 2001), 240–45; Gruenwald, *Apocalyptic*, 225–34.

38. In their commentary, Rebiger and Schäfer point out many parallels between Sefer ha-Razim and medieval Jewish magical texts, especially those from the Cairo Geniza. Most of these texts are not available in English translation, so I have not referred to them in the notes to my translation. For detailed discussions of the afterlife of Sefer ha-Razim, see Margalioth, *Sepher ha-Razim*, 29–46; and Rebiger and Schäfer, *Sefer ha-Razim*, 2:87–125. Add to these the Geniza fragment JTSL ENA NS 12.5, published by Alessia Bellusci, "A Geniza Finished Product for She'elat Ḥalom Based on *Sefer Ha-Razim*," *JJS* 67 (2016): 305–26, doi:10.18647/3281/JJS-2016. This page, written in Hebrew, dates to the twelfth–thirteenth century. It preserves a magical rite for finding a lost coin hoard by means of a dream. It quotes the list of the angels of the seventh camp of the first firmament from Sefer ha-Razim §107. These angels are in charge of dream interpretation. As a "finished product" that has been put to actual use, this fragment gives positive evidence that real practitioners used the rites in Sefer ha-Razim.

This Translation

The only previous translation of the complete text of Sefer ha-Razim into English is that of Morgan. He translated Margalioth's eclectic reconstructed base text, but without reference to the variants in the textual notes. Others have also published English translations of excerpts of the book.[39]

For all its flaws, Margalioth's eclectic critical text is overall quite good and there can be no doubt that he has correctly reconstructed the structure of Sefer ha-Razim and the general flow of its contents. But Schäfer and Rebiger have collected much new manuscript material and, crucially, have reconstructed a stemma of the manuscript evidence, showing how each source relates to the others and therefore providing much greater clarity about the place and importance of each manuscript for reconstructing the original text. They opt for a synoptic presentation of the manuscripts rather than attempting to produce a new reconstructed eclectic text.

Such an attempt would be worthwhile, but is beyond the scope of this translation. Instead, I have for the most part translated Margalioth's eclectic text, but in my textual apparatus I have given variant Hebrew, Judeo-Arabic, and Latin readings from the edition of Rebiger and Schäfer and from a few of Margalioth's notes. The manuscripts have numerous corruptions. It would serve no purpose to record obvious errors and omissions, of which there are many. I have ignored these. Often the manuscripts give variant readings that arguably make as much sense as the ones accepted by Margalioth for his eclectic reconstructed text. I have given these in the notes when they mattered for the translation. (Very occasionally I have preferred one of them for my base text over Margalioth's reading.) The English-only reader can thus see something approaching the full range of meaningful textual variation in the manuscripts. This reader should also be aware that sometimes bewildering variants in individual passages frequently look very similar in Hebrew and were thus easily confused as the manuscripts were copied.

I do not include minor variants such as the presence or absence of the conjunction *vav* ("and"), the word "all," or the definite article, as well as transposition of words and minor differences in pronoun suffixes, prepositions, verbal or noun number, and word order, unless these make a clear difference for the sense of the passage. When Margalioth's base text comes solely from one of his external sources which is unavailable to me, I have noted his reading but have translated another reading as my base text. In a few cases I have followed Margalioth's conjectural emendations that have no direct basis in any source. For the lists of angels I follow Margalioth's reconstruction.

The text of Sefer ha-Razim is repetitive and it is clear from the content and context that most or all of the manuscripts frequently drop phrases. In addition, Alemanno's reworking of the text in P tended to revise in the direction of succinctness. Thus the shorter reading is often not to be preferred. At the same time there appear to be many secondary

---

39. Michael A. Morgan, *Sepher Ha-Razim: The Book of the Mysteries*, SBLTT 25, Society of Biblical Literature Pseudepigraph Series 11 (Chico, CA: Scholars Press, 1983). Kimberly B. Stratton has published a translation of excerpts from the prologue and the first, fourth, and seventh firmaments. See Stratton, "The Mithras Liturgy and *Sefer ha-Razim*," in *Religions of Late Antiquity in Practice*, ed. Richard Valantasis, Princeton Readings in Religion (Princeton: Princeton University Press, 2000), 303–15. Lesses has also translated excerpts of the book (*Ritual Practices*, 233–35; 293–94, and 316). Philip S. Alexander translated three rituals from the book. See Alexander, "*Sefer ha-Razim* and the Problem of Black Magic in Early Judaism," in *Magic in the Biblical World: From the Rod of Aaron to the Ring of Solomon*, ed. Todd E. Klutz, JSNTSup 245 (London: T&T Clark, 2003), 170–90.

additions ("explicating pluses") in the manuscripts, although it is often difficult to be sure which longer readings are secondary. Given the corrupt state of the manuscripts, it is often impossible to reconstruct the specific details of a putative original text, but the general sense of the narrative can usually be recovered with reasonable confidence. We should bear in mind that magicians used the rituals and adjurations in Sefer ha-Razim. Surely used variant versions of them were in circulation. The manuscripts of this work may have reflected this variation from the beginning. In that case there was never an authoritative original text that we could reconstruct.

In the translation, superscript numerals in increments of five represent the lineation of Sefer ha-Razim in Margalioth's edition. He assigns separate lineations to the prologue and each of the seven firmaments. The siglum "§" followed by a number (in parentheses and superscripted) represents the paragraph divisions assigned to the work by Rebiger and Schäfer.[40]

My translation is literal, using the same English word for a given Hebrew word whenever possible. But I have also aimed for sufficiently idiomatic English that the text will make good sense to a nonspecialist reader. That said, Sefer ha-Razim is an esoteric work written in technical Hebrew and it deliberately cultivates an air of mystery. At times the exact meaning of a passage remains unclear even to specialists.

Bibliography

Alexander, Philip S. "Contextualizing the Demonology of the Testament of Solomon." Pages 613–35 in *Die Dämonen: Die Dämonologie der israelitisch-jüdischen und frühchristlichen Literatur im Kontext ihrer Umwelt*. Edited by Armin Lange, Hermann Lichtenberger, and Diethard Römheld. Tübingen: Mohr Siebeck, 2003.

———. "Incantations and Books of Magic." Pages 342–79 in vol. 3.1 of *The History of the Jewish People in the Age of Jesus Christ (175 B.C.–A.D. 135)*. By Emil Schürer. Edited by Geza Vermes, Fergus Millar, and Martin Goodman. Rev. ed. 3 vols. Edinburgh: T&T Clark, 1973–1987.

———. "*Sefer ha-Razim* and the Problem of Black Magic in Early Judaism." Pages 170–90 in *Magic in the Biblical World: From the Rod of Aaron to the Ring of Solomon*. Edited by Todd E. Klutz. JSNTSup. 245. London: T&T Clark, 2003.

Bellusci, Alessia. "A Geniza Finished Product for *She'elat Ḥalom* Based on *Sefer Ha-Razim*." *JJS* 67 (2016): 305–26. doi:10.18647/3281/JJS-2016.

Betz, Hans Dieter, ed. *The Greek Magical Papyri in Translation: Including the Demotic Spells. Volume One: Texts*. 2nd ed. Chicago: University of Chicago Press, 1992.

Bohak, Gideon. *Ancient Jewish Magic: A History*. Cambridge: Cambridge University Press, 2008.

Cohen, Martin Samuel. *The Shi'ur Qomah: Texts and Recensions*. TSAJ 9. Tübingen: Mohr Siebeck, 1985.

Davila, James R. *Descenders to the Chariot: The People behind the Hekhalot Literature*. JSJSup 70. Leiden: Brill, 2001.

———. *Hekhalot Literature in Translation: Major Texts of Merkavah Mysticism*. Supplements to the Journal of Jewish Thought and Philosophy 20. Leiden: Brill, 2013.

---

40. In the translation, citations of Margalioth and of Morgan by name alone refer to their notes to the relevant passages in Margalioth's edition and Morgan's translation.

Fodor, Alexander. "An Arabic Version of *Sefer Ha-Razim*." *JSQ* 13 (2006): 412–27. doi:10.1628/094457006780130411.

Gruenwald, Ithamar. *Apocalyptic and Merkavah Mysticism*. AGJU 14. Leiden: Brill, 1980.

Janowitz, Naomi. *Icons of Power: Ritual Practices in Late Antiquity*. Magic in History. University Park: Pennsylvania State University Press, 2002.

Lesses, Rebecca Macy. *Ritual Practices to Gain Power: Angels, Incantations, and Revelation in Early Jewish Mysticism*. HTS 44. Harrisburg, PA: Trinity Press International, 1998.

Levine, Lee. "Jewish Archaeology in Late Antiquity: Art, Architecture, and Inscriptions." Pages 519–55 in *The Late Roman-Rabbinic Period*. Edited by Steven T. Katz. CHJ 4. Cambridge: Cambridge University Press, 2006.

Margalioth, Mordecai. *Sepher ha-Razim: A Newly Recovered Book of Magic from the Talmudic Period Collected from Geniza Fragments and Other Sources*. Jerusalem: Yediot Achronot, 1966. [Heb.]

Morgan, Michael A. *Sepher Ha-Razim: The Book of the Mysteries*. SBLTT 25. Society of Biblical Literature Pseudepigraph Series 11. Chico, CA: Scholars Press, 1983.

Musajoff, Shlomo. *Merkavah Shelemah*. Jerusalem: Defus Solomon, 1921. http://www.hebrewbooks.org/7391.

Niggemeyer, Jens-Heinrich. *Beschwörungsformeln aus dem "Buch der Geheimnisse."* Judaistische Texte und Studien 3. Hildesheim: Olm, 1975.

Rebiger, Bill, and Peter Schäfer. *Sefer ha-Razim I und II: Das Buch der Geheimnisse I und II*. Vol. 1: *Edition*. Vol. 2: *Einleitung, Übersetzung und Kommentar*. 2 vols. TSAJ 125, 132. Tübingen: Mohr Siebeck, 2009.

Schäfer, Peter. *The Hidden and Manifest God: Some Major Themes in Early Jewish Mysticism*. SUNY Series in Judaica. Albany: State University of New York Press, 1992.

Schäfer, Peter, Margarete Schlüter, and Hans Georg von Mutius. *Synopse zur Hekhalot-Literatur*. TSAJ 2. Tübingen: Mohr Siebeck, 1981.

Stratton, Kimberly B. "The Mithras Liturgy and *Sefer ha-Razim*." Pages 303–15 in *Religions of Late Antiquity in Practice*. Edited by Richard Valantasis. Princeton Readings in Religion. Princeton: Princeton University Press, 2000.

Torijano Morales, Pablo A. *Solomon the Esoteric King: From King to Magus, Development of a Tradition*. JSJSup 73. Leiden: Brill, 2002.

Zsom, Dóra. "Another Arabic Version of *Sefer Ha-Razim* and *Ḥarba de-Moše*: A New *Sīfr Ādam* Manuscript." *The Arabist* 37 (2016): 179–201.

The Book of the Mysteries (Sefer ha-Razim)[a]

Prologue

(§2)1b[b]This is a book from the books of the mysteries[c] which was given[d] to Noah son of 'Lamech, son of Methuselah, son of Enoch, son of Jared, son of Mehalalel, son of Kenan, son of Enosh, son of Seth, son of Adam,[e] from the mouth of Razi'el the angel[f] in the year[g] that he entered the ark, before his entrance. (§3)And he wrote it[h] on a *sapphire stone very clearly*. And from it he learned[i] working of wonders and mysteries of knowledge and arrays of understanding and thoughts of humility 5and devices of counsel, to take up the searching out of the stages of the heights and to roam everywhere in the seven habitations, and to gaze at[j] all the constellations and to gain understanding of the custom of the sun, and to make clear[k] the searchings-out of the moon, and to know the highways of the *Great Bear, Orion, and the Pleiades*,[l] and to tell[m] what are

Jub. 10:11–14

Gen 5

Exod 24:10; Ezek 1:26; 10:1
Deut 27:8

Job 9:9

---

a. Sefer ha-Razim uses a number of Hebrew words that mean roughly "secret." I have translated each consistently with a single word. Following the precedent of Morgan, I translate the Hebrew word *raz* as "mystery." To be clear, by "mystery" I do not mean a mystical grasp of the intrinsically unknowable, as the term has been used in later Western esotericism. Rather, here it means secret knowledge that cannot be discovered through human effort and must be divinely revealed, but is not intrinsically unknowable by the human mind once revealed. The word *raz* is an ancient Persian word, but it was adopted into Hebrew in the book of Daniel and the Dead Sea Scrolls. This sense suits their usage of the word, as well as that of the *hekhalot* literature.

b. Paragraph 2; preceded by (§1): "In the name of YYY' God of Israel." G1; "The book of the mysteries." M2; "In the name of YYY' God of Israel I begin to write the book of Razi'el, the book of the mysteries" F; for N see the introduction.

c. "This is a book . . . mysteries" G1 M2 F N; omit G3; "This is the book of the mysteries" M7 TA. L opens with a paragraph summarizing the contents of the book.

d. "which was given to" G2 {M7} M2 P F N; "from the mouth of Razi'el the angel in the three hundredth year of the life of" G3; "which was revealed to Nuri'el from the mouth of Razi'el in the three hundredth year of the life of" M7; "which was revealed to" TA.

e. "Noah . . . Adam"; this genealogy suffers from numerous haplographies in the manuscripts.

f. "from the mouth of Razi'el the angel" omit G3 M7 TA.

g. "in the year"; "in the hour" P F N.

h. "And he wrote it"; "And you shall write it" G2 G3 M7 TA.

i. "he learned"; "you shall learn" G2 G3 M7 TA.

j. "to gaze at"; "to reckon with" M2 (gloss); "to turn in" P F N.

k. "make clear"; "inquire into" M2 P F.

l. "*the Pleiades*" or "*Draco*."

m. "to tell"; "to recognize" M2; "to know" G3 M7 TA.

The Book of the Mysteries (Sefer ha-Razim)

the names of the overseers of every single firmament and their kingdom[a] and how they can bring success to every matter, and what are the names of their attendants, and what is libated to them, and which is the proper time you[b] will be heard ¹⁰by them so as to do the whole will of anyone who draws near to them in purity;[c] (§10)to know from it[d] the working of death and the working of life, to understand the evil and the good, to search out seasons and moments, to know *the time to give birth and the time to die*, the time for hitting and the time for healing, to interpret dreams and visions, to stir up[e] battle and to quiet wars, and to rule over spirits and attack-demons,[f] to send them out so that they go like servants, to look at the four winds of the earth, to be made wise ¹⁵in the sound of thunder, to recount what is the working of lightning bolts, to tell what will be in every single new moon, to take up the business of every single year, whether for plenty or for famine, whether for produce or for dearth, whether for peace or for war, to become like one of the fearsome ones,[g] and to have insight into the heavens[h] on high.

(§11)From the wisdom of the mysteries of this book Noah learned and gained insight[i] to make gopher trees[j] into an ark, and to be put away secretly from the flood of the waters of the Deluge, to bring ²⁰with him (animals) two by two and seven by seven[k] and to collect[l] some of all food and of all edibles.[m] (§12)He put it in a box of gold[n] and he brought it first into the ark in order to know[o] from it the times of the day and to search out from it[p] the times of night and what is the proper time when he should stand to let fall a cry for help.[q] (§13)When he went out of the ark he kept on making use of it all the days of his life. At the time of his death he transmitted it to[r] Abraham, and Abraham to Isaac, and Isaac to Jacob, and Jacob to Levi, and Levi to Kohath, and Kohath to Amram and Amram ²⁵to Moses, and Moses to Joshua, and Joshua to the elders, and

Margin references: 1 Kgs 3:9; Qoh 3:2; Qoh 3:3; Job 38:35; Gen 6:14; Gen 6:19–7:3

a. "their kingdom"; "what is their work" M7 TA P F N.
b. "you"; or (with Morgan) "it" (i.e., prayer).
c. Paragraphs 4–9 appear only in L and are borrowed from version II (§§362–67). They recount the fall of Adam, his penitential prayer, and the coming of the angel Razi'el to him to reveal the contents of this book to him. N gives this material in Hebrew at §§15–20.
d. "to know from it"; "And you will understand ("penetrate" M7) the name from which it is to know" G3 M7; "to understand from it" TA.
e. "stir up"; "mix up" N.
f. "attack-demons"; "smiter-demons" G1 M2; "moments" P F.
g. "the fearsome ones"; "the seraphim" TA.
h. "into the heavens"; "into the songs" G1; "like the princes" TA; "into the princes" M2; "into the walls" or "into the chains" P F N; "into the treasuries" *Sefer Razi'el*.
i. "and gained insight"; omit G1 M2 P F N *Sefer Razi'el*.
j. "trees"; omit G1 M2 P F N.
k. "and seven by seven"; omit P F N.
l. "collect"; "prepare" M7.
m. "edibles"; + "from the knowledge of the wisdom of the mysteries of this book" M7.
n. "He put it in a box of gold" omit M7.
o. "in order to know"; "and he understood" TA.
p. "and to search out from it"; omit G3 TA; "and what are" M7; "and to remove from it" P F N.
q. "a cry for help"; "sleep" P F N.
r. "transmitted it to"; + "Shem (+ "his son" TA) and Shem transmitted it (omit "transmitted it" P) to" TA M2 P F N.

the elders to the prophets, and the prophets to the sages, and thus every single generation until King Solomon arose and the books of the mysteries[a] were revealed to him. He had great insight[b] into the books of understanding.[c] He ruled according to all his will over all the spirits and the attack-demons that roam[d] in the world and he bound and released, and sent out[e] and brought in, and built and was successful through the wisdom of this book. For many books were transmitted into his hand, but this one was found worthier and more honored and more difficult ³⁰than any of them. ⁽§¹⁴⁾Happy is the eye that looks into it! Happy is the ear that hearkens to[f] its wisdom! For in it are[g] the seven firmaments and all that is in them. From their camps it is learned to[h] have insight in everything and to succeed in every working, to reckon[i] and to do from the wisdom of this book.[j]

m. Avot 1.1

Wis 7:17, 20; Josephus, *A. J.* 8.44–49; Testament of Solomon; b. Giṭ. 68a–68b

The First Firmament

⁽§²⁸⁾¹The name of the first firmament is called "Heavens." In it are camps[k] full of wrath,[l] and seven thrones are ready there and upon them seven overseers[m] are enthroned. Encircling them are camps on each side and they listen to mortals in the hour that they carry out business, to everyone who learns to stand up[n] to pour libations[o] to their names and to invoke them by their letters[p] in the time (prayer) is heard,[q] so as to bring success. These seven overseers[r] rule ⁵the work of all these camps of angels so as to send them for every wish, to run and to succeed.[s]

PGM I. 171

a. "the books of the mysteries"; "mysteries of understanding" G3 M7 TA.
b. "and he had great insight into"; omit "great" G3 M7 TA; "and he greatly clarified in" G1.
c. "into the books of understanding"; "into the book of understanding" G3 M7; "into this book" TA.
d. "that roam"; "and the roamer-demons" M2 F N.
e. "and sent out"; "and had authority over" M2 P F N.
f. "hearkens to"; "has insight into" G1; "hears" M2 P F N.
g. "are"; "they clarify" G3; "are made fearsome" M7; "is the matter of" TA; "are made" M2 P F N.
h. "it is learned to" or "we shall learn to." "From their camps it is learned to"; "and the seven names of the seven ("the" M2 P N; "all the" F) overseers on high (+ "for them" G3)" G3 M7 TA M2 P F N.
i. "to reckon"; omit M2 F.
j. For §§15–20 (N only) see the relevant note to §3 above. N then gives Razi'el's continued description of the book, the transmission of the book from Adam to Solomon, and Solomon's use of it to dominate the demons (§§24–27).
k. "camps"; + "of angels" M7 TA P F N Sefer Razi'el.
l. "wrath" or "the sun."
m. "overseers"; "guardians" M7.
n. "who learns to stand up"; "who stands up (+ "upon them" P F) to learn" G3 M7 M2 P; "who stands up" (+ "upon them" N) TA N.
o. "to pour libations"; "at the business of" Sefer Razi'el.
p. "by their letters"; "by their signs" G1 G3 M2 P F N.
q. I follow Morgan's interpretation.
r. "overseers"; "guardians" M7.
s. Paragraph 29 is found only in L. It contains introductory comments about the seven overseers of the first firmament.

The Book of the Mysteries (Sefer ha-Razim)

The Seven Overseers of the First Firmament

(§30) These are the names of the seven[a] overseers who are enthroned on seven thrones. The name of the first is 'WRPNY'L; the name of the second is TYGRH; the name of the third is DNHL; the name of the fourth is KLMYY'; the name of the fifth is 'SYMWR; the name of the sixth is PSKR; the name of the seventh is BW'L. (§31) All of them were created [10]from fire and their appearances are like fire and their fire ignites, for they emerged from fire. And they[b] do not go out without permission to be busy with[c] the matter of a working until there goes out to them an utterance from the mouth of the seven overseers who are enthroned on thrones, who rule over them. For they are subservient to their will and by their permission they go about.[d] (§32) Every single one of them takes up his work[e] appointed to hasten[f] in everything (for) which they are sent, whether for good or for harm, whether for more or for less, whether [15]for war or for peace.[g] And all of them are called by name from the day[h] he was formed.

PGM IV. 972

The Seven Camps of Angels

(§33) And these are the names of the seven camps that attend to the seven overseers, for every single camp attends to one of the overseers.[i]

The Angels of the First Camp

(§36) These are the names of the angels of the first camp who attend 'WRPNYL: BWMDY DMN' 'NWK 'LPY 'MWK QṬYBY' PṬRWPY GMTY P"WR NRNTQ [20]RQHTY 'RWNH M'WT PRWKH 'QYL'H TRQWYH BRWQ SḤRWR' 'TNNY GYL'N TKT 'RNWB 'ŠMY YWṢṢ KPWN KRBY GYRŠWM PRY'N ŠŠM' 'BB' NTN'L 'R'L 'NYP TRW'WR 'BDY'L YWWN 'LWN MW'L LLP YḤSPT RḤGL RWM'PYYKTY 'RNY'L PWBWN KDY'L ZKRY'L 'GDLN MYG'L G'WPR KRTH KYLDH DYGL 'LNW TYRLY SBLH 'BY'L 'L KSYL SYQMH [25]ŠBH YWTNH R'LKH ḤLY'N 'PTY'L TY'MY'L 'L'L NTY'L 'PYKH TLGY'L N'NH 'STY'L.

(§37) These are the angels who obey in any matter in the first and the second[j] year of the enumeration of fifteen years of the reckoning of the kings of Greece.[k]

---

    a. "seven"; omit G3 TA M2 F.
    b. "they"—i.e., the subordinates of the seven overseers.
    c. "to be busy with"; "and not for any business of" P F.
    d. "to be busy ... they go about."; "for any matter until they receive permission from the mouth of God, exalted and lifted-up." TA. "they go about"; "they reign" G3; "they make you reign" M7; "they go with regard to any matter" P F.
    e. "his work"; "his reign" M7 L.
    f. "to hasten"; "to go" TA.
    g. Whether for more ... peace"; omit M2 (but glossed) P F N L.
    h. "by name from the day"; "by name. On high" M7.
    i. Paragraphs 34–35 are an addition found only in a gloss to M2 and in Sefer Razi'el. They reproduce material from §§38–39.
    j. "second"; "sixth" M7.
    k. Margalioth (24–25) notes that this is a reference to Roman indictions, periodic property tax assessments that were also used to date events. They originated in Roman Egypt in 287 CE on a five-yearly basis. A fifteen-year cycle began either in 297 CE or 312 CE. This passage must

The Book of the Mysteries (Sefer ha-Razim)

A rite of healing

(§38) If you seek to accomplish a matter of healing,[a] stand during the first or second hour in the night and take in your hand myrrh and frankincense. ³⁰It is placed on glowing coals of[b] fire for the name of the angel who rules over the first camp, who is called 'WRPNY'L. And recite[c] there seven times the seventy-two[d] angels who attend before him, and recite this:

PGM IV. 2460–2462; XIII 352–354

> (§39) I so-and-so son of so-and-so[e] seek from before you that you cause a successful healing by my hand for so-and-so son of so-and-so.

And anyone you seek shall be healed, whether in writing or by request.[f] And purify yourself from every impurity and cleanse your flesh[g] from all lust, and then you will succeed.

The Angels of the Second Camp

(§40)³⁵These are the names of the angels of the second camp who attend TYGRH: 'KSTR MRSWM BRKYB KMŠW 'ŠṬYB KRYT'L 'DYR GB' 'QRB' 'NBWR KBYR TYLH BRYTWR TRṬM NṬPY'L PRY'L TRWḤWN ŠLHBYN 'ŠLB' MŠTWB GRḤT' ḤGR' 'YṬMY'L ḤGL LGḤ MNYTY'L TNYMY'L 'YKRYT 'BRYT' RKYL'L ḤŠTK PPTŠ 'ŠTYRWP 'WDY'L 'ŠBYR ⁴⁰MLKY'L 'RWŠ DŠWW' HMK TRGH ZMBWT ḤṢNYPLPT ŠWW' 'ŠPWR 'RQ QNWMY'L NHY'L GDY'L 'DQ YMWMY'L PRWG DḤGY'L DGRY'L 'GRY'L 'RWNWR DWNRNY' DLKT TBL TLY'L 'LY'L MWT'R 'LPY'L PYTPR' LPWM 'WR ṬMR 'DLY'L 'SṬWRYN 'ZWTY 'YSṬWRṬY D'WBYT BRGMY DMWMY'L DYGR' 'BYB'L PRWṬY'L QWMY'L DGWGR' DLGY'L ⁴⁵PDWTY'L.

(§41)[h]These are the angels who are full of anger and wrath. And they are appointed over every matter of[i] battle and war. And they are ready to press hard[j] a man who is delivered to them. And there is no mercy in them, but rather (their nature is)[k] to take vengeance on and to punish whoever is delivered into their hand.[l]

---

have been written after the fifteen-year tax cycle had been established and had begun to be used as a dating method, i.e., no earlier than the mid-fourth century.

a. "to accomplish a matter of healing"; "for a healing" M2 P F.
b. "glowing coals of"; omit M2 P F.
c. "recite"; "invoke" TA M2 P F.
d. "seventy-two"; "seventy" M7 TA M2 JA.
e. "so-and-so son of so-and-so"; omit M2 P F N.
f. "whether in writing or by request"; "and if you seek to do so ("this" N)" M2 F N.
g. "and cleanse your flesh"; "and cleanse yourself" M7; "and cleanse yourself and remove yourself" M2 P F. TA omits "and cleanse . . . all lust."
h. Paragraphs 41–47 have a parallel in an Aramaic magic bowl. See Rebiger and Schäfer, *Sefer ha-Razim* 2:207.
i. "every matter of"; omit M2 P F JA.
j. "to press hard"; Margalioth adds "and to afflict to death." He takes this phrase from a very corrupt context in G10.
k. "but rather (their nature is)"; "(they are) hurrying" TA.
l. "to take vengeance on and to punish whoever is delivered into their hand"; perhaps instead read "and to afflict to death" here with G10.

203

The Book of the Mysteries (Sefer ha-Razim)

A rite to harm enemies

^(§42)And if you seek to send them against your enemy or against your creditor, or to overturn a ship[a] or to fell a fortified[b] wall or ⁵⁰to destroy and to harm any business of your enemies, whether you want to exile him or to fell him in bed or to dim[c] the illumination of his eyes or to bind his feet or to press him hard in every matter, ^(§43)take in your hand water from seven springs on the seventh of the month in the seventh hour in the day in seven earthenware jugs[d] that have not entered[e] into the light. And do not mix them together[f] with one another, but place them under the stars for seven nights. And on the seventh night ⁵⁵take for yourself saucers[g] of glass[h] for the name of your enemies and pour the water inside each and break the earthenware vessels and throw (them) to the four winds of heaven[i] and you shall recite this, facing the four winds:

PGM I. 234–236

PGM IV. 222, 3210

^(§44)HHGRYT, you who encamp in the east wind; ŠRWKYT, you who encamp in the north wind; 'WPLH,[j] you who encamp in the west wind; KRDY, you who encamp in the south wind, receive from my hand[k] at this time what I cast to you with regard to the name of so-and-so son of so-and-so, to break ⁶⁰his bones and to crush all his limbs and to break the majesty of his power like the breaking of[l] these earthenware jugs.[m] And let there be no healing for them, just as there is no healing for these earthenware jugs.[n]

And take the saucers of water[o] and invoke over each the names of these angels and the name of the overseer, TYGRH, and recite this:

^(§45)I deliver to you, angels of anger and wrath, so-and-so son of so-and-so so that you may strangle him and destroy him and his appearance, and fell him in bed, ⁶⁵and deprive him of his wealth, and cancel the thoughts of his heart, blow away his desire and his knowledge, and let him be ever more lacking until he reaches the point of death.[p]

a. "a ship"; + "into the heart of the sea" TA M2 P F.
b. "fortified'" "besieged" M7.
c. "dim"; "extinguish" M7; "hit" TA M2 F.
d. "jugs"; "vessels" M7 M2 P F N.
e. "have not entered into"; "were not made in" M7 TA M2 P F N.
f. "together"; omit M7 TA M2 P F N.
g. "saucers"; "a flagon" TA. The word translated "saucer" is a Greek word transliterated into Hebrew letters. Its basic meaning is a wide, flat bowl or vessel.
h. "glass"; "new glass" JA L.
i. "heaven"; "the world" M7 TA M2 P F N L.
j. 'WPLH; reading with the manuscripts rather than with Margalioth's 'WLPH.
k. "from my hand"; "my myrrh" M7; omit P F.
l. "like the breaking of"; "like" M7 TA M2 P F N.
m. "jugs"; "vessels" M7.
n. "And let there be … earthenware jugs"; omit G4 M7 M2 P F N.
o. "And take the saucers of water"; "And before you break them, take the vessels and the saucers" M7; "And take the flagon of water" TA; "and the complete saucer." P F.
p. Apart from G10, §45 is very poorly preserved in the manuscripts, with numerous haplographies. L translates a text close to that of G10. G10 (but not L) also contains the following

204

The Book of the Mysteries (Sefer ha-Razim)

(§46) And if you seek to exile him, recite this:

That you exile him and you ba[nish] him[a] from his children and his house [so that] nothing [re]mains to him.[b]

(§47) If he is your creditor, recite this:

That you shut his mouth[c] and you abolish his counsel and that he shall not come upon me[d] in his thought, and he shall not bring me within the words of his mouth,[e] and that I may pass in front of him and he shall not see me with his eyes.[f]

(§48) If it is concerning a ship, [70]recite this:

I adjure you, angels of anger and destruction, that you take your stand against the ship of the man so-and-so son of so-and-so and you do not allow him to go on a voyage from a single place,[g] and that there not come[h] to it a leading wind, and that you bring him to the sea[i] and you shake[j] him in its midst, and there not escape from it human being or cargo.[k]

(§49) If it is to fell a *fortified*[l] wall, recite this:

Isa 2:15

I adjure you, angels of perturbation and anger and wrath,[m] that you come in the vigor of your might [75]and you fell the wall of so-and-so son of so-and-so, and you strike it to the dust, and that it be overthrown *like the overthrow of Sodom and Gomorrah*,[n] and that you allow no one to place

Deut 29:23; Jer 49:18; cf. Jer 50:40; Amos 4:11

---

badly damaged text immediately following, some of which may be original: "And take . . . water and p[ou]r it on his door and break the sa[ucer]. . . ." There is also this marginal reading: "Another (reading). And if you seek to expel your enemy from this world in a hurry or to the underworld, write . . . the names on a clay vessel. . . ."

a. "and you ba[nish] him" G10; "and you drive him" M7; "and you expel him" TA M2 P F N; omit JA.
b. "[so that] nothing [re]mains to him" G10 only.
c. "his mouth"; "his eyes" M7; "his eyes and his mouth" M2 L.
d. "he shall not come upon me"; "I shall not come up" M7 TA P F N.
e. "and that he shall not bring me within the words of his mouth,"; omit M7 TA M2 P F N.
f. "with his eyes"; "and there shall come out of his mouth my good ("good things" M2)" TA P F N M2.
g. "from a single place"; omit M7 TA JA.
h. "come"; "go out" {M7} TA M2; M7 glosses "give."
i. "the sea"; "the heart of the sea" M7 TA N JA.
j. "shake"; "rebuke" M7 TA M2; "stir" TA.
k. "human being or cargo"; "anything" M2 L.
l. "*fortified*"; omit M7 TA M2.
m. "and anger and wrath"; omit M7 TA JA.
n. "*like the overthrow of Sodom and Gomorrah*"; + "and it shall smash(?) the cities of Gomorrah" M7; "as the fortresses of Sodom were overthrown, and let it be uprooted as the hills of Gomorrah were uprooted" JA. On the reading of M7, see Rebiger and Schäfer, *Sefer ha-Razim* 2:134 n. 76.

The Book of the Mysteries (Sefer ha-Razim)

stone upon stone in erecting it.[a] And if it is built in the day, let it be overthrown at night.

And pour it on the four corners of the house.[b]

(§50) If it is to fell[c] your opponent on (his) bed[d] or to destroy his appearance, or for any act of trouble, pour[e] the water[f] on his door.

(§51) If it is to exile him, pour[g] the water to the four winds of the world.

(§52) If it is 80to bind your creditor, throw the water[h] on his clothes.

(§53) If it is to sink a ship,[i] throw the glass[j] and its water, in the name of the ship and in the name of its owners,[k] into the midst of the ship.[l]

(§54) If it is to overthrow[m] a wall, dig at the four corners[n] of the wall and divide up the water into them. And do so in every single matter in purity and then you will succeed.[o]

The Angels of the Third Camp

(§56) These are the names of the angels who attend DNHL in the third camp: 85'WGRBBW 'WBŠ'L BRTWBY'L KLWBY'L RḤBY'L 'WHY'L KRBTWN KRB' D'YNWṬ 'YNYK 'BYRM 'TGL' 'WTWT 'ŠTNW'L 'ŠPR TGRY'L 'MYK'L 'TDŠW 'WRY'L 'RMWD 'STWN 'K'L 'N'WR 'SKYR' LBY'L 'LŠH ḤSNY'L LMWŠY 'DWT TYRWM 'LPY 'YMYK 'RGL' MYG'L 'LY'L MDNY'L.

(§57) 90'These are the angels who inform anyone who gains strength over[p] them in purity (about) what will come about on the earth in every single year, whether for plenty or for famine, whether rains shall multiply or be scarce, and whether there shall be a dearth, and whether there shall be produce, and whether locusts shall come,[q] and whether there shall be rivalry among the kings, and whether a sword shall come between the great ones of the kingdom, and whether death or tribulations shall fall[r] among mortals.[s]

---

a. "in erecting it"; "in its place" M7 F.
b. "And pour . . . the four corners of the house"; omit M7 JA; "And pour . . . the four angles of the wall" TA; "And pour . . . the winds of {the inside of} the house" M2.
c. "to fell"; "to alter" M7 TA.
d. "on (his) bed"; "or to fell him on (his) bed" M7 M2; "or to fell him with sickness" TA.
e. "pour"; "overturn" M7.
f. "the water"; "some of it" M7 G22; "some of the water" TA; "it" JA.
g. "pour"; "throw" M7 M2.
h. "the water"; "some of it" M2.
i. "a ship" + "in the heart of the sea" TA.
j. "the glass"; "the flagon" TA; "the saucer" M7; "the saucer of glass" M2.
k. "owners"; "owner" M7 M2.
l. "the ship"; "the sea" M7 JA; "the waters" TA.
m. "overthrow"; "fell" M7.
n. "corners"; "angles" M7 M2.
o. Paragraph 55 is found only in L. It gives instructions for additional malefic uses of the enchanted water.
p. "anyone who gains strength over them"; "all who busy themselves with them" M7.
q. "shall come," + "and whether the olive shall fall" M2 M7 JA L.
r. "and whether death or tribulations shall fall among mortals"; "and whether death shall fall among mortals or tribulation shall be sent among them" M7.
s. "and whether there shall be a dearth . . . among mortals"; "and concerning the fruit of

A rite to give foreknowledge

(§58)If you seek to know and to understand[a] what will happen ⁹⁵in every single year, take a hieratic document and write in hieratic and write with myrrh-ink every single word by itself. (§59)Take a new flask and put into it spikenard-oil[b] and throw all the written words inside it and stand facing the sun in the time that it goes out of its bridal chamber and recite:

> (§60)I adjure you, O Sun the illuminator of the earth,[c] in the name of the angels who give understanding and comprehension[d] of wise and closed-off things to men of ¹⁰⁰knowledge, that you carry out my request and you make known to me what will happen this year, and *do not hide from me anything.*

(§61)You shall adjure the adjuration for three days, three times, and on the third time you shall look at the oil.[e] See everything that floats on the surface of the oil: it is what shall be done[f] in that year. (§62)If two things float up, two shall happen; and if three things float up, three shall happen. And afterward you shall take the oil[g] and kindle it in the name of the angels ¹⁰⁵who attend to this camp. And as for all the rest of the texts, one should hide them in a wall or in a window. And so you shall do everything in purity and you shall succeed.

PGM II. 30, 60–61
PGM I. 278

Ps 19:5; Sh-R §208; *PGM* II. 78–80; III. 325; IV. 260–261; V. 237; VI. 4–5
Sh-R §§168, 213–14

Jer 38:14

The Angels of the Fourth Camp

(§63)These are the names of the angels who attend KLMYYH in the fourth camp: 'BRYH 'YMRHY DMN'Y 'MNHR Y'MNWK PṬKY' ṬWBY'L GWLY'L 'WPRY GMTY 'WRNY'L PRYKYHW Y'RN LṬMY'L 'WRYṬ TYMWGW 'NMRY 'LMYNY'L ¹¹⁰YKMṬW ṢṬRṬW ŠB'QNY BWRTY'S RSPWT KRSWN 'M'P WP'ṬN' 'Ḥ'L S'BY'L BLQYR PKHWR HSTR STRY'L 'LYSS ḤLSY'L ṬRSPW QRSṬWS MLKY'L 'RDQ ḤSDY'L 'ḤSP 'MY'L PRNWS GDY'L SBYB'L.

(§64)These are the angels who redirect[h] the mind of the king and the good-will of the great and the chiefs and ¹¹⁵the leaders[i] of the kingdom, and they direct and garland grace and benevolence with all who take it upon themselves to ask something from them in purity. You shall act forcefully and you will succeed.[j]

---

oaks, and concerning all produce and peace and quarrel, and concerning death and illness and life and healing" TA.
    a. "and to understand"; omit M7 M2 P N L.
    b. "spikenard oil"; "oil of olive-treaders" M7; "good spikenard oil" M2; "oil of rose" N var. L. Cf. the relevant note to §148 below.
    c. "the earth"; "the whole world ("[world]" G11) G11 M7 TA Sefer Razi'el.
    d. "and comprehension"; omit M7 TA M2 N.
    e. "at the oil"; + "—whether the oil blossoms" G11 (cf. N); + "and when the oil clears" JA.
    f. "shall be done"; "shall happen" M7 TA.
    g. "the oil"; + "in a lamp" G11 JA.
    h. "redirect"; "make to flee" M7.
    i. "and the chiefs, and the leaders"; "and the chiefs [and jud]ges" G11; "and the officials and judges" M7; "and the officials" TA.
    j. Paragraphs 65–73 are missing in M7.

The Book of the Mysteries (Sefer ha-Razim)

A rite to gain influence over others

^(§65)If you seek to bend[a] the mind of the king to your will or the captain of the army or a rich man[b] or an authority or a judge of a city[c] or all the inhabitants of the region, or the heart of a great or a rich woman, or the heart of a woman in her beauty,[d] take a lion cub[e] and slaughter it with a butcher knife of bronze and gather its blood[f] ¹²⁰and tear out its heart and put its blood inside it[g] and write the names of these angels in blood on the skin that is on its forehead and blot it out with old wine—three years old—and mix (it) with the blood. ^(§66)Take three of the *choice spices*—storax, myrrh, and a chain of musk[h]—and stand before[i] the planet[j] Venus, clean and pure, and put[k] the spices on the fire and take into your hand the cup in which are the blood and the wine and recite and invoke the name of the overseer and the names of the angels of his camp ¹²⁵twenty-one[l] times over the blood and over the wine. You shall recite in the presence of the planet Venus, the name of which is Aphrodite, three hundred (times)[m] and the angel ḤSDY'L,

PGM III. 425

PGM I. 10
Cant 4:14
PGM IV. 2460–2461;
XIII. 352–354

PGM IV. 2891

^(§67)I adjure you in the name of[n] the angels of the fourth camp who attend on KLMY' that you turn around to me king so-and-so and the heart of his army and the heart of[o] his attendants into my hand—I am so-and-so son of so-and-so—that I find grace and benevolence before him, and that he do my will and my request in every hour that I ask him.

^(§68)When you finish speaking the adjuration ¹³⁰twenty-one[p] times, look above and you will[q] see something like a glowing coal of fire descend into the blood and the wine.[r]

a. "seek to bend"; "want in purity to turn around" P F.
b. "rich man"; + "of a place" M2 F N; + "who is in a city" JA.
c. "of a city"; omit M2 P F N JA.
d. The text of the rest of §65 and of §§66–73 is missing in M7 (as above) M2 P F and displaced to §§77–85 in N (although I have collated N here with the other manuscripts). The text of TA is very corrupt. Paragraph 65 is well preserved only in G5, G11 (in damaged form), and JA. It also survives complete in L, but in a much-expanded form.
e. The translator of L seems not to have understood the Hebrew word for "cub." The Latin manuscripts offer "fetter," "leopard," and "white goat kid" as attempts at a translation.
f. "its blood"; + "in a silver bowl" G11 JA; + "in a vessel of gold" TA; + "in a new glass dish" L.
g. "inside it"; conceivably either the heart, the bowl, or the cup mentioned in §66.
h. "and a chain of musk"; "balsam, myrrh, and cinnamon" TA.
i. "before"; "beneath" TA.
j. "the planet"; literally, "the star." Likewise later in this paragraph.
k. "put"; "burn" TA.
l. "twenty-one"; "one and two" G5; "twelve" L.
m. This number "three hundred (times)" is omitted by TA JA N L and is found, written as a single Hebrew letter, only in G5. Perhaps, with Morgan, it should be deleted as a copyist's error. For other possibilities, see Rebiger and Schäfer, *Sefer ha-Razim* 2:217.
n. "in the name of"; + "the Creator of the world and in the name of" TA.
o. "his army and the heart of"; "his great ones and" TA.
p. "twenty-one"; "twelve" L.
q. "you will"; "if you" TA.
r. "the blood and the wine"; "the cup of wine and the blood, then it has done your will." TA (cf. L).

(§69) If you seek to come into the presence of the king or to any man or judge,[a] wash yourself[b] in running water and take some of the blood and some of the wine and spread it over your flesh and put the heart of the lion on your heart. (§70) If it is to turn around[c] the inhabitants of the region, take the heart of [135]the lion and conceal it within the region[d] and write on foil[e] the overseer and his camp and you shall recite this:

> (§71)[f] You angels who go around and roam about in the world,[g] turn around all the inhabitants of this region, great and small, old and young, poor and honored, and let fear of me and awe of me be upon them like the awe of the lion[h] over all the beasts.[i] Just as this heart is concealed[j] but I am speaking, so let all of them listen to me [140]and be unable to speak against me, all of the children of Adam and Eve.[k]   Job 1:7

(§73) And conceal[l] the heart in the center of the city and hide your face.[m] After three days let yourself be seen in the region. Put under the soles of your feet[n] some of the blood of the lion.

(§74) If you seek to bind the heart of a great or rich woman[o] to you, take some of the sweat of your face[p] in a new glass vessel and write[q] upon a tin

---

a. "to any man or judge"; "to an official" TA; "to the commander of the army or to a rich man in the city or to a ruler or to a judge" JA.

b. "wash yourself"; "immerse yourself" TA.

c. "it is to turn around"; "you seek to cause to do good to you all" TA.

d. "take the heart . . . region"; omit TA.

e. "on foil"; "on gold foil the name of" TA; omit N; "on silver foil the name of" JA. The word translated "foil" refers to a thin metal plate. The Hebrew word is used for the gold plate on the front of the high priest's turban, on which was inscribed "Holy to YHWH" (Exod 28:36–38; 39:30–31). Cf. the Phylactery of Moses, v. 3, in this volume.

f. Paragraphs 71 and 73 are largely reconstructed from JA, with attention to N, the much-expanded text of L, and the very fragmentary text of G5.

g. "who go around and roam about in the world,"; "who turn around the hearts of mortals" TA.

h. "the lion"; "a human being" TA.

i. "the beasts"; + "and like the awe of the eagle over all the birds" TA.

j. "concealed"; Margalioth retroverts a Hebrew word meaning "mute" here, possibly based on L. This fits the context well, but is speculative. In JA the Arabic word translates a Hebrew word meaning "conceal" in §62. The same Arabic word is used here and I retrovert and translate accordingly.

k. "Just as . . . Adam and Eve." omit TA. Here L adds §72, a paragraph added to the adjuration to bring in the goat-kid mentioned by the Latin of §65.

l. "conceal"; + "the foil and" TA JA L.

m. "and hide your face"; "and go and do not be seen in the region for three days" TA; omit JA. Margalioth reads "and hide your face for three days," based on N (cf. TA) and a lacuna in G5. The lacuna, however, is too small to accommodate the whole phrase. I reconstruct accordingly.

n. "your feet"; "your two heels" TA.

o. "to bind the heart of a great or a rich woman"; "to bring in a woman (who is) rich, great, and of distinguished birth and beautifully adorned" M7.

p. "the sweat of your face"; "the dripping of your nose" M7 M2 P F N; "the sweat that flows from your nose and your face" L. The same Hebrew word is translated as "sweat" or "dripping" according to context.

q. "and write" with M7 and TA; + "upon it" JA (with Margalioth); + "upon it and write" G5. The other manuscripts are corrupt and lack the relevant phrase entirely.

The Book of the Mysteries (Sefer ha-Razim)

PGM IV. 1255   *lamella*[a], the name of the overseer [145]and the names of the angels, and throw (it) inside it, and recite this over the sweat of your face:[b]

(§75)"I adjure you,[c] angels of grace[d] and angels of knowledge, that you overturn the heart of so-and-so daughter of so-and-so[e] so that she will do nothing apart from me.[f] And let her heart be with my heart as to love."[g] (§76)And take a new[h] bottle and hide it in a place where she comes in and goes out. "Just as a woman[i] returns to the babies of her womb, so shall this one, so-and-so, return to me, for love of me, from this day [150]and forever."[j] And do this[k] at the full moon.[l]

The Angels of the Fifth Camp[m]

(§89)These are the names of the angels who attend 'SYMWR in the fifth camp: BTW'R ŠKYNTTK 'DWM' TQW MQP' LHB' 'LY 'ZY ŠKNY'L KNWR BNŠ QRB' SRK ḤLŠY'L HRMN' 'BR HWD MLKYH PR'TWP 'D'T QWP MNMLK DYNMWR 'LPNṬWS DYDRYWK KLNH NYNḤY' DṢNḤY' MLGDM [155]DYMHN LYBRNK TTQHH 'PNY'L ZBYṬWR DKNSWR RMGDL LHTQWP 'LY GDGDL PRWṢ MSRWṢ KDYR MWS DYQN' NŠR TWB DRWMY'L DYR'Z DMWL' DYDY'L Ṭ'Y KRM 'TR 'QB HWNMWR' 'NQYW GZRY'L ṢBY'L ṢBYWD' YYQR 'DWT RGBY'L.

(§90)These are the angels who obey at night for speaking with the moon and with
1 Chr 10:13   the stars, [160]and *for consulting with a ghost*, and for speaking with the spirits.[n]

    a. "a tin *lamella*"; "a bronze leaf" L.
    b. "the sweat of your face"; "the dripping of your nose" M7 M2 P F N; "this sweat" L. Cf. the relevant note to §74 above.
    c. "I adjure you,"; "I adjure you, KLMY' the overseer, and I adjure you," M7.
    d. "grace"; "grace and charm" M7; "charm" M2 P F N. For the translation "charm," see the relevant note to §90.
    e. "so-and-so"; + "to love me" M7; + "to love me and to do what I want" P F N.
    f. "nothing apart from me"; "the word of so-and-so except by my hand and by my mouth" P F N.
    g. "as to love"; omit G5; "as to my love" M7 M2 JA.
    h. "new"; "glass" JA; "this glass" L.
    i. "a woman"; "she" P F N.
    j. The second sentence of §76 is missing in G5. This sentence appears as the first in M7 with some variants. The two sentences also appear in the latter order in TA, but the entire paragraph is in a substantially different form from the other manuscripts: "'And let my beloved be bound in her heart like the woman who loves the fruit of her womb, so let my love enter into her heart.' And you shall place the sweat in the *lamella* and you shall conceal it in a place where she goes out and comes in. Thus shall you do according to the working of the moon, in purity, and you shall succeed."
    k. "And do this" M7 JA; "And do it" TA M2 P F. Margalioth reads "and let this be written," which he reports to be the reading of Sefer Razi'el and Sefer Malbush. It is not found in any of the sources available to me.
    l. Manuscript N adds §§77–88 at this point. Paragraphs 77–83, 85–88 have a loose connection with the text of §§65–71, 73–76, and §84 seems to be inspired by the Latin of §72.
    m. The passage on the fifth camp, §§89–101, is missing in M7. The scribe comments: "This is the fifth camp. And I did not find the angels written. And I have not written anything but this, because I did not find any more."
    n. "and for *consulting* . . . spirits"; "concerning the business of love (and) alluring charm"

A rite for divination and necromancy

(§91)If you seek to speak with the moon and[a] with the stars concerning any kind of business,[b] take a white rooster and fine flour and slaughter the rooster[c] in running water.[d] (§92)And knead the fine flour[e] with blood and water and make[f] three[g] cakes and put them in the sun.[h] And write on them in blood[i] the name of the fifth camp and the name of the overseer and put the three of them on a table of myrtle wood[j] and recite facing the moon or facing the stars.[k] [165]Recite:

PGM IV. 35–45, 2190

> (§93)I adjure you that you bring near the astrological sign of so-and-so and his star to the star of so-and-so and his astrological sign for his love to be bound in the heart of so-and-so son[l] of so-and-so.

Sh-R §128

And recite:

Put some of your fire into this (man) so-and-so or this (woman) so-and-so, so that she leaves the house of her father and her mother for the love of this so-and-so son of (the woman) so-and-so.[m]

(§94)Take two of the cakes and put them with the rooster in a new bottle and seal its mouth with wax[n] and conceal the bottle in a place where the sun is not on it.

PGM VII. 915

(§95)If [170]it is for alluring charm,[o] take the remaining cake and crumble[p] it and put it inside old wine in a cup of glass and recite the names of the angels before the moon and the stars and recite this:

TA; + or "concerning the business of allure" M2 F. For the biblical and rabbinic background to "consulting a ghost," see Rebiger and Schäfer, *Sefer ha-Razim* 2:223–24. The terms translated "alluring charm" in the variant normally have the religious sense of "charity of benevolence." But in the context of love magic, they take on a sense of romantic attraction. For discussion, see Rebiger and Schäfer, *Sefer ha-Razim* 2:140 n. 124.

a. "with the moon and"; omit P F.
b. "concerning any kind of business"; omit TA M2 P F N.
c. "the rooster"; omit M2 P F; "it" N.
d. "in running water"; "in water" M2 P F; "within a vessel full of water" N; "in that vessel in which is water" L.
e. "fine flour"; "flour" TA M2 JA.
f. "And knead . . . make"; "And take the blood mixed with the water and knead the specified(? P) ("above-mentioned" F) flour and make from it" P F.
g. "three"; omit G5.
h. "in the sun"; "in oil" G5.
i. "in blood"; "with ink" JA.
j. "myrtle wood"; "new wood" TA; "wood" JA; L appears to combine both longer readings.
k. "the stars"; "Venus" TA.
l. "son"; "daughter" N.
m. "for his love . . . son of (the woman) so-and-so." P; "and she shall not eat and she shall not drink and she shall not sleep and she shall not rest until she does the will of so-and-so son of so-and so." TA JA. The manuscript tradition shows confusion on whether this spell involves male-to-female or male-to-male love. See Rebiger and Schäfer, *Sefer ha-Razim* 2:141 n. 130 and p. 222.
n. "wax"; "white wax" TA M2 JA L.
o. "charm"; "pious ones" TA M2 N and Margalioth. But cf. the relevant note to §90 above.
p. "crumble" (retroverted by Margalioth from JA; cf. §97); "crush" TA; "write" M2 F.

The Book of the Mysteries (Sefer ha-Razim)

(§96) I adjure you that you grant[a] grace and charm and mercies upon so-and-so out of the splendor, grace, charm, and mercies of your faces. I am so-and-so son of so-and-so, and let me find grace and charm and mercies and glory in the eyes of every person.[b]

(§97) And blow into the wind[c] and wash your face every sunrise for nine[d] days with the wine and with the cake crumbled[e] into it.

1 Chr 10:13

(§98) And if you want *to consult with a ghost*, stand facing[f] a grave and invoke the names of the angels of the fifth camp. And let there be in your hand oil and honey mixed together in a new glass saucer[g] and recite this:

(§99) I adjure you, spirit, the ram-bearer,[h] who encamps among the graves upon the bones of the dead, that you receive this offering from my hand and you do my will and you bring to me, to so-and-so, one who is dead, and that you make him stand and let him speak with me without dread.

PGM IV. 1033

And let him tell me true words, suppressing nothing, and let me not be in dread of him. And let him tell me my request that I require from him.[i]

(§100) And he should stand (there) at once. But if not, adjure again another time up to three times. And when he emerges, set before him the saucer[j] and afterward speak your words, and let there be in your hand a wand of myrtle.

PGM I. 72–73

(§101) And if you seek to release him, strike him three times[k] with the myrtle and pour out the oil and the honey and break the cup and throw the myrtle from your hand. And return home by a different path.[l]

(§102) And if you want to speak with the spirits, go out to the place of the killed[m] and call on the name of 'WBNYT RWNNYT:

PGM IV. 2207–2208; V. 332–333

a. "grant"; "pour" TA.
b. "every person" ("person" can also be understood as the name "Adam"); "every person and animal" M7; "all children of Adam and Eve" TA; "every Adam and Eve" (*sic*) N.
c. "And blow into the wind"; omit TA M2 JA L.
d. "nine"; "seven" TA JA; omit M2.
e. "crumbled" F JA; "crushed" TA P; "shaken" M2.
f. "facing"; "in the south of" M7.
g. "glass saucer"; "jug" TA; "glass ampoule (?)" F.
h. "the ram-bearer"; the word is Greek transliterated into Hebrew letters. It is a title of the Greek god Hermes, whose role included escorting the spirits of the dead to the underworld. M2 P F (cf. N) read "the spirit of the grave" followed by a nonsense-word *nomen barbarum*.
i. "suppressing nothing ... from him"; omit TA M2.
j. "saucer"; "jug" TA.
k. Reading "times" with TA rather than "wands" with Margalioth.
l. Paragraph 101 in Margalioth's edition is largely reconstructed from JA and sources not available to me. It is missing in M2 P F N, but the context surely requires something like it in this place. The Hebrew text of TA is somewhat different: "If you seek to release him, hit him three times and pour some of the oil and the honey on him and break the glass there. And you shall bring the myrtle stick in your hand and go by another way and throw it from your hands. And afterward you may enter your house."
m. "go out to the place of the killed"; omit M7 TA. The term "killed" is ambiguous. It could mean "murdered" or "executed" or it could be a dangerous place in which people died by accident. See Morgan, 39 n. 65; and Rebiger and Schäfer, *Sefer ha-Razim* 2:226.

212

The Book of the Mysteries (Sefer ha-Razim)

I adjure you[a] in the name of the angels who attend in the fifth camp and in the name of the overseer who is over them, whose name is 'SYMWR, that you hear me at this time and you send [190]me the spirit of ḤGRGYRWT,[b] and that it go according to my will wherever I send it and that it be obedient to me in everything until such-and-such a time.[c]

If you see a pillar[d] of smoke before you, speak your words and send (it) for every wish that you want.[e]

Sh-R §§111–12, 238

The Angels of the Sixth Camp

(§103)These are the names of the angels who attend in the sixth camp on PSKR: 'ZY'L 'RBY'L ṬRYPWN PWKBWS PSTMR LYNNY'L QRWNYDN ŠWKDWN [195]SLBYDM 'MY'L 'WZY'L PNY'L TRMY'L ḤMMY'L ṢRMY'L NYMMWS NWDNYY' B'RYB' ZWNNWN ḤSṬW'L SDRY'L HWPNY'WN QDMY'L KPNYY' 'RMY'L 'DMWN HRMWR ṢPLY'L SPRY'L QḤNY'L ŠBKYRY' 'RMWNYS ṬWPWMWS PṢṢY'L ḤṬPY'L PRSWMWN NḤLY'L.

(§104)These are the angels of might who are girded with vigor and valor[f] to run from place to place [200]and to fly into all the corners of the world to bring to a man one who flees[g]—a slave who has fled[h] or a thief who has fled.

A rite for apprehending fugitives

(§105)Take four bronze *lamellae* and write on every single one of them the name of the man and the name of his mother and the name of the overseer PSKR and the name of the angels who attend on him and recite:

> (§106)I deliver (him) over to you, angels of might, so that you shall seize so-and-so son of so-and-so in any place that he goes and in any place that he stays,[i] whether in a city or in a region,[j] whether [205]on the sea or on the dry land, whether at food or at drink, and that you make him fly like the

---

a. The "you" in this paragraph is the single spirit being addressed, reading with JA and M7. The other manuscripts have some confusion as to whether the adjuration addresses one or multiple spirits.

b. Morgan suggests that the name ḤGRGYRWT means "Hagar the proselyte" (cf. Gen 6). But this meaning has no obvious significance in this context.

c. "until such and such a time"; "for a year or two years" M7 JA; "in one year or two years" TA.

d. "a pillar"; "something like a pillar" M7.

e. "that you want."; + "And thus do everything in purity and you shall succeed." M7 TA JA (cf. N).

f. "vigor and valor"; "an arm" (i.e., strength) M2 P F N.

g. "to a man one who flees"; "a fleeing man" M7; "a man" TA.

h. "a slave who has fled"; + "or a debtor who has fled" M7.

i. G29 preserves a fragment of a Judeo-Arabic translation that is independent of the Judeo-Arabic translation in the other manuscripts. It begins at this point and reads as follows, giving a somewhat different version of §106: ". . . either in one of the villages or one of the cities or in part of the sea or in part of the dry land or he was seated eating or if seated drinking. And trouble his life and damage his livelihood like the unrest of . . . his son and make him homeless and do not overlook him in . . . not with . . . in . . . face compulsion, robbery . . . and his front if it was in a town or in a city." I am not sure of the translation of the last part of this fragment.

j. "or in a region"; "or outside" M2 P F N.

The Book of the Mysteries (Sefer ha-Razim)

flying bird, and you bring him against his will and that you not let him delay[a] one moment,[b] either in the day or at night.

And take (the) four bronze *lamellae*[c] and conceal them in the four winds of the world, whether in a city or in a region.

The Angels of the Seventh Camp

(§107)These are the angels who attend in the seventh camp on BW'L: [210]NWHRY'L DBB'L DYMTMR DB'L MḤŠYN "WR DY'N BBYT'L SRWR' 'HGYYH PRWPY'L MKSY'L 'LZY'L TKWRKS QRWMY'L RMY'L LḤSWN SLḤY'L 'ḤY'L 'KR 'WBR SRWGY'L YDW'L ŠMŠY'L ŠPṬY'L RḤBY' 'HMWD' MRMRYN 'NWK 'LPRṬ 'WMYGR' QRWKNS SRPY'L GDRY'L 'RDWD' PWRṬNY'L 'GMY'L RHṬY'L DYTRWN ḤZ'L PTW'L [215]GLGL' DMNṢR ZZY'L.

3 En. 17:6

(§108)These are the names of the angels who stand over the dream, to make wise anyone who draws near to them in purity[d] as to what the dream is and what its interpretation is.

A rite for mind-reading and dream interpretation

(§109)If the king calls you, or the chief of the city, or an authority, or your friend, and you seek to give him knowledge out of your wisdom, speak before him:

I will make known to you what is in your heart concerning me and what you think about me [220]and what you wish to do[e] and what is the interpretation of your dream.[f] Give me three days' time and I will make known to you all that is in your heart.

PGM I. 174–177; III. 263–265

(§110)Go out on the first day onto the seashore or on the bank of the river in the third[g] hour of the night and be wrapped in a new robe. Do not eat any small cattle[h] or anything that emits blood, and do not drink wine. And take myrrh and pure frankincense and put (them) on glowing coals of fire in a new earthenware[i] vessel. Set your face toward the water and you shall invoke the name of the overseer [225]with the name of the angels of the camp three times. You shall savor the sight of *a pillar*[j] *of fire* between heaven and earth. And recite this:

PGM XXXVI. 136

Sh-R §102; Exod 13:21

---

a. "let him delay"; "detain him to delay" M2 P F N.
b. "one moment"; omit M7 TA JA N.
c. "*lamellae*"; "hammered (plates)" TA.
d. "in purity"; + "so as to make the working that it undertakes succeed" M7.
e. "to do"; + "and what you dreamed" M7 TA JA.
f. "your dream."; + "Say to him:" M7 JA (cf. N).
g. "third"; "fourth" L.
h. "small cattle"; perhaps emend to "fish." Margalioth interprets the word as "small intestines" (cf. m. Ḥul. 3:1–3), but this interpretation does not fit the context as well as the other possibilities. For the possible meaning "legumes," see Rebiger and Schäfer, *Sefer ha-Razim* 2:230. Likewise in §119 and §227. Here M7 reads "vegetable," the corrected text of M2 reads "meat," and JA reads "animal meat."
i. "new earthenware"; "earthenware" M7 F N; "new" P L.
j. "You shall savor the sight of a pillar"; "You shall see a pillar" M2; "You shall see something like a pillar" M7 P F N JA L.

214

The Book of the Mysteries (Sefer ha-Razim)

(§111)I adjure you by him who *measured (the) waters in the hollow of his hand* and rebuked[a] the waters[b] so that they fled from before him, and who made flitting spirits in the air, the attendants of his presence, *an igniting fire. He rebuked the sea and it dried up,* and *the rivers he made into a desert.* In his name and by its letters[c] I adjure you, and in the name of the seven[d] angels of the seventh camp who attend on BW'L, that you make known to me ²³⁰what is in the heart of so-and-so son of so-and-so, and what is his wish, and what is the interpretation of his dream and what is his thought.

Isa 40:12
Ps 114:3
Ps 104:4
Nah 1:4
Ps 107:33

And so in the second and[e] the third night. You shall see that there shall be revealed to you a *pillar*[f] *of fire and cloud* over it[g] in the likeness of a man.[h] Ask it and it will tell you whatever you seek. (§112)If you seek to release it, throw some of the water to heaven[i] three times, from the sea or from the river by which[j] you are standing and recite under your breath:[k]

Sh-R §102; Exod 14:24

(§113)*Unseen Lord BW'L, once sufficing* ²³⁵*us, perfect shield-bearer,*[l] I release, I release (you). Sink down and return to your path.

PGM IV. 972

(§114)And recite this seven times. And do everything in purity and you shall succeed. (§115)'These are the names of the seven spirits[m] who attend in the firmament called Heavens. Peace.[n]

The Second Firmament

(§116)'The second firmament is called "Heaven of the Heavens."[o] In it are hoarfrost and smoke and *treasuries of snow and treasuries of hail* and angels of fire

Job 38:22

---

a. "rebuked"; "raged at" M7.
b. "the waters"; "the sea" TA.
c. "and by its letters"; omit M7 JA.
d. "the name of the seven"; perhaps emend to "the names of" with Morgan (since there are more than seven angels in this camp).
e. "the second and"; omit TA.
f. "a pillar"; "in a pillar" M7 TA; perhaps emend to "something like *a pillar*."
g. "over it"; "nearby" M2 F P.
h. "man"; "fire" M2 P F; "human being" M7 TA N JA.
i. "to heaven"; "to the air" TA.
j. "from the sea or by the river in which"; "in the place in which" M7.
k. "under your breath"; literally, "under your tongue."
l. The italicized phrase is a translation of a Greek phrase that has been transliterated into Hebrew letters. I follow the reconstruction of Morton Smith and James Coulter cited by Margalioth. The manuscripts are very corrupt and any reconstruction is speculative.
m. "spirits"; "stages" G12; "camps" JA.
n. "These are . . . Peace."; omit M7 TA P L; + quotations of Pss 104:24; 119:17; 27:7; and 119:35 M2 F N; "These are the seven stages of the firmament upon the first stage." G12. L omits §115.
o. Most manuscripts read "Heaven," but this is a corruption. That name has already been used for the first firmament. Read with P F (as corrected) N and cf. the end of §132. L reads "Firmament" (*Raquia*; an inexact Latin transliteration of Hebrew *raqiʿa*) for the name of this firmament. Only L assigns names to all seven firmaments. For the seven heavens in Jewish tradition, see Rebiger and Schäfer, *Sefer ha-Razim* 2:203–4.

The Book of the Mysteries (Sefer ha-Razim)

and angels of cold sweat and spirits of awe and spirits of fear. The firmament is full of dread, for in it are[a] angels beyond reckoning made into hosts upon hosts, and over them are princes and overseers.[b] (§117)In the firmament are twelve stages, and on every single ⁵stage stand angels in their glory and over them is *lofty one over lofty one* and they listen to the affairs of mortals for anyone who approaches them in purity.[c]

Qoh 5:7

Preparations for invoking the angels of the twelve stages of the second firmament

(§119)If you seek to ask something from any who stand on the stages of the second firmament, cleanse yourself for three weeks of days[d] from all tender fruit[e] and from all kinds of small cattle[f] and large cattle and from wine and from various fish and from all things that emit blood, and do not approach a woman in her impurity and you *shall not come to any dead* ¹⁰*people*, and do not go near a leper or one with a flux, and guard against chance pollution and a nocturnal emission, and keep your mouth from every evil word and from every sin, and sanctify yourself from all sin.

PGM I. 104, 290
Ezek 18:6
Lev 21:11
Lev 13–14, 15

The Angels of the First Stage

(§120)On the first stage these stand: ḤMRY'L HDRY'L RṢY'L HS'Y'L DMYMY'L ZBDY'L RNZY'L 'NŠ'L KṬBR'L.

(§121)The station of these is at the first stage. They stand in awe, wrapped in wrath, girded with fear, ¹⁵surrounded by quaking. Their covering is like a figure made of fire, their face is like an appearance of lightning, and their mouth is not silent from many words, but their voice is not heard. For their work is to quiet and startle and confound anyone who stands against whoever calls[g] to them in purity.[h]

Ezek 1:14

A rite for pacifying crowds or leaders

(§122)If you seek to quiet *a numerous crowd of people* or an authority or a judge or the inhabitants of the city or the inhabitants of the region, take a handful of ashes[i] from beneath[j] an idol[k] and recite over it backward[l] seven

Joel 2:2

---

a. "for in it are"; + "meteors and" TA.
b. "princes and overseers"; "black princes" M7.
c. L adds §118, which promises benefits from the invocation of these angels and urges the practitioner to approach them in a pure and proper ritual context. N has a shorter paragraph in this place, with related but not identical content, which seems to have been translated from Latin.
d. "three weeks of days"; the two manuscripts of L read "twelve days" and "twenty-two days."
e. "tender fruit"; Margalioth reads "fruit of the palm-tree" with Mafteaḥ Shelomo.
f. Cf. the relevant note to §110 above.
g. "calls"; "draws near" M7 M2 P F N.
h. "in purity"; omit G12 M7 TA.
i. "ashes"; "dust" G12 M7 TA L Mafteaḥ Shelomo.
j. After "beneath" Margalioth adds "the corner of," based on material not available to me. Morgan suggests we emend Margalioth's addition to "bread offering." But Morgan's suggested parallel with the burnt bread offered to Satan in T. Job 7 is imprecise and unpersuasive. The shorter reading of all the available manuscripts makes good sense and I have retained it.
k. "an idol"; "your shadow" G12; "the ladder" P F N; + "the ladder" M2; "the shadow of any staircase" L.
l. "backward"; or "out of order."

The Book of the Mysteries (Sefer ha-Razim)

times [20]the names of the angels written above (who are) on the first stage, and recite:

> (§123)I seek from you, angels of silence,[a] that you silence every mouth and heart of this whole place of the children of Adam and Eve[b] who stand against me in any evil matter. And let there go out from their mouth good things about me, and that I be vindicated in my court case and you do not give permission to any mouth to speak evil against me.

And sprinkle the ashes[c] whether in the city, whether in the region, whether before the authority, or whether before the judge, [25]and you shall be vindicated.

The Angels of the Second Stage

(§124)On the second stage these stand: 'ZZY'L ḤNN'L PṢṢY'L YŠ'Y'L DLQY'L 'RPD' MR'WT RYPYPYS 'MNY'L NḤMY'L PRZYRWM 'NB'L.

(§125)The station of these is on the second stage. They stand in vigor, filled with valor, surrounded by love, and opposite them[d] is burning fire. And they run and they bring near the astrological signs of mortals [30]to each other.[e]

A rite to make a woman fall in love

(§127)If you seek to put love of a man in the heart of a woman or to make a poor man get a rich wife,[f] take two bronze *lamellae* and write on them the names of these angels, on both sides of them, and the name of the man and the name of the woman, and recite this:

> (§128)I seek from you, the angels who rule[g] over the astrological signs of the children of Adam and Eve, that you do my will and you bring the astrological sign of so-and-so son of so-and-so near to the[h] woman so-and-so daughter of so-and-so, that he may bear grace and charm in her eyes. [35]And do not give her permission to belong to any man besides him.[i]
>
> (§129)And put one in a fiery furnace[j] and one in her ritual immersion pool. And

Sh-R §93

Sh-R §193; PGM IV. 1470–1471, 1494–1495, 1591–1593; 2930–2939

PGM IV. 1496–1523

---

a. "silence"; + "and fear" G12 M7 TA.
b. "the children of Adam and Eve"; "mortals" (literally, "the children of man/children of Adam") G12 TA Mafteaḥ Shelomo.
c. "ashes"; "dust" G12 M7 L Mafteaḥ Shelomo.
d. "opposite them"; "their body" P F.
e. "to each other"; Margalioth adds "for the sake of love" based on material not available to me. N adds §126 here, which applies the following ritual in §127 to the reconciliation of various interpersonal conflicts. It appears to be translated from Latin.
f. "to make a poor man get a rich wife"; "to marry a man to a woman who does not want him" M2 P F L.
g. "rule"; "are appointed" M7.
h. "near to the"; + "the astrological sign of the" TA P F N.
i. "besides him"; "besides me" M7 TA M2.
j. "furnace"; + "of the bathhouse" TA.

The Book of the Mysteries (Sefer ha-Razim)

PGM IV. 753
PGM IV. 57
Sh-R §167; Exod 19:15; PGM I. 291; IV. 897–898
PGM IV. 735

do so on the twenty-ninth[a] of the month when the moon is gone,[b] and take care and keep away from[c] a woman for three days, and from wine and from any meat.

The Angels of the Third Stage

(§130) On the third stage these stand: YHW'L D'YHW 'LY'L BRKY'L 'LY SPWM PNYMWR 'L'ZR GBLY'L KMŠY'L 'WDH'L Y'Ṣ'L RPPY'L ⁴⁰PSPY'L.[d]

(§131) The station of these is on the third stage, for their station is to agitate and to make quake the heart of mortals and to annul their plan and to abolish their thoughts. And they have fear and they go about with dread and they are expanders of rage,[e] and they are very harsh and mighty in valor. And dread is in front of them[f] and quaking is behind them. And they roar and cause quaking, going about and causing shaking. And their voice is like the sound of thunder and in their hand are staves of fire and their faces are like comets ⁴⁵of fire and fire goes out from their eyes[g] and all of them are ready[h] to abolish and[i] to annul.

A rite to abolish the plans or intentions of leaders

(§132) If you seek to abolish[j] from yourself the plan of a great man or the thought of the commander of the army or the plan of those going down to war, or any evil plan and evil thoughts, go out in the middle of the night, when the moon is full, alone[k] and pure[l] and wrapped in a new cloak. Stand under the moon and speak the names of the angels written above who stand on the third stage in ⁵⁰Heaven of the Heavens twenty-one times and recite:[m]

> (§133) Moon, O moon,[n] bring my words near before the angels who stand on the third stage.[o] Abolish[p] from me the thought of so-and-so son of so-

---

a. "twenty-ninth"; "twentieth" M2 P F; "twenty-eighth" N.

b. "gone"; "full" M7; "dismissed" TA.

c. "keep away from"; "keep pure of" M7 TA M2 P F N Mafteaḥ Shelomo.

d. A line of magical letters or "characters" is included after §130 in M7, N, Mafteaḥ Shelomo, the *Namenversion* fragment in G36, and in L. The characters are different in each source. For similar characters see *PGM* IV. 2706 and VII. 860, 922. See also §134 and the relevant note to §146 below.

e. "they are expanders of rage" M7; "and they expand in rage" G6. Margalioth reads "their appearance is in rage" based on material not available to me.

f. "in front of them"; "in their eyes" G6 M7.

g. "from their eyes" + "and ignites" M2; + "as though igniting" P F.

h. "ready"; "able" M7 TA{M2} P F N.

i. "to abolish and"; + "ready" M7 M2.

j. "to abolish"; "to thwart" P F N.

k. "alone"; "scrubbed" M2 P F; "barefoot" L. Margalioth suggests that we retrovert with L.

l. "and pure"; "and immersed and purify yourself" TA; "and purify yourself" M2 P F.

m. "Heaven of Heavens . . . and recite" omit G6 M7 N; "twenty-one times and recite" TA; "And you should say thus" L. Margalioth, whom I follow here, has combined the first two readings, which do not appear together in any one manuscript.

n. "Moon, O moon" TA. Margalioth finds the reading "Moon, moon, O moon" in material not available to me.

o. Moon . . . third stage"; omit G6 M7 M2 P F N L.

p. "Abolish"; "May they abolish" M7 TA; "I seek that you abolish" P F; "I adjure you that you abolish" Mafteaḥ Shelomo.

218

and-so and the plan of his heart and his plot, and let his mouth be silent from me and let his knowledge[a] perish and let his plan be annulled and let his heart be ruined.[b] And every time that he sees me[c] let him be filled with love[d] for me, and let him be turned into a friend of mine and let him not remember any hatred for me and let me find favor and charm[e] in his eyes.

(§134) And write ⁵⁵the angels and these characters[f] on a silver *lamella*[g] and put them *on the tablet of your heart*. And all the days that it[h] is on you, you shall succeed.

PGM I. 266–267; II. 60; VII. 193–195
Prov 3:3; 7:3

The Angels of the Fourth Stage
(§135) On the fourth stage these stand: ṢGRY'L MLKY'L 'WNBYB PGRY'L 'NNY'L KLNMYY' 'WMY'L MPNWR KWZZYB'[i] 'LPY'L PRYBY'L Ṣ'QMYH KDWMY'L 'ŠMD'[j] HWDYH YḤZY'L. (§136) The station of these is on the fourth stage. ⁶⁰They are girded with storm and the sound of their step is like the sound of bronze. They fly from the east and turn from the west[k] to the gate. They are swift as lightning and fire surrounds them. They separate sleep from mortals and it is theirs to cause good or to cause harm.[l]

A rite to cause insomnia
(§137) If you seek to make your enemy bereft of sleep,[m] take the head of a black[n] dog that saw no light in its days and take a strip of a cold-water pipe[o] and write on it these angels and recite this:

PGM IV. 2943–2966, 3255–3274 VII. 374–376
PGM VII. 397

> (§138) I transmit to you, angels of perturbation ⁶⁵who stand on the fourth stage, the soul and the breath and the spirit of so-and-so son of so-and-so,

a. "knowledge"; "thoughts" TA.
b. "ruined"; "torn" TA.
c. "And every time that he sees me"; "And if he sees me" M7 M2 P F N Mafteaḥ Shelomo; "until he sees me" TA.
d. "with love"; + "and mercies" P F N.
e. "and charm"; omit M7 TA M2 P F. For the translation of this word see the relevant note to §90.
f. See note on the characters in §130 above. The aside references to the characters in §134 and §152 imply that characters appeared in the original texts of §130 and §146. Cf. Rebiger and Schäfer, *Sefer ha-Razim* 2:240.
g. "a silver *lamella*"; "a silver cup" M7; "silver foil" TA M2 P F.
h. "it"; "the foil" M2 P F.
i. Morgan suggests that KWZZYB' refers to Shimon bar Kosiba (bar Kokhba), the failed messiah of the second Jewish revolt against Rome in 132–135 CE. If so, the form of the name is that reflected in the Talmud, meaning "(son of) a liar."
j. Morgan suggests that 'ŠMD' is a version of the name of the demon Ashmedai (cf. Tob 3:7–8).
k. "and turn from the west"; + "to the gate" G6; "to the west and they turn from the north to the south ("to the highest" M7)" M7 TA; "to the west and their face is from the north to the south" P F N; "to the stage and their face is from the north to the south" M2.
l. "and it is theirs to cause good or to cause harm" omit M7.
m. "to make your enemy bereft of sleep"; "to tear sleep from your enemy" M2 P F N.
n. "black"; omit M2 P F.
o. Margalioth plausibly reconstructs a transliterated Greek word from the corrupt readings of the manuscripts.

The Book of the Mysteries (Sefer ha-Razim)

that you may bind him with fetters[a] of iron and tie him to poles of bronze. Do not give sleep to his eyelids, nor slumber, nor deep sleep. Let him keep weeping[b] and crying out like a woman giving birth and do not give permission to a mortal to release him.[c]

PGM XXXVI. 370
Sh-R §236

(§139) Write this[d] and put it inside the mouth of the dog's head, and put wax over its mouth and seal it with a sealring[e] on which is a lion.[f] And go and conceal it 70behind his house or in a place[g] where he goes out and comes in.

(§140) If you seek to release him, bring it up from the place where it is concealed and remove its seal and take out the text and throw it into a fire, and at once[h] he shall go to sleep. And act with humility[i] and you will succeed.

The Angels of the Fifth Stage

(§141) On the fifth stage these stand: QWN'QRY'L PTWNY'L NQRY'L 'Y'L Y'BWTY'W BBSB'W BKPY MBWM SKTB'W 'MRY'L Y'L'L 75MKS'BW.

2 Chr 25:5
1 Sam 17:5

(§142) These are the ones who stand on the fifth stage. They *wear a buckler* and *a spear*, and *a bronze helmet*[j] on their heads, and *a coat of scale-mail* is their *clothing*. On their right and on their left is something like hailstones. (There is) quaking at their running and they walk around on rivers of fire, bearing torches[k] and hurrying to return an answer. And their mouth is not silent from roaring and their breath is like[l] a burning fire, and their fire ignites, and from the breath of their nose fire burns, for all their deeds are 80in[m] treasuries of fire, for they emerged from fire and their station is in fire.

A rite to light a stove in the cold

(§143) And if you seek to heat a stove in the cold,[n] take a lump of brimstone containing twenty-seven[o] shekels and divide it into the number of sections of the fire of the stove, and on every single one write with a bronze bar[p] the names of the angels who stand on the fifth stage, and recite:

PGM VII. 398

a. "with fetters"; "with bonds" G6 M7 TA N.
b. "keep weeping"; "keep barking like a dog" M2 P F N L (Mafteaḥ Shelomo variant reading).
c. "to release him"; + "apart from me" TA M2 P F N.
d. "Write this"; omit TA M2 P F N L.
e. "and put wax . . . a sealring"; "and seal it with wax with a sealring" M2 P F L.
f. "a lion"; "a form of a lion" TA M2 P F N L.
g. "or in a place"; omit M7 P.
h. "at once"; omit TA M2 M7 P F N.
i. "with humility"; "in purity and with humility" M7; "in purity" TA; "in humility and with purity" P F N L.
j. "*bronze helmet*"; "helmet of fire" M7 TA.
k. "torches"; "something like torches" M2 P F.
l. "their breath is like"; "from their breath is" M2 P F; "their breath is" M7 TA.
m. "in"; "like" P F.
n. "a stove in the cold"; The readings of the manuscripts are corrupt and vary widely. Margalioth's conjectural emendation is plausible and corresponds to the sense of L.
o. "twenty-seven"; "six" M7 TA Mafteaḥ Shelomo.
p. "bronze bar"; "iron pen" M7 Mafteaḥ Shelomo; "bronze pen" TA N L.

The Book of the Mysteries (Sefer ha-Razim)

(§144)I adjure you, angels of fire and angels of flame, by the king who is *a consuming fire*, that you stand with me ⁸⁵and you light the stove that is in the place of so-and-so.ᵃ Let anyone who enters into it be confounded by its heat.

Deut 4:24; 9:3

(§145)You (pl.) shall do this tried-and-true thingᵇ and you (sg.) will succeed. Take the brimstone and throw it in every single compartment of it and it shall be ignited in strength. On each day that you seek to ignite it, write (it) and throw (it) into the midst of it.

The Angels of the Sixth Stage

(§146)On the sixth stage these stand: 'BYHWD QṬYR ZLQY'L STRY'L ⁹⁰'DRK GḤLY'L TMKY'L SMKYH RB'Y'L YWQMY'L ŠMYHWD MHRY'L DWMY'L KRKWS QNZ QNY'L KNṬWN.ᶜ

(§147)These are the ones who stand on the sixth stage. They are bright with humility and their faces are full of glory. Their clothes are clothes white as light, they stand like *tall men*, they are fearsome as sages of the academy, they are enthroned on thrones of glory, true to the truth, and standing over the healing.

Num 13:32

A rite to heal someone who has had a stroke

(§148)If you seek ⁹⁵to heal a man who has had a stroke and is half-paralyzed by a spirit or by sorceries, take spikenard oil and honey,ᵈ three measures, and stand facing the sun as it rises, and invoke for seven days, three times a day, the name of the man and the name of his mother and the names of the angels who stand on the sixth stage. On the seventh day take him and make him stand naked facing the sun and pour oil over all his flesh, and let him be fumigated before the sun (with) *myrrh and frankincense* and *choice* ¹⁰⁰*spices*.ᵉ

PGM I. 278

PGM IV. §173–175
Cant 3:6; PGM V. 202; XIII. 352–354
Cant 4:14

(§152)Again write these angels of glory along with these charactersᶠ (as) an amuletᵍ on a silver *lamella*, and put (it) on his neck with asbestos and with

---

a. "and you light the stove that is in the place of so-and-so"; again, reading with Margalioth's conjectural emendation of the corrupt manuscripts.

b. The Hebrew word translated "tried and true thing" is a transliteration of a Greek word. Another interpretation of it that also fits the context here and in §197 is "illusion." See Rebiger and Schäfer, *Sefer ha-Razim* 2:240.

c. M7, TA, M2, N, Mafteaḥ Shelomo, and L each add a line of characters after §146. Cf. the relevant notes to §§130 and 134 above.

d. "spikenard oil and honey"; "oil of rose" M7 TA Mafteaḥ Shelomo; "oil of rose or spikenard oil or white honey" N; "oil of rose and white honey" L. In Hebrew "spikenard oil" and "oil of rose" look very similar. The manuscripts show some confusion between them here and in §§59, 164. The parallel in *PGM* I. 278 shows that they were used together as magical *materia*, which doubtless increased the confusion. For more on spikenard oil, see Rebiger and Schäfer, *Sefer ha-Razim* 2:243.

e. §§149–51 are found only in N and seem to be at least partly translated from Latin. They contain instructions for an additional adjuration in support of the stroke survivor. Some of this material also appears in §148 of L.

f. Cf. the relevant note to §146 above.

g. Margalioth reads "(as) an amulet" based on sources not available to me, although this is a plausible emendation of the corrupt reading of M7. TA reads "and write them."

incense of spices. Write [this]ᵃ on the twentieth of the month and you will succeed.ᵇ

The Angels of the Seventh Stage

(§153)On the seventh stage these stand: PTḤYH RZY'Lᶜ 'GRY'L HGDY'B 'DRWN KRQṬ' QṬYPWR 'BRY'L ŠTQY'L 'MY'L SYKBRDWM.

(§154)These are ¹⁰⁵the ones who stand on the seventh stage. Girded with vigor,ᵈ their might isᵉ like a lion.ᶠ Half of them resembles fire and half of them is cold like water.ᵍ They stand in their place and they are weakenedʰ from awe of them. They are wondrous in their deeds and there is no withstanding their form.ⁱ They come with stature and meteors of light in their eyelids. Those who stand beneath them cannot look at their appearances, and even those who stand above them are in dread ofʲ their appearances, for they turn ¹¹⁰to every side, and from above,ᵏ and to the four winds they go about.ˡ

A rite to protect a city from dangerous animals and floods

PGM VII. 370–373

(§155)If you seek to make fleeᵐ from the city every harmful animal or lion or wolf or bear or leopard, or river or sea that rises and floods houses, make a bronze imageⁿ in the likeness of one of themᵒ and makeᵖ an iron *lamella* and write on it, front and back, the names of the angels, and gird it upon it and conceal it at the entrance of the city,ᑫ and let its face be turned toward the north.

(§156)If it is a sea or a river you seek ¹¹⁵ to bind, so that it does not come in and destroy,ʳ make a stone image and write these angels with two bronze *lamellae* and put (them) under its heels. And make a staff of alabaster and put it on its shoulderˢ

    a. "write [this]" G13; "do (it)" TA.
    b. "(as) an amulet ... succeed"; omit M2 P F. "Write ... succeed."; "And he shall be healed. And this must be on the twentieth of the month." Mafteaḥ Shelomo; "And when seven days have been concluded, after these he will be as well as he ever was." L.
    c. This is the name Razi'el, the angelic revealer of Sefer ha-Razim according to the opening of the prologue (§2).
    d. "vigor"; "wind" or "spirit" M2 P F N.
    e. "their might is"; "and might" TA; "they are mighty" M3 P F.
    f. "like a lion" omit TA.
    g. "cold like water"; "like water" M7 M2 P F N; "hail" TA.
    h. "they are weakened"; The subject of the verb is unclear and the text may be corrupt.
    i. "their form"; "their character" M7; "their design" M2.
    j. "are in dread of"; "receive visitation from" M7.
    k. "and from above"; omit M7 TA M2 P F N.
    l. "they go about"; "of the world" M2 P F N.
    m. "to make flee"; "to thrust out" M7; "to remove" M2 P F N L.
    n. "a bronze image" omit G13 M7.
    o. "a bronze ... them"; "the likeness of what you want in stone" Mafteaḥ Shelomo.
    p. "and make"; + "in one of them" M2; + "like one of them" P F.
    q. "at the entrance of the city"; "in the city or the region" M2 P F N L.
    r. "to bind, so that it does not come in and destroy," reading with G13 (fragmentary) and M7. M2 P F read "that (omit M2) it not rise and destroy the face of the city." Margalioth reads "to bind, so that it does not come in and flood," based on material not available to me.
    s. "its shoulder"; "its two shoulders" M7 Mafteaḥ Shelomo.

with its right hand grasping the staff[a] and its left hand open[b] and its face facing the water.[c]

PGM IV. 2379–2382;
m. 'Abod. Zar. 3:1

The Angels of the Eighth Stage

(§158) On the eighth stage these stand: 'BRH BRQY'L 'DWNY'L 'ZRY'L BRKY'L 'MY'L QDŠY'L MRGY'L PRW'L PNY'L MRBNY'L MRNYS'L [120]ŠMY'L 'MNY'L MTN'L HWD HWD.[d]

3 En. 17:3

(§159) These are the ones who stand on the eighth stage. Their likeness is like *Hashmal*[e] of effulgence.[f] By their actions they speak. Quaking and fire are in their residence. They are full of dread,[g] they rule the spirits who roam the earth. And in a place where they are invoked[h] no evil spirit can appear.

Ezek 1:4, 27

A rite to protect a woman in childbirth from evil spirits

(§160) If you seek to thrust out an evil spirit so that it does not come to a woman at the time when she is giving birth and it does not kill her child, before [125]the woman becomes pregnant[i] write these angels on a gold *lamella* and put it in a silver pipe[j] and let it be on her. And at the time she gives birth take four silver[k] *lamellae* and write on them the angels, and put them in the four winds of the house[l] and no spirit shall arise.[m]

The Angels of the Ninth Stage

(§162) On the ninth stage these stand: GDWDY'L SKSY'L TRSWNY'L NṢḤY'L 'ṢD' RBNY' ḤLYL'L TWQPY'L SMKY'L PDH'L QRB' [130]ṢY'L PR'L PTḤY'L.

(§163) These are the ones who stand on the ninth stage: forceful ones in valor, flying in the air, their might is potency and the likeness of swords is in their hand, they are ready for battle, they grasp a bow, they hold a javelin, they leap higher than fire and they have horses of fire and juniper.[n] Their chariots are fire and there is fear of them everywhere they turn.

2 Kgs 2:11; 3 En. 6:1

---

a. "the staff"; "the head of the staff" M7 TA M2 P F L Mafteaḥ Shelomo.

b. "and its left hand open" omit M2 P F.

c. M7 reads "facing the earth." Paragraph 157 is found only in M2 F N. It reads "Blessed is the one who builds his stages in the heavens (Amos 9:6). Blessed is his name and his holiness."

d. The scribe of P accidentally omitted §158 and wrote it as §161. I have collated P here.

e. The word *Hashmal* appears only in Ezek 1:4, 27 in the Bible. Its meaning is uncertain, but its context in Ezekiel's vision of the heavenly world led later exegetes to infer that it was some sort of angelic or heavenly being.

f. "of effulgence"; "of adornment" M7; omit TA.

g. "full of dread"; "full of storm-wind"(?) M7; "full of ornamentation" TA.

h. "where they are invoked"; "where they are recognized" G13; omit TA; "where they speak" M2; "where they reside" P; "that disperses (them)" F.

i. "becomes pregnant"; "gives birth" TA.

j. "pipe"; "gate" M7; "amulet" TA.

k. "silver"; "bronze" M2 P F N L.

l. "winds of the house" G13; "angles of the house" (G15 ["the house"]) G15 M7 TA M2 P F; "corners of the house" N L; "angles" Mafteaḥ Shelomo.

m. "and no spirit shall arise"; omit G13 M7 Mafteaḥ Shelomo; "and no evil spirit shall come to her" TA. For §161, see the relevant note to §158 above.

n. "and juniper"; "and hail" TA.

A rite for invulnerability in battle

(§164) If you seek to be protected from arrow and from sword and from every wound of a man who goes down to war, take ¹³⁵seven leaves of a bay-laurel tree[a] and write these names on them, two on every single one of them, and put them in spikenard oil.[b] On the day that he goes out to war, let him pour (it)[c] on his flesh[d] and on his sword and his bow and his arrows. In addition write them on a silver *lamella* and put them in a bronze pipe. And let him gird (it)[e] over his heart, and no wound shall touch him.

The Angels of the Tenth Stage

(§165) On the tenth stage these stand: DKRY'L ḤRY'L ŠBQY'L ¹⁴⁰'TKY'L SMYK'L MRMW'L QN'L ṢPTP YH'L 'L ṢDQ 'KPP 'ZM'L MKMYK'L TRKY'L TBGY'L. (§166) These are the ones who stand on the tenth stage. They are commanded concerning[f] the truth and before them are multitudes and multitudes holding reed pens of fire. And they write documents unhindered and they make known merit to anyone who calls on their names to redeem and to save from tribute[g] and from the judgment of[h] the kingdom and from every death sentence.[i]

Rite to deliver a friend from legal difficulties

(§167) If you seek ¹⁴⁵to redeem your friend from an evil sentence and from any difficulty, purify yourself from all impurity and from sex with a woman for three days. Stand facing in the direction of the sun as it rises and invoke these names and recite:

> (§168) I seek from you, O great angel[j] called "sun" who ascends on the stages of the firmament, who looks on mortals, that you carry out my request and you bring[k] my words before the King of the kings of kings, the Holy One, blessed be he, for I pray to him concerning the business of so-and-so son of so-and-so, ¹⁵⁰who is in difficulty and under an evil sentence. You shall bring out from before him to him a good word and a time of rejoicing.[l]

---

a. "bay-laurel tree"; "juniper tree" N JA L.
b. "spikenard oil"; "good oil of roses" TA; "oil of roses" N. See also the relevant note to §148 above.
c. "let him pour (it)"; "let him pour some of it" TA; "let him plaster (it)" M2.
d. "his flesh"; "all his flesh" M7.
e. "gird (it)"; "fumigate (it)" TA; "cover (it)" P F.
f. "They are commanded concerning"; "Their position is over" G15 M7 TA JA L.
g. "from tribute"; "his soul from anguish and misery" M7 TA; "from chastisements of" P. The reading of M2 is meaningless, but it may be a corruption of the word for "land tax" or "tribute."
h. "and from the judgment of"; omit P.
i. "and from every death sentence"; "and from all business and (+ "from M7) a death sentence" M7 TA; "and from all wealth and a death sentence" M2.
j. "angel"; "king" M7 N L Mafteaḥ Shelomo.
k. "and you bring"; "and you introduce" M7.
l. "and a time of rejoicing" reading with M7. G13 is damaged and indecipherable. TA reads "and the spirits of"; M2 P F omit; Mafteaḥ Shelomo reads "and a time of refreshment and saving." Margalioth reads "and a time of refreshment" based on material not available to me.

/ *The Book of the Mysteries (Sefer ha-Razim)*

Let the ones who seek his harm be restrained[a] and let him be redeemed without injury.

Write these angels again on a bronze *lamella* and conceal it in the direction of the east, facing the sun when it rises. Do everything[b] in purity and you will succeed.[c]

The Angels of the Eleventh Stage

(§169)On the eleventh stage these stand: RPDY'L DMW'L M'RYNWS 155'MYN'L ṢHY'L 'QRY'L 'DNY'L RDQY'L ŠLMY'L 'STṬY'L SṬ'L 'GLGLTWN 'RMWT PRḤG'L NPPMYWT.

(§170)The station of these is on the eleventh stage. Awe is in their standing. They are supported in greatness,[d] causing camps of attendants to stand and sit on high. For at their order[e] angels of fire run back and forth, descending from greatness and ascending to ornamentation, flying and flying about. They are found[f] 160in their place ornamenting their Creator and psalming their Former.

A rite to restore a demoted leader to his former position

(§171)If you seek to set up in his position a king or an officer or an authority or a judge who has been demoted from his place, take oil and honey and fine flour and put (them) in a new glass saucer. Purify yourself from all impurity and do not eat unkosher meat and do not touch sex[g] with a woman for seven days. On the seventh day stand under[h] the moon in its fourteenth or fifteenth or sixteenth (day). And take the saucer 165into your hand, and write on it this camp[i] on high and invoke over it, facing[j] the moon, the names of the angels seven times, and recite:

PGM I. 41–42

> (§172)*I set down my supplication*[k] *before you*, O moon, who go about by day and by night, and your chariots are light, and in front of you and behind you are angels of benevolence. I adjure you by the King who brings you out and who brings you in when you wane and become full and stand in your place. So shall you make stand so-and-so son of so-and-so in his place and let him be glorified in the eyes of all who see him. 170Just as you have

Jer 38:26

---

a. "Let the ones who seek his harm be restrained"; "Let the ones who seek his harm stumble" M7; "everyone who seeks their harm" TA.
b. "everything"; omit TA M2 P F.
c. "and you will succeed"; omit P F L.
d. "They are supported in greatness"; reading with M7. Margalioth emends very speculatively to a phrase he takes to mean "Its great multitude is."
e. "For at their order"; "In their thousands" M2 F N.
f. "They are found"; "They glitter" M7.
g. "touch sex"; "have sex" M2 P F N.
h. "under"; "facing" TA M2 P F.
i. "and write on it this camp"; "and write it—this offering—" G16 (damaged) M7; "and the offering inside it" TA; "and write on it this offering" M2.
j. "facing"; "under" TA.
k. "*my supplication*"; + "and my prayer" M7; "my prayer" M2 F N.

The Book of the Mysteries (Sefer ha-Razim)

glory in the world, so put glory upon him in the eyes of all the children of Adam and Eve. Set him up in his position so that he may be a ruler as at first, and let him not turn aside from his place.

PGM VII. 915

(§173)Do this for him for three days and afterward make them into a cake and let it be dried out at night and let the sun not see (it). And let him eat it for three days[a] before the sun rises, and conceal the written[b] saucer in his house.

The Angels of the Twelfth Stage

(§174)On the twelfth stage these stand: 'STRYMY BR'WT BMR'WT DRWDY'L 175ŠDRY'L TLHBM BRG'L PY'L PP'L YKPTYNY KLPTWN BWBWKWK 'WMTWN 'RTMYKTWN 'ŠMYGDWN SPNYG PRNYG'L PSYKSWK T'GYŠWN 'RTLYDY.

(§175)The station of these is on the twelfth stage. (They are) encircled by righteousness and horns of effulgence are on their heads. Full of understanding, they understand how to sing psalms, standing divided into two groups, 180half of them singing and half of them responding antiphonally. Their tongue heals, their speech[c] binds up, and in anything for which they are invoked, you will succeed.[d]

A rite to cure a migraine headache or a cataract

PGM VII. 199–201, 201–202 XCIV. 39–60

PGM VII. 271
PGM IV. 735

(§176)If you seek to heal a migraine headache,[e] or to bind or rebuke a spirit of cataract,[f] take the fat that covers the brain[g] of a black steer[h] and write on it the names of these angels in purity. Put it in a silver[i] pipe[j] and tie it with seven colors[k] and put it beside the one with the headache. And keep 185yourself[l] from meat and from wine and from the dead and from a menstruating woman and from everything unclean.[m]

---

a. "for three days"; "on the third day" TA P F N L.
b. "written"; omit G13 M7 TA M2 P F L.
c. "their speech"; "their mention" or "their invocation" TA M2 P F L.
d. "and in anything . . . you will succeed"; and in anything for which they are invoked, there is healing" M7 TA; "and in anything that has a need (there is) healing" F.
e. "a migraine headache"; literally "a pain of half the head"
f. This word as found in TA M2 P F can mean either "cataract" or "glaucoma." The variant reading in G13 could be understood as "intestinal worms." N and L read "gout." See Rebiger and Schäfer, *Sefer ha-Razim* 2:159 n. 298 for details.
g. "the brain"; "the membrane of the brain" TA.
h. Like a number of the more unusual ingredients in the recipes of this book, this could be a code name for a type of plant. See Rebiger and Schäfer, *Sefer ha-Razim* 2:246.
i. "silver"; "bronze" M7.
j. "pipe"; "amulet" TA.
k. "with seven colors"; "with seven threads of seven colors" TA; "with a thread that is of seven colors" N L.
l. "keep yourself"; "let him keep himself" M7; "let him keep" M2 Mafteaḥ Shelomo; "and keep" P F.
m. Paragraphs 177–81 are found only in F and the other manuscripts of the *Umstellungtyp*. Paragraph 177 reads "I begin to write the seven firmaments." Paragraphs 178–81 correspond to §§28 and 116–17, 119, respectively.

The Third Firmament

(§182)The third firmament[a] is full of treasuries of misty cloud and from it spirits[b] go out and within it are camps of thunderclaps, and lightning bolts[c] go out from it. In it are three princes enthroned on their thrones and they and their clothing are in the likeness of fire, and the likeness of the thrones is like fire, and the fire glitters like gold. They rule over all the angels of fire (§183)and they are like fire. Their might and their voice are like a roar of ⁵the sound of thunder, and their eyes are like the beams of[d] the sun, and they rule over the wheels of flame[e] and glowing heat, and they have wings to fly, the shouting of their mouth is like horses, *their appearance is like torches*, they speak and cause quaking, they roar and make tremors, they glide on every wind and fly to every corner.

Nah 2:5

The Three Princes in Charge of the Third Firmament

(§184)[f]These are the names of the princes[g] who rule over the habitation that is the third firmament: the name of the first is YBNY'L; the name of the second is RHṬY'L; and the name of the third is DLQY'L. YBNY'L rules ¹⁰over every matter of fire, to make burn and to extinguish. RHṬY'L rules over every chariot of fire, to make it run and to make it stumble.[h] DLQY'L rules over flames of fire to kindle and to quench.

2 Kgs 2:11; 3 En. 6:1

The Angels Who Serve YBNY'L

(§185)[i]These are the names of the angels who attend on YBNY'L: Š'YPY'L 'DRY'L TDHDY'L B'ŠY'L ṬHPY'L RLBY'L BLNY'L THZRY'L 'ZY'L ¹⁵MNḤY'L MLTḤY'L DYBQY'L BRŠS'L SḤ'L TTB'L QSMY'L ṬSY'L QSṬSDY'L NMDY'L.

A rite to prevent a bathhouse from heating

(§186)If you seek to extinguish a bathhouse so that it does not light up and ignite, bring[j] a salamander and put it in old oil, three years old, in a glass[k] vessel, and do not put it on the ground. And invoke over it the name of the overseer and

---

    a. Manuscript B244 (Rebiger and Schäfer, *Sefer ha-Razim* 1:17 #1) gives the name of the third firmament as "Habitation," a traditional name for one of the seven heavens and a generic term for one of the heavens or firmaments in Sefer ha-Razim. See Rebiger and Schäfer, *Sefer ha-Razim* 2:159 n. 302 and 2:247. L gives the third firmament the name *Saaquyn*, an inexact transliteration for the Hebrew word meaning "Misty Cloud," another traditional name for one of the seven heavens.
    b. "spirits" or "winds."
    c. "camps of thunderclaps and lightning bolts"; "lightning bolts and thunderclaps" M2 P F L.
    d. "like the beams of"; "like the flame of" TA.
    e. "flame"; "gold" M2 P F N.
    f. F moves §§184–200 to §§300–314. I have collated its evidence here with §§184–200.
    g. "princes"; "overseers" M7; "princes and overseers" M2 P F.
    h. "to make it run and to make it stumble"; "and horses of fire to make understand and give insight" M7.
    i. N moves §§185–200 to §§301–14. I have collated its evidence here with §§185–200.
    j. "bring"; "take and bring" TA; "take" M2 P F N.
    k. "glass"; "new glass" M7 TA.

The Book of the Mysteries (Sefer ha-Razim)

the names of the angels who attend before him seven times backward[a] in the third hour in the night [20]and recite:

(§187)I adjure you, O salamander, in the name of YBNY'L and in the name of the angels of fire[b] who attend him, just as you were expelled from the fire, so may you expel and extinguish the fire from the igniting bathhouse of so-and-so son of so-and-so. (§188)And you, angels of fire, all of whose works are in fire, do not give permission to the fire that it should come and ignite this bathhouse. And stand at the gates of its chamber and come inside it and make it *like the cold of snow* and like *cold* [25]*water*.

Prov 25:25; *PGM* XIII. 298–303

Prov 25:13

Take the flask of oil and put some of it in every chamber in its four angles.[c]
(§189)If you seek to release the working, take some of the remainder of the oil and stand facing the sun and invoke the name of YBNY'L and the names of[d] the angels who attend him[e] and recite:

(§190)I adjure you, angel[f] of fire and angel of flame,[g] that you release what I have bound and you give permission to the angels who stand at the gates of the bathhouse of so-and-so son of so-and-so, [30]so that they may burn it and heat it as at first.

And take the flask of oil and pour it in every chamber in its four angles and it shall flame[h] and it shall ignite.[i]

The Angels Who Serve RḤṬY'L

(§192)These are the names of the angels who attend RḤṬY'L: 'GR' ZRGRY GNṬS T'ZM' LTSRP'L GDY'L TMNY'L 'QHY'L GWḤPNY'L 'RQNY ṢPYQW'L MWŠY'L SWSY'L HTNY'L ZKRY'L 'KNSP ṢDQY 'ḤSP [35]NKMR' PRDY'L QLYLY'L DRWMY'L.[j]

A rite to give racehorses stamina and speed

(§193)If you seek to make horses run when they have no vigor so that they shall not stumble in their running and they shall be fleet as the wind and no foot of any animal shall get ahead of them, and they shall bear grace and benevolence

PGM VII. 390–393

a. "backward" or "out of order."
b. "the angels of fire"; "the holy angels" P F; "the holy angels, angels of fire" N.
c. "put some of it in every chamber in its four angles"; "and put some of (omit "some of" P F L) it with your finger in the angles of every chamber" M2 P F N L.
d. "invoke the name of YBNY'L and the names of"; "and say: I adjure you, salamander, in the name of YBNY'L and" TA.
e. "attend him"; + "seven (["seven"] G13) times backward (or "out of order") in the third hour in the night" G13 M7.
f. "angel"; "angels" TA M2 P F N.
g. "and angel of flame"; omit TA; "and angels of flame" M2 P F.
h. "it shall flame"; omit TA; "it shall light up" G13 M7 M2; "the fire shall light up" P F N.
i. "and it shall ignite"; "and it shall burn" TA; + "as at first" P F. Paragraph 191 is found only in TA and it repeats the information about DLQY'L found in §184 but applies it to RḤṬY'L.
j. Mafteaḥ Shelomo includes a line of characters after §192.

The Book of the Mysteries (Sefer ha-Razim)

in their running, take a silver *lamella* and write on it the names of the horses[a] and the names of the angels and the name of the princes who are over them[b] and recite:

> (§194) I adjure you, angels of running who run among the stars, that you gird with vigor and valor [40]the race horses of so-and-so and his charioteer who races them, and let them run and not get tired and not stumble. Let them run as swiftly as an eagle,[c] and *let no animals stand in front of* them, and do not let any enchantment and sorcery arise against them.   Dan 8:4

And take the *lamella* and conceal it in the racecourse where you seek to win.[d]

The Angels Who Serve DLQY'L
(§196) These are the names of the angels who attend DLQY'L: NWRY'L 'ZLYBN [45]YLY'L MLKYH ḤYLY'L ḤRH'L ŠLQY'L ṢGRY'L PSKY'L 'QRY'L SMNY'L ṢBBY'L NḤLY'L TGMLY'L 'MYNW'L TLB'P QṬḤNY'L 'PRY'L 'NGY'L MŠRY'L 'MNGN'N.

A rite to create the illusion of fire
(§197) If you seek to show something tried and true[e] to your friend or to your neighbor—to fill a house with fire but to burn[f] nothing, take a root[g] of a wild plant and put it on hot coals of fire[h] and let its smoke ascend within the house and invoke [50]the names of the angels and the name of the overseer in charge of them, who is DLQY'L, while its smoke ascends, seven times. When the smoke is present,[i] all who see it shall savor the sight of fire.[j]

When you invoke the names of the angels, recite:

> (§198) I adjure you, O angels wrapped[k] in fire, by him who is entirely fire and his seat is on a throne of fire and *his attendants are fire that ignites*, and   Ps 104:4

---

    a. "horses"; + "or ("and" L) the names of their owners ("owner" M2 F)" P M2 F L.
    b. "the names of the princes who are over them"; "the name of the prince who is over them" G17 Mafteaḥ Shelomo; "the name of the prince, the overseer over them" M7; "the name of their (omit "their" L) overseer RHṬY'L" TA L; "the name of the overseer who is over them who is RHṬY'L" M2 F; "the name of the overseer who is RHṬY'L" N.
    c. "Let them run as swiftly as an eagle"; "Let them run as swiftly as the wind" G13 TA; "Let them be swift as an eagle and run like the wind" M2 P F L.
    d. "win."; + "And if you want to release them, take the *lamella* and throw it into the fire." M2 P F L. Paragraph 195 is found only in TA and it repeats the information about DLQY'L found in §184, even though it has already been applied to RHṬY'L in §191.
    e. Or "show an illusion." Cf. the relevant note to §145 above.
    f. "burn"; "ignite" M7 TA.
    g. "root"; emending G13 with Margalioth on the basis of Sefer Malbush.
    h. "a root . . . on hot coals of fire"; "a scorpion and throw it on fire" M2(!) P F N L.
    i. "is present"; "ascends" TA M2 P F N L.
    j. "shall savor the sight of fire"; perhaps emend to "shall see it as fire" (cf. TA JA: "it shall seem in their sight like fire").
    k. "wrapped"; "flying" M2 P F.

camps of fire attend before him; by his name[a] I adjure you that you show me this great [55]miracle and you fill this house with your fire, that I and anyone who is with me may see this great miracle, yet we shall not be in dread.

(§199)When you complete your words,[b] you see the house full of[c] fire. If you seek to quench it, speak the adjuration backward[d] and recite:

Angels of fire, extinguish it, extinguish it immediately! *Hurry! Hasten!*[e]

1 Sam 20:38

(§200)*How great are your works Y'Y, you have done all of them in wisdom.*[f]

Ps 104:24

The Fourth Firmament[g]

(§201)And the fourth firmament is stretched out in the wind of a storm and it stands on pillars[h] of fire and it is borne on cords[i] of flame. And it is full of storehouses of might, as well as treasuries of dewdrops. And swift angels are in all its corners, crowding one another,[j] *galloping, galloping*. And in it are seven rivers of fire and[k] water, and over them stand innumerable angels on each side. (§202)On one side angels of fire burn [5]like flames, and on the other side angels of cold are encircled by hail. These do not extinguish the others, nor do the others ignite these. These immerse in the rivers of fire and the others immerse in the rivers of water. And they answer and recite songs and[l] praisesongs to *the one who lives forever*, for he formed them to adorn his potency.[m]

Judg 5:22

Dan 4:31; 12:7

The Bridal Chamber of the Sun

(§203)In the firmament is the fine[n] bridal chamber of the sun, full of light[o] and entirely of fire. The angels of fire gird on might surrounding it[p] and they lead

a. Margalioth reads "by his great name," based on a reading that he reports finding in a printed edition of Sefer Razi'el.
b. "When you complete your words"; "When your words are sealed" M7; "When your words are finished" TA; "When you seal your words" M2.
c. "full of"; + "smoke and" M2 P F.
d. "backward"; or "out of order."
e. "*Hurry! Hasten!*"; "Suddenly! Abruptly!" M7; omit M2 JA.
f. Paragraph 200; omit M7 TA JA.
g. The section on the fourth firmament (§§201–16) is missing in two manuscripts of JA (G23 and G32). But the JA manuscript G27 preserves a fragment of §§203–6. L gives the name of the fourth firmament as *Mahon*, apparently Hebrew for "Habitation" or "Residence," traditional names for one of the seven heavens. Cf. the reading of B244 with reference to the third firmament (see the relevant note to §182 above).
h. "pillars"; omit M7; "a pillar" M2 P F.
i. Reading "cords" with TA. M7 reads "secrets." Margalioth reads "crowns," on the basis of material not available to me.
j. "crowding one another"; "crushing" M7; "glittering" TA.
k. "of fire and"; + "and seven of" TA.
l. "songs and"; "a song and" M7; omit M2 P F.
m. "his potency"; "his solicitudes" M2 P F N.
n. "is the fine"; "appears the" M2 P F N.
o. "light"; "effulgence" M2 P F N.
p. "surrounding it"; "made useful for it" F.

230

it during the day. ¹⁰In addition the angels of water have bodies like the sea and their voice is like the sound of valiant waters[a] in ornamentation of power. And they lead it at night.[b]

The Angels Who Lead the Bridal Chamber of the Sun during the Day

(§204)These are the names of the angels who lead it during the day: 'BR'SKS MRMR'WT MWKTY'L M'RYT ṢDQY'L YḤSY ḤṢY'L RB'L Y'BWK MY'L KRYMK' MRM'N PW'L GBRY'L 'ŠTWN TWQPY'L 'LY'L ¹⁵NPLY 'W'L QWDŠY'L HWDY'L NRWMY'L YRŠY'L MLKY'L 'GRYT'L LGHY'L MNWRY'L PL'W'L NWRY'L HRM'Y'L NSBRY'L.

These are the princes of the camps who lead the sun during the day.[c]

The Angels Who Lead the Bridal Chamber of the Sun during the Night

(§205)And these are the names of the angels who lead it at night: PRSY'L ṢRṢY'L 'GY'L NBYM'L 'MY'L YŠRY'L 'ŠM'W'L ²⁰ŠPṬY'L Š'W'L RDRY'L Š'SY'L LYBB'L BNRY'L ṢGRY'L MNH'L LMY'L PRY'L PDH'L LYBR'L RBṢ'L ḤMQY'L BGHY'L NBRY'L QṢPY'L R'DNY'L ḤTNY'L 'SPPY'L ḤLW'L ŠM'Y'L ZḤZḤ'L NKBRY'L PṢ'L QMNY'L ZH'L ḤDY'L.

These are the princes of the camps who lead it at night.[d]

A rite to see the sun in its chariot during the day

(§206) ²⁵If you seek to see the sun during the day sitting in the chariot and rising, keep watch and be careful and keep pure for seven days from all food and from all drink and from every unclean thing.[e] And on the seventh day stand facing it at the time when it is rising and fumigate yourself before it (with) *an incense of spices* weighing three shekels, and be adjuring the names of the angels who lead it during the day seven times. If you are not answered with these seven times, adjure them ³⁰again backward[f] seven times and recite:

> (§207)I adjure you,[g] O angels who lead the sun by the vigor of your might in the highways of the firmament to illuminate the world, by the one whose voice *makes the earth quake* and *who removes mountains* in his anger and makes the sea[h] seethe by his vigor and shakes the pillars of the world with his glance, and he bears everything[i] on his arm and he is *hidden from*

PGM XIII. 254–259

Exod 25:6

Hag 2:6, 21
Job 9:5
Deut 33:27

---

a. "waters"; + "hail" (*sic*) M2.
b. F places §§204–5 later as §§319–20. I have collated its readings here with §§204–5. N places §§204–8, 210–16 later as §§319, 324, 322–23, 325–31. I have collated its readings here, as usual, with §§204–8, 210–16.
c. "These are . . . the day."; omit M2 P F N.
d. M7 places §205 later as §209. I have collated it here with §205. "These are . . . at night." omit G18 M2 P F N. Paragraphs 206–11 are missing in M2 P F.
e. "from all food . . . unclean thing"; "from every unclean thing and from meat and wine" TA.
f. "backward"; or "out of order."
g. "I adjure you,"; "I seek," M7 N; "I seek from you" TA.
h. "the sea"; "the day" G13.
i. "and he bears everything"; "and he carries the world" TA.

Job 28:21	*the eyes of every living creature* and he is enthroned on the throne of the greatness of the kingdom of the glory of his holiness and he roams in the whole world.[a] ³⁵By his great, fearsome, valiant, magnificent, powerful, mighty, holy, strong, wonderful, secret, lifted-up, and illuminated name I invoke and I adjure you that you do what I want and my request at this time and moment and you turn aside the beam of the sun that I may see
Deut 5:4	it *face to face* as it is in its bridal chamber. But do not let me be kindled by your fire, and give me permission to do what I want.
Sh-R §58	⁽§²⁰⁸⁾As you finish adjuring, you will see it in its bridal chamber and you may ask it either for death or for life, ⁴⁰either for good or for harm. If you seek to release it, you shall invoke the adjuration[b] and recite:

I adjure you that you return the sunbeam to its place as at first so that the sun may go on its way.[c]

A rite to see the sun going by the north wind during the night

1 En. 72:5	⁽§²¹⁰⁾And if you seek to see the sun at night going[d] by the north wind, keep pure
Dan 10:2–3	for three weeks of days from all food and drink and from every unclean thing,
PGM XXXVI. 136	and stand ⁴⁵for a watch of the night, in the third hour,[e] and be wrapped up in white clothes[f] and speak the name of the sun and the names of the angels who lead it at night twenty-one times and recite:

	⁽§²¹¹⁾I adjure you, O angels who fly in the air of the firmament by him who sees but is not seen, by the king who reveals all enigmas and has seen all secrets, by the Dominion[g] who knows what is in the dark places and *he*
Amos 5:8	*turns the shadow of death to morning* and he ⁵⁰illuminates night like day, and all secrets before him are revealed like the sun, and *nothing is too*
Jer 32:17	*wonderful for* him.
	⁽§²¹²⁾[h]In the name of the holy king *who goes about on the wings of the*
Ps 104:3	*wind*, by the letters of the explicit name[i] revealed to Adam in the Garden of Eden, he who rules over the constellations, and the sun and the moon

---

a. "and he is enthroned . . . in the whole world"; "and his is the kingdom. Blessed be the name of the glory of his kingdom etc." TA.

b. "the adjuration"; + "backward" (or "out of order") M7; + "all of it" TA; + "from its beginning" N.

c. For §209 see the relevant note to §205 above.

d. "going"; "then you shall go" JA. Margalioth emends to "go" (impv.), but this does not fit the sense as well as "going" (applied to the sun). According to 1 En. 72:5, the sun takes a northern route after sunset to reach the east again.

e. "in the third hour" or "for three hours."

f. "white clothes"; "a white fringe" TA; "new clothing" JA.

g. "the Dominion" G19 N; "God" M7; omit TA; "Dominion and wise one" L. JA transposes "Dominion" and "king."

h. F places §§212–16 later as §§327–31. As usual, I have collated its readings here with §§212–16.

i. The term "explicit name" refers here to the four-letter divine name, YHWH, the Tetragrammaton. This name is frequently used in Jewish magical and mystical literature.

prostrate themselves before him like servants to their master.[a] In the name of the wondrous God I adjure you that you make known to me this great miracle that I seek, that I may see the sun [55]in its might in *the wheel of its chariots*[b] and that no matter of enigmas shall be too wonderful for me, and that I may see it *like full day* and I may ask from it my wish, and that it speak with me *as a man speaks* with *his friend*. Let it tell me the deep secrets and make known to me enigmas, but let it not attack me with anything bad.

Exod 14:25
Josh 10:13
Exod 33:11

As you finish speaking you shall hear the sound of thunder from the far north and you will see something like lightning going out and the earth shall glisten in front of you. (§213)And after you see this, prostrate yourself and fall on your face [60]to the earth and pray[a] this prayer:[d]

Sh-R §§60, 168

Hallowed east-rising Helios, good sailor, faithful guardian, trusty[e] *leader,*[f] *who long ago established the mighty*[g] *wheel, holy director, very powerful,*[h] *Lord, bright guide, absolute ruler, star-organizer,*[i] (§214)*I, so-and-so son of so-and-so*[j] *place my supplication before you that you appear to me without* [65]*dread*[k] *and you be revealed to me without* [65]*awe*[l] *and that you must not hide from me any matter and that you tell me in truth all that I seek.*

Jer 38:26; Dan 9:20

Jer 38:14

(§215)Stand on your feet and you shall see it in the north wind going eastward. Afterward turn your hands behind you and bow your head downward[m] and ask everything that you wish.[n] (§216)After you ask for it, lift up your eyes to the heavens and recite:

1 En. 72:5

'WRPLY'L, 'WRPLY'L, I adjure you by him who formed you for his effulgence and for his adornment to illuminate his world and gave [70]you

---

a. The text of §212 up to this point is very corrupt. Margalioth reconstructs from various sources. The text of L is close to his reconstructed text.
   b. "*its chariots*" or "*its chariot*" M7.
   a. "and pray"; "and speak" M7 TA.
   d. "this prayer"; + "in the name of heaven" M7; + "to the name of the sun" TA; + "This is the prayer" M2; + "in alignment with the sun. The prayer follows." L. The italicized prayer in §213 is certainly written in Greek transcribed into Hebrew letters, but the manuscripts are very corrupt and any specific reconstruction is speculative. I follow the transcription of Margalioth but I also note the variant possibilities he raises and the differences in the transcription of Morgan. For other attempts at a translation, see Rebiger and Schäfer, *Sefer ha-Razim* 2:257–59. For another prayer to Helios, see *PGM* XXXVI. 211–230.
   e. "trusty"; or "most high."
   f. "faithful guardian, trusty leader"; Morgan: "faithful leader of sunbeams, trusty one."
   g. "mighty" or "heavenly."
   h. "very powerful" or "poet."
   i. "star-organizer"; Morgan: "soldier."
   j. "so-and-so son of so-and-so"; omit M7; place after "my supplication" M2 F.
   k. "dread"; "awe" M7; "fear" TA M2.
   l. "awe"; "fear" M7.
   m. "bow your head downward" L; "turn your head downward" M7; "look to the ground" TA.
   n. "everything that you wish"; "every single thing" M7; "everything that you seek" TA.

The Book of the Mysteries (Sefer ha-Razim)

rulership over the day,[a] that you not harm me and you do not put me in dread, so that I may not be in dread and may not tremble and that you may turn on your way in peace. And I have released you[b] that you may not be delayed from going, *from now until forever*.

Ps 115:18

Amen. Selah.

The Fifth Firmament[c]

(§217)The fifth firmament is most ascendant, worthy in appearance, and in it are[d] clouds of effulgence. It is full of angels of majesty and within it they rumble with dread and their station is armies upon armies. They ornament the one who hews them from flame[e] and the sound of their running is like the agitation of the sea, and their walking is like wheels of earthquake.[f]

Ps 29:7

The Twelve Princes of the Fifth Firmament

(§218)There twelve princes of glory are enthroned on thrones of adornment,[g] and the likeness of their thrones is ⁵like the appearance of fire. They comprise four sides through the center of the firmament and they turn to the four winds of the world, three to each wind.[h] (§219)Angels run on their missions and from their roar the world quakes, from their breath lightning bolts go out, and they have wings of fire wrapped in the garlands of fire. And from the splendor of their faces the firmament glistens.[i] And they are appointed over the twelve months of the year and they understand what will happen in every single month. And apart from them nothing happens, for this they were formed (for) their station, ¹⁰each over his month, so that *they may make known to the months* what is coming in every single year.[j]

Isa 47:13

The Names of the Twelve Princes

(§220)These are the names of the twelve princes of glory of the fifth firmament: Š'PY'L DGHY'L DYDN'WR T'NBWN TRWRGR MWR'L PḤDRWN YLDNG 'NDGNWR MPNY'L ḤŠNDRNWS 'BRKY'L.[k]

    a. Margalioth reconstructs "by him who formed . . . the day" from material not available to me, but N and L have a text close to this.

    b. "I have released you" with M7 TA L. Margalioth reads "you release you." I cannot find this reading in the manuscripts and it does not make sense in Hebrew. Morgan emends to "I release you," but no manuscript has this reading.

    c. L gives the name of the fifth firmament as *Mahum*, perhaps a corruption of a Hebrew word for "Habitation" or "Residence," traditional names for one of the seven heavens. See also the relevant notes to §§182 and 201 above.

    d. "in appearance, and in it are"; "in appearance, they multiplied" M2; "in a hundred myriad" P F.

    e. "who hews them from flame"; "who forms them from flame" M7; "who forms them" TA.

    f. Reading "earthquake" with most of the Hebrew manuscripts and Sefer Razi'el. N reads "fire." Margalioth reads "thunder" with JA.

    g. "adornment"; "effulgence" TA.

    h. "three to each wind"; omit M2 P F N.

    i. "glistens"; "flashes" M7; "is split" P F; "spits" N.

    j. "year"; "month" M7.

    k. The manuscripts preserve a short and a long version (with variations) of this list of angels. The long version as excerpted in G41 reads as follows.

    "And these are the names of the twelve princes who stand over the twelve months of the

(§222)ᵃ"These areappointedᵇ over the twelve months of the year, from the month of Nisan to the month of Adar, each one in his month as they are written.

A rite to learn the month of your own death and other events

(§223) ¹⁵If you seek to know in which month you shall pass away from the world or what shall happen in any month, and in which month the rain shall happen and whether produce shall be abundant and whether the olive tree shall drop its fruit, and in which month kings shall array (for) war, and in which month death shall be abundant among mortals and among cattle, in which month illness shall fall among people, and whatever you wish, you will ask and you will know.ᶜ

PGM I. 188–189

(§224)If you want to know in which month you shall pass away from the world,ᵈ ²⁰take *lamellae* of refined gold,ᵉ and make from them twelve hammered (plates) and write on each one of them the name of the angelᶠ and the name of his month.ᵍ And take oldʰ good oil, seven years old, and throwⁱ all the hammered (plates) inside it and you shall adjure this adjuration over the oil seven times and recite:

(§225)ʲI adjure you, angels of knowledge and insight, by the one who said and the world came into being, in the name ofᵏ the magnificent and il-

---

year. The name of the first is Š'PY'L. The name of the second is DHGY'L. The n[ame of the thi]rd is DYDN'WR. The name of the fourth is T'NBW. [The name of the fif]th is TRWRGR. The name of the sixth is MWR'L. [The name of the seve]nth is PHDRWN. The name of the eighth is YLDNG. The name of the ninth is 'NDGNWR. The name of the tenth is MPNY'L. The name of the eleventh is HŠNDRNWS. The name of the twelfth is 'BRBY'L. Š'PY'L stands over the month of Nisan. DHGY'L stands over the month of Ayyar. DYDN'WR stands over the month of Sivan. T'NBW stands over the month of Tammuz. TRWRGR stands over the month of Av. MWR'L stands over the month of Elul. PHDRWN stands over the month of Tishri. YLDNG stands over the month of Marheshvan. 'NDGNWR stands over the month of Chislev. MPNY'L stands over the month of Tevet. HŠNDRNWS stands over the month of Shevat. 'BRBY'L stands over the month of Adar. And they are the ones who make known what shall be in every single month to anyone who purifies himself and asks of them and also in which month it shall come about. He shall understand and know."

JA is badly damaged, but probably read similarly. The Hebrew basis of L was probably similar, but L adds a thirteenth angel, "Romyel," over the intercalary additional month of Adar. M2 and Sefer Razi'el include a brief paragraph on the angels in Aramaic as §221. F places §§220, 222–28 as §§340–41, 344–49. As usual, I have collated its readings here with §§220, 222–28.

a. Paragraph 222 is omitted in M7 TA L.
b. "These are appointed"; "All of them are" M2.
c. The text of §223 is very corrupt in most of the manuscripts, but P and F preserve a coherent text. Margalioth's text is close to theirs.
d. "from the world"; "to your tomb" M7 TA; "[to] your [t]omb from the world" G20.
e. "refined gold"; "gold refined sevenfold" (G20 "[gold refined] sevenfold") G20 M7 M2.
f. "the angel"; + "on one side" M7.
g. "his month"; + "on one side" G20 M7.
h. "old"; omit M7 TA M2.
i. "throw"; "put" G20 M7 TA M2.
j. The manuscripts of §§225–28, 230 have many haplographies, corruptions, and longer readings. Again, P and F preserve a coherent text that is mostly followed by Margalioth.
k. "in the name of"; + "*God Most High, Creator of heaven and earth* (Gen 14:19)" TA.

The Book of the Mysteries (Sefer ha-Razim)

Isa 6:1

luminated God of truth, the exalted and lifted-up, strong and mighty, [25]powerful and wondrous king, God of all the creatures,[a] Rock of hosts, righteous, resplendent, upright, and faithful, and in the name of the one who stationed you over all the months of the year, *He who is enthroned in*

Ps 91:1

secret, the Most High who reveals mysteries[b] of secrets, He who rules over death and life, who is king forever and ever and ever, who is established everlastingly and everlastingly, by this great, intense, strong, dreadful, fearsome, wondrous, pure, holy adjuration I adjure you [30]that you make known to me the month of my passing away[c] in truth[d] and that you bring up a destiny for me regarding my request.[e]

PGM VII. 915

(§226) And put the oil beneath the stars for seven nights in a new glass vessel,[f] and the sun must not see it. And on the seventh night stand at midnight and look in the oil, and whatever hammered (plate) floats on the surface of the oil, you must see which month is written on it: in this month is your designated time to pass away.[g]

(§227) But before you do this working, purify yourself from all impurity for three weeks of [35]days and keep yourself from all small cattle[h] and from everything that emits blood and even fish. And you must not drink wine, and you must not go near a woman, and you must not touch a grave,[i] and be careful of a nocturnal emission. You must go about humbly and with prayer,[j] you must spend a long time in prayer and supplications, and prepare your heart for the fear of heaven[k], and you will succeed.

(§228) Take the oil after the working and be careful with it, for there is great healing in it. Make a signet ring of silver, pure from dross[l], and take all the

---

a. "the magnificent . . . creatures"; "In the name of *the God of all flesh* (Jer 32:27)" M7; "In the name of *the God of the spirits to all flesh* (Num 16:22)" TA.
b. "mysteries"; "storehouses" G20 M7 TA.
c. "my passing away"; "my death" G20 M7 TA.
d. "in truth" + "and all that I seek from you, you shall speak before me in truth" M7.
e. "to me regarding my request"; + "and all that you desire, write" G20 (damaged) M7.
f. "vessel"; omit P F N.
g. "your designated time to pass away"; "your death" M7.
h. For "small cattle" cf. the relevant note to §110 above. M7 reads "disgrace."
i. "you must not go near a woman, and you must not touch a grave"; "you must not touch a menstrually impure woman nor the dead nor swarming things" M7; "you must not have sex with a woman and you must not go near a menstrually impure woman nor the dead nor a grave" M2. L paraphrases but is closest to M2 without the reference to a menstrually impure woman.
j. "you must go about humbly and with prayer"; "strive greatly to do righteousness and give some of (omit "some of" M2) your bread to the poor and you must speak a prayer (omit "and you must speak a prayer" M2)" M7 M2.
k. "heaven"; + "and stay far away from every word of (omit "every word of" TA; omit "every" M2) falsehood and walk on the level" M7 TA M2.
l. "silver pure from dross" with Margalioth. The word translated "dross" appears to be a Greek word transliterated into Hebrew letters, but the manuscripts are corrupt and any reconstruction is speculative. Morgan reads it as a different Greek word that he takes to mean "pot-bellied." With his reading, translate the phrase "pure silver with a large hollow space within." L refers to the "head" of the ring, which could support Morgan's interpretation, but this may be a guess from context.

hammered (plates) and put (them) in the signet ring with ⁴⁰a white flower and with asbestos. Seal (it) and put (it) on your finger. No evil eye and no evil spirit shall come near you and no evil thing shall have authority in (your) house. And in the oil is great healing for the sick.ᵃ

PGM XIII. 354–356

The Sixth Firmamentᵇ

⁽§²³⁰⁾The sixth firmament—its treasuries are full of honeycomb and in it a place is prepared for the spirits of the righteous, and light and fire encircle it. In it are *double myriads of twice thousands* and hosts and camps standing in dread and in quaking. And on the head of every one of themᶜ is something in the likeness of a crown of fire. And their fire is in the likeness of gold. And bands of a host marchᵈ within it and their might is like *fire ⁵that cannot be blown out*. And they have fear from the aweᵉ of the rulers, for two princes rule over them: one to the west of the firmament and one to the east. ⁽§²³¹⁾Beforeᶠ the armies of the spirits are myriads of angelsᵍ formed from flame and burning like fire. Their bodies are like glowing coals of fire and their station is over glowing coals of fireʰ and they areⁱ agitated and quake to burst forthʲ with them with songs and praisesongs to the magnificent one of the ages who prepared them for the adornment of his worth and for the worth of his adornment.ᵏ

Sh-R §§237, 251; Ps 68:18

Job 20:26

The Two Angels Who Rule the Camps of the Sixth Firmamentˡ

⁽§²³²⁾¹⁰These are the two holy angels who rule over all the camps of the sixth firmament. The name of the first is 'PRKSY and the name of the second is TWQPYRS. And all the princes of the camps attend before them.ᵐ

The Chiefs of the Western Camps

⁽§²³³⁾These are the chiefs of the camps that are on the west of the firmament: WYWTN DWKMS'L KRH'L 'ŠRY'L BYW'L NRH'L GṢQY'L GR'YH ŠRY'L MSGY'L ¹⁵ḤNY'L 'WRPNY'L 'QWDW MWK'L 'LNYTK'L DM'L 'KZ'N ŠYR'YWM NHRY'L BHDRK ŠWPRY'L SDRKYN DBWB'WR 'MLY'L

---

a. "And in the oil . . . sick."; omit M7 TA M2. Paragraph 229 contains astrological material connected to angels and the days of the week and is found only in M2 and Sefer Razi'el.

b. L gives the name of the sixth firmament as *Zebul*, Hebrew for "High Abode," a traditional name for one of the seven heavens.

c. "one of them"; "angel" G33 G21 M7; "one of their appearances" P F N.

d. "march"; "burns" (*sic*) M7.

e. "the awe"; "the wrath" TA M2.

f. "Before"; "Before them" G21 (damaged) TA M2; "And their wings are" P F N.

g. "are myriads of angels"; "are myriads of myriads of angels" TA; "and much filled" M2; "Their hand are (*sic*) filled," P F; "full of blood" N.

h. "glowing coals of fire"; "streams of water" M7 TA.

i. "they are"; "the waters are" G21 M7 TA.

j. "to burst forth"; "to entreat: M7; "to rend" P.

k. "his adornment"; + "and the ones who stand for the glory of his potency" G21.

l. F moves §§232–38 to §§332–38 and N moves §§232–38 to §§353–60. In both cases, as usual, I have collated their evidence here.

m. "And all . . . before them." omit M7 TA. G21 is damaged but ends with "by their permission."

The Book of the Mysteries (Sefer ha-Razim)

TMPNYH BHḤML PRNYN 'MṢTY'L TYMNHRQ. Over these 'PRKSY rules, he who encamps to the west of the firmament.

The Chiefs of the Eastern Camps

(§234)And these are the chiefs of the camps that are to the east of the firmament: GWRY'L SNY'L 'ZRY'L ²⁰ŠRY'L 'LY'L MLKY'L MLMY'L ṢMY'L RNḤY'L 'QRY'L QŠTY'L 'BRKY'L ŠDRY'L SPYPY'L 'RM'T DMW'L MRY'L 'NNY'L NYPLY'L DRMY'L G'ŠY'L MNHR'L BHNYRY'L 'PŠRY'L QL'Y'L HDRNY'L DLRY'L Š'PY'L DLGLY'L 'DNNY'L ṬHRY'L DBRY'L HMNKY'L HNY'L ṬWBY'L. Over these TWQPYRS rules, he who encamps to the east of the firmament.

A rite to generate an illusion of bodyguards

(§235)²⁵If you seek to go on a journey (or) to war and you seek to return from the war or from the journey, or to flee from the city[a] and you seek that there should appear with you *a numerous crowd of people* and that all who see you shall be in dread of you as of one who has a militia with him, and that they are armed with sword and spear and all battle gear, (§236)before you go out of the city or from the place where you are staying, purify yourself from all impurity and cleanse your flesh from all[b] sin and guilt. Make for yourself a sealring of iron ³⁰and pure foil[c] of gold, and write the names of the overseers and the names of the chiefs of the camps on the third day in the month[d] and put (it) inside the sealring. Engrave on the sealring, apart from the foil, the likeness of a man and a lion. At the time that you go out to go from the place from where you go out to war and you see that men are going out to get you, take the sealring and put it inside your mouth and lift your eyes to heaven with a clean and pure heart and invoke the names of the overseers and the names of the chiefs that are ³⁵in the sixth habitation who attend before them and recite:

Joel 2:2

PGM IV 170

Sh-R §139

(§237)I adjure you angels of power and might, by the *powerful and mighty* right hand, by the vigor of his might and by the overpoweringness of his rulership,[e] by the God who was revealed at Mount Sinai with the chariots of double myriads, by the God whose attendants are a thousand thousand myriads, by the Lord who delivered Israel from Egypt with sixty myriads, by the one who lives forever, who spoke with Moses face to face, by the God who *reduces potentates* ⁴⁰*to nothing*, by the Rock in whose hand is enough[f] to save and to deliver, by the one who commanded and heated

Ps 24:8

Sh-R §§230, 251; Ps 68:18

Dan 7:10

Exod 12:37

Exod 33:11

Isa 40:23

---

a. "from the city"; + "or from the war" TA.
b. "from all"; + "blood and" M7.
c. Cf. the relevant note to §70 above.
d. "the third day of the month" or "on three days of the month; TA M2 Mafteaḥ Shelomo read "on the third of the month."
e. "and by the overpoweringness of his rulership"; "by the might of your days (emend to "of your right hand") YH'L *Most High, Creator of heaven and earth* (Gen 14:19) and the whole adjuration that we have written in the fifth firmament to the twelve overseers" TA.
f. "in whose hand is enough"; "the Almighty (cf. Jer 18:14) in whose hand is" M7 Mafteaḥ Shelomo. M2 has the corrupt reading "man in his hand."

up the camp of Sennacherib,[a] in his name and by its letters[b] I invoke and adjure you that you come and you stand with me to help me at this time in every place where I go, and that you appear with me as a great army in all your might and in the overpoweringness of your spears,[c] and that all who see me up close and from afar[d] and all who come to fight with me and to get me may be shattered[e] ⁴⁵before me from the abundance of the dread of your awe, and that they be unable to harm me and to get near me. *May there fall upon them awe and dread* and may awe of me fall upon them and upon all the children of Adam and Eve and upon every harmful animal, and may they be trembling and shaking before me.

2 Kgs 19:35//Isa 37:36; 2 Chr 32:21; T. Adam 4:6

2 Kgs 6:17; Matt 26:53
Exod 15:16

(§238)When you finish speaking the adjuration, you shall see before you something like smoke and misty cloud. Remove the sealring from your mouth and put it on your finger. When you come into your house and you want to release them, you shall return (it) into your mouth ⁵⁰and stand facing the sun and invoke the angels backward,[f] and afterward you must recite:

Sh-R §102

I release you; go on your way.
Then put the sealring on a finger.

The Seventh Firmament
The Glory of the Seventh Firmament

(§239)[g]The seventh firmament[h] is entirely sevenfold light
and from its light all the habitations glisten.[i]
In it the throne of glory is firm over four living creatures of glory.[j]
In it are treasuries of lives and treasuries of souls.
There is no reckoning or dissolution of the great illumination that is in it,
and the fulfilled illumination illuminates the whole earth.

---

a. "and heated up the camp of Sennacherib"; "and the waters were closed ("collected" Mafteaḥ Shelomo) on one side (cf. Gen 1:9 LXX; Exod 14:21)" M7 Mafteaḥ Shelomo; + "with fire" TA; + "and its kings" N; + "King of Syria" L.
b. "and by its letters"; "and by its signs" M7.
c. "and in the overpoweringness of your spears"; "with every weapon of battle" TA.
d. "and from afar"; + "be confounded by me" M7.
e. "and all who come . . . may be shattered"; "be confounded and shattered and fall" TA.
f. "backward"; or "out of order."
g. Paragraphs 239–59 have a parallel passage in the Shi'ur Qomah tradition and Margalioth made use of it in his reconstructed text, even though it does not come from a manuscript of Sefer ha-Razim. I cite the Shi'ur Qomah passage according to Schäfer, Schlüter, and von Mutius, *Synopse zur Hekhalot-Literatur*. It is found in §§966–67, 969.
h. G43 and L give the name of the seventh firmament as "*Arabot(h)*," a transliteration of the traditional Hebrew name of the seventh heaven.
i. "and from its light all the habitations glisten"; for "the habitations" G21 M7 M2 read "the springs" and TA reads "the luminaries." P F N read "and it enlightens and makes glisten all the habitations."
j. The four living creatures are described in Ezek 1:5–14. In Ezek 10 they are identified with the cherubim. The living creatures and the cherubim are traditional angelic inhabitants of the divine throne room in both Judaism and Christianity.

The Book of the Mysteries (Sefer ha-Razim)

> Angels are held in pillars of light
> and their light is like the light of Venus.
> And it is not extinguished,
> for [5]their eyes are like sparkles of lightning
> and their station is over light.

The Glory of God

> And they ornament in awe the one who is enthroned on the throne of glory,
> ([§240])for he alone is enthroned in his habitation of holiness.
> He seeks justice and paves the way for righteousness,
> He judges in truth and speaks in righteousness,
> and before him books of fire are opened

Dan 7:10
> and before him rivers of fire stretch.

Job 41:17
> *At his lifting up the gods are afraid,*[a]

Job 26:11
> and at his roar *the pillars vibrate,*

Isa 6:4
> and at his voice *the foundations of the thresholds totter.*
> And they[b] stand before him
> but they do not behold his likeness,[c]
> for [10]he is made secret from every likeness of an eye[d]

Exod 33:20
> and there is no one who may see him and live.
> ([§241])His likeness is hidden from all,

Sh-R §211
> but the likeness of all is not made secret from him.

Job 12:22
> *He reveals deep things from darkness*
> and knows what is in the secret places of gloom.

Dan 2:22
> For light encamps with him

Ps 104:2
> and he is enwrapped as with a garment of light.
> He is enthroned on the throne of light
> and around him is intense light.[e]

Ezek 1:5, 15–21
> ([§242])Living creatures and *ophannim*[f] bear him
> and they fly with their wings.

---

a. "*At his lifting up the gods are afraid*"; "From his fire the armies are afraid" P F N. Margalioth reads "dominions" for "gods," based on material not available to me. L reads "and before his fear the angels tremble."

b. For "they," Margalioth reads "his armies," based on the reading in Schäfer, Schlüter, and Mutius, *Synopse* §966.

c. "his likeness"; "the likeness of the face of him who tabernacles on the chariot" M7.

d. For "likeness of an eye" (the reading of all Hebrew manuscripts available to me) Margalioth reads "eye."

e. "and around him is intense light." This line is missing in the manuscripts of Sefer HaRazim available to me, but Margalioth reports that it is found in L6577 (see Rebiger and Schäfer, *Sefer ha-Razim* 1:20 [#8]). It also appears in Schäfer, Schlüter, and Mutius, *Synopse* §966. Some such line seems to be needed to make up the poetic couplet. TA omits "He is enthroned . . . intense light."

f. The *ophannim* appear in Ezek 1:15–21 and 10:6, 9–14, 16. The word *ophan* is one of the Hebrew words for "wheel." They seem to be animate elements of the architecture of a divine vehicle. In later tradition they are understood to be angelic inhabitants of the divine throne room. For the living creatures see the relevant note to §239 above.

The Book of the Mysteries (Sefer ha-Razim)

They have six wings apiece,
and with their wings they cover their faces[a]   Isa 6:2; Rev 4:6–8
and they put their faces down,
and to the four of them[b] ¹⁵they turn their faces.
Their faces do not rise up,[c] from their dread of him who is over them.[d]
Companies upon companies stand side by side before him
and they immerse in rivers of purity
and they wrap themselves in coverings of white[e] fire.
And they answer with humility in a strong voice,
Holy, holy, holy, Y"Y of hosts; the whole earth is full of his glory.   Isa 6:3
(§243)[f]And he anticipates all actions
and he was when there was no earth and heaven
and he is alone and there is no stranger with him.
The habitation is suspended on his arm,
and awe of him is in all habitations,
²⁰and fear of him among all angels.
For by the breath of his mouth[g] they were hewn out,
and for the adornment of his potency they were established.
He is unique and who will turn him back?[h]   Job 23:13
If he has commanded, there is no one to abolish,
for he is the King of kings of kings,
ruler over all the kings of the earth,
and lifted up among the angels of heaven.
He searches out hearts that are not yet formed,
and he knows thoughts that do not yet exist.

Concluding Benedictions

(§244)Blessed is his name
and may the worth of his adornment be blessed[i] forever and ever and
    everlastingly and everlastingly, eternally and eternally,

    a. The traits of the living creatures and the *ophannim* are combined with traits of the seraphim in Isa 6:2–3. A similar amalgamation of traits of the seraphim with the living creatures is found in Rev 4:6–8.
    b. Either the four living creatures (with Morgan) or the four directions of the compass (with Rebiger and Schäfer, *Sefer ha-Razim* 2:176).
    c. "Their faces do not rise"; "They do not raise their faces" TA M2.
    d. I follow Rebiger and Schäfer in reading this line with Schäfer, Schlüter, and Mutius (Rebiger and Schäfer, *Sefer ha-Razim* 2:176 and n. 479; Schäfer, Schlüter, and Mutius, *Synopse* §966). Margalioth adds "and from their awe," based on material not available to me. Margalioth's text could be translated, "Their faces do not rise up from their dread and from their awe. And behold, over them stand companies upon companies before him."
    e. "white"; omit M2 P F N.
    f. Margalioth's text of §243 is close to that of M7.
    g. "his mouth"; "his nostrils" M7.
    h. P ends here with the conclusion, "Behold, these are the ends of the hosts above who are in heaven and the heaven of the heavens."
    i. "Blessed is his name . . . be blessed"; "Blessed is he and blessed is his name and the worth of his adornment is" F N.

The Book of the Mysteries (Sefer ha-Razim)

	for there is no God besides him
Isa 44:6; Ps 18:32//2 Sam 22:32	[25]and apart from him there is no God.
	(§245)Blessed is his name in every single generation
	and may he be blessed in the habitations above.[a]
	(§246)[b]Blessed is his name by his might
	and may his invocation be blessed by the ornamentation of his power.
	For as is his name, so is his psalming, as it is said,
	as is your name, O God, so is your psalming to the ends of the earth.
Ps 48:11	*Righteousness fills your right hand.*
	And he draws pure ones near to fear him
	and he drives impure ones far away with the wrath[c] of his anger.
	He removes mountains with valiance and with might,
Job 9:5	*and they did not know when he overturned them in his anger.*
	He suspends the world like a grape cluster.
	[30]He carries everything that was and is and will be,
Dan 7:9	and is *the Ancient of Days*,
Prov 8:18	and with him is *wealth, riches, and righteousness*.[d]
Ezek 3:12	(§247) [e]*Blessed is his glory from his place*
	and may it be blessed with the ornamentation of his worth.
	He fills the heart of those who fear him with knowledge to search out
	and to know the power of the fear[f] of his name.
	§248)Blessed is his name in the seat of his adornment
	and may it be blessed by the adornment of his power.
Job 38:22	(§249)Blessed is his name in *the treasuries of snow*
Dan 7:10	and may it be blessed in the rivers of flame.
	(§250)Blessed is his name in the misty clouds of power[g]
	and may it be blessed in the clouds of effulgence.
	(§251)Blessed is his name by *the chariot of* [35]*double myriads*
Sh-R §§230, 237; Ps 68:18	and may it be blessed by *the twice thousands.*
	(§252)Blessed is his name by the chains of fire

a. §245 is missing in TA. It may have been lost by haplography (the scribe's eye skipping over identical text), but Morgan thinks it is a secondary prose gloss in this poetic passage.

b. I follow Margalioth's eclectic reconstruction of §246. The individual Hebrew manuscripts are corrupt, but L is translated from a Hebrew text very close to his.

c. "wrath"; "awe" M2 F N.

d. "with valiance ... *and righteousness*"; "and breaking proud ones, making poor and making rich, debasing and also exalting, merciful and gracious, visiting infertile women, bringing death and bringing life, supporting the fallen, redeeming and saving, knowing and a witness" TA.

e. Margalioth's text of §§247–59 is close, but not completely identical, to M7. L is translated from a text close to his. TA omits §247, 250–54, 256. The Hebrew manuscripts are corrupt and vary widely.

f. "fear"; "worth" M7.

g. "power"; "for his wonders" M2 F N. Margalioth reads "splendor," based on the parallel in Schäfer, Schlüter, and Mutius, *Synopse* §969.

and may it be blessed by the cords[a] of ignition.
(§253)Blessed is his name by the sounds of the thunderbolts
and may it be blessed by the sprint of lightning bolts.[b]
(§255)Blessed is his name in the mouth of all who are on the earth
and may it be blessed in *the abysses of the earth*. Ps 71:20
(§256)Blessed is his name in all the deserts
and may it be blessed in the waves[c] of the sea.
(§257)Blessed is his name alone by his throne
and may it be blessed[d] in the enthronement of his power.
(§258)Blessed is his name in the mouth of every soul
and may it be blessed in the song of every creature.
(§259)Blessed be Y"Y [40]forever. Amen and amen. Hallelujah![e]

a. "cords"; "secrets" M7.
b. Paragraph §254 is found only in M7. It reads, "Blessed be his name in his holiness, for his glory is the ornamentation of his power, *fearsome one of psalms, wonder-worker* (Exod 15:11)."
c. "waves"; "waters" M7.
d. "blessed"; "exalted" M7.
e. Paragraphs §§260–75 are found only in L. The final paragraph concludes: "Here ends the sixth book of the heavens, which is called Samayn." The concluding paragraph §276 is found only in M7. It reads, "The Book of the Mysteries, which was given to the first Adam and to Solomon the King, is completed. It is finished and completed. Praise be to the one who formed the world." After §259, TA continues with material unique to it in §§277–86 and the final paragraph concludes with: "The words of the Book of the Mysteries are finished. Blessed be he who says, 'Blessed be the Lord.'" After §259, M2 continues with material unique to it in §§287–91 and the final paragraph concludes with: "The Book of the Mysteries is completed with the help of the one who tabernacles (with) powerful ones." After §259, N continues with §292–95, which give the same text as §§28, 116–17, 119. At that point N and F continue with the rest of the *Umstellungtyp* recension.

The Prophecy of the Witch Sibyl (Prophetia Sibyllae magae) or "The Earth Was My Origin" (Mundus origo)
A new translation and introduction

by Johannes Magliano-Tromp

This Christian text, originally written in Latin, is designated as Prophetia Sibyllae magae ("The Prophecy of the Witch Sibyl") or Mundus origo, after its first words ("The earth was my origin"). It is a poem, in its preserved form consisting of 136 lines or verses, which are presented as a speech by the pagan prophetess Sibyl (or: *the* Sibyl). It portrays the prophetess as contrasting the magnitude of God's providential care for humankind with humankind's consistently ungrateful response. This response will lead to their condemnation at the final judgment, and to heavy punishment. Therefore, the prophetess calls upon humanity to live a life of faith, simplicity, and obedience to the divine commandments, in order to obtain forgiveness on that day.

In classical times, the Sibyl was highly renowned as a prophetess of doom, and as an advisor on how to act to avert the grand-scale catastrophes predicted by her. In Greek-speaking circles, a tradition of composing and transmitting Sibylline oracles was developed, in hexameters and archaizing language reminiscent of Homer. This tradition was adopted also by Jews, and later on by Christians. In the Latin world, the Sibyl features widely in the work of such prominent poets as Vergil and Statius.

The Sibyl played no conspicuous role in the earliest phase of Roman Christianity. However, one of Vergil's references to Sibylline prophecy came to be regarded by Christians as a pagan prophecy of Christ, which, together with the paramount position occupied by Vergil in the Roman school curriculum, must have contributed greatly to the revival of Christian interest in this genre, first through the works of Lactantius (flor. 303), then those of Augustine (354–430).

Mundus origo can be considered as one of the earliest examples of the creative adoption of the genre of Sibylline prophecy in the Latin church. Its main message is found in its contrast between God's providence for his creation on the one hand, and human ingratitude on the other—a gap that should logically lead to humankind's destruction in hell, but that can be bridged by God's gracious reaction to human belief in the creed and morals of the Christian church.

A special feature of this text is its insistence on the perfect identity of God, the Father, and God, the Son (the Son being his own Father), which is, from the point of view of orthodoxy, a heresy (see further below, under "Date and Provenance").[1]

Contents

The writing is well structured, and consists of eight distinct parts.

Part 1: introduction of the Sibyl and her oracles (vv. 1–33). In the first lines, the Sibyl

---

1. The term "orthodoxy" here refers to the stance on Christian dogma that eventually became standard in the Roman Catholic Church.

(whose name is not mentioned) presents herself as a prophetess who has often been inspired by God to utter his oracles. These oracles themselves contain truths that were known from the beginning of creation, when God conceived them. God created the world, but also destroyed it through the deluge; it was the same God who created the world, who also descended to the earth to be born from a virgin, and save humanity—creator, punisher, and savior are all the same God; Father and Son are the same God. Although God became man, he lost nothing of his divinity, and after his stay on earth, he returned to his heavenly abode. It is this God, then, who is the source of the Sibyl's prophecies.

Part 2: the Sibyl's prayer (vv. 34–52). The prophetess addresses God, both Father and Son, who are one, asking him why she is obliged to utter her prophecies, which contain truths that are known to God only. These truths concern the past, the present, and the future; the reasons why people act as they do; and the meaning of war, illness, and natural disasters. God, then, who knows why he created rivers of fire below the surface of the earth, also knows the evil secrets of people's hearts.

Part 3: the Sibyl's warning (vv. 53–59). Next, the prophetess addresses humankind, telling them that she herself would rather be burned twice on earth than put her soul at risk on the final day.

Part 4: the day of judgment (vv. 60–73). The day of judgment is described: humankind's sins will be punished by eternal fire, from which there is no escape, neither on account of earthly status, nor by means of witchcraft.

Part 5: salvation for the holy ones (vv. 74–82). The only ones to escape the horrors of the final judgment are the people who have lived a saintly life, the true servants of God, who have always recognized him as such, and have lived a life of prayer and faithfulness to the commandments.

Part 6: God's speech to the holy ones on the day of judgment (vv. 83–113). On the day of judgment, the Sibyl proceeds, God will speak to the faithful "with a good-natured breast"; the prophetess then quotes this future speech in full. God will relate how he created the earth and the heavenly bodies to shine upon it; how he constructed the human body, and filled it with spirit; also, how he made water, animals, and plants to provide humankind with pleasant food and drink. However, he will continue his speech by expressing his great disappointment with the ungratefulness of humans, for whom all this was designed and carried out. Instead of honoring the creator of all, people worship creatures as if these were gods. He will even ask the rhetorical question of why he has redeemed humankind with his own blood, if they do not recognize him as their only true God.

Part 7: the rapid approach of the end, and the need for repentance (vv. 114–132). Once again, the Sibyl addresses her audience, warning them that the day of judgment is rapidly approaching: the elements are already starting to show signs of wear and tear. She sets out that sinful behavior will destroy people in the end, but that there are also great rewards for those who will be saved on account of their faith and repentance, and by their leading a life of goodness, purity, and simplicity.

Part 8: conclusion (vv. 133–136). The Sibyl formally concludes her oracle, and expresses her hope that she may be found worthy of her soul being established into heaven. Her final thought is that life is limited and short.

Manuscripts and Versions

Mundus origo has been preserved in four manuscripts, preserved in Oxford (ninth century), Valenciennes (ninth century), Douai (eleventh century), and Prague (fifteenth century), respectively.[2] Three of these manuscripts were at the basis of the first edition of the text by Bernhard Bischoff, the four of them in the most recent, underlying the translation here presented.[3] Between these manuscripts, only a few and minor differences exist, suggesting that they all derive from one basic text.[4]

Mundus origo is always transmitted together with another Sibylline text, the Dicta Sibyllae magae ("The Sayings of Sibyl, the Witch"). This text, starting with the words "Non multi" ("There are not many gods"), is itself an elaboration of yet another text, In manus iniquas infidelium ("Into the wicked hands of the impious"). The writing last mentioned is a Latin translation of several fragments from the Sibylline Oracles. The Greek text of these fragments was provided by Lactantius in his *Inst.* 4.18, and the Latin text by Augustine in his *Civ.* 18.23.[5]

Nicoletta Brocca has argued that Mundus origo is a secondary addition to Non multi: the latter is sometimes transmitted without the former, but the former never without the latter.[6] However, it cannot be concluded from this that Mundus origo was also written later than Non multi; as a well-structured and unified text, it may have had an existence of its own before it was added to Non multi—the fact of the addition is in itself no evidence for the dating of Mundus origo (see further below).

There is reason to believe that the text represented by the available manuscripts was at home in France.[7] It is also clear, however, that the archetype was not the original text. The text contains many instances of faulty transmission, which are reflected in all manuscripts available, and must therefore have been characteristic of the basic text, too.[8] In quite some instances, this faulty transmission has led to incomprehensible and therefore untranslatable verses, that can sometimes be repaired by drastic conjecture only.

---

2. Bernhard Bischoff, "Die lateinischen Übersetzungen und Bearbeitungen aus den *Oracula Sibyllina*," in *Mélanges Joseph de Ghellinck, S. J.*, 2 vols. (Gembloux: Duculot, 1951), 1:121–47. In addition, vss. 17–22 are quoted in the ninth- or tenth-century Bern codex 184 of Vergil's work, on f. 244v (Bischoff, "Die lateinischen Übersetzungen," 123; according to Karl Wilhelm Müller, it concerns nine verses, of which he quotes vv. 17–19, which are in perfect agreement with the text of the other manuscripts. See Müller, *Analectorum bernensium particula III: De codicibus Virgilii, qui in Helvetiae bibliothecis asservantur* [Bern: Jenni, 1841], 9). According to Bischoff, other codices containing these lines are Vaticanus latinus 1581, f. 125v (twelfth century); Vaticanus latinus 1586, f. 77r (fifteenth century); and Paris BN latinus 2773, f. 24r–24v (eleventh century).

3. Bischoff was unaware of the Douai manuscript, although it had been cataloged. See Chrétien Dehaisnes, *Catalogue général des manuscrits des bibliothèques publiques des départements, VI: Douai* (Paris: Imprimerie nationale, 1878), 113. It was Nicoletta Brocca who signaled its existence in 2008. See Brocca, "La tradizione della Sibilla Tiburtina e l'acrostico della Sibilla Eritrea tra Oriente e Occidente, Tardantichità e Medioevo: Una 'collezione' profetica?," in *L'Antiquité tardive dans les collections Médiévales: Textes et représentations, VIᵉ–XIVᵉ siècle*, ed. Stéphane Gioanni and Benoît Grévins, Collection de l'Ecole française de Rome 405 (Rome: Ecole française de Rome, 2008), 225–60; cf. Brocca, in the reprint of that article as ch. 4 of *Lattanzio*, 301.

4. Bischoff, "Die lateinischen Übersetzungen," 138–39.

5. Bischoff, "Die lateinischen Übersetzungen," 122.

6. Brocca, *Lattanzio*, 302.

7. Valenciennes and Douai are located in the far northwest of France; the Oxford manuscript originates from Tours or its environments, in the center of France; only the fifteenth-century Prague manuscript has a Bohemian origin (Brocca, *Lattanzio*, 300).

8. Bischoff, "Die lateinischen Übersetzungen," 139; Johannes Magliano-Tromp, "*Mundus origo*: A New Edition of *Sibylla maga* (5th–9th Century)," in *The Embroidered Bible: Studies in Biblical Apocrypha and Pseudepigrapha in Honour of Michael E. Stone*, ed. Lorenzo DiTommaso, Matthias Henze, William Adler, SVTP 26 (Leiden: Brill, 2018), 671, doi:10.1163/9789004357211_036.

Genre, Structure, and Prosody

The text stands in the tradition of the Greek Sibylline oracles, a genre that was especially popular in the Roman Empire.[9] Sibyl is the name of the prophetess that, according to legend, lived in the formerly Greek parts of Italy, more precisely, in a cave in Cumae, near Naples. Her oracles were supposed to be written in books that were secret, and preserved by a special committee of the Roman Senate. They were predominantly political in nature, and dealt mainly with wars and natural disasters.

So great was Sibyl's fame that everywhere in the Roman Empire, especially in the Greek speaking parts, all kinds of separate sibyls emerged, turning the prophetess's name into a generic designation: *the* Sibyl. At the latest since the second century BCE, many books were written in her name, a substantial number of which were preserved by the Christian church, including at least one book of Jewish provenance.

In the Greek tradition, Sibylline oracles were written in hexameters, and in archaizing, Homeric language. Mundus origo also uses hexameters; as the Roman equivalent of Homer, Vergil is its model in language and style.[10]

It should be noted that the meter of the verses is often quite irregular.[11] This may partly be ascribed to the more lenient handling of the rules that was common, according to Peter Dronke, in seventh-century Spain.[12] However, it is also clear that the text's transmission has been defective, and this may also explain part of the irregularities—Dronke himself notes that in some lines, the transposition of a word or two suffices to restore a perfect meter.[13]

Another feature of the Sibylline genre is the acrostic in verses 77–83: the first letters of each line together form the word "CRISTUS." There seems to be no particular reason why exactly these lines were chosen to compose an acrostic, and it may simply be the playful application of a possibility. When Sibylline prophecy was introduced into the Latin church by Augustine, it was the acrostic of Sib. Or. 8:217–43 in particular that was popularized by his younger contemporary Quodvultdeus.[14] Thus, this kind of prophecy, and this literary technique, were probably associated with one another from the very start.[15]

Date and Provenance

Bischoff dated the writing to the fourth or fifth century on the basis of two arguments: its exceptional stance with regard to matters of Christology, and the careless way in which it treats the meter.[16]

The christological views that Bischoff intended are those of Sabellianism, or modalistic monarchianism.[17] According to this doctrine, associated with Noetus (flor. 200) and

---

9. For the following, see Rieuwerd Buitenwerf, *Book III of the Sibylline Oracles and Its Social Setting*, SVTP 17 (Leiden: Brill, 2003), ch. 1.3–4 and the literature cited there.

10. Jörg-Dieter Gauger, *Sibyllinische Weissagungen* (Düsseldorf: Artemis & Winkler, 1998), 436.

11. Bischoff, "Die lateinischen Übersetzungen," 145–46.

12. Dronke, "Hermes and the Sibyls: Continuations and Creations," in *Intellectuals and Poets in Medieval Europe*, Storia e letteratura 183 (Rome: Edizioni di storia e letteratura, 1992), 219–44, esp. 232.

13. Dronke, "Hermes," 243.

14. Dronke, "Hermes," 227–31; Jean-Michel Roessli, "Augustin, les sibylles et les *Oracles sibyllins*," in *Augustinus afer, Saint Augustin: Africanité et universalité*, ed. Pierre-Yves Fux, Jean-Michel Roessli, and Otto Wermelinger, 2 vols., Paradosis 45 (Fribourg: Editions universitaires, 2001), 263–86, esp. 278–80.

15. Gauger, *Sibyllinische Weissagungen*, 435–36.

16. Bischoff, "Die lateinischen Übersetzungen," 146.

17. Bischoff, "Die lateinischen Übersetzungen," 144–45.

Sabellius (flor. 215), the Father and the Son are distinguished from each other only in appearance: There is only one God, the Father, who took on the appearance of the Son when he descended to earth, but remaining the same God all the same. Although the representatives of this current generally upheld the incarnation of Christ (distinguishing them from certain gnostic trends), the Father and the Son are identical.

Obviously, this doctrine seeks to maintain the divinity and the humanity of Christ, as well as monotheism, and in that sense it can be regarded as a precursor of the Trinitarian creed.[18] However, it implied that the Father himself had suffered on the cross, and this so-called patripassionism was incompatible with what later became the victorious, and therefore orthodox view of the church.[19]

In Mundus origo, there are indeed numerous indications that the author identified the Father and the Son: It stresses as much in verses 15–21, 28–29, 62–64. Strikingly, the author even seems to distance himself from the biblical record, when he first says that even the Son does not know the timing of the final judgment (v. 61; cf. Matt. 24:36), but then has second thoughts, stating that the Son is the same as the Father, and should therefore also know the same things (vv. 62–64).

Bischoff, assuming that Sabellianism had disappeared by the fifth century, suggested that Mundus origo was written no later than the fifth century. Dronke, however, has denied the monarchian stance of Mundus origo, or at least that monarchian phrasings exclude a date later than the fifth century.[20] In this respect, he is probably right. Modalistic monarchianism is a mild heresy, insofar as it is opposed to gnosticism (denying the humanity of Christ) on the one hand, and Arianism (denying his divinity) on the other. Compared with those extremes, modalistic monarchianism is in the same camp as Trinitarianism. Given the very subtle differences within that party, a theological mistake is easily made, and the offhanded way in which the author rectifies the gospel's testimony about the Son's ignorance about the timing of the end, may sooner be a reflection of his theological naïveté, than the expression of heretical determination. In short, I agree with Dronke that the christological views of Mundus origo are no decisive argument for dating it.

With regard to the author's free handling of the meter, Dronke also disagrees with Bischoff, who had suggested that such lack of civilization could hardly be expected before the fourth century. Instead of criticizing the author of Mundus origo for its irregular meter, Dronke refers to the normal practice in seventh-century Spain, where it was not uncommon to take licenses with the classical tradition. He even goes so far as to suggest that the author's metrical habits betray his seventh-century Spanish background.[21]

Neither scholar attaches much value to the role possibly played by the faulty transmission of the text, even though Dronke notes that the meter of various verses can be restored by simply transposing a word or two.[22] Without meaning to say that the original

---

18. Reinhard M. Hübner and Markus Vincent, *Der paradox Eine: Antignostischer Monarchianismus im zweiten Jahrhundert*, Supplements to Vigiliae Christianae 50 (Leiden: Brill, 1999); see also Adolf Hilgenfeld, *Die Ketzergeschichte des Urchristentums urkundlich dargestellt* (Leipzig: Fues, 1884), 625.

19. In the rendering of their opponent Tertullian, *Prax.* 1: "He (i.e., Praxeas) holds that the Father himself descended into a virgin, was himself born from her, had suffered himself, in short, that he was himself Jesus Christ."

20. Dronke, "Hermes," 232–33.

21. Dronke, "Hermes," 232–33.

22. But, on the faulty transmission of the meter, cf. Bischoff, "Die lateinischen Übersetzungen," 145.

writing was composed in perfectly classical meter, I am not convinced that a less than perfect meter is a reliable indication of its provenance.

For dating the original writing, the only hard evidence is provided by the introduction of the Sibyl into the Latin church by Augustine, and the date of the oldest, but certainly not original manuscript. That means that Mundus origo was written somewhere between the fifth and ninth century.

Most available manuscripts stem from France (including the manuscript containing Non multi, but not Mundus origo), and quite possibly the archetype was originally written there, too; but this allows for no conclusions with regard to the location where the writing was originally composed. It must have been somewhere in western continental Europe.

Literary Context

For Romans in the first century CE, Sibyl was the prophetess par excellence, and she plays a conspicuous role in the works of the classical poets of that time, Vergil and Statius. Vergil himself composed a "Cumaean song," his fourth *Eclogue*, which was taken quite seriously by later Christians, because they read it as a messianic prophecy.[23] Mundus origo contains allusions to, and even quotations from Vergil; for instance, verse 30 is a literal quotation from *Ecl.* 4.17; verses 16–17 are strongly reminiscent of *Aen.* 8.319, and verse 74 of *Aen.* 8.720. In the context of Mundus origo, the quotations and allusions acquire an entirely new meaning—this so-called *cento* (or, "patchwork") technique was quite popular in the early church.[24]

Mundus origo is a relatively early example of the creative reception of Sibylline prophecy in the Latin church. Although educated Christians must have known her name through the works of Vergil and Statius, which were always in their educational program, the figure of the Sibyl as a prophetess of Christ was introduced by Augustine, who in turn had learned from her through the work of Lactantius. Augustine's younger contemporary Quodvultdeus wrote a sermon that became highly popular in the church of the West, and it contained the acrostic on Christ that even entered the Christmas liturgy (see the previous section). However, unlike In manus iniquas or Non multi, it was not a translation or adaptation of an existing Greek text, but an original composition.[25]

In the title of Non multi, the text to which Mundus origo is appended, the Sibyl is designated as a *maga*. Brocca has convincingly argued that this designation is secondary, and that the text originally must have read *magna*, "the great Sibyl."[26] However, it is quite likely that the reputation of the Sibyl contributed to the error. Whereas the masculine form, *magus*, "mage," can be used to designate either wise men or malignant sorcerers, the feminine *maga* refers exclusively to witches and black magic.[27] This matches the ambiguous appraisal of the Sibyl, both in Mundus origo and in the Sibylline tradition in general. The author of Mundus origo stresses the Sibyl's piety and chastity (v. 2), but also makes her confess her sinful nature (vv. 57–58, 65). This tension can easily be alleviated by

---

23. Henri de Lubac, *Exégèse médiévale: Les quatre sens de l'Ecriture; Seconde partie*, vol. 2, Théologie 59 (Paris: Aubier, 1964), ch. 8.5.
24. Karl Olav Sandnes, *The Gospel "According to Homer and Virgil": Cento and Canon*, NovTSup 138 (Leiden: Brill, 2011).
25. Dronke, "Hermes," 231, 235.
26. Brocca, *Lattanzio*, 312–15.
27. Extensively: Brocca, *Lattanzio*, 316–54.

seeing the confession of sins as part and parcel of a saintly life, but in many sources, the portrait of the Sibyl does contain some unfavorable traits, such as sexual licentiousness and telling lies (Sib. Or. 3:814–16; 7:151–62; note that the Sibyl in Sib. Or. 7:151–56 regards these as characteristic of her former way of life).[28]

Bibliography

Bischoff, Bernhard. "Die lateinischen Übersetzungen und Bearbeitungen aus den *Oracula Sibyllina*." Pages 121–47 in vol. 1 of *Mélanges Joseph de Ghellinck, S. J.* 2 vols. Museum Lessianum 13–14. Gembloux: Duculot, 1951.

Brocca, Nicoletta. "La tradizione della Sibilla Tiburtina e l'acrostico della Sibilla Eritrea tra Oriente e Occidente, Tardantichità e Medioevo: Una 'collezione' profetica?" Pages 225–60 in *L'Antiquité tardive dans les collections Médiévales: Textes et représentations, VIe–XIVe siècle*. Edited by Stéphane Gioanni and Benoît Grévins. Collection de l'Ecole française de Rome 405. Rome: Ecole française de Rome, 2008.

———. *Lattanzio, Agostino e la Sibylla Maga: Ricerche sulla fortuna degli Oracula Sibyllina nell'Occidente latino*. Studi e testi tradoantichi 11. Rome: Herder, 2011.

Buitenwerf, Rieuwerd. *Book III of the Sibylline Oracles and Its Social Setting*. SVTP 17. Leiden: Brill, 2003.

Dehaisnes, Chrétien. *Catalogue général des manuscrits des bibliothèques publiques des départements, VI: Douai*. Paris: Imprimerie nationale, 1878.

Dronke, Peter. "Hermes and the Sibyls: Continuations and Creations." Pages 219–44 in *Intellectuals and Poets in Medieval Europe*. Storia e letteratura 183. Rome: Edizioni di storia e letteratura, 1992.

Gauger, Jörg-Dieter. *Sibyllinische Weissagungen*. Düsseldorf: Artemis & Winkler, 1998.

Hilgenfeld, Adolf. *Die Ketzergeschichte des Urchristentums urkundlich dargestellt*. Leipzig: Fues, 1884.

Hübner, Reinhard M., and Markus Vincent. *Der paradox Eine: Antignostischer Monarchianismus im zweiten Jahrhundert*. Supplements to Vigiliae Christianae 50. Leiden: Brill, 1999.

Kurfeß, Alfons. "Prophezeiung der Magierin Sibylla (4./5. Jh.): Erster Versuch einer metrischen Übersetzung." *ZRGG* 3 (1953): 70–73.

Lightfoot, Jane L. *The Sibylline Oracles, with Introduction, Translation and Commentary on the First and Second Books*. Oxford: Oxford University Press, 2007.

Lubac, Henri de. *Exégèse médiévale: Les quatre sens de l'Ecriture*. Théologie 22, 41–42, 59. 4 vols. Paris: Aubier, 1959–1964.

Magliano-Tromp, Johannes. "*Mundus origo*: A New Edition of *Sibylla maga* (5th–9th Century)." Pages 670–85 in *The Embroidered Bible: Studies in Biblical Apocrypha and Pseudepigrapha in Honour of Michael E. Stone*. Edited by Lorenzo DiTommaso, Matthias Henze, and William Adler. SVTP 26. Leiden: Brill, 2018. doi:10.1163/9789004357211_036.

Müller, Karl Wilhelm. *Analectorum bernensium particula III: De codicibus Virgilii, qui in Helvetiae bibliothecis asservantur*. Bern: Jenni, 1841.

Roessli, Jean-Michel. "Augustin, les sibylles et les *Oracles sibyllins*." Pages 263–86 in *Augustinus afer, Saint Augustin: Africanité et universalité*. Edited by Pierre-Yves Fux, Jean-Michel Roessli, and Otto Wermelinger. 2 vols. Paradosis 45. Fribourg: Editions universitaires, 2001.

---

28. See further the comments on Sib. Or. 3:809–16 in Buitenwerf, *Book III*, 296–300.

Sandnes, Karl Olav, *The Gospel "According to Homer and Virgil": Cento and Canon.* NovTSup 138. Leiden: Brill, 2011.

Treu, Ursula. "Christliche Sibyllinen: Lateinische Sibylle (Mundus origo mea est)." Pages 616–19 in *Apostolisches Apokalypsen und Verwandtes.* Vol. 2 of *Neutestamentliche Apokryphen in deutscher Übersetzung.* Edited by W. Schneemelcher. 6th edition. Tübingen: Mohr Siebeck, 1997. Translated into English on pages 681–85 in *Writings Relating to the Apostles; Apocalypses and Related Subjects.* Vol. 2 of *New Testament Apocrypha.* Translated by R. McL. Wilson. Louisville: Westminster John Knox, 2003.

The Prophecy of the Witch Sibyl (Prophetia Sibyllae magae) or "The Earth Was My Origin" (Mundus origo)

Introduction of the Sibyl and Her Oracles

The earth was my origin, but my soul I took from heaven.
Sib. Or. 2:14 God shook my entire, untouched body.
Whenever my ample faith found it to be well and ready for it,
my songs have told me many an oracle.
Sib. Or. 2:4–5 5 The oracles that I write, God must know them.
God conceived my sayings in the castle of his heavenly home,
as soon as he finished his divine office and great task.[a]
He was God before the dawning of light, even before the chaos,
God was from the beginning without end, God, the creator of everything.
10 He discerned the friendly night from the chaos, which was removed,
and commanded that there should be day; and that day and night
would take turns with their lights; and he commanded the stars to set in motion
the cycles of things through which the ages renew themselves.[b]
He poured a flood over the earth, from above to below.
15 And God, having once again confined the waters within their shores,
Vergil, *Aen.* 8.319 was the first to descend from heaven to the earth,
as a man from <man>,[c] the child of an immaculate virgin,
John 19:5 always clad in purple, wearing his crown.
As his own Father, he came <near>[d] by being born,
20 and (they had) one spirit and one soul,
divided in name, but not in authority.
Matt 2:1–2 On the stars' directions, the mages called him by his name.
He descended as a lamb, he whom the world could hardly encompass.
He willed to assume the limbs of the human body,
25 but remained strong through his willpower. With a chaste body,
he could not grow old, even though he <advanced in age>.[e]

    a. Namely, creation. Short forms used are Bischoff = Bischoff, "Die lateinischen Übersetzungen"; Dronke = Dronke, "Hermes"; Kurfeß = Alfons Kurfeß, "Prophezeiung der Magierin Sibylla (4./5. Jh.): Erster Versuch einer metrischen Übersetzung." *ZRGG* 3 (1953): 70–73.
    b. Slightly emended by deleting *et* ("and") at the beginning of the line.
    c. Reading *de homine* instead of *de nomine* ("from name").
    d. Namely, to us, humankind; reading *propius* instead of *proprius* ("appropriately" or "individually"; Dronke).
    e. Reading *vergens* instead of *vegens* ("moving" or "hastening"), or *vigens* ("being vigorous").

As the one who is everywhere in charge, he removes the world's crimes.
And the offspring is himself the Father: both have one spirit,
one power, one will, and they are not divided with regard to their decisions.
30 *And he shall rule the pacified world with the virtues of his Father,*   Vergil, *Ecl.* 4.17
afterward returning to heaven and the golden palace of his Father.
Praise the Mighty One with all your soul and in a loud voice!
It is he who encompasses the ocean, who allows me to speak.

The Sibyl's Prayer

O Father, Highest God, <refuge>[a] and hope of your people,
35 O Highest Son of the Father, whose origin <is>[b] the seed of the Word,
who consult each other's spirit, as friends, about your commandments,
<Immortal God, why do the oracles that rise in my breast
speak secrets that are known to you only?>[c]
Our knowledge of the Highest One does not allow us the greater <things>:[d]
40 what may be, what may have been, and what will be, has to be revealed through prophecy—
which fear takes hold of whose hearts, which spirit accuses the conscience,
which fortune or noble power rules the rulers
(for the soul of kings, too, is moved by your authority),
so that peoples and nations fall, and no times of peace come about,
45 so that there are illness and fever, and the harmful heat from heaven,
so that there are eclipses of the moon and the sun,
so that the extended ocean <flows against>[e] the tides—
You, who have given names to the stars and signs to the heavenly bodies,
who commands the scorching floods to boil (in the innermost of the earth,
50 rivers are made that flow with blazing fire):
the fire of the sun too is known to the both of you only; you, who are able to know
the immortal meaning of all this, you also know the crimes we commit in our thoughts.

The Sibyl's Warning

O mortal man, tell me, What is on your mind, when you lose a part of your body?
"Highest God, just do not surrender me to blood and fire!"
55 As long as you save the soul that you will be losing from your body!

---

    a. Without an addition such as this, the line is far too short, and makes no sense (cf. Kurfeß); for "refuge" (*refugium*) in combination with "hope" (*spes*), see, e.g., Ps 91:2, 9; 94:22.
    b. Reading *est* instead of *es* (Bischoff).
    c. Reading *immortale dee cur* ("Immortal God, why") instead of *immortale iecur* ("immortal liver"; cf. Vergil, *Aen.* 6.598), and supplying an extra line to make sense of the rest of the words; for the Sibyl's reluctance to prophesy, cf. Sib. Or. 3:196–97, as well as Sib. Or. 3:1–4; 5:111, 286; for the secret nature of the knowledge revealed to her, see Sib. Or. 3:812; Tibullus, *Elegy* II 5.16–17, and, in Mundus origo itself, lines 61 and 117–118.
    d. Supplying *quae*.
    e. Reading *influat* instead of *inflet* ("swells").

The Prophecy of the Witch Sibyl or "The Earth Was My Origin"

I know that my figure will come back to me,
and I hope for the fire, and there is not enough fire for the blaze:
I bear the powerful ire and punishment, if I were to be burnt twice.
Fear him, whom the heavens serve, when he will stand up!

Sib. Or. 7:157

The Day of Judgment

Matt 24:36

60 That day will come, of which the High One knows the hour,
which he has not allowed us to know, and has concealed from his Son
(no, I shall not go so far as to say that, for he knows the day, too:
one who is his own Father, and does not differ from him,
he is able to know as well, because it is a power awarded[a] to him).
65 Then we shall all undergo all kinds of punishments for our deeds.
Then one will fear the Highest One, moan and shed tears,
when one sees the <nations>[b] being tortured in a whirlpool of flames,
and him who sets fire to men, and does not stop the punishment.
Then kingdoms are worth nothing, and royal dignities powerless,
70 neither purple nor colorful dress, nor a crown beset with varied gems,
nor <scepters>[c] confided to one's hands, or ages of rule.
Artful tricks are useless, a soothsayer cannot give succour.
Exhausted, everything collapses: honor, power, kingship.

Salvation for the Holy Ones

Vergil, *Aen.* 7.720

The Father himself, hidden behind the gate of his snow-white world,
75 he himself will cause an everlasting splendor to shine on his saints.
Everybody will be praying and imploring for the wrath to subside,
but only a few saintly people with a good heart will come together,
who have always served God the Father with an upright heart,
in whose <minds>[d] has lived the spirit of an eager pupil,
80 and who have wanted to fulfill the commandments with a sincere disposition,
who have always recognized you as God, and who have humbly prayed
with their voices, and have day and night made their moaning heard.

God's Speech to the Holy Ones on the Day of Judgment

Thus he will, with a good-natured breast, speak to you saints:
"Look at me, who has made the system of the heavens and the stars,
85 I have commanded the twin lights to shine on the world,
I have deposited the earth and the seas, and the animals of the deep,
I have distributed the joints over the limbs with my own hands.
I have augmented the body with bones, and (given) marrow to the bones,
and I have established the nerves, and veins full of blood;

---

a. Deriving *scita* from the verb *sciscere* ("to approve"); but the meaning is uncertain.
b. Reading *gentes* instead of *gemitus* ("groan"; Bischoff).
c. Reading *sceptra* instead of *scripta* ("written things"; Bischoff).
d. Reading *mente* instead of *mentes* (Bischoff).

The Prophecy of the Witch Sibyl or "The Earth Was My Origin"

90 I have formed a shiny skin, glueing it to the mud,
and I have inserted souls, and added senses to the mind;
I have given food to the animals, and nutrition for the body,
and I have given riches to the rivers, and fields and mines,
and pure fountains, and water suitable for the fountains,
95 cattle for plowing, small livestock, and species of birds,
I have included milk in the udders, separated from blood,
I have made plants to make the desert furrows green,
I have included the tender ears in spiked seed,
I have decorated the earth with flowers of all sorts,
100 I have provided the sweet lives of the bees and their homes,
I have commanded the round fruits to be full of juice,
I have given the vineyards, and made the <grapes for the branches>.[a]
These provisions I have made for mankind, and nothing invented was withheld from him.
I receive no gratitude, another gets the acknowledgments,
105 the work and the reward are conferred to the creatures made:
they worship mountains and stones, rams, bulls, and caves,
statues, fountains, altars, and a meaningless grave.
They augur the flight of birds, and confess the sun and the moon,
but hold the great maker of these works in contempt, and renounce him.
110 Look at me! Why did I redeem everybody with my own blood,
if they change the rule over mankind from their earthly abode?
Their desires meant more to them than their <fear>[b] of darkness.
But if someone wants his soul to be mine, he should continually be looking for me."

The Rapid Approach of the End, and the Need for Repentance

Accept the commandments with the right mind, and from a chaste body,
115 you who weep; approve of the things that merit reward.
The years are hastening, the ages are running toward the end
that God knows, but has kept me from knowing.
Only this <I know>[c] for a fact: the present and the future have to be prophesied.
For everything is decaying, the stars are falling apart,
120 the earth is dissolving, and the air is dressed in poverty,
because of a lack of vitality, all species become displeasing.
Their deeds weigh heavily on men; (his own) thoughts ruin the guilty one,
but he goes to perdition knowing that faith may cleanse his crimes.
Then every species will be restored. With regard to what he[d] brought forth out of himself,

---

a. Reading *uvasque in vitibus* for *venasque in corpore* ("veins in the body").
b. Reading *horror* instead of *honor* (Bischoff).
c. Reading *scio* instead of *saeculo* ("in the age" or "in the world"; Bischoff).
d. That is, God.

The Prophecy of the Witch Sibyl or "The Earth Was My Origin"

125 he will command that a pure splendor will shine (on it) forever,
and he presents chaste people with a mansion as a <reward>[a] for their deeds.
And under such a Lord there is no place for a rich man;
the poor man, who has believed from the depths of his heart, will be rich.
Sins find hell, and no rewards.
130 To do what is right in excess, that is the shortcut toward life;
to speak what is dear, what the great Maker <loves>;[b]
to regard as truth <what>[c] simple nature has reared.

Conclusion

Thus I, a mere mortal, have spoken the oracles I knew,
who, <as a worshiper>,[d] have not cut any throats, <calling>[e] them sacred.
135 If I am worthy, let him take my soul, and establish it in heaven.
The limited, short life of man passes with the years.

---

a. Reading *palmam* (grammatical direct object of the verb) instead of *palma* (grammatical subject).

b. Reading *diligit* instead of *collegit* ("collected"; Bischoff).

c. Reading *quodque* instead of *quoque* ("also"; Bischoff); the meaning of this line is particularly uncertain.

d. Reading *dicens cultrix* instead of *dies nec ultrix* ("day not vengeful"); but this corrupt line is presumably beyond repair.

e. See preceding note.

The Narration of Joseph
A new translation and introduction

by Anders Klostergaard Petersen

The Narration of Joseph (Latin: Narratio Ioseph) refers to a fragmentarily preserved text in the Sahidic dialect of Coptic. It was part of a poorly preserved codex, the other part of which contained an excerpt from the New Testament pseudepigraphal writing, the Acts of Andrew. The Narration of Joseph was first published in an article in 1961 by the Dutch scholar Jan Zandee.[1] Unfortunately, we hardly know anything about the origin of the text. It was bought by another Dutch scholar, the famous professor on gnostic religion, Gilles Quispel, on behalf of the University Library of Utrecht on January 7, 1956, from the inheritance of the similarly eminent Berlin Coptologist, Professor Carl Schmidt.

According to Schmidt's niece, it is likely that the documents had been bought by her uncle in Cairo shortly before his death in April 1938; but the exact provenance of the manuscript is lost in obscurity. In an article discussing the other text with which the Narration of Joseph had been juxtaposed, Quispel mentions that he had never come across any information in Schmidt's notes, a public announcement, or any rumor among antiquity dealers in Cairo about the existence of the collection of papyri that included this codex fragment.[2] Although regrettable, suffice it to say, that the Narration of Joseph was part of a miscellaneous codex, comprising an Old Testament as well as a New Testament pseudepigraphal text.

Contents

The extant part of the text revolves around the story recounted in Gen 37:15–35 how the brothers came to sell Joseph to a company of Ishmaelites. The narrative presupposes Jacob sending Joseph to Shechem to see how his brothers are faring and how the sheep are doing (cf. Gen 37:12–14). In Gen 37:14 Joseph arrives at Shechem but does not find his brothers. In his wandering to search for them he meets an anonymous person whose narrative function is to inform him that the brothers have proceeded to Dothan. In the Narration of Joseph, Joseph meets the anonymous person who—disguised in the shape of an old man—in fact, turns out to be the devil (cf. Gen 37:15). He tries to lead Joseph astray, but Joseph recognizes his true identity and rebukes him.

Dishonored by Joseph, the devil recedes to the brothers. He succeeds in stirring evil thoughts in them against their brother. When they see Joseph on his way to them, they decide because of his dreams (cf. Gen 37:18–20) to kill him, but Reuben prevents them (cf.

---

1. Zandee, "Iosephus contra Apionem: An Apocryphal Story of Joseph in Coptic," *VC* 15 (1961): 193–213. doi:10.2307/1582427.

2. Gilles Quispel, "An Unknown Fragment of the Acts of Andrew (Pap. Copt. Utrecht N. 1)," *VC* 10 (1956): 129.

Gen 37:21–22). Contrary to the Genesis base text (murder preceding throwing him into a cistern), the Narration of Joseph has the brothers come up with the idea of throwing Joseph into the cistern. Then follows another scene unknown from Genesis. Gad comes in the night and tries to kill Joseph by throwing stones down on him. Joseph, however, calls upon Judah for help. He intervenes and averts Gad's attempt to murder Joseph.

As the Ishmaelites arrive they notice the brothers in mutual quarrel. The brothers explain how their younger brother is the reason for the strife. The Ishmaelites—identified as two and named respectively Korah and his slave Apion—offer to solve the problem by buying Joseph into slavery. In the absence of Reuben (cf. Gen 37:29–30) as well as Judah (unlike in Genesis), the brothers consent and sell him for twenty shekels (cf. Gen 37:28).

Then follows a farewell scene that similarly diverges from Genesis by introducing an entirely new episode. Joseph humiliates himself by making excuses for his dreams. Unfortunately, at this point the text is fragmentarily preserved only. What follows is the brothers' attempt to conceal from Jacob how they have sold Joseph by giving him Joseph's garment soaked in the blood of a buck (cf. Gen 37:31–35). After a poorly preserved part of the story follows another narrative episode in which Joseph rebukes possibly Jacob or, more likely one of his brothers, by reminding him how one shall not swear oaths in the name of God. Similarly, although the text is difficult to discern at this point because of its fragmentary nature, Joseph adheres to creation theology referring to the sun, just as his wisdom is accentuated.[3] The very fragmentarily preserved end of the story seems to recount a great thirst in Egypt that Joseph comes to solve (cf. Gen 41, which speaks about hunger rather than thirst).

Manuscript

Although the text was published in 1961, it first came to the attention of the public in 1956, when Gilles Quispel published the first part of the quire that contained an unknown part of or addition to the pseudepigraphal New Testament text the Acts of Andrew.[4] Here it was designated the Act of Andrew (*te praxis ᵉnandreas*) referring to one episode only in a larger narrative on the apostle Andrew.[5] Quispel provided a translation of the excerpt from the Acts of Andrew, but also mentioned how this text has been preserved with another text following it and narrating a story related to the patriarch Joseph. Apart from this manuscript, we have no other knowledge of the text. It has not been preserved anywhere else, although it may have exerted influence on a later Coptic Christian text known as the Story of Joseph and His Brothers.[6]

As regards the codicological details, the Narration of Joseph is part of a quire comprising eight papyrus sheets containing four pages each. Both the front side (recto) as well as the back side (verso) of the pages were inscribed. With eight sheets that makes

---

3. Jan Dochhorn and Anders Klostergaard Petersen, "Narratio Ioseph: A Coptic Joseph Apocryphon," *JSJ* 30 (1999): 437–38, doi:10.1163/157006399X00091.

4. I am grateful to the director of the Utrecht State Library, Mr. Savenije, and in particular the leader of the Unit for Old Handwritings at the University Library, Dr. Koert van der Horst, for granting me access to the manuscript in 2007 and helping me with various details.

5. Quispel, "Fragment."

6. Carl Johann Joseph Wessely, "Geschichte von Ioseph und seine Brüdern," in *Griechische und Koptische Texte theologischen Inhalts V*, Studien zur Palaeographie und Papyruskunde 18 (Leipzig: Haessel, 1917), 22–29. For possible influence, see Dochhorn and Petersen, "Narratio," 443–45.

thirty-two pages altogether. The four exterior sheets, however, have been lost, implying that pages 1–8 and 23–32 are missing. Of the remaining four sheets, number 6 (counted from the outside) has also been lost, meaning that pages 11–12 and 21–22 have disappeared. Ultimately, of the original eight sheets only the two interior sheets, nos. 7 and 8, as well as sheet no. 5 have been preserved, leaving us with twelve pages.

Yet, these twelve pages have not all been inscribed, which makes it a little complicated to understand the current state of the manuscript. Only the verso and the recto side on the left half of the interior sheet (sheet no. 8) are inscribed (pages 15–16). The right half (pages 17–18) is neither inscribed nor numbered. This may cohere with the fact, already noted by Zandee, that the width of this page is only one third of a normal page and that it may, therefore, be difficult to use for writing.[7] Strangely enough there are some letters appearing on the back page of the inner sheet (page 16) on the right side and written upside down in a slightly greater size than the rest of the letters: *ešô/pee/ekô* or (*ekš*). It may well be, as suggested by Zandee, that these letters should be understood as a writing sample or test.[8] Potentially, however, they could also be magical letters indicating a distinct use of the codex at a later stage, but their exact use unfortunately remains in obscurity.

Another peculiarity of the quire is the reversed position of the recto- and verso-sides of the left leaf of the interior sheet (pages 15–16). The verso side on which the papyrus fibers run perpendicularly is turned toward the exterior, implying that page 15 constitutes the verso side and page 16 the recto side, also entailing that pages 10 and 21 appear at the back side of the papyrus sheet.

As pages 17–18 are not inscribed (the right half of sheet no. 8) they are not numbered either, implying that the quire—although consisting of thirty-two pages—in the actual counting of pages comprises thirty inscribed pages only, that is, including those that have been lost. This means that the actual page 19, therefore, is counted as page 17, wherefore we have pages 21–22 despite the fact that the actual pages 21–22 have been lost. The pages are numbered (numbers are readable on pages 9, 10, 13, 14, 17, 18, 21, and 22 in the upper either left or right corner) and contain at an average between forty-two and forty-five lines. This can be seen on the basis of the entirely preserved pages 17 (forty-five lines), 18 (forty-two lines), and the almost preserved page 14 (forty-two lines—one line is missing, but may be reconstructed).

The Narration of Joseph begins immediately after the end of the Act of Andrew at the bottom of page 15. The typographically marked connection to the previous story makes the beginning of the new story evident. Apart from the fragmentarily transmitted title ("Joseph" is the only word in the title that can be identified), only the first two lines, which constituted the beginning of the narrative, have been preserved. Subsequently, there is a gap of—based on a calculation of average lines per page—presumably between ten to fourteen lines. The first thirty-three lines on page 16 have been preserved, but are followed by another gap of approximately nine to twelve lines. Most likely the Joseph story constituted the remaining part of the quire, but we cannot know it for certain, since the relevant pages (23–30) have been lost.

The codex or quire is, as mentioned, characterized by the combination of an Old Testament apocryphal Joseph story with a New Testament apocryphon. Zandee mentions how the so-called miscellaneous anthology may be compared to the *synaxaria* used for

---

7. Zandee, "Iosephus," 194.
8. Zandee, "Iosephus," 194.

liturgical purposes in the Coptic Orthodox Church. They constituted calendars of saints organized according to the death day of the saint and were used in the church.[9] Additionally, there existed *lectionaria* composed of excerpts of Coptic Christian homilies also used for liturgical purposes and often being of a paraenetic character. Both the *synaxaria* and the *lectionaria* came into existence in the fifth century, which presumably is around the time the codex was made. As we shall see in the last section on the text's date and provenance, the *synaxaria* and *lectionaria* have played an important role in the dating of the writing as well as in assigning it a particular provenance.

Genre

The Narration of Joseph constitutes a narrative recounted in the third person and with a number of discursive parts in the form of embedded dialogues between the narrated figures of the story. It typifies that genre of Jewish literature that we in continuity with Geza Vermes have been accustomed to designate rewritten Bible, but which some scholars, including myself, prefer to name rewritten Scripture in order to avoid biblical anachronisms applied to a period in which the Bible had not yet come into existence.[10] One may, of course, discuss to what extent rewritten Scripture actually constituted a genre, whether seen from the actors' and/or observers' point of view, or simply exemplifies an excessive form of intertextuality, but I shall leave that discussion to another time.[11] Be that as it may, the Narration of Joseph typifies the phenomenon of rewritten Scripture, inasmuch as it uses Gen 37 as the basic narrative for its embellishments, additions, and rewritings, just as it follows the structure of its scriptural precedent quite closely. The focus on the sale of Joseph is not entirely without precedent. Jubilees has a parallel perspective, although it does not, contrary to the Narration of Joseph, ascribe a negative role to his dreams (cf. Jub. 34:10). To what extent the author or authors had an awareness of the changes imposed on the authoritative base text is difficult to tell, but the evidence points in the direction that the new text was simply held to provide the right interpretative key or, perhaps more adequately, the true version of the meaning of Scripture. At least, the text does not provide any indication of an awareness of its changes of or, even, polemics against the base text.

Similar to other writings classified as rewritten Scripture, the Narration of Joseph contains several elements added to the base text. When Joseph meets the anonymous

---

9. Zandee, "Iosephus," 200.

10. Vermes, *Scripture and Tradition in Judaism: Haggadic Studies*, StPB 4 (Leiden: Brill, 1961). See also George W. E. Nickelsburg, "The Bible Rewritten and Expanded," in *Jewish Writings of the Second Temple Period*, ed. Michael E. Stone, CRINT 2.2 (Assen: Van Gorcum; Philadelphia: Fortress, 1984), 89, doi:10.1163/9789004275119_004. For my own take on the discussion, see Anders Klostergaard Petersen, "Textual Fidelity, Elaboration, Supersession, or Encroachment? Typological Reflections on the Phenomenon of Rewritten Scripture," in *Rewritten Bible after 50 Years: Texts, Terms or Techniques? A Last Dialogue with Geza Vermes*, ed. József Zsengellér, JSJSup 166 (Leiden: Brill, 2014), 11–48, doi:10.1163/9789004271180_003; Petersen, "The Riverrun of Rewriting Scripture: From Textual Cannibalism to Scriptural Completion," *JSJ* 43 (2012): 475–96, doi:10.1163/15700631-1234123; and Petersen, "Rewritten Bible as a Borderline Phenomenon—Genre, Textual Strategy, or Canonical Anachronism?," in *Flores Florentino: Dead Sea Scrolls and Other Early Jewish Studies in Honour of Florentino García Martínez*, ed. Anthony Hilhorst, Émile Puech, and Eibert J. Tigchelaar, JSJSup 122 (Leiden: Brill, 2007), 285–306, doi:10.1163/ej.9789004162921.i-836.98.

11. Anders Klostergaard Petersen, ed., *Contextualising Rewritten Scripture: Different Approaches to the Rewriting of Scripture and the Attribution of Authority to Rewritings* (Leiden: Brill, forthcoming).

person of Gen 37:15, whose only narrative function is to inform him that the brothers have broken up from Shechem to Dothan, he is identified as the devil. It is quite common that rewritten Scripture identifies anonymous persons in the authoritative base text with figures known by the intended addressees. Whereas Josephus and Philo in their exposition of Gen 37 leave the figure in oblivion (*A. J.* 2:19–20; and *Ios.* 11–12), other texts such as Gen. Rab. 84:14 and the Syriac History of Joseph interpret the figure as an angel. In the latter text, the anonymous person is said to be an angel disguised as a shepherd.[12] Identifications of anonymous persons with the devil are found in other pseudepigraphal writings like the Testament of Job (2:9) and the Apocalypse of Moses (see, in particular, 15:1).

We see the same phenomenon of identifying anonymous persons in the base text with respect to the Ishmaelites in the Narration of Joseph. Their number is held to be two and they are named, respectively, Korah and Apion. The names are striking, a point to which I shall return in the discussion of the date and provenance of the text. For now, it suffices to say that similar to the identification of the anonymous person with the devil, the same interpretative pattern appears with regard to Korah and Apion.

The two other crucial points at which the Narration of Joseph diverges from the base text revolve around the role of Gad as well as Judah. Gad comes in the middle of the night to the cistern and tries to kill Joseph. We find a parallel in the Testament of Zebulun in which it is said that Judah watched over the cistern, since he feared that Simeon and Gad would kill Joseph (4:2). Similar to the Narration of Joseph, here Judah's role is emphasized as being especially protective to Joseph. Also in the aforementioned Syriac History of Joseph, Reuben tells Judah to watch over Joseph at the cistern (7:5).[13] The background text is Gen 37:26–27, where Judah suggests that they sell Joseph rather than killing him. In the base text there is no mitigating circumstance in Judah's proposal; but later texts could develop the motif in this direction, thereby granting Judah a more noble role in the narrative. In the Testament of Simeon, for instance, Simeon recounts how he became furious at Judah, because he had let go of Joseph (2:11; cf. Philo, *Ios.* 15).

Contrary to the Testaments of the Twelve Patriarchs, which retain the idea of Judah being involved in the brothers' violation of Joseph, the Narration of Joseph completely omits the fact that it was Judah who came up with the idea of selling Joseph. It also goes further in providing a positive picture of Judah by adding him to Reuben as being absent at the actual sale of the brothers: something that also runs counter to the scriptural base text (cf. Gen 37:29 as well as 37:26–27).

Finally, the Narration of Joseph shares with other rewritten Scriptural texts the idea—contrary to the base text—that some brothers more than others had a particular part

---

12. Kristian S. Heal, "The Syriac History of Joseph," *MOTP* 1:95, §§4:8–11; cf. the similar account in Ephraim Isaac, "The Ethiopic History of Joseph: Translation with Introduction and Notes," *JSP* 3, no. 6 (1990): 48, doi:10.1177/095182079000306. Similar angelologic interpretations are found in Tg. Ps.-J. Gen 37:15–17; and in Pirqe R. El. 38.

13. In my previous works on the Narration of Joseph I have used Isaac's "Ethiopic History" as a parallel text being unaware of the existence of the Syriac version (the same goes for Albert Marie Denis, who did not know the text either), which although comprising either a *Vorlage* to the Ethiopic rendition or a slightly alternative textual tradition, is differently recounted than the Ethiopic version. Denis, *Introduction à la litterature religieuse judéo-hellenistique*, 2 vols. (Turnhout: Brepols, 2000). For the parallel see Isaac, "Ethiopic History," 51. For differences mentioned between the Syriac and Ethiopic versions, see Heal, "Syriac History," 88–89.

The Narration of Joseph

in the violation of Joseph. In Joseph and Aseneth, for example, Gad, Dan, Asher, and Naphtali (the sons of Bilhah and Zilpah) are the main culprits whom the sons of Pharaoh try to instigate in an attack on Joseph and their father. The other brothers refuse to participate in the assault, and even Asher and Naphtali try to restrain Gad and Dan from pursuing the plan. Gad and Dan, on their side, are accentuated as the evil supporters and conspirators in the plan (Jos. Asen. 24–28; cf. the Ethiopic History of Joseph 49,[14] as well as Gen. Rab. 84:7; 137:1, although obviously not a piece of rewritten Scripture, but a Jewish midrash comprising older traditions with some undoubtedly dating back to Judaic religion). The negative role assigned to Gad is also found in the Testament of Zebulun in which Gad together with Simeon shows a particularly strong hatred toward Joseph (2–4). The strong animosity against his brother is explained in the Testament of Gad, where Joseph is said to have defamed Gad and the other sons of Zilpah and Bilhah before Jacob for having killed and eaten the best of the sheep. It is from within this tradition the strong hatred and obsessive attempt of Gad in the Narration of Joseph to kill Joseph make sense.

Date and Provenance

The origin of the Narration of Joseph is uncertain, but the most likely dating of the extant codex, based on an assessment of the handwriting, is sometime between the fourth and fifth century CE.[15] In his article on the Act of Andrew, Quispel also observed how the Joseph story must have been one episode only as part of a larger Joseph narrative—an observation compliant with the idea of the present quire being comparable to the *synaxaria* and the *lectionaria* of the Coptic Orthodox Church.[16] To anchor the Act of Andrew in a Christian monastic setting, Quispel mentions in passing how the Joseph story exemplifies "so typically a monk-story," but he never developed his view in detail.[17]

As already mentioned, the Joseph story was first published in an article by Zandee in 1961. Although he was prepared to consider the Jewish character of the text, he basically took over Quispel's understanding of the text in attributing it to Christian monastic circles: "The story of Joseph is a typical monk-story."[18] He had three primary reasons for this. First, since the fragmentary text constituted part of a so-called miscellaneous codex, it should be compared to the *synaxaria* and the *lectionaria*.[19] Second, in the story Joseph's meeting with the devil according to Zandee corresponds with similar narratives found in the *apophthegmata* literature, stories of the fathers, just as it shows correspondences to the Coptic hagiographic literature. Zandee, therefore, endorsed the view that "In our story Joseph is thought of in the same manner as christian (*sic*) authors consider their saints. Also this trait points to an adaptation of the Old Testament story by monks who

---

14. This element is toned down, verging on omission, in Heal, "Syriac History," §6:6, which only tells about how "the sons of the handmaidens" were especially mocking Joseph.

15. Zandee, "Iosephus," 193. In his dating of the handwriting Zandee follows Quispel, "Fragment," 136. Quispel also mentions that Paul Kahle, who must have seen the text in 1955, in a letter dated to February 3, 1955, stated his opinion that: "a fourth century date—or at the latest an early fifth century date—can be regarded as practically certain" (Quispel, "Fragment," 135).

16. Quispel, "Fragment," 130.

17. Quispel, "Fragment," 136 n. 4.

18. Zandee, "Iosephus," 200.

19. Zandee, "Iosephus," 200.

saw their ideal of piety incorporated in Joseph."[20] Third and finally, Zandee accentuated the motif of Joseph's humiliation before his brothers as typifying monastic exercises in self-abasement. At the same time, however, as he thought of the story as representing Christian hagiographic and monastic literature he acknowledged the existence of a number of Jewish motifs in the text which "points to our story being a christian (*sic*) adaptation of a Jewish original."[21]

Be that as it may, the Narration of Joseph is little known among scholars. It was not included in the Charlesworth edition of Old Testament pseudepigrapha (*OTP*), nor has it, until now, been part of the German *Jüdische Schriften aus der Hellenistisch-Römischer Zeit*,[22] just as it is not part of the Danish, French, Italian, or Spanish editions of the pseudepigrapha. Similarly, since its publication the text has hardly been mentioned in scholarship on apocryphal and pseudepigraphal literature.[23]

There is one very good reason for this disregard or lack of acquaintance with the text, which brings us back to the content. In the Genesis narrative it is said that a company of Ishmaelites came by (37:25–28) to whom the brothers eventually sold Joseph. In the Narration of Joseph the Ishmaelites are identified as Korah and his slave Apion. These names are far from coincidental. In Jewish tradition, Korah is known as the rebel par excellence against Moses and the Israelites (Num 16:1–40).[24] Similarly, Apion is the infamously passionate adversary of Judaism known from Philo's writing *On the Embassy to Gaius* and Josephus's *Against Apion*. Thus, in the text we have both the heretic and the enemy typifying intra- as well as intergroup risks and challenges.

By entitling the text *Iosephus contra Apionem* ("Joseph(us) against Apion"), Zandee assigned a witty name to the text, but it was also one that prevented it from coming to the attention of scholars. Scholars working on Philo's *On the Embassy to Gaius* or Josephus's *Against Apion* soon realized that the text has nothing to do with the Apion referred to by Philo and Josephus. Conversely, scholars on biblical pseudepigrapha and apocrypha hardly acknowledged the text, since by title it apparently belongs to the realm of Josephus and Philo scholarship. For this reason Jan Dochhorn and I in 1999 decided to rename the text from Zandee's attributed title Iosephus contra Apionem to Narratio Ioseph or the Narration of Joseph.[25] The aim was twofold. First, we wanted more scholars to become acquainted with the text. Second, we wanted a title that was more fitting to the actual content of the text.

Dochhorn and I had come across the text in 1998 by sheer serendipity. We found it fascinating and began to work on it. We soon came to the conclusion that something was wrong in the argument put forward, although in almost a casual remark only, by Quispel and subsequently elaborated by Zandee. Although it can easily be understood

---

20. Zandee, "Iosephus," 205.
21. Zandee, "Iosephus," 205.
22. I am currently preparing a commentary for the German series on the Narration of Joseph.
23. The only exceptions I know of are Harm Wouter Hollander, *Joseph as an Ethical Model in the Testaments of the Twelve Patriarchs*, SVTP 6 (Leiden: Brill, 1981); and Jan van der Vliet, "Satan's Fall in Coptic Magic," in *Ancient Magic and Ritual Power*, ed. Marvin Meyer and Paul Mirecki, RGRW 129 (Leiden: Brill, 1995), 412 n. 5, doi:10.1163/9789004283817_021; but neither of the two books has any extensive discussion of the Narration of Joseph.
24. For Korah as a polemic term in Second Temple Judaism, see Jonathan A. Draper, "'Korah and the Second Temple," in *Templum Amicitiae: Essays on the Second Temple Presented to Ernst Bammel*, ed. William Horbury, JSNTSup 48 (Sheffield: Sheffield Academic, 1991), 150–74.
25. Dochhorn and Petersen, "Narratio," 432.

how Coptic Christians would use the text in the fourth and fifth centuries and continue to make use of it, there is really nothing in the text warranting the Christian monastic context suggested by Quispel and Zandee. Whereas Zandee, contrary to Quispel, acknowledged that "the latter [sc. the Narration of Joseph] can be traced back to a Jewish origin" and even argues that the "document represents an intermediate stage on the way from Jewish apocryphal writings to christian (sic) hagiography,"[26] Dochhorn and I advocated that nothing in the text suggests the adoption of a Christian view, let alone an integration of Christian motifs. From our perspective the Narration of Joseph is a thoroughly Jewish text.[27] In order not to be misunderstood, let me emphasize that we did not exclude that the text was later used by Christians, as the juxtaposition of the Act of Andrew with the Narration of Joseph in the same codex amply demonstrates. Obviously, the text could have been used, read (in fact, it was used and read as the present quire clearly demonstrates), and even translated by Christians, but our conclusion was that the Christian users, whoever they were, did not make any alterations to the originally Jewish text apart from placing it in a new context together with the New Testament pseudepigraphic excerpt, the Act of Andrew.

By virtue of being a Coptic translation in the Sahidic dialect as well as appearing in combination with an excerpt from the Acts of Andrew, the text was certainly read and used by Christians, but again there is nothing, we argued, in the Narration of Joseph to prevent that Christians could have adopted the text in its Jewish form.[28] The fact that Christians adopted the Narration of Joseph only confirms a general phenomenon as regards the pseudepigrapha, namely that they have predominantly come to us "in a manuscript tradition copied and transmitted entirely by Christians."[29] The various parallels from the apophthegmatic and hagiographic literature adduced by Zandee to cast light on the text are certainly illuminating for understanding how Christians would interpret the writing at the time of its inclusion in the codex. The references, however, do not, we argued, shed light on the text when interpreted in light of its context of origin prior to its later Christian use.

All the motifs presented by Zandee as having Christian provenance may just as easily—or as Dochhorn and I, indeed, argued—may, in fact, more suitably be interpreted on the background of late Second Temple Judaism. Even Zandee himself seemed to vacillate in his view, since with respect to some of the motifs he at first explicitly attributed to the Christian monastic context, he later acknowledged their possible Jewish provenance. One example is the appearance of the devil. At first, Zandee identifies Joseph's confrontation with the devil with the *apophthegmata*'s recurrent portrayal of the anchorite being tempted by the devil appearing in disguise.[30] However, he later gives up his certainty about this relationship by acknowledging that the "original Jewish apocryphon might have already contained the idea that it was the devil who tried to seduce Joseph."[31]

---

26. Zandee, "Iosephus," 212, 213.

27. Dochhorn and Petersen, "Narratio," 432–33. I have subsequently retained our view in Petersen, "Narratio Ioseph: A Rarely Acknowledged Coptic Joseph Apocryphon," in *The Embroidered Bible: Studies in Biblical Apocrypha and Pseudepigrapha in Honour of Michael E. Stone*, ed. Lorenzo DiTommaso, Matthias Henze, and William Adler, SVTP 26 (Leiden: Brill, 2017), 809–23, doi:10.1163/9789004357211_042.

28. Dochhorn and Petersen, "Narratio," 433.

29. Davila, "Old Testament," 53. See also the more extensive elaboration of the argument in Davila, *The Provenance of the Pseudepigrapha: Jewish, Christian, or Other?*, JSJSup 105 (Leiden: Brill, 2005).

30. Zandee, "Iosephus," 201.

31. Zandee, "Iosephus," 207.

Correspondingly, Zandee points to the fact that the text polemicizes against a tactless use of the Tetragrammaton together with an oath (21:24-34.). He argues that "Joseph represents the rabbinic viewpoint of not taking an oath on the name of *JHWH*. This characteristic makes only sense in a Jewish writing and thus it can be a second indication that an original Jewish story is concerned here."[32] So, ultimately, is there a way that allows us to get closer to answering the question about the text's origin in, respectively, a Jewish or Christian context?

Before focusing our attention on this question, we need to acknowledge a recent scholarly development in the field subsequent to the debate referred to above about the text's provenance. During the last two decades there has been a growing acknowledgement of the difficulties in drawing clear-cut boundaries between Judaism and Christianity during the first centuries. There was considerably more criss-crossing, intertwinement, and exchanges between the two cultural and religious entities than scholarship traditionally has been prepared to recognize. There are scholars who have taken the argument to the extent to advocate the view that early Christ-religion, as I now prefer to call it in appreciation of its Judaic nature, in fact constituted a Judaism, one among a multiplicity of different types.[33]

Several scholars now subscribe to the view that Judaism and Christianity, in fact, did not become independent of each other until the fifth and, possibly, even later, the sixth and seventh centuries, when what we now term Judaism came into existence as the Judaism founded on the two Talmuds (the Yerushalmi and the Bavli) as the decisive interpretative filter through which the earlier rabbinic literature (for instance, Mishnah and Tosefta) and the Hebrew Bible were perceived.[34]

We do not need to enter this debate here. Suffice it to say that the certainty that used to exist in conceptualizing the relationship between Judaism and Christianity has been severely undermined and that we are standing at the beginning of a new era, one in which a different model for understanding the relationship between Judaism and Christianity is replacing the old one. Therefore, we need to be far more cautious in our assessments of what may be accorded a "Jewish" and a "Christian" tradition. The more so, since less clearly demarcated social groups such as "sympathizers," "Godfearers," "Judeo-Christ-adherents" of various types all contribute to muddling the picture even more. And these are groups that we know of, but surely there have been more groups that have fallen into oblivion. The reticence toward unambiguous demarcations between the two is also prompted by the fact that a considerably greater number of scholars reckon early Christ-religion to be a thoroughly Jewish or, as I now prefer to call it, "Judaic" phenomenon.[35]

---

32. Zandee, "Iosephus," 207.

33. Anders Klostergaard Petersen, "Unveiling the Obvious: Synagogue and Church—Sisters or Different Species?," in *Wisdom Poured Out like Water: Studies on Jewish and Christian Antiquity in Honor of Gabriele Boccaccini*, ed. J. Harold Ellens et al., DCLS 38 (Berlin: de Gruyter, 2018), 575–92, doi:10.1515/9783110596717-039.

34. For this whole debate, see the illuminating volume by Adam H. Becker and Annette Yoshiko Reed, eds., *The Ways That Never Parted: Jews and Christians in Late Antiquity and the Early Middle Ages*, TSAJ 95 (Tübingen: Mohr Siebeck, 2003); as well as Daniel Boyarin's seminal work. See Boyarin, *Border-Lines: The Partition of Judaeo-Christianity*, Divinations (Philadelphia: University of Pennsylvania Press, 2004). See also Anders Klostergaard Petersen, "At the End of the Road: Reflections on a Popular Scholarly Metaphor," in *The Formation of the Early Church*, ed. Jostein Ådna, WUNT 183 (Tübingen: Mohr Siebeck, 2005), 45–72.

35. Admittedly, the category is not perfect, since it suggests a certain confinement to the geographical

On the basis of such a change in scholarly perspective, it obviously may appear somewhat strange to spend so much ink on a debate that comes forward as being of a slightly anachronistic character. Yet, despite all the effort to untie and alleviate clearly demarcated boundaries—textual as well as scholarly—and to dissolve strongly conceptualized monolithic religious entities, it still makes sense to pose the question of origin and provenance. Although the anchoring of the text may not be turned into a sturdily understood difference between Christianity and Judaism, it remains sensible to ask in what type of Judaic religion the Narration of Joseph emerged. This question is related to a debate that more or less during the same period of scholarship as referred to above has taken place in the more specific field of apocryphal and pseudepigraphal research.

Whereas in James Charlesworth's *Old Testament Pseudepigrapha* there is a tendency to argue for the "Jewish" provenance of a great many pseudepigraphal writings without much further argumentative warranting, some scholars in the aftermath of this important publication have called for greater carefulness in assigning apocryphal and pseudepigraphal texts to a "Jewish" rather than a "Christian" background (since this debate has taken place predominantly independent of the previously mentioned discussion I here retain the terms used, but put them in quotation marks).[36]

The work of especially Robert A. Kraft, Richard Bauckham, and James Davila has made scholars working on Jewish and Christian pseudepigrapha far more alert to the problem in attributing distinctive works to a "Jewish" tradition. In the old days we would look for Christian motifs as well as motifs such as christological interpretation, typological use of Old Testament figures and themes, attacks on other forms of Judaic religion, allusions to crucifixion, virgin birth, and emphasis on allegedly Christian virtues, but as Davila in particular has emphasized, such motifs are far from ubiquitous, when one reads Christian homilies and related genres of say the fourth or the fifth century.[37]

In fact, it is often quite difficult to tell the difference between "Jewish" and "Christian" texts of the first several centuries, which only adds additional evidence to the viewpoint presented above about the fuzziness and ambiguity characteristic of "Christianity" and "Judaism" during an epoch in which the two came increasingly into existence as separate and autonomous entities. Therefore, we need, as perhaps most strongly argued by Davila, to change the cards for assigning particular works to a "Jewish" tradition, if no strong evidence points in that direction (such as, e.g., pre-Christ-religious manuscript attestation or transmission of traditions in other non-Christ-religious forms of Judaic religion).

---

area "Judah," which makes it difficult to see the obviousness for including diaspora forms of Judaism under this heading. I nevertheless adhere to the nomenclature in order to obtain a necessary terminological differentiation between Israelite (roughly the Hebrew Bible/Old Testament), Judaic (roughly Second Temple period and pretalmudic Judaism), and Jewish (talmudic and later forms of Judaism) religion, which are representative of distinctly different types of religion. See Petersen, "From Torah to Torahization: A Biocultural Perspective," in *Torah: Functions, Meanings, and Diverse Manifestations in Early Judaism and Christianity*, ed. William M. Schniedewind, Jason M. Zurawski, and Gabriele Boccaccini, EJL 56 (Atlanta: SBL Press, 2021), 343–66, here 344–46. doi:10.2307/j.ctv2cw0sj7.22.

36. For this discussion, see the important article by Robert A. Kraft, "The Pseudepigrapha and Christianity Revisited: Setting the Stage and Framing Some Central Questions," *JSJ* 32 (2001): 371–95; and for the tendency to overestimate the "Jewish" provenance of the pseudepigraphal literature, see, in particular, Richard Bauckham, "The Continuing Quest for the Provenance of Old Testament Pseudepigrapha," in *The Jewish World around the New Testament: Collected Essays*, WUNT 233 (Tübingen: Mohr Siebeck, 2008), 462–67, and esp. 465.

37. See Davila, *Provenance*, 77–119.

Such an idea is also in line with basic principles of new philology, which similarly calls for according the actual textual manuscript evidence primary significance over and against, however well-reasoned, conjecturally reconstructed texts.[38]

Having rethought the whole issue theoretically as well as methodologically, I am now far more inclined to think of the Narration of Joseph as a "Christian" text, thereby changing my mind with respect to my two previous works on the writing. I agree, for reasons in terms of basic philosophy of science, with Davila that it is theoretically more satisfying and exemplifies a methodologically more rigorous pursuit to move from "the known" to "the unknown." The fewer unknowns included in the ruminations, the better. Or to put it in a slightly different way, the burden of proof is heavier on those colleagues who opt for a Jewish provenance beyond the obvious current Christian one compared to those who take the actual manuscript situation as their default assumption for reconstructing the background of the work in question.[39]

Returning to the question of the Narration of Joseph. What we have at hand is, in fact, undoubtedly a Christian text in a Christian preserved codex collocating an Old Testament apocryphal story with a New Testament pseudepigraphal text.[40] I subscribe to Davila's point that: "granting that in many cases we simply cannot tell if a pseudepigraphon is of Jewish origin, it is better to exclude doubtful cases and base our reconstruction on what we know that we know. A false positive does more harm than a false negative: if we think we are studying ancient Judaism (or New Testament background) with a first-century-CE Jewish text and in reality it is a third-century-CE Christian composition, we pollute our corpus with erroneous information that distorts our understanding."[41]

Does this mean that I now return to Quispel's and Zandee's understanding of the Narration of Joseph as representative of a typical monk-story? Not at all. Their argument as well as the one put forward by Dochhorn and myself in 1999 are representative of a form of scholarship characteristic of that era, but also one that in my view has been surpassed. We have moved forward, and it would be futile not to change one's views in accordance with the best scholarship available. But what does this mean for the Narration of Joseph? In fact, here we have a test-case for seeing what the change in perspective is conducive to.

The story as it now stands is definitely a Christian work appearing in a Coptic quire together with an excerpt from the Acts of Andrew. Could it have a Jewish origin? Possibly; but I am no longer sure that we can show that with any certainty. I no longer see any reason why Christians of Egypt of the late fourth or fifth century should not have composed a work on Joseph and included it in a codex together with a Christian pseudepigraphal text. Surely, there are several resemblances to other undoubtedly non-Christ-religious Judaic

---

38. For this whole discussion, see Liv Ingeborg Lied and Hugo Lundhaug, eds., *Snapshots of Evolving Traditions: Jewish and Christian Manuscript Culture, Textual Fluidity, and New Philology*, TUGAL 175 (Berlin: de Gruyter, 2017), doi:10.1515/9783110348057.

39. Cf. Kraft, "Pseudepigrapha," 75.

40. Jeff W. Childers, "'You Will Find What You Seek': The Form and Function of a Sixth-Century Divinatory Bible in Syriac," in Lied and Lunghaug, *Snapshots*, 268: "We are reminded that when we detach ancient texts from the concrete artifacts in which they reside, we are liable to lose a critical dimension of the text's original significance."

41. James Davila, "The Old Testament Pseudepigrapha as Background to the New Testament," *ExpTim* 117, no. 2 (2005): 57, doi:10.1177/0014524605059; as well as the more elaborate argument in Davila, *Provenance*.

writings, but that does not necessarily make it of "Jewish" provenance. It only testifies to a much wider well of shared textual traditions from which a variety of Judaic forms of religion could draw. The fact that the text testifies to some interesting similarities to the Coptic Bohairic translation of the Bible (unfortunately the relevant Sahidic translation of Gen 37 is only very fragmentarily preserved—Gen 37:13–16, 19–22, 35, 36) points in the direction of Christian provenance. Again, that does not exclude, as Dochhorn and I in our 1999 article argued, that a clever Sahidic translator could have adapted the text to fit the Coptic Bible translation, but the evidence points in another direction.[42] True, as we contended back in 1999, Korah and Apion are not used in the extant text in any distinctively negative way against "Judaism"; but does that really make the text less Christian? I do not any longer think so. I do not any longer see a compelling reason why Christians of the late fourth or early fifth century in Egypt should not have been able to partake in a continuous riverrun of the Genesis Joseph narrative.[43]

Should we then just forget about the text and simply reckon it a Christian narrative? That would be a wrong conclusion. The text is abundant in interesting motifs as we saw in the discussion of genre. That makes it highly relevant for the study of the wider Jewish literature of antiquity—together with that strand of Judaic literature which we now designate Christian. To ascribe a Christian provenance to the Narration of Joseph does neither diminish its value for the study of Jewish pseudepigraphal literature, not does it make the text less interesting for general studies of ancient Judaism. For certain, scholars working on the figure of Joseph in post-Israelite Judaic religion should pay attention to the Narration of Joseph and reflect on its diverging traditions as well as those shared with other Judaic texts—Christ-religious ones, included.

Bibliography

Bauckham, Richard. "The Continuing Quest for the Provenance of Old Testament Pseudepigrapha." Pages 461–83 in *The Jewish World around the New Testament: Collected Essays*. WUNT 233. Tübingen: Mohr Siebeck, 2008.

Becker, Adam H., and Annette Yoshiko Reed, eds. *The Ways That Never Parted: Jews and Christians in Late Antiquity and the Early Middle Ages*. TSAJ 95. Tübingen: Mohr Siebeck, 2003.

Boyarin, Daniel. *Border-Lines: The Partition of Judaeo-Christianity*. Divinations. Philadelphia: University of Pennsylvania Press, 2004.

Childers, Jeff W. "'You Will Find What You Seek': The Form and Function of a Sixth-Century Divinatory Bible in Syriac." Pages 242–71 in *Snapshots of Evolving Traditions: Jewish and Christian Manuscript Culture, Textual Fluidity, and New Philology*. Edited by Liv Ingeborg Lied and Hugo Lundhaug. TUGAL 175. Berlin: de Gruyter, 2017.

Davila, James. "The Old Testament Pseudepigrapha as Background to the New Testament." *ExpTim* 117, no. 2 (2005): 53–57. doi:10.1177/0014524605059.

———. *The Provenance of the Pseudepigrapha: Jewish, Christian, or Other?* JSJSup 105. Leiden: Brill, 2005.

---

42. For this argument, see Dochhorn and Petersen, "Narratio," 444–49.

43. In this regard and for the change of my understanding of the text, I have been strongly influenced by especially Davila, *Provenance*, 77–84; together with the previously mentioned article by Kraft, "Pseudepigrapha." For the term "riverrun," see Petersen, "Riverrun."

Denis, Albert Marie. *Introduction à la litterature religieuse judéo-hellenistique*. 2 vols. Turnhout: Brepols, 2000.

Dochhorn, Jan, and Anders Klostergaard Petersen. "Narratio Ioseph: A Coptic Joseph Apocryphon." *JSJ* 30 (1999): 431–63. doi:10.1163/157006399X00091.

Draper, Jonathan A. "'Korah' and the Second Temple." Pages 150–74 in *Templum Amicitiae: Essays on the Second Temple Presented to Ernst Bammel*. Edited by William Horbury. JSNTSup 48. Sheffield: Sheffield Academic, 1991.

Heal, Kristian S. "The Syriac History of Joseph." *MOTP* 1:85–120.

Hollander, Harm Wouter. *Joseph as an Ethical Model in the Testaments of the Twelve Patriarchs*. SVTP 6. Leiden: Brill, 1981.

Isaac, Ephraim. "The Ethiopic History of Joseph: Translation with Introduction and Notes." *JSP* 3, no. 6 (1990): 3–125. doi:10.1177/0951820790003006.

Kraft, Robert A. "The Pseudepigrapha and Christianity Revisited: Setting the Stage and Framing Some Central Questions." *JSJ* 32 (2001): 371–95.

Lied, Liv Ingeborg, and Hugo Lundhaug, eds. *Snapshots of Evolving Traditions: Jewish and Christian Manuscript Culture, Textual Fluidity, and New Philology*. TUGAL 175. Berlin: de Gruyter, 2017. doi:10.1515/9783110348057.

Nickelsburg, George W. E. "The Bible Rewritten and Expanded." Pages 89–156 in *Jewish Writings of the Second Temple Period*. Edited by Michael E. Stone. CRINT 2.2. Assen: Van Gorcum; Philadelphia: Fortress, 1984. doi:10.1163/9789004275119_004.

Petersen, Anders Klostergaard. "At the End of the Road: Reflections on a Popular Scholarly Metaphor." Pages 45–72 in *The Formation of the Early Church*. Edited by Jostein Ådna. WUNT 183. Tübingen: Mohr Siebeck, 2005.

———, ed. *Contextualising Rewritten Scripture: Different Approaches to the Rewriting of Scripture and the Attribution of Authority to Rewritings*. Leiden: Brill, forthcoming.

———. "From Torah to Torahization: A Biocultural Perspective." Pages 343–66 in *Torah: Functions, Meanings, and Diverse Manifestations in Early Judaism and Christianity*. Edited by William M. Schniedewind, Jason M. Zurawski, and Gabriele Boccaccini. Atlanta: SBL Press, 2021. doi:10.2307/j.ctv2cwosj7.22.

———. "*Narratio Ioseph*: A Rarely Acknowledged Coptic Joseph Apocryphon." Pages 809–23 in *The Embroidered Bible: Studies in Biblical Apocrypha and Pseudepigrapha in Honour of Michael E. Stone*. Edited by Lorenzo DiTommaso, Matthias Henze, and William Adler. SVTP 26. Leiden: Brill, 2017. doi:10.1163/9789004357211_042.

———. "Rewritten Bible as a Borderline Phenomenon—Genre, Textual Strategy, or Canonical Anachronism?" Pages 285–306 in *Flores Florentino: Dead Sea Scrolls and Other Early Jewish Studies in Honour of Florentino García Martínez*. Edited by Anthony Hilhorst, Émile Puech, and Eibert J. Tigchelaar. JSJSup 122. Leiden: Brill, 2007. doi:10.1163/ej.9789004162921.i-836.98.

———. "The Riverrun of Rewriting Scripture: From Textual Cannibalism to Scriptural Completion." *JSJ* 43 (2012): 475–96. doi:10.1163/15700631-12341236.

———. "Textual Fidelity, Elaboration, Supersession, or Encroachment? Typological Reflections on the Phenomenon of Rewritten Scripture." Pages 11–48 in *Rewritten Bible after 50 Years: Texts, Terms or Techniques? A Last Dialogue with Geza Vermes*. Edited by Jószef Zsengellér. JSJSup 166. Leiden: Brill, 2014. doi:10.1163/9789004271180_003.

———. "Unveiling the Obvious: Synagogue and Church—Sisters or Different Species?" Pages 575–92 in *Wisdom Poured Out like Water: Studies on Jewish and Christian Antiquity in Honor of Gabriele Boccaccini*. Edited by J. Harold Ellens, Isaac Oliver, Jason von

Ehrenkrook, James Waddell, and Jason S. Zurawski. DCLS 38. Berlin: de Gruyter, 2018. doi:10.1515/9783110596717-039.
Quispel, Gilles. "An Unknown Fragment of the Acts of Andrew (Pap. Copt. Utrecht N. 1)." *VC* 10 (1956): 129–48.
Vermes, Geza. *Scripture and Tradition in Judaism: Haggadic Studies*. StPB 4. Leiden: Brill, 1961.
Vliet, Jan van der. "Satan's Fall in Coptic Magic." Pages 401–18 in *Ancient Magic and Ritual Power*. Edited by Marvin Meyer and Paul Mirecki. RGRW 129. Leiden: Brill, 1995. doi:10.1163/9789004283817_021.
Wessely, Carl Johann Joseph. "Geschichte von Ioseph und seine Brüdern." Pages 22–29 in *Griechische und Koptische Texte theologischen Inhalts V*. Studien zur Palaeographie und Papyruskunde 18. Leipzig: Haessel, 1917.
Zandee, Jan. "Iosephus contra Apionem: An Apocryphal Story of Joseph in Coptic." *VC* 15 (1961): 193–213. doi:10.2307/1582427.

The Narration of Joseph

(15:30) . . . . from Joseph. But it happened one day that Joseph [. . . .] (16:1) [. . . .]ᵃ in the form of an old man and said to him: "Joseph, where are you going?" And he responded and said to him: "I am on my way to my brothers." The devil (16:5) said to him: "Follow (me) and I shall [ta]ke you to them, because I know where they are." Joseph said to him: "Go away from me, for (16:10) I know who you are. You are the seducer ever since the fathers of my fathers. I will not follow you." But the devil was shamed out by Joseph (16:15) and left him. Gen 37:15–17

When the devil realized he had been put to shame by him, he quickly moved on and took dwelling with the brothers of Joseph (16:20). He led evil thoughts to stir up inside them against their brother. But as his brothers saw him coming, they said to each other: "See, the dreamer of dreams has come to us. Get up (16:25), come and let us kill him and see what his dreams will do to us." Judah and Reuben responded and said (16:30) to them: "Brothers, let us not put our hands on him, for it is a great infamy in order that God. . . ." (17:1) D[o] not. . . . . . His brothers, however, seized him and threw him down into a [cis]tern. But the cistern was empty (17:5). There was no water in it. Gen 37:18–20 Gen 37:21–22 Gen 37:24

In the middle of the night, however, Gad took stones and threw them down upon him with the aim in mind to kill him in the cistern (17:10). But Joseph exclaimed by saying: "My brother, Gad, leave me!" In contrast, Gad did not cease from (17:15) throwing stones down on him. And no single stone touched Joseph. When realizing, however, that no single stone touched him (17:20), he threw even more stones upon him. But Joseph shouted from down in the cistern: "My brother, Judah, help me!" (17:25). But Judah got up while sleeping among his herd of sheep. And he went to the cistern and found Gad throwing stones down upon him (17:30). But Judah restricted h[im] and. . . . in the middle. . . . But Jo[seph] cried out, saying: "Judah, restrain yourself (17:35); do nothing to him for the sake of me. For every sin comes from me and every strife arose with me." As he had said these things, they separated (17:40) themselves from him. They went away and sat down together with the herd of sheep until dawn.

It happened, however, that they quarreled among each other and (17:45) Korah, the Ishmaelite, came near together with his slave, Apion (18:1), with five of his camels loaded with perfume on their way to Egypt to do business there (18:5). But the Ishmaelite became attentive and saw them quarreling among Gen 37:25

---

a. Conjecture: "The devil appeared to him."

The Narration of Joseph

themselves and he said to them: "Certainly, I (18:10) quickly heard that you were brothers." And Joseph's brothers responded and said to him: "There is a young (18:15) slave boy here through whom all these strifes arose." And Korah, the Ishmaelite, went away, but saw that he was . . . a (18:20) slave. . . . "the price [tell] it to me and I shall remove the cause of the strife." Then (18:25) they took Joseph from the cistern, while Reuben was not there and neither Judah. And Gen 37:28 they gave him to Korah, the Ishmaelite, for (18:30) twenty shekels. They took, however, his garment and buried it in the ground. Then, he. . . . from them. And they went away, namely Korah (18:35) the Ishmaelite, and Joseph. Joseph, however, went to his brothers and humiliated himself before them and said [to them]: "Forgive me my dreams; I bid (18:40) you farewell; I beg you concerning our old father, for he is my lord. . . he. . . . for he wished. . .

Gen 37:31–35

. . . (21:1) the garment, and they butchered a young goat and [they se]nt it to their father saying. . . .: "Take and see. . . . if (21:5) you recognize this garme[nt]. . . to whom. . .ª Jacob, however, . . .ᵇ hand on it and [he] sa[id]: (21:10) "It is Joseph's. . ." And. . .ᶜ in great weeping, crying and saying: "This garment belongs t[o Jose]ph, my good son, this. . . . And they heard. . . . And they went to him. . . . And they answered. . . him (21:15). And he responded to them. . . . . . . Jacob. . . . . . (21:20) him. . . . And it happened. . . . And it happened. . in the da[y] that. . . . . ". . . my son. . . . ." ". . . in the days my son." But he. . . .

(21:25) And he swore an oath in the great name of God. But Joseph reproached him saying: "Do not swear this oath." But I looked out of (21:30) the windows in my house at him. My boy said to him: "In this way, [our] fathers used to swear. Therefore, also you [s]wear in this way. . . . . (22:1) and I went running down and went to them and I said to Joseph: ". . . . . me. . ." And he responded and said to me: ". . . . (22:5). . . of the sun. . . ." . . . . his wisdom. . . . . (22:10). . . But I said to him: "There is no other God. . . . . You shall not serve. . . . . But he said to me: ". . . . [they] think that. . . . (22:15). . . . But I. . . . . . (22:20). . . . . God. . . . . Joseph. . . . . hear. . . . . . . (22:25) and he said: ". . . . I found where my dear s[on]. . . . . Joseph from. . . . . But Joseph has gone. . . . . . of Korah, the Ishmaelite. . . . (22:30) and Apion his slave. . . . There was, however, a great thirst. . . Joseph answered and said: "May we. . . . all reach the cistern. . . . then I am very thirsty" (22:35) . . . . . . his slave fell forth. . . . .

a. Conjecture: "it belonged."
b. Conjecture: "put his."
c. Conjecture: "he burst out."

An Apocryphon about Aseneth
A new translation and introduction

by Richard Bauckham

Contents

In an extract from a lost work of Origen, preserved in the catena on Genesis (extract 1940 in Françoise Petit's edition of the catena[1]), he cites an "apocryphon" of the "Hebrews" as evidence that they knew that Potiphar (Gen 37:36; 39:1) and Potiphera (Gen 41:45, 50) were the same person. According to this apocryphon, Aseneth, daughter of Potiphar/Potiphera and later husband of Joseph, told her father that Joseph had not attempted to seduce her mother, as her mother had claimed. On the contrary, it was her mother who had attempted to seduce Joseph (cf. Gen 39). Her father was able to prove that this was the case and, now knowing Joseph to be a chaste man, he gave his daughter Aseneth to him in marriage (cf. Gen 41:45, 50). In doing so, he was also anxious to prevent any rumors about sexual misconduct in his house.

This narrative is used by Origen to explain the meaning of the biblical names Potiphera and Aseneth. The work from which the extract was taken was not his commentary on Genesis, which covered only Gen 1:1–5:1,[2] but apparently a series of notes (*excerpta*) on Genesis, including explanations of the Hebrew names.[3] (Other material of the same kind is preserved in other extracts from Origen in the catena on Genesis, including extract 1939, on the meaning of Joseph's new name Zaphenath-paneah in Gen 41:45.) It is clear that, in our extract, the etymological interpretation of the names, though doubtless dependent on Jewish sources,[4] does not derive from the apocryphon to which Origen refers. It is the story about Potiphar/Potiphera, Aseneth and Joseph (distinguished by bold print in the translation below) that he has taken from the apocryphon, apparently summarizing it in his own words.

---

1. Françoise Petit, *La Chaîne sur la Genèse: Édition Intégrale: IV: Chapitres 29 à 50*, Traditio exegetica graeca 4 (Leuven: Peeters, 1996), 255–56.

2. See Ronald E. Heine, "Origen's Alexandrian *Commentary on Genesis*," in *Origeniana Octava: Origen and the Alexandrian Tradition: Papers of the 8th International Origen Congress, Pisa, 27–31 August 2001*, BETL 164 (Leuven: Leuven University Press and Peeters, 2003), 63–73, esp. p. 65; Karin Metzler, "Weitere Testimonien und Fragmenta zum Genese-Kommentar des Origenes," ZAC 9 (2005): 143–48, doi:10.1515/zach.2005.9.1.143.

3. Robert Devreesse, *Les Anciens Commentateurs Grecs de l'Octateuque et des Rois (Fragments tirés des Chaînes)*, Studi e Testi 201 (Vatican City: Biblioteca Apostolica Vaticana, 1959), 29–30.

4. For Origen's indebtedness to rabbinic tradition in his interpretation of biblical Hebrew names, see Nicholas Robert Michael De Lange, *Origen and the Jews: Studies in Jewish-Christian Relations in Third-Century Palestine*, Cambridge Oriental Series 25 (Cambridge: Cambridge University Press, 1976), 117–21.

Manuscripts

Two manuscripts of the catena on Genesis (the Leningrad and Basel manuscripts) preserve a long version of this Greek extract from Origen, while three (Paris, Rome, and Patmos) contain an abridged version. All discussions of it until very recently referred only to the abridged version (best known in the edition in PG),[5] although Robert Devreesse already published some, but not all, of the additional material from the Basel manuscript in 1959.[6] Petit's edition was the first critical edition of both versions based on all the manuscripts. The translations below have been made from this edition.

Literary Contexts

There are two main features of the story Origen attributes to this apocryphon that can be identified also in other Joseph traditions. The first is the identification of Potiphar (Gen 37:36; 39:1) and Potiphera (Gen 41:45, 50) as the same person. We should note that in two major Jewish sources in Greek from the Second Temple period (LXX and Josephus) both Hebrew names are rendered by the same Greek form (*Petephrēs* in LXX, *Pentephrēs* in Josephus, with each form appearing as a variant reading in some MSS of the other work). But this does not necessarily imply that the two persons are being identified. In Josephus's case, both persons appear in his narrative (one in *A. J.* 2.39, 40, 54, 58, 78; the other in *A. J.* 2.91) in close proximity and are clearly distinguished. Later Jewish translations of the Bible into Greek (Aquila and Symmachus) transliterate the Hebrew names more literally and distinguish them: *Phoutiphar* and *Phoutiphari*, as Origen notes in another extract (1812) in the catena on Genesis.[7]

In fact, it is largely sources in Hebrew that make the identification of Potiphar with Potiphera, evidently on the grounds that the two names, while not identical, are similar. Jubilees, written in Hebrew in the second century BCE, describes Potiphar, on his first appearance in the narrative, as "a eunuch of pharaoh, the chief guard, the priest of the city of Heliopolis" (34:12; cf. also 40:10), combining the description of Potiphar in Gen 37:36; 39:1 with that of Potiphera in Gen 41:45, 50.[8] Genesis Rabbah (fifth-century CE or later), in an unattributed statement, also identifies the two persons (86:3; the identification is also assumed in 84:6). Like Origen, it undertakes to explain why the same person bore the two different, though similar, names by offering fanciful etymologies, though the explanation is quite different from Origen's. The Babylonian Talmud (b. Soṭah 13b) attributes to Rab the explanation that the man was called Potiphar before and Potiphera (a feminine form) after his castration (referring to a story of his castration by Gabriel that

---

5. The first discussion to take account of the long version was Anna Tzvetkova-Glaser, "Joseph and His Egyptian Family in the Interpretation of Origen and the Early Rabbis," in *Rewritten Biblical Figures*, ed. Erkki Koskenniemi and Pekka Lindqvist, Studies in Rewritten Bible 3 (Turku: Åbo Akademi University; Winona Lake, IN: Eisenbrauns, 2010), §1910.

6. Devreesse, *Les Anciens Commentateurs*, 38.

7. Petit, *La Chaîne*, 187-88.

8. Unfortunately, the references to Potiphar/Potiphera in Jubilees (34:12; 40:10; 44:24) are not extant in the Hebrew fragments of Jubilees from Qumran, and so we do not know whether the two names were assimilated or not. Tzvetkova-Glaser ignores Jub. 34:12 and fails to notice the combination of titles of Potiphar in 40:10, and so is able to conclude, erroneously, that Jubilees "presents Joseph's master and Joseph's father-in-law as two different persons" ("Joseph," 198). Ross Shepard Kraemer correctly notes that Jubilees identifies Potiphar and Potiphera, but erroneously claims that Targumim Neofiti I and Onqelos make the identification. See Kramer, *When Aseneth Met Joseph: A Late Antique Tale of the Biblical Patriarch and His Egyptian Wife, Reconsidered* (Oxford: Oxford University Press, 1998), 19, 314-16; see n. 10.

is also found elsewhere), thus agreeing with Origen's source that the name was changed, though the explanation of the change is different.[9] Jerome, in his *Hebrew Questions on Genesis* (on Gen 37:36; 41:45), based on Jewish sources, identifies Joseph's master with the father of Aseneth, but transliterates the Hebrew name in both cases as Phutiphar. Finally, the Greek Testament of Joseph, a work of uncertain provenance, presupposes the identification of Joseph's master with his father-in-law (18:3).

The targumim, however, notably fail to identify Potiphar and Potiphera, preserving the Hebrew text's differing descriptions of the two.[10] Nor is the identification made in Joseph and Aseneth (as 4:9 makes unequivocally clear), while later Christian sources such as the Palaea Historica and the Syriac History of Joseph show no sign of accepting the identification.[11] Thus, on the one hand, there was evidently a Jewish exegetical tradition of identifying Potiphar and Potiphera, which persisted from the second century BCE through to the medieval period, but it was by no means universally accepted. Explanations of the two names, on the other hand, differ from one source to another.

There is an obvious difficulty in supposing Potiphar and Potiphera to be the same person: the seeming contradiction between Potiphar's anger at Joseph's attempted adultery with his wife (as she alleges) and Potiphera's apparent willingness to let Joseph marry his daughter. This difficulty is precisely what the apocryphon reported by Origen attempted to resolve. It provides an example of a frequent practice in Jewish exegesis in antiquity: the creation of a story to explain a difficulty in the biblical text.

This story (of Aseneth's revelation of her mother's guilt and Joseph's innocence) is the second main feature that can be paralleled elsewhere. In this case, there is only one such parallel, in a late Hebrew midrash, known as Midrash Abkir, which is itself preserved only in excerpts. The text relates that, when Potiphar's wife accused Joseph, Potiphar wanted to kill him.

> Thereupon Asenath came to Potiphar secretly and related to him under oath the true state of affairs. Then God spoke to her as follows, "By thy life, because thou

---

9. Tg. Ps.-Jon. Gen 39:1; Jerome, *Qu. hebr. Gen.* ad 37:36; 41:45; Gen. Rab. 86:3. Only in b. Soṭah 13b is this story used to explain the two names.

10. Kraemer supposes that the identification must lie behind the targumim, when they translate Hebrew *sārîs* (traditionally translated "eunuch"), used of Potiphar in Gen 37:36; 39:1, not as "eunuch" but as "officer" or "chief" (*When Aseneth*, 316). Aseneth could not be the daughter of a eunuch. However, this argument is refuted by Kraemer's own quotation from Martin McNamara, who explains that the targumim *never* render *sārîs* as "eunuch" (except in Isa 56:3–4, where this is the obvious meaning). See McNamara, *Targum Neofiti: Genesis*, ArBib 1A (Edinburgh: T&T Clark, 1992), 174 n. 21 [not 171, as in Kraemer, *When Aseneth*, 321 n. 47]; cf. also Bernard Grossfeld, *The Targum Onqelos to Genesis*, ArBib 6 (Edinburgh: T&T Clark, 1988), 129 n. 12. This is a consistent translation policy, not adopted for the case of Potiphar in particular. The translation policy may well reflect accurately the fact that in Biblical Hebrew *sārîs* often means not "eunuch" but "high official" (see *DCH*). Targum Pseudo-Jonathan Gen 39:1 translates *sārîs* as "official" but adds the story of Potiphar's castration by divine decree. It does not, however, use this story to explain how he could have had a daughter (born before his castration), as is clear from its interpretation of Gen 41:45, 50, which explains that Aseneth was not really Potiphera's daughter. She was actually a daughter of Dinah (Joseph's sister) who had been raised by the wife of Potiphera (a tradition also found elsewhere).

11. The Syriac History of Joseph has an unparalleled story about Potiphar and his wife, after Joseph's elevation to pharaoh's vicegerent (chs. 24–27), but Joseph's marriage goes unmentioned. A full study of the treatment of the two names in Christian sources would need to examine patristic commentaries on Genesis, which I have not done.

hast defended him, the tribes that I wish to have originate from him will descend from thee."[12]

While the story reported by Origen makes Aseneth's revelation of the truth to her father the explanation for the latter's willingness to give her in marriage to Joseph, this story makes it the explanation of God's decision that she should marry Joseph and bear his children (the ancestors of two of the tribes of Israel). It is used to solve a different difficulty from the one that our apocryphon addresses: the problem of understanding why God should choose an Egyptian to be the foremother of two of the Israelite tribes. But the central episode (Aseneth's revelation of the truth to her father) is the same in both cases. In some form then the story that Origen attributes to the apocryphon of "the Hebrews" survived in Jewish tradition long after his time, just as the identification of Potiphar and Potiphera also did.[13]

Date and Provenance

There can be no doubt that Origen meant to refer to an apocryphal book in use among Jews. He uses the word *apocryphon* to refer to books not deemed canonical (and so read publicly) but otherwise similar to the biblical literature. The word cannot refer to an oral source.[14] However, since he gives only a summary of the story, we cannot be sure whether he read the work himself or merely heard its contents reported by one of his Jewish contacts. We cannot tell whether it was written in Hebrew, Aramaic, or Greek, nor whether Origen encountered it in Alexandria or in Caesarea. It is unlikely to be the same as the work called The Prayer of Joseph, from which Origen quotes elsewhere: the respective quotations suggest works of quite different character.[15] We do not know whether our apocryphon focused exclusively on Joseph or retold a larger portion of the biblical history. Of its date, we can say only that it was written before the third century CE.

---

12. Translation from Viktor Aptowitzer, "Asenath, the Wife of Joseph: A Haggadic Literary-Historical Study," *HUCA* 1 (1924): 256. He gives the Hebrew text in n. 43.

13. Another late source, *Sefer ha-Yashar*, has a variant of the story: An anonymous eleven-month-old male child witnessed the incident between Potiphar's wife and Joseph and was miraculously able to testify to the truth, convincing Potiphar of Joseph's innocence (Aptowitzer, "Asenath," 256 n. 43). James L. Kugel connects this variant story with Origen's version by mistakenly supposing that the latter also refers to an *anonymous* child. See Kugel, *In Potiphar's House: The Interpretive Life of Biblical Texts*, 2nd ed. (Cambridge: Harvard University Press, 1994), 64–65 n. 47. The illustrations in the Vienna Genesis (sixth century) include a scene where an infant in a crib witnesses the incident between Potiphar's wife and Joseph. See Joseph Gutmann, "Joseph Legends in the Vienna Genesis," in *Proceedings of the Fifth World Congress of Jewish Studies*, 5 vols. (Jerusalem: World Union of Jewish Studies, 1973), 4:181–85, esp. 182–83; Kugel, *In Potiphar's House*, 56–57. This is probably Aseneth, but it is also possible that the variant story attested in *Sefer ha-Yashar* lies behind the illustration.

14. Contra Tzvetkova-Glaser, who thinks he could be referring to an oral source ("Joseph," 200, 204). Tzvetkova-Glaser does not distinguish between the story Origen reports from the apocryphon and his explanation of the Hebrew names. The latter very plausibly comes from rabbinic oral tradition.

15. Marc Philonenko argues against Batiffol's proposal that the story about Aseneth comes from The Prayer of Joseph. See Philonenko, *Joseph et Aséneth: Introduction, Texte Critique, Traduction et Notes*, StPB 13 (Leiden: Brill, 1968), 39–40.

Bibliography

EDITIONS AND TRANSLATIONS

Petit, Françoise. Pages 255–56 (Fragment 1940) in *La Chaîne sur la Genèse: Édition Intégrale: IV: Chapitres 29 à 50*. Traditio exegetica graeca 4. Leuven: Peeters, 1996. (Critical edition of the texts of both versions [*editio princeps* of the long version]).

PG 12:135–36. (Text and Latin translation of the abridged version.)

Philonenko, Marc. Page 39 in *Joseph et Aséneth: Introduction, Texte Critique, Traduction et Notes*. StPB 13. Leiden: Brill, 1968. (French translation of the abridged version.)

Tzvetkova-Glaser, Anna. "Joseph and His Egyptian Family in the Interpretation of Origen and the Early Rabbis." Pages 197–205 (esp. p. 205) in *Rewritten Biblical Figures*. Edited by Erkki Koskenniemi and Pekka Lindqvist. Studies in Rewritten Bible 3. Turku: Åbo Akademi University; Winona Lake, IN: Eisenbrauns, 2010. (Text of both versions and English translation of the long version.)

STUDIES

Aptowitzer, Viktor. "Asenath, the Wife of Joseph: A Haggadic Literary-Historical Study." *HUCA* 1 (1924): 239–306.

De Lange, Nicholas Robert Michael. Page 129 in *Origen and the Jews: Studies in Jewish-Christian Relations in Third-Century Palestine*. Cambridge Oriental Series 25. Cambridge: Cambridge University Press, 1976.

Kraemer, Ross Shepard. Pages 230, 308 in *When Aseneth Met Joseph: A Late Antique Tale of the Biblical Patriarch and His Egyptian Wife, Reconsidered*. Oxford: Oxford University Press, 1998.

Tzvetkova-Glaser, Anna. "Joseph and His Egyptian Family in the Interpretation of Origen and the Early Rabbis." Pages 197–205 in *Rewritten Biblical Figures*. Edited by Erkki Koskenniemi and Pekka Lindqvist.Studies in Rewritten Bible 3. Turku: Åbo Akademi University; Winona Lake, IN: Eisenbrauns, 2010.

An Apocryphon about Aseneth

Long Version

The name *Phoutiphar* is contained in the name of the father of the woman who was married to Joseph.[a] Someone may think that this is a different man from the one who purchased Joseph. However, **the Hebrews have not held that opinion, but, learning it from an apocryphon, they say that the man who was Joseph's master became also his father-in-law. They also say that Aseneth, in the presence of her father, blamed her mother, since it was she who had designs on Joseph, not he on her, and it was because of the chastity of the man**[b] **that nothing happened to her. Somehow her (Aseneth's) father uncovered [*apopetasas*] something**[c] **and the act was proved. So, since she also knew of the purity of the man, he gave her to him in marriage, being eager also to show to the rest of the Egyptians, so that [there should be no rumors]**[d] **among them about what had happened, that no transgression of this kind had been committed in his house.**

It should be no surprise if she (Aseneth) was called "Calamity" [*sumptōsis*],[e] since she gave information against her mother about her moral lapse [*sumptōma*]. Nor (should it be surprising) if the expression "he shall uncover" [*apopetasei*] was added to the previous name of her father, since it was what he did afterward[f] that gave him the addition to his name.[g] This expression "he shall

Gen 39:6–19

Gen 41:45

---

a. Origen is referring to the two Hebrew names: *Pôtîphar*, the name of Joseph's master (Gen 37:36; 39:1) and *Pôtîpheraʿ*, the name of his wife Aseneth's father (Gen 41:45, 50). In the Hebrew consonantal text the latter has one letter more than the former. In LXX both names are rendered as *Petephrēs*, while Josephus calls both *Pentephrēs* (*Ant.* 2.39, 40, 54, 58, 78, 91, though some MSS have *Petephrēs*).

b. For Joseph's chastity (*sōphrosunē*), see also 4 Macc 2:2; Philo, *Ios.* 40, 57, 87; Josephus, *A. J.* 2.48, 50, 69; T. Jos. 4:1–2; 6:7; 9:2–3; 10:2–3; Jos. As. 4:7; Clement of Alexandria, *Paed.* 68.3; Origen, *Cels.* 4.46. It was a virtue especially associated with Joseph.

c. I.e., something that incriminated his wife.

d. A word or more seems to be missing from the Greek text here. For this translation, see Tzvetkova-Glaser, "Joseph," 205 n. 34.

e. Origen derives the name Aseneth (Hebrew 'Âsenat) from the Hebrew 'āsôn, "misfortune."

f. After Aseneth had informed against her mother, her father "uncovered" (*apopetasas*) something.

g. Origen means that the Hebrew name *Pôtîphar* became *Pôtîpheraʿ* through the addition of the Hebrew root *prʿ*, which means "to loose, to uncover." (For the meaning "uncover," which is not certainly used in Biblical Hebrew, see Jastrow, 1235.) This verb is used in Num 5:18, which says that the priest "shall let loose/uncover [*pāraʿ*] the head of the woman" accused

uncover," which is found in this example, points to the accusation of adultery brought against a woman by her husband. With reference to that accusation, Scripture says: *he shall uncover [apopetasei] the head of the woman)*.[a]

Num 5:18

Abridged Version

The name "Phoutiphar" is contained in the name of the father of the woman who was married to Joseph. Someone may think that this is a different man from the one who purchased Joseph. However, **the Hebrews have not held that opinion, but, learning it from an apocryphon, they say that the man who was Joseph's master became also his father-in-law. They also say that Aseneth, in the presence of her father, blamed her mother, since it was she who had designs on Joseph, not he on her. Also he gave her in marriage to Joseph, since he was eager also to show to the Egyptians that no transgression of this kind had been committed by Joseph in his house**.

---

of adultery. This may mean that he is to let loose (unbind) her hair, but the LXX (which has *apokalypsei* for *pāraʿ*) takes it to mean "uncover her head." Origen also adopts this meaning, translating *pāraʿ* as *apopetasei*. So he explains the addition (*prʿ*) to Potiphar/Potiphera's name from the fact that he "uncovered" something, and is then able to connect the expanded name also with Num 5:18. In Gen. Rab. 86:3, there is a different explanation of the name Potiphera, with reference to the verb *pʿr* used in the sense of "to uncover oneself."

a. This is not the LXX translation.

The Hebrew Testament of Naphtali
A new translation and introduction

by Vered Hillel

The Hebrew Testament of Naphtali is embedded in the medieval Chronicles of Jerahmeel (CJ) and is one of four different works that preserve traditions about Naphtali the son of Jacob—Hebrew Testament of Naphtali (Heb. T. Naph.), Greek Testament of Naphtali (T. Naph.), 4QTestament of Naphtali (4Q215) and Midrash Bereshit Rabbati (BR). The Hebrew Testament of Naphtali shares substantial material with T. Naph. (e.g., visions, lists of human body parts and their functions, exhortations to follow Levi and Judah), although in a very complicated manner, with each containing material not found in the other. The Hebrew Testament of Naphtali only indirectly relates to 4Q215 and BR in that they contain traditions about Naphtali that are shared with T. Naph. It seems that all four works stem from a common source often dubbed Original Naphtali.

Contents

The Hebrew Testament of Naphtali begins with Naphtali exhorting his sons to fear ADONAI[1] and warning them about their future apostasy and exile, which will result from their following the sons of Joseph instead of the sons of Levi and Judah. The patriarch then relates two dreams that confirm his prophecy. The first dream takes place while Naphtali is grazing his flocks. When his brothers and father enter the scene, Jacob instructs them to grab hold of their own portion. Each son, except for Joseph, seizes and rides on one of the luminaries. Joseph remains on earth refusing to join his brothers until a giant, winged bull with huge horns appears, which he mounts and rides about. During his time riding the bull, Joseph ascends to Judah, who is sitting on the moon, and physically removes ten of the twelve staves in his hand. The vision ends with the brothers being dispersed by a strong wind. In the second dream, Naphtali, his brothers and his father are by the Great Sea (Mediterranean) when an unmanned ship appears. Judah and Levi grab the two great masts and the remaining brothers, except Joseph, each grab an oar. After some cajoling from Jacob, Joseph takes the two steering oars from his father. As long as Joseph pays attention to the directions of Levi and Judah, everything goes well. However, eventually Joseph refuses to listen to Levi and Judah, and the ship crashes, causing the brothers to flee for their lives. The Hebrew Testament of Naphtali closes with another exhortation from Naphtali not to forsake ADONAI as did the seventy nations during the time of Abraham. Only Abraham and his descendants remained loyal to the creator. A list of body parts, culminating in the creator's life-giving breath, demonstrates the great wonders of the creator, making him worthy of adoration and obedience.

---

1. ADONAI indicates the use of the Tetragrammaton.

Manuscripts and Versions

Moses Gaster first drew scholarly attention to Heb. T. Naph. in 1893–1894 when he published a text that was preserved in a medieval manuscript of the Chronicles of Jerahmeel.[2] Solomon Aaron Wertheimer had published a version of Heb. T. Naph. a few years earlier in 1888. However, this version was little known because it was attached to his handwritten edition of *Pirkei Heichalot Rabbati* that was printed in the 1890s by Shmuel Dimant.

The Hebrew Testament of Naphtali is known in two recensions represented in four manuscripts. Recension 1 is known in three manuscripts that are identical in content and style, and recension 2 in one manuscript and is shorter and secondary:

RECENSION 1

A	thirteenth century	Oxford, Bodleian Heb. D11 [2792]
P	twelfth century	Paris
J	date unknown	First published from a Jerusalem manuscript by Solomon Aaron Wertheimer in 1888 as an appendix to *Pirkei Heichalot Rabbati*.[3]

RECENSION 2

Parma	thirteenth–fourteenth centuries	Biblioteca Palantina 2295 [1541] (De Russi 563)

The second recension was published by S. Wertheimer in *Batei Midrashot*, where it bears the title "*'gdh bbny y'jwv*" ("Haggadah of the Sons of Jacob").[4]

In his publication of the Hebrew text and English translation, Gaster collated a text based on MS A with readings from MSS P and J, inserting various readings, omissions, and corruptions into the footnotes.[5] He holds that MSS P and J are identical and that P is the best recension. R. H. Charles published Gaster's collated Hebrew text with some revisions in appendix II of his edition of the Greek text of the Testaments of the Twelve Patriarchs (T. 12 Patr.)[6] and the English translation in appendix 1 of his translation of

---

2. Moses Gaster, "The Hebrew Text of One of the Testaments of the XII Patriarchs," *Proceedings of the Society of Biblical Archaeology* 16 (1893–1894): trans. (1893): 33–49; text (1894): 109–17. The translation was subsequently published in Gaster, *The Chronicles of Jerahmeel or The Hebrew Bible Historiale* (London: Oriental Translation Fund, 1899; repr., with prolegomenon by Haim Schwarzbaum, New York: Ktav 1971), 88–94; and the text and translation in Gaster, *Studies and Texts in Folklore, Magic, Mediaeval Romance, Hebrew Apocrypha and Samaritan Archeology*, 3 vols. (London: Maggs Bros., 1925–1928; repr., New York: Ktav, 1971), trans. 1:69–91; text 3:22–30. The Hebrew text was published, with emendations, in Judah David Eisenstein, ed., *Otzar Midrashim: A Library of Two Hundred Minor Midrashim* (New York: Eisenstein, 1915), 2:236–38 [Heb.].

3. S. Wertheimer, ed., *Sefer Pirkei Heichalot Rabbati* (Jerusalem: Verthaimer, 1889), appendix [Heb.]. Text from MS J was reprinted with notes and commentary by his grandson Abraham J. Wertheimer, *Batei Midrashot*, 2 vols. (Jerusalem: Harav Kook, 1953), 2:193–98 [Heb.]. Abraham J. Wertheimer's publication combines midrashim from his grandfather's *Batei Midrashot* and *Leket Midrash*.

4. Solomon Aaron Wertheimer, *Batei Midrashot*, 4 vols. (Jerusalem: Lilienthal, 1894). Reprinted with commentary and notes in A. Wertheimer, *Batei Midrashot*, 2:199–203 [Heb.].

5. Gaster, "Hebrew Text."

6. R. H. Charles, *The Greek Version of the Testaments of the Twelve Patriarchs: Edited from Nine MSS Together with the Variants of the Armenian and Slavonic Versions and Some Hebrew Fragments* (Oxford: Clarendon, 1908), 239–44.

281

T. 12 Patr.[7] A revised edition of Charles's translation is printed in appendix 1 in the commentary on T. 12 Patr. by Harm W. Hollander and Marinus de Jonge.[8] An uncollated version of Heb. T. Naph. from the Oxford manuscript (A) is printed in the critical edition of the Chronicles of Jerahmeel (CJ) by Eli Yassif.[9] The translation in this volume follows MS A taking into consideration readings from MSS J and Parma and Gaster's collation of P since this manuscript was unavailable to me, and adopts the chapter and verse division from Charles's publication.[10]

The Hebrew Testament of Naphtali is extant in medieval Hebrew. Gaster emphatically claimed that all the writings in CJ are solely Hebrew writings and not translations.[11] While it has been shown for some portions of CJ that they are retroverted from other languages, Gaster's statement applies to Heb. T. Naph. A comparison of Heb. T. Naph. and T. Naph. demonstrates that there is no direct dependence of one text on the other and the many differences in the shared material—visions (Heb. T. Naph. 2–7; T. Naph. 5–7), list of body parts and their functions (Heb. T. Naph. 10:6; T. Naph. 2:8), and exhortations to follow Levi and Judah (Heb. T. Naph. 1:8, 7:6; T. Naph. 8:2)—indicate that they go back to a common Hebrew source.[12] Furthermore, Heb. T. Naph. adapts the story of Abraham and the seventy nations to demonstrate Naphtali's genealogical connection to Abraham and to legitimize his genealogy (9:1–10:2) just as the inclusion of Bilhah's genealogy in T. Naph. develops Naphtali's Abrahamic ancestry. Though developed differently, both documents equate Naphtali and his descendants with the house of Abraham, indicating some type of common source. Parallel material to the genealogy of Bilhah found in the so-called Testament of Naphtali from Qumran (4Q215), a late first-century BCE text written in Hebrew, and in an eleventh-century Hebrew work composed in the circles of Rabbi Moses the Preacher of Narbonne, Midrash Bereshit Rabbati (BR), only imply an ethnic identification, indicating "the existence of a developed Naphtali tradition in the period of the Second Temple" that had been "nurtured over the centuries" and eventually "reworked and remodeled in the Middle Ages."[13]

---

7. R. H. Charles, *The Testaments of the Twelve Patriarchs: Translated from the Editor's Greek Text and Edited, with Introduction, Notes and Indices* (London: Adam and Charles Black, 1908), 221–27; repr., *AOT* 2:361–63.

8. H. W. Hollander and M. de Jonge, *The Testaments of the Twelve Patriarchs: A Commentary*, SVTP 8 (Leiden: Brill, 1985), 446–50. The revision of Heb. T. Naph. was done by A. van der Heide.

9. Eli Yassif, *The Book of Memory That Is the Chronicles of Jerahme'el* (Tel Aviv: Tel Aviv University, 2001), 143–47 [Heb.].

10. Charles adopts the chapter divisions from Emil Kautzsch, *Die Apokryphen und Pseudepigraphen des Alten Testaments*, 2 vols. (Tübingen: Mohr, 1900), 2:489–92.

11. Gaster, *Chronicles*, xxi. One example of translations in CJ is the fragments of Pseudo-Philo's LAB, which were retroverted from Latin into Hebrew; see Daniel J. Harrington, "Pseudo-Philo," *OTP* 2:297–337, esp. 298. For the relation between CJ and LAB, see Harrington, ed. and trans., *The Hebrew Fragments of Pseudo-Philo's* Liber Antiquitatum Biblicarum *Preserved in the* Chronicles of Jerahmeel, SBLTT 3, Pseudepigrapha Series 3 (Missoula, MT: Society of Biblical Literature, 1974), 2–7.

12. See Marinus de Jonge, *The Testaments of the Twelve Patriarchs: A Study of Their Text, Composition and Origin* (Assen: Van Gorcum, 1953), 52–60, esp. 53; and Hollander and de Jonge, *Commentary*, 296. This has not always been the consensus and is still challenged by some scholars. For a history of the discussion see Vered Hillel, "Naphtali: A 'Proto-Joseph' in the Greek Testament of Naphtali" (Master's thesis, Hebrew University of Jerusalem, 2002), 42 n. 179; reworked and printed without the referenced footnote in *JSP* 16, no. 3 (2007): 171–201.

13. Michael E. Stone, "The Genealogy of Bilhah," *DSD* 3 (1996): 34–35, doi:10.1163/156851796X00309.

Genre, Structure, and Prosody

Hebrew Testament of Naphtali is of the testament genre, which usually includes the farewell discourse of a dying father to his gathered descendants. The genre *testament* can be defined either by its formal literary characteristics or by the nature of its content. The foremost literary characteristic is a testament's narrative framework. Typically, a testament begins with a third-person description of the setting of the farewell discourse in which a well-known biblical personage calls together his descendants and imparts vital knowledge and wisdom to them.[14] The Hebrew Testament of Naphtali fits this description: It opens with a short third-person narrative about Naphtali's advanced age and impending death,[15] and his calling together his descendants to address them. Essential features of the content of the testament genre are paraenesis (exhortation) and apocalyptic or future forecasting, the use of events from the patriarch's life to illustrate his words or to validate his predictions, revelation, or exhortation, and the frequent elaboration or adaptation of older stories to suit the purposes of the author. The Hebrew Testament of Naphtali uses the visions of earlier episodes in the patriarch's life to validate his exhortation to follow Levi and Judah and not Joseph (1:8; 7:6) and his prediction that in the future their sons will follow those of Joseph and not those of Levi and Judah and be led into apostasy and exile (Heb. T. Naph. 1:10; 7:4). Though 4Q215 from Qumran is called Testament of Naphtali, it is not a testament, as it exhibits none of the formal literary characteristics or the essential features of the content of the testament genre.[16] It is a genealogy.

The structure of Heb. T. Naph. is straightforward. The story is a third-person narrative in which the narrator relates the first-person account of Naphtali to his descendants.

1. Opening third-person narrative (1:1–9)
2. Naphtali's first-person narration (1:10–10:9)
   - Exhortation to fear ADONAI and to follow Levi and Judah and the prediction of future apostasy and exile for not heading the patriarch's words (1:5–10)
     - Dream 1: In the field tending flocks (2:1–3:13)
     - Dream 2: Beside the sea (4:1–6:8)
     - Jacob's interpretation of the dreams (7:1–6)
   - Exhortation not to forsake ADONAI (8:1–3a)
     - Narrative of Abraham and the seventy nations (8:3b–10:2)
   - Exhortation not to stray or worship other gods (10:3–4)
     - Reasons for worshiping the God of Abraham, the creator (10:5–9)
     - Exemplified by list of body parts and functions (10:6–8)
   - Exhortation in the form of a blessing (10:9)
3. Closing third-person comments (10:10)

---

14. On the genre *testaments*, see Vered Hillel, "Testaments," in *T&T Clark Encyclopedia of Second Temple Judaism*, ed. Daniel M. Gurtner and Loren T. Stuckenbruck, 2 vols. (London: T&T Clark, 2020), 2:766–68.

15. For clarification of Naphtali's impending death, see below.

16. For further information on the nontestamentary character of 4Q215, see Marinus de Jonge, "The *Testaments of the Twelve Patriarchs* and Related Qumran Fragments," in *For a Later Generation: The Transformation of Tradition in Israel, Early Judaism and Early Christianity*, ed. Randal A. Argall, Beverly A. Bow, and Rodney A. Werline (Harrisburg, PA: Trinity Press International, 2000), 63–77, esp. 69–72 and nn. 29–44.

The author sets the stage of Naphtali's advanced age and impending death (1:1) by adapting a list of the major characteristics of the stages of life from five years old to one hundred recorded in m. 'Abot 5:21. Naphtali is said to have passed through all of the stages of life, up to and including a "bent back" (ninety years old), but is not one hundred because at that age one is "as good as dead and gone completely from the world." After Naphtali warns his descendants not to follow Joseph but only Levi and Judah and predicts that in the future, they will indeed follow Joseph's sons and go into exile, he relates two dreams to substantiate his claims. After the first dream is completed and Naphtali relates it to his father, Jacob literally replies, "this dream will not ascend or descend" (3:13), meaning that the vision is insignificant, it is not important, because it has not been repeated.[17] The notion that two similar dreams or visions are necessary to assure their fulfillment is as old as Joseph's statement to Pharaoh that his two dreams are as one (Gen 41:25).[18] This is indeed the case in the two visions in Heb. T. Naph. and those in T. Naph. in which revelation of the meaning of the visions occurs only after the second vision is presented to Jacob.

The list of body parts and their functions (10:6–8) appears to have been drawn from different sources that are not known in any other texts. The first seven body parts, from the eyes to the tongue, have a prefixed *mem* and are followed by an imperfect verb. The next six, from the mouth to the liver, have a prefixed *bet* and are also followed by an imperfect verb. The functions of the stomach, feet, and kidneys are presented in the form of participles. The description of the lungs and their function is very obscure (*wry'h bry'h lnpš*, "with the lungs for breathing"). Various lists of body parts and their functions exist in rabbinic literature most often as a list of ten or twelve things that serve the soul,[19] but none of these lists are the source of those in Heb. T. Naph., nor do they shed any light on the obscure phrase about the lungs. The reading in MSS P and J *wbry'h bry'h lnpš* does not help clarify the phrase. There seems to be a word play with the root *r-'-h*, from which words such as lungs, creation, and health are drawn, and also with the word *nepesh*, which can mean soul or life, engendering the idea that lungs give health for life or for the soul through breathing. The closest comparable statement, which does not fit the context of Heb. T. Naph., is in b. Ḥul. 49a *ry'h šm'yrh 't h'nym* ("the lungs light up the eyes"). This passage may have prompted the emendation of the Hebrew text of Heb. T. Naph. in Otzar Midrashim to read *wbry'h mbry' lnpš* "and with his lungs giving health to his soul (or life)." The Hebrew Testament of Naphtali concludes that because each organ and function will always remain the same, a person is to pay attention to the creator who formed each individual from a "putrid drop" (Heb. T. Naph. 10:8). This phrase, known from m. 'Abot 3.1, is used in rabbinic literature to remind humans of their humble origins and to thwart pride.[20] The Hebrew Testament of Naphtali uses the

---

17. For the use of this phrase meaning insignificant, won't come to anything, see, e.g., b. Hullin 45b and y. Pes. 51a.

18. For information on the antiquity of this theory, see Th. Korteweg, "The Meaning of Naphtali's Visions," in *Studies on the Testaments of the Twelve Patriarchs*, ed. Marinus de Jonge, SVTP 3 (Leiden: Brill, 1975), 261–90, particularly 272–73, and n. 20.

19. B. Ber. 61a–61b lists thirteen body parts and their functions. The remainder of the references usually refer to ten or twelve body parts and functions, Lev. Rab. 4; Num. Rab. 18:11; Qoh. Rab. 7:19; Midr. Tehillim 103; Yalkut Shimoni on the Torah 464.3 and 4; Lekach Tov; Otzar Midrashim, *Othiot* of Rabbi Akiva, and Chuppat Eliyahu.

20. See also, e.g., Lev. Rab. 18.1; and "The Midrash on King Solomon, The Story of the Ant and the

phrases similarly to remind humans of their humble origin and their creator, which should cause the person to serve him.

Interestingly, either the Tetragrammaton is used for the name of the God of Israel or "the Holy One" or "the Holy One blessed be he." The Tetragrammaton is abbreviated in the text by a double yod (י״י) and rendered ADONAI in the translation. It appears until the introduction of the haggadah of Abraham and the seventy nations (8:3, after which only "the Holy One"/"Holy One blessed be he," appears). The exceptions are the introductory words, which use *Elohim* because it is a quote of Rachel's words in Gen 30:8, and the one occurrence of "Lord [*Adonai*] of heaven and earth" (9:2).

Date and Provenance

Since Heb. T. Naph. is embedded in the Chronicles of Jerahmeel, CJ is the starting point for determining the date and provenance of the Heb. T. Naph. Chronicles of Jerahmeel was essentially lost and is known only from its inclusion in a larger Jewish chronological anthology *Sefer Hazikronot* (*The Book of Memories*) compiled by Eleazar ben Asher HaLevi in the early fourteenth century somewhere in the Rhine provinces.[21] The author and provenance of CJ remain a mystery even though the composer identifies himself as Jerahmeel ben Shlomo (Oxford 2797, fol. 113a), who in turn has been identified with the eleventh- or twelfth-century Italian scholar and poet. Gaster, however, claims that the author of CJ relied on an older document dating to the sixth or seventh centuries that was written in Hebrew.[22] The most that can be stated from manuscript evidence is that Heb. T. Naph. is a Jewish document written in Hebrew sometime around the tenth or eleventh centuries, since MS P is from the twelfth century.

Internal evidence and comparison with documents that record similar traditions about Naphtali point toward a much earlier date and a possible Palestinian provenance. Gaster regarded Heb. T. Naph. as the original version of T. Naph.,[23] while Charles considered Heb. T. Naph. to be somehow related to the "primitive Hebrew text" from which T. Naph. was translated.[24] Similarly de Jonge has demonstrated that neither Heb. T. Naph. or T. Naph. is derived from one another but rely on a common source that he calls Original Naphtali, and Th. Korteweg has demonstrated that the visions in Heb. T. Naph., despite the manuscript evidence of a late date, are closer to Original Naphtali than the Greek T. Naph.[25] This places the date of source material for Heb. T. Naph. and T. Naph. to at least the first century CE since T. 12 Patr. is written sometime in the second century CE.[26] Though Heb. T. Naph. does not include the genealogy of Bilhah, both T. Naph.

Sealed Palace," in Eisenstein, *Otzar Midrashim*, 22.31 *byh hmdrš h"h*, 534. The terminology differs slightly between Heb. T. Naph. (*typh b'wš*h) and m. Abot 3.1 (*typh srûḥh*).

21. Anthologies, especially chronological anthologies such as *Sefer Hazikronot,* were common in medieval Jewish culture. Earlier chronicles, annals, and literary works were the primary raw material copied into these historical anthologies; see Eli Yassif, "The Hebrew Narrative Anthology in the Middle Ages," in *The Anthology in Jewish Literature*, ed. D. Stern (Oxford: Oxford University Press, 2004), 176–95; and specifically on *Sefer Hazikronot* with references to previous research and editions, see Yassif, "Introduction" in *Sefer Ha-Zikronot* (Tel Aviv: University of Tel Aviv, 2001), 11–68 [Heb.].

22. Gaster, *Chronicles*, lii.

23. Gaster, "Hebrew Text," 76.

24. Charles, *Text*, introduction §20, li–lii.

25. Korteweg, "Meaning," 281–82.

26. On the date and provenance of T. 12 Patr. and the extant form as a Christian composition, see Hollander and de Jonge, *Commentary*, 82–85.

and Heb. T. Naph. trace Naphtali's genealogy to Abraham, indicating a shared tradition, and the parallel material about the birth and naming of Bilhah in T. Naph. and 4Q215 takes the source material back to at least the first century BCE.

That Heb. T. Naph. is a Jewish document can be seen from its presence in CJ, its similarities with other Naphtali traditions in Jewish documents, and from a comparison of the visions in T. Naph., whose Hebrew source has been redacted to fit the Christian eschatological pattern in T. Levi and T. Jud. as an eschatological savior that represents the final restoration of Israel, as well as the salvation of the gentiles, and to present Joseph as a type of Christ in his first appearance on earth.[27] The Hebrew Testament of Naphtali shows no such Christian redaction. Other evidence that Heb. T. Naph. represents early Jewish traditions with no Christian interpolations are the similarities between the list of body parts and their functions as well as the haggadah of Abraham and the seventy nations, languages, divine patrons, and rabbinic literature and pseudepigrapha such as 1 Enoch and Jubilees. Thus, it can be stated that Heb. T. Naph. is a Jewish document that relies on sources and Naphtali traditions that can be traced to at least the first century BCE.

Literary Context
Though the setting of Heb. T. Naph. is the farewell speech of Naphtali, the focus of the testament, especially the visions, is on Joseph and his actions toward Levi-Judah, which cause Naphtali's descendants to rebel against ADONAI and go into exile. The two visions indirectly relate to Joseph's two visions (Gen 37:5–11), particularly the first vision involving the race for the luminaries and to Moses's use of bull and *re'em* in his blessings of the tribe of Joseph (Deut 33:13–17; Heb. T. Naph. 3:1–4). In contrast, T. Naph. connects Naphtali's biographical material to Jacob's blessing of Naphtali (Gen 49:21) as well as the biblical information of his birth and Bilhah's genealogy (T. Naph. 1:6–2:1).[28]

The Hebrew Testament of Naphtali and T. Naph. share a substantial amount of material, which mainly falls in three sections: the visions, list of body parts and functions, and admonitions to follow Levi and Judah. The two visions in Heb. T. Naph. are distinct and complete (chs. 2–4; 5–7). They are integrally related to one another and to the framework of the document. This correspondence between the two visions is significant, especially in light of the lack of coherence and meaning in the visions in T. Naph. The visions corroborate the patriarch's prophecy about his descendants' future apostasy, which occurs through the motif of a quarrel over leadership between Joseph and Levi-Judah. In both visions, Jacob summons his sons to a race. Levi and Judah seize the prize positions of leadership (sun and moon; two great masts), and Joseph refuses to participate until he receives an elevated position (a large bull; two steering oars). Joseph is the antagonist against the leadership of Levi and Judah, who lead his brothers into apostasy and exile. This is a clear reference to the division between the Northern and Southern Kingdoms of Israel. These two visions resemble one another so closely that they are as one dream (7:4–5) and therefore will be fulfilled.

Conversely, the visions in T. Naph. (chs. 5–6) are much shorter and not coherent or straightforward. It is not even clear if there are two visions or three.[29] Furthermore, these

---

27. See Hillel, "Proto-Joseph," 191–94, and nn. 74, 76, and 78.
28. The genealogy of Bilhah plays an important role in T. Naph. See Vered Hillel, "Why Not Naphtali?," in *Things Revealed: Studies in Early Jewish and Christian Literature in Honor of Michael E. Stone*, ed. Esther G. Chazon, David Satran and Ruth A. Clements, JSJSup 89 (Leiden: Brill, 2004), 279–88, doi:10.1163/9789047405467_024.
29. On the structure of the visions, see Vered Hillel, *The Testaments of the Twelve Patriarchs: Structure,*

visions omit all negative references to Joseph in keeping with the main purpose of the visions to illustrate Israel's eschatological salvation and to elevate the status of Levi–Judah and to emphasize their cooperation with one another. In the first vision (ch. 5) there is a race but no conflict between Levi–Judah and Joseph. To avoid any negative comments about Joseph, the vision ends after Joseph ascends into the heavens with no mention of his quarrel with Judah. In the second vision (ch. 6) there is no race and only a slight trace of a conflict (6:6). Though revelation comes to Jacob after the second dream (ch. 7), his insight does not stem from the correspondences between the two visions. These visions ostensibly make no sense without comparing them with their setting in Heb. T. Naph. The visions in T. Naph. demonstrate considerable redactional activity that disturbs the original coherence and meaning as a whole.

Analogous lists of body parts and their functions in Heb. T. Naph. (10:6) and T. Naph. (2:8) are another area of shared material that demonstrates a common source. Though the function of the lists in both testaments is similar, that is, the way in which the human body is formed should lead people to recognize the creator and this recognition should lead to worship of and obedience to him, there are many discrepancies. The most notable is the omission of "gall" from Heb. T. Naph. and its inclusion in T. Naph. and in all other lists of body parts and functions in Hebrew literature.[30]

The third area of shared material in Heb. T. Naph. and T. Naph. is the worship of the one true God, ADONAI, and the warning not to turn from him and to follow Levi and Judah. In Heb. T. Naph. Abraham warns his descendants to follow the God of their fathers and not to follow the nations of the earth who separated themselves from the Lord and followed their own angel. The Testament of Naphtali, reflecting argumentation and concepts represented in 1 En. 6–8, Jubilees, wisdom literature, and early Christian circles, warns his descendants not to reject God's order as did the gentiles, the Watchers, and Sodom but to remain in this "order unto good." In both testaments the patriarch warns his descendants to love and obey God, knowing all the while that they will not heed his warning and will eventually go into exile (Heb. T. Naph. 1:8–10; T. Naph. 4:1–5).

The haggadah of the seventy nations in Heb. T. Naph. (8:4–10:2) stems from a conflation of the Table of Nations in Gen 10 and Deut 32:8, which speaks of the Most High dividing humankind according to the "children of Israel" (cf. Gen 46:7). That each nation has a heavenly patron seems to stem from the reading in the LXX of Deut 32:8 as "the sons of God" (i.e., the angels) in connection with Gen 46:27, which is quite prevalent in Jewish tradition.[31] While the normal rabbinic count of nations is seventy with the number of languages correlating to the number of nations, there are variances. For example, Midrash Hagadol to Gen 10:1 mentions sixty nations and to 10:32 mentions seventy-two languages.[32] The seventy divine patrons may stem back to 1 En. 89:59, which mentions seventy shepherds (angelic princes

---

Source and Composition (Lewiston, NY: Mellen, 2013), 134–38 and notes there. On their meaning and function in T. 12 Patr., see Hillel, "Proto-Joseph," 190–96 and notes there.

30. For more information on lists of body parts in Hebrew, Greek, and Latin sources, see Hollander and de Jonge, *Commentary*, 304–5; and de Jonge, *The Testaments of the Twelve Patriarchs: A Study of Their Text, Composition and Origin* (Assen: Van Gorcum, 1953), 57–58.

31. See, e.g., Tg. Ps.-J Gen 11:7; Exod. Rab. 21:5; Lev. Rab. 29:2; Deut. Rab. 1:22; Song Rab. 8:14; and Mek. R. Ishmael, Shirah 2.

32. B. Sukkah 55b; Num. Rab. 14:12; Midrash Tehillim 68:6 [to Ps 68:12]; cf., m. Soṭah 7:5; b. Šabb. 88b. Another variation is found in, e.g., 3 Enoch, which refers to seventy-two princes of the kingdoms corresponding to the seventy-two nations of the world.

The Hebrew Testament of Naphtali

of the gentile nations) who ruled over Israel. Moreover, the haggadah of the Holy One descending with seventy angels to confound the languages of the seventy nations, leaving only the descendants of Shem through Abraham continuing to speak Hebrew (Heb. T. Naph. 8:4–6) is also found in Pirqei R. El. 24:10. This work dates to the first to third centuries CE according to the attributions to tannaitic rabbis, but the current scholarly consensus is that it was written in the early Islamic period.[33]

Genealogy of Bilhah

The Genealogy of Bilhah (4Q215, BR, and T. Naph.) only indirectly connects to Heb. T. Naph. through its shared material with T. Naph.[34] All three texts tell the same story and have a similar structure. Unfortunately, 4Q215 is very fragmented—it starts in the middle of a sentence and the ends of the lines are missing—limiting comparison with the analogous texts of T. Naph. and BR. Nevertheless, 4Q215 is important because it transmits a version of the genealogy that is older than the other two witnesses, making it possible to show that R. Moses must have had a Hebrew or Aramaic source document that, at a number of points, was closer to 4Q215 than to T. Naph. The most telling point is that 4Q215 and BR contain parallel material that is missing from T. Naph. Both Midrash Bereshit Rabbati and 4Q215 contain two narrative events: the first recounts the genealogy, birth, and naming of Bilhah (BR 74:12–16; 4Q215 1–5) and the second tells the story of how Laban gave Zilpah to Leah and Bilhah to Jacob (BR 74:17–18; 4Q215 7–11; cf. Gen 29:24, 29). The Testament of Naphtali recalls the first event (1:9–12) but not the second.

All three documents state that Bilhah and Zilpah are sisters and that their father is the brother of Deborah, Rebecca's nurse. He was taken captive and ransomed by Laban, who gave him his servant as a wife. She birthed two daughters, the first was named Zilpah after the city related to his captivity and the second was Bilhah according to her eagerness to suckle when she was born. The Testament of Naphtali drops out at this point in the story and BR and 4Q215 continue with a narrative about Laban giving Zilpah to Leah and Bilhah to Rachel (Gen 29:24, 29).

Midrash Bereshit Rabbati, 4Q215, and Testament of Naphtali[35]

BERESHIT RABBATI	QUMRAN 4Q215	GREEK TESTAMENT OF NAPHTALI
[12]...There are those who say that		[1:6a] I was born from Bilhah

---

33. Rachel Adelman, *The Return of the Repressed: Pirqe de-Rabbi Eliezer and the Pseudepigrapha*, JSJSup 140 (Leiden: Brill, 2009), 35–42; Katharina E. Keim, *Pirqei deRabbi Eliezer: Structure, Coherence, Intertextuality*, Ancient Judaism and Early Christianity 96 (Leiden: Brill, 2017), 40–43.

34. Michael E. Stone, "4QTestament of Naphtali," in *Qumran Cave 4.XVII, Parabiblical Texts, Part 3*, ed. George Brooks, DJD XXII (Oxford: Clarendon, 1976), 73–82; Stone, "Qumran Corner: Testament of Naphtali," *JSJ* 47, no. 2 (1996): 311–21, doi:10.18647/1902/JJS-1996; Stone, *Genealogy*.

35. The translations of BR and T. Naph. are mine. The text of BR is from Ch. Albeck, ed., *Midrash Bereshit Rabbati* (Jerusalem: Mekixe Nirdamim, 1940), 119 [Heb.]; and T. Naph. is from Marinus de Jonge, *The Testaments of the Twelve Patriarchs: A Critical Edition of the Greek Text*, PVTG 1 (Leiden: Brill, 1978), 113–14. The translation of 4Q215 is from Stone, "4QTestament," 80.

The Hebrew Testament of Naphtali

the father [13]of Bilhah and Zilpah	line 1with 'Aḥiyot, Bilhah's father	1.9and my mother is Bilhah,
		the daughter of Rotheus,
was the brother of Deborah	[lacuna] Deborah	brother of Deborah,
the nurse of Rebecca	who nursed Reb[ecca.	the nurse of Rebecca
and 'Aḥotay was his name.		
		who was born on the very same day as was Rachel.
		10Rotheus was of the family of Abraham, a Chaldean, godfearing, freeborn, and noble.
Before he took [14]a wife, he was taken captive.	2And he went into captivity.	11And having been taken captive
Laban sent and redeemed him	And Laban sent and redeemed him,	he was bought by Laban
and gave him his maidservant to wife.	and he gave him Hannah, one of [his] maidservants [lacuna]	and he gave him Aina his maidservant to wife.
	3first Zilpah [lacuna]	
She bore him a daughter		12She bore him a daughter,
and he called her name [15]Zilpah	And he made her name Zilpah,	and he called her name Zilpah
after the name of the city	after the name of the city	after the name of the village
to which he was taken captive.	to which he was taken captive [lacuna]	where he was taken captive.
	4And she conceived,	
She bore another daughter.	and she bore Bilhah my mother.	Next, she bore Bilhah,
and he named her Bilhah,	And Hannah called her name Bilhah	
		saying,
		My daughter hastens after something new,
for when she was born,	for when she was born [lacuna]	for when she was born,
16she hastened to nurse.	5hastening to nurse,	she hastened to nurse.

289

The Hebrew Testament of Naphtali

He said	and she said,
"How my daughter hastens!"	"How my daughter hastens!"
	And she called (her) Bilhah again [lacuna]
	⁶vacat
And when Jacob went to Laban's, ¹⁷Aḥotay, their father was dead.	⁷And when my father Jacob came to Laban, fleeing from before Esau his brother and when [lacuna]
	⁸father of Bilhah, my mother.
And Laban took Ḥavah (Hannah) his maidservant and her two daughters	And Laban brought Hannah, my mother's mother and her two daughters, [lacuna]
and gave Zilpah, the older, to Leah ¹⁸his older daughter as a maidservant	
and Bilhah, the younger, to Rachel his younger daughter	⁹ [lacuna] and one to Rachel. And when Rachel was barren [lacuna]
	¹⁰ Jaco]b my father and gave him Bilhah my mother
	and she bore Dan [my] brother [lacuna]

There are a few points worth noting. The first are the variations of the names for Deborah's brother: 'Aḥotay in BR (13), 'Aḥiyot in 4Q215 (line 1), and Rotheus in T. Naph. (1:9); and for Zilpah's and Bilhah's mother: Ḥavah in BR (17), which can also be read as Hannah in the manuscript of BR, Hannah in 4Q215 (lines 2 and 4) and Aina in T. Naph. (1:11).[36] The Greek names are good equivalents of the Hebrew, though there are difficulties, especially with the "R" of Rotheus. The difficulties with the correspondence between the Hebrew and Greek variations of the names, caused Michael Stone to conclude that the names point to a shared tradition.[37]

---

36. On the names of Deborah's brother see Albeck, *Bereshit Rabbati*, 119; Martha Himmelfarb, "R. Moses the Preacher and the Testaments of the Twelve Patriarchs," *AJSR* 9, no. 1 (1984): 55–78, esp. 62 and n. 16, doi:10.1017/S0364009400000805; and Stone, "Genealogy," 26–27. On the reading in BR, see Albeck, *Bereshit Rabbati*, 119.

37. Stone, "Genealogy," 27 and nn. 18–19; 29–30 and n. 28.

The two Hebrew texts agree on the explanation of Zilpah's name but differ with the Greek. Testament of Naphtali states that Zilpah was named after the village in which (*en hē*) 'Aḥotay was located when he was taken captive. Whereas the Hebrew texts both indicate the village to which 'Aḥotay was taken captive. All three texts explain Bilhah's name by a play on words stemming from the Hebrew root *b-h-l*, meaning "to hasten," and give the etymology of her name in the description of the baby's behavior and the parent's subsequent exclamation, though the order in Heb. T. Naph. and BR differ from T. Naph. The Hebrew texts explain that Bilhah hastened (*mitbahelet*) to nurse and her parents (father in BR and mother in Heb. T. Naph.) exclaimed how she hastens; how eager she is (Heb. T. Naph. *mitbahelet*; BR *behulah*). The play on words is not immediately clear in the Greek, but as Hollander and de Jonge have pointed out, *balla* is Greek for *blhh* and *speudein* ("to hasten, be eager") is the usual translation of *bhl* in the LXX.[38]

Original Naphtali

The brief comparison of the four works (Heb. T. Naph., T. Naph., 4Q215, and BR) that preserve traditions about Naphtali son of Jacob demonstrates their reliance on an earlier source, dubbed Original Naphtali, which may or may not have been a testament. De Jonge correctly points out that both Heb. T. Naph. and T. Naph. have been so thoroughly redacted that it is very difficult, if not almost impossible, to define the contents of Original Naphtali.[39] Nonetheless, based on subject matter and argumentation, it is possible to posit that the visions, the lists of body parts and their functions, and the exhortations to follow Levi and Judah were contained in Original Naphtali. The development of Abrahamic ancestry in Heb. T. Naph. (the haggadah of Abraham and the seventy nations) and in T. Naph. (the genealogy of Bilhah) also indicates that some type of reference to Abraham's lineage was part of Original Naphtali.[40]

Bibliography

Adelman, Rachel. *The Return of the Repressed: Pirqe de-Rabbi Eliezer and the Pseudepigrapha*. JSJSup 140. Leiden: Brill, 2009.

Albeck, Ch., ed. *Midrash Bereshit Rabbati*. Jerusalem: Mekixe Nirdamim, 1940. [Heb.]

Charles, R. H. *The Greek Version of the Testaments of the Twelve Patriarchs: Edited from Nine MSS Together with the Variants of the Armenian and Slavonic Versions and Some Hebrew Fragments*. Oxford: Clarendon, 1908.

―――. *The Testaments of the Twelve Patriarchs: Translated from the Editor's Greek Text and Edited, with Introduction, Notes and Indices*. London: Black, 1908.

Gaster, Moses. *The Chronicles of Jerahmeel or The Hebrew Bible Historiale*. London: Oriental Translation Fund, 1899. Repr., with prolegomenon by Haim Schwarzbaum. New York: Ktav, 1971.

―――. "The Hebrew Text of One of the Testaments of the XII Patriarchs." *Proceedings of the Society of Biblical Archaeology* 16 (1893–1894): trans. (1893): 33–49; text (1894): 109–17.

Hillel, Vered. "Naphtali: A 'Proto-Joseph' in the Greek Testament of Naphtali." *JSP* 16, no. 3 (2007): 171–201.

---

38. Hollander and de Jonge, *Commentary*, 300 nn. 1, 12. On Bilhah's name in midrash, Stone points out a similar etymology in midrash haggadah to Gen 33 ("Genealogy," 31–32 and n. 32).

39. De Jonge, *Text*, 53–60; Korteweg, "Meaning," 281–82.

40. See Hillel, "Proto-Joseph," 197–98.

———. *The Testaments of the Twelve Patriarchs: Structure, Source and Composition.* Lewiston, NY: Mellen, 2013.

———. "Why Not Naphtali?" Pages 279–88 in *Things Revealed: Studies in Early Jewish and Christian Literature in Honor of Michael E. Stone.* Edited by Esther G. Chazon, David Satran, and Ruth A. Clements. JSJSup 89. Leiden: Brill, 2004. doi:10.1163/9789047405467_024.

Himmelfarb, Martha. "R. Moses the Preacher and the Testaments of the Twelve Patriarchs." *AJSR* 9, no. 1 (1984): 55–78. doi:10.1017/S0364009400000805.

Hollander, Harm W., and Marinus de Jonge. *The Testaments of the Twelve Patriarchs: A Commentary.* SVTP 8. Leiden: Brill, 1985.

Jonge, Marinus de. *The Testaments of the Twelve Patriarchs: A Critical Edition of the Greek Text.* PVTG 1. Leiden: Brill, 1978.

———. *The Testaments of the Twelve Patriarchs: A Study of Their Text, Composition and Origin.* Assen: Van Gorcum, 1953.

Keim, Katharina E. *Pirqei deRabbi Eliezer: Structure, Coherence, Intertextuality.* Ancient Judaism and Early Christianity 96. Leiden: Brill, 2017.

Korteweg, Th. "The Meaning of Naphtali's Visions." Pages 261–90 in *Studies on the Testaments of the Twelve Patriarchs.* Edited by Marinus de Jonge. SVTP 3. Leiden: Brill, 1975.

Stone, Michael E. "The Genealogy of Bilhah." *DSD* 3 (1996): 20–36. doi:10.1163/156851796X00309.

———. "Qumran Corner: Testament of Naphtali." *JJS* 47, no. 2 (1996): 311–21. doi:10.18647/1902/JJS-1996.

Wertheimer, Abraham J. *Batei Midrashot.* 2 vols. Jerusalem: Harav Kook, 1953. [Heb.]

Yassif, Eli. *The Book of Memory That Is the Chronicles of Jerahme'el.* Tel Aviv: Tel Aviv University, 2001. [Heb.]

The Hebrew Testament of Naphtali

Naphtali the son of Jacob, the wrestlings of God. Gen 30:8

1 ¹When Naphtali grew old (sixty) and came to a ripe old age (seventy) and completed his (years of) strength (eighty), and accomplished the (years of) customary[a] feebleness[b] (ninety), he began to charge his children, saying to them, "My children, come and draw near and receive the commands of your father." ²And his sons answered and said to him, "Behold, we are listening in order to fulfill everything that you command us." ³And he said to them, "I do not command you about money or about gold or even about all the provisions that I leave to you (here) under the sun. Nor do I command you something difficult that you may not be able to accomplish, but I speak to you about an easy matter that you can achieve." ⁴And his sons answered and replied a second time, saying, "Speak, our father, because we are listening." Cf. Ps 90:10

⁵He said to them, "I give you no command except concerning the fear of Adonai; him you must serve and to him you must cling." ⁶They said to him, "And what does he need with our service?" He said to them, "He does not need any creature, but creatures of his world need him. Indeed, he did not create his world for naught, but so that they will fear him and that no one will do to his neighbor what he does not want for himself." ⁷They said to him, "Our father, have you seen us departing in any respect from your ways or from the ways of our fathers, to the right or to the left?" ⁸He said to them, "Adonai and I are witnesses for you that it is just as you say. But I fear the future to come lest you stray after the gods of strange nations or walk in the practices of the peoples of the lands, and lest you join the children of Joseph, (instead of) only the children of Levi and the children of Judah." ⁹They said to him, "Why do you command us this way?"[c] ¹⁰He said to them, "Because I know that in your future the sons of Joseph will turn away from following Adonai, the God of your fathers, and will cause the children of Israel to sin and to be exiled from the good land into another land, just as we have been exiled through him to enslavement in Egypt. Deut 13:5; 10:20
Qoh 3:14
Cf. Lev 19:18
Cf. T. Levi. 19:3

2 ¹"Moreover, I will explain to you the vision that I saw while grazing the flock. ²I looked and saw my twelve brothers shepherding with me in the field; T. Naph. 5:1–7

---

a. Lit., *mšpṭ*, "judgment, sentence."
b. Lit., *šwh*, "bent back."
c. Lit., "What do you have in mind to command?"

and behold, our father came and said to us, 'My children, run and grab hold, each one before me, of whatever comes up as his portion.' ³And we answered and said to him, 'And what should we grab? Look, we don't see anything except the sun and the moon and the stars.' ⁴And he said to them, 'Take hold of whatever you can.'ᵃ When Levi heard this, he took a staff in his hand and leapt upon the sun, sat upon it and rode it. ⁵When Judah saw this, he did also; he grabbed a staff and jumped on the moon and rode upon it. ⁶Likewise the nine tribes, each one of them rode on his star and his planet in the heavens. Only Joseph remained alone on the earth. ⁷Jacob, our father, said to him, 'My son, why have you not done as your brothers?' He said, 'My father, what do they who are born of woman (have to do with) the heavens, since in the end they will have to stand on the earth?'"

3 ¹"While Joseph was saying this, behold, a giant bull stood near him, and the bullᵇ had large wings like the wings of a stork and his huge horns like the horns of the *re'em*.ᶜ ²And Jacob said to him, 'Get up Joseph, my son, and ride on him.' ³And Joseph got up and rode on the bull. And Jacob our father departed from us. ⁴For about four hoursᵈ Joseph was boasting on the bull, sometimes walking and running, and sometimes flying up with him until he came near Judah. And Joseph extended the rod that was in his hand and began to hit Judah his brother. ⁵And Judah asked him, 'My brother, why do you hit me?' ⁶He said to him, 'Because in your hand are twelve staffs and I only have one. Now give themᵉ to me and there will be peace.' ⁷But Judah refused to give them to him. So Joseph beat him until he had taken from him the ten that did not belong to him, and there remained in Judah's hand only two of them. ⁸Then Joseph said to them, to his ten brothers, 'Why do you run to Judah and Levi? Depart from following them and follow me.' ⁹And when his brothers heard Joseph's words, they departed from Levi and Judah as one man to follow Joseph. And no one remained with Judah except for Benjamin and Levi only. ¹⁰When Levi saw this, he dejectedly went down from the sun. ¹¹Joseph said to Benjamin his brother, 'Aren't you my brother? Come with me too!' But Benjamin refused to go with Joseph his brother. ¹²And it happened toward the end of the day that a mighty wind separated Joseph and his brothers, so that no two were left together. ¹³And after I saw this vision, I told it to Jacob my father, and he said to me, 'My son, this dream is insignificant,ᶠ because it has not been repeated.'"

4 ¹"However, not much time passed before I saw another vision. ²All of us were standing with our father Jacob on the shore of the Great Sea,ᵍ when, behold,

---

a. This sentence is inserted from MS Parma for clarity.
b. Lit., "he."
c. The *re'em* is known for its enormous size and horns, and great strength (e.g., Num 23:22; 24:8; Job 39:9–12; b. B. Bat. 73b).
d. MSS P J "two hours," Parma "one hour."
e. MSS P J "ten of them."
f. Lit., "will not ascend or descend." See introduction.
g. Mediterranean. T. 12 Patr. 6:1 refers to the Sea of Jamnia.

a ship[a] sailed in the middle of the sea without a sailor or pilot[b]. ³Our father said to us, 'Do you see what I see?' We answered, 'Yes, we see it.' ⁴He said to us, 'Do whatever you see me do!' Jacob our father, took off his clothes and threw himself in the sea. And we all (jumped in) after him. ⁵And Levi and Judah went first and jumped into it and Jacob with them. ⁶And behold, in the boat were all the good things that are in the world. ⁷Then Jacob our father said to them, 'Look at what is written on the mast; for there is no boat that the name of the owner is not written on the mast.' ⁸Then Levi and Judah looked and saw and behold, written on the mast was 'this ship belongs to the son of Berachel[c] and all the good that is in it.' ⁹When Jacob our father heard this, he rejoiced, bowed and lifted up thanks to the Holy One blessed be he, saying 'It is not enough that he blessed me on the earth, but he has also blessed me on the sea.' ¹⁰Immediately he said to us, 'My sons, steel yourselves,[d] and whatever each of you takes, that will be his part (i.e., job).' ¹¹Instantly, Levi leapt onto the great mast that was in the ship[e] and sat on it. ¹²Following him, Judah jumped onto the second mast that was near Levi, and he also sat on it. ¹³My remaining brothers each took hold of his oar, and Jacob our father seized the two steering-oars[f] by which to straighten (the course of) the boat, but Joseph remained alone. ¹⁴Our father said to him, 'Joseph my son, take hold of your oar, even you!' But Joseph was not willing. ¹⁵When our father saw that Joseph was not willing to take hold of his oar, he said to him, 'My son, come here and take one of the steering-oars that is in my hand and steer the boat, and your brothers will row with the oars until you reach land.' ¹⁶And he taught us, each one of us, saying, 'In this way you should guide the boat, and you will not be afraid of any waves of the sea or wind or storm that may rise against you.'"

T. Naph. 6:2

Cf. Gen 26:29

5 ¹"When he had finished giving us instructions, he disappeared from before us. ²Joseph seized hold of both steering-oars, one on his right and one on his left, and the rest of my brothers were rowing, and the boat sailed, floating over the surface of the water. ³Levi and Judah were sitting on the two masts to see which way the ship was to go. ⁴As long as Joseph and Judah were of one mind, so that Judah pointed out to Joseph which way was good and Joseph steered the boat in that direction, the boat continued peacefully without hindrance. ⁵In the meantime, a quarrel occurred between Joseph and Judah, and Joseph did not direct the boat according to his father's words or according to Judah's

---

a. The text uses the words *spina* ("ship/boat") and *onîa* ("ship") interchangeably referring to the same vessel.

b. Lit., "any person."

c. Meaning: "he whom God has blessed." In T. Naph. 6:2 the inscription reads "the ship of Jacob."

d. The word comes from the same root (*g-b-r*) as "man" giving a hermeneutical reading of the antiquated phrase "be a man!"

e. Lit., "it."

f. For more information on boats with double-side oars and the term *kabarnitin*, see Daniel Sperber, *Nautica Talmudica* (Ramat-Gan: Bar-Ilan Press; Leiden: Brill, 1986), Merchant Ships, 5.1 Merchant Oared-Galley, 86–91, esp. 88 n. e and 90 and n. 8.

directions, and the boat went in a roundabout way, and the waves of the sea smashed it onto the rock, until it was broken up."

6 ¹"Then Levi and Judah came down from the masts to flee, each for his own life, and also the rest of my brothers, every one of us, fled for our own lives toward the land. And then Jacob my father came and found us strewn about, one here and one there. ³He said to us, 'What is with you my sons? Perhaps you did not guide the ship correctly, as I ordered you?' ⁴And we said to him, '(By) the life of your servants, we did not stray from anything that you commanded us, but Joseph transgressed in this matter that he did not straighten out the (course of) the boat as you ordered or as Judah and Levi instructed him in jealousy of them.' ⁵And he said to us, 'Show me where it is.' And he saw and behold the tops of the masts were visible and she (the ship) was floating on the surface of the water. ⁶And my father whistled, and we all gathered around him. ⁷And first he threw himself into the sea and restored the boat, and ⁸then he admonished Joseph and said to him, 'Do not further, my son, the deceptive jealousy of your brothers, because through you, they almost, all of them, lost their lives.'"

7 ¹"When I explained this dream to my father, my father clapped his hands and groaned, and his eyes trickled tears. ²And I waited[a] till I was ashamed, but he did not say a word to me. ³So I took the hand of my father to embrace and kiss it, and I said to him, 'Oh servant of ADONAI, why do your eyes weep?' ⁴He said to me, 'My son, because of the repetition of your vision my heart has sunk, and my body is shocked due to my son Joseph, whom I loved more than all of you. As a result of the wickedness of my son Joseph, you will be sent into exile and scattered among the nations. ⁵Because both your first and second visions are the same, they are one vision. ⁶Therefore, I command you not to unite with the sons of Joseph but only with Levi and Judah.'"

> T. Naph. 7; T. Levi 8:18–19; Aramaic Levi 7b (4:13)

8 ¹"'Moreover, I tell you that my lot will fall in the finest of the middle of the land, and you will eat and be satisfied from its choice delights. ²I warn you that you should not despise your abundance[b] and you should not rebel and not disobey the commands of ADONAI who satisfies you with the best things of his earth. ³And do not forsake ADONAI your God, the God of your fathers, whom my father Abraham chose when the people[c] were scattered in the days of Peleg. ⁴For at that time the Holy One came down from his highest heaven and brought seventy ministering angels, Michael in the lead. ⁵He spoke and commanded every one of them to teach the seventy families, the offspring of Noah, seventy languages. ⁶Immediately the angels descended and carried out the command of their creator. And the holy language, the Hebrew language, only remained with the house of Shem and the house of Eber and the house of Abraham my father who is one of their descendants.'"[d]

> Tg. Ps-J. Gen 11:7; Deut 32:8 LXX
>
> Tg. Ps-J. Gen 11:8; Pirqe R. El. 24.10
>
> b. 'Abod. Zar. 2b; Jub. 12:25–26

a. The word is difficult to read in A, but is supplied from P and J.
b. Lit., "you should not kick your fatness."
c. Lit., "generations."
d. Lit., "children's children."

9 ¹"And on that day Michael brought forth a message from the Holy One, blessed be he, and said to the seventy nations, to each one individually, ²'You know the rebellion that is with you and the sedition that you have conspired against the God of heaven and earth. And now choose you today whom you will serve and who will be your advocate in heaven.' ³Nimrod the wicked answered and said, 'For me there is none greater than he who in an hour taught me and my nation the language of Cush.' ⁴Put and Egypt and Tubal and Yevan and Meshech and Tiras answered similarly and thus all the nations chose its own angel and not one of them mentioned the name of the Holy One, blessed be he. ⁵But when Michael said to Abraham our father, 'Abram, whom do you choose and whom will you worship?' Abram[a] answered, 'I choose and select only him who spoke, and the world came into being, who created me in my mother's womb, body inside of body, and placed in it spirit and soul. Him I choose and to him I will cling, me and my seed all the days of the world.'"

Gen 10; Deut 32:8; cf. Gen 46:27

Gen 10:8
Gen 10:6
Gen 10:2

Josephus, A. J. 1.155

10 ¹"Then the Most High separated the nations and apportioned and allocated to every nation their portion and lot. ²And from that time, every nation on earth separated from the Holy One, except for the house of Abraham alone that remained with the creator of the world to worship him, and after him Isaac and Jacob. ³Therefore my sons, I implore you not to stray or worship another god, but only (worship) him whom your fathers have chosen. ⁴For you should surely know that there is no one like him and there is no one who can do (anything) like him or like his works, in heaven or on earth, and there is no one who can work wonders like his mighty deeds. ⁵You can comprehend part of his power[b] in the creation of mankind—how many amazing wonders there are in each person. ⁶He created each person from his head to his foot.[c] With his ears he hears, and with his eyes he sees, and with his brain he understands and with his nose he smells and with his trachea he produces his voice, and with his esophagus he takes in food and water, and with his tongue he speaks and with his mouth he completes (the formation of his voice).[d] With his hands he does his work, and with his heart he understands, and with his spleen he laughs, and with his liver he becomes angry. His stomach grinds, and with his feet he walks, and (his) lungs for breathing,[e] and with his kidneys he is counseled. ⁷And not one of his organs will exchange its purpose, but each (remains) in its own (function). ⁸For this reason, it is fitting for a person to direct his heart to all of these: who it is that has created him and who it is that formed him from a putrid drop[f] in the womb of a woman, and who it is that has delivered him out into the atmosphere of the world and given him eyesight for seeing

T. Naph. 2:8

m. 'Abot 3.1

---

a. J adds "our father."
b. The reading is from MS P. MS A has *rwḥw*, "his spirit."
c. "To his foot" is implied in MS A and written in MS P.
d. The mouth completes the process of speaking by pronouncing the words; see b. Šabb. 33b.2; b. Ber. 61a–b; Qoh. Rab. 7.19. Alternatively, an Aramaic reading of *gamor* renders the translation "the mouth learns or teaches by verbal expression."
e. The Hebrew here is obscure and has been translated in a manner that reflects the surrounding context.
f. See explanation in introduction.

The Hebrew Testament of Naphtali

and feet for walking, and who causes him to stand upright and brings him to his full strength[a] and (who) has prepared for him good deeds in the place of understanding[b] and placed[c] in him a living soul and a pure spirit from himself. [9]Blessed is the person who does not defile the holy spirit of God that has been placed and breathed inside of him. And blessed is the one who returns it to the creator as pure as the day it was entrusted to him."

[10]Up to here are the words of Naphtali the son of Israel with which he admonished his sons, words as sweet as honey.[d]

---

a. Lit., "to normal health (possibly "to his creator") and to his defined place." Charles translates the phrase "brings him nigh to his Creator and to his place" (*Translated*, 227).

b. For clarification, see b. Ber. 10a "What is meant by all his benefits (Ps 103:2)? Rabbi Abbahu said: God placed her breasts (near her heart), the place (that is the source) of understanding."

c. Lit., "threw."

d. Lit., "with honey, as sweet as his palate."

Fragments of the Assumption of Moses and the Testament of Moses
A new translation and introduction

By Richard Bauckham

Sources and Questions

In two of the ancient lists of apocryphal works ascribed to Old Testament persons two Moses apocrypha are listed: the Testament of Moses and the Assumption of Moses (see texts A6 and A7). These are the only explicit references to a work called the Testament of Moses in ancient literature, but there are a handful of other explicit references to the Assumption of Moses (texts A1–A5). The lists are generally reliable, and there is no reason to doubt that there were two distinct works with these titles. The list attributed to Nicephorus (A6) assigns different lengths to them. The explicit allusions to the Assumption of Moses in patristic texts provide a little information about its contents, which included a dispute between the archangel Michael and the devil over the body of Moses (texts A1, A2, A3). This was of particular interest to patristic writers because the New Testament letter of Jude alludes rather enigmatically to such a dispute, evidently expecting its readers to know the story (v. 9). Many modern scholars have inferred that the Assumption of Moses was Jude's source. But there are also many other ancient sources, mostly extracts from exegetical works that have not as such survived, that claim to report the story to which Jude 9 alludes. There was evidently more than one story about the contest between Michael and the devil, and some scholars have argued that Jude's source was not the Assumption of Moses, but the Testament of Moses.

The matter is complicated by the existence of a fragmentary but substantial Latin text of a Moses apocryphon in a sixth-century manuscript in the Biblioteca Ambrosiana in Milan, published by Antonio Ceriani in 1861.[1] (For the sake of clarity I shall refer to this as the Milan Fragment, but use the now common abbreviation T. Mos. for references to chapter and verse.) Ceriani identified the text as the Assumption of Moses, on the apparently strong basis that Pseudo-Gelasius quotes in Greek from the Assumption of Moses words that occur in Latin translation in the Milan Fragment (1:14; see text A4). Some scholars still maintain this identification, notably Johannes Tromp in his edition of and commentary on the Milan Fragment.[2] But beginning with R. H. Charles (who nevertheless still called his translation of and commentary on the fragment The Assumption of Moses), many scholars hold that the work of which the Milan Fragment is a large part is actually the Testament of Moses.[3] (Reasons include the fact that it fits

---

1. On this *editio princeps* of the Milan Fragment see Johannes Tromp, *The Assumption of Moses: A Critical Edition with Commentary*, SVTP 10 (Leiden: Brill, 1993), 90–92.
2. Tromp, *Assumption*.
3. The fullest argument to this effect is probably that of Ernest-Marie Laperrousaz, "Le Testament de Moïse (généralement appellé "Assomption de Moïse"): Traduction avec introduction et notes," *Sem 17*

well into the genre of testament in ancient Jewish literature.)[4] Those who argue that the Testament of Moses was the source of Jude 9 suppose that the lost ending of this work, not preserved in the Milan Fragment, which breaks off before the end, contained a story of the dispute between Michael and the devil different from the one in the Assumption of Moses, but preserved in some of the other sources that claim to tell the story that Jude knew.[5] Clearly the issues are complex. They include the date and provenance of the two works as well as their relationship to Jude 9 and to the Milan Fragment.

The collection of translated texts provided below is the largest such collection to have been assembled. It includes all the texts from antiquity that might be evidence of the contents of either the Assumption or the Testament of Moses. (For the sake of completeness I have also included a few that refer or allude to other, otherwise unknown Moses apocrypha.) The discussions in the rest of this introduction will focus on attempting to identify which texts provide the most reliable evidence of the content and character of the Assumption and the Testament respectively. I shall also offer a new hypothesis about the relationship between the two works.

The Assumption of Moses

The Alexandrian theologians of the third and fourth centuries—Clement, Origen, and Didymus (if text A3 is correctly ascribed to him)[6]—knew a work called the Assumption of Moses (*Analēpsis Mōseōs*). It included a story of a contest between Michael and the devil that all three of these writers identified with the story to which verse 9 of the New Testament Epistle of Jude alludes.[7] Their allusions to the work by name tell us nothing else about it, but in view of its title we can be virtually certain that it was the source of the story both Clement and Origen tell of how, at the time of his death, Moses was seen in two forms, one (the body) buried and the other (the spirit) taken up to heaven (texts B1, B2). Two other short passages about Moses, ascribed by Clement of Alexandria to "the initiates" (texts C1, C2), may plausibly be derived

---

(1970): i–xi, 1–140. See also Samuel E. Loewenstamm, "The Death of Moses," in *Studies on the Testament of Moses*, ed. George W. E. Nickelsburg, SCS 4 (Missoula, MT: Scholars Press, 1976), 185–217.

4. Another fragmentary text that appears to have taken the form of a testament of Moses is 1Q22. Its possible relationship to the Assumption of Moses and the Testament of Moses discussed in this chapter has not been investigated.

5. I argued this view in Richard Bauckham, *Jude, 2 Peter*, WBC 50 (Waco, TX: Word, 1983); and in Bauckham, *Jude and the Relatives of Jesus in the Early Church* (Edinburgh: T&T Clark, 1990). There are assessments of my arguments in James R. Davila, *The Provenance of the Pseudepigrapha: Jewish, Christian, or Other?*, JSJSup 105 (Leiden: Brill, 2005), 150–51; Fiona Grierson, "The Testament of Moses," *JSP* 17 (2008): 265–80, doi:10.1177/0951820708091897; and John Muddiman, "The Assumption of Moses and the Epistle of Jude," in *Moses in Biblical and Extra-Biblical Tradition*, ed. Axel Graupner and Michael Wolter, BZAW 372 (Berlin: de Gruyter, 2007), 169–80, doi:10.1515/9783110901368.169. In the present chapter I have modified my position in some ways, as a result of a fresh examination of the evidence, while still holding that the source of Jude 9 was the lost ending of the work preserved in the Milan Fragment, which I identify as the Testament of Moses.

6. On the question of authenticity, see Peter Russell Jones, *The Epistle of Jude as Expounded by the Fathers—Clement of Alexandria, Didymus of Alexandria, the Scholia of Cramer's Catena, Pseudo-Oecumenius, and Bede*, Texts and Studies in Religion 89 (Lewiston, NY: Mellen, 2001), 4–5.

7. It is unfortunate that Clement's commentary on Jude is extant only in the sixth-century Latin translation by Cassiodorus. It consisted of "outlines" rather than a full commentary, but it is possible that Clement said more about the Assumption of Moses than Cassiodorus thought appropriate to retain. On this issue see Jones, *Epistle of Jude*, 2–3.

from the Assumption of Moses, since Clement does not refer to any other apocryphal work about Moses.

It is important to note that the word "assumption" (*analēpsis*) need not imply either that Moses escaped death and was taken up bodily into heaven (like Enoch and Elijah) or even that his body was taken up to heaven after his death (as in later traditions about the Virgin Mary). Philo speaks of the death and burial of Moses while also claiming that his spirit was taken up to heaven (*Mos.* 2.288–291), apparently using the very word "being taken up" (*analambanomenos*) in that sense. So the title Assumption of Moses is quite consistent with what is described in texts B1 and B2, where Moses's spirit is seen ascending to heaven while his body is buried.[8]

Bishop Evodius of Uzala (in Africa), writing in 414 CE (text B3), alludes to what is clearly the same story as Clement and Origen tell about the burial and assumption of Moses, but details in his version show that he has not derived it from those authors or at least not from their extant works. So it is of considerable interest that he gives what is evidently the title of his source (which he is careful to say is not authoritative): the Secrets of Moses or the Secret Words of Moses (the Latin *secretis* could mean "secret words"). The title could be an allusion to Deut 29:28 (Evv 29:29). The same title occurs in a reference by Pseudo-Gelasius (text C3), which will be discussed shortly. But it also connects with Clement's attribution of esoteric information about Moses to "the initiates" (*mustoi*; texts C1, C2). Clement is referring to those Christians he called "gnostics," who were able to receive and understand esoteric teaching, something not expected of ordinary Christians. In texts C1 and C2 he may be referring to them as readers or even as authors of esoteric knowledge about Moses. Very likely he refers to the same book that Evodius calls the Secret Words of Moses. It could be that this is an alternative title for the Assumption of Moses. After all, that work could hardly have treated only the death, burial, and assumption of Moses. Its length according to the Stichometry of Nicephorus (text A6) must imply a much broader content.

An illuminating parallel is the self-description of several of the Nag Hammadi Gospels as the "secret sayings" or "secret teaching" of Jesus (Gospel of Thomas, Book of Thomas, Apocryphon of James, Apocryphon of John, Gospel of Judas). The claim is that they contain the esoteric teaching of Jesus, given to and transmitted by favored disciples, distinguished from his public teaching recorded in the widely known Gospels. It is teaching for the select company of initiates who can appreciate it. Similarly, the Secret Words of Moses was plausibly a book containing the esoteric teaching of Moses, distinguished from his public teaching in the books of the Pentateuch.[9] Such a work would appropriately end, as Deuteronomy does, with an account of the end of Moses's life, but one that reveals much more about it than was generally known. (Compare the extended account of the ascension of Jesus at the end of the Apocryphon of James.)

Apart from the three Alexandrian theologians (A1–A3) and the two lists of Old Testament apocrypha (A6, A7), the only ancient writer to refer by name to a work called the Assumption of Moses is the author of an ecclesiastical history that used to be attributed to Gelasius of Cyzicus (A4, A5). It contains an account of the proceedings of the Council

---

8. Tromp, *Assumption*, 281–85.

9. See also 4 Ezra 14:26 (cf. 45–46), which distinguishes between the twenty-four books of the Hebrew Bible and the seventy other Scriptures that Ezra is to "deliver in secret to the wise."

of Nicaea (325 CE) that is generally considered to be historically worthless.[10] The quotations from the Assumption of Moses occur in a debate between the bishops at the council and an Arian philosopher. The debate is unlikely to be authentic but its source, if any, is unknown. It is noteworthy that these references to the Assumption of Moses and a contiguous one to the Secret Sayings of Moses (text C3) are the only references to apocryphal sources in the whole of this work. There is no reason to think that the author himself was familiar with them. He must have drawn them from sources in which they were used to counter Arian views. We cannot therefore depend on the accuracy of the attributions. The author could have confused different Moses apocrypha. It is usually argued that the Secret Sayings of Moses cannot be the same work as the Assumption of Moses because the reference to it follows immediately the first reference to the Assumption of Moses. The author cannot have thought they were the same work, but he could have drawn the two quotations from different sources without knowing that these were alternative titles for the same work.

The first of the two quotations attributed to the Assumption of Moses corresponds closely to a sentence near the beginning of the Milan Fragment (T. Mos 1:14). It demonstrates that the Milan Fragment was translated from Greek and it is the only clear allusion we have to anything in the Milan Fragment. Not surprisingly it has been taken as proof that the Milan Fragment is part, probably the major part, of the Assumption of Moses. Some who think that the Milan Fragment is the Testament of Moses propose that the Assumption of Moses was a revised version of the Testament of Moses, or that it was appended to the Testament of Moses and the two sometimes treated as one work.[11] It is also possible that the words of Moses quoted here in Pseudo-Gelasius were borrowed by the Assumption of Moses from the Testament of Moses. We have to admit that there are various possibilities and the evidence is elusive. But since this passage of Pseudo-Gelasius is the only evidence for identifying the Milan Fragment as the Assumption of Moses, we must be cautious about relying on a potentially unreliable witness.

In the case of the second quotation (or pair of quotations; text A5) there is no difficulty in attributing it to the same work that the Alexandrian theologians knew as the Assumption of Moses. We know that that work included a contest between Michael and the devil over the body of Moses. In the context, evidently about creation, in Pseudo-Gelasius, the two quotations from Michael make the point, against Phaedo the Arian, that the Holy Spirit, being equally divine, took part in the work of creation with the Father and the Word. They are not as such scriptural quotations, though they seem to be based on passages of the Psalms (Pss 103[104]:30; 32[33]:6; cf. also Jdt 16:14). It is odd that the bishops quote this obscure apocryphon, which turns out to be unknown to Phaedo, rather than the scriptural passages, but perhaps the point is to display their learning by contrast with Phaedo's ignorance. In any case, we should not suppose that in the Assumption of Moses Michael was quoting Scripture. (At the time of Moses's death the Psalms had not been written.) The quotations have been taken from a speech of Michael to the devil.

---

10. Colm Luibhéid, *The Council of Nicaea* (Galway: Galway University Press, 1982), 69 n. 2: "A virtually unanimous scholarly consensus has decreed that nothing in this work is to be accepted which cannot be corroborated elsewhere."

11. Robert H. Charles, *The Assumption of Moses* (London: Black, 1897), xiii; Emil Schürer, *The History of the Jewish People in the Age of Jesus Christ (175 B. C.–A. D. 135)*, ed. Geza Vermes, Fergus Millare, and Martin Goodman, rev. ed. (Edinburgh: T&T Clark, 1986), 286–87; Bauckham, *Jude and the Relatives*, 268–70.

It would make very good sense if Michael were responding to the claim made by the devil in texts D4, D5a, and D7a: "The body is mine, for I am the master of matter." Michael will have rejected this claim by asserting that God created everything and so is the master of everything. Moreover, the "spirit" who created the world was not the rebellious spirit, the devil, but the Spirit of God, the Holy Spirit. The devil has no right to possession of the material world that God made. So we can with reasonable assurance trace one of the traditions preserved in the scholia on Jude 9 (section D of the texts) back to the Assumption of Moses. As we shall see in the next section, it is unlikely that any other material in these scholia derives from the Assumption.

There is also a further link between this particular tradition in the scholia and Origen's comment on the Assumption (text A2). The scholia say that the devil made his claim "wishing to deceive." Origen says that, replying to the devil, Michael said that the serpent who deceived Eve was inspired by the devil. Presumably Michael was discounting the devil's deceptive claim by pointing out that the devil had been a deceiver from the beginning. So there is a good fit between these scholia (D4, D5a, D7a) and two of the very few texts that explicitly cite the Assumption of Moses and disclose something of its content (A2, A5).

The Assumption of Moses seems to have had a very distinctive version of the debate between Michael and the devil. The devil's claim to be "the one who rules over matter [$hul\bar{e}$]" strongly suggests that there is a polemic against dualism, probably of a broadly "gnostic" kind.[12] The use of the word "matter" is crucial for distinguishing this text from the claim made by the devil in Matt 4:9 and from the description of him as "the ruler of this world" in a number of early Christian works.[13] It belongs to a dualism of spirit and matter, such that the devil does not claim the spirit of Moses but only his body. The devil does not explicitly claim to be the demiurge, the creator of this world, but his claim closely parallels the description of Ialdabaoth as the ruler over the matter of Chaos and all that was subsequently made from it (Orig. World 100.4, 28).

This is very different from the contest described in Jude 9, with its background in Zech 3:1-2. There the devil (Satan) plays his traditional role of accuser in a judicial context, not a power who claims to rule the material world and thereby owns Moses's body. The Alexandrian theologians recognized the common theme of a debate between Michael and the devil over the body of Moses.[14] The comments of Clement (A1) and Didymus (A3) show that they recognized two accounts of the same event, not necessarily that they thought one writing the source of the other. But Origen (A2) thought that Jude knew the Assumption of Moses. Since he doubtless thought that the Assumption was written long before Jude, it was a not unnatural inference. But it is much more likely that, if there is a direct literary relationship, the Assumption of Moses was dependent on Jude. The author will have taken over the basic idea of the contest from Jude and filled

---

12. Loewenstamm speaks of "the author's struggle with the dualistic doctrines of a crystallizing Gnosticism" ("Death," 211).

13. See Alan F. Segal, "Ruler of This World: Attitudes about Mediator Figures and the Importance of Sociology for Self-Definition," in *Aspects of Judaism in the Graeco-Roman Period*, vol. 2 of *Jewish and Christian Self-Definition*, ed. E. P. Sanders (London: SCM, 1981), 245-68.

14. It is uncertain whether the Assumption of Moses contained Michael's words, "May the Lord rebuke you!" The authors of texts D4 and D7a are commenting on Jude 9 and may themselves have made a link between the devil's claim, derived from the Assumption of Moses, and Michael's words, derived from Jude 9.

it out with antignostic content. This would indicate that the Assumption is a Christian work dating from the second century CE.

Finally, it is possible that text G4 relates to the Assumption of Moses. It is not likely that Gal 6:15 is a quotation from a source, but it is quite possible that a Christian work attributed to Moses put these words on Moses's lips. They could be one of his "secret sayings."

The Dispute over the Body of Moses: Traces of the Testament of Moses?

For early Christian exegetes Jude 9 was an enigmatic text that cried out for explication. The exegetical works in which several of them attempted to explicate it have not survived, but we do have many scholia, collected in catenae ("chains"), that report what they said. A scholion is a short extract from a larger work, usually unattributed. From the sixth century onward scholia were collected in catenae to form continuous commentaries on biblical books, although the collected comments usually represent a variety of different interpretations of the biblical verse in question.[15] A scholion is sometimes itself a combination of more than one earlier scholia in abbreviated form (e.g., texts D5, D7). The commentaries on Jude by Pseudo-Oecumenius (D2) and Theophylact (D9) are similar to catenae, largely reproducing earlier exegetical comments.[16] The contents of the scholia on Jude 9 collected in section D are quite repetitive, but the variations in the reports of the same tradition can be significant.

It is very likely that one or more of the exegetes from whose works some of these scholia have been excerpted knew a story about the contest between Michael and the devil that was told in an apocryphal work that was also Jude's source. But we should not assume that all these exegetical comments have a source of that kind. It was common for Jewish and Christian exegetes in antiquity to use their ingenuity to produce a plausible story that could explain an obscure biblical text. A clear example of a comment that reflects nothing more than the exegete's ingenious guesswork is text D6, which imagines the contest took place in the context of the transfiguration of Jesus and, supposing the devil's "slander" to be blasphemy against God, attributes to the devil a totally implausible charge against God (see also D7d).

The tradition that recurs in many of these scholia and probably has the best claim to preserve the story that Jude knew is the one in which the devil charges Moses with murder. The version in Pseudo-Oecumenius reads:

> It is said that Michael the archangel took care of the burial of Moses. For the devil would not accept this, but brought an accusation because of the murder of the Egyptian, on the grounds that Moses was guilty of it, and because of this would not allow him to receive honorable burial (text D2; cf. D3, D5b, D7c, D8, E2).

This is the only scholion (apart from D9) in which the anonymous exegete indicates that he is quoting a source, probably a written one.[17] Theophylact, copying Pseudo-Oecumenius, expands his statement to read, "In apocryphal books it is said" (D9). He probably had no more information about the source, but his interpretation of Pseudo-

---

15. On Cramer's *Catenae*, see Jones, *Epistle of Jude*, 5–6.
16. On Pseudo-Oecumenius, see Jones, *Epistle of Jude*, 6.
17. *legetai* ("it is said") usually indicates a written source.

Oecumenius is probably right. In some other scholia that parallel this one in Pseudo-Oecumenius, the story is continued:

> The angel, not tolerating the slander against him (Moses), said to the devil, "May God rebuke you!" (D3; cf. D5b, D7c).

It is notable that Jude 9 does not have the phrase, "not tolerating the slander against him," but says rather that Michael "did not presume to condemn him for slander." This is the point that Jude wishes to make: that even the archangel Michael, contending with the devil himself, did not take on himself the divine prerogative of pronouncing judgment. This is an inference that Jude himself has drawn from the story reported in the scholia. That story is very plausibly his source.

This account of the devil accusing Moses of murder is never found combined with the attribution to the devil of the claim. "The body is mine, for I am the master of matter" (D4, D5a, D7a), which I have suggested plausibly comes from the Assumption of Moses known to the Alexandrians and Pseudo-Gelasius. Text D5, which reports both traditions, clearly understands them to be alternative explanations of the devil's "slander," found in different sources. The account of the devil's attempt to shame Moses as a murderer can therefore be attributed, not to the Assumption of Moses, but to the Testament of Moses, and the latter can be considered Jude's source.

It is unlikely that any of the other material in the scholia on Jude 9 can be attributed to either of these apocryphal works. Since the scholia limit themselves to explaining Jude, they do not describe the death or assumption of Moses, but the account I have assigned to the Testament of Moses implies that his body was buried by the archangel Michael. One version of this account says that Michael was sent "to remove the body" (D4, D5a), meaning that he was to transfer it to a grave that no one saw and that was to remain unknown (Deut 34:6).

There are two accounts of the contest (texts E1, E2) that do place it in a larger narrative context, including narrating the burial of the body by Michael.[18] Text E2 adds little to the accounts in the scholia, but E1 is considerably fuller. Here the legal dispute over the body of Moses has been replaced by physical combat. Michael appears in his traditional role as the "chief captain" of the heavenly armies (cf. Rev 12:7), while the devil has lost his traditional role as an accuser bringing charges in court. Instead he is called Samuel. The name is undoubtedly a corruption of Samma'el, a name by which the devil is known in the Ascension of Isaiah (1:8; 7:9; §11:41), where he is also called Malkira and Beliar. The name also appears in 3 Baruch (4:7; 9:7) in connection with the devil's role in the fall of Adam. Otherwise it seems to be unknown in Christian literature,[19] but significantly appears in rabbinic traditions about the death of Moses, where Samma'el is the evil angel of death who tries but fails to take Moses's soul (not body; Deut. R. 11:10; Midrash Petirat Moshe 11). Furthermore, the account seems to be quite independent of Jude 9. Whereas Jude understands Michael's words, "The Lord rebuke you!," to mean that he leaves it to God to "rebuke" the devil, this account specifically says that Michael does rebuke the

---

18. For a fuller discussion of these texts, see Bauckham, *Jude and the Relatives*, 245–54.
19. Samma'el appears, along with other names drawn from Jewish angelology, in four Nag Hammadi treatises: the Apocryphon of John, the Hypostasis of the Archons, On the Origin of the World and the Trimorphic Protennoia.

devil. That Michael defers to God's unique prerogative of judgment is probably an inference that Jude himself made, not explicit in his source, and so it is plausible that this chapter of the Palaea is dependent ultimately on the same Jewish source that Jude knew. At the same time, the fact that the contest is in this text alone a military rather than a verbal and legal conflict indicates that it has not preserved its ultimate source very faithfully. Not much weight can be given to it in attempting to reconstruct Jude's source.

Three scholia, not yet discussed, form a distinct category because their author is given, and they are longer than most scholia (F1, F2, F3). (F4 is merely an abbreviated version of F1; note also that D7b is also dependent on F1.) These comments of Severus of Antioch (d. 538) have almost nothing in common with the traditions so far discussed. There was a widespread idea that after death groups of good and bad angels contended for the soul,[20] but Severus's idea that the dispute over the body of Moses (not his soul) was intended by God to instruct the people about the dispute to which their souls will be subject after death (F1) is obviously no more than Severus's own homiletical use of the story in Jude 9, dependent on nothing more than Jude 9 itself. The allegorical interpretations of the "body" of Moses, which Severus reports in text F2, are similarly no more than ingenious attempts to interpret Jude 9 in the absence of any other information about the contest. Perhaps Severus deliberately eschewed apocryphal sources.

But in text F1 he (or perhaps the scribe who extracted this passage from its context in a work of Severus) explicitly cites "the apocryphal book that contains the more detailed account of the genesis or creation," undoubtedly a reference to Jubilees (characterized by its opening material, as Genesis itself is).[21] What is ascribed to this apocryphal work is the account of Moses's burial, given as an interpretation of Deut 34:5-6. A scribe who knew that Jubilees is a narrative that parallels that of the Pentateuch could have guessed it was likely to be the source of a more detailed account of Moses's death than Deuteronomy provides. This reference to Jubilees has been taken as evidence that the Assumption of Moses was copied together with Jubilees as a kind of sequel to it.[22] But in fact the account of Moses's burial here has nothing in common with those in texts B1–B3, which derive from the Assumption of Moses. Could it come from the Testament of Moses? The fact that Severus knows nothing about the dispute over Moses's body that does not come from Jude 9 makes it very unlikely that he knew the Testament himself. The idea that a luminous cloud hid Moses's death and/or burial from the bystanders is found in Josephus, *A. J.* 4.326, and in the Samaritan work Memar Marqah 5:3. It might have occurred in the Testament of Moses, but there is no good evidence for that.

In conclusion, the content of the source of Jude 9, plausibly the Testament of Moses, is probably preserved in texts D2, D3, D5b, D7c, D9, E2, and perhaps E1. Its accounts of the dispute over the body of Moses, in which the devil accused Moses of murdering the Egyptian, and of Michael's burial of the body tell a story that is different from and incompatible with the story told in texts that probably derive from the Assumption of Moses: A2, A5, B1, B2, B3, D4, D5a, D7a. Charles attempted to combine information from all these sources and more into a single, rather complicated narrative.[23] But the result is

---

20. Richard Bauckham, "The Dispute over Abraham," *MOTP* 1:53–58.

21. On the title "Leptogenesis" for the Book of Jubilees, see Robert H. Charles, *The Book of Jubilees or the Little Genesis* (London: Black, 1902), xv–xvi.

22. Montague Rhodes James, "Moses (Apocalypse, Testament, Assumption)," in *The Lost Apocrypha of the Old Testament: Their Titles and Fragments* (London: SPCK, 1920), 50.

23. Charles, *Assumption*, 105–10.

incoherent. We should recognize that there were two different stories of the dispute over Moses's body and his burial. One was undoubtedly in the Assumption of Moses. The other, which makes a fitting conclusion to a work in the testament genre, very probably was in the Testament of Moses and was the source on which the Letter of Jude draws.

The Relationship between the Testament of Moses and the Assumption of Moses: A New Hypothesis

It is generally agreed that the Milan Fragment must have ended with an account, however brief, of the death and burial of Moses. But which account? Is the Milan Fragment the Assumption of Moses or the Testament of Moses?

It has sometimes been argued that the references to the death of Moses in the Milan Fragment (T. Mos. 1:15; 3:13; 10:12, 14) imply a normal death, not an assumption.[24] But as I have already explained, the kind of "assumption" that is described in texts B1–B3 (very likely dependent on the Assumption of Moses) does not preclude death. According to those texts, Moses died, his body was buried, and his spirit was "assumed" into heaven. But one reference to Moses's death in the Milan Fragment is problematic. In 10:12, Moses speaks of the time that will elapse "from my death [and?] assumption until his (God's) coming." The Latin *morte receptione mea*[25] is translated by Tromp, who defends the reading as original and takes the two nouns to be in apposition, as "my death, my being taken away." In his view the Milan Fragment is from the Assumption of Moses and ended with a story of the death of Moses and the assumption of his spirit into heaven. Laperrousaz, who identifies the Milan Fragment as the Testament of Moses, also defends the originality of both nouns and argues that *receptio* refers to the reception of Moses by the earth at his burial, citing 11:5, where the verb *recipio* is used in that sense.[26] But according to neither proposal is the reception or assumption *identical* with Moses's death and so one would expect *morte et receptione mea*, "my death and reception/assumption." The most likely explanation is that the word *receptione* was originally a marginal note by a scribe or reader, later incorporated into the text. If the Milan Fragment is of the Testament of Moses, the scribe who added the word *receptione* need not have known the Assumption of Moses. He could have known the story of Moses's assumption and burial from Clement of Alexandria or Origen. He thought the word "death," while not incompatible with that story, deserved further explication. In that case, the text of 10:12 does not provide evidence either that the Milan Fragment is from the Assumption of Moses or that it represents a text of the Testament of Moses that has been revised to form part of the Assumption of Moses.[27]

So the references to the death of Moses in the Milan Fragment provide no clear indication whether it is from the Testament of Moses or the Assumption of Moses. Chronology is more helpful. Clement of Alexandria's references to the Assumption by name provide a *terminus ad quem* for the work at about 190 CE. Other considerations, already discussed, suggest that it is later than the first century CE: the antidualist polemic and, if the Secret Words of Moses is another title for the same work, the parallel with

---

24. E.g., Charles, *Assumption*, 7, 44.
25. This is a correction of the manuscript reading *morte receptionem*.
26. Laperrousaz, "Le Testament," 41–46.
27. I suggested this as a possibility but argued that it is unlikely in Bauckham, *Jude and the Relatives*, 269–70.

gospels from Nag Hammadi that purport to record the "secret sayings" of Jesus, which date from the second–third centuries. One other possible indication of date concerns the story of the double Moses, found in Clement, Origen, and Evodius, relating that Moses's body was buried in the earth but his spirit was escorted by angels up to heaven. This quite closely resembles the accounts of the death of Abraham, found in recension A of the Testament of Abraham (20:11–12),[28] and the death of Job, found in the Testament of Job (52:2–12). It is notable that in the latter case Job's three daughters are privileged to see Job's soul being taken up to heaven, just as Joshua sees Moses's ascent in the account that probably derives from the Assumption of Moses. Unfortunately, the provenance and date of these two works are debated. While it has been common to consider them originally Jewish works, it is also widely recognized that the versions we have contain Christian features.[29] The relationship between these three accounts of the assumption of an eminent figure from the biblical past may repay investigation and suggest a common milieu of origin.

So it is very likely that the Assumption of Moses was composed in the second century CE. In that case it cannot be the source of Jude 9 and it cannot be the work known to us in the Milan Fragment. Most scholars assign the latter to the early first century CE, at least in its final form.[30] William Loader has recently argued for a date not long after 63 BCE,[31] but the proposals of Solomon Zeitlin in 1947 and Klaus Haacker in 1969 for dating the work in the second century CE (the latter in connexion with a Samaritan provenance) have received no support.[32] It follows that the work attested by the Milan Fragment is very likely the Testament of Moses and was the source of Jude 9. In that case the Assumption of Moses could have been dependent on the Testament of Moses or it could have derived the notion of a contest between Michael and the devil from Jude 9 alone, as I suggested above.

However, it is possible that the Assumption was not only dependent on the Testament but was based on a specific passage in the Testament. Early in the work Moses addresses Joshua thus:

> You, however, receive this writing, which serves to acknowledge the trustworthiness of the books which I will hand to you, and you must order them, embalm them, and put them in earthenware jars in a place which he made from the beginning of the creation of the world, so that his name be invoked, until the day of repentance, in the visitation with which the Lord will visit them in the fulfilment of the end of days. (T. Mos. 1:16–18)[33]

The sentence is somewhat obscure. "This writing" is undoubtedly the Testament itself, or, more precisely, the prophecy that Moses addresses to Joshua in 2:3–10:10 (cf. 10:11; 12:1).

---

28. The account in recension B of T. Ab. (14:7–8) looks like an abbreviated version.

29. Davila, *Provenance*, 197–99, 201–7.

30. For various specific proposals, see Schürer, *History*, 281–82 n. 9. The argument of George W. Nickelsburg for an original dating in the Maccabean period and a later redaction in the early first century CE need not be discussed here. The case for a date in the early first century CE is presented by J. Priest, "Testament of Moses," *OTP* 1:920–21; Tromp, *Assumption*, 116–17.

31. William Loader, "Herod or Alexander Jannaeus? A New Approach to the *Testament of Moses*," *JSJ* 46 (2015): 28–43.

32. See Schürer, *History*, 281 and n. 8.

33. This translation is from Tromp, *Assumption*, 7, 9.

But what are the books (plural) that Joshua is to embalm and store in jars? They can hardly be the same as the "writing," though some have understood the passage in that sense.[34] Probably they are the books of the law (cf. Deut 31:24–26) and the place God made "from the beginning of the creation of the world" is Mount Zion, which later Jewish tradition regards as the first part of the world to be created (b. Yoma 54b).[35] It is there that God's name will be invoked until the eschatological visitation. But this meaning is far from clear. Joshua could have deposited the books of the Torah in the tabernacle, beside the ark of the covenant (as the Levites were to do, according to Deut 31:26) but he could not have placed them in the temple on Mount Zion. Moreover, as Tromp remarks, "It is not easy to understand why the books of the law should be embalmed and stored in jars, apparently without anyone being able to consult them."[36] The passage can easily be read as an example of the notion, common in apocalypses, that a book revealed to a seer long ago has been kept secret until revealed in the end times (e.g., Dan 8:26; 12:9; 1 En. 82:1–2). Both Tromp and Stone think that this is what is intended, and that it is Moses's prophecy, given in the Testament, that is to be preserved in secret.[37] But the passage, as it stands, clearly distinguishes "this writing" from the "books" that are to be preserved in a secret place. It was open to a reader in antiquity to suppose that the Testament here refers to secret teachings of Moses, not contained in the Testament itself, but written in books that Joshua is to seal up in jars and deposit in an unknown hiding place. I suggest that this is how the author of the Assumption of Moses, otherwise known as the Secret Words of Moses, understood the text. His own writing purported to be those secret books.

This hypothesis has the advantage of providing an explanation for Pseudo-Gelasius's attribution to the Assumption of Moses of words found in the Milan Fragment at 1:14, a little before the reference to the secret books in 1:16–18. We can suppose that the Assumption of Moses based its opening section on these verses of the Testament. In order to introduce its revelation of Moses's secret teaching it quoted his remarkable claim that God foresaw him "from the beginning of the world to be the mediator of his covenant." So these words appeared in both the Testament and the Assumption.

Bibliography

EDITIONS AND TRANSLATIONS

Adler, William. "*Palaea Historica* ('The Old Testament History')." *MOTP* 1:585–672.
Bonwetsch, G. Nathanael. "Die Mosessage in der slavischen kirchlichen Litteratur." *NAWG* (1908): 581–607.
Charles, Robert H. Pages 105–10 in *The Assumption of Moses*. London: Black, 1897.
Cramer, John A., ed. *Catenae Graecorum Patrum in Novum Testamentum*. Vol. 8: *In epistolas catholicas et apocalypsin*. Oxford: Oxford University Press, 1844.
Denis, Albert-Marie, ed. Pages 61–67 in *Fragmenta Pseudepigraphorum Graeca*. PVTG 3. Leiden: Brill, 1970.

---

34. Michael E. Stone, *Secret Groups in Ancient Judaism* (New York: Oxford University Press, 2018), 132.

35. Charles, *Assumption*, 7. Tromp seems to think that the books in 1:16 are the books of the law, but that the reference shifts in 1:17 to the "writing," the prophecy that Moses is about to give to Joshua (*Assumption*, 144–46).

36. Tromp, *Assumption*, 146.

37. Tromp, *Assumption*, 147–48; Stone, *Secret Groups*, 134.

[Gelasius of Cyzicus]. *Anonyme Kirchengeschichte (Gelasius Cyzicenus CPG 6043)*. Edited by Günther Christian Hansen. GCS 9. Berlin: de Gruyter, 2002.

James, Montague Rhodes. Pages 17–18 in *The Testament of Abraham: The Greek Text Now First Edited with an Introduction and Notes*. TS 2.2. Cambridge: Cambridge University Press, 1892.

Jones, Peter Russell. *The Epistle of Jude as Expounded by the Fathers—Clement of Alexandria, Didymus of Alexandria, the Scholia of Cramer's Catena, Pseudo-Oecumenius, and Bede*. Texts and Studies in Religion 89. Lewiston, NY: Mellen, 2001.

Laperrousaz, Ernest-Marie. "Le Testament de Moïse (généralement appellé "Assomption de Moïse"): Traduction avec introduction et notes." *Sem* 17 (1970): i–xi, 1–140. (Edition on pages 26–62.)

Renoux, Charles. PO 47, no. 210/2. In *La Chaîne Arménienne sur les Épîtres Catholiques. IV: Sur 2–3 Jean et Jude*. Turnhout: Brepols, 1996.

Vassiliev, Athanasius, ed. *Anecdota Graeco-Byzantina*. Moscow: Imperial University Press, 1893.

Zaccagni, Lorenzo Alessandro (Laurentius Alexander Zacagnius). Page 561 in *Collectanea Monumentorum Veterum Ecclesiae Graecae ac Latinae*. Vol. 1. Rome: Press of the Sacred Congregation for the Propagation of the Faith, 1698.

STUDIES

Bauckham, Richard. Pages 65–76 in *Jude, 2 Peter*. WBC 50. Waco, TX: Word, 1983.

———. Pages 235–80 in *Jude and the Relatives of Jesus in the Early Church*. Edinburgh: T&T Clark, 1990.

Davila, James R. Pages 149–54 in *The Provenance of the Pseudepigrapha: Jewish, Christian, or Other?* JSJSup 105. Leiden: Brill, 2005.

Denis, Albert-Marie. Pages 432–60 in vol. 1 of *Introduction à la littérature Religieuse Judéo-Hellénistique*. 2 vols. Brepols: Turnhout, 2000.

Dochhorn, Jan. "Der Tod des Mose in der Assumptio Moesis." Pages 167–85 in *Modebilder: Gedanken zur Rezeption einer literarischen Figur im Frühjudentum, frühen Christentum und der römisch-hellenistischen Literatur*. Edited by Michael Sommer, Erik Eynikel, Veronika Niederhofer, and Elisabeth Hernitschek. WUNT 390. Tübingen: Mohr Siebeck, 2017.

Grierson, Fiona. "The Testament of Moses." *JSP* 17 (2008): 265–80. doi:10.1177/09518207 08091897.

James, Montague Rhodes. "Moses (Apocalypse, Testament, Assumption)." Pages 42–51 in *The Lost Apocrypha of the Old Testament: Their Titles and Fragments*. London: SPCK, 1920.

Loewenstamm, Samuel E. "The Death of Moses." Pages 185–217 in *Studies on the Testament of Abraham*. Edited by George W. E. Nickelsburg. SCS 6. Missoula, MT: Scholars Press, 1976.

Muddiman, John. "The Assumption of Moses and the Epistle of Jude." Pages 169–80 in *Moses in Biblical and Extra-Biblical Tradition*. Edited by Axel Graupner and Michael Wolter. BZAW 372. Berlin: de Gruyter, 2007. doi:10.1515/9783110901368.169.

Renoux, Charles. "L' Assomption de Moïse: D'Origène à la chaîne Arménienne sur les Épîtres Catholiques." Pages 239–49 in *Recherches et Tradition: Mélanges Patristiques Offerts à Henri Crouzel, S. J.* Edited by André Dupleix. Théologie Historique 88. Paris: Beauchesne, 1992.

Ruwet, Jean. "Les 'Antilegomena' dans les Oeuvres d'Origène." *Bib* 24 (1943): 18–58, here 53–54.

Schürer, Emil. Pages 284–87 in vol. 3.1 of *The History of the Jewish People in the Age of Jesus Christ (175 B. C.–A. D. 135)*. Edited by Geza Vermes, Fergus Millare, and Martin Goodman. Rev. ed. Edinburgh: T&T Clark, 1986.

Stokes, Ryan E. "Not Over Moses' Dead Body: Jude 9, 22–24 and the *Assumption of Moses* in Their Early Jewish Context." *JSNT* 40 (2017): 192–213. doi:10.1177/0142064X177400.

Taube, Moshe. "The Slavic *Life of Moses* and Its Hebrew Sources." *Jews and Slavs* 1 (1993): 84–119.

Tromp, Johannes. Pages 270–85 in *The Assumption of Moses: A Critical Edition with Commentary*. SVTP 10. Leiden: Brill, 1993.

———. "Origen on the *Assumption of Moses*." Pages 323–40 in *Jerusalem, Alexandria, Rome: Studies in Ancient Cultural Interaction in Honour of A. Hilhorst*. Edited by Florentino García Martínez and Gerard P. Luttikhuizen. JSJSup 82. Leiden: Brill, 2003.

Turdeanu, Emil. "La *Chronique de Moïse* en russe." *Revue des études slaves* 46 (1967): 35–64. doi:10.3406/slave.1967.1933.

Fragments of the Assumption of Moses and the Testament of Moses

A. Texts That Refer Explicitly to a Work Entitled the Assumption of Moses

A1. Clement of Alexandria, Hypotyposes in Epistulam Judae[a]

When Michael the archangel, disputing with the devil, argued about the body of Moses.[b] This corroborates the Assumption of Moses.[c]

Jude 9

A2. Origen, De Principiis 3.2.1[d]

We must now see how, according to the Scriptures, the enemy powers, or the devil himself, contend with the human race, inciting and instigating to sin. In the first place in Genesis the serpent is reported as having deceived Eve, and with regard to this, in the Ascension[e] of Moses (a book to which the apostle Jude refers in his letter) *Michael the archangel, disputing with the devil about the body of Moses,*[f] says that the serpent, inspired by the devil, was the cause of the transgression of Adam and Eve.

Gen 3:1–6

Jude 9

A3. (Pseudo-?) Didymus of Alexandria, In Epistulam Judae Enarratio[g]

(Didymus is arguing against those who claim that the devil is evil by nature, not merely by will.) Nor is the devil an earthly substance. For at one time he had divine glory and holy knowledge of God, although, having changed, he has fallen from such greatness. So from the common understanding that we have of all rational beings that they have free will, and that a change has taken place

---

a. Latin text in Charles, *Assumption*, 107.

b. The quotation conforms to the Vulgate Latin.

c. Some have argued that the Latin (*hic confirmat assumptionem Moysi*) should be translated, "This confirms the assumption of Moses," referring to the event, not the book (e.g., Tromp, *Assumption*, 27). But Jude 9 does not refer to or even imply an "assumption" of Moses (whether of body or spirit). Clement must mean that the story of a contest over the body of Moses occurred in the book Assumption of Moses.

d. Latin text in Jan Dochhorn, "Der Tod des Mose in der Assumptio Moses," in *Modebilder: Gedanken zur Rezeption einer literarischen Figur im Früjudentum, frühen Christentum und der römisch-hellenistischen Literatur*, ed. Michael Sommer et al., WUNT 390 (Tübingen: Mohr Siebeck, 2017), 171.

e. The Latin term *ascensio*, used here in Rufinus's Latin version of Origen, is equivalent to the Greek *analepsis*.

f. The words correspond to Jude 9 in the Vulgate Latin.

g. Latin text in PG 39, cols. 1814–15.

in the devil, it is evident that his nature is not evil. The one who transcends all wickedness is not of this kind, although those who oppose this consideration object[a] to the present epistle and to the Assumption of Moses, on account of the place where it is indicated that a word of the archangel about the body of Moses was directed to the devil. For not only from this testimony but from the whole divine Scripture his fall is revealed. Jude 9

A4. Pseudo-Gelasius of Cyzicus, Historia Ecclesiastica 2.17.17[b]
(Bishop Eusebius of Caesarea is speaking) As it is written in the book of the Assumption of Moses, Moses, having summoned Jesus the son of Nave (i.e., Joshua the son of Nun) and disputing with him, said, "And God foresaw me before the foundation of the world to be the mediator of his covenant. T. Mos. 1:14

A5. Pseudo-Gelasius of Cyzicus, Historia Ecclesiastica 2.21.7, 19[c]
(Bishop Protogenes of Sardica is speaking:) And in the book of the Assumption of Moses, *Michael the archangel, disputing with the devil*, says, "For from his Holy Spirit we were all created." And again he says, "From the face of God the Spirit went forth and the world was made". . . . (The Arian philosopher Phaedo responds:) As for the Assumption of Moses, which you quote and of which you have just spoken, I have never heard of it until now. Jude 9 / Ps 103(104):30 / Ps 32(33):6; Jdt 16:14

A6. Stichometry of Nicephorus[d]

1 Enoch	4800 lines
2 Patriarchs	5100 lines
3 Prayer of Joseph	1100 lines
4 Testament of Moses	1100 lines
5 Assumption of Moses	1400 lines
6 Abraham	300 lines
7 Eldad and Modad	400 lines
8 Of Elijah the Prophet	316 lines
9 Of Zephaniah the Prophet	500 lines
10 Of Zechariah the father of John	500 lines

Pseudepigrapha of Baruch, Habakkuk, Ezekiel and Daniel

---

a. Latin *praescribant*. Jones translates the verb differently as "plead as a pretext," but Dochhorn has "Einwände erheben" (Jones, *Epistle of Jude*, 68; Dochhorn, "Der Tod des Mose," 172). The opponents maybe argued that, since the devil is evil by nature and has no free will, he cannot be held to be guilty of any offence.

b. Greek text in *Anonyme Kirchengeschichte (Gelasius Cyzicenus CPG 6043)*, ed. Günther Christian Hansen, GCS 9 (Berlin: de Gruyter, 2002), 58.

c. Greek text in Hansen, *Anonyme Kirchengeschichte*, 69–70.

d. Greek text in Dochhorn, "Der Tod des Mose," 173.

A7. Synopsis of Pseudo-Athanasius[a]

1 Adam
2 Enoch
3 Lamech
4 Patriarchs
5 Prayer of Joseph
6 Eldad and Modad
7 Testament of Moses
8 Assumption of Moses
9 Psalms of Solomon
10 Apocalypse of Elijah
11 Vision of Isaiah
12 Apocalypse of Zephaniah
13 Apocalypse of Zechariah
14 Apocalypse of Ezra
15 History of Jacob

B. Texts about the Assumption of Moses

B1. Clement of Alexandria, Stromateis 6.15.2–3[b]

It is therefore reasonable that Jesus the son of Nave (i.e., Joshua the son of Nun) should have seen Moses being taken up[c] in two forms, the one with angels, while the other was honored with burial in the clefts of the mountains. Jesus saw this sight from above, when he was lifted up, with Caleb, by the Spirit. But they did not both see it in the same way, for one of them descended more quickly, since he bore much weight, while the other descending after him, subsequently told of the glory he had seen, since, being purer than the other, he was able to perceive more.

[Deut 34:6 MT; Josephus, A. J. 4.326]

B2. Origen, In Jesu Nave Homiliae xxvi 2.1[d]

Finally, in a certain book in which, though it is not in the canon, a figure of this mystery is described, it is related that two Moseses were seen, one alive in the spirit, the other dead in the body. No doubt, in this it is indicated that, if you consider the letter of the law, empty of all the things we have mentioned above, that is the Moses who is dead in the body. But if you are able *to remove the veil* of the law and to understand that the law is spiritual, that is the Moses who lives in the spirit.

[2 Cor 3:16]

---

a. Greek text in Dochhorn, "Der Tod des Mose," 173.
b. Greek text in Albert-Marie Denis, *Fragmenta Pseudepigraphorum Graeca*, PVTG 3 (Leiden: Brill, 1970), 65.
c. Greek *analambanomenon*.
d. Latin text in Charles, *Assumption*, 108.

B3. Evodius of Uzala, Epistula ad Augustinum 158.6[a]
In the secret books (*apocrypha*)[b] and in the Secrets (or Secret Words) of Moses himself—a writing that lacks authority—(it is said that) when he went up the mountain to die, it came about through the power of the body that there was one body that was committed to the earth and another that was associated with an angel as its companion.

C. Other Probable Allusions to the Assumption of Moses
C1. Clement of Alexandria, Stromateis 1.23.1[c]
The parents gave the child a certain name, but he was called Joachim. He also had a third name in heaven after his assumption,[d] so the initiates say: Melchi.

LAB 9:16

C2. Clement of Alexandria, Stromateis 1.23.1[e]
The initiates say that (Moses) killed the Egyptian with a word only, as Peter killed Ananias and Sapphira.

Exod 2:12
Acts 5:1–11

C3. Pseudo-Gelasius of Cyzicus, Historia Ecclesiastica 2.17.18[f]
In the book of the Secret[g] Sayings of Moses, Moses himself prophesied about David and Solomon. About Solomon he prophesied thus: "And God shall pour upon him wisdom and righteousness and full knowledge, and he shall build the house of God."

1 Kgs 3:12

D. Jude 9 and Other Patristic Comments on It
D1. Jude 9
But when Michael the archangel, in debate with the devil, disputed about the body of Moses, he did not presume to condemn him for slander,[h] but said, "May the Lord rebuke you!"

D2. Pseudo-Oecumenius, In Epistulam Judae 9
It is said that Michael the archangel took care of the burial of Moses. For the devil would not accept this, but brought an accusation because of the murder of the Egyptian, on the grounds that Moses was guilty of it, and because of this would not allow him to receive honorable burial.

Exod 2:12

---

a. Latin text in Denis, *Fragmenta*, 65.

b. The Latin word *apocryphon*, from the Greek *apokryphon*, though at this date it was beginning to acquire the meaning "false," here has its proper meaning of "secret," in the sense of books too sacred or precious to be openly read.

c. Greek text in Denis, *Fragmenta*, 64.

d. Greek *analēpsin*.

e. Greek text in Denis, *Fragmenta*, 64.

f. Greek text in Hansen, *Anonyme Kirchengeschichte*, 58–59.

g. The translation "mystical" (as in James, *Lost Apocrypha*, 51) is misleading.

h. Some versions translate these words (*ouk etolmēsen krisin epenenkein blasphēmias*), "did not dare to bring a slanderous accusation against him" (NIV).

Fragments of the Assumption of Moses and the Testament of Moses

D3. A Scholion in Cramer's Catena (183, lines 18–22)

When Moses died on the mountain and Michael was sent to remove the body,[a] the devil slandered Moses and proclaimed him a murderer because he struck the Egyptian. The angel, not *tolerating the slander against him, said to the devil,* "*May* God *rebuke you!*"

Exod 2:12
Jude 9

D4. A Scholion in Cramer's Catena (160, line 27–161, line 3)[b]

(**Greek**) (Jude) is showing the Old Testament to be in agreement with the New, since both were given by the one God. For the devil resisted, wishing to deceive, saying, "The body is mine, for I am the master of matter," and was answered by the angel, "*May the Lord rebuke you!*", that is, *the Lord of the spirits and of all flesh*. For this reason, a little before, he said that *Jesus saved a people from the land of Egypt*, the God of the Old and New Testament. Glory to him!

Jude 9
Num 16:22; 27:16 LXX
Jude 5

(**Armenian**) (Jude) refers to this event in order to show that the Old (Testament) is in agreement with the New, and that it is by the one God that the two have been given, those whose *glories these people insult*. Again in fact, *in their madness*, they have taken material things for God. This signifies that Satan wished to deceive, when he said, "This body belongs to me, because I am the master of matter." This is why he heard from the angel, "*May the Lord rebuke you!*", which signifies that the Lord is *the Master of spirits and all flesh*. If one reflects on these words, (Jude) here affirms something even more important: it is the one whose supremacy these people reject *who saved his people from the land of Egypt*, the one God of the Old and New Testament, to whom be glory for ever. Amen.[c]

Jude 8
Jude 8
Jude 9
Num 16:22; 27:16 LXX
Jude 5

D5. A Scholion on Jude 9[d]

(**D5a**) When Moses died on the mountain, the archangel Michael was sent to remove the body. But the devil resisted, wishing to deceive, saying, "The body is mine, for I am the master of matter,"

(**D5b**) or slandering the holy man because he struck the Egyptian and proclaiming him a murderer. The angel, not tolerating the slander against the holy man, said to the devil, "*May* God *rebuke you!*"

Exod 2:12
Jude 9

---

a. Tromp translates *metathēsōn to sōma* as "to transfer the body to heaven," but the meaning must be that Michael is to remove the body from the spot where Moses died and bury it elsewhere, in an unknown grave (*Assumption*, 276). See text E1, where this is explicit.

b. The scholion appears in Pseudo-Oecumenius, *In Jud.* 9. The Armenian version of this scholion is in Charles Renoux, *La Chaîne Arménienne surotres Catholiques, IV: Sur 2–3 Jean et Jude*, PO 47, no. 210/2 (Turnhout: Brepols, 1996), 154–57 (Armenian text and French translation). It is possible that the Armenian version preserves details that have dropped out of the extant Greek text.

c. My translation from the French in Charles Renoux, "L' Assomption de Moïse: D'Origène à la chaîne Arménienne sur les Épîtres Catholiques," in *Recherches et Tradition: Mélanges Patristiques Offerts à Henri Crouzel, S. J.*, ed. André Dupleix, Théologie Historique 88 (Paris: Beauchesne, 1992), 243–46. I have also consulted the translation in Renoux, *La Chaîne*, 155, 157.

d. Greek text in Charles, *Assumption*, 110; Denis, *Fragmenta*, 67.

D6. A Scholion in Cramer's Catena (161 lines 4–8)[a]

Michael, since he lacked the authority, did not bring upon him (the devil) the punishment appropriate to blasphemy, but left him to the judgment of his Master. For when he brought Moses onto the mountain where the Lord was transfigured, then the devil said to Michael, "God lied in bringing Moses into the land that he swore he should not enter."

Matt 17:2–3
Deut 34:4

D7. A Scholion on Jude 9[b]

(**D7a**) For the devil resisted, wishing to deceive, saying, "The body is mine, for I am the master of matter," and was answered by, "*May the Lord rebuke you!*", that is, the Lord who is *Master of all the spirits*.

Jude 9
Num 16:22; 27:16

(**D7b**) Others say that God, wishing to show that after our departure hence demons oppose our souls on their upward course, permitted this to be seen at the burial of Moses.[c]

(**D7c**) For the devil also slandered Moses, calling him a murderer because he smote the Egyptian. Michael the archangel, not tolerating the slander, said to the devil, "*May the Lord God rebuke you, devil!*"

Exod 2:12
Zech 3:2 OG

(**D7d**) He also said this, that God had lied in that he brought Moses into the land that he swore he should not enter.

Deut 34:4

D8. A Scholion on Jude 9 Preserved in an Armenian Catena[d]

The children of Israel, raised among the Egyptians who deified and worshiped everything, even contemptible objects, saw Moses shining, more than any man, with a glory manifested by extraordinary signs and a face that the grace of God made shine with glory. Fearing that they should come, in the manner of the Egyptians, to worship his corpse or even his name, the providence of God allowed, in his patience, that after the departure (of Moses) the devil should claim his body, under the pretext of a sin, in order to divert them, when they saw it, from giving it too great honors. Although he had taken the part of the people, the angel did not, however, put an end to the arrogance of the Evil One, but *said, "May the Lord punish you."* And since he removed the body from their eyes, they were encouraged not to consider either the name or the body of the prophet a god. On the basis of this event let us also understand Paul's word, "*Death reigned from Adam to Moses.*" In fact, the one who had fought against Adam and triumphed over him was here vanquished, after being humiliated, the one whom Adam, his adversary according to the spirit, had not been able to resist. As for the body (of Moses), (the Evil One) was deprived of it, thanks to the intervention of the angel who came to his aid. He removed the sentence (of death) and the obstacle created by the victory of (the Evil One). And showing

Exod 34:29–35

Jude 9

Rom 5:14

---

a. This scholion is also in Pseudo-Oecumenius, *In Jud.* 9.
b. Greek text from Bodleian MS Arch.E.5.9 in Montague Rhodes James, *The Testament of Abraham: The Greek Text Now First Edited with an Introduction and Notes,* TS 2.2 (Cambridge: Cambridge University Press, 1892), 18.
c. With this sentence, cf. text F1.
d. Renoux, *La Chaîne,* 160–63 (Armenian text and French translation).

D9. Theophylact of Ohrid, Expositio in Epistulam Judae

In apocryphal books[b] it is said that Michael the archangel took care of the burial of Moses. The devil did not accept this, but brought an accusation because of the murder of the Egyptian, on the grounds that Moses was guilty of it, and because of this would not allow him to receive honorable burial.

Exod 2:12

E. Other Accounts of the Dispute over Moses's Body
E1. Palaea Historica 121[c]

Concerning the death of Moses. Moses said to Jesus the son of Nave (i.e., Joshua the son of Nun), "Let us go up onto the mountain." ²And when they had gone up, Moses saw the land of promise, and he said to Jesus, "Go down to the people and tell them that Moses is dead." ³And Jesus went down to the people, but Moses came to the end of his life. ⁴And Samuel (i.e., Sammael) tried to bring his body down to the people, so that they might make it a god. ⁵But Michael the chief captain by the command of God came to take it and remove it, ⁶Samuel resisted him, and they fought. ⁷So the chief captain was angry and rebuked him, saying, "*May the Lord rebuke you, devil!*" ⁸In this way the adversary was defeated and took flight, ⁹but the archangel Michael removed the body of Moses to the place where he was commanded by Christ our God, and no one saw the burial place of Moses.

Deut 34:1–4

Josh 5:14; Dan 8:11

Zech 3:2 OG

Deut 34:6

E2. Slavonic Life of Moses 16

But at the end of the same year in the twelfth month, on the seventh day, that is, in March, Moses the servant of God died and was buried on the fourth day of the month September on a certain mountain by the chief captain Michael. For the devil contended with the angel and would not permit his body to be buried, saying, "Moses is a murderer. He killed a man in Egypt and hid him in the sand." Then Michael prayed to God and there was thunder and lightning and suddenly the devil disappeared; but Michael buried him with his own hands.[d]

Deut 34:5–6

Josh 5:14; Dan 8:11

Exod 2:12

---

a. My translation from the French in Renoux, "L' Assomption," 246–47. This French differs somewhat from the translation in Renoux, *La Chaîne*, 161, 163.

b. Theophylact's exposition of Jude, including this section, reproduces that of Pseudo-Oecumenius, but these opening words ("in apocryphal books") are an addition (cf. text D2).

c. Greek text in Athenasius Vassiliev, *Anecdota Graeco-Byzantina* (Moscow: Imperial University Press, 1893), 257–58. Chapter and verse numbers follow William Adler, "Palaea Historica ('The Old Testament History')," *MOTP* 1:647.

d. This translation is from James from the German translation in Bonwetsch, "Die Mosessage," 607, but I have amended the opening words according to the suggestion of Turdeanu. See James, *Lost Apocrypha*, 47–48; G. Nathanael Bonwetsch, "Die Mosessage in der slavischen kirchlichen Litteratur," *NAWG* (1908): 607; Emil Turdeanu, "La Chronique de Moïse en russe," *Revue des études slaves* 46 (1967): 55, doi:10.3406/slave.1967.1933.

F. Comments of Severus of Antioch, with a Related Scholion
F1. Letter to Thomas, Bishop of Germanicia[a]

Here [in Deut 34] by means of a bodily image God set forth a mystery that occurs concerning the soul. For when the soul separates from the body, after its departure hence both good angelic powers and a very evil band of demons come to meet it, so that according to the quality of the deeds, evil and good, that it has done, either one group or the other may carry it off to the appropriate place to be guarded until the last day, when we shall all be presented for judgment, and led away either to eternal life or to the unending flame of fire. God, wishing to show this also to the children of Israel by means of a certain bodily image, ordained that at the burial of Moses, at the time of the dressing of the body and its customary depositing in the earth, there should appear before their eyes the evil demon as it were resisting and opposing, and that Michael, a good angel, should encounter and repel him, and should not rebuke him on his own authority, but retire from passing judgment against him in favor of the Lord of all, and say, *"May the Lord rebuke you!"* in order that by means of these things those who are being instructed might learn that there is a conflict over our souls after their departure hence and that it is necessary to prepare oneself by means of good deeds in order to secure the angels as allies, when the demons are gibbering jealously and bitterly against us. And when the divine image had appeared before their eyes it seems that then some cloud or shining of light came upon that place, obscuring it and walling it off from the onlookers, so that they might not know his grave.[b] Therefore also the holy Scripture says in Deuteronomy, *And Moses the servant of the Lord died there in the land of Moab by the word of the Lord. And they buried him in the land of Moab, near the house of Phogor, and no one saw his death or his grave,[c] until this day.* These things, it is said, are found in the apocryphal book that contains the more detailed account of the genesis or creation.[d]

[Jude 9]

[Deut 34:5–6 LXX]

F2. Letter to Thomas, Bishop of Germanicia[e]

Some have said that the Jews called the law itself the body of Moses, and that, when he revealed the law to the children of Israel, the devil opposed and acted against him, hindering the giving of the law, disputing and saying that the people were not worthy to receive it. So Moses, taking the lead, put to flight the opponent by shouting, *"May the Lord rebuke you!"* But others called the

[Jude 9]

---

a. Greek text in John A. Cramer, ed., *Catenae Graecorum Patrum in Novum Testamentum*, vol. 8: *In epistolas catholicas et apocalypsin* (Oxford: Oxford University Press, 1844), 161, lines 20–162, line 17. But the last sentence, not in Cramer's *Catenae*, is preserved in the catena of Nicephorus, quoted in James, *Testament*, 17. (Albert-Marie Denis points out that James erroneously ascribes it to the catena of Nicetas; Denis, *Introduction à la littérature Religieuse Judéo-Hellénistique*, 2 vols. [Brepols: Turnhout, 2000], 1:443 n. 37.)

b. This sentence corresponds to text F3.

c. These three words appear to be a correction (following Deut 34:6) incorporated into the text.

d. That is, Jubilees. On the title "Leptogenesis" for the Book of Jubilees, see Charles, *Book of Jubilees*, xv–xvi.

e. Greek text I, Cramer, *Catenae*, 162 lines 17–30. The extract is from the same letter, apparently following shortly after text F1.

Fragments of the Assumption of Moses and the Testament of Moses

people he was leading the body of Moses, and said that, as they were coming out of the land of Egypt, the devil opposed and resisted, saying to Moses, as if in a legal trial, that his body, that is, the people, was not worthy to receive liberation from the Egyptians. Michael hindered and put a stop to his opposition by crying out, "*May the Lord rebuke you!*"

Jude 9

F3. Treatise against Alexandria[a]

(Jude) says, "*He did not dare to bring* the *condemnation of blasphemy against him, but said* only, '*May the Lord rebuke you!*'" That is, since he was a blasphemer and fighter against God from the beginning, from the time when he was infected with the apostasy, and after that deceived Adam through cunning, contesting the commandment of God, (Michael) *did not dare to give a condemnation and verdict of blasphemy, but said, "May the Lord rebuke you!"* For the matter of the verdict and condemnation he reserved for the judge, that is, Christ.

Jude 9

Gen 3:4–5
Jude 9

F4. A Scholion from a Catena on the Pentateuch[b]

Indeed, it is said in an apocryphal and secret book where there is a more detailed treatment of created(?), we read that, when Moses died, a shining cloud surrounding the place of burial so touched the eyes of the bystanders that no one could see either the dying lawgiver or the place where his corpse is concealed.

G. Allusions to Moses Apocrypha That Are Otherwise Unknown

G1. Epiphanius, Panarion (Adversus Haereses) 9.4.13[c]

The angels, as the tradition that has come to us has it, buried the body of the holy Moses and did not purify themselves, but the angels were not profaned by the holy body.

G2. On the Origin of the World (NHC, II,2) 102.7–9[d]

You will find the function of these names and the masculine power in the Archangelikē of Moses the Prophet.[e]

---

a. Greek text in Cramer, *Catenae*, 162 lines 31–163, line 7.
b. Quoted in Latin by Charles, *Assumption*, xlviii; from Johan A. Fabricius, *Cod. Pseud. V. T.*, 2:121–22. This text is evidently dependent on the latter part of text F1.
c. Greek text in Denis, *Fragment*a, 66.
d. On the Origin of the World is a modern title given to this gnostic treatise that appears without a title in this Nag Hammadi codex. This translation is by Hans-Gebhard Bethge and Orval S. Wintermute, "On the Origin of the World," in *The Nag Hammadi Library in English*, ed. James M. Robinson (Leiden: Brill, 1977), 164.
e. The reference is to the masculine and feminine names of the seven androgynous powers, created by Ialdabaoth, who are the "powers of the seven heavens of Chaos." The feminine names are said to be found in the First Book of Noraia. There undoubtedly was a gnostic Book of Noria (a name given to Noah's wife; Epiphanius, *Haer.* 2.1.3), and so there is no reason to doubt that the Archangelikē of Moses the Prophet was also an existing book.

G3. Epiphanius, Panarion (Adversus Haereses) 39.5.1
Now, they (the Sethians) have composed certain books, attributing them to great people: they say there are seven books attributed to Seth; other, different books they entitle *Foreigners*; another they call a *Revelation* attributed to Abraham, and full of all evil; others attributed to Moses;[a] and others attributed to other figures.[b]

G4. Euthalian Apparatus[c]
From an apocryphon of Moses, once only,[d] "Neither circumcision nor uncircumcision is anything, but new creation."[e]

Gal 6:15

---

a. These may well include the Archangelikē of Moses the Prophet (see text G2). No other gnostic works attributed to Moses are known.

b. This translation is from Bentley Layton, *The Gnostic Scriptures* (London: SCM, 1987). 189.

c. Lorenzo Alessandro Zaccagni, *Collectanea Monumentorum Veterum Ecclesiae Graecae ac Latinae* (Rome: Press of the Sacred Congregation for the Propagation of the Faith, 1698), 1:561, quotation XI.87. George Syncellus attributes the same quotation to an Apocalypse of Moses, while Photius says it occurs "among the apocrypha of Moses"; see Denis, *Introduction*, 466–67.

d. The meaning is that this work is cited only once in the Pauline corpus.

e. The first part of the quoted sentence appears also in Gal 5:6, but the Euthalian list does not indicate a quotation in that verse.

The Sword of Moses (Ḥarba de-Moshe)
A new translation and introduction

by Yuval Harari

The Sword of Moses (Ḥarba de-Moshe) is one of the two Jewish magical treatises that have survived from antiquity and in many respects it is the more significant one.[1] It presents a broad assortment of magical practices for accomplishing various goals, all based on the use of a magical "sword" of words, which Moses brought down from heaven. This practical information—the broadest extant collection of Jewish magical recipes from the first millennium—and the vast list of holy names upon which the execution of these instructions is based are enveloped in a theoretical framework. It is exactly this framework that makes the Sword of Moses such a significant record, as it outlines the cosmology in which magical activity grounded its rationale and meaning. All of these components, drawn in part from the Magical Sword literature, were redacted by the author into a magical treatise, that is to say, into a coherent text that demonstrates its logical development, even though not free of difficulties, from beginning to end.

Structure, Genres and Contents

The Sword of Moses is primarily a book of magical recipes.[2] But unlike other such collections of recipes (known mainly from the Cairo Genizah and later from medieval manuscripts), this operative information is introduced by a literary-theoretical section.[3] Thus, one may divide the treatise into three main parts: (A) controlling the sword; (B) the

---

1. The other book is Sefer ha-Razim (The Book of Mysteries). See Mordechai Margalioth, *Sepher ha-Razim: A Newly Recovered Book of Magic from the Talmudic Period Collected from Geniza Fragments and Other Sources* (Jerusalem: Yediot Aharonot, 1966) [Heb.]; Bill Rebiger and Peter Schäfer, *Sefer ha-Razim I und II; Das Buch der Geheimnisse I und II*, vol. 1: *Edition*; vol. 2: *Einleitung, Übersetzung und Kommentar*, 2 vols., TSAJ 125, 132 (Tübingen: Mohr Siebeck, 2009); James R. Davila, "The Book of the Mysteries (*Sefer ha-Razim*)," in the present volume. Cf. Philip S. Alexander, "*Sefer ha-Razim* and the Problem of Black Magic in Early Judaism," in *Magic in the Biblical World: From the Rod of Aaron to the Ring of Solomon*, ed. Todd E. Klutz, JSNTSup 245 (London: T&T Clark, 2003), 170–90. On Jewish magic in antiquity see Gideon Bohak, *Ancient Jewish Magic: A History* (Cambridge: Cambridge University Press, 2008), with a discussion of Sefer ha-Razim on 170–75; cf. Yuval Harari, *Jewish Magic before the Rise of Kabbalah* (Detroit: Wayne State University Press, 2017), with a discussion of Sefer ha-Razim on 275–84.
2. The following discussion is a concise, updated version of the detailed study in Yuval Harari, *The Sword of Moses: A New Edition and Study* (Jerusalem: Academon, 1997), 51–135 [Heb.].
3. On types of Jewish instructional literature of magic see Harari, *Jewish Magic*, 255–90.

This introduction to and translation of the Sword of Moses were first published in Yuval Harari, "The Sword of Moses (*Ḥarba de-Moshe*): A New Translation and Introduction," *Magic, Ritual, and Witchcraft* 7 (2012): 58–98. It is reprinted here in an updated and slightly revised version with permission of the University of Pennsylvania Press, for which I am grateful.

sword of names; and, (C) the operative section. The beginning of the first section and the end of the last function as the opening and the conclusion of the treatise as a whole.

A. Controlling the Sword
The Opening: On the Origin and the Authority of Magical Knowledge
The Sword of Moses begins with a description of a four-leveled heavenly hierarchy of thirteen princes (*sarim*, archangels). Four of them are at the bottom, "who are appointed over the sword... and over the Torah." Five more princes are located above them, and then three others that are elevated even further. At the top, heading the whole structure, 'HYW PSQTYH sits, before whom all the angels "kneel and bow down and prostrate themselves... every day" after they are dismissed from bowing before God. Each of the princes rules over thousands of thousands of chariots of angels, the least of whom has control over all those who are situated beneath him.

This hierarchical structure of heavenly forces has significant operative importance. According to the concept of power in the Sword of Moses, when one adjures 'HYW PSQTYH, not only does that highest prince become bound to the adjurer but so too do all the princes under his authority. This is actually the aim of the ritual for ruling over the sword, as detailed in the rest of this section, in which the adjurer gains control over the sword by invoking the princes one by one, from the bottom of the heavenly hierarchy to its top. Typical to magical activity, successful adjuration of the angels requires knowledge of their names, which are indeed manifest throughout the depiction of their heavenly positions.

By stating that the four lower princes are appointed over both the sword and the Torah, the author of the Sword of Moses aspires, at the very beginning of the book, to link these two corpora, projecting the halo of the latter over the former. The author tightens this binding by demonstrating that the sword (like the Torah) is given from the mouth of God, an idea that will be further alluded to in the description of the relationships between Moses, the princes, and God (below). The manifest claim that the origin of the magical knowledge incorporated in the treatise is divine serves, of course, to establish the theoretical as well as operative authority of this knowledge.[4]

The question of the operative efficacy of the knowledge suggested in this book requires further explanation. Ancient Jewish magic was based on the view that, through rites and charms, a person can gain control over angels (or other metaphysical entities) and force them to act for his/her own benefit.[5] How could a person possess such power? Why would a spell make any impression on the angels? The Sword of Moses answers this question: God commanded them to do so, by requiring their obedience to one who adjures them by his names as a tribute of honor to him. Thus, simply and incisively the Sword of Moses solves (or better dissolves) the ever-perplexing question

---

4. Cf. on this issue, Michael D. Swartz, *Scholastic Magic: Ritual and Revelation in Early Jewish Mysticism* (Princeton: Princeton University Press, 1996), 173–205. For a similar process of formation of authority in magical treatises from the Greco-Roman world, see Hans Dieter Betz, "The Formation of Authoritative Tradition in the Greek Magical Papyri," in *Jewish and Christian Self-Definition*, vol. 3, ed. Ben F. Meyer and E. P. Sanders (Philadelphia: Fortress, 1982), 161–70.

5. Cf. Yuval Harari, "Jewish Magic: Principles, Acts, Objectives," in *Khamsa Khamsa Khamsa: The Evolution of a Motif in Comtemporary Israeli Art*, ed. Shirat-Miriam Shamir and Ido Noy (Jerusalem: Mayer Museum for Islamic Art, 2018), 183–89.

of the coexistence of heavenly omnipotence and earthly magic. The Lord himself is the patron of human magic.[6]

The narrative that opens the book further ties the command given to the angels by God to the constitutive event of Moses's ascent to receive the Torah. According to the Sword of Moses, upon Moses's return to earth he brought both the Torah and the sword down from heaven. This idea echoes the talmudic tradition about Moses's ascent on high (b. Šabb. 88b–89a) and manifests explicitly what the rabbis only implied: the "gifts" given to Moses by the angels were actually words, namely charms by which they could (and still can) be adjured and controlled. The Moses of the Sword of Moses is, thus, an archetype of the magician. He is the one who brought heavenly, magical knowledge down to his people, and according to the pattern of knowledge-power that was set in heaven concerning him, so too can his successors act.[7]

The Rite for Controlling the Sword

According to the Sword of Moses, magical activity has two stages. First, control over the sword has to be gained, and only upon achieving that may a person execute its power. To control the sword one has to engage in a three-day ritual, which combines purification, prayer, and adjuration. To yield its desired result, the whole rite should be performed in secrecy.

Purification, which is a common requirement throughout ancient Jewish magical literature, is to be achieved through bathing, abstaining from nocturnal pollution, and from any contact with unclean objects, as well as by eating only pure bread with salt and by drinking only water.[8]

The Sword of Moses views the daily prayer (*tefilat ʿAmidah*) and especially the *Shomeʿa Tefilah* benediction (in which one pleads for the acceptance of the prayer) as forceful situations that can (and should) be employed in the service of magical aims. Three times a day, during their daily prayers, the person who strives toward controlling the sword should add adjurations to their prayer or combine them with it. Thus, spell and prayer are interwoven as two complementary modes of performative speech. Three times a day, during the *ʿAmidah* prayer, adjurations of the thirteen princes should be performed. Also, on these occasions two adjuratory prayers that address God should be recited.[9] One encourages him to bind the heavenly princes to the adjurer and to carry out all their desires; the other asks for his protection, lest the adjurer be swept away by fire (apparently cast upon them by the adjured angels).

The adjuration of the thirteen archangels is the core and the climax of the entire rite. The adjurer turns to them by name, one by one, according to their status (lowest

---

6. At the same time it seems that according to the Sword of Moses, God is beyond the limits of the efficacy of human magic. See Harari, *Sword of Moses*, 67–70.

7. On this topic see further Yuval Harari, "Moses, the Sword and *the Sword of Moses*: Between Rabbinical and Magical Traditions," *JSQ* 12 (2005): 293–329, doi:10.1628/094457005783478315.

8. On abstinence and purification in early Jewish magic and mysticism, see further Swartz, *Scholastic Magic*, 153–72; Rebecca M. Lesses, *Ritual Practices to Gain Power: Angels, Incantations, and Revelation in Early Jewish Mysticism*, HTS 44 (Harrisburg, PA: Trinity Press International, 1998), 117–60; James R. Davila, *Descenders to the Chariot: The People behind the Hekhalot Literature*, JSJSup 70 (Leiden: Brill, 2001), 75–125.

9. On the magical genre of adjuratory prayers, see Peter Schäfer and Shaul Shaked, *Magische Texte aus der Kairoer Geniza*, 3 vols., TSAJ 64 (Tübingen: Mohr Siebeck, 1994–1999), 2:10–14.

to highest), and adjures them to surrender to him. The actual result of their surrender is the transmission into his hands (as in the case of Moses) of the power to control the sword and to use it.

The adjuration of the princes clearly rests, both ideologically and textually, on the narrative that begins the book. Together they constitute the (Hebrew) foundation of the whole section. The author himself, who extended this structure, also integrated the Aramaic units into this section. The most striking one is the narrative of the heavenly "swift messenger" (*sheliḥa qalila*) who was sent by God to reveal his mysteries on earth and of the difficulties that the messenger confronted while trying to find a suitable recipient for them. Through this unit, moral requirements are linked to the very possibility of controlling the sword and employing it.

B. The Sword of Names

The second section of the Sword of Moses is a huge accumulation of *nomina barbara* (about 1,800 words, including three short legible texts that are also conceived as magical names). This is the sword related to in the first section. It comprises various groups of letter combinations—such as names that end with YH or with EL; names followed by the name ṢB'WT; names organized alphabetically; and names that follow the pattern, A son of B—that were assembled into the sword by the author. These lists as well as the way in which they are arranged in the sword testify to the attention invested in the latter's creation. It seems to be the result of the redaction and expansion of magical formulas, together with spells, lists of angels' names, and a few legible texts.

C. The Operative Section

The last section of the book is a list of about 140 magical recipes. It was assembled from various magical sources that were possessed by the author, who, after having added at least a few recipes of his own, redacted and tied them to the sword. Each of the recipes in the list requires either the recitation or transcription of a precise segment of the sword in order. Thus, the sword is cut into 137 sequential sections, according to the list of recipes.[10]

The two first recipes specify such a broad range of aims that they also seem to have a rhetorical function. All the other recipes are dedicated to specific objectives. Together they cover a very wide range of human needs and aspirations. Most of the recipes are organized in groups. The most prominent is the group for healing (arranged from the head downward) that is located at the beginning of the section. Other groups concern causing harm, war and governance, agriculture, rescue from distress, self-protection, and enhancing both memory and knowledge. This collection of recipes as well as a few pairs, where the latter recipe suggests the nullification of what was achieved through the former, attest to the practical interest that the redactor had in this list and in the book as a whole. The broad range of aims listed in this section—love and sex, grace and favor in the eyes of others, divination, control over spirits, and financial success are but a few examples that might join the above-mentioned ones—indicates the breadth of support offered by practitioners of magic to their communities and the extent to which magical activity penetrated day-to-day life.

---

10. In a few cases recipes share the same sequence of names from the sword.

The operative section (and the book as a whole) ends with a general instruction and a strict warning regarding inappropriate use of the sword. In such cases, the book concludes, "angels of anger and rage and wrath and fury" may attack and destroy the adjurer. Tremendous power is concealed in the sword that was given from the mouth of God and transmitted to Moses, but such is also its peril. Its use by an amateur could end very violently.

Manuscripts, Versions, and Editions
A. The Full Version
The complete version of the Sword of Moses is found in relatively late manuscripts that all belong to the same textual branch. The earliest known version is found in MS Geneva, Bibliothèque de Genève, Comites Latentes 145, pp. 60–84 (hereafter MS Geneva).[11] The manuscript, which comprises about six hundred pages of a long compilation of magical treatises and recipes entitled *Sefer Shoshan Yesod ha-Olam*, was written by Rabbi Yosef Tirshom, probably in Turkey or in Greece at the beginning of the sixteenth century.[12] This version is transcribed in my current edition of the treatise, translated herein.

As early as 1896 Moses Gaster published a transcription and a translation of the Sword of Moses as well as a study of the treatise.[13] His edition was based on a manuscript from his own collection (Gaster 177), whose correlation with MS Geneva was later indicated by Gershom Scholem and Meir Benayahu.[14] A close examination of the two manuscripts exposed clear intertextual evidence for the reliance of the former upon the latter.[15]

Three more manuscripts of the treatise are found in the Department of Manuscripts of the Jewish National and University Library in Jerusalem. They are all handwritten copies of Gaster's printed edition from the beginning of the twentieth century.[16] Regarding textual issues, then, there is no reason to consult any of the links in this textual chain except the initial one.

B. Genizah Fragments of the Sword of Moses
A few pages of the book as well as some magical fragments that rely on it are found in the Cairo Genizah. All of them are highly important in the history of this treatise (and of its magical information), though far less so for textual issues.[17]

---

11. This manuscript, formerly known as Sassoon 290, has been digitized and is available online: www.e-codices.unifr.ch/en/list/one/bge/clo145.

12. See the detailed discussion in Meir Benayahu, "The Book *Shoshan Yesod ha-Olam* by Rabbi Yoseph Tirshom," in *Temirin: Texts and Studies in Kabbalah and Hasidism*, ed. Israel Weinstock (Jerusalem: Mossad Harav Kook, 1972), 1:187–269 [Heb.]. Benayahu also included in his article the index that is found at the beginning of the manuscript, which comprises some 2,100 indications of magical recipes.

13. Gaster, "The Sword of Moses," *JRAS* (1896): 149–98, doi:10.1017/S0035869X00023455; repr., *Studies and Texts in Folklore, Magic, Mediaeval Romance, Hebrew Apocrypha and Samaritan Archaeology*, 3 vols. (London: Maggs Bros., 1925–1928; repr., New York: Ktav, 1971), 1:288–337; 3:69–103.

14. Benayahu, "*Shoshan Yesod ha-Olam*," 196–97. MS Gaster 177 (currently located in John Rylands University Library, Manchester), which is discussed by Benayahu, also included MS Gaster 178 (currently located in the British Library, London; marked: Or. 10678) in which the Sword of Moses is found.

15. Harari, *Sword of Moses*, 13–14.

16. These copies, MSS Jerusalem, Israel National Library, Heb. 82330, 82647, 83675, were created by Eliyahu Mizrahi Dehuki, a Jerusalem kabbalist of Kurdish origin. On Dehuki and his interest in practical Kabbalah see Yuval Harari, "Three Charms for Killing Adolf Hitler: Practical Kabbalah in WW2," *Aries* 18 (2017): 191–94, doi:10.1163/15700593-01702002.

17. For a detailed discussion of these fragments see Yuval Harari, "*The Sword of Moses*: Genizah Fragments," *Ginzei Qedem—Genizah Research Annual* 10 (2014): 29–92 [Heb.].

The main evidence comes from six double-sided pages of the book, all written by the same person and dated to the eleventh to the mid-twelfth centuries.[18] Two of the pages contain fragments from the first section ("Controlling the 'Sword'"), including the beginning of the "Swift Messenger" narrative and part of the adjuration of the thirteen princes. Three more pages are consecutive parts of the sword of names. The sixth page contains the beginning of the list of recipes. The text is almost identical to that in MS Geneva. The main significance of this version is the contextual evidence that it offers. Historically, it testifies to the existence of a relatively early version of the treatise. Concerning the function of the text, it points to its practical, amuletic use. This is demonstrated by the adjuration of the princes, in which the general indication NN (found in the later version) was replaced by a personal name: Mariot son of Nathan.[19]

Four more Genizah fragments attest another three copies of the book. One of them spans one bifolium (four pages) and contains a relatively broad part of the opening section ("Controlling the Sword").[20] Parts of a third copy are preserved in two narrow strips of paper, the surviving portions of a single manuscript that was cut vertically from top to bottom. Each of the strips includes only a quarter or so of each original line. Together, they cover excerpts from all three sections of the treatise.[21] The last copy of the book is attested by another strip of paper. It includes tiny portions of the concluding part of the book—the last recipes and the warning at its end.[22]

Two more Genizah fragments that contain recipes from the Sword of Moses attest to the intention of its practical use. MS Cambridge, CUL Jacques Mosseri VI 13.2 is a relatively early manuscript (early eleventh century), comprising three written pages in which recipes 50, 55–56, and 111–115 are copied. The novelty of this recension is that after each of the recipes, the required formula from the sword is cited in full (along with its indication by its opening and closing words). Yet another step in the direction of easing the use of the practical information in the treatise was made by the scribe of MS Cambridge, CUL T-S NS 70.130. On this single page, part of which is dedicated also to gematria, four recipes from the treatise occur in this order: numbers 85, 25, 46, 56. In this case the compiler, who for some reason picked out these particular recipes from the list, omitted the indications of the opening and closing words of the required formulas altogether and cited the sequence of names in full at the end of each recipe. This copy differs widely from MS Geneva with respect to both the language of the recipes and the names from the sword.

---

18. Five of the fragments are found in the Jewish Theological Seminary Library in New York and one in Cambridge University Library. Their signatures—according to the textual order—are: JTSL ENA 2643.5; JTSL ENA NS 2.43; JTSL ENA NS 2.42; CUL T-S NS 89.11; JTSL ENA 3373.3; JTSL ENA 2842.31.

19. On this phenomenon in other books of magic recipes, see Ortal-Paz Saar, "Success, Protection and Grace: Three Fragments of a Personalized Magical Handbook," *Ginzei Qedem* 3 (2007): 101*–35*; Gideon Bohak, *A Fifteenth-Century Manuscript of Jewish Magic, MS New York Public Library, Heb. 190 (Formerly Sassoon 56): Introduction, Annotated Edition and Facsimile*, 2 vols., Sources and Studies in the Literature of Jewish Mysticism 44 (Los Angeles: Cherub, 2014), 1:14 [Heb.].

20. Fascimiles of this fragment—MS Cambridge CUL T-S A45.23—have been published in Simon Hopkins, *A Miscellany of Literary Pieces from the Cambridge Genizah Collections*, Cambridge University Library 3 (Cambridge: Cambridge University Library, 1978), 74–77.

21. Manuscripts Cambridge, CUL T-S AS 143.417, Jacques Mosseri VI 32.3. On torn strips in the Cairo Genizah, see Gideon Bohak, "Reconstructing Jewish Magical Recipe Books from the Cairo Genizah," *Ginzei Qedem* 1 (2005): 9*–29*.

22. Manuscript Cambridge, CUL T-S Ar 49.34.

Two more fragments deserve attention. One is a torn, perforated sheet of paper, with very small characters covering one side. Its first three lines have no parallel in the treatise. From line 4, however, the text parallels recipes numbered 56–61 in MS Geneva despite numerous differences. I believe that these recipes were copied, not from the treatise itself, but from some earlier textual layer of which the author made use.[23] The other fragment mentions "the sword of Moses" in its title and belongs to the Magical Sword literature (below).[24]

C. Magical Sword Literature

Located in MS Geneva as well as in two medieval Ashkenazi manuscripts (New York, JTSL 8128 and Oxford, BL 1531) are fragments of what I call Magical Sword literature. I believe that they are late representations of an early textual layer of which the redactor of the Sword of Moses made use. Common to each of them is the employment of the term *sword* to indicate the magical formula, which in some of them is also ascribed to Moses. Although the relationship between most of these fragments and the Sword of Moses is apparent, it seems that the creative way in which the textual layer they represent was handled on its way into the Sword of Moses makes them irrelevant for the study of the original form of this book.[25]

Language and Redaction

The Sword of Moses was redacted from texts in both Hebrew and Aramaic. The language of the magical recipes in the operative section is Babylonian Aramaic in which many Hebrew words are embedded. Aramaic is also the language of the few legible texts at the beginning and the end of the sword. In contrast, the opening section of "Controlling the Sword" combines broad texts in both languages. Its framework, which comprises most of it, is written in Hebrew. This part is a heterogenous text that was composed by the author out of materials that the author possessed (the narrative source) as well as practical instructions that the author contributed. Into this Hebrew framework, the author also integrated two Aramaic units: the story of "the swift messenger" and some more practical instructions that depend upon both this story and the Hebrew source. The dependence of the Aramaic unit upon the Hebrew one attests that this section is not a mere assemblage of textual units but rather the result of mindful and creative work of redaction. The author, who preferred practical efficacy over literary considerations, merged narrative units with units of adjuration and added additional instructions to them. Most of the latter were written in Hebrew, but some are also in Aramaic.

The last element that should be indicated is a sequence of names in the sword that are derived from a Greek spell. This spell occurs again at the end of the sword, this time in Aramaic.[26] The Aramaic version of the spell also occurs in a fragment of the Magical Sword literature, which (as mentioned above) I believe to have predated the Sword of Moses. The translation of the Greek spell, then, took place before the redaction of this

---

23. MS Cambridge, CUL T-S AS 147.194.
24. MS New York, JTSL ENA 2124.28.
25. For transcriptions and a discussion of these texts, see Harari, *Sword of Moses*, 139–52; Peter Schäfer, Margarete Schlüter, and Hans Georg von Mutius, *Synopse zur Hekhalot-Literatur*, TSAJ 2 (Tübingen: Mohr Siebeck, 1981), §§598–622, 640–50. Cf. Gaster, *Studies and Texts*, 1:88–93; 3:330–36.
26. See Claudia Rohrbacher-Sticker, "From Sense to Nonsense, from Incantation Prayer to Magical Spell," *JSQ* 3 (1996): 24–46.

book, and it is quite clear that while merging the (highly faulty) Hebrew transliteration of the Greek original version, its redactor could not understand its meaning.

Date and Provenance

The exact dating of the Sword of Moses as well as its sources is hard to determine. The Genizah fragments testify to its existence in the eleventh to twelfth centuries. R. Hai Gaon mentioned both its name and its opening words in his famous *responsum* to the sages of Kairouan (today's Tunisia) at the very beginning of the eleventh century.[27] The question is, how much earlier was it compiled? Gaster's dating of the Sword of Moses to the first to fourth centuries is hard to justify.[28] It seems more reasonable that the book stemmed from the (later) era of magical treatises, such as Pishra de-Rabbi Hanina or Havdala de-Rabbi Akiva. Although there is no hard proof for the date of origin of any of these compositions (including the Sword of Moses), scholars tend to agree that they were compiled during the third quarter of the first millennium.[29] This seems plausible to me too. However, at the current stage of research, it is impossible to date the book more specifically within this period or even to justify these very time limits beyond any doubt.

Determining the place of composition of the Sword of Moses, that is to say where its Hebrew and Babylonian Aramaic components were interwoven into its current format, is also difficult. Nevertheless, if my assumption, based on textual analysis of the book, that the practical instructions in the section of Controlling the Sword were written by the compiler is correct, then the compilation as a whole probably originated in Eretz Israel. These instructions are written in Hebrew, and it is unlikely that a Babylonian Jew would use it as his own language, interweaving his words between sources partly written in Babylonian Aramaic.

Literary and Practical Context

The Sword of Moses is deeply rooted in the Jewish world of the second half of the first millennium as it brings together rabbinical, liturgical, mystical, and magical elements. It draws its authority from the famous rabbinic tradition, which it echoes, about the "gifts" that Moses received from the angels during his ascension on high (b. Šabb. 88b–89a and parallels). Its concept of purity, mentioned in the opening section without any specifications, seems to rely on (rabbinical) halakhic principles. The daily 'Amidah prayer appears to be a standard liturgical routine for both the writer and his expected readership. The heavenly picture reflected in the book—the hierarchical structure of the archangels, the numerous hosts of angels gathered in chariots under their authority, and the heavenly

---

27. Simcha Emanuel, *Newly Discovered Geonic Responsa* (Jerusalem: Ofeq Institute, 1995), 121–46 (esp. 131–32) [Heb.]. On this *responsum*, see Harari, *Jewish Magic*, 334–38.

28. Gaster, *Studies and Texts*, 1:311.

29. Joshua Trachtenberg, followed also by Lawrence Schiffman and Michael Swartz, dated the book to the Geonic period (second half of the first millennium). See Joshua Trachtenberg, *Jewish Magic and Superstition: A Study of Folk Religion* (New York: Atheneum, 1970), 124, 315; Schiffman and Swartz, *Hebrew and Aramaic Incantation Texts from the Cairo Genizah: Selected Texts from Taylor-Schechter Box K1, Semitic Texts and Studies 1* (Sheffield: JSOT Press, 1992), 20. For the dating of *Havdala de-Rabbi Akiva* and *Pishra de-Rabbi Hanina*, see Gershom Scholem, "Havdalah de-Rabbi Aqiba: A Source of the Jewish Magical Tradition from the Geonic Period," *Tarbiz* 50 (1980/1981): 243–81 [Heb.]; Franco M. Tocci, "Metatron, 'Arcidemonio' e Mytrt (Μιθρας?) nel *Pisra de-R. Hanina ben Dosa*," in *Incontro di Religioni in Asia tra il III e il X secolo d. C., Atti del Convegno Internazionale*, ed. Lionello Lanciotti, Civiltà Veneziana, Studi 39 (Firenze: Olschki, 1984), 79–97.

worship of God, who dwells in his palaces—correlates with the one that emerges from the Hekhalot and Merkavah writings. The same also holds true for the names of the angels and of God, as well as for the hymn embedded in the prayer to God (called QWSYM).[30] In any event, these correspondences should be regarded as signs of acquaintance on the author's part with the heavenly cosmology that is also drawn in the early Jewish mystical writings, rather than the direct influence of these writings upon him or as evidence of his belonging to the circles of *yordei ha-merkavah* ("descenders to the chariot").

Concerning its magic, the Sword of Moses rests on a long-standing tradition of utilizing rites and spells to gain control over angels and to exploit them in the service of the adjurer. The earliest literary consolidation of this tradition known to us is found in the Book of the Mysteries (Sefer ha-Razim). However, that book differs from the Sword of Moses in both its theoretical and operational views as well as the way in which the practical material is organized within the theoretical framework.

The connections between the Sword of Moses and the vast corpus of Babylonian magic bowls are loose, too.[31] The "swift messenger," who in this book narrates the episode of being sent down to earth by God, also appears in one of the bowls, but apart from that one can hardly detect specific links, either textual or operative, between these sources.[32] This is also the case regarding non-Jewish magic sources, both Babylonian and Greco-Roman.[33]

The use of the technical term *sword*, typical to the Sword of Moses, binds it to Jewish traditions that relate to the tongue as a sword, on the one hand, and to the Greek term *xifos*, which functions in the very same way in a spell entitled *Xifos Dardanou* (the Sword of Dardanos) found in the Greek magical papyri, on the other. Nevertheless, one should not assume Greco-Roman influence over the author of the book, who actually takes a small step—in a characteristically magical direction—beyond Jewish traditions, both rabbinic and mystical, concerning the power of "the sword of the tongue."[34] This step is reflected considerably already in the Magical Sword literature, on which, as noted, the author relied and in which both the ideas of the magical sword of words (along with some short formulations of it) and its attribution to Moses can be found.[35] Guided by a

---

30. On these hymns, see Meir Bar-Ilan, *The Mysteries of Jewish Prayer and Hekhalot* (Ramat Gan: Bar-Ilan University Press, 1987) [Heb.]; Naomi Janowitz, *The Poetics of Ascent: Theories of Language in a Rabbinic Ascent Text*, SNY Series in Judaica (Albany: State University of New York Press, 1989).

31. On the Aramaic incantation bowls, see, e.g., the following recent surveys (with further bibliography): Bohak, *Ancient Jewish Magic*, 183–93; Harari, *Jewish Magic*, 234–51; Dan Levene, "Curse or Blessing, What's in the Magic Bowls?," *Parke Institute Pamphlet* 2 (Southampton: University of Southampton, 2002); Michael G. Morony, "Magic and Society in Late Sasanian Iraq," in *Prayer, Magic, and the Stars in the Ancient and Late Antique World*, ed. Scott Noegel, Joel Walker, and Brannon Wheeler, Magic in History (University Park: Pennsylvania State University Press, 2003), 83–107; Shaul Shaked, "Magic Bowls and Incantation Texts: How to Get Rid of Demons and Pests," *Qadmoniot* 129 (2005): 2–13 [Heb.]; Shaked, James N. Ford, and Siam Bhayro, *Aramaic Bowl Spells: Jewish Babylonian Aramaic Bowls*, vol. 1, Magical and Religious Literature of Late Antiquity 1 (Leiden: Brill, 2013).

32. For the swift messenger, see Dan Levene, *A Corpus of Magic Bowls: Incantation Texts in Jewish Aramaic from Late Antiquity* (London: Kegan Paul, 2003), 93–96.

33. Although a piece of a Greek spell is embedded in the Sword of Moses, it is absolutely clear that at the time of the latter's compilation its author did not understand the spell. This occurrence, then, cannot serve as a case of professional borrowing from the Greek tradition. Cf. Rohrbacher-Sticker, "From Sense to Nonsense."

34. See Harari, "Moses," 298–309.

35. Cf. above, n. 25.

unique proficient view, the author first expanded the relatively short sword—known in the Magical Sword literature—exponentially, by incorporating various lists of names to compose the version found here, and then linked it to his list of recipes. This collection of instructional information was probably also a result of the transmission of magical knowledge and not merely of personal, genuine invention.

The Sword of Moses was undoubtedly a renowned book of magic in Babylonia in the late Geonic period. This is evident from the way it is referred to by R. Hai Gaon in his *responsum* to the sages of Kairouan. From the Cairo Genizah we can learn that it was also known, desired, and copied in Egypt at the beginning of the second millennium. The fragments we have available attest not only to the attraction of the treatise from a theoretical point of view but also to the belief in its inherent power as a (personalized) apotropaic text and to the practical interest in the operative information embedded in it.

Although we cannot trace the exact lines of its transmission during the next few centuries, the interest in the Sword of Moses seems to have been retained. Indeed, unlike other magical treatises found in the genizah, we cannot point to any interest stirred by it among the medieval Ashkenazi pietists; nevertheless, it did find its way to the significant sixteenth-century compilation *Sefer Shoshan Yesod ha-'Olam*. It seems to have drawn only scant attention during the early modern period, but at the beginning of the twentieth century it was still attractive enough to be handcopied from Gaster's printed edition by a Jerusalem kabbalist.[36] Thus, even though one can hardly detect precise imprints of the Sword of Moses in the theoretical or the operative development of Jewish magic, it certainly remained a vital source of authoritative information for those experts who knew it, copied it into their manuals, and used it for the benefit of their clients.

The Translation

The Sword of Moses demonstrates a wide range of linguistic difficulties: syntactical errors and misspellings, interpolations and disruptions, peculiar forms and sheer scribal mistakes. Only in rare cases could I account for the philological considerations that led me to the suggested solution. However, keeping in mind Gaster's absolute silence concerning his own considerations, which in some cases are hard to follow, I did try to give the reader a sense of the original text as far as the framework of this edition enables it.

Bibliography

Alexander, Philip S. "*Sefer ha-Razim* and the Problem of Black Magic in Early Judaism." Pages 170–90 in *Magic in the Biblical World: From the Rod of Aaron to the Ring of Solomon*. Edited by Todd E. Klutz. JSNTSup 245. London: T&T Clark, 2003.

Bar-Ilan, Meir. *The Mysteries of Jewish Prayer and Hekhalot*. Ramat Gan: Bar-Ilan University Press, 1987. [Heb.]

Benayahu, Meir. "The Book *Shoshan Yesod ha-Olam* by Rabbi Yoseph Tirshom." Pages 187–269 in vol. 1 of *Temirin: Texts and Studies in Kabbalah and Hasidism*. Edited by Israel Weinstock. Jerusalem: Mossad Harav Kook, 1972. [Heb.]

Betz, Hans Dieter. "The Formation of Authoritative Tradition in the Greek Magical Papyri." Pages 161–70 in vol. 3 of *Jewish and Christian Self-Definition*. Edited by Ben F. Meyer and E. P. Sanders. Philadelphia: Fortress, 1982.

---

36. See above, n. 25.

Bohak, Gideon. *Ancient Jewish Magic: A History*. Cambridge: Cambridge University Press, 2008.

———. *A Fifteenth-Century Manuscript of Jewish Magic, MS New York Public Library, Heb. 190 (Formerly Sassoon 56): Introduction, Annotated Edition and Facsimile*. 2 vols. Sources and Studies in the Literature of Jewish Mysticism 44. Los Angeles: Cherub, 2014. [Heb.]

———. "Reconstructing Jewish Magical Recipe Books from the Cairo Genizah." *Ginzei Qedem* 1 (2005): 9*–29*.

Davila, James R. *Descenders to the Chariot: The People behind the Hekhalot Literature*. JSJSup 70. Leiden: Brill, 2001.

Emanuel, Simcha. *Newly Discovered Geonic Responsa*. Jerusalem: Ofeq Institute, 1995. [Heb.]

Gaster, Moses. "The Sword of Moses." *JRAS* 28 (1896): 149–98. doi:10.1017/S0035869X00023455. Repr., pages 288–337 in vol. 1 and pages 69–103 in vol. 3 of *Studies and Texts in Folklore, Magic, Mediaeval Romance, Hebrew Apocrypha and Samaritan Archaeology*. 3 vols. London: Maggs Bros., 1925–1928. Repr., New York: Ktav, 1971.

Harari, Yuval. "Jewish Magic: Principles, Acts, Objectives." Pages 183–89 in *Khamsa Khamsa Khamsa: The Evolution of a Motif in Comtemporary Israeli Art*. Edited by Shirat-Miriam Shamir and Ido Noy. Jerusalem: Mayer Museum for Islamic Art, 2018.

———. *Jewish Magic before the Rise of Kabbalah*. Detroit: Wayne State University Press, 2017.

———. "Moses, the Sword and the *Sword of Moses*: Between Rabbinical and Magical Traditions." *JSQ* 12 (2005): 293–329. doi:10.1628/0944570057 83478315.

———. "*The Sword of Moses*: Genizah Fragments." *Ginzei Qedem—Genizah Research Annual* 10 (2014): 29–92. [Heb.]

———. "The Sword of Moses (*Ḥarba de-Moshe*): A New Translation and Introduction." *Magic, Ritual, and Witchcraft* 7 (2012): 58–98.

———. *The Sword of Moses: A New Edition and Study*. Jerusalem: Academon, 1997. [Heb.]

———. "Three Charms for Killing Adolf Hitler: Practical Kabbalah in WW2." *Aries* 18 (2017): 171–214. doi:10.1163/15700593-01702002.

Hopkins, Simon. *A Miscellany of Literary Pieces from the Cambridge Genizah Collections*. Cambridge University Library 3. Cambridge: Cambridge University Library, 1978.

Janowitz, Naomi. *The Poetics of Ascent: Theories of Language in a Rabbinic Ascent Text*. SUNY Series in Judaica. Albany: State University of New York Press, 1989.

Lesses, Rebecca M. *Ritual Practices to Gain Power: Angels, Incantations, and Revelation in Early Jewish Mysticism*. HTS 44. Harrisburg, PA: Trinity Press International, 1998.

Levene, Dan. *A Corpus of Magic Bowls: Incantation Texts in Jewish Aramaic from Late Antiquity*. London: Kegan Paul, 2003.

———. "Curse or Blessing, What's in the Magic Bowls?" *Parke Institute Pamphlet* 2. Southampton: University of Southampton, 2002.

Margalioth, Mordechai. *Sepher ha-Razim: A Newly Recovered Book of Magic from the Talmudic Period Collected from Geniza Fragments and Other Sources*. Jerusalem: Yediot Aharonot, 1966. [Heb.]

Morony, Michael G. "Magic and Society in Late Sasanian Iraq." Pages 83–107 in *Prayer, Magic, and the Stars in the Ancient and Late Antique World*. Edited by Scott Noegel, Joel Walker, and Brannon Wheeler. Magic in History. University Park: Pennsylvania State University Press, 2003.

Rebiger, Bill, and Peter Schäfer. *Sefer ha-Razim I und II; Das Buch der Geheimnisse I und*

II. Vol. 1: *Edition*. Vol. 2: *Einleitung, Übersetzung und Kommentar*. 2 vols. TSAJ 125, 132. Tübingen: Mohr Siebeck, 2009.

Rohrbacher-Sticker, Claudia. "From Sense to Nonsense, From Incantation Prayer to Magical Spell." *JSQ* 3 (1996): 24–46.

Saar, Ortal-Paz. "Success, Protection and Grace: Three Fragments of a Personalized Magical Handbook." *Ginzei Qedem* 3 (2007): 101*–35*.

Schäfer, Peter, Margarete Schlüter, and Hans George von Mutius. *Synopse zur Hekhalot-Literatur*. TSAJ 2. Tübingen: Mohr Siebeck, 1981.

Schäfer, Peter, and Shaul Shaked. *Magische Texte aus der Kairoer Geniza*. 3 vols. TSAJ 42, 64, 72. Tübingen: Mohr Siebeck, 1994–1999.

Schiffman, Lawrence H., and Michael D. Swartz. *Hebrew and Aramaic Incantation Texts from the Cairo Genizah: Selected Texts from Taylor-Schechter Box K1*. Semitic Texts and Studies 1. Sheffield: JSOT Press, 1992.

Schlüter, Margarete. "The Eulogy חכם הסתרים ואדון הרזים in Heikhalot Literature." *Jerusalem Studies in Jewish Thought* 6 (1987): 95–115.

Scholem, Gershom. "Havdalah de-Rabbi Aqiba: A Source of the Jewish Magical Tradition from the Geonic Period." *Tarbiz* 50 (1980/1981): 243–81. [Heb.]

Shaked, Shaul. "Magic Bowls and Incantation Texts: How to Get Rid of Demons and Pests." *Qadmoniot* 129 (2005): 2–13. [Heb.]

Shaked, Shaul, James N. Ford, and Siam Bhayro. *Aramaic Bowl Spells: Jewish Babylonian Aramaic Bowls*. Vol. 1. Magical and Religious Literature of Late Antiquity 1. Leiden: Brill, 2013.

Swartz, Michael D. *Scholastic Magic: Ritual and Revelation in Early Jewish Mysticism*. Princeton: Princeton University Press, 1996.

Tocci, Franco M. "Metatron, 'Arcidemonio' e Mytrt (Μιθρας?) nel *Pisra de-R. Hanina ben Dosa*." Pages 79–97 in *Incontro di Religioni in Asia tra il III e il X secolo d. C., Atti del Convegno Internazionale*. Edited by Lionello Lanciotti. Civiltà Veneziana, Studi 39. Firenze: Olschki, 1984.

Trachtenberg, Joshua. *Jewish Magic and Superstition: A Study in Folk Religion*. New York: Atheneum, 1970.

The Sword of Moses

[60]   In the name of the great and holy God

(There are) four angels who are appointed over the sword given from the mouth of 'H WH YH WH HYH, the Lord of the mysteries,[a] and who are appointed over the Torah, and they observe the depth of the mysteries of the lower and upper (realms). And these are their names: ŠQD ḤWZY, MRGYW'L, and HDRZYWLW, ṬWṬRYSY.

And above them there are five princes, holy and powerful, who ponder the mysteries of 'HY HY YHY in the world for seven hours a day. And (they) are appointed over a thousand thousands of myriads and a thousand chariots hastening to carry out the will of 'HY HY HYH, the Lord of lords and the honorable God. And these are their names: MHYHWGṢY, PḤDWTTGM, 'SQRYHW, ŠYTYNYḤWM, QTGNYPRY. And (concerning) every chariot over which they are appointed, the prince of each and every one of them marvels and declares: *Is there a figure to his troops?* And the least (angel) in these chariots[b] is a prince greater than all those four (above-mentioned) princes.

Job 25:3

And above them there are three (more) princes, chiefs of the host of 'H YWH WYW WYW, the Lord of all, who causes his eight palaces (*hekhalot*) to shake and be in commotion every day with tumult and quaking. And they have authority over all of his handiwork, and beneath them there are double those chariots. And the least in (these) chariots is a prince greater than all those (five) princes. And these are their names: 'SSHY, ŠṬRYS, HWYH,[c] SHWTGY'YH.

The prince and master who is (the) king, named 'HYW PSQTYH, who sits, and all the heavenly hosts kneel and bow down and prostrate themselves on the ground all together before him every day, after they are dismissed from prostrating themselves before NQṢ ŠL'H HW 'WHH, the Lord of all.

---

a. For this epithet, see the English section in, Margarete Schlüter, "The Eulogy חכם הסתרים ואדון הרזים in Heikhalot Literature," *Jerusalem Studies in Jewish Thought* 6 (1987): 95–115.

b. The original is written in the singular.

c. The name ŠṬRYSHWYH, which occurs later in the book, is erroneously divided.

I am deeply grateful to the late Prof. Shaul Shaked as well as to Dr. Geoffrey Herman and Dr. Mathew Morgenstern for their remarks and suggestions, which were of tremendous benefit for the final shape of this translation. I am also exceedingly indebted to Prof. Michael Sokoloff, for I can hardly imagine breaking my way through the third part of the treatise had it not been already studied by him for his *Dictionary of Jewish Babylonian Aramaic of the Talmudic and Geonic Periods* (Ramat Gan: Bar-Ilan University Press; Baltimore: Johns Hopkins University Press, 2002).

And when you adjure him he is bound by you and he binds for you <all those three princes and their chariots and> all those five princes and all the chariots that are under their authority and the four angels that are under them; for he, and all those princes have been ordered so, to be bound by Moses, son of Amram, to bind for him all the princes who are under their authority. And they may not tarry upon their adjuration or turn from it this way or the other, (but) should give all who adjure them power over this sword <and reveal to them> its mysteries and hidden secrets, its glory, might, and splendor. And they may not tarry because the decree of 'BDWHW HWH ṢL 'LYH 'L YH is issued upon them, saying: Do not impede any mortal [61] who will adjure you and do not treat him otherwise than what you were decreed with regard to my servant Moses, son of Amram, for he adjures you by my ineffable names and it is to my names that you render honor and not to him. But if you impede him I will burn you for you have not honored me.

Exod 6:20

Exod 6:20

And each and every one of them gave him (i.e., Moses) a word[a] by which the world is manipulated. The words were the words of the living God and the king of the world. And they said to him: If you wish to manipulate this sword and to hand it down to the generations which will come after you, one who prepares himself to manipulate it should sanctify himself (free) from nocturnal pollution and from (ritual) impurity for three days and should only eat and drink in the evening.[b] And he should (only) eat bread made by a pure man or by his own hands with clean salt and (only) drink water.[c] And no one should be aware that he is doing this deed for the purpose of manipulating this sword, because these are the secrets of the world and they must be carried out in secrecy, and they are (only) to be transmitted to humble people.

And on the first day of your seclusion, perform ablution(s) and you need not (do it) again. And pray three times a day[d] and after each prayer say this prayer: Blessed are you QWSYM our God, king of the world, the God who opens daily the gates of the east and cleaves the windows of the orient and gives light to the whole world and to those who dwell in it with the abundance of his mercies, with his mysteries and his secrets; and who taught his people, Israel, his mysteries and secrets and revealed to them a sword by which the world is manipulated, and said to them: When you come to use this sword, by which every desire is fulfilled, and every mystery and secret are revealed, and every miracle and marvel and wonder are performed, say such and such before me, and recite such and such before me, and adjure such and such before me. I shall immediately accede and be reconciled to you and will give you authority over this sword[e] to carry out every request with it. And the princes will accede to you and my holy ones will reconcile themselves to you and they will instantly

---

a. For this meaning of the Hebrew *davar* see Harari, "Moses," 321–27.
b. Lit. "and he should neither eat nor drink but from one evening to the other."
c. On purification and asceticism in the Sword of Moses, see Yuval Harari, *Sword of Moses*, 90–91.
d. Apparently the daily *'Amidah* prayer, which has to be recited three times a day. On the role of liturgical prayer in the magical practice of the Sword of Moses, see Harari, *Sword of Moses*, 92–101 and cf. below, §§77, 127.
e. Lit. "by this sword."

The Sword of Moses

fulfill your wish and deliver my mysteries to you and will reveal my secrets to you and will teach you my words and will make my wonders manifest to you. And they will abide by you and will serve you like a disciple before his master. And your eyes will be enlightened[a] and your heart will behold and perceive all that is hidden, and your stature will be increased. Unto[b] you I call SWQYM, king of the universe,[c] you are the one who is called YHWGH HW 'L YH king of the world; you are the one who is called P'ZWGH WH WW 'L YH merciful king; you are the one who is called ZHWT GYHH 'L YH gracious king; you are the one who is called ṢHBRWHW HWH 'L YH living king; you are the one who is called SPṬHWTHW 'L YH humble king; you are the one who is called QGYWHY HW HY 'L YH righteous king; [62] you are the one who is called ŠHRW SGHWRY 'L YH lofty king; you are the one who is called SPQS HPYHWHH 'L YH flawless king; you are the one who is called QTTHW GTHY 'L YH honest king; you are the one who is called PTRYS HZPYHW 'L YH mighty king; you are the one who is called R'PQ ṢYWYHYH 'L YH chosen king; you are the one who is called ḤWSH YHWHY 'L YH proud king; you are the one who is called WHW HW HY HY 'HYH WH YH YH WH YH WH YW HY HYW YH, you listen to my prayer for you are one who listens to prayer. And bind your servants, the princes of the sword, for me for you are their king, and fulfill for me my every wish since everything is in your hand, as it is said:

Ps 145:16 *You open your hand and satisfy every living being with favor.*

I adjure you 'ZLY'L who is called HWDY ZHY HW HWH, 'R'L who is called SQRYSYHYH, Ṭ'NY'L who is called 'TRṢ 'HYH YH, ṬP'L who is called GWPQY HWH 'HYH, and the mightiest of all: HLYKYH being YWPY'L, MYṬṬRWN who is called GHWDPṬHW HH YHH HDR MRWM, MRŠWT MLKY[d] YDY'L who is called SGHWH HYH, R'ŠY'L who is called MHWPTQYHH YY, ḤNY'L who is called RHW PGTYH, HNY'L who is called PHWṢPNYGYH, 'ŠR'L who is called THMWTYHYHYH, WYŠDY'L who is called QNYTY PṢYH, 'ŠH'L who is called YHWT NṬHY HYH, 'MWDY'L who is called RWPNYGYH WSSYH, W'ṢR'L who is called ŠHGNWTGYHH, to be bound to me and to subordinate the sword to me so that I may use it as I wish and receive shelter under our Lord[e] in heaven. In this honorable, great and awesome name HW HY HHY HW HH 'H WH YH YH HWY HW HY HW HWH YHW Y' HW HW YH YHW HY HW Y' YH WH HW Y' HW HWY HYW HW YH WH YH HW HWH YHY HW YH 'HYH MHWH, the twenty-four letters upon the crown, (I adjure you) to deliver to me by this sword the mysteries of the upper and lower (realms and) the secrets of the upper and lower (realms), and let my wish be fulfilled and my words obeyed and my request accepted. By means of the explicit uttering of the adjuration through this worthy name, the most honorable (name) in this world by which

---

a. Lit. "will shine."
b. This is the beginning of the formula that should be recited before God.
c. The Hebrew phrase may also be translated "the eternal king."
d. The legible Hebrew words: "glory of the height, from the domain of my king" seem to function as components of MYṬṬRWN's name.
e. Lit. "in the shadow of our Lord." Cf. Ps 91:1–2.

all the heavenly hosts[a] are bound and chained, which is HH HH HWH HHYY YWHH 'H WH NYH HWH PH WHW HYH ṢHW 'H WH HYH HH WH [63] YH WH YH SYH WH YH WYH blessed be he, (I adjure you) neither to tarry nor harm me, or cause me to tremble or be afraid. In the name of the name which is revered by your king and whose terror rests upon you, and who is called PRZMWTGYH SRḤWQTYH HYGNYTYH ṬRSNYHYH QRZMTHW ṢGYH YH WH HYH HW HY H' HWH HWH 'HH HHY 'H WH HWH HYH 'H WH YH YHH YHW YHY 'W HH 'H HH H' HYH 'H ZQRYDRYH accomplish for me that which I adjured you, and serve me as a master. For it is not by one greater than you that I adjure[b] you but by the Lord of all, by his name through which you and all the heavenly hosts are held, caught, tied up (and) chained. And if you tarry I will hand you over to the Lord, to the holy one blessed be he and to his ineffable name, whose anger and rage and wrath burn in him and who honors all his creation through one of its (i.e., the ineffable name's) letters, and who is called ZRWGDQNṬ' QṢWPṢḤTYH 'HWH SQTY GYH GYGYM HYGYH HW YH HNYH HWH QLṢG; so that if you tarry he will eradicate you and you will be sought after but not found.[c] And protect me from my impetuosity and from harming my body[d] in the name of ḤZQ'Y 'HYH WH YH HH YHH YH WH HH YH HYH 'HYW YH HYW YHY WHWY HY HWY YH QQHWH SQQHWH the guardian of Israel. Blessed are you SWQYM, sage of the secrets, divulger of the mysteries and the king of the world.

I heard a voice in the firmament, the voice of the master of the firmament who spoke[e] and said: I want a swift messenger who would <go> to man. (And) he said: And if my mission is carried out my sons will be exalted by my sword <that> I transmit to them for it is the foremost of all my mysteries and it became manifest[f] by the hand of wondrous[g] seers. *For so will my word be*, and it is said: *My word is like fire, says the Lord*, (thus) said PGNYNYNWGSYH God of heaven and earth. And I, me, 'SSY 'SS and 'SYSYH and 'PRGSYH, the swift messenger, good in (carrying out) my mission and hurried to perform my delegation ascended before him. And the Lord of all commanded me: Go and obey[h] people who are pious, good, decent, and righteous, and trustworthy, whose heart(s) are not divided and whose mouth(s) are free of duplicity, and who do not deceive with their tongues, and whose lips do not lie, whose hands do not grab [64] and whose eyes do not intimate, who do not hasten to evil, who are corporeally removed from every defilement, detached from every uncleanness, separated from any pungent (food), and who do not approach a woman. And

Isa 55:11
Jer 23:29

    a. The original is written in the singular.
    b. Lit. "adjured."
    c. Cf. Ezek 26:21.
    d. The Hebrew phrasing may also be translated "from the pain of my body."
    e. Cf. Harari, *Sword of Moses*, 145.
    f. It is also possible to read "and it arrived (at the world)."
    g. The Aramaic phrase may also indicate secret, invisible seers. See Marcus Jastrow, *A Dictionary of the Targumim, the Talmud Babli and Yerushalmi, and the Midrashic Literature* (London: Luzac, 1903), s.v. "*pryš*," 1228.
    h. Other possible readings are "be known to" or "be heard by."

The Sword of Moses

as the master of all commanded me, I, 'SSY 'SS and 'SYSYH and 'PRGSYH, the swift messenger, descended to earth. And when I was passing along I said (to myself): Who among human beings[a] possesses all these (virtues)? I shall go and rest upon him. And I searched my mind and thought to myself that there was no human being who could do something like this. I sought but I did not find and I did not stumble upon one. And the master of all imposed a vow upon me by his mighty right (hand)[b] and the glory of his splendor and a crown of glory[c] HWH WYH 'QN HY DRYH ṬHR QRWNNYH YH WH HH HHW HY YH D', a vow of his mighty right (hand). And the master of all imposed a vow upon me and put me under an oath and I did not fall down. Then, I, 'SSY 'SS and 'SYSYH and 'PRGSYH, stood up to be strengthened in the covenant of the will of N, son of N in the name of QMBGL 'QMH WH ZRWMTYH YHY KRWQ ZNWTYH YRPHW ḤTYH QṢY WṢYḤṢ YHṢ YHṢ.

This is the great and honorable name that was given to the son of man[d] YH BYH 'Ṣ 'H B'H HWY HW HW WH Y' HW ZH WH WH 'H YH YHW HH YHW YHW 'QP HY HH YY'H HH H'H HW'H HHWH HYY HW HW HY holy mighty mighty selah. Recite it after your prayer.[e] And these are the names of the angels that serve the son of man: MYṬṬRWN, SGDDTṢYH and MQṬṬRWN, SNGWTYQT'L, and NGYQTG'L, and YGW'TQTY'L, and 'NTGQS'L, and 'NTWSSTY'L, and MYK'L SRWG, and GBRY'L ŠQTKNYH, and HDQRWNTY'L, and 'NHSG'L, YHW'L, TYZRT, NSY'L, and SYGSṬH'L, and 'NPY, QQPY'L, and NHR, GSGNHY'L, and YKNY, 'TYH'L, and 'QTQLYQ'L, YNH, GYTNY'L YH. In the same manner you shall serve me, N, son of N, and receive my prayer and my request which I desire and introduce it to the presence of YHWH HH SHH 'HH HH WH WH, the holy one, blessed be he, in whose name I adjure (you) and impose a vow upon you, like a bird who gets into the nest. And mention my merit before him and through words of supplication grant atonement for my sins at this very moment and do not tarry, in the name of SH HH WH WYH YH WYH WH WH WYHH WYH 'H HHWY 'HW Y' HY HY HW HW YHW HH HWH YH WH blessed be he Sabaoth Sabaoth selah, may his servants sanctify him and sweetly adore him[f] and say *holy holy holy* is the Lord of this holy name, *whose glory fills the whole world*. And do not impede,[g] in (the power of) the decree of HW HYH YH HW YY YHW HY HY [65] HWH HY HW HH HHYH HY HWH HYH HWYH YHW HHW HH HHWY YHW 'HW HH YH 'HH 'YH 'Y 'H 'Y 'H WH YH who lives eternally.

Isa 6:3

And in the name of DYṬYMYN QYRWY'S WHW 'RQM GNLY'WS QWSMWS QLYQS 'SQLYṬTR' 'YLY 'LY MWPY SPR' SṬGD'GS ṬL'SY QṬM

    a. The translation offers a correction of illegible Aramaic phrasing.
    b. Lit. "by the right side of his might."
    c. The letters *hwd* can be read either as "glory" or as the first name in the sequence that follows.
    d. The Hebrew-Aramaic idiom *bar adam* is peculiar and rare. It might also refer to a certain figure known by this appellation.
    e. Apparently the daily *'Amidah* prayer. Cf. above, p.337 n. d.
    f. The genizah fragment JTSJ ENA NS 2.11, p. 43 reads here "and humble (ones) adore him."
    g. The Aramaic phrase also bears the meaning "and do not tarry."

The Sword of Moses

'NT PRGW PYGH DYHY MYTQ'S NPL' (= "wonderful") TṬ' DWNYṬ' TTMN'S ṬWP DWGZ MṬYG' MHW WHWṬR ZYQQTYHW 'HWNY YHW YH 'L ḤYNQYH PPṬY HY'S SPṢPNṬR;[a] and in the name of SMRT SMS PṢṢ 'DWNWḤT HWSYH 'LYWN (= "supreme") YH HW'Y 'W HYH PY PY 'YTYH WBṢRS MṢRPYH TSQYHW BŠTQṢR the great, from whom nothing is hidden, who sees and is not seen; and in the name of ṬYRQṬTYH who is dominant over heaven (and) who is called YHW YHW WH YH YH 'H 'YW WH NYHW HYH HY HY YHY WHY HWH YHW HYH HYH WH HWH HH WYH YYH WHY HY YHW HY the great and exalted name, which the king of the world speaks out of his mouth in another manner: YHW 'H YH WHHH YH WH YH YHW HH YH HW HWW HY HY HH HY HW HW' HW HYH HWYH YH WH YH WH YH YH HY HY HY 'HH 'HY HW HH YH YHY HW HWH YHW HW HH YYHW HH YYW; (in these names I adjure) you, the swift messenger: Do not tarry and (do not) tremble, and come and carry out for me, I, N, son of N, all my needs, in the name of YHW HHYW YHW 'HYW HHW HW HYH HHY HWH YH WH HHY YH HW HYW HYH WHWṬR QTNGYH ZW QWSSYH 'HWNYH 'L (= "God") HY NQTS'L YH HWH NYGGHH PSQTRH HY HWH YH ZRWMTH HYH WBR ŠṬH HY HHYH the great, who sees and is not seen; 'HWH, the sense of which was revealed to all the heavenly hosts, and by the sense of which I adjure you for thus it was transmitted to Moses, son of Amram, from the mouth of the master of all YHWH WH'H HWH YHWH HYH HW HHNYHH YH HY HY HW HH YHWH SH HH WHYH WHH HWH YH YH YHY LNHH YH YH 'H TBYNW 'YH YHWŠ 'HYŠH W'GRYPṬ YHW ṢB'WT YHWH YHWH ṢB'WT is his name. Blessed are you God, Lord of the mighty (and) master of the mysteries.[b]

Exod 6:20

And which are (the) letters that ŠQD ḤWZY gave him (i.e., Moses)?—he said to him: If you wish to become wise and to use this sword, call me and adjure me and strengthen me and fortify me and say: I adjure you ŠQD ḤWZY in a great, holy and marvelous, pure and precious, mighty and awe-inspiring mystery, and this is its name: YRWNYQ' 'QPTH HNH NHH YRK YDKYRWHW YH YH ṢYQ'Ṣ. By these letters[c] I adjure you[d] to surrender to me and to make me wise and to bind for me the angels who subjugate the sword in the name of the revealer of the mysteries. Amen.

Write with ink on leather and carry them (i.e., the letters of adjuration) with you (during the) three [66] days while you purify yourself and say the following adjuration before your prayer and after your prayer:[e] MARGYY'L—(these letters) were given to him (i.e., Moses):[f] HY HW HYH WHY HWH YHW YHWH

---

a. For this formula, transliterated in part from the original Greek, see Rohrbacher-Sticker, "From Sense to Nonsense," 33–46.
b. Cf. above, p. 336 n. a.
c. The given "by these signs" is in all probability an error.
d. Lit. "I adjured you."
e. Cf. above, p. 337 n. c.
f. A newly discovered Geniza fragment of the Sword of Moses (Cambridge University Library, T-S A45.23) led me to reinterpret the following obscure paragraph. The translation suggested hereby differs from my previous one. See Harari, "Genizah Fragments," 54–57 [Heb.].

The Sword of Moses

HW HYH HW HWYH WHW HHYHW YWH HHWNYH HY 'W HYH WH WH WH YH WH YHWH YHWH YHWH YHW YHW YHW GNYNYH WHH; ṬRWṬRWSY—(these letters) were given to him:[a] 'HW HWH 'HY HWH 'HWYH YH' HWH YH YH HWH HWD' 'H WHH HY HWH W'HYH HWYH 'HH WYH WH HY 'HYH YHYH YWH HY 'H 'H YH 'HH WYHWH HYH 'HY HYH YHYH 'H HYH 'YH; HDRWYZLW—(these letters) were given to him: HHW' HH YH YH 'W HYW HH' YHWH 'H HH 'WY HH'H WYH 'HYH 'WH' HYH WYH HH YH HWH' HYH HH WH YHH WHHYH HWHY HWHH WYHH; MHYHWGṢYY—(these letters) were given to him: YHH HHY WHH WYHH HHY YHH HH WHWH HWH 'HYH YHW HH WH YH HYH YH H' HWH YHW YH H' HWY H' YH 'H HW YYH HWY HH HH WH 'H WH 'HYH YH YHWH HW HWH HY HWH; PḤDWTTGM— (these letters) were given to him: H' HYH YHW YH H' HWY H' WH 'H HY WH WWH HYW HH YH WYH YHW YH HWYYH HWYH "H HYWRH HYW H' WHHWH H'HNYHH; 'SQRYHW —(these letters) were given to him: B'H BHYN 'SWNYHH ŠMGYHH HWY YHH YH HW WHWYH HWY HY WH HY YWH HW HWH YHY HW YHY HYWHY HHWH HHYH HHYWY WYWHH WYHH 'L HYH 'H HYH H'H 'H HY 'HWY 'HWYH; ŠYTYNYḤWM—(these letters) were given to him: 'H 'H WYH H'L WH HYH 'L HHY WHH'L HYHY'L 'LHYH HYH 'HWY WYH 'HHW YH WHY HYH 'H H' HYH 'L HHW'L HHY 'H' QMM'H HL'L; QTGNYPYY—(these letters) were given to him: H' HW' W'H 'LH' SMH 'H 'LH' SY'H WHH 'H YHH 'WHH 'HH' WMYṢHW HYH MYTYH "LDHWY WYH HW HW 'L LYH HW HY WH'Y WH'W YH H' HW WHY WHY WYH 'HH HWH HYW YH YHH YH HY HYH YH WYH WH 'H 'Š 'HY ŠYH; 'SQWHHYY—(these letters) were given to him: 'HW YH YHY ŠYH YHZYH YHW YHH 'H WH 'HWH 'HYH 'HW YH YH YHH ŠNY HWH MKNWSYHH YH HWH HWY H' MSKPNHYH [67] YH HY'; SṬRYSHWYH—(these letters) were given to him: HWY H' DYYH' 'HYŠ HWH SQQ HWH HYH 'HY HWH QNQSHYH HWH YHH YHD 'H 'H WHYH 'H YH WHYH WD HYH YHW HH YHW HYH HWH YHHYHWH HYH YH; SHWTG'YH—(these letters) were given to him: YH HY??? Y??YHW YW HYWY YHH WH HHW YYHH HH HH HY HHWH YYH HYW 'H YH' HH 'LHW HYH QHYH WYWHH 'YWY HY HH STYHW HH YY HWH YHW HY YHWH YHW HYHY YHWHYH YW YH YH HWH YHWH HH HYH YH WYH HYH YHW YHW HY HW; 'HPSQTYH—(these letters) were given to him: HW LYH HYH HHWH 'H WH HHYHYHW HWH WH 'HW HYH YHW HW DYH YH 'HH WHH YH WH WHH HY HWH WHYH WH HYH ZHYH WHW HYHYH HWH 'H HY 'W HH 'HYHH YHH WY WYH YH WHY HW HY HWH.

And they (i.e., the thirteen angels) did not hide from him (i.e., Moses) any word[b] and letter of these ineffable names and they did not give him a substitute for even one of their letters, for thus were they com-

a. Corrected from "to me." This is also the case regarding all the following angels, except ŠYTYNYḤWM.

b. The primary meaning of the Hebrew phrase is "anything." However, another possible meaning of *davar*, "a word" (cf. above, p. 337 n. a.), as well as the occurrence of "letters" immediately following, imply the reading "any word."

The Sword of Moses

manded by the Lord of the secrets[a] to transmit to him this sword and these names, which are the secrets of the sword. And they said to him: Command the generations that will follow you to recite this one blessing before praying,[b] so that they will not be swept away by fire: Blessed be 'YZW' 'YZWNS who accompanied Moses; may he accompany me, whose name is 'HWṢWṢYH RP'WZTYH RPW'TZYH ZHWGYHYH HQṢṢYH 'NTWTYHWH GDWDYHWH WYNY'ṬṬWQTZYH PṢ'PY PY 'ZYH ṬHRWGSGYH ŠDYH QTṢYH RHWMY HWH TGPMṢYH 'HYWPSQTYH TYŠMṢYHYH MṢHWGTHYH 'BHYTYZYH QPHWHY RPṬGWT RPRPṬR YMRṬRYH QBRSYH NKD QTSNYH MRP'YRYH GNṬSRD HWH DYD'RR'H QDYDHH QGYṢHH WDYN'WṢYH 'PSWNYH 'Y PY LY M'SSWN PRQWMYH 'Y PY QWḤZYH 'YRWNYH 'YPRWNSYH 'PSY?W'H 'HYH 'H DY; send me 'ḤRY'WSSHW YHW QTSHHYH who makes the cherubim move and may they help me. Blessed are you QWSYM (who rules) over the sword.

Whoever wishes to manipulate this sword should recite his (daily) prayer and upon reaching *Shome'a Tefila*[c] he should say: I adjure you the four princes ŠQDḤWZY, MRGYY'L and ṬRWṬRWSY and HDRWYZLW, servants of HDYRYRWN [68] YHWH HRYRYRWN HWHY HDYH DYHYRWN HWH, to accept my adjuration (even) before I pray and my supplication (even) before I entreat, and to fulfill for me everything I desire through this sword just as you did for Moses, in a mighty and glorious, miraculous name, which is HW HYH HWH SPR HWH HYH YHWH WH YH WHW YWHH 'HWSHH YHH QQS HWH. And he should (then) call the five (princes) who are above them and say: I adjure you MHYHWGṢYY PḤDWTTGM 'SQRYHW ŠYTYNYḤWM QTGNYPYY HDWDY WHWH YD GBRY'L YH HW HDYRYRWN to accept my adjuration (even) before I adjure you and to be bound by me and to bind for me these four princes and all the encampments of the chariots of the princes over whom you are appointed, to fulfill for me my desire through this sword by this beloved name: 'HY HWH YH WH 'Y 'W HHY HWHY ŠHWSHH YWH HW HWW YH YHH YWH HYY. And he should call the three (princes) who are above them and say: I adjure you 'SQWHHY ŠṬRYS HWYH SHWTGY'YH, the beloved ones of[d] ZRHWDRYN who is HDYRYRWN, to be bound by me and to bind for me MHYHWGṢYY PḤDWTTGM 'SQRYHW ŠYTYNYḤWM QTGNYPYY ŠQD ḤWZY MRGYY'L HDRWYZLW who are under your authority, to fulfill for me my desire through this sword by this unique name: HH HWH HWY ŠQṢD HŠH HY 'W HW HH YHH PTṬGHW HH YH YHW HW HYY WHY YHNYH WNHHYH MTGMHWH HYQHH WHY H' ṢR MQWQṢṢYH HYH WHY HH TS HWW HYH YHW HY HYH

---

a. The given "Lord of the hidden" is apparently a mistake for "Lord of the secrets." Cf. above, p. 336 n. a.

b. The original is written in the singular.

c. *Shome'a Tefila* ("You who hearken unto prayer") is the sixteenth benediction (out of nineteen) in the daily *'Amidah* prayer (cf. above, p. 337 n. d.). See also the reference to *Ḥonen ha-Da'at* ("You who grants wisdom," the fourth benediction) in §127 below.

d. The appellation "the beloved ones of" (written in one word in Hebrew) is marked as a name in the manuscript by the placement of a typical sign above it, apparently by mistake.

WYH TYH ZYH THWHY. And he should hold the head prince of them all and say: I adjure you 'HYWPSQTYH strong and powerful, the head of all the heavenly hosts, to be bound by me, you, yourself, and not your messengers, and to bind for me these princes who are with you, to fulfill for me my desire through this sword by a name that is irreplaceable:[a] YHWWH 'HH HWH HHY HH 'YH HYH HW HWH YHWHY HW HY WHYH WHH 'HWHY HHY 'H WHWHY YH WH 'H WH 'H YW HY HW HY HYH HH WH YHW HWY HWY HHWH YHW YHW, for you are beloved and he (i.e., the Lord) is beloved and I, too, am from the seed [69] of Abraham who is called beloved.[b] Blessed are you YHWH king of the mysteries and Lord of the secrets, who hearkens unto prayer.

And he should not touch or use this sword until he has carried out these things; and afterward he may perform everything that he desires according to that which is written (i.e., in the last part of the treatise), each matter according to its proper order.

And this is the sword:[c] TWBR TSBR 'KN ṬṬH MYṬS. . . . Thus, in the names and appellations of you all, you who are powerful everywhere, there is none like you, hurry, and make haste and bring me 'SSY 'SS W'SSYS W'PRGSYH YRWNYQ' YRK YRṢ YHṢ YQṢ so he may fulfill for me my every desire in the name of Y'W YHWHH YH HYH 'WZRWS 'WZWRWS SWMRT' . . .

[70–74] . . .[d]

Holy angels, superior to all the hosts of HWHY HWYH HYWHH WHH YH 'H YHH, who arise from the throne that is set for them before him, in order to be bound to those who subjugate the sword (and) to fulfill for them their desire. In the name of the master of all the holy ones who are the heads of all the angels, creator of the world QLTYR' 'LY 'LY MPY MQRNS the one who seals the earth and the height(s), creator of human beings, his servants, DHW HWH 'H WH YH WH HH superior, God, through whom (i.e., the angels)[e] I am visible in the world, QLWTMY MQR'M ṢPHWYY ŠŠNWHYY, you, (the angels) who are superior [75] to me everywhere, the master of all requires[f] of you to carry out for me the thing that I desire, for you can accomplish every desire in heaven and on earth, in the name of YHW HY HWHY HWH 'HW WHY YH HH WH HHY YWHY HY 'HY HY HWH YHW HWH YHW HW YYH YHW YHW HH HHH YHW HWHH YHY HW HWH HW'H

---

a. The Hebrew phrase can also mean "by a priceless name."

b. Cf. Midrash Sifre on Deuteronomy 352. See Reuven Hammer, trans., *Sifre: A Tannaitic Commentary on the Book of Deuteronomy*, YJS 24 (New Haven: Yale University Press, 1986), 364–68; and the parallels indicated in Harari, *Sword of Moses*, 88 n. 31.

c. Most of the sword of words is a huge collection of *nomina barbara*, which will not be transliterated here. Only two sections of the sword that are intelligible, one at the beginning and the other one at the end, will be translated. See further the discussion on the structure of the sword and the clusters of "names" it comprises in Harari, *Sword of Moses*, 115–21.

d. Here follows an extensive sequence of *nomina barbara*, which comprises most of the sword.

e. On a contextual level, the Aramaic plural "through whom" is peculiar. However, grammatically it makes sense as referring to the angels.

f. The Aramaic "I desire" is erroneous.

The Sword of Moses

HWWH YH HW HW WD HHW YWHYH HH YWHY HWH 'HYH 'HW HWH YWHW HY HHW 'HY 'HH HWH HW HHY HH YH HH WH HH WYH HH 'WHH HHYHH HH HH HHW YHH YH HY HHY HHY HHWH HHY HWH 'HH YHW 'L 'L YHW, as it is written in the Scripture: *I am the Lord, this is my name* .[a]

Isa 42:8

[1] If at a full moon[b] you wish[c] to seize and to bind a man and a woman so that they will be with each other, and to annul spirits and blast-demons and satans, and to bind a boat, and to free a man from prison, and for every thing, write on a red plate from TWBR TSBR until H' BŠMHT.[d] [2] And if you wish to destroy high mountains[e] and to pass (in safety) through the sea and the land, and to go down into fire and come up,[f] and to remove kings, and to cause an optical illusion, and to stop up a mouth, and to converse with the dead, and to kill the living, and to bring down and raise up and adjure angels to abide by you, and to learn all the secrets of the world, write on a silver plate, and put in it a root of artemisia, from TWBR TSBR until H' BŠMHT. [3] For a spirit that moves in the body, write on *magzab*[g] from TWBR until MNGYNWN. [4] For a spirit that causes inflammation, write from MGNYNWN until HYDRST'. [5] For a spirit in the whole body, write from HYDRST' until H' BŠMHT. [6] For a demon, write from H' BŠMHT until Y'WYHW. [7] For (a spirit of) terror,[h] write from Y'W YHYW until YY YY YY. [8] For diphtheria(?),[i] say over rose oil from YY YY YY until 'WNTW and he should drink (it).[j] [9] For an (ear?) ache,[k] recite[l] in his ear on the painful side from 'WNTW until HWTMY'S. [10] For any kind of eye pain, say over water for three days in the morning from HWTMY'S until MSWLS and he should wash his eyes with it. [11] For a cataract, say over sesame oil from MSWLS until PSMY and he should rub (his eye with it) for seven mornings. [12] For grit (in the eye), say over powdered *kohl*[m] pertaining to his name from

---

a. Isaiah's words may also be phrased "Me, YHWH is my name."

b. The words "in full moon" are apparently interpolated here by mistake.

c. The original is written in the 3rd sg.

d. This is the way that the author indicates the precise section of the sword to be recited in each and every recipe.

e. Cf. Sokoloff, *Dictionary*, s.v. "*pgr*'," 887.

f. Cf. §113.

g. Both the etymology and meaning of the Aramaic *magzab* are unclear. It is an object large enough to write upon and small enough to be carried on the body (as attested in §95; cf. §35).

h. For this spirit see also Joseph Naveh and Shaul Shaked, *Amulets and Magic Bowls*, 2nd ed. (Jerusalem: Magnes, 1987), B1:3 with the note on p. 127. Cf. Naveh and Shaked, *Amulets*, B13:13; and see Sokoloff, *Dictionary*, s.v. "*srwdt*'," 830.

i. The Aramaic *askarta* apparently denotes a throat disease that involves choking. See Sokoloff, *Dictionary*, s.v. "*škrt*'," 149; Jastrow, *Dictionary*, s.v. "*škr*'," 94.

j. Lit. "place it in his mouth."

k. The location of this recipe among those that relate to head problems as well as its suggested treatment implies that it deals with an earache. However, the original Aramaic might also be a slight miswriting of the word "tooth" and thus meaning "For a tooth(ache)."

l. The Aramaic verb also bears the meaning "to whisper." Both meanings, however, denote the pronunciation of a charm.

m. *Kohl* is a blue powder used for painting the eyelids.

PSMY until SYṬWN and he should apply (it) for three mornings. [13]For blood that runs from the head, recite over his head from SYṬWN until QWRY for three mornings on which you wash your hands before you get out of your bed. [76] [14]For *Palga* spirit,[a] say seven times over a vessel full of water and seven times over sesame oil from QWRY until HYMY <I adjure you *Palga* spirit . . .> to be removed and to get out of N, son of N. Amen amen selah. And pour (the water from) that bucket over his head and rub him with that oil. Do that to him (three times in the course of) three days and write for him in an amulet from "I adjure you" until "Amen amen selah"[b] and hang (it) on him. [15]For hemicrania (spirit) and for a spirit that cuts the (skull?) bone,[c] write from HYMY until ŠDY and hang (it) on him. [16]For a spirit that blocks up(?) the bone, write from ŠDY until 'HYH and hang (it) on him. [17]For an earache, say in his left ear from ŠDY until 'HYH backward. [18]For deafness, say over intestines of *shelifuta* while it is cooked in *ydy* oil from 'HYH until RWS and place it in his ear when it has dissolved slightly. [19]For a boil and *sifta*[d] and *shimta* and an infected pustule and *rigsha* and a man's member that is tied (impotence) and *ḥazozita*, and for wet or dry *ḥafofiata* and sore spots that occur on a person, say over olive oil from RWS until SŠTWMTY'L and rub it with your left hand. [20]For jaundice, say over water in which pellitory are boiled from SŠTWMTY'L until YY'ZNY' and he should drink (it). [21]For pain in a nostril and for a nostril spirit, recite over *ydy* oil from YY'ZNY' until YYHQLTYH and pour it into his nostril. [22]For pain in the stomach and for pain in the intestines, say over water from YYHQLTYH until YYSWSWGYH and he should drink (it). [23]For scabs, say over water in which oleander <leaves> are boiled from YYSWSWGYH until YYQRMTYH and he should bathe in it. [24]For *hazorta* and *tarsana* and (problems concerning) the testicles, say from YYQRMTYH until HWTMZ. Say (it) once over them and once over olive oil and rub him for three days (with the oil) and do not let any water come near them. [25]For (a person who was hurt by) an evil sorcerer, say from HWTMZ until GYPRY' over seven unglazed jugs filled[e] with water from the river and pour (it) over his head. [26]For (the case of drinking) uncovered (liquids?),[f] spit spittle into his mouth and say over his mouth or over a cup of *shekhar*[g] from GYPRY' until HLYWHW and he should drink (it) and see what comes out of his mouth. [27]For a person bitten by a snake or any reptile[h] that causes damage, say over the place of his wound or over vinegar from HLYWHW until 'M'WS and he should drink (it). And

---

a. For *Palga* spirit, see b. Pesaḥ. 111b. The name *Palga* derives from the word "to split." Thus, the harm caused by this spirit may be identified with a migraine or cerebrovascular accident paralysis.

b. I.e., the recited formula. Cf. Harari, *Sword of Moses*, 37 nn. 155 and 156.

c. The placement of this recipe, which probably refers to bones problem, may imply that pain of the skull is concerned.

d. This word as well as all the other undecipherable terms in this section apparently denotes some kind of skin disease.

e. The original word is a scribal mistake.

f. The original Aramaic is uncertain.

g. The Aramaic word denotes an alcoholic beverage other than wine.

h. Cf. Sokoloff, *Dictionary*, s.v. "*ryḥš*," 1076.

also against any reptiles and distress charms[a] this charm, from HLYWHW until 'M'WS, (is beneficial). [28]For a woman who sees (menstrual) blood not at the proper time, say over the shell of an ostrich egg from 'M'WS until Y'WS and roast (it) in the oven and tie [77] (it) on her.[b] [29]For every pain in the mouth, say over flour when it is purified[c] from Y'WS until RTBN and he should adhere (it) in his mouth. [30]For *shukhta* and *ashḥata*,[d] say over wine from RTBN until SSṬN and he should drink (it). [31]For (an aching) sciatic nerve, write on a leather sheet from SSṬN to YKṢRṢ and also recite (it) over olive oil and he should rub that amulet with that olive (oil). And also smear his aching thigh (with the oil) and hang that amulet on him. [32]For strangury (i.e., retention of urine), say over a cup of wine from YKṢRS until TPSMT and he should drink (it). [33]For hemorrhoids, take a flock (of wool)[e] and put salt in it and dip it in oil and say over it from TPSMT until YGLWN' and he should carry (it) on him. [34]For a person who has swelling and also (for) one who has gonorrhea,[f] say over water in which pellitory are boiled from YGLWN' until 'HRWNY' and he should drink (it). [35]For *nishma*,[g] you may write on *magzab* from 'HRWNYY' until 'PNGYKYS and he should put it upon the place of the *nishma*. Everything that is like that will be cured. [36]Or you may take a rope(?)[h] made of wool and dip it in *ydy*[i] oil and say over it from 'HRYNYS until 'PNGYKYS and he should put it on the place of the *nishma*. [37]For heavy blows[j] and for a wound caused by an iron knife and any wound that it should not inflame, say over white naphtha from 'PNGYKYS until QYS' and he should rub (it) on the place of his wound. [38]For cough and stomach ache, say over the choicest *ydy* fat from QYS' until 'TQS and he should drink (it). [39]For a (diseased) gall bladder and excrement (problems), say over water in which grapes are boiled from 'TQS until 'LYHW and he should drink (it). [40]For the liver of a sick person, say over *shatita*[k] made of water lentils from 'LYHW until 'TNWHY and he should take (it) and sleep a little. [41]For a (diseased) spleen, say <over> a large cup of wine from 'TNWHY until MYBN'S and he should drink (it). And do that for him for three days. [42]For a spirit that dwells in a woman's womb, say over camphor oil[l] from MYBN'S until TWSY and put it on her with a flock of

---

a. I.e., charms for sending reptiles to cause injury to someone or for causing him distress.

b. Lit. "on him."

c. The original is miswritten. Cf. Sokoloff, *Dictionary*, s.v. *nšyp*," 779.

d. Both words denote ailments. While the former apparently indicates some kind of skin disease or pus exuding from an infection, the latter is uncertain.

e. See below, §42.

f. The Aramaic is difficult. It seems to indicate a genital disease.

g. The exact meaning of this word, which occurs in three different forms in this book, is uncertain.

h. The uncertain Aramaic is apparently a mistake.

i. For *ydy* "oil" (or "fat"), see further §§18, 21, 38, 86.

j. Lit. "for destruction."

k. *Shatita* was a certain kind of porridge made of ground grains or dried fruits. See Sokoloff, *Dictionary*, s.v. "*štyt*," 1185.

l. Cf. Sokoloff, *Dictionary*, s.v. "*kpwr*," 594. See also, however, Jastrow, who suggests "oil of pitch" (Jastrow, *Dictionary*, s.v. "*kwpr*," 624).

wool. [43]For a woman that miscarries, say over a cup of wine or over *shekhar*[a] or water from TWSY until ŠQBS and she should drink[b] (it) for seven days. And even if she sees blood, say (it) over a cup of wine and she should drink (it) and her fetus will live. [44]For a man whose hair does not grow, say over nut oil from ŠQBS until SLGY and he should smear (it). [45]To adjure a (heavenly) prince, write on a laurel leaf: I adjure you, the prince whose name is 'BRKSS[a] in the name of SLGYY until YGṬWS, to <hasten?> and come to me and to reveal to me [78] everything I need (to know) from you and do not tarry. And the one bound by you will descend and reveal himself to you. [46]To remove a magistrate from his prominent position, say over dust from an ant hill from YGṬWS until QTNQ and throw it toward him. [47]To cure a sore, take him (i.e., the patient) to the riverbank and say over him: I adjure you sore in the name of QTNQ until NT'LSS to depart and be annulled and pass from N, son of N. Amen amen sela. And he should go down and immerse himself seven times in the river and when he comes up write him (in) an amulet from "I adjure you" until "sela,"[d] and hang (it) on him. [48]For *burdes*(?),[e] write on a red copper plate from NT'LSS until MYBN'S and hang (it) on him. [48a][f]And if <you wish> no rain to fall[g] on your roof, write from MYBN'S until 'S'. [49]And if you wish to see the sun, take a *dby* stone[h] and a web of a male date palm and stand opposite the sun and take(?)[i] a stone called *atrophinon* and thorns of the bramble[j] and say from 'S' until H'HWN and you shall see him as a man dressed in white and he will answer you whatever you ask him, and he will even make a woman follow you. [50]A person who wishes to descend into a fiery furnace should write on a silver plate from H'TWN[k] until B'TYR and he should hang (it) on his thigh and descend. [51]And if you see a king or a ruler and you wish him to follow you,[l] take a *sora*-vessel of water and put in it a root of artemisia and a root of purslane and a root of *artakles* and say over it from B'TYR until 'HSWTY and place (it) on coals of fire in an unglazed clay (vessel) and put on it olive leaves, and everyone upon whom you decree will come to you, and even if it concerns a woman. [52]And if you wish to reverse them, take spring water

a. Cf. §26.

b. The original is written in the masculine (here as well as in the following sentence).

a. For *abraxas/abrasax* see William M. Brashear, "The Greek Magical Papyri: An Introduction and Survey; Annotated Bibliography (1928–1994)," *ANRW* 18.5:3577, doi:10.1515/9783110875720-013.

d. I.e., the spoken spell mentioned above.

e. The meaning of the Aramaic is uncertain.

f. This prescription was skipped while enumerating the recipes in the manuscript (apparently for the preparation of the index). It is identified here as 48a in order to keep in line with the original numbering.

g. The Aramaic is erroneous.

h. The Aramaic is miswritten both here and in the next occurrence of the word. The translation is based on the close parallel in Harari, *Sword of Moses*, 140, §144.

i. The original "and say" is syntactically impossible. It seems that the occurrence of the abbreviation for the Hebrew "and say" in the next line misled the scribe.

j. On the use of the bramble (*'wrdyn', wrdyn'*) in magical activity, see b. Šabb. 67a with Bohak, *Ancient Jewish Magi*, 411–14.

k. The correct form is H'HWN.

l. The meaning of the following is apparently the fulfillment of one's request.

and say over it from 'HSWTY until 'PWNY and cast (it) toward them. [53]For everything (i.e., any charm) you wish to untie, say over water from 'PWNY until 'GTŠ[a] and cast (it) over him (i.e., the bewitched person) and also write (the formula) in an amulet and hang (it) on him. And also (you can use it) to release a man from prison. [54]To catch fish, take unglazed sherds[b] and place olive leaves upon them and say over them from 'NTŠ {and place} until 'TQNZ and place (them) at the riverbank. [55]To make a woman follow you, take some blood of yours and write her name[c] on a new lamp when she comes and say toward her from 'TQNZ until 'TWMY. [56]To make a man follow you, take a new sherd and dip (it) in black myrrh and say over it pertaining to his name from 'TWMY until PNKYR and go and depart and do not look backward. [57]For trees that do not produce fruit, write on a new sherd from PNKYR until BRY and bury it among the roots of the trees[d] that [79] do not have[e] (fruits) and water all those trees. And do the same (also) for a date palm that does not produce fruit. [58]For white rot[f] that afflicts fruit, write on a new sherd from BRY until BRTY' and bury (it) in the water canal (cistern?)[g] on that plot of land. And also say <these words> over water and ash and salt and water the earth. [59]For a *merubya* spirit,[h] write on a plate of tin from BRTY' until 'WZWRWWS. And also recite (it) in his ear seven times and spit while you recite. And also say (it) over a jug of water seventy times and let him drink of it. [60]For a person bitten by a rabid dog, write on the hide of a donkey that has been peeled from its carcass from 'WZWRWWS until 'NSTRHWN. And remove his clothes and say (it) over sesame oil and let him rub (it) all over his body and let him put on different clothes, and hang that hide on him. [61]For fever or sons of fever,[i] write on the membrane of the brain of a ram or a buck from N'STRHWN until M'DMWG and hang (it) on him. [62]For someone who is walking on the way and gets lost, he should say over the four corners of his *uzar*[j] from S'DMWG <until> 'QWTG and it (i.e., the way) becomes straight.[k] [63]If you wish to borrow something from someone, say over lily oil or over *aqusa* oil or over *suta* oil from Q'WTG until 'LYHWS. [64]One more,[l] if you wish a woman to follow

a. The correct form is 'NTŠ. Cf. the next recipe and the lists of names in Harari, *Sword of Moses*, 33.
b. The original is written in the singular. The preposition occurs twice in the plural ("on them").
c. The original is written in the masculine. Further masculine forms in the recipe ("he comes," "toward him") are also translated in the feminine.
d. The original is written in the singular. The following preposition is in the plural.
e. The original seems to be an awkward Hebrew-Aramaic phrase.
f. The Aramaic term indicates a fruit disease being compared to the whiteness of milk.
g. The Aramaic term apparently relates to the irrigation system.
h. *Merubya* seems to correlate with *meruba*, *merubin* that occur in the incantation bowls as names of a certain kind of evil spirit. See Sokoloff, *Dictionary*, s.v. "*mrwb*", 705.
i. Fever and sons of fever are perceived as evil personae that cause the disease. The "sons of fever" were probably those that caused a less severe fever.
j. The meaning of the original is uncertain. Gaster's suggestion, "belt," which reads a Hebrew word with an Aramaic suffix, seems implausible.
k. In the original the last word ("and it becomes straight") occurs as part of the name.
l. This phrase probably relates to §55, which is designated for the same purpose.

you,[a] take some of your blood[b] and write (with it) on her gate your name and her name and write on your gate her name and your name and say in front of her gate from 'LYHWS until GSKY'. [65]And if you wish to know (whether) you succeed in your journey or not, take a *gila'a* lettuce[c] whose leaves are spread out and stand in front of the sun and say from GSKY' until 'SDWS and watch: if its leaves are withered and bent you should not go, but if it is in its natural state you should go and you shall succeed. [66]If you wish to release a man from prison, say once in front of him and once in front of the sun and once in front of the prison[d] from 'SDWS until YQWTNY. [67]To (disperse an) assembly,[e] take dust from your house and say over it seven times in the paths of the town from YQWTNY until 'QTDS, and also take <dust> from the paths of the town and say likewise over it and throw (it) within your house. [68]If you wish to kill a person, take mud from the two banks of the river and make a figure and write his name on it. And take seven thorns from a withered date palm and make a bow of *ḥuskaniata* wood and strands of horse hair and put the figure in a cloth bag[f] and stretch the bow over it[g] and shoot it and say over every thorn from 'QTDS until PRSWSY may N, son of N be injured, and he will be removed from you.[h] [69]If you wish to send a sore[i] (to afflict someone), take [ ] of seven people and put (it) in a new clay vessel and go out of the town and say over it from [80] PRSWSY until 'BNSNS and bury it in a place that has not been trodden over by a horse. And after that take some earth from above that clay vessel and scatter (it) in front of him (i.e., the person to be afflicted) or on the threshold of his house. [70]To send a dream against someone, write on a silver plate from 'BNSNS until QYRYW'S and place (it) in the mouth of a cock and slaughter it while it is placed in its mouth and turn its mouth around and place it between its thighs and bury (it) at the bottom part of a wall. And put your heel on its place and say thus: in the name of [ ][j] may the swift messenger go and torment N, son of N in his dreams until my will is fulfilled. [71]If a snake follows you, say toward it from QYRYW'S until 'YLWHŠ and it will wither. [72]And if <you wish> to detain a ship at sea, say over a sherd or a stone from 'YLYHŠ until 'SNWRPY and throw (it) toward it into the sea. [73]And if you

    a. The original is written in the masculine.
    b. The original is miswritten.
    c. *Gila'a* lettuce possibly indicates round-leaved lettuce. See Jastrow, *Dictionary*, s.v. "*gyl*'," 238.
    d. Lit. "in front of a weapon." It seems more plausible, however, that the original should have been in front of "the house of weapon," i.e., the prison.
    e. The original is uncertain. Cf., however, Sokoloff, *Dictionary*, s.v. "*kynf*'," 575. The location of this recipe between one for releasing a man from prison and the aggressive ones that follow suggests that it too has an aggressive inclination; possibly for the sake of juridical or physical self-defense.
    f. The original seems to be a miswriting of either "rough cloth" or "moneybag."
    g. The original is miswritten.
    h. The two Aramaic words meaning "and he will be removed from you," which close the recipe are awkwardly marked by the scribe as initials. They suggest that the deed is directed against an oppressor.
    i. For the demonization of sores, see §47 above.
    j. The words, possibly the names written on the silver tablet, which also had to be recited, are missing.

wish to release it, say over earth or over a clod from 'SNWRPY until NPṬGNS and throw (it) into the water and when it dissolves[a] it is released to travel. [74]If you wish to close an oven or basin or a pot so that (foods) will not be put (in them)[b] say over earth from NPṬGNS until SPṬSY' in front of them and throw (it) toward them. [75]If you wish to untie them, spit your spittle before them and say from SPṬSY' until SGMS[c] and they will be (released for) cooking. [76]If you wish to cross over the sea as on dry land, say over the four corners of a scarf in the fringes.[d] Hold one corner (of the scarf) in your hand and another corner will go before you, and say from GSMS until 'PSWMT.[e] [77]If you wish to curse a person, say while you pray, in (the benediction called) *Makhni'a Zedim*[f] may 'SQWHḤYY strike(?)[g] N, son of N in the name of 'PSWMT until QHWHYHWṬ. [78]And if you wish to speak with the dead, say in his left ear from QHWHYHWṬ until 'HYŠWNY [ ][h] and until 'ZRYQY and throw (it) into their holes.[i] [79]If you wish to kill a lion or a bear or a hyena[j] or any harmful animal, say over earth <from under>[k] your right foot from 'ZRYQY until NNHYH and throw (it) toward them. [80]If you wish to (magically) bind them, say over earth from under your left foot from NNHYH until HYṬG'Y and throw (it) toward them. [81]If you wish to open a door, take the root of *zirdeta* reed and place (it) under your tongue and say in front of the door from HYṬG'Y until BYRQS.[l] [82]If you wish to kill an ox or cattle, say in its ear from BRQS until TMYMS. [83]If you wish to inflame (fire of love) in (someone's)

    a. The original verb can also relate to the spell by which the ship was detained, meaning "and when the spell is untied."
    b. Another possible translation of the original: "so that they will not become ritually unclean," is implausible in this context. The next recipe makes clear that this charm is aimed at preventing the utensils from being used for cooking.
    c. The relevant name in the sword is GSMS (Harari, *Sword of Moses*, 34, §76). See also the next recipe.
    d. The original is miswritten. Cf. §91, where the fringes of a belt are indicated.
    e. The instruction to recite the formula seems to have been integrated into the text at this point either by mistake or as a deliberate correction of what is missing above. It should appear as part of the ritual to be performed over the four corners of the scarf where it says "and say" but no formula is indicated.
    f. *Makhni'a Zedim* ("You who overpower the evil ones") is the twelfth benediction of the daily *'Amidah* prayer.
    g. In the original, the name 'SQWHḤYY is followed by another one: YGWPṬ. However, as the sentence lacks a verb it is possible that this name is actually a miswriting of the Hebrew "will strike him." If that is the case, then the adjurer should turn to 'SQWHḤYY, who is mentioned among the thirteen archangels as 'SQWHḤYY, and adjure him to strike N, son of N.
    h. Due to a scribal error at this point, both the end of the recipe concerned with speaking with the dead and most of the one that follows it are missing. Thus, §78 actually comprises the beginning and the end of two consequent recipes and indicates two consequent formulas—from QHWHYHWṬ until 'HYŠWNY and from 'HYŠWNY until 'ZRYQY.
    i. See the previous note.
    j. In the context of lions and bears, the original is probably the Aramaic term for hyena. However, the Hebrew for viper should also be considered.
    k. Cf. the next recipe.
    l. The correct form is BRQS, as found in both the next recipe and the correlative formula in the sword (Harari, *Sword of Moses*, 34).

heart,[a] say over a piece (of meat)[b] from TMYMS until BDRQS[c] and put it by him and he should eat it. [84]If you wish to make someone demented, say over an egg from BRDQS until 'HYTY and give (it) to him [81] into his hands. [85]If you wish to destroy someone's house, say over a new sherd from 'HYTY until Š'YLS and throw (it) into his house. [86]If you wish to banish someone, say over *ydy* oil from Š'YLS until 'SPKL and smear (it) on the doorpost of his gate.[d] [87]If you wish to make someone hated (by others), say over let blood from 'SPKL until 'ZMRS and pour (it) on his threshold. [88]If you wish (to cause) a woman to abort, say over a jug of water from 'ZMRS until YZY'WS and pour (it) on her threshold.[e] [89]If you wish to make someone sick, say over olive oil from YZY'WS until N'STG and he should rub (it). [90]If <you wish> to know concerning a sick person whether he will die or recover, say in front of him from N'STG until LHRTN. If he turns (his) face to you he will recover and if (he turns his face) to the wall he will die. [91]If you wish to hold a lion by its ear, say from LHRTN until DWDY'H, and tie seven knots in the fringes of your belt and say (the formula mentioned) over each and every knot and hold it. [92]If you wish for your fame to go forth in the world, write <in> an amulet from DWDY'H until 'PTYGWNNY' and bury it at your gate. [93]If you wish the earth to contract before you,[f] say over a single *zirdeta* reed from 'PTYGWNNY' until YWLWYHW. [94]If you wish (a person) to be cured from hemorrhoids and not to be sick again, take a pit of *hana shiraʿa* (fruit)[g] and roast (it) in the oven and say over it from YWLWYHW until 'PYWN and mix it with olive oil and let him take (and put) a little[h] on it and it will become better. [95]For every (kind of) dripping(?),[i] write on *magzab* from 'PYWN until KRY'K and let him hang (it). [96]For poison, grind *palgagi* cumin[j] <and> write (with it?) on an egg[k] and put (it) in wine and say over it from KRY'K until HYPRW and let him drink (it). [97]For hailstones that descend[l] from the sky, take a ring of iron and lead and hang (it) on something tall at any place that you wish and say over it from HYPRW until GRWMY. [98]If you wish to enter before a king

    a. The original is miswritten.
    b. The original Aramaic may also denote a certain meat dish or a piece of bread.
    c. The correct form is BRDQS, as found both in the next recipe and in the correlative formula in the sword (Harari, *Sword of Moses*, 34).
    d. The original is miswritten. The correct words may also denote "the threshold of his gate."
    e. Lit. "his threshold."
    f. The practical meaning of the contraction of the earth is the shortening of the journey.
    g. The precise meaning of the Aramaic *hana shiraʿa* is uncertain. However the "pit" indicates that it is some kind of a fruit (unless the words are miswritten).
    h. I assume that the original is a miswriting for "a little." Otherwise the recipe as a whole makes no sense (even though the phrase itself is legible: "and let him take and put an amulet on it").
    i. The given word is uncertain and so is its meaning. It presumably derives from a word that denotes "a drop" in the Aramaic of the targumim. See Jastrow, *Dictionary*, s.vv. "*rys*," "*rsys*," 1484.
    j. Lit. "cumin of *palgagi*."
    k. It is plausible that the formula that should be written on the egg is the one to be recited over the wine.
    l. Lit. "when it comes."

or the nobles, say over lion skin while it is dipped in black myrrh and clear wine from GRWMY until ŠHRYWMY and carry[a] (it) on you. [99]For blight that afflicts the field, take a tendon and soak it in turnip water in the night between Wednesday and Thursday and on the next day sprinkle that water on that field and say from ŠHRYWMY until QHTṬY. [100]For worms that afflict the fruit, take a worm from the mud and put (it) in a tube and say over it from QHTṬY until STGMY and shut the opening (of the tube) with pitch[b] and bury (it) in that plot of land. [101]To release a man from prison, say over residue of gum arabic[c] and over *tuhala* dates from STGMY until 'YY and let him eat (it). [102]For land that does not produce fruit, take eight jugs from eight houses and fill them with water from eight canals and put salt into them from eight houses and say over them from 'YY until 'SH'L eight times and sprinkle over each corner (of that plot of land) two jugs (of water) and break those jugs over eight paths. [103]For a sick person who is weak[d] and you do not know why he is weak,[e] boil *shikhra*[f] in water and say over that water from 'SH'L until LWQY and let him drink (it) when he is thirsty. [104]To stir up a battle, take dust from under your left foot and say over it from LWQY until QBQZY'L[g] and throw it toward them and they will separate and take up weapons[h] and fight. [105]If you wish to impose your terror over all people, write on a lead plate from QBZQY'L until GTHWṬY'L and bury (it) in a synagogue on the western side. [106]If you wish light to shine for you when it is dark, write on a sheet from GTHWṬY'L until ZRWQZ"L and carry[i] (it) on you whenever you desire. [107]If you wish to tie eyes (from afflicting evil), write on a leather sheet and place (it) in a vessel[j] (made) of palm leaves under the stars from ZRWQZ"L until BTQNŠY'L[k] and do not speak while you write. [108]If you wish to send a sword and it will fight for you, say over a new knife (made) entirely of iron from BTQŠNY'L until TŠHWHY'L and cast it toward them. [109]If you wish them to kill each other, say over a knife (made) entirely of iron from TŠHWHY'L until KLLYSTNY'L and bury it with the bottom part[l] in the ground and put your heel on it (while) in the ground and they will kill each other until you take it <out of> the ground. [110]And if you wish them to calm down, take dust from under your right foot and say backward what you have said and throw (it) toward them and they

---

a. Lit. "and hold." Cf. §§106, 112.
b. The original is miswritten.
c. The given word is miswritten.
d. The word apparently denotes the deterioration of the sick person's condition or even his/her passing.
e. This is a case when the lack of a precise diagnosis prevents the implementation of a more focused treatment.
f. See §26.
g. The correct form is QBZQY'L, as found in both the next recipe and the correlative formula in the sword (Harari, *Sword of Moses*, 34).
h. Lit. "tools of war."
i. Lit. "and hold." Cf. §§98, 112.
j. The original is written in the plural.
k. The correct form is BTQŠNY'L, as found both in the next recipe and in the correlative formula in the sword (Harari, *Sword of Moses*, 35).
l. The "bottom part" of the knife is apparently the hilt.

will calm down. [111]And if an adversary lays hold of you and wishes to kill you, bend the little finger of your left hand and say from KLLYSTNY'L until KTRYHY'L and he will run away from you like a man who runs away from his killer. [112]To cause an optical illusion, say over a lion's hide from KTRYHY'L until HDGSWM'Y'L and carry[a] (it) on you and no one will see you. [113]If you fall <into> fire[b] and you wish to ascend out of it, say from HDGSWM'Y'L until SMQTY'Y'L and you will ascend safely. [114]If you fall into a deep pit without knowing, say while you fall from SMQTY'Y'L until HMGG'Y'L and nothing will harm you. [115]If you are drowning[c] in a deep river, say from [83] {SMQTY'Y'L until} HMGG'Y'L until MŠQWNY'Y'L[d] and you will come out safely. [116]If a rock or a landslide falls on you and you are (trapped) under it, say from MŠQWNYN'Y'L[e] until QNY'YS'Y'L and you will escape safely. [117]And if the authorities lay hold of you, bend the little finger of your left hand and say from QNY'YS'Y'L until BKLHWH'Y'L[f] before the king or the judge and he will kill the people who have seized you. [118]If a band of marauders attacks you, turn toward the west and say from BKLHWH'Y'L until QDŠYG'Y'L[g] and they will become like stones and will not move. [119]And if you wish to untie them, face toward the east and say backward what you have said. [120]And if you walk in valleys or mountains and there is no water to drink, raise up your eyes to heaven and say from QDŠYG'Y'L until PYZQHY'Y'L[h] and a spring of water will be opened for you. [121]If you are hungry,[i] raise up your eyes to heaven and spread out your arms to heaven and say from PZQHY'Y'L until QRSRNHY'L and a prince will stand before you and will give you bread and meat. [122]And if you wish to summon the prince of man to you, say over your scarf from QRSRNY'L[j] until HBQŠPHY'L and the one bound by you will de-

    a. Lit. "and hold." Cf. §§98, 106.
    b. The given word is unclear.
    c. Lit. "drowned."
    d. This is no doubt a scribe error. The required formula is from HMGG'Y'L until MŠQWNY'Y'L.
    e. The correct form is MŠQWNY'Y'L, as found both in the previous recipe and in the correlative formula in the sword (Harari, *Sword of Moses*, 35).
    f. The phrase "and you will escape safely ... BKLHWH'Y'L" is written in the margin. Having realized that he had skipped over the end of §116 and §117 in its entirety, the scribe added the missing section in the margin and indicated its place in the text with a common sign. Nevertheless, he did not erase the name BKLHWH'Y'L, which he had mistakenly written right after the name MŠQWNY'Y'L, probably because he considered it inappropriate to cross out a holy name (in other cases he did erase surplus words which he had mistakenly written; see the next note.). Thus, the name BKLHWH'Y'L occurs twice in the text—first, by mistake, after MŠQWNY'Y'L, and then in its correct position at the end of §117. It is copied here only once.
    g. The words "before the king or before the judge," which occurred appropriately in the previous recipe, were copied again by mistake at this point. They were eliminated with a line by the scribe.
    h. This name occurs three times, each in a different form: here, in the next recipe and in the sword. The scribe apparently considered the current form to be correct, since he also wrote it in the margin of the line where it occurs in the sword.
    i. The original is miswritten.
    j. The correct form is QRSRNHY'L, as found both in the previous recipe and in the correlative formula in the sword (Harari, *Sword of Moses*, 35).

The Sword of Moses

scend and he will come to you[a] and whatever you desire (to know) he will tell you. [123] And if you wish to remove him, say before him backward what you have said and he will go. [124/5] If[b] you wish that any heavenly prince will teach you what he knows,[c] call 'HYWPSQTYH and adjure him in the third hour of the night (with the words:) "in the name of the master of all the holy ones" until the end of the sword, send to me (the desired angel) and he will reveal to me and teach me all that he knows[d] and (then) he will flee.[e] [126] If you wish to walk upon water[f] so that your foot will not sink, take a lead plate and write on it <from> HBQŠPHY'L <until> Š'STŠHY'L and place it in your belt and say (the formula written) while you are walking. [127] If you wish to become wise, mention (during) three sequent months starting at the beginning of the month Nisan in Ḥonen ha-Da'at[g] from Š'STŠHY'L until 'GPTNSHY'L, may the gates of wisdom be opened to me so that I shall contemplate them. [128] If you wish to learn immediately everything that you may hear, write on an egg laid on the same day from 'GPTNSHY'L <until> QNYNSHW'L and erase (it) with undiluted wine in the morning and drink (it) and taste nothing for three hours. [129] If you wish to make someone forget all that he knows, write, pertaining to his name, on a laurel leaf[h] from QNYNSHW'L until 'WBRYHW'L and bury (it) under his threshold. [130] If you wish to send an evil demon against your enemy, take a green locust and say over it from 'WBRYHW'L until QSGHNHW'L[i] and tie to it (a piece of) wormwood and let it fly away. [131] To send[j] a spirit, take a bone of a dead person and dust from below him in a jar[k] and tie it up in a (piece of) linen [84] rug (together) with saliva[l] and say over it from QSGHNHW'L

---

a. Cf. §45.

b. Both numbers 124 and 125 occur in the margin and the next recipe is marked 126. Thus, one recipe is missing. In any case, recipe 124/125 requires the recitation of the closing section of the sword, which mentions 'HYWPSQTYH, the highest angel in the heavenly hierarchy, who is described at the beginning of the treatise (most probably composed by the compiler, himself). Thus, its appropriate position in the list of recipes should be close to its end, near §137. It was apparently located here due to its content, which broadens the option of acquiring angelic knowledge suggested in the previous recipe. See the discussion on this recipe in Harari, *Sword of Moses*, 128–29.

c. Lit. "will teach you that which is in his hand."

d. See the previous note.

e. I prefer to read the original as a Hebrew word integrated into the text rather than as an Aramaic one, which means "to tremble." The occurrence of Hebrew words in the list is not infrequent and it seems more likely that the adjurer wishes to dismiss the angel after having heard from him what he needed to know, rather than to make him tremble. Cf. §§122–23.

f. Lit. "in the water."

g. Ḥonen ha-Da'at is the fourth benediction of the weekday 'Amidah prayer. Cf. p. 343 n. c.

h. The original is miswritten. For writing on a laurel leaf, see also §45.

i. Neither this name nor any possible miswriting of it appears in the sword of names. It thus seems that some of the original names in the sword have been omitted. See Harari, *Sword of Moses*, 36, n. 140.

j. The original is miswritten.

k. The original Aramaic means "molar" (or tooth), which is unlikely in this context. It is more plausible, then, to read it as a close miswriting of "jar."

l. The exact denotation of the original is hard to discern.

The Sword of Moses

until MRGHMHW'L,[a] pertaining to his name, and bury (it) in a cemetery. [132]For (catching) thieves, say: May thieves and robbers be bound and surrender in the name of MRGWHMHW'L until 'ṬṬHSHW'L,[b] and while reciting (it) put your little finger in your ear {while reciting (it)}. [133]And when you wish to release them, say from Y'WYHW[c] and remove your hand from your ear. [134]To close up your house against thieves, say over a jug of water from 'ṬṬHSHW'L until MPGSRHW'L and sprinkle (it) all around your roof. And (it is effective) also for sealing a town. [135]To seal a house from marauders, take dust from a nest[d] of ants and carry (it) around your roof and while carrying (it) around say <from> MPGSRHW'L until "in the name of the master of all the holy ones."[e] [136]To seal yourself from an evil spirit, say in the name of TWBR TSBR until HYDRST', I, N, son of N, will pass in peace and not in harm.[f] And (act the same way) also to excommunicate them (i.e., the evil spirits) whenever you encounter them. [137]And for all other things that are not referred to explicitly, (say from) "in the name of the master of all the holy ones" until the end of the sword. And upon each amulet that you may write from the sword write on top (of it) "in the name of the master of all the holy ones."

<. . . In order>[g] that the deed (performed) through this sword[h] might be put into effect and he (i.e., the one who wishes to use the sword) will come forth to manipulate[i] it and all these deeds (suggested above), and they will be transmitted to him for the sake of manipulating them just as they were

  a. This name occurs in three different forms—here, in the next recipe and in the correlative formula in the sword.
  b. In the original, the name was written with double-S ('ṬṬHSSHW'L) and then one was assigned by the scribe as a surplus without being erased. The form 'ṬṬHSHW'L also occurs in §134 and in the correlative formula in the sword.
  c. The formula to be recited is not clear. The name that opens it is not found in the sword and neither is its end included. Actually, the formula required in the next recipe (§134) begins with the name that ends the one required in §132. Bearing in mind the technique of saying a formula backward in order to reverse the act accomplished through reciting it forward (e.g., §§109–10, 118–19, 122–23) it seems reasonable that the current recipe required the recitation of the previous formula from end to beginning. However, the name Y'WYHW does not occur in the formula indicated.
  d. The original is miswritten.
  e. In the original the words are mixed up. Cf. correlative phrase of the sword and §137.
  f. The original is uncertain but apparently denotes harm. Cf. Sokoloff, *Dictionary*, s.vv. "*hzyq*," "*hyzyq*," 374.
  g. Due to the incoherent syntax of this paragraph, the suggested reading is uncertain. The words "[in order] that the deed (performed) through this sword will be put into effect" can also be understood as the end of the previous sentence and not as a beginning of a new phrase. In that case one should read: "And for all other things that are not referred to explicitly, (say from) 'in the name of the master of all the holy ones' until the end of the sword. And upon each amulet that you may write from the sword write on top (of it) 'in the name of the master of all the holy ones' so that the deed (performed) through this sword might be put into effect." Nevertheless, it seems to me that at this point, toward the end of the treatise, the compiler returns to speaking about the use of the sword in general, and the preliminary rite for having control over it in particular. Thus, I believe that the beginning of this sentence, which related the importance of carrying out the preliminary ritual before trying to make a concrete use of the sword, is missing in our text. See Harari, *Sword of Moses*, 132–33.
  h. The original is miswritten.
  i. The original is miswritten.

transmitted to Moses, son of Amram, may divine peace rest upon him. But he who acts not (in accordance with the prescribed action) in his act and will come forth to manipulate it, angels of anger and rage and wrath and fury rule over him and torment his body and all (the limbs) of his body cause him to be cold. And these are the names of the princes who lead them: the name of the prince who is appointed over the angels of anger —MZPWPY'S'Y'L is his name; and the name of the prince who is appointed over the angels of rage {is}—ṢQṢWRWMTY'L is his name; and the name of the prince who is appointed over the angels of wrath—QSW'PPGHY'L is his name; and the name of the prince who is appointed, <over the angels of> fury—N'MWSNYQTTY'L is his name. And there is no number to the angels that are under their authority and all of them rule over him and his body will be made disfigured.[a] May the Lord guard you from all evil. Amen.

End of the sword with the help of *God dreaded in the great council of the holy ones.*

Exod 6:20

Ps 89:7

---

a. The original is miswritten. Cf. Dan 3:29.

The Phylactery of Moses
A new translation and introduction

by Roy D. Kotansky

The so-called Phylactery of Moses is a text inscribed on a single, small (9.1 cm. × 5.6 cm.) sheet of copper found in Akrai, Sicily sometime in the early nineteenth century. Although it is not necessarily a text claiming to be written by Moses himself, its authority rests in the fact that it identifies itself, foremost, as the very protective amulet that Moses himself used before the presence of the Lord, in his ascent upon Mt. Sinai (or Mt. Horeb). But its pseudepigraphic value depends not only upon its Mosaic utility, but also in the fact that at the heart of the amulet's text stands an authoritative citation of Deut 32— albeit in a somewhat corrupt and truncated form, a citation not from the Septuagint (LXX), but from an early Aquilan translation. The passage preserves the so-called Song of Moses, a song that the great lawgiver presents "in the hearing of all the assembly of Israel" (Deut 31:30), before his death on the eve of Israel's entrance into the Promised Land. In this sense, then, Moses is perhaps also the phylactery's author in the mindset of its original compiler, and in the mindset of its compositional history, insofar as Moses is considered the putative author of the book of Deuteronomy, as one of the Five Books of Moses that constitute the Torah (see further n. 16, below).

The Phylactery of Moses is, properly speaking, a *lamella*—a magical amulet engraved onto a thin metal sheet (usually of gold or silver, but occasionally of copper) and worn about the body for general protection. Accordingly, it is a "phylactery," from the Greek *phylaktērion*, a common noun in the magical literature for any protective charm but one usually engraved. In the Greek text of Matt 23:5, the plural *ta phylaktēria* is also applied to the Jewish *tefillin* that the scribes and the Pharisees "make large" (*platynousin*) by presumably flattening them out as beaten metal foil. Ultimately, the use of such a thin sheet of metal, as ours, for protection derives from Exod 28:36 (LXX; cf. 39:30–31) where Aaron is commanded to inscribe the phrase "Holy to the Lord" (*hagiasma kyriou*) on a "pure gold leaf" (*petalon chrysoun katharon*), in order to protect him in the wilderness sanctuary (see further vv. **1, 3**, below, with notes).

The text of the Phylactery of Moses preserved on this *lamella* is not complete and certainly does not represent the original version of the composition, which may have been much longer and fuller. Its lacunose condition, especially at the beginning, suggests only fragments of a once complete magical narrative, or *historiola*, whose contents can only be surmised. In fact, it looks as if we possess, at best, only exiguous remnants of the whole story, namely its beginning and end verse: v. **1**[1] describes the "phylactery" that Moses used to protect himself in the presence of the divine, presumably on Mt. Sinai (or

---

1. Note that the versification (in bold font) is according to the translational sense of the text. It is different from the original line numbering, which corresponds to the Greek text as inscribed on the amulet.

Horeb)[2]—see vv. **4, 11**—whereas v. **2** describes the withdrawal of the "Spirit of Holiness" and Moses's subsequent departure from God's presence. In between these two verses there must have once stood a complete story narrating Moses's interaction on the holy mountain in the company of the Lord. The nature of the preserved text tantalizingly suggests that during the prophet's interaction with the divine, he is supernaturally vested with magical or occult power by God himself (cf. also Exod 4:1–9, 17, 30–31).

There is also a confusing repetition of key phrases and entire verses that suggests considerable corruption in the original manuscript. This may have resulted, for example, from the careless insertion into the body of the text of marginal variants mean to supplant or supplement the original readings. Or, these may have been interlinear remarks, glosses, or variants unintentionally duplicated in the text. Further, outright instructional materials erroneously inserted into the body of the text mar the continuity of the storyline, as if the copyist had worked from a magical handbook and unknowingly copied ritual portions of the spell along with the actual magical narrative and the accompanying words of empowerment.[3] In any event, the whole produces a haphazard disunity that may have, fortuitously, augmented the tablet's theoretical value in that the repetition might be seen to preserve a kind of cadenza of magical phrases, the iteration of which makes the whole spell look and sound more forceful.

For instance, it becomes clear from a cursory reading that vv. **1–3** in the narrative, lacunose as they are in the present state of the text's transmission, are mirrored somewhat by the following vv. **4–6**, especially in regard to the first verse of each section: "A phylactery that Moses used to protect him in the Holy of Holies (and) to lead him into the splendor of the supernatural" (**1**) corresponds to "A phylactery of Moses when he went up on Mt. Sinai . . . to receive the *kasty*-amulet" (**4**). Then, the whole of vv. **4–9**, which constitutes this title, with instructions, followed by the body of the amulet proper, is duplicated yet again, in vv. **11–14**, with a similar incipit: "A phylactery of Moses when he went up on Mt. Sinai to receive the golden tablet, to receive the *keset*-amulet" (**11**).

From this alone, one can hypothesize the editorial intention, if not necessarily the end-product, of this otherwise wayward compositional whole. The incipit, for example, may have meant to have been read as follows, had the program of editorial emendations been properly implemented (with the underlined material deriving from vv. **4, 11**):

---

2. Horeb (as opposed to Sinai) is likewise the "mountain of God" (cf. Exod 3:1—the incipit of the burning bush episode), where Moses is vested with magical powers. The traditions of Horeb versus Sinai may represent the results of two competing source-critical traditions, with Sinai belonging to the Yahwistic (J) and Priestly sources (P) and Horeb belonging to the Elohistic (E) and Deuteronomistic (D) sources; see G. I. Davies, "Sinai, Mount" in *ABD* 6:47–49, esp. p. 47. Giuseppe Veltri wishes to connect this with *merkavah* or *hekhalot* ascent literature; but here it is the mountain, not heaven, that is attained. See Veltri, "Jewish Traditions in Greek Amulets," *Bulletin of Judaeo-Greek Studies* 18 (1996): 35.

3. It is not, however, as F. P. Rizzo argues (followed by Michael Zellmann-Rohrer) that the phylactery itself is a "handbook"—its small size, material, and amuletic nature disallow this—but that it errantly reproduces instructions previously copied out of a papyrus spellbook, with some evident misappropriation (see the relevant note to v. **3**, below). But all amulets ultimately derive from such formularies (or handbooks). See Rizzo, "I 'formulari di Mosé' in uno documento acrense: Paure e speranze dell' uomo tardo-antico," *Atti dell' Accademia di Scienze Lettere e Arti di Palermo* 15 (1994–1995): 1–63; Zellmann-Rohrer, "GEMF 26 (GMA 32)," in *Greek and Egyptian Magical Formularies*, vol. 1: *Text and Translation*, ed. Christopher A. Faraone and Sofía Torallas Tovar, California Classical Studies 9 (Berkeley: University of California Press, 2022), 343–45.

"A phylactery of Moses which he used when he went up on Mt. Sinai to get the ṣiṣi- (or: keset-) amulet, to protect him in the Holy of Holies, to lead him into the splendor of the supernatural."

These passages, then, seem to overlap one another textually. For a restored version of the Phylactery of Moses, see the end of the translation below.

Text

The text of the Phylactery of Moses is preserved in a single manuscript: a small copper, or copper-alloy, tablet, height 9.1 cm.; width 5.6 cm, formerly housed in the Syracuse Museo Archeologico Nazionale (no inventory number given) but now lost. Although reported to be of bronze, apparently no tests were conducted to identify the metal used. Since copper routinely oxydizes to a green patination, and since copper is the "pure" metal usually adopted for use as amulets, it seems likely that this amulet is copper but has been misidentified as bronze. Bronze is a copper-tin alloy. In the ancient magical handbooks, phylacteries made of metal are to be written on gold, silver, copper, tin, or (occasionally) lead or iron—all pure earth metals that are not alloyed. No instructions in the ancient magical literature prescribe the engraving of amulets onto bronze.

As mentioned above, the text shows evidence of having been copied, somewhat haphazardly, from an earlier papyrus formulary, for some of the title and rubrics from the instructional part of its papyrus *Vorlage* have made their way onto the amulet itself. This suggests an older transmissional history of the phylactery that, here to date, has not survived our present manuscript record. Repetitions, too, in the text (above) suggest an older history of transcription. The tablet, broken down the middle and with its lower right corner missing, had been folded many times before engraving so as to create ruling-lines with which to write. The surface of the tablet, as Karl Preisendanz observed, shows an unusual amount of wear, as if overly handled in modern times or in antiquity. It may have been venerated as a kind of reliquary, or holy object, by its original owner(s), in which case it would not have been rolled up and inserted into a capsule, which is usually the case with such *lamellae*.

Original Language, Date, and Provenance

The original language would seem to be Greek, as the Aquilan insertion restored in lines 19–22 (of the amulet proper) might tend to prove; the inserted text represents an early counter-Septuagintal rendition of the Hebrew Bible popular with, and in use among, certain Jewish communities. Aquila's floruit was around the first quarter of the second century CE (perhaps ca. 128 CE, or earlier), but as Dominique Barthélemy observes, Aquila's work can be seen as the culmination of at least one hundred years of Jewish translational activity.[4]

---

4. See Barthélemy, *Le Devanciers d'Aquila: Première publication intégrale du texte des fragments du Dodécaprophéton*, VTSupp 10 (Leiden: Brill, 1963), passim; cited by Leonard J. Greenspoon, "Aquila's Version," *ABD* 1:320–21. Further, Sidney Jellicoe, *The Septuagint and Modern Study* (Oxford: Clarendon, 1968), 76–82; Natalio Fernández Marcos, *The Septuagint in Context: Introduction to the Versions of the Bible* (Leiden: Brill, 2000), 109–22; Roy Kotansky, "Phylactery of Moses," in *Greek Magical Amulets: The Inscribed Gold, Silver, Copper, and Bronze Lamellae*, part 1: *Published Texts of Known Provenance*, Abhandlungen der Nordrhein-Westfälischen Akademie der Wissenschaften, Sonderreihe Papyrologica Coloniensia 22.1 (Opladen: Westdeutscher Verlag, 1994), 128, doi:10.1007/978-3-663-20312-4_32; and for

Further evidence for an original composition in Greek is the fact that the text presents a number of terms that stem primarily from the world of Greek magic: the words *phylaktērion* (lines 1, 8, 23 of the amulet), *magos*, "sorcerer" (lines 10, 26, 33), *katadesmos*, "binding spell" (lines 10–11, 26); and the phrases *hēmerinos pyretos*, "daily fever" (lines 30–31), *ophthalmou baskaneia*, "evil eye" (line 31), *aitēsimon agatha*, "requesting good things" (line 32), *diaphylaxon tonde*, "protect so-and-so" (lines 15–16), and so on.

Conversely, under the supposition that the Aquilan section is, in itself, already a translation of a putative Hebrew original and that the text seems to represent a kind of magical composition in which, for starters, the Aquilan citation can be seen as an older insertion become corrupt, it is not impossible to see at least parts of the text deriving from a Semitic milieu. It is difficult to assess the apparently transliterated Hebrew terms in the non-Aquilan sections, such as the Greek spellings of *seisei* (lines 24–25) and *kasty* (lines 9, 25), which look like Aquilan literalisms outside of the strictly Aquilan section preserved in lines 19–22 (the quotation of Deut 32:1–3). See notes to the translation, below. The whole presents a fascinating crux that cannot be easily resolved here.

The original date of the composition of the amulet must be viewed not only in the context of its use of the Aquilan version, but also alongside the paleographic issues and how this text stands in relation to the fact that it shows a lot of wear and tear from excessive handling in antiquity, something that may account for the injunction within the text that the tablet should be handed down to no one but one's legitimate heirs. This mandate recorded more than once on the tablet enhances the prospect that the amulet was highly venerated within the family who owned it and that it was possibly handed down for posterity within subsequent generations. Hence, the actual writing of the tablet may belong to a period much older than the archaeological context in which it was discovered, uncertain as that may be. In this respect, the amulet can be seen as an heirloom artifact kept in the household for centuries before eventual burial with the last surviving family member.

The paleographic hand preserved on the Acre copper *lamella* can be dated from the late second century to the third century CE, although it is not impossible that the amulet could date to as late as the early fourth century CE.[5] In any case, paleographic dating cannot be equated with the original composition of the text, for our exemplar will represent but one manuscript (here, on metal) of a text that enjoyed an earlier compositional history. How early can only be guessed at, but under the supposition that the translation attributed to "Aquila" may represent a translational tradition earlier than his own floruit in the second century, it is possible, but hardly provable, that the original composition of the Phylactery of Moses extends somewhat earlier than the time of Aquila. In view of the fact, however, that Irenaeus has already begun to cite Aquila's translation by around 180 CE (in *Adversus Haereses*, apud Eusebius, *Hist. Eccles.* 5.8), it seems that the translation of "Aquila the Pontic" was widely available for reading before the last quarter of the second century CE.

It remains noteworthy that the citation of Aquila preserved in the amulet is so corrupt, more corrupt indeed than its non-Aquilan surrounding text, to suggest that it

---

detailed commentary on the Greek text of Deut 32:1–3 vis-à-vis the Hebrew, esp. "Appendix 2: The New Fragment of Aquila," 149–54. See further n. c, to v. 7, below.

5. Assuming the hand matches the archaeological context, and it is not an heirloom artifact; on the paleographic dating, see Kotansky, "Phylactery of Moses," 128.

enjoyed a history apart from, and independent of, the text in which it was embedded. It is obvious that the hoary citation that is meant to represent Moses's departing words of blessing to the people of Israel came to stand as a magical formula of healing, easily corrupted by the presence of words rare and possibly difficult to understand in popular vernacular. To these words accrued other incantatory phrases (vv. **7–8**) more common to the later magical tradition—all this to such an extent that it hardly seems likely that the writer of the amulet, as a whole, understood the text of Aquila in vv. **9–10** as meaningful Greek, at all. The words had become, over time, magical formulas, or *voces magicae*, and this was indeed how they came to be understood by modern scholars before the most recent edition.[6] This can only mean that the Aquilan formula once circulated independently, perhaps mostly in oral form, as an exorcistic formula within Greek-speaking Judaism, long before it was incorporated into the text of our amulet, with its introductory phrases of praise, utility, and safeguarding. It is remarkable, too, that the Greek text that preserves this older, incantatory blessing of Moses from Deuteronomy is not from the Greek translation of the LXX, but from one of the alternative, reputedly Jewish, Greek versions that reached full maturation in the second century CE.

The amulet was uncovered at Akrai (founded ca. 664 BCE; Latin Acrae, modern Palazzuolo Acreide), forty-three kilometers from Syracuse, Sicily, sometime in the early nineteenth century, during early excavations, probably of Baron Gabriele Iudica (1760–1835), and was first published rather unreliably by Børge Thoracius in his *Monumentorum Siculorum speciminis secundi particula prima* and then more critically by Preisendanz in 1931 (but only published after WWII) and further in another edition by L. Bernabò Brea in 1956.[7] The most recent edition, used here, is that of Roy Kotansky, with introduction, translation, commentary, and the identification of the new Aquilan fragment found therein.[8] The translation here is an adaptation of Kotansky's as well. A number of new, and somewhat tendentious, readings by Michael Zellmann-Rohrer cannot be confirmed from the poorly published photo by Brea and have not been incorporated into the present text.[9] The amulet was formerly housed in the Syracuse, Museo Archaeologico Nazionale (no inv. number) but is apparently long lost, as mentioned.

Theological Importance

The Phylactery of Moses provides an excellent example, albeit in truncated form, of how a theological story, or *historiola*, the term so often used of magical narratives, was employed for supernatural benefit. Here a lost narrative about Moses and his ascent upon Mt. Sinai, and his subsequent encounter with God, was believed to hold such traditional magical power that it could be applied to later-age bearers for protection, healing, and

---

6. See Kotansky, "Phylactery of Moses." For a similar misunderstanding of once intelligible words as "magic," note Roy D. Kotansky, "A Bronze Medallion in Madrid: Cross-Cultural and Material Transmission of an Amuletic Tradition from Syria to Sicily," in *Magic and Religion in the Ancient Mediterranean World: Studies in Honor of Christopher A. Faraone*, ed. Radcliffe G. Edmonds III, Carolina López-Ruiz, and Sofía Torallas-Tovar (London: Routledge, 2024), 295–324.

7. Thorlacius, *Monumentorum Siculorum speciminis secundi particula prior* (Hauniae, 1829); Achille Vogliano and Karl Preisendanz,"Laminetta Magica Siciliana," *Acme* 1 (1948): 73–85; Brea, *Akrai*, Società di storia patria per la Sicilia orientale, Monografie archeologiche 1 (Catania: Cartotecnica, 1956), 170–71, no. *52, Tav. 39 (52).

8. Kotansky, "Phylactery of Moses."

9. Zellman-Rohrer, "GEMF 26 (GMA 32)," 343–45; Brea, *Akrai*.

a variety of spiritual benefits. At the simplest level the magic works on the principle of *similia similibus*, "like-by-like" healing: just as Moses used the amulet to "protect" himself in the Holy of Holies, so too will the wearer of the present charm—and subsequent generations—be protected in their day-to-day lives. Even though the supernatural protection that Moses originally sought before the presence of God and his mountain, in the wearing of the amulet, served a higher goal, its putatively numinous and divine power could nonetheless be carried over for a more ephemeral purpose for the present holder, so much so that unearthly injuries produced by malicious sorcery, harmful (or erotic) binding-spells, or spirit possession, could be rendered entirely null and ineffective.

The heart of the Phylactery of Moses is the utterance of the prophet's own words encapsulated in the somewhat garbled version of the Aquilan citation of Deut 32 (discussed further below). It is Moses's expressions of blessings, called "the words of this song" in Deut 31:30 (the speech's incipit [cf. 32:44–47]), that characterize the dynamics of the amulet, overall. They represent words of power from the mouth of Moses, God's prophet, to whom was given the very utterances of the Law. They prove, in effect, to be formulas of a magical incantation, as it were, incantatory at least in the eyes of the amulet's designer and its wearer—words that promise to be not "idle," but rather "life-giving" (Deut 32:47), and language that is promissory of granting inheritance and great benefaction.

Thus at a different, and perhaps deeper, level the Phylactery of Moses can be seen to serve as the very protective device that Moses himself used before God on Sinai. The amulet claims as much. It is immaterial that the advertisement in the amulet's incipit alleging that it was the very magical device that Moses used can hardly be true. Art imitates life here. It is intended in its colorful theological description that the phylactery identify itself as the venerated object that Moses had first acquired and then owned, and that this amulet had been handed down since biblical times, from generation to generation, as a kind of sacral priestly heirloom to be held in eventual perpetuity by the very possessing family in ancient Acre who left it in the ground for our discovery at Palazzulo Acreide. This is the power of magical narrative and its pseudepigraphic attribution. The Phylactery of Moses is his phylactery because it is the actual talisman that Moses employed so many centuries ago to protect him from God's glory and to initiate him into his power. Moses was both the original owner of the phylactery and its first user, no matter who the true manufacturer was—perhaps it was God himself, who in a similar fashion had written for Moses the tablets of the law with his own hand (Exod 32:15–16).

The ancient owner of the charm now stands under the tradition of the protective aegis of Moses, the greatest pre-Christian biblical magician of all of ancient Judaism, perhaps in some ways even greater than Solomon. Just as such *historiolae* in Christian contexts routinely narrate biblical accounts of Jesus, here too, we see in a primarily Jewish narratival setting, the presentation and elevation of a quintessential biblical hero, a magus par excellence, as a figure of great historical and storytelling power.

In another respect, despite the use of perhaps later magical accretions to the Deuteronomic Song of Moses herein cited, it is noteworthy that the Phylactery of Moses contains a more religious orthodoxy in its text of healing, if one may bring up the age-old conundrum concerning the modern-day dichotomy envisioned between magic and religion. Among the so very many known magical Jewish texts of this genre, including, for example, the Prayer of Jacob, and countless others, whether Greek, Aramaic, Hebrew, or Coptic, the Phylactery of Moses is remarkable in its complete absence of any angelology in its magical application. The ubiquitous and often redundant use of angel-names in Jewish magical texts is altogether missing in the Phylactery of Moses. This can hardly be unintentional. It is as if, despite the use of a few incongruent magical names in lines 14–16 of the Greek text, the author found in the prayerful incantation of the Song of Moses, and in the citation of the divine name several times ahead of it, enough biblical power to eschew any need for the intervention of angelic names or epithets. Moses and his God are power enough for the efficacy of this wonderful amulet.

Literary Context

The most remarkable feature of the Phylactery of Moses is its citation of the Aquilan version of the Greek Old Testament, and the occasional allusions to Aquilan-like language in much of the amulet's text. But this most obvious of relationships to canonicity does not stop there, for additional allusions to biblical language and themes permeate the text, the most noteworthy of which are the apparent references to living long and lengthy days in lines 34–36 of the Greek text of the amulet. Here, in the somewhat restored version of the Greek, we find allusions to repetitive Septuagintal phrases, such as "in order that you might live" (cf. Deut 4:1; 6:24; 8:1; 11:8; 16:20; 30:6, 19), and "that your days may be long" (Deut 4:40; 5:16, 33; 6:2; 11:9; 17:20; 32:47).[10] Such language may reflect the general tenor of the Song of Moses in Deut 32, a text that, albeit punitive and retributive in nature, yields to promise and hope, as Moses himself comments upon the meaning of the very words that he had just spoken: "Take to your heart all the words with which I am warning you today, which you shall command your sons to observe carefully, even all the words of this law. For it is not an idle word for you; indeed it is your life. And by this word you shall prolong your days in the land, where you are about to cross over the Jordan to possess it" (Deut 32:46–47 NASB).

Whereas the Phylactery of Moses presupposes Moses's role as a famous *magos*, no specific reference is made to the biblical accounts of his powers before Pharaoh, and elsewhere, accounts narrated throughout the text of Exodus. Moses's encounter with the Lord (YHWH), beginning in Exod 3 with the Burning Bush epiphany on "Horeb, the Mountain of God," and extending through the whole of the book with its numerous references to mountain meetings with the divine, or some powerful aspect of God, forms the evident backdrop to the lost *historiola* of the phylactery's narrative. Obviously, the repetitive, and often contradictory, references to Moses before God, either on the mountain or at the foot of the mountain of Horeb or Sinai, make a single, hallmark biblical citation difficult to come by. The reader is expected to understand the various traditions lying behind Moses's encounter before the awesome glory of God, and to take for granted his subsequent investment of power by the divine.

In terms of its relation to other apocryphal Greek texts, the Phylactery of Moses stands in the same tradition of such religio-magical pseudepigraphic books as the "Monad," or Eighth Book of Moses (see below), and the so-called Prayer of Jacob.[11] For this latter text (= *PGM* XXIIb), an invocation of the Jewish creator God, we do find some remarkable parallels with our text, such as the invocation of the one who sits "upon the mountain of Holy Sinaios" (line 8; see notes, below); the invocation of divine names

---

10. With reference to stereotypical formulas in the Greek text of Deuteronomy in light of John W. Wevers, *Text History of the Greek Deuteronomy*, MSU 13 (Göttingen: Vandenhoeck & Ruprecht, 1978), see Kotansky, *Greek Magical Amulets*, 147–48. For further examples of parallels, see the notes below.

11. James H. Charlesworth, "The Prayer of Jacob," in *OTP* 2:715–23.

(*Sabaōth, Adōnai*, line 9, and line 15, where *Sabaōth* is called the "secret name"); the effort of the spell to bestow blessings, such as wisdom, power, and sundry good things (lines 14, 17, 18, 19); and in its overall language of prayer and supplication. The Prayer of Jacob, however, uses much more angelic language than biblical; as noted above, the Phylactery of Moses is noteworthy for its almost Sadducean deprivation of angelological belief; there is not any hint of a folklore of angels at all.

The Eighth Book of Moses (*PGM* XIII.1–734) is a lengthy tractate containing a ritual preparation for a number of magical operations.[12] Although generically a recipe book presuming the same kind of magical background as our text, it bears little in common with the Phylactery of Moses other than its namesake. As Morton Smith observes:

> The attribution to Moses was due partly to the text's contents . . . partly to Moses' fame as a magician. . . . The compiler of *PGM* XIII was both a composer and collector of "Mosaic" texts. He himself had written one called "The Key of Moses" (l. 229) . . . [and] he cites "The Archangelic (Teaching?) of Moses," Moses' "secret moon prayer," and "The Tenth Hidden (Book?) of Moses."[13]

The Archangelic Teaching (?) of Moses, as Smith notes, is also cited among the Nag Hammadi codices (II.5.102), about which Smith writes, " [this] may be reflected by a medieval manuscript which quotes an 'archangelic hymn' given to Moses for use as a phylactery."[14] In other words, we see a tradition here much like that found in respect of our Phylactery of Moses: texts, secrets, and laws given to Moses by God. The otherwise distinctly non-Mosaic invisibility spell, From the Diadem of Moses (*PGM* VII. 619–627). may also represent such a handed-down recipe of patriarchal pedigree. In the Hebrew language, we find similarly titled pseudepigraphic works, such as the Ḥarba de-Moshe ("the Sword of Moses"), which like the Greek material, represents a magic work fathered onto the great patriarch, Moses, by virtue of his role as a magician.[15]

The tradition of Moses and the gold leaf engraved with "Holy to the Lord" that Aaron wears, in accordance with the commands of Exod 28:36 (see above), is also echoed remarkably in the thirteenth-century Canterbury Amulet (Canterbury Cathedral Library, Additional MS 23): "Through this ineffable name of yours, inscribed with the Tetragrammaton by the hand of Moses onto the holy (gold) leaf of veneration that Aaron your priest, by your decree, raised up to his forehead" (*per hoc / ineffabilem nomen tuum quod aaron tuus sacerdos / tuo iussu per manus moysi in lamina / sacre venerationis scriptum tetragrama/ton in fronte sua detulit*), col. 4, lines 23–25 (my trans.).[16] This remark of Moses's "leaf of veneration" (*lamina venerationis*) suggests an enduring tradition reminiscent of the Acre *lamella*'s own sense of spiritual and material self-worth that contributed to its likely overhandling in antiquity and to its guarded transmission down through the sacred

---

12. Translated by Morton Smith, "PGM XIII," *GMPT*, 172–89; and by Todd E. Klutz, "The Eighth Book of Moses," *MOTP* 1:189–235.

13. Smith, "PGM XIII," 172 n. 2.

14. Smith, "PGM XIII," 193–94 n. 136.

15. Ḥarba de-Moshe is translated by Yuval Harari in this volume.

16. See Don C. Skemer, *Binding Words: Textual Amulets in the Middle Ages*, Magic in History (University Park: Pennsylvania State University Press, 2006), Appendix I, 285–304, esp. 292. Here Moses is called the actual writer of the gold tablet, which may by extension apply to the Phylactery of Moses.

familial line (sc., *gonimois*—"[for] your offspring [only]," v. **13**), a lineage that may well have claimed Levitical ancestry through one of the greatest of biblical leaders, Moses.

Bibliography

Bohak, Gideon. *Ancient Jewish Magic: A History*. Cambridge: Cambridge University Press, 2008.

Brea, L. Bernabò. Pages 170–71, no. *52, Tav. 39 (52) in *Akrai*. Società de storia patria per la Sicilia orientale, Monografie archeologiche 1. Catania: Cartotecnica, 1956.

Calhoun, Robert Matthew. *Paul's Definition of the Gospel in Romans 1*. WUNT 2/316. Tübingen: Mohr Siebeck, 2011.

Faraone, Christopher A. *The Transformation of Greek Amulets in Roman Imperial Times*. Philadelphia: University of Pennsylvania Press, 2018.

Horst, Peter W. van der. *Jews and Christians in Their Graeco-Roman Contexts*. WUNT 196. Tübingen: Mohr Siebeck, 2006.

Kotansky, Roy D. "Phylactery of Moses." No. 32, pp. 126–54 in *Greek Magical Amulets: The Inscribed Gold, Silver, Copper, and Bronze Lamellae*. Part 1: *Published Texts of Known Provenance*. Abhandlungen der Nordrhein-Westfälischen Akademie der Wissenschaften. Sonderreihe Papyrologica Coloniensia 22.1. Opladen: Westdeutscher Verlag, 1994. doi:10.1007/978-3-663-20312-4_32.

———. "Textual Amulets and Writing Traditions in the Ancient World." Pages 507–54 in *Guide to the Study of Ancient Magic*. Edited by David Frankfurter. RGRW 189. Leiden: Brill, 2019. doi:10.1163/9789004390751_020.

Peterson, Erik. "Das Amulett from Acre." *Aegyptus* 33 (1953): 172–78.

Rizzo, F. P. "I 'formulari di Mosè' in uno documento acrense: Paure e speranze dell' uomo tardo-antico." *Atti dell' Accademia di Scienze Lettere e Arti di Palermo* 15 (1994–1995): 1–63.

Thorlacius, Børge. *Monumentorum Siculorum speciminis secundi particula prior*. Hauniae, 1829.

Veltri, Giuseppe. "Jewish Traditions in Greek Amulets." *Bulletin of Judaeo-Greek Studies* 18 (1996): 33–47.

Vogliano, Achille, and Karl Preisendanz. "Laminetta Magica Siciliana." *Acme* 1 (1948): 73–85.

The Phylactery of Moses

1 A [phyla]ctery[a] that [Mos]es[b] used to [protec]t[c] him in the Holy of Holies[d] (and) to introduce him into the splendor of (the) supernatural.[e]

---

a. Or, "amulet" (*phylaktērion*, a "protective charm"); in Aramaic this is a *qāmêā*[c].

b. An Aramaic-Greek bilingual phylactery mentions the tradition of giving an amulet to Moses on Mt. Horeb: "I adjure you . . . by the signet ring that the king of angels gave to Moses on Horeb . . . in ancient times." See Roy D. Kotansky, Joseph Naveh, and Shaul Shaked, "A Greek-Aramaic Silver Amulet from Egypt in the Ashmolean Museum," *Mus* 105 (1992): line 27, pp. 9, 12, 19, with commentary. On Moses receiving magic traditions, in addition to the law, from God, note Armand Delatte, *Anecdota Atheniensia*, I: *Texts grecs inédits relatifs à l'histoire des religions*, Bibliothèque de la Faculté de Philosophie et Lettres de l'Université de Liège 36 (Liège: Vaillant-Carmanne; Paris: Champion, 1927), 1:29–30, lines 26–27; 1–6. A large pseudepigraphic literature exists on Moses as magician, going back to the Pentateuch. See Scott B. Noegel, "Moses and Magic: Notes on the Book of Exodus," *JANES* 24 (1996): 45–59; John G. Gager, *Moses in Greco-Roman Paganism*, SBLMS 16 (Nashville: Abingdon, 1972), 134–61; Gager, "Moses the Magician: Hero of an Ancient Counter-Culture?," *Helios* 21 (1994): 179–88; Smith, "PGM XIII," 172 n. 2.

c. Reading [*phylax*]*e* = [*phylax*]*ai* with Vogliano, rather than [*stērix*]*ai*, "to strengthen."

d. In the LXX the Holy of Holies is usually the *sanctum sanctorum* of the Jerusalem Temple. But here it must have in mind Moses entering the tabernacle that God commanded from Sinai for Moses to build; see, e.g., Exod 25:7 (LXX). The tabernacle sanctuary contains the invisible presence of God on his elaborate Cherubim throne with the holy Ark. Although in the book of Exodus, the sanctuary is a *hagiasma* ("sanctuary") or *skēnē* ("tent"), it is also referred to as the "Holy of Holies" (e.g., Exod 26:33–34). Moses needs protection from the awesome Shekinah glory of God (cf. *doxa*, "glory," in line 3, below). Since there are biblical traditions of Aaron needing special accoutrements to enter the Holy of Holies, including the enigmatic "oracular (?) breast-plate," or *log(e)ion* (Exod 28:15, 22 LXX), and since this *logion* is also mentioned in Lev 8:8–9 (LXX) in conjunction with the gold leaf (*petalon*) worn as a headband by Aaron, it is easy to envision Moses's phylactery here as a gold leaf, too. And that seems to be what is implied by the mention of the gold leaf in v. **3**, below (with n. b. to v. 3). See further Abigail Booth, "Sacred Writing and Magic Metal: The High Priest's Holy Crown as a Protective Amulet," *Studia Antiqua* 20, no. 1 (2021): 23–37.

e. Or, "to lead him into the glory of the divine," or, "to draw him into the glory of the occult

---

We are grateful to Springer Nature for permission to reprint a revised version of the English translation of the Phylactery of Moses, originally published as Roy Kotansky, "Phylactery of Moses," in *Greek Magical Amulets: The Inscribed Gold, Silver, Copper, and Bronze Lamellae*, part 1: *Published Texts of Known Provenance*, Abhandlungen der Nordrhein-Westfälischen Akademie der Wissenschaften, Sonderreihe Papyrologica Coloniensia 22.1 (Opladen: Westdeutscher Verlag, 1994), 126–54.

2 [Th]e Spirit of Holin[ess] withdrew,[a] ⁽⁵⁾and after these things he turned away.[b]

(or 'the magical')" (*eis tēn doxan physikou*). Preisendanz took this as a reference to Moses's initiation into the office of the magician, but the verb here, "to lead; draw; bring" (*agagein*), is probably simply a verb of motion (cf., e.g., Exod 3:12 [LXX]; Vogliano and Preisendanz, "Laminetta Magica Siciliana," 80). "Glory of the divine" here could be a variant of "glory of God" (Exod 24:16 [LXX]) or "glory of the Lord" (Exod 24:17 [LXX]). So Erik Peterson, "Das Amulett from Acre," *Aegyptus* 33 (1953): 172–78. The text's *physikou*, "of the numinous," "of the divine," i.e., "belonging to the occult laws of nature" (LSJ, s.v. "*physikos*," def. III), is commonly used simply "of nature," "physical," but as a noun can also mean "a (natural) philosopher," hence Preisendanz's extension, "magician," that is, an "occult philosopher," in which case the sense here is "to initiate him into the glory (or 'reputation?') of a magus." This, however, would belie the sense of protection needed. Of course, Moses's presence before the Lord intends to invest him with supernatural powers, nonetheless. Veltri aptly compares *physikou* to a Jewish magic name transcribed in Hebrew, "the spirit of PSQWN," in a Geniza magic text (T.-S. K 1.144, fol. 3a/17) and to PSQWN as a name of Meṭaṭron. See Veltri, "Jewish Traditions in Greek Amulets," 35; text in Peter Schäfer and Shaul Shaked, *Magische Texte aus der Kairoer Geniza*, 3 vols., TSAJ 64 (Tübingen: Mohr Siebeck, 1997), 2: no. 22.

a. The conclusion of a lost portion of narrative, which must have contained a description of Moses's encounter with the "splendor of the supernatural," and its subsequent withdrawal. For the concept of "spirit of holiness," cf. T. Levi 18:11: "and he will grant to the saints to eat from the tree of life, and the spirit of holiness will be upon them"; Rom 1:4 ("in power, according to a spirit of holiness"). See further Robert Matthew Calhoun, *Paul's Definition of the Gospel in Romans 1*, WUNT 2/316 (Tübingen: Mohr Siebeck, 2011), 137–38, with n. 121, also citing Odes of Solomon 19:4.

b. Preisendanz assumes the loss of Moses's own magic power after the spirit of God departs. It is more likely that this refers to the simple departure of Moses from the scene at the end of the narrative.

3 Make[a] a [s]pell on a gold leaf[b] (six [letters]): "*Sabaōth.*"[c] [It is necessary] to make an offering with frank[i]ncense (and) myrrh.[d]

4 A phylactery of Moses when he went up on Mount Sinai[e]

a. This and the following sentence preserve actual instructions from a magical formulary inadvertently copied into the text of the amulet itself, not that the amulet itself is a magical formulary, as argued by F. P. Rizzo, "I 'formulari di Mosé' in uno documento acrense: Paure e speranze dell' uomo tardo-antico," *Atti dell' Accademia di Scienze Lettere e Arti di Palermo* 15 (1994–1995): 1–63; cf. Christopher A. Faraone, *The Transformation of Greek Amulets in Roman Imperial Times* (Philadelphia: University of Pennsylvania Press, 2018), 18, 255, 270, 296 n. 90, 401 n. 74. In other words, the copyist working from a magical instruction book wrote onto the *lamella* instructions to be carried out by the practitioner in the actual making of the amulet and attendant rituals.

b. The spell (or "formula," Greek *logos*) on a gold leaf (*petalon chryson*) follows instructions commonly found in magical handbooks for writing inscribed "leaves" or *lamellae*. Note *PGM* VII. 382; XII. 197, 199; etc. Because the practitioner seems to have misunderstood the text he was copying, he wrote his amulet onto bronze (or, copper, rather). Clearly the instructions intended a gold leaf to be engraved, and this principally with the name of "Sabaōth," etc. What we have instead, fortunately, is the core text of the amulet (lines 7–10, below) along with all the pertinent virtues and history of the amulet and its intended uses included. This, of course, renders the text more valuable and revered to both ancient and modern readers alike. That said, the manufacture of a gold leaf with the name of the Lord on it (*Sabaōth*) echoes the tradition of Aaron making a pure gold leaf (*petalon chrysoun*), engraved "holy to the Lord," to be worn in the Holy of Holies (cf. Exod. 28:36; cf. 39:30, 31; and comments in the introduction, above). Here "Sabaōth" competes with Exodus and other traditions that suggest that the Tetragrammaton (YHWH) be engraved on the plaque. On an Aramaic silver *lamella* from Tiberias, we read of the names HW' YZWT YH YH [Y]H written on the frontlet; with reference to the "Tannaitic" quotation in b. Šabb. 63b and b. Sukkah 5a, mentioning R. Eleazar b. Yose's claim of seeing the gold plate (*ṣiṣ*) in Rome engraved with "*qodeš* to God" (note line 11, below, with note). See Joseph Naveh and Shaul Shaked, *Magic Spells and Formulae, Aramaic Incantations of Late Antiquity* (Jerusalem: Magnes; Hebrew University, 1993), amulet 17, pp. 50–57, esp. p. 52, lines 2–4; p. 54; see also no. 27, line 1, pp. 91, 93 and the note on the "(gold) foil" in *Sefer ha-Razim* §70, in this volume.

c. *Theta* (*-th*) is only a single letter; hence, six letters to the name. In the body of the amulet to be inscribed, beginning in line 14 of the Greek text with "*Iaō Sabaōth*," etc., obviously more than *Sabaōth* was to be written. Clearly, the text here has been abbreviated. Indeed, if the doublet that constitutes lines 9–13 of the Greek original were deleted, then this instruction for making a gold leaf—despite the mention of "six letters"—would be followed naturally by the amulet's text proper, beginning in line 14 of the Greek, "Make a spell on a gold leaf: '*Iaō Sabaōth Adōnaie* . . . protect so-and-so,'" etc. On these magic names of Jewish derivation, see the relevant note to v. 7, below.

d. As restored by Preisendanz. Again, we have additional instructions copied directly from the handbook onto the copper *lamella* itself. Cf. *PGM* IV. 2873–74; V. 202; XIII. 20–21 (offerings in the Key of Moses including frankincense of Helios and myrrh of Selene). In *Sefer ha-Razim* §38 and §110, we read of myrrh and frankincense being burned over coals, while an angelic incantation is invoked; cf. also Matt 2:11, on gold, frankincense, and myrrh offered to the Christ-child. As Preisendanz notes, this may refer to the "fumigation" or consecration of the metal leaf; cf. *PGM* VII. 741–55; and S. Eitrem, "Die magischen Gemmen und ihre Weihe," *Symbolae Osloenses* 19 (1939): 57–85, doi:10.1080/00397673908590338.

e. A kind of doublet of line 1, as mentioned above. For the name of the mountain, the Greek writes, corruptly, *seilamōnai*. The parallel below, in line 24 of the Greek original, reads "on Mount *Sei[n]a*" + *bein* (so Kotansky), with the second syllable possibly a corrupt form of "ascend," repeated; or, one could read *Sei(na)* [*l*]*abein*, "on Mount Sin(ai), to receive." Evidently a form of *Seina*, "Sinai" was intended (or, a corruption with Mt. Salmon; cf. Judg 9:48). A similar reference to Sinai, written [*S*]*inaios* in Greek, occurs in the magic Prayer of Jacob, line 8. See James H. Charlesworth, "Prayer of Jacob," *OTP* 2:721 n. l.

... to re[c]eive the *kasty* ("magic band").[a]

5 [(10)]By carrying [i]t, you shall fear neither a sorcerer,[b] nor a binding-spell, nor an [ev]il spiri[t],[c] nor anything whatsoever.[d]

6 But carry [i]t in purity[e] —it is something that you should not hand over to anyone except your offs[p]ring:[f]

    a. The Greek has simply *kastu* (or, *kasty*), evidently a kind of amulet. For discussion, see Kotansky, "Phylactery of Moses" (Appendix I), 148–49. The Greek is an exact transliteration of the translation of Aquila's (and Theodotion's) rendering of the rare Hebrew *qeset*, "writing case" in Ezek 9:2, 11, here perhaps a type of amulet-case, or capsule. Alternatively, Ezek 13:18, 20's *keset*, a similar word rendered "magic band(s)," may be closer, in that the so-called *to Hebraikon* version glosses these *kesatôt* as *phylaktēria*, "amulets" (phylacteries). See Frideric Field, *Originis Hexaplorum quae supersunt: Sive veterum interpretum Graecorum in totum Vetus Testamentum fragmenta*, 2 vols. (Oxford: Clarendon, 1867–1871), lxxi. The whole may contribute to the knotty question of the magic *kestos* that Aphrodite wears in *Il.* 14.214, a long-time *crux interpretum*. See Christopher A. Faraone, *Ancient Greek Love Magic* (Cambridge: Harvard University Press, 1999), 97–102, esp. p. 98 n. 4.

    b. The first two elements here imply the potential workings of harmful magic against the wearer of the charm. The first term, *magos*, is the common word for a "magician," usually (but not exclusively) pejorative. See Fritz Graf, *Magic in the Ancient World*, Revealing Antiquity 10 (Cambridge: Harvard University Press, 1997), 20–30, 31, 34, 49; Roy D. Kotansky, "The Star of the Magi: Lore and Science in Ancient Zoroastrianism, The Greek Magical Papyri, and St. Matthew's Gospel," *Annali di Storia dell' Esegesi* 24, no. 2 (2007): 379–421, esp. 392–93. This word may have in mind, too, the catalog of forbidden practices in the Mosaic decrees of Deut 18:10–11 where the difficult Hebrew word *'ôb* is glossed *magos* in the Syro-Hexapla. See Roy Kotansky, *Greek Magical Amulets: The Inscribed Gold, Silver, Copper, and Bronze Lamellae, Part I; Published Texts of Known Provenance*, Papyrologica Coloniensia 22.1 (Weisbaden: Westdeutscher Verlag, 1994), 141. The second word here, "binding-spell" (*katadesmos*), refers to curses written on lead tablets to harm one's rivals or enemies. See John G. Gager, *Curse Tablets and Binding Spells from the Ancient World* (Oxford: Oxford University Press, 1992); Esther Eidinow, "Binding Spells on Tablets and Papyri," in *Guide to the Study of Ancient Magic*, ed. David Franfurter, RGRW 189 (Leiden: Brill, 2019), 351–87.

    c. Greek *pneuma ponēron*, the particularly Hellenistic Jewish expression as found, e.g., in Luke 7:21; 8:2 (var.); and Acts 19:12; cf. also *PGM* XIIIa. 3; and Robert W. Daniel and Franco Maltomini, *Supplementum Magicum I* (Opladen: Westdeutscher Verlag, 1990), 31, 4 (both Christian). See also the gold *lamella* from Rome, which may be a calque on the Hebrew (*rwḥ r'h*, "evil spirit") behind LXX 1 Reg. 16:14–15 (a Davidic exorcism of King Saul) and Tob 6:8 (Rec. B); in Kotansky, *Greek Magical Amulets*, 25, 1, with commentary, 101–2.

    d. For the connection of esoteric teaching given to Moses on Sinai, in reference to fearless might over demonic powers, note the great *phylaktērion*, Cod. Paris. 2316, F. 316ʳ, given in R. Reitzenstein, *Poimandres: Studien zur griechischen-ägyptischen und frühchristlichen Literatur* (Leipzig: Teubner, 1904), 291–303, esp. 292: "An archangelic hymn, which God gave to Moses on Mt. Sinai, and said to him, 'Take, carry this hymn and you shall be fearless before all demonic apparitions.'"

    e. For similar injunctions, cf. *PGM* IV. 2230 ("carry it in purity"); X. 38; XII. 277 ("having consecrated it, carry it in purity"); II. 149; IV. 899.

    f. The notion of secrecy and keeping the text within one's familial or spiritual heritage is common in magic. Cf. *PGM* I. 193 ("Therefore, hand down these things to no one, except your legitimate son, alone"); IV. 872 ("teach it to no one"); IV. 851–52 ("Hand down the Rite of Solomon to no one"); IV. 2517–18 ("keep it secret, son"); XII. 94 ("child . . . you shall guard this in a holy manner, handing it down to no one, except your fellow mystics in your sacred rites"). Here, however, we should observe that, in reference to the fact that this text shows an

7 "*Iaō Sabaōth Adōnaie Seilam Abla/*[(15)]*natha[n]alba*,[a]
O World of the World,[b] protect (him/her), so-and-so.[c]

8 "*Abrasax [T]rō Ypszasssooch*, 'called dry land' *zoo.e*
[magic signs] *oooochoabria[.]s Iaō ou ei eie Iēou
Thaththa Elaa Phtha ōō*.[d]

9 "The [(20)]heaven will be da[r]k<en>ed, [a]nd I will speak,
And let the earth [h]ear the wor<ds of my mo>uth,
10 As fi<ne> dew upon the grass, and as gentle showers upon the herb,
Because <I have called> the name of the L(or)d."

(Deut. 32:1–3 Aquila).[e]

---

unusual amount of wear from handling (see introduction, above), this mandate was probably properly followed, as this will explain how the text was worn down by constant handling through subsequent generations within the owner's own family.

a. This series of magical names begins the text of the Phylactery of Moses, proper. *Iaō Sabaōth Adōnaie* represents the common "Lord God of Hosts" from the Hebrew Bible, used often in magical and gnostic texts as three separate divine names; cf. e.g., Charlesworth, "Prayer of Jacob," 721, with nn. l, q, and r; Roy D. Kotansky, "Kronos and a New Magical Inscription Formula on a Gem in the J. P. Getty Museum," *Ancient World* 3 (1980): 181–88: "*Iaō, Sabaōth, Adōnaie*, the three great ones." On the underlying Hebrew, cf. Roy D. Kotansky, Péter Kovács, and Péter Prohászka, "A Gold Lamella for Migraine from Aquincum," *Journal of Ancient Judaism* 6 (2015): 127–42, esp. 136–39. *Seilam* is a shortened form of *Se(mes)eilam*, "Eternal Sun"; and *Ablanathanalba* is a widespread palindromic name (a name that reads the same forward and backward) of uncertain meaning.

b. Greek, *kosme kosmou*, is seemingly a mistake for the namesake of the famous tractate, *Kore Kosmou*, "Pupil/Girl of the World" in the *Corpus Hermeticum*, which contains mystic teachings of Isis on the creation of the world. See A. D. Nock and A. J. Festugière, eds., *Corpus Hermeticum*, IV: *Fragments Extraits de Stobée (XXIII–XXIX)* (Paris: Les Belles Lettres, 1980), frag. XXIII, 1–50. Or, as argued in Kotansky, this may be an Aquilan-like literalism for Hebrew *ôlam le-ôlam*, "forever and ever," whose root can be understood as "world, creation" (*Greek Magical Amulets*, 142). In either case, we understand here an invocation of, or sympathetic allusion to, the creation of the world as a means of bringing about protection and healing for the wearer of the charm. The use of Hebrew words alongside Greek (here and elsewhere in the notes below), especially within the context of Aquilan-like translational techniques, suggests a tradition of interpretive glossing found in other magical texts. See Roy D. Kotansky, "A Hexagonal Aquamarine Gem with New Hermeneutical Glosses," *Mus* 135 (2022): 285–319 (esp. 312 n. 70, on our Phylactery of Moses); and Kotansky, "An Invocation on an Obsidian Gem with Hermeneutical Glosses," *Mus* 132 (2019): 259–87. The Phylactery of Moses would benefit from closer scrutiny of this technique in the light of Origen's *Hexapla* (see nn. a and b to v. 4, above).

c. "Protect so-and-so" reflects the careless copying of a formulary, where "so-and-so" (Greek *tonde* = *ton deina*) represents the place in the actual amulet where the owner's name was supposed to be inserted (cf. *PGM* IV. 1193, etc.). The positioning of this common formula of protection here creates a "like-by-like" association between the bearer of the amulet and Moses, who also found protection before God's presence (lines 1–2) in the erstwhile *historiola*, given in fragmentary form above.

d. These lines appear to contain a mixture of magic names (e.g., *Abrasax*, numerically equivalent to 365; *Iaō* + *Iēou*, with *eie*, perhaps Hebrew "I am" in Exod 3:14 [cf. Kotansky, "Obsidian Gem," 278]; and *Phtha* = Egyptian Ptah, the creator god of Memphis) and garbled Greek, with perhaps an allusion to the LXX text of Gen 1:10 ("and God called the dry land, 'earth'"). If so, this would go well with the notion that this section invokes the powers of creation for protection.

e. These vv. **9–10** (lines 19–22 in the original Greek) preserve a new Aquilan fragment of

The Phylactery of Moses

11 A phylactery of Moses[a] when he went up on Mount Sinai ⁽²⁵⁾to [r]eceive the golden tablet (*ṣiṣi*),[b] to receive the magic band (*keset*).
12 By carrying [i]t,[c] you shall fear neither a sorcerer, no[r] a binding-spell, No[r] an evil-spirit, nor anything whatsoever.
13 But carry i[t] in [p]urity—it is something that you should not hand [o]ver to anyone except your offspring:

14 "*Iaō Sab/*⁽³⁰⁾*a[ōth]* <. . .>."[d]

15 For fever, or [fo]r daily [fever], or for the Evil Ey[e], [or for] requesting good things.[e]

16 [By carrying it], you shall [fe]ar [neither] a sorcerer, nor an [evil] spir[it], [nor] an [ap]parition.[f]

Deut. 32:1–3, as identified and discussed more fully in Kotansky, "Phylactery of Moses, Appendix 2," in *Greek Magical Amulets*, 149–54. As transcribed onto our copper leaf, however, the verses could hardly have been understood as anything other than magic words along with the invocations of v. **8** (lines 14–22, of the original). The corrupt nature of the verses shows the antiquity of this original text, for it must have undergone considerable copying for it to have reached this level of corruption. The use of rare, poetic, or obscure words by Aquila may have contributed to its misunderstanding.

a. As mentioned in the introduction, this is a repetition, yet again, of previous verses, this time those closer to vv. **4–7** (Greek lines 8–14a) than to vv. **1–3** (Greek lines 1–6). The phylactery proper here, though, terminates with the citation only of the first two words of the quoted invocation: "*Iaō Sabaōth*" (below, in v. **14** = Greek lines 29–30).

b. This phrase, not in the earlier doublets, seems to be a variant on "to receive the *kasty*" that follows. The Greek reads simply, "to receive the *seisei*," a word we take to be a transliteration of Hebrew/Aramaic *ṣiṣ/ṣiṣah*, "plate, foil," a reference to the gold tablet of v. **3**, above.

c. See above, vv. **5–6**, for the doublet contained in these verses.

d. A truncated citation of the amuletic invocation proper that is contained more fully, above, in vv. **7–10**.

e. A kind of amulet title, again copied unwittingly from the magical handbook used as the scribe's *Vorlage*. Such titles, or subtitles, usually come at the beginning of the magical text and describe the promised virtues of the amulet. Here the titular promises read wholly like a scribal intrusion into the text, for nothing in the earlier doublets mentions fever or the evil eye, but rather sorcery, binding-spells, and evil spirits. But here the intrusive material works to expand the effectiveness of the spell. The third element about requesting good things, however, reads in the next verse rather more congruently with the concluding verses of the spell and operates well with the general timbre of the text overall, which describes Moses's final words of blessing to the people of Israel before they enter the Promised Land. For fever amulets, cf. P. J. Sijpesteijn, "Amulet against Fever," *CdE* 57 (1982): 377–81 (with additional literature); Daniel and Maltomini, *Supplementum Magicum I*, nos. 2–4, 9–14, 18–19, 21–23, 25, 28–31, 34–35, etc.; Kotansky, "Textual Amulets and Writing Traditions," 547–49. For the evil eye, see Campbell Bonner, *Studies in Magical Amulets Chiefly Graeco-Egyptian* (Ann Arbor: University of Michigan Press, 1950), 96–98; Daniel and Maltomini, *Supplementum Magicum I*, no. 6, line 8; Bernhard Kötting, "Böser Blick," *RAC* 2:473–82; Roy D. Kotansky, "'Beware the Evil Eye': A Closer Glance at a Recent Title," *Mus* 131 (2018): 217–37. For request spells, cf. *PGM* XII. 144; XIII. 287.

f. Here the repeated verse from earlier omits the reference to a "binding-spell" (and to "anything whatsoever") and includes, at the end, a mention of an apparition (Greek *phantasia*), a reference to a ghost or demonic visitation (cf. *PGM* IV. 2699–701; VII. 579, etc.).

17 You shall live lo[ng days] ⁽³⁵⁾having [l]earned [these things].ᵃ

18 You shall live a lo[ng life, having] freedom from [an evil dem]on.ᵇ

Restored Version:
I. A phylactery of Moses that he used when he went up on Mt. Sinai to get the *ṣiṣi-* (or: *keset-*) amulet, to protect him in the Holy of Holies, (and) to lead him into the splendor of the supernatural. < . . . then > the Spirit of Holiness withdrew, and after these things he turned away.

II. "*Iaō Sabaōth Adōnaie Seilam Ablanathanalba*, O World of the World, protect (him/her), so-and-so. *Abrasax [T]rō Ypszasssooch*, 'called dry land' *zoo.e* [magic signs] *oooochoabria.s Iaō ou ei eie Iēou Thaththa Elaa Phtha ōō*. The heaven will be darkened, and I will speak, and let the earth hear the words of my mouth. As fine dew upon the grass, and as gentle showers upon the herb, because I have called upon the name of the Lord."

III. Make the spell on a gold leaf. It is necessary to make an offering of myrrh with frankincense.

IV. By carrying it you shall fear neither a sorcerer, nor a binding-spell, nor an evil-spirit, nor an apparition, nor anything whatsoever. But carry it in purity; it is something that you should not hand over to anyone except your offspring. You shall live long days having learned these things. You shall live a long life, having freedom from an evil demon.

V. (Also) for fever, or for daily fever, or for the evil eye, (and) for requesting good things.

---

a. Presumably, all the things pertaining to the Phylactery of Moses including the important *historiola* about the phylactery's procurement, albeit a narrative mostly lost in this copy of the amulet.

b. For the restoration of these lines, based in part on parallels from Deuteronomy (e.g., Deut 30:20; 32:27, 47; etc.), see discussion in Kotansky, *Greek Magical Amulets*, 147–48. The noun *adeia*, used of freedom from an evil demon, seems to represent another Aquilan word. In the famous passage of Isa 61:1, the LXX's *aphesis* used of the "emancipation" or "setting free" of captives (Hebrew *drwr*) is rendered rather *adeia* (as also in Jer 34:9 Hexapla = LXX 41:9).

Jannes and Jambres
A new translation and introduction

by W. B. Henry and T. M. Erho

Perhaps the best-known parabiblical character in antiquity, Jannes, the great Egyptian magician, rose to prominence in Jewish, pagan, and Christian circles around the turn of the era, being named early on in the Damascus Document (5.18–19), Pliny the Elder's *Natural History* (30.11), and pseudo-Paul (2 Tim 3:8).[1] Many traditions[2] developed about him and an initially unnamed brother, eventually dubbed Jambres,[3] the most significant strand being the narrative found in the book or apocryphon Jannes and Jambres.[4] Underlying this work, set against the backdrop of the exodus, is the persistent theme of the mortality of all terrestrial beings and the absolute sovereignty of the God of heaven, that of the Hebrews/Jews, who will ultimately punish those who oppose him and do not behave morally.

Contents

Despite the fragmentary state of the text and variance between witnesses, much of the basic narrative can be reconstructed. The apocryphon opens with the mother of the eponymous brothers receiving an alarming dream (p. 1). Upon learning its details, Jannes realizes that it foretells his own death and a simultaneous calamity for Egypt in three years' time (p. 2). He has a fortified garden built, but an earthquake and storm damage it, and he runs to his library (pp. 2–3). When two heavenly emissaries indicate in a dream that they will remove Jannes from his house fourteen days later, he bids his mother farewell and flees to Memphis after giving his brother Jambres a series of instructions (pp. 4–6). When in Memphis, Jannes announces that he is giving his daughter away in marriage to Jambres (pp. 6–7). After the festivities, Jannes issues further instructions to his brother before being called away to counter the miracles that Moses and Aaron are performing before Pharaoh. He is at first successful, but, falling ill, realizes that he is opposing God

---

1. Although the character is modeled on the generic references to the Egyptian magicians in Exodus (7:11, 22; 8:7, 18; 9:11), the individual figure and his name are purely extrabiblical (at least from the Jewish perspective).

2. These traditions have been collected by Albert Pietersma, *The Apocryphon of Jannes and Jambres the Magicians: P. Chester Beatty XVI (with New Editions of Papyrus Vindobonensis Greek inv. 29456 + 29828verso and British Library Cotton Tiberius B. v f. 87)*, RGRW 119 (Leiden: Brill, 1994), 3–47. A recent addition is the Coptic Exodus Apocryphon translated by Frederic Krueger in this volume.

3. In Latin, Jambres is known as "Mambres," and his brother's name is usually "Iamnes." On the various forms of these names, see Pietersma, *The Apocryphon of Jannes and Jambres the Magicians*, 36–42.

4. The full initial title (p. 1) is "Book of Tales of Jannes and Jambres." The so-called Gelasian decree of the sixth century includes "Penitence of Iamnes and Mambres" in a list of apocryphal books; see Ernst von Dobschütz, *Das Decretum Gelasianum de libris recipiendis et non recipiendis in kritischem Text herausgegeben und untersucht*, TUGAL 38.4 (Leipzig: Hinrichs, 1912), 12.

in opposing Moses and Aaron and must now die. He then engages in another conversation with Jambres (pp. 7–9). After his death, the predicted calamity, the destruction of Pharaoh and his army in the Red Sea, takes place (p. 10). This event prompts Jannes's mother to visit him, but upon realizing that she is speaking with a specter and her son is in fact dead, she also dies (pp. 11–12). When Jambres has attended to her burial, he performs necromancy and summons the spirit of his brother (p. 12). The very fragmentary final part of the text is a speech of Jannes's ghost, detailing the horrors of hell and how no earthly creature, no matter how great or powerful, can escape death, and urging his brother to live an upright life.

Manuscripts and Versions

Jannes and Jambres is preserved in the original Greek in four Egyptian papyri assigned to the third and fourth centuries CE.[5] An extensive fragment of an Ethiopic translation also exists, as well as a short excerpt in Latin.[6]

- The most important Greek manuscript is the fourth-century codex B (P. Chester Beatty CBL BP XVI), housed in the Chester Beatty in Dublin. Its provenance is unknown. Parts of nine damaged leaves survive, each with writing on both sides.[7]
- Next in importance is V (P.Vindob. G 29456 + 29828 + 180 + 28249 v), a third-century copy on the back of a roll of unknown provenance now in the papyrus collection of the Austrian National Library in Vienna.[8] The two largest fragments, A and B, each representing a single column, overlap pp. 5–6 and 7–8 of codex B, one column being lost between them. Fragments C and D belong to the final part of the book, with fragment C overlapping p. 17 of codex B.

---

5. There is nothing to suggest that the Greek is a translation from another language.

6. There is no complete and up-to-date critical edition. Pietersma, *Apocryphon of Jannes and Jambres the Magicians*, includes, along with the first edition of B (91–261), most of V (263–74), and the Latin fragment as given in the London manuscript (275–81). The remainder of V was first published by Pietersma, "Two More Fragments of the Vienna *Jannes and Jambres*," *BASP* 49 (2012): 21–29. H was first published by Georg Schmelz, "Zwei neue Fragmente des Apokryphons über die Zauberer Jannes und Jambres," in *Atti del XXII Congresso Internazionale di Papirologia, Firenze, 23–29 agosto 1998*, ed. Isabella Andorlini et al., 2 vols. (Florence: Istituto Papirologico "G. Vitelli," 2001), 2:1207–12; and O by S. Beresford, "5290: *Jannes and Jambres*," in *The Oxyrhynchus Papyri Volume LXXXII*, ed. N. Gonis et al., Graeco-Roman Memoirs 103 (London: Egypt Exploration Society, 2016), 1–6. Martina Hirschberger has provided a text and German translation based on earlier editions but including many new proposals, some of which merit serious consideration. See Hirschberger, "Die Magier des Pharao: Das *Buch der Worte von Jannes und Jambres* in seinem Kontext," in *Jüdisch-hellenistische Literatur in ihrem interkulturellen Kontext*, ed. Martina Hirschberger (Frankfurt: Lang, 2012), 229–65. The Ethiopic fragment was first published in Ted M. Erho and W. Benjamin Henry, "The Ethiopic *Jannes and Jambres* and the Greek Original," *APF* 65 (2019): 176–223; this article also includes new editions of large parts of the Greek taking the new evidence into account (194–212) and a discussion of the order of the material (212–15). There are comments on various textual points in W. B. Henry, "Notes on *Jannes and Jambres* (P. Chester Beatty XVI)," *ZPE* 198 (2016): 59–67; a further set is being prepared for publication.

7. The designations of the fragments contributing to each page are specified in the headings in the translation below.

8. The front, used first, carries the Vienna Hermetica. For an edition and French translation of this text, see Jean-Pierre Mahé, *Hermès Trismégiste*, vol. 5: *Paralipomènes* (Paris: Les Belles Lettres, 2019), 307–30. There is an English translation in M. David Litwa, *Hermetica II: The Excerpts of Stobaeus, Papyrus Fragments, and Ancient Testimonies in an English Translation with Notes and Introductions* (Cambridge: Cambridge University Press, 2018), 171–74.

- H (P.Heid. inv. G 1016), a small fragment of a single leaf of a fourth-century codex of unknown provenance, kept in the papyrus collection of the University of Heidelberg, overlaps pp. 8–10 of B. There is text on both sides.
- O (P.Oxy. LXXXII 5290), the outer half of a fourth-century codex leaf, was found in the rubbish dumps of Oxyrhynchus (modern Bahnasa) in the 1905–1906 excavation season. It forms part of the collection of the Egypt Exploration Society, now kept in the Bodleian Art, Archaeology and Ancient World Library in Oxford. There is text on both sides, representing a fuller version of part of p. 11 of B.
- A thirteenth-century bifolium containing parts of an Old Ethiopic version translated directly from the original Greek is found in the Roger Schneider *Nachlass* at the Walda Masqal Centre of the Institute for Ethiopian Studies in Addis Ababa (Schneider ms. frag. 19). While the exact provenance of this fragment is uncertain, it most likely came from the Tigray Region of northern Ethiopia. The first leaf of the bifolium covers the entirety of pp. 6–7 of B, as well as parts of both pp. 5 and 8, allowing for the reconstruction of much of the lost Greek text in this section. No precise textual overlap has been identified in the Greek for the second Ethiopic leaf, but its contents are of similar character to pp. 17–18 of B.[9]
- The Latin excerpt is transmitted, together with an Old English translation, in an eleventh-century manuscript in the British Library in London, Cotton Tiberius B V Part I f. 87r. There is a twelfth-century copy of the Latin, thought to be drawn from the London manuscript, in the Bodleian Library in Oxford, Bodl. 614 ff. 47v–48r.[10] The opening corresponds closely to p. 12 of B, and the speech of Iamnes from the underworld corresponds in part to the fragmentary p. 13 of B.

From the surviving Greek evidence, it seems clear that multiple versions of the book circulated, as, for example, the conversation between Jannes and his mother in O is significantly longer than B can accommodate. The Ethiopic bifolium may reinforce this notion: while the first Ethiopic leaf accords closely with the extant Greek text, the second, though doubtless containing an equally literal rendering of the same *Vorlage*, lacks any direct parallel in B.[11] Given the fragmentary character of all the surviving witnesses, how many versions of the book existed in antiquity and the extent to which they differed from one another cannot be ascertained.[12]

Date and Provenance

The proliferation of traditions about Jannes and Jambres in the early centuries of the Common Era complicates the dating of the apocryphon, as most of the preserved references to these figures do not relate to this work. While the earliest physical evidence for the

---

9. For this reason, a translation of the entirety of the second Ethiopic leaf is provided below.
10. For the Latin text of both copies, see Andy Orchard, *Pride and Prodigies: Studies in the Monsters of the* Beowulf-*Manuscript*, rev. ed. (Toronto: University of Toronto Press, 2003), 181 (§37), and for the Old English text, with a parallel translation, 202–3 (§37).
11. As the Greek of the part in question is preserved in a highly fragmentary form, it is not clear how much weight can be placed on this argument.
12. P.Mich. inv. 4925 v, a genealogical fragment seemingly mentioning both Jannes and Jambres that had been assigned to the early part of the book, probably belongs instead to the large corpus of external traditions about the brothers. Cf. Erho and Henry, "Ethiopic *Jannes and Jambres*," 213 n. 32. It should not be brought to bear upon this question.

book, the fragments of a roll in Vienna (V), offers a *terminus ante quem* in the third century, a more precise or earlier dating is less easy to substantiate. Pseudo-Paul's statement that "Jannes and Jambres opposed Moses" (2 Tim 3:8) does not comport with the extant narrative, in which Jannes leaves his brother behind and goes to oppose the miraculous acts being performed by Moses and Aaron single-handedly (p. 7). The absence of Jambres from these events, moreover, seems integral to the apocryphon, as, with the exception of his necromancy ritual, he functions purely as a passive secondary character, the primary addressee of his brother's speeches; moreover, his involvement in the confrontation before Pharaoh would seemingly place him in a position similar to that of Jannes as a direct antagonist of the God of the Hebrews inescapably doomed to Hades, rather than one for whom penitence and change remain possible. Similar comments apply to a fuller account given by the second-century Greek philosopher Numenius of Apamea (frag. 9).[13] Numenius, like pseudo-Paul, has Jannes and Jambres acting together to counter Moses. However, the philosopher also mentions that the two were able to undo the most violent of the disasters that Moses brought against Egypt, a scenario conflicting with the biblical account in which, after some initial successes (Exod 7:11, 22; 8:7), the magicians fail to replicate the plagues (Exod 8:18). In the apocryphon, there is almost no interest in the plagues, and Jannes's "doing as many things as they (Moses and Aaron) were doing" (p. 5), followed by his incapacitation (cf. Exod 9:11), might be construed as his total success in the magical showdown. Numenius may have known a related form of the tale, but it is unlikely that this aligned closely with the narrative of the apocryphon.[14] While Origen demonstrates knowledge of this story of Numenius in *Against Celsus* (4.51), in his *Commentary on Matthew* (*Comm. ser. Matt.* 117 [GCS 38:250]), the Alexandrian directly refers to a secret or apocryphal book entitled "Iamnes and Mambres." No details are provided with respect to its exact contents, but this is the first reference to such a book rather than scenarios of uncertain length and character involving the brothers. The *Commentary on Matthew*, written around 248, more likely than not alludes to the same work as is found in the papyri, the earliest of which dates to the same century. The apocryphon itself, however, may be somewhat earlier.

Nothing in the extant content of Jannes and Jambres is manifestly Christian, and a Jewish origin for the work seems probable. Pseudo-Paul's statement about the magicians would have placed no constraints upon a Jewish author in the composition of such a tale, whereas some attempt to align with it might be expected of Christians, unless they belonged to a community which either rejected or was unfamiliar with 2 Timothy.[15] The narrative setting suggests a connection to the Egyptian diaspora.

Sources generally remember Jannes and Jambres as a duo, magicians of seemingly equal merit, an equivalence hardly in keeping with the preserved narrative of the apocryphon, with which they normally lack any familiarity.[16] In the apocryphon, only Jannes

---

13. See Édouard des Places, *Numénius: Fragments* (Paris: Les Belles Lettres, 1973), 51.
14. See Fabienne Jourdan, "Numénius et les traditions juives: La confrontation de Moïse avec Jannès et Jambrès (Num. 18 F = fr. 9 dP)," *Semitica et Classica* 14 (2021): 39–57.
15. The third-century Vienna fragments were copied not in a codex but on the back of a roll that already had a Hermetic text on the front, but nothing can be read into this choice: while the codex is the book form usually associated with Christianity, there are numerous cases in which a used roll received a Christian text on the back. See, e.g., Peter Malik, "P.Oxy. VIII.1079 ($\mathfrak{P}^{18}$): Closing on a 'Curious' Codex?," *NTS* 65 (2019): 99 n. 21, adding P.Oxy. LXXXVI 5534.
16. Cf. Pietersma, *Apocryphon of Jannes and Jambres the Magicians*, 25–35; and Krueger on the Coptic Exodus Apocryphon in this volume.

appears to be in the king's employ, and he alone is summoned to Pharaoh's court to combat Moses and Aaron. Jambres does ultimately perform necromancy with the aid of Jannes's magical book in order to bring up the spirit of his brother for their climactic conversation, but his skillfulness in the art is nowhere indicated, and it is not suggested before that point that he is a magician. It may be of significance, therefore, that two of the earliest writers to reference some form of the legend, Pliny the Elder (*Nat.* 30.11) and Apuleius (*Apol.* 90.6), include Jannes in lists of famous magicians without his brother, in contradistinction to virtually all later sources.[17] This comes closer to reflecting Jannes's preeminence in the apocryphon, and could point toward the work's circulation close to the turn of the era, though this admittedly strains very meager evidence.

If the text derives from the Egyptian diaspora, it is possibly relevant that Philo of Alexandria denounces a mythological interpretation of Gen 6:1–4 in his tractate *On the Giants*, in part due to its similarities to Greek myths about the giants and Titans. Such an interpretation may have been common in his day.[18] If so, and if the contents of the second Ethiopic leaf belong to the original Jannes and Jambres narrative, this may be the conceptual background against which the Jewish giants of Enochic fame could straightforwardly be given the names of Greek heroes. But the circulation of mythological interpretations of this type can hardly be restricted to Philo's time if they existed.

The contents of the apocryphon thus offer no firm clues as to its period of origin. Although it is arguably anti-Egyptian, the work's composition should not be tied to a particular crisis (such as Trajan's 115–117 campaign), and dates in the first two centuries CE, or even slightly before the turn of the era, remain plausible.

Literary Context

While the biblical exodus narrative looms behind the tale of Jannes and Jambres, its tangible impact is negligible and most elements that do appear are subtly different. For example, Jannes, seemingly by himself, counters the miraculous signs performed by Moses without failure (p. 7), whereas in the biblical account a group of magicians succeeds in replicating only three miracles (Exod 7:11, 22; 8:7) before becoming overmatched (Exod 8:18; 9:11). Perhaps the most direct resemblance to a passage in Exodus follows immediately thereafter, as the great magician becomes tormented with a bad sore, the one plague said to have affected the magicians (Exod 9:11). Apart from this, however, the plagues do not appear in the extant sections of Jannes and Jambres at all. The Exodus account itself only otherwise seems to be referenced in the drowning of the Egyptians in the Red Sea (p. 10). Thus, while Exodus lies in the background of Jannes and Jambres, it serves as a well-known backdrop for the narrative rather than a major source upon which the author relied in composing the tale.

Another biblical passage, the Septuagintal rendering of Ezek 32:17–22, probably influenced the formulation of part of Jannes's speech at the end of the book. This section mentions a series of terrestrial elites—kings of Egypt, Egyptian nobles, the tallest humans, and, in at least one version of the speech, giants—whose spirits reside

---

17. The Damascus Document (5.18–19) also mentions Yoḥanah alongside a nameless brother.

18. See Michael Tuval, "'Συναγωγὴ γιγάντων' (Prov 21:16): The Giants in the Jewish Literature in Greek," in *Ancient Tales of Giants from Qumran and Turfan*, ed. Matthew Goff, Loren T. Stuckenbruck, and Enrico Morano, WUNT 360 (Tübingen: Mohr Siebeck, 2016), 54.

in hell despite their earthly power while alive, introducing each with a "Where is?" question followed by a rhetorical "Did not he/they die?" The Ezekiel passage similarly records a series of figures who were once great upon earth, including giants, kings, and commanders, concluding with the pronouncement that Pharaoh and his compatriots will join them in death and Hades, just as they do in Jannes and Jambres. As exemplified in the giants' rhetorical "You are greater than whom?" (Ezek 32:21 LXX), the overarching theology of this section, according to which even great earthly creatures all perish and none match God's power, likewise mirrors the perspective of the apocryphon.

Except possibly for the Book of the Watchers,[19] direct influence from other Jewish writings cannot be discerned in the surviving text of Jannes and Jambres. However, there are several striking similarities to the Book of Giants. Both texts focus on the antagonists, two brothers who are elites of their races. Each of the pairs encounters dreams foretelling their own demise and the corporate destruction of their races by water, in the Deluge or in the Red Sea. If the content of the second Ethiopic leaf belongs to the original layer of textual composition, then giants named after foreign heroes feature in both works (the Babylonian Gilgamesh in the Book of Giants and the Greek Acamas and Ajax in Jannes and Jambres) alongside others with names of varying origins. Each then also includes giants' wives, a notion never explicitly raised in other early Jewish writings,[20] and the instigation of some form of giganticide relating to an action involving one of these. Their theological outlooks are likewise closely congruent, being concerned with the sovereignty of God over all earthly creatures, who are mortal and will face divine punishment regardless of their terrestrial might.

While the author was likely immersed in the Greco-Egyptian world, he exhibits no meaningful knowledge of Greek myth.[21] Still, the names of Ajax and Acamas belong to heroes, those of semidivine parentage, and may have been selected for this reason. The Jewish Watchers, the sons of heaven, beget giants through intercourse with the daughters of men on earth, a lineage effectively analogous to that of Greek heroes in general and a cross-cultural equation aided by their description as "renowned men" in the Septuagintal rendering of Gen 6:4. Other elements in this part of Jannes and Jambres occasionally come close to duplicating something from Greek mythology, such as the idea of giants throwing rocks (see e.g., Hesiod, *Theog.* 715–716), but such generic resemblances are probably coincidental. In any case, the part of the text translated on the second Ethiopic leaf is exceptional, and if it is set aside, there is no clear evidence of classical influence in the apocryphon.

---

19. It is not clear whether the reference in the second Ethiopic leaf to the insatiable giants who drink blood derives from 1 En. 7:4–5, the Book of Giants, or some other tradition. The surviving fragments of the Book of Giants are translated in this volume.

20. The idea would seem to be assumed in a fragment of pseudo-Eupolemus quoted by Eusebius, *Praep. ev.* 9.18.2, where Abraham's ancestry is traced back to the giants.

21. The author of the text translated on the second Ethiopic leaf may have known Eratosthenes's 250,000 stadia calculation for the circumference of the earth; see Erho and Henry, "Ethiopic *Jannes and Jambres*," 192.

Bibliography

Beresford, S. "5290: *Jannes and Jambres*." Pages 1–6 in *The Oxyrhynchus Papyri Volume LXXXII*. Edited by N. Gonis, F. Maltomini, W. B. Henry, and S. Slattery. Graeco-Roman Memoirs 103. London: Egypt Exploration Society, 2016.

Erho, Ted M., and W. Benjamin Henry. "The Ethiopic *Jannes and Jambres* and the Greek Original." *APF* 65 (2019): 176–223. doi:10.1515/apf-2019-0010.

Henry, W. B. "Notes on *Jannes and Jambres* (P. Chester Beatty XVI)." *ZPE* 198 (2016): 59–67.

Hirschberger, Martina. "Die Magier des Pharao: Das *Buch der Worte von Jannes und Jambres* in seinem Kontext." Pages 213–65 in *Jüdisch-hellenistische Literatur in ihrem interkulturellen Kontext*. Edited by Martina Hirschberger. Frankfurt: Lang, 2012.

Pietersma, Albert. *The Apocryphon of Jannes and Jambres the Magicians: P. Chester Beatty XVI (with New Editions of Papyrus Vindobonensis Greek inv. 29456 + 29828verso and British Library Cotton Tiberius B. v f. 87)*. RGRW 119. Leiden: Brill, 1994. (Further bibliography may be found here.)

———. "Two More Fragments of the Vienna *Jannes and Jambres*." *BASP* 49 (2012): 21–29. doi:10.2143/BASP.49.0.3206595.

Schmelz, Georg. "Zwei neue Fragmente des Apokryphons über die Zauberer Jannes und Jambres." Pages 1199–1212 in vol. 2 of *Atti del XXII Congresso Internazionale di Papirologia, Firenze, 23–29 agosto 1998*. Edited by Isabella Andorlini, Guido Bastianini, Manfredo Manfredi, and Giovanna Menci. 2 vols. Florence: Istituto Papirologico "G. Vitelli," 2001.

NOTE: for a summary of an additional manuscript of the Ethiopic version of Jannes and Jambres, which came to our attention too late to translate in this chapter, see the appendix at the end of this volume. Some details of this chapter have been corrected in light of new information in this manuscript.

Jannes and Jambres

Page 1 (1abcd3h4c→)
Book of Tales of Jannes and Jambres

In Memphis in the time of King Pharaoh [. . .] a beautiful young woman [. . .] intimate friend of King Pharaoh [. . .]

[. . .] dwells [. . .] King [. . .] mother [. . .] son J[a— . . .] has seen [. . .]: for [.] saw [. . .] and four-obol [. . .] full [. . .] iron saw coming [. .], and that he came to a cypress, and he sawed it and left three spans and [.] raised it, [and .] eight days the cypress [. . .]

Jannes, hearing of the dr[eam and being dis]heartened and [seeing] hi[s] mother [.], asked her to g[o] to her own place, instructing her not to [. . .] "For many [phantoms are] dis[played . . .] like human beings [. . . their] eyes [.]

Page 2 (1abcd3h4c↓)
[. . .] and [. . .] and their mouth not [.] their [.] is not seen speaking [and] their [feet] do not touch the ground [. . ."]

[. . .] (she) [g]oing [. . .] (he) [.]ing [. . . Jam]bres, (he) ann[ounced . . .] his mother [. . .] told [hi]m [th]at h[is mother . . .] "and I am [the cy]pre[ss,] and the human being [. .] saw [is] an angel of God. [. .] sawing the cypress he let [.] three [s]pans, after three years I [will] di[e]; but if I [.] this critical time, I am blessed. But gr[eat] torment [will come t]o Egypt when I di[e."]

Jannes [to]ld all [the craf]tsmen, builders, and architects to build a wall around the garden, and when it was built he left it [. . .] Their father [. . .]

Page 3 (2a→)
[. . .] all [. . .] having convened [. . .] wise men and [. . .] seven [days] he entert[ained i]n the [. .] and seeing [. .] the planting flourishing (and) the [.] already providing shade, he [was] glad; and when [eveni]ng came, he ordered [. . .] under a cer[tain] apple-tree. And [.] him[a] a great earthquake happ[ened]

---

a. Or "there."

The translations of the second leaf of the Ethiopic fragment and of pp. 6–8 and much of pp. 17–18 of the Greek are based on the editions published in Ted M. Erho and W. Benjamin Henry, "The Ethiopic *Jannes and Jambres* and the Greek Original," *APF* 65 (2019): 176–223. We are grateful to Walter de Gruyter GmbH for permission to reprint this material. The edition of the whole announced in the same article (p. 176) is at an advanced stage of preparation. We thank SBL Press for permission to publish this translation of the full text here in advance of the appearance of the edition.

Jannes and Jambres

and [.] from heaven [. .] thunder, so that some [cypre]sses were uprooted from the garden. The[n] Jannes ran into the library where [his] powers were

Page 4 (2acf↓)
[…] omen […] and finding […] Egypt […] the bo[ok…] commanded […] came […] clothed […] two having […] him, and saying, "The lord of the earth [himsel]f and overseer [of al]l sent us to lead you away [. .] thus a companion of corpses [. . fo]rever." [But] taking pity, [the] two white-clad (figures) sai[d . .] will be still in hi[s hom]e [for another] fourteen [days and th]en […]

Page 5 (4abdefg→)
to you." He, when wak[ing…] and recalling the […] and seeing Jambr[es…] (he) […] said […] king […] magicians […][a]

"[…] Do not trouble yourself any more, then, […] mother, lest [you] become exasperated […] I shall send to [you] daily so that I know your affairs and you mine. I gave orders to Jambres my brother too to care for you faithfully."[b] And he went up to her and kissed her, suppressing his tears. But when she had left, he let out tears like a river. And he sent out, begging all his friends to show care for his mother.

Summoning[c] his brother, he t[rave]led to Memphis, taking [the] book. And he said [to him,] "Jambres,[d] […][e] writ[-]

Page 6 (4abdefg↓)
[and] keep it in secret and [take care not to come out] on the day on which [the king] and the chiefs of Egypt come out [to pursue] the people of the Hebrews nor to [go] along with them, but [plan] to be unwell and sa[ve your own] soul from death and from [the destruction of the Egyp]tians which the God of the hea[vens[f] will carry out according to his word on behalf of the children of the Hebrews whom the Egyptians caused to die in the river. And when the ti]me of [my de]ath [comes], go [every day to] our mother [and send me] letters, and when [the three years are completed, te]ll her, '[The] king [comman]ded him [to remain] for another [three years,' so that our] mother [will not] go [to Memphis and find out that I have] died. [But if she compels you to say,] sa[y], 'He is [impure] and cannot [be seen until] he is purified.'" And sending word f[rom Memphis,] he [con]vened [all] the [chiefs of] Egypt [and said to] the[m, "I am giving away my] dau[ghter] to [my] brother

---

a. Part of the gap can be supplied from V frag. A, which begins here. It has "[…] know, mo[ther…] me to remain in the […] three magicians [.] wi[sdom…] and stand over […] And agreeing," in which "magicians" corresponds to "magicians" in B.
 b. V has "to pr[ovi]de for you, to care for you faithfully."
 c. V has "t[aking] along."
 d. V has "'Brother'" in place of "[to him], 'Jambres.'"
 e. The first leaf of the Ethiopic fragment begins about here.
 f. V frag. A ends here.

Page 7 (3abce1ef→)

in marriage and I am celebrating the [wedding for] seven [da]ys. And you will rej[oice] together with us, dear brothers. [And] after [a hundred] days, I depart from you [to Hades." And after making merry for the] seve[n days of the wedding, Jannes instructed his] brother [Jambres concerning his] chil[dren and concerning his wife] and mo[ther not to neglect her] nor [to abandon] he[r for one hour so that she will not be pained, but to go to her every day. And when he had] completed [his speech, am]bassadors were present [from the king, sa]ying, "Come quickly [and op]pose[a] Moses the Hebrew: [for he is] mak[ing si]gns so that everyone is amazed." And Jannes,[b] having come to the king [Pharaoh,][c] opposed Moses and his [brother] A[aron, d]oing as many things as they [were doing.] But [when] his death neared, tor[mented] by a bad sore in his bottom and not finding a bottom remedy, he sent word to the king, saying, "This is God's [mi]racle that is operating for them. Therefore I, wishing to oppose the [power of God,][d] depart to death." [And] Jannes called his brother [ag]ain [and] entreated him concerning his mother

Page 8 (3abce1ef8d↓)

not to pain h[er]: "But remember that she took a risk in life in giving birth to us.[e] Do not then be occupied about money [and] forget our mother. Get ready[f] [. . .]"[g] [. . .] and [.] breathe little." [. . .] his brother [. . .] and [. . .] Jannes . . . said, "S[uc]h indeed (is) the [. . .] and not [. . .] giving to [. . .] for the morrow [. . . ,] and the [. . .] being observed [. . .] (Jannes) questioned (Jambres): "Of what kind [is] the hour now [. .] setting of [.] star?" A[nd] he replied, ["." And he (Jannes)] said, "Such indeed (is) the hour of sinful and deceitful hea[rts,] which do not remem[ber] the hour of dea[th]." And he (Jannes) said to him, "Co[me ou]t and see how great (a part) is left of the d[a]y." And he (Jambres) said to him, "None." And Jannes said, "So great indeed (is) the [day] of every woman who will tur[n a]way from [the] bed of her own [hus]band a[nd] have intercou[rse] with another, Jambres [my] brother. Now my sou[h]

Page 9 (2h3g↓)

is destroyed[i] and [. . .] my whole body is dist[urbed .] his brother Jambres [. . .] and Jannes[j] [. . .]the oaths which [.] made [.] swear [. . .] your [.] and took away [. . .] and Jannes in dis[tress . . .] said [. his] brother [. . .] be brought [. . .] a

---

a. V frag. B begins here.
b. V appears to have omitted the word.
c. V omits the word.
d. V has different wording in the first part of the speech: "this is [. . . ,] I cannot [. . .]."
e. V has "in our being born of her."
f. The first leaf of the Ethiopic fragment ends here.
g. V has in the fragmentary part that follows "for now the breath [. . .] deny, for to[day . . .] breathe little; [. . .] his brother [. . .] he said," before breaking off.
h. H ↓ begins here.
i. H ↓ has "[is dis]turbed and destroyed."
j. H ↓ has "the fam[ous]" in the next line where B is not preserved, and no intelligible text after that.

Jannes and Jambres

hundred [beasts of burd]en, [.] ki[ds [. . .] a hundred [. .]asses [. . .] a hundred camels a[nd . . .] place [. . .] held [. . .] them [. . .]

Page 10 (2h3g→)
[. . .] and noise [. . .] and mour[ned . .] hi[s] brother [. . .[a] k]ing with the [. . .] came to pursue the p[eople of the Heb]rews and perished [. . .] in the Red[b] Sea [. . .] Egypt [. . .] and the people [of the Hebrews, and there wa]s wailing [. . .] Egypt. Jambres [. . .] his own [.] and the [. . .]

Page 11 (5abcfp↓)
hear [.] Jannes [. . .] king, [.] comfort[ed . . .] other friends. [But the mother] cri[ed out sa]ying "Did my son J[a— . . ." . . .] the mother [. . .] wishing to kiss him.[c] He went away from her and stood at a distance, [say]ing to her: "Keep away [from me],[d] mother: because of the sacred rites, [and especially] because of the fire, I cannot draw near to you. There is [now] much [perplexity] for you, [mother]:[e] for you are [not] able [to see] me [now] because of the sacred rites. When [you are purifi]ed, you will see, [but not now]." [She] said: "Will I too [be purified], child?" [He said:] "You will invoke [in his name] the [Most High and] you will be purified [. . .] you will see [me]." She [said, . looking] toward him: "[Go away], man, (you) who are misleading me." [He said:] "I, Jannes, [your son,] went astray [from the liv]ing God and op[posed] his power. [Do not then say] such a thing, m[other]." The [mother] said to him, [. . .] "Why then did you answer now [rebuking] me so ha[rshly]?" Jannes said [to her:] "I seemed har[sh to you], mother, [ordering you] not to touch me: [for] you did [not] come [with] power [over what I speak of . . .] by other [. . .] Invoke the[n the Mo]st [High] God so that [you may be] pu[rified] as you wish and [see me]

Page 12 (5abcfp→)
[. . .] I have seen corpses and none [. . .] to you, child. Stay here [. . .] changed, and to your appearance [. . .] child. You are a corpse: for [your . . .] and your lips do not move [. . .] your ankles do not touch [. . ."]

[. . .] breath [. . .] his mother and[. . .] tomb of his brother [. . .] her [.] dead and p[erforming .] all the customary rites he buried h[er . . .] the mother, Jambres opening the [books] of magic, performed necromancy and brought up from [Hades] the image of his brother, and Jannes answer[ing] said to the brother Jambres "Wh[y .] did you become [.] and [. . .] not [. . ."] And Jambres

---

a. H → has in this fragmentary part "[bro]ther [. . .] was purified [. . .] Therefore much t[ime . . .] her son [. . .]."
b. H → has no usable text after this point.
c. The following stretch is better preserved in O, whose fuller text is translated here.
d. B has only "Keep away."
e. B diverges from this point on: "And she [.] said: '[. . .]' Answering, [he sa]id: 'You took the trouble, mother, to come to me, busy[ing yourself .] not [. . .] they have rep[roa]ched me [. . .] I will come to [you.' . . .] and [his] mother [. . .] wondered [. . .] him [. . . de]mon, for [.] had chosen [. . .] astray [. . .]" The latter part of this gives the end of the conversation and the narration that follows, not represented in O.

[.] "Why not [. . .] and [.] weep and my hou[se .] I was deprived [. . .] and all [. . .] and [.] gave [.] and money [. . .] made [. . .] then [. . ."]

Page 13 (6abcfg↓)[a]
[. . .] opened [. . . dwe]lling-place [. . .] cubits [. . .] cubits [. . .] nor [. . .] you burn [. . .] bad [. . .] for [. . .] nor make merry [.] you [. . .] nor [. . .] drew near [. . .] and we go down [. . .] is not conceded to us [. . .] difficult, from which [. . .] we [for]get [. . .] and friends and [. . .] for the gates of [. . .] deaf and [. . .]

Page 14 (6abcfg→)
[. . .] bene[- . . .] made [. . .] eternity nor [. . .] stone [. . .] other [. . .] do not touc[h . . .] but [. . .] us [. . .] but if [. . .] the world [. . .a]nd unab[le . . .] de-stroy[ed . . .] our limbs [. . .] full of darkness [. . .] being burnt by [. . .] nothing [. . .] themselves [. . .] hand over [. . .] and [. . .]

Page 15 (7abcefij↓)
[in] Hades nor kin[g . . .] excels the b[eggar . . .] equality righteous [. . . st]ood against [. . .] earth [. . .] the power[ful . . .] torture [. . .] worship [. . .] worshiped ido[ls . . .] when collapse occurs [. . . ru]in together with the idols [. . .] the idols neither those rever[ing . . .] God the king [. . .] and in Hades no one [. . .] borrow[ed . . .] and not [. . .] this as long as [. . .] drug [. . .] not swear falsely [. . .] not [. . .] creditor [. . .], my [br]other [. . .] where [. . .] are punished from [. . .] take. You, so far as you c[an . . .

Page 16 (7abcefij→)
[. . .] other [. . .] children nor the [. . .] soul unworthily of you [. . .] prostitute not at all worse [. . .] most pleasant is sinning and [. . .] (a female) wishing [. . .], brother J[ambr]es [. . .] not [. . .] not later [. . .] but pain [. . .] you will hand over [. . .] woman [. . .] worthless a[nd . . .] that in Hades [. . .] nor [. . . prostitu]te [. . .] clothes [. . .] children [. . .]

Page 17 (5deghko6ei↓ + V frag. C)
[. . .] of Egypt the ch[iefs . . .] Didn't they all d[ie? . . .] Where is first [. . . —]est of hu[man beings . . .] did not weig[h . . .] Where are the sons [. . .] in Egypt and through the [. . .] herself [. . .] knew [. . .] kings of E[gypt . . . r]eigned. Didn't even the[y die? . . .] the lea[f] of the olive [. . .] and weav[- . . .] died. Where [. . . Didn't even] she die[b] [. . .] king [. . .] son [. . .] of human beings [. . .]

Page 18 (5deghko6ei →)
[. . .] and [. . .] died [. . .] tallest of human beings [. . .] he died. You see [. . .] out of the [. . .] for he knew [. . .] He, going down [. . .] died. These [. . .] and

---

a. The order of the material in the fragmentary final leaves is uncertain in some places.

b. V frag. C continues a little further, with another example of the "Didn't even [. die?]" refrain. V frag. D, which comes earlier in the same column, is similar in content: "[of] human beings [. . . Didn't] even [. . .] Didn't [even . . .] thunderb[olt . . .] Didn't [even . . .]."

kille[d . . .] came before him [. . .] in the sky [. . .] cedars [. . . Did]n't even [. . .] and [. . .] Didn't even [. . . —]self [. . .]

Latin excerpt

Mambres opened the magic books of his brother Iamnes and performed necromancy and brought out from the underworld the ghost of his brother. The soul of Iamnes responded to him saying: "I, your brother, died not unjustly, but indeed justly, and the judgment of God went against me since I was wiser than all wise magicians. And I stood by the two brothers Moyses and Aaron who made signs and great prodigies. For this reason I died and was brought down from the middle to the underworld, where there is great burning and a lake of perdition from which there is no ascent. And now, my brother Mambres, take heed to yourself in your life so that you are generous to your sons and friends, for in the underworld there is nothing good, only sadness and gloom. And once you are dead and have come to the underworld, your dwelling-place among the dead will be two cubits wide and four cubits long."

Ethiopic fragment, leaf 2

"that he (could) carry water in a bucket (which fit) in its mouth fifteen (units) in measure, and an axe of iron (weighing) 600,000 talents. But later even he died!

"Where are Amān and Bārān, the giants who devoured men like locusts and wild animals and cattle and birds? They drank <blood>[a] and despoiled the Orient because they (could) not be satisfied. However, Bapares, their father, lifting a stone of a thousand talents, threw it by his own strength into the height(s) of heaven. And noontime descended, and he ran that same day 250,000 stadia and returned before the sun set. And where is he? Did he not die? Even he and his wife and his children died!

"Where is Acamas, whose eyes were huge? Did he not, while they were sleeping, raise up mountains with his belly? And since the dust storm was drawn out, he placed in a <bowl> his eyes in 4,200 pieces, but it did not concern him, for his eyes <were> heavy. And did not even he die?

"Where is the great Aklu, the gigantic? When walking, twenty cubits (of earth) adhered to his feet from the weight of his steps. And when therefore it happened one time (that) he drank water from the river, it decreased the water (by) five cubits. Did not even he die?

"Where is the great Akaryās, the gigantic, who walked in the depths of the (Za)Banṭes(a)[b] Sea and the water reached (only) up to his breasts? To this one (belonged) footsteps of 500,000 cubits, and, because of his wife's adultery, he killed 103 gian[ts. And] this one killed [ ]sa[ ]s the gigantic and cast his body into the Great Sea. But afterward even he died!

a. This word is added on the basis of the probable parallel to 1 En. 7:4–5.
b. It is unclear from the Ethiopic text whether the name of the sea is Banṭes, Banṭesa, Zabanṭes, or Zabanṭesa.

"Where is Yotāmār, son of Māriket, who in his intelligence understood the hours and minutes of the day and of the night, and the months of the years, and the signs given? And much (else) he investigated. Did not even he die?

"Where is Ajax, the great and mighty, the marvelous, the gigantic, who left the eastern frontier running and [. . .]?"

A Coptic Exodus Apocryphon
A new translation and introduction

by Frederic Krueger

This hitherto unknown OT apocryphon in the Sahidic dialect of Coptic (no doubt depending on a Greek *Vorlage*) exhibits strong similarities to Jewish historical novels about the Maccabean revolt or other (pseudo-)historical tales of brave Jewish resistance to a heathen king and his army. Our text chooses the Egyptian setting of the exodus and describes a confrontation between Pharaoh's army and the Israelites in which the latter appear less like a band of refugees on the run, and more like a defiant rebel force who have fortified themselves and represent a credible threat reminiscent, for example, of the Maccabees or Judith's followers defying the Seleucid or Assyrian king respectively. Their fearless leader in our case must, of course, be Moses who is referred to as a "young lad" and "the Hebrew" by the Egyptians. The free retelling of the exodus story and the likely focus on Moses as the national hero of the Jews invite comparison with Artapanus's Moses romance as well. Substantial parts of the text are furthermore so similar to parts of the History of the Captivity in Babylon, also a Jewish OT apocryphon surviving in Coptic, that a direct dependency of one work on the other is to be assumed. Similarly close parallels suggest an influence of our tale on a later Constantinian legend in Coptic. The most surprising feature of our text is the prominent role assigned to the infamous Egyptian magicians Jannes and Jambres, who, oddly enough, seem to be put in charge of the Egyptian army as if they were generals. The only witness, an approximately fourth-century papyrus fragment, marks the first direct appearance in Coptic literature of their legend, best known from roughly contemporary Greek manuscripts of the Apocryphon of Jannes and Jambres (Jan. Jam.; see W. B. Henry and T. M. Erho in this volume) from the third and mainly fourth century. Both tales must have been transmitted at this time by Egyptian Christians. In light of the absence of earlier manuscripts of either tale, this could have been their original *Sitz im Leben*. However, certain arguments suggest a Jewish *Urtext* of Jannes and Jambres, making such a transmission history plausible for this related Coptic tale as well, especially considering how closely it resembles well-known Jewish tales of the Hellenistic and early Roman periods.[1]

---

1. The present introduction both expands upon (in terms of interpretation) and heavily condenses (in terms of philological and papyrological commentary) the observations published in Frederic Krueger, "Pharaoh's Sorcerers Revisited: A Sahidic Exodus Apocryphon (P.Lips. Inv. 2299) and the Legend of Jannes and Jambres the Magicians between Judaism, Christianity, and Native Egyptian Tradition," *APF* 64 (2018): 148–98. I am grateful to Walter de Gruyter Publishing for permission to include a revised version of my translation in that article here.

Contents

The preserved part of the tale begins with Pharaoh consulting with his courtiers or advisors about a crisis brought on by a certain large population, who are obviously the children of Israel. They are currently "encamped in the east," suggesting the flight during the exodus, but considering the genre conventions discussed below, perhaps with a more defiant, paramilitary character of the Hebrews than we would expect. Pharaoh is clearly worried and entertains genocidal plans against the Hebrews to "eradicate them from the land," although he first sends scouts to ascertain their exact numbers. Upon their return, Pharaoh is told that they number a million, and that they are led by "this young lad" who can be none other than Moses.[2] It is said, "those who are his own (i.e., the Hebrews) he has taken away from those who are not his own (i.e., the Egyptians)," and it is predicted that he is going to "shut the desert" against the pursuing Egyptians.

Alarmed at this ominous news, Pharaoh proceeds to write a "furious letter," commanding his messengers to go to Memphis and bring him "Jannes and Jambres, the Two Sons (i.e., of Balaam), the priests of Heliopolis." Clearly, Pharaoh hopes that, if anyone, these mighty sorcerers would be able to oppose Moses and his (magical?) abilities to "shut the desert." Jannes and Jambres follow their king's summons and arrive at Pharaoh's location on the same day.

After a large gap of between half and two thirds of a page, which we would certainly expect to include Pharaoh giving his instructions to Jannes and Jambres, the other side of the fragment shows a massive assembly of the Egyptian army, obviously called by Pharaoh, possibly further encouraged by Jannes and Jambres, to attack the Hebrews. The first item we can partially read are ten thousand "pure" unidentified things; eight hundred trumpeters; six hundred of the best chariots (a quotation of Exod 14:7); there are Cataphracts (the heavily armored horsemen typical of the armies, e.g., of the Parthians and Sassanids that were adapted by the Roman military and are thus highly anachronistic in a tale set in Pharaonic Egypt) whose number is lost but may be estimated at a hundred based on the size of the lacuna. The attack force then takes on a peculiarly magical character, no doubt owing to the expertise brought in by Jannes and Jambres: there are hundreds of captive teachers (i.e., lesser/assistant magicians?) and "eight pure little boys" whose purpose is "to speak magic"—Jannes and Jambres appear to have complemented the regular army by a special magician contingent that they trust will be enough against

---

2. The most difficult translation problem posed by the Coptic text is whether or not *šēre koui* "little boy" is to be taken literally. While I previously favored a literal meaning, especially since "eight pure little boys" recur on the next page, in this instance probably referring to actual children, the Jewish literary context that I now consider of prime importance for any interpretive effort probably demands a conventional adult hero figure, a Moses in the style of Artapanus, suggesting that a nonliteral meaning such as a derogatory "youngster" is intended here (which could have been expressed by Greek *neanias* in the lost original). The same Greek word may have been used with different nuances in the original, or the translator may have used the same Coptic phrase to translate two different Greek words with two different meanings. Considering the close parallels between our text and the History of the Captivity in Babylon (see below), we can probably assume that Moses is a *šēre koui* in the same sense that Jeremiah is a *šēre šēm*, also "little boy" or "young man," which in Jeremiah's case is used to define a part of the population "from twenty years and under"; see Karl Heinz Kuhn, "A Coptic Jeremiah Apocryphon," *Mus* 83 (1970): 298. The parallels found in the Christian *Historia Eudoxiae* (see below) prove, furthermore, that *šēre šēm* in the former and *šēre koui* in our text are equally identical in meaning when the reference is to "little boys."

the one "young lad," that is, Moses, the great magician of the Hebrews. Jannes and Jambres now give orders to "go, find the Hebrew (i.e., Moses) and bring him . . . ," at which point the fragment breaks off.

It is unclear how central Jannes and Jambres, who dominate the scene accidentally preserved by our fragment in the surprising role as military leaders, ultimately are to the overall tale (we can probably expect at the very least their spectacular defeat at the hands of Moses). It was, however, probably much more minor than in Jannes and Jambres, considering the genre conventions discussed below.

Manuscripts and Versions

At present, the only known witness is the papyrus fragment assigned the inventory number P.Lips. Inv. 2299 of the *Papyrus- und Ostrakasammlung* at the Leipzig University Library, which I edited with extensive commentary in 2018 (see n. 1). The fragment, preserving the bottom sixteen and fifteen lines respectively of the only folio surviving from a papyrus codex, measures 10.2 cm (height) by 11.8 cm (breadth), representing at most the lower half, but considering the oblong format of many early Coptic manuscripts, perhaps only about the lower third of the page. Holes of varying size and a large vertical tear across the fragment frequently obstruct legibility on both sides. Four small fragments of the same manuscript have thus far not yielded any identifiable words, although recent work by the collection's papyrus conservator Jörg Graf suggests that two of them can be attached to the papyrus at its heavily damaged beginning (this joining would however be a very minor addition unlikely to improve transliteration or translation in a meaningful way). Since Coptic literature is overwhelmingly translation literature from Greek and both Jannes and Jambres and most of the Jewish works that our tale resembles were written in Greek, a lost Greek *Vorlage* seems all but certain for our tale as well.

Genre, Structure, and Literary Context

In an early report in a 2016 issue of *Welt und Umwelt der Bibel*, I still entertained my original working hypothesis, also strongly suggested by the title of the article, that, analogous to the Geʿez manuscript discovered by Ted Erho (see Henry and Erho in this volume), we are dealing with a Coptic witness to Jannes and Jambres itself, though certain incompatibilities with the latter's plot already suggested that it would have to be "eine andere Version der Geschichte" ("a differing version of the story").[3] In the 2018 full edition and commentary, however, I made sure to emphasize what had emerged as obvious in the meantime: that it is "clearly a hitherto unknown tale, different from *ApoJJ* [Jannes and Jambres]."[4] Nevertheless, the combined discussion of both tales in my article, which covered the Jannes and Jambres tradition more broadly, has misled at least one scholar to conclude that they are one and the same, hence the need to reiterate on this occasion that they are certainly not.[5] As I have shown in my article, Jannes and Jambres is a relatively

---

3. Ted Erho, Frederic Krueger, and Matthias Hoffmann, "Neues von Pharaos Zauberern: Äthiopische und koptische Textzeugen zum apokryphen Text 'Jannes und Jambres,'" *Welt und Umwelt der Bibel* 80 (2016): 70–72, 71.

4. Krueger, "Pharaoh's Sorcerers Revisited," 154.

5. Jens Herzer, "Haben die Magier den Verstand verloren? Jannes und Jambres im 2. Timotheusbrief," in *Religion als Imagination: Phänomene des Menschseins in den Horizonten theologischer Lebensdeutung; Festschrift für Marco Frenschkowski*, ed. Lena Seehausen, Paulus Enke, and Jens Herzer (Leipzig: Evangelische Verlagsanstalt 2020), 136.

traditional court tale, possibly of Christian but probably Roman-period Jewish origin, in which the conventional Jewish hero who uses his influence at the court of the gentile king is exchanged for one of the gentile oppressors himself: Jannes, who is humanized to an extent that has surprised biblical scholars but that becomes understandable as a local Egyptian influence when we compare the many Heliopolitan priest-magicians who star in the pagan Egyptian tales from which Jannes and Jambres lifts both its general perspective and tone, as well as a number of specific plot elements.[6] The Coptic apocryphon, on the other hand, and this occurred to me only after the publication of my article, has different, though not entirely unrelated genre affinities: As briefly indicated above, our tale seems to share a good bit of its narrative structure and several details with some well-known Jewish historical novels of the Hellenistic and early Roman periods about the Maccabean revolt or other (pseudo-)historical tales of brave Jewish resistance to a heathen king and his army, such as 1–2 Maccabees and Judith. As in Jannes and Jambres, as well as 3 Maccabees (which, similar to the latter, comes very close to having the Egyptian king himself as its repenting heathen protagonist), the choice of the Egyptian setting suggests that, unless we are dealing with a Christian composition based on the Jewish model (which is certainly possible), the Greek *Urtext* of our tale was likewise written by an Egyptian Jew for the Jewish diaspora in Egypt during the Hellenistic or early Roman period, whereas the similar stories of 1 Maccabees and Judith were written in Palestine and thus make use of a local rather than an Egyptian setting.[7] Despite the Egyptian ground held in common with Jannes and Jambres and 3 Maccabees, the conventions of those tales resembled by our story in all other regards suggest that one of the Egyptians was probably not the protagonist this time, be it Jannes and Jambres or Pharaoh, but the fearless leader of the Jewish rebels, that is, Moses, the prominently mentioned "Hebrew" and "young lad" who leads the Jews. This focus on Moses as a resourceful quasi-military leader (if that may indeed be inferred from the situation described) defying the plots of Pharaoh and his courtiers and achieving victory in war suggests that we are dealing with a kind of "Moses romance" similar to the famous one written by Artapanus, and for the same Egyptian Jewish community. In fact, one might even suggest that our tale shows us not exactly the conventional pursuit of the Hebrews but rather the Egyptian response to the military campaign which Artapanus's tale suggests Moses might lead against the Egyptians, a notion which, oddly, Artapanus mentions only to drop it again.[8] His Moses never raises that army, But perhaps ours did? We also do well to remember that Artapanus has widely been suspected as having invented, or significantly shaped, the legend of Jannes and Jambres the magicians (see Henry and Erho in this volume), who, while suspiciously absent from Artapanus's own novel, make a big appearance in

---

6. Krueger, "Pharaoh's Sorcerers Revisited," 161–69. For an excellent overview of the theme of Egyptian-foreign magical contests in ancient Egyptian literature, to which my analysis of the native Egyptian element in the Jannes and Jambres legend is much indebted, see Franziska Naether, "Magical Practices in Egyptian Literary Texts: In Quest for Cultural Plurality," in *Cultural Plurality in Ancient Magical Texts and Practices: Graeco-Egyptian Handbooks and Related Traditions*, ed. Ljuba M. Bortolani, Svenja Nagel, and Joachim F. Quack, Orientalische Religionen in der Antike 32 (Tübingen: Mohr Siebeck 2019), 27–41.

7. On these and similar Jewish tales and their social context see Lawrence Wills, *The Jewish Novel in the Ancient World* (Ithaca, NY: Cornell University Press, 1995).

8. As noted by John J. Collins, "Artapanus," in *OTP* 2:901 h2: "The suggestion that Moses led an army against Egypt does not fit with what follows."

A Coptic Exodus Apocryphon

ours.[9] As stated previously, our tale exhibits numerous close parallels to various other historical novels about Jewish defiance to heathen kings and their armies as well. To illustrate this, the following table summarizes what seem to me more or less obvious correspondences between 1 Maccabees, Judith, and our tale. I assign capital letters to the relevant elements where they first appear and reuse that letter for identification where that element recurs in another tale, regardless of which elements actually occur in which order in that tale. Square brackets contain speculations on elements that, while not preserved in the Coptic fragment, seem likely enough to at least entertain their original presence based on the related tales.

1 MACCABEES	JUDITH	COPTIC EXODUS APOCRYPHON
The Seleucid king wants to force the Jews to worship Greek gods (A).	The Assyrian king wants to force the whole world to worship him as a god (A).	[Does Pharaoh also want to force the Jews to worship him or his gods (A)?]
It is reported to the king that the refusing Jews are hiding in camps in the wilderness (B).	The king gets very angry at the Jews' disobedience (E). He must first depart to Persia for war (D).	The Egyptian king (I) sends scouts who report back to him about the situation, size, and leadership of the Jewish rebels in their camp (B). Pharaoh wants to "destroy them from the earth" (C).
The resulting attacks let the rebels fear that "they will quickly destroy us from the earth" (C).	Upon his return he sends summons to his nobles (F). He puts a general (K), Holofernes, in charge of an army.	The Israelites "shut the desert" against the Egyptians (M). Pharaoh becomes furious (E).
The king departs for Persia to collect taxes to finance his war (D).	Detailed description of army (G): "120,000 foot-soldiers and 12,000 cavalry" as well as donkeys (P).	
Upon his return he is told about new exploits of the rebels.	The general sends scouts who report back to him about the situation, size, and leadership of the Jewish rebels in their camp (B).	He writes a letter summoning his court magicians (F), Jannes and Jambres, as leaders of the army (K). [Will they be beheaded (L)?].
"The king was enraged when he heard this" (E). He writes letters summoning his nobles (F). Detailed description of army (G): "The number of his forces was 100,000 foot-soldiers, 20,000 horsemen (H), and 32 elephants."	Holofernes promises that the king's army will "destroy them from the face of the earth" (C). Holofernes is beheaded by Judith (L). The Israelites "close the mountain passes" (M).	Detailed description of army (G): "... foot-soldiers, 10,000 ... and 800 trumpeters (J), 600 of the best chariots ... 100? armored horsemen (H), 140,000 ..." with donkeys (P), hostages (N), and children (O).
Many similar descriptions of armies, in one instance of the Ptolemaic king of Egypt (I), often mentioning trumpets (J).		

---

9. Albert Pietersma, *The Apocryphon of Jannes and Jambres the Magicians: Edited with Introduction, Translation, and Commentary*, RGRW 119 (Leiden: Brill, 1994), 3–11.

One of these armies is led by the two generals (K) Gorgias and Nicanor. Nicanor is beheaded (L). The Jews use their knowledge of the landscape to their advantage, enemies are "shut in" or "locked out" of besieged cities (M). Jewish hostages (N) are used as bargaining chips, sometimes children (O).

Our work furthermore shares a number of close similarities with the History of the Captivity in Babylon (CAVT 227; Clavis Coptica 0032), another Jewish OT apocryphon that has survived only in Coptic (and, in this case, a subsequent Arabic translation).[10] The translations are based on Karl Heinz Kuhn's edition yet sometimes modified.[11] The translation of the exodus apocryphon sometimes differs slightly from the complete translation offered below in order to highlight the corresponding choice of words between both texts. Correspondences range from, in my opinion, very obvious to merely tentative.

HISTORY OF THE CAPTIVITY IN BABYLON

The pleased Nebuchadnezzar summons his generals:
"Now when Chelchiane had said this, her word pleased the king. He commanded that Cyrus and Amesaros, the generals of his army, be brought to him. They came (and) stood before the king."[12]

COPTIC EXODUS APOCRYPHON

The displeased Pharaoh summons his "generals":
"When Pharaoh heard these things, he forthwith wrote a furious letter, say[ing], '[G]o to Memphis! Bring ye [Jan]nes and Jambres, the two sons, the priests of Heliopolis!' And on that day [did] Jann[es and] Jambres come to Pharaoh [. . .]"

---

10. For a recent overview and bibliography see Alin Suciu, "2.6.1 Textual History of the History of the Captivity in Babylon," in *Textual History of the Bible*, ed. Armin Lange, http://dx.doi.org/10.1163/2452-4107_thb_COM_0202060100. On the Coptic manuscripts specifically, none of which can securely be dated before the ninth century, see Suciu, "2.6.2 Coptic," in Lange, *Textual History of the Bible*, http://dx.doi.org/10.1163/2452-4107_thb_COM_0202060200. No less than three additional Coptic manuscripts, two Fayyumic and one Sahidic, were recently identified by Vincent Walter at the Leipzig University Library that also houses our papyrus (this is surely coincidental as provenance and date are completely different). I am grateful to Walter, for informing me of his finds and introducing me to the pertinent literature, as well as Korshi Dosoo, who initially brought this text to my attention in a completely different context.
11. Kuhn, "Coptic Jeremiah Apocryphon."
12. Kuhn, "Coptic Jeremiah Apocryphon," 133.

A Coptic Exodus Apocryphon

Nebuchadnezzar's army assembles to attack Jerusalem:
"Seven hundred and seventy thousand foot-soldiers with their swords drawn in their hands, seventy thousand cataphracts, seventy thousand clad in breastplates of iron mounted on the horses, seventy thousand chariots with twelve strong men occupying the chariot at once, sixty thousand men-at-arms to his right and left. They amounted to twelve million one hundred and seventy thousand in number."[13]

Pharaoh's army assembles to attack the Hebrews:
"... foot-soldiers and ten thousand [...] pure ... and eight [hundred?] trumpeters, and six hundred of the best chariots at the rate of fourteen (men) per chariot, and [a hundred?] cataphracts, and a hundred and forty thousa[nd ...] ... hundred teachers as hostages, and eight pure little boys to speak m[ag]ic (?) and [...] hundred asses saddled with saddles of gold."[14]

Nebuchadnezzar has the Hebrews counted:
"They found that there were one million eight hundred thousand people."[15]

Pharaoh has the Hebrews counted:
"They counted [the(ir?)] myriads and said: 'They are one million (...)'"

Jeremiah is a "youngster":
"O king live for ever, if thou dost want the prophet of God who sent thee to us, he is a youth. Behold all the youths of this place, file them past, all of them from twenty years and under..."[16]

Moses is a "youngster":
"They are a hundred times ten thousand under the leadership of this youth."

Teachers, children, and magic:
"Now there were some of the little children of the Hebrews in the school of the Chaldeans (...) And there was a child among them whose name was Ezra (...)";[17] (Ezra performs water miracle); "Now when the teacher of the school saw him, he bowed down (and) reverenced Ezra (...)"[18]

Teachers, children, and magic:
"(...) hundred teachers as hostages, and eight pure little boys to speak m[ag]ic (?)"

Ezra removes the Hebrew children from the Babylonian school:
"Ezra brought the children of the Hebrews out of the school of the Chaldeans."[19]

Moses removes the Hebrews from the Egyptians:
"(...) and those who are his own he has ta[ken away fr]om those who are not his own!"

13. Kuhn, "Coptic Jeremiah Apocryphon," 291.
14. Note that "saddled with ... of gold" in the Exodus Apocryphon and "clad in ... of iron" in the History of the Captivity in Babylon are both expressed by the words *hēk (h)ᵉn ... ᵉn* (word for metal).
15. Kuhn, "Coptic Jeremiah Apocryphon," 295.
16. Kuhn, "Coptic Jeremiah Apocryphon," 298.
17. Kuhn, "Coptic Jeremiah Apocryphon," 309.
18. Kuhn, "Coptic Jeremiah Apocryphon," 310.
19. Kuhn, "Coptic Jeremiah Apocryphon," 312.

Cyrus has Hebrews brought to him for punishment: "They brought the Hebrews (and) gave them hard blows."[20]	Jannes and Jambres, on Pharaoh's orders, issue orders for Moses's capture: "And now [go], find the He[brew a]n[d] br[ing him (. . .)]"

In addition to these more or less direct parallel formulations, there is a pervasive affinity to Exodus in the History of the Captivity of Babylon. The situation of the Hebrews is constantly compared to that of their forebears as they were led out of Egypt. Specifically, the way that God punishes Babylon by "shutting up the heaven and the earth"[21]—thunderstorms, darkness during the day, and devastating earthquakes ensue—when the new king Cyrus refuses to let the Hebrews go, and instead enslaves them even more brutally, is very clearly modeled after the Pharaoh of the hardened heart and the plagues of Egypt. Does this notorious interest in the exodus indicate that the History of the Captivity in Babylon used our text as an inspiration and sometimes even as a source for certain passages, resulting in the parallels listed above? Conceivably, but not necessarily. Comparing the Babylonian exile to the exodus is hardly original and does not require recourse to extracanonical elaborations like ours. If, as it seems, both works are based on lost Greek originals of the Hellenistic or early Roman period, we do not know which is the older. We do, however, know which was the more popular: Our exodus apocryphon with its sole surviving fragment cannot have been anywhere near as well known as the History of the Captivity in Babylon or the closely related Paraleipomena Jeremiou (Bar 4), widely considered to be derivative of the former.[22] These were very popular texts among Jews and Christians that were transmitted for many centuries in many manuscripts in many languages and dialects. To boot, the notion that Jannes and Jambres led the Egyptian army during the exodus is otherwise completely unknown in the Jannes and Jambres tradition. In fact, it contradicts the plot of Jannes and Jambres (see Henry and Erho in this volume), where they purposely stay away from the pursuit of the Hebrews, again suggesting that our tale was not widely known. For these reasons, I would cautiously suggest that the influence might rather run in the opposite direction and that our exodus apocryphon took inspiration and whole passages from an early version of the History of the Captivity in Babylon. The previously noted numerous allusions to the exodus in this work may have played a part in that inspiration.

Similarly close, if not closer parallels can be demonstrated between our tale and yet another historical novel preserved only in Coptic, a legend about Emperor Constantine and a fictitious sister of his, the so-called Historia Eudoxiae (Clavis Coptica 0201). This story tells—once again in a very novelistic fashion with little regard for historicity—of the heroes' feats in Christianizing the empire, defeating the Persians, and rediscovering the Holy Sepulchre in Jerusalem. It has been suggested that the text, preserved in seventh-century manuscripts, is reacting to the recent recovery of Jerusalem and the cross after the Persian invasion at that time, but there are reasons to believe the work, possible

---

20. Kuhn, "Coptic Jeremiah Apocryphon," 318.

21. Kuhn, "Coptic Jeremiah Apocryphon," 316 and 317 as well as elaborated narratively on the following pages. Compare perhaps in our text "He is going to sh[ut th]e desert against us."

22. On the relationship between the two, in addition to the scholarship reviewed by Suciu, "Textual History," see P. Piovanelli, "In Praise of 'The Default Position,' or Reassessing the Christian Reception of the Jewish Pseudepigraphic Heritage," *NTT* 61 (2007): 233–50.

A Coptic Exodus Apocryphon

redaction notwithstanding, is older, perhaps as old as the fifth century, which would still probably make it younger than our Coptic manuscript and certainly its Greek original.[23] If our tale really is originally a Jewish pseudepigraphon of the Hellenistic or early Roman period, it must have inspired the decidedly Christian Historia Eudoxiae, not the other way around. Among the many similarities to our tale, note in particular the identical use of "pure little boys" for ritual purposes and the military use of magicians in both the Egyptian and the Persian armies (I cite Pearson's translation):

COPTIC EXODUS APOCRYPHON	HISTORIA EUDOXIAE
Jannes and Jambres, on Pharaoh's orders (or having further enticed him?), issue orders to capture the miracle-working Moses: "And now [go], find the He[brew a]n[d] br[ing him (...)]"	The Persian generals persuade the kings to attack the Romans and capture the miracle-working Constantine: "(t)he commanders of the army of the Persian kings spoke in the presence of the [kings], saying to them the following: 'Our lords, kings of the land of Persia, listen to your servants speaking in the presence of your majesties. If you desire to rise up and fight with the king of the Romans, give us permission and we will bring him bound to your chariot as a dog to the capital city of the kingdom, in order that the entire world might again know that no king is such a lord as (those of) the kingdom of the Persians. For we have found out why he was saved on the day we surrounded him. The cloud came and seized him from our hands because he knows the magical potions of the Christians. Thus he worked his arts and saved himself from our hands..."[24]
The Egyptian army takes along teachers and children to provide countermagic: "... hundred teachers as hostages, and eight pure little boys to speak m[ag]ic (?)"	The Persian army takes along magicians to teach them countermagic: "... But now there are with us some magicians who can take note of everything that he will do with his arts, and teach us about them."[25]

23. Birger A. Pearson, "Introduction," in *Eudoxia and the Holy Sepulchre: A Constantinian Legend in Coptic*, ed. Tito Orlandi, Testi e documenti per lo studio dell'antichita, serie copta 67 (Milan: Cisalpino-Goliardica, 1980): 162–66. It seems unlikely that the story significantly postdates the Council of Chalcedon in 451 when Jerusalem received patriarchal control over Palestine, something that is generally taken for granted, even anachronistically, in Coptic literature, with no awareness that prior to Chalcedon, the bishop of Caesarea had metropolitan jurisdiction over Palestine. The *Historia Eudoxiae*, however, is oddly aware of this historical fact, suggesting an early date of composition. I am grateful to Alin Suciu for bringing this issue to my attention.

24. Pearson, "Introduction," 45.

25. Pearson, "Introduction," 45.

A Coptic Exodus Apocryphon

Pharaoh summons his "generals":
"When Pharaoh heard these things, he forthwith wrote a furious letter, say[ing], "[G]o to Memphis! Bring ye [Jan]nes and Jambres, the two sons, the priests of Heliopolis!" And on that day [did] Jann[es and] Jambres come to pharaoh [...]"

Pharaoh's army assembles to attack the Hebrews:
"... foot-soldiers and ten thousand [...] pure ... and eight [hundred?] trumpeters, and six hundred of the best chariots at the rate of fourteen (men) per chariot, and [a hundred?] cataphracts, and a hundred and forty thousa[nd...] hundred asses saddled with saddles of gold."

Pharaoh's trumpeters:
"eight [hundred?] trumpeters"

The Persian kings summon their general:
"And the Persian kings immediately ordered Canopus,[26] the commander-in-chief of their army, to gather his chariots and his horsemen and infantry [to] march forth [against] Romania."[27]

Constantine's army assembles to meet the Persians:
"But when the great king Constantine heard (about it) he gathered together his soldiers and counted them. They numbered a hundred-twenty myriads (1,200,000) in all, bearing the sword."[28]

Constantine's military entourage for his sister:
"make ready for her four generals and forty thousand soldiers and four chariots for the general and three for the royal virgin ... and much cattle"[29]

The Persian army:
"to gather his chariots and his horsemen and infantry"[30]

Constantine's trumpeters:
"The king had two trumpets of refined gold ... A blast would be given on the first trumpet, and the generals would gather together and the provincial commanders. And on (a blast of) the second trumpet, the courtiers and tribunes and chief officials of the king's court would gather."[31]

---

26. Note the Egyptian name. An echo of our exodus tradition?
27. Pearson, "Introduction," 45. "Romania" is the Roman empire.
28. Pearson, "Introduction," 45.
29. Pearson, "Introduction," 63.
30. Pearson, "Introduction," 45.
31. Pearson, "Introduction," 61.

Pharaoh's chariots and gold-saddled asses: "six hundred of the best chariots (...) hundred asses saddled with saddles of gold."

Constantine's golden mule-drawn chariot: "the king gave command and his favorite chariot was brought, the one in which he had come to Jerusalem, made entirely of gold. It had four white mules yoked to it"

The Egyptian army is threatened by the desert:
"He is going to sh[ut th]e desert against us"

The Roman and Persian armies are threatened by the desert:
"They remained opposite each other three months. And the Persians and the Romans ran out of water . . . (the Persians) are dying of thirst in this desert, [they] and their kings and their cattle."[32]

Pharaoh has the Hebrews counted:
"They counted [the(ir?)] myriads and said: 'They are one million (...)'"

Constantine has his army counted:
They numbered a hundred-twenty myriads (1,200,000) in all"[33]

Pharaoh needs "pure little boys" for countermagic:
"and eight uncorrupted small children to speak m[ag]ic (?)"

Constantine and the archbishop need "pure little boys" to enter the Holy Sepulchre:
"send to Zion and bring us twelve uncorrupted[34] small children"[35]

So much for the Jewish and Christian works that look like they inspired and/or were inspired by our tale. The way in which our tale freely transforms events and characters from both canonical (Exodus) and noncanonical (Jannes and Jambres, perhaps Artapanus) exodus narratives to conform them to the literary form represented by 1 Maccabees and Judith, while also lifting passages from the History of the Captivity in Babylon (if not the other way around), raises the important but as yet unanswerable question to what extent the rest of the story conforms with or deviates from either point of orientation. Unlike these major connections, the following comparanda, which now appear as more circumstantial to the greater structure, were already noted in my 2018 article.

The report made to Pharaoh that the "young lad" leading the Hebrews has taken away *netenouf ne* "those who are his own" (i.e., the Hebrews) from *netenouf an ne* "those who are not his own" (i.e., the Egyptians) might invite a diagnosis of New Testament, and specifically Johannine language: The phrase *netenouf* (± *tērou*) *ne*, "(all) his own," occurs seven times in the Sahidic NT, and it is particularly characteristic of the Gospel of John, where it occurs four times (John 1:11; 8:44; 10:4; 13:1). Such a deliberate use of NT language could potentially be explained by a Christian reading of Exodus in which Moses is understood as prefiguring Jesus. However, there is reason to suspect that this

---

32. Pearson, "Introduction," 47.
33. Pearson, "Introduction," 45.
34. *aphthartos*, the same word used in our tale. It probably means that the children are virgins and therefore ritually pure.
35. Pearson, "Introduction," 71.

impression is misleading, and not only because the phrase "his own (people)" occurs in non-Christian contexts as well: Another NT attestation of the phrase in question (2 Tim 2:19: *pjoeis gar afsoun netenouf ne* = *egnō kyrios tous ontas autou* "The Lord knows those who are his") is, in the Greek, an almost literal quotation of Num 16:5 (not attested in Sahidic) *egnō ho theos tous ontas autou*. Considering the general influence by the book of Numbers to be discussed momentarily, it seems probable that if there is an intertextual reference at all, it is to Num 16:5 rather than to John (although the fourth-century Christian readership of our manuscript may well have interpreted it as the latter).

Pharaoh summoning Jannes and Jambres to oppose Moses in a contest involving magic clearly mirrors their *locus classicus* in Exod 7:11, but the overall situation is more similar to King Balak summoning the magician Balaam to curse the Hebrews for him in Num 22. This influence is no doubt facilitated, perhaps even motivated, by the fact that Jannes and Jambres were believed to be "the two sons" of Balaam and were accordingly identified with the latter's unnamed youths in Num 22:22, for instance, in Targum Pseudo-Jonathan, where we also find Jannes and Jambres interpolated into Exod 1:15.[36] Here they interpret a dream of Pharaoh's, explaining that a Hebrew child will be born that will prove Egypt's downfall, thus offering further motivation for his genocidal intentions (shared by Pharaoh in our tale, where a similar prediction is made to him concerning "this young lad", though in this case *prompting* the summoning specifically of Jannes and Jambres rather than *following* from their initial presence):

> And Pharaoh said (that while) he slept, he saw in his dream that all the land of Egypt was placed on one balance of a weighing-scales, and a lamb, the young (of a ewe), on the other balance of the weighing-scales; and the balance of the weighing-scales on which the lamb (was placed) weighed down. Immediately he sent and summoned all the magicians of Egypt and told them his dream. Immediately Jannes and Jambres, the chief magicians, opened their mouths and said to Pharaoh; "A son is to be born in the assembly of Israel, through whom all the land of Egypt is destined to be destroyed."[37]

---

36. *pišēre snau* is used by our MS as though it were a veritable nickname: "Jannes and Jambres, the two sons, the priests of Heliopolis." Among the witnesses to Jannes and Jambres, P.Mich.Inv. 4925 verso seems to refer to Jannes and Jambres as *his* (scil. Balaam) *two sons*," [*d*]*uo huious autou* (line 8); see the edition by Georg Schmelz, "Zwei neue Fragmente des Apokryphons über die Zauberer Jannes und Jambres," in *Atti del XXII Congresso Internazionale di Papirologia: Firenze, 23–29 agosto 1998*, ed. Isabella Andorlini, 2 vols. (Istituto papirologico "G. Vitelli": Firenze 2001), 1199–1212, and pls. XLVIa, b, c. On Balaam's reinterpretation as advisor to pharaoh see Judith R. Baskin, *Pharaoh's Counsellors: Job, Jethro, and Balaam in Rabbinic and Patristic Tradition*, BJS 47 (Chico, CA: Scholars Press, 1982), 75–113.

37. Michael Maher, trans., *Targum Neofiti 1:Exodus and Targum Pseudo-Jonathan; Exodus*, ArBib 2 (T&T Clark: Edinburgh, 1994), 162. Balaam and/or Jannes and Jambres are often encountered as pharaoh's advisors, warning him against Moses's destiny as Egypt's doom; see Pietersma, *Apocryphon*, 26–27. Exegetical elaborations like the ominous dream interpreted through pharaoh's counselors, reminiscent of the story of Joseph, may have arisen out of growing dissatisfaction with the canonical reason for pharaoh's mass infanticide (simple fear of population growth in the slave population); see Klaus Koch, "Das Lamm, das Ägypten vernichtet: Ein Fragment aus Jannes und Jambres und sein geschichtlicher Hintergrund," *ZNW* 57 (1966): 79–93, esp. 87. Note that, as pointed out by Pietersma, this interpolation found in Targum Pseudo-Jonathan is not, in fact, taken from Jannes and Jambres (it is actually more reminiscent of our fragment, though obviously still not identical with its version of events; *Apocryphon*, 50–51). Similar to the adaptation of pagan Egyptian court tale traditions in Jannes and Jambres, it is likely that the image of a lamb signifying Egypt's doom in a prophecy made to the pharaoh of the Exodus represents the ad-

Other characteristics of the tale as preserved by our fragment are very reminiscent of the book of Numbers as well: One of the first things legible on the recto is the report made to Pharaoh that [the Israelites] *tooute ᵉmpeeft*[*e*] "are gathered in the east." This expression corresponds exactly to the Sahidic Septuagint's frequent use of *tooute* to render the meaning of Greek verbs like *stratopedeuō* and *prostithēmi* that are used to denote the gathering of the Hebrews, often specifically their temporary encampment on their way to Canaan after the exodus, including repeatedly the book of Numbers. The detailed "accountant's style" by which our tale delights in giving the precise *numbers* of so-and-so many hundreds and (tens of) thousands of soldiers, horsemen, trumpeters, chariots, donkeys and assistant magicians, might appear reminiscient of Numbers as well, although the genre affinity discussed above suggests that it is chiefly inspired by the similar detailed descriptions of armies in 1 Maccabees and similar related tales, especially the near-identical description of Nebuchadnezzar's army in the History of the Captivity in Babylon.

Date and Provenance

Analysis of the language, a so-called prestandardized Sahidic exhibiting both markedly southern, that is, (Sub-)Akhmimic, as well as markedly northern, that is, "Crypto-Bohairic" features, together with codicological and palaeographical observations, places our manuscript in close proximity with the earliest Coptic manuscripts such as the Nag Hammadi codices, yielding a likely date between the third to fifth centuries.[38] Considering the dense attestation of the closely related Jannes and Jambres in no less than five mainly fourth-century Greek manuscripts, it seems reasonable to suggest a fourth-century date for P.Lips. Inv. 2299 as well. While the provenance of this papyrus was completely unknown to me when I published my edition, I am now glad to be able to present substantial new information that I owe to the efforts of the curator of the *Papyrus- und Ostrakasammlung*, Almuth Märker. She made me aware of an unpublished 2001 MA thesis by Ivo Gottwald, who had gone through old allotment protocols preserved in the *Zentralarchiv* at the Staatliche Museen zu Berlin, Preußischer Kulturbesitz as well as the *Cabinet Numismatique* at the Bibliothèque Nationale et Universitaire de Strasbourg to determine which Leipzig papyri had been acquired via the German Papyrus Cartel between 1903 and 1913.[39] On July 6, 1910, the Strasbourg protocol 26/4 notes the sale to Leipzig of several fragments including what is clearly our papyrus, described as "small fragments; among these a small Latin piece of parchment and a Coptic literary piece wherein Pharaoh appears, thus apparently biblical, ca. fourth century CE. Furthermore:

---

aptation of the Egyptian apocalypse Oracle of the Lamb (known also to many Greek authors) in which a divine lamb foretells Egypt's horrible devastation to King Bocchoris, who was in turn widely believed to be the pharaoh of the exodus; see the sources cited in Krueger, "Pharaoh's Sorcerers Revisited," 188–90.

38. On the issue of how to account for the different kinds of dialectal impurity of the Sahidic encountered in the Nag Hammadi codices, see Wolf-Peter Funk, "Toward a Linguistic Classification of the 'Sahidic' Nag Hammadi Texts," in *Papers from the Sections*, vol. 2 of *Acts of the Fifth International Congress of Coptic Studies: Washington, 12–15 August 1992*, ed. David W. Johnson (Rome: CIM, 1993), 163–77; and Funk, "The Linguistic Aspects of Classifying the Nag Hammadi Codices," in *Les textes de Nag Hammadi et le problème de leur classification*, ed. Louis Painchaud and Anne Pasquier, Bibliothèque Copte de Nag Hammadi 3 (Presses Université Laval: Quebec, 1995), 107–47. For a detailed treatment of these issues see Krueger, "Pharaoh's Sorcerers Revisited," 174–76.

39. Gottwald, "Vier Leipziger Homer-Papyri" (MA thesis, Universität Leipzig, 2001).

A small lead tablet containing a love spell."[40] According to the protocol, this lot was bought for 50 piastres from a mediator (so not the original finder/owner), a certain Sa'id Sam'ani in the Middle Egyptian city of Mallawi, which is situated just a few kilometers southeast of al-Ashmunayn, ancient Hermopolis. Other protocols suggest further acquisitions that were bought and indeed found in this area of Middle Egypt: Protocols from the year 1908 list two parchment leaves from around the third century containing verses of Menander that were bought with some Coptic literary pieces for 487.5 piastres from a nameless "trader in Mallawi" (the same Sa'id Sam'ani or a contact of his?); these were allegedly found in al-Sheikh Ibada, ancient Antinoopolis, across the river from Hermopolis. Hermopolis itself is in turn named by Strasbourg and Berlin protocols from May 27, 1904 as the finding place of the content of thirty-two boxes of papyri including literary pieces by Homer and Ulpian that were bought for 731.25 piastres from a certain Hagi Magran. Potentially of interest may also be the acquisition through Rubenson from an unnamed source for 440 piastres of a box full of papyrus fragments, two of which were literary, and one of which was specifically dramatic, of around the fourth century, which were found "perhaps (in) Behnesa," ancient Oxyrhynchus farther north in Middle Egypt, according to the protocols for July 25, 1906. In light of the rather homogenous picture emerging from the above acquisitions that were made within a very few years, it seems extremely likely that, like the other Greek and Coptic literary papyri often of the third to fourth century listed above, P.Lips. Inv. 2299 also hails from one of these major cities in Middle Egypt of the Roman period: Hermopolis or nearby Antinoopolis are likely candidates, and we should not rule out Oxyrhynchus.

Bibliography

Koch, Klaus. "Das Lamm, das Ägypten vernichtet: Ein Fragment aus Jannes und Jambres und sein geschichtlicher Hintergrund." *ZNW* 57 (1966): 79–93.

Krueger, Frederic. "Pharaoh's Sorcerers Revisited: A Sahidic Exodus Apocryphon (P.Lips. Inv. 2299) and the Legend of Jannes and Jambres the Magicians between Judaism, Christianity, and Native Egyptian Tradition." *APF* 64 (2018): 148–98. doi:10.1515/apf-2018-0008.

Kuhn, Karl Heinz. "A Coptic Jeremiah Apocryphon." *Mus* 83 (1970): 95–135 and 291–350.

Naether, Franziska. "Magical Practices in Egyptian Literary Texts: In Quest for Cultural Plurality." Pages 27–41 in *Cultural Plurality in Ancient Magical Texts and Practices: Graeco-Egyptian Handbooks and Related Traditions*. Edited by Ljuba M. Bortolani, Svenja Nagel, and Joachim F. Quack. Orientalische Religionen in der Antike 32. Tübingen: Mohr Siebeck, 2019.

Pietersma, Albert. *The Apocryphon of Jannes and Jambres the Magicians: Edited with Introduction, Translation, and Commentary*. RGRW 119. Leiden: Brill, 1994.

Wills, Lawrence. *The Jewish Novel in the Ancient World*. Myth and Poetics. Ithaca, NY: Cornell University Press, 1995.

---

40. "Kleine Fragmente; darunter ein kleines lateinisches Pergamentstück und ein koptisches lit. Stück, worin Pharao vorkommt, also wohl biblisch, etwa 4. Jh. n. Chr. Ferner: kleine Bleitafel, einen Liebeszauber enthaltend."

A Coptic Exodus Apocryphon

P.Lips. Inv. 2299 Recto:
[...] he [said], "Hasten t[o ...] encamped in the eas[t ...] ... three ... [... (5) ...] ... you return to the/so that (?) [... pro]ceed to wipe ... [... wip]e (?) them out, eradicate them f[ro]m the lan[d ...]" They counted [the(ir?)] myriads and said: "They are a hundred times ten thousand under the leadership of this young man. He is going to sh[ut (10) th]e desert against us, and those who are his own he has ta[ken away fr]om those who are not his own!" When Pharaoh heard these things, he forthwith wrote a furious letter, say[ing], "[G]o to Memphis! Bring ye [Jan]nes and Jambres, the two sons, the priests (15) of Heliopolis!" And on that day [did] Jann[es and] Jambres come to Pharaoh [...]

(between half and two-thirds of a page missing)

Verso:
[...] break the (? or: ... yourself in/as the ?)" ... [...] ... [...] ... (5) ... foot-soldiers[a] and ten thousand [...] pure ... and eight [hundred?] trumpeters, and *six hundred of the best chariots* at the rate of fourteen (men) per chariot, and [a hundred?] (10) armored horsemen, and a hundred and forty thousa[nd ...] ... hundred teachers as hostages, and eight pure little boys to speak m[ag]ic (?) and [...] hundred asses saddled with saddles of gold. [They said], namely Jannes and Jambres, "And now [go], (15) find the He[brew a]n[d] br[ing him. ...

Exod 14:7

---

a. Only after my edition appeared did I begin suspecting that this poorly legible word might be *rᵉmᵉnrat* = Greek *pezos* "foot-soldier"; thanks to the parallel passage in the History of the Captivity in Babylon (see introduction), I am now certain of this. What should be *tau* at the end of the word looks rather like *upsilon*, however, so perhaps it is a defective spelling for *rᵉmᵉnratou*, which would be closer to *rᵉmratou*, the form used in the History.

Fragments of Elijah Apocrypha
A new translation and introduction

by Richard Bauckham

There are two extant works attributed to Elijah. The work that is now commonly called the Apocalypse of Elijah is extant in four Coptic manuscripts (three in Sahidic and one in Akhmimic Coptic), none of which preserve the complete text but that together very probably preserve the whole of a work that, at the end of the Akhmimic manuscript (the only one to preserve the end of the work) has the title Apocalypse of Elijah. There is also a small Greek fragment that shows the work was originally written in Greek. Nevertheless, it will be referred to here as the Coptic Apocalypse of Elijah in order to avoid confusion, because, as we shall see, there seems to have been another Apocalypse of Elijah in Greek, which we shall call the Greek Apocalypse of Elijah. In strictly generic terms, the Coptic Apocalypse of Elijah is a prophecy rather than an apocalypse. There is no revelation by a supernatural being to a seer in visions or in a heavenly ascent. Following a homiletic introduction, the work is a prediction of the events of the last days, with particular emphasis on the career of the Antichrist (called "the Lawless One" and "the Shameless One") and those who will oppose him. Elijah appears within the narrative, along with Enoch, as a figure who, returning from heaven, takes part in these eschatological events. Apart from the subscript title, there is no indication that Elijah is the prophet who speaks throughout. But the work was evidently known as ascribed to Elijah. The codex that contains the Akhmimic version also contains part of an Apocalypse of Zephaniah.[1] In the list of Old Testament apocrypha in the Stichometry of Nicephorus, the eighth and ninth items are "Of the prophet Elijah" and "Of the prophet Zephaniah." Their contiguity both here and in the Akhmimic manuscript suggests that they were known as a pair and that it is the Coptic Apocalypse of Elijah to which the Stichometry refers. (However, the 316 stichoi assigned to it here is a little longer than the Coptic Apocalypse.)[2] The Catalog of Sixty Canonical Books inserts the "Vision of Isaiah" between the "Apocalypse of Elijah" and the "Apocalypse of Zephaniah."

In the past the Coptic Apocalypse of Elijah has been thought to be a Christian redaction of a Jewish work or at least to embody material from an older Jewish Apocalypse of Elijah. But the work as we have it is undoubtedly Christian and the attempt to get behind it to older, purely Jewish material is hazardous. David Frankfurter has argued in detail that it is an Egyptian Christian composition from the late third century.[3]

---

1. In my view this is probably a different work from the Apocalypse of Zephaniah quoted by Clement of Alexandria, *Str.* 5.11.77.
2. Wintermute, "Apocalypse of Zephaniah," *OTP* 1:499.
3. Frankfurter, *Elijah in Upper Egypt: The Apocalypse of Elijah and Early Egyptian Christianity*, SAC (Minneapolis: Fortress, 1993). See my review of this book, reprinted in Richard Bauckham, *The Jewish World Around the New Testament: Collected Essays I*, WUNT 233 (Tübingen: Mohr Siebeck, 2008), 35–38.

The other extant work attributed to Elijah is Sefer Eliyyahu, called by some scholars the Hebrew Apocalypse of Elijah.[4] Unlike the Coptic Apocalypse of Elijah, this is generically an apocalypse. The angel Michael takes Elijah on a rapid cosmic tour and then reveals to him the events of the last days. Elijah sees in a vision the resurrection of the dead, their judgment, paradise, and the New Jerusalem. He does not appear as an actor in the events. The only significant point of contact with the Coptic Apocalypse is that both include a physiognomic description of the Antichrist (called Gīgīt in the Hebrew Apocalypse), but the two descriptions have little in common. Historical allusions date this work to the seventh century CE, and, as with the Coptic Apocalypse, hypotheses of an older version that has been reworked to produce the form of the text we have are difficult to substantiate. However, the two main components—the cosmic tour and the eschatological prophecy and vision—have little connection and so may originally have been distinct.

In addition to these two apparently complete works, there are a variety of quotations and fragments that are ascribed to Elijah in ancient sources. Most were collected in the invaluable publication by Michael Stone and John Strugnell, who provided critical texts and translations of six fragments.[5] (Five of these had already been identified by Montague Rhodes James in 1920.)[6] In the present collection I have omitted two of their six fragments (for reasons explained below) and added three others. Stone and Strugnell were undogmatic about the source(s) of the fragments, remarking only that they believed "in antiquity there was at least one Elijah apocryphon," while observing some recurring features linking the fragments with both the Coptic and the Hebrew apocalypses.[7] James had been more ambitious:

> It is quite probable, I think, that the original Apocalypse [of Elijah] contained all the ingredients that the fragments show us, descriptions of hell-torments, eschatological prophecy, descriptions of Antichrist and didactic matter. But neither of the extant Apocalypses can be supposed to represent the old book faithfully. The Coptic has been Christianized, the Hebrew abridged, and additions made to both.[8]

At the opposite extreme, Hedley Sparks concluded:

> From the evidence available . . . it looks as if there were several apocrypha, bearing the name of Elijah, circulating in the early centuries. They may have been different recensions of the same basic material: they may have been completely independent. We have no means of knowing.[9]

---

4. For an English translation, see John C. Reeves, "Sefer Elijah," in *Trajectories in Near Eastern Apocalyptic: A Postrabbinic Jewish Apocalyptic Reader*, RBS 45 (Atlanta: Society of Biblical Literature, 2005).

5. Stone and Strugnell, eds., *The Books of Elijah Parts 1-2*, SBLTT 18 (Missoula, MT: Scholars Press, 1979). Part 1 contains six "Fragments of the Elijah Literature"; part 2 contains the three recensions of the Greek Life of Elijah, along with an account of the Armenian Short History of Elijah the Prophet.

6. James, *The Lost Apocrypha of the Old Testament: Their Titles and Fragments* (London: SPCK, 1920), 53–61, 92.

7. Stone and Strugnell, *Books of Elijah*, 1.

8. James, *Lost Apocrypha*, 61.

9. Sparks, "The Apocalypse of Elijah: Introduction," *AOT*, 757. Frankfurter agrees, but thinks that the comments of Didymus the Blind suggest that there was "a Greek Elijah apocryphon containing a tour of hell" (*Elijah*, 55).

Whether the fragments derive from one or more than one Elijah apocrypha and how they might be related to the Coptic and Hebrew apocalypses are questions to which we shall return after discussing each of the fragments in detail.

However, it will be useful to adduce at this point the best evidence that, besides the Coptic apocalypse, there was another apocalyptic work attributed to Elijah in antiquity. In the exegetical works of Didymus the Blind, who presided over the catechetical school in Alexandria during the fourth century, there are three relevant comments:

(1) For just as it is true to say of God that no one says to him, "What are you doing?," so also of the shameless and impudent king. This shameless one can at once take on the appearance of the Antichrist. For also in the Prophecy of Elijah concerning him a young woman is to rise up and accuse him in that way, calling him "shameless."[10]

(2) I have read in an apocryphal book that Enoch and Elijah are the two sons of oil, which is probably on account of their preeminence over other people.[11]

(3) For also in Hades there are different regions. There is a place of rest and another of condemnation. This is recounted in the Apocalypse of Elijah.[12]

The first passage is a clear reference to the story of Tabitha in the Coptic Apocalypse of Elijah 4:1–5. The second passage, commenting on the phrase "sons of oil" (i.e., anointed ones) in Zech 4:14, is probably a reference to the story of Enoch and Elijah as it is told in the Coptic Apocalypse of Elijah 4:7–19. The latter passage does not use the phrase "sons of oil," but Didymus will have observed that it clearly casts Enoch and Elijah in the role of the two witnesses of Rev 11:3–13. These, in turn, are said to be the two olive trees of Zech 4:11–13 (Rev 11:4), called the "sons of oil" in Zech 4:14. So Didymus means that he found their identification as Enoch and Elijah in "an apocryphal book" that is most likely to be the Coptic Apocalypse of Elijah.[13] Didymus doubtless knew the original Greek text of this apocalypse. It is notable that he calls it, not the Apocalypse, but the Prophecy of Elijah, which is what generically it is.

Bärbel Krebber proposes that Didymus's third reference is to the Coptic Apocalypse of Elijah 5:27 ("The Righteous One and the [. . . .] will see the sinners in punishment, along with those who persecuted them and those who delivered them over to die"), but this is not plausible.[14] The latter refers to the fate of sinners after the last judgment,

---

10. Didymus the Blind, *Comm. Eccl.* 235.28 (on Eccl/Qoh 8:4a–5a), in Johannes Kramer and Bärbel Krebber, eds., *Kommentar zu Eccl. Kap. 7–8,8*, vol. 4 of *Didymos der Blinde: Kommentar zum Ecclesiastes (Tura-Papyrus)*, Papyrologische Texte und Abhandlungen 16 (Bonn: Habelt, 1972), 136.

11. Didymus the Blind, *Comm. Zach.*, in Louis Doutreleau, *Didyme l'Aveugle: Sur Zacharie*, SC 83 (Paris: Cerf, 1962), 1:374–76.

12. Didymus the Blind, *Comm. Eccl.* 92.5–6 (on Eccl/Qoh 3:16), in Michael Gronewald, ed., *Kommentar zu Eccl. Kap. 3–4,12*, vol. 2 of *Didymos der Blinde: Kommentar zum Ecclesiastes (Tura-Papyrus)*, Papyrologische Texte und Abhandlungen 22 (Bonn: Habelt, 1977), 130.

13. The identification of the two witnesses of Rev 11:3–13 as Enoch and Elijah was widespread in early Christianity; see Richard Bauckham, "The Martyrdom of Enoch and Elijah: Jewish or Christian?," *JBL* 95 (1976): 447–58, repr. with additional material in Bauckham, *Jewish World*, 3–25. In principle, therefore, Didymus could be referring to some other apocryphal work. But since we know that he knew the Coptic Apocalypse of Elijah, this is the obvious source.

14. Krebber, "Die Eliasapokalypse bei Didymos," in Kramer and Krebber, *Kommentary zu Eccl.*,

whereas Didymus is explicitly speaking about the places where the righteous and the wicked dead are at the present time.[15] He must have known an apocalypse in which Elijah was a seer taken on a tour of the places of the dead. This is a known category of Jewish and Christian apocalypses.[16] It is notable that Didymus calls this work the Apocalypse of Elijah, distinguishing it from the work he calls the Prophecy of Elijah. There was evidently a Greek Apocalypse of Elijah, known in Egypt in the fourth century, and so we are justified in considering whether any of the other fragments of Elijah apocrypha derive from it.

Fragment 1

The Apocalypse of Elijah to which Didymus refers must have been one of those apocalypses in which the seer was shown the places where the dead spend the intermediate state between death and the last judgment. It depicted these as regions of Hades, the general term for the world of the dead prior to the last judgment. Moreover, although some Jewish and Christian works depict the dead as merely anticipating their future state after the last judgment, the righteous in restful joy, the wicked in dread of their future punishment (4 Ezra 7:75–101; Pseudo-Hippolytus, *De universo*; cf. 1 En. 22), Didymus in the context is discussing Jesus's parable of the rich man and Lazarus, in which the rich man is already suffering torments in Hades (Luke 16:23). So the Apocalypse of Elijah would have been one of those apocalypses that depicted the wicked dead as already being actively punished at the time when the seer received his revelation (e.g., Apocalypse of Zephaniah, Apocalypse of Paul, Latin Vision of Ezra, *Gedulat Moshe*).

Fragment 2

The apocryphal Epistle of Titus is a Latin work that used to be thought to derive from Priscillianist circles in Spain in the fifth century, but the current view is that it originated in Cyprianic circles in North Africa in the late fourth century.[17] It is wholly concerned with requiring strict adherence to celibacy by those who have vowed to live in that state, and its many biblical and apocryphal quotations and allusions are selected with that purpose in view. The quotations are often quite free and not all of the sources of the apocryphal quotations can be identified, but there is no reason to think that the author simply invented any of them.[18]

149–50. The translation is from Frankfurter, *Elijah*, 326. For it not being plausible, see Frankfurter, *Elijah*, 46.

15. He is discussing the parable of the rich man and Lazarus (Luke 16:19–31).

16. See esp. Martha Himmelfarb, *Tours of Hell: An Apocalyptic Form in Jewish and Christian Literature* (Philadelphia: University of Pennsylvania Press, 1983); Richard Bauckham, "Visiting the Places of the Dead in the Extra-Canonical Apocalypses," in *The Fate of the Dead: Studies on the Jewish and Christian Apocalypses*, NovTSup 93 (Leiden: Brill, 1998), 81–96, doi:10.1163/9789004267411_005.

17. For Priscillianist circles, see Aurelio De Santos Otero, "The Pseudo-Titus Epistle," in *Writings Related to the Apostles, Apocalypses and Related Subjects*, vol. 2 of *New Testament Apocrypha*, ed. Wilhelm Schneemelcher and Robin McL. Wilson (Cambridge: Clarke, 1992), 54. For Cyprianic circles, see Giulia Sfameni Gasparro, "L'Epistula Titi discipuli Pauli de dispositione sanctimonii e la tradizione dell'enkrateia," *ANRW* 2.25.6:4551–64; Jean-François Cottier, "L'Épître du Pseudo-Tite," in vol. 2 of *Écrits Apocryphes Chrétiens*, ed. Pierre Geoltrain and Jean-Daniel Kaestli, Bibliothèque de la Pléiade 516 (Paris: Gallimard, 2005), 1135.

18. This is the view of this Elijah fragment taken by Joseph Verheyden, "Les Pseudépigraphes d'Ancien Testament: Textes Latins; À Propos d'une Concordance," *ETL* 71 (1995): 398–401. Frankfurter thinks that

It is likely that the quotation is actually an abbreviated version of Elijah's tour of the punishments in Gehenna. Usually, in the apocalyptic tours of hell, the seer sees the different kinds of punishment one by one and learns what category of sinners is suffering in each case immediately after seeing each punishment. Typically, on seeing a punishment, the seer asks the angelic guide, "Who are these?," and receives a reply in the form, "These are the ones who. . . ." In the passage in the Epistle of Titus, the narrator (Elijah) first describes all the types of punishments and then explains what sort of sinner suffers each category. There is no conversation with an angel. There is a partial parallel to this method of narrating and explaining the punishments in Acts of Thomas 56. Here a young woman who has made a temporary visit to Hades between her death and her resuscitation by Thomas, describes four categories of hanging punishments. Her guide then explains to her what sort of sinners suffers each. But this is not a full-scale apocalypse. It is part of an episode within a long narrative, so there is a good reason for the more summary presentation.[19] In the Epistle of Titus the summarizing approach goes further, eliminating the angelic guide. That this is a summarized form of a more expansive tour of hell is even more apparent when we observe that, after describing six hanging punishments (12:10b–11a) and before explaining them, the narrator adds: "Some virgins are roasted on a gridiron, and some souls are fixed in eternal torment" (12:11b). Other tours of hell describe, first, a series of hanging punishments and then go on to describe a series of other punishments, often including fire. The author of the Epistle of Titus has selected just one of these further punishments (virgins on a gridiron) and then summarized all the other punishments in his source with the inclusive reference to souls who are "fixed in eternal torment."

The author's selection from his source can also be seen to serve his particular purpose in quoting it. Among the hanging punishments, sexual sins are prominent, though they are not the only type of sin. This is quite typical of hanging punishments in other tours of hell.[20] But from the other punishments, inflicted on sinners guilty of many other sorts of sins, which presumably occurred in his source, the author has selected only the case of virgins roasted on a gridiron. Moreover, unlike all the other punishments he describes, this one is not explained. We are not told of what the virgins are guilty. The author of the Epistle of Titus doubtless wants his readers to think of Christian women who were vowed to a life of chastity and broke their vow. (He is particularly concerned about cases of a man and a woman in a "spiritual marriage.") But it may well be that the source specified young women who did not preserve their virginity until marriage, a category of sinners that occurs in other tours of hell.[21] Consequently, the author has not included the explanation of this punishment that he found in his source.

---

the author of the Epistle of Titus associated traditional material with Elijah because "Elijah was understood to be an authority on such matters" (*Elijah*, 56). It is not clear to me why he resists identifying the Epistle of Titus's source with the "Greek Elijah apocryphon containing a tour of hell" that he thinks we have "good reason" to postulate on the basis of Didymus's evidence (55).

19. See also Gedulat Moshe (Greatness of Moses) 13:10–16 (translated in *MOTP* 1:714–25), where Moses sees eight different hanging punishments that are then explained to him by his guide Nasargiel, the prince of Gehenna. The man in black who shows the young woman around the punishments in hell in Acts of Thomas 55–57 is probably also the angel in charge of them.

20. Himmelfarb, *Tours of Hell*, 85–92.

21. Himmelfarb, *Tours of Hell*, 103–4.

Therefore there is no need to think that the author of the Epistle of Titus has invented anything in his quotation.[22] He has merely selected and summarized. It is true that the specific punishment of roasting on a gridiron is not paralleled in other tours of hell, but many of the punishments in hell were modeled on the kinds of punishments that were inflicted on criminals in the Roman Empire and, as Saul Lieberman points out, the gridiron was one such punishment.[23]

In their edition of Elijah fragments, Stone and Strugnell print, along with this fragment from the Epistle of Titus, three Hebrew tours of hell that cannot be called versions of the fragment but have been considered especially close to it and perhaps derived from the work from which it was taken. The first two are somewhat varying versions of a story about Rabbi Joshua ben Levi, who is shown the punishments in hell by Elijah the prophet.[24] (The second version is translated as Tractate on Gehinnom 5:5–15 in *MOTP* 1:739–40.) The third text is an account of a visit to hell by the prophet Isaiah, who saw the wicked and their punishments in the five "courts" or "compartments" of Gehenna.[25] (This is translated as In What Manner Is the Punishment of the Grave 6–10 in *MOTP* 1:744–45.) This text has a much more tenuous connection with Elijah in that a copy of it from the Cairo Geniza carries a scribal note claiming it was excerpted from Seder Eliyyahu Rabbah. But it does not appear in any printed editions of that work.[26] The Rabbi Joshua fragment describes a series of hanging punishments (respectively four and six in the two versions) followed by a variety of other kinds of punishment. In the Isaiah fragment, Isaiah sees three hanging punishments, preceded by one other kind and followed by one other kind.

Another brief tour of hell in medieval Hebrew literature should also be mentioned here, because Elijah features in the same role as he plays in the story of Rabbi Joshua ben Levi. It is a midrash of unknown source found in an appendix to the responsa of the thirteenth-century Rabbi Meir of Rothenburg. In the course of the narrative Elijah takes a man to see the punishments in Gehenna (as well as the rewards of the righteous in the Garden of Eden). The four punishments described include two hanging punishments (men hanging by their genitals, women hanging by their breasts). Elijah explains the sins for which the sinners are being punished.[27] The midrash is an expansion of the story told in y. Ḥag. 2:2 (77d) and y. Sanh. 6.6 (23c), but the latter cannot be the sole source of its account of the punishments, since it features only two of those found in the unknown midrash, including a certain Miriam said by one rabbi to be hanging by her breast, but by another to have the hinge of the gate of Gehenna in her ear.[28]

Lieberman argued that the Elijah fragment in the Epistle of Titus has more in common with these Hebrew visions of hell than it does with the Christian apocalypses that

---

22. Here I differ from Himmelfarb, *Tours of Hell*, 36.

23. Lieberman, "On Sins and Their Punishments," in *Texts and Studies* (New York: Ktav, 1974), 46 n. 101.

24. Stone and Strugnell, *Books of Elijah*, 16–21. For the appropriateness of Rabbi Joshua ben Levi in this role, see Jean-Marc Rosenstiehl, "Les Révélations d'Élie: Élie et les tourments des damnés," in *La Littérature Intertestamentaire: Colloque de Strasbourg (17–19 Octobre 1983)*, Bibliothèque des Centres d'Études Supérieures Spécialises (Paris: Presses Universitaires de France, 1985), 101–3.

25. Stone and Strugnell, *Books of Elijah*, 20–23.

26. Himmelfarb, *Tours of Hell*, 31.

27. Lieberman, "On Sins," 39–40; Himmelfarb, *Tours of Hell*, 30–31. There is a French translation of this text in Rosenstiehl, "Les Révélations," 103–5.

28. Lieberman, "On Sins," 33–34; Himmelfarb, *Tours of Hell*, 29–30.

feature hanging punishments (Apocalypse of Peter, Acts of Thomas 55–57, Apocalypse of Paul, etc.),[29] and this view received partial support from Martha Himmelfarb.[30] Although comparing the various hanging punishments and their respective types of sinners in the various apocalypses that include them is a complex matter, those in the Epistle of Titus quotation do have clear affinities with those in the Hebrew visions.[31] The appearance of Elijah in two of the Hebrew visions is probably less significant. There is a difference between being the visionary to whom the punishments are shown and being the guide who shows someone else around and explains the punishments. Since Elijah was the only man (apart from Enoch) who ascended to heaven without dying, his many roles in rabbinic lore included revealing heavenly knowledge.[32] His role as a guide to the punishments in hell could be simply an aspect of that. Nevertheless, it might preserve a trace of a memory of an apocalypse in which Elijah was himself the seer and narrator.

Himmelfarb offers a family tree to explicate the relationships between these various tours of hell that include hanging punishments.[33] She envisages an unknown Jewish source of a "core of hanging punishments" for the Apocalypse of Peter, the Elijah fragment in the Epistle of Titus, and the Isaiah fragment, which she considers ancient, depend.[34] The later texts (Joshua ben Levi fragment, unknown midrash, and Gedulat Moshe) she thinks are dependent on the Isaiah fragment (as well as on the story in the Palestinian Talmud). She raises the alternative possibility that the Jewish texts borrowed, in the medieval period, from the later Christian apocalypses, such as the Apocalypse of Paul, but shows that this hypothesis cannot account for the evidence.[35]

I think that Himmelfarb's proposal needs to be reconsidered. If we tabulate the texts, as in table 1, the most obvious conclusion is that the Elijah fragment is the earliest of the Jewish texts and the source of the Joshua ben Levi fragment (two versions), the Isaiah fragment, and the unknown midrash (which is also dependent on the story in the Palestinian Talmud). The Gedulat Moshe represents an independent tradition that has more in common with the accounts of hanging punishments in the Christian apocalypses. Thus it seems that the Elijah fragment in the Epistle of Titus derives from a Jewish apocalypse on which the Hebrew tours of hell (with the exception of the Gedulat Moshe) were also dependent.

Fragment 3: "Eye Has Not Seen . . ."

In 1 Cor 2:9 Paul appears to cite as Scripture words that are not found in the Hebrew Bible or the Septuagint: "What eye has not seen, nor ear heard, and what has not gone up into the heart of a human, the things that God has prepared for those who love him." Origen claimed that these words occurred in "the secret writings [*secretis*] of Elijah the prophet."[36] The anonymous writer known as Ambrosiaster, writing in the late fourth century, may have been dependent on Origen, directly or indirectly, but it is notable that

---

29. Lieberman, "On Sins," 47.
30. Himmelfarb, *Tours of Hell*, 34–36.
31. See table 4 in Himmelfarb, *Tours of Hell*, 87–88.
32. See Kristen H. Lindbeck, *Elijah and the Rabbis: Story and Theology* (New York: Columbia University Press, 2010), 116–35.
33. Figure 2 in Himmelfarb, *Tours of Hell*, 133.
34. Himmelfarb, *Tours of Hell*, 136–37.
35. Himmelfarb, *Tours of Hell*, 134–36.
36. This passage is extant only in the Latin translation.

he calls the source the Apocalypse of Elijah among the secret books (*apocryphis*). Jerome disputed that Paul used an apocryphal source, arguing that the apostle was paraphrasing the Hebrew text of Isa 64:3[4], but he admitted that the words Paul quotes do occur in the Ascension of Isaiah and the Apocalypse of Elijah. He is correct about the Ascension of Isaiah, which includes the exact words of Paul's quotation (11:34), though only in the Latin and Slavonic versions (see appendix text 7, below). But it is not clear whether he had ever seen a text of the Apocalypse of Elijah. Like Ambrosiaster, he knows the title Apocalypse of Elijah, which Origen does not give (at least in the extant text), but may simply be relying on Origen for the information that it contained Paul's quotation. Later writers (Euthalius Diaconus, Photius, and George Syncellus) speak only of a "secret writing" (*apocryphon*) or "secret writings" of Elijah, showing their dependence on Origen.[37]

The context of Origen's comment is important. He is commenting on the fact that, in Matt 27:9–10, a quotation is ascribed to the prophet Jeremiah that cannot be found in the canonical book of Jeremiah, though it does correspond broadly to Zech 11:13. To solve this problem he suggests either that "Jeremiah" is a scribal error for "Zechariah" or "that there is some secret writing of Jeremiah in which it was written." Clearly he does not know such an apocryphon but is making an intelligent guess. He then defends this suggestion against those who might object to the idea that a New Testament author should quote an apocryphal book by citing two examples in which, he thinks, Paul certainly does so. These two examples are distinguished from the suggestion about Matt 27:9–10 in that in these cases he knows the apocryphal work from which Paul quotes and knows that the quotation can be found in it. Just as he knows that there is a book of Jannes and Jambres, in which the two Egyptian magicians are given those names, so he also knows that "the secret writings of Elijah the prophet" contain something like 1 Cor 2:9. The failure to give an exact title in this case probably shows a lack of interest in the matter, but should not discredit the information.

Origen cannot have known that Paul was quoting an Elijah apocryphon, since versions of the saying Paul quotes appear frequently in early Jewish and especially early Christian literature (see appendix for examples). But Origen evidently did know that something like Paul's quotation appeared in an Elijah apocryphon. Unfortunately he does not actually quote this apocryphal work and so we cannot tell how close it came to Paul's quotation. It may have had only the first part of the saying ("what eye has not seen, nor ear heard, and what has not gone up into the heart of a human"), which occurs more frequently in the literature than the rest of the saying in Paul's version or corresponding words.

The Epistle of Titus may provide some support for Origen's claim. As we have seen, this work contains a lengthy quotation from a "tour of hell" in which Elijah was the seer (frag. 2). The same epistle begins by assuring "the holy and pure" of the Lord's promise to give them "what eyes have not seen nor ears heard and what has not gone up into the heart of a human." While this could be dependent on 1 Cor 2:9, there is clear evidence that these words were known independently of Paul (appendix text 2, below). So it is possible that the author of the Epistle of Titus found them in the same Elijah apocryphon from which he quoted our fragment 2 (and see also frag. 4 for another possible reminiscence of that work in the Epistle of Titus).

In the majority of occurrences, the saying "Eye has not seen . . ." was used to refer to the blessings the righteous will receive in the eschatological age. This is true in the Epistle

---

37. Stone and Strugnell, *Books of Elijah*, 66–67.

of Titus and in many of the texts to be found in the appendix (1, 2, 3, 4, 7, 9, 11, 12, 13, 14, 15, 16, 17), though it was also used for the revelation of esoteric knowledge, especially in gnostic texts (5, 8, 10). If it occurred in the same Elijah apocryphon as our fragments 1 and 2, we can assume that it had the former significance. We may suppose that Elijah, viewing the places of rest where the righteous dead await the last judgment, was told that in the future they will obtain "what eye has not seen, nor ear heard, and what has not gone up into the heart of a human."

Fragment 3a

Here we must consider the possibility that Clement of Alexandria, *Protr.* 10.94.4–95.1, quotes precisely the passage of an Elijah apocryphon to which Origen alludes. If we had only Clement's text, we might understand it in the following way. He first quotes an unknown source: "But the holy ones of the Lord will inherit the glory of God and his power." Then he addresses to Paul, the "blessed one," the question, "Tell me, O blessed one, what kind of glory?," and answers it by quoting from 1 Cor 2:9 the words, "that eye has not seen nor ear heard and that has not gone up into the heart of a human" (in Greek his words are close but not identical with Paul's). Then he either resumes quoting his unknown source or composes freely the conclusion: "And they shall rejoice in the kingdom of their Lord forever. Amen."

Several points about Clement's literary usage should be noted. First he habitually uses the epithet "blessed" for writers of Scripture (David, Paul) as well as apostles (Peter, Paul) and other holy men (John the Baptist). Second, he uses an interjected question in the same way elsewhere (*Protr.* 1.9.1; 6.68.1, 70.1). So the question should not be understood as part of the scriptural quotation. Third, although the use of "amen" looks as though it must mark the end of an apocryphal text Clement has quoted, adding "amen" after "forever" is something Clement does elsewhere without indicating a literary conclusion of any kind (*Paed.* 1.4.11.2).

However, we cannot reach a conclusion about this passage without taking into account the parallels to it in the Testament of Our Lord in Galilee and the Apostolic Constitutions. The former is a close parallel to everything in Clement that follows the introduction to the quotation down to the amen, with the exception of the interjected question. The parallel in the Apostolic Constitutions shows the influence of 1 Cor 2:9 ("which God has prepared for those who love him"),[38] but also a substantial amount of agreement with the passage in Clement that dependence on 1 Cor 2:9 cannot explain. It seems unlikely that these two texts are dependent on Clement, since the *Protrepticus* is not the sort of work to which someone would go for eschatological information and this passage is not a prominent one within the *Protrepticus*. The most likely explanation is that they are dependent on the source from which Clement quoted. In that case Clement's quotation must be a single passage consisting of these words: "But the holy ones of the Lord will inherit the glory of God and his power. [Glory] that eye has not seen nor ear heard and that has not gone up into the heart of a human. And they shall rejoice in the kingdom of their Lord forever." The "blessed one" Clement addresses must be the eminent person to whom this apocryphal work was ascribed.

---

38. The phrase "those who love him" seems peculiar to 1 Cor 2:9 and texts dependent on it. Among the texts in the appendix, it occurs only in texts 7, 16, 17, and 18.

That person could be Elijah, and it could be that this is the work to which Origen referred and thought to be the source of Paul's quotation. But we cannot be at all sure of that. As noted, the saying "that eye has not seen nor ear heard and that has not gone up into the heart of a human" was widely known, and there were many apocryphal works available in Alexandria in the late second and third centuries. A significant point to note is that the work quoted by Clement was certainly a Christian work (a non-Christian Jewish work would not refer to "the holy ones of the Lord" and distinguish "the Lord" from "God"). But, of course, an Elijah apocryphon could be Christian, as the Coptic Apocalypse of Elijah is.

Fragment 4: Elijah the Heavenly Scribe

Epistle of Titus 9:3 has been understood to refer to the apocalypses Enoch was believed to have written, recounting events of the antediluvian period. The reference to Elijah could then envisage a narrative of the eschatological events written by Elijah in an apocalypse. But more probably Enoch appears here in his role as the heavenly scribe who records the sinful and righteous deeds of all people in preparation for the last judgment (Jub. 10:17; 2 En. 53:2–3; T. Ab. B11). This writer restricts Enoch's scribal activity to "the earlier acts of humanity" and gives Elijah the role of recording the deeds of the new (Christian) people who are called, like Elijah, not merely to righteousness, but to holiness (i.e., for this author, chastity). In that case there is no reference here to the writing of a prophecy by Elijah, but the information about Elijah may well come from an apocryphal source (of which this writer knows many). The role of heavenly scribe is ascribed to Elijah hardly anywhere else, but there is a trace of it in the Babylonian Talmud (b. Qidd. 70a).[39] The author of the Epistle of Titus is not likely to have invented it. His source is plausibly the same as the one from which he quotes a vision of the punishments in hell seen by Elijah (frag. 2). Perhaps in this work Elijah was told that, after his ascension to heaven, he would be given the role of heavenly scribe, recording people's deeds. That these people will be Christians may be the interpretation given to the passage by the author of the Epistle of Titus.

Fragment 5: Portrait of the Antichrist

In 1917 François Nau published the last two pages of a biblical manuscript in Greek from the thirteenth century in which several fragments about the Antichrist are collected.[40] They are taken from Pseudo-Methodius, John Chrysostom, commentaries on passages of Scripture, and, finally, "secret sayings [*apokruphois*] that Elijah the prophet spoke about the Antichrist." The physical description of Antichrist that follows is closely paralleled in several other sources[41] and differs almost entirely from other such descriptions elsewhere in apocalyptic literature,[42] including the Coptic Apocalypse of Elijah (3:14–18) and the Hebrew Apocalypse of Elijah.[43]

---

39. See Lindbeck, *Elijah*, 47–48, 184–85.
40. Nau, "Methodius, Clément, Andronicus," *JA* 9 (1917): 453–62.
41. Three of these are included in the translations of frag. 5 below. Others (all in later Arabic and Ethiopic sources) are less complete: see Stone and Strugnell, *Books of Elijah*, 32–35 and the comparative table on pp. 36–37. Cf. also Jean-Marc Rosenstiehl, "Le Portrait de l'Antichrist," in *Pseudépigraphes de l'Ancient Testament et Manuscrits de la Mer Morte*, by Marc Philonenko et al. (Paris: Presses Universitaires de France, 1967), 50–52.
42. Rosenstiehl, "Le Portrait," 46–50.
43. Reeves, "Sefer Elijah," 33.

There is no reason to doubt that the compiler of the collection of extracts about Antichrist found this description of Antichrist in a work, written in Greek, ascribed to Elijah. But was this the same work as that to which our fragments 1 and 2 belonged? The natural home for a description of Antichrist is in a passage of eschatological prophecy, which is where this portrait of Antichrist is found in the Testament of Our Lord and the Testament of Our Lord in Galilee. But, so far as we can tell from fragments 1–2 of the Greek Testament of Elijah, the latter was an account of a vision in which Elijah was shown the places of the dead. A parallel might be found in the Greek Apocalypse of Ezra, where, in the course of touring the punishments in hell, Ezra sees "a man restrained with iron bars," who turns out to be Antichrist. When Ezra asks about him, he is given a physiognomic description and a brief account of his (presumably future) career on earth (Gk. Apoc. Ezra 4:25–43). However, it is odd that Ezra needs to be given a description of the man he sees, and it is likely that the whole passage about the Antichrist has been secondarily attached to the narrative of the tour of hell.[44]

It is entirely possible that the Greek Apocalypse of Elijah to which fragment 1 refers contained eschatological prophecy as well as revelation of the places of the dead. Another possibility is that fragment 5 derives from a form of the Greek original of the Coptic Apocalypse of Elijah in which the description of the Antichrist differed from that in our Coptic manuscript. It is notable that both in the Coptic Apocalypse (3:14) and in the Syriac version of the Testament of Our Lord (11) the description of the Antichrist is introduced by reference to "his signs," as it is also in the Hebrew Apocalypse of Elijah.

Fragment 6: Wake Up, Sleeper

The quotation in Eph 5:14b has usually been thought to be from an early Christian baptismal hymn.[45] It is explained as addressed to an individual who is being baptized. The second-person singular address makes it difficult to understand how it could have been used as a hymn in any other context. The imagery (waking from sleep, rising from death, light of Christ) seems appropriate to baptism, but it must be said that, although there is evidence for the association of baptism with resurrection (Col 2:12), there is no clear evidence from this early period for the association of baptism with light. Moreover, the introductory formula, "Therefore it is said" (or perhaps "Therefore he [God] says"), is used in Eph 4:8 to introduce a quotation from Scripture (cf. also Jas 4:6). It is questionable whether an early Christian hymn would be cited as though it were inspired Scripture, though Ephesians itself does refer to Spirit-inspired songs (5:19).

More promising is the observation that the passage could be based on Isa 26:19 and Isa 60:1–2 (although this is not incompatible with the idea that it belongs to a hymn).[46] The view that it is cited *as* a quotation from Isaiah is not plausible, because even allowing for the technique of adapting the words of Scripture to the purpose and context for which it is cited, the quotation itself is too different from the Isaianic texts. However, establishing that it is based on those texts can help us discern what sort of a work it is quoted from. That it is based on Isa 26:19 and Isa 60:1–2 is particularly plausible if we

---

44. In the related Latin Vision of Ezra, a passage about Antichrist appears in a quite different context (71–79), but the portrait of Antichrist it includes is different from that in the Greek Apocalypse of Ezra.
45. E.g., Andrew T. Lincoln, *Ephesians*, WBC 42 (Dallas: Word, 1990), 318–19.
46. Thorsten Moritz combines both notions. Moritz, "Tradition in Eph 5.14," in *A Profound Mystery: The Use of the Old Testament in Ephesians*, NovTSup 85 (Leiden: Brill, 1996), 97–116, doi:10.1163/9789004267312_007.

suppose the author was dependent on the Hebrew of these passages, rather than (as most scholars suppose without argument) the Septuagint. The two passages are linked by the key word "rise" (*qûm*), which is the first word in Isa 60:1 and whose Greek equivalent (*egeire*) is also the first word of the quotation in Ephesians. The quotation can be seen as a paraphrase of Isa 60:1–2 interpreted by reference to Isa 26:19 (which supplies the images of rising *from sleep and from death*).[47] The third line is closely based on Isa 60:2b ("YHWH shall rise upon you and his glory will be seen on you").

The two Isaianic passages are poetic, but they are prophecy, not hymns. The key to understanding how they are used in the Ephesians quotation, which previous scholars have missed, is to notice to whom they are addressed. Isaiah 26:19 is in part addressed to "those who dwell in the dust," while Isa 60:1–2 is entirely addressed to Zion. So might not the Ephesians quotation be addressed, not to an individual person, but to a collective, the people of God? It is true that the addressee is grammatically masculine, whereas Zion and Jerusalem in Greek are both feminine, but the passage can easily be understood as addressed, like Isa 26:20, to "my people" (*laos mou*), which is masculine in Greek as in Hebrew.

The quotation is therefore a prophecy addressed to Israel, the people of God, who, as commonly in the later chapters of Isaiah, are called to recognize the arrival of their salvation and restoration. As such it belongs to a genre of such prophecies from the late Second Temple period: the Apostrophe to Zion (4Q88; 11Q5 [11QPs^a] 22; 11Q6 [11QPs^b] 6); Pss. Sol. 11; and 1 Bar 5, all of which are based on Isa 60 and related passages in Isaiah. First Baruch 5:5 calls on Jerusalem to "arise" (*anastēthi*), while Pss. Sol. 11 prays that the Lord may "raise up" (*anastēsai*) Israel (cf. Eph 5:14: *anasta*).

The first two of these passages are psalms, the third a prophetic oracle, but there are close resemblances between all three. So the work from which Ephesians quotes could be a psalm, but the way in which it is quoted as authoritative Scripture suggests that it was more likely a prophecy ascribed to a biblical prophet. However, there is a difficulty in the fact that the quotation appears to be Christian ("Christ will shine on you"). Would a pseudepigraphal text ascribed to a biblical prophet but written by a Christian be likely to be, already at the time of Ephesians, known and respected as an authoritative writing? The solution may lie in the fact that the Isaianic basis of the text has "the Lord" (YHWH) where the text of the quotation has "Christ." This is a christological reading of a biblical YHWH text of the kind that is not uncommon in the New Testament. But in this instance the substitution of "Christ" for "the Lord" could be the work of the author of Ephesians, who has adapted the Jewish text in this way. (Note that Eph 4:8 quotes a significantly adapted form of Ps 68:18.)

The earliest quotation of Eph 5:14 is of considerable interest. It is clear that Clement of Alexandria understands the passage to be spoken by "the Lord." This does not mean he took it to be a saying of Jesus, as has been commonly supposed.[48] Rather, he understands it to be the words of a prophet speaking in the Lord's name. Earlier in the same work he writes that in the early history of Israel God spoke to the people by miraculous signs (the burning bush and the pillar of fire).

---

47. See also Dan 12:2.
48. E.g., Alfred Resch, *Agrapha: Aussercanonische Schriftfragmente*, TUGAL 15.3/4 (Leipzig: Hinrichs, 1906), 32.

But since flesh is more honorable than a pillar or a bush, after those signs prophets raised their voices, the Lord himself speaking in Isaiah, he himself in Elijah, he himself in the mouth of the prophets (*Protr.* 1.8.3).

The fact that, after Isaiah, always the favorite prophet for Christian writers, Clement singles out Elijah for mention by name among the other prophets, is striking, and might perhaps be an indication that he knew an apocryphal work ascribed to Elijah.

However, it is unlikely that the three additional lines that Clement adds to the quotation from Ephesians are drawn from the original source of the quotation.[49] If they were, they would show that that work was thoroughly Christian, but the content is more obviously attributable to Clement himself. Thus, elsewhere in the *Protrepticus*, Clement speaks of Christ as "the sun of righteousness," quoting Mal 4:2 (*Protr.* 11.114.3); he uses the phrase "before the morning star" (from Ps 109:3 LXX) to refer to Christ's existence at the beginning (*Protr.* 1.6.3); and he speaks of being enlightened by the "rays" of Christ (*Protr.* 11.113.3, 115.4). The rhetorical procedure by which he expands the quotation from Eph 5:14 with three parallel descriptions of Christ shining is similar to his procedures elsewhere (e.g., 9.82.6–7).

Only once in patristic literature is the quotation in Eph 5:14 attributed to Elijah. This somewhat obscure passage in Epiphanius (*Pan.* 42.12.3) appears to treat the source, Elijah, as part of the Old Testament. This would make more sense if it were said of Isaiah, because Epiphanius could have recognized that the quotation is based on Isa 60:1–2. So it has been suggested that "Elijah" here is a scribal error for "Isaiah" (ΗΛΙΑΣ for ΗΣΑΙΑΣ).[50] This would bring Epiphanius into line with Hippolytus, who in one place (*Comm. Dan.* 4.56.4) ascribes the quotation to Isaiah. Alternatively, "Isaiah" in Hippolytus could be a scribal error for "Elijah." It has to be said that the evidence for connecting this fragment with Elijah is weak.

Several later writers (Euthalius Diaconus, Photius, George Syncellus) claim that the quotation is from the Apocryphon of Jeremiah.[51] This is likely to be a guess. These writers knew that there was such an apocryphon, from which some patristic writers appear to quote, but they did not know the work themselves. It is notable, however, that Clement of Alexandria, Origen,[52] Hippolytus, Epiphanius, and these later writers all agree in attributing the quotation to a prophet, though Severian and Theodoret of Cyrrhus considered the source to be a Christian hymn, referring to 1 Cor 14:26 to maintain that such a hymn could be inspired and so cited as an inspired authority.[53]

Fragment 7

This is from one of two late recensions of the Lives of the Prophets.[54] The reference can hardly be merely to the text of 1 Kgs 19:11–18, but it could presuppose an interpretation

---

49. On these lines, see Franz Joseph Dölger, *Sol Salutis: Gebet und Gesang im christlichen Altertum*, Liturgiegeschichtliche Forschungen 4/5 (Münster: Aschendorff, 1925), 365–70.

50. Stone and Strugnell, *Books of Elijah*, 76.

51. Texts in Stone and Strugnell, *Books of Elijah*, 78–79.

52. Origen, *Selecta in Ps.* (Ps 3:6) (PG 12.1128A), attributes the quotation to "the prophet."

53. Thomas Kingsmill Abbott, *A Critical and Exegetical Commentary on the Epistles to the Ephesians and to the Colossians*, ICC (Edinburgh: T&T Clark, 1897), 158.

54. On the recensions of the Lives of the Prophets, see Albert Marie Denis, *Introduction à la littérature religieuse judéo-hellénistique, 1: Pseudépigraphes de l'Ancien Testament* (Turnhout: Brepols, 2000), 585–93.

Fragments of Elijah Apocrypha

of that text that understood Elijah's encounter with God on Mount Horeb to be the occasion for the revelation of much greater "mysteries" than the words of God actually recorded in that text. The wind, the earthquake, and the fire (1 Kgs 19:11–12) could be understood to refer to revelations of the other world. This would be consistent with the way other biblical texts were elaborated in apocalyptic literature.[55] So this reference in the Epiphanian Life of Elijah may well presuppose knowledge of a literary work in which such revelations to Elijah were described.

The Hebrew Apocalypse of Elijah begins with Elijah asleep under a broom tree and an angel awaking him (1 Kgs 19:5–6). It continues "Michael, 'the great prince' of Israel, revealed this mystery [i.e., an account of the end of days] to the prophet Elijah at Mount Carmel." There seems to be a confusion here between Mount Carmel and Mount Horeb, but before Michael begins to predict the events of the end time, a section intervenes in which "a wind from the Lord" lifts up Elijah and transports him in turn to three of the four edges of the world where he sees the mysteries of the other world, including the punishment of sinners.[56] Perhaps this "wind from the Lord" was inspired by 1 Kgs 19:11.

Other Suggested Fragments

Stone and Strugnell, in their collection of fragments of Elijah apocrypha, include a passage about the military forces of Antichrist that is twice quoted by Hippolytus (*Antichr.* 15, 54).[57] (There seems to be no trace of it anywhere else, despite the frequency of accounts of Antichrist's career in Christian apocalypses and related literature.) Hippolytus attributes it to "another prophet" (i.e., other than Jeremiah). The only reason for Stone and Strugnell to include it is that James guessed that it came from the Apocalypse of Elijah.[58] He did so because he thought, on the basis of our fragment 5, that this apocalypse included material about Antichrist.[59] If we cannot be sure that our fragment 5 comes from the same work as others of our collection of fragments, then the basis for James's intelligent guess is weakened. It could be supported by Hippolytus's attribution of our fragment 6 to Isaiah, if this is a transcriptional error for Elijah (see above), but this too is no more than a possibility. Consequently, it is hard to justify James's guess.

Stone and Strugnell's fragment 6 is a story about Elijah that Epiphanius (*Pan.* 26.13.228) attributes to gnostics.[60] It tells how, at the time of his assumption to heaven, Elijah was assailed by a female demon who claimed to have been impregnated by him, without his knowledge, and had children by him. There is no reason to think the source of this story was an Elijah apocryphon, and it is quite out of character with the fragments in the present collection.

---

55. E.g., Abraham's vision in Gen 15:7–19; see Richard Bauckham, "Early Jewish Visions of Hell," in *The Fate of the Dead: Studies on the Jewish and Christian Apocalypses*, NovTSup 93 (Leiden: Brill, 1998), 72–73, doi:10.1163/9789004267411_004.

56. Reeves, "Sefer Elijah," 31–32. On this passage, see Bauckham, "Early Jewish Visions" (1998 ed.), 57–59.

57. Stone and Strugnell, *Books of Elijah*, 84–85. It is also discussed in Wilhelm Bousset, *The Anti-Christ Legend: A Chapter in Christian and Jewish Folklore*, trans. A. H. Keane (London: Hutchinson, 1896), 27–28; Denis, *Introduction*, 1278; Charles E. Hill, "Antichrist from the Tribe of Dan," *JTS* NS 46 (1995): 99–117, doi:10.1093/jts/46.1.99.

58. James, *Lost Apocrypha*, 92.

59. James, *Lost Apocrypha*, 61.

60. Stone and Strugnell, *Books of Elijah*, 88–89.

Frankfurter calls attention to two passages in recensions of the Life of Elijah "that show the existence of a tradition in which Elijah received revelations."[61] One of these is our fragment 7, the other is in another late recension of the Life of Elijah, the Dorothean recension. It calls Elijah

> the first of humans to give humans an example of traversing heaven, the first of humans to set an example of having a share of the earth for a dwelling and traversing the whole heaven, who was mortal and contested with the immortals, who walked on the earth and as a spirit traversed heaven with angels, who by means of sheepskin gave double gifts to his disciple Elisha [2 Kgs 2:9–14], the long-lived and unaging man.[62]

Frankfurter thinks this refers to events during Elijah's lifetime, but probably it is merely a high-flown description of Elijah's ascension to heaven itself, portraying him as the first human who both lived on earth and also ascended through the whole heaven. So it does not presuppose any tradition of revelations made to Elijah.[63]

The Greek Apocalypse of Elijah

In antiquity, as well as the Coptic Apocalypse of Elijah, there was an apocalypse in which Elijah was shown the places of the dead, where the righteous are at rest and the wicked are being punished (frag. 1), though the content need not have been limited to this. Of the other fragments, the one we can be most confident comes from this apocalypse is fragment 2, which portrays Elijah taken on a tour of hell, where he sees the variety of different punishments inflicted on different categories of sinners. This clearly aligns the apocalypse with others that included similar tours of hell. Fragment 3 could well come from the same work and preserve the words in which Elijah was told of the future destiny of the righteous after the last judgment. Fragment 3a may be a quotation from precisely that part of the apocalypse, but nothing in our sources associates it with Elijah. Fragment 4 could plausibly be an allusion to the same apocalypse of Elijah that is quoted in fragment 2. It would mean that Elijah was portrayed not only as a visionary touring the places of the dead, but also, following his ascension, as a heavenly scribe recording the people's deeds.

If fragment 5 comes from the same Greek Apocalypse of Elijah, then the work included eschatological prophecy, in which God or an angel gave Elijah an account of the events of the last days. This is entirely possible, but we should note that the evidence for connecting this fragment with Elijah is weak, and this is even more the case with fragment 6.

Was the Greek Apocalypse of Elijah a Jewish composition, a Christian composition, or perhaps a Jewish composition edited by a Christian? We lack the evidence to distinguish the last two possibilities. Fragment 3a is undoubtedly Christian and fragment 4 may be, but none of the other fragments need be. The most significant evidence lies in the relationship between fragment 2 and the Hebrew visions of hell, discussed above. Elijah's tour of hell resembles those in the Hebrew sources more closely than it does

---

61. Frankfurter, *Elijah*, 60.
62. Translation adapted from Stone and Strugnell, *Books of Elijah*, 94, 96.
63. This is probably also true of the passage from Aphraates quoted by Frankfurter, *Elijah*, 60.

those in Christian literature. While this does not rule out the possibility of a Christian origin, it is probably most easily explained if the Greek Apocalypse of Elijah was transmitted in Jewish as well as Christian circles, and indeed survived in Jewish circles when it was apparently forgotten in Christian traditions. Perhaps it was even known in a Hebrew version.

If fragments 3a and 6 are not from the Greek Apocalypse of Elijah, then the earliest attestation of the work is Origen's (frag. 3). But a Jewish apocalypse of this kind could be considerably older. It might even be the earliest Jewish tour of the punishments in hell.

A Cosmic Tour?

I reserve for this separate discussion a more adventurous proposal that I think should be considered, though it is certainly more speculative than the conclusions reached in the previous section. The first main section of the Hebrew Apocalypse of Elijah (Sefer Eliyyahu) has a brief account of a cosmic tour by Elijah. It has all the marks of a distinct unit inserted into the text, since it divides the introductory statement about Michael's revelation of the events of the last days from the beginning of Michael's predictions. Michael plays no part in the cosmic tour:

> A wind from the Lord lifted me [Elijah] up and transported me to the southern part of the world, and I saw there a high place burning with fire where no creature was able to enter. Then the wind lifted me up and transported me to the eastern part of the world, and I saw there stars battling one another incessantly. Again the wind lifted me up and transported me to the western part of the world, and I saw there souls undergoing a painful judgment, each one in accordance with its deeds.[64]

This is a tour to the edges of the world, though a remarkably brief one, and the various sights Elijah sees can be identified from their resemblances to what Enoch sees in his cosmic tours in the Book of the Watchers, though the points of the compass and the descriptions vary significantly. The high place in the south must be the central of Enoch's seven mountains (1 En. 18:6–8; 24–25), which are protected by mountains of fire (18:9; 24:1). The stars Elijah sees in the east must be the seven erring stars of 1 En. 18:13–16; 21:3–6. The place of the dead that Elijah sees is in the west, like Enoch's Sheol (1 En. 22), but there is a very significant difference: unlike Enoch, Elijah sees the souls of the wicked already being punished.

Apart from our fragment 2, this is the only text in which Elijah is said to see the punishments of the wicked after death. Also significant is the phrase "each one in accordance with its deeds," which suggests that Elijah saw a variety of punishments corresponding to the various sins of the souls,[65] just as he does in our fragment 2. Another point of connection is that the dead are called "souls" in both cases. This

---

64. Reeves, "Sefer Elijah," 32.
65. The phrase is used with reference to the punishments in Gehenna in Apoc. Pet. 13:3. For more detail about the use of this phrase, see Richard Bauckham, "The Apocalypse of Peter: A Jewish Christian Apocalypse from the Time of Bar Kokhba," in *Fate of the Dead*, 195–98, doi:10.1163/978900 4267411_010.

is unusual in tours of hell, though it is also found in the Apocalypse of Zephaniah (2:8; 10:3), and, significantly with reference to the hanging punishments, in Acts of Thomas 56.[66]

It is possible, therefore, that the passage in the Hebrew Apocalypse of Elijah is a brief summary of a cosmic tour that was described at much greater length in the Greek Apocalypse of Elijah. In that case, Elijah's visit to the places of the dead in the Greek Apocalypse will have been part of a wider tour of the other world, as Enoch's was. This would place the Greek Apocalypse of Elijah on the earlier side of a major transition in the way the world was envisaged in apocalypses. The mysterious and inaccessible places to which Enoch was taken by angels in the Book of the Watchers were all located at the furthest extremities of the flat circle of the earth, not above or below it. But in the first and second centuries CE a new cosmology altered the form of the cosmic tour in the apocalypses. Most of the places Enoch saw at the edges of the world were relocated to the seven heavens above the earth, and apocalyptic seers were now escorted upward through the heavens to view the secrets contained in them, as well as sometimes being taken down to the place of the dead below the earth. Apocalypses such as 2 Enoch, 3 Baruch, and the Gedulat Moshe illustrate this new cosmology. Elijah's cosmic tour in the Hebrew Apocalypse of Elijah is an anomalous survival of the old apocalyptic cosmology. Not only is this explicable if it derives from the Greek Apocalypse of Elijah, but also that apocalypse can probably be dated to the first century CE at the latest. It would probably be somewhat earlier.

If the Greek Apocalypse of Elijah belongs on the earlier side of this cosmological transition, in its conception of the state of the dead it belongs on the later side of another transition. This is a transition in the understanding especially of the present state of the wicked dead. Instead of merely waiting in dread of the punishments they knew to be awaiting them at the last judgment, from around the first century CE they came to be understood as already being punished with the kind of punishments that are depicted in the tours of hell.[67] This new view can be seen in such works as the Apocalypse of Zephaniah and the Apocalypse of Paul.[68] In that case, the Greek Apocalypse of Elijah would seem to have been both a late example of the old cosmology and an early example of the new view of the state of the dead.

---

66. The dead are "souls" in 1 En. 22:3–13, but are not there being punished.
67. On these transitions, see Bauckham, "Visiting the Places of the Dead," 81–93.
68. Almost all the works studied in Himmelfarb, *Tours of Hell*, belong in this category. The Apocalypse of Peter, in its original form, preserved in the Ethiopic version, is an exceptional case, because it has made use of a tour of hell in which the seer saw the punishments of the wicked happening in the present and refunctioned it as a prophecy of the punishments of the wicked after the last judgment.

Fragments of Elijah Apocrypha

Table 1. Hanging Punishments in Jewish Texts

ELIJAH	JOSHUA A	JOSHUA B	ISAIAH	MIDRASH	MOSES
		1. noses			
1. genitals	1. hands (genitals?)	2. hands (genitals?)	2. genitals	1. genitals	
2. tongues	2. tongues	3. tongues	1. tongues		5. tongues
3. eyes	3. eyes	6. eyes			1. eyes
4. upside down		4. feet			4. feet
5. *breasts*		5. *breasts*	3. *breasts*	2. *breasts*	6. *breasts*
6. hands					3. hands
	4. ears				2. ears
					7. *hair*
					8. *feet*

Note: Italics indicate punishments explicitly of women.

Bibliography

EDITIONS AND TRANSLATIONS OF THE FRAGMENTS

(* indicates the texts on which my translation is based)

Fragment 1

*Gronewald, Michael, ed. Pages 130–31 in *Kommentar zu Eccl. Kap. 3–4,12*. Vol. 2 of *Didymos der Blinde: Kommentar zum Ecclesiastes (Tura-Papyrus)*. Papyrologische Texte und Abhandlungen 22. Bonn: Habelt, 1977.

Fragment 2

Cottier, Jean-François. "L'Épître du Pseudo-Tite." Pages 1133–71 in vol. 2 of *Écrits Apocryphes Chrétiens*. Edited by Pierre Geoltrain and Jean-Daniel Kaestli. Bibliothèque de la Pléiade 516. Paris: Gallimard, 2005.

*De Bruyne, Donatien. "*Epistula Titi, discipuli Pauli, de dispositione sanctimonii*." *RBén* 37 (1925): 58. doi:10.1484/J.RB.4.04753.

———. "Nouveaux Fragments des Actes de Pierre, de Paul, de Jean, d'André, et de l'Apocalypse d' Élie." *RBén* 25 (1908): 153–54.

De Santos Otero, Aurelio. "The Pseudo-Titus Epistle." Pages 53–74 in *Writings Related to the Apostles, Apocalypses and Related Subjects*. Vol. 2 of *New Testament Apocrypha*. Edited by Wilhelm Schneemelcher and Robin McL. Wilson. Cambridge: Clarke, 1992.

*Hamman, Adalbert, ed. Cols. 1534–35 in *Patrologia Cursus Completus: Series Latina: Supplementum 2*. Paris: Garnier, 1960.

Stone, Michael, and John Strugnell, eds. Pages 13–26 in *The Books of Elijah Parts 1–2*. SBLTT 18. Missoula, MT: Scholars Press, 1979.

Fragment 3

Cottier, Jean-François. "L'Épître du Pseudo-Tite." Pages 1133–1171 in vol. 2 of *Écrits Apocryphes Chrétiens*. Edited by Pierre Geoltrain and Jean-Daniel Kaestli. Bibliothèque de la Pléiade 516. Paris: Gallimard, 2005.

*De Bruyne, Donatien. "*Epistula Titi, discipuli Pauli, de dispositione sanctimonii.*" RBén 37 (1925): 48. doi:10.1484/J.RB.4.04753.

De Santos Otero, Aurelio. "The Pseudo-Titus Epistle." Pages 53–74 in *Writings Related to the Apostles, Apocalypses and Related Subjects*. Vol. 2 of *New Testament Apocrypha*. Edited by Wilhelm Schneemelcher and Robin McL. Wilson. Cambridge: Clarke, 1992.

Guerrier, Louis, and Sylvain Grébaut. Pages 141–236 in *Le Testament en Galilée de Notre-Seigneur Jésus-Christ*. PO 9. Paris: Firmin-Didot, 1913.

*Hamman, Adalbert, ed. Cols. 1522–1523 in *Patrologia Cursus Completus: Series Latina: Supplementum 2*. Paris: Garnier, 1960.

*Klostermann, Erich, ed. *Origenes*. Page 250 in vol. 11. GCS 38. Leipzig: Hinrichs, 1933.

*Marcovich, Miroslav. Pages 139–40 in *Clementis Alexandrini* Protrepticus. Supplements to Vigiliae Christianae 34. Leiden: Brill, 1995.

Resch, Alfred. Pages 25–29 in *Agrapha: Ausserkanonische Schriftfragmente*. TUGAL 15.3/4. Leipzig: Hinrichs, 1906.

*Stone, Michael, and John Strugnell, eds. Pages 41–73 in *The Books of Elijah Parts 1–2*. SBLTT 18. Missoula, MT: Scholars Press, 1979.

Wajnberg, Isaak. "Apokalyptiker Rede Jesu an seine Jünger in Galiläa." Pages 47*–66* in *Gespräche Jesu mit seinen Jüngern nach der Auferstehung*. Edited by Carl Schmidt. TUGAL 3.13. Leipzig: Hinrichs, 1919.

Fragment 4

Cottier, Jean-François. "L'Épître du Pseudo-Tite." Pages 1133–71 in vol. 2 of *Écrits Apocryphes Chrétiens*. Edited by Pierre Geoltrain and Jean-Daniel Kaestli. Bibliothèque de la Pléiade 516. Paris: Gallimard, 2005.

*De Bruyne, Donatien. "*Epistula Titi, discipuli Pauli, de dispositione sanctimonii.*" RBén 37 (1925): 54–55. doi:10.1484/J.RB.4.04753.

De Santos Otero, Aurelio. "The Pseudo-Titus Epistle." Pages 53–74 in *Writing Related to the Apostles, Apocalypse and Related Subjects*. Vol. 2 of *New Testament Apocrypha*. Edited by Wilhelm Schneemelcher and Robin McL. Wilson. Cambridge: Clarke, 1992.

*Hamman, Adalbert, ed. Col. 1530 of *Patrologia Cursus Completus: Series Latina: Supplementum 2*. Paris: Garnier, 1960.

Fragment 5

Cooper, James, and Arthur John Maclean. Pages 57–58 in *The Testament of Our Lord: Translated into English from the Syriac*. Ante-Nicene Christian Library. Edinburgh: T&T Clark, 1902.

Guerrier, L., and Sylvain Grébaut. Pages 141–236 in *Le Testament en Galilée du Notre-Seigneur Jésus-Christ*. PO 9. Paris: Firmin-Didot, 1913.

James, Montague Rhodes. Pages 151–54 in *Apocrypha Anecdota: A Collection of Thirteen Apocryphal Books and Fragments*. TS 2.3. Cambridge: Cambridge University Press, 1893.

———. Pages 57–58 in *The Lost Apocrypha of the Old Testament: Their Titles and Fragments*. London: SPCK, 1920.

*Nau, François. "Methodius, Clément, Andronicus." *JA* 11.9 (1917): 415–71. See pp. 453–55, 458, 462.

Rosenstiehl, Jean-Marc. "Le Portrait de l'Antichrist." Pages 45–60 in *Pseudépigraphes de l'Ancient Testament et Manuscrits de la Mer Morte*. By Marc Philonenko, Jean-Claude Picard, Jean-Marc Rosenstiehl and Francis Schmidt. Paris: Presses Universitaires de France, 1967. See pp. 50–52.

Stone, Michael, and John Strugnell, eds. Pages 26–39 in *The Books of Elijah Parts 1–2*. SBLTT 18. Missoula, MT: Scholars Press, 1979.

Wajnberg, Isaak. "Apokalyptiker Rede Jesu an seine Jünger in Galiläa." Pages 47*–66* in *Gespräche Jesu mit seinen Jüngern nach der Auferstehung*. Edited by Carl Schmidt. TUGAL 3.13. Leipzig: Hinrichs, 1919. See pp. 61–62*.

Fragment 6

*Marcovich, Miroslav. Page 126 in *Clementis Alexandrini* Protrepticus. Supplements to Vigiliae Christianae 34. Leiden: Brill, 1995.

Resch, Alfred. Pages 32–34 in *Agrapha: Aussercanonische Schriftfragmente*. TUGAL 15.3/4. Leipzig: Hinrichs, 1906.

*Stone, Michael, and John Strugnell, eds. Pages 76–81 in *The Books of Elijah Parts 1–2*. SBLTT 18. Missoula, MT: Scholars Press, 1979.

Fragment 7

*Stone, Michael, and John Strugnell, eds. Pages 96–97 in *The Books of Elijah Parts 1–2*. SBLTT 18. Missoula, MT: Scholars Press, 1979.

EDITIONS AND TRANSLATIONS OF OTHER ELIJAH PSEUDEPIGRAPHA

Buttenwieser, Moses. *Die Hebräische Elias-Apokalypse und ihre Stellung in der apokalyptischen Litteratur des rabbinischen Schrifttums und der Kirche*. Leipzig: Pfeiffer, 1897. (Edition.)

Doutreleau, Louis. *Didyme l'Aveugle: Sur Zacharie*. Vol. 1. SC 83. Paris: Cerf, 1962.

Frankfurter, David. *Elijah in Upper Egypt: The Apocalypse of Elijah and Early Egyptian Christianity*. SAC. Minneapolis: Fortress, 1993. (Translation of the Coptic Apocalypse of Elijah on pp. 299–338.)

Herbert, Máire, and Martin McNamara. *Irish Biblical Apocrypha*. Edinburgh: T&T Clark, 1989. (Translation of The Two Sorrows of the Kingdom of Heaven on pp. 19–21.)

Kramer, Johannes, and Bärbel Krebber, eds. Pages 136–37 in *Kommentar zu Eccl. Kap. 7–8,8*. Vol. 4 of *Didymos der Blinde: Kommentar zum Ecclesiastes (Tura-Papyrus)*. Papyrologische Texte und Abhandlungen 16. Bonn: Habelt, 1972.

Kuhn, K. H. "The Apocalypse of Elijah." *AOT*, 753–73.

Pietersma, Albert, Susan Turner Comstock, and Harold W. Attridge, eds. *The Apocalypse of Elijah Based on P. Chester Beatty 2018*. SBLTT 19. Missoula, MT: Scholars Press, 1981.

Reeves, John C. "Sefer Elijah." Pages 29–39 in *Trajectories in Near Eastern Apocalyptic: A Postrabbinic Jewish Apocalyptic Reader*. RBS 45. Atlanta: Society of Biblical Literature, 2005. (Translation.)

Rosenstiehl, Jean-Marc. *L'Apocalypse d'Élie: Introduction, Traduction, et Notes*. Textes et Études 1. Paris: Guethner, 1972.

Schrage, Wolfgang. "Die Elia-Apokalypse." Pages 195–288 in vol. 5 of *Apokalypsen*. Edited by Werner Georg Kümmel. JSHRZ 5. Gütersloh: Mohn, 1980. doi:10.14315/9783641248130. (Translation.)

Wintermute, Orval S. "Apocalypse of Elijah." *OTP* 1:721–53. (Translation.)

STUDIES (ALL FRAGMENTS)

Dehandschutter, Boudewijn. "Les Apocalypses d' Élie." Pages 59-68 in *Élie le Prophète: Bible, Tradition, Iconographie: Colloque des 10 et 11 Novembre 1985.* Edited by Gerard F. Willems. Leuven: Peeters, 1988.

Denis, Albert-Marie. "L'Apocalypse d'Élie (Fragments) et les écrits aux titres parallèles." Pages 609-31 in *Introduction à la littérature religieuse judéo-hellénistique, 1: Pseudépigraphes de l'Ancien Testament.* Turnhout: Brepols, 2000.

Frankfurter, David. Pages 44-57, 60-61 in *Elijah in Upper Egypt: The Apocalypse of Elijah and Early Egyptian Christianity.* SAC. Minneapolis: Fortress, 1993.

James, Montague Rhodes. "Elijah. Apocalypse." Pages 53-61 in *The Lost Apocrypha of the Old Testament: Their Titles and Fragments.* London: SPCK, 1920.

Krebber, Bärbel. "Die Elias apokalypse bei Didymos." Pages 159-61 in *Kommentar zu Eccl. Kap. 7-8,8.* Vol. 4 of *Didymos der Blinde: Kommentar zum Ecclesiastes (Tura-Papyrus).* Edited by Johannes Kramer and Bärbel Krebber. Papyrologische Texte und Abhandlungen 16. Bonn: Habelt, 1972.

Schürer, Emil. Pages 799-803 in vol. 3.2 of *The History of the Jewish People in the Age of Jesus Christ (175 B. C.-A. D. 135).* Edited by Geza Vermes, Fergus Millar, and Martin Goodman. Rev. ed. Edinburgh: T&T Clark, 1979.

Stone, Michael, and John Strugnell, eds. *The Books of Elijah Parts 1-2.* SBLTT 18. Missoula, MT: Scholars Press, 1979.

Wintermute, Orval S. "Elijah, Apocalypse of." *ABD* 2:466-69.

STUDIES (FRAGMENT 1)

Lührmann, Dieter. "Alttestamentliche Pseudepigraphen bei Didymos von Alexandrien." *ZAW* 104 (1992): 231-49. doi:10.1515/zatw.1992.104.2.231. See pp. 245-48.

STUDIES (FRAGMENT 2)

Bauckham, Richard. "Early Jewish Visions of Hell." *JTS* 41 (1990): 355-85. Repr., pages 49-80 in *The Fate of the Dead: Studies on the Jewish and Christian Apocalypses.* NovTSup 93. Leiden: Brill, 1998. doi:10.1163/9789004267411_004. See pp. 57-60.

Himmelfarb, Martha. *Tours of Hell: An Apocalyptic Form in Jewish and Christian Literature.* Philadelphia: University of Pennsylvania Press, 1983.

Lieberman, Saul. "On Sins and Their Punishments." Pages 29-56 in *Texts and Studies.* New York: Ktav, 1974.

Rosenstiehl, Jean-Marc. "Les révélations d'Élie: Élie et les tourments des damnés." Pages 99-107 in *La Littérature Intertestamentaire: Colloque de Strasbourg (17-19 Octobre 1983).* Bibliothèque des Centres d'Études Supérieures Spécialises. Paris: Presses Universitaires de France, 1985.

Sfameni Gasparro, Giulia. "L'Epistula Titi discipuli Pauli de dispositione sanctimonii e la tradizione dell'enkrateia." *ANRW* 2.25.6:4551-64.

Verheyden, Joseph. "Les Pseudépigraphes d'Ancien Testament: Textes Latins: À Propos d'une Concordance." *ETL* 71 (1995): 383-420.

STUDIES (FRAGMENT 3A)

Ruwet, Jean. "Clément d'Alexandrie: Canon des Écritures et Apocryphes." *Bib* 29 (1948): 77-99, 240-68. See 248-57.

STUDIES (FRAGMENT 5)

Ford, Josephine Massyngbaerde. "The Physical Features of the Antichrist." *JSP* 14 (1996): 23–41. doi:10.1177/095182079600001403.

Rosenstiehl, Jean-Marc. "Le Portrait de l'Antichrist." Pages 45–60 in *Pseudépigraphes de l'Ancient Testament et Manuscrits de la Mer Morte*. By Marc Philonenko, Jean-Claude Picard, Jean-Marc Rosenstiehl, and Francis Schmidt. Paris: Presses Universitaires de France, 1967.

STUDIES (FRAGMENT 6)

Hanson, Anthony Tyrrell. Pages 142–43 in *The New Testament Interpretation of Scripture*. London: SPCK, 1980.

Moritz, Thorsten. "Tradition in Eph 5.14." Pages 97–116 in *A Profound Mystery: The Use of the Old Testament in Ephesians*. NovTSup 85. Leiden: Brill, 1996. doi:10.1163/9789004267312_007.

Noack, Bent. "Die Zitat in Ephes. 5,14." *ST* 5 (1952): 52–64.

Ruwet, Jean. "Les 'Agrapha' dans les Œuvres de Clément d'Alexandrie." *Bib* 30 (1949): 133–60. See p. 143.

STUDIES ("EYE HAS NOT SEEN . . .")

(These are studies of the saying that do not necessarily discuss the attribution to Elijah.)

Berger, Klaus. "Zur Diskussion über die Herkunft von I Kor.II.9." *NTS* 24 (1978): 270–83. doi:10.1017/S0028688500007906.

Ellis, Earle E. Pages 204–8 in *Paul's Use of the Old Testament*. London: Oliver & Boyd, 1957.

Feuillet, André. "L'Enigme de I Cor., II,9." *RB* 70 (1963): 52–74.

Gathercole, Simon. Pages 237–45 in *The Composition of the Gospel of Thomas: Original Language and Influences*. SNTSMS 151. Cambridge: Cambridge University Press, 2012.

Gathercole, Simon. Pages 283–85 in *The Gospel of Thomas: Introduction and Commentary*. TENTS 11. Leiden: Brill, 2014.

Hartog, Paul. "1 Corinthians 2:9 in the Apostolic Fathers." Pages 98–125 in *Intertextuality in the Second Century*. Edited by D. Jeffrey Bingham and Clayton N. Jefford. The Bible in Ancient Christianity 2. Leiden: Brill, 2016. doi:10.1163/9789004318762_009.

Ponsot, Hervé. "D'Isaïe, LXIV, 3 à I Corinthiens, II, 9." *RB* 90 (1983): 229–42.

Prigent, Pierre. "Ce que l'œil n'a pas vu, 1 Cor. 2,9: Histoire et préhistoire d'une citation." *TZ* 14 (1958): 416–29.

Ruwet, Jean. "Origène et l'Apocalypse d' Élie: À Propos de 1 Cor 2,9." *Bib* 30 (1949): 517–19.

Sevrin, J.-M. "'Ce qu l'œil n'a pas vu . . .': 1 Co 2,9 comme parole de Jésus." Pages 307–24 in *Lectures et relectures de la Bible: Festschrift P.-M. Bogaert*. Edited by J.-M. Auwers and A. Wénin. Leuven: Leuven University Press; Peeters, 1999.

Sparks, Hedley Frederick Davis. "1 Kor 2 9 a Quotation from the Coptic Testament of Jacob?" *ZNW* 67 (1976): 269–76.

Trevijano Etchevería, R. "La Valoración de los Dichos No Canónicos: El Caso de 1 Cor. 2.9 y Ev.Tom log. 17." Pages 406–10 in *Papers Presented to the Eleventh International Conference on Patristic Studies Held in Oxford 1991: Historica, Theologica et Philosophica, Gnostica*. Edited by Elizabeth A. Livingstone. Studia Patristica 24. Leuven: Peeters, 1993.

Tuckett, Christopher M. "Paul and Jesus Tradition: The Evidence of 1 Corinthians 2:9 and

Gospel of Thomas 17." Pages 55–73 in *Paul and the Corinthians: Studies on a Community in Conflict; Essays in Honour of Margaret Thrall*. Edited by Trevor J. Burke and J. Keith Elliott. NovTSup 109. Leiden: Brill, 2003. doi:10.1163/9789004268272_004.

Verheyden, Joseph. "Origen on the Origin of 1 Cor 2,9." Pages 491–511 in *The Corinthian Correspondence*. Edited by Reimund Bieringer. BETL 125. Leuven: Leuven University Press; Peeters, 1996.

Williams, H. H. Drake, III. "No Eye Has Seen, No Ear Has Heard of Divine Wisdom." Pages 157–208 in *The Wisdom of the Wise: The Presence and Function of Scripture within 1 Cor, 1:18–23*. AGAJU 49. Leiden: Brill, 2001.

Fragments of Elijah Apocrypha

Fragment 1. Places of the Dead
Didymus the Blind, Commentary on Ecclesiastes 92.5-6
(on Eccl/Qoh 3:16)
For also in Hades there are different regions. There is a place of rest and another of condemnation. This is recounted in the Apocalypse of Elijah.

Fragment 2. Punishments in Gehenna
Epistle of Titus 12:8-12[a]
You, the one who believes that all these things shall be and who knows that different sentences will be pronounced on the wicked: In the same member with which a person has sinned they will also be tortured.[b] 9Indeed, the prophet Elijah testifies that he had a vision: **The angel of the Lord,** he says, **showed me a deep valley, which is called Gehenna, burning with sulphur and bitumen.** [Isa 34:9] **10In that place are many souls of sinners and it is there that they are tormented with different kinds of torture. Some suffer in hanging by their genitals, others by their tongues, some by their eyes, others in hanging head downward. 11Women will be tormented in their breasts, and young men in hanging by their hands.**[c] **Some virgins are roasted on a gridiron, and some souls are fixed**[d] **in eternal torment. 12By these various punishments the acts of each are made manifest. Thus those who suffer pain in their genitals are adulterers and pederasts. Those who hang by their tongues are blasphemers and false witnesses. Those whose eyes are burned**[e] **are those who have fallen because they have looked with craving at damnable acts. Those who hang head downward are those who hate the righteousness of God, evil-minded people, none of them in harmony with**

---

a. Lines 397-417 in De Bruyne's edition. Chapter and verse numbers are those of Cottier, "L'Épître du Pseudo-Tite."

b. On this notion, see Bauckham, *Fate of the Dead*, 214-15.

c. Perhaps a euphemism for the penis: see Himmelfarb, *Tours of Hell*, 89-90.

d. Lieberman ingeniously suggests the translation "fixed [i.e., roasted] on a spit" ("On Sins," 46). But I think the meaning is more likely that they are constrained to suffer the same punishment forever.

e. De Bruyne plausibly suggests that the translator erroneously used the Latin verb *cremare* ("to burn") to translate the Greek verb *kremannymi* ("to hang up, suspend"). Donatien De Bruyne, "*Epistula Titi, discipuli Pauli, de dispositione sanctimonii,*" *RBén* 37 (1925): 69, doi:10.1484/J.RB.4.04753. This was already suggested by James, *Lost Apocrypha*, 55.

their brother. ¹³Deservedly therefore they are burned with the punishments to which they are sentenced. ¹⁴As for the women who are condemned to be tortured in their breasts, they are those who have wantonly surrendered their bodies to men, and so the men will be nearby in tortures hanging by their hands for the same reason.

Fragment 3. "Eye Has Not Seen . . ."
Origen, On Matthew 27:9 (Series Commentariorum 117)

I suspect either that there was a scribal error and Jeremiah was written in place of Zechariah or that there is some secret writing of Jeremiah in which it was written. . . . But if anyone thinks they are offended when I say this, let them take care lest this is prophesied somewhere in the secret books of Jeremiah, knowing that the apostle [Paul] also cites certain writings of secret things, as when he says in one place: *What eye has not seen nor ear heard*. For this is found written in no canonical book, but in the secret writings of Elijah the prophet. Similarly his statement, *As Jannes and Jambres resisted Moses*, is not found in books used for public reading, but in the secret book that is entitled the book of Jannes and Jambres.

[1 Cor 2:9]
[2 Tim 3:8]

Jerome, Epistula 57 ad Pammachium 9

In this passage [1 Cor 2:9] certain people are accustomed to follow the absurdities of apocryphal writings, and say that the testimony has been taken from the Apocalypse of Elijah, although in Isaiah according to the Hebrew text it may be read thus: *From eternity they have not heard nor with their ears perceived. Eye has not seen, O God, apart from you, the things you have prepared for those who wait for you.*[a] The Septuagint translated this very differently: *From eternity we have not heard nor have our eyes seen a god apart from you, and your true works, and you will do mercy for those who wait for you.*[b] We understand from where he took the testimony, but the apostle did not render it word for word, but in a paraphrastic manner he indicated the same sense with different words.

[Isa 64:3(4)]
[Isa 64:3(4)]

Jerome, Commentary on Isaiah 17 (on Isa 64:3[4])

[In addition to the argument of *Epist. 57*, he says:] For the Ascension of Isaiah and the Apocalypse of Elijah have this testimony.

Ambrosiaster, Commentary on the Pauline Epistles *(on 1 Cor 2:9)*

But as it is written, "What eye has not seen nor ear heard, and what has not gone up into the heart of a human, the things that God has prepared for those who love him." This is written in the Apocalypse of Elijah among the secret books [*apocryphis*].

---

a. This is the Vulgate translation of Isa 64:4: *A saeculo non audierunt, neque auribus perceperunt. Oculus non vidit, Deus, absque te, quae praeparasti exspectantibus te.*

b. Jerome's translation here varies a little from the text of Isa 64:3 in Rahlfs's edition of the LXX.

Fragments of Elijah Apocrypha

Epistle of Titus 1:1[a]
Great and honorable is the divine promise that the Lord with his own mouth has promised to the holy and pure, that he would give them **what eyes have not seen nor ears heard and what has not gone up into the heart of a human**, and that they would be forever and ever an incomparable and invisible[b] people.

Fragment 3a
Clement of Alexandria, *Protrepticus 10.94.4–95.1*
Hence the Scripture rightly proclaims to those who have believed: **But the holy ones of the Lord will inherit the glory of God and his power.** Tell me, O blessed one, what kind of glory? [Glory] **that eye has not seen nor ear heard and that has not gone up into the heart of a human. And they shall rejoice in the kingdom of their Lord forever.** Amen. O people, you have the divine promise of grace, and you have heard, on the other hand, the threat of punishment. Through these the Lord saves, teaching humanity by fear and grace.

Testament of Our Lord in Galilee (Ethiopic) 11 (end)
The Lord will rise up to judge his people, in order to render to each of them according to their works and according to the words that they have spoken, on the way of righteousness. As for the righteous, who have walked in the way of righteousness, **they will inherit the glory of the Lord and his power. And his strength will be given to them, which no eye has seen nor ear heard. And they will rejoice in my kingdom.**[c]

Apostolic Constitutions 7.32.5

Matt 25:46

1 Cor 2:9

Then the wicked *shall depart into eternal punishment, but the righteous shall go into eternal life,* **inheriting those things that eye has not seen nor ear heard and that has not gone up into the heart of a human,** *which God has prepared for those who love him.* **And they will rejoice in the kingdom of God that is in Christ Jesus.**

Fragment 4. Elijah the Heavenly Scribe
Epistle of Titus 9:3[d]

Jub. 10:17; 2 En. 53:2–3; T. Ab. B11

O holy dispensation of God to make provision for the age to come, so that Enoch, who was counted among the first people, was commissioned to write the earlier acts of humanity, and Elijah, the holy one, would record the deeds of the later new people.

---

a. Lines 2–6 in De Bruyne's edition.

b. Perhaps *inconspicibilis* ("invisible"?) should be corrected to *incorruptibilis* ("incorruptible").

c. Based on the French translation in Louis Guerrier and Sylvain Grébaut, *Le Testament en Galilée de Notre-Seigneur Jésus-Christ*, PO 9 (Paris: Firmin-Didot, 1913), 187, and the German translation in Isaak Wajnberg, "Apokalyptiker Rede Jesu an seine Jünger in Galiläa," in *Gespräche Jesu mit seinen Jüngern nach der Auferstehung*, ed. Carl Schmidt, TUGAL 3.13 (Leipzig: Hinrichs, 1919), 66*. Cf Stone and Strugnell, *Books of Elijah*, 46. The Ethiopic text is in Guerrier and Grébaut, *Le Testament*, 187, and reprinted in Stone and Strugnell, *Books of Elijah*, 47.

d. Lines 271–274 in De Bruyne's edition.

Fragment 5. Portrait of the Antichrist
Codex Parisinus Graecus 4, fol. 228ʳ
It is contained in secret sayings that Elijah the prophet spoke about the Antichrist, in what form he is to appear at that time: **his head a flame of fire; his right eye mingled with blood; but the left shining, having two pupils; his eyelids white; his lower lip large; his right thigh thin and his feet broad; and the big toe of his foot has been broken**.

Testament of Our Lord (Syriac) 11–12
And these are the signs of him: **his head as a flame of fire, his right eye mingled with blood, but the left is green, having two pupils; his eyebrows white, his lower lip large, but his right thigh lean, his feet broad, broken and thin is his great finger (*or* toe)**. He is the scythe of devastation. Therefore I say unto you, children of the light, that the time is at hand, and the harvest is ripe that sinners should be harvested in judgment.[a]

Testament of Our Lord (Latin) (Codex Treverensis 36)
His head like a flame of fire, his eyes like a cat's, but the right will be mixed with blood and the left joyful and having two pupils; the eyebrows white, the lower lip larger, the right thigh lean, the shin-bone thin, the feet broad, his big toe will be broken. He is the scythe of desolation and to many he will represent himself as the Christ.

Testament of Our Lord in Galilee (Ethiopic) 6
This is his sign: **his head is like a flame of fire, his right eye is mingled with blood, his left eye is dead, the two pupils of his eyes are white between the eyelids, his lower lip large, his feet wide, the toes and the joints of his feet are twisted**. He is the scythe of destruction. The time has come, the harvest is near, he will harvest for punishment those who are destined for it. To many he will represent himself as the Christ. He will praise himself and his deeds and he will confirm the thoughts of his heart.[b]

Fragment 6. Wake Up, Sleeper
Ephesians 5:14b
Therefore it says:

> Wake up, you that sleep,
> and rise from the dead,
> and Christ will shine on you.

---

a. Translation from Montague Rhodes James, *Apocrypha Anecdota: A Collection of Thirteen Apocryphal Books and Fragments*, TS 2.3 (Cambridge: Cambridge University Press, 1893), 153; and James Cooper and Arthur John Maclean, *The Testament of Our Lord: Translated into English from the Syriac*, Ante-Nicene Christian Library (Edinburgh: T&T Clark, 1902), 57–58.

b. Translation based on the French translation in Guerrier and Grébaut, *Le Testament,* 183, and the German translation in Wajnberg, "Apokalyptiker Rede," 61–62*.

Fragments of Elijah Apocrypha

Clement of Alexandria, Protrepticus 9.84.1–2
The Lord does not grow weary of admonishing, terrifying, exhorting, arousing, and warning. In fact he wakes from sleep and raises up from the darkness itself those who have gone astray.

Isa 26:19; Dan 12:2	**Wake up, you that sleep**, he says,
Isa 26:19; 60:1	**and rise from the dead,**
Isa 60:2	**and Christ the Lord will shine on you,**
Mal 4:2	the sun of the resurrection,
Ps 109:3 LXX	the one who was begotten before the morning star,
	the one who bestows life with his own shining rays.[a]

Epiphanius, Panarion 42.12.3
From where did the apostle get the passage, **Therefore it says**, other than, plainly, from the Old Testament? This passage is found in Elijah. And from where did Elijah proceed? But he was one of the prophets who conducted their lives under the rule of the law, and he proceeded from the law and the prophets. If in Christ he prophesied, **Wake up, you that sleep, and rise from the dead, and Christ will shine on you,** then the prototype was fulfilled through Lazarus and the others.

Hippolytus, Commentarium in Danielem 4.56.4
And Isaiah says, **Wake up, you that sleep, and rise from the dead, and Christ will shine on you.**

Hippolytus, De Antichristo 65
The prophet says, **Wake up, you that sleep, and rise from the dead, and Christ will shine on you.**

Fragment 7. Very Great Mysteries
Pseudo-Epiphanius, Life of Elijah

1 Kgs 19:10   For after he had been a zealot and a strict guardian of the commandments of God and had been reckoned worthy of the greatest mysteries and divine
2 Kgs 2:11   revelations,[b] he was taken up to heaven in a fiery chariot.

---

a. The last three lines are probably not part of the quotation, but Clement's own addition.
b. For this meaning of *charisma*, see *PGL*, s.v. G.6.

APPENDIX

Other Early Examples of "Eye Has Not Seen . . ."[a]

The following collection does not include passages that explicitly quote 1 Cor 2:9.

Text 1. 1 Corinthians 2:9
But, as it is written, "What eye has not seen, nor ear heard, and what has not gone up into the heart of a human, the things that God has prepared for those who love him."

Text 2. Pseudo-Philo, *Biblical Antiquities* 26:13a
And when the sins of my people have reached full measure, and their enemies have acquired power over their house, I will take these stones and the former stones together with the tablets, and I will put them back in the place from which they were brought at the beginning. And they will be there until I remember the world and the inhabitants of the earth. And then I will take these and many other, much better ones, from what eye has not seen nor ear heard and what has not gone up into the heart of a human, until the like should come to be in the world.[b]

Text 3. 1 Clement 34:7–8
So let us also, being gathered together in concord in our conscience, earnestly cry out to him with one mouth, so that we may share in his great and glorious promises. [8]For he says, "Eye has not seen nor ear heard, and it has not gone up into the heart of a human, what great things he has prepared for those who wait for him."

---

a. The fullest (but certainly not complete) collection of such examples is in Stone and Strugnell, *Books of Elijah*, 41–73; see also Klaus Berger, "Zur Diskussion über die Herkunft von I Kor.II.9," *NTS* 24 (1978): 270–83, doi:10.1017/S0028688500007906. The following can be added: Arabic Apocalypse of Peter in Alphonse Mingana, *Woodbrooke Studies: Christian Documents in Syriac, Arabic and Garshuni*, 7 vols. (Cambridge: Heffer, 1927), 3:224; Apocalypse of St John Chrysostom 39 in John M. Court, *The Book of Revelation and the Johannine Apocalyptic Tradition*, JSNTSup 190 (Sheffield: Sheffield Academic, 2000), 80–81; Vision of Tungdal in Jean-Michel Picard and Yolande de Pontfarcy, *The Vision of Tungdal* (Dublin: Four Courts, 1989), 153; The Mission of Mar Adda and Pattek the Teacher (Sogdian version) in Samuel N. C. Lieu and Iain Gardiner, eds., *Manichaean Texts from the Roman Empire* (Cambridge: Cambridge University Press, 2004), 112.

b. My translation from the Latin text in Howard Jacobson, *A Commentary on Pseudo-Philo's* Liber Antiquitatum Biblicarum, 2 vols., AGJU 31 (Leiden: Brill, 1996), 1:41.

Other Early Examples of "Eye Has Not Seen . . ."

Text 4. 1 Clement 11:7
Therefore if we do what is righteous in the sight of God, we will enter his kingdom and receive the promises that ear has not heard nor eye seen and that have not gone up into the heart of a human.

Text 5. Gospel of Thomas 17
Jesus said, "I will give you what eye has not seen, and what ear has not heard, and what hand has not touched, nor has it ascended to the heart of man."[a]

Text 6. Martyrdom of Polycarp 2:3b
And the fire of their inhuman torturers to them was cold, for they held before their eyes the flight from the fire that is eternal and never quenched, while with the eyes of the heart they gazed upon the good things that are kept for those who wait, things that ear has not heard nor eye seen and that have not gone up into the heart of a human, but which were shown to them by the Lord, for they were no longer humans but already angels.

Text 7. Ascension of Isaiah 11:34
And he [the angel] said to me, "This is enough for you, Isaiah, for you have seen what no other son of flesh has seen, what eye has not seen nor ear heard and what has not gone up into the heart of a human, what great things God has prepared for those who love him."[b]

Text 8. Dialogue of the Savior (CG III,5) 139:20–140:4
Matthew said, "Tell me, Lord, how the dead die, and how the living live." The Lord said, "[You have] asked me for a word [about that] which eye has not seen, nor have I heard about it, except from you."[c]

Text 9. Prayer of the Apostle Paul (CG I,1) A.25–34
Grant what no angel-eye has [seen] and no archon-ear <has> heard and what [has not] entered into the human heart, which came to be angelic and (came to be) in the image of the psychic God when it was formed in the beginning, since I have faith and hope.[d]

Text 10. Gospel of Judas 47:10–13
Jesus said, "[Come], and I will teach you about . . . which no man will see. For a great, limitless aeon exists, whose measure no generation of angels has seen.

---

a. Translation from Simon Gathercole, *The Gospel of Thomas: Introduction and Commentary*, TENTS 11 (Leiden: Brill, 2014), 283.

b. My translation from the Latin in Paolo Bettiolo et al., eds., *Ascensio Isaiae: Textus*, CCSA 7 (Turnhout: Brepols, 1995), 233. This passage is also in the Slavonic version, but lacking in the Ethiopic.

c. Translation by Harold W. Attridge, "The Dialogue of the Savior (III, 5)," in *The Nag Hammadi Library in English*, ed. James M. Robinson (Leiden: Brill, 1977), 236.

d. Translation by Dieter Mueller, "The Prayer of the Apostle Paul (I,1)," in Robinson, *Nag Hammadi Library in English*, 28.

In it is [the] Great and Invisible Spirit, whom no angel's eye has seen; nor has the thought of a mind received it; nor has it been called by any name.[a]

Text 11. Martyrdom of Peter 10
Therefore you also, brothers, having taken refuge in him and learning that in him alone you exist, will attain those things of which he says to you, "What neither eye has seen nor ear heard and what did not go up into the heart of a human." So we pray for those things you have promised to give us, immaculate Jesus.[b]

Text 12. Clement of Alexandria, *Protrepticus* 12.118.4
Then you will behold my God and be initiated into those holy mysteries and enjoy the things that are hidden in heaven, which are kept for me, which eye has not seen and which have not gone up into the heart of anyone.[c]

1 Cor 2:7

Text 13.1 Clement of Alexandria, *Stromata* 4.22.114.1
For the gnostic are prepared the things that eye has not seen nor ear heard and that have not gone up into the heart of a human.[d]

Text 14. Tertullian, *De spectaculis* 30.7
To see such sights, to enjoy such rejoicings—what praetor or consul or quaestor or priest will out of his generosity offer to you? Yet these things are in some sense already ours through faith, presented by the imagination of the spirit. But of what kind are those things that eye has not seen nor ear heard and that have gone up into the heart of a human? They are of more value, I believe, than the circus, the theatre or amphitheatre, or any stadium.[e]

Text 15. Tertullian, *De resurrectione carnis* 26.7
So also in Isaiah, "You shall eat the good things of the earth," [meaning that] the good things of the flesh will be perceived, which are waiting for it when, in the kingdom of God, it will be refashioned and made angelic and will obtain the things that eye has not seen nor ear heard and which have not gone up into the heart of a human.[f]

Isa 1:19

---

a. Translation from Simon Gathercole, *The Gospel of Judas: Rewriting Early Christianity* (Oxford: Oxford University Press, 2007), 88.

b. My translation from the Greek text in Stone and Strugnell, *Books of Elijah*, 51.

c. My translation from the Greek text in Miroslav Marcovich, *Clementis Alexandrini* Protrepticus, Supplements to Vigiliae Christianae 34 (Leiden: Brill, 1995), 171.

d. My translation from the Greek text in Annawies van den Hoek and Claude Mondésert, *Clément d'Alexandrie: Les Stromates; Stromate IV*, SC 463 (Paris: Cerf, 2001), 244.

e. My translation from the Latin text in Marie Turcan, *Tertullien: Les Spectacles* (De spectaculis), SC 332 (Paris: Cerf, 1986), 328.

f. My translation from the Latin text in Ernest Evans, *Tertullian's Treatise on the Resurrection* (London: SPCK, 1960), 72.

Text 16. Pseudo-Hippolytus, *De universo* (end)
You too will participate with these people and with those good persons who are going to attain the ascension to the immeasurable heaven and you will see the kingdom. For God will reveal those things that are now hidden, which neither eye has seen nor ear heard and which have not gone up into the heart of a human, which God has prepared for those who love him.[a]

Text 17. Testament of Jacob 8:8 (Bohairic)
And he showed me all the resting-places and all the good things prepared for the righteous, and the things that eye has not seen, nor ear heard, and have not come into the heart of men, that God has prepared for those who love him and do his will on earth (for, if they end well, they do his will).[b]

Text 18. Acts of Thomas 36
But we speak about the world above, about God and angels, about Watchers and saints, about the ambrosial food and the drink of the true vine, about clothing that endures and does not grow old, about things which eye has not seen nor ear heard, neither have they entered into the heart of sinful men, which God has prepared for those who love him.[c]

---

a. My translation from the Greek text in Karl Holl, *Fragmente vornicänischer Kirchenväter aus den* Sacra Parallela, TUGAL 20.2 (Leipzig: Hinrichs, 1899), 143. Only fragments of this work survive but this is very probably the end of the text; see William J. Malley, "Four Unedited Fragments of the *De Universo* of the Pseudo-Josephus Found in the *Chronicon* of George Hamartolus (Coislin 305)," *JTS* NS 16 (1965): 20–21. The authorship is debated. Charles E. Hill argues for Tertullian. See Hill, "Hades of Hippolytus or Tartarus of Tertullian? The Authorship of the Fragment *De Universo*," *VC* 43 (1989): 105–26, doi:10.2307/1584133.

b. Translation from K. H. Kuhn, "The Testament of Jacob," *AOT*, 448.

c. Translation by Han J. W. Drijvers, "The Acts of Thomas," in Schneemelcher and Wilson, *Writings Related to the Apostles*, 354.

The Somniale Danielis and the Lunationes Danielis
A new translation and introduction

by Lorenzo DiTommaso

The enduring popularity of the biblical figure of Daniel throughout late antiquity and the Middle Ages generated a galaxy of apocryphal Jewish, Christian, and Islamic writings.[1] These writings consist of three basic types: (1) legends about Daniel or figures associated with him; (2) apocalyptic prophecies that are pseudonymously attributed to Daniel; and (3) prognostic texts, also attributed to him.[2] Most important among the Daniel prognostica are the Somniale Danielis, an alphabetical dreambook,[3] and the Lunationes Danielis, a type of lunary or "moon-book."

1. The Somniale Danielis

Oneiromancy is the practice of interpreting dreams to foretell the future. Dream interpretation was common throughout the ancient Near East. It was also part of daily life in Greece and Rome.[4] One of the few dreambooks from classical antiquity that has survived is the *Oneirokritikon* of Artemidorus Daldianus (second century CE), which he compiled from material in earlier books and the experiences of dream diviners.[5]

---

1. Lorenzo DiTommaso, *The Book of Daniel and the Apocryphal Daniel Literature*, SVTP 20 (Leiden: Brill, 2005).

2. According to Matthias Heiduk, the lead editor of *Prognostication in the Medieval World*, prognostication is "a collective term to describe all methods of predicting the future." See Heiduk, Klaus Herbers, and Hans-Christian Lehner, eds., *Prognostication in the Medieval World: A Handbook*, 2 vols. (Berlin: de Gruyter, 2021), 109. This definition, however, smooths over important distinctions among the various species of prediction. It does not, for example, differentiate between eschatological speculation and divination. Such distinctions are not solely modern: while medieval manuscript codices often contain collections of prophectic-apocalyptic texts or prognostic works, only rarely are works of both types bound in the same codex.

3. Johann Albert Fabricius included the *Somniale Danielis* in his pioneering volume, *Codex pseudepigraphus Veteris Testamenti: Collectus, castigatus, testimoniisque, censuris et animadversionibus illustratus* (Hamburg: C. Liebezeit, 1713).

4. Steven M. Oberhelman, "Traditions and Practices in the Medieval Eastern Christian World," in Heiduk, Herbers, and Lehner, *Prognostication in the Medieval World*, 390, doi:10.1515/9783110 499773-018.

5. See most recently Peter Thonemann, *An Ancient Dream Manual: Artemidorus' The Interpretation of Dreams* (Oxford: Oxford University Press, 2020); and the essays in Gregor Weber, ed. *Artemidor von Daldis und die antike Traumdeutung: Texte – Kontexte – Lektüren*, Colloquia Augustana 33 (Berlin: de Gruyter, 2015), doi:10.1515/9783110407402.

Origin, Date, and Provenance

The Somniale Danielis was composed in Greek in the fourth or fifth century CE.[6] It translated into Latin no later than the eighth century, and then from the Latin into all the major vernacular languages of the West.[7] The Somniale remained popular until the middle of the sixteenth century, when interest shifted to the *Oneirokritikon* of Artimedorus and other Byzantine dreambooks, which had been recently rediscovered in their original Greek.[8]

Although the Somniale Danielis was composed in the late-antique Greek East, it is a medieval Latin work in terms of its reception, dissemination, and contribution to lived experience. Lorenzo DiTommaso and László Sándor Chardonnens record 229 western manuscript versions of the work.[9] One hundred sixty-three versions are in Latin, fifteen in German, thirteen in French, nine in Welsh, eight in Old English, eight in Italian, seven in Middle English, and one version each in Czech, Icelandic, Irish, and Spanish.[10] The earliest manuscripts are in Latin and date from the ninth century (see below); the latest date from the seventeenth and eighteenth centuries, overlapping the early printed editions of the work.[11] Only two late copies of the Somniale are extant in the original Greek.[12]

Literary Features and Content

The definitive literary feature of the Somniale Danielis is that it lists the subjects of the dreams in alphabetical order.[13] Each entry consists of a dream that is followed by a

---

6. Max Förster, "Das älteste kymrische Traumbuch (um 1350)," *Zeitschrift für celtische Philologie* 13 (1921): 58; and Franz Drexl, "Das Traumbuch des Propheten Daniel nach dem cod. Vatic. Palat. gr. 319," *Byzantinische Zeitschrift* 26 (1926): 290–314, doi:10.1515/byzs.1926.26.1.290. On the arguments for a fourth-century date, see Oberhelman, "Prolegomena to the Reconstruction of the Archetype of the Greek *Somniale Danielis*," in *Sogni e visioni nel mondo indo-mediterraneo*, ed. Daniela Boccassini, Quaderni di studi indo-mediterranei 2 (Alessandria: Orso, 2009), 114.

7. Förster, "Das älteste kymrische Traumbuch," 59–60; Oberhelman, "Prolegomena"; and Steven R. Fischer, *The Complete Medieval Dreambook. A Multilingual, Alphabetical Somnia Danielis Collation* (Bern: Lang, 1982), 7, all pin the Latin translation to the seventh century. But in my view an early eighth-century date fits the manuscript evidence and corresponds with the Carolingian revival of learning.

8. László Sándor Chardonnens, "Mantic Alphabets in Late Medieval England, Early Modern Europe, and Modern America: The Reception and Afterlife of a Medieval Form of Dream Divination," *Anglia* 132 (2014): 641–75, doi:10.1515/ang-2014-0072; and Chardonnens, "Dream Divination in Manuscripts and Early Printed Books: Patterns of Transmission," in *Aspects of Knowledge: Preserving and Reinventing Traditions of Learning in the Middle Ages*, ed. Marilina Cesario and Hugh Magennis (Manchester: Manchester University Press, 2018), 23–52.

9. DiTommaso and Chardonnens, "Conspectus of the Western Manuscripts and Early Printed Books of the *Somniale Danielis*," in *Dream Interpretation in the Global Middle Ages*, ed. Valerio Cappozzo, Reading Medieval Sources (Leiden: Brill, forthcoming).

10. A few manuscript versions of the Somniale are extant in non-western translations, specifically Armenian, Hebrew, Polish, and possibly Arabic; for details, see DiTommaso and Chardonnens, "Conspectus."

11. DiTommaso and Chardonnens, "Conspectus," record 103 early printed versions of the Somniale. The earliest, in Latin, dates from ca. 1475.

12. Berlin, Staatsbibliothek zu Berlin—Preußischer Kulturbesitz, Ms Phillipps 1479 (xv), fols. 4v–10v [314 dreams, alphabetical sequence A–Σ]; and Vatican City, Biblioteca Apostolica Vaticana, Pal. gr. 319 (xv–xvi), fols. 31r–48r [486 dreams, A–Ω].

13. Although the Somniale groups dreams by subject in alphabetical order, the order is not maintained within each letter-grouping. Thus, those dreams whose subjects begin with the letter "A" appear in approximate alphabetical order or no order at all, followed by the collection of dreams under the letter "B," and so on. This arrangement is known as the "A-order" and is attested in early medieval glossaries.

short, unambiguous interpretation. The two parts are joined by a transitive verb, usually *significare*, that identifies the dream as a portent.[14]

Entries normally consist of between six to ten words, and sometimes less. This economy of expression gives the Somniale an index-like appearance in manuscript that is amplified in cases where two or three versions are written in tall columns across a single page. The size of the initial letter of the first entry for each letter of the alphabet is usually magnified, while the initial letters of the subsequent entries under the same letter are often rubricated or struck through. Such visual features rendered the Somniale easy to consult and handy to use.

While many manuscript versions of the Somniale Danielis contain the full alphabetic sequence of dreams, from A to Z in the Latin,[15] other versions cover only part of the alphabet. Sometimes this is accidental, in that one or more manuscript pages have been lost. In most cases, however, the reason for its abbreviated list of dreams is unknown. A few versions contain two or even three alphabetical sequences of dreams, while others list the dreams in alphabetical disarray.[16]

The number of dreams varies greatly among the manuscripts. Some versions contain under one hundred dreams, while others include six hundred dreams or more.[17] The median number of dreams among all the versions is around three hundred, although this figure is more statistical than diagnostic. In general, the later a version, the more dreams it contains. But there are many exceptions to the rule. Significantly, the manuscripts do not exhibit an evolutionary trajectory from shorter earlier versions to longer later ones.[18]

The attribution to Daniel, the famous interpreter of dreams in the Bible, is early and consistent among the manuscripts.[19] The attribution is conveyed by the title of the work, (Som(p)niale or Som(p)nia Danielis), in its *incipit* or *explicit*, and/or by means of a prologue of variable length and content that prefaces many of the manuscript versions and printed editions. The prologue explains that Daniel is one of the Jewish captives whom King Nabuchodonosor has exiled to Babylon (2 Kgs 25), where he has compiled a list of dream interpretations that God has revealed to him.[20]

Whether the medieval users of the Somniale Danielis always connected the dreams and their interpretations is unclear. Sometimes the pairing makes logical sense. A dream

---

14. In some later versions a *punctus* or *punctus eleuatus* stands in for the verb.
15. Alphabetical sequences among the vernacular languages vary slightly from the Latin.
16. In a few longer versions, the same dream is listed twice and accorded differing interpretations.
17. The most dreams in a manuscript version, 903, appears in three very late and essentially identical copies: Rome, Biblioteca Casanatense, Ms.792 [*olim* D.VI.23] (Italy, xvii), fols. 59r–89v; Rome, Biblioteca Nazionale Centrale, Ms.Prov.Claustr.Varia III (Italy, xvii–xviii^{in}), fols. 451r–475v; and Toledo, Archivo e Biblioteca Capitulares de la Catedral, BCT 103-14 (Spain, xvii), pp. 1–50. The runner-up, with 716 dreams, is also late: Oxford, Oxford University, All Souls College, MS 81 (England, xv–xvi), fols. 205r–211v.
18. Also notable is the fact that the later versions of the Somniale do not accrue supplemental information, in contrast with some other apocryphal works.
19. Joseph is the other great dream-interpreter of the Bible. Among the later books that are ascribed to him is the *Somniale Ioseph*, whose interpretations are keyed to the letters of the alphabet. See DiTommaso and Chardonnens, "Conspectus," for a list of manuscripts and a bibliography.
20. For example: *Ego sum Daniel unus de filiis Israel qui captiui ducti sunt de Iherusalem in Babilonem; haec omnia a Domino cepi et nihil de meo ipso addidi* ("I am Daniel, one of the sons of Israel who was led captive from Jerusalem to Babylon; I have received all these things from the Lord and added nothing of my own"). First-person prologues preface other post-classical Daniel apocalyptic and prognostic writings, as well as the revelatory visions of the biblical Daniel (8:1–2; 9:1–4a; and 10:2–4).

The Somniale Danielis and the Lunationes Danielis

about a hen and her chicks (123) foretells plenty and hence good business.[21] Likewise, a dream that one is in exile portents danger (268), while the image of a mouse and a lion together signifies security (175). But why would a dream about sitting on a foal warn of deception in business (25), or one about animals speaking among themselves signal future trouble (38)? No doubt some of the cultural contexts that would make such links logical to contemporary readers have been lost. But it is difficult to imagine any scenario in which a dream where one's arms are cut off might signify good fortune ahead (293), or where one's beheading foretells wealth (256).

Textual Features

The hallmark textual feature of the Somniale Danielis is the diversity in the number, sequence, and subjects of the dreams and their interpretations across the full range of the manuscript evidence.[22] The textual fluidity of the work is clear even in its earliest versions, which date from the ninth through the eleventh centuries:[23]

- *London, British Library, Harley MS 3017 (Fleury or Nevers, ix), fol. 1ra–vb: 76 dreams [alphabetical sequence D–N] (Latin)[24]
- *Uppsala, Universitetsbiblioteket, C.664 (northern Italy, ix$^{2/2}$), pp. 101–111: 312 dreams [alphabetical sequence D–Z] (Latin)
- Leiden, Universiteitsbibliotheek, SCA 49 (Germany, x), fol. 79v[25]
- Vienna, Österreichische Nationalbibliothek, Cod. 2723 (Mondsee, x), fols. 124v–130v: 241 dreams [two alphabetical sequences: A–C, L–V; C–Z] (Latin)
- Munich, Bayerische Staatsbibliothek, Clm 14377 (Germany, x–xi), fols. 105va–106vb: 124 dreams [alphabetical sequence A–C, I–R] (Latin)
- Vatican City, Bibliotheca Apostolica Vaticana, Pal. lat. 235 (x–xi), fols. 39vc–40r: 54 dreams [alphabetical sequence A–F] (Latin)
- Vatican City, Bibliotheca Apostolica Vaticana, Ross. 144 (x–xi), fols. 25v–26v: 41 dreams [alphabetical sequence S, A–C] (Latin)
- Vienna, Österreichische Nationalbibliothek, Cod. 271 (Tegernsee, x^{ex}–xi^{in} [ca. 1000]), fols. 76va–77vb: 158 dreams [alphabetical sequence A–Z] (Latin)
- London, British Library, Sloane MS 475 (perhaps England, xi^{in}), fols. 217v–218r: 29 dreams [alphabetical sequence A–B] (Latin)
- Vercelli, Biblioteca Capitolare Eusebiana, LXII (2) (xi^{in}), fols. 218rb + 219va–b: 110 dreams (Latin) [alphabetical sequence A–O]

21. The examples are drawn from the translation below.
22. See DiTommaso and Chardonnens, "Conspectus," for the number of dreams and alphabetical sequence in each manuscript version.
23. As proposed by Lawrence T. Martin, based on only three manuscripts, but now confirmed by the evidence of the "Conspectus." See Martin, "The Earliest Versions of the Latin *Somniale Danielis*," *Manuscripta* 23 (1979): 131–41, doi:10.1484/J.MSS.3.951.
24. An asterisk (*) indicates that the codex also contains a lunary (below, §2). Vatican City, Bibliotheca Apostolica Vaticana, Reg. lat. 567, dates from the eleventh century, but its Lunationes Danielis (fols. 30v–31r) and Somniale Danielis (fols. 34r–37r), which are scribbled in the page margins, are in a later hand.
25. Undertext, now erased and difficult to read. An illness lunary is written across the top two thirds of the page, while the beginning of a Somniale occupies the lower third. The codex ends thereafter.

- London, British Library, Cotton MS Titus D.XXVI [& XXVII]²⁶ (Winchester, xi²/⁴ [ca. 1020–1030], fols 11v–16r: 159 dreams [alphabetical sequence A–I, L–V] (Latin)
- Berlin, Staatsbibliothek zu Berlin—Preußischer Kulturbesitz, Ms lat. fol. 35 (Germany, xi), fols. 1ra–2ra: 122 dreams [alphabetical sequence A–C, I, L–S] (Latin)
- London, British Library, Cotton MS Tiberius A.III (Canterbury, this part xi), fols. 27v–32v: 302 dreams [three alphabetical sequences: A–I, L–V; C–U; S] (two versions: Latin with Old English gloss)²⁷
- London, British Library, Cotton MS Tiberius A.III (Canterbury, this part xi), fols. 38r–39v: 96 dreams [alphabetical sequence A–V] (Old English)
- London, British Library, Cotton MS Tiberius A.III (Canterbury, this part xi), fol. 42r–v: 26 dreams [in no discernable alphabetical order] (Old English)

The textual diversity is reflected across the totality of western manuscripts of the Somniale Danielis.²⁸ It is so great that the relationship among the versions cannot be illustrated by means of a traditional stemma, nor can the versions be classified into text-groups.²⁹ Likewise, one cannot reconstruct a hypothetical lost Greek Urtext or isolate the "most important" early manuscripts.³⁰ Although some manuscript versions of the Somniale were copied from others, and a few late manuscripts were transcribed from early printed books, the overall impression is one of persistent and pervasive textual plasticity.

Accordingly, the Somniale Danielis is better understood as a "work" rather than a "text," and its manuscript exemplars as versions of a notional construct—"the alphabetical dreambook attributed to Daniel"—rather than copies of a literary object. Virtually every manuscript version is textually unique within the notional parameters of the work.³¹ For this reason, the individuals who wrote the Somniale on skin (and later paper) must be considered as more than copyists. This in turn suggests a high level of scribal autonomy that persisted over many centuries and in diverse geographic and social contexts. Unfortunately, little is known about these individuals. The earliest versions of the Somniale Danielis are products of abbeys, but this is true for medieval manuscripts in general. Modern critical scholarly enquiry on the Somniale Danielis has concentrated on

---

26. Cotton MS Titus D.XXVI and Cotton MS Titus D.XXVII were once part of a single manuscript that began with D.XXVII.

27. This version of the Somniale is translated below.

28. DiTommaso and Chardonnens, "Conspectus," do not seek to identify textual micropatterns among the manuscript versions, but some exist, notably in the vernacular traditions. A close examination of such patterns might reveal local trajectories in the transmission history of the work.

29. Contra the claim of E. O. G. Turville-Petre, "An Icelandic Version of the Somniale Danielis," in Nordica et Anglica. Studies in Honor of Stefán Einarsson, ed. Allan H. Orrick (Janus linguarum, series maior, 22; The Hague: Mouton, 1968), 19–36, that by the tenth century the Somniale existed in "two distinct versions" (21).

30. Contra Maria Jennifer Falcone, "Dream Books and Treatises on Dream Interpretation in the Medieval Western Christian World," in Heiduk, Herbers, and Lehner, Prognostication in the Medieval World, 762, doi:10.1515/9783110499773-049.

31. Half the Welsh versions are textually similar, while several German exemplars can be classified into text-versions. On the latter, see Klaus Speckenbach, "Die deutsche Somniale Danielis-Rezeption" in Träume und Kräuter: Studien zur Petroneller 'Circa instans'-Handschrift und zu den deutschen Traumbüchern des Mittelalters, ed. Nigel Palmer and Klaus Speckenbach, Pictura et poesis 4 (Cologne: Bohlau, 1990), 128–51.

the earliest specimens and issues of origin.[32] But most versions date from the thirteenth, fourteenth, and fifteen centuries (which is again true for medieval manuscripts overall) and are often bound in codices containing other prognostic and divinatory works, which suggest purpose and function.

Theology and Anthropology

A late-antique Jewish origin of the Somniale Danielis is ruled out by the lack of manuscript evidence as well as the rabbinic strictures against prognostic speculation and divination. There is also the striking absence of Jewish (and Christian) content in the work, notwithstanding its attribution to the prophet Daniel and a prologue that situates the Somniale in the biblical narrative.[33]

This lack of theological content supports the argument that the Somniale Danielis emerged out of the oneirocritical tradition of the eastern Roman Empire.[34] While it would be incorrect to label the dreambooks of classical antiquity as "irreligious" or, even worse, "secular" (those associated with Asclepius have religious connotations, and the belief that dreams are avenues for the transmission of divine information was widespread), they are not theological. This fact alone does not disprove the possibility of a Christian origin of the Somniale, which could be established if the work's attribution to Daniel were demonstrated to have been present in its original, late-antique Greek version. But the absence of manuscripts predating the ninth century renders the point moot. Whatever its origin, the Somniale Danielis was likely a Christian document by the fifth century, and certainly so by the time that it entered the medieval Latin tradition in the eighth century.

Anthropologically, the Somniale Danielis is a work with two personalities. On the one hand, the business of dream interpretation is intimate. The Somniale would have been consulted privately, either by literate persons who wished to interpret their own dreams or by individuals whose professions included interpreting dreams for others. The work certainly had no liturgical use or public function. On the other hand, the practice of dream interpretation is impersonal. Anyone could consult the Somniale to interpret their dreams, and its interpretations applied to everyone. A dream of X signified Y for knave and knight alike. The universal anthropology of the Somniale enabled it to transcend geographic, linguistic, cultural, and social barriers, and, along with its ease of use, must be accounted at least partly responsible for its widespread distribution throughout the medieval West.

Only two barriers had the potential to impede the creation, distribution, and use of the Somniale Danielis. The first barrier was official hostility to dream interpretation.[35]

---

32. This said, the recent scholarship has expanded the scope of the investigation to the reception of the work in later contexts and printed versions as well as its cultural influence. For bibliographies of editions, translations, and studies for each manuscript version, see DiTommaso and Chardonnens, "Conspectus."

33. Dream 42 in the translation below ("To see the sky in flames signifies that some evils will befall the whole world") might be an allusion to the Revelation of John or, more generally, the eschaton. Dream 301 speaks of "praying to the Lord." But such dreams do not appear in every version.

34. Some early versions contain references to classical figures, for example Hercules and the emperor (dreams 130 and 132 in the translation below).

35. So Jesse Keskiaho, "Paying Attention to Dreams in Early Medieval Normative Sources (400–900): Countering Non-Christian Practices or Negotiating Christian Dreaming?," *Early Mediaeval Europe* 28 (2020): 3–25; and Michele Grazia, "*In somnis peccare*: La repressione dell'attività onirica nei Libri Penitenziali," *Archivio Giuridico* 153 (2021): 857–904. Note also Roberta Antognini's review of *Dizionario*

John of Salisbury (late 1110s–1180), for example, challenged the work's attribution to Daniel.[36] The text of the Somniale is also crossed out in a few manuscript versions.[37] But the case for censorship has been grossly overstated. In reality, official proscription of dreambooks was late, local, and intermittent. The best argument against church censure of the Somniale is the large number of manuscript versions that have survived, their broadcast distribution across western Europe, and the fact that many were scribed in abbeys and monasteries.

The other barrier, the European Enlightenment, eventually proved to be insurmountable. The evolution of the scientific method, and the revolution in the understanding of the universe and humanity's place in it, gradually pushed oneiromancy, magic, alchemy, divinatition, and similar practices from mainstream intellectual society to its margins.[38]

2. The Lunationes Danielis

Lunar hemerologies or lunaries are a species of prognostic literature that forecast auspicious days for specific actions or events, keyed to the thirty days of the lunar month.[39] In Greek the form is called a *selendromion*. Lunaries can appear in stand-alone format or be embedded in larger compositions.

Fifteen types of lunaries are known, although only seven or eight regularly appear in the manuscripts.[40] One type of lunary specifies the good and bad days to let blood. Another type records the best days to apprehend fugitives. Still others are concerned with dreams or thunder, while one type correlates a child's future character and fortune to the day of the month when they are born. The longest type is the collective or general lunary, which records felicitous and infelicitous days for a range of actions. Some collective lunaries include brief quotations from the Bible (usually the Psalms) or notations about the days of the month when biblical figures were born or died.[41]

---

dei sogni nel Medioevo, by Valerio Cappozzo, in *Renaissance Quarterly* 74 (2021): 688–90, doi:10.1017/rqx.2021.78. She asserts that the name of Daniel is "often omitted from the incipit of the manuscripts to avoid censorship from the church, for which oneiromancy was considered superstitious and therefore forbidden," and so concludes that "the attribution of the *Somniale* is difficult" (689).

36. *Policraticus* II.17.97–98, cited in Roy Michael Liuzza, *Anglo-Saxon Prognostics. An Edition and Translation of Texts from London, British Library, MS Cotton Tiberius A.iii* (Anglo-Saxon Texts 9; Cambridge, England: D. S. Brewer, 2010), 41 n. 152.

37. See DiTommaso and Chardonnens, "Conspectus," for the examples.

38. A bridge of sorts is the Somniale Danielis of Vatican City, Bibliotheca Apostolica Vaticana, Pal. lat. 1880 (Germany, xv[med]), fols. 259r–271r, copied by the German physician Ulrich Ellenbog (ca. 1435–1499). Ellenbog did not subscribe to the mantic value of dreams, but used dream images for diagnostic medical purposes, as he explains in the medical treatise following the Somniale in this manuscript.

39. Lunaries chart the course of a synodic month, from new moon to new moon, which has a period of a little over 29.5 days (rounded up to 30 days). The sidereal month runs slightly over 27.5 days (rounded up to 28 days) and is the basis for prognostic works featuring the mansions of the moon. Bede knew the difference between the two (*De temporum ratione* 36.8–12). See further Irma Taavitsainen, *Middle English Lunaries: A Study of the Genre*, Mémoires de la Société Néophilologique de Helsinki 47 (Helsinki: Sociéte´ Néophilologique, 1988), 45–48.

40. Timothy Paul Grove, *Christ Came Forth from India: Georgian Astrological Texts of the 17th, 18th and 19th Centuries*, Eurasian Studies Library 15 (Leiden: Brill, 2020), 424. See also Laurel Means, "Electionary, Lunary, Destinary, and Questionary: Toward Defining Categories of Middle English Prognostic Material," *Studies in Philology* 89 (1992): 367–403.

41. Paris, Bibliothèque nationale de France, lat. 3528 (France, ca. 1470), fols. 117v–118r, is an interesting

Origin, Date, and Provenance

As with dreambooks, lunaries are a feature of literary cultures throughout the ancient Near East.[42] Their probable point of origin is Babylon, with its long history of astronomical investigation. Lunaries are also part of the classical tradition. The earliest known example, in Greek, appears in Hesiod's *Works and Days* (eighth century BCE).[43]

The Lunationes Danielis is the stand-alone lunary that was known throughout medieval Christendom. It was among the most popular and widely circulated prognostic texts of the Middle Ages.[44] Many hundreds of manuscript copies are preserved in Greek, Latin, and virtually every western vernacular language, as well as in manuscripts in many nonwestern languages.

There is no reason to assume that the road from the classical lunary to the medieval Lunationes Danielis ran through early Judaism. Lunaries are unknown in the Bible, Second-Temple Jewish literature, and the rabbinic writings.[45] Excepting the notices about biblical figures and brief biblical quotations in the collective lunaries, the Lunationes is also devoid of Jewish (and Christian) content.[46]

The Greek manuscripts of the Lunationes Danielis are all late and therefore of minimal use in reconstructing its early history.[47] The oldest extant manuscript copies are written in Latin and date from the late eighth or ninth centuries:[48]

---

case. It contains a list of the biblical names and events linked to each day of the moon, or what remains of a collective lunary when the prognostications have been removed.

42. For examples in Babylonian and Egyptian literature, see Stefan Weinstock, "Lunar Mansions and Early Calendars," *JHS* 69 (1949): 57–60, doi:10.2307/629462.

43. Lines 765–828. An abbreviated lunary is embedded in Vergil's *Georgics* (ca. 29 BCE), lines 1.276–286. On classical lunaries, see Franz Cumont, "Les présages lunaires de Virgile et les 'Selenodromia,'" *L'Antiquité classique* 2 (1933): 259–70.

44. Means, "Electionary," 376.

45. The Qumran text 4Q318 (4QZodiac Calendar and Brontologion) must be considered a unique outlier rather than the tip of a hidden iceberg of an otherwise unknown tradition of early Jewish prognostication. The Testament of Shem, which some consider to be Second Temple text, exhibits all the characteristics of a late-antique composition.

46. These notices and quotations are not original but represent additions by late-antique Greek or Syriac Christians to an inherited classical model. The point is underscored by the Syriac Book of Medicines, a compendium that preserves Mesopotamian and Greco-Roman material, including multiple lunaries, some of which date from the fifth to the seventh centuries. See E. A. Wallis Budge, *Syrian Anatomy, Pathology and Therapeutics, of "the Book of Medicines"* (London: Oxford University Press, 1913), 2.535–37 and 537–38 (illness lunaries), 556–57 (travel lunary), and 559–65 (comprehensive lunary), and Siam Bhayro, "The Reception of Galen's *Art of Medicine* in the Syriac *Book of Medicines*," in *Medical Books in the Byzantine World*, ed. Barbara Zipser, Studi Online 2 (Bologna: Eikasmós Online, 2013), 123–44. The lunar prognostic in §§17–20 of *Peri Diosēmeiōn* (*De Ostentis*), by John the Lydian (490–ca. 560), is organized by the twelve zodiacal signs instead of the thirty days of the month and is not a lunary.

47. Grove records two hundred printed editions of lunaries, as well as twenty-five Greek manuscript copies and one Latin specimen that was translated from the Greek. Of the Greek manuscripts, one dates from the eleventh century and others from the thirteenth to nineteenth centuries (*Christ Came Forth*, 424–46).

48. For lists of manuscripts, see Christoph Weißer, *Studien zum mittelalterlichen Krankheitslunar: Ein Beitrag zur Geschichte laienastrologischer Fachprosa* (Würzburger medizinhistorische Forschungen 21; Würzburg, 1982), and Lászlo Sándor Chardonnens, "Handlist of Dream Divination and Lunar Prognostication in Western Manuscripts and Early Printed Books up to 1550" <https://radboud.academia.edu/LaszloSandorChardonnens/>, revised 14 February 2022 and accessed 15 May 2022.

- Paris, Bibliothèque nationale de France, lat. 10756 [*olim* Bern, Burgerbibliothek, Cod. 611][49] (Eastern France, this part viii$^{1/2}$), fol. 68va–b (illness lunary)
- St. Gallen, Stiftsbibliothek, Cod. Sang. 44 (St-Gallen, viii$^{4/4}$ [ca. 780]), pp. 226–228 (illness lunary)
- St. Gallen, Stiftsbibliothek, Cod. Sang. 1395 (France, this part viii–ix), fol. 468br–v (thunder lunary)
- Paris, Bibliothèque nationale de France, lat. 11218 (Burgundy, ix$^{1/4}$ [ca. 800]), fol. 101ra–b (illness lunary)
- Vatican City, Bibliotheca Apostolica Vaticana, Reg. lat. 846 (ix$^{1/4}$), fol. 114vb–c (bloodletting lunary)
- Munich, Bayerische Staatsbibliothek, Clm 14725 (Northeast France, ix$^{1/4}$), fol. 25r (illness lunary) and 25r (dream lunary)
- Karlsruhe, Badische Landesbibliothek, Aug. perg. 172 (ix$^{1/3}$), fol. 76v (illness lunary)
- Bern, Burgerbibliothek, Cod. 417 (this part ix$^{2/4}$ [ca. 826]), fols. 15r–16r (lunary)[50]
- Vatican City, Bibliotheca Apostolica Vaticana, Pal. lat. 1449 (Lorsch, ix$^{1/2}$), fol. 9r (bloodletting lunary)
- Bern, Burgerbibliothek, Cod. 611 (this part ix$^{3/4}$), fols. 19v–20r (birth lunary)
- San Lorenzo de El Escorial, Real biblioteca, L.III.8 (Senlis, ix$^{3/4}$ [860–870]) fols. 184r–186v (collective lunary)[51]
- Vatican City, Bibliotheca Apostolica Vaticana, Pal. lat. 485 (Lorsch, ix$^{3/4}$ [860–875]), fols. 13v (illness lunary) and 15v (bloodletting lunary)
- St. Gallen, Stiftsbibliothek, Cod. Sang. 751 (perhaps northern Italy, ix$^{2/2}$), pp. 175a–176a (bloodletting lunary), 176a–b (illness lunary), 376 (collective lunary), 428b (bloodletting lunary), and 428c–429 (birth lunary)
- *Uppsala, Universitetsbiblioteket, C.664 (northern Italy, ix$^{2/2}$), p. 23 (illness lunary)[52]
- *London, British Library, Harley MS 3017 (Fleury or Nevers, ix), fols. 58v (illness lunary) and 58v–59r (birth lunary)
- Lucca, Biblioteca Statale [*olim* Biblioteca Governativa], Ms. 296 (ix), fol. 109r (dream lunary)
- Paris, Bibliothèque nationale de France, NAL 1616 (perhaps Brittany, ix), fols. 10v–12r (collective lunary)[53]
- Reims, Bibliothèque Carnegie de Reims, MS 443 (ix), fol. Br–v (dream lunary)
- Munich, Bayerische Staatsbibliothek, Clm 14221 (Germany, ix$^{4/4}$–x), fol. 16v (bloodletting lunary)
- Berlin, Staatsbibliothek zu Berlin—Preußischer Kulturbesitz, Ms Phillipps 1790 (ix–x), fols. 40r (birth lunary), 40r (combined illness and dream lunary), 40v–41v (illness lunary), 41v (illness lunary), and 42r–v + 70r (dream lunary)

---

49. Fols. 62–69 of this manuscript were once part of Bern, Burgerbibliothek, Cod. 611, a composite codex containing material from the fifth and seventh centuries (as the undertext in palimpsests) and material from the eighth and ninth centuries. The manuscript is described by Florian Mittenhuber, Gerald Schwedler, and David Ganz, https://www.e-codices.unifr.ch/en/description/bbb/0611/Mittenhuber.

50. I have not been able to verify this information by autopsy.

51. A later hand has crossed out the attribution to Daniel in this specimen.

52. An asterisk (*) indicates that the codex also contains a version of the Somniale Danielis.

53. Adam Łajtar and Vincent W. J. van Gerven Oei identify a lunary in Old Nubian that is very similar to this copy. See Łajtar and van Gerven Oei, "An Old Nubian Lunary with a Greek Addition from Gebel Adda," *Mus* 133 (2020): 13–30, doi:10.2143/MUS.133.1.3287659.

Several conclusions may be tendered from our knowledge of ancient lunaries in general and the earliest Latin manuscripts of the Lunationes in particular. (1) The Lunationes Danielis is a Christianized work that emerged in the eastern Mediterranean world in the fourth or fifth centuries CE. (2) Its original language was Greek or, less likely, Syriac. (3) The Lunationes entered the Latin (western) tradition during the first half of the eighth century, around the same time as the Somniale Danielis. (4) It did so, however, independently from the Somniale, since their literary association in manuscripts does not appear to have occurred before the tenth century.[54] (5) The association with the Somniale was likely enabled by the Lunationes's ascription to Daniel. (6) The process of association occurred within the Latin tradition of transmission and reception, rather than in later vernacular environments. (7) The inclusion of two or more types of Lunationes in a single codex or codicological unit also occurred within the early Latin tradition.

Literary Features and Content

The defining literary features of the Lunationes Danielis are its prognostic formula and the thirty days of its forecast coverage. Entries consist of the word for "moon" (in Latin *Luna* or its abbreviation *L* or *Ł*) plus a notation for the specific day of the month (*i, ii, iii* . . . or *prima, secunda, tertia* . . .), followed by the prognosis for that day (e.g., *Luna prima. Bona est.*). Other than those of the collective type of lunary, the entries are usually brief, no more than five or six words. Early copies of the Lunationes Danielis are written as a narrow column of text, one entry per line, like an inventory. Some manuscripts present two or even three lunaries that are disposed in tall parallel columns across a single page. Later copies tend to be written in continuous text across the page from margin to margin.

The Lunationes exhibits several titles in manuscript, including *lunare, lunarium, lunaris*, and *lunationes*, or their vernacular equivalents. The subject of the forecast (birth, bloodletting) is often stated in its title.[55] The text's brevity and inventorial presentation contributed to its utility, as did the practice of rubricating the initial letter of the word "Luna" for each of the thirty days.

The attribution of lunaries to Daniel is not as routine as with the Somniale, perhaps because the biblical figure is not assocated with the moon.[56] Even so, the attribution is more than common enough to justify the title Lunationes Danielis, which is extant across the earliest Latin manuscript copies.[57] This association with Daniel is underscored by

---

54. Only two of the twenty early manuscript codices that contain the Lunationes also preserve a version of the Somniale.

55. Weißer, *Studien zum mittelalterlichen Krankheitslunar*.

56. Hence manuscript copies of the Lunationes are occasionally associated with other figures, including Adam, Esdras (Ezra), Bede, and Merlin (DiTommaso, *Book of Daniel*, 259–77).

57. Pablo A. Torijano attributes the Lunationes to "David and Solomon" ("The Selendromion of David and Solomon," in *MOTP* 1:298–304). His study, however, is based solely on nine late Greek manuscripts, of which only one is so attributed. The ascription to Solomon occurs more regularly in the French manuscript tradition. The website JONAS (https://jonas.irht.cnrs.fr/), which is maintained by the Institut de recherche et d'histoire des textes, references two dozen manuscript copies of a 'Lunaire de Salomon' in Old French or more rarely Occitan. Caution is warranted, however: not only does the webiste associate the title with other types of moon prognostics, but many of the formal lunaries it does list under the title are in fact unattributed. On the Lunaire de Salomon, see Tony Hunt, "Les pronostics en anglo-normand: Méthodes et documents," in *Moult obscures paroles: Études sur la prophétie médiévale*, ed. Richard Trachsler, Culture et civilisations médiévales 39 (Paris: Presses de l'Université de Paris-Sorbonne, 2007), 38–42.

the fact that copies of the Lunationes often appear in the same manuscript codex with the Somniale, and that in many instances a dream Lunationes immediately precedes or follows the Somniale. More extraordinary still are those manuscripts where a Lunationes is positioned between the Somniale's prologue and its roster of dreams, in effect creating a single composition under the name of Daniel and governed by its prologue.[58] No text besides the Lunationes shares the Somniale's prologue in this manner.

Unlike the Somniale Danielis, which is best construed as a notional work, the Lunationes Danielis is a literary text in the classic mold. It exists in several classifiable types, some of which exhibit different versions. Also unlike the Somniale, it appears that the textual relationship among the manuscript copies of the Lunationes and its types could be represented stemmatically, although this remains to be proven.

Theology, Anthropology, and Sociology

The Lunationes Danielis shares with the Somniale Danielis a lack of Jewish or Christian vocabulary or ideas, apart from its signature ascription to Daniel.[59] One assumes that the Lunationes was used for the same purposes as the Somniale and would have had the same audience. Carine van Rhijn convincingly argues for the pastoral use of prognostic texts such as the Lunationes.[60] But prognostication, generally speaking, was popular throughout the Middle Ages. Among other things, forecasting the future gave knowledge and a sense of power to those who could read.

Prognostic texts are often held up as examples of esoteric works or scientific literature.[61] But both labels are problematic when applied to the Lunationes Danielis and the Somniale Danielis. Strictly speaking, esoteric texts are meant for a small group of persons with a specialized interest or knowledge, and are not intended for widespread distribution.[62] The Lunationes and the Somniale, by contrast, circulated widely throughout the medieval West from the early Middle Ages well into the age of print. Neither work contains an internal injunction against transmission, and both presume an anthropology that is universal rather than local, sectarian, or otherwise restricted.

By some criteria, the Lunationes and the Somniale might be considered examples of premodern scientific literature.[63] But the invincible credulity on the part of the intended

---

58. Examples are listed in DiTommaso and Chardonnens, "Conspectus." See, for example, Vatican City, Bibliotheca Apostolica Vaticana, Pal. lat. 235 (x–xi), fol. 39v. This early manuscript contains a version of the Somniale Danielis and three Lunationes, which are arranged in such a fashion as to suggest a continual work (see the discussion in DiTommaso, *Book of Daniel*). In the same vein, note the combined Somniale and collective lunary in Cambridge, Cambridge University Library, Ee.1.1 (England, xiii/xiv), fols. 1v–2v, and the combined Somniale and dream lunary in the private Petroneller "Circa instans" manuscript (Austria, xv$^{2/2}$), fols. 145v–152r. More remarkable still is the copy of the Lunationes Danielis at Basel, Universitätsbibliothek, L.III.3, fols. 2r–v, which is unattached to a Somniale yet bears the title COMPVTATIO SOMNIALVM DANIELIS PROPHETAE.

59. Phrases such as "give praise to God" (e.g., the eighth day of the month in the translation below) are not integral to the earliest manuscript copies of the text.

60. Van Rhijn, "Pastoral Care and Prognostics in the Carolingian Period: The Case of El Escorial, Real Biblioteca di San Lorenzo, MS L III 8," *RBén* 127 (2017): 272–97.

61. Cf. Torijano, "Selendromion of David and Solomon."

62. As opposed to esotericism, which is a pattern of thought or discourse; see Kocku von Stuckrad, *Western Esotericism: A Brief History of Secret Knowledge* (London: Equinox, 2005), 1–11.

63. One criterion is the manipulation of existing knowledge to solve problems. Another is the universality of the claims of both works. Cf. volume 1 of Lynn Thorndike, *A History of Magic and Experimental Science during the First Thirteen Centuries of Our Era* (New York: Macmillan, 1923).

users that is presumed by both works makes the label "scientific" inappropriate.[64] Despite the fact that lunar and dream forecasts are easily falsifiable, the many hundreds of extant manuscript versions of the Lunationes or the Somniale exhibit no evidence of the critical testing and empirical verification that are integral aspects of true scientific enquiry. Instead, and for over seven centuries, these versions faithfully reproduced variations of the same kinds of forecasts.

Bibliography

Angelidi, Christine, and George T. Calofonos, eds. *Dreaming in Byzantium and Beyond*. Farnham: Ashgate, 2014.

Berriot, François. *Exposicions et significacions des songes et Les songes Daniel: Manuscrits français de la Bibliothèque nationale de Paris et de la Staatsbibliothek de Berlin, XIVe, XVe et XVIe siècles*. Travaux d'humanisme et renaissance 234. Geneva: Droz, 1989.

Bühler, Curt F. "Two Middle English Texts of the *Somnia Danielis*." *Anglia* 80 (1962): 264–73.

Cappozzo, Valerio. *Dizionario dei sogni nel Medioevo: Il* Somniale Danielis *in manoscrittti letterari*. Biblioteca dell' "Archivum Romanicum" 466. Firenze: Olschki, 2018.

———, ed. *Predicting the Past: Worldwide Medieval Dream Interpretation*. Reading Medieval Sources. Leiden: Brill, forthcoming.

Chardonnens, László Sándor. *Anglo-Saxon Prognostics, 900–1100: Study and Texts*. Brill's Texts and Sources in Intellectual History 153.3. Leiden: Brill, 2007.

———. "Dream Divination in Manuscripts and Early Printed Books: Patterns of Transmission." Pages 23–52 in *Aspects of Knowledge: Preserving and Reinventing Traditions of Learning in the Middle Ages*. Edited by Marilina Cesario and Hugh Magennis. Manchester: Manchester University Press, 2018. doi:10.7765/9781526107015.00009.

Dinzelbacher, Peter. *Vision und Visionsliteratur im Mittelalter*. Monographien zur Geschichte des Mittelalters 23. Stuttgart: Hiersemann, 1981.

DiTommaso, Lorenzo. "Greek, Latin, and Hebrew Manuscripts of the *Somniale Danielis* and *Lunationes Danielis* in the Vatican Library." *Manuscripta* 47/48 (2003–2004): 1–42. doi:10.1484/J.MSS.2.300288.

———. *The Book of Daniel and the Apocryphal Daniel*. SVTP 20. Leiden: Brill, 2005.

DiTommaso, Lorenzo, and Lászlo Sándor Chardonnens. "Conspectus of the Western Manuscripts and Early Printed Books of the *Somniale Danielis*." In *Dream Interpretation in the Global Middle Ages*. Edited by Valerio Cappozzo. Reading Medieval Sources. Leiden: Brill, forthcoming.

Epe, Andreas. *Wissensliteratur im angelsächsischen England: Das Fachschrifttum der vergessenen* artes mechanicae *und* artes magicae*; Mit besonderer Berücksichtigung des* Somniale Danielis*; Edition der (lateinisch-) altenglischen Fassungen*. Münster: Verlag Tebbert, 1995.

Fischer, Steven R. *The Complete Medieval Dreambook: A Multilingual, Alphabetical Somnia Danielis Collation*. Bern: Lang, 1982.

Förster, Max. "Die altenglische Traumlunare." *Englische Studien* 60 (1925–1926): 58–93.

———. "Vom Fortleben antiker Sammellunare im englischen und in anderen Volkssprachen." *Anglia* NS 67/68 (1944): 1–171.

Gejrot, Claes. "Daniel's Dreams: An Edition and Translation of a Medieval Latin Book

---

64. For one view on the distinctions between premodern and modern science, see Steven Weinberg, *To Explain the World: The Discovery of Modern Science* (New York: Harper, 2015).

of Dreams." Pages 173–202 in *Symbolae septentrionales: Latin Studies Presented to Jan Öberg*. Edited by Monika Asztalos and Claes Gejrot. Scripta minora 2. Stockholm: Sällskapet Runica et Mediævalia, 1995.

Gregory, Tullio, ed. *I sogni nel Medioevo: Seminario internazionale Roma, 2–4 ottobre 1983*. Lessico Intellettuale Europeo 35. Rome: Edizioni dell'Ateneo, 1985.

Grub, Jutta. *Das lateinische Traumbuch im Codex Upsaliensis C 664 (9.Jh.): Eine frühmittelalterliche Fassung der lateinischen Somniale Danielis-Tradition; Kritische Erstedition mit Einleitung und Kommentar*. Lateinische Sprache und Literatur des Mittelalters 19. Frankfurt am Main: Lang, 1984.

Heiduk, Matthias, Klaus Herbers, and Hans-Christian Lehner, eds. *Prognostication in the Medieval World: A Handbook*. 2 vols. Berlin: de Gruyter, 2021.

Kruger, Stephen F. *Dreaming in the Middle Ages*. Cambridge Studies in Medieval Literature 14. Cambridge: Cambridge University Press, 1992.

Liuzza, Roy Michael. *Anglo-Saxon Prognostics: An Edition and Translation of Texts from London, British Library, MS Cotton Tiberius A.iii*. Anglo-Saxon Texts 9. Cambridge: Brewer, 2010.

Martin, Lawrence T. "The Earliest Versions of the Latin *Somniale Danielis*." *Manuscripta* 23 (1979): 131–41. doi:10.1484/J.MSS.3.951.

———. *Somniale Danielis: An Edition of a Medieval Latin Dream Interpretation Handbook*. Europäische Hochschulenschriften 375. Lateinische Sprache und Literatur des Mittelalters 10. Frankfurt am Main: Lang, 1981.

Means, Laurel. "Electionary, Lunary, Destinary, and Questionary: Toward Defining Categories of Middle English Prognostic Material." *Studies in Philology* 89 (1992): 367–403.

———. *Medieval Lunar Astrology: A Collection of Representative Middle English Texts*. Lewiston, NY: Mellen, 1993.

Miller, Patricia Cox. *Dreams in Late Antiquity: Studies in the Imagination of a Culture*. Mythos. Princeton: Princeton University Press, 1994.

Oberhelman, Steven M. *Dreambooks in Byzantium: Six* Oneirocritica *in Translation, with Commentary and Introduction*. Aldershot: Ashgate, 2008.

———. "Prolegomena to the Reconstruction of the Archetype of the Greek *Somniale Danielis*." Pages 107–24 in *Sogni e visioni nel mondo indo-mediterraneo*. Edited by Daniela Boccassini. Quaderni di studi indo-mediterranei 2. Alessandria: Orso, 2009.

———. "Traditions and Practices in the Medieval Eastern Christian World." Pages 386–99 in *Prognostication in the Medieval World: A Handbook*. Edited by Matthias Heiduk, Klaus Herbers, and Hans-Christian Lehner. 2 vols. Berlin: de Gruyter, 2021. doi:10.1515/9783110499773-018.

Önnerfors, Alf. "Zur Überlieferungsgeschichte des sogenannten Somniale Danielis." *Eranos* 58 (1960): 142–58.

Palmer, Nigel, and Klaus Speckenbach. *Träume und Kräuter: Studien zur Petroneller "Circa instans"-Handschrift und zu den deutschen Traumbüchern des Mittelalters*. Pictura et poesis 4. Cologne: Bohlau, 1990.

Semeraro, Martino. *Il "Libro dei sogni di Daniele": Storia di un testo "proibito" nel Medioevo*. Il libri di Viella 29. Rome: Viella, 2002.

Suchier, Walther. "Altfranzösische Traumbücher." *Zeitschrift für französische Sprache und Literatur* 67 (1956/1957): 129–67.

Svenberg, E. *Lunaria et zodiologia latina, edidit et commentario philologico instruxit*. Studia graeca et latina Gothoburgensia 16. Göteborg: Acta Universitatis Gothoburgensis, 1963.

Taavitsainen, Irma. *Middle English Lunaries: A Study of the Genre*. Mémoires de la Société Néophilologique de Helsinki 47. Helsinki: Sociéte´ Néophilologique, 1988.

Torijano, Pablo A. "The Selenodromion of David and Solomon" *MOTP* 1:298–304.

Weißer, Christoph. *Studien zum mittelalterlichen Krankheitslunar: Ein Beitrag zur Geschichte laienastrologischer Fachprosa*. Würzburger medizinhistorische Forschungen 21. Würzburg: Wellm, 1982.

Wittmer-Butsch, Maria Elisabeth. *Zur Bedeutung von Schlaf und Traum im Mittelalter*. Medium Aevum Quotidianum 1. Krems: Medium Aevum Quotidianum, 1990.

Note on the Translations

As Roy Liuzza observes, the Somniale Danielis is a "strikingly polymorphous work; no two copies are identical."[65] Although this is not wholly accurate (some manuscript versions are copies of others), the great majority of specimens are idiosyncratic versions of a composition whose coherence is more notional than textual, as discussed above. Therefore, any version that is selected as a basis for a translation of the Somniale (rather than a translation of the specific version) should strive to be as representative of the work as possible, within the limitations of the evidence. To this end, I chose the Somniale that is preserved in London, British Library, Cotton MS Tiberius A.III, fols. 27v–32v. Dating from the eleventh century, it is one of the earliest surviving specimens; of these, it has the second greatest number of dreams (302).[66]

This version is also one of the more important. MS Cotton Tiberius A.III is a miscellany from Christ Church in Canterbury, England. It contains a trove of Old English (Anglo-Saxon) compositions, as well as Latin works with and without Old English glosses. Among its contents are multiple prognostic works, including three versions of the Somniale and no less than ten copies of the Lunationis Danielis, of several different types.[67] One of the latter, a collective or general lunary (fols. 32v–35v), is translated below. Both it and the Somniale Danielis that I have selected are written in Latin, with interlinear glosses. After its forecasts for the thirtieth day of the month, this Lunationes adds "Here end the dreams of Daniel the prophet," essentially making it and the Somniale before it a single work under one title.[68]

---

65. Liuzza, *Anglo-Saxon Prognostics*, 42.

66. See the list of these manuscripts above. Photographs of the manuscript are available at https://www.bl.uk/manuscripts/FullDisplay.aspx?ref=Cotton_MS_Tiberius_A_III.

67. For details and bibliography, see Liuzza, *Anglo-Saxon Prognostics*.

68. For discussion, see above, note 58, and the paragraph to which it refers.

Somniale Danielis[a]

On the variety of dreams, in alphabetical order, by the prophet Daniel[b]

(1)[c] [A][d] To see birds in dreams and to fight with them signifies[e] strife.
(2) To snare birds signifies wealth.
(3) To see birds taking something from you signifies harm.
(4) To see asses or kids signifies a crime in business.
(5) To bear arms in dreams signifies protection.
(6) To see asses eating signifies toil.
(7) To see asses crying or running free signifies strife with an enemy.
(8) To see boiling waters signifies evil speech from one's enemies.
(9) To see trees bearing fruit signifies desired profit.
(10) To climb trees signifies honor obtained.
(11) To see clear air signifies success in business.
(12) To see oneself beset by beasts signifies that one will be overcome by enemies.
(13) To bend a bow or loose an arrow signifies toil or anxiety.
(14) To see a ring in a dream signifies money.
(15) To take a ring signifies safety.

   a. Emendations are made silently. Variants are ignored except in a few instances where the meaning of the Latin text in this version is unclear.
   b. DE SOMNIORVM DIVERSIITATE SECVNDUM ORDINEM ABCHARII DANIELIS PROPHETE (rubricated). This version of the Somniale lacks a prologue.
   c. The dreams are not numbered in the manuscript. Their enumeration in this translation is for reference only.
   d. This version contains three dream sequences. The first sequence runs from dreams 1 to 249 and includes dreams about subjects beginning (in Latin) with the letters A–I and L–V. (Early versions of the Somniale omit the letters J and W, which did not exist when it was translated into Latin, and conflate U and V. The letter K played next to no role in medieval Latin.) The second sequence, spanning dreams 250–270, contains dream-subjects beginning with the letters C–U, while all the entries in the third sequence, dreams 271–302, begin with the formula "Si uideris." The first letters of each dream in all three sequences are rubricated.
   e. The verb or verbal phrase used to express that a dream "signifies" (*significare*) differs among the manuscript versions, and even among the 302 dreams of this version. While such differences are important for a literal translation of a specific version of the Somniale, they are less so for a representative translation of the work as whole. As a result, I translate the word as "signifies." In addition, excepting the dreams in the third sequence ("Si uideris"), I depersonalize their subjects (e.g., dream 9, from "If he sees trees bearing fruit . . ." to "To see trees bearing fruit . . ." or "Seeing trees bear fruit . . .").

(16) To give a ring signifies harm.
(17) To handle gold in a dream signifies success in business.
(18) To drink absinthe signifies much strife.
(19) To drink vinegar in a dream signifies illness.
(20) To drink agrimony signifies awful news.
(21) To be dressed in white or bright clothes signifies joy.
(22) To see oneself plowing signifies great toil ahead.
(23) [B] To shave one's beard signifies harm.
(24) To see trousers in dreams signifies safety.
(25) To sit on a foal signifies deception in business.
(26) To see oneself senseless signifies illness.
(27) To have mighty arms signifies bounty.
(28) To see oneself taming beasts signifies the esteem of enemies.
(29) To see beasts running signifies disturbance.
(30) To wash oneself in a bath signifies anxiety.
(31) To see oneself bearded signifies distinction.
(32) To have a white surplice signifies joy.
(33) To have a colored surplice signifies terrible news.
(34) To see war or barbarians signifies that joy will be revealed publicly.
(35) To eat butter signifies good news.
(36) To see oxen grazing signifies struggle in business.
(37) To see oxen sleeping signifies evil in business.
(38) To see beasts speaking signifies serious trouble.
(39) [C] To be wearing an outer garment signifies safety.
(40) To accept a crown of any substance signifies joy.
(41) To see oneself as blind signifies hindrance.
(42) To see the sky in flames signifies that evils will befall the whole world.[a]
(43) To see cucumbers or gourds signifies illness.
(44) To eat dry wax signifies strife with quarrelsome people.
(45) To sees doves signifies sadness.
(46) To see oneself in prison signifies trouble or slander.
(47) To have a white head in a dream signifies wealth.
(48) To shave one's head signifies harm.
(49) To wear new shoes in a dream signifies wealth from an unexpected source.
(50) To wear old shoes signifies deception.
(51) To gather or craft nails signifies toil.
(52) To see dogs barking or attacking signifies that enemies seek to overpower you.
(53) To see dogs playing signifies gratitude.
(54) To wash the head signifies freedom from all fear and danger.
(55) To accept new cheese signifies wealth.
(56) If something is salted, that signifies strife.
(57) To see camels, and oneself attacked by them, signifies harm.

a. Perhaps an allusion to the Revelation of John or, more generally, the eschaton.

(58) To see oneself eating coals signifies that one will be slandered by enemies.
(59) To see lattices, or one enclosed by them, signifies that one will be scandalized or arrested.
(60) To write or read a sheet of paper signifies terrible news.
(61) To vomit food signifies harm.
(62) To vomit ointment signifies strife.
(63) To see oneself unable to run signifies impediment.
(64) To sit on a cart signifies great strife.
(65) Wax or candles signifies joy.
(66) To converse with a dead person signifies wealth.
(67) To sleep with one's sister signifies harm.
(68) To sleep with one's mother signifies safety.
(69) To sleep with a virgin signifies anxiety.
(70) To sleep with one's own wife signifies anxiety.
(71) To accept books on any subject, or to read or hear them read, signifies a time of happiness.
(72) To see oneself multiplied signifies a grave accusation ahead.
(73) Guards signify deception.
(74) To touch bells, psalteries, or strings signifies strife.
(75) To see a harp signifies safety in business.
(76) To speak with a dead person signifies great wealth.
(77) To see flashes signifies wealth.
(78) [D] One's teeth falling out signifies that a parent will die.
(79) One's lower teeth falling out, with blood or without pain, signifies estrangement from parents.
(80) To sacrifice in one's house signifies multiplicity of joy.
(81) To see one's house to collapse signifies harm.
(82) To see one's house collapse and be destroyed signifies harm.
(83) To see one's house burn signifies mortal peril.
(84) To eat sweets signifies that one will suffer many crimes.
(85) To dress in a wide-sleeved garment[a] signifies wealth from grain.
(86) To see dragons signifies honor.
(87) [E] To sit on a white horse signifies a positive outcome.
(88) To sit on a black horse signifies anxiety.
(89) To sit on a fallow horse signifies damage.
(90) To sit on a bay horse signifies advancement.
(91) To sit on a chestnut horse signifies bad business ahead.
(92) To see horses running loose, or be attacked by them, signifies harm.
(93) To see oneself drunk signifies illness.
(94) To see eunuchs signifies harm.
(95) To see a fierce elephant signifies accusation.
(96) To handle ivory signifies hindrance.
(97) To buy or sell ivory signifies much sadness.
(98) [F] To handle wheat in a dream signifies prosperity in business.

a. A dalmatic.

(99) To see oneself struck by iron signifies worry.
(100) To handle iron in any form signifies illness.
(101) To see one's face in something signifies long life.
(102) To have a handsome face signifies assistance and honor.
(103) To have a dirty face signifies the oppression of many accusations.
(104) To see a turbulent river signifies misfortunes ahead.
(105) To handle grain signifies illness.
(106) To see one's brother or sister signifies terrible sores.
(107) To see a ditch and fall into it signifies accusation.
(108) To see a spring appear in one's house signifies bounty or joy.
(109) To see ants signifies great strife.
(110) To see a river flowing through one's house signifies danger.
(111) To see phantoms signifies wealth from an unexpected source.
(112) To see a fig tree signifies strife with troublesome people.
(113) To see a black fig signifies sadness.
(114) To see a leaf with wine and drinking it signifies illness.
(115) To take leaves with new wine and drinking it signifies a time of happiness.
(116) To see philosophers in argument signifies harm.
(117) To see sons or daughters born signifies bounty.
(118) [G] To see oneself as a gladiator signifies terrible harm.
(119) To bear and use a sword signifies anxiety.
(120) To await men bearing arms signifies very great strife ahead.
(121) To lose a jewel from a ring signifies loss.
(122) A hen laying an egg signifies wealth but with anxiety.
(123) To see a hen with her chicks signifies prosperity in business.
(124) To see heathens fighting and be attacked by them signifies strife and danger.
(125) To rejoice in a dream signifies sadness.
(126) Hail in a dream signifies sadness.
(127) To see hail in a dream signifies cruel sadness.
(128) [H] To see he- or she-goats signifies advancement.
(129) To have guests signifies envy.
(130) To see Hercules signifies a friendship ahead.
(131) To kill a man signifies protection.
(132) [I] To be made emperor signifies some honor.
(133) To walk around a plaza or a palace signifies anxiety.
(134) To see fire in any place signifies peril.
(135) To swim in a river signifies anxiety.
(136) To bathe in a fountain signifies wealth.
(137) To wash oneself in the sea signifies joy.
(138) To wash in a dirty whirlpool signifies accusation.
(139) To fall into the sea signifies wealth.
(140) To fall into a pond signifies joy.
(141) To fall into a dirty whirlpool signifies accusation.
(142) To see and play with children signifies a time of happiness.
(143) To see sick people signifies trouble.

(144) To see oneself waiting in a theater or amphitheater signifies confusion.
(145) To walk in an orchard signifies great anxiety.
(146) To see oneself painted on a tablet signifies long life.
(147) [L] To be girded with a belt signifies protection.
(148) To lose the moon signifies a loss of faith.
(149) To be girded with a golden moon signifies envy.
(150) To be girded with a divided moon signifies strength.
(151) To see a clear moon signifies envy.
(152) To see two moons signifies envy.
(153) To see a bloody moon signifies harm.
(154) To see the moon in the sky either fall or rise signifies toil.
(155) To see a white moon signifies wealth.
(156) To see a colored moon signifies harm.
(157) To handle lard signifies a parent will die.
(158) To see linen clothing being washed signifies harm.
(159) To be dressed in linen clothing signifies some sort of sickness.
(160) To see a lion running signifies success in business.
(161) To see a lion sleeping signifies wickedness in business.
(162) To be attacked by a lion signifies dissension among enemies.
(163) To see oneself bound signifies an impediment.
(164) To handle lanterns signifies illness.
(165) To see lanterns signifies safety.
(166) To throw stones signifies sickness.
(167) To quarrel in a dream signifies prosperity in business.
(168) To see one's bed well-prepared signifies clarity.
(169) [M] To see a smooth sea signifies success in business.
(170) To see fish of the sea signifies much anxiety ahead.
(171) To see one's hands defiled signifies evil deeds.
(172) To see one's mother either dead or alive signifies joy.
(173) To see himself magnified but with less joy signifies loss.
(174) To see a woman with flowing hair signifies dissension.
(175) A mouse and lion in a dream signifies safety.
(176) To travel signifies deception.
(177) To see a dead person signifies joy.
(178) To kiss a dead person signifies living life.
(179) To see soldiers signifies joy.
(180) To wash the hands signifies great annoyance.
(181) To gather harvests signifies joy.
(182) To accept honey signifies care not to be deceived by another.
(183) [N] To see ships signifies good news.
(184) To gather nuts signifies strife.
(185) To see a nest of birds signifies struggle in business.
(186) To see snow signifies joy.
(187) A cloud upon the earth signifies nothing good at all.
(188) To have a wedding signifies harm.
(189) To walk around with bare feet signifies harm.

Somniale Danielis

(190) [O] To hear an organ playing signifies joy ahead.
(191) To make a speech signifies a more fortunate time ahead.
(192) To handle someone's bones signifies hatred.
(193) To handle work signifies impediment.
(194) To handle olives signifies wealth.
(195) To see sheared sheep signifies harm.
(196) To give a kiss signifies harm.
(197) [P] To see rain signifies joy.
(198) To receive maidens signifies a happy time.
(199) To see oneself as hirsute signifies an increase in danger.
(200) To fall into a pit signifies an accusation.
(201) To accept money signifies strife.
(202) To cry in a dream signifies joy.
(203) To accept a palm signifies honor.
(204) To accept white bread signifies an accusation.
(205) To accept wax bread signifies new friendships ahead.
(206) To accept barley bread signifies joy.
(207) To prepare one's house for a woman signifies bounty.
(208) To accept porridge signifies wealth with worry.
(209) To see a bridge signifies safety.
(210) To see pigs signifies illness.
(211) To wash one's feet signifies anxiety.
(212) To handle lead signifies illness.
(213) [Q] To see or sit in a white chariot signifies a problem in business.
(214) To see any four-legged beast signifies anxiety.
(215) To sit in a white chariot signifies honor.
(216) To see a four-footed beast talking signifies the enmity of a king.
(217) [R] To see laughter or grins signifies sadness.
(218) To see a rose signifies health.
(219) To see resin or sulfur signifies great troubles.
(220) To see kings signifies a departure from the world.
(221) To accept a royal messenger is a great sign.
(222) To go ashore signifies toil.
(223) To go down from the shore signifies a good time.
(224) To see frogs signifies anxiety.
(225) [S] To see two suns signifies honor.
(226) To see a shining sun signifies joy.
(227) To see either the sun or moon signifies happiness in a judgment.
(228) To see many stars signifies happiness.
(229) Blood running from one's side signifies harm.
(230) To sit on a ladder signifies deceit.
(231) To be attacked by a serpent signifies an enemy ahead.
(232) To sit in a dream signifies illness.
(233) [T] To hear or see thunder signifies good news.
(234) To see storms signifies wealth.
(235) To see darkness signifies illness.
(236) To weave on a loom and see either joy or sadness signifies good news.

Somniale Danielis

(237) To make a statement signifies protection.
(238) To see an earthquake signifies that one will let something go.
(239) To see oneself measuring signifies anxiety
(240) [V] To see vines full of ripe fruit signifies joy.
(241) To harvest grapes signifies a pleasure in one's life.
(242) To be flogged in a dream signifies good things ahead.
(243) To go hunting signifies wealth.
(244) To see oneself getting dressed signifies mirth.
(245) To see oneself attacked by a bear signifies the treachery of an enemy.
(246) To drink wine signifies illness.
(247) To have smart clothing signifies joy.
(248) To travel or walk on a muddy road signifies grave injury.
(249) To take a wife signifies harm.
(250) [C][a] To see one's hair signifies growth.
(251) To see one crown among others signifies death.
(252) To wash with a man signifies failure.
(253) To sin with another signifies illness.
(254) To speak or walk with a nobler person signifies advancement.
(255) To see onions signifies eye illness ahead.
(256) [D] To see oneself beheaded signifies wealth.
(257) [I] To wash oneself in a bath signifies anxiety.
(258) To see oneself in prison signifies harm.
(259) To wash in a fishpond signifies mirth.
(260) To wash in a river signifies joy.
(261) To fall into a fountain signifies accusation.
(262) [L] To see oneself bound signifies harm.
(263) [N] To see oneself swim signifies harm.
(264) [O] To see oil signifies joy.
(265) To see a garden signifies harm.
(266) [P] To gather apples signifies trouble.
(267) [Q] To see oneself flying signifies a change of place.
(268) To see oneself in exile signifies major crimes ahead.
(269) [V] To see sour grapes signifies strife.
(270) To see claws signifies anguish.
(271)[b] If you dream that you see two moons—this signifies joy and happiness.
(272) If you see yourself falling from a high location—this signifies good fortune to a poor person and bad to a rich person.
(273) If you see a dragon flying over you—this signifies treasure.
(274) If you see that your face is beautiful—this signifies joy.
(275) If you see yourself walking into or out of beautiful water—this signifies safety.
(276) If you see yourself walking into or out of beautiful water—this signifies nothing good ahead.

a. The second dream sequence begins here.
b. The third dream sequence begins here. Note the change to the second person.

Somniale Danielis

(277) If you see yourself girded with a sword—this signifies safety.
(278) If you see yourself finding precious jewels—this signifies stories.
(279) If you see many goats—this signifies vanity.
(280) If you see yourself judging others—this signifies good things or honor is in store.
(281) If you see many dogs—this signifies that you should beware your enemies.
(282) If you see yourself kissing your neighbor—this signifies good.
(283) If you see much bread—this signifies joy.
(284) If you see bees attack or injure you—this signifies that others will disturb your life.
(285) If you see bees flying into your house—this signifies abandonment.
(286) If you see a snake coming toward you—this signifies that you should beware evil women.
(287) If you see an eagle flying—this signifies that your wife will die.
(288) If you see yourself washing in hot water—this signifies bodily harm ahead.
(289) If you see yourself washing in cold water—this signifies bodily health ahead.
(290) If you see or find many coins—this signifies stories, mockery, or curses.
(291) If you see yourself taking something from a dead person's hand—this signifies money will come to you.
(292) If you see your house burning—this signifies that you will find money.
(293) If you see your arms cut off—this signifies good.
(294) If you see yourself having much clothing—this signifies that your enemy will be in your power.
(295) If you see that you have a gold ring—this signifies honor.
(296) If you see yourself vomit—this signifies your thoughts will be scattered and your counsel ignored.
(297) If you see your neck bound—this signifies caution lest you do evil.
(298) If you see yourself falling into darkness from a high position—this signifies anguish or injury.
(299) If you see yourself desiring your neighbor's wife—this signifies an evil pain in the body.
(300) If you see yourself sleeping with your wife—this signifies good.
(301) If you see yourself praying to the Lord—this signifies that much joy will come to you.
(302) If you see yourself building a house—this signifies that your wealth will increase.

Lunationes Danielis[a]

On the observation of the moon and the things to heed.[b]

The first day of the month.[c] It is useful for doing all things. The boy born on this day will be illustrious, clever, wise, and learned, but in danger from water—if he survives, he will have a long life. The girl will be without stain, chaste, kind, lovely, pleasing to men, and balanced in judgment, but long bedridden later in life. She will have a sign in the mouth or on the eyebrow. The sick will languish for a long time. Dreams will be joyful, since they forecast nothing bad, though rarely good. All day is good for letting blood.

The second day of the month. It is useful for doing all things, and for buying, selling, or boarding a ship. The boy born on this day will be wise, kind, clever, and fortunate. The girl, likewise. The sick will recover promptly. Dreams will not come to pass. It is not a good day for letting blood.

The third day of the month. It is unsuitable for starting work, except for pruning, taming beasts, or castrating swine. Do not plant a garden: weeds will grow. Stolen property will be found swiftly. The sick will either recover quickly or else endure long peril. The boy born on this day will be spirited and greedy for foreign things; he will rarely grow old and not die a good death. The girl, likewise, and industrious; she will desire many men and not be an old woman. Dreams are empty. It is not a good day for letting blood.

The fourth day of the month. It is useful for undertaking all tasks and sending boys to school. Fugitives will be found promptly. The sick will die quickly or else barely survive. The boy born on this day will be a fornicator; he will be wealthy if he survives to age twelve. He will have danger. The girl, likewise. Dreams, good or bad, are portentous. It is a good day for letting blood from the sixth hour to the ninth hour.

The fifth day of the month. Do not give oaths, because of perjury. Fugitives will be swiftly found dead or returned bound. Stolen property will be found

---

a. This lunary immediately follows the Somniale in the manuscript. Emendations are made silently, and variants are ignored except in a few instances where the meaning of the Latin text in this version is unclear. As with the Somniale above, I have aimed for a representative translation of a collective lunary using this manuscript version as a base rather than a strict translation of the version. To this end I have slightly depersonalized the text.

b. This composite or general lunary contains forecasts for deeds, births, illness, dreams, and bloodletting for each day of the month. The order in which they are presented slightly varies from each forecast day to the next.

c. The "L" in the word "Luna" for each day is rubricated.

with difficulty. The boy born on this day will barely survive past five years and will often die useless. A girl will die the worst death because she will be a sorceress and potionmaker. The sick will die. Dreams are portentous. It is not a good day for letting blood.

The sixth day of the month. Stolen items will be found. The sick will languish long but gently. The boy born on this day will be bold, great, and clever in many things. He will be fortunate if he survives past nineteen. He will have a sign on his right hand. The girl will be chaste, pleasing to men, and pleasant in all good things. Dreams are certain: do not reveal them. It is not a good day for letting blood.

The seventh day of the month. It is good for letting blood, administering medicine, or taming or castrating beasts. Fugitives will be found. Stolen property will be located. The boy born on this day will be prudent, strong, educated, learned, and love truth. He will have a sign on his face. The girl will be talkative and pleasing to men. She will have a sign on the right brow and left breast. The sick will be cured with medicine. Dreams are certain, though often delayed. It is a good day for letting blood until the evening.

The eighth day of the month. It is good for planting seed or transporting bees. Stolen property will not be found. The boy born on this day will be obscure, strong, and in great danger from water. He often will have a sign on his right side. The girl will have a sign on her right brow. She often will be great, and useful and modest. She will not be content with one man. Dreams will quickly come to fruition; give praise to God. The sick will die quickly. All day is good for letting blood.

The ninth day of the month. It is good for all undertakings and for creating a garden. Fugitives will be found promptly. The sick will recover without delay. The boy born on this day will be favored, clever, strong, and calm; he will be in danger until his seventh year. He will have a sign on his right hand. He will be wealthy if he lives to thirty years. The girl will be zealous, thankful, useful, chaste. She will have the same sign as the boy. Dreams will quickly come to fruition: conceal them. It is not a good day for letting blood.

The tenth day of the month. It is good for doing all things and for entering a new house or sending boys to school. The boy born on this day will be careless and industrious in his early life. The girl will be kind, a spinner of wool, and continue to do better throughout her life. The sick will either die quickly or arise promptly. Dreams are meaningless. It is a good day for letting blood from the sixth hour until the evening.

The eleventh day of the month. It is useful for soliciting favors, felling trees, or bringing in bees. The boy born on this day will be passionate, skillful, and spirited; he will do better later in life. The girl will have a sign on the face and on the breast. She will be wise, chaste in her later years, but not die a good death. The sick will either languish long or arise promptly. Dreams will come to pass within four days. It is not a good day for letting blood.

The twelfth day of the month. It is useful for all works, and for sowing, bringing home a wife, or departing on a journey. The boy born on this day will be good and amiable. He will have a sign on his right hand or his knee. The girl will have a sign on her breast. She will be lovely but not enjoy a long life. The sick will either languish long or die. Dreams are certain: be sure. All day is good for letting blood.

The thirteenth day of the month. It is dangerous for undertaking anything; do not argue with friends. Fugitives will be found promptly. The boy born on this day will be spirited. He will have a sign around the eyes. He will be bold, grasping, proud, and self-involved; he will not live long. The girl will have a sign on the neck or on the thigh. She will be proud, spirited, and careless of her body with many men; she will die quickly. The sick will either recover promptly or languish long. Dreams will come to pass within nine days. It is a good day for letting blood from the sixth hour until the evening.

The fourteenth day of the month. It is good for all good things, and for purchasing slaves, taking a wife, or sending boys to school. The boy born on this day will be a merchant. He will have a sign around the eyes or on the thigh. He will be bold, proud, and self-involved, he will not live long. The girl will have a sign on the neck. She will be proud and rash and desire many men; she will die quickly. The sick will either recover promptly or languish long. Dreams will come to pass in a short time. It is a perfect day for letting blood.

The fifteenth day of the month. It is not safe for testifying. The boy born on this day will be dangerous. He will have a sign on his right shoulder, kind, and hospitable. He will be susceptible to iron or while in water. The girl will be modest, industrious, chaste, and pleasing to men. The sick will either recover within three days or be in danger. Dreams will do no harm. It is not a good day for letting blood.

The sixteenth day of the month. It is not good for anything, except that thieves will be swiftly proclaimed dead. The boy born on this day will be hospitable, efficient, steadfast, and continue to do better in his later years. He will have a sign on his face. The girl will have a sign on the right side. She will be clever and loved by all. The sick, as above. Dreams will come to pass only after a long time and will be painful. It is a good day for letting blood.

The seventeenth day of the month. No day is more fortunate for all undertakings and for sowing or sending boys to school. The boy born will be dangerous, amicable, clever, wise, learned, bold, and honest. The girl will be learned with words, useful in all things, chaste, and wealthy. The sick will suffer for a long time. Dreams will come to pass promptly. It is not a good day for letting blood.

The eighteenth day of the month. It is useful for doing all things, and for bringing a spouse into the home or boys to the house or to school. The boy born on this day will be unconquerable. He will have a sign around the knee. He will be restless, proud, and talkative. The girl will have a sign like the boy. She will be chaste, industrious, and a servant; she will be better in her later years. The sick will arise promptly. Dreams will be fulfilled within ten days. All day is good for letting blood.

The nineteenth day of the month. It is useful for doing all things. The boy born on this day will be kind, clever, wise in many things, and continue to get better over time. He will have a sign on the brow. The girl will be as the boy; she will be unsatisfied with one man. The sick will recover promptly with medicine. Dreams will be revealed within five days. It is not a good day for letting blood from the first hour to the ninth hour.

The twentieth day of the month. It is useless for all things. The boy born on this day will be a farmer and clever. A girl likewise; she will spurn men. The sick will languish a long time and not arise quickly. Dreams are not to be believed. It is not a good day for letting blood.

The twenty-first day of the month. It is not useful for doing things, excepting gladiators, and something given will not be returned. Stolen property will be quickly found. The boy born on this day will be industrious, merciful, learned, and do well. The girl will have a sign on the neck or the right breast. She will be industrious, chaste, loved in all things, and content with one man. The sick will recover with difficulty or die quickly. Dreams are empty. It is a good day for letting blood until the third hour.

The twenty-second day of the month. It is useful for buying slaves. A boy born on this day will be a healer. Likewise for a girl; she will be poor. The sick will be comforted promptly. It is a useful day for letting blood. Dreams are certain, if held in one's memory.

The twenty-third day of the month. It is useful for doing all things. The boy born on this day will be popular. The girl will be spirited. The sick will either languish a long time or die promptly. Dreams are not portentous, or else held in the heart. It is a good day for letting blood until the sixth hour.

The twenty-fourth day of the month. It is useful for undertaking things. The boy born on this day will be combative. The girl will be strong. The sick will die promptly. Dreams mean nought. It is a good day for letting blood in the morning.

The twenty-fifth day of the month. It is useful for undertaking a hunt. The boy born on this day will be eager. The girl will be eager and a spinner of wool. The sick will recover within three days. Dreams will come to pass within nine days. It is a good day for letting blood from the sixth hour until the ninth hour.

The twenty-sixth day of the month. The boy born on this day will be mindful. The girl will be quick. The sick will die promptly. Dreams, as above. It is a good day for letting blood from the third hour until the ninth hour.

The twenty-seventh day of the month. The boy born on this day will be prudent. The girl will be honest and wise. A sick person will live. Dreams are portentous but will do no harm. All day is good for letting blood.

The twenty-eighth day of the month. The boy born on this day will be industrious and credulous in all things. The girl will be obedient and faithful. The sick will recover promptly. Dreams, as above. It is a good day for letting blood from the ninth hour until the evening.

The twenty-ninth day of the month. The boy born on this day will be credulous and eminent. The girl will be wise and wealthy. Dreams are good and certain. It is a good day for letting blood.

The thirtieth day of the month. The boy born on this day will be most fortunate and kind. The girl will be fortunate and gentle. The sick will suffer but survive. Dreams will come to pass within three days—meanwhile, beware. It is not a good day for letting blood.

Here end the dreams of Daniel the prophet.

The Syriac Apocalypse of Daniel
A new translation and introduction

by Matthias Henze

The Syriac Apocalypse of Daniel, or "The revelation that was revealed to Daniel in the land of Persia and Elam," as the text is referred to in the superscript of the manuscript, is a little-known Syrian Christian pseudepigraphon. It embellishes the biblical story of Daniel, who in the opening scenes serves at the court of several foreign monarchs. The main part of the work is devoted to a long vision of Daniel about the end of time that culminates in the New Jerusalem. Biblical Daniel has had a remarkable reception history in Judaism and Christianity.[1] Our text joins the ranks of the many postbiblical apocalypses attributed to the biblical seer. Since its original publication a little over two decades ago, the Syriac Apocalypse of Daniel has received only sparse attention. And yet, it is a remarkable composition, not only for what it tells us about early Syriac Christianity but also because of its intriguing exegetical tropes and numerous apocalyptic motifs.

Contents and Composition

Like biblical Daniel, which it closely follows, the Syriac Apocalypse of Daniel consists of two parts, a narrative frame in chapters 1–13, in which the points of connection with the biblical book are especially obvious, and an eschatological vision in chapters 14–40, in which Daniel sees the end of time unfolding, beginning with the revolt of the peoples of the north and leading up to the final judgment of all peoples and the messianic banquet on Mount Zion.

The work begins with a superscript, "By the power of God we record the revelation that was revealed to the prophet Daniel in the land of Persia and Elam," and it concludes with a postscript that mimics the language of the superscript, "Here ends the awesome revelation that was revealed to the prophet Daniel in the land of Elam and in Persia." There are no obvious breaks or lacunae in the text, so that we can assume with some degree of confidence that the work is preserved intact.

The Syriac Apocalypse of Daniel is a carefully structured composition. At the beginning Daniel introduces himself in the first-person singular as the narrator of the book. He first tells of his adventures at the court of Nebuchadnezzar. When the Babylonian king is defeated by the Assyrian King Sennacherib (*sic*), Daniel flees to King Cyrus and convinces the Persian monarch to conquer Babylon. Cyrus follows Daniel's advice, retrieves the temple implements that Nebuchadnezzar had brought from Jerusalem, and

---

1. Lorenzo DiTommaso, *The Book of Daniel and the Apocryphal Daniel Literature*, SVTP 20 (Leiden: Brill, 2005), 87–230; also Mariano Delgado, Klaus Koch, and Edgar Marsch, eds., *Europa, Tausendjähriges Reich und Neue Welt: Zwei Jahrtausende Geschichte und Utopie in der Rezeption des Danielbuches* (Fribourg: Universitätsverlag; Stuttgart: Kohlhammer, 2003).

The Syriac Apocalypse of Daniel

deposits them, with the exception of Solomon's throne, at "Mount Silai" in Elam. Cyrus is then assassinated by a magus named Gemath, until Gemath himself is killed and his kingdom overthrown by King Darius. It is at Darius's court that Daniel has his long vision that occupies the latter portion of the text.

The vision begins in chapter 14 with a revolt of the people of the north. Daniel goes through and describes in some detail the events of the end time. The final woes that befall the world lead to the arrival of a grotesque warrior figure who is born of the tribe of Levi. This figure is followed by the false messiah, possibly an antichrist figure (assuming that the warrior and the false messiah are two distinct figures). After a period of terror, the false messiah will be defeated by the angel of peace. God appears on Mount Zion, followed by the arrival of the true Messiah, the resurrection of the dead, the pilgrimage of all peoples to Jerusalem, the final judgment, when all people appear before the Messiah who is enthroned in the new Jerusalem, and the final Passover banquet on Mount Zion.

The composition of the work can be outlined as follows:

PART 1: THE NARRATIVE FRAME
          Superscript
Chapter 1   Daniel introduces himself: he has recorded what he saw during the time of Darius the Mede, King of Persia, and Alpachtan, King of Babylon
Chapters 2–4   Daniel at the court of King Nebuchadnezzar
Chapter 5   Sennacherib (*sic*) defeats the Babylonians; Daniel flees to King Cyrus and urges him to conquer Babylon
Chapters 6–8   Cyrus takes Babylon and deposits the temple vessels at Mount Silai
Chapter 9   Gemath the magus kills Cyrus and reigns for six months
Chapters 10–12   Daniel at the court of King Darius, son of BGDT, king of Persia
Chapter 13   Daniel's visions (transitional chapter from narrative frame to vision)

PART 2: DANIEL'S VISION
Chapter 14   The revolt of the peoples of the north marks the beginning of several calamities, including the breakdown of the natural and social orders
Chapter 15   The first wave of calamities and natural disasters is followed by an interim period of superficial peace
Chapters 16–18   More end time calamities and natural disasters
Chapters 19–20   These lead directly into the last days
Chapter 21   The birth of a monstrous warrior of the tribe of Levi
Chapters 22–24   The advent of "the crooked serpent, the false messiah," the deceiver: his birth, physiognomy, and deeds; he is destroyed by the pacifying angel
Chapter 25   An interim period of fear and silence
Chapters 26–29   Theophany on Mount Zion
Chapters 30–32   The advent of the Messiah
Chapter 33   The new Jerusalem is built
Chapters 34–36   Three trumpet calls announce the resurrection of the dead
Chapter 37   The pilgrimage of all nations to Mount Zion
Chapter 38   The Messiah sits on the throne in the new Jerusalem: the final judgment
Chapter 39   The just and righteous enter Jerusalem
Chapter 40   The Passover banquet on Mount Zion
          Postscript

One of the more intriguing aspects of this text is the many exegetical tropes and apocalyptic motifs that are here woven together. For example, after King Cyrus deposits the Jerusalem temple treasure at Mount Silai, we read of a certain magus called GMT, who assassinates the Persian king and seizes the throne for half a year, before he himself is assassinated by his nobles. This magus is most likely Gemath, or possibly Gaumata, of whom we read in the Bisitun inscription (GWM[T] . . . MGWSH') and who is also mentioned as Cometes in Justin's epitome of Gnaeus Pompeius Trogus's lost *Universal History*.[2] The vision portion of the apocalypse includes an intriguing description of the false messiah. His arrival is preceded by the brief appearance of a warrior figure of the tribe of Levi (ch. 21).[3] On his skin he will have images of several weapons of war, and between his eyes he has a horn whose tip is broken off and from which a snake appears. The false messiah appears and declares of himself, "I am the Messiah!" (ch. 22). Much attention is given to his physiognomy. He comes with armies of supporters, and the gates of the north are opened, until he is defeated by the pacifying angel and his band of other angels.

Manuscripts and Editions

The Syriac Apocalypse of Daniel survives in two manuscripts. The first, and only complete manuscript is Harvard MS Syr 4. The apocalypse appears toward the end on fols. 117 recto–122 verso. The manuscript is a collection of ascetical writings. Almost two-thirds of the manuscript is devoted to the works of John of Dalyatha. It also includes excerpts from John bar Penkaye, Evagrius Penticus, Basil the Great, and others.[4] In his edition of the letters of John of Dalyatha, Robert Beulay observes that one of the copyists is named in the margin of the Harvard manuscript, Rabban Malke of Beth Sbirino, who died in 1490.[5] This would imply that the manuscript dates from the fifteenth century. Our English translation is based on the Harvard manuscript. More recently, a second manuscript has come to light, CFMM 281, from the Hill Museum and Manuscript Library (HMML) at Saint John's University in Collegeville, MN. This Syriac manuscript comes from the Deir al-Zafaran monastery and dates to the year 1475 CE.[6] The Syriac Apocalypse of Daniel is the last of four texts preserved

---

2. Sebastian Brock, "Two Editions of a New Syriac Apocalypse of Daniel," *JAC* 48–49 (2005):7. See also the story of the false Smerdis in Herodotus, *Hist.* 3.61–79. For the Bisitun inscription, see Jack Martin Balcer, *Herodotus and Bisitun: Problems in Ancient Persian Historiography*, Historia 49 (Stuttgart: Steiner, 1987), 49–69.

3. Menachem Ben-Sasson, "'The Vision of Daniel' from the St. Petersburg Genizah," *HTR* 115 (2022): 331–62, doi:10.1017/S0017816022000220.

4. For a description of the manuscript, see Alexander Golitzin, "A Monastic Setting for the *Syriac Apocalypse of Daniel*," in *To Train His Soul in Books: Syriac Asceticism in Early Christianity*, ed. R. Darling Young and M. J. Blanchard, CUA Studies in Early Christianity 4 (Washington, DC: Catholic University of America Press, 2011), 66, doi:10.2307/j.ctt284w2x.8. Golitzin goes on to argue that the Syriac Apocalypse of Daniel stems from a monastic setting and that it was written by a monk "to remind his fellow monks of the meaning of their vows" (68). Alison Salvesen in her review may be correct in her response that a monastic connection with the apocalypse, if it existed at all, is most likely "in the final stages of its redaction or in its reception." See Salvesen, review of *To Train His Soul in Books: Syriac Asceticism in Early Christianity*, ed. R. Darling Young and M. J. Blanchard, *Church History* 82, no. 2 (2013): 421, doi:10.1017/S0009640713000188.

5. John of Dalyatha, *La collection des lettres de Jean de Dalyatha: Édition critique du texte syriaque*, ed. and trans. Robert Beulay, PO 39.3 (Turnhout: Brepols, 1978), 16; Golitzin, "Monastic Setting," 66 n. 2.

6. Yuhanna Dolabani, *Catalogue of Syriac Manuscripts in Za'faran Monastery*, ed. Gregorios Ibrahim,

in the manuscript (201 recto–218 verso). It is preceded by a West Syriac life of Mary; a homily on Mary and Joseph by Ephrem of Nisibis; and a homily on the assumption of Mary by Timotheos, Metropolitan of Gargar. The Syriac text of the HMML manuscript is virtually identical with the text of the Harvard manuscript, but it is incomplete. The manuscript only contains chapters 1–14 and 15–23 (following Henze's chapter division), with one page missing in between.

The hitherto unknown Syriac Apocalypse of Daniel has been edited twice. The first edition is by Miron Slabczyk, *Apokalipso de Danielo Profeto en la Lando Persio kaj Elamo*.[7] A short introduction in Esperanto is followed by the Syriac text and translation, again in Esperanto, on facing pages. There is a short index of names at the end. The second edition, which appeared only a year later, is by Matthias Henze, *The Syriac Apocalypse of Daniel*.[8] In the introduction Henze lists other apocalypses attributed to Daniel, goes over the main introductory matters, and offers a brief literary analysis of the text. This is followed by the Syriac text, an annotated English translation, a photographic reproduction of the manuscript, and several indices. The manuscript does not divide the text into verses and chapters. Slabczyk introduces a division of the entire text into twenty-seven chapters, whereas Henze renumbers the textual units of the apocalypse and divides the entire text into forty chapters.[9]

Genre

The superscript in the manuscript calls the text a "revelation," or "apocalypse" (Syr. *gelyana*') that was "revealed" to Daniel.[10] The text fits well the modern understanding of the apocalypse as a distinct literary genre as defined by John J. Collins: "'Apocalypse' is a genre of revelatory literature with a narrative framework, in which a revelation is mediated by an otherworldly being to a human recipient, disclosing a transcendent reality which is both temporal, insofar as it envisages eschatological salvation, and spatial, insofar as it involves another, supernatural world."[11] As already noted, the Syriac Apocalypse of Daniel consists of two parts, a narrative framework and a detailed, apocalyptic vision that is concerned with the orderly unfolding of the final installment of history. Following biblical Daniel, the human recipient of the apocalyptic teachings is Daniel, and what he learns certainly concerns a "transcendent reality," in both the temporal and the spatial sense. Angels are mentioned, but there is no interpreting angel who accompanies Daniel and explains to him what he sees. Daniel disappears in the vision part of the book, and he is not mentioned again until the postscript. There is also no heavenly ascent. The Syriac Apocalypse is thus a historical apocalypse that shows little interest in cosmology and the heavenly realm.

Dar Mardin: Christian Arabic and Syriac Studies from the Middle East 27 (Piscataway, NJ: Gorgias, 2009), 83–84, doi:10.31826/9781463218546.

7. Slabczyk, *Apokalipso de Danielo Profeto Profeto en la Lando Persio kaj Elamo: Sirian tekston, Esperantan tradukon kaj komentarion prepares* (Vienna: Arkado eldonejo, 2000).

8. Henze, *The Syriac Apocalypse of Daniel: Introduction, Text, and Commentary*, STAC 11 (Tübingen: Mohr Siebeck, 2001).

9. Marcus Vinícius Ramos has produced a Portuguese translation of the text. See Ramos, "The Book and the Manuscript: Text, Translation and Commentary of the Syriac Apocalypse of Daniel" (PhD diss., University of Brasília, 2014).

10. Alexander Kulik, "Genre without a Name: Was There a Hebrew Term for 'Apocalypse'?," *JSJ* 40 (2009): 540–50.

11. Collins, *Apocalypse: The Morphology of a Genre*, SemeiaSt 14 (Missoula, MT: Scholars Press, 1979), 9.

Date and Provenance

There is no external evidence relating to the date or place of composition of the Syriac Apocalypse of Daniel. Both have to be determined based on internal evidence only, which proves to be a challenge. In many apocalypses from late antiquity, the transition from narrative frame to vision provides some clues about the text's date of composition, as it is here that the authors often insert allusions to contemporary events before the text moves on to actual prophecies of what is expected to come. In the Syriac Apocalypse of Daniel this moment is reached in chapters 13–14. But unfortunately there are no historical allusions, veiled or direct, here or elsewhere in the text, to any historical data. The apocalypse is atypical in that it lacks any clear reference to recognizable historical events, individuals, or places.

Instead of providing a historical allusion, the apocalyptic portion of the text begins with the revolt of the people of the north (ch. 14). With the arrival of the false messiah and his entourage a few chapters later, the gates of the north are opened and a multitude of armies, among them the Agogites and Magogites, are released to terrorize the world (ch. 22). The motif of the gates of the north is well known from other Syriac writings, chief among them the Syriac Alexander Legend, which was composed in 629–630 CE in northern Mesopotamia and that was a source for other Syriac apocalypses.[12] Assuming that our author also used the Alexander Legend, the *terminus a quo* for the composition of our text would be the early seventh century CE. The most important and influential Christian apocalypse in Late Antiquity is Pseudo-Methodius, written in 690–691 CE. The influence of Pseudo-Methodius on subsequent Syriac apocalypses can hardly be overestimated. And yet, the Syriac Apocalypse of Daniel shows no signs of familiarity with it, and none of the major motifs and none of Pseudo-Methodius's distinct vocabulary reoccurs in our text.[13] The easiest explanation is to assume that the author of the Syriac Apocalypse did not know Pseudo-Methodius, presumably because Pseudo-Methodius had not yet been composed. If this is correct, then this would mean that the *terminus ante quem* for the composition of our text would be the late seventh century CE. The Syriac Apocalypse of Daniel would then have been composed in the middle of the seventh century CE.

Even less can be said about the provenance of the text. An East Syrian origin seems unlikely. Instead, a West Syrian, possibly Melkite milieu seems more plausible.[14] But this has to remain conjectural.

Original Language

There are good reasons to assume that, unlike other Syriac apocalypses that were translated from Greek into Syriac, the Syriac Apocalypse of Daniel was originally written in Syriac.[15] The Syriac does not show any obvious signs that the text was translated from Greek, nor are there any Greek calques. The apocalypse draws heavily on the Bible

---

12. Henze, *Syriac Apocalypse*, 12–13.
13. Henze, *Syriac Apocalypse*, 14–15.
14. Henze, *Syriac Apocalypse*, 16–17; Brock, "Two Editions," 17. Slabczyk does not assign any date of composition but suggests that the author was a Byzantine Greek, from one of the Greek islands (*Apokalipso de Danielo Profeto*, 10). This hypothesis regarding the origin of our text is based on the recurring references to the seas and the inhabitants of the islands.
15. Argued by Henze, *Syriac Apocalypse*, 8–9; followed by Golitzin, "A Monastic Setting," 67; and Brock, "Two Editions," 9.

through paraphrase, allusions, and a few quotations. The biblical text that is used is that of the Peshitta, the Syriac translation of the Bible, not the Septuagint. And similarly, personal names, such as the name of the Assyrian king Asarhaddon in chapter 5, follow the spelling in the Peshitta, not that of the Septuagint.

Literary Contexts

The Syriac Apocalypse of Daniel has multiple literary contexts. One is that of the Hebrew Bible. The language of the apocalypse closely imitates that of the Bible. The author writes in the biblical idiom. The biblical references in the margins of this translation are only beginning to map the intricate web of biblical paraphrases and allusions, and more could be added. Since the Syriac Apocalypse of Daniel presents itself as a sequel to biblical Daniel, this attempt to stay close in language, expression, and motifs to the Bible does not surprise.

A second context is that of early Jewish literature, and specifically of the Jewish apocalyptic literature of the Second Temple period. There are numerous points of connection between our text and significantly earlier Jewish apocalypses such as 1 Enoch, 4 Ezra, and 2 Baruch, for example, regarding the corruptible nature of this world, the preexistence of the Messiah, and the resurrection of the dead. Particularly striking are similar phrases with 4 Ezra and 2 Baruch, works that are also transmitted in Syriac.[16] The similarities between these early Jewish works and our apocalypse raise a number of intriguing methodological issues. One concerns our modern translations. In its received form, the Syriac Apocalypse of Daniel is clearly a Christian work. In the messianic passage in chapter 31, for example, we read that the Messiah is identified as Jesus. "Then will be revealed the splendor of Jesus." In the next chapter, all of creation rejoices before the Messiah: "the plains and all that is in them will rejoice before the Messiah, Jesus our Lord" (chapter 32). Apart from the fact that the Messiah is identified explicitly as Jesus, he is also referred to in the Syriac as *malka meshiha*, which could be rendered "Christ the King" or, more literally, "the King Messiah." Sebastian Brock comments, "While it is true that this phrase of Jewish origin is already taken over by Aphrahat and is quite often found in Syriac liturgical texts, the Christianizing rendering ["Christ the King"] here distances the reader from the possibility that the terminology might be deliberately used here to counteract Jewish messianic speculation that seems to have been around in the early seventh century."[17] Brock's comment raises an important point, namely how to translate a text that is rooted in the Jewish tradition and uses Jewish modes of expression but that is clearly a Christian text. The translation below is mindful of Brock's plea and is intended to emphasize the Jewish roots of the language, whenever appropriate.

A third context, finally, is that of the Syriac literature of the sixth and seventh centuries CE. Some relevant parallels are noted in the margins of the translation, but more systematic work needs to be done.

---

16. Notice the similar conclusion reached by Florentino García Martínez, who comments on "The Little Daniel," a related Daniel apocryphon (see discussion below), and its similarities with the early works associated with Daniel, including the Aramaic Pseudo-Daniel texts from Qumran: "The Jewish work (or works) on which ["The Little Daniel"] is based, perfectly concur with the apocalyptic writings of the first centuries." See García Martínez, *Qumran and Apocalyptic: Studies on the Aramaic Texts from Qumran*, STDJ 9 (Leiden: Brill, 1992), 160. Considerably less convincing is DiTommaso, who seeks to minimize the similarities between the Syriac Apocalypse of Daniel and 4 Ezra (*Book of Daniel*, 119–21).

17. Brock, "Two Editions," 16.

While the Syriac Apocalypse of Daniel is loosely connected to a host of texts of different times and genres, the only sustained literary link is with another Syriac apocalyptic text also attributed to Daniel. The text in question bears the title "Again, [the book of] the small Daniel on our Lord and on the end." It survives in a single manuscript of the twelfth century from the British Library, Add. 18,715, and was first edited and translated by Hans Schmold in a 1972 dissertation at the University of Hamburg.[18] The text, The Young Daniel, which is shorter than the Syriac Apocalypse of Daniel, overlaps significantly with the apocalypse. In his edition of the apocalypse, Henze notices and comments on the close parallels and concludes that the two Daniel apocrypha "are clearly related to each other." He concludes: "The two texts preserve variant accounts of the same apocalypse."[19] In his extensive study of the apocryphal Daniel literature, Lorenzo DiTommaso disputes that there is any connection between the two Syriac texts, let alone that they go back to a common *Urtext*, as Henze suggests. DiTommaso writes: "even a cursory survey of the contents of the vision portions of both texts demonstrates that they are different texts. Given these points and the problems with Henze's argument, there is simply nothing that would permit his bold conclusion that 'the two texts preserve variant accounts of the same apocalypse.' My feeling is that these two Syriac Daniel apocrypha are fundamentally unrelated and that any points of contact are a result of shared traditions or an independent dependence on sources."[20]

DiTommaso's assertion that we are dealing with two independent texts that are unrelated is curious, to say the least, since a synoptic reading of the Syriac makes plain the extensive verbatim agreements between them. The point is made well by Brock, who observes that there is "a very close correspondence" between the two texts.[21] In his review article, Brock translates some sections of the two works in parallel columns and puts the verbal agreement in italics.[22] Then, in a more recent study, Brock translates all of The Young Daniel into English and again comments on the extensive parallels with the Syriac Apocalypse of Daniel.[23] Having dismissed, perhaps a bit too easily, the possibility that one text is dependent on the other, Brock concludes that "it is evident that both texts must go back to a common source." He then goes on to suggest, albeit tentatively, that the common source also dates from the seventh century, without describing it any further.[24] There is no doubt that Brock is much closer to the mark than DiTommaso. The extensive parallels between the two Daniel apocryphas will prove to be of central importance for any further work on the Syriac Apocalypse of Daniel.

---

18. Schmold, "Die Schrift 'Vom jungen Daniel' und 'Daniels letzte Vision': Herausgabe und Interpretation zweier apokalyptischer Texte" (PhD diss., University of Hamburg, 1972). Claudio Balzaretti published an Italian translation and emphasized the common passages with the Syriac Apocalypse of Daniel. See Balzaretti, "L'Apocalisse del giovane Daniel (Syr Dan)," *Rivista di storia e letteratura religiosa* 42 (2006): 109–29.

19. Henze, *Syriac Apocalypse*, 11.

20. DiTommaso, *Book of Daniel*, 121–23.

21. Brock, "Two Editions," 9.

22. Brock, "Two Editions," 10–15.

23. Sebastian Brock, "'Young Daniel': A Little Known Syriac Apocalyptic Text; Introduction and Translation," in *Revealed Wisdom: Studies in Apocalyptic in Honour of Christopher Rowland*, ed. John Ashton, AGJU 88 (Leiden: Brill, 2014), doi:10.1163/9789004272040_019, with further bibliography.

24. Brock, "Young Daniel," 269.

Bibliography

Balcer, Jack Martin. *Herodotus and Bisitun: Problems in Ancient Persian Historiography*. Historia 49. Stuttgart: Steiner, 1987.

Balzaretti, Claudio. "L'Apocalisse del giovane Daniel (Syr Dan)." *Rivista di storia e letteratura religiosa* 42 (2006): 109–29.

Ben-Sasson, Menachem. "An Interreligious 'Encounter' in Four Visions of Daniel." Pages 614–44 in *Religious and Intellectual Diversity in the Islamicate World and Beyond. Volume II. Essays in Honor of Sarah Stroumsa*. Edited by Omer Michaelis and Sabine Schmidtke. Leiden: Brill, 2024.

———. "'The Vision of Daniel' from the St. Petersburg Genizah." *HTR* 115 (2022): 331–62. doi:10.1017/S0017816022000220.

Berger, Klaus. *Die griechische Daniel-Diegese: Eine altkirchliche Apokalypse; Text, Übersetzung und Kommentar*. StPB 27. Leiden: Brill, 1976.

Brock, Sebastian. "The Small/Young Daniel Re-Edited." Pages 250–84 in *The Embroidered Bible: Studies in Biblical Apocrypha and Pseudepigrapha in Honour of Michael E. Stone*. Edited by Lorenzo DiTommaso, Matthias Henze, and William Adler. SVTP 26. Leiden: Brill, 2018. doi:10.1163/9789004357211_017.

———. "Two Editions of a New Syriac Apocalypse of Daniel." *JAC* 48–49 (2005): 7–18.

———. "'The Young Daniel': A Little Known Syriac Apocalyptic Text: Introduction and Translation." Pages 267–85 in *Revealed Wisdom: Studies in Apocalyptic in Honour of Christopher Rowland*. Edited by John Ashton. AGJU 88. Leiden: Brill, 2014. doi:10.1163/9789004272040_019.

Collins, John J., ed. *Apocalypse: The Morphology of a Genre*. SemeiaSt 14. Missoula, MT: Scholars Press, 1979.

Delgado, Mariano, Klaus Koch, and Edgar Marsch, eds. *Europa, Tausendjähriges Reich und Neue Welt: Zwei Jahrtausende Geschichte und Utopie in der Rezeption des Danielbuches*. Fribourg: Universitätsverlag; Stuttgart: Kohlhammer, 2003.

DiTommaso, Lorenzo. *The Book of Daniel and the Apocryphal Daniel Literature*. SVTP 20. Leiden: Brill, 2005.

García Martínez, Florentino. *Qumran and Apocalyptic: Studies on the Aramaic Texts from Qumran*. STDJ 9. Leiden: Brill, 1992.

Golitzin, Alexander. "A Monastic Setting for the *Syriac Apocalypse of Daniel*." Pages 66–98 in *To Train His Soul in Books: Syriac Asceticism in Early Christianity*. Edited by R. Darling Young and M. J. Blanchard. CUA Studies in Early Christianity 4. Washington, DC: Catholic University of America Press, 2011. doi:10.2307/j.ctt284w2x.8.

Henze, Matthias. "Seeing the End: The Vocabulary of the End Time in the *Syriac Apocalypse of Daniel*." Pages 554–68 in *The Embroidered Bible: Studies in Biblical Apocrypha and Pseudepigrapha in Honour of Michael E. Stone*. Edited by Lorenzo DiTommaso, Matthias Henze, and William Adler. SVTP 26. Leiden: Brill, 2018. doi:10.1163/9789004357211_029.

———. *The Syriac Apocalypse of Daniel: Introduction, Text, and Commentary*. STAC 11. Tübingen: Mohr Siebeck, 2001.

———. *Syrische Danielapokalypse*. JSHRZ 1.4. Gütersloh: Gütersloher Verlagshaus, 2006.

Kulik, Alexander. "Genre without a Name: Was There a Hebrew Term for 'Apocalypse'?" *JSJ* 40 (2009): 540–50.

Ramos, Marcus Vinícius. "The Book and the Manuscript: Text, Translation and Commentary of the Syriac Apocalypse of Daniel." PhD diss., University of Brasília, 2014.

Salvesen, Alison. Review of *To Train His Soul In Books: Syriac Asceticism in Early Christian-*

ity, ed. R. Darling Young and M. J. Blanchard. *Church History* 82, no. 2 (2013): 420–22. doi:10.1017/S0009640713000188.

Schmold, Hans. "Die Schrift 'Vom jungen Daniel' und 'Daniels letzte Vision': Herausgabe und Interpretation zweier apokalyptischer Texte." PhD diss., University of Hamburg, 1972.

Silva José, Sara Daiane da. "O Anticristo do *Apocalipse Grego* e do *Apocalipse Siríaco de Daniel*." Pages 248–54 in *La Antigüedad Grecolatina en Dabate*. Edited by Julián Macías. Buenos Aires: Rhesis, 2014.

Slabczyk, Miron. *Apokalipso de Danielo Profeto en la Lando Persio kaj Elamo: Sirian tekston, Esperantan tradukon kaj komentarion prepares*. Vienna: Arkado eldonejo, 2000.

Ubierna, Pablo. "Syriac Apocalyptic and the Body Politic: From Individual Salvation to the Fate of the State; Notes on Seventh Century Texts." *Imago Temporis. Medium Aevum* 6 (2012): 141–64.

The Syriac Apocalypse of Daniel

2 Bar. 1:1; 3 Bar. 1:1
Matt 24:15; 4Q174 (4QFlor) 1–3 ii 3–4; Josephus, *A. J.* 10.186–281; Liv. Pro. 4

By the power of God we record the revelation that was revealed to the prophet Daniel in the land of Persia and Elam.

Daniel Introduces Himself

Dan 6:1; 9:1; 11:1

4Q174 1–3 ii; Matt 24:15

Pesher Dan 9:26
Jer 25:9; 27:6; 28:14; 43:10

1 In the kingdom of Darius the Mede who ruled Persia, and in the kingdom of Alpahtan,[a] king of Babylon, I have seen these visions, I, the prophet Daniel. These prophecies were revealed to me after the visions that I had seen (previously), as well as the prophecy that was revealed to me by the Holy Spirit in the years of Nebuchadnezzar, king of Babylon, who had come up against the land of Judah and the holy city Jerusalem, as he had been commanded by God, to besiege it and to bring distress upon it.

Daniel at the Court of King Nebuchadnezzar

2 Kgs 25:1
Dan 1:2; 5:2; 2 Kgs 25:14; Ezra 1:7–11; 5:14; 6:5; Jer 27:16–19, 21; 28:3, 6; 52:18; Bar 1:8; 1 Macc 4:49–51; Josephus, *A. J.* 11.14; Treatise of the Vessels
1 Kgs 7:50; 2 Kgs 25:15–17; 1 Chr 28:17; Jer 52:19; Neh 7:70
Exod 25:10–16; 30:27; 38:1–7; 40:6, 29; Lev 4:7; 1 Kgs 7:48
Exod 25:31–37; 30:27; 31:8; Lev 24:4; Num 3:31; 8:1–4; 1 Kgs 7:49; 1 Chr 28:15; Zech 4:2; Sir 26:17; 1 Macc 1:21; 4 Ezra 10:22; Heb 9:2
Exod 26:30–33, 37; 36:36; 1 Chr 18:8; Sir 26:18
Exod 28:6–14; 39:4–5
Exod 28:21; 39:14
Exod 28:31–43; 39:1–31;
Exod 28:17–21; Ezek 28:13; Sir 45:6; 2 Bar. 6:7

2 King Nebuchadnezzar came up against the land of Judah and laid siege[b] to it, and God delivered it into his hands. He plundered, destroyed, and captured it, and brought it into captivity. And he took the treasure that was in the temple of God, and all the service implements of the sanctuary, the gold and silver, cups and bowls, the beautiful basins[c], forks and pitchers, the table of the altar, the seven-branched lampstand, the golden inner pillars of the tabernacle, and that great ephod that the high priest used to wear, which had twelve stones on its shoulders with the names of the sons of Jacob inscribed on them, and the vestments, the precious stones, sapphires[d] and crystals that were in the sanctuary from the years of King David and Solomon, his son after him, and the entire treasure

a. The personal name of the otherwise unknown Babylonian king is fully vocalized in the manuscript; perhaps from the Aramaic word for "governor," Ezra 5:3, 6; 6:6; Dan 3:2, 3; 6:8 [Evv 6:7].
b. The Syriac word is difficult to read; cf. 2 Kgs 25:1.
c. The word *mizraq* is Hebrew (e.g., Exod 27:3; 38:3; Zech 14:20). It is not attested in Syriac but in Jewish Aramaic; cf. Brock, "Two Editions," 16–17.
d. The Syriac has the singular.

of King Solomon and of all the kings who were after him in Jerusalem, as well as the great golden throne on which King Solomon used to sit. King Nebuchadnezzar took away the booty and spoil of Jerusalem, the women and children, cattle and beasts, garments and fine ornaments along with the silver and gold. He took away his glorious implements with him and brought them to the land of Babylon.

1 Kgs 10:18–20; 2 Chr 9:17–19

Matt 9:16

2 Kgs 25:13–17; Treatise of the Vessels

3 We were in captivity and exile, I, Daniel, and all the young men of my age, Judean men. We were chosen to serve in the king's palace and to stand in the king's palace according to rank. The great God of my fathers gave me a spirit of wisdom, a spirit of knowledge, and a spirit of understanding. I excelled in every kind of wisdom more than all those of my age who were with me in the land of Babylon and of the Chaldeans, because I kept the commandments of my God, and also because I did not relax in (keeping) his laws and judgments. I revealed and explained what would happen in the land of Babylon and concerning everything that had happened to the former kings who were in the land of Babylon in those days.

Dan 1:10; Gal 1:14

Jdt 9:12; T. Dan 1:9; T. Jos. 1:4; 2:2; 6:6–7; T. Jud. 19:3; T. Sim. 2:8; 4 Macc 12:17

Dan 1:17; 2:21; 4:5–6 [Evv 4:8–9]; 5:11; Isa 11:2; Wis 7:7; Sir 39:6; 4 Ezra 5:22

Dan 2:48; 4:6

4 Ezra 7:89; 2 Bar. 44:14; 46:5

4 I was standing at the gate of the king of Babylon, in the royal house of the Chaldeans. None of the wise men and the Chaldeans and those who conceal judgment[a] prevailed over me in the land of Babylon. For I revealed and explained (the vision) concerning the statue whose head was gold and whose feet were iron, and concerning the stone that shattered it, and concerning (the vision of) the tree that was uprooted and its roots cut off, and concerning (the vision of) the palm of a hand that wrote on the wall of the royal palace. All the prophecies and visions were revealed to me while my accusers, the Chaldeans, threw me into the lions' den. Yet the God of my fathers sent an angel and shut the lions' mouth, and they did not destroy me, but they cut down my enemies and their children. When Nebuchadnezzar went insane and Belteshazzar his son[b] ruled after him and took over the Chaldean kingdom, he invited his nobles, his lords, his wives, and his concubines to recline,[c] and he brought in the golden and silver service implements, the cups and bowls[d] of the house of the Lord in Jerusalem, which Nebuchadnezzar, king of Babylon, had brought from the house of God. The king of Babylon drank wine from them, he and

Dan 2:31–34

Dan 4:11–12 [Evv 4:14–15]

Dan 5:5

Dan 6:23–25

Dan 4

Dan 5:2–4

a. The Syriac has the singular; the obscure phrase may be a pun on the Aramaic for "Chaldeans" (Dan 2:5, 10; 3:3; 4:4; 5:7).

b. Following the Peshitta, our text consistently confuses the names Belteshazzar, the name given to Daniel (Dan 1:7; 2:26; 4:8–9; 10:1) and Belshazzar, who, according to Daniel, is the son of Nebuchadnezzar (Dan 5:12).

c. Lit. "he made them recline at table" (cf. Mark 6:39).

d. Emended, following ch. 2, and Exod 25:33–34; 37:19.

The Syriac Apocalypse of Daniel

his wives and his concubines, and blasphemed the living God. Then the palm of the hand of anger appeared and wrote on the wall what would befall the king. And the living God became angry with him.

Sennacherib Defeats the Babylonians

5 King Sennacherib came up from Assyria, from the city of Nineveh, and took possession of the entire land that was King Belteshazzar's, and he ruled in it. Then his son Esarhaddon ruled over Assyria[a] and Nineveh after him.

At that time the Babylonian and the Chaldean men drew near and slandered me before Sennacherib, king of Assyria. He sought to carry me off and kill me. Then it was revealed to me by God the Most High that it was Satan who had incited him against me. And so I withdrew to Persia[b] to the royal palace of King Cyrus. While I was there among the Persians, God gave me honor and friendship with King Cyrus. I was brought before him and told King Cyrus about everything that Nebuchadnezzar, king of Babylon, had done in the land of Judah and among the citizens of Jerusalem, and about the spoil and booty that he had brought with him from there, and about the golden cups and the beautiful[c] implements of the temple of the Lord that Nebuchadnezzar, king of Babylon, had brought from the land of Judah, and about the golden throne on which King Solomon used to sit, and about the precious stones and the sapphires,[d] and about the beautiful jewels that used to be kept in the treasury of King Solomon, which he had taken as spoil and carried to Babylon.

I urged King Cyrus the Persian that he should march against the land of Babylon, fight against it and capture it, and that he should seize the treasures and implements of the sanctuary that King Nebuchadnezzar had brought to Babylon and that had remained there.

Cyrus takes Babylon and Deposits the Temple Vessels at Mount Silai

6 The great King Cyrus arose with an army of horsemen and with many chariots of the Persians and Elamites. They went and besieged Babylon. They breached its walls and demolished its towers. They captured it and entered into it and destroyed it.

---

a. Lit. "the place of Assyria."
b. Lit. "the place of the Persians."
c. The word is difficult to read in the MS.; cf. Dan 1:13.
d. The Syriac has the singular, "and about the precious stone and the sapphire."

King Sennacherib fled from (the city) and went to his former land, to Assyria and Nineveh. The great King Cyrus entered Babylon and walked around in it and in the entire treasury of the king of Babylon. He plundered Babylon and led it into captivity, and he took the golden and silver implements and all the service implements that King Nebuchadnezzar had brought from the kings of Judah, and the entire treasure and the booty of the kings of Babylon that was found among the Chaldeans and Babylonians. King Cyrus took them.

7 I, Daniel, was wise (and I knew) all the implements. I showed Cyrus the Persian king (the implements) that were among the Chaldeans and Babylonians, all of the implements that had come from Jerusalem to the land of Babylon. And King Cyrus handed those implements over to his chief eunuch, the service implements, the cups and bowls, buckets and basins, forks and pitchers, and that table of the altar, the seven-branched lampstand, and the jewels of beryl that were attached to it, the precious jewels, and also the pearls, columns, and the golden dishes of the tabernacle, and the great ephod that the high priest used to wear, which had twelve stones on its shoulders with the names of the sons of Jacob inscribed on them, and the vestments from the time of King David, and that golden throne on which King Solomon used to sit. Everything that was found in Babylon that King Nebuchadnezzar had brought, King Cyrus carried from Babylon and brought it to Elam and Persia. Babylon was subjugated to Persia and Elam, as I had foretold Belteshazzar regarding the palm of the hand that had written for him some of the words of God on the palace's wall, that his kingdom would be given to the Medes and Persians, because they had drunk from the implements of the house of God.

8 And as they were going up from Babylon to Persia and Elam, King Cyrus handled these implements with great reverence. And God showed him that he should go and deposit them in the mountain of Elam, in the mountain called Silai[a] after the name of Mount Sinai, so that they would be kept (there) until the last time. He also wrote on the clean face of a stone and put (it) together with them. Only on that golden throne on which King Solomon used to sit the king showed mercy and left it in the treasury.

---

a. The word is vocalized in the MS.; etymology and origin remain obscure.

Gemath the Magus Kills Cyrus and Reigns for Six Months

9 Gemath the magus rose in the middle of the night, killed King Cyrus, and seized the kingdom in Persia[a]. I was afraid and fled to the provinces of Persia and Elam, lest he kill me, for I had been close to King Cyrus, lest I would have to go and show him the mountain in which those implements were deposited that King Cyrus had brought from Babylon. For he (Gemath) had entered the treasury of King Cyrus and had found King Solomon's golden throne. Gemath brought it out, sat on it, and became boastful and blasphemous. And God showed me that that kingdom was to remain for a short while. The kingdom of Gemath the magus (who ruled) after Cyrus the Persian (lasted) six months, and his nobles plotted against and killed him. Darius bar Bagdath bar Artaban[b] seized his kingdom and assumed the authority of Cyrus, king of Persia, and stood in the gate of the kings.

Daniel at the Court of King Darius, Son of BGDT, King of Persia

10 King Darius wrote a letter about me to all Persian provinces and found me in the great city of Elam. I got up and came to the Gate of King Darius[c]. Then he began to pressure me to go and show him the implements of the sanctuary that Cyrus the Persian had put away, for he had seen the throne of King Solomon that King Nebuchadnezzar had brought from Jerusalem to Babylon and that King Cyrus had brought up to Persia, for he had seen its splendor and its beauty, whose likeness no human hands could fashion. He forced me to go and show him where that treasure was put away.

11 At that time God sent a heavenly angel who struck King Darius and took away the light of his eyes. He became very afraid and was shaken. It was shown to him in a nocturnal vision that, on account of the evil thoughts he had thought, he should go and take the implements of God's treasure. And it was shown to him in the vision that he should go to Jerusalem, go up to the house of the Lord, and worship there, and there the light of his eyes would be returned to him. The great King Darius sent and called for me that I should go with him to Jerusalem.

    a. See Bisitun inscription of King Darius (Balcer, *Herodutus and Bisitun*, 49–69).
    b. The vocalization of his name is uncertain; no historical figure of that name is known. The name is possibly modeled after "Darius the Mede" in Dan 6:1 [Evv 5:31]; 11:1.
    c. The "Gate of King Darius" would have been in Ecbatana (Old Persian, "gathering place"), the capital of the Median Empire; cf. 1 Esd 6:23.

Then we went up to Jerusalem with a mighty army, with many chariots, horsemen, and soldiers. We came up to Jerusalem, to the place of the house of my fathers, but we found Jerusalem ravaged and void of its inhabitants and deserted by its residents. We found there some of my kinsmen, but I did not find anyone of my own age who had been there during my time, during those days before (Jerusalem) had been carried into captivity. King Darius entered (the city) and walked into the sanctuary. Also, I bathed him in (the pool of) Shiloah, and he believed in the God of my fathers. He worshiped in the sanctuary, his eyes were opened, and he saw the light. Praising the living God, he walked through all the streets of Jerusalem.

12 King Darius called all the elders who had grown old that could be found, and the priests who were left from King Nebuchadnezzar's sword, and the old men who had grown old in their years. He inquired of them, and they reported to him about the treasure that King Nebuchadnezzar had taken from there, about its beauty, and about the temple implements. Whatever King Darius inquired of those elders, they reported to him truthfully. They persuaded him about each matter in its place, and he gave them generous gifts. Everything that I had reported to them in Persia and Elam about Jerusalem he found to be true. Darius led with him some of the priests and of the scribes, and they went to Persia and Elam. As they were going, King Darius took control of many cities and conquered them, and great provinces, and many places came under his rule. And he acquired the land of the water.[a]

Daniel's Visions

13 I went with him to Persia and Elam. There great prophecies were revealed to me.[b] And I revealed surpassing visions without end and without number, mysteries and seasons and signs and wondrous visions. I pointed out the times when the days of the age are ending, and the end of the consummation, that the Holy Spirit showed Daniel in Persia and Elam in the days of King Darius, what is yet to be and what is hidden to be revealed at the end of days, at the end of the seasons, and at the consumption of (?).[c] In seven weeks, in the season of seasons, and at the consummation of times

---

a. The phrase "land of the water" remains obscure; possibly an error for "land of the Medes." The Medes are mentioned in Dan 5:28; 6:1, 9, 13, 16; 8:20; and 9:1; and, outside of Daniel, in Gen 10:2; 2 Kgs 17:6; Isa 21:2; Jer 25:25; 51:11, 28; Tob 1:14. The term would then explain why Darius has the surname "the Mede."

b. The Syriac uses the rare phrase "it was revealed over"; see Brock, "Two Editions," 16–17.

c. The word in the Syriac is corrupt.

The Syriac Apocalypse of Daniel

<table>
<tr><td>1Q27 1 i 3–4; 4Q416 2 iii 9, 14, 18; 4Q417 1 i 6, 8–11; 2 i 6–9, 18; 4Q418 77 2</td><td>there will be the day and the mystery to be. A wondrous vision will be revealed at the consummation of times, and at the end of days, at the end of the seasons, and also at the consummation of the judges of Zion, and at the consummation of Jerusalem. The wise and those who keep the covenant will understand this book and at the end of ends will be moved by it.</td></tr>
<tr><td>Tob 14:5; 4 Ezra 3:14; 11:44; 12:9; 14:5; 2 Bar. 12:4; 27:15</td><td></td></tr>
<tr><td>Dan 9:12; Mic 3:11; Bar 2:1</td><td></td></tr>
<tr><td>Dan 1:4; 11:33, 35; 12:3, 10; Hos 14:10; Amos 5:13; 4 Ezra 8:62; 12:37–38; 14:45–47; 2 Bar. 28:1; 70:5; 1 En. 93:10, 13; 99:10</td><td></td></tr>
</table>

The Revolt of the Peoples of the North

Isa 52:1; Rev 1:3; 22:7; 4 Ezra 8:27; 2 Bar. 48:22

14 The peoples from the north will rebel, and there will be much commotion and a great earthquake on the face of the earth.

Dan 8:26; 12:4, 9; Rev 10:4; 22:7, 10; 2 Bar. 20:3

Dan 12:13; T. Mos. 1:17–18

Deut 28:49; Jer 10:22; Ezek 38–39; Joel 2:1–11; Zech 14:2; 4 Ezra 13:5; Josephus, *B. J.* 7.245

Mark 13:8; 4 Ezra 4:42; 9:3; 2 Bar. 27:7; Qur'an Sura 22:1–2; 99:1–3

And there will be these signs:
Like the sound of angels
and like the tumult of armies from heaven it will be heard.
There will be a great uproar from heaven
until the high mountains will be made level with the plains.

Matt 24:4–31; Mark 13:5–27; Luke 21:7–33; 1 En. 75:3; 82:16, 19; 4 Ezra 4:52; 5:1, 13; 6:12, 20; 7:26; 8:63; 9:1–6; 13:32; 2 Bar. 72:2; Jub. 2:9; Sib. Or. 2:154; 3:796

1 En. 40:10; 108:5; 2 En. 17:1

Isa 13:4; 17:12; Zeph 1:5

Isa 40:4; Ezek 38:19–20

Then the four winds of heaven will be gathered, one to the other,
and there will be a great and mighty battle;
also, the corpses of the slain will be gathered like mounds.
The western horn will rise and break the winds of heaven,
and it will hold fast until the ends of days.

Jer 49:36; Ezek 37:9; Zech 2:6; 6:5; LXX Zech 2:10; Dan 7:2; 8:8; 11:4; Matt 24:31; Rev 7:1–3; 4 Ezra 13:5; 2 Bar. 64:3; 1 En. 18:2; 76:14; 77:1–3; 1QH^a 9:9–11; Pseudo-Methodius VIII.1; Josephus, *B. J.* 6.300; LAE 38:3

Matt 24:6; Mark 13:7

Dan 8:5; Young Daniel 9:6

Ezek 39:6

Signs will appear on earth,
and trepidation on the islands;
fire will be burning on them day and night.

Isa 50:3; Joel 2:31; Rev 6:12

Isa 13:10; 24:23; Ezek 32:7; Joel 3:4 [Evv 2:31]; 4:15 [Evv 3:15]; Amos 5:20; 8:9; 1 En. 80:4–8; Sib. Or. 3:801–3; 4:56–57; Ascen. Isa. 4:5; T. Mos. 10:5; T. Levi 4:1; Matt 24:29; Luke 21:25; Acts 2:20; Rev 6:12–14; Qur'an Sura 81:1–4; 82:2–5

Matt 10:21; Mark 13:7–8; 4 Ezra 5:9; 6:24; 9:3–4; 1 En. 100:1

There will be these signs in those times:
the sun will be wrapped as if in sackcloth,
and the moon will be clothed as if in blood.
The earth and the sea will shake,
and many people will fall.
In those times error will be on earth:
a son will renounce his father, a brother his brother,
and a friend will deceive his friend.

2 Kgs 17:20; 24:20; Jer 7:15

Jer 15:2; 24:10; 28:8; Ezek 7:15; 14:21; Sir 39:29; Matt 24:7; Rev 6:8; 18:8

God will chastise the earth.
In those days there will be a great famine and pestilence,

much hail, heat, blight, and the sword.
Locust and crawling locust will devour the grass of the land.

In those days there will be a great darkness that will cover the earth,
a thick darkness the generations.
The earth will conceive deceit
and will travail and give birth to iniquity.
Dew will be withheld from heaven
and rain from the clouds.
Heavenly fire will devour the stones of the earth and set fire in the northern regions;
it will be burning day and night
and devour dust and roots and stones and trees.

In those days the earth and the sea will be in uproar.
Peoples will rise against peoples,
kingdom against kingdom,
and cities against cities.
The strong of the earth will rebel, one against the other.

In those days angels will go out to the four winds of heaven
to bring about the requital of anger from the midst of the earth.
They will begin to strike and to destroy with sword and with pestilence,
and with trials of various kinds.

The First Wave of Calamities and Natural Disasters

15 After this there will be stillness on earth,
and peace will abound.
Those who dwell in the world will be established.
The earth will be constrained by its inhabitants,
and the seas and the islands will be filled with residents.
Habitations and dwellings will become towns,
and commercial centers will grow.
Earth and sea will be adorned with towns and commercial centers,
as well as with palaces and buildings.
Towns will be built on the mountains
and walls and towers on the plains.

The Syriac Apocalypse of Daniel

Then, suddenly, the winds of the heavens will be in commotion,
and heavenly angels will walk on earth. Gen 6:1–4; Jude 14–15; 1 En. 6:2–7; 14:3; Jub. 5:1–2; Philo, *Giants* 2.358; Josephus, *A. J.* 1.31; CD-A 2:17–19; 1QH^a 17:38–19:5; 4Q530–533, 534–536
The earth will be constrained by its inhabitants
and the sea and the islands by their settlers.
They will be given a deceitful sign and a deceiving spirit, Matt 24:11; Mark 13:5–6; John 8:44; 1 Tim 4:1; Rev 12:9; 20:10; T. Reu. 2:1, 8–9; T. Ash. 6:2; 1QS 3:18–21
and in every place and city corrupt palaces and buildings will abound.

At that time the winds of the seas will be turned around,
and dust will be falling down from heaven upon the earth; Deut 28:24; Mark 13:25
mountains will be drizzling ash for many days. Exod 19:18; Pss 104:32; 144:5; Rev 8:8
The days of the months will be short,
and the days of the year will hasten. 1 En. 80:2; 4Q385 3 2–7; 4 Ezra 4:26, 34; 2 Bar. 20:1–2; 83:1; LAE 19:13; Matt 24:22; Mark 13:20
The courses of the sun and the moon will be changed,
and those times will be shown to be false. 1 En. 80:4–5; 4 Ezra 5:4; Ascen. Isa. 4:5

The winds of heaven will be bound and will not blow, Gen 8:1; Rev 7:1; 4 Ezra 11:2
and these clouds of the firmament will be held back
and will not traverse (the sky). Jer 10:13; 51:16
The rain will not come down from heaven,
and the sun's light will fade,
and its light will become like the light of *Sîn*, that is, the moon. Isa 13:10; Ezek 32:7; Joel 2:2, 10; Matt 24:29; Rev 8:12; Herodotus, *Hist.* 7.37.2
The light of the moon will not be seen,
and the stars will not shine. Job 25:5; Isa 13:10; Ezek 32:7–8
Darkness and gloom will seize the face of the earth. Exod 10:22
Evil will abound on earth among those who dwell in the world. Isa 60:2; Joel 2:2; Amos 5:20
The earth will withhold its fruit and the mountains their vegetation. Ezek 17:9; 2 Bar. 10:9

More End-Time Calamities and Natural Disasters

16 A sound will be heard from heaven:
there will be horrors and chasms in the mountains,
there will be terrors and commotion here and there, Isa 66:15–23; Ezek 38–39; Joel 4:9–21 [Evv 3:9–21]; Zech 14; Mark 13:7–27; Rev 20–22
with the light of lightnings and in the sound of thunders. Isa 34:4
The clouds of heaven will be rolled up.
Heavenly angels will appear on earth like human beings. Gen 6:1–4; Jude 14–15; 1 En. 6:2–7; 14:3; Jub. 5:1–2; Philo, *Giants* 2.358; Josephus, *A. J.* 1.31; CD-A 2:17–19; 1QH^a 17:38–19:5; 4Q530–533, 534–536

At that time a pillar of fire will appear from heaven
and will reach to the ground.   Exod 13:21–22; Num 14:14; Joel 2:30; Rev 10:1; Wis 18:3; Sib. Or. 3:250; 1 En. 18:11; 21:7
The earth will be dark for many days:
the sun will not rise, nor the moon traverse (the
   sky),   Isa 13:10; Job 9:7; Rev 6:12; 8:12
and the stars will not be seen.   Mark 13:24

In these times the towns of the sea will be covered,
and the cities will be engulfed in the seas.   Isa 28:2; 66:12; Jer 47:2
Many places will be struck by snakes.
Also, many people will go (down) by the sword,   Matt 26:52
and many cities will be subdued into paying tribute.   Josh 16:10; Judg 1:30, 33, 35; Pseudo-Ephrem, "Sermon on the End of the World," lines 161–164; Pseudo-Methodius XI.12
Villages and hamlets will burn with fire.
In these times wrath will abound on earth
and deception will increase in the world.
Sin will abound on earth,
and evil will put forth its head.
Only some, a few, will be left in the midst of the
   earth.   Isa 11:11; 17:5–6; 28:5; 30:17; Amos 3:12; 5:3, 15; Zeph 2:9; 3:12–13; 4 Ezra 6:25; 7:28; 13:17–20, 48–50; 2 Bar. 29:4
Winds and misfortunes will abound
and will go forth to cause trouble on earth and to
   corrupt it.

In those times wisdom will abound on earth:
false prophets and deceiving teachers
will teach all kinds of things.   Mark 13:22; 1 Tim 6:20

Who will be there in those days of wise men and scribes, those (mentioned) above, who will resemble the kingdom of heaven? This kingdom will not be revealed to them; rather, it will be hidden from them. The truth will be revealed to those who seek it.

17 In those days there will be tumult day and night.   Matt 24:7; Mark 13:8; Luke 21:11; 4 Ezra 9:3
High palaces will fall,   Isa 30:25
and many people will perish,
high buildings will be cast down
and will become graves for their inhabitants.

Many villages will be tossed into the sea,
and their inhabitants will go out in the flood.   Dan 9:26

In those times there will scarcity on earth and much
   oppression.
People will be robbing and plundering what does not
   belong to them.   Mic 2:2; Ps 109:11; Ezek 7:21; Mark 3:27; 2 Bar. 27:11
Error will abound on earth: Gen 6:5

The Syriac Apocalypse of Daniel

Rom 1:25	true things will be deemed lies,
	and lies will be believed.
Isa 28:15; Jer 9:5; 2 Thess 2:11; 2 Tim 3:13	Truth will vanish from the earth.
	The kings of the earth will lie, and its judges will be
Mic 7:3	changed
	in order to change a righteous judgment for dishon-
1 En. 91:7; 4 Ezra 11:41–42; 2 Bar. 48:31–35	est richness.
	The world will be hard pressed by its sins.
	All of its dwellings and towns will be in uproar,
	and villainy will appear on the walls of their towers.
	(People) will be filled with falsehood
	and will talk fornication and injustice.
	In laziness they will hasten
	to repay injustice for righteousness
	and evil for goodness.
	Also, their kings will be carried off,
	and their truth will be shown to be a lie,
	their money (coinage) will be rejected,
	and their pride will be diminished.
1 En. 69:17; 4 Ezra 6:24; Sib. Or. 4:15; Pss. Sol. 17:19; T. Mos. 10:6; T. Levi 4:1	**18** In those days the springs on earth will be wanting,
Isa 19:5–6	the fountains of the earth will fail,
Isa 42:15; 44:27	and deep rivers will dry up.
	Summer days will be in winter,
	winter days in summer,
Syriac Alexander Poem l. 663–664	and the days of the year will be altered .
	Division will fall on earth,
	zeal and rebellions in the earthly dwellings.
	A son will silence his father in the court of law,
	and a daughter-in-law will strive against her mother-
Mic 7:6; Matt 10:35; Luke 12:53	in-law and will drive her out.
Isa 40:12	In those days the land will be measured in a span
	and a cubit (of land) will be bought for a mina.
	Wrathful punishment will come upon the earth.
	The area of one khor (of seed) will yield (only) one seah,
	and one thousand vines of the vineyard will yield
Isa 5:10; 1 En. 10:19; 2 Bar. 29:5; Irenaeus, *Haer.* 5.33.3	one measure of wine.
	They will sow much but will not reap,
	and beget children but will not rear (them).
	A man will do business day and night,
Lev 26:20, 26; Deut 28:29–31; 4 Ezra 5:12	yet he won't have enough food.
	Fathers will bury (their) sons

and also sons (their) fathers,
as (it was) during the years of previous generations.

In those days the islands will be dashed into the sea   Matt 18:6; 21:21; Mark 11:23; Luke 17:2; Rev 8:8
and those who travel by the sea and the islanders
    will be cut off.

The Last Days

19 Then the times will be fulfilled
and the last days will draw near.

There will be these signs:
the sun's light will fade,
the moon will be restrained from its course,
also, the firmament will conceal its face.   Isa 13:10; Ezek 32:7–8; Amos 8:9; 1 En. 80:2–8; Matt 24:29; 4 Ezra 5:5

When the last days will begin to draw near,   2 Bar. 29:3; 39:7
great signs will suddenly begin to appear:
a great earthquake will be on earth,
a strong and severe noise in the firmament of
    heaven,
and a great calamity on earth;   Pseudo-Ephrem, "Sermon on the End of the World," line 366
it will be heard from sea to sea   Ps 72:8; Mic 7:12; Zech 9:10; Sir 44:21
and from the ends of heaven to the ends of the earth.   Deut 4:32; Matt 24:31
The clouds of the firmament will be torn,   Job 37:11; 4 Ezra 4:50
and an immense fire will settle between the four   Jer 49:36; Ezek 37:9; Zech 2:6; 6:5; LXX Zech 2:10; Dan 7:2; 8:8; 11:4; Matt 24:31; Rev 7:1–3;
    winds of heaven,   1 En. 18:2; 76:14; 77:1–3; 4 Ezra 13:5; 2 Bar. 64:3; 1QH^a 9:9–11; Pseudo-Methodius VIII.1;
and it will burn the mountaintops four times on a   Josephus, B. J. 6.300; LAE 38:3
    single day.
    Exod 24:17; Deut 4:11; 5:23; Jer 51:25; Rev 8:8

Angels will appear in Zion
and holy ones in Jerusalem.   Gen 6:1–4; Jude 14–15; 1 En. 6:2–7; 14:3; Jub. 5:1–2; Philo, Giants 2.358; Josephus, A. J. 1.31;
Angelic hosts will appear on the waves of the sea.   CD-A 2:17–19; 1QH^a 17:38–19:5; 4Q530–533, 534–536
Then great fear will dwell in the sea,
trembling will fall on the islands,
and a great earthquake in all the dwellings of the
    earth.   Ps 104:4; Dan 10:6; Heb 1:7; 4 Ezra 8:22; 13:10; 2 Bar. 21:6; Jos. Asen. 14:9; 1 En. 17:1;
Then heavenly angels will appear like fire   2 En. 1:3–5; Apoc. Abr. 11:1–3; Apoc. Zeph. 6:11–15; Gen. Rab. 78:1
and will burn many people who are on their way.
Then the earth and the sea will be stirred up,   Acts 2:2–3
and strong and powerful winds will be blowing.   Isa 50:3; Joel 2:31; Rev 6:12

    Isa 13:10; 24:23; Joel 3:4 [Evv 2:31]; 4:15 [Evv 3:15]; Ezek 32:7; Amos 8:9; Zech 14:7;
20 In those days the sun will be wrapped as if in   1 En. 80:4–8; Sib. Or. 3:801–3; 4:56–57;
    sackcloth,   Ascen. Isa. 4:5; T. Mos. 10:5; T. Levi 4:1; Matt 24:29; Luke 21:25; Acts 2:20; Rev 6:12–14;
and the moon will be clothed as if in blood,   Qur'an Sura 81:1–4; 82:2–5

The Syriac Apocalypse of Daniel

Isa 34:4; Ezek 32:7-8; Joel 2:10; 4:15 [Evv 3:15]; Mark 13:24-25; Rev 6:12-13; T. Mos. 10:5-6; Lactantius, *Epit.* 71	and the stars fall like leaves from the trees. Like guardians of fire
Ezek 28:14	arrows and spears will be hurled over the earth.
Ezek 39:9; Hab 3:11; Zech 9:14	Then all people and all tongues will be frightened and shaken, and suddenly, great calamities
Zech 14:4	and chasms will be on earth:
Ps 2:8-9; Dan 7:23; Mic 4:13; Hab 3:9	the earth will be torn to pieces like a garment as far as the great abyss.
Num 16:31-32	Many people will also be swallowed alive in the midst of the earth.
Jer 4:24; Ps 46:3-4 [Evv 46:2-3]	Then mountains will be shaken from their places, hills will be moved from their sites.
Exod 13:21-22; Num 14:14; Joel 2:30; Rev 10:1; 1 En. 18:11; 21:7; Wis 18:3; Sib. Or. 3:250	Then pillars of fire will appear from heaven,
Gen 15:17; Ps 21:10 [Evv 21:9]; Pr Azar 1:26, 66; 3 Macc 6:6; 4 Macc 16:3, 21; 4 Ezra 4:48; Young Daniel 7:57	and a fiery furnace from the midst of the clouds. And there will appear in the firmament of heaven something like horses of fire,
2 Kgs 2:11; Sir 48:9; Rev 9:17-19	and like chariots of war, holding an iron sword and a spear of war.

The Birth of a Warrior of the Tribe of Levi

21 It will be in those days that a woman will bear a boy from

Gen 49:17; Pseudo-Methodius XIV.6, 10; Hippolytus, *Antichr.* XIV	the tribe of the house of Levi. And these signs will appear on him: on his skin will be images like the weapons of war: the details (?) of a breastplate,[a] a bow, a sword, a spear, an iron dag-
Isa 6:6; Rev 19:12; 4 Macc 8:12	ger, and war chariots. His face will be like the face of a burning
Sir 43:4	furnace, his eyes like burning coals. Between his eyes he has
Dan 8:5-8	a single horn, whose tip is broken off, and something that has the appearance of a snake is coming out of it.

The Advent of the False Messiah

22 When these signs will begin to take place, then the advent

2 Thess 2:7-8; Pseudo-Ephrem, "Sermon on the End of the World," lines 355-524	of the heartless one[b], the crooked serpent, the false messiah, will begin to appear. He will come from the extremities of the
Isa 27:1	land of the East to deceive those who dwell in the world. He
Matt 24:5, 24; Mark 13:6, 22; Luke 21:8; 2 Thess 2:4-9; Rev 13:4, 13; Apoc. El. (C) 3:1; Ascen. Isa. 4:2-12	will say of himself, "I am the Messiah!" He will issue from a snake's belly, from the intestines of an adder. With him will come many guards and mighty angels.
Syriac Testament of the Lord 11; Apoc. El. (C) 3:15-17; Apoc. Dan. 9:15-26	These are his signs and the terrifying appearance of his stature:
Gen 49:12; Prov 23:31	his head is large, his hair is red (or: "glistening"),

a. The Syriac is unclear.
b. Lit. "the one stripped of heart."

his eyes are blue,[a] and his neck is strong.
His sides[b] are raised, his chest is broad,   Lev 14:9; Prov 30:13
his arms are long and his fingers short.
He has two horns in (next to?) his ears,[c]
and he has excessive flesh in his ear,
also, his flesh is lacking.[d]
His appearance is furious, stupendous, and wrathful,
the appearance of his stature is also stupendous.

He will appear like lightning in heaven   Zech 9:14; Matt 24:27; Luke 17:24;
and like a torch in the camp.   2 Bar. 53:8–10; Pseudo-Ephrem, "Sermon on the End of the World," lines 425–426
With him (will be) fiery chariots and war camps.
Faster than a leopard are his horses,
and more shameless[e] than the evening wolves are his messengers.   Hab 1:8
His stature is great and lofty   Dan 2:31; 3:1–5
and floats over the mountains,
equal to the clouds in the heaven.   Dan 4:10, 20
With him (will come) a host of serpents and encampments of Indians.   Pseudo-Methodius V.2; VI.5

Then the gates of the north will be opened before him,   Syriac Alexander Poem I, 424–504; II, 432–520; III, 492–586; Pseudo-Ephrem, "Sermon on the End of the World," lines 197–225
and the army of Mebagbel[f] will come out
and the multitude of the Agogites and Magogites,   Ezek 38:2; Rev 20:7–10; Josephus, *A. J.* 1.123; Qur'an Sura 18; 21: 95–96; 3 En. 45:5; Sib. Or. 3:319–20, 512–13, 663–65
enormous in their statures,
powerful in their strength,
and abounding in their camps.   Matt 16:27; 2 Thess 1:7
They will seize the world, the expanse of the earth,
so as to march from sea to sea   Ps 72:8; Mic 7:12; Zech 9:10; Sir 44:21
and from the ends of the heaven to the ends of the heaven.   Deut 4:32; Matt 24:31

23 These are the deeds and signs he will perform:
he will be running in front of his troops and his camp,
and mountains and hills will be running rapidly.
He will rise with the sun at sunrise,
and precede it in its settings

---

a. "blue," literally, "steel gray"; cf. Young Daniel 9:11.
b. "sides;" cf. Young Daniel 9:11, "his eyebrows."
c. The Syriac is probably corrupt; possibly "he has two openings in his ears," or, with Young Daniel 9:12, "he has two horns in his ears."
d. The Syriac is difficult to read.
e. Young Daniel 9:15 also reads "more shameless," though Brock emends to "swifter" ("Young Daniel," 285).
f. "The army of Mebagbel," possibly a proper name; cf. Ezek 38:2–6.

The Syriac Apocalypse of Daniel

and hold it back, so it cannot traverse (the sky).
And he will say to the moon to stand still, and it will stand still and not move.

Josh 10:12–13; Apoc. El. (C) 3:6–8; b. 'Abod. Zar. 25a

He will stretch out his hands to the firmament of clouds
and hold back the rain and the dew.
And he will make the clouds of the firmament stand still, so that they will not move;
and he will command the winds, and they will not blow.
He will turn the deep rivers backward.
He will stand in the sea up to his knees:
its animals live in fear,
and the dragons that live in (the sea) will be greatly frightened.

4 Ezra 6:51–52; Apoc. Dan. 9:1–6

Three times on a single day he will run from sea to sea

Ps 72:8; Mic 7:12; Zech 9:10; Sir 44:21

and from the ends of the heaven to the ends of the heaven.

Deut 4:32; Matt 24:31

He will stretch out his long arms
and gather in the birds of heaven, the beasts, and birds of prey,
and yet his hosts and camps will not be filled.

Isa 33:20; Lam 2:4
Pseudo-Methodius XIV.1

24 He will pitch his tent opposite Zion,
and his tent will be opposite Jerusalem.
The peoples will see him and be afraid,
and tribes will be frightened.
The islands of the sea will live in fear,
thinking that he is the Messiah.
Many who follow him will go astray,

Matt 24:24; Rev 13:13

for he will do many signs and wonders.

Apoc. El. (C) 3:12–13; 4:31; Pseudo-Ephrem, "Sermon on the End of the World," lines 423–424

But he is unable to raise the dead.
His kingdom and his power will last a season, seasons, and half a season,

Dan 7:25; 12:7; Rev 12:14

that is, three years and six months.
He will begin to set up horrors (i.e., idols) in Zion[a]

Dan 9:27; 11:31; 1 Macc 1:54; Matt 24:15; Mark 13:14

and alien worship in Jerusalem.
He will receive a curse from heaven,

Dan 11:23

and he will act deceitfully with evil deceit toward those who are close to him.

1 En. 40:8; 52:5; 53:4; 54:4; 56:2; 60:24; T. Dan 6:2, 5; T. Ash. 6:6; T. Ben. 6:1

Then the angel of peace will come forth from the presence of the Mighty Lord, with great power and heroic strength.

---

a. The Syriac is corrupt; following here the emendation of Brock, "Two Editions," 16 n. 11.

With him (will be) angels, men of war, who will seize him in the land of the South, on the pathways of the Great Sea. They will strike him with an unquenchable fiery sword from his head to his knees, and they will split him into two. They will toss him to the side of the sea, like a great mountain that has fallen, and like a rock that is thrown down.[a] His end and his destruction will be in the sea. All of his armies and soldiers will be swallowed by the sea, and they will perish.

Jub. 10:28; 13:10

Sib. Or. 5:512–13; 11Q14 (11QMelch) 9–15; 1QM xv–xix; Gk. Apoc. Ezra 4:3; T. Levi 3:3; 18:12; T. Jud. 25:3; T. Sim. 6:6; T. Dan 5:10–11; T. Zeb. 9:8

Rev 12:18–13:10; 1 En. 60:7–9, 24; 4 Ezra 6:49–52; 2 Bar. 29:4

An Interim Period of Fear and Silence

25 Then fear will dwell on earth,
and a great shuddering will seize all travelers and residents of the islands.
Many people will die in fear and trembling.
Many of the towns will be ruined, and their buildings will fall,
and many provinces will be destroyed over their inhabitants.
The land will be deserted without residents
and the seas and the islands by their inhabitants.
Towns and cities will be laid waste and be left deserted.
Ten villages will gather together to live (at) the mountain, at the mountain base.
The way of the sea will be cut off,
and the paths of the villages and the crossings will be torn up.

Jub. 6:5

Jer 48:8–9; Jdt 2:24

Isa 17:2, 9; Lam 1:1, 7

Ps 77:20 [Evv 77:19]; Isa 9:1; 43:16; 51:10; Bar 3:30–31

Wild animals will abound in the mountains and over the people,
like evening wolves they will threaten people,
lying in wait to tear (them) apart.
And many towns and cities will become abodes for wild animals:
jackals will build a home in royal palaces and lofty buildings,
hawks and birds will glide in and break into them,
and lowly and few people will be left.
They will be dwelling on the mountaintops
in great dread and much fear.

Lev 26:22; Isa 11:8; 4 Ezra 5:8; 2 Bar. 73:6

Ezek 22:27; Zeph 3:3; Hab 1:8

Isa 13:22; 34:11–15; 35:7; 43:20; Jer 9:11; 10:22; 49:33; 51:37; Mal 1:3; Ps 44:19

Job 39:26

There will be stillness on earth for half a short week.
They will understand the number of years,

Dan 9:27

---

a. On the defeat of the false messiah, see 2 Thess 2:8; Ascen. Isa. 4:14.

The Syriac Apocalypse of Daniel

and the consummation of the times and of the signs,
   they will understand at the time when it will happen.

4 Ezra 11:44; 14:10-12 The end will draw near to the end of the world,
2 Tim 3:1; 2 Pet 3:3 when the time of the final days will draw near.
   It will be at the consummation of the last time of the end of the world:
1 En. 16:1; T. Benj. 11:3; 2 Bar. 59:8; 69:4; 83:7
Isa 24:19-20 the earth will be split and burst open,
1 Sam 2:8; Ps 75:3; Job 38:4 the pillars of the lower earth will be broken off,
Job 3:21; Prov 2:4; 10:2; Sir 3:4; Tob 4:9; and the storehouses of fire will be opened:
Matt 6:19, 21; 4 Ezra 4:35, 41; 5:42; 7:85, 95; the mountains and hills will be overthrown within it,
2 Bar. 14:12; 21:23; 30:2 and they will be cast into deep chasms.

Who will be (there) on that day to command,
   and who will be found at that moment
Matt 24:30; Apoc. El. (C) 3:2 when the great and awesome cross of the God of
Deut 10:17; Ps 136:2-3; Ezra 7:12; Dan 2:37,   gods and Lord of lords will appear?
47; LXX Dan 3:18, 34; LXX 4:37; Ezek 26:7;
Zech 14:9; Rev 11:15-18; 15:3-4; 17:14; 19:16;
1 En. 9:4; Pr Azar 1:68

Theophany on Mount Zion

26 And it will be on that day
   that the Lord will command the four winds of
       heaven to blow with great movement,
   with movement and with strong gusts.
Jer 49:36; Ezek 37:9; Zech 2:6; 6:5; LXX Zech Then strong and dreadful clouds will be gathered
2:10; Dan 7:2; 8:8; 11:4; Matt 24:31; Rev 7:1-3;   from all the ends of heaven,
4 Ezra 13:5; 2 Bar. 64:3; 1 En. 18:2; 76:14; and heavenly angels (will appear) on top of them.
77:1-3; 1QH^a 9:9-11; Pseudo-Methodius
VIII.1; Josephus, B. J. 6.300; LAE 38:3
Rev 10:1; 14:14-16 A swift race, they will seize the four winds of the world
   and hurl much lightning and strong and dreadful thunder.
   They will terrify the entire world.
   The clouds of the firmament will be emptied out.
   Fiery sparks and blazing flames will be thrown from between the clouds
   unto the earth and will burn without pause.
   All the ends of the earth will be shaken and agitated.
Dan 3:4, 7, 29; 5:19; 6:25; 7:14; 4 Ezra 3:7; Upon all peoples, nations, and tongues,
Jdt 3:8; Rev 5:9; 7:9; 10:11; 13:7; 14:6; 17:15; great fear will fall and trembling will seize those
Origen, Cels. 8.2; Justin, Dial. 119   who dwell by the seas and those who live in the wilderness.

Then they will flee from the west to the east,
   and from the east to the west,
Ps 107:3; Isa 24:17-18; 43:5-6; Ezek 12:15; and from the north to the south,
Zech 7:14; Luke 13:29; Jub. 36:10; T. Levi 10:4 and from the south to the north.
Num 11:1; Ps 79:5-6; Isa 30:27, 30; 66:15; Jer And from every place and from every quarter
15:14; Lam 1:12; Ezek 22:20; Sir 45:19; Pss.   fire of anger will meet and seize them.
Sol. 17:4

More powerful winds will trouble them,
mighty lightning will frighten them,
and strong thunder will agitate them.

    Exod 19:16; Rev 4:5; 8:5; 11:19; 16:18; 2 Esdras 16:10; Sib. Or. 5:345, 433; Ahiqar 6:26

Who will be (there) on that day,
and who will be found at that moment,
when the God of gods and Lord of lords appears,
the mighty Lord, the warrior of the kingdom?

    Deut 10:17; Ps 136:2–3; Ezra 7:12; Dan 2:37, 47; LXX Dan 3:18, 34; LXX 4:37; Ezek 26:7; Zech 14:9; Rev 11:15–18; 15:3–4; 17:14; 19:16; 1 En. 9:4; Pr Azar 1:68

27 (The earth) will shake before him on that day
    from its poles below;
furthermore, the heavens will shake from their
    pillars on that day.

    1 En. 18:3; Heb 12:26–27

The mountains will be turned over,
and the hills will melt like wax before fire.
All the islands of the sea will be cut off,
they will be sought but no longer be found.

    Pss 68:3 [Evv 68:2]; 97:5; Ezek 22:21–22; Mic 1:4; Jdt 16:15; Wis 16:22–23; 4 Ezra 13:4; 1 En. 1:6; 52:6

Then the springs of water will fail,

    Isa 19:5–6

and deep rivers will be turned around (to flow)
    backward.
They will hasten in fear before the great King of
    heaven and earth,

    Gen 14:22; Ezra 5:11; Tob 10:13; Jdt 9:12

the master of all servants.

And it will be on that day
that darkness will cover the earth

    Isa 8:22; 60:2; Add Esth 11:8

and clouds the nations.
The earth will tremble before him
and run like lead in water[a].

    Exod 15:10; 1 En. 48:9

Strong thunders will be everywhere,
and powerful and stupendous lightning will not be
    silenced.
Dark and dreadful clouds will traverse the earth.
Angelic chariots will be racing over the mountains,
and heavenly angels will appear like fire on swift
    chariots.

    2 Kgs 2:11; Sir 48:9

The earth's strength will not be able to stand before
    him,
nor the heavens endure before him.

    2 Pet 3:12

With the sound of strong thunders, a dreadful
    earthquake, and much rebuke, with the flash-
    ing of much lightning and the sounds of severe
    thunders,

    2 Sam 22:8; Ps 18:16 [Evv 18:15]

---

a. For "in water" the manuscript gives the alternate reading "in fire" in the margin.

the heart of all people will be weakened in fear and trembling.
They will not be able to stand on that day before the strength of his vigor.

All flesh will fall asleep on that day,
and nothing that creeps on the face of the earth will be left at that moment.
On that great and mighty day,
the earth will totter,
the sea will dry up,
the earth will shake.
They will run and be agitated,
and great horrors will take place in the depths of the earth.
And (there will be) a great and mighty vision on the heavenly firmament.

28 Then the heaven and the heaven's heaven will burst open,
and all the firmaments will give place.

Then Adonai Seba'oth,
God of gods, Lord of lords, and King of kings,
the Great and Awesome One,
(will come down) from heaven with strong and mighty strength,
in majestic beauty, on clouds of light,
and on a chariot of holy waters,
with marvelous strength,
and with a burning flame and a fiery flame,
and with angels, men of war.

His voice will be heard from many heights,
and he will speak with a powerful fire and a burning flame.
Fiery chariots will surround him and encampments of holy angels.
He will walk on wings and will place his chariot on the clouds.
He will bend the heaven and descend,
and clouds (will be) under his feet.
The earth will see him and shake before him,
and mountains will melt like wax.
Furthermore, the depths and all the earth—
as with a cloak it will be spread out over them.
The waters will see him and be shaken,

the waves of the great sea will rise over the mountaintops that are in it.	Isa 30:25
Many clouds will sprinkle fire.	Ps 77:18 [Evv 77:17]; Ezek 1:4
The repositories of fire will be opened	
and the storehouses of the wind that are hidden in the firmament.	Ps 135:7; Jer 10:13; 51:16; 1 En. 60:11; 69:23; 2 En. 40:11; 4 Ezra 4:35, 41; 5:37; 7:32, 35, 80, 101; 2 Bar. 14:12; 21:23; 30:2
What used to be concealed in the depths will be revealed before him, on that day.	
Then, on that day, the earth will be purified in the fire like (molten) lead,	
and (the skies) will be rolled up like a scroll.	Isa 34:4; Rev 6:14; Sib. Or. 3:82–83; 8:233, 413; Gos. Thom. 111
Furthermore, the light of the stars will pass	
and fall like leaves from the trees.	
The sun and the moon will not shine,	Job 25:5; Isa 13:10; Ezek 32:7; Joel 2:2, 10; Matt 24:29; Rev 8:12: 4 Ezra 7:39; Herodotus, *Hist.* 7.37.2
and the firmament, which held back rain and dew, will be opened and flow on that day.	
The angels of the depths below will hold out their hands,	
and the heavenly pillars will be weakened.	Deut 10:17; Ps 136:2–3; Ezra 7:12; Dan 2:37, 47; LXX Dan 3:18, 34; LXX 4:37; Ezek 26:7; Zech 14:9; Rev 11:15–18; 15:3–4; 17:14; 19:16; 1 En. 9:4; Pr Azar 1:68
29 Then the God of gods, Lord of lords, and King of kings,	
Adonai Seba'oth, the mighty Lord,	
will appear completely on Zion.	Ps 84:7
He will establish the cherub of the sanctuary on Zion	Exod 25:17–22; 1 Sam 4:4; 2 Sam 6:2; 22:11; 1 Kgs 6:23; 2 Kgs 19:15; 1 Chr 13:6; Pss 18:11 [Evv 18:10]; 80:2; 99:1; Isa 37:16
and the throne of righteousness on the mountains of Jerusalem.	
Furthermore, the (?) of the King Messiah from heaven will appear on earth.[a]	Jub. 31:20; 1 En. 62:2–3
Seraphim of splendor will be standing before him,	Isa 6:2; 1 En. 61:10; 2 En. 20:1; 21:1; 22:2
and majestic angels will be ministering before him.	
He will make his divine presence[b] settle on the mountains of Jerusalem.	2 Chr 6:18; 7:1; Jdt 9:8; Sir 36:18; 2 Macc 14:35; 3 En. 5–7
He will abide (in Jerusalem) and sanctify her,	
and the shadow of his wings will cover her	Ruth 3:9; Pss 17:8; 36:8 [Evv 36:7]; 57:2 [Evv 57:1]; 63:8 [Evv 63:7]
and make the splendor of his countenance shine upon her;	
his right hand, a mighty strength, will overshadow her.	

a. The relative particle "of" in front of "the King Messiah" as well as the fact that the verb "will appear" is in the fem. sg. suggest that the subject of the sentence dropped out.

b. "Divine Presence"—Syriac škîntā'. Cf. *shekinah*, which has the same sense in Postbiblical Hebrew.

The Syriac Apocalypse of Daniel

The Advent of the Messiah

30 Then there will be the advent of the King Messiah in great glory.

His name is before the sun,

Ps 147:4; Prov 8:22–26; 4 Ezra 6:1–6; and before the moon his dominion and his kingdom.
1 En. 48:2–3; 62:7; Enuma Elish 1.1–2

With him the just and the righteous will come,

1 Thess 3:13; 2 Thess 1:7; Jude 14; 1 En. 39:6; and they will appear with holy clouds at the beginning of the revelation of his advent,
70:4; 4 Ezra 7:28; 13:52; 14:9

like a mighty one and like a warrior, strong in battle.

Fire will devour before him, and a flame will burn around him,

Exod 24:17; Deut 4:24; 9:3; 32:22; Ps 50:3; it will be running before him and burn up his enemies.
Isa 29:6; Joel 2:3; Amos 7:4

It will be devouring stones and trees on earth,

and it will be burning water, iron, and bronze.

It will have dominion over the mountains and the springs of the rivers,

and there is no one who will be left.

Two iron gates will be opened before the Lord of lords,

Ps 24:7–10; 3 Macc 6:18; Acts 12:10

Isa 45:2; Ps 107:16 the brazen bars will be broken down,

Job 14:18 and mountains will be pounded like dust.

Darkness will flee before him,

and the night will be swallowed up by his light.

The gates will be opened and the pillars of the earth will appear.

1 Sam 2:8; Job 9:6; 1 En. 57:2

Ps 89:48; Qoh 8:8; Hos 13:14; Wis 16:13; He will cut off death's power,
Acts 2:24; 1 Cor 15:54–56; Heb 2:14; Rev 20:6

and sin will be sought but will not be found.

Ps 21:6 [Evv 21:5]; Hab 3:3 **31** Then the splendor of Jesus will be revealed in great glory,
1 En. 50:4; 4 Ezra 7:42, 87, 91; 2 Bar. 21:23–25

and his greatness and the wonder of his advent will appear.

The mountains will see (him) and rejoice;

Ps 98:4; Isa 49:13 the hills will exult,

Ps 98:8; Isa 55:12 the rivers will clap (their) hands,

Ps 96:11 the sea will rejoice in its fullness.

The clouds and the thick darkness will be covered with light

and will sprinkle dew.

The earth will see his countenance and rejoice,

the islands will see his glory and be enveloped in joy.

The mountains will see him in the world[a] and lift up their slopes

---

a. The Syriac has the plural.

and run and dance to meet him.   Ps 114:4; 1 En. 51:4
The sea will see him and rejoice,
and its waves be lifted up higher than the mountains
 to give him praise and honor.
The winds will remain silent
and will go out to meet him in joy.
32 Then the earth will stand firm and will not
 move,   Pss 24:2; 104:5
the winds will be still and will not blow,
and the sea will be calm and will not be agitated.   Ps 107:29
The glory of the Messiah will appear.
Then the mountains will bear peace,
and the hills will be clothed in righteousness.   Ps 72:3; Jer 31:23
Then those who live in the wilderness will exult,   Isa 35:1; 42:11; 51:3
and the plains and all that is in them will rejoice
before the Messiah, Jesus our Lord.
Peace will flourish in the world,   Lev 26:6; Ezek 34:25; Sir 1:18
and righteousness will be abundant on earth.   Pss 72:7; 92:13 [Evv 92:12]; Prov 11:28

Mountains will be flowing with milk,
and hills will gush with honey.   Jer 11:5; Joel 3:18; 2 Esd 2:19
Springs of milk will be flowing down from the
 mountaintops,
and fountains of oil will gush from the foot of the
 mountains.   Exod 3:8, 17; 13:5; Num 14:8; Deut 6:3; 11:9; 26:9, 15; Jer 11:5; 32:22; Ezek 20:6, 15; Joel 3:18
Streams of water will flow in the wilderness   Isa 32:2; 41:18
and glorious rivers in dry places.   Isa 35:6; 43:20
Fountains of clear water will gush in the desolated
 and deserted land.
The cedar and the olive tree will sprout on Mount
 Zion,   Ezek 17:22–24
and all around Jerusalem myrtle and cypress
and blossoming trees[a].   1 En. 28–30
Streams of water (and) rivers will be running on the
 mountaintops of Zion.   Isa 30:25; Zech 14:8; 2 Esd 16:60

The New Jerusalem Is Built

33 Then the new Jerusalem will be built,   Isa 65:18; Rev 3:12
and Zion will be completely inhabited.   Isa 54:11–14; Ezek 40–48; Zech 2:4–5; Tob 13:8–17; Rev 21:1–22:7
The mighty Lord will build Zion,
and his holy Messiah will shine in Jerusalem.   Rev 21:23; Jub. 1:17, 26–29; 25:21; 1 En. 90:28–39
Mighty men will build her walls,
and holy angels will complete her towers.
With stones of justice she will be built,

---

a. The Syriac has the singular.

The Syriac Apocalypse of Daniel

and with jewels of righteousness she will be completed.
The Messiah will be the architect
and the angel of peace her builder;
she will be built as an eternal building.

Her light will be seen to the ends of the earth;
on holy mountains and on shining clouds she will be completed.
Jerusalem will be pure and glorious,
as holy clouds carry her.
The world will shine in her splendor.

She will have seven walls.
Twelve gates will be opened in Jerusalem,
and they will write on them the names of the sons of Jacob.
Holy angels will stand on her walls
and righteous guards on her towers.
Peace will be over her gates,
and they will be opened and never again be shut.
They will be opened for those entering in harmony and those going out in peace.
She will become a fortitude of righteousness.
A fiery trumpet will sound in her,
and all the hymns of the righteous will be heard from within her.

Three Trumpet Calls Announce the Resurrection of the Dead

Margin references:
- Isa 54:11–12; Tob 13:16; Rev 21:11, 18–20
- 1 En. 40:8; 52:5; 53:4; 54:4; 56:2; 60:24; 3 En. 33:1; T. Dan 6:5; T. Ash. 6:5; T. Benj. 6:1; T. Mos. 10:1–2
- Isa 60:3; Rev 21:24
- Ezek 48:33–34; Rev 21:21; 5Q15 i 10; 11Q19 xxxix 11–16; xl 11–14
- Ezek 48:30–35; Rev 21:12–13
- Rev 21:25; Isa 60:11; 1QM xii 13–15

34 Then joy will be on earth
and happiness on the firmament of heaven.
The first horn will call from the height of heaven,
a great trumpet will sound from Jerusalem.
Its sound will be heard from the ends of the earth to the depth below.

Then the earth and its power will be opened,
and its foundations below will appear.
The sea will be opened,
and its springs below be revealed.
The pillars of the earth will be revealed,
and its poles below will appear.
The firmament of the darkness below on which the earth is set
and the sea and the springs of fire will be revealed,
and the storehouses of the wind will be opened.

Margin references:
- 4 Ezra 6:23; Matt 24:31; 1 Cor 15:52; 1 Thess 4:16; Rev 4:1; 8:7
- 2 Sam 22:8; Ps 18:16 [Evv 18:15]
- Job 38:4–6
- Jer 10:13; 51:16; Ps 135:7; 1 En. 60:11; 69:23; 2 En. 40:11; 4 Ezra 4:35, 41; 5:37; 7:32, 35, 80, 101; 2 Bar. 14:12; 21:23; 30:2

Nothing will be left at that hour that will not be revealed.   Mark 4:22; Luke 8:17
It will appear on earth and in the sea, on high and in the deep
and in Sheol, and in the depth, and at the ends of the firmament below.

35 Then a second horn will call from heaven,
a great trumpet will sound from Jerusalem.   Rev 8:8
Then the earth will travail and will raise
every form and shape of the bodies that had been stored in it.   1 Cor 15:35; 2 Bar. 50:2
It kept them like a most trusted deposit[a]—   1 En. 51:1
all the limbs that have come into being from the beginning of the world
until that day on which the (world's) end is completed,
every corpse that was corrupted   4 Ezra 4:11; 7:96, 111; 14:13; 2 Bar. 21:19; 28:5; 40:3; 74:2
and that was brought from region to region
and from place to place,
and was mixed with the earthly element,
was corrupted by fire and its strength,
and by wind and its strength
and in the sea and on dry ground.

The earth is the mother of all.   Wis 7:1; 4 Ezra 10:7, 9–10
It will keep everything incorrupt,
and it will return it like a great deposit.
For there is nothing that will not be revealed on that day.   1 En. 51:1; 2 Bar. 49:2–3; 50:2; Ephrem, "Sermon on the Fear of God and on the End," lines 502–515
The earth will deliver and yield every corpse
and (all) shapes of human limbs,
from water and fire
and from upon high and from the depth,
and from the darkness and from the mountains,
and from heights and from hills,
and from the springs.

Every form and the shapes of human limbs
that were corrupted on the face of the earth will be gathered on that day.

36 Then a third horn will call from heaven,
a great trumpet will sound from Jerusalem.   Rev 8:10, 12
Then all those who are asleep will be awakened,   Dan 12:2; 1 Thess 4:13; 1 En. 49:3; 91:10; 92:3; 2 Bar. 21:24; LAB 3:10; 19:12

a. Lit. "the deposit of deposits."

and those who lie in the dust will rise,
and those lying in darkness will come out into the light.

Then the sealed and hidden (graves) in the earth will be opened,
and those lying in the dust will come out at the appointed hour.[a]
The graves and heaps (of stones) will be opened on that day,
and those who are lying (in them) will rise and walk on the face of the earth.
With one voice they will raise their hands and offer praise—
all who were dead but live,
who lay down but rose,
who slept but were awakened,
who were cast down but were released.

Their voice will be heard from the sea and the islands
and from the mountaintops and hills,
and from many plains
and from the four winds of the world.
And all of them will say with one voice,
"Holy, holy, holy is the mighty Lord.
There is none like you and nothing like your works.
The whole earth is full of your glory.
Your great works will glorify you and your wondrous powers."
They will exalt your great and terrifying name,
those who were dead but live,
who lay down but rose,
who slept but were awakened.

The Pilgrimage of All Nations to Mount Zion

37 Then all peoples will gather in Zion
and the nations in the gates of Jerusalem,
all the just and righteous,
all who fear the name of the mighty Lord,
and those who do what pleases him,
and all of Abraham's seed,
the sons of Jacob, the chosen ones,
and all the exiles of Israel,

---

a. Lit. "in one hour."

all who were scattered in all the winds of heaven and
    shores of the sea
and at the fringes of the earth's sea.
They will gather together and come on that day,
from the east and from the west
and from the north and from the south,
and from the end of the earth,
and from all the islands of the seas
and from the mountains, and from the hills, and
    from the plains.

Roads will be trodden in the sea,
there will be paths in the deep seas.
All the elect will be passing through
to gather in Jerusalem,
as it was when (God) led them out of the land of
    Egypt:
mountains will be leveled before them and hills will
    be broken down,
as it was at the (Red) Sea in the days of Moses when
    they were passing through.
There will be a cleared road,
they will not go around the Euphrates and Tigris, the
    deep rivers.
They (the rivers) will be cut into twelve roads,
and they will be crossing in sandals.
Their waters will be silent and stand (still)
and will not flow to change the roads on which they
    will be (standing).
And the just and righteous will pass through,
all of Abraham's seed,
the exiles of Israel
and all those who fear the name of the mighty Lord,
and those who do the word of his mouth.

The Messiah Sits on the Throne in the New Jerusalem: The Final Judgment

38 Then countless peoples and nations will be
    coming,
and countless tribes from every place and from
    every mountain.
They will be holding in their hands branches of palm
    trees and of olive trees,
of cypresses and beautiful blossoms,
delightful flowers and sweet-smelling reeds.
They will be shouting and praising the great King of
    the ages.

The Syriac Apocalypse of Daniel

<table>
<tr><td>Dan 3:7; 4:1; 6:25; Jer 50:41; Rev 10:11</td><td>All peoples and nations and kings and nobles will worship him,</td></tr>
<tr><td>2 Kgs 19:21; Ps 9:14; Isa 1:8; 3:16, 17; 10:32; 62:11; Jer 4:31; Lam 1:6; 2:1, 8, 10; Mic 1:13; Zeph 3:14; Bar 4:14; Matt 21:5; John 12:15</td><td>and all flesh will worship and give praise at the gates of daughter Zion.
Furthermore, they will gather together to the light of his splendor.</td></tr>
<tr><td>1 Kgs 6:24-27; Ps 18:10; Ezek 28:14, 16; 41:18</td><td>He will set up the cherub of the sanctuary on Mount Zion</td></tr>
<tr><td>Pss 89:14; 97:2; Isa 9:7; Rev 21:2-3</td><td>and the throne of righteousness in the New Jerusalem.</td></tr>
<tr><td>Dan 7:13; Ps 8:5 [Evv 8:4]; 9:20 [Evv 9:19]; Matt 19:28; 25:31; Rev 3:21; 1 En. 61:8; 62:5</td><td>The great Messiah, the Son of Man, will sit on it and will judge the peoples in righteousness and the nations in uprightness.</td></tr>
<tr><td>John 5:27; 2 Thess 1:7-10; 1 En. 69:27-29; Pseudo-Methodius XI.5-7</td><td>He will hold (dominion) and will rule forever and ever,</td></tr>
<tr><td>Dan 7:13-14</td><td>and (from) generation to generation.
All the ends of the earth will worship him.
A mighty fire will be around Zion,</td></tr>
<tr><td>Job 41:11; Isa 4:5; 60:11; Ezek 43:2-3; Zech 2:5; Rev 21:25</td><td>and fiery sparks will be burning around Jerusalem.</td></tr>
<tr><td></td><td>All peoples and nations will gather together there,
all the just and righteous</td></tr>
<tr><td>Pss 61:6 [Evv 61:5]; 102:16 [Evv 102:15]; Isa 59:19; Mic 6:9; Rev 11:18; 15:4; Bar 3:7</td><td>and all who fear the name of the mighty Lord.</td></tr>
</table>

The Just and Righteous Enter Jerusalem

<table>
<tr><td></td><td>39 They will gather together and will enter into (the city) uncovered[a] and with joy
to receive what they have been promised.
And they will rejoice in the joy of Zion
and in the exultation of Jerusalem.</td></tr>
<tr><td>Zech 2:5</td><td>They will enter through its fiery walls,</td></tr>
<tr><td>Prov 6:28; Isa 43:2</td><td>and set their feet on the fiery sparks.
The fire will turn into dew under their feet,
and the fiery sparks will turn into holy water.</td></tr>
<tr><td></td><td>All the just and righteous will enter
and all who fear the name of the mighty Lord and do his will.
Everyone among them will enter the gate of his father's house</td></tr>
<tr><td>Num 16:14; 36:2; Deut 4:21; 15:4; Jer 12:14</td><td>and will go to the portion of his tribe.
But all who cannot enter the fiery gate</td></tr>
<tr><td>Matt 8:12; 22:13; 25:30; Luke 13:28</td><td>will gnash their teeth outside.
Jerusalem will be glorious and excellent and free.</td></tr>
</table>

a. Lit. "with uncovered heads."

"Abode of Peace" and "Town of Peace" she will be
    called.
But the uncircumcised and unclean will not enter
    into her.

Her citizens will live in her with joy.
They will be trusting and will inherit her land as an
    everlasting covenant.
Further, night will no more be over her,
nor will the sun or the moon set over her,
nor will it need the light of the sun,
not even (that of) the moon,
but the light of the mighty Lord
and the splendor of the Messiah will be shining over
    her forever and ever.

The Passover Banquet on Mount Zion

40 Then the mighty Lord will gather all the elect
    of Israel
and all the scattered of Judah
and all of Abraham's seed,
and they will celebrate a banquet for Zion
and a feast for Jerusalem,
a Passover, and joy, and glory,
a banquet of peace
in the days of the Messiah, at the redemption of
    Zion,
indeed, at the gathering of the exiles of Israel
and all of the just and righteous.

We beg from the Messiah our Lord, that he deem us worthy to stand at his right side, and to mingle us among the company of his holy ones, among the ranks of his friends, those who have loved him and kept his commandments, in his grace and his abundant mercy, forever and ever. Amen.

Here ends the awesome revelation that was revealed to the prophet Daniel in the land of Elam and in Persia.

Isa 1:26; 60:14; 62:4; Jer 23:6; Ezek 48:35; Zech 8:3

Isa 52:1; Rev 21:27; 22:15

Gen 9:16; 17:7, 13, 19; 2 Sam 23:5; Ps 105:10; Isa 61:8; Jer 24:5; 50:5; Sir 44:18; 45:7, 15; Bar 2:35; 1 Macc 2:54; 4 Ezra 3:15

Isa 24:23; 60:19; Zech 14:6–7; Rev 22:5; 4 Ezra 7:39, 42; 4Q542 1 i 1

Isa 60:1, 20; Rev 21:23; Bar 5:1–4; Sib. Or. 3:787; 5:420–27; T. Dan 5:12–13; 4 Ezra 7:42; Pesiq. Rab Kah. 21:5

Deut 30:4; Isa 60:4; Jer 32:37; Ezek 34:13; 36:24; Matt 24:31; Mark 13:27

2 Chr 20:7; Ps 105:6; Isa 41:8; Jer 33:26; 4 Macc 18:1; Jub. 31:7; T. Levi 8:15; Pss. Sol. 9:17; 18:4

Isa 25:6; Matt 8:11–12; 22:1–14; Luke 14:15; 4 Ezra 2:38; T. Isaac 6:22; 3 En. 48A:10

Ps 110:1; Matt 25:33; Acts 2:33–34; 5:31; 7:55–56; Rom 8:34

Ps 122:8; Isa 41:8; John 15:14–15; Jub. 19:9; Mek. Exod. 14:15, 35b

Exod 20:26; Neh 1:5; Dan 9:4; John 14:15, 21; 2 John 1:6

1 Tim 1:2; Heb 4:16; 2 John 1:3; Wis 3:9; 4:15; 2 Esdras 2:32

Pseudo-Methodius XIV.13–14

Armenian 4 Ezra

Introduction by Vered Hillel
Translation by Michael E. Stone

The Armenian translation of 4 Ezra (Arm) is a major reworking or revision of 4 Ezra that has had a widespread and influential impact in Armenian literature. The Apocalypse of Ezra (4 Ezra) was written after the destruction of the temple in 70 CE and is typified by its dialogic visions between Ezra and an angel and by its focus on theodicy. The Armenian translation, which was not known in Western scholarship until the twentieth century, is extant as a Christian composition translated from a reworked fifth-century Greek text and is one of seven more or less complete versions of 4 Ezra that survive in translation: Latin, Syriac, Ethiopic, two Arabic, Armenian, and Georgian. The Armenian version is notable for its wide divergences from the texts witnessed by the other versions of 4 Ezra. Many of Arm's revisions change the conceptual or theological meaning of the text while others are simply stylistic preferences. Armenian's primary literary and editorial techniques are discussed below.

Manuscripts and Versions

Armenian 4 Ezra was first published in the West in 1805 in the Armenian Bible of Johannes Zohrabian.[1] The text in the Zohrab Bible was reprinted by Sargis Yovsēpʻianc̔ in 1896, translated into English by James Issaverdens in 1901 and into German in 1910 by Bruno Violet.[2] In 1979 Michael E. Stone published a critical edition with a new English translation based on twenty-two manuscripts.[3] These manuscripts separate into two families, I = H and II = W ψ (ψ represents all other manuscripts). Though neither families I or II are descendants of one another, they do share a common ancestor. Manuscript H is the best single witness to the text, and W is the best witness of family II.[4]

Subsequent to publication of the critical edition, six further manuscripts became known (Aa–Ff).[5] These six manuscripts were collated for chapters 3 and 4 and published

---

1. Zohrabian, *The Scriptures of the Old and New Testaments* (Venice: Mekhitarist Press, 1805) [Armenian].

2. Yovsēpʻianc̔, *Uncanonical Books of the Old Testament* (Venice: Mekhitarist Press, 1896), 251–99 [Armenian]. Issaverdens, *The Uncanonical Writings of the Old Testament Found in the Armenian Manuscripts of the Library of St. Lazarus* (Venice: St. Lazarus, 1901), 364–501. Violet, *Die Esra-Apokalypse (IV Esra)*, vol. 1: *Die Überlieferung*, GCS 18 (Leipzig: Hinrichs, 1910).

3. Stone, *The Armenian Version of IV Ezra*, University of Pennsylvania Armenian Texts and Studies 1 (Missoula, MT: Scholars Press, 1979). We are grateful to Professor Stone for permission to reprint this translation here. The catalog information for these twenty-two manuscripts is on pp. 6–11. Cf. Albertus Fredrik J. Klijn, *Die Esra-Apokalypse (IV Esra)*, GCS (Berlin: Akademie-Verlag, 1988).

4. The relationship between the text forms and a stemmatic representation is found in Stone, *Armenian Version*, 11–14.

5. Manuscripts Aa–Ff are found in Onnik Eganyan, Andranik Zeytʻunyan, and Pʻaylak Antʻabyan,

by Stone in *A Textual Commentary on the Armenian Version of IV Ezra*.[6] With the exception of Ff, these manuscripts belong to family II and do not affect the stemma, or the text presented in the critical edition. Manuscript Ff is exceptional because of its age (thirteenth century), its character similar to H and W, and number of unique corruptions, as well as being found in a miscellany copied in Rome, which was not an important locale for Armenian studies. An additional fifteen manuscripts (Gg–Uu) have come to light since the publication of the *Textual Commentary* in 1990. These fifteen new manuscripts have not been thoroughly studied for their textual character and require further study before they can be included into the stemma. However, probes of select sections of Hh show that it belongs to family II and diverged from the archetype before the ancestor of W ψ. Manuscript Hh is significant because it is the oldest known manuscript of Arm (twelfth century) and the first copy of 4 Ezra to be found in a nonbiblical manuscript.[7] All but two known copies of Arm (Ff and Hh) are in Bible manuscripts, intimating that it was closely associated with the transmission of the Bible.

A	Jerusalem, Arm. Patriarchate 1933	Bible	1645 CE
B	Rome, Cod. Vat. Arm. 1	Bible	1625 CE
C	Venice, Mekhitarist 1182	Bible	1656 CE
D	Venice, Mekhitarist 1270	Bible	Fourteenth–fifteenth century CE
E	Venice, Mekhitarist 229	Bible	1655 CE
F	Venice, Mekhitarist 623	Bible	1648 CE
G	Jerusalem, Arm. Patriarchate 1934	Bible	1643–1646 CE
H	Erevan, Matenadaran 1500	Miscellany	1272–1288 CE
I	Erevan, Matenadaran 2732	Bible	Seventeenth century CE
J	Erevan, Matenadaran 200	Bible	1653–1658 CE
K	Erevan, Matenadaran 201	Bible	1660 CE
L	Erevan, Matenadaran 354	Bible	Fourteenth century CE
M	Erevan, Matenadaran 205	Bible	Seventeenth century CE
N	Erevan, Matenadaran 351	Bible	1619 CE
P	Jerusalem, Arm. Patriarchate 1927	Bible	1653 CE
Q	Jerusalem, Arm. Patriarchate 1928	Bible	1648 CE
R	London, Brit. & For. Bib. Soc.	Bible	ante 1667 CE
S	London, British Library or 8833	Bible	Seventeenth century CE
T	New Julfa, All-Savior Church 15	Bible	1662 CE
V	New Julfa, All-Savior Church 16	Bible	Seventeenth century CE
W	Jerusalem, Arm. Patriarchate 2558	Bible	Seventeenth century CE
Z	Jerusalem, Arm. Patriarchate 2561	Bible	Seventeenth century CE
Aa	Erevan, Matenadaran 188	Bible	1641–1643 CE
Bb	Erevan, Matenadaran 189	Bible	1649–1650 CE
Cc	Erevan, Matenadaran 191	Bible	1663 CE

Grand Catalogue of the Armenian Manuscripts of the Maštocʽ Matenadaran, vol. 1 (Erevan: Academy of Sciences, 1984) [Armenian].

6. Stone, *A Textual Commentary on the Armenian Version of IV Ezra*, SBLSCS 34 (Atlanta: Scholars Press, 1990), 309–27.

7. For information on these fifteen new manuscripts, see Michael E. Stone, "7.2.6 Armenian," in *Textual History of the Bible*, ed. Armin Lange, doi:10.1163/2452-4107_thb_COM_0207020600.

Armenian 4 Ezra

Dd	Erevan, Matenadaran 203	Bible	1666 CE
Ee	Erevan, Matenadaran 204	Bible	Seventeenth century CE
Ff	Erevan, Matenadaran 142	Miscellany	1269 CE
Hh	Erevan, Matenadaran 5607	Miscellany	Twelfth century CE
Ii	Erevan, Matenadaran 4070	Miscellany	1550–1553 CE
Jj	Erevan, Matenadaran 2628	Bible	1635 CE
Kk	Erevan, Matenadaran 2669	Bible	1641 CE
Ll	Erevan, Matenadaran 2587	Bible	1648 CE
Mm	Erevan, Matenadaran 6281	Bible	1667 CE
Nn	Erevan, Matenadaran 2732	Bible	Seventeenth century CE
Oo	Erevan, Matenadaran 3705	Bible	Seventeenth century CE
Pp	Erevan, Matenadaran 350	Bible	1700 CE
Qq	New Julfa, All Savior Church 3	Bible	1654 CE
Rr	New Julfa, All Savior Church 2	Bible	Seventeenth century CE
Ss	Venice, Mekhitarist 3	Bible	1648 CE
Tt	Venice, Mekhitarist; Kurdian 37	Bible	1638 CE
Uu	BL	Bible	1661 CE

Text-critical and philological studies have shown that the revisions in Arm existed for the most part in a Greek text that was edited and reworked by a Christian before it was translated into Armenian and most likely preserve fragments of ancient Ezra literature.[8] Moreover, this analysis accords with the tendency of Armenian translations of ancient documents to remain remarkably faithful, and at times even servile, to the rendition of their originals.

Characteristics of the Armenian Translation

Armenian 4 Ezra is typified by extensive revisions that involve the addition and omission of substantial passages, the replacement of many verses and groups of verses by alternate text, the rearrangement of the structure and contents of many passages, as well as numerous minor changes in the text. The Armenian also has a propensity for fixed linguistic formulas (e.g., 6:17B; 7:78; 14:8) and prefers certain words and tends to avoid others. This reworking creates a unique interpretation that is at variance with the other versions. The ensuing descriptions of Arm's idiosyncratic readings follow the two categories set out by Stone in *Textual Commentary*, xiv–xvii: (1) clear conceptual or theological points—expansions, translation of the name *Adam*, omission of *evil heart* and Messiah, *good things*, *prepared*, angels, Antichrist, and divine and human will; and (2) editorial techniques repeatedly employed—reordering of material, formulaic lists, Semitisms, quotations and allusions to the Bible and cross-references to 4 Ezra, and the addition of *after this/that* and *again*.

Expansions

The expansions in Arm are for the most part concerned with issues of theodicy and are embedded in dialogic passages. Some of the expansions are schematic lists that em-

---

8. Michael E. Stone, "Some Features of the Armenian Version of IV Ezra," *Mus* 79 (1966): 387–400; repr., in *Selected Studies in Pseudepigrapha and Apocrypha with Special Reference to the Armenian Tradition*, SVTP 9 (Leiden: Brill, 1991), 282–95; Stone, *Fourth Ezra: A Commentary on the Book of Fourth Ezra*, Hermeneia (Minneapolis: Fortress, 1990), 8.

bellish those occurring in the Apocalypse of Ezra. The most prominent expansions in Arm are:

5:6A–12E	Messianic woes; eschatological prophecy about the Antichrist.
5:35A–36D	Limits of human knowledge.
6:1A–1L	Dialogue between Ezra and an angel on the fate of the people; prophecy of the Antichrist; the secret of redemption revealed.
6:20A–20D	Messianic woes; Antichrist; judgment.
6:41A–41B	Description of creation.
6:54A–54D	The creation of Adam and Eve; Adam's willful disobedience.
8:1A–2B	Reasons for sin; free will of humankind; God's mercy, forgiveness, and foreknowledge.
8:41A–B	The fate of humans.
8:62A–62O	The purpose of creation; the reasons for sin.
9:16A–16I	The fate of humans; Ezra's vision of the Most High.
13:40A–40D	The return of the multitude.

Translation of "Adam"

The Armenian translation avoids the use of the name Adam, with two exceptions, 4:30 and 7:118. All further occurrences in the other versions have either been omitted and the context rephrased (3:10, 21, 26; 6:56; 7:11) or changed to "man, human" (3:5; 6:54A; 7:70, 116). The change of the name Adam to "man" could simply be a play on the Hebrew word *adam*, which can be translated either Adam or "man, human." Similar phrases in the Apocalypse of Esdras 2:10–11, 5:9, 6:16 and the Apocalypse of Sedrach 4:3 use the Greek word *anthrōpos*. These similarities do not indicate that the Armenian translator faithfully rendered *anthrōpos* from the Greek original, as this would imply that the other versions read "man" instead of "Adam," and this is not the case. Nor does such a translation imply that the translator knew Hebrew, as the translation "man, human" could simply be dependent on an onomastic list such as was common in the ancient world.

The context of the five omissions demonstrates that they are not due to scribal error but are deliberately rephrased. The reasons for the avoidance of the use of the proper name Adam are not completely clear. They may be a result of reliance on an onomasticon such as *Onomastica Sacra* (a Late Antique work on the meaning of proper nouns in the Bible) or they may be a commonsense interpretation for ideological or theological reasons. These changes may have been influenced by Arm's tendency to blame humanity for the introduction of evil into the world and for its continued action. In Arm, the parlous state of the world is not a result of Adam's sin, but of Israel's rejection of Torah and God's subsequent rejection of Israel (3:22; 5:12C; 6:1E; 7:11). The Armenian also avoids the idea that the world was created for Israel, stating that it was created for humankind (7:10; cf. 11–12).

Omission of "evil heart"

Audacious statements about the *evil heart* of humanity or the evil inherent in the world are prominent in the book of 4 Ezra, which stops just short of saying that God created the evil heart. The Armenian version on the other hand removes all culpability from God and stresses human responsibility for evil and its formulation. The Armenian methodically represses all references to *evil heart*, either by omitting them (3:20–21, 26; 4:4, 30; 7:48, 92) or by transforming the text (3:22; 4:27; 7:11). For example, 3:22 addresses the question of how God could have allowed the evil heart to exist in humans alongside Torah. The Armenian omits *evil heart* and modifies the text, changing the sense of the verse so that God is exonerated from any responsibility in the creation of evil, and Israel is indicted for disobedience due to rejection of the Torah.

The question of theodicy is taken up again in the expansion in 8:62E–O, which concludes that the cause of evil is not the creator, but rather humanity, who did not use creation well and offended their creator (8:62N). Additionally, Armenian expansions in 7:135, 139–140 and 8:1A–1D, which strongly emphasize God's mercy, graciousness, forgiveness, and foreknowledge, indicate that humankind has free will to choose their actions. The idea of free will conflicts with the idea of inherent evil. The Armenian is not so much interested in the idea of the evil heart, as much as in avoiding its deterministic implications.

Omission of "Messiah"

The Armenian translation omits the word *Messiah* or *son* from passages in which the Messiah is called the *son* or *servant of God* in other versions: "God's anointed" is used in 7:28, "the Most High" in 13:32, "mysteries of the Most High" in 13:52, and simply "with me" in 14:9, whereas 7:29 and 13:37 omit the term altogether. Furthermore, Arm completely omits 7:29–31, which recounts eschatological events that describe how the Messiah will come and will rejoice for four hundred years with the survivors of the messianic woes. Then the Messiah and all humanity will die, the earth will revert to primordial chaos, and silence will reign for seven days, after which new creation, resurrection, judgment, and reward and punishment follow. Thus, Arm omits the ideas about the death of the Messiah and the subsequent new creation and announces that the resurrection will immediately follow the coming of God's anointed. This omission makes the eschatology of Arm more palatable to a Christian point of view.

Good Things

Armenian 4 Ezra uses the Armenian word *barik'* (*good things*) as a term for eschatological rewards where different expressions are found in the other versions. The term *good things* is used in 4:39; 5:40; 7:14, 17, 95, 120, 122, 128; 8:5; and 62K. Sometimes the term is inserted into the Arm text when it is clearly absent in the other versions, and at other times, Arm draws on the assumed meaning of the verse as found in the other versions and rephrases it to focus on eschatological reward (e.g., 4:39). These eschatological rewards that are "stored up for the saints" (7:122) are described in the highest epithets; they are prepared before the world existed (7:14) and they are indescribable (7:120).

Prepared

The Armenian version also has a predilection for the term *prepared* in connection with the eschaton (7:14, 36, 37, 38, 61, 77, 95, 120, 123; 8:5, 59; 9:9; 14:15; cf. 7:70, 93). It is introduced frequently where it does not occur in the other versions, except for three instances, 8:52 where *prepare* also occurs in other versions and 7:14 and 7:77 where *prepare* corresponds to a similar, but not identical, verb in the other versions. In most occurrences, the term is a gloss added to another word designating eschatological reward and punishment. Armenian and Arabic alone present the concept that paradise is *prepared* (7:38).

Angels
Armenian introduces exclusive ideas about angels that are not found in the other versions; an angelic demiurge is mentioned in 5:23, the righteous are reckoned with the angels in 7:96, and in 8:62I angels, like humankind, have the wisdom to know good and evil. In other instances, Arm explicitly inserts an angel into the text where they are only implied in the other versions (5:44, 56; 12:40, 51).

Antichrist
The Antichrist is not mentioned in the other versions of 4 Ezra but does occur several times in the Armenian translation. While the actual word "Antichrist" does not occur in the Armenian text, the idea or role of the Antichrist is quite prominent. The Antichrist is called the "spirit of error," who will work signs and lead people astray (6:1H, cf. 5:6A; cf. 1 John 4:6; 1 Tim 4:1; 1QS 1.23–24; 4.16, 20) and "Rebellion" who will corrupt many (6:24; cf. 2 Thess 2:3).

Divine and Human Will
The idea of human and divine will occurs quite often in Armenian 4 Ezra, but it parallels the other versions only once, in 8:28. The Armenian version contrasts divine and human will in 8:26–33 and refers to God's will as creative or revealed will, "will of the Most High" (5:23; 6:1C, 1D) and as "your [God's] will" (8:32, 33). Human free will is mentioned in 8:1B; 6:54C; and 9:16A. Humans have a choice, they can act according to their own will, either righteously or wickedly, or in accord with God's will or against it. Furthermore, the same Armenian word *kamk'* (*will*) is used for God's will, human will, and bodily desires (the will of the body), which lead humans to act against God's will (7:45; 8:62E, 62F).

Reordering of Material
The phenomenon of rearranging the elements of verses or passages is widespread in Arm (e.g., 4:24, 50; 5:13; 9:9). Often Arm subsumes all elements dealing with the same subject into a single, contrasting sentence (e.g., 5:1, 23; 6:22) and reformulates typical Hebrew contrasting parallelism of A:B C:D as A+C: B+D (e.g., 7:36). Armenian also tends to render first-person speech found in the other versions into third-person divine speech (e.g., 5:41; 7:27, 28, 130).

Formulaic Lists
Armenian 4 Ezra is deeply concerned with the messianic woes that feature eschatological signs such as corruption of the cult and ritual (e.g., 5:9; 9:3; 13:34), fighting and strife between individuals and groups (e.g., 5:9; 6:24), and cataclysmic earthly events (e.g., 5:6B–9; 6:20A–C). These woes are presented in formulaic lists of individuals and groups of people among whom conflicts will arise (5:6, 9; 6:24; 13:31). Each list corresponds to single phrases in the other versions, but is notably expanded in Arm. Such formulaic lists relating to an eschatological drama are found in other ancient literature (e.g., Matt 10:21, 24; 24:7, 21; Isa 19:2; 2 Chr 15:6) and are characterized by a peculiar literary style that usually begins with some form of the phrase "And in those days sons will rise up against fathers ... sons, " and so on. While the four lists in Arm are quite typical in their formulaic representation, their expanded rhetoric makes them longer and more complex than other similar lists. Formulaic lists of this sort corroborate Arm's penchant for stringing together homogenous list-like material (e.g., 6:20A–C; 7:33). Furthermore, signs of the

end, well known in Jewish and Christian sources, occur elsewhere in passages that are peculiar to Arm, for example, 5:1–2; 6:20A–20C; 9:3.

Semitisms

Another editorial technique distinctive to the Armenian translation is the readings in which Arm uses a participle or infinitive in the instrumental case together with a finite verb. This construction reflects the manner in which the Armenian translation of the Bible renders Greek translations of the Hebrew infinitive absolute and finite verb (see e.g., 3:34; 4:2, 13; 6:24; 8:37; 9:11; 13:8, 11). This construction is used by the Armenian version in instances where it does not appear in any other version of 4 Ezra.[9]

Quotations and Allusions to the Bible and Other Places in 4 Ezra

The Armenian version often quotes or alludes to biblical verses or to other places in 4 Ezra in material exclusively found in translation. The quotations and allusions are concentrated in the first part of the book, where most of the editorial interpolations in Arm occur. Other than the references to Genesis, which are due to the prominence of the theme of creation, the citations are from various verses scattered throughout the Old and New Testaments. Note that the allusions and citations from the New Testament, particularly from Paul, indicate that the reworking was Christian. Such quotes, allusions, and cross-references are indicated in the translation.

Addition of "After This/That" and "Again"

The addition of the connecting phrases "after this/that" and "again" is a stylistic feature of Arm. In the majority of the cases, the addition of "after this/that" is distinctive to Arm and does not correspond to anything in the other versions. Such phrases are found in 3:3 (H), 5, 19 (HW); 5:10; 6:1C, 1I; 9:25; 13:38. The word "again" occurs twenty times in Arm, nine of which occur in material peculiar to the Armenian translation (3:12; 4:18, 51; 5:15, 43; 6:36, 53; 8:6; 13:1).

Relation to Apocryphal Literature

The Armenian translation of 4 Ezra, specifically the expansions, is one of six writings in the Esdras/Sedrach tradition that purport to be a discussion between an angel and Ezra on the fate of humans:[10]

1. Greek Apocalypse of Esdras[11]
2. Greek Apocalypse of Sedrach
3-4. Latin Vision of Ezra (short and long versions)[12]

---

9. The use of Hebraisms is addressed in Michael E. Stone, "A Hebraism in the Armenian Version of 4 Ezra," *Language Studies: Avi Hurvitz Festschrift* 11–12 (2008): 213–16 [Heb.].

10. This section on Esdras/Sedrach literature is drawn from the discussion on this literature in Michael E. Stone, *Ancient Judaism: New Visions and Views* (Grand Rapids: Eerdmans, 2011), 161–66.

11. Otto Wahl, *Apocalypsis Esdrae, Apocalypsis Sedrach, Visio Beati Esdrae*, PVTG 4 (Leiden: Brill, 1977). For English translations, see Michael E. Stone, "The Greek Apocalypse of Ezra," *OTP* 1:561–79; and S. Agourides, "Apocalypse of Sedrach," *OTP* 1:605–13.

12. Short version: Otto Wahl, *Apocalypsis Esdrae, Apocalypsis Sedrach, Visio Beati Esdrae*, PVTG 4 (Leiden: Brill, 1977). For an English translation, see J. R. Mueller and G. A. Robbins, "Vision of Ezra," *OTP* 1:581–90. Long version: Pierre-Maurice Bogaert, "Une Version longue inédite de la 'Visio Beati Esdrae,'

5. Armenian Questions of Ezra[13]
6. Armenian Expansions of 4 Ezra, which are additional expanded passages in the Armenian version of 4 Ezra.

All six works are united by their relationship to the Apocalypse of Ezra, particularly in their dialogical literary form, as revelatory dialogue is a predominant feature of 4 Ezra. Furthermore, these six works address topics drawn from 4 Ezra, such as questions about the purpose and nature of creation, the reasons for sin, the cataloguing of messianic woes, and concern for the fate of the righteous. Additional features are shared by some of the books. For example, the Vision of Ezra (both versions) and the Greek Apocalypse of Esdras include the hanging punishments material, but the short version of the Vision of Ezra does not include the description of the Antichrist, which is included in the long version, the Greek Apocalypse of Esdras, and the Armenian expansions. The Armenian version is most closely related to the Greek Apocalypses of Esdras and of Sedrach, with which Arm shares multiple readings (e.g., Arm 3:5; 4:2, 12; 5:36A and 36B). It is highly unlikely, however, that there is any direct literary dependence between Arm and these two apocalypses.

Date and Provenance

The mid-fifth century CE is the *terminus ad quem* for Arm. The creation of the Armenian alphabet is said to have taken place in the beginning of the fifth century, and there is evidence that Arm was translated soon after that. The fifth-century Armenian author dubbed Agathangelos excerpts material peculiar only to the expansions in Arm. For example, History of the Armenians §267 preserves phrases that depend on the extant Armenian version of 4 Ezra 5:36.[14] This verse in Arm contains an expanded list of things that are destined to be revealed, while Agathangelos's text, which lists God's creations, clearly alludes to phrases found only in Arm's expanded list and not in the other versions. Literary allusions to Armenian 4 Ezra (5:13; 9:23–24, 26–27; 10:20; 14:24–26, 38–40) preserved in the *Homily on the Church* of John of Jerusalem §§20–21, a late fourth- or early fifth-century document probably translated into Armenian in the sixth century, substantiate the fifth century date for Arm.[15] Additionally, inner developments of the Armenian text forms and parallels in related Ezra literature (see above, "Relation to Apocryphal Literature") confirm the antiquity of the translation.[16]

---

dans le Légendier de Teano (Barberini Lat. 2318)," *RBén* 94 (1984): 50–70. For an English translation, see Richard Bauckham, "The Latin Vision of Ezra," *MOTP* 1:498–528.

13. Michael E. Stone, "A New Edition and Translation of the *Questions of Ezra*," in *Solving Riddles and Untying Knots: Jonas C. Greenfield Festschrift*, ed. Ziony Zevit, Seymour Gittin, and Michael Sokoloff (Winona Lake, IN: Eisenbrauns, 1995), 293–316; repr. in *Apocrypha, Pseudepigrapha and Armenian Studies: Collected Papers*, OLA 144 (Leuven: Peeters, 2006), 374–98. For an English translation, see Stone, "Questions of Ezra," *OTP* 1:591–99.

14. The text of Agathangelos can be found in Robert W. Thomson, ed., *History of the Armenians: A Facsimile Reproduction of the 1909 Tiflis Edition*, Classical Armenian Text Reprints (Delmar, NY: Caravan Books, 1980). The English translation is in Thomson, *The Teaching of St. Gregory*, rev. ed., Avant: Treasures of the Armenian Christian Tradition 1 (New Rochelle, NY: St. Nersess Armenian Seminary, 2001), 67–68.

15. Michel van Esbroeck, "Une Homélie sur l'Eglise attribuée à Jean de Jérusalem," *Mus* 86 (1973): 283–304.

16. Inner Armenian text forms are developed by Stone in "Some Features."

Bibliography

Bogaert, Pierre-Maurice. "Une Version longue inédite de la 'Visio Beati Esdrae,' dans le Légendier de Teano (Barberini Lat. 2318)." *RBén* 94 (1984): 50–70. doi:10.1484/J.RB.4.01084.

Eganyan, Onnik, Andaranik Zeyt'unyan, and P'aylak Ant'abyan, *Grand Catalogue of the Armenian Manuscripts of the Maštoc' Matenadaran*. Vol. 1. Erevan: Academy of Sciences, 1984. [Armenian]

Issaverdens, James. *The Uncanonical Writings of the Old Testament Found in the Armenian Manuscripts of the Library of St. Lazarus*. Venice: St. Lazarus, 1901.

Klijn, Albertus Fredrik J. *Die Esra-Apokalypse (IV Esra)*. GCS. Berlin: Akademie-Verlag, 1988. doi:10.1515/9783110851953.

Stone, Michael E. "7.2.6 Armenian." In *Textual History of the Bible*. Edited by Armin Lange. doi:10.1163/2452-4107_thb_COM_0207020600.

———. *Ancient Judaism: New Visions and Views*. Grand Rapids: Eerdmans, 2011.

———. *The Armenian Version of IV Ezra*. University of Pennsylvania Armenian Texts and Studies 1. Missoula, MT: Scholars Press, 1979.

———. *Fourth Ezra: A Commentary on the Book of Fourth Ezra*. Hermeneia. Minneapolis: Fortress, 1990.

———. "Some Features of the Armenian Version of IV Ezra." *Mus* 79 (1966): 387–400. Repr., pages 282–95 in *Selected Studies in Pseudepigrapha and Apocrypha with Special Reference to the Armenian Tradition*. SVTP 9. Leiden: Brill, 1991.

———. *A Textual Commentary on the Armenian Version of IV Ezra*. SBLSCS 34. Atlanta: Scholars Press, 1990.

Thomson, Robert W. *The Teaching of St. Gregory*. Rev. ed. Avant: Treasures of the Armenian Christian Tradition 1. New Rochelle, NY: St. Nersess Armenian Seminary, 2001.

Violet, Bruno. *Die Esra-Apokalypse (IV Esra)*. Vol. 1: *Die Überlieferung*. GCS 18. Leipzig: Hinrichs, 1910.

Wahl, Otto. *Apocalypsis Esdrae, Apocalypsis Sedrach, Visio Beati Esdrae*. PVTG 4. Leiden: Brill, 1977.

Yovsēp'ianc', Sargis. *Uncanonical Books of the Old Testament*. Venice: Mekhitarist Press, 1896. [Armenian]

Zohrabian, J. *The Scriptures of the Old and New Testaments*. Venice: Mekhitarist Press, 1805. [Armenian]

Armenian 4 Ezra

3 ¹ I, Salathiel, who was also called Ezra, ²was in Babylon in the thirtieth year of the captivity of Judaea and of the destruction of Jerusalem. I was distressed on my bed and I was considering the destruction of Zion and the building of Babylon. ³And then indeed I was amazed in my heart[a] and began to speak terrible words to the Most High, ⁴and I said, "Lord my God! Did you not make the heavens and the earth and everything that is in them?[b] ⁵And after that you created man[c] with your incorruptible hands and you blew into him the breath of life and he became . . . before you ⁶And you placed him in the paradise of delight that your right hand planted. ⁷ᴬTo him you gave a command, so that he might know the Lord, and he transgressed that and was vanquished. On account of this at once you justly decreed death on him and on all the peoples who were to come forth from him, ⁸who transgressed the laws of your holy commandments. ⁷ᴮFor from him there came forth peoples, nations, and families without number. ⁹You brought the flood upon them and you destroyed them. ¹¹You had mercy upon your servant, Noah, and on his account upon his sons; and together with all his house he found favor before you, because he was pleasing to you.[d] ¹²And again the earth caused humankind to increase from his seed, and likewise they acted impiously before you even more than their fathers; ¹³and they constantly acted wickedly. You chose one just man among them, whose name was Abraham. ¹⁴You loved him and you showed him alone, by himself, the end of times. ¹⁵And you made a covenant with him to make his seed increase like the stars of heaven in multitude and like the sand by the shore of the sea without number. And so you gave him a son, Isaac and to Isaac, Jacob. ¹⁶And to Jacob (you gave) Joseph, together with the other eleven, and because of Joseph you led the fathers into Egypt, and you nourished them for many years. ¹⁷And after that you brought them forth by the hands of your

Exod 20:11; Ps 146:6 [Evv 145:6]

Gen 2:7

Gen 6:8–9

Gen 22:17; Hos 1:10

---

a. Or: "soul."
b. The phrase "the heavens . . . in them" is unique to Arm. It recurs in an almost identical verse solely in Arm 6:38.
c. Other versions read "Adam."
d. The other versions preserve a relatively different text of this verse. The phrase "and on his account" is not found in any other version, but reflects the same idea as Jub. 5:19.

Translation from Michael E. Stone, *The Armenian Version of IV Ezra*, University of Pennsylvania Armenian Texts and Studies 1 (Missoula, MT: Scholars Press, 1979). We are grateful to Professor Stone for permission to reprint this translation with minor modifications here.

servant Moses, and you led them into the wilderness and nourished them for forty years, and after that you led them into the land that you promised to your servant Abraham. [19]And you gave them Law and they did not observe (it). After that, for many years you gave them judges to judge and instruct them to observe your Law until Samuel, the prophet, who called upon your name.[a] [22]And because the infirmity remained in them, your Law departed from their hearts[b] [23]until you set up a ruler over them, David your servant. [24]To him you also said to build Jerusalem again in your name and to offer you sacrifices in it. After him, you raised up his son Solomon, whom you commanded to build the temple in a night vision; and (you commanded) all the people to say prayers and offer sacrifices in it. [25]And when this took place . . . the people that dwelt in the city sinned.[c] [27]And because of them you delivered the city into the hands of the heathen who were around it.[d]

[28]"While we were in our land, I used to say to myself, 'Is it that the inhabitants of Babylon have acted better and is Zion spurned because of that?' [29]But when I came here, I saw many impieties without number and behold, during these thirty years my soul has seen very many disobedient people. Therefore, my heart is astounded [30]when I consider how you tolerate the lawless and are merciful to the impious, and (how) you destroyed your people and were merciful to your enemies. [31]Is it that Babylon did anything better than Zion? [32]Or has some foreign nation known you more than Israel? Which nation has believed in your covenant like Jacob, [33]whose fruit has not been revealed? I traveled extensively among the nations and I found those who do not remember your commandments to be satiated. [34]Now, if you were to weigh our wickedness and the heathens', in the weight of the pans it would be discovered to which side it[e] inclines. [35]When did the inhabitants of this earth not sin before you? What people observed your commandments? [36]Perhaps you will find a few persons, but nowhere a (whole) people.

4 [1]And after I had considered this, an angel was sent to me whose name was Uriel. [2]He began to speak to me and said, "Your heart has been greatly amazed at this life in your desire to understand the way of the Most High." [3]And I said, "I beseech you, make me understand." He answered and said to me, "I was sent to set three similitudes before you and to show you three ways. [4]If you will tell me one of them, I will relate to you those things about which you desired to know."

[5]I replied and said, "Speak my lord!"

And he said to me, "Go, weigh the weight of fire for me or the heaviness of the wind, or bring me back the day that has passed."

---

a. Verses 16–19 are patterned after Ps 105 and Neh 9.

b. Arm changes the meaning of the verse to refer to an indictment of Israel for disobedience instead of a reference to the evil heart.

c. Arm omits 3:26 because it deals with Adam's sin and the evil heart.

d. The phrase "and because of them" is found only in Arm and sets up an explicit causal relationship between the sin of the people mentioned in 3:25 and the destruction of the city in 3:27.

e. That is, the balance.

⁶I replied and said, "Who of humankind can do this, that I should do (it)?"

⁷And he said to me, "But if I had asked you how many chambers are there in the heart of the sea, or how many heads are there of the channels of the deep, or how many paths are there above the firmament, or how many exits are there of hell, or how many entrances are there to paradise; ⁸then you would say to me, 'I have not descended into the sea, nor in the beginning have I been in the deep, nor have I ascended above the heavens, nor have I descended to the portals of hell, nor have I entered paradise.' ⁹Now, I did not ask you this, but about fire and wind and the day, to which you are accustomed and from which you cannot be separated. ¹⁰For those things that have been nurtured with you, you are unable to know; ¹¹How then can you understand the very great ways of the Most High, for the way of the Most High is beyond understanding? You are corruptible and inhabit a corruptible life, you cannot know the ways of the incorruptible." ¹²I replied and said to him, "It would be better for us if we had not been born than, having lived in impiety and having been delivered over into suffering, not even to know why we suffer."

¹³He replied and said to me, "Hear a parable! The forest of the trees of the field went forth; it made a plan and said to its fellows, ¹⁴'Come, let us go and make war against the sea so that it draws back before us and let us make another forest in it.' ¹⁵Again, the waves of the sea planned to go to fight with the forests of the field, to prepare another place for themselves. ¹⁶Their plan was in vain: fire came and consumed the forest. ¹⁷Similarly also, sand intervened and held the waves back. ¹⁸Now if you were a judge, which of them would you acquit or alternatively, which of them would you condemn?"

¹⁹I said, "Both of them, for in vain did they make a plan, since the earth was given to the forests, and a place to the sea, for the sand to hold the waves at bay."

Arm 4 Ezra 6:41B

²⁰And he said to me, "You have judged well. Why then did you not discern that which I said to you? ²¹Just as the earth was given to the forests, and a place of sand to the waves, so knowledge of earthly matters was given to those who are upon the earth and cognizance of the heavenly to those in the heavens."

²²And I said, "I ask you, lord, why then was such a mind given to me, to consider things such as these? ²³For it profits me not to ask what is above all, but it is good to know this—the calamities that we experience daily. Now, Why is Israel delivered into the hands of heathen and the people that God loved delivered into the hands of the wicked, and the Law of our fathers forgotten and the written covenants nowhere to be found?

²⁴And we live here like locusts that have no Law, nor commandments, nor covenants, and we depart this world without having become worthy of mercy.ᵃ ²⁵What still further shall we receive, we over whom his name is pronounced?"

²⁶He answered and said to me, "Now, while you are indeed here you shall see and having come close you shall be amazed, for this world is hastening to

---

a. Arm has adapted a phrase like Latin *pertransimus de saeculo ut locustae* ("we depart from the world like locusts"), split it into two elements, reversed the order and then expanded each of them separately.

Armenian 4 Ezra

pass away, [27]since it is not able to bear the evil of its time because the people of this world[a] are full of every wickedness.[b] [28-29]Therefore, too, the threshing floor[c] will pass over them; for if the harvest will not first come upon them, neither will that which is the fruit of goodness reach the righteous. [30]Come, consider! If the little transgression[d] of Adam perpetrated that much evil, having increased evil thenceforth upon the earth, what sort of destruction shall it prepare (for those) who act wickedly?"

[33]I replied and said, "How long will this be?" [34]And he said to me, "You are not wiser than the Most High if you would make the end arrive immediately, for you hasten because of yourself alone, but the Most High is long-suffering because of many. [35]For, concerning that, the souls of the just asked the Most High and said, 'How long shall we be here? When will the reward of our time come?' [36]The Lord[e] answered them and said, 'Be patient until the appointed times will be filled.' [37]For he has measured the times in a measure and has weighed the eternities on a scale and has counted the hours by number: he will not move nor will he arouse until the appointed hour arrives.

[38]I replied and said, "I beg of you, lord! [39]Is it (due to) the Most High's abundant mercy that he is patient for the sake of us wicked ones, not bringing the end; but is he long-suffering for our sake, delaying the just so that they do not enjoy the good things that he has promised them?"

[40]He replied and said, "It is indeed thus, as you have understood; but it will come in its time. For just as a pregnant woman cannot give birth before the appointed time, if the ninth month is not completed, [42]and just as the woman hastens to reach the time to be delivered from the pangs and the travail of the birth, so the chambers of the earth too, hasten to restore the fruit that was entrusted to it. [43]Accordingly, when the time comes you will see and recognize that concerning which you wished to know."

[44]And I asked him and said, "I beseech you, lord, if I have found favor before you and if I am worthy, [45]reveal to me concerning the time, whether the greater part has passed or is (yet) to be."

[47]And he said to me, "Stand at the right-hand side and I will show you the form of a parable."

[48]And I stood up and he showed me a burning furnace; and it came to pass that when the flame was ended, smoke went forth. [49]And after a moment there came a cloud full of water and it poured down very fierce rain, and after the passing of the rain—dew.

[50]And he said to me, "Consider that, for just as the fire is greater than the smoke and the rain than the dew, so the portion of the time which has passed is greater."

a. Or: "age."

b. The sentence has been changed from a pronouncement of dualistic despair of this world to an indictment of the moral sins of human beings.

c. Or: "threshing."

d. Reworded to avoid "evil seed" or "evil heart" and may also be responsible for the omission of the rest of 4:31 and 4:32.

e. The angel Remiel is the speaker in the other versions. This change, coupled with the addition of "the Most High" in verse 35, makes God the sole actor in Armenian.

⁵¹Again I beseeched him and said, "Who of us, then, will be alive? Who of us will be in those days? What sign will there be of those times?"

⁵²He replied and said to me, "I can tell you about the signs, but I was not sent to tell you about your life."

5 ¹"Hear concerning the signs! Behold, days are coming and in those days humankind shall be amazed at very great wonders and the truth of faith shall hide from uprightness. ²And after the increase of impiety, there will be certain people upon the earth who speak perverse things with lying words and with varied fabrications: certain ones having erred in hypocrisy through the sanctity of worship, having seized upon incontinence. ³And this earth,ᵃ which you see formerlyᵇ . . . will become a wilderness, without rest and pathless.

⁴If God will permit, you will see wonders. After the third vision, the earth shall be disturbed and suddenly the sun shall appear by night, and the moon by day. ⁵And blood shall drip from wood, and speech shall be heard from stone, and peoples shall fight with peoples; ⁶ᴬand workers of signs shall hold power, and tellers of tales shall be mighty; ⁶ᴮand at that time, the sea shall often be moved in various places, and there shall be abysses and the atmospheres shall be changed; and the birds of heaven shall change their places,ᶜ ⁷and the sea of Sodom shall swarm with fish; ⁸and fire shall be sent forth often, and a signᵈ shall be born of women, ⁹and in sweet waters saltiness shall be found; and humans shall fight with one another, sons with fathers and fathers with sons, mothers and daughters opposed to one another, siblings with siblings, friends with acquaintances, nations with nations, peoples with peoples, priests with priests, and ministrants with ministrants; and they shall hide the just commandment of the Most High and falsehood shall be mighty in them, and wisdom shall depart from the saints.   *Mark 13:7–8, 12*

¹⁰And after that, they will seek and they will not find, for hatred shall increase and falsehood shall be frequent, and their fathers shall be arrogant and the upright shall be few. ¹¹ᴬAnd a land will ask its neighbor and say, 'Has anyone gone over you who held to the faith and spoke the truth, ¹¹ᴮor did justice, or hated wickedness, or has belonged to the portion of the truth,ᵉ or has done mercy or has hated rapine, ¹¹ᶜor has sought the Most High with all their heart; or did anyone love their friend in holiness?' ¹¹ᴰIt will answer and say, 'No one   *Lev 19:18; Deut 6:24;*
of that sort is found on me.' ¹²ᴬAt those times humankind shall hope to receive   *Matt 19:19*
something from the Most High; they shall seek and they shall not receive; ¹²ᴮthey shall toil laboriously and they shall not rest; they shall be oppressed and shall not enjoy the works of their own hands; they shall walk and their path shall not be straight. ¹²ᶜThey shall be seized at the end of time by pains and by grief and by mourning, for not only did they change the Law, but also

---

a. Or: "land."

b. Arm is incomplete at this point.

c. The two additional phrases, "and at that" and "various places," and their correspondence to T. Mos. 10:6 may indicate the antiquity of the text behind the Arm translation.

d. Or: "portent."

e. Arm text has no meaning as it stands. The translation has been reconstructed from the Greek and may be compared with 1QM 13:9–10.

the Most High himself, upon the earth . . .[a] [12D]Because of that, evil will come upon them and the Most High will reign manifestly and he will come and will change them; and the Most High will show glory from himself in them [12E]when he will requite them with punishment. Just as they thought arrogantly, so will he dishonor them. [13]I was commanded to say these signs to you. If again, once more, you petition the Most High with fasting and tears for about seven days, you shall hear even greater things than these."

[14A]And when I awoke, having heard this, I thought about (it). I became afraid and the nature of my body was weakened, my strength departed from me and my soul was close to fainting. [14B]I considered that none of us can be saved, and we die like animals in which there is no wisdom,[b] and we are tortured in eternal torments. When I considered this intensely, I was worried. [15]The angel Uriel came again and strengthened me; he set me up and stood me on my feet and said to me, "Do not be sad, for that which the Most High will do in the days of the end has been shown to you before its time. You have found grace from God."

[16]And it came to pass after this, Pʻałałtiēl who was the leader of people came to me and said to me, "Why has the beauty of your face become thus disfigured? [17]Do you not know that he entrusts Israel to you in this land of our sojourning? [18]Stand up quickly and eat bread, lest you die and leave us, like a shepherd who (leaves) his flock in the power of evil wolves."

[19]And I said to him, "Go away from me and do not approach me for seven days!"

And he went from me according to this pronouncement. [20]And I, weeping and lamenting and relating my sins, fasted for seven days even as the angel had commanded me.

[21]And it came to pass after the seven days were completed, again the thoughts of my heart greatly spurred me on. [22]And my heart received a spirit of understanding and I began to say these words before the Most High, [23]and I said, "O Lord! You are he, who, by the will of the Most High, made and prepared everything, and by your wisdom you conduct everything and you requite each according to his ways. You, Lord, out of all the woods of trees chose for yourself the vine,[c] [24B]out of all flowers—the lily, [26]out of all birds—the dove, out of all quadrupeds—the sheep, [25]out of all the multitude of waters—the Jordan River, out of all cities—the city of Zion, [24A]out of all the dwellings of the earth—the land of sanctity; [27]and out of all the people, you chose for yourself the seed of Abraham and the Law, chosen by you above[d] everything, which you bestowed upon your beloved people. [28]And now, my Lord, long-suffering one who does not remember sins, why did you deliver your people, upon whom your name is named, into the power of an abominable and impious nation and (why) did you thus scatter the seed that you loved among the heathens; [29]and it was trampled underfoot like the dust of the earth, beneath

---

a. The last four words of the verse are corrupt.
b. Lit., "in which there is in them no"; see introduction on Arm's stylistic use of Semitisms.
c. Lit.: "material." The Arm is a mistranslation of the Greek *hylē*.
d. Or: "of."

their feet? ³⁰(If) you indeed hated your people because of the evil of their deeds, they ought to have been punished at your hands."

³¹And it came to pass, as I was speaking all this with him, the angel who had spoken with me before, on the previous night, was sent to me. ³²And he said to me, "Listen to me and be attentive, observe and I shall speak further before you."

³³And I answered and said, "Speak, my lord, so that your servant may hear!" And he said to me, "Why is your heart so astounded as to come to say such words before the Most High? Did you love Israel more than the Most High?" 1 Sam 3:9

³⁴And I said, "No, lord, but I spoke in affliction, because my reins continually importune me[a] and seek to understand the paths of the Most High, and to investigate one portion of his judgments."

³⁵ᴬAnd he said to me, "Do not investigate that which is above you, and do not examine that which is concealed from the children of humankind, and keep to yourself whatever is said to you, and do not investigate the paths of the Most High lest you stray from him, for you have no need of the hidden things." Sir 3:21–22; 4 Ezra 4:2

³⁵ᴮAnd I said, "Then why was I born and (why) was my mother's womb not my tomb? For I would not have seen the destruction of Jacob and the death of Israel, and the fullness of the heathen who did not know God." And he said to me, "Do not struggle to know those things that are unknown. Behold! Let me ask you (some) things, perhaps you can tell me (them)." And I said, "Tell me!"

³⁶ᴬAnd he said, "Tell me the number of those who are going to be born and going to die, and of those who are and who are going to be and who are going to die! Relate to me the breadth of the sea and the multitude of the fish, or the heights of the heavens, or the hosts of stars, or the circuits of the sun, or the orbits of the stars, or the forms of the firmament, or the breadth of the earth, or weight of dust! ³⁶ᴮReckon for me the number of the hairs of your body, or the blinking of your eye, or the power of hearing, or the multitude of sight, or the preparation of smell, or the touches of hands, or the running of veins! ³⁶ᶜOr will you find the imprints of feet, or the appearance and measure of breath, or its form, or its color, or the nest of wisdom, or the wisdom of birds, ³⁶ᴰor the variety of creeping things that are on dry land and that are in the waters, which are hostile to one another, the running without feet, or the blowing of the winds? And gather for me the dispersed and scattered drops of rain, and make green the flowers that have withered. ³⁷Open for me the closed chambers of the earth and bring close to me the winds that are enclosed and shut up in them, or show me the form of a wind, or the appearance of souls, and then you shall understand the paths of the Most High and you shall know the variety of his ways."

³⁸And I was amazed at these words and I said, "O, lord, lord! Who of humankind can do or know that, if not he whose dwelling is not with humankind?"

⁴⁰And he said to me, "Just as you cannot do or say one of them, so you will be unable to investigate the wisdom of the Most High, or to know the variety

---

a. In a biblical context the Armenian word translated "reins" indicates the seat of emotion as "kidneys" do in Hebrew. A more modern understanding, but less accurate translation, is "my emotions implore me."

of his ways,[a] or to find out his judgments and the end of his love that he has promised to give to his beloved ones, or the good things from him that eye has not seen and ear has not heard and have not occurred to humankind and humankind has never considered, which God has prepared for his beloved ones."

1 Cor 2:9

⁴¹I replied and said, "Behold, as you said to me, this has been promised to those who served with sanctity and those who will be pleasing to him. What shall we sinners do, for we acted wickedly before knowing this and, behold, we are going thither empty and devoid?"

⁴²And he said to me, "His judgment is like a crown. Just as it is not diminished by its slowness, so it does not advance by its swiftness."

⁴³Once more, again I said to him, "Indeed, can he not make those who have passed away and those who are and those who will be, at one time, so that this world may pass away without delay and judgment may come and each person may learn what is prepared for them?"[b]

⁴⁴ The angel replied and said to me, "I know that according to the time the Most High has determined also to make that which is going to be in (its) time, and the creatures cannot hasten, just as has been fixed by the Most High; for it[c] cannot sustain all at the one time."

⁴⁵And I replied, "How did the Most High say that he would restore all human creatures? For if he said that he will raise up, at that time, all whom he will find—the living together with the dead—and when they will rise up, he will gather them all together and receive them all into that world, and it will sustain (them), why now could this world not hold them all at one time?"

⁴⁶And he said to me, "Ask a woman's womb and say to it, 'If you have to bear ten (children), why do you not bear them all together, but one after the other?'"

⁴⁷And I said to him, "It will be unable to do this."

⁴⁸He answered and said to me, "Thus, too, the earth cannot do this, for it is like a womb and (its) times (are) determined and it has been commanded to be obedient.[d] ⁴⁹For, just as a child cannot give birth, nor when she is an old woman can she give birth, so too the earth cannot act before the time."

⁵⁰I replied and said to him, "Since I have found grace before you, let me ask you one more thing. For, if indeed the earth is a womb and we are from it, now was it young or old?"

⁵¹And he said to me, "Ask her who gives birth ⁵²and say, 'Why are those whom you bore (latterly) unlike the former ones, but lesser in stature and weaker in strength?' ⁵³And the womb will say to you, those who are born in youth are (of) one strength and those who (are born) in old age of another.' ⁵⁴Consider too, that you are weaker than the former ones ⁵⁵and those who will

---

a. Arm addition clearly drawn from 5:37.

b. The latter part of the verse is an addition unique to Arm. The phrase "this world ... and" is drawn from 4 Ezra 4:26.

c. That is: the earth.

d. Some phrases in this expansionary text of Arm are difficult. As a result, the translation is based on the other versions.

Armenian 4 Ezra

be after you (weaker) than you as if, indeed, the earth were in old age and its youth had passed."

⁵⁶I replied and said to the angel, "I ask of you, lord, do not turn away (your) face from me, who am asking you about many things, but command me further to learn from you that concerning which I wish to ask."

6 ¹ᴬAnd he said to me, "Ask what your soul desires and I will tell you those things that it is right for you to know."ᵃ

¹ᴮAnd I said, "I beseech you, hear me patiently! Our fathers believed patiently, because he showed himself to them manifestly—to Enoch, Noah, Abraham, Isaac, Jacob, Moses, Aaron, and all his holy ones. ¹ᶜAnd after all them, the people had the book of the Law and from it they learned to do the will of the Most High. ¹ᴰBut now the Most High does not speak manifestly, and the holy ones have been removed from here, and the covenants have been burned: How shall this undisciplined people know the will of the Most High?"

¹ᴱHe replied and said to me, "The Most High will come and act and teach, but this people is stiff-necked and uncircumcised in everything and of little faith until the end, for evil will come upon them." — Acts 7:51

¹ᶠAnd I said to him, "How will the Most High come, or when will his coming be?" ¹ᴳAnd he said, "First of all, he will come after a little time in the form of a son of man, and he will teach hidden things: and they will dishonor him and they will be rejected and they will do themselves evil. And after that, acts of wickedness will increase; ¹ᴴthe spirit of error will lead them astray, to flatten the mountains with anger and to work signs so as to lead astray certain of the holy ones. ¹ᴵAfter that, the Most High shall come again in a vision of great glory and he shall put an end to the spirit of error and he shall rule, and he shall requite the holiness of the holy ones and the wickedness of the impious. ¹ᴶThen all wicked families of the people shall lament and it will avail them nothing, because they were rejected by him. ¹ᴷBehold! I have told you every secret: let it be as a seal for you! Therefore, I command you to consider (it) until the times are completed. ¹ᴸBecause the Most High prepared (it) before the existence of the dwelling of the earth, and before the weighing of the exits of this world, and before the existence of the multitude of the breezes, ²and before the sounding of the noise of thunder, and before the shining orders of stars, and before the establishment of the pavements of the garden, ³and before the appearance of its beauty, and before the strengthening of the power of earthquake, and before the gathering of the unnumbered cohorts of angels, ⁴and before the elevation of the firmament of the heavens, and before the foundation of the firmament of dry land, ⁵and before the consideration of this world, and before the sealing of the reward of recompense (of those) who observed the truth of faith." — 1 John 4:6; 1 Tim 4:1; 1 QS 1.23–24; 4.16, 20

¹¹I replied and said, "Since I have found grace before you, ¹²show me the sign that is going to take place at the end of time!"

¹³ᴬAnd he said to me, "Since you enquire into and investigate the ways of the Most High, arise, stand on your feet!"

---

a. The expansive passage in 6:1A–1L is unique to Arm. It is clearly a Christian addition patterned after the three visions of 4 Ezra as well as its literary, dialogue form.

Armenian 4 Ezra

¹⁷ᴬAnd I arose (and) stood up, and he said to me, ¹³ᴮ"If you hear the sound of a cry, ¹⁴and if the place upon which you are standing shakes, ¹⁵do not fear; for his word is about to come to its fulfillment. ¹⁶The earth will tremble and shake while you are being spoken with." And after I (*sic*) had said that, behold, the glory of the Lord illuminated the place on which I was standing.

¹⁷ᴮAnd then there was the sound of speech, and its voice was like the sound of a great multitude or like that of the waters of many streams cascading down a slope, and it said to me, ¹⁸"Behold! Days will come when I shall wish to visit the inhabitants of earth. ¹⁹I shall see the injustice of the unjust, and the wickedness of the wicked, and the apostasy of the apostates, and those who made my people stumble. And when the suffering of my servants will be full ²⁰ᴬand when I wish to bring near the end of this life of yours, this sign shall take place: Falsehood shall be beloved and envy shall be born, wickedness shall be roused and justice shall be hated, incontinence shall increase and modesty shall be withheld, war shall grow and peace shall diminish, ²⁰ᴮmercy shall be despised and avarice shall be glorified, the suffering of my holy ones shall be increased and the pride of the wicked shall be multiplied. ²⁰ᶜBecause of this there will be famine and earthquake and flood in various places, and there will be a sign in the heavens and fearsome things shall appear in the atmosphere, and on earth, signs in many places; ²¹one-year-old children shall speak, and those who will be pregnant shall bear grace[a] and it shall live and grow; ²²and suddenly sown places shall be found empty, without seed, ²⁴and cities shall rise up against cities and laws against laws; sons shall kill fathers, brothers—brothers, peoples—peoples, beloved ones—beloved ones, families—families; and Rebellion shall come secretly, he shall surely come in my name, with a new mutation of my indescribable glory and power;[b] and he shall corrupt many and become mighty, and he shall subject those who believe in him. And after these signs, this[c] too shall be in many cities and in villages and in provinces, the waters shall stop and shall not go from those days even for three hours.[d] ²⁰ᴰAnd after the completion of these signs, books shall be opened upon the face of the heavens, and then my glory shall appear; ²⁶and they shall see those who fly to me on high, all my holy ones; and everyone who is found worthy of me shall live and shall be glorified and shall be brighter than the sun. Then the hearts of the inhabitants of the world shall be turned to a different wont; ²⁷and evil shall be destroyed and taken away, and deceit shall pass away, and faithlessness shall be ashamed, ²⁸and faith shall flower; the truth shall be revealed that until now remained without fruit for so many years, falsehood shall perish, and incorruptibility shall appear and corruptibility shall come to an end; and thus the end of this world shall arrive."

²⁹And when he had said this to me, the glory of God appeared to us like a vision of brightness. And the place on which I was standing shook a little, and I began to be disturbed and I was unable to bear the glory and fear seized me.

Marginal references:
4 Ezra 9:3; 2 Bar. 27:7, 70:9; Matt 24:7
4 Ezra 13:31
Isa 19:2 LXX

---

a. The word "grace" is a corruption.
b. "Rebellion" is used as a title for the "Antichrist"; see 2 Thess 2:3.
c. Or: "a wind."
d. The expanded list of conflicting groups in this verse is analogous to material in 5:9.

And the angel came and strengthened me ³⁰and said to me, "Fear not and be not afraid. You are blessed ³²for you have found grace from the Almighty. I have known the uprightness of your heart and the sanctity of your soul, which you have had from your youth. ³³And because of that, you were worthy of the word of God and of the secret of lengthy times. ³¹Fast yet another seven days, and even more than this shall be revealed to you."

³⁵And it came to pass after this, I fasted yet another seven days. ³⁶And again my heart was disturbed and I began to say before the Most High ³⁸and I said, "Lord, my God, you made the heavens and the earth and everything which is in them, ⁴⁰you commanded light to shine, you separated (it) from darkness and you called it day. And that which was mixed ⁴¹ᴬwith the multitude of waters and with the earth you divided; and you distinguished the earth, separately. One part of the waters you set apart in the lower depths and fixed the earth upon it, and the other part you established above the heavens below that, like a ceiling, you stretched and delimited the firmament. ⁴¹ᴮAnd you circumvallated the gathering of the waters that remained and held (them) back with sand; for previously they were a mixture with one another, over which the spirit was moving and that was dark; and the earth had not yet appeared because the word of man did not yet exist. You commanded the rays of light to come forth, by which your wondrous acts might be seen. This (was) on the first day.

⁴²"But on the second day you separated the firmament of the heavens and elevated it on high and you commanded the lower waters that one part should separate from another, so that one part of them might take up its lot above and the other part might remain below.

⁴³ "Again, on the third day (in?) that which remained, you established the earth, to bring forth from it herbs for grain and flowers of grass and plants of fruit-bearing trees. ⁴⁴And the earth brought forth a diverse multitude, grain as the nourishment of strength and fragrant smells for the sweetness of the palate and the fruit of the trees for sweet eating.

⁴⁵ "On the fourth day you commanded the sun to exist and to illuminate and to nourish the growth and that was put forth by the earth; likewise, also to illuminate the darkness of night and to distinguish the changes of hours and the successions of times.

⁴⁷ "But on the fifth day you said to the earth to bring forth the crawling animals (that possess) a breath of life, and the various kinds of birds. And a multitude of forms became ordered, arranged by beautiful colors and by various sorts of appearances, for variety. ⁴⁸In the same way the sea too brought forth the multitude of fish, the large ones among them to serve as satiation by being eaten and the small ones for the eye's pleasure in their movement.

⁵³ "And again, on the sixth day, by the word of your command the earth brought forth the quadrupeds, the reptiles, and the birds. ⁵⁴ᴬAnd after these, with a lordly hand, you created their master, the human; and you planted paradise like a city and you placed him within. ⁵⁴ᴮAnd like someone for his son, you produced everything for enjoyment for him, both in sweetness and in pleasure. So you decorated paradise with all forms and you gave it as a heritage into the hands of him whom you created from dust and vivified by breath. ⁵⁴ᶜAnd from his ribs you created the woman to dwell with him, to be a companion

Armenian 4 Ezra

Exod 20:11; Ps 146:6 LXX [Evv 145:6]

Gen 1:6-8; 4 Ezra 6:41

Gen 1:1-5; 4 Ezra 6:39-40

4 Ezra 3:5

515

Armenian 4 Ezra

for him, a fabricator of the race of humankind. You adorned him with human will; you set him up as ruler and king of everything, which, through you, had come into existence upon the earth. ⁵⁴ᴰBut you did not make him needful of any earthly instrument and like a glorious and choice writing you gave him the commandment, which he cast from (his) hands. He went forth from the paradise of delight; he was alienated from incorruptibility; he became deserving of toil; by a command he was delivered into the hands of death. He was dust and he returned to dust and from him we were all begotten.

Gen 3:19; 4 Ezra 3:7

⁵⁵"I have said all this before you, ⁵⁶for you said concerning the heathen that they are nothing and will be reckoned as nothing and are likened to shattered glass and to useless drops of rain. ⁵⁷How do the heathen rule over your chosen people and the seed of your servant Abraham, to trample the seed ⁵⁸of your people whom you called chosen, whom you took as your own and named for yourself, to whom you promised to give a portion of inheritance, the good land of promise? You delivered the people and the promised land into the hands of reprobate heathen. ⁵⁹For, if you promised to give (it) to your people, how have the heathen, who did not receive the promise, taken it as a portion of inheritance and, led into exile in sojourning, we are subject to them; and the heathen rule over us?"

7 ¹And it came to pass when I finished these words, that angel who had previously spoken with me was sent to me ²and he said to me, "Ezra, rise up and hear what I am going to speak with you!"

³I stood up and said, "Speak!" And he said to me, "If there was a sea in a broad place ⁴and its entrance was narrow, for it was deep and like a narrow river, ⁵if someone wanted to enter the sea and to rule over it, then if he did not first pass through the narrow, how could he enter its broadness? ⁶Or again, (if there was) a town decorated and beautified with all decorations and all good things ⁷and its entrance was narrow and thin and rough, as if (there was) fire on the right side and very deep water on the left side, ⁸and only one path passed between the fire and the water, so that there was not room for anyone else, but only a path for a person's feet; ⁹if that city will be indeed given to a person as an inheritance, unless they who should wish to inherit it pass through the narrow (place), they cannot take up the inheritance."

¹⁰And I said, "That is the case. "He replied and said to me, "Similarly, a portion of inheritance will be given to Israel. ¹¹For God made this world for the sake of humankind, and he filled it with every produce and he gave them the Law by which they might be educated and rule a good and modest and blameless kingdom; but they did not observe (it), but abandoned itᵃ and the Most High decided to abandon those who had revolted against him.ᵇ ¹²Because of that, the entrances of this world are narrow and difficult, hard and full of suffering. ¹³For, if they will first enter upon the narrow and thin path of this world, ¹⁴and having entered, they are not long-suffering, they will not receive the good things that have been prepared for them, which existed before this world. ¹⁵But you,

a. Or: "him."
b. Or: "it."

be not disturbed because you are mortal, ¹⁶and be not upset because you are corruptible, but having attained that which is close, consider also that which will be in the future."

¹⁷And I said, "Then, therefore, the just will inherit the good things and on that account they sustain well the passage through the narrow and thin path. ¹⁸But have those who are weak and did not live their lives with holiness and know not the trial of afflictions become distant from eternal goodnesses?"

¹⁹And he said to me, "I also say to you. You are not better than the Most High nor as sweet as God nor more loving of humankind than he. ²⁰Let those who transgress the commandment of the Lord perish rather than the Law of God be despised. ²¹The Most High assuredly commanded humans what they should do to live and what they should observe not to be punished. ²²But they renounced everything and in addition to all this, they said that the Most High does not exist nor does the requital of good and of evil deeds. They perverted their paths ²⁴and they abandoned his Law and they despised his commandments and they rejected his covenant and they disbelieved his holy words and they dishonored his elect ones. ²⁵Because of this, hear Ezra! Emptiness to the empty and fullness to the full!

²⁶"Behold, a time will come when that sign that was predicted to you will come to pass, and the city that is now unseen will be revealed, and every knee will crawl upon the earth, ²⁷and everyone who will be found blameless shall see the glory of the Most High. ²⁸Then God's anointed will appear manifestly to humankind and he will make those happy who persisted in faith and in patience. ³²And through the voice of God all those who were buried in the earth shall arise ³³and stand before the Almighty for judgment. And the life that is unseen shall arrive, ³⁴and corruptibility will pass away and compassion will come to an end, and mercies will become superfluous and the gates of penitence will be blocked; long-suffering will be gathered to itself and faith will show its fruit. ³⁵And after deeds—their rewards; and justice will flower. ³⁶And then the place of the rest for the holy will be revealed and the true paradise of delight, and opposite them, furnaces of fire and eternal tortures and the undying worm that has been prepared for the lawless and the wicked. ³⁷And then the Most High will say to the righteous, 'See the place of your rest that was prepared for you from the beginning of creation and enter henceforth, be at rest and caper like calves that have been released from bonds!' He will say to the impious and the wicked, 'Look and comprehend me, whom you did not serve or whom you rejected or whose Law you despised. ³⁸Look at what there is before you, the delight prepared for the righteous, and for you wicked, the fire and the eternal tortures.' ³⁹The day of judgment will be thus: The sun will not be giver of light, nor the shining moon, nor the twinkling stars,[a] ⁴⁰nor shade-giving clouds, nor thunder significative of the times, nor the refreshing wind, nor water for quenching thirst, nor sweetly mixing air; not evening for rest from toils, nor night for cessation of labors, nor health for satisfaction of labor; not midday for eating of food, nor winter for the labor of preparation

Isa 66:24

---

a. Throughout this list Arm adds descriptive glosses that are usually comprehensible, but occasionally (e.g., "significative of the times"; 7:40) their meaning is not readily perceptible.

of the earth; ⁴¹not spring for the birth of earth and trees, not summer heat, not autumn to care for fruit from dampness, not hail from the violence of the air, not fire for the destruction of dragons, not rain for the growth of trees, not dew for the comfort of plants, ⁴²not morning that signals the light of day, not lamp of night and revealer of darkness, but only a crown of glory and joy for the just, while for the wicked the undying fire and eternal darkness and unending torment. ⁴⁴This is the judgment."

⁴⁵I answered sighing and said to him, "Blessed are those who endure for a short time on account of the glories of exaltation and wretched are we because for a little time we did the will of our bodies and we are given over into the eternal torments and we are punished continually in the undying fire. It were better had we not been born! ⁴⁶Who is there of fleshly creatures who has not sinned or who is there of those who are born who has not transgressed his commandment? ⁴⁷As I see, for few that world is for joy and for many for torments. ⁴⁸For all of us in common are contaminated with wickedness. We have walked in the paths of destruction and the ways of death and we have become distant from the truth of life."ª

⁴⁹He answered and said to me, ⁵¹"You said that the just are few and the impious are many. Now listen to this!

⁵²"If you had precious stones, then, according to their value, you would range everything and (all) materials. Would you reckon what is worthless to be like them, or like lead, or dust, or like some other thing?"ᵇ

⁵³And I said, "No!"

⁵⁴And he said to me, "Say to the earth, ⁵⁵'Why, just as you give birth to much dust, do you not put forth gold in the same way?' ⁵⁶It will answer you and say, 'Because dust is more common than iron, and iron than lead, and lead than tin, and tin than copper, and copper than silver, and silver than gold, and gold than precious stones.' ⁵⁷Choose, therefore, and see which is precious and desirable."

⁵⁸And I said, "Who does not know that the lesser and the rarer is desirable?"

⁵⁹And he said to me, "Just as the rarer and the lesser seems desirable to men, ⁶⁰so a few righteous are precious to the Most High and he rejoices over the few who glorified his name upon earth and by whom his name is praised and extolled. Therefore, the righteous will flourish and will be glorified before God, ⁶¹but the foolish multitude is like a vapor and is readied for the flaming fire, and their faces will be shamed and dishonored."

⁶²And while he spoke of this with me, I was sighing and was disturbed and I felt weak, and I said, "Oh, earth! Why did you bear humankind, ⁶⁴for they will be given over into eternal torments? ⁶⁵Therefore, let the race of humankind mourn and let the beasts of the field rejoice; let all offspring of rational beings wail and let every quadruped be happy! ⁶⁶It is much better for them than for us, for they do not hope for resurrection nor do they await judgments. ⁶⁷Of what profit is it for us if we rise up for judgments and for unending torments?

---

a. This verse has been adapted to avoid all reference to the evil heart.

b. The parable is obscured by the omission of the comparison of a large number of precious stones opposed to a small quantity of less valuable material.

⁶⁹Would that there were no resurrection for us, for then we would be saved from eternal torments."

⁷⁰And while I was considering this, he said to me, "From the beginning of creation, before the existence of humankind upon the face of the earth, the prescient Most High prepared in advance the place of delight and that of torment.[a] ⁷¹Understand, therefore, ⁷²that they had the Law through which they might be delivered and they did not observe (it) but despised (it). ⁷³What answer will they have to give on the day of the end? ⁷⁴For the Most High was long-suffering for such a long time and they, by despising, destroyed their own souls."

⁷⁵ I answered and said to the angel, "I beg of you, lord, tell me whether after death, when he requires of each of us our soul, we shall go to the place of torments or shall we be at rest; shall we be punished forthwith or on the day of judgment?"

⁷⁶He answered and said, "I shall tell you this too. Do not reckon yourself with those worthy of death, ⁷⁷for a treasury full of goodnesses has been prepared for you and those like you, which will not be revealed to you until the end of time. ⁷⁸Listen, therefore! Concerning that about which you enquired, such is the pronouncement. When a commandment of death issues forth, before a person gives up the ghost, then at once the spirit is separated from the body and goes to the place of its determination. ⁸⁹And if one is full of good deeds and, having observed the commandments of the Most High even at the time in which they were in the corruptible dwelling, they served immaculately with the body in constancy during all the time of toils, ⁹¹they will be joyous and rejoice in the rest in the sevenfold path: ⁹²the first path: with great toil they labored against all sins; ⁹³the second path: having seen the tortures prepared for sins; ⁹⁴the third path, of the testimony that God gave on their behalf, that with great faith they observed the Law that was given to them; ⁹⁵the fourth path, in which the prepared good things are revealed to them and how they are preserved in great peace, having ministered with the angels; ⁹⁶the fifth path, (in which) they are glorious with joy for they have been stripped of corruptibility and thenceforth are reckoned with angels, to inherit the endless light; ⁹⁷the sixth path, in which they are shown how their face shines like the sun and are not darkened thenceforth by corruptibility; ⁹⁸the seventh path, which (is) higher than all the paths, in which they are bright with assuredness and not shamed through boldness, but rejoicing they hasten to see the countenance of God, as they served without blemish during their lives, by which they will be honored too and also will receive the reward of recompense. ⁹⁹These are the paths of the souls of the righteous.

⁷⁹"But the souls of the impious and those who did not observe the commandments of the Most High and despised his Law and detested his servants ⁸⁰shall not enter the place of eternal rest, but the souls, as soon as they have been separated from the body, shall enter with sadness and toils upon seven paths to eternal torments: ⁸¹The first path—because they abandoned the Law and changed the Law and the faith of the Most High; ⁸²the second path—because they did not wish to turn and repent while they were in this world; ⁸³ the

---

a. The expansion here is surely based on 6:1L–6:10.

third path, in which they are afflicted by seeing the rest of the righteous and their own torments; ⁸⁴the fourth path, the eternal fire that awaits them at the end of time; ⁸⁵the fifth path, in which they see the souls of the others who are pleasing to the Most High and preserved by angels in ministry and in exceeding peace; ⁸⁶the sixth path, by means of which they see henceforth the prepared kingdom of the holy ones and their own complete destruction; ⁸⁷the seventh path, which is above all the paths, in which those are consumed and destroyed by shame and dishonor who are encompassed by fear when they see the paths of the Most High, before whom they sinned while they were alive in the body and (that) they are going to be punished before the righteous ones."

¹⁰⁰I answered and said, "Will time be granted to the souls to see how they will be punished after their taking leave of the body?"[a]

¹⁰¹And he said to me, "Time will be granted, not of tranquility but of torments; for the souls of sinners are shut up in these places of torment and are guarded by punishing angels until the day of rebuke and judgments and requital of good and evil."

¹⁰²I also said, "I beg of you, permit me also to ask this. Now, on the day of judgment, will the righteous be able to have the impious excused or to pray on their behalf; ¹⁰³like fathers for sons, or sons for fathers, or brothers for brothers, or family for family, or loved ones for loved ones?"

¹⁰⁴He answered and said to me, "Let no one be deceived in this, for on the day of judgment there is impartiality and all truth shall be sealed. For just as one will not send somebody to die in his place, or to sleep, or to be ill, or to eat, or to drink; ¹⁰⁵ so at that time no one can pray for anyone or have someone excused from torments. Each person will be interceded for by their own deeds."

¹⁰⁶ I answered and said to him, "How do we find that Abraham prayed to God for the sake of Lot and for the sake of his house, and Moses for the sake of our fathers who sinned in his days, ¹⁰⁸and David on account of the smiting of the people, and Solomon on account of the sanctuary, ¹⁰⁹and Elias for the sake of the coming of rain, and Elisha for the sake of the life of the dead, ¹¹⁰and Hezekiah for the sake of the people in the days of Sennacherib and for the sake of his health, and others for the sake of others? ¹¹¹For if when corruption was rampant and the wickedness was increasing, righteous men sought of God on behalf of wicked and received,[b] why should this not happen then?"

¹¹²He answered and said to me, "In this world, if the just will ask they will receive, for repentance is of profit to those for whose sake they intercede. ¹¹³For this world is not (that) of consummation nor of glory; but in that world of life, in which the order of penitence passes away, ¹¹⁴and corruption is ended, and filthiness is undone, and faith is abolished, and righteousness increases, and truth sprouts forth, ¹¹⁵no one can attain mercy who on account of their deeds of transgression is in torments of judgment."

¹¹⁶And I said to him, "Did I not make this pronouncement to you from the beginning, that it were better if humankind had not been born upon the earth

---

a. Arm's adaptation of this verse to explain that souls will view their punishment derives from Arm's placing of the seven rewards before the seven punishments.

b. That is: response.

than if they are straightway destroyed? ¹¹⁷What profit will there be for humans if they will attain many days, and that life will be sorrowful and they await torments after death? ¹¹⁹What profit will there be to us sinners that resurrection is promised after death and we have done deeds deserving of death? ¹²⁰What profit will there be for us that indescribable goods have been prepared for the righteous, and for us sinners—shame? ¹²¹What profit will there be for sinners that there are storehouses of glory for the righteous, and we have strayed through evil? ¹²²What will be our relationship with the hope of good things that are stored up for the saints? We have gone along the toilsome path.[a] ¹²³What does it advantage us if the heavenly garden will be prepared for those who are blameless, the fruit of which is incorruptible, in which are unending delight and joy; ¹²⁴and we shall not enter there? ¹²⁵And when the faces of the righteous will shine like the sun, our faces will be darkened like a dark night. ¹²⁶And indeed we never considered while alive what we will have to suffer after death. ¹¹⁸Oh, Adam! What have you done? You alone sinned, but the affliction was not yours alone, but common to all who were descended from you."

¹²⁷He answered me and said to me, "Let them labor upon the earth to abandon evil, ¹²⁸so that they might not suffer that which I said, but by driving out evil they might receive good. Now it is for humans ¹²⁹to choose life and death, because Moses said this to them. ¹³⁰And they did not believe him and all prophets after him nor God who spoke with them."

¹³²I replied and said, "I know and believe thus, that in mercy the Most High is merciful, ¹³³and in pity he takes pity upon those who turn to him. ¹³⁴He is long-suffering of those who sin, ¹³⁵and generous, because he is quick to be gracious and to forgive sins. What value is it to the Most High if so many souls whom he made will perish and only a few souls will live? ¹³⁶I know that he is greatly merciful: ¹³⁷if he were not merciful, all men could not live. ¹³⁸Likewise he is also gracious: if he were not gracious, and (did not) alleviate our sins through his love of humankind, all flesh could not live. ¹³⁹He is a judge who judges and reproaches and after the reproach, he pardons. For if not, he would condemn and punish the rebellious multitude; no one would remain of all the multitude except the few. And where would his mercy be which he promised, or pity, or sweetness, or love of humankind? Whom would that benefit, if not the miserable sinners? Is it for that reason he created so many souls, that he might destroy (them)? God forfend! Is he not full of knowledge? Would he not know what humans would do, before their birth, and is he not familiar with every thing before it happens?"[b]

8 ¹ᴬ He answered and said to me, "Speak not that which is above you and do not dissemble before God; consider that which is permitted you. ¹ᴮHe made this world for the sake of many but that one, for the sake of few. For, although his prescience is abundant, still he granted humans free will, the knowledge of (their) actions, so that they might know what to do so that they are not punished and what to do and be punished. ¹ᶜWhy are those who have the same

Sir 3:21-22

---

a. Arm reworks the section from 7:120 to the end, drawing inspiration from 7:66 and 7:77.
b. The idea that the existence of mercy implies pardon for sinners also occurs in Pr. Man. 7.

body and the same passion of emotions not like the righteous? ¹ᴰNot only did they not walk in their paths, but they also despised them and abhorred their conduct. Therefore the Most High will preserve few for that (future) world. ²ᴬI shall tell you also one parable and you respond to me. If you were to ask the earth, as it were, to give you soil that will bear for you a precious and valuable appearance, ²ᴮand it gave you soil that produced various sorts of appearance, little of (that) like the valuable and twice as much of (that like) the worthless, would you not sit down and select the valuable for yourself and cast away the worthless? ³Consider whether the parable is true." And I said, "It is correct."

⁴And I began to speak to myself, "Oh, my soul, take delight as you wish, and earth (*sic*) humble (your) mind, that you may hear ⁵and proceed where you wish not, for the good things of delight were not given nor prepared for you, but only this brief time of life." ⁶And I decided again to say some words before the Most High, (as to) how he would give us seed of produce in which there might be fruit, or how would each corruptible place bear the produce of good deeds and live, or would he not give (this)? ⁷We are the work of his hands and therefore we are deserving of his mercy, ⁸for here he brings us to life. It is evident in whose (pl.) womb he continually creates our bodies and provides sustenance, similarly also through the distribution of various kinds of seeds, wine, and oil; through fire and water; through a period of nine months in a dwelling, in the mother's womb, the child is born: by wisdom it is a provider for him, ⁹and it preserves him carefully and when in its time, it yields up and gives the child ¹⁰whom he had commanded to come into being and be born, (he commands him) to suck milk for some time. ¹¹And after this (he commands) him to conduct himself through his wisdom and to be nurtured by the products of his fruit. ¹²And he instructs him through his Law, and gradually makes wisdom grow in him and knowledge of all evil things and those that are not of the same sort. ¹³And after all this, he kills him; thus he has authority over his works. ¹⁴But then, if he destroys him whom he had formed for so long a time, and had caused to be born with labor and pains, and nurtured with difficulties, and instructed by easy stages, of what profit is it?" ¹⁵And while I was thinking this, I opened my mouth and began to beseech the Most High and to say, "Lord, Lord, like God have mercy upon your work and upon your creations, and be of aid to your possessions; and even more to your people, on whose account I mourn;[a] ¹⁶and to your inheritance, on account of which I am saddened; and to the people of Israel, on whose account I mourn; and to the seed of Abraham, on whose account I am disturbed. ¹⁷You regard us and you reckon our sins. ¹⁸For I have heard of the great mercilessness that will be in the future, because of our arousing anger. ¹⁹Therefore, Maker of All, long-suffering Most High, listen to my voice and attend to my words which I speak in prayer before you."

Prayer of Ezra
²⁰"You who have dwelt for eternity, whose eyes assuredly see and search out everything, and his upper chambers are on high; ²¹whose throne is indescrib-

---

a. This verse, down to "possessions" has no parallel in any other version. The phrase "I opened . . . to say'" closely resembles 9:28.

Armenian 4 Ezra

able and glory inexpressible; around whom are multitudes of hosts of angels and they serve (him) with awe ²²and by his command and word he turns the spirits into fire; ²³whose word is immovable and mighty—it orders everything, each in its fashion; whose command is very strong and order fearsome; whose look dries up the deeps and (whose) threatening word splits the earth—everything that he wishes he creates from nothing, that which has come into being he changes by (his) might; whose truth testifies; ²⁴ listen to the voice of your servant and attend to the supplication of your minister; give ear to my words. ²⁵While I am alive, let me speak. ²⁶Regard not the downfall of those who do not have the willpower to observe your commandments and have been overcome by thoughts of evil, but have mercy as beneficent one and savior and have pity as regulator, you who alone are without sin. Indeed, we beg of you, regard not the transgressions of your people, but those who uprightly served you with truth. ²⁷Have pity! Do not requite the wicked according to their deeds but have pity for the sake of those who fearfully observed your covenant. ²⁸And do not consider concerning those who have gone wickedly before you, but remember those who willingly knew fear of you. ²⁹And desire not to destroy those who have made their customs like those of the animals, but with your pity regard ³⁰your servants who have placed hope in your glory. ³¹For we and those before us have willingly done (deeds) deserving of death; you, Lord, lover of men, were called long-suffering because of us. ³²For, although we were beneath such a good deed and did nothing according to your will, but went after abomination of the body, you had pity to be merciful and then you were called Merciful. ³³For the holy ones by your will acted with holiness and do not need mercy, for they have the reward of recompense for their own works. ³⁴What are we men that you should be angry with us? ³⁵In truth there is no one born upon the earth who has not sinned. ³⁶In this let your pity be known, when you have mercy upon and pardon us and forgive our impieties that do not have the substance of good deeds."

³⁷The Lord answered me and said to me, "If the sinners will indeed return to me with all their hearts, ³⁸I will not think to requite (them) according to their former sins, but as I shall find and judge (them) at the end of their giving up of the ghost; and I shall be as happy over those who return to good deeds ³⁹as I shall be happy over my righteous ones.

⁴¹ᴬ"Liken me to a simple farmer; just as a farmer plows, sows as much as he wishes and desires, and tends each (plant) as is necessary in its season; although certain of them are weak and close to destruction, he tends to those for which it is necessary. ⁴¹ᴮAnd if he, by care, overcomes he is exceedingly happy, for that which wished to be weak was strengthened. But if the care at the due time was of no avail, he will uproot it sadly. Such will also be the case with regard to humans who (are) upon the earth. The Most High will be long-suffering toward them for, if they who act wickedly will repent instead of that and will do good things, they will live, but if not—they will be punished."

⁴²I answered and said, "Since you have permitted me to speak once before you, I beseech you, say to me, your servant. ⁴³The farmer's seeds, if they do not receive rain in due measure, wither and dry up; ⁴⁴in the same fashion also humankind, if they will not be granted mercy by you, cannot live. ⁴⁵Therefore,

Ps 104:4

Deut 30:10

Armenian 4 Ezra

Lord, have pity upon this people of yours and be compassionate to your inheritance; you show compassion on your possessions, works of your hands."

⁵⁰He answered and said to me, "The humans who have inhabited this world will be exceedingly wretched because they walked with much arrogance, and knowledge concerning the future time was found in none of them. ⁵¹But you, consider concerning yourself and be concerned about the glory of those who are like you. ⁵²For you the true garden is opened and the tree of true life is planted, that (future) life is prepared, delight is readied, the city is built, the rest is arranged, the goodness adorned. ⁵³Sickness is sealed off from you, death is taken away from you, hell has been put to shame, corruption is driven away from you. ⁵⁴Every toil is separated from you, treasuries of immortality are revealed to you. ⁵⁵Beseech no longer concerning the destruction of this people, ⁵⁹for just as there is prepared for you that which I stated before, so thirst and torments are readied for them. ⁶⁰And I made humankind that they might observe my commandments and avoid eternal death, and they always embittered me. ⁶¹Because of this, my judgment is close."

⁶²ᴬI replied, I spoke with the Lord and I said, "I beseech you,ᵃ speak with this wretched people, that they may hear from you and believe, that they may fear and repent and not perish, but be saved. ⁶²ᴮFor if someone else should speak perhaps they would not have faith and this is a human being."

⁶²ᶜAnd the Lord answered and said, "I myself always revealed myself to my servants who were pleasing to me; I spoke with those who were worthy of me, but to the others I made myself known through humans. ⁶²ᴰI am the Lord who tests the heart and the reins and I know humankind and what is in them before they come from the womb. I know (that) if I should speak with them face to face, they will not obey, but will be even more strongly disobedient."

Jer 1:5

⁶²ᴱI answered the Lord and I said, "I ask of you, Most High, why was there not given to us a heart such that we should know only the good, and we should do it alone and we should desire it alone, and it should be sweet for us to know it alone? ⁶²ᶠAccordingly, since we received the knowledge of evil, why do we desire that which you hate? ⁶²ᴳWhy indeed did you create it at all, that we should have it and through it we might sin?"

⁶²ᴴThe Lord answered and said, "I made humankind, not that they might perish, but that they might live this life with honor and inherit that (future) life. ⁶²ᴵAnd, like to my angels, I gave them wisdom to know what is good and what is evil. ⁶²ᴶAnd I honored them and gave them the authority to do whatever they desired and I made subject to them all things that are under heavens that they might rule over them. ⁶²ᴷAnd I gave Law and commandments how they might be able to live and how they might obtain immortal goods. ⁶²ᴸAnd they received these great goods and authority from me. That which was created well, they did not use well and they sinned. Not that I created anything evil, but everything that I created was very good: each thing that existed, existed for its own purpose, just as iron existed, not that it might kill, but that it might work the ground and fulfill the needs of all humankind. ⁶²ᴹBut humankind did not remain in that same state in which they were created, but they undertook

Sir 39:16, 21

---

a. The same phrase occurs at the start of the addition in 6:1B.

that which was not made for good. Thus also in other things, that which had come into being for good, they changed to evil. [62N]The cause was then not he who creates things well, but they who do not use them well; they offended their creator. Therefore torments await them. [62O]For all should be guided by those things that have come into being through me so that they might know me. They too, who do not enjoy them, have known me. Cease, therefore, and care nothing concerning them."

[63]I replied and said, "I beg of you, Lord, who bear not resentment, my soul does not have temerity to question you. Listen to your servant concerning that—you revealed the multitude of the signs to me, and you did not say when it will be or at what time."

9 [1]He replied and said to me, "By measuring, signal for yourself the coming of the signs, and it shall be when you will see that all are close to consummation, [2]then apprehend the end. First, the signs that were spoken must take place and thus, the coming of the end. [3]When the time approaches there will be disturbances of peoples, quaking of the places of the heathen, deceptions of leaders, trembling of saints, persecutions of priests, turning aside of the holy faith, doubt of the people, disorder of the heathen, tribulation of the city, flaming forth of fire in various places, great shaking, different sorts of separations, flooding of cities and villages, going astray of abominable demons. [4]Then you shall understand that the end is near. [8]And he who will be found worthy of me at that time, will be saved and will see my salvation and the new earth and my borders that I sanctified before eternity and prepared for mine as an inheritance. [9]And then the despicable shall see and lament and be amazed, who now see my paths. Therefore, prepared judgment is established for them, [10–11]because they did not know the benefits of my Law, to observe everything that was written in it. [13]But you, do not mingle yourself with such as the flame of fire will consume."

[14]I replied and said, [16]"Lord, I have said many times and now I say, [16A]those who perish are many and those who are saved are few, and they with great difficulty. [16B]Who can carefully prepare himself thus, as even your Law commands?"

[16C]The Lord answered and said, "I commanded nothing above humans nor anything impossible; but I say to you briefly, just as you wish to be honored by your servant, you too do the same to the living God, and that which seems evil to you, do not to your neighbor.[a] [16D]And just as you like to be benefited if you are beloved, you too do the same, for if it seems pleasant to experience this from your brother, you too do (the same) to him, for I commanded you that which is yours. [16E]For as is the will, so are the deeds and as are the deeds, so is the reward. [16F]The imperceptive and foolish sort will perish and the precious and the pearls will be saved, for I do not want the multitude of the sinners as I desire the few holy ones. [16G]This will be thus, and thus it will be established and thus it has been determined by me and nothing of them will pass away until my judgment will take place at the end of my word."

---

a. That Torah is given to humans to assure their salvation is a typical view of Arm (7:72; 3:20).

¹⁶ᴴAnd it came to pass when the Lord stopped speaking with me, I saw the glory of the Most High, exceedingly great, brighter than the sun. Then, while fear still possessed me and trembling at the immeasurable glory, the angel who had spoken with me at first came to me. ¹⁶¹And he strengthened me and he brought back my astonishment to me and said to me, "Fear not and tremble not, for you have found great grace before God. ²³And fast yet seven more days, ²⁴having gone to the field where there will be neither house nor shelter nor anything else except only flowers and eat nothing except of the flowers of the field where you will be. ²⁵And beseech the Most High tirelessly and after that I will come to you."

²⁶And, according to his speech, I went to a field in the place which is called Ardap' by name and sat there upon the flowers and ate of them; and the eating of them was sweet to me and satisfying and increased my strength. ²⁷And it came to pass after some days, while I was reclining upon the grass and again my heart was disturbed in me as formerly, ²⁸my mouth was opened and I began to speak before the Most High and to say, ²⁹"O Lord God, who are the creator of all souls. You surely appeared to our fathers in the desert land when they were coming forth from Egypt, passing through an arid and barren desert, and you said to them, ³⁰'Listen children of Israel and attend to my words, seed of Jacob. ³¹Behold I plant my Law, if it produces fruit in you I will be praised in you.' But our fathers did not observe your Law; because of that they perished. ³⁶Likewise, we too who received your Law transgressed and acted lawlessly. ³⁷But your Law did not perish but remained in its glory."

³⁸And while I was saying this to myself, I lifted my eyes and I saw from the right, and behold a woman was lamenting and cutting herself and crying exceedingly loudly, tearing her garments and casting ashes about her head. ³⁹And I left my previous discourse upon which I was (engaged); considering (it), I was amazed that a woman was seen in such a place. Turning to her I said to her, ⁴⁰"Why are you crying and why are you lamenting bitterly?"

She answered and said to me, ⁴¹"Permit me, sir, to bewail myself and to continue to mourn, for I am exceedingly embittered in my soul and am full of tribulation."

⁴²And when I said, "What happened to you? Tell me!"

⁴³She said to me, "I, your handmaiden, was barren and I did not bear a child although I lived with my husband for thirty years. ⁴⁴And I continually, day and hour in those thirty years, begged the Most High by day and by night. ⁴⁵And it came to pass after thirty years, God hearkened to your maidservant and looked at my tribulation and he saw my distress and he gave me a son; and I and my husband and all my fellow-citizens rejoiced in him and we glorified God. ⁴⁶And we nurtured him with great travail. ⁴⁷And it came to pass when he grew up and matured, we wished to take a wife for him and we prepared a day of festivity.

10 ¹"And it came to pass when my son came to his nuptial couch, he fell down and died. ²And we removed the light and we set up immeasurable mourning in the place of great festivity. And all my (fellow) citizens arose to comfort me because of him. And after (their) greatly comforting me, I desisted until the night of the following day. ³And it came to pass, when everyone had ceased comforting me, I too was silent. And I arose by night, I fled and I came here, as you see me in this field, [4]intending to return to the city no more, but to stop here, neither to eat nor to drink but continually to mourn and fast until I die."

[5]And, abandoning my discourse upon which I was (engaged), I replied angrily to the woman and said, [6]"That which you know, you know better than all women. Do you not see our mourning, [7]which came upon Zion who is the mother of us all? Jerusalem indeed groans, both sad and exceedingly afflicted: and now do you not mourn her more? [8]For we are all in sorrow and in grief of contrition, but you are sad because of your one son. [9]Ask the earth and it will say to you that it ought to mourn, [10]for that great multitude which was born of it returned to corruption. [11]Now, who should mourn, she who lost such a great multitude or (should) you lament because of one? [12]If you should say, 'The earth's sadness is not like my mourning, for I lost the fruit of my womb whom I bore with pains; [13]but the earth goes according to its ways, its present grief has departed and gone just as it came.' And I say to you, [14]'Just as you bore with labor, so also the earth from the beginning gave humankind to its creator.' [15]Now, therefore, keep your (place) in yourself and bear patiently the afflictions that have come upon you. [16]For your son too will arise in his time and you will be renowned among women. [17]Return therefore, to the city to your husband."

[18]And she said to me, "I will not do that and I will not enter the city, but I will die here."

[19]And I spoke to her again and said, [20]"Do not do this thing, but be persuaded for the sake of the sadness and be consoled for the sake of the city of Jerusalem. [21]Therefore, also look at her, for our sanctuary is contaminated and the altar is destroyed [22]and the praises ceased and our splendor is destroyed and the light of the candles extinguished and the ark of our covenant taken into captivity, our sanctuary is defiled and we are alienated from the name that was called over us, our free men are insulted and our priests have wept and our Levites have fallen into slavery and our wives were violated and our young men were killed and our mighty ones were given over to subjection; [23]and more than everyone, Zion was rejected like a worthless vessel and her glory was taken away and we were delivered over into the hands of those who hate us. [24]But you, cast away the multitude of sorrow from yourself and expel the numerous pains from yourself, for the Almighty will be reconciled with you and the Most High will give you respite from your pains and troubles."

[25]And it came to pass as I was speaking with her, her face rejoiced exceedingly and her appearance became like lightning and her form so fearsome to those near her that my heart was exceedingly terrified at it and thinking, I said, "What is this?" [26]And suddenly she called out with a loud sound, she screamed with fear so that the earth shook at her voice. [27]I saw and behold, the woman no longer appeared to me, but a builded city upon strong foundations. I was terrified and I cried out loudly and said, [28]"Where is the angel Uriel who came to me on the previous day? For he made me come to this place of wonders and in the end my prayers became a great outrage for me."

[29]And while I was saying this, the angel came and saw me [30]and behold, I was lying like one dead and my understanding was in disorder. He grasped my right

hand and strengthened me and set me upon my feet and said to me, [31]"What happened to you and why are you troubled? Why are your understanding and the thoughts of your heart disordered?"

[32]And I said, "Why did you abandon me? for I acted according to your words and came to this place and, behold, I saw that which I am unable to understand."

And he said to me, [33]"Stand up like a man and I will instruct you."

And I said, [34]"Speak, lord, but only do not abandon me, lest I die in vain. [35]I have seen that which has not been seen and I have heard that which I knew not [36]unless my mind wandered and my soul was astounded. [37]Now, I beg you, tell your servant about these wonders."

[38]He replied and said to me "Listen to me and I shall instruct you and shall tell you concerning that which you fear. Because of this the Most High has revealed many secrets to you, [39]for he has seen your uprightness, that you sorrow indefatigably because of the people and you mourn exceedingly over Zion. [40]These are the matters: [41]the woman who appeared to you a little time ago—you saw she was mourning and you began to console her. [42]Now therefore, you shall no longer see her in the form of a woman but she shall she appear to you (as) a builded city. [43]And that she told you concerning the sadness of her son—[44]This woman whom you saw is that Zion which you now see as a builded city. [45]And that she said to you, 'I was barren for thirty years,' for she passed many years in this world and when she came to be and was built, sacrifice was <not> offered in her.[a] [46]And it came to pass after that, Solomon built the city and the temple and offered sacrifice in it. When was it? When the barren woman gave birth. [47]. . . with toil—that was the settlement of Jerusalem. [48]And when she said to you, 'My son entered to his nuptial couch; he died,'—that sadness took place which was the downfall of Jerusalem. [49]You saw that she was mourning for her son and you began to comfort her on account of her sorrows that had come upon her. [50]When the Most High saw that you cared about her wholeheartedly, he showed you the brilliance of her glory and the beauty of her splendor. [51]Because of that I said to you that you should remain in a field where no house was built. [52]I knew that the Most High wished to show you all this [53]and therefore I told you to come to this place where there was no construction of a foundation. [54](where) the work of human construction could not stand in the place where he was going to show you the city of the Most High.

[55] "But you, fear not and let your heart be not terrified but enter and see the brilliance of the city or greatness of the construction, as much as your eye could see. [56]And after this you will hear as much as hearing of your ears is able. [57]For you were more blessed than many and were pleasing to the Most High as few. [58]Remain here also tomorrow night, [59]and I will show you as many dream visions as the Most High will show you, which things are going to befall the inhabitants of the earth in the days of the end."

[60]And I fell asleep for two nights as the angel commanded me.

---

a. The word "not" is restored from the other versions to provide a clear sense to the verse.

Armenian 4 Ezra

11 ¹And it came to pass on the second night[a] and behold, an eagle came forth from the sea that had twelve wings and three heads. ²And it lifted up its wings and flew through the whole earth and all the winds of heaven blew and were gathered to it. ³And I saw other wings sprouting from its wings and those became small and tiny wings. ⁴But the heads of the eagle were in silence, and the middle head was larger than the others: nevertheless it too was resting in silence with them. ⁵And behold it raised up its wings to rule over the earth and its inhabitants. ⁶And I saw how everything that was under the heavens was subject to it and none of the creatures that were upon the earth opposed it. ⁷And I saw that the eagle arose and stood on its feet and said, ⁸"Do not all desire to be awake at one time,[b] but let each one fall asleep in its place and let it awake in its time; ⁹and let the heads be preserved for the end."

¹⁰And I saw and behold, the voice did not issue from its head but from the middle of its body: ¹¹and I counted its additional wings and these were eight. ¹²And I saw that one wing arose from its right side and ruled over all the earth. ¹³And when this had happened, (its) end came upon it so that its place was not visible at all and the second arose and ruled and lasted for a long time. ¹⁴And after the rule, (its) end came upon it so that it perished like the first one. ¹⁵And a voice came to it and said, ¹⁶"Hear your good news, you who possessed the earth for such a long time before you perished. ¹⁷No one after you will hold power for as long a time as you, but not even half of your (time)."

¹⁸And the third one arose and it held power and it too perished like the first one, ¹⁹And thus each of its wings held rule and likewise perished. ²⁰And I saw the other wings and these arose in their own time from the right side to hold power; a certain one of them held (it) and immediately perished ²¹and a certain one of them arose and was unable to hold power.

²²And after that I saw that the twelve wings had perished and two of the remaining wings, ²³and nothing remained on the limbs of the eagle except the three hidden heads alone, ²⁴and six wings. Of these, two were set apart and went (and) rested by the head to the right side and four remained in their place. ²⁵And I saw that the four wings planned to rise up and rule; ²⁶and then I saw one that, although it arose, immediately perished. ²⁷And I saw and behold there remained two of them that planned to increase and to rule. ²⁹And while they were planning that, one of the hidden heads . . . which was the larger. ³⁵And then it took both heads with it. ³¹And the head turned around with the body and ate the remaining wings that wished to rule. ³²And that head ruled the whole earth and subdued its inhabitants with great toil and tyrannized the habitations of the earth more than the violence of the wings.

³³And I saw after that, the middle head perished like the other wings. ³⁴And two heads remained and in the same way they ruled the earth and its inhabitants. ³⁵I saw that behold, the head that was on the right ate and spoiled that of the left side.

a. The phrase "and I saw a dream" found in the other versions has fallen out of the text here.
b. Or: "to watch everything at one time."

³⁶And I heard a voice that said to me, "Look before you and see what you see." ³⁷I saw and behold, a lion roused up from the forest. It called and roared and cried out in a human voice and I heard that it said to the eagle, ³⁸"Listen to me and I will speak with you. Thus says the Most High, ³⁹'Did not you remain of the four beasts whom I made to rule over my earth, that through them the end of times might come? ⁴⁰And you came fourth, you overcame them and you tyrannized continually because of them with great toil. You conducted this world for such a long time with guile ⁴¹and judged not the earth in truth; ⁴²you did violence to the meek and harmed the humble; you hated the true things and loved lies; you destroyed the fortifications of the mighty and broke down the walls of those who did not sin against you. ⁴³And your outrages ascended to the Most High and your arrogances to the Mighty One. ⁴⁴And the Most High looked at his times and behold, they were finished. ⁴⁵Because of that you shall surely perish, O eagle, and your worthless wings and your evil heads and your cruel talons and all your wicked body; ⁴⁶so that the earth may rest and all the world be relieved to be delivered from your violence, to hope for the judgment and mercy of him who made it.'"

12 ¹And it came to pass when the lion spoke these words with the eagle ²and behold, the head that remained perished and the two wings that were under it rose up and were transferred to rule and their rule was full of corruption and disorder. ³And then they also perished and all of the body of the eagle was burned and the earth was greatly amazed.

And I awoke from the great surprise and the abundant fear and I said to my soul, ⁴"Truly you made me investigate the paths of the Most High. ⁵And behold, my soul and my spirit are undone, I am exceedingly weak and there is no strength in me due to the great fear by which I was frightened this night. ⁶Now I will beseech the Most High that he may strengthen me until the end."

⁷And I said, "Lord, Lord! If I have found favor in your eyes and if indeed I was blessed often by you and if indeed my request has ascended to before your countenance, ⁸strengthen me and make known to your servant the oracles and matters and the interpretation of the terrible dream that I saw, that you may fully comfort my soul, ⁹since you made me worthy to show me the end of years and the consummation of times."

And he said to me, ¹⁰"This is the interpretation of the dream that you saw: ¹¹the eagle that went up from the sea is the fourth kingdom that was revealed to your brother Daniel; ¹²but it was not revealed to him in the way that I now reveal (it) to you. ¹³Behold days will come and a kingdom will arise upon the earth and it will be more terrible than all the kings that were formerly. ¹⁴In it there will reign twelve kings, one after the other, ¹⁵but the second of the kings will hold (power) more times than the twelve. ¹⁶This is the interpretation of the twelve wings that you saw. ¹⁷And the voice that you heard that spoke, which spoke forth not from the head but from its body, ¹⁸that is the matter: that in the time of that kingdom there will be not a few differences; it will come close to perish and it will never fall but will be set up (and) established in (its) former rule. ¹⁹And that you saw the numerous remaining wings springing up around its great wings, ²⁰this is that matter: there will arise eight kings from it whose times will be fleeting and seasons swift. Two of them will perish [21]at the approach of the time. And at the division into two of its kingdom, four will be preserved for the time when the consummation of the time will desire to approach them; the two will be preserved for the end. [22]And that you saw three silent and quiescent heads in it, [23]this is that matter: at its end the Most High will raise up three kings and they will renew many things. They will rebuke the earth [24]and its inhabitants with great toil, more than everyone who existed previously. Therefore they were named the heads of the eagle. [25]They will be the chief ones of their kingdom and they will fulfill its end. [26]And that you saw the great head destroyed and annihilated: one of them will die through torments, [27]and a sword shall devour the two who remain. [28]And simultaneously with them, at the end it too will fall by sword.[a] [29]And that you saw the two remaining wings transferred to the head of the right side, [30]these are those matters that the Most High has preserved for its end, whose rule is worthless and full of disturbances.[b]

[31] "As you looked at the lion and you saw (it) issuing forth from a lair, awakened and aroused from sleep; roaring and crying out it spoke with the eagle and rebuked its injustices according to all the words that you heard. [32]It is the anointed one whom the Most High will send at the times of the end from the family of David. He himself will spring forth and come and speak with it and rebuke its impieties and will speak concerning its injustices and will set curses before it. [33]And he will bring it to his judgment alive and when he will rebuke it, then he will destroy it. [34]And he will save the remnant of his[c] people with pity and he will transform those who remain in his[d] borders and he will rejoice them until the end of the judgment will come, about which he spoke in the beginning. [35]This is what you saw and this is its interpretation. [36]You alone were worthy to learn the secrets of the Most High.

[37] "Write that which you saw in a book and place it in a safe place. [38]And you shall instruct the wise of your people in this and you shall place it in a fitting place and you shall enlighten the wise through it and those who fear me whose hearts you know, that they receive it to preserve these secrets. [39]But you, remain here seven more days so that I may show you that which the Most High wishes to reveal to you." [40]And the angel departed from me.

And it came to pass when the people heard that seven more days had passed and I had not yet returned to the city, all the people—from small to great—gathered and came to me and said, [41]"What did we sin against you and in what did we transgress that you abandoned us and remained here in this place?[e] [42]You alone remained for us from all the prophets, like a bunch of grapes from the vintage, like a candle in a dark place, like a single harbor of salvation. [43]Was not this evil that came upon us enough, [44]but will you too abandon us as well?

---

    a. The first part of this verse was lost to homoeoteleuton in Arm, Arabic[1] and Ethiopic[1].
    b. The Armenian to this verse is very obscure and cannot be reflected in the English translation.
    c. Or: "its."
    d. Or: "its."
    e. A popular hendiadys.

How much better were it for us to be scorched and burned in fire with Zion, ⁴⁵for we are no better than her dead!" And as they said this they wept loudly.

⁴⁶I answered and said to them, "Be of good courage, house of Jacob, ⁴⁷for memory of us remains before the Most High and the Mighty One will not forget us for ever; ⁴⁸and I did not abandon you but I came to this place to beseech the Lord concerning the ruin of Zion and to seek mercy on account of our tribulation. ⁴⁹And now, let each of you go to his house and I will come to you after these days." ⁵⁰And the people went to the city as I said to them. ⁵¹And I sat in the field for seven days as the angel had commanded me and I ate of the flowers and of the grasses of the field, and they were nourishment for me during those days.

13 ¹And again I saw in the night vision. ²And I saw a great wind from the direction of the sea, which moved all its waves. ³And that wind itself brought one like a man out of the heart of the sea and the man was running and flying against them together with the clouds and wherever he turned his face and looked, everything upon which he looked trembled. ⁴And where the word of his mouth reached, all who heard his voice were melted and consumed, as wax melts when it comes near to fire.

⁵And I saw after that, there was an assembly of a multitude of men without number from the four corners of the earth to fight against the man who ascended from the sea. ⁶And I saw how he hewed out the great mountain for himself and entered into it. ⁷And I sought to find the land and the place whence it was hollowed out and I was not able.

⁸After that I saw and behold, all of those who had assembled to him to fight against him were greatly frightened, but nonetheless they indeed fought. ⁹And when he saw many men coming up to him at a run, he did not raise his hands against that multitude to take up a weapon or any other instrument of war, but I only saw in the fight ¹⁰that a flame of fire streamed forth from his mouth and from his lips like the flash of flame. ¹¹And he rushed swiftly upon the multitude (which was) prepared to fight and he burned (them) suddenly all together until there existed nothing at all of the innumerable multitude except the dust of ashes and the smell of smoke. I saw and I wondered to myself.

¹²And after this I saw a man descending from a mountain and summoning still another peaceful multitude to himself. ¹³And many men came to him to see;[a] some of them were joyous and some sorrowful; some (were) bound and others of them led those who were bound.

And I woke up from the multitude of the host and I beseeched the Most High and I said, ¹⁴"Lord, from the beginning you showed your servant these wonders of yours and reckoned me worthy to accept my supplication. ¹⁵Therefore, now too make the interpretation of this dream known to me. ¹⁶As I think with my own mind, these will be those who will remain in those days: then woe to those who remain in that![b] ¹⁹I see very great troubles and numerous tribulations as this dream shows. ²⁰Now then, were it more profitable to attain

a. Or: "be seen."
b. That is: time.

that time or to pass away like a cloud and not to see that which is going to happen at the end of time?"

The angel replied and said to me, ²"I shall tell you the interpretation of this dream, but both concerning those who remain ²²and concerning those of whom he has spoken, at the end of times, these are the matters: ²³blessed are those who will be found in those days, who will observe the faith in patience and truth and mercy. ²⁴Know therefore that those who remain are more blessed than those who have passed away. ²⁵But this is the interpretation of the dream: The man whom you saw who ascended from the sea, ²⁶that is he whom the Most High will send after many times and through him he will save his creation and he will bring back those who remain. ²⁷And that you saw a fiery breath that went forth ²⁸and that he had no weapon in (his) hand nor any instrument of war and that he overcame the multitude who were about to charge, who came to fight with him, this is that matter: ²⁹For behold, days will come when the Most High will wish to save those who are upon the earth. ³⁰Amazement shall come upon all the inhabitants of the earth. ³¹They shall think to fight with one another—place with place, nation with nation, kingdom with kingdom, peoples with peoples, leaders with leaders, priests with priests: the faith of worship shall be split into various sides. ³²And it shall come to pass when these signs happen that I told you, the Most High shall appear with great power. He is that man whom you saw, that he ascended from the sea. And some of the heathen will destroy the images of their abomination, ³³and when they shall hear about him they shall draw apart so as not to fight with one another. ³⁴And they will be assembled at one time, an innumerable multitude of all the inhabitants of the earth, to serve the Lord faithfully, and at the approach of the end they will be separated from one another. This is the multitude that you saw that desired to come and fight with him. ³⁵But he will stand upon the peak of the mountain that is Zion. ³⁶For he will come from Zion and will appear to all those who are ready. ³⁷And he will rebuke the impiety of others and their evil deeds and he will show them the judgment by which he will judge them. ³⁸And after that, without labor he will destroy them. ³⁹And that you saw him gathering another peaceful multitude: ⁴⁰ᴬthese are those who, having been gathered by the despicable heathen, were led away, and some of the seed of Abraham were mixed with them.[a] ⁴⁰ᴮThis is the assembled and peaceful multitude. And the Most High will show more signs to those who are patient and he will preserve them."

⁴⁰ᶜAnd I said, "That generation[b] will be more blessed than this people."

⁴⁰ᴰAnd he said to me, "It will be thus as you saw and (as) it was interpreted to you."

⁵¹And I said to him, "Lord, make this further known to me! Why did I see a man ascending and coming from the sea?"

⁵²And he said to me, "Just as no one can see or investigate or know the abysses of the depths, thus now no one upon the earth will be able to recognize or know the mysteries of the Most High except in the time of the glorious rev-

---

a. Verses 40A–D resemble 13:40–50 and replace a narrative about the return of the ten (or nine and a half) tribes found in the other versions.
b. Or: "nation."

elation. ⁵³This is the interpretation of the dream that you saw and concerning that, to you alone upon the earth has it been revealed. ⁵⁴You, who took pains for the sake of his name and his Law, abandoned your own cares and sought on account of his people and beseeched ⁵⁵that you might conduct (your) life with wisdom and knowledge. ⁵⁶Because of that he showed you all of this, for after another three days I shall speak to you and wonders shall appear to you."

⁵⁷And like one strolling, I walked in that place in the field and I praised the omnipotent God, ⁵⁸that he thus nurtures and directs and does not despise the race of men. And I was there for three days.

14 ¹And it came to pass on the third day, I was sleeping under an oak tree ²and behold, a voice came forth opposite me, from a thorn bush and said to me, "Ezra, Ezra!" And I said, "Here I am." And when I said this I stood upon my feet and he said to me, ³"I indeed appeared from this thorn bush and spoke with Moses when the people were in servitude in Egypt. ⁴I sent him and I brought forth my people from Egypt and I led them to Mount Sinai and I kept him with me for many days. ⁵And I showed him many wonders and I revealed to him the secrets of the times and I made known to him the end of times and I commanded him to speak ⁶open words freely and whatever (is) hidden.[a] ⁷And now I say to you. ⁸These signs that I indicated previously and the dream that you saw and the interpretation that you learned, preserve in your heart. ⁹For you will be raised up from among men and henceforth you and whoever is like you will be with me until the consummation of the times.[b] ¹³Therefore, give instruction concerning your house and admonish your people and comfort their miserable ones and instruct their wise. ¹⁴Take leave, therefore, of the corruptible life and separate the confounded thought from yourself and set human heaviness apart from yourself and cast away care and vexatious thought from yourself and hasten to transfer from this world. ¹⁵(As to) the prepared evils that you just now saw—you shall see again yet worse than this. ¹⁶For in the measure that this life passes, in that measure do evils increase upon the inhabitants of the earth. ¹⁷Truth that was with God and men will be very distant; falsehood and hatred shall draw near. Behold, the eagle that you saw in the vision hastens to come."

¹⁸I replied and said, "Let me speak a little before you, Lord. ¹⁹Behold, I am going as you commanded me and I will instruct the people who are present, but who will instruct him who will be born at another time? ²⁰For this earth is in darkness and its inhabitants are without light. ²¹Because your Law was burned and after this, no one will know the deeds of your wonders nor the commandments that you commanded. ²²For, if I have found grace before you, cast a holy spirit into me and I will write everything that took place from the beginning in this world and as much as was written in your Law. Perhaps men will be able to find the path and those who wish, to live in purity of way."

a. The verse is corrupt.
b. The absence of 14:10–12 may be due to corruption or to Arm's tendency to avoid fixed, predetermined times.

²³He replied and said to me, "Go assemble the people and say to them that they should not seek you during forty days. ²⁴And prepare numerous tablets for yourself and take Darian and Arabian, Hermian and Elkana and Et'en with you, those five for they will be prepared to write. ²⁵And you shall come in due order and I will kindle a candle of wisdom in your heart and it will not pass away until the completion of that which you are to write. ²⁶And when you will finish this, there is some of it that you shall reveal and there is some of it that you shall teach to the wise secretly, in hiding. Tomorrow at this hour, begin to write!"

²⁷And I went as the Lord commanded me and I assembled all the people and I said to them, ²⁸"Hear, O Israel, these words of mine! ²⁹Our fathers indeed sojourned in Egypt formerly and they were delivered from there. ³⁰And they received the law of life that they did not observe, which you also transgressed. ³¹And a land was given to you as an inheritance and in your land both you and your fathers acted wickedly and you did not observe the paths that the Most High commanded you, ³²and the just Judge. And in time he took away from you that which had been given. ³³And now you are here and your brothers are further within than you. ³⁴If you will set in your heart and instruct and make your heart obedient you shall be preserved alive. ³⁵For judgment will come after death when we shall live once more. Then the name of the righteous shall be revealed. ³⁶Now, let no one come near to me henceforth and let no one seek me for forty days."

³⁷And I took the five men with me as he had commanded me and I went to the field and I remained there. ³⁸And it came to pass on the following day and behold, the sound of a voice called me and said, "Ezra, Ezra! Open your mouth and swallow what I am giving you." ³⁹And I opened my mouth and behold, a goblet was given to me and its color was like water. ⁴⁰And I took (it) and I drank and when I had drunk my heart poured forth wisdom and my mind increased in understanding and my spirit kept memories. ⁴¹And my mouth was opened and it was not closed. ⁴²And the Most High gave wisdom to the five men and in turn they wrote the spoken signs in a script that they knew not. And they sat there for forty days, and they wrote by day ⁴³and by night they ate bread; and I talked by day and by night I desisted. ⁴⁴And in forty days they wrote ninety-four books. ⁴⁵And it came to pass after the forty days were completed, the Most High spoke with me and said, "The first thing that you wrote, make known openly and the worthy will read it. ⁴⁶And the second you shall keep to teach to the wise of the people. ⁴⁷For in them are proverbs of wisdom and a spring of understanding, a river of knowledge." And I did so.

⁴⁸In the fourth year of the week of years after five thousand years of creation of the world and two months of days, Ezra himself was taken up and elevated to company of those like him.

I wrote all this and became the scribe of the Most High.

Two Pseudo-Philonic Works
A new translation and introduction

by Sze-kar Wan

Both De Jona and De Sampsone hew closely to the biblical text of Jonah and Judges, pausing only for apologetic asides, moral exhortations, or interpretive comments. Preserved only in a literal Classical Armenian translation, the originals were composed in Greek in a style favored by Greek-speaking Jews and intended to be delivered as homilies in the synagogue. In language and structure both works bear some resemblance to the writings of the first-century CE Jewish philosopher Philo of Alexandria but were not written by him. Both works touch on issues popular with other Second Temple Jewish writings such as the Wisdom of Solomon, Paul's Epistle to the Romans, and 4 Maccabees. As such they open a window into the formative stages of Judaism and Christianity at the beginning of the Common Era.

Contents

De Sampsone covers only three episodes of the Samson story: the annunciation of his birth, his killing of a young lion, and his wager with the wedding guests (Judg 13–14). The abruptness of the prologue along with allusions to other parts of the Samson story—the fall of Samson at the hands of the unnamed Delilah (1.1–6; Judg 16:15–19; cf. 13:5) and Samson's last request for strength (4.1–3; Judg 16:28)—might raise the suspicion that parts of the original sermon have been lost.[1] But the line "without preparation" found in both the superscription and postscript suggests that De Sampsone was composed and delivered extemporaneously and was never intended to be a complete commentary.

The prologue (§§1–4) poses an overarching question: How could a perfect God appoint as judge an imperfect Samson beset by impetuosity and moral failings?[2] The answer: the sovereign God can turn human failure into success. Samson's power is given before birth, not as a compensation for doing justice but as grounds for it (§3), and it can be withdrawn due to transgression. Even after Samson asks for forgiveness, he is granted not his full power but a dribble of it, "because it would not be right to crown a defeat" (4.6; cf. Judg 16:28–30). So, Samson succeeds in driving out the hated foreigners in spite of his weaknesses (46.2–3).

In the first episode, the homily follows the annunciation story but for a few asides (§§5–19). Why do the three angels accept Abraham's invitation to a meal (Gen 18:5), but

---

[1]. See discussion in Folker Siegert, *Drei hellenistisch-jüdische Predigten I*, WUNT 20 (Tübingen: Mohr Siebeck, 1980), 6–7.

[2]. This division between appearance and reality is mirrored by Samson's loss of power: His hair might be shorn by a sense-perceptible shearer (Judg 16:19), but his real strength is cut off by an intelligible barber (§1).

the angel here refuses to eat with Samson's father Manoah (Judg 13:16)? It is because Manoah's invitation comes after the birth announcement and is therefore mere gratitude, whereas Abraham's invitation, issued before the birth prophecy, betrays true hospitality (§14). As to why the angel refuses to reveal his name, it is because he does not wish to usurp the honor that is due God alone, the preacher suggests (§§15–16).

The gender role reversal prompts a brief discussion. The birth announcement is made to a woman who relates it to her husband (7.2–3), the angel shows his full glory to the wife but to Manoah merely "an unthreatening form and a gentle face," and upon the angel's visit the man is frightened by having encountered the divine while the "wise and determined" woman consoles him (18.4–8). All this demonstrates that the wife has superior knowledge in contrast to Manoah's ignorance (§§11–13; 17.4–5).

Samson's killing of a young lion (§§20–28) paves the way for his battle of wits with the wedding guests. The preacher asks if God should be faulted for Samson's transgressions since he is endowed with the divine spirit. Three answers, two apologetic and one theological, are given. First, Samson's fleshly desires are stronger than his human spirit (§20). Second, because the spirit Samson receives is one "of power but not of justice or wisdom," Samson alone bears full responsibility (§§24–26). The theological answer is based on the sovereignty of God, "who is capable of . . . (turning) Samson's waywardness into a punishment of the foreigners" (§23).

The final episode centers on the wager between Samson and the wedding guests (§§29–46). Samson's riddle, "Out of the eater came the food, and out of the strong came the sweet" (Judg 14:14), occasions a tribute (§31), while the bride's duplicity gives rise to a tirade against women and foreigners (§§33–35). The bride is forced to trick Samson, but she is nevertheless culpable since she has been deceiving Samson from the start (§§38–40). That justifies Samson's slaughter of thirty men in Ashkelon to pay off his debts (Judg 14:19; §§43–45).

Following the biblical book of Jonah, De Jona unfolds also in three acts. The prologue (1.1–4 [1–4]) lays the theological foundation that God is the mastermind of the world, skipper of a well-constructed ship, and all mortals should recognize and worship God as such. The first act (2.1–26.5 [5–102]; Jonah 1–2) begins with a call to condemn the Ninevites (2.1–3.2 [5–9]), representatives of gentiles guilty of ingratitude toward the creator and of wickedness against each other (4.1–5.6 [10–19]). Failure to worship the creator as the cause for human immorality was a common theme among Greek-speaking Jews (Wis 13:1–19; Rom 1:18–32). Anticipating the Ninevites' repentance, the preacher calls the foretelling of doom deliverance because God will use the occasion to rescue wayward foreigners out of a "love for humanity" (Greek *philanthrōpia*).

The sermon then follows the flight of Jonah to his lengthy prayer in the belly of the sea monster (Jonah 1:1–2:9). Jonah is depicted as throwing himself into the sea to save his fellow passengers (14.2–3 [59]), as opposed to being cast overboard (Jonah 1:15; see, however, 12.5 [51]). Jonah's self-sacrifice segues into a discussion of God's love for humanity, a constant since creation (25.1–8 [91–98]) and basis of Jonah's confession (19.1–26.5 [69–102]; Jonah 2:2–9).

Jonah's prophecy of destruction and Nineveh's repentance in the second act (27.1–39.6 [103–157]; Jonah 3) occasion two long speeches. The first (30.1–36.3 [115–40]) establishes the chief sin of the Ninevites as their failure to worship God as creator even though creation makes that plain (31.1–35.2 [118b–35]). As a result of God's universal love for humanity the city is delivered (38.5 [151]). The second speech (39.1–6 [152–57]) is a thanksgiving prayer that proves God's love for humanity supersedes prophetic determinacy.

In the final act (40.1–53.3 [157–219]; Jonah 4), Jonah's complaint for being compelled to pronounce a failed prophecy (41.2–45.4 [161–81]) solicits two lengthy responses from God. The first reaffirms God's love for all humanity (46.2–48.7 [183–96]), and the second poses the question if universal love might not contradict divine power (49.2–53.3 [198–219]). Since God is always in favor of love for humanity, that takes precedence over both justice and power.

Authorship

Both works have been attributed to Philo, and both are included in a collection of Classical Armenian translations of Philo's writings.[3] The extant manuscripts of De Jona even include Philo as part of its title. The saying "It is customary for envy to follow the footstep of the great" found in De Sampsone 20.1 has been attributed, erroneously, to Philo's *De gigantibus*.[4] Both works share with Philo his fondness for the ornate Asiatic Greek style and his penchant for citing the views of other exegetes using the diatribal formula "someone might say" (e.g., De Sampsone 38).[5]

There are sound reasons to doubt Philonic authorship, however. Philonic exegesis is absent in both sermons. In one occasion, the preacher calls a field a "symbol" of truth, for the seed sown therein "allegorizes" the woman's pregnancy (De Sampsone 9.3), but this is closer to a commonplace metaphor than the type of allegorical interpretation frequently found in Philo's writings. Philo, by contrast, uses symbolic exegesis in the service of his grand allegory of the soul, and that is wholly absent in these sermons.[6] Moreover, popular myths such as the sun as a disk (De Jona 33.5 [128]) or the earth supported by columns (De Jona 33.4 [127]) that are left intact would doubtlessly have been allegorized by Philo. The most decisive argument against Philonic authorship is the portrayal of God as changeable (De Jona 46.8 [186]), which contradicts the basic Philonic tenet of the immutability of God.[7]

Evidence speaks against the same author for both sermons. Their similar Greek and biblical interpretation was common among other Greek-speaking Jews, but their stylistic and theological divergence points to different authors. Stylistically, De Jona is composed in lengthy, elevated speeches, whereas De Sampsone is composed of short comments

---

3. Johannes B. Aucher, *Philonis Judaei paralipomena Armena* (Venice: San Lazzaro, 1826).

4. The citation is preserved in Greek. See James R. Royse, *The Spurious Texts of Philo of Alexandria: A Study of Textual Transmission and Corruption with Indexes to the Major Collections of Greek Fragments*, ALGHJ 22 (Leiden: Brill, 1991), 89–92.

5. So David M. Hay, "Philo's References to Other Allegorists," SPhilo 6 (1979–1980): 41–75. Hay limits his discussion to Philo's citation of other allegorical interpreters, but his observations can in fact be generalized to cover Philo's references to other literalist and physical (Stoic) interpreters.

6. See Jean Daniélou, *Philon d'Alexandrie*, Les temps et les destins (Paris: Fayard, 1958); Thomas H. Tobin, *The Creation of Man: Philo and the History of Interpretation*, CBQMS 14 (Washington, DC: Catholic Biblical Association of America, 1983).

7. For the question of Philonic authorship, see also Siegert, *Drei hellenistisch-jüdische Predigten*, 2; Siegert and Jacques de Roulet, *Pseudo-Philon prédications synagogales: Traduction, notes et commentaire*, SC 435 (Paris: Cerf, 1999), 33–34. It is debatable whether the contrast between the sense-perceptible barber and the intelligible Satan (De Sampsone 1) betrays Philonic usage. It is probably more accurate to suggest Middle Platonism as a common denominator.

in an episodic structure.[8] Theologically, both works trade on the divide between Jews and outsiders, but whereas the foreigners of De Sampsone are objects of scorn, devoid of redeeming qualities, the same are delivered in De Jona ostensibly because of their contrition but more fundamentally because of God's love for humanity.

These diametrically opposite attitudes toward gentiles are the result of irreconcilable conceptions of God. In all instances in the two sermons love for humanity resides exclusively with God.[9] But whereas in De Sampsone only Samson and his parents are possible recipients of God's love (De Sampsone 3.1, 2, 4; 4.6, 7; 6.1; 9.5; 11.1), which otherwise has no universal application beyond Israel, in De Jona God's *philanthrōpia* is shown generously to foreigners. The Ninevites will be shown God's love in spite of Jonah's attempt to thwart it (7.6 [27]). He later relents by giving himself up for his fellow passengers, but he does so as God's disciple (13.1 [54]; 14.2 [58]; cf. 15.2 [61]). Jonah's mission, in spite of his attempted escape from it, is in fact a demonstration of such love (15.3–4 [62]). God's love for the Ninevites is massively shown when their contrition is accepted and their destruction averted (35.3 [136]; 35.6 [138]; 38.4 [150]; 39.3 [153]). De Jona makes a convincing case, in fact, for taking God's *philanthrōpia* in the literal sense of "love for *all* humanity" (50.1 [205]; 53.2 [218]), but it is this transgression of traditional bounds that forms the central bone of contention between Jonah and God (e.g., 23.4–5 [87–88]; 25.1 [91]; 42.1 [163]). The different interpretations of boundaries to God's love for humanity place the onus on those who see the same author responsible for both sermons.

Audience and Setting

Both works were clearly composed by Jewish authors for a Jewish audience. The sharp distinction between those who acknowledge the creator God and those who do not would make sense only for a Jewish audience. The intended audience was familiar with the biblical stories, so much so that only allusions were needed to make a point. The prologue of De Sampsone, for example, only needs to allude to Samson's source of strength (Judg 13:5; 16:17) and reasons for his downfall (Judg 16:4–22), and Jonah's condemnation of Nineveh is proleptically called deliverance, anticipating what the audience already knew (De Jona 2.2–3.1 [7–8]).

Oral markers in De Sampsone such as the speaker directly addressing the audience (2.1; 10.1; 35.1; 38.1), its episodic structure, and its faithfulness to the biblical story all point to its origin as an impromptu homily delivered "without preparation" to a Greek-speaking synagogue.[10] Oral features in De Jona are no less pronounced (1.2 [2]; 1.4 [4]; 6.1 [20]; 7.5 [26]; 8.3 [30]; 9.2 [33]), but the commentarial nature of the work and the skillful attention to textual details (e.g., on *katastrephō* in 48.2–7 [191–196]) point to synagogue teaching as a likely setting.[11] If the Alexandrian synagogue was the

---

8. Though how much this has to do with the impromptu character of De Sampsone is unclear.

9. In this regard, both writings stand in the apologetic tradition of the Letter of Aristeas, according to which God is the sole author of love for all human beings, who are capable of love as imitation of God (§§208, 257) or divine endowment (§290). Philo compares *philanthrōpia* to piety (*Virt.* 51), so that perfect virtue is conditioned on *philanthrōpia* (*Abr.* 107–118). In contrast, Josephus equates *philanthrōpia* to Roman *clementia* (*A. J.* 12.124; *B. J.* 2.399) and attributes it to Herod (*A. J.* 14.298). He concedes *philanthrōpia* can be divinely centered (*A. J.* 1.24), so that the Torah is not just a Jewish but also a universal authority (*A. J.* 16.42). See Ulrich Luck, "Philanthrōpia," *TDNT* 9:109–10.

10. See also Siegert and de Roulet, *Pseudo-Philon prédications synagogales*, 20.

11. See footnote on the discussion of *katastrephō* in the translation.

setting for Philo's lengthy Allegorical Commentary, the case is even stronger with the shorter, more straightforward commentary of De Jona.[12] If these hypotheses bear out, De Sampsone and De Jona would likely be the only Greek-speaking synagogue homilies in existence.[13]

Literary Genre

De Jona and De Sampsone have been called encomia or hagiographies of Jewish heroes.[14] Compared to classic encomia such as Xenophon's *Agesilaus*, however, De Sampsone and De Jona make no attempt to hide unsavory details of their protagonists.[15] De Sampsone does stress Samson's youth, his power, and his cleverness in dealing with his enemies, and it elaborates on his miraculous birth. But Samson is introduced at the outset as an imperfect hero whose infatuation with a foreign woman would lead to his demise. He is defeated not so much by his enemies as by his lustful desires. Jonah is introduced as someone who attempts to flee not just from God but especially from his own knowledge of God. He is then presented as a selfish figure more interested in his own reputation and personal comfort than in countless human lives. A common thread uniting the two homilies is that God can make use of flawed instruments to realize higher purposes. If

---

12. Hartwig Thyen, *Der Stil der jüdisch-hellenistischen Homilie*, FRLANT NS 37 (Göttingen: Vandenhoeck & Ruprecht, 1955). Philo gives us a glimpse of a diaspora synagogue: See *Spec.* 2.61–63; *Mos.* 2.215–16; *Hypothetica* = Eusebius *Praep. ev.* 8.7 359D. Philo of course did not make the modern distinction between preaching and teaching. On the basis of these observations, Ervin R. Goodenough has argued, persuasively, that his exposition was intended for gentiles, while the verse-by-verse allegorical commentary was intended for a Jewish audience. See Goodenough, "Philo's Exposition of the Law and His *De vita Mosis*," *HTR* 26 (1933): 116, 118, doi:10.1017/S0017816000005071.

13. Based on the practice of reading the book of Jonah, along with Isa 57:14–58:4, after the Torah on Yom Kippur (b. Šabb. 24a; 116a), Muradyan and Topchyan have theorized that De Jona might have been a homily prepared for that occasion. Gohar Muradyan and Aram Topchyan, "*Pseudo-Philo, On Samson* and *On Jonah*," in *Outside the Bible: Ancient Jewish Writings Related to Scripture*, ed. Louis H. Feldman, James L. Kugel, and Lawrence H. Schiffman, 3 vols. (Philadelphia: Jewish Publication Society, 2013), 751.

14. So Siegert and de Roulet, *Pseudo-Philon prédications synagogales*, 21; and Muradyan and Topchyan, "Pseudo-Philo," 751.

15. In *Agesilaus*, Xenophon chronicles Agesilaus's life (chs. 1–2) before enumerating and discussing his virtues one by one (chs. 3–11). An encomium can go beyond the merely epideictic or panegyrical to the judicial, as is the case with Gorgias's *Encomium of Helen*, which defends Helen's virtues by dismissing charges of adultery against her. Among Jewish writings, 4 Maccabees and Philo's lives of the patriarch are clearly encomia. Fourth Maccabees chronicles the lives of the martyrs and the virtues they exemplify through their deaths. Philo's *De Abrahamo*, to pick but one example, includes not only biographical narratives of the patriarch but also such well-known topoi of the genre as *eudaimonismos* ("happiness or blessedness," *Abr.* 115) and *synkrisis* ("[superiority by] comparison," 178–99), while bypassing episodes that might compromise the character of Abraham, e.g., Sarah and Hagar (Gen 16 and 21) and Abimelech (Gen 20–21). See Anton Priessnig, "Die literarische Form der Patriarchenbiographien des Philon von Alexandrien," *MGWJ* NS 37 (1929): 143–55; and Robert Hamerton-Kelly, "Sources and Traditions in Philo Judaeus: Prolegomena to an Analysis of His Writings," *SPhilo* 1 (1972): 12. Priessnig's is a comprehensive study that classifies all of Philo's biographies of patriarchs, but his discussion of *De Abrahamo* is sufficient for our purpose. By Hellenistic times, the encomium attained enough of a fixed form that rhetorical handbooks could stipulate specific rules for its composition; so, e.g., Rhet. Her. 3–4; Cicero's *Part. or.* 21; Quintillian, *Inst.* 3.7.3; cf. Aristolte, *Rhet.* 1 which dates to an earlier period. According to Quintilian, *Inst.* 3.7.10–18, encomia in praise of persons should include not only the heroes' virtues but also signs and wonders, as well as other extraordinary events, attending their birth, life, and death. See Philip L. Shuler, "Encomium," *ADB* 2:505–6.

at the end good is nevertheless achieved, it is a testimony not to the heroes but to the sovereignty of God.

What sets De Jona and De Sampsone apart, unlike such well-known encomia as 4 Maccabees and Philo's *De Abrahamo*, is their relatively strict adherence to the biblical narrative no matter how tangential they seem in an encomium. The beasts of Nineveh covered in sackcloth (Jonah 3:8), for example, occasion a full explanation: "(the animals) prayed in their own way: supposing that they shared in the damnation, they stood before them in prayer" (De Jona 37.7 [146]). De Sampsone similarly raises the question why Samson's mother receives news of his birth when Isaac's birth is announced to his father Abraham (De Sampsone 7.1), to which the answer lies with the extraordinary wisdom of Samson's mother. These questions are resolved to show how consistent and just the biblical text is.

In sum, De Jona and De Sampsone are biblical commentaries structured much like Philo's Allegorical Commentary. As has long been shown, the start of the Allegorical Commentary (such as his *Legum allegoriae*) is tied closely to the biblical text, but subsequent treatises introduce his philosophical ideas gradually by incorporating biblical texts from outside Genesis.[16] De Jona and De Sampsone follow the same commentarial tradition, the difference being that their main biblical texts happen to be biographical narratives instead of the Torah.

Date and Provenance

Since both works rely exclusively on the Septuagint, they must have been composed some time after the second century BCE. Affinities to Philo's writings in form make first-century Alexandria a likely place of origins. Other considerations contribute to this hypothesis. The critique against gentiles for not knowing God even though the goodness of God can be known through creation (De Jona 33.1 [125]; cf. also 4.2–6 [11–14]; 27.3 [105], 33.2–6 [126–29]) bears striking resemblance to the same critique found in Wisdom of Solomon (13:1–9), which was likely produced in first-century Alexandria.[17] The apostle Paul made a similar statement but grants gentiles the actual knowledge of God (Rom 1:19–23), suggesting that he was modifying a form that had become standard in Greek-speaking Judaism.[18]

Possible contacts with early Christian thoughts can be entertained. The casting of Jonah overboard, presented as an act of self-sacrifice (De Jona 13.1 [54]; 14.1 [58]), could be taken as a form of substitutionary atonement (cf. 12.3 [49]), except the preacher explicitly suggests a mixed motive of altruism and selfishness. The annunciation of Samson's birth to his parents follows the well-established pattern of the three angels visiting Abraham (Gen 18:1–15), but the author of De Sampsone is also at pains to point out differences between the two accounts. Most striking, the unnamed woman is singled out in the commentary as already pregnant with Samson when the angel meets her a second time in a "sown field" (9.3). That the husband is given no role in her pregnancy up to this point in the narrative might well suggest that she is sown with a divine seed. The emphasis on

---

16. Maximillian Adler, *Studien zu Philon von Alexandreia* (Breslau: Marcus, 1929).

17. See the introduction in David Winston, *Wisdom of Solomon: A New Translation with Introduction and Commentary*, AB 43 (Garden City, NY: Doubleday, 1979).

18. See Hans Bietenhard, "Natürliche Gotteserkenntnis der Heiden? Eine Erwägung zu Röm 1," *TZ* 12 (1956): 275–88; Robert Jewett, *Romans: A Commentary*, Hermeneia (Minneapolis: Fortress, 2007), 153–54. For a possible critique against Roman custom, which would strengthen the first-century date in Alexandria, see Siegert and de Roulet, *Pseudo-Philon prédications synagogales,* 163–64.

Two Pseudo-Philonic Works

Samson's gift of power endowed before birth, not as a result of doing justice but a motive for it, was a common enough topic in Greek-speaking Judaism, but its presence in a context rich with possible christological elements might indicate contact with Christianity.[19] There is no evidence of direct polemics in either sermon against the nascent Jesus-followers, certainly nothing that rises to the level of Celsus. If there were contacts they were amicable. But it remains an intriguing possibility that conversation had started.

Manuscripts, Versions, and Translation

Presence of grammatical constructions at home in Greek but alien to Classical Armenian[20] points to the Hellenophile School as the milieu in which the two works were translated.[21] The Armenian text was first published by the Mekhitarist Johannes B. Aucher,[22] who considered both Philonic.[23] Aucher's edition is based mainly on manuscripts from Venice and Jerusalem, and Hans Lewy's attempt to replace it with supplementary manuscripts from Erevan has not been successful.[24] The current translation is based mainly on Aucher's text, with deviation registered in notes. In the case of De Jona, Lewy's critical text is also consulted, though Aucher's reading is generally preferred.[25]

Aucher's text is accompanied by a literal Latin translation that faithfully reproduces the idiosyncrasies of the Armenian but often fails to clarify the text itself.[26] Still, Aucher's understanding of the Armenian is helpful toward the punctuation and division of the text. Folker Siegert was the first to translate the two homilies into a modern language, German. Siegert also collaborated with Jacques de Roulet to publish a French translation with comments and critical notes.[27] The two homilies are now available in English in a translation by Gohar Muradyan and Aram Topchyan accompanied by copious notes.[28]

---

19. See Siegert and de Roulet, *Pseudo-Philon prédications synagogales,* 38 and n. 2; and their comments on De Sampsone 19 and 24 for a comparison of Samson to Christ.

20. For example, the infinitive with accusative case and participial agreements.

21. For history and characteristics of the Hellenophile School, during which a profusion of Greek literature was translated into Classical Armenian, see Hakob Manandyan, *The Hellenophile School and Its Periods of Development*, Azgayin matenadaran 119 (Vienna: Mekhitarist Press, 1928); Nerses Akinean, *Armenian Literature and the Viennese Mekhitarist School*, Handes Amsorya 46 (Vienna: Mekhitarist Press, 1932), 272–92. A short discussion of the Armenian translator of De Jona in the context of the Hellenophile school can be found in Hans Lewy, *The Pseudo-Philonic De Jona, Part I*, Studies and Documents 7 (London: Christophers, 1936), 9–16.

22. *Philonis Judaei paralipomena Armena. De Sampsone* appears on pp. 549–77, and *De Jona* on pp. 578–611, with an appendix on p. 612. Included in the same volume are Philo's *Quaestiones in Genesim I–IV, Quaestiones in Exodum I–II*, and a short fragment *De Deo*, which is likely Philonic. Four years earlier Aucher had published a volume that included the Philonic works, *De providentia I–II* and *De animalibus*.

23. The two sermons have always been regarded as Philonic by Armenian commentators who incorporated them in standard lectures on Philo's writings. See Muradyan and Topchyan, "Pseudo-Philo," 751–52.

24. For discussion of the manuscript tradition, see Lewy, *De Jona*, "Introduction," 4–8; Abraham Terian, *Philonis Alexandrini De animalibus: The Armenian Text with an Introduction, Translation and Commentary*, Studies in Hellenistic Judaism 1 (Chico, CA: Scholars Press, 1981), 14–24; and Siegert and de Roulet, *Pseudo-Philon prédications synagogales*, 18–19.

25. Lewy, *De Jona*, 1–43, with notes on 45–49.

26. See criticism by Lewy, *De Jona*, "Introduction," 1–3.

27. Siegert, *Drei hellenistisch-jüdische Predigten*; Siegert and de Roulet, *Pseudo-Philon Prédications synagogales*.

28. Muradyan and Topchyan, "Pseudo-Philo," 750–803.

Bibliography

Adler, Maximillian. *Studien zu Philon von Alexandreia*. Breslau: Marcus, 1929.

Akinean, Nerses. *Armenian Literature and the Viennese Mekhitarist School*. Handes Amsorya 46. Vienna: Mechitarist Press, 1932. [Modern Western Armenian]

Aucher, Johannes B. *Philonis Judaei paralipomena Armena*. Venice: San Lazzaro, 1826.

Awetikʿean, Gabriēl, Xačʿatowr Siwrmēlean, and Mkrtičʿ Awgerean. *Norbaṙgirkʿ Haykazean Lezowi*. 2 vols. Venice: San Lazzaro, 1836–1837.

Bietenhard, Hans. "Natürliche Gotteserkenntnis der Heiden? Eine Erwägung zu Röm 1." *TZ* 12 (1956): 275–88.

Daniélou, Jean. *Philon d'Alexandrie. Les temps et les destins*. Paris: Fayard, 1958.

Goodenough, Erwin R. "Philo's Exposition of the Law and His *De vita Mosis*." *HTR* 26 (1933): 109–25. doi:10.1017/S0017816000005071.

Hamerton-Kelly, Robert. "Sources and Traditions in Philo Judaeus: Prolegomena to an Analysis of His Writings." *SPhilo* 1 (1972): 3–26.

Hay, David M. "Philo's References to Other Allegorists." *SPhilo* 6 (1979–1980): 41–75.

Jewett, Robert. *Romans: A Commentary*. Hermeneia. Minneapolis: Fortress, 2007.

Lewy, Hans. *The Pseudo-Philonic De Jona, Part I*. Studies and Documents 7. London: Christophers, 1936.

Luck, Ulrich. "*Philanthrōpia*." *TDNT* 9:107–12.

Manandyan, Hakob. *The Hellenophile School and Its Periods of Development*. Azgayin matenadaran 119. Vienna: Mechitarist Press, 1928. [Modern Eastern Armenian]

Muradyan, Gohar, and Aram Topchyan. "*Pseudo-Philo, On Samson* and *On Jonah*." Pages 750–803 in *Outside the Bible: Ancient Jewish Writings Related to Scripture*. Edited by Louis H. Feldman, James L. Kugel, and Lawrence H. Schiffman. 3 vols. Philadelphia: Jewish Publication Society, 2013.

Priessnig, Anton. "Die literarische Form der Patriarchenbiographien des Philon von Alexandrien." *MGWJ* NS 37 (1929): 143–55.

Royse, James R. *The Spurious Texts of Philo of Alexandria: A Study of Textual Transmission and Corruption with Indexes to the Major Collections of Greek Fragments*. ALGHJ 22. Leiden: Brill, 1991.

Shuler, Philip L. "Encomium." *ABD* 2:505–6.

Siegert, Folker. *Drei hellenistisch-jüdische Predigten I*. WUNT 20. Tübingen: Mohr Siebeck, 1980.

———. *Philon von Alexandrien: Über die Gottesbezeichnung "wohltätig verzehrendes Feuer."* WUNT 46. Tübingen: Mohr Siebeck, 1988.

Siegert, Folker, and Jacques de Roulet. *Pseudo-Philon prédications synagogales: Traduction, notes et commentaire*. SC 435. Paris: Cerf, 1999.

Terian, Abraham. *Philonis Alexandrini De animalibus: The Armenian Text with an Introduction, Translation and Commentary*. Studies in Hellenistic Judaism 1. Chico, CA: Scholars Press, 1981.

Thyen, Hartwig. *Der Stil der jüdisch-hellenistischen Homilie*. FRLANT NS 37. Göttingen: Vandenhoeck & Ruprecht, 1955.

Tobin, Thomas H. *The Creation of Man: Philo and the History of Interpretation*. CBQMS 14. Washington, DC: Catholic Biblical Association of America, 1983.

Winston, David. *The Wisdom of Solomon: A New Translation with Introduction and Commentary*. AB 43. Garden City, NY: Doubleday, 1979.

Armenian Pseudo-Philo's *De Sampsone*
Without Preparation

«549» 1.1 Now as he was swept away by the torrents of sensuality[a] and plunged into the abyss of desire, he could no longer look up but has himself become possessed by lust. 1.2 As if reproached by a judge, he was forced by a woman to tell the truth, 1.3 for the woman hoisted sensuousness as a stake to which she nailed his lusts like straps and hung the trapped man with them. 1.4 After she hung him high, she softened him with seductive, sweet, and fanciful words and «550» penetrated into the young man's inner entrails with torture of lust. Incapable of resisting what would have been easy in sober judgment because of lust, he began to reveal unutterable thoughts and say, *No razor should come upon my head*. 1.5 The woman shamelessly made him sleep on her lap[b] and called a barber. After first shaving off from him his decency, she shaved off his strength as well. 1.6 Accompanying the sense-perceptible shearer was the intelligible[c] barber, Satan, who along with his long hair cut off his strength and made him one of the sinful human beings.

[Judg 16:17; cf. 13:5]
[Judg 16:19]

2.1 For the accomplishment of great things, strength is needed, but wisdom is necessary for us to relate a story of miraculous events. 2.2 Since in receiving power Samson shows the magnificence of the deeds, let us seek wisdom for ourselves from him who gave him strength, in order to set before our listeners wisely what Samson accomplished with his strength. 2.3 If in our account[d] we show ourselves ignorant and unskillful regarding the true deeds, we would not diminish Samson's strength but calumniate God's grace.

3.1 From among his other wonderworks, God works one other: Either he demonstrates his strength, or proclaims his love for humanity,[e] or manifests his sovereignty, or teaches his patience, or announces the blessings reserved for the enjoyment of the just, or pronounces judgment reserved for sinners. 3.2 For since

---

a. Arm. *gijowt'own*, lit. "humidity, moistness," carries the derivative sense of "lustfulness or sexual impurity," hence "Sinnenlust" (Siegert) and "passions charnelles" (Siegert and de Roulet). "Ductility" (Muradyan and Topchyan) might be too literal in this context. In the notes, the following short forms are used: Siegert for Siegert, *Drei hellenistisch-jüdische Predigten*; Siegert and de Roulet for Siegert and de Roulet, *Pseudo-Philon prédications synagogales*; Muradyan and Topchyan for Muraydyan and Topchyan, *Pseudo-Philo*.

b. Lit., "knees" following the LXX.

c. The common contrast between sense-perceptible and intelligible roughly corresponds to that between literal and allegorical. Philo made use of that contrast copiously in his writings.

d. Lit., "with words."

e. Here and below, the Greek is *philanthrōpia*.

through Samson God demonstrates his full might[a] and his love for humanity, he made it known by the gifts that God gave to him even before his birth. 3.3 For if he had found favor «551» with the living God after he was born, it would have been clear that he had received his strength as recompense for righteous deeds. 3.4 Because he was newly conceived and was concealed in the mother's womb,[b] and the gift from above had come into being before the receiver's birth, the grace and gift of love for humanity is not the result of righteous deeds.

4.1 He demonstrated his power again in that he granted him all-conquering strength;[c] 4.2 he convincingly demonstrated the domination of his work[d] by giving him mastery over foreign peoples. 4.3 Is it not clear that those who vanquish servants of foreign gods also vanquish with them their superior protectors? 4.4 The (veracity) of the reception[e] one knows to be conclusive and irrefutable through the gifts that he gave him. 4.5 He again showed his discretion this way: So long as he kept the commandments in their entirety, God granted him his gifts in full. When he breached the commandment, however, he did not nullify[f] the gifts in him but exacted from him a punishment for his transgressions. 4.6 Then he returned to his love for humanity, but he did not grant him all the gifts, because it would not be right to crown a defeat. 4.7 Instead, he provided a drop of grace to vacate the verdict of death poised to be sentenced out of his utmost love for humanity «552» and to prevent his grace from extinguishing completely. 4.8 But in order not to deviate from the discussion with which we have concerned ourselves, or to expend words for other purposes, let us return forthwith to the promised discussion and to the events in the beginning.

5.1 Samson's parents had lived with each other for a long time. They sought a fruit of their union but found none, 5.2 for her womanly soil had become irreparably infertile:[g] though it received the seed it produced no fruit. 5.3 Just as the aridity and infertility of the earth are in need of God's visitation and a stream of water over it, so also the soil of a woman, when it refuses the fruit, is in need of divine spring and grace. 5.4 A good and sublime overseer like a highly skillful farmer would pluck up and pull out what remains a hindrance in its present condition[h] and make the ground tilled and pliable for the sower, but it is divine grace that will grant to nature[i] the completion[j] of the seed itself.

Judg 13:2

---

a. Greek *aretē*.
b. Lit., "in the birth pangs of the mother."
c. Lit., "strength conquering that of all."
d. Greek *energeia*.
e. Presumably referring to Samson's reception of strength as gift.
f. The Arm. *tʻołowm* likely translates the Greek *aphiēmi* ("to give up" in transitive sense), thus making Siegert and de Roulet's "Dieu n'annule pas sa grâce" preferable to Muradyan and Topchyan's "God did not leave the gifts to Samson."
g. The Arm. *taragowsim* likely translates the Greek *aporeō*, "to be lacking." Gabriēl Awetikʻean, Xačʻatowr Siwrmēlean, and Mkrtičʻ Awgerean, *Norbaṙgirkʻ Haykazean Lezowi*, 2 vols. (Venice: San Lazzaro, 1836–1837) (hereafter cited as ASA).
h. I.e., the current state of infertility, but that is inferred from the context.
i. "Nature" (Greek *physis*) was a common euphemism for womb among Greek-speaking Jewish writers. Among its meanings are "origin, birth" and "sex." The same usage is found in 6.1; 13.2, and elsewhere.
j. Or "perfection," which is the state of the seed producing fruit.

Judg 13:3

6.1 Now the humanity-loving God, seeing the impotence of this human nature, sent an angel appearing as if he were a messenger of good tidings announcing the good news of a child to the barren woman. In truth, however, by invisible power he ordered the nature to receive what had not yet been sown. 6.2 For thus, I believe, he commanded the man to be born and to be a gift as the voice of God and the angels' service, because he was ready to carry out his service by means of divine commands.[a] «553» 6.3 In order that the God of the universe would not engage some foreigner for his service, he imparts it from above to those who do not arrive[b] (at it on their own), so that the mother would receive an announcement of the one about to be born. 6.4 He restores to the parents, by means of childbirth,[c] the honor of a child's coming into being. 6.5 And it was no small matter that the shame of childlessness be erased by the birth of a child. He himself the master craftsman[d] employed[e] the announcement of a child for the salvation of the whole people.

7.1 I must marvel, just as physicians who carry out human healing more by wisdom than by art examine the nature of the bodily ailments by gauging the strength of the patient before prescribing[f] healing medicines, God likewise heals the illness of those whose souls are ailing by not prescribing simple or artless healing.

Judg 13:3

7.2 Why, in the case of barren Sarah, did Abraham receive the good news of childbirth, whereas here the woman receives the messenger of the good news? 7.3 That is because there the husband was more ready than the wife in matters of faith, but here Manoah's wife was more ready to believe.

Judg 13:4, 14

8.1 After the angel delivered the good news to the woman and ordered (her) to abstain from intoxication, he impregnated the soul with good hope before making the womb (so in reality). 8.2 When her husband returned, the wife told (him) of the visit of God and the vision of the angel, saying she did not know who he was who appeared in the vision or where he dwelled. 8.3 "But I saw a vision," she said, "of the majesty[g] of an angel's exalted form with a resplendent and fantastic appearance, «554» 8.4 for I had no other way of knowing whence came what I saw, and I guessed at his nature and origins.[h] 8.5 By his magnificence[i] he looked like a man of God; by the luminous resplendent face (he looked like) a citizen of heaven, as if wearing beams of light."

Judg 13:6

a. Translating the Arm. literally. Various attempts to make sense of the instrumental case have proved unsatisfactory, including taking "divine commands" as the object of "carry out" (Muradyan and Topchyan), "selon des orders divins" (Siegert and de Roulet), and "aufgrund göttlicher Gebote" (Siegert).
b. Lit., "they discover/find," but reading with Siegert the Greek *heuriskō,* which can mean "to invent, make."
c. Lit., "as to some instruments of childbirth."
d. Lit., "artist," in the sense of someone who puts the whole thing together. Here "master craftsman" comes close to Muradyan and Topchyan's "artisan," though without the negative connotations of the latter. Siegert opts for "Bildner," and Siegert and de Roulet have "qui met tout en forme."
e. Lit., "received." The underlying Greek *paralambanō* has the sense of taking matter upon one's own hand, hence "undertake, use, or employ" (LSJ).
f. Lit., "offering"; same word used in the following phrase.
g. The underlying Greek might be *semnotēs* "majesty" (Siegert from ASA).
h. Lit., "dwelling."
i. Lit., "greatness."

Armenian Pseudo-Philo's De Sampsone

9.1 Upon hearing this, Manoah was overjoyed in spirit by the expectation of a child, and he marveled at the glorious news in his ears. He called fervently for the angel to return, wishing to see and hear him for himself. 9.2 Anticipating his prayer, he gave a command and (the angel) again appeared to the woman in the sown field where she was sitting. 9.3 This, then, was a symbol of truth, for her field was also sown; the seed of the exterior field allegorizes it. 9.4 Drawing from the speedy angel himself and adding it to her own run, the woman ran with bird-speed and reached her husband. The angel, quick and (capable of) flying through air and faster than the moon and the sun, stood (there) and waited all that time for the woman's husband. 9.5 This is indeed how God sowed gentleness and love for humanity into him. 9.6 This is not surprising, for if a human was made according to the image of the divine appearance, an infinitely greater[a] divine likeness was imparted to faces of angels. 9.7 For the closer to God they dwell, the closer they resemble his image.[b]

Judg 13:8
Judg 13:9
Judg 13:10

10.1 I have prolonged this discourse of yours,[c] beloved, to sing praises, for our praise (of angels) is a praise for divinity. 10.2 For anyone who praises the well-proportioned beauty of an image marvels much more at living nature itself, from which art «555» imitates to offer a work of the image. 10.3 That is why though I am heaping praises on the image, its face does not bear archetypal beauty.

11.1 Now that God's love for humanity has been shown, as well as the obedience of the angel, the readiness of the woman, the compliance of the man—they were all together, he who gave the order and they who received the order—once again I marvel at the gentle and artful administration of the angel. 11.2 That is because the second time he did not appear (in the same manner) as the first. He did not present himself to Manoah the same way he had appeared to his wife 11.3 but instead came and stood visible to human eyes, not like the radiance of the sun that strikes anyone gazing at it with its rays. Here he appeared to Manoah with measured visibility, artfully, as I said, and appropriately.[d] 11.4 For where there are promises, gifts, and recipient, there must be (corresponding) increase commensurate with the greatness of the gift, so that one might receive great faith from the great one. 11.5 Where it has to do with an ordinary word or a simple command, a nonthreatening appearance would be necessary for what is said, lest fear would conceal the memory of the commands. 11.6 Rather, it seems to me better that the appearance of the angel be divided into two natures, to the woman and to the man as they were able to see (it each in their own way). 11.7 Let me offer Scripture as witness that he appeared in two ways. 11.8 Concerning the woman as she described the nature of the vision, she says, *A man of God came to us and his appearance was like the appearance of an angel.* 11.9 But what of the man? It says, *Manoah did not know that he was an angel of the Lord.*

Judg 13:6
Judg 13:16

12.1 So if that is the case, (on account of) the knowledge of the woman, (the angel showed) his unconcealed[e] appearance and terrifying immensity, but (on

---

a. Doublet "great very" here translated with intensification.
b. Lit., "much more to his image are their proximities."
c. Taking the second-person suffix -*d* literally; contra Muradyan and Topchyan.
d. I.e., appropriately for the occasion; lit., "usefully toward things."
e. Lit., "simple, clear, pure."

account of) the ignorance of the man, (he showed) an unthreatening[a] form and a gentle countenance. The gentle one, and he is said to be truly[b] gentle, is the very one who «556» was sent in service of the woman earlier the first time. 12.2 Just as a servant would deliver good news of victory against enemies to the king, the angel thus delivered the good news that (the bond of) her barrenness had been loosened[c] for the woman—12.3 hence the first (appearance) to the woman. Then the second time, when he was called by the man, he was not arrogant and did what was not proper for him: he did not hesitate to wait. 12.4 Afterward, when the husband came without meeting him in his proper glory, he asked him, insolently, who he was and where he was from: "Have you made this visit the first time or, according to the words of the woman, the second time?" Without accusing Manoah of arrogant impudence or censuring him for excessive questions, he began to give instructions to his questioner this way.

13.1 "I, who am seen by you now and was seen by your wife, have come to announce to you a good news of a creation.[d] 13.2 For he, overseer of all who are afflicted, who alone can relieve misery of anguish and command nature, because he saw your marriage fruitless due to the disobedience of nature, has sent me for two things: that I open the closed doors of nature and that I fulfill your longing for a child. 13.3 Now what must those who receive grace do in return?[e] 13.4 To keep the command of the blessed: namely, for the mother to refrain from intoxication and for the one to be created[f] (to refrain) from razor. 13.5 Being clear-headed and sober, the woman will give birth to one destined for great deeds. The man must not let anything come upon the child who is the head of his people. 13.6 He should wear his head of hair as a symbol of the multitude, for the powers of all the people are stored up in this body. «557» 13.7 The head of his people must remain pure and perfect, and the symbol of a multitude be uncut. 13.8 As long as he remains this way, the multitude of his people (will remain) as one body, (as) a tower being guarded by the one to be born; it will be undefeated and indestructible. 13.9 But if the head of the child is corrupted or his head of long hair shorn, the powers of the multitude, whose storehouse is this man, will disappear."

14.1 After Manoah heard this, he thanked him who made him a promise and gave his pledge[g] to keep the command. He then invited the angel to a meal. 14.2 When one observes this, one must be astonished by the variety of the just: there is a great difference from the small to the middling, and from the middling to the supremely just. 14.3 Why did Abraham invite the angels to eat before he received the promise, but Manoah, after receiving (it)? 14.4 It is because Manoah

---

a. Lit., "empty, vacant."
b. Lit., "greatly."
c. Lit., "untying of the being-barren nature."
d. The underlying Greek seems to be *ktisma* "creature, creation," which would comport with the following discussion of "nature" and birth; in 13.4, the child to be born is called "the one to be created." Siegert has "growth" (*Zuwachs*), Siegert and de Roulet have "offspring" (*progeniture*), while Muradyan and Topchyan opt for "gift."
e. Lit., "What must they who receive grace payment give as grace payment?"
f. That is, the child Samson who is yet to be born.
g. Lit., "testimony."

gave the invitation as recompense for the gift; he received first before giving thanks. Abraham, however, offered his repast as a sign of hospitality; he gave first before receiving. 14.5 What each of the two gave was good, but they were not equivalent.[a] One welcomed strangers out of gratitude, the other out of his natural inclination. 14.6 That is why, with Abraham, they entered his tent and gave the appearance of eating the food.

14.7 One might ask, If they passed by without eating the food, how was the food placed before (them) consumed? 14.8 Because angels were full of fire, they consumed the food with fire via a vision.[b]

15.1 He declined Manoah's invitation but advised him that his offer of hospitality «558» be to God. 15.2 After heeding his advice of sacrificing to God, he once again wanted to honor also the angel. So he asked, "*What is your name, so at least we might remember you?*"[c] 15.3 He once again showed that his honor was God and reckoned glorification of God to be his honor. So he said, "*Why do you ask for my name? It is wonderful.*"

Judg 13:16

Judg 13:17

Judg 13:18

O divine discourse in heaven, where the prophet teaches the host of angels wisdom of the Lord! 16.1 He did not say Michael or Gabriel or the power has spoken, lest he should usurp the divine name for himself. 16.2 Instead, what did he say? "It is wonderful." It is clear that this angel, sometimes and in various ways, makes (his own name) great by changing according to the needs of mortals. 16.3 Second, to demonstrate again his faithfulness anew, the angel said mentioning the name of the Most High and Most Excellent would be inappropriate and changed his own. He demonstrated that they err in his honor. He thus left off the knowledge (of his own name). 16.4 When one undertakes the knowledge of his changing name, the knowledge preserves the glory of God, the infallible spirit, 16.5 for he who remains in his eternal glory, along with his kingdom, is always found to be immutable by his worshipers.

17.1 After this, he provided a sacrifice, and (the angel) stayed until the gift of sacrifice had been offered to God. 17.2 Then he joined the sacrifice in a chariot of the honored one in his ascent[d] to the heavens, being borne aloft by the flame of the sacrifice. 17.3 Therefore it is necessary for the angel to show Manoah his worth and to divide the miracle into a beginning and «559» an end. 17.4 In dividing his own nature into two—to the woman in the beginning he appeared as a frightening terror and, at the end to the man, he appeared formidable—17.5 to persuade the woman by his form to accept the beginning of things, and to make the man believe in (their) completion by means of the sacrifice, and to show the vision as proof of the coming miracle.

Judg 13:20

18.1 After Manoah had placed upon the stone everything that would go into the sacrifice, the angel touched it with the tip of his staff, and it instantly burst into flame. 18.2 When Manoah saw the sacrifice so kindled and the angel ascending in the flame while guiding the sacrifice heavenward, from the wonders of his

---

a. Lit., "did not have equal measure."
b. Whether the food was actually consumed by fire or, as Muradyan and Topchyan suggest, it only appeared to have been consumed, is left unclear by the pithiness of the text.
c. The LXX has "we might glorify you."
d. The Greek is likely *anabasis* ("ascent"), according to ASA 1.650a.

Exod 33:20 face he turned to fear. 18.3 It occurred to his virtuous mind, for he was acquainted with the Scripture that said, *No one will see my face and live.* 18.4 Thinking that he had seen the God of the universe, he thought he would lose his own life.[a] The woman, however, encouraged him, addressing the frightened man with wisdom and courage as follows. 18.5 "Has this vision," she said, "become bad, husband, something that was good for a wicked man?[b] The sacrifice of one who has been condemned to death would not be accepted. 18.6 A lovely sight would (still) be, for the wicked, a vision of the good. If the humanity-loving (God) has been benevolent[c] to us with the vision itself and the acceptance of our offering, what would be his intention to condemn to death the one who honored (him), after receiving the sacrifice as pledge and guarantee for his deliverance?"

18.7 A new wonder can be seen that the man is filled with fear, but the woman with courage. Even though he should have comforted and consoled his fearful wife, he himself was comforted «560» for being frightened. As for the woman, who should have received healing when frightened, she comforted and consoled the frightened man with words as if with medicine. 18.8 It was not for nothing that someone had said different souls inhabit outward appearances[d]—a feminine soul (inhabiting that) of a man and (a soul) that befits a man wearing the form of a woman.

19.1 So the woman was given the good news, the man was persuaded, the angel passed through and left, the sacrifice reached the high heaven, and having been helped by all this the woman bore for him Samson, a salvation[e] for a suffering people and a monument to the praiseworthy valor of his life. 19.2 So he appeared like the others; he was superior to them in ways he presented himself to the others.

Judg 13:25 On him the spirit served in the place of his soul, and his body was more indestructible and more impervious than diamond. 19.3 As his narrators testify, he was unharmed and felt no pain to blows with all kinds of iron. He struck anyone who struck him and injured in return anyone who injured him.[f] 19.4 Samson was guarded by the spirit, in order that, in not waging war against anyone, so to speak, he would give no opening to others who in conquest (of him) desired the glory of a tyrant. 19.5 He was not harmed by anyone who wished to strike him, and he was not injured by any of his enemies' arrows. He rose up against those who wished (him) harm by turning their deceit around into their own harm.

20.1 As it is said, it is customary for envy to follow the footstep of the great,[g] and as the character of life is truly perfect, the deeds ascribed to him are (also)

---

a. Lit., "that his own life would become lifeless."

b. Armenian makes no distinction between the masculine and the neuter, but since "wicked" in the next sentence refers to a condemned man and a wicked man, I have sided with Muradyan and Topchyan against Siegert to take wicked as masculine.

c. Lit., "the philanthropic one has been philanthropic."

d. Lit., "appearing faces."

e. "Savior" might provide a smoother reading; so Muradyan and Topchyan and Siegert. I opt for the literal translation here to provide a better parallel to "monument" in the next phrase.

f. The original is compact: "He became a strike to the striker against him, injuring in return the injurer."

g. Whether this means "great men" or "great deeds" is open to interpretation, since Armenian does not distinguish between the masculine and the neuter. I decided to leave that ambiguity in place.

perfect. «561» 20.2 The weak human nature does not seem to hold fast the greatness of God's gift. That is why at the time even though manly Samson had received a spirit and his body was growing in strength, he proved[a] to be weak in spirit,[b] which was more timorous than his carnal desire. 21.1 For in the puberty of his power, when both—the power of his wholesome body and desire of the soul—are fully developed simultaneously, at that time, I think, his soul yearned deeply for sexual relation with a woman, for his flesh was overflowing. 21.2 At the height of his power, a part of which was for insemination, he wanted to sow a part of his seeds in the ground, so that his offspring would become a strength of paternal strength and be offered up as a seed. 21.3 Therefore, no children are suitable for this purpose on account of their immaturity, nor old men of account of their fading virility, but Samson was just at the right age for this— 21.4 with the flowers of youth on his face like beautiful flowers on mossy grounds and in gardens, which was borne by proud, delectable, and delicate smiles in his eyes and rays of the sun coloring his cheeks. 21.5 (But this was) not like the beauty flowering on virgins and women, but that of those who have endured strong labor and at the same time been tanned by the sun in their hard work. 21.6 The contour of his eyebrows resembled the curve of the crescent moon before it is rounded out.[c]

22.1 When love (shone) on his face like the glow of the sun, some foreign woman came on the scene. The woman was (beautifully) constituted in a feminine form. 22.2 He (thus) turned his gaze to a foreign land as one bound and trapped by a vision. «562» 22.3 When his eyes took in a compliant quarry and the vision fed his desires incessantly, it inflicted a wound inside in his soul. 22.4 Wounded, the soul crushed[d] thoughts of piety, and converted his graceful nature[e] of modesty and reverence to shamelessness.   *Judg 14:1*

23.1 Some of the wise say that he was delivered in a passion to the foreigner by the will of the divinity in order to open up a way for him to inflict losses on the foreigners, but others say that the divinity does not want to save by means of lawlessness, 23.2 for he had the sovereignty to manage both—to force him into a lawful marriage and to punish the foreigners lawfully. But because self-willed Samson was besotted with the foreign woman, God who is capable of all things turned Samson's waywardness into a punishment of the foreigners.

24.1 Others, reading with half-understanding but not being able to examine either divine power or Scripture for gain, propose that Samson's transgression was an accusation against the spirit, for it says that he sinned while he had the spirit. 24.2 Those who presume to say this deserve God's double punishment, because they intentionally blasphemed against Scripture and because, not knowing the truth, they besmirched Scripture by finding what was good

---

a. The underlying Greek may well be *elenchō*, "to prove" as in a legal proceeding, thus derivatively "to reprove, to put to shame."

b. The use of *šowčʻ* here seems to refer to Samson's human spirit, as opposed to the divine spirit; for the latter the Armenian translator consistently uses *hogi;* contra Muradyan and Topchyan: "he was reproached by the spirit for being weak."

c. Lit., "until the crescent, transformed from the inside, forms a full circle."

d. Lit., "was struck from."

e. Likely from Arm. *goy* "being, existence, substance," not *goyn* "color."

as wicked. 24.3 If he had received the spirit of justice and prudence, the accusation would be just. But if he had received (just) the spirit of power, what (then)? 24.4 (The spirit) of justice would prevent sins, but not (the spirit) of power. But if Samson did not receive the first when he received this spirit, why do you ignore the man but accuse the spirit of power while exacting deeds of justice (from him)? 24.5 The spirit being accused could say, not without reason, «563» "We are a variety of gifts under the sovereignty of the good and the great one. The nature of each gift is different, and the gifting of every blessing is limited. 24.6 For to someone is sent the gift of wisdom, to another knowledge and intelligence, to another strength and power, and to yet another the fear of the Lord."

Isa 11:2

25.1 Now if he had received the gifts of all the spirits, the man would have to appear sinless. But if he received from a spring and from the great sea a drop of grace, how could he discover the whole from just one of the parts he received? 25.2 If so, we could be persuaded by examples. Our ancestor Abraham received the spirit of justice, and he showed that he was full of goodness, because he believed in the living one. 25.3 Joseph received (the spirit) of self-mastery[a] and proved himself in the presence of her who was an occasion rife with carnality[b] by overcoming the pleasure of carnal desire. 25.4 Simeon and Levi received the spirit of zeal, and they showed it by killing the Shechemites. Judah received (the spirit) of righteous judgment, and he proclaimed it by indicting his daughter-in-law. 25.5 Samson had (the spirit) of power, and he proved it most perfectly by his deeds. 25.6 Now if against those who were strong it was weak,[c] the spirit would deserve the accusation for it was (meant) to show power using Samson as an instrument. But if the spirit remained strong as a gift but others vanquished Samson by deceit, why do we place an unjust accusation on the spirit?

Gen 15:6, etc.

Gen 39:7–20

Gen 34:25–26

Gen 38:24

26.1 "Yes," (the critic)[d] says, "when Samson sinned, it would have been proper for the spirit to depart «564» in order that it would not be a helper to a transgressor." 26.2 But (if so,) where would the fulfillment[e] of the divine promise be found? Have you not become the fiercest enemy of divine Scripture? 26.3 The child's parents had received the promise of power—God had sent (it) and the angel had served (it)—and before he had demonstrated any deeds of power, his lust surrendered[f] to the maiden. 26.4 If the spirit, on account of Samson's lust, had gone somewhere with the power, we would not come to know the promise. 26.5 Are they not sharpening their tongue against divinity himself

---

a. The likely underlying Greek *sōphrosynē* means "moderation, self-control, temperance, chastity, etc."

b. Lit., "full in flesh." Muradyan and Topchyan take it to refer to Joseph, but since the next phrase mentions Joseph's conquest of his carnal desires, it seems better to apply it to the occasion of temptation.

c. Adopting Aucher's conjecture.

d. Muradyan and Topchyan are correct in taking the statement as a citation of the "enemies of Scripture"; contra Siegert.

e. Lit., "deed."

f. The Arm. *matnim* in the passive voice means "to give oneself up, to surrender" to (Arm. *i*) someone. Here "lust" is a synecdoche for Samson.

and naysaying Scripture by claiming, "Samson did not receive a spirit of power and the gift was written up superfluously, for if he had received (it), we would have seen it through his exploits in every incident"? 26.6 So, slander of the impious is found everywhere, but Scripture cannot be slandered or abandoned to sophistic arguments.[a] It speaks instead to pious and honest people. This is an apologia of the spirit but let us return to Samson and to the divine narrative.

27.1 He was in the prime of his life at an age of rigor, and youth was blossoming on his body. He was a treasure stronger than a human being. 27.2 Gifted with the strength of his body he was traveling with his parents. The town to which Samson came with his parents was called Timnah. 27.3 When they were on their way there, Samson made a detour to a vineyard where he enjoyed the sight of its fecundity. (There) he saw a young lion couching under bunches of grapes. 27.4 He roused it by falling upon it as if he were getting ready to fight not a young lion but a puppy. 27.5 A worthy spectacle was the fight between the lion exhibiting strength in its mane on its neck and Samson «565» who manifested his age of power on features of his face. 27.6 As they tussled—for irrational animals are ferocious but rational human beings are valiant and powerful—the lion, as was its wont when hunting its usual prey, opened its maw to seize its prey and advanced with its body raised. 27.7 As brave warriors discover that they could destroy their enemies with (their) arrogance, so Samson the brave warrior defeated the lion due to its own dreadfulness. 27.8 Since the brave man knew that the maw, which is the lion's weapon for everything, would be open on two sides he divided his hands, with the left on the inside of its mouth and the right by the lion's nostrils and lips. 27.9 By force he opened it wider still; he was so exceedingly strong that he tore the beast through the middle. 27.10 When he tore the beast apart, the tear passed through the neck, scarcely stopping when it was halted by the lion's stomach. 27.11 To proclaim this, Scripture says, *Ripped it as he would rip a kid, and there was nothing in his hands.*

Judg 14:5

LXX Judg 14:6

28.1 And so he ripped apart the lion and left it dead on the ground. Then he returned to join his parents again. 28.2 He did not reckon his exploit to be so wonderful that he should let his parents know. 28.3 After such an exploit he appeared firm and silent without any wound, and he betrayed no fear by the color of his face, nor did he reveal his exploit by his soul's agitation or signal labor through bodily weariness. 28.4 As if he had done nothing, he was quiet with unshakable control; he showed his color because of courage. «566» 28.5 It seems to me that filled with the spirit of power and bright with divine gifts, he was already contemplating the future riddle of the lion and he wished to conceal the invention of the riddle.

29.1 After he returned, the desire for the vision of the lion entered him. When he came to the same place, he saw the young lion swarming with bees. 29.2 For the bees, upon seeing the maw in the form of an opening, discovered a hollow into the stomach of the beast as if in rock. Gradually migrating inside through the mouth of the young lion, they had constructed a honeycomb. 29.3 When he saw the multifaceted splendor of the bees' construction, he made

---

a. Arm. "words of artists," but the Arm. *ban* likely translates the Greek *logos*, "argument."

Judg 14:14 — something more splendid than the honeycombs, a riddle: 29.4 Drawing food "out of the one that eats" and taking "honey out of the strong," he composed, as it would become apparent, into a riddle, which he posed at the wedding banquet as follows:

30.1 "People who honor the present banquet! Since in this occasion it is appropriate to delight not only the body with food but also the soul with words, I will at the start of merriment propose to you who are here a riddle that is not fabricated but based on truth. 30.2 But because we are discussing truth, a penalty will be imposed on the riddler if the audience prove wiser by solving (it). 30.3 (On the other hand,) a profit will be returned to him if he triumphs by outwitting you[a] with one riddle. 30.4 The riddle in and of itself is entertaining, but a wager under (these) conditions will be more splendid. For listeners who would lose the bet[b] (to me), the hunt for answer would be more pleasant;[c] for the riddler who fears losing, (on the other hand,) a double delight awaits after his victory. 30.5 So, what is the profit «567» for the winners and what is the damage for the loser? Listen, there are thirty of you solving the riddle, but I who propose the riddle am one. 30.6 If I am (more) capable (than) the many of you in power, each one of you would owe me the victor a long tunic as compensation, but if you solve this concealed and hidden riddle, I would be a debtor to each of your bodies individually. 30.7 In losing each of you will pay a single penalty in accordance with the wager, providing dress for one body, but I would be doomed to adorn many, who each is a single body in the winner's party. 30.8 So, what is this riddle? Pay attention: *Out of the eater came the food,*

Judg 14:14 — *and out of the strong came the sweet.*"

31.1 You pose the problem well, Samson! You made the first known by the strength of the second and the weak by the strong. 31.2 *Out of the eater came the food* is easy to understand, for goats and sheep eat and produce food, namely milk. 31.3 But *out of the strong came the sweet* is unsolvable.[d] This is most wise and artful, proposing the easy first to entrap his audience before twisting its easiness with the difficulty of the second. The easy one lures (them) into a trap, while the strong one seizes the deceived in it. 31.4 You, therefore, forwarded your riddle as proof not only of strength but also of wisdom.

32.1 Upon hearing this, those who had come to Samson's wedding in joy were ready to solve the riddle, before they could ascertain the riddle or truly understand the depth of the riddle. (So) they accepted the proposed invitation to the wager. 32.2 For caught between two evils, «568» wishful thinking[e] and intoxication, they were more than determined (to win) the wager. Intoxication did not let them reflect on or thoroughly examine the matter first, and wishful thinking has already triumphed and handed them the victory before thinking. 32.3 For by nature everyone expects the best and goes forward by striving[f] to

---

a. Lit., "by considering in your thoughts."
b. Lit., "be defeated with a profit."
c. Lit., "he investigates diligently the word more pleasantly."
d. Lit., "without understanding."
e. Lit., "hope."
f. Lit., "by contest, struggle."

exceed[a] their hope, especially those who inundate their reasoning with alcohol. 32.4 For when the mind has sunk into intoxication and succumbed to warring animalistic impulses, it drags down the irrational animality of the heart as if into an abyss. 32.5 After it has erased all thoughts, it wakes and rushes to a decision in such an animalistic fashion that it is imprisoned in its own action.

33.1 Samson, however, was unable to entrap (them), because the woman intervened and violently tore up the trap laid by him. 33.2 The hunter, she wove a trap of her own to ensnare, and the hunted, she set free by shredding the net. 33.3 Such, O Samson, is the foreigner woman: ready anytime to copulate and to pretend to love[b] faithfully. In her soul, (however,) she wars against him with whom she copulates[c] and she divides her inheritance among foreigners. 33.4 Though she is peaceful in her flesh, she is rebellious in her soul. Alas, what is more, she does nothing peaceful but everything warlike. 33.5 She lets nobody be saved without plotting against the one she is meant to protect. 33.6 She cunningly devises her plot, so that whoever receives what appears to be beneficial will (in fact) receive covert death-bearing fruits. 33.7 Just as those who mix poison with food demonstrate that their culinary art deceives, «569» those who take the poison prove the evil deed of the same woman.

34.1 Do you see the deception of the mind? Were you, O Samson, deprived of victory by a woman? 34.2 From now on see to it that you not trip over a second stone and fall. Rather, do not strike the same stone a second time. Do not be ignorant of and forget what you have learned in nature. 34.3 Come now, be more careful and stable in the future! Violent and horrible, O Samson, is the female gender. She can emasculate[d] a man and make (him) feminine and vanquish bodily power using the deception of lust on the soul. 34.4 Only for them is it easy to vanquish the race of strong men, for they go to war not with weapons or manly valor, but their face is their weapon, their word is their sword, and their flatteries and caresses (are) their fire. 34.5 What is most surprising of all is that they win when we make peace with them. If we are angry at something, we can vanquish (them) again, but if we reckon them sweet and compliant, we will be overwhelmed. 34.6 Above all, however, although they are swifter than any arrow,[e] they cannot shoot one who is not willing. 34.7 Their arrows would appear ineffective and useless, if we on our own do not rouse or agitate them against ourselves. 34.8 How so? The beautiful feminine face came by as something brilliant, but it would become a useless weapon if it is disregarded. 34.9 If you simply bypass it, you will be unharmed. But if you provoke it, return a glance with a glance,[f] and win the woman's attention with your face,[g] then the opposite happens, namely, your mental attention «570» is struck.[h] Defeated by her weapon, you will let (the

---

a. Lit., "vanquish."
b. Lit., "to give a semblance of love."
c. A simplification of "with whom she shares in mixing of flesh."
d. Lit., "castrate," which is the meaning of the Latin root of "emasculate."
e. A run-on phrase, "in order to be shot to wound," is left out of the translation.
f. Lit., "build a glance upon a glance."
g. Lit., "win the woman's face with yours."
h. Lit., "receives its strike itself."

arrow) strike[a] your own heart. 34.10 So our swords are an empty and a useless weapon: we use them against ourselves, drawing them toward ourselves.

35.1 Let none of the audience accuse me of misjudging myself or of being overzealous beyond measure. 35.2 I have lingered in this disquisition[b] not to exonerate Samson or, again, to show the irrational man to be rational with the words I have spoken. But I will first make an accusation against the foreigners and show their devious intentions; then my discourse will help us. 35.3 For the vices of the ancestors are a preservation of later generations' chaste prudence, because life is one, the natures of humanity are the same, traps are similar, and everyone's vices are the same. 35.4 Concerning these things (this) discourse is beneficial. Even though our words have to do with the man from the beginning, they are beneficial to later generations that live in the same deceptions.[c] 35.5 They might discover this discourse to be a curative antidote for the deadly poison. 35.6 Now, then, since we were ready to tell the story about the riddle but the amazement of the examination at the foreign woman had intervened and cut off the narrative, let us return to where we left off.

36.1 In the morning, after they had shaken off their drunken stupor, they set their mind to the wisdom of the riddle but came up with no solution. 36.2 Since they were unable to solve it,[d] they came to the conclusion that it was the cleverest of the riddles. Because it was unintelligible to them the excessive wisdom «571» seemed to be unsolvable. 36.3 Three days they sought to solve it[e] and (three) sleepless nights passed. On the fourth day, they turned to Samson's wife, 36.4 and this is a true concession[f] of defeat and an impudent entreaty for a shameless victory. 36.5 How? They went to the woman and asked, "Woman, we are your city, your parents, your homeland. 36.6 The land you see and your properties are all adjacent to all of us. But by an agreement through a relative you have lain with a foreigner. 36.7 So, (be sure) you do not respect one part more than so many parts, and that your love for the foreigner is not stronger than your love for your parents! 36.8 Samson has posed a riddle to us, and we are battling with him for riches, for in this one proposal stands the (prospective) loss[g] of the industriousness of our labors and ignominy[h] of defeat. 36.9 Because the glory is common (to us all), let us defeat the foreigner. Humiliation of defeat will be common as well, because if all the citizens bear shame, a part of shame will come upon you also.

37.1 "Do not crown the foreigner over your parents. Do not honor this man with our humiliation. And do not see Samson's face bright and cheery but wish

---

a. Lit., "you will have sprouting forth."
b. Adopting Aucher's proposal of emending the text to read *i žaṙagrowt'eann* ("in the disquisition") Aucher, 570 n. 1; see also Muradyan and Topchyan, 802 n. 24; contra Siegert, 74 n. 777.
c. Lit., "who living by means of the same deceptions are being arranged in life."
d. Lit., "Not understanding it."
e. The underlying Greek is likely *zēteō*, "to seek, to solve (a problem)."
f. Lit., "acknowledgment of truth."
g. Lit., "trial, misfortune, calamity."
h. Lit., "injury," but since the first half of sentence expresses material loss, the second half might refer to the psychological.

your parents' sad and gloomy. 37.2 If you wish not to trust our words but rather wish to be an accomplice of this man, you will suffer all the consequences and we will suffer none. 37.3 Should you give only to them a place of honor, we will reimburse (our) loss of the wager from your ancestral properties and impose death on you for your disloyalty. 37.4 This way, «572» we will lose nothing, because the loss (from the wager) will be reimbursed from your properties and the gloominess with which we will be afflicted owing to our defeat will be alleviated by your death." Judg 14:15

38 Perhaps someone from the audience might say, "But if they made such a threat[a] against the young woman, it is no longer right to blame her for valuing her own interest more highly than another's." 38.2 Read the Scripture in truth! You who criticize those who blame the woman will find yourself the woman's enemy. 38.3 Those who accepted the riddle had occupied themselves for three days in search of a solution, and (only) after the third day did they change course and dash to her. 38.4 She, however, had tempted Samson from the first day on. Before the others put pressure (on her), she put pressure (on him), and before they asked (her) for a favor, she had (already) asked that (he) do her a favor. 38.5 This is how her devious machination came upon Samson. She carried out her work not out of compulsion but rather because of her nature. 38.6 Even though all of us are in doubt regarding our question, (we can be certain that) the woman's evil deed of knavery has earned her the word "robbery," because it was (evident) in everything. 38.7 If someone asked her for a favor she would grant it, but when she was asked she escalated her wickedness to complete the deceit to betray Samson and to crown the uncircumcised. Judg 14:17a

39.1 Now, in order that we not let this discussion go unwitnessed and that I denounce the woman's knavery that I promised, I will offer you the same Scripture itself as witness. 39.2 Consider what the foreigners asked from the woman and when, and what the woman wanted and when she began to ask (for it). 39.3 If so, let us first resolve the foreigners' (words): *They were not able to solve the riddle* «573» *on the third day, and they said to Samson's wife, use soft speech to trick your husband.* 39.4 But if it happened after the third day, on the fourth day, when they asked (her) to betray Samson, she must have begun the betrayal at that time. 39.5 So, what did she do and when did she begin the betrayal? Let us hear the same Scripture because she confesses: *And the woman wept over him for seven days, on which there was a banquet for them.* 39.6 But if this is the case, the first three days belonged to her own wickedness and four were for begging. 39.7 Therefore, this must be said: she who had begun the deceit (even) before the squabble betrayed her husband without any compulsion. Judg 14:14–15

Judg 14:17

40.1 What shall I say, nefarious, abominable woman! You wish to hear the riddle not to enjoy the composition or to learn wisdom from your spouse, but to betray him who had spoken, to strip the crown from him who composed it with wisdom. 40.2 Are you not utterly shamed by the bridal candle, and have you no regard for the bridal wreath as a symbol of nuptial union? 40.3 Have you no regard for the kindness of your husband, and are you not shamed by the very table, the wedding banquet that Samson prepared for you? 40.4 But you

---

a. Lit., "they threatened ... threats."

dissolved the nuptial union before the banquet was finished and you betrayed your husband before doffing the crown. 40.5 Because of you the wedding bed became an enemy to the one who adorned it, and you made the nuptial songs into dirges in places of mourning. 40.6 That is why you did not guard the nuptial bed after seven days, as it was the custom of a wedding, but you utterly destroyed the wedding by dissolving the marriage union.

Judg 14:10
Judg 14:20

41.1 So, as the deception become potently effective,[a] the conqueror «574» was vanquished and the deceivers became victorious when they began to solve the proposed riddle. 41.2 In order to get back at Samson by any means necessary,[b] they stood together and answered, *What is sweeter than honey, and stronger than a lion?* 40.3 When Samson heard this and (knew) whence came the deception, he said, "Men, this riddle is solved, but the victory belongs to the woman, not to the men, for *If you had not plowed with my heifer, you would not have solved[c] my riddle.*

Judg 14:18a

Judg 14:18b

42.1 What wisdom, once more![d] What, again, a wonderful riddle! They would not be able to know it fully if their deeds had not clearly shown its meaning.[e] 42.2 What do you say, Samson? *If you had not plowed with my heifer, (you) would not have understood[f] my riddle.* 42.3 What does it wish to signify? It seems to me that it surpasses us, even if we are to study it, but it is fitting that Samson's riddle is incomprehensible to foreigners but is understood by us who belong to the same race. 43.4 Since we do not investigate for stratagem of deception, as they do, but for divine gratitude, we scrutinize it for the memorial[g] of wisdom. Make known to us seekers why you mention "heifer" and what is "a plowing heifer." 43.5 For we see the heifer not "plowed" but "plowing." Why do you call one who has plowed a "plower"? 43.6 O the beautiful and the wise, you made known what was hidden. The female heifer, being in the middle, became the foreigners' plower when they pressed and forced her to exert herself urgently: *Use soft speech to trick your husband,* but she plowed you. 43.7 So beautifully and artfully expressed by you! From there (the foreigners) made haste and with violence, rushing *to plow with my heifer.*

Judg 14:18b

Judg 14:15

«575» 43.1 After they had given (him) this answer, he made restitution of the wager that had been snatched away by them in their victory in another way. 43.2 Since this foreign people are one, he dressed those nearby while he killed their faraway relatives.[h] 43.4 Because they must be dressed in black for the dead, he dressed them splendidly from their possessions. 43.4 Just as only one of the blood brothers was clothed, he dressed the victor by stripping the innocent one. 43.4 In so doing, however, he did not kill gratuitously[i] or senselessly—let no one accuse the wise one— 43.6 but to be humanity-loving on

Judg 14:19

---

a. Lit., "becoming strong it vanquished."
b. Or "in full."
c. Lit., "discovered," but *gtanem* translates the LXX *euriskō,* which has the sense of "to solve."
d. Lit., "second wisdom."
e. Lit., "word" or Greek *logos,* in this context the rational explanation of the biblical text and the object of "shown."
f. Now corresponding to LXX Codex B; the earlier citation corresponds to Codex A.
g. Following Aucher in changing the locative *yišataki* to an accusative.
h. I.e., he gave the spoils to the victors; the spoils are garments.
i. Lit., "in vain," which might translate the Greek *eikē.*

account of the threat against the woman by the foreigners who forced her to betray Samson by threatening to burn down the woman's house. 43.7 Now that they were victorious and the house had been saved from incineration, he lit a blaze in midst of the foreigners with his sword of fire, lest the cheaters benefit from their victory. 44.1 He performed justly and (in accordance with) what is the will of the divine writings, for even the writing somewhere says clearly, *One who digs a hole will fall into it.*

Judg 15:4–5

Qoh 10:8

44.2 For fair-minded Samson, it seems to me, no less astonishing than his proposed riddle are his heroic exploits. 44.3 For he who defeated and destroyed thirty warriors with so much of his own valiant nature but did not render their dresses useless by a blood bath could well have destroyed the house of one of those who threatened it, 44.4 making their devious[a] victory a cause for a massacre. «576» But if he had done that, he would have been considered being fearful of losing[b] the wager and transgressing the terms of the bet.

45.1 Now, since he was wise, he saw how he could avoid losses[c] while staying true to the wager. He took the cost of the wager from other things to make up for the payoff[d] to the winner, as I say, with no losses. 45.2 Although those who won by trickery deserve a severe penalty, it would be inappropriate for the defeated party to exact revenge on the victors at this time, at the moment of his defeat. 45.3 He who was beaten fulfilled the predetermined wager. After the time to exact a penalty had passed, Samson did this. After he had paid the wager to them, fulfilled his responsibility, and submitted himself to the agreed-upon promises of the wager, he found at a later time (an occasion) to exact revenge on the cheaters. 45.4 He did not cheat at the time of the wager, (lest) he be slandered as faithless. Nor did he let (the matter) go afterward, (lest) he be known as cowardly. Instead, as it befits a wise and altogether just man, he gave without suffering loss, and in seizing[e] (properties) from others he was neither ignoble nor ungrateful. 45.5 When he himself was defrauded, he did not exact revenge in exchange; when he exacted revenge, he did not defraud. He just waited for a while.

46.1 To wait for things that arrive to the spiritually endowed, they with his own spirit foresee every opportunity. 46.2 When the time came, he exacted revenge on the foreigners at the suitable moment. After this, he drove the cheaters out. 46.3 The expulsion was due to his own strength, but (he succeeded) rightly because he knew the arrival of the (favorable) time.[f] 46.4 Because it had not been suitable (to do) what he wanted, it was necessary for his character to forget quickly the bridal bed and the wedding, and to bear arms against all those who wore those robes as a symbol of his wedding. 46.5 Even though every foreign race is exceedingly disdainful and ungrateful by nature, it would not be appropriate for the just one to appear as participating in such ingratitude.

Without preparation on Samson.

    a. Lit., "not pure."
    b. Lit., "from the loss."
    c. Lit., "be preserved unharmed."
    d. Lit., "demand from the wager."
    e. So presumably; literally "cutting." Another MS reads "restoring."
    f. The contrast is keyed on the parallel construction *hiwrmē zōrowt'enēn* ("because of his own strength") and *i žamanagēn egeal* ("because of the time that is coming").

Armenian Pseudo-Philo's *De Jona*

«578» 1.1 (1) Some who read the prophets marvel at their benefit for humanity, and some admire their prophecy. 1.2 (2) I, however, praise also those who praise, for I see him who is indeed to be praised above all spirit-breathed prophets.[a] He is superior to the chosen ones in the same way that a lyre player (is superior) to a lyre, a master-builder to the house, a helmsman to a skiff, or one who vests any operation with intelligence and skill to any tool of craft. 1.3 (3) For just as there the body would be useless if it has no soul that moves it, so too the master-builder if he does not receive a mind for his masterpiece. 1.4 (4) That is why I believe the legislation to be like a ship constructed from on high: the skipper of all sits on it while it is sailing, piloting this world justly[b] for sake of the salvation of everyone. He pilots by administering the needs of all things, wherever it is and whatever it is.

Gen 10:11 «579» 2.1 (5) Now he who pilots every city saw from high above that Nineveh was descending into a depraved way of life, and it was also the beginning of cities.[c] Like an able physician he sought a suitable medicine for the city's illness to arrest the spread of the disease and, with his help, to forestall the danger. 2.2 (6) The remedy had a reputation opposite to deliverance, (however,) for in desiring to save and preserve it, he sent a prophet to threaten the city with destruction, to teach, methinks, the art of the very same doctor. (7) Just as the most skillful of them who promise to deliver the sick might set them straight by fire and water, 2.3 so, too, the all-wise who alone is the savior builds compassion of deliverance by pronouncing destruction and ruin.

---

a. Following Siegert against Aucher's punctuation (which Muradyan and Topchyan follow), which puts a full stop after "I, however, praise also those who praise." The explanatory note beginning with "for indeed" (Greek *kai gar*), which takes up the rest of 1.2, is meant to compare the relationship between, on one hand, the praises of the prophet and authors of said praises and, on the other, the prophets and the author of their prophecy, that is, God. This requires reading the plural "them" in 1.2 as a singular "him"; the Armenian translator consistently confuses the plural and the singular. The following short forms are used here: Siegert for Siegert, *Drei hellenistisch-jüdische Predigten*; Aucher for Aucher, *Philonis Judaei paralipomena Armena*; Muradyan and Topchyan for Muradyan and Topchyan, *Pseudo-Philo*; Lewy for Lewy, *Pseudo-Philo*.

b. The underlying Greek might well be *orthōs* "rightly, justly."

c. The pronoun *sa* ("he, she, or it") could refer to "God" (so Muradyan and Topchyan) or Nineveh (Siegert). I take the latter since the next sentence speaks of arresting the spread of Nineveh's disease, presumably to other cities.

3.1 (8) For their deliverance, the humanity-loving one[a] looks for a partner, a common man[b] who is one of their own and is regarded as a servant (of God). It is not as though he did not know the future—for who gave knowledge to prophets? (He did so) in order to make the second (act) more wonderful than the first. 3.2 (9) He entrusted the deliverance of lives only (to him) by sending a human being for the deliverance of human beings. He healed him first by reprimanding the healer, for just as they were ill in their way of life, the prophet, too, was weakened[c] in his knowledge of God, when he thought he could escape from the inescapable God.

Dan 2:21

4.1 (10) Now the Lord, approaching him as he was wont to do since days of yore, says to him this way: "Do you, prophet, see the city of Nineveh that has been given by me in abundance whatever is (needed) for the happiness of its inhabitants? 4.2 (11) Do you see the luxuriant sheaves of grain, the land more fertile «580» than any other land, flourishing with fecundity owing to the mild and sweet air that surrounds it? They cannot complain about cold weather, frequent torrent, or unnaturally scorching sun.[d] 4.3 (12) Now why do they deny me the gratitude that is my due? I am not demanding too much compensation for so much beneficence, am I? Just words of gratitude![e] 4.4 Indeed, they have become so ungrateful as not only to do away with gratitude but also to become ignorant of their gift-giver. 4.5 (13) Why do they need the heaven to be luminous, the clouds (to produce) rain, the earth to be fruitful, the trees to sprout forth, the moon to appear bright, and the sun to radiate beams for their ungrateful souls? 4.6 What they received, I believe, they have rendered useless: 14 They did not see the world with eyes (given) for knowledge of the architect, they closed their ears off to words of piety,[f] and they wagged their own tongue to blaspheme my divinity.[g]

5.1 (15) "If they made up for the evil against me with benevolence toward one another, it could perhaps be forgivable, but their culpability[h] toward human beings surpassed their culpability toward God. 5.2 (16) Just as their lifespan is divided into ages—old age, adulthood, and childhood—so their sins are also divided into ages. Their youths hunt after pleasure of the flesh, the able-bodied who have grown into manhood commit[i] robbery with their strength, and their women, who surpass one another in beauty, adorn themselves to lay traps. 5.4 (17) Even the deeds of gray-haired men are unacceptable. When their age

Qoh 7:26

---

a. Since the motif of God's love for humanity runs through the entire sermon and functions almost like a technical term, I am highlighting the etymology of the Greek by consistently translating the adjective *philanthrōpos* as "humanity-loving" and the noun *philanthrōpia* as "love for humanity."

b. Lit., "a man from the many" (Greek *tōn pollōn*), that is, one of the hoi polloi.

c. Adopting Lewy's conjecture.

d. Lit., "sun hotter than nature itself."

e. The phrase "Just words of gratitude!" belongs grammatically to the rhetorical question that precedes and stands in apposition to "compensation." But I have followed Siegert in making it into an independent exclamation for emphasis.

f. Lit., "from piety of words."

g. Lit., "they moved their own tongue against me in mention of (my) divinity with wickedness."

h. Lit., "accusation."

i. Lit., "to conduct oneself toward robbery."

took away their strength and robbed (them of) their beauty «581» and gave (them) reason to make up for their loss, they cultivated it for wickedness, equipping themselves to defraud each other. 5.5 (18) Now if they are not ready to show gratitude toward me or goodwill toward one another, they are a burden to the elements, on which their senseless conducts are nurtured. 5.6 (19) Now, what do I wish, prophet? Proclaim destruction to this city: A most painful death will visit (it) so that in the meantime they should not live in pleasure with (any) expectation for the future."

6.1(20) As the prophet heard this, since he had devoted himself[a] to his art—that is, I mean, his prophecy—he saw that the city (would remain) whole even after the proclamation. And as if he had not been serving the Lord but had acquired prophecy by himself, he fled from the city to which he was commanded to go. 6.2 (21) He was altogether most foolish, supposing he could flee from the creator of the universe. The overseer of the universe let the man who thought he was fleeing God (do it), inasmuch to reproach the prophet as to manifest his power and to make the proclamation to the city stronger, so that the city to which extermination was proclaimed might escape and be delivered from danger. 6.3 (22) He was not able to, because it was an impossibility for him to escape the overseer of the universe. He fled instead, ridding[b] himself of the knowledge of the future, and hurled himself into the open sea.

7.1 (23) As he walked toward the sea perplexed, he came across a trireme there. Waving to the sailors, he said, "O Sailors, where are you going? Where are you sailing the skiff off to? Do me a favor:[c] take me on board!" «582» 7.2 (24) When they named the city and agreed, they stretched out and pulled up on board the trouble of the sea and him who would become a danger to the sailors. 7.3 Because the prophet, herald to the city, was in waves of agitation when he boarded the skiff because of his prophecy, 7.4 (25) they took in a stone that had received the proclamation, and they undertook the sea voyage against themselves. Instead of (the sailors') piloting the skiff above the waves, the waves, searching (for the prophet),[d] billowed over them. 7.5 (26) So, I suppose, contriving his own total forgetfulness, (the prophet) had left the deck of the ship and sunk into its belly; (thus) with a heart of sadness he had given himself up to forgetfulness. 7.6 (27) Since the sea did not see[e] him who had gone out from it, it prayed and was frightened. The elements, however, nobler than a servant, raised the sea against the prophet; they begrudged the salvation of the fugitive, because he did not wish love for humanity on the Ninevites.

Jonah 1:5

---

a. Lit., "having gazed, looked up"; both Muradyan and Topchyan and Siegert have "recalled." The underlying Greek might well be *prosechō*, which can mean "to devote oneself to (a thing)" (LSJ). The aorist participle refers to what Jonah had been trained for.

b. Contra Muradyan and Topchyan, who take the participle as a passive. Since Jonah is said to have foreseen the city's eventual salvation in 6.1, his flight constitutes an active evasion of his own prophecy.

c. Lit., "Be a useful thing to me."

d. The Arm. *yowzeal* can mean "agitating" or "agitated," but the personification of the sea ("it prayed and was frightened") and the elements ("nobler than a servant," "it begrudged") in the ensuing context requires an explicit attribution of intentionality.

e. Following Lewy's (45) suggestion of reading the Greek *eide* ("it saw") for *eiche* ("it had").

8.1 (28) Thereupon the skipper left the helm and the sailors the other tasks, and they stretched out their hands in prayer. In spite of their prayer the storm did not subside, nor did the boat calm down; instead, the howling of the waves became stronger, and the winds blasted ever more violently and they competed against one another for the destruction of the sailors. 8.2 (29) Torrents covered the boat, and the winds were sweeping away those on the skiff before sinking it. Little wonder perhaps, for the heat of the storm was inside the boat and it sought parching wind over the sea. 8.3 (30) Now, why did the storm not cease? Just as, I think, a great conflagration that seizes a forest will not «583» extinguish, but if someone removes the wood from the forest, the fire will, upon being extinguished, vanish. 8.4 (31) In the same way, the heat of the storm would be a raging inferno as long as the prophet was there, but when he was away, there would be a sign of peace.

9.1 (32) The skipper of the ship who was paying attention to the sea and was entrusted with the command of the ship sensed that someone was sleeping through such commotion, for the sound of the snoring of his nostrils was his enemy,[a] as it happens to those in deep sleep. 9.2 (33) For, I believe, when the mouth is closed and the other senses are shut down, the breath is compressed and comes out through the nostrils. So compressed, the narrow channel likewise wheezes when it is filled with air. That is usually what happens in the throat. 9.3 (34) The prophet, however, was snoring not so much because he was compelled by nature as he was summoned by a verdict to a rebuke for his sinning. 9.4 (35) Presently the captain approached him and said, "Man, are you so carefree that you are sleeping? Has sleep seized you so deeply that you could not be awakened by the crashing of these waves or the upheaval of the skiff? 9.5 Arise, stand up, and shake off your sleep. Pray to your god! 36 Do you not see that before you came on board we were sailing happily, but after you came on board we are in danger? 9.6 Do you not see the sea is bursting higher than the air and the storm is clutching our boat? 37 So why is it that all are at work while you stand idle? 9.7 If you are counting on relying[b] on our labor and are demanding[c] (that you) be delivered by others' labor, we will perish, betrayed by (your) lazy indifference."

LXX Jonah 1:5

10.1 (38) So the prophet woke up and went up to the deck of the boat, and saw the storm cloud, «584» the billowing waves, the violent winds, the lamentation of the people, and the weeping of the children. All the souls stood only a short way from death.[d] 10.2 (39) Looking around from above as if from some summit, he saw the magnitude of the misery and knew[e] that it was on account of his sins that the sea was roiling. Nevertheless, he hid by forgetting;[f] he consoled himself[g] by reckoning the danger to be not merely his own but

---

a. The LXX describes Jonah snoring, whereas the MT simply has him sleeping.
b. Lit., "to be sufficient."
c. Lit., "requiring, compelling, obliging."
d. Lit., "By a little space all the souls stood imprisoned by death."
e. Lit., "he thought, supposed."
f. Adopting Lewy's emendation from *hamareal* ("reckoning"), which is assimilated to *hamareal* of the following sentence, to *arareal* ("doing, making").
g. Following Lewy's emendation of reading the last three words of §39 (*tesanel ew mxit'arel*, "to see and to care") as *tesanelov mxit'arec'aw* ("he cared by seeing").

common to all. 10.3 (40) For human beings are accustomed to suffering pains more easily when many people take part in a community. That creates equality; the misfortune of one becomes the remedy of comfort for others.

11.1 (41) Now the helmsmen of the boat understood that prayers could be thwarted by sins, and (so) they conducted an enquiry into the deeds of every individual. After they had examined others for their accounts of life debts, they turned to the prophet. Coming to him, they sought an examination of his conducts. 11.2 (42) "Who are you?" they said, "And from where did you come to us? What are your heart's thoughts? What are you struggling with in your soul? 11.3 What are the conducts in your life? You are weak in body but a burden to the boat. We fear you might sink our boat by weighing it down with your deeds." 11.4 (43) So said the captain and all others. The prophet, however, disclosed (only) what was beneficial to himself but maintained his silence on what he knew to be harmful. 11.5 He mentioned (he was) a servant of the Lord but was silent on his circumventing the Lord's command or the flight. 11.6 (44) But he who alone cannot be deceived set the whole human knowledge before him with incontrovertible evidence, for from the commotion «585» of those on board and from the interrogation of the seafarers came a question, and from the question came the casting of lots, and from the lot he who had been unknown to people was found and bound. 11.7 (45) This is highly appropriate, for where a judge was human, he[a] (could) defeat the judge's[b] verdict by concealing (himself), but where God was the supreme judge, he was unable to be deceptive. 11.8 (46) What now? By means of lots, God became a judge to the pious people: in an open (casting of lots) each is moved by whom he likes and raises one's hand, whereas in secret (casting), no one has one's own authority[c] and (God) delivered[d] him in secret.

12.1 (47) Now as God judged the man and delivered him into the hand by lot, they took him and delivered him into the hands of his judge who would punish him. As Scripture says, *What should we do to you, so this sea would calm down for us?* 12.2 (48) "It is you who are the cause of this storm, and the lot convicts you. We, however, my friend,[e] do not thirst for murder or, like those who are savages by nature, execution of a human being. We only wish to break up this evil that traps us on all sides. 12.3 (49) Now if there is a way for us and for you to reach land and the skiff be delivered whole and we are preserved, no one will begrudge anyone who harms nobody's life. But if keeping you alive (means) we must die, then we reckon the survival of the many is preferable to[f] one person's death. 12.4 (50) The darkening heaven above us,

---

a. I.e., the prophet.
b. Lit., "judges'"; the switch between singular and plural is frequent; I have kept it singular for consistency.
c. Lit., "with no own authority."
d. Or "betrayed," as in revealing Jonah's identity and his culpability. The underlying Greek could well be *paradidonai*, "to deliver (someone to the authorities)" or "to arrest." Similarly in the next sentence, 12.1 (47).
e. Lit., "O man."
f. Lit., "honorable instead of."

Armenian Pseudo-Philo's De Jona

the beloved earth and its land are our witnesses; the element of the sea that stirred up this storm over (us) is a witness. 12.5 (51) Look indeed at the misery delivered in this storm! It is not at all because of (our) pilfering and barbarous character «586» that we are hurling this man overboard, or because we crave after his baggage. To escape alive from a hostile, unknown hand and (to avoid) a terrible and a miserable death of this ship is (our) pressing concern,[a] not this luggage. 12.6 (52) Strange man, our ship will not take you. Change to another ship as you wish. May there be (someone) to save you when you depart from this ship! With luck you will board another ship to which you go. You have come to us in the most inopportune time. 12.7 Maybe an angel from the abyss or perhaps a dumb *ketos*[b] might be entrusted with your soul! 53 So, may you not be blamed for the annihilation of our ship or we be responsible for the death of your soul."

13.1 (54) They demanded an answer from the man. Now since the disciple of the humanity-loving God[c] did not gain life from others' deliverance, he offered (life) from his own death. 13.2 (55) Upon hearing a humanity-loving voice from a humanity-loving mouth, he said to those longing for life who were praying: 13.3 (56) "Because you are setting me up as judge of your lives, your interest will not be hurt by my judgment, for although I have the form of a judge, I am dressed in the contingency of an accused. 13.4 (57) If you had not hung this judgment[d] on me, I would want to benefit greatly from others' misfortune. But because you who are in danger are trusting your adversary to do justice, I will protect the givers' trust to my last breath."

14.1 (58) "What now, prophet? Why do you hesitate? Why do you pursue deliverance? Make yourself die and you, though trapped, will overcome the trap. 14.2 Since «587» you cannot secure life, erect now a monument of love for humanity on the ship even as you die, and show (yourself) a pious prophet, since you are a deserter from pious prophecy." 14.3 (59) So saying while they were on the high seas, he gave himself to the raging sea.

15.1 (60) Miserable, pious ones, was the calamity, that a man—after making a beginning for deliverance, being entrapped by necessity, and being cornered by the lot, God, and people—became a judge (condemning) himself to death,[e] and in becoming a caretaker of others' deliverance, he renounced his own. 15.2 (61) We must, therefore, admire the Lord's love for humanity, for he arranged[f] that both—the prophet who deserved condemnation for his flight

a. Lit., "compels" without an object. The underlying Greek is probably *anankazō*, "to compel, to constrain" but also "to apply compulsion" when used absolutely.

b. The Arm. *kitos* is a transliteration of the Greek *kētos*, "sea monster," which is different from the MT *dāg gādôl* ("big fish"). Given the ambiguity, it seems best to leave the word in Greek untranslated.

c. Contra Siegert. Here I follow Lewy's emendation and apply this and the next two occurrences of "humanity-loving" to God rather than to Jonah.

d. I.e., Jonah is expected to make a judgment.

e. Lit., "judge of his own death."

f. Rejecting Lewy's suggestion of reading the participle as an infinitive. The Arm. *orošem* might well translate the Greek *diakrinō*, which means "to arrange, set in order," as well as "to decide, judge, evaluate." The preacher appears to be using the passengers' confession (hinted at in Jonah 1:5) to adumbrate the eventual repentance of the Ninevites.

from his (duty of) proclamation because death was closing in from all sides and those who condemned gratuitously—confess their sins. 15.3 (62) In so doing, the humanity-loving one wished not only to pity the miserable man but also to prepare him for his own service in the future. 15.4 After locking him up in ineluctable dangers, (God) performed (for him) a benevolence so (the prophet) by said benevolence (done) for him might learn God's love for humanity and never become jealous of the Ninevites—himself having been saved by (God's) love for humanity.

16.1 (63) Now after having healed both diseases and having educated the man—that no one should regard God as ignorant or oppose his love for humanity—he prepared for him a vessel that was passing swiftly around, a *ketos*, which he took to be a deadly beast but was (in fact) deliverance and a guardian of deliverance. As the prophet was swimming, the *ketos* drew (him) into itself like breath and it conceived (him) alive inside its belly. «588» 16.2 (64) So the belly of the *ketos* became the abode of the submerging prophet, with (its) eyes like a mirror of exterior appearances and the movement of its fins like (that of) a royal carriage.

17.1 (65) O prophet, how great it was to move with the speed of a carriage when the *ketos* rushed toward you and swallowed you! What king could be said to look so profoundly into the abyss of the world as you, as the invisible became visible? 17.2 (66) To whom among mortals would the ends of the earth become so visible as to you, when the sea's abyss was displayed as a theater? 17.3 For whom had a craftsman (ever) contrived a machine so innovative, so perfect, as (the one with which) you (could) inspect[a] everything while you the onlooker were visible to no one.

Jonah 2:1

18.1 (67) Since the prophet was hidden in the belly of the beast in appearance, he was in truth protected by the right hand of God, he prayed inside the *ketos*, as we said; (so) he used the beast's mouth for prayer. 18.2 (68) It was an uncanny spectacle to behold the *ketos* becoming an intercessor for the prophet's deliverance. It opened its mouth to lift a prayer to God, lending its tongue for articulation of words, 18.3 being played by the prophet's fingers like a musical instrument by a musician.

Jonah 2:2–9

19.1 (69) The prayer of the supplicant was as follows: "If you wanted to make me experience great torment, I see the measure of my sins and they deserve the full weight of punishment. 19.2 (70) For you wanted to put a stop to my sins up to this point, only to teach (me) to accept the principle of love for humanity that belongs to you,[b] so that, (even though) I have been separated from the sights of all, I should not be cast out from your sight, or that «570» my mouth not be rendered mute, (even if) it has become mute to everyone (else). 19.3 I will gaze at you with the eyes of my whole heart and move my whole tongue to intercede on my own behalf, for you have left it free for me. 19.4 (71) Because you listen to those culpable of sins. When supplicants are permitted to see the king and their gifts are received, that is the principle of love for humanity for them. 19.5 To me, you have granted not only the power of speech but even a

---

a. Lit., "you (could) look intently by inspection."
b. Lit., "beginning," translating the Greek *archē* ("principle"). The same for 19.4.

defense speech for my own deliverance. 19.6 (72) For if you were to sentence me to death, what is more powerful than this wild beast? 19.7 Or, if you were to bury me in a grave, what is deeper than the sea's depth? For when the whole world collapses, it will be buried in this grave.

20.1 (73) "I have therefore waylaid my (own) deliverance. But since the judge is humanity-loving, he brought about[a] a form of deliverance instead of pains,[b] thus proclaiming his abundant love for humanity. Though he had compassion on me, I did not go unpunished. 20.2 Now after you have thrust me into all this, you show your compassion like a sovereign. 20.3 (74) First, I saw the sea stirred up above me and the boat sinking because of me. Then the judgment of those who were onboard with me who made a judgment on my deliverance. Then the condemnation of the lot and the hurling of my body overboard like a useless vessel. After all that, the attack of this frightful beast that could slay with terror before killing. 20.5 (75) But these are perhaps calamities that can be seen, but the distress from (this) strict confinement, «590» invisible to all human beings, is borne witness by no one except him who is enduring (it). 20.6 (76) For who will see him sinking inside the *ketos*? Who will show compassion to him who cannot be seen? And, further still, who will stretch out his right hand to seize and snatch the drowning man from the maw of the wild beast?

21.1 (77) "For I, who fled from land to the sea, from the sea to the boat, and from the boat to the empty belly of the beast, was[c] intercepted and found out to be a fugitive even before my flight, 21.2 (78) because I did not escape the stars.[d] I cannot find food (here), yet I cannot escape.[e] Being held in this tight spot, my misfortune has turned into a parable and the prophet's calamity has become a legend. 21.3 (79) For is not what is seen like a parable or legend? For it is as if I were imprisoned in a belly, concealed and locked under a copper deck behind an iron wall, (so) I can remain motionless and (still) see the whole world. 21.4 (80) The life of the *ketos* has morphed into me. Seeing to (my) nourishment, the beast gave me permission for the use of its own womb.[f] Look, I send forth my prayers out of its mouth, I see out of its eyes, and I move using its fins. In the confinement of this beast, I am not so much struck down as I am happily enjoying myself: 21.5 (81) I see the world as if in a mirror, and I see the grace toward me more clearly[g] than in the mirror.

22.1 (82) "Because you wanted only to instruct me through fear, you placed me in a stronghold and opened up for me the face of the *ketos* to the outside view, for it is a solid machine, a wrath to those that (would be) nightmares in darkness

---

a. Lit., "multiplied."
b. The underlying Greek is likely *pathos* ("pain").
c. Following Lewy's emendation (47 n. 2).
d. Is this a reference to the drawing of lots that doomed the prophet?
e. Lit., "change places."
f. Lit., "nature," but the underlying Greek *physis* was frequently used in Greek-speaking Judaism as euphemism for womb; see, e.g., De Sampsone 5.4 and note on "nature." See 16.1; 25.7–8; 26.2 where the *ketos*'s swallowing of Jonah is described as a conception and pregnancy and its spewing him on dry land as a rebirth.
g. Adopting Lewy's (45) correction from the Greek *energesteron* ("active") to *enargesteron* ("clear").

to all.[a] 22.2 (83) I owe «591» you praise for two things: that I escaped[b] the teeth of the *ketos* that carries me, and that I was beyond the destructions of all wild beasts. 22.3 (84) Now listen to the prayer of us both, this instrument of our voice that makes use of prayer on our behalf. Let me be delivered from this dark prison and grant this *ketos* the freedom to feed, for it does not have sufficient food for me,[c] being prevented from taking nourishment because of me.[d]

23.1 (85) "I know I have disregarded my order and provoked the severest penalty,[e] but after being punished I am chastened. 23.2 (86) I have learned not to flee from the eye that sees all and that encompasses all with its vision, and not to ignore the divine voice. 23.3 So persuaded, I will become a memorial of your power in the holy Scripture for those who will read of the flight of the prophet who had taken this ship, (this) torture chamber the *ketos*. 23.4 (87) May this come upon mortal ears: Your redeeming hand and mouth ready for sinners, a refuge for fugitives, your love for humanity for those who must read this. 23.5 (88) So many punishments come from you, but (in you) are loving acts for humanity (also) gathered. You punish the sinner with righteous judicial wrath, but you also care for him with kingly love.

24.1 (89) "Who among us, upon learning that one could not flee from God, would consider fleeing? Who, after I have sunken into the *ketos* and returned from the ferocity of the wild beast unscathed, would (not)[f] «592» believe that the most luminous of all, by means of the *ketos* whose ferocity he tamed and softened, had nourished the man without air? 24.2 (90) For he sustains terrestrial lives on land and aquatic lives in the sea and supplies the need of our nostrils for air by wind.

Gen 6–8

25.1 (91) "So already in the first age was your love for humanity toward Noah known. For, when you dissolved the whole world in water and buried all that had been living in it, in order that you not be overcome by (your own) artistry of wisdom, you even kept a man whole in midst of the flood, granting him an ark as ship and establishing his providence as helmsman—so that he who was preserved might become the start of the second age. 25.2 (92) A memorial to the second age (was established) by an unjust fire to the patriarchs who overcame

Dan 3:19–30

Babylonian tyrants with their pious deeds. 25.3 (93) One who thinks of the king of the present age, who adds to old miracles with new, will have greater faith in deeds when encountering the present miracles. 25.4 (94) For no mortal who has overcome the flame would still ask how a just man can remain standing unperturbed and unshakable in the worldwide storm, (or) how the sea was split

Exod 14:22
Dan 6:16–23

for the Hebrews to walk straight through, or how pious people played with wild animals. 25.5 (95) They will regard me, who was seeking an ideal of rebirth in my sleep, a witness to all these events, and they will find me trustworthy regarding their own lives and find an ideal of truth. «593» Having seen a part, they will

---

a. The text is unclear, but the preacher seems to be praising the *ketos* as a protective stronghold against wild animals.
b. Emending the text to an aorist first-person singular.
c. Alternative proposed by Aucher: "It does not have sufficient food (for itself)."
d. Lit., "because of us."
e. Lit., "punishment of penitents."
f. "Not" supplied by Lewy, though the sentence still makes sense without it.

believe you in totality. 25.6 (96) For if he could open up the entrails of the wild beast and deliver its living breath whole after it had been summoned out of its body, how could he not deliver him whole who was made from earth and was given back to earth as a down payment? 25.7 (97) Regarding this extraordinary birth of a child—who at once breathed and was strengthened, not by anyone present there or by a doctor's intervention of the breathing condition, but by your holy hand inside—this will be made convincing by us. For nothing hinders your power inside. 25.8 (98) My mysterious conception inside the *ketos* will be a testimony to what a natural pregnancy is like."

26.1 (99) So as he remained in his prayer, God was moved to compassion[a] by his prayer. Forgetfulness came upon the *ketos*, for it was commanded to spew Jonah out onto dry land. 26.2 Upon seeing the world like a rebirth, he worshiped God and once again took up his former (order of) proclamation. 26.3 (100) Just as a wild horse, in my view, would run after much spurring on (even though) it is harnessed against its will, so the prophet became gentle and mild, after much peregrination and after he understood that he was dealing with the inescapable Lord. 26.4 (101) Not only did he hasten but he himself was transformed into the same message. Three days' journey he completed in one[b]—with the only concern of communicating the voice of God, the proclamation, to the inhabitants of Nineveh—in order not to waste the limited time that had been allotted for healing[c] the Ninevites' illness on the traveler's tardiness. 26.5 (102) Sweating and with alacrity, free of rebelliousness, he reached the people.

«594» 27.1 (103) He stood on a high place and proclaimed: "Inhabitants of this place, draw back the curtains to the nuptial chamber, and strip the wreath off the bridegrooms! Throw the crowns away! Mourn not for the dead but for the living! 27.2 (104) For the Lord of the universe has cut short your lifespan. Your time has been decided for you: your city has three days![d] What is the reason? You are not ignorant, for you yourselves know, as I (now) proclaim to you. 27.3 (105) You do not know God and you give no thanks for God's gifts. You violate[e] oaths. You buy justice and you corrupt judges with bribes. You insult the poor but worship wealth acquired through unjust means. You chase after illicit lust (106) and you defile marriages. You shame the beauty of maidens but want to show femininity in men. You change betrothals and you carry off others' betrothed. You purport to instruct jurisprudence, yet you kindle unjust flame 27.4 (107) by persecuting the living, stripping the corpses, defrauding (others') deposits (with you) while demanding what you have not deposited, ready (yourselves) for an unworthy punishment of second judgments before paying the just penalty of the first. 27.5 No thinking on your part is free of wickedness; everything you say, everything you do, everything you teach others issues from wickedness."

Jonah 3:4

a. Lit., "compassion fell upon God."
b. Lit., "he completed a single, simple task."
c. Lit., "eliminating."
d. The preacher here follows the LXX; the MT has "forty days."
e. Lit., "you change"; Aucher proposes an alternative reading of *koxēkʻ* ("you trample (on)").

28.1 (108) When the Ninevites heard the prophet, they agreed with the urgent[a] message and believed the prophet because they were open to prudence.[b] 28.2 They believed his message because he could recount «595» their deeds even though he was not from their city. 28.3 (109) For he who could recount their deeds without ever having seen them could, by means of said prophetic gift, also predict the future and what would befall them. 28.4 (110) (So) the Ninevites assembled men and women, elders and sovereigns, ministers and kings, lords and dignities of all kinds, gathering (them all) in one place. In the gloomy assembly hall, they made the following announcement:

29.1 (111) "Perhaps, (fellow) citizens, you are gathering together to show honor,[c] in hopes that the sovereign might recognize evidence of (your) just cause and commute the judge's death sentence. 29.2 (112) For honor (shown) to the king by his servants before a death sentence attests to the loyalty of the honoring souls, but submission offered under threat demonstrates thoughts of deceit and flattery, not of love. 29.3 For (the prophet) seems (to want) only to honor but not,[d] as we are now doing, to cure our problem of gratitude. 29.4 (113) He, however, is only mortal, one of those who fall under the laws of the king who passed the death sentence to our city. It is (therefore) right to come together to render to the judge honor that[e] testifies to the loyalty of the honoring souls. 29.5 (114) There is no reason to stop our prayer to the teacher, for (his messenger) is in no position to vacate the validity of the law. (If he could,) he would be a legislator and the Lord of lords.

30.1 (115) "Let us pray, dear friends, to God, the Lord of the universe, for no law can undo the power of our prayer. Let us seek the Lord of the law with our prayers. 30.2 (116) For although those with partial authority execute the condemned and «596» the law that governs all areas sentences the condemned, they carry out not their own will but the king's. 117 If this is the case, we can pray so until the great king wishes to save those who pray. We do not struggle against others' will, for all depends on the king's will. 30.4 (118) Therefore let us examine what we have ignored that should be done in accordance with the will of God, for those of us contemplating the matters[f] might find out that our own conducts make the message credible.

31.1 "How might we find out that our conducts are pleasing to God? We will look at what is inside us and we will find what we seek. 31.2 (119) When one

---

a. Here following Lewy's emendation of reading *andandał* ("urgent").

b. Lit., "because of pertinent thought."

c. Adopting Siegert's (28 n. 211) suggestion that the Armenian *antʻanal i patiw* translates the Greek *syntrechein eis timēn* "to come together for honor or deference." The same goes for the same phrase in 29.4.

d. "Not" inserted by Lewy.

e. Inserting *or* ("that") as suggested by Lewy, the antecedent of which is "honor"; see also 29.2.

f. Reading *zaynosikʻ . . . orkʻ ditenn* ("these things . . . those who contemplate") as a word-for-word translation of the Greek *tauta . . . hoi theōrountes*. Contra Muradyan and Topchyan, who take the plural *zaynosikʻ . . . orkʻ ditenn* and *arʻnen* as singular and referring to Jonah, which would require taking Jonah as the direct object of the subjunctive verb *gtcʻnwkʻ* ("we might find out"). But since in the following line (31.1), the same subjunctive is connected with *varsn* ("the conducts"), I take that to be the sense here as well.

renounces one's own ways[a] and repents, one will see its opposite: one[b] incurs the death sentence, the other relieves the threat. Now, what can encourage our boldness,[c] dear people, more than the truth to be found?

32.1 (120) "First of all, we received God's grace to take part in human nature, but after birth, we became envious of animals; though created rational, we turned into the nature of irrational animals. 32.2 For just as one recognizes only one's food but has no comprehension of the feeder, so we enjoy the fruits of the earth but do not recognize the one who brings forth the fruit. 32.3 (121) Even though he supplies to us, by his generous hand, with not only what was (needed) for food but also what was (intended) for enjoyment and happiness, he never demanded anything from us, leaving (us) alone till now. 32.4 He did not wish to do to us what we do to animals, even when we show ourselves to be like animals. 32.5 (122) For when we put food in front of animals, we demand «597» their service in exchange. But if after being fed they offer no benefit to the feeder, the food for the animals is reckoned as loss to the feeder. 32.6 (123) For having granted us not only the gift of food but also the gift of life, he fed the city till this day but has been given no feeder's benefit. 32.7 (124) What benefit, you say? Which father from among our forefathers instructed his own sons? 32.8 Who showed gratitude on the wedding day? Who at childbirth reciprocated the gift of beauty to the creator? And on which altar has God been praised?

33.1 (125) "We, however, cannot say we have no capacity to know God or see the incorruptible with corruptible eyes, for he who is invisible has an unbearable[d] glory. 33.2 (126) Though he will make allowance for our frailty, he (nevertheless) grants us his own exquisite knowledge. He remains in his own glory without being seen, but he gave us eyes for vision into himself. 33.3 He gave us elements of the world—the heaven, the sun, the moon, the morning star, and harmony of the myriad stars—so that even if we do not see the creator himself, we can (still) know him through what were created with ingenuity. 33.4 (127) Does it not make God visible, when he laid this heaven above the air and set it on invisible columns? 33.5 (128) Does the sun not reveal the charioteer? Though it is moderate in size,[e] it is driven[f] over the whole world by an invisible hand. Though its burning nature «598» is confined inside a disk, it (nevertheless) radiates in rays that warm all those in need of it. 33.6 (129) However, the rays of the creator God, the disk that cannot be encircled,[g] fill and encircle the

---

a. Lit., "one moves away from oneself."
b. The Arm. *sa ... na* ("this ... that") likely renders the Greek *men ... de*.
c. Behind the Arm. *hamarjakowtʻiwn* likely stands the Greek *parrēsia* (ASA).
d. Siegert has *unsichtbar* ("invisible"), followed by Siegert and de Roulet and Muradyan and Topchyan. The Arm. *antaneli* (lit., "unsupportable, heavy, burdensome") is often a translation of either the Greek *aphorētos* ("unbearable, unendurable" or "irresistible") or *achōrētos* ("immense, immeasurable"; ASA). The latter is how Aucher takes it (*ingens*, "great"). Nowhere does the Arm. mean "invisible," however, unless we emend the text to read *antesaneli* ("invisible"). In alluding to the weight of glory, the preacher might well be thinking of the etymological meaning of the Hebrew *kābôd*, which means both "glory" and "weight." Cf. Paul's phrase "eternal weight of glory" (*aiōnion baros doxēs*) in 2 Cor 4:17.
e. Lit., "with a moderate nature."
f. Lit., "being spread it is spread."
g. Both Siegert and Muradyan and Topchyan follow Lewy's emendation in making "the

world, stretching the rays over it, thereby manifesting God in connection with the artwork[a] hung high in inaccessible heights.

34.1 (130) "If this were not enough to manifest (God), it might be worthwhile fixing our gaze on another thing made by God day after day. 34.2 (131) What is this star of the night that begins to be conceived as if out of thin air? 34.3 It has such firm intelligence from the creator that it would wax day after day, then again wane by the same measure, (132) so that it might not wax so excessively as to give off more than its proper measure of beams or wane (so much) as to be (re)born late; it might mix beams born earlier with those of later[b] births so that, at its demise, it might reach (re)birth. 34.4 (133) When the moon gives way to the sun, night changes into day, days into seasons, (just as) division of seasons into months, months into days, days into hours, and daytime into equal nighttime. 34.5 (134) The nature of the sea, the seafarers' (navigation) of their journey by the movement of the stars, «599» the filling up of rivers from on high or the springs' issuing forth from deep below, the production of vegetation in the fields, and trees' fruit-bearing—34.6 all things are measured by season, regulations, and proper degree, so as to produce nothing that is not suitable; all things are terminated by giving way to the birth of others. Does all this not demonstrate the Lord of the universe?

35.1 (135) "However, we who have demonstrated only our human forms but not thoughts, even though we received rationality for the sake of knowledge and honor, have made this honor of the Lord into shame. 35.2 Having seen such a world we did not understand the creator of the world; having seen such a ship of perfection we did not understand the skipper. 35.3 (136) Therefore, since we know his love for humanity, let us now at least acknowledge that we recognize him, so we might be saved by God's love for humanity and obtain deliverance, so we might enjoy one thing, that our spirits will receive a good praise for repentance. 35.4 (137) Since a death-bearing message has been rightly proclaimed to this city, let us, as much as we are able, proclaim a salvific message in response. 35.5 What is a salvific message? *Call for a fast and a prayer to* Jonah 3:5 *goodness.* 35.6 (138) For surely[c] he who sent this annihilation to us will, at least for once, give way when he is seized by the force of his own love for humanity. He might be severe toward the sinner, but he is gentle toward supplicants.

36.1 (139) "If no one dares to lift up his hands in prayer for shame of his own conduct, we will compel the prophet himself to be our intercessor. 36.2 (140) We will speak to the proclaimer: 'If you are a servant of God, lend us «600» your voice. Show us your abundant prophetic gift without envy or jealousy. 36.3 Pray as a partner of our life that we might be delivered by our equal partnership with you, and (that) our city might remain unconsumed and unharmed

---

disk that cannot be encircled" in the direct object of "fill and encircle." In that case, the sentence would read: "However, the rays of the creator God fill and encircle the disk that cannot be encircled, stretching the rays over the world."

a. The Arm. consists of the preposition *z-* with *arowestē* ("artwork")—not "creator" (contra Siegert)—in the ablative case, hence "concerning, with reference to, or in connection with the artwork."

b. Lit., "other."

c. Reading *irōkʻ* with Lewy.

owing to your entrance. Be a wall around our city and an armor of protection for its citizens!'"

37.1 (141) After they had said this, they dismissed the assembly, and they made their own way home, each renouncing their pride. Their renunciation was as follows. 37.2 (142) The king exchanged the throne of his power for sackcloth, the judge put away the scepter, token[a] of his power, the master gave the slave freedom, the elder put ashes on his gray hair, and the matron plucked out her long-flowing hair. 37.3 (143) Curtain was ripped out[b] from the bridal chamber, the bridal lamp and candelabra were extinguished, and lamentation and wailing were heard instead of songs. Virgins mourned their unfulfilled hopes, youths their youthfulness, and children in their indistinct voice what was incomprehensible, death. 37.4 (144) The refrain of their lamentation was: *How will anyone know (if) perhaps God (could be) prayed to?*[c] 37.5 (145) According to Scripture, they clothed themselves with such humility, arranging their souls in such orderly fashion, that the cattle became a defender through their prayers and that they distinguished themselves with their worthy supplications.[d] 37.6 (146) It is right that they remained (in prayer),[e] for though they were not partners in human transgressions (because they that did not possess intellect could not lay claim to rational understanding), they were associated with (the humans') illness and destruction of the city would surely fall on them as well. 37.7 So, they prayed in their own way: supposing that they shared in the damnation, they stood before them in prayer.

«601» 38.1 (147) But why must we speak of the animals' integrity? At the time the characters of the humans have changed: fathers no longer had any tenderness toward their children, wives toward their husbands, or servants toward their masters. Instead, they denied their children and drove the animals from their stables. 38.2 (148) They not only renounced all pleasures, but even drove away from their sight the women to whom they were attached. 38.3 (149) No more table in proper form[f] (could) be seen, or throne, or pleated dress, or beloved gold; instead, for everyone the ground was bed, delight and enjoyment, throne, and household items.[g] 38.4 (150) By these they supposed they might either kindle[h] the

Jonah 3:9

Jonah 3:7–8

---

a. Following Lewy (47) in taking the Arm. *xratown* ("counsel"; Greek *symboulos*) as a misreading of the Greek *symbolon* ("symbol, token").

b. Doublet lit. "untie" or "dissolve."

c. Lit., "will be prayed to."

d. This refers to the animals' not drinking or feeding, i.e., fasting, and their being covered in sackcloth, which the preacher evidently took to be a form of prayer (cf. 37.7). Hence, "animals" should be the subject of the infinitive *linel* ("to be") and *datel* ("to judge" but here "to distinguish").

e. Lit., "they stood remained justly." Both Siegert and Muradyan and Topchyan take it to refer to the animals' eventual survival, but the rest of the paragraph is a description and explanation why the animals joined the Ninevites in prayer. They are also described in 37.7 as: "They *stood* before them in prayer."

f. Lit., "in its form."

g. Following Muradyan and Topchyan's proposal of reading the Greek *ta endon* ("what is in the household") for the Arm. *i mēj* ("in middle"), which seems preferable to inserting "dust" into the text (so Lewy and Siegert).

h. Conjecture. Lewy suggested adding "encounter," which Siegert follows; Muradyan and Topchyan suggest "gain."

love for humanity of the humanity-loving Lord or receive their condemnation that came with the proclamation for their sins. So, they put on their precious raiment, with a view that if the prophecy of the proclamation prevails, it could be reckoned as their burial dress, but should the Lord's love for humanity grant life to the supplicants, they would (already) be resplendent in their raiment when they feast. 38.5 (151) That was what happened.[a] When the time for the death sentence had passed and they unexpectedly saw themselves (alive),[b] they gave God thanksgiving.

Jonah 3:10

39.1 (152) Calling again for a second assembly, they entrusted elders with a speech of thanksgiving. 39.2 They came forward and, when the assembly insisted, spoke the following after leaving behind sorrow and terror. (153) "So far as we were concerned, dear ones, we were dead. Having condemned ourselves, we were left to die with this city; 39.3 (yet) we live because of the Lord's love for humanity. 39.4 If that is so, it is proper «602» to offer thanksgiving to him from whom we received life as a share of grace. 39.4 (154) If one buys a slave at a price, one acquires the benefit of bodily service. It would (therefore) be utterly wicked not to offer our souls to our buyer who has purchased us from death to life. 39.5 (155) No master would grant time to the slave's service or would acquire him for a portion of the service for his debt and grant the rest as gift. For us, however, the Lord of the universe has granted us the time of life. 39.6 (156) Because we have been granted access to his generosity, we are in a position to be his witness. For, if after we disobeyed and were ignorant of him, he still provided nourishment (to us) as a generous father, how much more blessing will he bestow (us) if we are devout and acknowledge (him)?" 157 This being the case, they were determined, nobly and honestly, to repay the goodness with piety.

40.1 The prophet, after delivering his pronouncement to the Ninevites, did not stay in the city, nor did he leave for the surrounding areas of the city. Instead, he fled from the people to wait for their calamity from afar, to look for an observation post to watch the inescapable spectacle. 40.2 (158) His seat was in the shade covered with pumpkin[c] branches, a well-shaded and comfortable contrivance for him. 40.3 While he waited to see the city being incinerated, however, he saw it wearing a crown.[d] 40.4 (159) At that moment there was as if an exchange of miseries (had taken place): what had been the prophet's happiness became the Ninevites', while the Ninevites' utter sadness came around to the prophet. 40.5 (160) The deliverance of the city could not gladden him to the same extent as the nonfulfillment of his prophecy had depressed him.

Jonah 4:5–6

41.1 Now, when he caught sight of the Ninevites, saw their dance, «603» and heard the harmony of their instruments and their applauses,[e] he wept and said:

a. Following Lewy in reading *i dēp ełew* ("it happened") and taking it as start of 38.5 (151).
b. Following Lewy (46) in supplying "life" to the text.
c. Arm. *ddmeni* = Greek *kolokynthē*, a round gourd or pumpkin.
d. Or "wreath." Arm. *psakakir* might translate the Greek *stephanēphoros*, according to Muradyan and Topchyan. Presumably this refers to the festivities the Ninevites stage to celebrate their deliverance.
e. Siegert takes the participle *hareal* to refer to Jonah, but the Arm. expression *cap's cap'i harkanel* ("to applaud, to praise") probably refers to the Ninevites' merrymaking.

41.2 (161) "This is why I fled, not supposing to flee from the all-seeing eye but to protect my honor and dignity. 41.3 I discerned that he sent a death sentence not for killing and threatened ruin not to bring down sudden destruction,[a] but to build. 41.4 (162) I knew the peace of God toward those who supplicate in prayers. He does not stand tears or resist the lamentations of the afflicted. 41.5 He utterly changes sadness from the face and grants to those who beseech (him)[b] a reprieve from the death sentence.

42.1 (163) "I fled to proclaim not only God's love for humanity on earth but also his power on the sea: How I was transported being carried in a belly as if sitting in a carriage, how I had a dangerous and murderous *ketos* as bodyguard, how as a carefree spectator sitting in midst of a dangerous endeavor I became the *ketos*'s driver, out of my judgment I reached and saw the sources of the sea with clear and discerning sight. 42.2. (164) With my puny eyes, I saw the bottom of abysses, rocks that took roots among the waves, the light that sparkled for the amusement of the sea animals, the boiling waves, the playfulness of marine lives, and all forms of animals. 42.3 (165) I received a new world instead, after I fled the human one. (166) I was a swimmer in the company of aquatic lives, I was fed in the torrents like a marine animal, and I breathed in humid rather than dry air, drawing breath from the *ketos*'s palate. I danced with the leaping beast and ran with the swimmer. 42.4 (167) Each time I was carried to the surface of the sea above the billows, I beheld a world as strange and new through the *ketos*'s eyes. «604» And each time I fell through the sea and was placed on the floor of the abysses, I enjoyed myself with a contest against the beast. 42.5 (168) How the seafloor standing inside the abyss forced open, by tremor,[c] the gate of torrents to let in an abundance of torrential water in all directions! 42.6 (169) The Leviathan set its body against the torrents and stopped the chasm with its rotund body, sitting (there) like a fearless champion and letting in only as much water to surge upward as its body would allow. 42.7 (170) Not only that but (I also saw) from where are the unknown rivers born, from what source spring these torrential flows, where they are consumed, and how potable water is mixed with salt water. 42.8 (171) How terrifying is the appearance of the sea monsters![d] It bears resemblance to that of land (animals), but it has a nature four times as ferocious. Sometimes they would be loving and affectionate toward one another; at other times they would unleash their teeth on each other. All this I saw in my peregrination.

43.1 (172) "All these are wonderful for me as well: How the heavy weight remains on the sea without the liquid nature dissolving the hard and firm, 43.2 (173) and how the ocean enclosed the earth from the outside, surrounding it like a wall to prevent ferocious creatures[e] that are said to dwell beyond it from coming into our earth, (but) never flooded the dry land even though it gushed forth around the earth. 43.4 (174) But more wonderful than all this is that the

a. Arm. *hastatem*, "establish, confirm," likely translates the Greek *ephistēmi* (ASA), which carries the hostile sense of an army attacking enemies suddenly or by surprise (LSJ).
b. Lit., "grants to the beseeching words."
c. Lit., "shaking the place."
d. Lit., "ketoses."
e. Lit., "wild natures."

divinity reduced the agitation of our trouble by setting its power as limit and constraint[a] to everyone's own predilection,[b] by regulating excess, by hemming in «605» matter with the sea's edge, and by providing a place of stability to all in confusing wandering. 43.5 (175) It was for the sake of being their witness that I fled and for the sake of seeing them that I was pursued, so that it was for the sake of God's censure of me that I received accusation."

44.1 (176) You fled, man[c] of God. Speak, now that you lived again! You fled from God, but what place would you find that is free from God? 44.2 Have you not read from the Torah: *Did not my hand lay the foundation of the earth, and my right hand fashion the heaven?* 44.3 (177) So even if you were to pass beyond the earth or ascend above the heavenly vault, could you hide from the creator of these things? 44.4 It is indeed impossible to surpass human limits or to escape from the eyes that see all. 44.5 (178) Just as an assured and clever hunter who knows his quarry pretends a withdrawal[d] from the hunted, leaving the hunted animal alone and letting it escape, to change[e] the flight into a nonflight and, after it has run, to lay a trap to ensnare the quarry. In the same way, the hunter of human beings brought the fugitive, after a long sea voyage, back to land. He was hunted down by the trap of prophecy.

45.1 (179) "It was not in vain that I became a messenger to everyone. It was not in vain that I flew by the *ketos*'s flippers and undertook the sea journey to see everything. Instead, I who was the fugitive, seeing the obedience[f] of all to God, will become a teacher of (how) not to flee from God. 45.2 (180) For will he who cannot (even) flee the limits of the sea flee God? Will he disobey God, when (even) the waves of the sea obey (him)? 45.3 Will he reject the commandment of the divinity, when (even) the marine Leviathan obeys the commandment of God? (181) Who would not want to save a city of human beings, when (even) the beast did not refuse to save the world «606» by holding back the swirling waves with its own body[g] against the abyss and the tremor of bottom?[h] 45.4 Does the prophet not want (this) on account of the people?"[i] So lamented the prophet.

46.1 (182) So the redeemer of all, because he delivered the Ninevites from death using his healing art, came also to the prophet in order that he might see his malady. 46.2 (183) "Why are you sad, prophet? For your sad countenance betrays the sadness of your soul, and your form demonstrates[j] your disposition.

Isa 48:13

Jonah 4:9-10

a. Lit., "doorkeeper."
b. Lit., "determination, resolution."
c. Lit., "head."
d. Lit., "wandering."
e. Lit., "fence in, shut up."
f. Lit., "seeing the persuasion of all by God." Since the context contrasts rejecting God's commandment to the Leviathan's obedience (45.3), I am translating *hawanowtʻiwn* as "obedience" and the verb as "obey."
g. Lit., "form."
h. Lit., "foot of a mountain."
i. The meaning of this last sentence is unclear; something seems to have dropped out of the text.
j. Lit., "accuses, charges," but the underlying Greek *elenchō* means both "to reveal" and the more juridical sense of "to prove, convince, demonstrate."

46.3 Even though an old wound had weighed down your spirit,[a] this is the time to doff[b] the old sadness and not to don a new sadness. 46.4 (184) Do you not see that those who formerly deprived (me) of gratitude owing to ignorance, as a result of the second birth and the new life because of the proclamation,[c] now render praise to me alone? 46.5 So why do you not rejoice in the change of their character? And why do you not join in their thanksgiving? 46.6 (185) If you grumble at the piety of these people, you are unjust. If you are envious of the salvation of those on whom compassion was shown, you are inhumane. If you are troubled by the nonfulfillment[d] of the proclamation, the accusation, prophet, is against me, not you, 46.7 (186) for you preached not whatever you wished but what you were commissioned (to preach).[e] I am the autocrat who sent them the threat. 46.8 I possess the authority to change,[f] even to overturn, laws and to commute a death-sentence. After I commissioned your proclamation in truth, I transformed and turned (it) into love for humanity.

47.1 (187) "A body cannot overstep its own predetermined[g] limits, for if it trespasses them, it deprives the sovereignty of others' space. 47.2 Besides, are not all the creatures each in their own proper legitimate space? All «607» boundaries, however, are signs of a singular lordship. 47.3 (188) What space will it damage, or of whose sovereignty will it deprive a space, if it trespasses its limits, as said before? 47.4 For he who was there from the beginning has full sovereignty over his own property,[h] so that subsequent changes to others' spaces are (just) leases. 47.5 (189) If this is the case, that the two areas here are under one lord, veracity of the pronouncement and deliverance of the Ninevites, then I have exchanged the accolade (that would have accompanied) the veracity of the pronouncement for the praise (that came with) the deliverance of this city.

48.1 (190) "Perhaps you object, prophet, 'Why did you humiliate me, move my tongue for falsehood, and acquire honor with my shame?' 48.2 (191) You might understand your word this way, but I will convince you, prophet, that I not only rescued those who were in danger, for that was my intention, but also did not carry out this plan to humiliate you. 48.3 (192) Read your proclamation, and I will show you it is not destructive: *Three days[i] more and Nineveh will be overturned.* Is this not what you proclaimed? 48.4 (193) Now if (Nineveh) had not turned around and changed their wicked ways to good, LXX Jonah 3:4

---

a. Lit., "worked care in your spirit."

b. Following Lewy's (46) ingenious proposal of reading the underlying Greek as *ekdysasthai* ("to doff") instead of *eklysasthai* ("to loosen") as reflected in the Armenian *lowcanel*. That would provide a neat contrast to the Arm. *zgenowl* ("to wear, to don") in the next clause.

c. Muradyan and Topchyan suggest that the second birth and proclamation are those of Jonah's while the new life is that of the Ninevites'. Though that is possible, the Arm. text does not switch between a second-person and a third-person demonstrative marker. I have therefore kept the translation neutral.

d. Lit., "falsehood."

e. I follow Aucher's punctuation against Lewy and Siegert. The first full clause of §186 seems best to explain the rationale of what comes before.

f. Lit., "move."

g. Lit., "separated, determined, decided."

h. Following Lewy's proposal.

i. The MT has "forty days."

I would have misused[a] your proclamation and you really would have been found a liar. 48.5 (194) But if your message signified a turnaround and if the hearers embraced a turnaround, why do you suffer so grievously even though your proclamation has been fulfilled? 48.6 (195) But, it says,[b] their city was not destroyed, nor were the houses and city walls; their heart and behaviors were turned around by piety and what was about to be destroyed was restored, for I do not desire stones and buildings to be overturned.[c] «608» 48.7 (196) For the overturning of walls would be[d] easy enough, since they can fall from the onslaught by enemies with their war machines, but to turn the soul from evil to good—(only) a divine hand can move and change it."

49.1 (197) Perhaps because he did not believe that he had completed and was discharged from his task[e] by such verbal arguments, the Lord destroyed his shade, denuded the pumpkin bush, and made the prophet lament in tears. 49.2 When he lamented the plant, (God) appeared and responded: (198) "The pumpkin plant is beautiful to you, prophet, but the human race is beautiful to me. 49.3 Your pumpkin plant covered your head, growing upward from the inside and spreading outward above; human beings, (too,) are adorned with godly virtue[f] by drawing words of piety from within. 49.4 (199) You wanted the divine power to keep the ground moist, so that the leaves of the pumpkin plant would not dry out and be stripped bare. 49.5 But for me, Do I not (wish to) prevent the souls from drying out, lest the bodies perish? 49.6 (200) You wanted the divine power to be idle but make your judgment by examining your (own) misfortune. What compassion you have toward this plant! 49.7 The shade of your pumpkin plant is lovely, is it not? (201) Natural was its luxuriant foliage, with branches interwoven together[g] to give you shade. 49.8 It was this way by itself, so that you, prophet, cannot say that the pumpkin plant grew because of your labor, or that your night watches counted toward the plant's growth. 49.9 (202) (Yet) you cannot bear to see the defoliation of this flourishing, blooming pumpkin plant. The first night bore this plant, but the second night «609» destroyed (it). 49.10 (203) Now, regarding your plant, which you did not plant or irrigate, or enclosed with a circular fence with any skill, but

---

a. Following Lewy's suggestion that the underlying Greek is *katechraomai* ("to use" or "to misuse").

b. Rejecting Lewy's emendation to "you say"; it seems clear that the author is engaged in a figurative dialogue with contemporary readers and that the third-person singular refers to Scripture.

c. Lit., "to be turned around." This odd argument, that the nondestruction of Nineveh in fact fulfills Jonah's initial prophecy, seems to be based on a clever manipulation of the double meaning of the Greek *katastrephō* (LXX Jonah 3:4; Hebrew *hāpak*) "to overthrow" as well as "to turn around, to direct" (LSJ). That enables the preacher to use "turnaround" (Arm. *šrǰem*, Greek *strephō* or *katastrephō*, and their corresponding noun forms) both in the positive sense of conversion or repentance (numerous times in 48.4–7) and, here and in 48.7, in the negative sense of destruction as originally intended in the LXX and the MT.

d. Lit., "has."

e. Lit., "were free from things."

f. Presumably to be adorned with godly virtue is the human analog to a plant growing upward. This is reflected in Siegert's translation: "people develop godly life."

g. Lit., "through branches in position one after another in order."

only supported with a guard so it would cover and shade you—this is the extent of your labor on the plant— (204) but now you, so ready to find delight in a tree, are in sorrow because what delighted you has disappeared. 49.10 Therefore, is it right, prophet, to be unconcerned with a city not of plants but of rational human beings?

50.1 (205) "Since you wanted to teach about the humanity-loving (God):[a] if you (are) a humane redeemer (embodying) love for humanity toward inanimate objects, can I be known as inhumane toward human beings? 50.2 (206) Do you consider how many infants I have given from here to fathers, how many newborns I have taught to call their parents 'fathers,' 50.3 how many women in throes of[b] their labor pains have I preserved safe and sound, and how many of those being sought for execution have I hidden by shielding them behind a reedy fence?[c] 50.4 (207) The exterior face of your pumpkin plant, constructed for[d] incessant nourishment, resembled a kind of wall to you, while on the inside it provided for you the pleasantness of a bedewed house. 50.5 (208) I have compassion for this plant that perished[e] before its time, considering it with fatherly sorrow. In the same way, I transformed the acute birth pangs of pregnant women into sensuous joy and with (those born) I populated their city. 50.6 So, shall I lay waste this area and command that this human city be destroyed, when you could not suffer the loss of (even) a shade?

51.1 (209) "Ask a farmer—since you went into the country after fleeing the city— «610» if anyone would be pitiless toward cultivated and fruit-bearing plants or would put an axe to a useful tree, or if anyone would save oneself the trouble of (cultivating) a plant,[f] so it would take root, or would casually rip out what has just been planted. 51.2 (210) When faced with a plant that is not growing,[g] would he not at least[h] lavish more caring efforts to care for its nature and to stimulate (its growth) with remedy of care? 51.3 The more damage it sustains from the outside, the more labor would the farmer (expend) nurturing it, (until) it could gather its own strength and transform its fruitlessness into fecundity. 51.4 (211) Do you not see how farmers would water plants that are drying out by digging a narrow trench for the water to pass through easily, or they would care for[i] those (plants) they hardly irrigate by making a hole around the tree so the water could gather there? 51.5 (212) Do you not see how they would elevate low crawling branches from the ground and raise them artfully with reed, so they could hold up the weight of fruits, or

---

a. Following Lewy's emendation of the text.
b. Arm. *šnorh* translating the Greek postposition *charin*, lit., "thanks to, on account of, because of."
c. Unlike Siegert and Muradyan and Topchyan, I fail to detect any reference to children in this sentence.
d. "for" inserted by Lewy.
e. Lewy's conjecture.
f. Lit., "holding back the trouble from a plant."
g. Lit., "When faced with the vegetative nourishing nature diminishing." The context does not favor the preacher's singling out edible plants for discussion in this one instance.
h. Accepting Lewy's correction of reading *gonea* ("at least").
i. Lit., "warm."

how they would graft the fruitful plants? 51.6 Why do they do this? To prevent their labor from proving futile.

52.1 (213) "Now, if farmers do not shred their own labor to pieces but preserve it whole, shall I shred[a] the message proclaimed to them by shredding the Ninevites? 52.2 (214) Indeed they now show an abundance of humility![b] They who refused to honor the true savior are now willing to honor their would-be destroyer. 52.3 Why could they not soften the judge's death sentence in gaining something redemptive? «611» 52.4 (215) I think that is the case with a farmer, and I will convince (you) with this example. He despaired[c] of the fecundity (of a plant) and would rip up what he planted. Upon seeing bud[d] bursting forth, (however,) he granted the tree safety on account of the fruit. 52.5 (216) And how just would that be! For a tree would be cut down for rottenness but saved for its fecundity. 52.6 At one time, the Ninevites were infertile with regard to piety: they did not know the fruit of divine justice, and they gave the honor of the creator to this world. 52.7 (217) Now, however, they do not give thanks to nature for the fruits or worship the heating (power) of the elements; instead, they confess that they honor the fruit-giver instead of the fruits and worship the architect himself instead of the world.

53.1 (218) "To those who changed their conducts, how can I keep the death sentence of the proclamation unchanged? 53.2 If we sent a merciless word on account of the people's deplorable conducts, on account of their pious conducts now we must send a word of love for humanity. 53.3 (219) Just as on account of their previous conducts they deserved a severe pronouncement, so conversely on account of their repentance (they deserve a pronouncement) of love for humanity."

a. Accepting Lewy's emendation.
b. Lit., "sweetness, gentleness, meekness."
c. Following Lewy's reading of the underlying Greek as *apēlpisen* ("he despaired").
d. Adopting Lewy's reading; Aucher's text has "fruit."

II. Thematic Texts

Justinus's *Book of Baruch*
A new translation and introduction

by Todd E. Klutz

The early Jewish-Christian writing known as Justinus's (or Justin's) *Book of Baruch* (*JBB*) is preserved only in a single manuscript, a fourteenth-century bombycinus found at a Mount Athos monastery in 1841 by Constantinus Minoides Mynas and consisting of a larger heresiological treatise.[1] The heresiological work, originally divided into ten books but with the first three missing, was interpreted by Mynas as especially similar to the *Contra Celsum* and on that basis was attributed, despite its anonymity, to Origen (ca. 185– ca. 253). Now known to English-speaking scholars as books 4–10 of the Refutation of All Heresies, the text of Mynas's manuscript became a site of scholarly disputation soon after its introduction to the public, the identity of the work's anonymous author dominating critical inquiry from the outset. Attribution to Origen was reinforced in 1851 when the same text was (re)combined by Emmanuel Miller with additional material preserved in five other manuscripts,[2] all of them self-ascribed to Origen and dating from the fourteenth to the sixteenth centuries; but as early as 1688, and partly on the basis of authorial self-characterization in the material added later by Miller to the Mynas text, scholarly readers of Origen's writings had already expressed doubts about the authorship of some of the material in these manuscripts, and in the years directly following the publication of Miller's edition a wide range of other attributions were proposed—Tertullian, Didymus the Blind, and the fourth-century Arian bishop Aetius among others—until Johann Joseph Ignaz von Döllinger argued that the most likely candidate was Hippolytus of Rome (ca. 170–ca. 236), fierce critic of the Roman bishop Kallistos and eventual martyr.[3]

The literary result of Miller's editorial work was a partially preserved doxographical treatise whose first of ten books treats influential Greek and other pagan philosophies; whose second and third books have long been lost but probably dealt with Hellenistic and Near Eastern mystery cults; and whose last six books (4–10) are devoted almost entirely to beliefs and practices conceptualized as heretical and as having their origins in paganism rather than the teaching of holy Scripture. Within the tripartite structure just summarized, Justinus's *Book of Baruch* is located in book 5, where the composition in question is quoted verbatim at many points but paraphrased at others, the overarching

---

1. Labeled Parisinus Supplément grec 464 (hereafter the Parisinus), the manuscript was deposited soon after its discovery in the Bibliothèque royale; see M. David Litwa, trans. *Refutation of All Heresies*, WGRW 40 (Atlanta: SBL Press, 2016), xxvii.

2. On which see Miroslav Marcovich, ed., *Hippolytus: Refutatio omnium haeresium*, PTS 25 (Berlin: de Gruyter, 1986), 1–3.

3. For the additional material, see Litwa, *Refutation*, xxvii; and Marcovich, *Hippolytus*, 8–10. Döllinger, *Hippolytus und Kallistus, oder, die Römische Kirche in der ersten Hälfte des dritten Jahrhunderts* (Regensburg: Manz, 1853).

purpose being to acquaint the audience with the myth and ritual practices spread by a certain Justinus, unmentioned in ancient sources other than the Refutation but portrayed by our heresiologist as the purveyor of a particularly noxious variety of "gnostic" thought.

In scholarly opinion from the time of Miller's edition of the Refutation to the present, the doxographical framework and sequence within which Justinus's book is embedded has remained largely unaltered. But in a few areas pertinent to understanding *JBB*, scholarship has developed in significant ways that inform the translation and contextualization offered below. For instance, although Döllinger's proposal of Hippolytan authorship for the Refutation eventually acquired the authority of received scholarly opinion, its credibility was greatly tarnished in 1995 and 2003 by Allen Brent and J. A. Cerrato,[4] respectively, whose studies exposed the links between Hippolytus and the Refutation to be far too tenuous for carrying the weight of the prevailing attribution.[5] Building on those studies and related contributions to the discussion, the introduction to M. David Litwa's 2016 edition of the Greek text of the Refutation with a new English translation advises readers to accept the anonymity of the ancient author and resist the appeal of "conventional attributions based on questionable evidence."[6] This new and admirably cautious position on the matter is well defended in Litwa's edition and given additional support in several substantive reviews of that work.[7] What has been demonstrated in those contexts, therefore, need not be restated here; but since the main insight of the new perspective is accepted by the present writer, at least one of its most direct consequences is signaled below wherever reference needs to be made to the author of the Refutation, whose anonymity is consistently acknowledged at those points by labeling him either AR, short for "author of the Refutation," or other appellations avoiding the name Hippolytus.

Structure, Content, and Prosody

As implied above, no serious study of *JBB* can advance far without considering at least some of the problems and questions surrounding the Refutation and its author. Why that is the case is worthy of further clarification. In the first place, although most interpreters of *JBB* agree that much of its content is presented in the form of a verbatim copy of a source known to the AR, it is clear that other parts of what the AR attributes to the so-called gnostic Justinus have not been copied directly from a source but rather are more in the form of a paraphrase of Justinus's teachings. The latter material is no less valuable or interesting for being paraphrased rather than directly quoted; but for purposes of understanding the literary structure and rhetorical force of the substantial volume of quoted material, the distinction is important and has potential for enriching our understanding of *JBB*. To that end, the following observations focus on a particular

---

4. Allen Brent, *Hippolytus and the Roman Church in the Third Century: Communities in Tension before the Emergence of a Monarch-Bishop*, Supplements to Vigiliae Christianae 31 (Leiden: Brill, 1995); and J. A. Cerrato, *Hippolytus East and West: The Commentaries and the Provenance of the Corpus* (Oxford: Oxford University Press, 2002).

5. Litwa, *Refutation*, xxxiv–xxxix.

6. Litwa, *Refutation*, xl.

7. See, e.g., Paul-Hubert Poirier, "A New Edition of the *Elenchos* of Pseudo-Hippolytus: David Litwa's *Refutation of All Heresies*," *LTP* 74.3 (2018): 447–53, esp. 450–53; and Miguel Herrero de Jáuregui, review of *Refutation of All Heresies*, by M. David Litwa, *Gnosis: Journal of Gnostic Studies* 3 (2018): 118–22, esp. 118–19, 122, doi:10.1163/2451859X-12340052.

feature in the block of quoted material whose implications—not previously entertained in the scholarly sources to my knowledge—illuminate the structure, identity, and content of *JBB*.

The feature in question is a schematic structure, more precisely, an *inclusio*, that becomes discernible in the core block of quoted material (5.26.1–33) when orientating discourse near its beginning (5.26.1) is compared with similar but partly new orientational information at its end (5.26.33). The grammatical constituents of the shared motifs are small in number, but the absence of one of them in the rest of the AR's treatment of Justinus gives the collocation as a whole no small measure of salience. To be precise, just as the cosmic figure called "Good" is distinguished at the outset from the characters of both Elohim and Edem by his possession of foreknowledge, so also the same figure is characterized near the end of *JBB* as possessing a corresponding power of "forecreation" or "preproduction," whereby he was able to preproduce the entire creation (presumably in and through an act of his mind) that had not existed previously.[8]

While the character of the Good is mentioned at several other key junctures in *JBB*, he is considerably less salient in the text's plot of narrated actions than either Elohim or Edem. But more than anything else, what makes the constituent features of the *inclusio* just noted stand out are, first, the occurrence in both passages of the semantic field of things being uniquely known or somehow done beforehand—in both cases the knower/doer is the Good—a motif without parallel in other passages of *JBB*; and second, largely by means of a folk etymology that exploits the phonemic features of Greek prepositions and adverbs signifying time relatively prior to subsequent time, the unique power of the Good to know and do "priorly" is given as evidence of his identity being the same as that of the ancient Mediterranean phallic deity Priapus. With this unanticipated identification being delayed to the very end of *JBB*, and thus located much later than orientating information about key characters in a story would normally be expected, the core narrative of *JBB* is able to conclude with a fabulous surprise that audiences would probably long remember, a storytelling achievement far more likely to be the fruit of a gnosticizing imagination like that of Justinus than of an antagonistic critic such as the AR. Further consequences of this feature will be given attention below.

In addition to facilitating a proper appreciation of the storytelling art evidenced by *JBB*, awareness of the *inclusio* device just noted can help the modern reader both to recognize the boundaries of the core story that the AR has apparently copied (and perhaps largely preserved) from his so-called *Sondergut* or other sources, and thus also to distinguish that story from other material in which the AR either paraphrases Justinus's teaching or explicitly distances himself from it. As for the boundaries of the narrative core, the orientating information regarding the three unreproduced sources of all things (5.26.1)—the Good, Elohim, and Edem—marks the beginning of the story while the subsequent identification of the Good with Priapus (5.26.33), as the one who precreated everything that exists, is additional orientating knowledge that rounds off the narrative and immediately precedes a shift from quoted source material to paraphrase (5.26.34–5.27.4).

---

8. As discussed below, in the context of *JBB* the usage of "Edem" is probably motivated partly to connote the biblical Eden; but since it has additional potential to convey meaning associated with the ground, soil, earth, and downward directionality, it is rendered by the hyphenated form "Eden-Groundland" in the new translation.

Justinus's Book of Baruch

Once the boundaries, transitions, and stylistic distinctions just mentioned are duly recognized, nearly all of the material presented in the Refutation about Justinus and his *Book of Baruch* becomes easy to summarize in the form of a general outline. More particularly, apart from the AR's brief preview of Justinus in 5.5 and the condensed summary of *JBB* in the Refutation's final book (10.15.1–7), the given blend of paraphrase, quoted material, antagonistic evaluation and other commentary relating to Justinus can be outlined as follows:

A. Polemical introduction of Justinus by the AR (5.23.1–3)
B. Direct citation of the oath used in Justinus's ritual of initiation, and brief comment by the AR on the effects of the oath on initiates (5.24.1–2a)
C. The AR's extradiegetic abstract of *JBB* with special reference to Justinus's alleged plagiarism of pagan myth transmitted by Herodotus (5.24.2b–3)
D. The AR's paraphrase of the Herodotean story alleged to be the (unacknowledged) source of Justinus's entire myth (5.25.1–4)
E. Our only extant version of Justinus's *Book of Baruch*, presented in the form of quoted material and implicitly focalized at several points as originating not in the consciousness of the AR but rather in that of Justinus (5.26.1–33)
F. Examples provided by the AR of Justinus's universalizing equation of select referents in his own myth (e.g., Elohim and Edem) and those widely known from Greek mythology (e.g., the eagle and Ganymede) and Jewish biblical prophecy (5.26.34–37)
G. An alternative version of Justinus's initiatory oath presented as directly quoted material, followed by the AR's interpretative summary of the oath's purificatory and other transformative effects (5.27.1–3)
H. The AR's summary of Justinus's interpretation of Hos 1:2 (LXX) as encapsulating Justinus's "whole mystery," and of the treacherous plot of the maternal angel Naas to prevent the true interpretation of the prophetic text from being understood (5.27.4)
I. The AR's negative appraisal of *JBB* and other teaching attributed to the same figure as heretical, evil, and polluting (5.27.5)

Because Justinus is introduced in the third person by the AR throughout section A (i.e., 5.23.1–3) and appraised, along with his several writings and devoted readers, in overtly negative terms in that context, previous translators and other careful readers of *JBB* correctly understand that segment as standing outside the textual boundaries of the larger mythic narrative, however blurry the identity of the latter may seem to first-time readers. For that reason and in line with Willis Barnstone's 2003 translation, Ref. 5.23.1–3 is not included in the new translation below.[9]

However, because the initiatory oath of secrecy in 5.27.1–3 is presented by the AR as a verbatim citation taken directly from *JBB*, both that segment and a similar oath formula cited earlier (5.24.1) are included in the new translation, with both of those versions inviting comparison to the encounter of Elohim with the Good in 5.26.15–17a. Like the versions of the oath in 5.24.1 and 5.27.1–3, all the other material outlined above in sections B through I (5.24.1–5.27.5) is presented in the rendering below along with headings intended to distinguish *JBB*, as an embedded narrative possessing its own

---

9. Barnstone, "The Book of Baruch," in *The Gnostic Bible*, ed. Willis Barnstone and Marvin W. Meyer (Boston: Shambhala, 2003), 124–33.

literary integrity, from its stylistically variegated immediate co-text in the Refutation. The inclusion of nearly all the textual material presented by the AR as relevant to *JBB* and its author is regarded here as an essential aid to understanding both what Justinus's book is, in terms of the particular literary form in which it has been preserved, and how it was interpreted and used in its early contexts of reception.

In the outline sketched above, the lengthiest and most fully elaborated segment by far is the core narrative corresponding to point E (Ref. 5.26.1–33), extending to a length greater than all the other segments combined, and presented as a direct citation or verbatim copy of the gnostic Justinus's own mythic composition. As suggested above and observed by others, the narrative attributed by the AR to Justinus possesses entertainment value for audiences of diverse times and places; so it is scarcely surprising that many of the story's modern scholarly interpreters have given ample space to summarizing its plot or even retelling it in full. In varying degrees, the several summaries of *JBB* now available can help first-time readers to orientate themselves to the text and are even essential to certain types of scholarly inquiry; but because they invariably display little or no interest in reading the text with the aid of critical theories of story structure or narrative discourse in general, they miss opportunities for a richer interpretation. Relying largely on theories of story structure explained by Michael Toolan and John Yorke, a few comments on the narrative structure of *JBB* may prove useful to readers of the translation provided below.[10]

Yorke's concept of "exposition," nearly identical in substance to Toolan's concept of "orientation," is well illustrated at the very outset of *JBB* (Ref. 5.26.1), a typical location for information about a story's *dramatis personae*.[11] In that context special attention is given to three characters: namely, a cosmic source/principle called "Good" and briefly characterized as male, a second masculine source/principle called "Elohim," and a feminine source/principle called "Edem" and "Israel," the third being characterized as passionate, double-minded, and having the mixed form of a maiden from the groin up but down below the shape of a snake. Of these three figures only the Good is portrayed as having the attribute of foreknowledge. Further orientating information about the Good in particular is given subsequently by the narrator, but not until much later, in the form of an aside following the denouement of the whole story, a noteworthy instance of strategic delay given further attention below.

The English noun "source" is used both in the comments above and in the translation below because it hints, appropriately, at the potential of all the action and commentary following the orientational material just summarized to be construed as flowing very naturally from the collocation of the three named characters. Indeed, it is not an exaggeration to say that those same three figures come to be portrayed in *JBB* not only as ontological sources of all the created things mentioned subsequently in the narrative but also as the conceptual sources of folk psychology and cultural logic that drive forward the story and discourse of *JBB* as a whole. What happens in *JBB* is easily seen as a natural consequence of what is. To see clearly how this discursive logic is realized, attention needs to be turned here from elements of orientation such as those

---

10. See Toolan, *Narrative: A Critical Linguistic Introduction*, 2nd ed., Interface (London: Routledge, 2001), 143–71; and Yorke, *Into the Woods: How Stories Work and Why We Tell Them* (London: Penguin, 2013), 4–44.

11. Yorke, *Into the Woods*, 36.

just considered to what many narrative theorists call "complicating action" and the "midpoint climax."[12]

Having acquired the orientational knowledge summarized above regarding Elohim and Edem/Israel, audiences familiar with a range of scriptural traditions from ancient Israel are unlikely to be surprised by the initial instance of complicating action following the introduction of the three sources. With Edem/Israel, for instance, having already been defined not only as "female" but also as possessing a singularly mixed and visually striking form, the male Elohim sees her and, aroused to desire by her appearance, approaches her. Edem/Israel fully reciprocates Elohim's desire and, with neither of the two having foreknowledge of the complications soon to result from their union, they come together and generate twenty-four angels, twelve of them subservient to their father and twelve to their mother.

The full group of twenty-four angels being collectively equated with paradise, the twelve subservient to the father in particular use beautiful earthy material from the upper regions of Edem/Israel to create "the human being," while other animals are made from Edem's serpentine parts. Both the male human being Adam and the female Eve receive powers directly from Elohim and Edem/Israel, with soul from Edem and spirit from Elohim being invested in each member of the new couple. Like the two cosmic sources of their souls and spirits, moreover, but also in obedience to a command that they "increase and multiply and inherit the earth," Adam and Eve contribute to a program of reproduction leading to a completion of created order.

Once that point in the plot is reached, however, the complications in the action take a downward turn, in both the literal and the metaphorically extended senses of the word. Perhaps a hint of the troubles is evident in the narration of the human being's creation by the twelve paternal angels: while those twelve occupy themselves with the presumably good work of fashioning Adam and Eve, where are the other twelve, the angelic assistants of mother Edem/Israel? Our narrator has nothing to say on the matter. But what he does go on to narrate, as the next complication in the story, is a partitioning of the twelve maternal messengers into four dominions, throughout which the latter twelve circulate in a rotational system of astral government that continuously floods the world with famines, diseases, and other physical misfortunes now and forevermore.

Once that complication is underway, the ensuing actions in the plot continue their downward trajectory until a midpoint climax is reached in the story. Elohim decides to ascend to the heights of heaven to compare their contents with those of his creation below but leaves behind his spouse Edem since her earthy constitution was ill-suited to a journey upward. However, once Elohim reaches the peak of his heavenly ascent, he sees a light greater than any in his own creation, hears a voice inviting him to enter into the presence of the Good, and has a transformative visionary experience which in certain particulars is a paradigm for the initiation required of Justinus's followers. Thus, when the Good instructs Elohim against undoing the inferior creation below and to remain seated at the Good's right hand, Elohim is persuaded to allow the world below to continue under the administration of Edem and her servants. But just as importantly, since Elohim is now firmly settled above with the Good, his lengthening absence from Edem is experienced by the latter as an act of abandonment, for which Edem retaliates by ordering two of her messenger-servants (Babel/Aphrodite and Naas) to torment the

---

12. Toolan, *Narrative*, 149–55; and Yorke, *Into the Woods*, 37–41.

spirit of Elohim in human beings by stirring up separations, divorces, adulteries, and other painful experiences similar to those of her desertion by Elohim.

The intensification of conflict between Elohim and Edem having no immediate resolution but serving instead as an instance of midpoint climax, the next cycle of complications sees the emergent arc of decline become a more precipitous fall. In response to the punishments organized by Edem, Elohim sends one of his own messenger servants, Baruch, to bring aid to Edem's human victims, in each of whom the spirit of Elohim still resides. Notwithstanding an initial effort by Baruch to protect Adam and Eve, the maternal messenger Naas succeeds at sexually seducing Eve and using Adam for pleasure as if he were a young female slave. Baruch is then sent to Moses, to unnamed Israelite prophets, and to Herakles (as "a prophet from the uncircumcised") in the hope that they might enable humans to resist Naas and turn to the Good, but with Baruch's mission being thwarted in each instance by Naas's power to pervert the message and seduce the people.

By this point in the story, all hope would seem to have been lost. Baruch is sent by Elohim on one final mission, however, the setting for it being Nazareth "in the days of King Herod," where Baruch finds the twelve-year-old boy Jesus tending sheep. Baruch tells Jesus the story of Elohim and Edem, and exhorts him both to tell human beings the story about Elohim's exemplary ascent to the Good and to join Elohim and Baruch by effecting his own ascent to the Good. Jesus obeys Baruch; resists an attempt by the maternal messenger Naas to seduce him; and, after undergoing a crucifixion caused by a spurned and hostile Naas, ascends as a spirit to the Good, leaving his body and soul below for their mother Edem.

In the narration of Jesus's triumph over Naas and his ascent to the Good, the plot of *JBB* comes to a clear resolution, a denouement in which a semidemonic angel is overcome, its downwardly oriented mother is left below in a hellish world partly of her own making, and a fully human hero exemplifies a paradigmatic ascent superior to that of his forerunning but conjugally faithless father Elohim. But despite all the complications having now been resolved, and as noted briefly above, the narrator turns from his story's resolution to provide a final piece of orientating information about the Good, a type of information typically provided near the beginning of a piece of narrative discourse, moreover, and whose withholding can sometimes give its eventual disclosure highly unsettling effects. Delayed to the very end of *JBB*, the disclosure given in the final complex of clauses in the text is that the Good is none other than the phallic (and thus hypermasculine) deity Priapus, a revelation having great potential to be construed not merely as orientational but indeed as strikingly *reorientational*. As a result of withholding this startling new information to the very end, extra meaning is created that breaks the boundaries of the orientation category and corresponds more closely to the type of narrative element often labeled *evaluation*, whereby commentary given by one intratextual voice or another concerning the narrated action serves to guide the extratextual audience toward the desired interpretation of the story as a whole.[13]

As for what a preferred interpretation might look like in this connection, the following reflection is offered as a working hypothesis. In brief, by comparison with the previous discovery of the Good by Elohim (5.26.15–16)—an event presented as having the mixed consequences of being paradigmatic for the salvation of human males and

---

13. See Toolan, *Narrative*, 151–56.

females, but also entailing a permanent separation of Elohim from his spouse Edem that occasions universal suffering for the world of human beings produced through the original couple's previous union (5.26.24a)—Jesus's combination of faithfulness to the paternal angel Baruch (5.26.31a), successful resistance to the seductive schemes of the maternal angel Naas (5.26.31b), and ascent from the cross to the hypermasculine Good sets forth the ultimate paradigm of salvation and reward for both male and female human beings (5.26.32). The correspondence between Yorke's concept of a midpoint climax on the one hand and Elohim's actions of ascending to the Good and abandoning Edem on the other hand would seem to cohere with such a reading and may even be considered as support for it. But in the present context, no attempt to infer a global significance from the narrative structure of *JBB* as a whole can claim to be more than a provisional conjecture.

Cultural Context and Literary Genre

Although it is not untrue to say that *JBB* is in some sense a Jewish-Christian work, such a description should not be construed as denying or even downplaying the richly hybridized complexity of *JBB*'s full range of literary and other cultural associations. Comments on particular instances of intertextuality and related comparative matters are addressed at appropriate points in the notes accompanying the translation below; but a few matters of more general interest are best treated here.

The prominence of the Good in *JBB* points to the importance of considering what his eventual identification as Priapus might mean. The characterization of the Good as masculine, in the orientating material of *JBB*'s opening clauses, could easily have enabled early audiences to be less surprised than modern readers at the identification. Priapus's long association in the Greek and Roman worlds with fertility is explicitly invoked at the end of *JBB* where reference is made to his popular image as carrying fruit, an image having potential in Justinus's story to connote the metaphorical fruitfulness of the mind of the Good, in his preproducing of all things prior to their realization through the union of Elohim and Edem. But in addition to the fruitfulness of his mind, and at least equally important for interpreting *JBB*, there is the matter of Priapus's famously large penis,[14] whose representation in popular statuary and a wide range of written material instantiates a popular Roman model of machismo consistent not only with Justinus's masculine figure of the Good but more particularly with a willingness and ability to provide protection against various dangers.[15] An allusion to Priapus in one of Martial's Priapic compositions combines the motifs of the enormous phallus, fertility, and apotropaic reputation in short compass:

> From our little field to you, eloquent Juvenal,
>   look, we send you Saturnalian nuts.
> The other fruits have been given to sexy girls
>   by the extravagant prick of the guardian god.[16]

---

14. On which see C. A. Williams, *Roman Homosexuality*, 2nd ed. (Oxford: Oxford University Press, 2010), 18, 94–99.

15. Williams, *Roman Homosexuality*, 18; and Amy Richlin, *The Garden of Priapus: Sexuality and Aggression in Roman Humor* (New Haven: Yale University Press, 1983), 63, 67, 127.

16. Martial, *Epigr.* 7.91, cited in Richlin, *Garden*, 127.

Of the several registers attested in the extensive collection of Priapic poetry known as the *Carmina Priapea*, the most prevalent variety consists of protective threats against thieves, constituting 46.3 percent of all the pieces in the collection according to Amy Richlin.[17] Both Priapus, as a deified phallus, and the use of apotropaic phalli in children's amulets and similar material objects were so popular in late republican and early imperial Rome that the male organ seems to have been assigned the potency of something like a magicoritual weapon.[18] Accordingly, just as domestic homes and gardens could be protected against thieves by a statue of Priapus, with his conspicuous member signaling to any intruder a consequent humiliation by one variety or another of penetrative dominance, so also those who imitate the paradigmatic ascent of Elohim and Jesus in *JBB* can find protection in the heavenly domain above—in the presence of the masculine Good, the transcendental referent of all the diverse conceptualizations of Priapus—against the destructive workings of a vengeful Edem and her servants Naas and Babel/Aphrodite in the world below.

As just implied but also suggested at several points in *JBB*, the Good is conceptualized as being located at the very top of a cosmic hierarchy, on a vertical axis that, although its presence is never explicitly asserted, is assumed almost from the beginning of the text to its end and thus deserves far more attention than it has been given in scholarly discussion. By briefly exploring how this assumed axis is realized in *JBB*'s narration of select interactions between the Good, Edem, Elohim, and other characters, a long-recognized difficulty in translating the name of the story's female source/principle (Edem/Eden) can be seen afresh as part of a larger image schema that promises to yield new insight into Justinus's understanding of gender and the embodied males and females in the social world of his historical audience.

The envisaged image schema, consisting of the assumed vertical axis just mentioned, is hinted at clearly for the first time when Justinus describes the material substance for the creation of the human being, in the forms of Adam and Eve, as having been taken not from the beastly parts of Edem—parts already identified earlier as located specifically "below" her groin and having the nature of a snake—but instead from above her groin, implied in context to be identical with the most pleasant parts of the land. The so-called beastly and lower parts of Edem, however, do make a contribution to a different but related process in this creation story in so far as they supply the raw material for the fashioning of the various beasts and animals of the emerging order. In this same cycle of narrated action, moreover, an early hint can be discerned to the effect that the name Edem, in reference to the text's lone female source/principle, has strong potential to be interpreted as meaning more than a simple reference to Eden as the place of the Genesis garden; for the name "Edem" is sandwiched in this context by parallel references to "the earth" (i.e., land, soil, or ground) whose effect is to suggest that the two nouns are being used with overlapping and closely related meanings, an association strongly reinforced in subsequent segments of *JBB* and anticipated in a few passages of the LXX.

While the loanword 'edem is attested in several ancient Jewish sources as a transliteration corresponding to "Eden" in the Hebrew text of Gen 2–3 and a few other passages in Jewish Scripture,[19] its usage and occurrences in *JBB* have potential to give it the character

---

17. Richlin, *Garden*, 120.
18. Richlin, *Garden*, 63, 121–22.
19. See Gen 2:8, 10; and 4:16.

of a folk-etymologizing device whose fuller significance would arise from the morphological similarities between the masculine Hebrew noun 'ādām (meaning "ground" or "land") and the feminine cognate 'adāmāh (meaning "earth" or "arable ground"). The possibility of a confused but none the less meaningful connection in the mind of Justinus has been suggested previously by at least two respected commentators, and the capacity of the different Hebrew noun forms to convey overlapping meanings has been defended by a prominent Hebraist;[20] but the consequences for interpreting the name of Justinus's female source principle have not been considered in relation to the vertical axis inferred here. The translation adopted below is persuaded that the combined evidence in *JBB* both for the existence of the vertical axis and for the equation of "Edem" and "earth" (i.e., gē, in contrast to "heaven") warrants a new English translation of the loanword-name "Edem" as strongly connoting an area at the bottom of the axis. Thus, instead of rendering the word by either "Edem" or "Eden," the approach taken here is to use a fresh hyphenated name that acknowledges the relevance of "Eden" but also renders more palpable the Hebrew word-group's associations with the ground beneath the heavens. For that purpose the name "Eden-Groundland" will be used. To see why such as a strategy can be helpful, a few more references in *JBB* to Eden-Groundland need to be considered.

Between the overtones of verticality in the description of Edem's body (5.26.7) and the subsequent narration of Elohim's ascent to the Good (5.26.14), additional hints are given as to Edem's assumed identity and her relative position, both spatially and in terms of status, in the sacred cosmography of *JBB*. But the hints can be recognized more easily if the more overt evidence in the ascension narrative is considered first. In brief, having just described Elohim's motion as an unmistakably vertical ascent "to the heights of heaven," Justinus explains the given instance of upward movement as being partly the result of Elohim's having an innate quality of upwardness, in contrast to Edem whose decision not to follow her spouse skyward is explicitly attributed to her identity as "earth" (gē, 5.26.14), whose location relative to "the heights of heaven" is assumed to lie at the bottom of the axis connecting the two. Eden-Groundland, therefore, whose previously implicit identification as "earth" is now overt, is now also to be seen as possessing an innate disposition of downwardness.

The additional hints between the representation of Edem's body and the ascension narrative are located, first, in Justinus's comments on the procreation mandate of Gen 1:28 LXX (Ref. 26.9b) and, second, in the ensuing etiological account of the origins of natural and environmental misfortune (26.11–13). In the former, the equation of Eden-Groundland and "the earth," implicit back in 26.7 but explicit later, in 26.14, is conveyed explicitly through the narrator's clarification that the command to "inherit the earth" means to inherit Eden-Groundland, the cumulative effect of the repetition being nothing less than a foregrounding of the equation by the end of 5.26.14. As for the etiology of physical adversities in 5.26.11–13, its juxtaposition with the ascension narrative in 5.26.14 contributes to a spatially oriented contrast that puts semantic flesh on the conceptual backbone of the vertical axis just inferred: to be precise, in contrast to father Elohim and

---

20. The two commentators are Jarl Fossum, "Gen. 1,26 and 2,7 in Judaism, Samaritanism, and Gnosticism," *JSJ* 16.2 (1985): 218; and Miroslav Marcovich, "Justin's *Baruch*: A Showcase of Gnostic Syncretism," in *Studies in Graeco-Roman Religions and Gnosticism*, ed. Miroslav Marcovich (Leiden: Brill, 1988), 93–119, esp. 94. For the Hebrew, see Mitchell J. Dahood, "Zacharia 9,1, 'ÊN 'ĀDĀM," *CBQ* 25 (1963): 123–24; and KBL, s.v. "ādām IV."

his band of twelve angelic assistants, all of whom undertake the vertical journey toward the heights of heaven (5.26.14), the twelve angelic servants of Eden-Groundland execute the will of their mother by engaging in perpetual motion described by the narrator no less than four times as circular, consonant with the zodiacal scheme inferred by other interpreters of this segment, resulting in a ceaseless flood of misfortune interanimated with planar changes in the four rivers of earth/Groundland, and thus by extension being horizontal rather than vertical in character.[21]

Other details regarding the image schema just described will emerge in the course of treating different themes below, but those summarized above should be sufficient for establishing the existence of a vertical axis on whose pegs the key characters of *JBB* can either climb or be permanently stationed. But just as importantly, by plotting both the key spatial locations of the schema and the gender associations of the main characters in a manner that consistently associates masculinity with UP and femininity with DOWN, the narrator of *JBB* is able to produce a larger conceptual structure that has just as much to do with symbolic gender as it does with vertical orientation. In addition to facilitating the metaphorical assumption that masculine is UP and feminine is DOWN, the larger structure can be construed still more abstractly as entailing inter alia that GENDER IS A VERTICAL AXIS. More concretely, however, and since the zodiacal system outlined above has the character of a two-dimensional plane at the axis's base, where the circular motions of the maternal angels realize the will of mother Eden-Groundland, a couple of additional metaphors can be deduced from Justinus's framework: namely, MASCULINE MOTION IS VERTICAL, and FEMININE MOTION IS HORIZONTAL (and perhaps also circular). To what extent this whole scheme is maintained to the end of *JBB* is an important question addressed below in a note on Justinus's representation of Jesus.

In so far as both Elohim and Eden-Groundland are described at different points in *JBB* as moving through space (albeit in different ways), the theme of motion contributes to an important feature in the characterization of the Good, who although he is seen (by Elohim, e.g., at the peak of his ascent) and utters authoritative commands, is never characterized as moving. In that regard, the Good in *JBB* strongly resembles "the One who is truly at rest" in the Nag Hammadi tractate Allogenes (NHC XI 3 59.22–23), a transcendent figure denominated by the first-person narrator of that text as "the Good" and experienced at the peak of Allogenes's soul flight as a vision of light. Seen collectively as a triad, moreover, the three "source" figures in *JBB* display similarities with a trio of beings described in another Nag Hammadi text, namely Zostrianos, whose portrayals of "the Invisible Spirit," Kalyptos (the knowledge of the Invisible Spirit's knowledge), and the androgynous female Barbelo (Zost. 80.19–83.19) have prompted scholarly comparison with divine triads in a wider range of sources from around the same era, most notably the Middle Platonists Philo of Alexandria (ca. 20 BCE–50 CE) and Numenius of Apamea (second century CE).[22] In *Deus* 30–36, for instance, Philo attributes to the divine creator

---

21. For the zodiacal scheme, see, e.g., Litwa, *Refutation*, 341 nn. 401–404.

22. See in particular Philo, *Deus* 30–36. As noted by Litwa, the relevance of Numenius for contextualizing the source/principle triad of *JBB* in particular is argued by J. Montserrat-Torrents. See Litwa, *Refutation*, 335 n. 386; Montserrat-Torrents, "La philosophie du Livre de Baruch de Justin," *StPatr* 18 (1985): 253–61. On Numenius's value for comparative study of a wider range of ancient sources contemporary with *JBB*, see Richard T. Wallis, "Soul and Nous in Plotinus, Numenius and Gnosticism," in *Neoplatonism and Gnosticism*, ed. Richard T. Wallis, Studies in Neoplatonism 6 (Albany: State University of New York, 1992), 461–82, esp. 466–73.

universal knowledge superior to that possessed by any other figure, refers to an elder "son of God" who—similar to Elohim in *JBB* after his ascent—abides with the creator and is imperceptible by intellect, and describes a "younger son of God" perceptible by external sense and associated with the flux of matter in created time and space (similar to Eden-Groundland in all respects except for gender).

In the surviving fragments of Numenius, whose evident acquaintance with allegorical exegesis of Jewish Scripture has sometimes been read as evidence of Philonic influence,[23] a blend of Pythagorizing Platonism and Near Eastern religious ideas is set forth that resembles the hospitable sympathies of *JBB* at too many points for even a short survey of them to be attempted here.[24] For anyone interested in comparative study of *JBB*, however, a careful reading of John Dillon's discussion of Numenius might recommend for special attention Numenius's dualistic conceptualization of his divine triad, with its eternal monad being designated "the Good" and distinguished from a coeternal dyad consisting of demiurge (analogous in some but not all respects to the *JBB*'s Elohim) and world soul (analogous in similar degree to Eden-Groundland).[25] Additionally, and to anticipate a widely neglected feature of *JBB* highlighted in the notes accompanying the translation below, Numenius's emphasis on the solitary, empirically detached, and individuating nature of mystical ascent to the Good would be another theme offering high potential for comparative illumination of Justinus's composition.[26]

Date and Provenance

As *JBB* is preserved only in a single manuscript of the Refutation of All Heresies, the original setting of its composition cannot be treated responsibly without considering the implied context of the Refutation as a whole and the fourteenth-century manuscript now known as Parisinus Supplément grec 464. As for the Refutation as a whole, although the case for its composition by Hippolytus of Rome is now burdened by heavy liabilities, the repeated use of first-person reference in the anonymous heresiographer's invective against his opponent Kallistos (Ref. 9.11.1–12.26)—reputed leader of the church in Rome from 217 to 222 CE—continues to be taken as good evidence for the historical situation assumed by his composition. In brief, since the ten books of the Refutation include little or nothing that conflicts with the situation implied specifically in the text's anti-Kallistos discourse, our author is still best seen as having lived in Rome, his Refutation showing no sign of having been completed long after Kallistos's death in 222 CE.[27]

---

23. Or even as evidence of a philosophical genealogy in which Numenius mediates influence from Philo to Plotinus, a thesis noted but dismissed by John M. Dillon, *The Middle Platonists: A Study of Platonism 80 B. C. to A. D. 220*, rev. ed. (London: Duckworth, 1996), 378–79.

24. Dillon, *Middle Platonists*, 363, 379.

25. On the Good's nature as Being, Numenius produced a Hermetic-style treatise in six books, *On the Good*, which survives only in fragments; Dillon, *Middle Platonists*, 363. For the demiurge and world soul, see Dillon, *Middle Platonists*, 371–75; Numenius's conceptualization of the demiurge and world soul as neither separate entities nor successive emanations, but rather as a coeternal dyad, has the character of a metaphysical representation of what is presented in *JBB* as the myth of Elohim's conjugal union with Eden-Groundland.

26. See, e.g., the material cited by Dillon (*Middle Platonists*, 372) from frag. 2 in Édouard des Places, *Fragments de Numénius* (Paris: Les Belles Lettres, 1973): "one must remove oneself far from the things of sense and consort solitarily with the Good in its solitude, where there is neither man nor any other living thing . . . but some unspeakable and truly indescribable wondrous solitude."

27. Litwa, *Refutation*, xl–xli.

A *terminus post quem* of around 222 CE for the completion of the Refutation, however, entails by itself almost nothing about how many years earlier *JBB* and the seven other so-called gnostic writings excerpted by the AR may have been produced. In this connection the status of *JBB* as one of the eight different writings now widely understood to have been transmitted to the AR in the form of a single collection, a "gnostic *Sondergut*," is important to the extent that it entails a prior process of collecting and copying the eight previously separate and notably diverse writings. But how many years earlier and where that process may have occurred remains highly uncertain, though the apparent unavailability of the *Sondergut* to the AR's precursors, especially Irenaeus of Lyons and Clement of Alexandria, and the AR's substantial knowledge of church communities and conflicts in Rome can be considered at least circumstantial evidence of a Roman origin for the *Sondergut*.

However, since the present analysis joins other recent studies in viewing the assumed *Sondergut* as allowing the AR's own interpolations to be distinguished at most points from his substantial volume of earlier source material,[28] the present task requires the evidence just summarized regarding the Refutation to be reframed in the light of contextually relevant details pertaining more particularly to *JBB* (Ref. 5.26.1–33) and its immediate literary co-text (i.e., Ref. 5.23–28). As it happens, two considerations in that regard suggest a Roman provenance, albeit inconclusively, while evoking a place in cultural history around the middle of the second century CE or not long afterward. The very striking identification of the transcendent Good as the phallic deity Priapus (5.26.33), for instance, can be richly illuminated by an abundance of comparative materials—most notably, Catullus, Ovid, Martial, Horace, and the *Carmina Priapea*[29]—potentially all of which reflect in one degree or another an urbanized Roman environment from the late Republic to the late first century CE.[30] Thus, while few interpreters if any would defend a date of composition for *JBB* as early as the first century CE, an audience for whom an unexplained reference to Priapus could be used to clarify the abstract metaphysical concept of the Good is unlikely to have stood far away from the milieu in which Priapus enjoyed his greatest renown. A similar impression emerges from the comparative comments above on Numenius, whose *floruit* is dated by a consensus of scholarly opinion at around the middle of the second century CE and whose lecturing activity outside Apamea is more likely to have taken place in Rome than in other centers of learning such as Alexandria or Athens.[31]

A substantial body of evidence not mentioned above—most especially, *JBB*'s appropriation of a wide assortment of passages from Jewish Scripture and the New Testament, as well as comparative material in several of the broadly gnostic texts discovered at Nag Hammadi (i.e., in addition to the two already cited, Allogenes and Zostrianos)—could be used in a fuller treatment of *JBB* to produce a more nuanced picture of its context of production; and select pieces of that larger body are given attention at appropriate points below in the notes on the translation. But to the knowledge of the present writer, none of the relevant external evidence militates against the impression *JBB* was most probably composed in Rome around the middle of the second century.

---

28. See, e.g., Litwa, *Refutation*, li–lii.
29. On the contextual proximity of each to the others, see Richlin, *Garden*, 143.
30. On an urban Roman setting and a first-century CE date for the *Carmina Priapea* in particular, see James Uden, "The Vanishing Gardens of Priapus," *HSPC* 105 (2010): 189–219, esp. 190 n. 3.
31. See Dillon, *Middle Platonists*, 361.

Manuscripts and Modern Editions

The lone manuscript in which *JBB* is preserved, as noted at the outset of the present chapter, has the distinction of being the only extant witness to books 4–10 of the Refutation, constituting far more than half of that treatise's total bulk. For purposes of understanding how the Greek textual base of the translation below has been established, the most important feature of the Parisinus is that its text has been correctly diagnosed by the well-known philologist Miroslav Marcovich as afflicted by "huge textual gaps, countless word omissions, displacement of words and even entire clauses, intrusive marginal glosses, and above all many scribal errors."[32] Since numerous instances of those types of ailments are singled out for surgery in the part of Marcovich's edition corresponding to the text of *JBB* (Ref. 5.26.1–33), the quality of his handling of the textual problems throughout the Refutation as a whole is a matter requiring at least brief comment here.

Before completing his critical edition, Marcovich had published extensively on the Refutation and displayed a pronounced fondness for textual emendations. While many of these are either helpful or even necessary for making sense of the text, a great many others have been assessed by scholarly reviewers as indicative of an unjustified confidence on the part of a critic who imagines he knows better what an ancient text should say than its author.[33] In balance, the combination of relevant information about previous scholarship and of helpful emendations in Marcovich makes his work indispensable for critical study of the Refutation;[34] yet his edition should not be relied upon uncritically as the basis of a new translation.[35] Accordingly, the Greek text assumed by the translation below has been established by relying on the unamended text of the Parisinus wherever intelligible meaning can be wrestled from it, by comparing Marcovich's edition with that of his less interventionist precursor Paul Wendland (the latter serving as the basis for the translation),[36] and by giving special attention to previously proposed emendations wherever their potential impact on translation is weighty.

The approach to establishing the Greek text for the translation below, therefore, is essentially the same as that taken in the excellent new edition published by Litwa; but since Litwa's Greek text lacks an apparatus and is not presented as a new critical edition, it has not been followed slavishly here. As for the issue of emendations, a representative sample has been taken chiefly from Marcovich for critical evaluation in the notes accompanying the translation.

Bibliography

Abramowski, Luise. "Female Figures in the Gnostic *Sondergut* in Hippolytus's *Refutatio*." Pages 136–52 in *Images of the Feminine in Gnosticism*. Edited by Karen L. King. SAC. Philadelphia: Fortress, 1988.

Barnstone, Willis. "The Book of Baruch." Pages 119–33 in *The Gnostic Bible*. Edited by Willis Barnstone and Marvin W. Meyer. Boston: Shambhala, 2003.

Broek, Roelof van den. "Gospel Traditions and Salvation in Justin the Gnostic." *VC* 57 (2003): 363–88. doi:10.1163/157007203772064568.

---

32. Marcovich, *Hippolytus*, 6–7.
33. Poirier, "New Edition," 450.
34. Litwa, *Refutation*, xxx–xxxi; and Poirier, "New Edition," 450.
35. Litwa, *Refutation*, xxxi.
36. Paul Wendland, ed., *Refutatio omnium haeresium*, Hippolytus Werke 3, GCS 26 (Leipzig: Hinrichs, 1916).

---. "Justin the Gnostic." Pages 656–58 in *Dictionary of Gnosticism and Western Esotericism*. Edited by Wouter J. Hanegraaff. Leiden: Brill, 2006. doi:10.1163/1873-8338_dgwe_DGWE_185.

Buckley, Jorunn Jacobsen. "Transcendence and Sexuality in the Book of Baruch." *HR* 24, no. 4 (1985): 328–44. doi:10.1086/463012.

Clivaz, Claire, and Sara Schulthess. "On the Source and Rewriting of 1 Corinthians 2.9 in Christian, Jewish, and Islamic Traditions (*1 Clem* 34.8; *GosJud* 47.10–13; a ḥadīth qudsī)." *NTS* 61 (2015): 183–200. doi:10.1017/S0028688514000307.

Haenchen, Ernst. "Das Buch Baruch: Ein Beitrag zum Problem der christlichen Gnosis." *ZTK* 50 (1953): 123–58.

Litwa, M. David, trans. 2016. *Refutation of All Heresies*. WGRW 40. Atlanta: SBL Press, 2016.

Marcovich, Miroslav, ed. *Hippolytus: Refutatio omnium haeresium*. PTS 25. Berlin: de Gruyter, 1986. doi:10.1515/9783110858235.

McMahon, John H., trans. "The Refutation of All Heresies." *ANF* 5:25–403.

Montserrat-Torrents, J. "La philosophie du Livre de Baruch de Justin." *StPatr* 18 (1985): 253–61.

Olender, Maurice. "Éléments pour une analyse de Priape chez Justin le Gnostique." Pages 874–97 in vol. 2 of *Hommages à Maarten J. Vermaseren*. Edited by Margreet B. de Boer and T. A. Eldridge. 3 vols. EPRO 68. Leiden: Brill, 1978. doi:10.1163/9789004295438_022.

Orbe, Antonio. "La cristología de Justino gnóstico (Hipol., Ref. V 26, 29–32)." *EstEcl* 47 (1972): 437–57.

Simonetti, Manlio. "Note sul Libro di Baruch dello gnostico Giustino." *Vetera Christianorum* 6 (1969): 71–89.

Wendland, Paul, ed. *Refutatio omnium haeresium*. Hippolytus Werke 3. GCS 26. Leipzig: Hinrichs, 1916.

Justinus's *Book of Baruch*[a]

The Oath Used in Justinus's Ritual of Initiation

24 [1] "If you are wanting to know," says Justinus, "*what eye has not seen nor ear heard, nor has ascended over the human heart,*[b] swear by the one above all things—the Good,[c] the Highest—to guard what is inexpressible, the secret parts of the teaching. For indeed even our Father, when he saw the Good and was initiated by him, guarded the inexpressible things of the secret and swore, as it is written, '*The Lord swore and will not regret doing so.*'"

1 Cor 2:9

Ps 110:4 (LXX 109:4)

The Refutation's Abstract of Justinus's *Book of Baruch* and Its Herodotean Source

24 [2b]But so that we might not have to go through the greater number of their writings, we shall illustrate the unspeakable mysteries of Justinus from only one book of his, a work that, in his opinion, is especially praiseworthy. [3]Now that volume is entitled *Baruch*; and by means of it we shall make known one myth in particular among the many set out by Justinus. Although the myth is in Herodotus,[d]

---

a. Because all of the material translated here is taken from book 5 of the Refutation of All Heresies, only the chapter and verse divisions are given in the segmentation of the present translation. The divisions used here are the same as those employed in the critical editions of Wendland (*Refutatio*) and Marcovich ("Justin's *Baruch*"). Short forms used in this chapter are Barnstone for Barnstone, "Book of Baruch"; Cruice for Patrice François Marie Cruice, *Philosophumena sive haeresium omnium confutatio: Opus Origeni adscriptum* (Paris: Excursum in typographeo Imperiali, 1860); Duncker and/or Schneidewin for Luwig Duncker and Friedrich Wilhelm Schneidewin, eds., *S. Hippolyti episcopi et martyris Refutationis omnium haeresium: Librorum decem quae supersunt* (Göttingen: Dieterich, 1859); Litwa for Litwa, *Refutation*; Marcovich for Marcovich, "Justin's *Baruch*"; McMahon for John H. McMahon, trans., "The Refutation of All Heresies," ANF 5:25–403; Miller for Miller, *Origenis Philosophumena*; Wendland for Wendland, *Refutatio*.

b. The reason the Good is described here as not having ascended over the human heart is that, in contrast both to Elohim and to Justinus's human initiates, the Good is inherently superior to all else and thus has no need of ascent or any other type of motion. The fine study by Claire Clivaz and Sara Schulthess, although it includes no mention of either *JBB* or the Refutation and is largely genealogical in interest, contextualizes a corpus of ancient comparative texts whose use of a shared extracanonical source has great potential for illuminating the portrayal of the Good here and elsewhere in *JBB*. See Clivaz and Schulthess, "On the Source and Rewriting of 1 Corinthians 2.9 in Christian, Jewish, and Islamic Traditions (*1 Clem* 34.8; GosJud 47.10–13; a ḥadīth qudsī)," NTS 61 (2015): 183–200, doi:10.1017/S0028688514000307.

c. Against MacMahon's "Him who is good above all," which requires grammatical discord between the article and substantive, Marcovich and Litwa are followed here by repeating the singular article from the previous noun phrase and emending the plural adjective to the singular; hence "the Good," i.e., the highest of the three divine principles introduced later in the text.

d. For the story in question, see Herodotus 4.8–10, whose tale of an encounter between Herakles and a viper-maiden is used to anticipate the ensuing portrayals of the female source

Justinus changes it around and then narrates it to his pupils as something strange. From that myth he builds for himself the whole structure of his teaching.

25 ¹Now Herodotus says that Herakles, after driving the oxen of Geryon from Erytheia, came into Scythia and, being sleepy from the journey, reclined at a certain desert spot and slept for a short time. But while he slept, the horse on which he was seated throughout his long journey vanished. On being aroused from his sleep, he started to do a search over the whole desert in an effort to find the horse. ²He strays far from the horse; yet he finds in the desert a certain maiden, half woman, and asks her if perchance she might have seen the horse anywhere. The maiden says she has seen it but will not show it to Herakles unless he first goes along with her for a friendly session of intercourse. ³Now her upper parts as far down as the groin were those of a maiden, but all her body below the groin was something frightful in appearance like a snake. In eagerness, however, to find out about his horse, Herakles is won over by the beast; for he had sexual intercourse with her and made her pregnant, and after the sexual exchange he prophesied to her that she had by him in her womb at the same time three children who would become famous. ⁴And he ordered her who would bear them[a] that she must give to the offspring the names Agathyrsus, Gelonus, and Scytha. In exchange for this he received from the beast-like maiden his horse and, winning back the oxen[b] as well, he rode off.

The Refutation's Transition from the Herodotean Source to Justinus's Book

25 ⁴ᵇNow the myth in Herodotus of what happened after these things is tedious, so away with it for now. But what the opinions are of Justinus, who transfers this legend into an account of the generation of all things, we shall explain.

The Refutation's Extended Excerpt of Justinus's *Book of Baruch*

26 ¹This is what he says: There were three unreproduced[c] sources of all things[d]—two masculine, one feminine. Of the masculine sources, the first[e] is

---

Eden-Groundland and Herakles in Justinus's narrative, the latter being described as "prophet from the uncircumcised" (5.26.27).

a. Against MacMahon's "on bringing forth," the participle for giving birth here has the article and is therefore very unlikely to have an adverbial nuance.

b. Against MacMahon, "oxen" should be used here to preserve the lexical string with "oxen" earlier in the passage. The effect of this is that Herakles had lost not only his horse but also the oxen he was driving, and that his favor to the maiden functioned as part of a contract that ultimately enabled him to regain all his lost property.

c. "Unreproduced" (*agennētos*), rather than "unbegotten" (MacMahon) or "unborn" (Litwa), is used here chiefly to preserve the lexical correspondence to "produced" (*egeneto*) in the immediately ensuing reference to "all reproduced things."

d. Litwa and MacMahon's phrase "principles of the universe" misses the target at least twice; for several aspects of the ensuing co-text, esp. the metaphors "roots and streams," suggest that the idea of "sources" is closer than the abstract concept of "principles" is to the sense of Greek *archai* in this context. Singular "universe," moreover, would be more appropriate for rendering *kosmou* than for the plural phrase actually used here, namely *tōn 'olōn* ("all things"), whose occurrence in the ensuing co-text is appropriately coreferential with another plural substantive, namely "the things that exist" (*ta onta*).

e. The Greek noun added here by Marcovich (and included by Litwa) coheres with the

called Good, that one alone being spoken of thusly and having foreknowledge of all things; the other, the father of all reproduced things, lacks foreknowledge[a] and is invisible. The feminine source, on the other hand, in addition to being likewise without foreknowledge, is passionate, double-minded, double-bodied, similar in every way to the maiden in Herodotus's myth, down to the groin a maiden, but below that a snake, so Justinus says. ²And this maiden is called "Eden-Groundland"[b] and "Israel." These three are, he says, the sources of all things, roots and streams from which the things that exist have come to be; and other than these three there was nothing.

Now when the father—"Elohim"[c] this father is called, says Justinus—first beheld that semimaiden Eden-Groundland, he fell into a lust for her, being as he is without foreknowledge; and with no lesser passion did Eden-Groundland begin to lust after Elohim. This lust brought them together into that singular type of favor that is love. ³From that manner of getting together the father produced for himself by Eden-Groundland twelve messengers; and the names of the father-messengers are these: Michael, Amen, Baruch, Gabriel, Esaddaios . . .[d] ⁴Listed here in similar fashion are the names of the mother-messengers that Eden-Groundland made; these are Babel, Achamoth, Naas-Snake, Bel, Belias, Satan, Sael, Adonaios, Kauithan, Pharaoth, Karkamenos, Lathen. Of the twenty-four, the father-messengers assist the father, and everything they do is in accord with his will; whereas the mother-messengers assist the mother, Eden-Groundland. ⁵Now the whole crowd of all these messengers together, Justinus says, constitutes the garden about which Moses says, "God planted a garden in the eastern quarters of Eden," that is, right in the face of Eden-Groundland so that she might see the garden continually. ⁶Allegorically,[e] the messengers in this garden are called "trees," and

---

presence of the article and makes excellent sense if rendered as "the first" (i.e., the first of the two male sources).

a. Contra Marcovich, Litwa, and other modern editions (e.g., Cruice and Schniedewin), who at this point add a phrase describing the second male principle as "unknown," the unamended text of the Parisinus is accepted here. The additional phrase would anticipate an utterance attributed subsequently to Elohim (5.26.37), but its absence here in 5.26.1 causes no damage requiring the proposed emendation.

b. The rendering of the Hebrew loan-word *edem* as the name "Eden" has solid support from considerations of Genesis intertextuality, usage in comparative Greek sources (e.g., the LXX and Philo), and coherence with the widely attested role of Priapus (equated with the Good in 5.26.33) as a protector of gardens. But as discussed above in the introduction, the usage of "edem" in this context also looks very much like a folk-etymology intended to associate *JBB*'s designated female source with the ground, with earthy (as opposed to heavenly) material, and thus with downwardness. Hence the hyphenated name above.

c. The Greek word here is a transliteration of the word used with great frequency in the Hebrew Bible to denote the God of Israel.

d. Where the names of the remaining seven messengers of the father once followed Esaddaios (i.e., El Shaddai), our sole textual witness has a lacuna.

e. Marcovich inserts at this point a postpositive sentence connector that explicitly frames the ensuing clause(s) as serving to explain those immediately preceding; but the less explicit quality of the unamended text at this point is not objectionably ambiguous, and both Litwa and Barnstone rightly reject the addition.

the tree of life is the third member of the father-messengers, namely Baruch; whereas the tree known as that of pleasure and pain is the third member of the mother-messengers, namely Naas-Snake. For Justinus takes the things of Moses to mean something along those lines, saying that Moses spoke about these things in a roundabout way because not everyone has room for the truth.[a] [7]But once, Justinus continues, the garden had come into existence from the gratifying intercourse of Elohim and Eden-Groundland, the messengers of Elohim took material not from the beastly parts of Eden-Groundland but rather from above the groin—from the most pleasant[b] parts of the land,[c] from the humane and civilized regions—and they made a human being. Whereas from the beastly parts, says Justinus, come the wild beasts and all the other animals. [8]They therefore made the human being to be a symbol of their unity and good will, and deposited their own powers in him, Eden-Groundland providing the soul and Elohim the spirit. In this way the human being Adam becomes something like a seal, both a memorial of the love between Eden-Groundland and Elohim, and an everlasting symbol of their marriage. [9]In this same way Eve too comes into being, says Justinus, just as it is written in Moses, as an image and a symbol, a seal to keep Eden-Groundland in mind forever; and thus both a soul from Eden-Groundland and a spirit from Elohim were likewise deposited in the Eve-image.[d]

And then commandments were given to them: *Increase and multiply yourselves, and thus take over the earth*, which is to say, Eden-Groundland—for that is how Justinus wishes they had been written— [10]and so in marriage Eden-Groundland transferred to Elohim all of her wealth, as much substance as was hers. Whence, says Justinus, in imitation of that first marriage, wives transfer a marriage payment to their husbands up to the present day, trusting in a certain divine and patrimonial custom that originated in Eden-Groundland's payment to Elohim.

Gen 1:28

[11]Now everything having been created—heaven and earth and the things therein—and just as it is written by Moses, the twelve messengers of the mother were divided into four dominions; and after each of those four is

---

a. Here and at several other points in *JBB*, by interpreting select teachings of Moses as prefiguring (and thus also cohering with) his own teachings, Justinus assumes a posture toward his Jewish scriptural precursors closer to that attested, e.g., in Treat. Res. 48.5–13 than to that evinced in Disc. Seth 63.26–34.

b. The use of "(most) *pleasant*," as a rendering of the Greek superlative adjective, captures at least part of the effect produced by the lexical string initiated by the immediately preceding reference to "the knowledge of *pleasure* and pain" (5.23.6), a string obscured in the renderings by MacMahon ("the knowledge of *good* and evil . . . the most *beauteous* earth") and Litwa ("the Knowledge of Good and Evil . . . the most beautiful earth").

c. The metaphor at play here might be summed up as, "the subdivided place called Eden-Groundland is a human body."

d. The characterization of Adam and Eve in these lines as twin-like, with each of them being a receptacle of both a male principle (i.e., spirit from Elohim) and a female principle (soul from Eden-Groundland), strikingly resembles the conceptualization of individual males and females who have benefited from "the bridal chamber" as described in Gos. Phil. 65.1–26.

a river named:[a] the Pison, the Geon, the Tigris, and the Euphrates.[b] These twelve messengers circulate themselves into the four domains and, being closely twined together,[c] superintend the order of the cosmos, imposing on the cosmos a certain oriental kind of despotic authority[d] from Eden-Groundland. [12]Yet they do not stay forever in their own places but rather go around as if in a circular dance, moving from place to place and yielding to each other[e] at set intervals of time[f] the places assigned to them. Now whenever Pison rules over a place, famine and trouble and distress come about in that part of the land; for the regime administered by these messengers/envoys is ungenerous and miserly. [13]From each fourth of them, moreover, and in accord with the power and nature of each, come likewise phases of illness and hordes of ailments.[g] In line therefore with such governance over the four quadrants, and like the aforementioned rivers, this flood of evil continues to surge round the cosmos without pause, in agreement at all times with the will of Eden-Groundland.

[14]Now the necessity of all this evil has originated from some such cause as follows.[h] Elohim, having prepared and constructed the world out of his satisfying union with Eden-Groundland, wanted to ascend into the uppermost parts of the heavenly realm and to see that none of the things belonging to the created order were in short supply, bringing his messengers along with him.

---

a. Contra MacMahon, Barnstone, and Litwa, all of whom construe the four regions as having been named after the four rivers, considerations of morphology—e.g., *potamos* ("river") is in the nominative and *ekaston* ("each") is in the accusative—and the sequencing of information in the antecedent co-text suggests that the rivers were named after the four dominions, a noteworthy consequence being that the Genesis intertext (LXX Gen 2:10–14) is being recast by Justinus as an aetiological account of how the familiar rivers acquired their respective names.

b. The close association here of rivers and phenomena seen to be closely connected to the feminine is widely attested in ancient Mediterranean texts, a noteworthy parallel being the Nag Hammadi tractate entitled the Testim. Truth 30.18–31.5.

c. The meaning of the circumstantial participle here is sufficiently clear without the addition of Marcovich's conjectured reciprocal pronoun (adopted by Litwa and translated "with each other"), which is rejected here, therefore, as unnecessary.

d. MacMahon's phrase "viceregal authority," while credible from a lexical and comparative perspective (see, e.g., Flavius Philostratus, *Vit. soph.* 1.22.3), overlooks the potential for negative connotations in Greco-Roman discourse about oriental imperial powers, potential seemingly realized in the immediately ensuing characterization of Edem's envoys in 5.26.12b–13.

e. The reciprocal pronoun added to the Parisinus at this point by Marcovich and incorporated by Litwa is required for grammatical coherence and thus accepted here.

f. Taking the pair of time-related nouns as a hendiadys that instantiates a single temporal concept ("intervals of time"), as opposed to Litwa's "set times *and* intervals."

g. In Marcovich's edition, three additions are proposed: a preposition, a noun, and a verb (the first two of which are accepted by Litwa, "*In* each of the four . . . the power and nature of each *river*"), none of which is required for the rendering above.

h. Contra MacMahon but in accord with Litwa, the noun phrase at the end of the clause ("some such cause") is best construed as referring not to antecedent discourse but rather to ensuing events, and thus as introducing a new stage in the narrative rather than concluding the action directly preceding.

For he was, by nature, of an upward disposition, whereas Eden-Groundland was earthly by nature;[a] and since she therefore had no interest in following her companion upward,[b] he left her down in the realm below.[c]

15 Thus, when Elohim arrived at the uppermost level of heaven and saw a light superior to what he himself had constructed, he said, "Open the gates for me so that I can enter and extol the Lord; for I was accustomed to thinking that I am Lord." 16 A voice from the light was given, saying, "This is the gate of the Lord; the righteous enter through it"; and immediately the gate was opened. Without his attendants the Father was now with the Good and saw *what eye has not seen nor ear heard, nor has ascended over the human heart*. 17 At which time the Good then says to him, *Sit at my right hand*; and the Father replies to the Good, "Give me permission, Lord, to put an end to the world I have made, for my spirit is all tied up now in human beings and I want to take it back." 18 The Good then replies to him, "No such evil can you do while you are here with me; for it was from the sensual pleasure of intercourse that both you and Eden-Groundland made the world. Let Eden-Groundland, therefore, have the created order for as long as she wishes;[d] but as for you, you must stay here with me."

1 Cor 2:9
Ps 110:1

19 At that same moment, because Eden-Groundland realized she had been abandoned by Elohim and been caused such distress, she made her own messenger-attendants stand by her while she beautified herself in the hope that Elohim might descend to her in lust.[e] 20 However, once Elohim was overwhelmed by the Good and stopped going down to her, Eden-Groundland gave orders to Babel—also known as Aphrodite—to stir up adulteries and marital separations so that, just as Eden-Groundland had become separated from Elohim, so also the spirit of Elohim—still among human beings—might be punished grievously with the same kinds of separations and thus suffer the same things as Eden-Groundland when she had been abandoned below.

a. The complement of the verb in this clause is nominal and makes appropriate sense either as a predicate noun ("earth") or, as preferred above, as having adjectival force ("earthly")

b. Where the Greek syntax of the Parisinus is both simple and clear (as reflected in the translation above and in both Litwa and Barnstone), Marcovich emends the text by revising one verb and inserting another to signal (create?) a parallel to the subsequent characterization of Naas in 5.26.31; but since the resultant sense in 5.26.14 ("for being earthly, and although she wanted to follow her companion upward, *she was not able*") acquires too little value for the price of anomalous morphology, increased syntactical complexity, and unnecessary change in word order, the proposal is not accepted here.

c. The contrast between up and down in these clauses is foregrounded and contributes much to the assumed vertical axis of metaphorically extended meanings discussed above in the introduction.

d. The characterization of the Good here as protecting Eden-Groundland against the violent passion of Elohim anticipates the subsequent identification of the Good as Priapus (5.26.33), the phallic deity famous not only in connection with fertility but also for protecting gardens and homes against thieves.

e. The same axis of verticality highlighted in the immediately preceding co-text is carried forward and given still greater prominence in the present segment.

²¹ And so, Eden-Groundland proceeds to give great authority to her third messenger, the aforementioned Naas-Snake,[a] so that he might chastise[b] with all kinds of chastisements the spirit of Elohim that was still among human beings; but also that, through the same spirit, Elohim himself—the one who, in breach of the covenants she had made with him, abandoned his companion—might be chastised.

Now Elohim the father, having seen these things, sends out Baruch—the third of his own messengers—for the purpose of assisting the spirit that was still among all human beings; ²²and Baruch, once he had arrived, stationed himself in the midst of Eden-Groundland's messengers—in the very center, that is, of paradise, since the messengers in whose midst he stood *are* paradise—and commanded the man, *From every tree that is in paradise, you may eat for your sustenance; but from the tree of the knowledge of pleasure and pain, you may not eat*, which same tree is Naas-Snake. Now the point of all this was that the man should listen to the other eleven messengers of Eden-Groundland since, whereas the eleven admittedly have passions, they are not characterized by lawlessness. Naas-Snake, however, did indeed have a lawless nature; ²³for he approached Eve, deceived her, and seduced her into adultery,[c] all of which is lawless to the core. He also approached Adam and kept him for use as a receptive boy-partner,[d] which is the very same kind of lawlessness. Whence have come acts of adultery and sodomy to the present time.

Gen 2:16–17

From that time onward, and from a single source that came from the father, both vices and virtues have exercised great strength over human beings; ²⁴for when he ascended to the Good, the father pointed out a way for those who likewise wish to ascend, but when he withdrew from Eden-Groundland he instigated a whole world of ills against the spirit of the father that was still among human beings.

a. The translation above, "her third messenger . . . Naas-Snake," is a rendering of words not found in the Greek text of the Parisinus but rather proposed by Marcovich, adapting suggestions made in previous editions (e.g., Wendland, Schneidewin and Duncker) and followed recently by Litwa in the light of information available in the antecedent co-text of the present passage (esp. 5.26.4).

b. The grammatical subject of this purpose clause is unexpressed and could be taken either as Naas (so above), and thus as male, or as Eden-Groundland and thus female (as in MacMahon's "Edem . . . that she might chasten"); but both the authority given to Naas in this context and the same character's sexually aggressive behavior in the ensuing action conform to ancient Mediterranean stereotyping of males and support the rendering "he" rather than "she" in this context. Litwa's rendering of the Greek subjunctive as an English infinitive allows ambiguity where it is unnecessary.

c. The last of the three clauses in this sequence, like the first two, attribute all the agency in the action to Naas; thus, Litwa's "he committed adultery with her" has potential to connote a reciprocity on the part of Eve that the grammar of the Greek text does not allow.

d. Litwa's rendering "treated him as his young lover" is an attempt to translate a sequence of Greek words that include an emendation approved earlier by Marcovich and going back to Cruice. Against Litwa's suggestion, however, the emendation he adopts at this point (*paidika*) would put Adam in the position not of the active "lover" but instead in the role of the passive recipient, a dynamic captured more than adequately by the unamended reading of the Parisinus. On some of the lexical and other issues bearing on translation, see K. J. Dover, *Greek Homosexuality*, with forewords by Stephen Halliwell, Mark Masterson, and James Robson (London: Bloomsbury, 2016), 16–17.

Accordingly, Baruch was sent to Moses, through whom he spoke to the sons of Israel so that they might turn themselves toward the Good. ²⁵But through the presence of the soul given by Eden-Groundland and residing within Moses—as indeed it resides within all human beings—the third messenger of the mother (Naas-Snake)[a] cast shadows of darkness over the commandments of Baruch and caused his own orders to be obeyed instead; on account of which the soul remains stationed against the spirit, and the spirit against the soul.[b] For the soul is Eden-Groundland whereas the spirit is Elohim, each of the two being individually within all human beings, both females and males.

²⁶After these events, Baruch was sent forth again, this time to the prophets, so that by the prophets the spirit still dwelling among human beings might listen and escape Eden-Groundland and her wicked forgery, just as Elohim the father had escaped. But by means of the very same strategy and through the presence of the soul that was still dwelling among humanity along with the spirit of the father, Naas-Snake dragged down the prophets in the same manner. All of them tumbled down, and they did not follow the words of Baruch that Elohim had enjoined.

²⁷Finally, Elohim chose a prophet from among the uncircumcised—namely, Herakles—and sent him to fight the twelve messengers of Eden-Groundland and liberate the father from the twelve wicked messengers of creation. These are the twelve contests that Herakles fought, in order, from the first to the last: lion, hydra, boar, and the others in succession;[c] ²⁸for these are the gentile names they were called, people say, since the time of the maternal messengers' activity. But just when it was looking as if Herakles had won the contest, Omphale-Navel, also known as Babel[d] and Aphrodite, enfolds herself tightly around Herakles, drags him down,[e] strips him of his power—his power having been the commandments of Baruch which Elohim had commanded—and reclothes him in her own mantle,[f] that is, the power of Eden-Groundland, the power

---

a. In the Parisinus a lacuna directly follows "the third," which has been followed by the conjectural addition "angel of Eden/Groundland" in all editions of the text from Cruice to Litwa, with the name of the third angel "Naas" being added by Wendland directly after the ensuing article and included in subsequent editions. Both the existence of the lacuna and the strong contextual grounds for the proposed addition justify its adoption here.

b. As noted by Litwa the comparative text most similar in wording to the passage above is Gal 5:17, whose conflict between "spirit" and "flesh" has perhaps been revised deliberately to cohere with the difference between "spirit" and "soul" as elaborated in *JBB*. For additional comparative sources, see Litwa, 347 n. 418.

c. On the "labors of Herakles," see in particular Hesiod, *Theog.* 288–333, which includes reference to cave-dwelling Echidna, "half dancing-eyed nymph with pretty cheeks, half horrible serpent" (298–303), a text anticipating the Herodotean legend represented earlier by the AR (5.24.3–5.25.4) as the source of Justinus's myth; and Euripides, *Herc.fur.* 348–428.

d. I.e., the first-mentioned messenger offspring of Mother Eden-Groundland (5.26.4).

e. Similar to some of the verticality discourse earlier in *JBB*, and against Litwa's reduction of the action in this context to a work of seduction ("Babel . . . seduced him"), the compound verb used by the narrator to signify the action of Babel-Aphrodite on Herakles connotes downward motion.

f. Contra Litwa ("Herakles, instead, put on her own personal attire"), the unexpressed grammatical subject of the verb in this action is best understood as the same as that in the preceding three main narrative clauses, i.e., Omphale-Navel, who in addition to seducing

Justinus's Book of Baruch

below. And in this way both the prophecy about Herakles and his labors came likewise[a] to be imperfect.

[29] But in the end, during the days of Herod the king, Baruch is sent, having been commissioned by Elohim yet again; and once he had arrived in Nazareth, he found Jesus, the son of Joseph and Mary, a twelve-year-old child herding sheep, and Baruch told him everything that had happened from the beginning, from the time of Eden-Groundland and Elohim, but also about the things that happened afterward.[b] [30] He said, "All of the prophets prior to you tumbled down; do therefore try not to fall down, Jesus, son of man, but preach this word to human beings and tell them both about the father and about the Good, and ascend to the Good and settle yourself there with Elohim, the father of us all."

[31] Jesus listened to the envoy and said, "I shall do all these things," and he preached accordingly. Naas-Snake therefore wanted to drag down this one also but he wasn't able to do so;[c] for Jesus stayed faithful to Baruch. And so, because Naas-Snake wasn't able to drag down Jesus, he was enraged and caused him to be crucified. But Jesus, leaving the body of Eden-Groundland at the tree, ascended to the Good; and he said to Eden-Groundland, *Woman, now you* [John 19:26] *have your son completely*, that is, the soulish man of clay; whereas Jesus himself, after putting his spirit into the hands of the Father, ascended to the Good.

Now the Good is Priapus, who prior to all of this caused everything that exists. It is for this very reason that he is called Priapus, because he had caused all things priorly;[d] [33] on account of which he stands, Justinus says, in every temple, being honored by every creature and, on the main roads, holding ripened fruits above his head, the crops of creation, of which he was the originary cause in so far as he had prepared the creation previously before anything existed.

Herakles emasculates him symbolically by attiring him in feminine clothing; on the feminizing effect of a man being attired in women's clothing in the Roman world, see Williams, *Roman Homosexuality*, 141.

a. I.e., just like the interventions attempted via Moses and the prophets as narrated in the antecedent co-text (5.26.24b–26); but since the traditions about the labors of Herakles eventually led to his becoming idealized in early imperial Stoic and Cynic schools as an exemplar of their doctrines (see, e.g., Epictetus, *Diatr.* 1.16; 3.26; 4.10; H. J. Rose, "Heracles," *OCD*, 499), the narration of his failure has potential to elevate the contrasting success of Jesus, at the end of Justinus's story, even more than the prior failures of Moses and the prophets of Israel do.

b. The words "but also ... afterward" are largely based on a helpful emendation proposed by Miller and followed by subsequent editions; but Marcovich goes beyond those changes by supplying an additional reference to "the Good" directly following the reference to Elohim, an addition that anticipates a reference to the Good shortly afterward but that is not essential for textual cohesion or coherence.

c. This final brief clause, concerning the inability of Naas to seduce Jesus, is based on an addition proposed by Wendland and adopted by Marcovich and recent translators (e.g., Litwa), the justification for the change being that the ensuing clause about Jesus's faithfulness to Baruch makes more sense as an explanation of Naas's weakness against Jesus than as an explanation of Naas's desire to seduce him.

d. On the contribution of this surprising equation of the Good and the well-known phallic deity to the structure and force of *JBB* as a whole, see the discussion above under the heading "Structure, Content, and Prosody," where the widely recognized features of Priapus most relevant to the present story are judged to be his Platonized hypermasculinity and his (at least partly consequent) ability to provide protection against the chaotic powers of Eden-Groundland and her messengers.

The Refutation's Summary of Other Teachings by Justinus

34Therefore, says Justinus, whenever you hear people saying that the swan came upon Leda and produced a child from her, see the swan as Elohim and Leda as Eden-Groundland.[a] And whenever people say that the eagle came upon Ganymede, see the eagle as Naas-Snake and Ganymede as Adam. 35And whenever they say that the gold came upon Danae and produced a kid from her, see the gold as Elohim and Danae as Eden-Groundland. In this same manner they likewise try to teach all discourses of this sort,[b] by comparing legends that are similar to each other.

36So, whenever a prophet says, *Hear, O heaven, and lend me your ears, O earth, the Lord has spoken*,[c] "heaven" signifies the spirit of Elohim that is within the human being, says Justinus, and "earth" is the soul[d] that along with the spirit is within the human being; and "the Lord" is Baruch, 37and "Israel" Eden-Groundland. For Eden-Groundland too, in addition to Israel, is called Israel, the companion of Elohim. "Israel," says Elohim, "does not know me; for had she known me, that I am with the Good, she would not have punished—through ignorance of the father—the spirit that henceforth is among human beings."

Isa 1:2

Alternative Version of the Oath Presented in Refutation 5.24.1

27 ¹In this same first book entitled *Baruch*, an oath also is written which is sworn by those about to hear these mysteries and thus be initiated with the Good. This same oath, Justinus claims, our father Elohim swore when he was with the Good; and he did not regret the swearing, concerning which it is written, Justinus says, *The Lord swore and will not regret doing so*. ²Now the oath is as follows: "I swear by the one above all things, by the Good, to guard these mysteries and to divulge them to no one, nor to turn back from the Good to the created thing." Once someone swears this oath, they enter the presence of

Ps 110:4 (LXX 109:4)

---

a. A story possibly older than Homer and retold in various ways across the centuries, the version assumed here having Zeus approach Leda (daughter of Thestius, king of Aetolia, and Tyndareus) in the shape of a swan to produce an egg from which came Helen, the eventual wife of Menelaus in the *Iliad* and *Odyssey*, a version preserved in Justinus's time by a work attributed to the second century BCE mythographer Apollodorus (see *Bibliotheca* 3.126) among others; see H. J. Rose, "Leda," *OCD*, 590–91.

b. As indicated by the shifts from singular to plural ("they . . . try to teach"), from Justinus as narrator to the voice of the AR, and from particular myths to general hermeneutics, the style of discourse has changed by this point from directly quoted excerpt to summary; hence the segmentation implied by the heading placed just before 5.26.34.

c. Critical comparison of the biblical intertext, LXX Isa 1:2, and its use in the present context strengthens the impression given elsewhere in *JBB* that its ideological orientation is relatively individualizing, the references in Isaiah to tangible collectives such as Judah, my people, Jerusalem, other cities, and the metaphorical children in a family (Isa 1:1–8) being without comparably group-oriented analogues in Justinus's narrative. Appropriation of the same Isaianic text in Clement of Alexandria, *Strom.* 4.26.169, as implied by Litwa, shows several noteworthy affinities with Justinus and, on a continuum between the collective and the individual, lies closer to Justinus than to Isaiah.

d. The noun phrase here is conjecturally lengthened by Marcovich so as to mean "the soul of Edem," recalling a concept introduced back in 5.26.8 and resulting in a parallelism with the immediately preceding reference to "the spirit of Elohim," a stylistic enhancement resisted here since it is unnecessary for an adequate reading of the text.

the Good and see *what eye has not seen nor ear heard, nor has ascended over the human heart,*[a] and they drink from the living water, which to them is a bath, as they think of it, a well springing up with living water.

1 Cor 2:9
John 4:10

Paraphrase of Justinus's Interpretation of the Alternative Oath

³ Now since a separation between water and water, Justinus says, is preserved everywhere by the expanse in the middle, water below the firmament is from the evil creation, in which the soulish humans of clay are bathed; but above the firmament is the living water of the Good,[b] in which the spiritually living human beings bathe, and in which Elohim also once bathed and, having finished his bath, he did not change course.

⁴ And so, Justinus notes, wherever the prophet says that he must take for himself *a wife of fornication since, by continuing to fornicate, the land will fornicate itself away from following after the Lord*, this is about Eden-Groundland separating from Elohim. By means of such things, claims Justinus, the prophet clearly utters the entire mystery; but on account of the wickedness of Naas-Snake, he is paid no attention.

Hos 1:2

The Refutation's Concluding Appraisal of Justinus's Writings

⁵ In this very same manner they likewise transmit other prophetical utterances by means of numerous books; but preeminent for them is the book entitled *Baruch*, in which the reader will learn the entire plot of their myth. Therefore, beloved, although I have met with a great many heresies, I have met with none more severely evil than this one. ⁶ In truth, and as the well-known saying can be taken up against him, his followers ought to imitate his Herakles and clean out the cattlestall of Augeas,[c] the very gutter into which Justinus's supporters have fallen, never to be made clean thereafter nor able even to raise their heads.

The Refutation's Transition from Justinus to Simon the Magician

28 ¹ In so far then as we have set forth the attempts of Justinus the pseudo-gnostic, it seems good to set out in the ensuing books the heretical opinions coming after him as well, and to leave not even one of them unrefuted. A juxtaposing of their own words is sufficient for a warning, even if it is solely[d] the secrets and mysteries among them that are examined, concerning which the fools are barely initiated even after much hard work. Let us then see also what Simon says.

---

a. See the note above on 5.24.1 regarding the citation of this same intertext in the alternative version of Justinus's initiatory oath.

b. Here the cosmology assumed in Gen 1:6–7 is interpreted in a manner that reinforces the image schema of verticality, already seen at many previous points in *JBB*, whereby DOWN is conceptualized as evil and UP is equated with good.

c. A rhetorically cunning allusion to the famous labors of Herakles, a web of intertexts appropriated by Justinus for his own purposes (see above at 5.26.27), but used against him in the present context by the AR.

d. Marcovich proposes that the adverb *monon* be deleted in this clause ("even if it ... is the secrets") and that the cognate adjective *monōn* be inserted into the preceding clause ("Only a juxtaposing of their own words"), an emendation that, since it weakens the coherence of the protasis without improving the sense of apodosis, is not accepted here.

The Fifteen Signs before Judgment
A new translation and introduction

by Brandon W. Hawk

The Fifteen Signs before Judgment lists the portents on the fifteen days leading up to the eschaton. Composed in the early medieval period, this eschatological work is similar to earlier lists of events leading up to Judgment Day. The textual tradition of the Fifteen Signs is highly variable, and multiple versions circulated during the Middle Ages. Lists are extant in Latin, Hebrew, and Armenian, as well as most Western European languages. Versions of the Fifteen Signs were also embedded in many later Latin and vernacular pieces of literature.

Contents
As is obvious from the title, the Fifteen Signs presents an enumeration of the phenomena expected to occur on each of the fifteen days leading up to Judgment Day. Inspired by earlier biblical and apocryphal literature, the text foretells signs such as the rising of the seas, the burning of the seas, the leveling of the waters and earth, a bloody dew, the destruction of buildings, battling rocks, earthquake, the falling of stars, the resurrection of the dead, and the burning of the earth. Individual versions differ in their details and arrangements of the portents, but the signs remain generally similar across the textual families. Many versions include a brief preface that identifies Jerome as the one who discovered these signs in "the annals (or chronicles) of the Hebrews." Some versions include additional extended prefaces or conclusions about the Judgment Day.

Manuscripts and Versions
The most important witnesses of the Fifteen Signs tradition survive in Latin, Hebrew, and Armenian, from which were translated various other versions. The Latin versions are earliest, although there are no compelling criteria available that enable us to discern the language of composition. Considering the wealth of evidence in Latin and Western European languages, the most plausible explanation is that the Fifteen Signs was composed in Latin and later adapted into other versions as well as translated into other languages, including Hebrew, Armenian (which is a translation, but the source language is uncertain), Slavic, and many other European vernaculars. There is, however, still room for doubt, and precise relationships between Western and Eastern versions remain uncertain.

William W. Heist provided the most comprehensive study of the legend, as well as a representative list of over one hundred textual witnesses in Latin and European vernacular languages.[1] More recent assessments and identifications, especially of the

---

1. Heist, *The Fifteen Signs before Doomsday* (East Lansing: Michigan State College Press, 1952); see

Hebrew, Armenian, and Slavic versions, have called Heist's conclusions into question.[2] Lorenzo DiTommaso has identified around six hundred textual witnesses to the Fifteen Signs tradition; these require more study before the full range of relationships may be determined.[3] Nonetheless, within the mass of evidence from Western Europe, the general picture remains concerning Heist's identification of three major Latin recensions: Pseudo-Bedan, Damian, and Comestor versions. Later recensions proliferated from the thirteenth century onward, but these three earliest versions form the bases for such developments. As Concetta Giliberto aptly suggests: "Such groupings of the versions of the Fifteen Signs list into different families are not to be interpreted as strict and rigid classifications, but rather as a kind of systematisation of the material of the Fifteen Signs, which allows us to compare similarities and differences among the lists, and to shed light on their possible relationships."[4] In what follows, we should be aware of the macroscale while also acknowledging that there is much variation in individual instances at the microscale.[5]

The Pseudo-Bedan recension of the Fifteen Signs probably represents the earliest Latin version. Heist believed it to be from the twelfth century, but more recent research has provided evidence for an earlier date. An important witness, and the reason for its pseudonymous authorial attribution, is the florilegium known as the *Collectanea Pseudo-Bedae*, which is very likely Hiberno-Latin.[6] No surviving manuscript of this collection has been identified, but the florilegium was printed by Johann Herwagen in his 1563 edition of Bede's works and reprinted by Jacques-Paul Migne in his *Patrologia Latina*.[7] The contents of the *Collectanea* indicate its likely composition in the British Isles (possibly in Ireland) in the ninth century.[8] The Latin Pseudo-Bedan version of the Fifteen Signs certainly circulated more widely by the year 1100: it appears, for example, in

---

his appendix A (204–12) for an annotated list of texts consulted, and appendix B (213–14) for a list of additional witnesses known but not used for his study. See also lists in Bernard Lambert, *Bibliotheca Hieronymiana Manuscripta: La tradition manuscrite des oeuvres de Saint Jérôme*, 4 vols., Instrumenta Patristica 4 (Steenbrugge: Abbatia S. Petri, 1969–1972), 3B:652–55; John J. Machielsen, *Clavis Patristica Pseudepigraphorum Medii Aevi*, 5 vols. (Turnhout: Brepols, 1990–2004), 2: nos. 411 and 927; Christof Gerhardt and Nigel F. Palmer, eds., *Das Münchner Gericht von den 15 Zeichen vor dem Jüngsten Gericht: Nach der Handschrift der Bayerischen Staatsbibliothek Cgm 717; Edition und Kommentar*, Texte des späten Mittelalters und der frühen Neuzeit 41 (Berlin: Schmidt, 2002), 59–67; and Lorenzo DiTommaso, "Pseudepigrapha Notes III: 4. Old Testament Pseudepigrapha in the Yale University Manuscript Collection," *JSP* 20 (2010): 14–15, doi:10.1177/09518207103823.

2. For an overview, see Brandon W. Hawk, "The *Fifteen Signs before Judgment* in Anglo-Saxon England: A Reassessment," *Journal of English and Germanic Philology* 117 (2018): 443–57, doi:10.5406/jenglgermphil.117.4.0443.

3. Discussed via private correspondence.

4. Giliberto, "The Fifteen Signs before Doomsday in Cotton Vespasian D. xiv: Role and Conceptualisation," in *Practice in Learning: The Transfer of Encyclopaedic Knowledge in the Early Middle Ages*, ed. Rolf Bremmer Jr. and Kees Dekker, Mediaevalia Groningana 16 (Leuven: Peeters, 2010), 287–88 n. 16.

5. Cf. comments in Hawk, "*Fifteen Signs*."

6. Martha Bayless and Michael Lapidge, eds., *Collectanea Pseudo-Bedae*, Scriptores Latini Hiberniae 14 (Dublin: Dublin Institute for Advanced Studies, 1998).

7. Johann Herwagen, ed., *Opera Bedae Venerabilis presbyteri Anglosaxonis*, 8 vols. (Basel: Herwagen, 1563), 3:647–72; and PL 94:555. See Peter Jackson, "Herwagen's Lost Manuscript of the *Collectanea*," in Bayless and Lapidge, *Collectanea Pseudo-Bedae*, 101–20.

8. Michael Lapidge, "The Origin of the *Collectanea*," in *Collectanea Pseudo-Bedae*, ed. Bayless and Lapidge, 1–12.

an autograph manuscript of the Liber Floridus (Ghent, University Library 92, compiled ca. 1090–1121) and in Eton, Eton College Library 21 (Bk. 2. 8; ca. 1100, Peterborough). Notably, these witnesses and contemporary manuscripts like them demonstrate that even earlier exemplars must have existed.

The Italian monk and cardinal Peter Damian (d. 1072/1073) included another early version of the Fifteen Signs in his *Epistolae* 92 and 93, both composed around 1062. The text of the Fifteen Signs in both letters is the same.[9] This recension, now known as the "Damian" type, is similar to the Pseudo-Bedan version but differs in its arrangement and some details. The earliest, most authoritative manuscripts of Damian's *Letters* survive from the late eleventh century:[10]

> Rome, Biblioteca Apostolica Vaticana, Vat. lat. 3797
> Rome, Biblioteca Apostolica Vaticana, Urb. lat. 503
> Montecassino, Biblioteca dell'Abbazia, Cod. Cassinensis 358
> Montecassino, Biblioteca dell'Abbazia, Cod. Cassinensis 359

All of these manuscripts were copied within a few decades of Damian composing his letters and therefore constitute some of the earliest surviving material witnesses to the Fifteen Signs legend.

The French theologian Peter Comestor (d. 1178) included a version of the Fifteen Signs in his encyclopedic *Historia scholastica*, completed around 1170.[11] This comprises the third major Latin recension. Again, in comparison with the earlier versions, there are some notable parallels, but the arrangement and details differ substantially. Over 250 manuscripts of Comestor's *Historia scholastica* survive, but the earliest is Paris, Bibliothèque nationale de France, lat. 16943 (ca. 1183), copied within several years of Comestor's death.[12]

From his work collecting versions of the Fifteen Signs (and despite his dubious claims about the origins of the legend), Heist indicates that, in Western Europe at least, "all of the main lines of development had reached a comparatively stable form by the twelfth century."[13] After that period, the Fifteen Signs was translated into numerous Western European languages during the medieval period (discussed below), and certain manuscripts preserve hybrid versions. For example, we might compare two of the earliest identified vernacular translations, in late Old English (London, British Library, Cotton Vespasian D.xiv, ca. 1150, southeast England) and in Old Frisian (Oldenburg, Niedersächsisches Staatsarchiv, Bestand 24–1, Ab. Nr. 2, ca. 1300). Both of these translations are based on the Pseudo-Bedan version, but they contain interpolations and influences from the Damian version (in the Old English) and Comestor version (in the

---

9. For this reason, I translate only the text from *Epistola* 92, as in Peter Damian, "Epistula 92," PL 145835–42.

10. See list of manuscripts in Kurt Reindel, ed., *Die Briefe des Petrus Damiani*, Monumenta Germaniae Historica, Die Briefe der deutschen Kaiserzeit 4.1 (Berlin: Weidmann, 1949), 1:33–39.

11. Peter Comestor, *Historia Scholastica*, PL 198:1611.

12. Maria C. Sherwood-Smith, *Studies in the Reception of the* Historia Scholastica *of Peter Comestor*, Medium Ævum Monographs NS 20 (Oxford: Society for the Study of Medieval Languages and Literature, 2000), 14–15.

13. William W. Heist, "The Fifteen Signs before Judgement: Further Remarks," *Mediaeval Studies* 22 (1960): 203.

Old Frisian).[14] Jacobus de Voragine (ca. 1230–1298) included a conflation of Damian's and Comestor's versions into his massive compendium of saints' lives known as the *Golden Legend*, compiled around 1260, which served as the basis for many vernacular translations in the later Middle Ages.[15] These versions were picked up, used, and criticized by a number of scholastic authors like Hugo de Novocastro (ca. 1270–1323) and Guiral Ot (1285–1349), while the authenticity and legitimacy of the legend was questioned by a number of Dominicans like the medieval editors of Thomas Aquinas (1225–1274) and Hugo of Prato (ca. 1262–1322).[16] These and other instances demonstrate the difficulties of categorizing individual iterations of the Fifteen Signs as well as the fluidity of the general tradition.

Such variance is also witnessed in the Hebrew version of the Fifteen Signs. Michael E. Stone first edited and translated this text, from a fourteenth-century manuscript from the Rhineland, Oxford, Bodleian Library, Cod. Heb. d.11.[17] Its text type is independent of the Latin and Armenian versions included here. While Stone demonstrates that this Hebrew text is translated from Latin, its details differ substantially from the Pseudo-Bedan, Damian, and Comestor types, which are generally reflected in the Latin and Armenian versions. It contains a unique, expansive preface with both biblicizing and classicizing elements. The Hebrew translation must therefore rest on and gives special witness to another aspect of the Latin tradition.

Another set of fluid textual versions appears in Armenian witnesses to the Fifteen Signs tradition.[18] Stone has edited and translated three recensions from four manuscripts:

Recension I: Jerusalem, Patriarchal Library, 1729 (1741, Lim)[19]
Recension II: Jerusalem, Patriarchal Library, 1861 (1669, New Julfa);[20] and British Library, Harley 5459 (1689)[21]
Recension III: Erevan, Matenadaran M2188 (15th century)[22]

---

14. Giliberto, "Fifteen Signs before Doomsday in Cotton Vespasian D. xiv"; and Giliberto, "Fifteen Signs of Doomsday of the First Riustring Manuscript," in *Advances in Old Frisian Philology*, ed. Rolf H. Bremmer Jr., Stephen Laker, and Oebele Vries, Amsterdamer Beiträge zur älteren Germanistik 64 (Amsterdam: Rodopi, 2007), 129–52.

15. J. G. Graesse, ed., *Jacobi a Voragine, Legenda aurea: Vulgo historia lombardica dicta*, 3rd ed. (Breslau: Koebner, 1890), 6–7; and William Granger Ryan, trans., *Jacobus de Voragine, The Golden Legend: Readings on the Saints*, 2 vols. (Princeton: Princeton University Press, 1993), 1:8.

16. See Robert E. Lerner, "Sign Theory: Some Scholastic Encounters with 'The Fifteen Signs before the Day of Judgement,'" *Journal of Ecclesiastical History* 73 (2022): 720–36, doi:10.1017/S0022046921002177.

17. Stone, *Signs of Judgement, Onomastica Sacra and the Generations from Adam*, University of Pennsylvania Armenian Texts and Studies 3 (Chico, CA: Scholars Press, 1981), 42–57 (see introduction at pp. 12–13).

18. Stone, *Signs of Judgement*, 3–40; see also Stone, "Jewish Tradition, the Pseudepigrapha and the Christian West," in *The Aramaic Bible: Targums in Their Historical Context*, ed. D. R. G. Beattie and M. J. McNamara, JSOTSup 166 (Sheffield: Sheffield Academic, 1994), 432–35.

19. Stone, *Signs of Judgement*, 3–40.

20. Stone, *Signs of Judgement*, 3–40.

21. Michael E. Stone, "Two Unpublished Eschatological Texts," *JSP* 18 (2009): 297–302, doi:10.1177/0951820709106105.

22. Michael E. Stone, *Armenian Apocrypha Relating to Angels and Biblical Heroes*, EJL 45 (Atlanta: SBL Press, 2016), 4–9.

As Stone writes, "The Armenian version clearly belongs to the same branch of the stemma as pseudo-Bede, Comestor and Damian, but it is not identical with any single one of them."[23] In fact, each recension includes its own idiosyncrasies of correspondence to and divergence from the major Latin versions. Armenian recension I is primary (based on linguistic and textual considerations), and it corresponds to the Latin Pseudo-Bedan and Comestor types in most signs and arrangement (except for a few details). Recension II, however, is longer and differs from the Latin versions and Armenian recension I to a greater extent. In particular, the framework of recension II is secondary and contains more traditions found in other Armenian literature. The text of recension II in Harley 5459 contains some unique features, in the form of substantial divergences or additions of details. Recension III shows even more extensive differences from the Latin and other Armenian witnesses. It includes a unique frame, relating the signs to the coming of the antichrist and later Christ (at the beginning), as well as the coming of Christ and the Jews proclaiming their belief in him (at the end). Other major differences of Armenian recension III concern the arrangement and details of the signs: in some cases, it is parallel with recensions I and II, and with the Pseudo-Bedan version, but in other cases it contains special parallels with the Comestor version or unique elements. As yet there is no way to date the Armenian versions definitively, but it is clear that they are copies of earlier texts. For this reason, it is safe to assume that all of the Armenian versions were composed at least by the late medieval period, and perhaps earlier.

Witnesses to Slavic translations of the Fifteen Signs survive in several late medieval and early modern Cyrillic and Glagolitic manuscripts.[24] These witnesses include the following:[25]

Plovdivski zbornik (Cyrillic): Plovdiv, Ivan Vazov National Library, Bosnensko sborniče 116 (54) (seventeenth century), fols. 101r–108r

Berčićev zbornik no. 5 (Glagolitic): Saint Petersburg, National Library of Russia, sign. Bč 5, fols. 15v–16v[26]

Vinodolski zbornik (Glagolitic): Zagreb, Archive of the Croatian Academy of Sciences and Arts, sign. III a 15 (fifteenth century), fols. 43r–v

Libro od mnozijeh razloga (Cyrillic): Zagreb, Archive of the Croatian Academy of Sciences and Arts, sign. IV a 24 (1520), fols. 52r–54r[27]

Zbornik duhovnog štiva (Glagolitic): Zagreb, Archive of the Croatian Academy of Sciences and Arts, sign. IV a 48 (fifteenth century), fols. 73r–v[28]

---

23. Stone, *Signs of Judgement*, 5.

24. I am indebted to Josip Vučković for his notes about Slavic manuscripts, texts, and scholarship, as well as for providing summaries and preliminary translations of these versions of the *Fifteen Signs* into English, via private correspondence.

25. See Josip Vučković, "Interpolacija stihova iz pjesme *Svit se konča* u izlaganju o Posljednjem sudu iz Berčićeva zbornika br. 5," *Ricerche slavistiche* NS 2, no. 62 (2019): 332–33.

26. See Svetlana Olegovna Vialova, *Glagoličeskij sbornik XV v. Rossijskaja nacional'naja biblioteka: Sobranie Ivana Berchicha, f. 67, Berchich No. 5. Glagoljski zbornik 15. st. Ruska nacionalna biblioteka; Zbirka Ivana Berčića, f. 67, Berčić br. 5. Knjiga 2*, Monumenta glagolitica Archiodioecesis Iadertinae 20.2 (Zadar: Sveučilište u Zadru—Stalna izložba crkvene umjetnosti, 2016).

27. See Milan Rešetar, *Libro od mnozijeh razloga: Dubrovački ćirilski zbornik od g. 1520*, Srpska akademija nauka i umetnost 15 (Beograd: Srpska kraljevska akademija, 1926); and Mateo Žagar, ed., *Libro od mnozijeh razloga 1520: Latinički prijepis s komentarima* (Zagreb: Matica hrvatska, 2020).

28. See Rudolf Strohal, *Stare hrvatske apokrifne priče i legend* (Bjelovar: Weiss, 1917), 90–97.

Grškovićev zbornik (Glagolitic): Zagreb, Archive of the Croatian Academy of Sciences and Arts, sign. VIII 32 (sixteenth century), fols. 17r–v

The text in *Grškovićev zbornik* relies on the version in Jacobus de Voragine's *Golden Legend*, while the version of the Fifteen Signs in the *Libro od mnozijeh razloga* is part of a prose translation of an Italian poem titled *El giudizio generale*.[29] The texts in the *Zbornik duhovnog štiva* and *Berčićev zbornik no. 5* constitute prefaces to a longer work titled *Sud gospodina Boga* ("The Judgment of the Lord God"); these two, along with the free-standing text in the *Vinodolski zbornik*, contain some details similar to the Damian and Comestor types, but they also diverge in significant ways.[30] The *Libro od mnozijeh razloga* is from Dubrovnik, whereas the Glagolitic witnesses are from the Zadar archipelago, Kvarner Gulf and Istria, all in present-day Croatia. The text in the *Plovdivski zbornik* does not correspond specifically to any one text type in the other languages, although, curiously, it is closest to Armenian recension III in some aspects of its ordering of signs and specific details included; it also includes a preface attributing the signs to the prophet Daniel and a sixteenth day relating the appearance of angels blowing trumpets and the Final Judgment.[31] Notably, the Plovdiv manuscript is dated to the seventeenth century but includes a chronicle covering events up to 1539, and the contents more generally represent texts that already existed earlier than the sixteenth century; it possibly originates from present-day Bosnia and Herzegovina. The Plovdiv manuscript contains the only version of the Fifteen Signs to be identified in a manuscript with Slavic Orthodox contents, as all of the others contain Catholic contents.[32] Such witnesses speak to the need for further research on the Slavic sources and their relationships to the recensions in Latin and Armenian.

Taking all of this evidence into account, there is no clear way to determine the original language of the Fifteen Signs at present. The Latin versions provide the earliest material witnesses, but that does not preclude the possibility that there was an earlier form of the text in another language. All three Armenian recensions are certainly translations from another language, but Stone admits that "The question of the original language of the Armenian version remains without solution."[33] It is possible that the Latin and Armenian versions derive from a common antecedent, such as a Greek version—but no evidence for that possibility is forthcoming. It is just as possible that the Armenian recensions derive from Latin; again, there is no solid evidence to refute or corroborate the possibility. The Hebrew version is clearly based on a Latin antecedent, but it is uniquely distinct compared to the major known Latin versions. The Slavic versions similarly provide evidence that they are based on Latin texts, although their precise relationships to Latin versions have yet to be traced.

The following translations include the three major Latin versions (Pseudo-Bedan, Damian, and Comestor) in parallel, the Hebrew version, and the three Armenian recen-

---

29. See Nakaš, "*Skazanije i pripovidjenije od Suda velikoga*."
30. See Lejla Vučković, *Interpolacija stihova iz pjesme* (Sarajevo: Forum Bosnae, 2016).
31. For facsimile with transcription, see Nakaš, *Plovdivska bosanska knjiga*, 206–20; for discussion of the manuscript, see 321–34; and Nakaš, "*Skazanije i pripovidjenije od Suda velikoga* (*Libro od Mnozijeh Razloga* 49–56)," *Croatica: časopis za hrvatski jezik, književnost i kulturu* 45, no. 65 (2021): 109–24.
32. See Nakaš for a full study of the manuscript (*Plovdivska bosanska knjiga*).
33. Stone, *Signs of Judgement*, 14. Cf. similar assessments in his more recent works, Stone, "Two Unpublished Eschatological Texts," 297–98; and Stone, *Armenian Apocrypha*, 4–5.

sions in parallel. I am grateful to Michael Stone and to Sage Publishers and SBL Press for allowing me to reprint his translations of the Hebrew and Armenian versions, along with the addition of notes about biblical sources and parallels.

Genre and Structure

In general, the Fifteen Signs is what DiTommaso calls an "apocalyptic oracle." It is not an apocalypse in the strict definition of the genre; nor is it as focused as many works of apocalyptic eschatology. It does contain a prophetic view of apocalyptic events leading up to the final eschaton, but it is not presented as a visionary experience related through the perspective of a specific figure. In fact, in the prologue about Jerome finding these signs (which accompanies many versions), the Fifteen Signs is presented as an apocalyptic oracle, aligned as it is with historical chronicles. The title of this work evoking "fifteen signs" is something of a misnomer, since it contains many more than fifteen. The work is more an enumeration of the many signs on fifteen days leading up to Judgment Day than it is of fifteen signs. In this regard, it aligns with a variety of other apocalyptica (see the section "Literary Context" below).

Other features make the Fifteen Signs stand out from classical apocalypses and help to align it with the category of apocalyptic oracles. For example, it lacks a number of features of classical apocalypses. There are no *ex eventu* prophecies or other specific historical allusions (adding to the difficulty of determining a particular date, provenance, and literary context for the composition). Stone notes the odd absence of "cosmic or super-human protagonists"; as he says, "strangely, the text preserves no hint of belief in an Anti-Christ . . . no messiah or savior and no angels" so common in late antique and medieval apocalyptica.[34] Some of these elements do, of course, appear in the frameworks for Armenian recensions II and III: Gabriel appears at the end of recension II, while recension III begins with the evocation of Antichrist and Christ and ends with Christ's appearance with angels. But these are later, expansive additions unique to these versions.

The structure across versions is rather obvious, as it is divided into fifteen distinct days as a framework for the various portents. The climax is the final lead-in to the Judgment Day. Occasionally, in some texts, a sixteenth day is added to emphasize the judgment. There is no obvious explanation for or consensus about the justification for the structure of fifteen days.

Date and Provenance

The origins of the Fifteen Signs are difficult to determine with such a vast number of witnesses as well as textual and linguistic iterations that have not yet been fully assessed. This is especially the case because we are still uncertain about the relationships between the Latin, Hebrew, and Armenian versions—within each tradition as well as taken together. Concerning the date, what can be said for certain rests on the earliest datable witnesses, which are no earlier than the eleventh century. While scholars generally agree that the *Collectanea* containing the Pseudo-Bedan version was likely compiled in the ninth century, there is still uncertainty without any material witness. A definite *terminus ad quem* for the composition of the Fifteen Signs, therefore, is Peter Damian's incorporation of the text into his *Epistolae* 92 and 93 around 1062.

---

34. Stone, *Signs of Judgement*, 18.

A provenance for the legend is equally elusive. Because of certain Irish evidence, Heist claimed that the Fifteen Signs was the product of Irish scribes.[35] He pointed to the tenth-century Irish poem *Saltair na Rann* as the mediating text between the seven-day arrangement of signs in the Apocalypse of Thomas and the formulation in the Fifteen Signs. Considering the number, types, and languages of witnesses identified since Heist's study, his view of an Irish text as a mediator is now questionable. Proposed connections with the Apocalypse of Thomas and Fifteen Signs are general and largely based on common apocalyptic imagery rather than definite parallels. The few distinct parallels across the two apocrypha (for example, earthquakes and falling stars) are common motifs gleaned from signs in the Bible. Martin McNamara has surveyed the Irish evidence, and it is certain that the Fifteen Signs tradition was influential in Ireland, and that it was likely there at an early point in the history of the text's transmission.[36] While Heist's view of these developments is now in doubt, parallels between the various texts deserve further attention; only further work on the relationships between the early instances of the legend will provide a clearer understanding of the origins.

It has long been obvious that the *Pseudo-Bedae Collectanea* is the product of insular learning in the British Isles. Many of the contents of the florilegium are Irish motifs, and pieces of the collection have parallels in Hiberno-Latin, Irish, and Old English literature.[37] Because the Pseudo-Bedan version of the Fifteen Signs in this collection is likely the earliest, the conclusion that the tradition began in an insular milieu is a plausible one. Even such speculations as this must be tempered until the mass of witnesses are assessed in a more comprehensive manner.

The Armenian versions raise questions concerning date and provenance. Much depends upon as yet indeterminate relationships between Latin and Armenian versions. As with considerations of the original language, there are too many possibilities without any direct evidence to preclude or accept any single explanation.

Literary Context

The Fifteen Signs legend, as noted, has affinities with earlier biblical and apocryphal apocalyptic traditions. Significant parallels appear in the Hebrew Prophets (especially Isaiah), the Synoptic Apocalypse, Revelation, Sibylline Oracles, 4 Ezra, Seventh Vision of Daniel, and Apocalypse of Thomas. In his edition and translation of the Armenian and Hebrew versions, Stone provides a robust commentary, citing many parallels and potential sources.[38] Some of the images included in the versions of the Fifteen Signs are so common (like the blowing of trumpets, widespread fire, and the new heavens and new

---

35. Heist, *Fifteen Signs*.
36. McNamara, "The Signs before Doomsday in Irish Tradition," in *The Apocrypha in the Irish Church* (Dublin: Dublin Institute for Advanced Study, 1975), 128–32; McNamara, "Apocalyptic and Eschatological Texts in Irish Literature: Oriental Connections?," in *Apocalyptic and Eschatological Heritage: The Middle East and Celtic Realms*, ed. Martin McNamara (Dublin: Four Courts Press, 2003), 94–97; and McNamara, "The (Fifteen) Signs before Doomsday in Irish Tradition," *Warszawskie Studia Teologiczne* 20 (2007): 223–54. See also Caitríona Ó Dochartaigh and John Carey, "Introduction," in *The End and Beyond: Medieval Irish Eschatology*, ed. John Carey, Emma Nic Cárthaigh, and Caitríona Ó Dochartaigh, 2 vols. Celtic Studies Publications 17 (Aberystwyth: Celtic Studies Publications, 2014), 2:549–65; and Emma Nic Cárthaigh, "Fifteen Signs of Doomsday in the *Liber Flavus Fergusiorum*," in Carey, Nic Cárhaigh, and Ó Dochartaigh, *End and Beyond*, 2:753–60.
37. See essays and commentary in Bayless and Lapidge, *Collectanea Pseudo-Bedae*.
38. Stone, *Signs of Judgement*, 34–40 and 50–57.

earth) as to evade any specific parallels, since they appear pervasively throughout many biblical and noncanonical apocalyptica. Such parallels deserve further attention, as they may lead to a better understanding of the sources and literary contexts of the Fifteen Signs. In the following translations, I do not cite all of the various potential parallels, as many of them require further explanations or caveats, but only the most significant, mainly from the Bible.

Despite parallels in Christian apocalyptica, none of the portents in the Fifteen Signs is obviously Christian, and many are found in the Hebrew Bible. Because of the conventional nature of such signs, none are necessarily drawn from the New Testament or Christian literature. The Hebrew version is the only one that includes quotations with clear verbal parallels. In fact, these quotations in the Hebrew version and other biblicizing elements—like specific references to specific biblical locations (Mount Tabor and the Valley of Jehoshaphat)—are significant because they seem to be added by the translator, whereas other versions include only allusions or more general parallels to the Bible. Some versions invoke biblical authority either in direct relation to the Hebrew Bible, as in the quotation of Isa 66:16 in the preface to the Hebrew text, or more generally, as in the evocation of scriptural genres in the framework of Armenian recension II.[39] Both Armenian recensions II and III include Christian elements, but these must be later interpolations in the tradition. All of this leaves open the possibility that the Fifteen Signs might have ultimately derived from a Jewish context before its Christian appropriation. In this respect, we might recall the curious reference to Jerome finding these signs in Hebrew annals or chronicles.

The later reception of the Fifteen Signs provides further information about its importance in the context of medieval European culture. This reception includes hundreds of iterations in Latin, as well as hundreds more in vernacular languages across Europe. Some of the earliest vernacular translations include Old English in the twelfth century;[40] Old French in the twelfth century;[41] and Old Frisian in the thirteenth century.[42] In the middle of the twelfth century, the legend was incorporated into an Anglo-Norman play titled *Jeu d'Adam*. Because of the widespread popularity of Jacobus de Voragine's *Golden Legend*, hundreds of Latin and vernacular versions from the late medieval period ultimately rely on that work. Noteworthy translations that have received scholarly attention include late medieval versions in Irish, Welsh, Old Norse, French, German, and Slavic (as discussed).[43] The Fifteen Signs also made its way into later medieval historical chroni-

---

39. See Stone's remarks in *Signs of Judgement*, 14–15.
40. Giliberto, "Fifteen Signs before Doomsday in Cotton Vespasian D. xiv."
41. Erik van Kraemer, ed., *Les quinze signes du Jugement dernier, poème anonyme de la fin du XIIe ou du début du XIIIe siècle publié d'après tous les manuscrits connus avec introduction, notes et glossaire*, Commentationes humanarum litterarum 38.2 (Helsinki: Societas Scientiarum Fennicae, 1966); and Reine Mantou, ed., *Les quinze signes du Jugement dernier, poème du XII e siècle, édition critique*, Extrait des Mémoires et Publications de Société des Sciences, des Arts et des Lettres du Hainaut 80.2 (Hainaut: Société des sciences, des arts et des lettres, 1966).
42. Giliberto, "Fifteen Signs of Doomsday of the First Riustring Manuscript."
43. For Irish, see Whitley Stokes, "Fifteen Tokens of Doomsday," *Revue Celtique* 28 (1907): 308–26; and Nic Cárthaigh, "Fifteen Signs." For Welsh, see William W. Heist, "Welsh Prose Versions of the Fifteen Signs before Doomsday," *Speculum* 19 (1944): 421–32, doi:10.2307/2853480. For Old Norse, see James W. Marchand, "Early Scandinavian Variants of the Fifteen Signs before Doomsday," *Acta Philologica* 31 (1976): 177–32. For French, see William W. Heist, "Four Old French Versions of the Fifteen Signs before the Judgment," *Mediaeval Studies* 15 (1953): 184–98; and Heist, "Further Remarks." For German, see

cles—bringing the legend into alignment with its self-proclaimed origin in annals—as in the fifteenth-century French Chronique Anonyme Universelle.[44] Unsurprisingly, the eschatological signs were incorporated into art and drama, as they appear in late medieval manuscript illustrations (as in the *Chronique Anonyme*), stained glass windows, and cycle plays, which must have given even wider audiences knowledge of the Fifteen Signs.[45]

The popularity of the Fifteen Signs did not end with the early modern period. Heist demonstrated the use of the legend in two sixteenth-century polemical works.[46] C. H. Conley identified the Fifteen Signs as a source for various portents throughout Shakespeare's plays *Julius Caesar* and *Hamlet*.[47] Mark Z. Christensen has discussed the presence of this legend in post-Colombian Maya manuscripts from the Americas.[48] All of these instances attest to the enduring and widespread influence of the Fifteen Signs well beyond the European Middle Ages.

Bibliography

EDITIONS AND TRANSLATIONS

Bayless, Martha, and Michael Lapidge, eds. *Collectanea Pseudo-Bedae*. Scriptores Latini Hiberniae 14. Dublin: Dublin Institute for Advanced Studies, 1998.

Collectanea Pseudo-Bedae. PL 95:539–62.

Comestor, Peter. *Historia Scholastica*. PL 198.

Damian, Peter. "Epistula 92." Pages 14–26 in vol. 3 of *Die Briefe des Petrus Damiani*. Edited by Kurt Reindel. Monumenta Germaniae Historica, Die Briefe der deutschen Kaiserzeit 4.3. Wiesbaden: Harrassowitz, 1989.

———. "Epistula 92." PL 145:835–42.

Davis, Lisa Fagin. *La Chronique Anonyme Universelle: Reading and Writing History in Fifteenth-Century France*. Studies in Medieval and Early Renaissance Art History 61. Turnhout: Brepols, 2014.

Giliberto, Concetta. "The Fifteen Signs before Doomsday in Cotton Vespasian D. xiv: Role and Conceptualisation." Pages 285–309 in *Practice in Learning: The Transfer of Encyclopaedic Knowledge in the Early Middle Ages*. Edited by Rolf Bremmer Jr. and Kees Dekker. Mediaevalia Groningana 16. Leuven: Peeters, 2010.

Gerhardt and Palmer, *Das Münchner Gericht von den 15 Zeichen*. On all of these vernacular versions, see Heist, *Fifteen Signs*, passim, with earlier bibliography there.

44. Lisa Fagin Davis, *La Chronique Anonyme Universelle: Reading and Writing History in Fifteenth-Century France*, Studies in Medieval and Early Renaissance Art History 61 (Turnhout: Brepols, 2014), 224–35.

45. See Clifford Davidson, "The Signs of Doomsday in Drama and Art," *Historical Reflections/Réflexions Historiques* 26 (2000): 223–45.

46. William W. Heist, *Sermon Joyeux and Polemic: Two Sixteenth-Century Applications of the Legend of the Fifteen Signs*, University of North Carolina Studies in the Romance Languages and Literatures 73 (Chapel Hill: University of North Carolina Press, 1968).

47. Conley, "An Instance of the Fifteen Signs of Judgment in Shakespeare," *Modern Language Notes* 30 (1915): 41–44, doi:10.2307/2916899.

48. Christensen, *The Teabo Manuscript: Maya Christian Copybooks, Chilam Balams, and Native Text Production in Yucatán* (Austin, Texas: University of Texas Press, 2016), 138–71; and Christensen, *Aztec and Maya Apocalypses: Old World Tales of Doom in a New World Setting* (Norman: University of Oklahoma Press, 2022), 69–114.

———. "The Fifteen Signs of Doomsday of the First Riustring Manuscript." Pages 129–52 of *Advances in Old Frisian Philology*. Edited by Rolf H. Bremmer Jr., Stephen Laker, and Oebele Vries. Amsterdamer Beiträge zur *älteren* Germanistik 64. Amsterdam: Rodopi, 2007.

Graesse, J. G. Theodor, ed. *Jacobi a Voragine, Legenda aurea: Vulgo historia lombardica dicta*. 3rd ed. Breslau: Koebner, 1890.

Heist, William W. "Four Old French Versions of the Fifteen Signs before the Judgment." *Mediaeval Studies* 15 (1953): 184–98.

———. "Welsh Prose Versions of the Fifteen Signs before Doomsday." *Speculum* 19 (1944): 421–32. doi:10.2307/2853480.

Herwagen, Johann, ed. *Opera Bedae Venerabilis presbyteri Anglosaxonis*. 8 vols. Basel: Herwagen, 1563.

Kraemer, Erik von, ed. *Les quinze signes du Jugement dernier, poème anonyme de la fin du XIIe ou du début du XIIIe siècle publié d'après tous les manuscrits connus avec introduction, notes et glossaire*. Commentationes humanarum litterarum 38.2. Helsinki: Societas Scientiarum Fennicae, 1966.

Mantou, Reine, ed. *Les quinze signes du Jugement dernier, poème du XII e siècle, édition critique*. Extrait des Mémoires et Publications de Société des Sciences, des Arts et des Lettres du Hainaut 80.2. Hainaut: Société des sciences, des arts et des lettres, 1966.

Marchand, James W. "Early Scandinavian Variants of the Fifteen Signs before Doomsday." *Acta Philologica* 31 (1976): 177–32.

Nakaš, Lejla. *Plovdivska bosanska knjiga*. Sarajevo: Forum Bosnae, 2016.

Nic Cárthaigh, Emma. "The Fifteen Signs of Doomsday in the *Liber Flavus Fergusiorum*." Pages 753–60 in vol. 2 of *The End and Beyond: Medieval Irish Eschatology*. Edited by John Carey, Emma Nic Cárthaigh, and Caitríona Ó Dochartaigh. 2 vols. Celtic Studies Publications 17. Aberystwyth: Celtic Studies Publications, 2014.

Rešetar, Milan. *Libro od mnozijeh razloga: Dubrovački ćirilski zbornik od g. 1520*. Srpska akademija nauka i umetnost 15. Beograd: Srpska kraljevska akademija, 1926.

Ryan, William Granger, trans. *Jacobus de Voragine, The Golden Legend: Readings on the Saints*. 2 vols. Princeton: Princeton University Press, 1993.

Stokes, Whitley. "The Fifteen Tokens of Doomsday." *Revue Celtique* 28 (1907): 308–26.

Stone, Michael E. *Armenian Apocrypha Relating to Angels and Biblical Heroes*. EJL 45. Atlanta: SBL Press, 2016.

———. *Signs of Judgement, Onomastica Sacra and the Generations from Adam*. University of Pennsylvania Armenian Texts and Studies 3. Chico, CA: Scholars Press, 1981.

———. "Two Unpublished Eschatological Texts." *JSP* 18 (2009): 293–302. doi:10.1177/0951820709106105.

Strohal, Rudolf. *Stare hrvatske apokrifne priče i legende*. Bjelovar: Weiss, 1917.

Vialova, Svetlana Olegovna. *Glagoličeskij sbornik XV v. Rossijskaja nacional'naja biblioteka: Sobranie Ivana Berchicha, f. 67, Berchich No. 5. Glagoljski zbornik 15. st. Ruska nacionalna biblioteka, Zbirka Ivana Berčića, f. 67, Berčić br. 5. Knjiga 2*. Monumenta glagolitica Archiodioecesis Iadertinae 20.2. Zadar: Sveučilište u Zadru—Stalna izložba crkvene umjetnosti, 2016.

Žagar, Mateo, ed. *Libro od mnozijeh razloga 1520: Latinički prijepis s komentarima*. Zagreb: Matica hrvatska, 2020.

The Fifteen Signs before Judgment

STUDIES

Christensen, Mark Z. *Aztec and Maya Apocalypses: Old World Tales of Doom in a New World Setting*. Norman: University of Oklahoma Press, 2022.

———. *The Teabo Manuscript: Maya Christian Copybooks, Chilam Balams, and Native Text Production in Yucatán*. Austin, Texas: University of Texas Press, 2016.

Conley, C. H. "An Instance of the Fifteen Signs of Judgment in Shakespeare." *Modern Language Notes* 30 (1915): 41–44. doi:10.2307/2916899.

Davidson, Clifford. "The Signs of Doomsday in Drama and Art." *Historical Reflections/ Réflexions Historiques* 26 (2000): 223–45.

DiTommaso, Lorenzo. "Pseudepigrapha Notes III: 4. Old Testament Pseudepigrapha in the Yale University Manuscript Collection." *JSP* 20 (2010): 3–80. doi:10.1177/09518207103823.

Gayk, Shannon. "Apocalyptic Ecologies: Eschatology, the Ethics of Care, and the Fifteen Signs of the Doom in Early England." *Speculum* 96 (2021): 1–37. doi:10.1086/711658.

Gerhardt, Christof, and Nigel F. Palmer, eds. *Das Münchner Gericht von den 15 Zeichen vor dem Jüngsten Gericht: Nach der Handschrift der Bayerischen Staatsibibliothek Cgm 717; Edition und Kommentart*. Texte des späten Mittelalters und der frühen Neuzeit 41. Berlin: Schmidt, 2002.

Hawk, Brandon W. "Biblical Apocrypha as Medieval World Literature." *The Medieval Globe* 6, no. 2 (2020): 49–83. doi:10.17302/tmg.6-2.2.

———. "The *Fifteen Signs before Judgment* in Anglo-Saxon England: A Reassessment." *Journal of English and Germanic Philology* 117 (2018): 443–57. doi:10.5406/jenglgermphil.117.4.0443.

Heist, William W. *The Fifteen Signs before Doomsday*. East Lansing: Michigan State College Press, 1952.

———. "The Fifteen Signs before Judgement: Further Remarks." *Mediaeval Studies* 22 (1960): 192–203.

———. *Sermon Joyeux and Polemic: Two Sixteenth-Century Applications of the Legend of the Fifteen Signs*. University of North Carolina Studies in the Romance Languages and Literatures 73. Chapel Hill: University of North Carolina Press, 1968.

Lerner, Robert E. "Sign Theory: Some Scholastic Encounters with 'The Fifteen Signs before the Day of Judgement.'" *Journal of Ecclesiastical History* 73 (2022): 720–36. doi:10.1017/S0022046921002177.

McNamara, Martin. "Apocalyptic and Eschatological Texts in Irish Literature: Oriental Connections?" Pages 75–97 in *Apocalyptic and Eschatological Heritage: The Middle East and Celtic Realms*. Edited by Martin McNamara. Dublin: Four Courts Press, 2003.

———. "The (Fifteen) Signs before Doomsday in Irish Tradition." *Warszawskie Studia Teologiczne* 20 (2007): 223–54.

———. "The Signs before Doomsday." Pages 128–32 in *The Apocrypha in the Irish Church*. Dublin: Dublin Institute for Advanced Study, 1975.

Nakaš, Lejla. "Skazanije i pripovidjenije od Suda velikoga (*Libro od Mnozijeh Razloga* 49–56)." *Croatica: časopis za hrvatski jezik, književnost i kulturu* 45, no. 65 (2021): 109–24.

Steel, Karl. "Woofing and Weeping with Animals in the Last Days." *Postmedieval* 1 (2010): 187–93. doi:10.1057/pmed.2010.24.

Stone, Michael E. "Jewish Tradition, the Pseudepigrapha and the Christian West." Pages 431–49 in *The Aramaic Bible: Targums in Their Historical Context*. Edited by D. R. G. Beattie and M. J. McNamara. JSOTSup 166. Sheffield: Sheffield Academic, 1994.

Vučković, Josip. "Interpolacija stihova iz pjesme *Svit se konča* u izlaganju o Posljednjem sudu iz *Berčićeva zbornika br. 5*." *Ricerche slavistiche* NS 2, no. 62 (2019): 317–40.

Wagner, Daniela. *Die Fünfzehn Zeichen vor dem Jüngsten Gericht: Spätmittelalterliche Bildkonzepte für das Seelenheil*. Berlin: Reimer, 2016.

The Fifteen Signs before Judgment Day

Latin Versions

Pseudo-Bedan type, *Collectanea*

Jerome found in the annals of the Hebrews the fifteen signs of the fifteen days before the day of judgment.

Damian type, *Letter 92*

However, concerning the fifteen signs that will occur on the same number of days preceding the day of judgment, I do not consider it a waste to insert what I have learned to be reported by blessed Jerome, in his very own words. Indeed, just as I do not certainly accept the strength of the authority in these words, so neither do I wholly reject their fidelity. This matter, therefore, just as it has come to us, has been inserted simply in this manner, as also for the ancient Hebrew peoples—for whom the terror of divine judgment has increased—it may be made known from their pages. It says:

Comestor type, *Historia Scholastica*

So Jerome found in the annals of the Hebrews the signs of fifteen days before the day of judgment; but he does not say whether these days are going to be continuous or interrupted.

The Fifteen Signs before Judgment Day

¹On the first day, the sea will rise to the height of forty cubits[a] above the height of mountains and will be like a wall, and the rivers likewise.

¹Sign of the first day: all the seas will be raised to the height of fifteen cubits above the highest mountains (and) they will not damage the land but will stand like sea walls.

¹On the first day, the sea will rise forty cubits above the height of mountains, standing in its place like a wall.

Exod 14:22, 29
Gen 7:20

²On the second day, they will descend to the deep, so that one can barely see their height.

²Sign of the second day: all the seas will prostrate to the uttermost deep, so that human eyes can barely see them.

²On the second, it will descend, so that one can barely see it.

³On the third day, they will be level, just as they were at the beginning.

³Sign of the third day: all the seas will be restored to their ancient state, just as they were created at the beginning.

³On the third, all the beasts of the sea appearing above the sea will give roars as far as the heavens.

⁴On the fourth day, the fish and all the beasts of the sea will be gathered above the waters and will give cries and groans, whose meaning is known to none except God.

⁴Sign of the fourth day: all the beasts and all that move in the waters of the sea will be gathered and lifted above the Great Ocean, in contention together, bellowing and roaring; men will not know what they might say or what they might think, but God knows such, for whom all things live to render service. These four signs are about the sea and the three following are about the lower and upper air.

⁴On the fourth, the sea will burn, and the waters.

Jub. 23:18

---

a. Genesis 7:20 indicates that the biblical flood raised the waters fifteen cubits, but most of the versions of the Fifteen Signs indicate forty cubits for the eschatological flood on the first day; a few versions do indicate fifteen cubits, presumably because of influence from Genesis. Cf. the preface to the Hebrew version, where it mentions the biblical flood and fifteen cubits, but then also indicates forty cubits in the raising of the seas on the first day.

623

The Fifteen Signs before Judgment Day

	⁵On the fifth day, the waters themselves will burn from the rising to the setting (of the sun).	⁵Sign of the fifth day: all the birds of the heavens will gather in the plains, each kind in its own order, (and) these birds will be talking and crying together, neither eating nor drinking, fearing the coming of the judge.	⁵On the fifth, the grass and trees will give a bloody dew.
4 Ezra 5:5	⁶On the sixth day, all the grass and trees will give a bloody dew.	⁶Sign of the sixth day: streams of fire will arise against the appearance of the firmament, running from the setting to the rising of the sun.	⁶On the sixth, buildings will fall down.
	⁷On the seventh day, all buildings will be destroyed.	⁷Sign of the seventh day: all the stars wandering and stationary will strew fiery heads, as is seen in comets, and (be) a sign for the world and its inhabitants.	⁷On the seventh, the rocks will strike against each other.
	⁸On the eighth day, the rocks will fight each other, and each will divide itself into three parts, and each part will strike against another.	⁸Sign of the eighth day: there will be a great earthquake, so that no man is able to stand, nor any animal, but all will be cast down.	⁸On the eighth, there will be a general earthquake.
Ezek 38:20; 4 Ezra 9:3	⁹On the ninth day, there will be an earthquake, like there has not been since the beginning of the world.	⁹Sign of the ninth day: all stones great and small will be split into four parts, and each part will strike against the other parts, and no man will understand that sound, except God alone.	⁹On the ninth, the earth will be leveled.
Isa 40:4	¹⁰On the tenth day, all the hills and valleys will be turned back into a plain, and the earth will be level.	¹⁰Sign of the tenth day: all the trees of the woods and all the blades of grass will flow with a bloody dew.	¹⁰On the tenth, men will emerge from caves, and will go as if insane, nor will they be able to speak mutually.

¹¹On the eleventh day, men will emerge from their caves, and they will run around as if insane, and each one will not be able to answer the others.[a]	¹¹Sign of the eleventh day: all the mountains and hills and all human buildings previously built will be reduced to dust.	¹¹On the eleventh, the bones of the dead will rise, and will stand above the graves.	Ezek 37:12; Matt 27:52
¹²On the twelfth day, stars and tokens will fall from the sky.	¹²Sign of the twelfth day: all the animals of the earth will come from the forests and the mountains to the plains roaring and bellowing, neither eating nor drinking.	¹²On the twelfth, the stars will fall.	Isa 34:4; Matt 24:29; Rev 6:3; 8:10; 4 Ezra 5:5
¹³On the thirteenth day, the bones of the dead will be collected, and they rise as far as the grave.	¹³Sign of the thirteenth day: all graves will lie open from the rising to the setting of the sun, and the corpses will rise as far as the mouth of the grave.	¹³On the thirteenth, the living will die, so that they might rise with the dead.	Ezek 37:12; Matt 27:52
¹⁴On the fourteenth day, all men will die, so that they might rise together with the dead.	¹⁴Sign of the fourteenth day: the whole human race, those who were still to be found, will quickly go down from the dwellings and places in which they will be, neither understanding nor speaking, but running around as if insane.	¹⁴On the fourteenth, heavens and earth will burn.	
¹⁵On the fifteenth day, the earth will burn as far as the edge of hell, and afterward will be the Day of Judgment.	¹⁵Sign of the fifteenth day: (all) living humans will die, so that they will rise again with the dead who had died long before. The end, that is, the Day of Judgment.	¹⁵On the fifteenth, there will be new heavens, and a new earth, and all will rise.	

a. Men hiding from God in caves out of fear of judgment appears in Isa 2:10, 19, and 21, and could be the context for the reversal of their hiding through their exit from the caves; cf. the tenth day of the Hebrew version, which states that men will hide in caves and quotes Isa 2:21 and 19, thus aligning this sign more closely with the Bible.

Hebrew Version

Fifteen Signs before the Day of Judgment from The Book of Jerahmeel

And the waters increased to fifteen cubits above the mountains in the days of the Flood for thus everything was filled with the sins of men and thus will it happen on the Day of Judgment as happened in the Flood. For on the Day of Judgment the Holy One will judge his world as it says, *For by fire will the Lord execute judgment*. And the fire will increase to fifteen cubits above Mount Tabor, (and above the highest) of all mountains, the mountain called Olympus. For, from that mountain the Greeks made the reckoning of the Olympiads. For, each four years they would ascend Mount Olympus and they would write their victories in the dust of the soft earth which was on the mountain.[a] And the wind did not blow upon it because of its height for the atmosphere had no control over it. The birds of the heavens too do not flutter over it and people did not ascend it unless they placed a sponge soaked with water in their eyes and their nostrils because of the air.[b]

Fifteen days before the Day of Judgment there will be portents in the heavens and on the earth, and there will be great distress such as has not been from the time of existence of nations upon the earth. And the earth will quake and the mountains will melt and the tumult of the seas will roar in (its) streams, which a man shall relate to his son in fear of his heart that the Day of the Lord is close upon all the nations, that is the Day of the Lord which his anger will not contain and all flesh will not be saved except by repentance of abandoning its evil; and he will return to the Lord.

And these are the fifteen signs on fifteen days, each individual one on its day.

¹On the first day, the sea will issue forth from the limit of its boundary over all its shores and the water will rise to forty cubits above the highest mountains and will stand like a wall.

²On the second day, it will subside and dry up until (it is) few.

³On the third day, the great sea-monsters which are in the sea will be visible

---

a. This passage is meant to link biblical knowledge about Mount Tabor with classical knowledge about Mount Olympus as the highest mountain. It also evokes classical notions of reckoning time, which are appropriate for considering the timing of Judgment Day. Stone notes that the passage is rather forced, indicating the interpolation of this prefatory material with the Hebrew translation of a Latin text.

b. These details about Mount Olympus are parallel to similar statements in Isidore of Seville's *Etymologies* XIV.iv.13, which relates that the mountain "with its lofty peak rises up to such heights that neither clouds nor wind are perceived on its peak."

The Hebrew version and the Armenian recensions I and II are reprinted from Michael E. Stone, *Signs of Judgement, Onomastica Sacra and the Generations from Adam*. University of Pennsylvania Armenian Texts and Studies 3. Chico, CA: Scholars Press, 1981, 42-57, 3-40, and 4-9, reprinted by permission of the author. Armenian recension IIa is reprinted from Michael E. Stone, "Two Unpublished Eschatological Texts," *Journal for the Study of the Pseudepigrapha* 18, no. 4 (June 1, 2009): 293–302, reprinted by permission of SAGE Publications. Armenian recension III is reprinted from Michael E. Stone, *Armenian Apocrypha Relating to Angels and Biblical Heroes*, EJL 45 (Atlanta: SBL Press, 2016), 4–9, reprinted by permission of SBL Press.

because of the lack of water, and they are the *balaenas*,[a] and they low with their voice to the heavens.   Jub. 23:18

⁴On the fourth day, all the waters in the seas and lakes and rivers will become dry and dry up, and human, beast, and bird will thirst and groan.

⁵On the fifth day, human, beast, and bird will weep for water until they drip blood from their eyes and all the trees and the grasses will drip blood.   4 Ezra 5:5

⁶On the sixth day, there will be sounds and lightning and thunder and winds.

⁷On the seventh day, all the stones will be smashed and melt.

⁸On the eighth day, *the earth* will *rock and reel and the foundations of the heavens* will *tremble*.   2 Sam 22:8

⁹On the ninth day, the houses will fall and the terraces will fall and the trees and stone will cry out as a human cry.

¹⁰On the tenth day, men *will enter into the clefts of the cliffs and holes of the ground because of the terror of the Lord*.[b]   Isa 2:21, 19

¹¹On the eleventh day, the bones of men will be aroused from their graves and will be cast and dragged through the streets.   Jer 22:19; Ezek 37:12; Matt 27:52

¹²On the twelfth day, the stars and the luminaries will fall, and *the heavens will be rolled up as a book*, and the earth *will wear out like a garment*, and the graves will be opened, and the trumpets will be blown, and *many will awake*.   Isa 34:4; Matt 24:29; Rev 6:3; 8:10; 4 Ezra 5:5

Isa 34:4

Ps 102:26

¹³On the thirteenth day, they will die and *all flesh* will *perish together*.   Ezek 37:12; Matt 27:52

¹⁴On the fourteenth day, heaven and earth will be burnt and melt in the great fire and be destroyed.   Dan 12:2

Job 34:15

¹⁵On the fifteenth day, the new heavens and the new earth will be created, and *those wise who dwell in the dust shall awake and will shine like the brightness of the firmament*, and *like the sun as it rises in its might*.   Dan 12:2–3

¹⁶And they shall be gathered in the midst of the holy city Jerusalem, and *eye to eye they will see the return of the Lord to Zion*. And they will be gathered to the valley of Jehoshaphat for their judgment and then they will all be created with a new spirit and a new soul and a new creation, and they will come before the king, the Lord.   Judg 5:31

Isa 52:8

Joel 4:12

Ps 98:6

---

    a. Stone observes that this this phrase is added as an explanation of the sea-monsters and relates it to the Latin *belluae marinae* ("beasts of the sea") in the fourth day of the Pseudo-Bedan and Comestor versions. This is one instance that demonstrates the reliance of the Hebrew version on a Latin text.

    b. This sign in the Hebrew version is a reversal of the usual portent in other versions, which state that men will emerge from their caves rather than hide in them; the Hebrew version thus aligns this sign more closely with the Bible, especially by quoting Isa 2:21 and 19.

Armenian Recensions

RECENSION I	RECENSION II	RECENSION IIA	RECENSION III
And other doctors say, "We have read in the books of the Jews that there are going to be fifteen signs on fifteen days before the Judgment."	Concerning the coming of the Son of God and the end of the world, or in what fashion is the terrible Judgment. Now, we who hope for the coming of Christ our God, by the witness of the Sacred Scriptures, and by the word of Apostles and Prophets, and by the witness of the holy Gospel of Christ, (know) that in this fashion is the destruction of the world going to be at the last time. There are fifteen signs before the coming of Christ.	That which Yovhannes the doctor pronounced concerning the destruction of this world and concerning the Day of the Judgment and concerning the coming of Christ our God. We hope for the coming of Christ our God by the witness of the Sacred Scriptures and by the word of the Apostles and Prophets, and by the witness of the Gospel of Christ, that in this fashion will be the destruction of the world for the last time. There are fifteen signs before the coming of Christ.	Concerning the fifteen signs that are going to take place after the destruction of the Antichrist before the coming of Christ. After the destruction of the Antichrist there will remain forty days until the end of the world and the coming of Christ. After twenty-five days, on fifteen other days signs will commence, one sign on each day.
¹On the first day, the sea will rise forty cubits above the highest mountains and it will stand like a wall around the	¹On the first day, the sea will rise forty cubits above the mountains according to the measure of the Flood, and it will	¹The first: the seas will rise fifty cubits above Mount Masis[a] (more than) in the great flood. It stands like a wall; it does not	¹The sign of the first day will be thus: the seas in their places will rise up fifteen cubits (higher) than the highest mountains and

Exod 14:22, 29

a. Mount Masis is the traditional name for Mount Ararat.

world like a sign that God is able to destroy the earth as by a flood.	stand like a wall around the world that they might see and wonder and know that God is able to make this earth pass away through a flood.	drip upon the world, so that all will see and wonder and know that the Lord is able to make this world pass away through water.	will not go forth from their place, but the waters will stand like a wall. Gen 7:20
²On the second day, the sea will go down to a depth until it will be seen with difficulty.	²On the second day, the sea will go down to a depth of the dry land and no more water will be seen.	²The second day: the sea descends that the depths dry up and water is no longer visible.	²The sign of the second day: all the seas will become low and they will descend to the depths so that they will be barely able to see them.
³On the third day, very great whales, having come forth upon the face of the waters, will cry up to the heavens.	³On the third day, very great fish and whales having come forth, perish upon the sand. They will cry loudly and die and, having rotted, will make this world stink.	³The third day: fish and very great whales perish upon the sand. They cry loudly and roll over and having rotted they make this world stink.	³The sign of the third day: everything will return to its first form, as it was created formerly. Jub. 23:18
⁴On the fourth day, plants and shoots shall drip dew of blood.	⁴On the fourth day, trees and plants and all shoots shall drip dew of blood and dry up.	⁴The fourth day: trees and plants and all shoots will drip blood and dry up.	⁴The sign of the fourth day: all animals and those things which swarm in the sea's waters assemble upon the face of the sea, and like (a woman) in childbirth, they will raise up their voices, and they will call out and bellow, having apprehended their end. 4 Ezra 5:5

	⁵On the fifth day, all buildings shall be destroyed.	⁵On the fifth day, all buildings are destroyed.	⁵The fifth day: all buildings are destroyed.	⁵The sign of the fifth day: all the birds of the heavens shall gather in one place and weep and neither eat nor drink, knowing that their end has come.
	⁶On the sixth day, rocks shall be smitten against one another.	⁶On the sixth day, mountains and rocks smite against one another with a fearful thundering and are destroyed.	⁶The sixth day: the mountains and rocks crumble.	⁶The sign of the sixth day: fiery rivers will rise up from the west running over against the face of the firmament, as far as the east.
	⁷On the seventh day, the sea and the earth will be burnt with fire.	⁷On the seventh day, the sea and the earth will be burnt with fire.	⁷The seventh day: seas, heaven and earth will burn like fire.	⁷The sign of the seventh day: all the planets and the fixed stars will be scattered through their fiery tent.
Ezek 38:20; 4 Ezra 9:3	⁸On the eighth day, there will be a general earthquake.	⁸On the eighth day, there will be a general earthquake.	⁸The eighth day: there will be a general earthquake.	⁸The sign of the eighth day: the earth will shake mightily, so that no human will be able to stand, nor any living creature, but all will fall onto the ground.
Isa 40:4	⁹On the ninth day, all mountains and valleys will be leveled.	⁹On the ninth day, all mountains and valleys will be leveled.	⁹The ninth day: the few men who will remain wander around like animals. They can no longer speak with one another and all of them die.	⁹The sign of the ninth day: all very great and small stones will be split into four parts and each part strike against the other.

The Fifteen Signs before Judgment Day

¹⁰On the tenth day, men who are in the caves and caverns of the ground having come forth, they will go around like madmen and will be unable to speak with one another.ᵃ	¹⁰On the tenth day, men. . . .ᵇ	¹⁰The tenth day: all lands are leveled, all mountains crumble and are made low and all valleys will be filled up.	¹⁰The sign of the tenth day: all forest trees and green grasses shall drip bloody dew.	
¹¹On the eleventh day, the dead come outside their graves.	¹¹On the eleventh day, all die. They fall outside their graves.	¹¹The eleventh day: the bones and dust of the dead fall in every place.	¹¹The sign of the eleventh day: all the living beings of the earth,ᶜ mountains and all human buildings will crumble and turn into dust.	Ezek 37:12; Matt 27:52
¹²On the twelfth day, stars shall appear to have fallen from heaven.	¹²On the twelfth day, stars shall appear to fall from heaven.	¹²The twelfth day: fiery rivers glitter.	¹²The sign of the twelfth day: all the animals of the earth shall assemble in the field. They shall bellow and neither eat nor drink.	Isa 34:4; Matt 24:29; Rev 6:13, 8:10; 4 Ezra 5:5
¹³On the thirteenth day, all men shall die.	¹³On the thirteenth day, all men shall die.	¹³The thirteenth day: the stars are shaken.	¹³The sign of the thirteenth day: all the graves from the rising of the sun to the setting of the sun will be opened and the corpses will be stood up at the edge of the graves.	Ezek 37:12; Matt 27:52

   a. Men hiding from God in caves out of fear of judgment appear in Isa 2:10, 19, and 21, and could be the context for the reversal of their hiding through their exit from the caves; cf. the tenth day of the Hebrew version, which states that men will hide in caves and quotes Isa 2:21 and 19, thus aligning this sign more closely with the Bible.
   b. This recension is missing the rest of the tenth sign.
   c. Stone suggests that this phrase is only here because of dittography from below (day 12).

The Fifteen Signs before Judgment Day

¹⁴On the fourteenth day, there will be a new heaven and earth, and all the dead shall rise.	¹⁴On the fourteenth day, the heavens and earth shall be burnt like atmosphere.	¹⁴The fourteenth day: all creatures will burn and melt.	¹⁴The sign of the fourteenth day: all the human race who will be alive in (their) places and in their dwellings, having gone forth shall go around running like madmen.
¹⁵On the fifteenth day, the heavens and the earth shall be burnt, that is to say the atmosphere.	¹⁵On the fifteenth day, there will be a new heaven and earth.	¹⁵The fifteenth day: there will be new heavens and new earth.	¹⁵The sign of the fifteenth day: all men shall die so they may go forth to greet the dead.
	¹⁶Then Gabriel, the archangel, by God's command sounds the blast of the trumpet over the Pit of our Illuminator, "Behold, Christ is coming, rise up before him." Then the saints arise.	¹⁶Then divine grace shines and all creatures are adorned like flowers and will be united in form and nature. Like the divinely planted Garden, thus this earth will be paradisiacal and renewed and prepared and awaits the coming of the Son of God. But when the fire burns and cleans this earth it is renewed and becomes paradisiacal. For three days it awaits thus and after the third day a command goes forth (from) the throne of	¹⁶Then Christ shall come and all angels with him and the deniers and the Jews, and they shall say, "This is the Christ whom we crucified in Jerusalem. Now we truly see him and see the sign of the nails." And they shall smite themselves greatly because of that.

Matt 25:31

The Fifteen Signs before Judgment Day

Divinity and He sends the archangel Gabriel and he summons with a fearsome and dreadful sound.

And when he calls out this with a dreadful sound, all the earth trembles and is split and the souls from Adam up to that day are sent chased away. They put on their bodies like a garment.

And when Gabriel calls out, "Arise, O dead since Adam. Behold, Christ is coming, rise up, ascend before him."[a] And human bodies that were drowned in the sea and eaten by fish, and others who have been eaten by wild beasts and reptiles, and others who have decomposed in the earth and been consumed by worms and turned to dust.

And all souls and bodies are united and live and become a new man. But each person's garment is their deeds: the body

---

a. It is difficult to tell whether this quotation should end after the first sentence ("Arise ... Adam") or the second ("Behold ... him"). Stone does not indicate the close of the quotation, but it seems likeliest that Gabriel's speech should encompass both commands, since the rest of the passage is descriptive.

of the righteous is covered in light, it sends out rays like the sun.

The sinners are covered by their own deeds like a blackened cloud and gloomy darkness covered with mist and smoke. Thus they are not abandoned by the fogginess of a black cloud, which a person sees like the light of the sun. Thus the evil deeds of sinners do not abandon (them) so that they might see the light of the Divinity, for they are not worthy of seeing the glory of God.

Old Testament Pseudepigrapha Known Only by Title

by Liv Ingeborg Lied and Matthew P. Monger

References to writings ascribed to figures known from biblical texts and narratives are abundant in Jewish, Christian, Manichean, Muslim, and other texts from late antiquity and the Middle Ages. One category of such references mentions writings that survive neither as extant documents nor as excerpts or quotations of any substantial length. This entry provides a brief overview of potential Old Testament pseudepigrapha known only by title in sources dated to the period before the seventh century CE. We will also discuss some obvious methodological challenges facing the study.

The Old Testament pseudepigrapha (OTP) make up a category of writings that since the early eighteenth century has conventionally been defined in scholarship as Jewish and Christian writings—commonly claimed to be books—associated with or attributed to the name, life, or career of a figure known from the Hebrew Bible/Old Testament.[1] These books are assumed to have been composed in the first centuries before and after the turn of the Common Era, but have not been identifiable to modern scholars as part of either the Hebrew Bible or the Apocrypha or Deuterocanonical writings of the Christian West. This conventional definition implies that the category "OTP" is primarily a research category invented for analytical and exegetical purposes—it refers neither to books materially circulating together as a collection, nor to writings conceptually identifiable as such before the eighteenth century. When exploring extant textual materials from Jewish, Christian, Manichean, Muslim, and other provenances, there is no empirically

---

1. For the label, see Johann A. Fabricius, *Codex pseudepigraphus Veteris Testamenti: Collectus, castigatus, testimoniisque, censuris et animadversionibus illustratus* (Hamburg: Liebezeit, 1713). Cf. James A. Sanders, "Introduction: Why the Pseudepigrapha?" in *The Pseudepigrapha and Early Biblical Interpretation*, ed. James H. Charlesworth and Craig A. Evans, JSPSup 14 (Sheffield: JSOT Press, 1993), 13–19, esp. 14–15; Annette Yoshiko Reed, "The Modern Invention of 'Old Testament Pseudepigrapha,'" *JTS* NS 60 (2009): 403–36; Hindy Najman, "Interpretation as Primordial Writing: Jubilees and Its Authority Conferring Strategies," *JSJ* 30 (1999): 379–410, esp. 403–5; and cf. Eva Mroczek, *The Literary Imagination in Jewish Antiquity* (Oxford: Oxford University Press, 2016). In scholarship, the pseudepigrapha are typically imagined as books, i.e., as relatively substantial and distinct blocks of text, identifiable as discrete entities and as circulation units. The book-category can be applied to texts of various length. Important here is that the textual entity is a discrete, identifiable circulation unit. See, e.g., Michael E. Stone, "The Book(s) Attributed to Noah," *DSD* 13 (2006): 4–23, esp. 16; Liv Ingeborg Lied, "Text—Work—Manuscript: What Is an Old Testament Pseudepigraph*on*?," *JSP* 25 (2015): 150–65, doi:10.1177/0951820715621202. The assumption of a book format matters to the understanding of the category "pseudepigrapha" as such. Cf. the major modern editions, e.g., *APOT*, title page, iii; James H. Charlesworth, *OTP* 1:ix, xv–xvi, xxv; Richard Bauckham and James R. Davila, "Introduction," *MOTP* 1:xvii–xxxviii. Cf., furthermore, Mroczek, *Literary Imagination*. This entry does not mention book titles mentioned in the Hebrew Bible or in the New Testament. These books are discussed by Davila in "Quotations from Lost Books in the Hebrew Bible," *MOTP* 1:673–87.

identifiable division between OTP and other narratives set in the biblical story world. The accounts that we have are probably better interpreted as sources of a continuing interpretation, development, and narrative expansion of the lives and deeds of biblical figures, some of which have been labeled OTP.[2] The implication for the present entry is that although the selection described here exceeds the limits of traditional pseudepigrapha, the criteria of the conventional definition, which are arguably artificial, will to some extent have to be retained in order to single out potential cases.

This entry concerns pseudepigrapha that are known only by title. This means that the writings presented here are by necessity *postulated* books, known only through the medium of another writing. These books, thus, are not accessible in the shape of their own, assumed, textual contents. They exist as claimed textual objects. Since these claimed books are known by title, we may assume that they existed as conceptions of books, as cognitive placeholders. In the cases where the same title appears in several different sources from the period we address, we may also assume that there was a shared, historically circulating conception of that book at the time. Many of the books mentioned only by title in our sources are assumedly primarily fictitious, in the sense that they are serving fiction as literary devices, never circulating as anything else than imagined books, in that particular literary context. Other books may once have existed also as material documents, or as layout units in manuscripts, and could thus be considered "lost," but this information is often not available to us.[3] In yet other cases, the situation may be more complex. For instance, a book that initially was serving as a narrative device could later

---

[2]. For the purpose of writing this entry, we subscribe to a narrow definition of pseudepigrapha, in the sense that we have included only the potential OTP known only by title that are associated with or ascribed to a figure. The well-known modern edited volumes of OTP often also include various narrative expansions set in "biblical times." Hence, the potential would be there for this entry to include postulated books such as the potential Book of the Words of Truth and Reprimand mentioned as the outcome of Enoch's vision about the destiny of the Watchers in 1 En. 14:1. See Lawrence H. Schiffman, "Pseudepigrapha in the Pseudepigrapha: Mythical Books in Second Temple Literature," *RevQ* 21.81, no. 3 (2004): 429–38, esp. 432. For the Miscellanies, assumedly containing a lament for Sitis (T. Job 40:14), and The Miscellanies of Eliphas, containing the insulting words of Elihu (T. Job 41:6); claimed books by Philo of Alexandria, such as potential books missing from *Questions and Answers on Exodus*, from *Drunkenness* and from *Dreams*, see James R. Davila, "Wish List of Lost Books," https://paleojudaica.blogspot.com/2005/07/wish-list-of-lost-books-michael-pahl.html. For the so-called Book of the Covenant, mentioned by Didymus the Blind, *Commentary on Genesis*, e.g., 126,24–26, see James C. VanderKam, "The Book of the Covenant," in *MOTP* 1:28–32. For the claimed Book of the Stranger, Book of Questions, and Apocalypse of the Stranger associated with Adam and Eve and mentioned by Theodore bar Koni (*Liber Scholiorum* xi,63), and the Book of Remedies, mentioned in some manuscripts of m. Pesaḥ. 4.9, see Davila, "Wish List of Lost Books." However, this category of OTP would be impossible to pin down given the continuing interpretative flow of later Jewish, Christian, Manichean, and Islamic texts in particular. Expanding on the events of biblical times is precisely what many of these texts tend to do, e.g., in the form of chronographical and hagiographical treatises, as well as in commentaries and homilies. An attempt to draw lines between these categories of writings would be based on criteria in a modern research discourse, not on any identifiable divide in the available sources.

[3]. A layout unit is a section of text in a manuscript that is demarcated by paratextual or nonverbal layout features. The term could in principle be used for book-length entities and for shorter units. We apply it here for book-length units. That they are lost has been a central assumption and a key discourse in previous research. See in particular Montague R. James, *The Lost Apocrypha of the Old Testament: Their Titles and Fragments* (London: SPCK, 1920); but also James H. Charlesworth, "Introduction for the General Reader," *OTP* 1:xxi–xxxiv, esp. xxi–xxii.

be ascribed textual contents. Likewise, a book may fruitfully be described as fictitious in one context although a similarly named extant text is circulating elsewhere.[4]

Old Testament pseudepigrapha known only by title occur in extant lists of Scriptures, or in prose accounts listing and describing books. References to potential OTP known only by title also occur in manuscript marginalia and in the context of narrative prose texts. In this entry, we take the extant lists of Scriptures known from Greek, Latin, Syriac, Slavonic, and Armenian manuscript sources as our primary point of departure for establishing potential examples.[5] In addition, we will discuss some particularly interesting cases attested in narrative prose texts. This presentation is not meant to be exhaustive. Instead, we offer some important cases and a discussion of methodological issues related to the study of them.[6]

Potential Old Testament Pseudepigrapha Known Only By Title
Eldad and Modad

A book ascribed to Eldad (Elad) and Modad (Modat/Medad/Medat/Meldat), the two elders mentioned in Num 11:26–29, is noted in several of the lists of scripture that have come down to us from Greek, Armenian, and Slavonic traditions. It appears in the Stichometry of Nicephorus (assumedly ninth century), in the synopsis of Pseudo-Athanasius (possibly sixth century), in the addition to the List of Sixty Books (probably seventh century), in the list included in Mechithar of Aïrvank's Armenian chronicle (fourteenth century), as well as in the Slavonic 1073 Svjatoslav Miscellany and the Taktikon by Nikon of the Black Mountain (eleventh century).[7] All these lists identify the book as "apocryphal," or "secret."[8] According to the Stichometry of Nicephorus, this book consisted of no more than four hundred lines (*stichoi*). If this is correct, we must envision a relatively short book. A book of Eldad and Modad is mentioned also in the Shepherd of Hermas (2.3.4), offering a brief, potential, quote or paraphrase: "'The Lord is near to those who turn to him,' as it is written in the book of Eldad and Modat, who prophesied to the people in the wilderness."[9] The origin and character of this quote are debated, though, and no other certain paraphrases of the claimed book are known.[10]

---

4. Cf. the discussion in the latter part of this entry. See also Liv Ingeborg Lied, Marianne Bjelland Kartzow, and Esther Brownsmith, "Books Known Only by Title," *JSP* 32 (2023): 303–22, doi:10.1177/095182072311617.

5. Cf. also the convenient overview in Albert-Marie Denis, *Introduction aux pseudépigraphes grecs d'Ancien Testament*, SVTP 1 (Leiden: Brill, 1970), xiv–xv.

6. Due to the artificial character of the category OTP, any attempt to create a comprehensive list of OTP known only by title would be nonsensical.

7. The Armenian and Slavonic lists are known to the authors of this entry only through secondary literature. See, e.g., Denis, *Introduction*, ix–xvi; Andrei Orlov, *Selected Studies in the Slavonic Pseudepigrapha*, SVTP 23 (Leiden: Brill 2009), 3; Slavomír Čéplö, "Books Known Only by Their Names from Booklists in the Slavia Orthodoxa," in *Unruly Books: Rethinking Ancient and Academic Imaginations of Religious Texts*, ed. Esther Brownsmith, Marianne Bjelland Kartzow, and Liv Ingeborg Lied (forthcoming).

8. See further, James, *Lost Apocrypha*, xiii–xiv.

9. Translation in J. B. Lightfoot and John R. Harmer, *The Apostolic Fathers: Greek Texts and English Translations of Their Writings*, ed. and rev. Michael W. Holmes, 2nd ed. (Grand Rapids: Baker, 1992), 345.

10. Cf. James, *Lost Apocrypha*, 38–40; Denis, *Introduction*, 142–45; James R. Davila, "A Worst-Case Scenario (Eldad and Modad)," https://web.archive.org/web/20190502192456/https://www.st-andrews.ac.uk/divinity/rt/otp/abstracts/eldad. See also, Richard Bauckham, "Eldad and Modad," *MOTP* 1:244–56. Bauckham argues that the New Testament letter of Jas 4:4–8 quotes from Eldad and Modad without naming the source.

The Book concerning the Giant Named Ogias

Among the apocryphal books listed in the Latin Gelasian Decree (probably sixth century) is "The book concerning the giant named Ogias, who according to the account of the heretics fought with the dragon after the flood, apocryphal."[11] The Gelasian Decree ascribes this book to "heretics," and categorizes it as apocryphal. It has been suggested that the book should be identified with the Manichean Book of Giants, and this remains a possibility given the shared focus on giants and battle in both books.[12] The fragments of a Book of Giants among the Dead Sea Scrolls are well known, and traditions about giants were certainly kept alive in Jewish and Christian milieus.[13] Even though these accounts of giants are many, and the giant Ogias appears in several accounts,[14] the mention in the Gelasian Decree is the only reference to a *book* about this particular giant.[15] No excerpts or paraphrases of such a book are extant, nor is such a book referred to by this title in any other list or literary source known to us.[16]

Lamech

A book of Lamech, probably Lamech the father of Noah, is listed among the apocryphal books in the List of Sixty Books, and also occurs in Slavonic in the Taktikon and in the so-called Pogodin's Nomokanon (fourteenth century). Although it is evident that various narratives about Lamech have been circulating, and that story clusters made their way into other compositions, no *book* of Lamech is extant.[17]

The Book, concerning the Daughters of Adam, of Leptogensis

In its list of apocryphal books, the Gelasian Decree mentions a book entitled Liber de filiabus Adae Leptogeneseos, apocryphus.[18] This title has been interpreted as a reference

---

11. *Liber de Ogia nomine gigante qui post diluvium cum dracone ab hereticis pugnasse perhibetur, apocryphus.*

12. Cf. W. B. Henning, *The Book of Giants: The Fallen Angels and Their Giant Sons* (London: Forgotten Books, 2007), 54, 71–72; John C. Reeves, *Jewish Lore in Manichean Cosmogony: Studies in the* Book of Giants *Traditions*, HUCM 14 (Cincinnati: Hebrew Union College Press, 1992), 21–22. See also the introduction to the Book of Giants by James R. Davila and the introduction to the Manichean Book of Giants by Prods Oktor Skjærvø in this volume.

13. Florentino García Martínez, *Qumran and Apocalyptic: Studies on the Aramaic Texts from Qumrân*, STDJ 9 (Leiden: Brill, 1992), 97–115; Reeves, *Jewish Lore*, 51–164. See also the translation of the Aramaic Book of Giants by Loren T. Stuckenbruck in this volume.

14. Cf. Robert A. Kraft, "Og and the Giants," http://ccat.sas.upenn.edu/rak//courses/735/Parabiblical/jamesog.htm.

15. For the name and identification of the figure(s) Ogias/Og/Ohya/'Ohyah, see Reeves, *Jewish Lore*, 42 n. 85.

16. Cf. James, *Lost Apocrypha*, 40–42; Denis, *Introduction*, xiii; J. T. Milik, "Problèmes de la littérature hénochique à la lumière des fragments araméens de Qumrân," *HTR* 64 (1971): 330–78; Henning, *Book of Giants*, 54, 71–72.

17. For the debates about the Genesis Apocryphon and a potential book of Lamech, see Nahman Avigad and Yigael Yadin, *A Genesis Apocryphon* (Jerusalem: Magnes, 1956), 38; Richard C. Steiner, "The Heading of the *Book of the Words of Noah* on a Fragment of the Genesis Apocryphon: New Light on a 'Lost' Work," *DSD* 2 (1995): 66–71 esp. 69–71. Narratives of Lamech are included and developed, e.g., in the Cave of Treasures and the *Palaea Historica*. See Davila, "Lost Book Found/Update (7 September 2011)," https://paleojudaica.blogspot.com/2006/08/lost-book-found-regular-readers-will.html. See further James, *Lost Apocrypha*, 10–11; Denis, *Introduction*, xiii.

18. According to the critical edition in Ernst von Dobschütz, *Das Decretum Gelasianum de libris*

to Jubilees.[19] However, the manuscripts of the Gelasian Decree show a wide range of variants for this title and there is good reason to question whether Jubilees as a whole is what is referred to here. Some Latin manuscripts omit the word *filiabus*, thus pointing to a Book of Adam, while others omit the word *Leptogenesis*, making the connection to Jubilees tenuous.[20] If we accept the title as it is given in the critical editions, it could also be interpreted as referring to a book concerning the daughters of Adam, *of* Leptogenesis, but not itself identifiable as Leptogenesis.[21] The title could be a book about the daughters of Adam, a book excerpted from, associated with, or otherwise placed in the tradition of Leptogenesis.

No book named Liber de filiabus Adae is extant. Still, a possibility that has been given some attention in scholarship is that the title may be associated with a tradition that transmitted names given to the women who were daughters of Adam and/or married to his sons and the first patriarchs found in Greek, Syriac, Hebrew, Arabic, and Armenian contexts.[22] The names of the women in these sources are ultimately derived from Jubilees and are directly associated with Jubilees/Leptogenesis in some of the manuscripts, but they circulated independently of Jubilees.[23] Today, these names are extant as notes, glosses, lists, and brief prose catalogs, and it is possible that this has always been their primary form of circulation. We may not rule out, though, that someone has conceived of them as (belonging to) a book related to, but not identical with, Jubilees/Leptogenesis.

Book(s) of Noriah

In the *Panarion* (26,1,3–4), Epiphanius of Salamis mentions a book of Noriah, identified in this context as the wife of Noah.[24] According to Epiphanius, framing his account using

---

recipiendis et non recipiendis in kritischem Text herausgegeben und untersucht, TUGAL 38.4 (Leipzig: Hinrich, 1912), 12.

19. Cf., e.g., Charlesworth, "Introduction for the General Reader," *OTP*, xxii. The name *hē leptē Genesis, ta lepta Genesis*, was often applied in Greek sources to Jubilees, potentially, a section or a different format of Jubilees—imagined as "a detailed Genesis," or "details of Genesis." Cf. Simon Franklin, "A Note on a Pseudepigraphal Allusion in Oxyrhynchus Papyrus No. 4365," *VT* 48 (1998): 95–96, doi:10.1163/1568533982722009.

20. On the variance of the manuscripts for this entry in the Gelasian Decree, see Matthew P. Monger, "The Book of the Daughters of Adam in the Gelasian Decree," forthcoming.

21. See Jean-Baptiste Frey, "Apocryphes de l'Ancient Testament, généralités sur le sens du mot apocryphe et sur les apocryphes," *DBSup* 1:354–57; Denis, *Introduction*, 12, 160.

22. For an overview and discussion see Tal Ilan, "Biblical Women's Names in the Apocryphal Traditions," *JSP* 11 (1993): 3–67, doi:10.1177/095182079300001101; and W. Lowndes Lipscomb, "A Tradition from the Book of Jubilees in Armenian," *JJS* 29 (1978): 149–63. Cf. Matthew P. Monger, *The Names of the Wives of the Patriarchs: A Study of Transmission and Reception in Early Jewish, Christian, and Muslim Sources* (forthcoming).

23. The title of the list in the Syriac BL Add 12,154 f. 180r reads "The names of the wives of the patriarchs according to the book that among the Hebrews is called Jubilees."

24. The name Noriah/Noraia apparently referred to various, possibly overlapping, female figures in late antiquity, such as the daughter of Adam and Eve, the sister/wife of Seth. The name also circulates in variant versions, such as Norea/Orea/Oraia/Horaia/Nora/Nuraita/Nuhraita, as well as Naamah. See Birger A. Pearson, "Revisiting Norea," in *Images of the Feminine in Gnosticism*, ed. Karen L. King, SAC (Philadelphia: Fortress, 1988), 265–75, esp. 265–66; and Pearson, "The *Book of Allogenes* (CT,4) and Sethian Gnosticism," in *Gnosticism, Platonism and the Late Ancient World: Essays in Honour of John D. Turner*, ed. Kevin Corrigan and Tuomas Rasimus, Nag Hammadi and Manichaean Studies 82 (Leiden: Brill, 2013), 105–16, esp. 112–13. The Norea-figure is also known from the extant Thought of Norea (NHC IX 2). This name/figure is known from several sources both before and after the assumed date of

the typical heresiological rhetoric, this book is a forged nonsensical book, ascribed to a nonsensical name and blending mythology and falsehood, telling a story about the various ways in which Noriah delayed the building of Noah's ark (26,1,7–9). A First Book of Noraia/Book of Noraia is mentioned also in the Nag Hammadi treatise On the Origin of the World (NHC II 102.10–11).[25] According to this treatise, the book contains the names of the female entities associated with the seven androgynous forces of the heavens. On the Origin of the World 102.24–25 also refers to an Account [Logos] of Oraia, potentially conceived as the same books as the Book of Noraia, a Book of Solomon, as well as an Archangelic (Book) of the Prophet Moses (II 102.9), and the Seventh Universe of the Prophet Hieralias (II 112.24). All these claimed books are mentioned and probably function in the text as reference works, as archives of knowledge in which the reader may find more detailed accounts.[26]

Books of Seth

Several accounts from late antiquity mention books and writings ascribed to Seth,[27] the son of Adam and Eve. Books ascribed to Seth are mentioned, for instance, by Epiphanius (*Panarion* 26, 8.1; 40.7.4) and by (Pseudo-)Chrysostom in *Commentary on Matt.* 2:2. Epiphanius refers in general terms to "many books" of Seth. Since some writings ascribed to Seth are indeed extant, for instance in the Nag Hammadi codices, some of the books mentioned by Epiphanius may in fact be available to us.[28]

One writing ascribed to Seth in heresiological literature that is likely to be available only in the form of a title, surviving primarily as a conceived, postulated book, is the so-called Paraphrase of Seth, mentioned in *Refutation of All Heresies* (Hipp.) 5.17. According to this brief account, the Paraphrase of Seth contains all the secret tenets of the Sethians, providing an overview of their entire doctrine to be consulted by the interested reader.

The so-called Tablets, or Pillars of Seth, mentioned in Josephus, *A. J.* 1.70, is another postulated writing ascribed to Seth. According to Josephus, these inscribed pillars, one in stone and one in brick, contained received wisdom concerning the heavenly bodies and their order. This wisdom was inscribed on these pillars in order to be preserved beyond

---

composition of the Nag Hammadi treatises. Cf. Pearson, "Revisiting Norea," 265–66; and Steven M. Wasserstrom, "Jewish Pseudepigrapha in Muslim Literature: A Bibliographical and Methodological Sketch," in *Tracing the Threads: Studies in the Vitality of Jewish Pseudepigrapha*, ed. John C. Reeves, EJL 6 (Atlanta: Scholars Press, 1994), 87–114, esp. 97–99.

25. It is not clear if the Noraia of On the Origin of the World is identifiable as Noah's wife or some of these other figures of the antediluvian world mentioned by this or a similar name. Note that the treatise, On the Origin of the World, is not named in the codex, but commonly referred to as such in scholarship.

26. Cf., e.g., James, *Lost Apocrypha*, 12; Robert A. Kraft, "The Pseudepigrapha in Christianity," in Reeves, *Tracing the Threads*, 55–86, esp. 67; Denis, *Introduction*, 301.

27. Also, Sith/Sethel.

28. Cf. The Three Steles of Seth (NHC VII 5), The Second Treatise of the Great Seth (NHC VII 2), as well as the Gospel of the Egyptians, which is ascribed to Seth. Cf., e.g., M. Tardieu, "Les livres mis sous le nom de Seth et les Séthiens de l'hérésiologie," in *Gnosis and Gnosticism: Papers Read at the Seventh International Conference on Patristic Studies (Oxford, September 8th–13th 1975)*, ed. M. Krause, NHS 8 (Leiden: Brill, 1977), 204–10, doi:10.1163/9789004437159_022; John C. Reeves, *Heralds of That Good Realm: Syro-Mesopotamian Gnosis and Jewish Traditions*, Nag Hammadi and Manichaean Studies 41 (Leiden: Brill, 1996), 37. Cf. further for later Armenian texts associated with Seth and Adam, Michael E. Stone, *Armenian Apocrypha Relating to the Patriarchs and Prophets* (Jerusalem: Israel Academy of Sciences and Humanities, 1982), esp. 4–6. Cf. also the passage in Pseudo-Chrysostom mentioned above. Alexander Toepel, "The Apocryphon of Seth," *MOTP* 1:33–38. Cf., furthermore, the discussion of method, below.

the antediluvian world. Stone and brick were chosen as writing materials to prevent the inscribed texts from being destroyed by either fire or water.[29] Again, the Tablets of Seth are fruitfully understood as fictitious, serving the narrative account where we find it.[30]

The Hymnal of the Daughters of Job

Chapters 46 to 51 of the Testament of Job contain a description of the inheritance of Job's three daughters.[31] According to T. Job 46–47, these three daughters inherit heavenly ribbons that they wrap around their bodies. The ribbons make each of them ecstatically utter a hymn, patterned on a heavenly model, which is eventually written down. The hymn of Hemera, named "The Spirit" by some modern interpreters of the Testament of Job, was written down on her garment, or alternatively on her stele/gravestone.[32] "The Hymns of Kassia" contains an account of the creation of the heavens, alternatively hymns entitled "The Creation of the Heavens."[33] The glory of the father, alternatively, "The Glory of the Father," is recorded in "The Prayers of Amaltheias-Keras," the prayers uttered by the third daughter.[34] According to T. Job 51:3–4, the hymns/prayers are written down. Testament of Job 51:3 may suggest that the daughters took notes for each other.[35] Testament of Job 51:4 further claims that their uncle, Nereos, then recorded "a complete book of most of the contents of hymns that had issued from the three daughters."[36]

The hymnal of the daughters of Job is as far as we know mentioned only in this particular narrative context. It is very likely to be fictitious, serving the narrative account of which it is a part in the Testament of Job. The passage in the Testament of Job is renowned for its description of ecstatic speech, and for casting women in the role as mediators of revealed knowledge. Seeing a potential reference to female scribes is rare, and hence interesting, as is the description of the special circumstance of Nereos's recording of the book in the presence of the holy angel/Holy Spirit.

---

29. Cf., furthermore, the account of a book of memorial, mentioning the name of Seth in particular (although not being ascribed to him), in 4Q416 (4QSapiental Work A^b) I, 14–16.

30. It is possible that the Nag Hammadi text, the Three Steles of Seth, was interpreted as the tablets ascribed to Seth mentioned by Josephus.

31. Commonly named Hemera, Kassia, and Amaltheia/Amaltheias-Keras.

32. Named "The Spirit" by Robert A. Kraft, *The Testament of Job according to the SV Text*, Texts and Translations 5, Pseudepigrapha Series 4 (Missoula, MT: Society of Biblical Literature; Scholars Press, 1974), 82–83; followed by R. P. Spittler, "Testament of Job," *OTP* 1:829–68, esp. 866. For the location of the writing, see Spittler, "Testament of Job," 866; Berndt Schaller, "Das Testament Hiobs," in *Unterweisung in lehrhafter Form*, ed. Werner Georg Kümmel, vol 3.3 of *Jüdische Schriften aus hellenistisch-römischer Zeit* (Gütersloh: Gütersloher Verlagshaus, 2001), 301–88, esp. 369 and n. g; Gesa Schenke, "Testament of Job (Coptic Fragments)," *MOTP* 1:160–75, esp. 174.

33. Kraft, *Testament of Job*, 83.

34. Potentially, "The Prayers of Amaltheia's Horn," or "the unchangeable prayers" (cf. Spittler, "Testament of Job," 866; and Schenke, "Testament of Job," 175).

35. Alternatively, they explained the speech of their sister. The interpretation of this verse varies (Cf. Kraft, *Testament of Job*, 83, followed by Spittler, "Testament of Job," 866, and Schenke, "Testament of Job," 175).

36. So Spittler, "Testament of Job," 866. Or, potentially, he did not (Kraft, *Testament of Job*, 83). In the Coptic version, he expressly did not, due to their specific character, being the splendors of God (so Schenke, "Testament of Job," 175). For a translation and discussion of the Slavonic version, see Maria Cioată (Haralambakis), *The Testament of Job: Text, Narrative and Reception History*, LSTS 80 (London: T&T Clark, 2012), esp. appendix C.

Books in the Service of Lineage and Preservation of Wisdom

In its account of the death of Jacob, Jubilees says, "He gave all his books and the books of his fathers to his son Levi so that he could preserve them and renew them for his sons until today" (Jub. 45:16).[37] The transmission of books from one generation to the next is a frequently occurring literary topos in Jewish and Christian texts of (late) antiquity and beyond.[38] In many accounts, as in the case of Jub. 45:16, above, these books are not named or further identified, serving *en bloc*, as inherited wisdom and evidence put down in writing.[39] In other accounts, the book in question is not further named, but explicitly associated with the one who puts it down in writing, as in 1 En. 82:1–2, where Enoch passes down books to Methuselah, and in Jub. 10:13–14 where Noah writes down all his knowledge about healing in a potential book of Noah and passes it down to Shem.[40] On some occasions, longer lists or narrative prose catalogs of such books appear. In 2 En. 33:9–10, the handwritings of the fathers, Adam, Seth, Enosh, Kainan, Maleleil and Ared, are handed over to Enoch. Such lists of books probably served to display the continuity in the transmission of wisdom.[41] In yet other cases, such as in the Cologne Mani Codex, these books are further identified by genre as the Apocalypses of Adam, Sethel, Enosh, Shem, and Enoch. As John C. Reeves and David Frankfurter have suggested, it is likely that the function of these claimed apocalypses is primarily to ensure a lineage of authoritative revelatory figures, locating Mani at the culmination of it.[42]

Some figures appear more often than others. Books associated with Enoch or claimed to be written down by Enoch are mentioned particularly often in this capacity, as are books of other antediluvian figures such as Adam, Noah, Lamech, and Seth.[43] Books ascribed to other important biblical figures, such as Jacob, Levi, Moses, and the major prophets may serve similar narrative purposes.

More OTP Known Only by Title?

The above selection of entries is based on the criterion that these potential books are known only by title, allowing for the briefest quotes and paraphrases of the books' contents. If we had cast our net wider, including books that are named but also described by one or more paragraph-length paraphrases of some of its contents, more books could have been added. A primary example of such a book would be the Gospel of Eve, named,

---

37. Translation by James C. VanderKam, *The Book of Jubileess: A Critical Text*, CSCO 511, Scriptores Aethiopici 88 (Leuven: Peeters, 1989), 299–300.

38. Cf., e.g., Jub. 10:14; 4Q213a (4QAramiac Levi^a) I, 1–8; 4Q542 (4QTestament of Qahat) II, 9–11; 4Q543 (4QVisions of Amram^a) I,1 ; T. Mos. 1:15–18. Cf. Schiffman, "Pseudepigrapha in the Pseudepigrapha," 433–38.

39. The fact that they are written accounts matters. Cf. Najman, "Interpretation as Primordial Writing," 381–84; cf. furthermore, Mladen Popovic, "Pseudepigraphy and a Scribal Sense of the Past in the Ancient Mediterranean: A Copy of the Book of the Words of the Vision of Amram," in *Is There a Text in This Cave? Studies in the Textuality of the Dead Sea Scrolls in Honour of George J. Brooke*, ed. Ariel Feldman, Maria Cioată, and Charlotte Hempel, STDJ 119 (Leiden: Brill, 2017), 308–13, esp. 308, 312–13.

40. For the long-standing debate about the potential Book of Noah, see Stone, "Book(s) Attributed to Noah"; and Martha Himmelfarb, "The Book of Noah," *MOTP* 1:40–46.

41. Cf., e.g., Najman, "Interpretation as Primordial Writing," 385; Stone, "Book(s) Attributed to Noah," 14.

42. Reeves, *Heralds*, 17; Frankfurter, "Apocalypses Real and Alleged in the Mani Codex," *Numen* 44 (1997): 60–73, esp. 61, doi:10.1163/1568527972629876. See also Reeves's chapter in this volume on the alleged apocalypses cited in the Cologne Mani Codex.

43. Cf., e.g., Reeves, *Heralds*, 37; Frankfurter, "Apocalypses," 63, 65–66.

quoted, and refuted by Epiphanius in *Panarion* 26.2.6–7.[44] Other examples are the books of Abramos mentioned by Vettius Valens (*Anthologiae* 2.28.1–3).[45]

A wider list could also have included potential books, sometimes presented as such in scholarship, based on the description in textual accounts as "Words of," "Prophecy of," or "A report has it." Examples of such potential books are the alleged Apocryphon of Eber,[46] or the Prophecy of Ham, the latter mentioned by Clement of Alexandria (*Strom.* 6.6; 53.5).[47] These occurrences were not included in this entry, because their status and format as written accounts are not clear. We acknowledge that "Words of . . ." is a conventional title formula, appearing in the titles of several of the books of the Hebrew Bible.[48] "Prophecy of . . ." may equally imply a book format. Still, when the phrase is all that is available to us, we considered these cases to be too uncertain to be included, since accounts identified as such may simply be references to narratives where words are uttered.

Finally, this entry ends its exploration in the seventh century. This chronological limit is of course artificial, since the mention of books associated with biblical figures certainly continues well beyond the seventh century. In fact, there is a profusion of such books in later accounts.[49] By way of example, scrolls of Abraham and Moses, of unclear identification, are mentioned in the Qur'an (e.g., Sura 53:36–37; and 87:18–19), and later Islamic tradition describes writings attributed to Adam, Seth, Enoch, Abraham, and Moses.[50] The eighth-century Chronicle of Zuqnin refers to books of Seth, as does the thirteenth-century Book of the Bee. The Book of the Bee also ascribes writings to Enosh (29.19–20). According to Reeves, a claimed Book of Enoch also appears in the Mandean Right Ginzā, and potential books of Shem are mentioned in the Book of Asaph, as well as in Karaite sources.[51] An Apocalypse of Enoch is mentioned by Michael Rabo's in his twelfth-century, Syriac, *Chronicle* (11:22).[52] It is not known to what it refers. In the Armenian The Names, Works, and Deaths of the Holy Prophets 17, books of Nathan and Agapa, Sadok, Ak'ia and Salamut are mentioned;[53] and the Zohar refers to books of Adam and of Enoch.[54]

Notes on Method: Critical Remarks

The single most striking trait of the initial selection of claimed books presented as OTP known only by title in this entry is that it does not include books ascribed to the most

---

44. Cf., James, *Lost Apocrypha*, 8; Denis, *Introduction*, 302.
45. James E. Bowley, "The Compositions of Abraham," in Reeves, *Tracing the Threads*, 215–38, esp. 231–32.
46. Cf. Gilles Dorival, "Le patriarche Héber et la tour de Babel: un apocryphe disparu?" in *Poussières de christianisme et de judaisme antiques: Études reunites en l'honneur de Jean-Daniel Keastli et Éric Junod*, ed. Albert Frey and Rémi Grounelle (Lausanne: Éditions du Zébre, 2007), 181–201; James C. VanderKam, "The Apocryphon of Eber," *MOTP* 1:47–52.
47. Cf. James, *Lost Apocrypha*, 15; Kraft, "Pseudepigrapha in Christianity," 65; and furthermore, the discussion below.
48. Cf. Steiner, "Heading," 66–67.
49. Cf. Reeves, *Heralds*, 38.
50. Cf., Matthew P. Monger, "Books Known Only by Reference in the Qur'an," in Brownsmith, Kartzow, and Lied, *Unruly Books*; Bowley, "Compositions of Abraham," 218–19.
51. Reeves, *Heralds*, 38, 53; Stone, "Book(s) Attributed to Noah," 12.
52. Sebastian P. Brock, "Apocalypses," in *Gorgias Encyclopedic Dictionary of the Syriac Heritage*, ed. Sebastian P. Brock, Aaron M. Butts, and George A. Kiraz (Piscataway, NJ: Gorgias, 2011), 25–27, esp. 26.
53. Stone, *Armenian Apocrypha*, 173, cf. 175.
54. Schiffmann, "Pseudepigrapha in the Pseudepigrapha," 437–38.

well-known biblical figures. Indeed, accounts from late antiquity are ripe with references to books ascribed to all the major patriarchs, kings, prophets, and some other salient figures from the biblical narrative.[55] Books ascribed to Adam, Enoch, and Moses are particularly frequent, occurring, for instance, in most of the surviving Christian lists and catalogs of "apocryphal" or "false" scriptures. Such claimed books may also be mentioned *en bloc* for instance in heresiological literature,[56] and books ascribed to these figures are attested in Jewish, Christian, Manichean, and Muslim narrative texts—across manuscript and linguistic traditions.[57] These postulated books have not been treated as OTP known only by title here, although some of the titles mentioned in these accounts may well be so,[58] because it is impossible to verify whether or not the titles refer to a known work, or something else.

This situation invites some interesting methodological reflections. First of all, there is no one-to-one relationship between a title mentioned in one context and an extant text in another.[59] This means that in principle we do not know whether a title mentioned in a list or in another account is identifiable with surviving textual contents. Most of the major biblical figures have books ascribed to them, but due to the profusion of extant books associated with them, for instance, in relatively late Armenian and Slavonic traditions,[60] and due to the fragmentary survival of many such writings from late antiquity, the task of identifying those that are known only by title is incommensurable and methodologically problematic. The implications are, for instance, that a book mentioned in a narrative account, serving as a literary device in that context, may share its name with a book that is extant somewhere else and still be fruitfully interpreted as an imaginary book in the narrative context in which it appears. This may, for instance, be the case with the references to a Book of Enoch in the Greek Testaments of the Twelve Patriarchs, where the book serves as a testimony against the wicked, while the paraphrased contents do not match known Enochic books.[61] Another case that exemplifies the same dilemma is the case of the Testament/Assumption of Moses. The List of Sixty Books, the Stichometry of Nicephorus, the synopsis of Pseudo-Athanasius, as well as the Taktikon and the 1073 Svjatoslav Miscellany mention both a Testament and an Assumption of Moses.[62] A partly preserved Latin text is extant in the manuscript Biblioteca Ambrosiana C 73 Inf. The identification of this extant text is widely debated in scholarship. The text may be identifiable as one of them, both, or neither of them.[63] If so, one, none, or both are eligible as OTP known only by title.[64]

---

55. The category of prophets includes figures described as such in later, Christian traditions, such as Baruch.

56. E.g., Const. ap. VI.16.

57. Cf., e.g., Martha Himmelfarb, "Some Echoes of *Jubilees* in Medieval Hebrew Literature," in Reeves, *Tracing the Threads*, 115–42; Schiffman, "Pseudepigrapha in the Pseudepigrapha," 437; Wasserstrom, "Jewish Pseudepigrapha in Muslim Literature"; Reeves, *Heralds*.

58. As, e.g., the so-called Book of the Mystical Words of Moses (cf. James, *Lost Apocrypha*, 51).

59. Cf. Davila, "Worst-Case Scenario."

60. Stone, *Armenian Apocrypha*, xi–xii; Orlov, *Selected Studies*, 3–7.

61. T. Sim. 5:4; T. Levi 10:5; T. Dan 5:6; T. Naph. 4:1; T. Benj. 9:1, and potentially, T. Levi 14:1; T. Jud. 18:1.

62. The Assumption of Moses is also mentioned in several other accounts from late antiquity. See Richard Bauckham, *Jude and the Relatives of Jesus in the Early Church* (Edinburgh: T&T Clark, 1990), 263. Also cf. Bauckham's chapter on the Assumption and Testament of Moses in this volume.

63. See, in particular, Richard Bauckham, *Jude and the Relatives of Jesus*, 235–80, esp. 238; James R. Davila, *The Provenance of the Pseudepigrapha: Jewish, Christian, or Other?*, JSJSup 105 (Leiden: Brill, 2005), 149–54. The Latin fragment is translated by J. Priest, "Testament of Moses," *OTP* 1:919–34.

64. In some cases, a writing that originates as a fictitious writing may later be associated with a circulating book-entity. This may well be the case with Baruch's epistle to Babylon, mentioned in 2 Bar. 77:19,

Second, it is evident that titles, figures, and books are often confused—in the past as they are today. Some books, for instance, the book today commonly referred to as Jubilees/Leptogenesis/Parva genesis (or parts of it), has been associated with many other names, such as the Life of Adam, the Apocalypse of Moses, The Testament of the Protoplasts, and potentially Jewish Histories.[65] Books associated with the same figure, such as books ascribed to the figures Baruch, Ezra, or Moses, respectively, were sometimes confused. Likewise, the same book title may refer to different books, as is the case with the title, the Apocalypse of Elijah. The same personal name may also refer to different figures, as for instance the name Zecharias/Zacharias. Materials associated with these Zecharias figures were assumedly mixed up in late antiquity and the Middle Ages.[66] It is possible, also, that heresiologists mixed books up in their accounts. It has been debated whether Hippolytus mixed up the name of Seth with the name of Shem when naming the Paraphrase of Seth, discussed above.[67] And finally, we cannot trust the surviving lists either. As noted above, there are a wide range of variants in the manuscripts of the Gelasian Decree for the entry that refers to the Book of the Daughters of Adam.[68] Further, according to Montague R. James, some manuscripts of the Gelasian Decree read *Testamentum Iacobi*, while others read *Testamentum Iobi*.[69]

Third, and finally, it is possible that smaller sections of books never circulating alone as independent books have been perceived as such in modern scholarship. It is well known that smaller sections, such as stories, prayers, and hymns, were sometime assigned titles, for instance, as an aid to readers to ease the retrieval of particular passages.[70] For sure, some of these smaller entities may have circulated independently, as part of different larger compositions and compilations, or as a book in a compendium of works, and if so, they deserve treatment as such.[71] However, some of them are probably better

---

which may have inspired the later Syriac manuscript tradition, which regularly copied two epistles of Baruch appended to Jeremiah, not one as is commonly found in other traditions.

65. George Syncellus 4.19–22; Anastasis of Sinai, *On the Hexameron* 7. Cf. O. S. Wintermute, "Jubilees," *OTP* 1:35–142, esp. 41; James, *Lost Apocrypha*, 7; William Adler, "Jacob of Edessa and the Jewish Pseudepigrapha in Syriac Chronography," in Reeves, *Tracing the Threads*, 143–71, esp. 146–47. Materials from Jubilees were also ascribed to Josephus and to Asaph (Adler, "Jacob of Edessa," 147). It is well known that what is potentially the same book circulated under several names in late antiquity and the Middle Ages. This is the case, e.g., with the Life/Death/Testament, and potentially, Repentance/Penitence, of Adam (Stone, *Armenian Apocrypha*, 45–46). This situation is not only a historical phenomenon. Scholars continue to rename books today, as is the case with, e.g., the Story/Apocalypse of Zosimus/The History of the Rechabites/Account of the Blessed Ones. See, e.g., Chris A. Knights, "A Century of Research into the Story/Apocalypse of Zosimus and/or the History of the Rechabites," *JSP* 15 (1997): 53–66, esp. 53, doi:10.1177/095182079700000150; Davila, *Provenance*, 207–9.

66. E.g., Zechariah ben Jehoiada, the priest; Zechariah ben Berechiah, the prophet; Zechariah ben Iddo, the prophet; and Zacharias the father of John the Baptist. See Sheldon H. Blank, "The Death of Zechariah in Rabbinic Literature," *HUCA* 12–13 (1937–1938): 327–46. The list of Sixty Books refers to an "Apocalypse of Zacharias." It is not clear to which book this is supposed to refer.

67. Reeves, *Heralds*, 55 n. 53.

68. Monger, "Book of the Daughters of Adam."

69. James, *Lost Apocrypha*, 19.

70. See Stone's "Biblical Paraphrases," in *Armenian Apocrypha*, 81–126.

71. For independent circulation, see, e.g., the Story of Shamuni in some Syriac manuscripts (e.g., British Library Add 12,172 and Add 14,732). Part of a larger composition may be the case with some of the writings associated with Adam; e.g., the Horarium (of Adam). See Stone, *Armenian Apocrypha*, 39–57; and Richard Bauckham, "The Inquiry of Abraham (A Possible Allusion to the Apocalypse of Abraham)," *MOTP* 1:59–62, esp. 59–60. As a compendium, e.g., the books of 1 Enoch; *potentially* the sections of the Genesis Apocryphon (so, Steiner, "Heading," 69).

perceived simply as a subsection and as an integral part of the narrative of another book, which has subsequently been misinterpreted in later scholarship. This might be the case with the claimed book of Lamech, presented above, as well as with an alleged Prayer of Joseph.[72] Potentially, it may also provide a fruitful interpretation of some of the potential books of Noah, such as the section of the Genesis Apocryphon referred to as "[Copy of the] Book of the Words of Noah."[73]

Bibliography

Adler, William. "Jacob of Edessa and the Jewish Pseudepigrapha in Syriac Chronography." Pages 143–71 in *Tracing the Threads: Studies in the Vitality of Jewish Pseudepigrapha*. Edited by John C. Reeves. EJL 6. Atlanta: Scholars Press, 1994.

Avigad, Nahman, and Yigael Yadin. *A Genesis Apocryphon: A Scroll from the Wilderness of Judaea*. Jerusalem: Magnes, 1956.

Bauckham, Richard. "Eldad and Modad." MOTP 1:244–56.

———. "The Inquiry of Abraham (A Possible Allusion to the Apocalypse of Abraham)." MOTP 1:59–62.

———. *Jude and the Relatives of Jesus in the Early Church*. Edinburgh: T&T Clark, 1990.

Bauckham, Richard, and James R. Davila. "Introduction." MOTP 1:xvii–xxxviii.

Blank, Sheldon H. "The Death of Zechariah in Rabbinic Literature." HUCA 12/13 (1937–1938): 327–46.

Bowley, James E. "The Compositions of Abraham." Pages 215–38 in *Tracing the Threads: Studies in the Vitality of Jewish Pseudepigrapha*. Edited by John C. Reeves. EJL 6. Atlanta: Scholars Press, 1994.

Brock, Sebastian P. "Apocalypses." Pages 25–27 in *Gorgias Encyclopedic Dictionary of the Syriac Heritage*. Edited by Sebastian P. Brock, Aaron M. Butts, and George A. Kiraz. Piscataway, NJ: Gorgias, 2011.

Čéplö, Slavomír. "Books Known Only by Their Names from Booklists in the Slavia Orthodoxa." In *Unruly Books: Rethinking Ancient and Academic Imaginations of Religious Texts*. Edited by Esther Brownsmith, Marianne Bjelland Kartzow, and Liv Ingeborg Lied. Forthcoming.

Davila, James R. *The Provenance of the Pseudepigrapha: Jewish, Christian, or Other?* JSJSup 105. Leiden: Brill, 2005.

———. "Quotations from Lost Books in the Hebrew Bible." MOTP 1:673–87.

Denis, Albert-Marie. *Introduction aux pseudépigraphes grecs d'Ancien Testament*. SVTP 1. Leiden: Brill, 1970.

Dobschütz, Ernst von. *Das Decretum Gelasianum*. Leipzig: Hinrich's, 1912.

Dorival, Gilles. "Le patriarche Héber et la tour de Babel: Un apocryphe disparu?" Pages 181–201 in *Poussières de christianisme et de judaisme antiques: Études reunites en l'honneur de Jean-Daniel Keastli et Éric Junod*. Edited by Albert Frey and Rémi Grounelle. Publications de l'Institut romand des sciences bibliques 5. Lausanne: Zébre, 2007.

Fabricius, Johann A. *Codex pseudepigraphus Veteris Testamenti: Collectus, castigatus, testimoniisque, censuris et animadversionibus illustratus*. Hamburg: Liebezeit, 1713.

Franklin, Simon. "A Note on a Pseudepigraphal Allusion in Oxyrhynchus Papyrus No. 4365." VT 48 (1998): 95–96. doi:10.1163/1568533982722009.

---

72. See James, *Lost Apocrypha*, 25; Avigad and Yadin, *Genesis Apocryphon*, 38; Steiner, "Heading," 71.
73. Steiner, "Heading," 69; Stone, "Book(s) Attributed to Noah," 6.

Frankfurter, David. "Apocalypses Real and Alleged in the Mani Codex." *Numen* 44 (1997): 60–73. doi:10.1163/1568527972629876.
Frey, Jean-Baptiste. "Apocryphes de l'Ancient Testament, généralités sur le sens du mot apocryphe et sur les apocryphes." *DBSup* 1:354–57.
García Martínez, Florentino. *Qumran and Apocalyptic: Studies on the Aramaic Texts from Qumrân*. STDJ 9. Leiden: Brill, 1992.
Henning, W. B. *The Book of Giants: The Fallen Angels and Their Giant Sons*. London: Forgotten Books, 2007.
Himmelfarb, Martha. "The Book of Noah." *MOTP* 1:40–46.
———. "Some Echoes of *Jubilees* in Medieval Hebrew Literature." Pages 115–42 in *Tracing the Threads: Studies in the Vitality of Jewish Pseudepigrapha*. Edited by John C. Reeves. EJL 6. Atlanta: Scholars Press, 1994.
Ilan, Tal. "Biblical Women's Names in the Apocryphal Traditions." *JSP* 11 (1993): 3–67. doi:10.1177/095182079300001101.
James, Montague R. *The Lost Apocrypha of the Old Testament: Their Titles and Fragments*. London: SPCK, 1920.
Knights, Chris A. "A Century of Research into the Story/Apocalypse of Zosimus and/or the History of the Rechabites." *JSP* 15 (1997): 53–66. doi:10.1177/09518207970000150.
Kraft, Robert A. "The Pseudepigrapha in Christianity." Pages 55–86 in *Tracing the Threads: Studies in the Vitality of Jewish Pseudepigrapha*. Edited by John C. Reeves. EJL 6. Atlanta: Scholars Press, 1994.
———. *The Testament of Job according to the SV Text*. Texts and Translations 5. Pseudepigrapha Series 4. Missoula, MT: Society of Biblical Literature; Scholars Press, 1974.
Lied, Liv Ingeborg. "Text—Work—Manuscript: What Is an Old Testament Pseudepigraph*on*?" *JSP* 25 (2015): 150–65. doi:10.1177/0951820715621202.
Lied, Liv Ingeborg, Marianne Bjelland Kartzow, and Esther Brownsmith. "Books Known Only by Title." *JSP* 32 (2023): 303–22. doi:10.1177/095182072311617.
Lightfoot, J. B., and John R. Harmer. *The Apostolic Fathers: Greek Texts and English Translations of Their Writings*. Edited and revised by Michael W. Holmes. 2nd ed. Grand Rapids: Baker, 1992.
Lipscomb, W. Lowndes. "A Tradition from the Book of Jubilees in Armenian." *JJS* 29 (1978): 149–63.
Milik, J. T. "Problèmes de la littérature hénochique à la lumière des fragments araméens de Qumrân." *HTR* 64 (1971): 330–78.
Monger, Matthew P. "The Book of the Daughters of Adam in the Gelasian Decree." Forthcoming.
———. "Books Known Only by Reference in the Qur'an." In *Unruly Books: Rethinking Ancient and Academic Imaginations of Religious Texts*. Edited by Esther Brownsmith, Marianne Bjelland Kartzow, and Liv Ingeborg Lied. Forthcoming.
———. *The Names of the Wives of the Patriarchs: A Study of Transmission and Reception in Early Jewish, Christian, and Muslim Sources*. Forthcoming.
Mroczek, Eva. *The Literary Imagination in Jewish Antiquity*. Oxford: Oxford University Press, 2016.
Najman, Hindy. "Interpretation as Primordial Writing: Jubilees and Its Authority Conferring Strategies." *JSJ* 30 (1999): 379–410.
Orlov, Andrei. *Selected Studies in the Slavonic Pseudepigrapha*. SVTP 23. Leiden: Brill, 2009.
Pearson, Birger A. "The *Book of Allogenes* (CT,4) and Sethian Gnosticism." Pages 105–16 in

Gnosticism, Platonism and the Late Ancient World: Essays in Honour of John D. Turner. Edited by Kevin Corrigan and Tuomas Rasimus. Nag Hammadi and Manichaean Studies 82. Leiden: Brill, 2013. doi:10.1163/9789004254763_008.

———. "Revisiting Norea." Pages 265–75 in *Images of the Feminine in Gnosticism.* Edited by Karen L. King. SAC. Philadelphia: Fortress, 1988.

Popović, Mladen. "Pseudepigraphy and a Scribal Sense of the Past in the Ancient Mediterranean: A Copy of the Book of the Words of the Vision of Amram." Pages 308–13 in *Is There a Text in This Cave? Studies in the Textuality of the Dead Sea Scrolls in Honour of George J. Brooke.* Edited by Ariel Feldman, Maria Cioată, and Charlotte Hempel. STDJ 119. Leiden: Brill, 2017.

Priest, J. "Testament of Moses." *OTP* 1:919–34.

Reed, Annette Yoshiko. "The Modern Invention of 'Old Testament Pseudepigrapha.'" *JTS* NS 60 (2009): 403–36.

Reeves, John C. *Heralds of That Good Realm: Syro-Mesopotamian Gnosis and Jewish Traditions.* Nag Hammadi and Manichaean Studies 41. Leiden: Brill, 1996.

———. *Jewish Lore in Manichean Cosmogony: Studies in the* Book of Giants *Traditions.* HUCM 14. Cincinnati: Hebrew Union College Press, 1992.

———, ed. *Tracing the Threads: Studies in the Vitality of Jewish Pseudepigrapha.* EJL 6. Atlanta: Scholars Press, 1994.

Sanders, James A. "Introduction: Why the Pseudepigrapha?" Pages 13–19 in *The Pseudepigrapha and Early Biblical Interpretation.* Edited by James H. Charlesworth and Craig A. Evans. JSPSup 14. Sheffield: JSOT Press, 1993.

Schaller, Berndt. "Das Testament Hiobs." Pages 301–88 in *Unterweisung in lehrhafter Form.* Edited by Werner Georg Kümmel. Vol. 3.3 of *Jüdische Schriften aus hellenistisch-römischer Zeit.* Gütersloh: Gütersloher Verlagshaus, 2001.

Schenke, Gesa. "Testament of Job (Coptic Fragments)." *MOTP* 1:160–75.

Schiffman, Lawrence H. "Pseudepigrapha in the Pseudepigrapha: Mythical Books in Second Temple Literature." *RevQ* 21.81, no. 3 (2004): 429–38.

Spittler, R. P. "Testament of Job." *OTP* 1:829–68.

Steiner, Richard C. "The Heading of the *Book of the Words of Noah* on a Fragment of the Genesis Apocryphon: New Light on a 'Lost' Work." *DSD* 2 (1995): 66–71.

Stone, Michael E. *Armenian Apocrypha Relating to the Patriarchs and Prophets.* Jerusalem: Israel Academy of Sciences and Humanities, 1982.

———. "The Book(s) Attributed to Noah." *DSD* 13 (2006): 4–23.

Tardieu, M. "Les livres mis sous le nom de Seth et les Séthiens de l'hérésiologie." Pages 204–10 in *Gnosis and Gnosticism: Papers Read at the Seventh International Conference on Patristic Studies (Oxford, September 8th–13th 1975).* Edited by M. Krause. NHS 8. Leiden: Brill, 1977. doi:10.1163/9789004437159_022.

Toepel, Alexander. "The Apocryphon of Seth." *MOTP* 1:33–38.

VanderKam, James C. "The Apocryphon of Eber." Pages 47–52 in *MOTP* 1.

———. *The Book of Jubilees: A Critical Text.* CSCO 511. Scriptores Aethiopici 88. Leuven: Peeters, 1989.

———. "The Book of the Covenant." *MOTP* 1:28–32.

Wasserstrom, Steven M. "Jewish Pseudepigrapha in Muslim Literature: A Bibliographical and Methodological Sketch." Pages 87–114 in *Tracing the Threads: Studies in the Vitality of Jewish Pseudepigrapha.* Edited by John C. Reeves. EJL 6. Atlanta: Scholars Press, 1994.

Wintermute, O. S. "Jubilees." *OTP* 2:35–142.

BLOG POSTS AND ONLINE RESOURCES

Davila, James R. "Lost Book Found/Update (7 September 2011)." https://paleojudaica.blogspot.com/2006/08/lost-book-found-regular-readers-will.html.
———. "Wish List of Lost Books." https://paleojudaica.blogspot.com/2005/07/wish-list-of-lost-books-michael-pahl.html.
———. "A Worst-Case Scenario (Eldad and Modad)." https://web.archive.org/web/20190502192456/https://www.st-andrews.ac.uk/divinity/rt/otp/abstracts/eldad/.
Kraft, Robert A. "Og and the Giants." http://ccat.sas.upenn.edu/rak//courses/735/Parabiblical/jamesog.htm.

Appendix: Summary of the Complete Ethiopic Version of Jannes and Jambres

by T. M. Erho

In June 2024, after the second *Old Testament Pseudepigrapha: More Noncanonical Scriptures* volume had already reached the proofs stage, a complete copy of the Ethiopic translation of Jannes and Jambres emerged.[1] It had been photographed the previous month within a thick sixteenth-century miscellany manuscript belonging to the Tigrayan monastery of Dabra Hāllēluyā, in which the apocryphon covers five densely written folios toward the rear.[2] Although the corruptness of the text and the difficulty of the particularly slavish Ethiopic rendering of its Greek *Vorlage* precluded the establishment of a reliable English translation in time to be included in this volume, the importance of this find—the first recovery of a complete Hellenistic Jewish literary text in many decades—suggested that it should be addressed in some form in the present anthology devoted to the Old Testament Pseudepigrapha.[3] Hence, a synopsis, rather than a full translation, is presented below.

Synopsis

Entitled "The Book of Jannes and Jambres," the text opens by introducing the first of the two brothers, a man beloved by Pharaoh because of his great wisdom. The narrative immediately shifts to a terrifying dream seen by the brothers' mother, concerning a large city and many trees, one of which is felled by a man with an iron saw. Upon the dream being recounted to him, Jannes sends his mother back to her house, telling her not to visit him any more and describing for her the special characteristics of human-like phantoms. He then summons his brother Jambres and outlines for him both the dream and its interpretation, which foretells his own death three years in the future and a simultaneous calamity for Egypt.

Thereafter, Jannes has a great wall built around his garden and has it filled with plants, creating a delightful paradise that he is eager to share with the Egyptian nobles. However, a violent earthquake and thunderstorm uproot many trees, sending Jannes running to his library for insight into this event. Finding an explanation in one of his books, he throws it away and orders his garden destroyed, rendering the formerly luscious area a desolate haunt of animals. After sending for Jambres, Jannes falls asleep and has a vision of two

---

1. Research for this contribution was funded by the European Union (ERC, consolidator grant agreement no. 101044300, project "BeInf—Beyond Influence: The Connected Histories of Ethiopic and Syriac Christianity," at Universität Hamburg [2022–2027]).

2. The manuscript was photographed by Denis Nosnitsin, who also made the initial identification of Jannes and Jambres among its contents. Nosnitsin is preparing an article on various aspects, especially codicological, of this unusual miscellany codex.

3. A comprehensive edition and translation will appear in the announced SBL Press Writings from the Greco-Roman World volume on Jannes and Jambres being prepared by W. B. Henry and T. M. Erho.

Appendix: Summary of the Complete Ethiopic Version of Jannes and Jambres

men clothed in white who declare that they have been sent by God to take him away to the place of the dead, ultimately stating that they will return for him in fourteen days. Awakening, he starts weeping, and tells Jambres the dream when he arrives. Jannes then informs his mother that Pharaoh wants him to be the master magician in Memphis, and once again urges her not to visit him, making preparations instead for her well-being during his absence.

Jannes and Jambres then set out together for Memphis, during which time the former instructs the latter not to join Pharaoh and his posse when they pursue the Hebrews and to keep news of his forthcoming death from their mother, enjoining secrecy on his brother in both matters. Sometime later, Jannes throws a feast for the marriage of his brother and his daughter, at which he issues further instructions to Jambres for the well-being of his family after his demise, particularly for that of his mother. During this event, officials from Pharaoh arrive and demand that the master magician come and counter the miracles and signs performed by Moses and Aaron, which he does successfully.

Jannes, however, is then struck by a terminal illness. When he is in the throes of death pains, his brother comes to him, and the two converse as the hours of the day slip away. At its end, Jannes perishes, and, in his immediate angst, Jambres attempts to commit suicide, an action halted by the timely intervention of the brothers' friends. Jambres then mourns for seven days.

Sometime later, the mother wishes to see Jannes again, and although she is initially put off by Jambres, he thereafter forgets about her, in direct disregard of his deceased sibling's repeated pleas. After Pharaoh and his cohorts go out to pursue the Hebrews and are drowned in the Red Sea, great lamentation arises throughout Egypt, prompting the mother to fear that Jannes has perished along with them. Despite the multiple prior warnings, she consequently sets out at night for Memphis, encountering a group of phantoms that look like priests on her journey. The spirit of Jannes is among them, and when the mother recognizes him, he tries to convince her once more to go back to her home. She, however, cannot be dissuaded, and correctly ascertains that she is conversing with a phantom and not a living person on the basis of her son's description of the special characteristics of such entities several years earlier. The spirit of Jannes flees, and, although he pleads with her not to follow him, the mother does so and dies. Finding her corpse at Jannes's tomb, Jambres buries her with the customary rites and mourning, and then uses magical books to perform necromancy and raise the spirit of his brother from hell for one final conversation. Jannes initially inquires about the crestfallen state of his living brother, which the latter ascribes to the loss of his sibling, who had made him a complete man.

The spirit of Jannes then begins a lengthy monologue affirming that his death was just, because, although the wisest man in Egypt, he had opposed the one ruler, God.[4] Going on to say that he has descended to hell, he describes its many torments, including darkness, fire, heat, and thirst. Asserting that only the righteous (those who fear God) experience joy and rest in the afterlife, Jannes declares that all those in hell, equals there regardless of their dissimilar statuses in the mortal realm, would trade anything to escape its horrors, but that this is impossible. Only those who do good upon earth are spared this terrible fate through the intervention of God.

---

4. While the preceding narrative appears to hew to the basic progression found in P. Chester Beatty XVI, materials in this speech manifest different sequences in places.

Appendix: Summary of the Complete Ethiopic Version of Jannes and Jambres

Jannes illustrates at length the fact that even the most illustrious terrestrial figures condemned to hell cannot raise themselves out of it. Pharaoh, his predecessors, and all the nobles of Egypt, who possessed so much on earth, all died and encountered the unquenchable fire. So too did many other eminent figures who performed notable deeds and made significant discoveries, among them Hephaestus, Zeus, Isis and Serapis, Aphrodite, Athena, Hermes, Ares, Apollo, Dionysus, Demeter, Heracles, Asclepius, and Adonis. None of these have been able to save their bodies from death or liberate their spirits from the fires of hell, nor have the greatest of the antediluvian giants, whose physical statures and exploits were even more prodigious. In fact, upon being divinely afflicted with an illness, the most powerful of all of these terrestrial creatures, one of the giants, acknowledged the superiority of God during his lifetime.

While noting that there are many other such figures whose names he has heard in hell, Jannes begins to bring his monologue to a close. Reiterating the horrors of hell and the tortures that sinners endure there, he indicates that he has both written down and told Jambres everything. After urging his brother to be merciful and just, Jannes briefly describes the blessed, idyllic abode of the righteous.[5] Jannes exhorts Jambres to be good a final time and disappears, as his guardians must now return him to hell.

As a result of this paranormal encounter, Jambres immediately begins to take actions to reform his life. He destroys the sacrifices on his brother's grave and then summons his family, friends, and acquaintances in order to read to them from some books. Afterwards, he engages in a systematic attempt to burn books of magic, idolatrous statues, and the homes of those possessing such vile artifacts. This attracts the attention of the citizenry and Pharaoh's remaining children, who undertake an inquiry into these activities. Questioning Jambres about his sudden and impassioned antagonism toward magic, they receive the reply that his brother Jannes counseled him to perform these actions and revealed to him a new path toward eternal wealth. Jambres also gives Pharaoh's children a book in which everything Jannes had said and done was written, so they summon a priest to read it to them. Upon learning from this book that their father is in hell being tormented, they rend their garments and declare that Pharaoh brought this terrible fate upon himself. The royal family then issues a decree commanding that idolatrous temples and statues throughout Egypt are to be destroyed and anyone worshiping them or sacrificing to the dead is dispossessed or aggrieved in worse ways.

Jambres then begins to give away his possessions and to teach Pharaoh's children about the new righteous way of life to which he has turned. Instructing them about the sovereignty and uniqueness of the one God and the existence of immortal souls, as well as about divinely loved human characteristics, including meekness, mercy, and compassion, he also outlines a long series of types of individuals who will be tortured in hell, among them blasphemers, unbelievers, murderers, lesbians, adulterers, fraudsters, enchanters, sorcerers, liars, and unjust arbitrators. Jambres additionally teaches that God is timeless, existing before evil, and that those who dwell in hell should not be loved.

The men of Memphis, however, desirous of continuing to worship gods at a big stone altar where many statues remain, implore Pharaoh's children to exempt these from the general destruction. Jambres enters the discussion and declares that it cannot be so, but

---

5. This passage probably constitutes a Christian interpolation in whole or part, as it seems narratively incompatible with the rest of the text and contains certain phraseology closely associated with Christian tradition, e.g., "kingdom of heaven" and "water of life."

Appendix: Summary of the Complete Ethiopic Version of Jannes and Jambres

encounters strong resistance on the basis that the well-being of the city might be undermined if its protective deity is destroyed. Taking another tack, Jambres inquires who this god is, eventually getting the response that it is an angel who guards the city. He then asks who commands that angel, a question to which Pharaoh's children respond with the correct answer of God, earning plaudits from their teacher. Having thereby won the argument concerning that deity, Jambres is then queried about the river-god Nilus and his children and once more gets Pharaoh's children to realize and acknowledge God's superiority. He then demands that the statues be demolished.

After this transpires, the Memphites rise up angrily against Jambres, bitterly complaining that the Hebrews took all their possessions and now through the evil counsel of the two brothers their security is threatened, as the protective god of the city and the Nile god are no more. They seek to kill Jambres and those associated with him, but are persuaded to delay this action temporarily on account of the imminence of the Nile flooding season; if the river does not rise sufficiently, the murderous plot can be resumed. Of course, the Nile and other Egyptian rivers fill up in accordance with the season, legitimating Jambres's position. In fact, a perfect flooding season occurs, resulting in an unprecedented harvest and an even better one the following year. This abundance causes the recalcitrant Egyptians to change their ways, blessing Jambres and deciding to worship God.

Index of Modern Authors

Citations to footnotes are represented by superscript letters and numbers.

Abbott, Thomas Kingsmill, 413[53]
Adam, Alfred, 12[16]
Adams, W. Y., 24[9], 24[11]
Adelman, Rachel, 288[33]
Adhami, Siamak, 161[g]
Adler, Maxmillian, 541[16], 645[65]
Adler, William, 318[c]
Akinean, Nerses, 542[21]
Albeck, Hanoch, 64[12], 288[35], 290[36]
Alexander, Philip S., 188[19], 196[39], 322[1]
al-Nadim, Ibn, 10[7], 11, 102, 105
Andersen, F. I., 22[6–7], 26, 31–33
Andreas, F. C., 92, 156[d], 158[g]
Angel, Joseph, 64[16]
Aptowitzer, Viktor, 276[12–13]
Asmussen, Jes P., 92[12], 95, 98[38], 162[i]
Attridge, Harold W., 430[c]
Aucher, Johannes B., 538[3], 542[22], 552[c], 556[b], 558[g], 560[a], 568[c], 569[e], 571[d], 577[e], 580[d]
Avigad, Nahman, 638[17], 646[72]
Awetikʿean, Gabriēl, 545[g]

Baillet, Maurice, 59[3]
Balcer, Jack Martin, 461[2], 472[a]
Balzaretti, Claudio, 465[18]
Bang, Willy, 170[2], 176[g]
Bar-Ilan, Meir, 330[30]
Barnstone, Willis, 586[9], 596, 598[a], 600[e], 602[a], 603[b]
Barthélemy, Dominique, 358[4]
Baskin, Judith R., 397[36]
Bauckham, Richard, 192[30], 266[36], 300[5], 305[18], 306[20], 307[27], 403[43], 404[16], 414[55–56], 416[65], 416[67], 424[b], 503[12], 635[1], 637[10], 644[62–63], 645[71]

Baumgarten, Joseph M., 10[9]
Bayless, Martha, 610[6], 616[37]
Becker, Adam H., 265[34]
BeDuhn, Jason D., 107[85], 108[87–88], 124[74], 127[179]
Bellusci, Alessia, 195[38]
Benayahu, Meir, 326[12], 326[14]
Ben-Sasson, Menachem, 461[3]
Beresford, S., 373[6]
Berger, Klaus, 429[a]
Bettiolo, Paolo, 430[b]
Betz, Hans Dieter, 190[25], 323[4]
Beyer, Klaus, 412, 593
Bhayro, Siam, 330[31], 440[46]
Bietenhard, Hans, 541[18]
Bischoff, Bernhard, 246[2–5], 246[8], 247[11], 247[16–17], 248[22], 252[a], 253[b], 254[b–d], 255[b–c], 256[b–c]
Black, Matthew, 120[152]
Blank, Sheldon H., 645[66]
Bledsoe, Amanda M. Davis, 44[10]
Bohak, Gideon, 191[28], 322[1], 327[19], 327[21], 330[31], 346[j]
Böhlig, Alexander, 9[3]
Bonner, Campbell, 370[e]
Bonwetsch, Nathaneal, 318[d]
Booth, Abigail, 365[d]
Bousset, Wilhelm, 414[57]
Bowley, James E., 643[45], 643[50]
Boyarin, Daniel, 265[34]
Boyce, Mary, 92, 95[28], 95[30], 100[49], 127[181]
Brandt, Wilhelm, 9[4]
Brashear, William M., 346[c]
Brea, L. Bernabò, 360[9]

655

Index of Modern Authors

Brent, Allen, 584[4]
Brocca, Nicoletta, 246[3], 246[6-7], 249[26-27]
Brock, Sebastian, 461[2], 463[14-15], 464[17], 465[21-24], 468[c], 473[c], 481[e], 482[a], 643[52]
Brownsmith, Esther, 637[4]
Buitenwerf, Rieuwerd, 247[9], 250[28]
Burns, Dylan M., 13[18]

Calhoun, Robert Matthew, 366[a]
Carey, John, 616[36]
Čéplö, Slavomír, 637[7]
Cerrato, J. A., 584[4]
Chardonnens, László Sándor, 434[8-11], 435[19], 436[22], 437[28], 438[32], 439[38], 440[48], 443[58]
Charles, R. H., 281[6], 282[7], 282[10], 285[24], 298[a], 302[11], 306[21], 306[23], 307[24], 318[d], 320[b]
Charlesworth, James H., 362[11], 367[e], 369[a], 635[1], 636[3], 639[19]
Childers, Jeff W., 267[40]
Christensen, Mark Z., 618[48]
Cioată, Maria, 641[36]
Cirillo, Luigi, 15[b]
Clark, Larry, 183[b]
Clivaz, Claire, 598[b]
Cohen, Martin, 188[17]
Colditz, Iris, 56[66], 95, 153, 172[13]
Collins, John J., 3[1], 47[23], 389[8], 462[11]
Comestor, Peter, 611[11], 612–14
Conley, Heist, 618[47]
Contini, Riccardo, 9[3]
Cooper, James, 427[a]
Cottier, Jean-François, 404[17], 424[a]
Court, John M., 429[a]
Cramer, John A., 304[15], 319[a], 319[e], 320[a]
Cruice, Patrice François Marie, 598[a], 600[a], 604[d], 605[a]
Cumont, Franz, 440[43]

Dahood, Mitchell J., 592[20]
Damian, Peter, 611[9], 612–15
Daniel, Robert W., 368[c], 370[e]
Daniélou, Jean, 538[6]
Davidson, Clifford, 618[45]
Davies, G. I., 357[2]
Davila, James, 98[38], 193[35], 194[36], 195[37], 264[29], 266[37], 267[41], 308[29], 322[1], 324[8], 635[1], 636[2], 637[10], 638[17], 644[59], 644[63]

Davis, Lisa Fagin, 618[44]
De Bruyne, Donatien, 424[a], 424[e], 426[a], 426[d], 636[2]
De Lange, Nicholas Robert Michael, 273[4]
Delatte, Armand, 365[b]
Delgado, Mariano, 459[1]
Denis, Albert Marie, 261[13], 314[b], 315[a], 315[c], 315[e], 316[d], 319[a], 320[c], 321[c], 413[54], 414[57], 637[5], 637[7], 637[10], 638[16-17], 639[21], 640[26], 643[44]
De Santos Otero, Aurelio, 404[17]
Devreesse, Robert, 273[3], 274[6]
Dilley, Paul, 105[73]
Dillon, John M., 594[23-26], 595[31]
Dimant, Devorah, 66[21]
Dimant, Shmuel, 281
DiTommaso, Lorenzo, 433[1], 434[9-11], 435[19], 436[22], 437[28], 438[32], 439[37], 442[56], 443[58], 459[1], 464[16], 465[20], 610[1], 615
Doak, Brian R., 44[11], 64[14]
Dobschütz, Ernst von, 372[4], 638[18]
Dochhorn, Jan, 258[3], 258[6], 263[25], 264[27-28], 267, 268[42], 312[d], 313[a], 313[d], 314[a]
Dolabani, Yuhanna, 461[6]
Dölger, Franz Joseph, 413[49]
Döllinger, J. J. I. von, 583[3], 584
Doran, R., 47[24]
Dorival, Gilles, 643[46]
Dover, K. J., 604[d]
Draper, Jonathan A., 263[24]
Drexl, Franz, 434[6]
Drijvers, Hans J. W., 432[c]
Dronke, Peter, 247[12-14], 248[20-21], 249[25], 252[a], 252[d]
Drower, E. S., 11[12]
Duling, D. C., 49[30], 188[19]
Duncker, Luwig, 598[a]

Eidinow, Esther, 368[b]
Eisenstein, Judah David, 281[2], 285[20]
Eitel, Ernst, 154[d]
Eitrem, S., 367[d]
Emanuel, Simcha, 329[27]
Erdal, Marcel, 177[b], 178[c-d]
Erho, Ted M., 65, 373[6], 374[12], 377[21], 379, 386, 388[3], 389, 393
Esbroeck, Michel van, 503[15]
Evans, Ernest, 431[f]

Index of Modern Authors

Fabricius, Johann Albert (Johannes Albertus), 102[62], 320[b], 433[3], 635[1]
Falcone, Maria Jennifer, 437[30]
Faraone, Christopher A., 368[a]
Festugière, A. J., 369[b]
Field, Frideric, 368[a]
Fischer, Steven R., 434[7]
Fodor, Alexander, 186[5]
Förster, Max, 434[6-7]
Fossum, Jarl, 592[20]
Frankfurter, David, 13[18], 401[3], 402[9], 404[14], 404-5[18], 415[61], 415[63], 642[42-43]
Franklin, Simon, 639[19]
Frey, Jean-Baptiste, 639[21]
Fröhlich, Ida, 90[4], 101[57], 101[59], 110[101], 123[162]
Funk, Wolf-Peter, 398[38]

Gabain, Annemarie von, 176[g], 181[g], 182
Gager, John G., 365[b], 368[b]
Ganz, David, 441[49]
García Martínez, Florentino, 50[32], 112[119], 464[16], 638[13]
Gardner, Iain, 9[2-3], 15[b], 92[12], 93[17], 93[20-21], 99[43-45], 102[63-64], 105[73], 106, 107[85], 108, 109[81], 110[107], 110[109], 111[112], 112[121], 114, 118[145], 121[157], 124[74], 155[e], 160[k], 429[a]
Gaster, Moses, 281[2], 285[5], 282[11], 285[22-23], 326[13], 328[25], 329[28], 331, 347[j]
Gathercole, Simon, 430[a], 431[a]
Gauger, Jörg-Dieter, 247[10], 247[15]
George, Andrew, 42[5]
Gerhardt, Christof, 610[1], 618[43]
Gerven Oei, Vincent W. J. van, 441[53]
Gignoux, Phillipe, 163[c], 164[b]
Giliberto, Concetta, 610, 610[4], 612[14], 617[40], 617[42]
Goff, Matthew, 42[7], 64[10-11], 64[15], 102[59], 115[130], 122[160], 123[165]
Golitzin, Alexander, 461[4], 463[15]
Goodenough, Ervin R., 540[12]
Gottwald, Ivo, 398[39]
Graesse, J. G., 612[15]
Graf, Fritz, 368[b]
Grébaut, Sylvain, 426[c], 427[b]
Greenfield, Jonas C., 17[c], 17[f]
Greenspoon, Leonard J., 358[4]
Grierson, Fiona, 300[5]

Grossfeld, Bernard, 275[10]
Grove, Timothy Paul, 439[39], 440[47]
Gruenwald, Ithamar, 10[9], 191[28], 195[37]
Guerrier, Louis, 426[c], 427[b]
Gutmann, Joseph, 276[13]

Hagen, Joost L., 18[1], 19[2]
Halperin, D. J., 19[2]
Hamerton-Kelly, Robert, 540[15]
Hamilton, James, 179[c]
Hammer, Reuven, 342[b]
Hansen, G. C., 313[b-c], 315[f]
Harari, Yuval, 188[18], 322[1-3], 323[5], 324[6-7], 325[15-17], 328[25], 329[27], 330[31], 330[34], 335[a], 335[c-d], 337[e], 339[f], 342[b-c], 344[b], 346[h], 347[a], 349[c], 349[j], 350[c], 351[g], 351[k], 352[e], 352[j], 353[b], 353[i], 354[g], 363[15]
Harmer, John R., 637[9]
Harrington, Daniel J., 282[11]
Hawk, Brandon W., 610[2], 610[5]
Hay, David M., 538[5]
Heal, Kristian S., 261[12-13], 262[14]
Heiduk, Matthias, 433[2]
Heine, Ronald E., 273[2]
Heist, William W., 609[1], 610, 611[13], 616[35], 617[43], 618[46]
Hendel, Ronald, 44[9]
Henning, W. B., 41[3], 51[36], 51[39], 56[71], 59[2], 61[6], 90[5], 92[11-12], 94[26], 96, 97[32], 98[37], 98[41], 101, 102[61], 104[69], 106, 107[84], 108[87], 109[91], 112[123], 114, 118[148], 119, 121[158], 123[166], 125, 128[182], 137[b-c], 139[e], 140[f], 141[c], 142[f], 143[b], 143[d-f], 144[a], 144[c-d], 145[a], 145[f], 145[h], 145[j], 147[a], 148[a-b], 148[d], 148[f], 148[h], 150, 151[a], 152[b-c], 154[d], 155[a], 155[c-d], 155[f], 156[a-b], 156[d], 157, 158[c], 158[f], 158[h-i], 159[c], 159[f], 159[g], 159[i], 160[d], 160[f-h], 160[j], 161[d-f], 162[a-d], 162[g], 163[a], 163[d-f], 164[a], 165[a-b], 170[2], 178[a], 638[12]
Henrichs, Albert, 9[2-3], 12[16], 93[17]
Henry, W. Benjamin, 65, 373[6], 374[12], 377[21], 379, 386, 388, 393
Henze, Matthias, 462[8], 463[12-15], 465[19]
Herbers, Klaus, 433[2]
Herrero de Jáuregui, Miguel, 584[7]
Herwagen, Johann, 610[7]
Herzer, Jens, 388[5]
Hilgenfeld, Adolf, 248[18]

657

Index of Modern Authors

Hill, Charles E., 414[57], 432[a]
Hillel, Vered, 282[12], 283[13], 286[27-29], 291[40]
Himmelfarb, Martha, 290[36], 404[16], 405[20-21], 406[22], 406[26-28], 407[30-31], 407[33-35], 417[68], 424[c], 642[40], 644[57]
Hirschberger, Martina, 373[6]
Hoek, Annawies van den, 431[d]
Hoffman, Matthias, 388[3]
Holl, Karl, 432[a]
Hollander, Harm Wouter, 263[23], 282[8], 282[12], 285[26], 287[30], 291[38]
Hopkins, Simon, 327[20]
Hübner, Reinhard M., 248[18]
Hunt, Tony, 442[57]
Hutter, Manfred, 113[124-26], 121[155], 125, 139[a], 140[h], 157[d-e], 159[f]

Ilan, Tal, 639[22]
Isaac, Ephraim, 261[12-13]
Issaverdens, James, 496[2]

Jackson, A. V. William, 91, 109[100], 110[104], 110[109], 112[122], 113[127]
Jackson, Peter, 610[7]
Jacobson, Howard, 429[b]
James, Montague Rhodes, 306[22], 315[g], 317[b], 318[d], 319[a], 402[6], 402[8], 414[58-59], 427[a], 636[3], 637[8], 637[10], 638[16-17], 640[26], 643[44], 643[47], 644[58], 645[65], 645[69], 646[72]
Janowitz, Naomi, 189[20], 330[30]
Jastrow, Marcus, 337[g], 343[i], 345[l], 348[c], 350[i]
Jellicoe, Sidney, 358[4]
Jones, F. Stanley, 104[4]
Jones, Peter Russell, 300[6-7], 304[15-16], 313[a]
Jonge, Marinus de, 282[12], 283[16], 285[26], 287[30], 288[35], 291[38-39]
Jourdan, Fabienne, 375[14]
Jullien, Christelle, 10[8]
Jullien, Florence, 10[8]

Kartzow, Marianne Bjelland, 637[4]
Keskiaho, Jesse, 438[35]
Kiel, Yishai, 141[e]
King, Karen L., 104[65]
Klijn, A. F. J., 9–10[4], 49[63]
Klimkeit, H.-J., 178[b]
Klutz, Todd E., 190[25], 363[12]
Knights, Chris A., 645[65]

Köbert, Raimund, 9[3]
Koch, Klaus, 397[37], 459[1]
Koenen, Ludwig, 9[2], 13[19], 15[a], 16[c], 93[19]
Konai, Theodore bar, 10, 11[13], 12, 109[100], 110[104], 110[109], 112[122]
Korteweg, Th., 284[18], 285[25], 291[39]
Kósa, Gábor, 61[6], 92[14-15], 102[60], 108[90], 109[91], 109[94], 111[112], 124[172]
Kosman, Admiel, 45[14]
Kotansky, Roy, 358[4], 359[5], 360[6], 360[8], 362[10], 365[b], 367[e], 368[a-c], 369[a-b], 369-70[d], 370[e], 371[b]
Kötting, Bernhard, 370[e]
Kovács, Péter, 369[a]
Kraemer, Erik von, 617[41]
Kraemer, Ross Shepherd, 274[8], 275[10]
Kraft, Robert A., 266[36], 267[39], 268[43], 638[14], 640[26], 641[32-33], 641[35-36], 643[47]
Krebber, Bärbel, 493[14]
Krueger, Frederic, 372[2], 375[16], 386[1], 388[3-4], 389[6], 398[37-38]
Kugel, James L., 276[13]
Kuhn, Karl Heinz, 387[2], 391[11-12], 392[13], 392[15-19], 393[20-21], 432[b]
Kulik, Alexander, 462[10]
Kurfeß, Altons, 252[a], 253[a]

Łajtar, Adam, 441[53]
Lambert, Bernard, 610[1]
Laperrousaz, Ernest-Marie, 299[3], 307[26]
Lapidge, Michael, 610[6], 610[8], 616[37]
Larsen, John Møller, 10[4]
Layton, Bentley, 321[b]
Le Coq, Albert, 91, 94, 170[1], 183[a]
Lee, Ralph, 65[19]
Lehner, Hans-Christian, 433[2]
Lentz, Wolfgang, 101[56]
Lerner, Robert E., 612[16]
Lesses, Rebecca Macy, 185[2], 189[20], 196[39], 324[8]
Levene, Dan, 330[31-32]
Levine, Lee, 193[32]
Lewy, Hans, 542[21], 542[24-26], 560[a], 561[c], 562[e], 563[f-g], 565[c], 565[f], 567[c], 567[g], 568[f], 570[a], 570[d-e], 571[g], 572[c], 573[a], 573[g-h], 574[a-b], 577[b], 577[e], 577[h], 578[a-b], 579[a], 579[d-e], 579[h], 580[a], 580[c-d]

Index of Modern Authors

Lieberman, Saul, 406[23], 406[27-28], 407[29], 424[d]
Lied, Liv Ingeborg, 267[38], 267[40], 635[1], 637[4]
Lieu, Samuel N. C., 9[2-3], 15[b], 92[12], 93[17], 93[20-21], 99[43-45], 100[48], 102[63-64], 108, 110[107], 110[109], 121[157], 429[a]
Lightfoot, J. B., 637[9]
Lincoln, Andrew T., 411[45]
Lindbeck, Kristen H., 407[32], 410[39]
Lipscomb, W. Lowndes, 639[22]
Litwa, M. David, 373[8], 583[1], 583[3], 584[5-7], 593[21-22], 594[27], 595[28], 596[34-35], 598[a], 598[c], 599[c-e], 600[a], 600[e], 601[b], 602[a], 602[c], 602[e-h], 603[b], 604[a-d], 605[a-b], 605[e-f], 606[c], 607[c]
Liuzza, Roy Michael, 439[36], 446[65], 446[67]
Loader, William, 308[31]
Loewenstamm, Samuel E., 300[3], 303[12]
Lubac, Henri de, 249[23]
Luck, Ulrich, 539[9]
Luibhéid, Colm, 302[10]
Lundaug, Hugo, 267[38], 267[40]
Luttikhuizen, Gerard P., 10[4]

Machielsen, John J., 610[1]
Maclean, Arthur John, 427[a]
MacMahon, John H., 598[a], 598[c], 599[a-d], 601[b], 602[a], 602[d], 602[h], 604[b]
Mahé, Jean-Pierre, 373[8], 397[37]
Malik, Peter, 375[15]
Malley, William J., 432[a]
Maltomini, Franco, 368[c], 370[e]
Manandyan, Hakob, 542[21]
Mantou, Reine, 617[41]
Marchand, James W., 617[43]
Marcos, Natalio Fernández, 358[4]
Marcovich, Miroslav, 431[c], 583[2-3], 592[20], 596[32], 598[a], 598[c], 599[e], 600[a], 600[e], 602[c], 602[e], 602[g], 603[b], 604[a], 606[b-c], 607[d], 608[d]
Margalioth, Mordecai, 185[1], 186, 187[14], 188, 190[22], 190[24], 191[28], 192[31], 193[34], 195[38], 196, 197[40], 202[k], 203[j], 204[j], 209[j], 209[m], 210[k], 211[o], 212[k-l], 214[h], 215[l], 216[e], 216[j], 217[e], 218[e], 218[m-n], 219[o], 220[n], 221[a], 221[g], 222[r], 224[l], 225[d], 229[g], 230[a], 230[j], 232[d], 233[a], 233[d], 234[a-b], 234[f], 235[c], 235[j], 236[l], 239[j], 240[a-b], 240[d-e], 241[d], 241[f], 242[b], 242[e], 242[g], 322[1]

Marsch, Edgar, 459[1]
Martin, Lawrence T., 436[23]
Martini, Raymundus, 64[13]
McNamara, Martin, 275[10], 616[36]
Means, Laurel, 439[40], 440[44]
Metzler, Karin, 273[2]
Migne, J.-P., 102[61], 610
Milik, J. T., 11[11], 41[2], 44, 48[27], 49, 50[32-33], 55[63], 59[1], 59[3], 60[4], 62[7], 65[17-18], 66[20-21], 94, 98[38], 102[59], 171, 177[d], 638[16]
Miller, Emmanuel, 583, 598[a], 606[b]
Mimouni, Simon Claude, 10[4]
Mingana, Alphonse, 429[a]
Mittenhuber, Florian, 441[49]
Mondésert, Claude, 431[d]
Monger, Matthew P., 639[20], 639[22], 643[50], 645[68]
Montserrat-Torrents, J., 593[22]
Morano, Enrico, 41–42[3], 50[34], 56[66], 61[6], 94–95, 98[33], 101[56], 112, 116[137-38], 117[142], 118[46], 120[153-54], 121[156], 121[159], 123[164], 123[167], 124[170], 124[173], 126[176], 126[178], 128[128], 137–41, 142[d], 142[f], 143[e], 143[g], 144[d], 145, 146[g], 147, 148[d], 148[h], 149[a-b], 150, 151[b], 152–60, 161[d], 162–64, 166–69
Morgan, Michael A., 196[39], 197[40], 199[a], 200[b], 201[q], 208[m], 212[m], 213[b], 215[d], 216[j], 219[i-j], 233[d], 233[f], 233[i], 234[b], 236[l], 241[b], 242[a]
Moritz, Thorsten, 411[46]
Morony, Michael G., 330[31]
Mroczek, Eva, 635[1]
Muddiman, John, 300[5]
Mueller, Dieter, 430[d]
Mueller, J. R., 502[12]
Müller, Friedrich W. K., 91[9], 100[49]
Müller, Karl Wilhelm, 246[2]
Muradyan, Gohar, 540[13-14], 542[23], 542[28], 544[a], 545[f], 546[a], 546[d], 547[c], 548[d], 549[b], 550[b], 550[e], 551[b], 552[b], 552[d], 556[b], 560[a], 560[c], 562[a], 562[c], 570[f], 571[d], 571[g], 573[e], 573[g-h], 574[d], 577[c], 579[c]
Mutius, Hans Georg von, 188[17], 239[g], 240[b], 240[e], 241[d], 242[g], 328[25]

Naether, Franziska, 389[6]
Najman, Hindy, 635[1], 642[39], 642[41]

Index of Modern Authors

Nakaš, Lejla, 614[29], 614[31-32]
Nau, François, 410[40]
Naveh, Joseph, 343[h], 365[b], 367[b]
Newington, Samantha, 46[22]
Nic Cárthaigh, Emma, 616[36], 617[43]
Nickelsburg, George W. E., 43[8], 260[10], 308[30]
Niggemeyer, Jens-Heinrich, 189[20]
Nock, A. D., 369[b]
Noegel, Scott B., 365[b]

Oberhelman, Steven B., 433[4], 434[6-7]
Ó Dochartaigh, Caitriona, 616[36]
Orchard, Andy, 374[10]
Orlov, Andrei, 637[7], 644[60]

Palmer, Nigel F., 610[1], 618[43]
Panaino, Antonio, 162[h]
Pearson, Birger A., 19[3], 20[4], 394[23-25], 395[27-31], 396[32-35], 639-40[24]
Pedersen, Nils Arne, 10[4], 102, 105[73], 106
Pennington, A., 20[5], 21-22, 26, 32-33, 35-36
Petersen, Anders Klostergaard, 258[3], 258[6], 260[10-11], 263[25], 264[27-28], 265[33-34], 266[35], 267, 268[42-43]
Petit, Françoise, 273[1], 274[7]
Philonenko, Marc, 276[15]
Picard, Jean-Michael, 429[a]
Pietersma, Albert, 46[19], 327[2-3], 373[6], 375[16], 390[9], 397[37]
Piovanelli, P., 393[22]
Places, Édouard des, 375[13]
Plumley, J. M., 18-22, 23[8], 24[10-11], 25, 30, 34
Pognon, Henri, 11[13]
Poirier, Paul-Herbert, 584[7], 596[33-34]
Polotsky, Hans J., 102, 105[73], 106, 112[121]
Pontfarcy, Yolande de, 429[a]
Popovic, Mladen, 642[39]
Preisendanz, Karl, 358, 360[7], 365[e], 366[b], 367[d]
Priessnig, Anton, 540[15]
Priest, J., 308[30], 644[64]
Prohászka, Péter, 369[a]
Puech, Émile, 41[2], 59[3], 60, 66[21], 68[a]
Pulleyblank, Edwin, 100[50]

Quick, Laura, 45[14]
Quispel, Gilles, 257[2], 258[5], 262[15-17], 263-64, 267

Ramos, Marcus Vinícius, 462[9]
Rebiger, Bill, 185[2-4], 186[5-6], 187[8-11], 187[13], 188[15-16], 190[22-23], 191[28], 192[31], 193[32-33], 195[38], 196-97, 203[h], 205[n], 208[m], 210[n], 211[m], 212[m], 214[h], 215[o], 219[f], 221[b], 221[d], 226[f], 226[h], 227[a], 233[d], 240[e], 241[b], 241[d], 322[1]
Reck, Christiane, 92, 95[28], 95[30], 141, 143[4], 146[j], 150
Reed, Annette Yoshiko, 48[28], 265[34], 635[1]
Reeves, John C., 10[5-6], 11[10], 12[15], 13[17-18], 13[20], 15[b-d], 16[a], 16[d], 16[g], 17[b-d], 17[i], 41[2], 48[26], 59[3], 90[4], 94, 98[38-39], 104[67], 106[77], 108[86], 121[158], 152[a], 171[8], 177[d], 402[4], 410[43], 414[56], 416[64], 638[12-13], 638[15], 640[28], 642[42-43], 643[49], 643[51], 644[57], 645[67]
Reindel, Kurt, 611[10]
Reinink, G. J., 9-10[4]
Reitzenstein, R., 368[d]
Renoux, Charles, 316[b-c], 317[d], 318[a]
Resch, Alfred, 412[48]
Rešetar, Milan, 613[27]
Rhijn, Carine van, 443[60]
Richlin, Amy, 590[15-16], 591[17-18], 595[29]
Rizzo, F. P., 357[3], 367[a]
Robbins, G. A., 502[12]
Roberts, C. H., 23[8], 24[10]
Robinson, S. E., 193[33]
Rohrbacher-Sticker, Claudia, 328[26], 330[33], 339[a]
Röhrborn, Klaus, 176[g]
Rölling, Wolfgang, 45[14]
Römer, Cornelia, 13[19], 15[a], 16[c], 93[19]
Rose, H. J., 606[a], 607[a]
Rosenstiehl, Jean-Marc, 406[24], 406[27], 406[41-42]
Rouillard-Bonraisin, Hedwige, 45-46[17]
Roulet, Jacques de, 538[7], 539[10], 540[14], 541[18], 542[19], 542[24], 542[27], 544[a], 545[f], 546[a], 546[d], 548[d], 571[d]
Royse, James R., 538[4]
Rudolph, Kurt, 10[8]
Ryan, William Granger, 612[15]

Saar, Ortal-Paz, 327[19]
Salvesen, Alison, 461[4]

Index of Modern Authors

Sanders, James A., 635[1]
Sandnes, Karl Olav, 249[24]
Schäfer, Peter, 185[2-4], 186[5-6], 187[8-11], 187[13], 188[15-16], 190[22-24], 191[28], 192[31], 193[32-33], 193[35], 195[38], 196–97, 203[h], 205[n], 208[m], 210–11[n], 211[m], 212[m], 214[h], 215[o], 219[f], 221[b], 221[d], 226[f], 226[h], 227[a], 233[d], 239[g], 240[b], 240[e], 241[b], 241[d], 242[g], 322[1], 324[9], 328[25], 366
Schaller, Berndt, 641[32]
Schenke, Gesa, 641[32], 641[34-36]
Schiffman, Lawrence, 329[29], 636[2], 642[38], 643[54], 644[57]
Schlüter, Margarete, 188[17], 239[g], 240[b], 240[e], 241[d], 242[g], 328[25], 334[a]
Schmelz, Georg, 373[6], 397[36]
Schmidt, Carl, 93, 112[131], 257
Schmidt-Glintzer, Helwig, 91[10], 100[48], 101
Schmold, Hans, 465[18]
Schniedewin, Friedrich Wilhelm, 598[a], 600[a]
Scholem, Gershom, 326, 329[29]
Schulthess, Sara, 598[b]
Schürer, Emil, 302[11], 308[30], 308[32]
Schwedler, Gerald, 441[49]
Seeman, Chris, 44[9]
Segal, Alan F., 303[13]
Sfameni Gasparro, Giulia, 404[17]
Shaheen, A. Moeiz, 24, 25[12]
Shaked, Shaul, 324[9], 330[31], 343[h], 365[b], 366[e], 367[b]
Sherwood-Smith, Maria C., 611[12]
Shuler, Philip L., 540[15]
Siegert, Folker, 536[1], 528[7], 539[10], 540[14], 541[18], 542[19], 542[24], 542[27], 544[a], 545[f], 546[a-b], 546[d], 546[g], 548[d], 550[b], 550[e], 552[d], 556[b], 560[a], 560[c], 561[e], 562[a], 565[c], 570[c], 571[d], 571[g], 572[a], 573[e], 573[g-h], 574[e], 577[e], 578[f], 579[c]
Sijpesteijn, P. J., 370[e]
Sims-Williams, Nicholas, 116[134], 139[c], 143[b-c], 149[a]
Skemer, Don C., 363[16]
Skjærvø, Prods Oktor, 40[1], 41[3], 47–48, 50[34], 51[37], 52[44], 56[66], 56[71], 98[35], 100[53], 101[55], 104[68], 105[72], 105[74], 106[77], 106[80], 107[83], 108[88-89], 111[113], 111[115], 112[123], 118[147-50], 127[180], 142[e], 143[d], 146[k], 158–59[i], 638[12]
Slabczyk, Miron, 462[7], 463[14]

Smith, Morton, 363[14], 365[b]
Sokoloff, Michael, 343[e], 343[h-i], 344[h], 345[c], 345[k-l], 347[h], 348[e], 354[f]
Sparks, Hedley, 402[9]
Speckenback, Klaus, 437[31]
Sperber, Daniel, 295[f]
Spittler, R. P., 641[31-32], 641[34-36]
Steiner, Richard C., 638[17], 643[48], 645[71], 646[72-73]
Stokes, Whitley, 617[43]
Stone, Michael E., 17[c], 17[f], 282[13], 288[34-35], 290[36-37], 291[38], 309[34], 309[37], 402[5], 402[7], 406[24-25], 408[37], 410[41], 413[50-51], 414[57], 414[60], 415[62], 426[c], 431[b], 496[3-4], 497[6-7], 498[8], 502[9-11], 503[13], 503[16], 505, 612[17-22], 613[23-24], 614[33], 615[34], 616[38], 617[39], 626[a], 627[a], 631[c], 633[a], 635[1], 640[28], 641, 642[40-41], 643[51], 643[53], 644[60], 645[65], 645[70-71], 646[73]
Stratton, Kimberly B., 196[39]
Strohal, Rudolf, 613[28]
Stroumsa, Guy G., 11[11], 90[4]
Strugnell, John, 402[5], 402[7], 406[24-25], 408[37], 410[41], 413[50-51], 414[57], 414[60], 415[62], 426[c], 429[a], 431[b]
Stuckenbruck, Loren T., 41[2], 42[4], 43[8], 47[25], 54[53], 59[3], 60[4], 61[6], 63[8], 64[9], 65[17], 66[22], 68[a], 90[4], 94[22], 98[33], 98[38-39], 98[41], 121[158], 123, 145[g], 146[a], 171[10], 177[e-f], 638[13]
Stuckrad, Kocku von, 443[62]
Suciu, Alin, 391[10], 393[21], 394[23]
Sundermann, Werner, 41[3], 61[6], 62, 91[9], 92[12], 93[18], 94–96, 99[42-44], 99[47], 102[60], 104[67], 107[84], 108, 113[128], 116[135], 125, 128[182-83], 137, 139, 140[d], 145[d], 146[b-c], 146[e], 146[i], 156[a], 156[c], 156[f], 157[a], 158[d], 160[f], 160[j], 162[a], 171
Swartz, Michael D., 323[4], 324[8], 329[29]

Taavitsainen, Irma, 439[39]
Tardieu, Michel, 9[2], 104[66], 106[80], 640[28]
Terian, Abraham, 542[24]
Thomas, Joseph, 94[4], 108[8]
Thomson, Robert W., 503[14]
Thonemann, Peter, 433[5]
Thorlacius, Børge, 360[7]
Thorndike, Lynn, 443[63]
Thyen, Hartwig, 540[12]
Tobin, Thomas H., 538[6]
Tocci, Franco M., 329[29]

Index of Modern Authors

Toepel, Alexander, 640[28]
Toolan, Michael, 587[10], 588[12], 589[13]
Topchyan, Aram, 540[13-14], 542[23], 542[28], 544[a], 545[f], 546[a], 546[d], 547[c], 548[d], 549[b], 550[b], 550[e], 551[b], 552[b], 552[d], 556[b], 560[a], 560[c], 562[a], 562[c], 570[f], 571[d], 571[g], 573[e], 573[g-h], 574[d], 577[c], 579[c]
Torijano Morales, Pablo A., 188[19], 442[57], 443[61]
Trachtenberg, Joshua, 329[29]
Tromp, Johannes, 246[8], 299[1-2], 301[8], 307, 308[30], 308[33], 309[35-37], 312[c], 316[a]
Turcan, Marie, 431[e]
Turdeanu, Emil, 318[d]
Turville-Petre, E. O. G., 437[29]
Tuval, Michael, 46[18], 376[18]
Tzvetkova-Glaser, Anna, 274[5], 274[8], 276[16], 278[d]

Uden, James, 595[30]

VanderKam, James C., 43[8], 636[2], 642[37], 643[46]
Vassiliev, Athensius, 318[c]
Veltri, Giuseppe, 357[2]
Verheyden, Joseph, 404[18]
Vermes, Geza, 260[10]
Vialova, Svetlana Olegovna, 613[26]
Vincent, Markus, 248[18]
Visotzky, Burton, 10[9]
Vliet, Jan van der, 263[23]
Vogliano, Achille, 360[7], 365[c], 365[e]
Vučković, Josip, 613[24-25]
Vučković, Lejla, 614[30]

Wahl, Otto, 502[11-12]
Wajnberg, Isaak, 426[c], 427[b]
Waldschmidt, Ernst, 101[56]
Wallis, Richard T., 593[22]
Wallis Budge, E. A., 440[46]

Wasserstrom, Steven M., 640[24], 644[57]
Weinberg, Steven, 444[64]
Weinstock, Stefan, 440[42]
Weißer, Christoph, 440[48], 442[55]
Wendland, Paul, 596[36], 598[a], 604[a], 605[a], 606[c]
Wertheimer, S., 281[3-4]
Wessely, Carl Johann Joseph, 258[6]
Wevers, John W., 362[10]
Wilkens, Jens, 61[6], 126, 170[3-6], 171[7-10], 172[11-13], 173[14], 176[a-d], 176[f], 177[d], 178[e-f], 178[i], 179[a-b], 179[d], 180[b-c], 180[e-j], 181[a-h], 182[a-c], 183[c]
Williams, Alan V., 93[16], 109[95], 109[98]
Williams, C. A., 590[14-15], 605[f]
Wills, Lawrence, 389[7]
Winston, David, 541[17]
Wintermute, O. S., 43[8], 192[29], 320[d], 401[2], 645[65]
Wright, Archie T., 64[9]
Wurst, Gregor, 114

Yadin, Yigael, 638[17], 646[72]
Yassif, Eli, 282[9], 285[21]
Yorke, John, 587[10-11], 588[12]
Yoshida, Yutaka, 92[15]
Yovsēpʻiancʻ, Sargis, 496[2]

Zaccagni, Lorenzo Alessandro, 321[c]
Žagar, Mateo, 613[27]
Zandee, Jan, 257[1], 259[7-8], 260[9], 262[15], 262[18-19], 263[20-21], 264[26], 264[30-31], 265[32], 267
Zellman-Rohrer, Michael, 357[3], 360[9]
Zieme, Peter, 42[6], 50[34], 51, 55, 57, 90[1], 94[24], 96[31], 100, 101[58], 116[138], 119-20, 121[159], 123, 125, 170[3], 181[8]
Zohrabian, Johannes, 496[1]
Zsom, Dóra, 186[5]

Index of Scripture and Other Ancient Texts

Hebrew Bible

Genesis

Ref	Pages
1:1–5	515
1:1–5:1	273
1:6–7	608[b]
1:6–8	515
1:9 LXX	239[a]
1:10 LXX	369[d]
1:28	601
1:28 LXX	592
2–3	591
2:7	505
2:8	591[19]
2:10	591[19]
2:10–14 LXX	602[a]
2:16–17	604
3:1–6	312
3:4–5	320
3:19	516
4:16	591[19]
5	199
5–10	65
5:24	51, 70, 141
5:25	2
6	39, 213[b]
6–8	568
6:1–4	2, 43, 44, 47, 51, 90, 376, 476, 479
6:2	51, 56, 139
6:3	44, 147
6:4	46, 377
6:5	39, 51, 85, 477
6:8–9	505
6:11	39
6:11–12	51, 74, 85
6:14	200
6:19–7:3	200
7:8–9	55
7:20	623, 626, 629
8:1	476
9:16	495
10	297
10:2	297, 473[a]
10:6	297
10:8	297
10:8–9	46
10:11	560
14:5	46
14:19	235[k], 238[e]
14:22	485
15:6	552
15:7–19	414[55]
15:17	480
16	540[15]
17:7	495
17:13	495
17:19	495
18:1–15	541
18:5	536
20–21	540[15]
21	540[15]
22:17	505
26:29	295
27:39	475
29:24	288
29:29	288
30:8	293
31:5	473
31:29	473
31:42	473
32:9	473
34:25–26	552
37	260, 261
37:5–11	286
37:12–14	257
37:13–16	268
37:14	257
37:15	257, 261
37:15–17	271
37:15–35	3, 257
37:18–20	257, 271
37:99–22	268
37:21–22	258, 271
37:24	271
37:25	271
37:25–28	263
37:26–27	261
37:28	272
37:29	261
37:29–30	258
37:31–35	258, 272
37:35	268
37:36	268, 273, 274, 275
38:24	552
39	273
39:1	274
39:6–19	278
39:7–20	552
41	258
41:25	284, 294
41:32	294
41:45	273, 274, 275, 278
41:50	273, 274, 278[a]
46:7	287

663

Index of Scripture and Other Ancient Texts

46:27	287, 297	25:6	231	26:22	483
49:12	480	25:7 LXX	365[d]	26:26	478
49:17	480	25:10-16	468		
49:21	286	25:17-22	487	**Numbers**	
		25:31-37	468	3:31	468
Exodus		25:33-34	469[d]	5:18	279
2:12	315, 316, 317, 318	26:30-33	468	8:1-4	468
3	362	26:33-34 LXX	365[d]	11:1	484
3:1	357[2]	26:37	468	11:26-29	637
3:8	489	27:3	468[c]	13	44
3:12 LXX	366[e]	28:6-14	468	13:22	45
3:14	369[d]	28:15 LXX	365[d]	13:32	221
3:17	489	28:17-21	468	13:32-33	44
4:1-9	357	28:21	468	13:33	46, 47
4:17	357	28:22 LXX	365[d]	14:8	489
4:30-31	357	28:31-43	468	14:9	481
6:20	335, 339, 355	28:36	363, 367[b]	14:14	477, 480
7:11	372[1], 375, 376, 397	28:36 LXX	356	15:17	486
7:22	372[1], 375, 376	28:36-38	209[e]	16:1-40	263
8:7	372[1], 375, 376	30:27	468	16:5	397
8:18	372[1], 375, 376	31:18	468	16:14	494
9:11	372[1], 375, 376	32:15-16	361	16:22	316, 317
10:1-20	475	33:11	233, 238	16:31-32	480
10:22	475, 476	33:20	192, 240, 550	22	397
12:37	238	34:29-35	317	22:22	397
13:5	489	36:36	468	23:22	294[c]
13:21	192, 214	37:19	469[d]	24:8	294[c]
13:21-22	477, 480	38:1-7	468	27:16 LXX	316, 317
14:7	387, 400	38:3	468[c]	36:2	494
14:21	239[a]	39:1-31	468		
14:22	568, 623, 626, 628	39:4-5	468	**Deuteronomy**	
14:24	192, 215	39:14	468	1:28	46
14:25	233	39:30-31	209[e], 356, 367[b]	1:29	44[13]
14:29	623, 626, 628	40:6	468	2:10-11	45
15:10	485	40:29	468	2:19-21	45
15:11	243[b]			3:11	45, 46
15:16	239	**Leviticus**		4:1	362
18:4	473	4:7	468	4:11	479
19:15	218, 224	8:8-9 LXX	356[d]	4:21	494
19:16	485	13-14	216	4:24	221, 488
19:18	476	15	216	4:31	230
20:11	505, 515	16:7-10	53, 73	4:32	479, 481, 482
20:26	495	19:18	293, 509	4:40	362
24:10	199	21:11	192, 216	5:4	232
24:16 LXX	366[e]	24:4	468	5:16	362
24:17	479, 488	26:6	489	5:23	479
24:17 LXX	366[e]	26:20	478	5:33	362

664

Index of Scripture and Other Ancient Texts

6:2	362	34:5–6 LXX	319	14:19	537, 558
6:3	489	34:6	305, 314, 318, 319[c]	14:20	558
6:24	362, 509			15:4–5	559
8:1	362	**Joshua**		16:4–22	539
9:2	45	5:10	318	16:15–19	536
9:3	221, 488	5:14	318	16:17	539, 544
10:17	484, 485, 486, 487	10:12–13	482	16:19	536[2], 544
10:20	293	10:13	233	16:28	536
11:8	362	14:8	486	16:28–30	536
11:9	362, 489	16:10	477		
12:7	230			**1 Samuel**	
13:5	293	**Judges**		2:8	484, 488
15:4	494	1:30	477	3:9	511
16:20	362	1:33	477	4:4	487
17:20	362	1:35	477	16:14–15	368[c]
18:10–11	368[b]	3:14–16	493	17	45
26:9	489	5:22	230	17:5	192, 220
26:15	489	5:31	627	17:26	470, 473
27:8	199	9:48	367[d]	17:36	470, 473
28:24	476	13–14	536	20:38	230
28:29–31	478	13:2	545	21:11	46[21]
28:49	474	13:3	546	21:15–22	45, 46
29:23	192, 205	13:4	546	21:22	46
29:28	301	13:5	536, 539, 544, 548		
30:4	493, 495	13:6	546, 547	**2 Samuel**	
30:6	362	13:8	547	6:2	487
30:10	523	13:9	547	17:10	486
30:19	362	13:10	547	22:8	485, 490, 627
30:20	371[b]	13:11	548	22:9	486
31:24–26	309	13:14	546, 548	22:11	487
31:26	309	13:15	548	22:13	486
31:30	356, 361	13:16	537, 547, 549	22:32	242
32	356, 361, 362	13:17	549	23:5	495
32:1–3	359, 369, 369–70[e]	13:18	549		
32:8	297	13:20	549	**1 Kings**	
32:8 LXX	287, 296	13:25	550	3:9	200
32:22	488	14:1	551	3:12	315
32:27	371[b]	14:5	553	6:23	487
32:44–47	361	14:6 LXX	553	6:24–27	494
32:46–47	362	14:10	558	7:48	468
32:47	361, 362, 371[b]	14:14	537, 554	7:49	468
33:13–17	286	14:14–15	557	7:50	468
33:17	294	14:15	557, 558	8:37	475
33:27	231	14:17	557	10:18–20	469
34:1–4	318	14:17a	557	10:20	472
34:4	317	14:18a	558	19:5–6	414
34:5–6	306, 318	14:18b	558	19:10	428

19:11	414	6:2–4	192	28:15	478
19:11–18	413	6:3	241, 338, 492	29:6	488
19:11–12	414	6:4	240	30:17	477
		6:6	480	30:25	477, 487, 489
2 Kings		8:6	473	30:27	475, 484
2:9–14	415	8:22	485	30:27–28	486
2:11	223, 227, 428, 480, 485	9:1	483	30:30	484
6:17	239	9:2	492	32:2	489
17:6	473[a]	9:7	494	33:20	482
17:20	474	10:17	475	34:4	476, 480, 487, 625, 627, 631
18:13–19:37	470	10:32	494		
19:4	470, 473	11:2	469, 552	34:9	424
19:15	487	11:8	483	34:11–15	483
19:16	470, 473	11:11	477	35:6	489
19:21	494	11:11–13	492	35:7	483
19:35	192, 239	11:15	493	35:11	489
19:36	471	13:3	46	36–37	470
19:37	470	13:4	474	37:4	470, 473
24:20	474	13:7	486	37:16	487
25	435	13:10	474, 476, 477, 479, 487	37:17	470, 473
25:1	468, 468[b]			37:26	192, 239
25:13–17	469	13:22	483	37:38	470
25:14	468	14:9	45, 46	40:3–4	493
25:15–17	468	16–17	23	40:4	474, 493, 624, 630
25:17	471	17:2	483	40:12	192, 215, 478
		17:5–6	477	40:23	238
Isaiah		17:9	483	41:8	492, 493, 495
1:1–8	607[c]	17:12	474	41:18	489
1:2	607	19:1	486	42:8	343
1:2 LXX	607[c]	19:2	475, 501	42:11	475, 489
1:8	494	19:2 LXX	514	42:14–16	493
1:19	431	19:5–6	478, 485	42:15	478
1:26	495	21:2	473[a]	43:2	494
2:2–5	492, 493	22–23	23	43:5–6	484
2:10	625[a], 631[a]	23:15	473	43:5–7	493
2:15	205	23:17	473	43:16	483, 493
2:19	625[a], 627, 631[a]	24:17–18	484	43:16–21	493
2:21	625[a], 627, 631[a]	24:19–20	484	43:20	483, 489
3:2	46	24:23	474, 479, 495	44:6	242
3:16	494	25:6	492, 495	44:27	478
3:17	494	26:7	493	45:2	488, 493
4:5	494	26:19	411, 412, 428	47:13	192, 234
5:10	478	26:20	412	48:13	576
6	194	27:1	56, 480	48:20–21	493
6:1	236	28–29	23	49:12	493
6:2	192, 241, 487	28:2	477	49:13	488
6:2–3	241[a]	28:5	477	49:19	475

Index of Scripture and Other Ancient Texts

Reference	Page
49:24–25	46
50:3	474, 479
51:3	489
51:10	483
52:1	474, 495
52:8	627
52:11–12	493
54:11–12	490
54:11–14	489
54:16	486
55:11	337
55:12	488
57:14–58:4	540[13]
59:19	493, 494
60	412
60:1	412, 428, 495
60:1–2	411, 412, 413
60:2	428, 476, 485
60:3	490
60:4	493, 495
60:11	490, 494
60:14	495
60:19	495
60:20	495
61:1	371[b]
61:8	495
62:4	495
62:11	494
64:3 [Evv 64:4]	408, 425
65:18	489
66:12	477
66:15	484
66:15–23	476
66:16	617, 626
66:24	517

Jeremiah

Reference	Page
1:5	524
1:13–15	475
3:3	475
4:24	480
4:31	494
7:15	474
9:5	478
9:11	483
10:13	476, 487, 490
10:22	474, 483
11:5	489
12:14	494
13:6	473
15:2	474
15:14	484
18:14	238[f]
22:19	627
23:6	495
23:29	337
24:5	495
24:10	474
25:9	468
25:25	473[a]
27:6	468
27:16–19	468
27:21	468
28:3	468
28:6	468
28:8	474
28:14	468
30:3	492
31:23	489
32:22	489
32:17	232
32:27	236[a]
32:37	493, 495
33:26	492, 493, 495
34:9 Hexapla	371[b]
35:5	471
38:14	207, 233
38:26	225, 233
40:1	22
40:2	22
41:9 LXX	371[b]
43:10	468
47:2	477
48:8–9	483
48:19	192, 205
49:33	483
49:36	474, 475, 479, 484, 492
50:5	495
50:41	494
51:11	473[a]
51:16	476, 487, 490
51:25	479
51:28	473[a]
51:37	483
50:40	205
51:44	470
51:58	470
52:18	468
52:19	468

Ezekiel

Reference	Page
1	193, 194
1:4	192, 223, 487
1:5	192, 240
1:5–14	239[j]
1:13	486
1:14	216
1:15–21	192, 240
1:26	199
1:27	223
3:12	242
7:6	473
7:15	474
7:21	477
9:2	368[a]
9:11	368[a]
10	194, 239[j]
10:1	199
10:6	240[f]
10:9–14	240[f]
10:16	240[f]
12:15	484
13:18	368[a]
13:20	368[a]
14:21	474
17:9	476
17:22–24	489
18:6	192, 216
20:6	489
20:15	489
20:47	475
21:7	486
22:20	484
22:21–22	485
22:27	483
26:7	484, 485, 486, 487
26:7–9	470
26:21	337[c]
28:13	468
28:14	480, 494

28:16	494	2:4–9	475	3:10	574
32:7	474, 476, 479, 487	2:10	476, 480, 487	4	538
32:7–8	476, 479, 480	2:15–16	492	4:5–6	574
32:12	46	2:20	475	4:9–10	576
32:17–22 LXX	376	2:25	475		
32:21	46	2:30	477, 480	**Micah**	
32:21 LXX	377	2:31	474, 479	1:4	485, 486
32:27	44[12], 46	3:4 [Evv 2:31]	474, 479	1:13	494
34:13	493, 495	4:18 [Evv 3:18]	489	2:2	477
34:25	489	4:9–21 [Evv 3:9–21]	476	3:11	474
36:24	493, 495	4:12 [Evv 3:12]	627	4:1–4	492, 493
37:9	474, 475, 479, 484, 492	4:15 [Evv 3:15]	474, 479, 480	4:13	480
				6:9	493, 494
37:12	625, 627, 631	**Amos**		7:3	478
37:12–13	492	3:12	477	7:6	475, 478
38–39	474, 476	4:7	475	7:8	492
38:2	481	4:11	205	7:12	479, 481, 482
38:2–6	481[f]	5:3	477		
38:15	475	5:8	232	**Nahum**	
38:19–20	474	5:13	474	1:4	192, 215
38:20	624, 630	5:15	477	1:5	486
39:6	474	5:20	474, 475, 476	1:5–6	493
39:9	480	7:1–3	475	2:4	192
39:18	46	7:4	488	2:5	227
39:20	46	8:2	473		
40–48	489	8:9	474, 479	**Habakkuk**	
41:18	494			1:8	481, 483
43:2	486	**Jonah**		2:3	473
43:2–3	494	1–2	537	3:3	488
48:30–35	490	1–4	540[13]	3:9	480
48:33–34	490	1:1–2:9	537	3:11	480
48:35	495	1:5	562, 565[f]		
		1:5 LXX	563	**Zephaniah**	
Hosea		1:7	564	1:5	474
1:2	608	1:8	564	2:9	477
1:2 LXX	586	1:9	564	3:3	483
1:10	505	1:11	564	3:12–13	477
2:1	470, 473	1:15	537	3:14	494
9:7	475	2:1	566		
13:14	488	2:2–9	537, 566	**Haggai**	23
14:10	474	3	537	1:10	475
		3:4	569	2:6	231
Joel		3:4 LXX	577, 578[c]	2:21	231
1:4	475	3:5	572		
2:1–11	474	3:7–8	573	**Zechariah**	23
2:2	216, 238, 475, 476, 487	3:8	541	2:4–5	489
2:3	488	3:9	573	2:5	494

Index of Scripture and Other Ancient Texts

2:6	474, 475, 479, 484, 492	22:22 [Evv 22:21]	294	98:6	627
2:10 LXX	474, 475, 479, 484, 492	24:2	489	98:8	488
		24:7–10	488	99:1	487
3:1–2	303	24:8	238	102:16 [Evv 102:15]	493, 494
3:2 OG	317, 318	27:7	215[n]		
4:2	468	29:7	234	102:26 [Evv 102:25]	627
4:11–13	403	32:6	302, 313	103:2	298[b]
4:14	403	33:16	46	103:30	302, 313
6:5	474, 475, 479, 484, 492	36:8 [Evv 36:7]	487	104	194
7:14	484	42:3	470, 473	104:2	192, 240
8:3	495	44:19	483	104:3	232, 486
9:10	479, 481, 482	46:3–4 [Evv 46:2–3]	480	104:4	215, 229, 479, 523
9:14	480, 481	48:11	242	104:5	489
10:1	475	50:3	488	104:6	486
10:11	493	57:2 [Evv 57:1]	487	104:24	215[n], 230
11:13	408	61:6 [Evv 61:5]	493, 494	104:32	476
14	476	63:8 [Evv 63:7]	487	105	506[a]
14:2	474	68:3 [Evv 68:2]	485	105:6	492, 493, 495
14:4	480	68:12	287[32]	105:43	493
14:6–7	495	68:18	192, 237, 238, 242, 412	107:3	484, 493
14:7	479	71:20	243	107:16	488
14:8	489	72:3	489	107:29	489
14:9	484, 485, 486, 487	72:7	489	107:33	192, 215
14:20	468[c]	72:8	479, 481, 482	109:3 LXX	413, 428
		74:14	56	109:4 LXX	598, 607
Malachi		75:3	484	109:11	477
1:3	483	77:17 [Evv 77:16]	486	110:1	495, 603
3:10	486	77:18 [Evv 77:17]	487	110:4	598, 607
3:20 [Evv 4:2]	413, 428	77:20 [Evv 77:19]	483, 493	114:3	215
		79:5–6	484	114:4	489
Psalms		80:2	487	115:18	234
2:8–9	480	84:3	470, 473	119:17	215[n]
8:5 [Evv 8:4]	494	84:7	487	119:35	215[n]
9:3 [Evv 9:2]	492	89:7	355	122:8	495
9:14 [Evv 9:13]	494	89:14	494	135:7	487, 490
9:20 [Evv 9:19]	494	89:48	488	136:2–3	484, 485, 486, 487
11:6	486	90:10	293		
17:8	487	91:1	236	144:5	476, 486
18:9 [Evv 18:8]	486	91:1–2	336[e]	145:1	492
18:10 [Evv 18:9]	486, 494	91:2	253[a]	145:10	492
18:11 [Evv 18:10]	487	91:2	253[a]	145:16	336
18:16 [Evv 18:15]	485, 490	92:13 [Evv 92:12]	489	145:6 LXX [Evv 146:6]	505, 515
18:32 [Evv 18:31]	242	94:22	253[a]		
19:5	46, 207	96:11	488	147:4	488
21:6 [Evv 21:5]	488	97:2	494		
21:10 [Evv 21:9]	480	97:5	485, 486	**Job**	
22:15 [Evv 22:14]	486	98:4	488	1:6	43

669

1:7	209	**Canticles**		3:18 LXX	484, 485, 486, 487
2:1	43	3:6	221	3:19–30	568
3:21	484	4:14	208, 221	3:29	484
9:5	231, 242			3:34 LXX	484, 485, 486, 487
9:6	488	**Qohelet/Ecclesiastes**			
9:7	477	3:2	200	4	469
9:9	199	3:2–3	192	4:1	494
12:22	192, 240	3:3	200	4:4 [Evv 4:7]	469[a]
14:18	488	3:14	293	4:5–6 [Evv 4:8–9]	469
20:26	237	5:7	216	4:6 [Evv 4:9]	469
23:13	192, 241	7:26	561	4:8–9 [Evv 4:11–12]	469[b]
25:3	334	8:8	488	4:10 [Evv 4:13]	74, 481
25:5	476, 487	10:8	559	4:11–12 [Evv 4:14–15]	469
26:5	46			4:20 [Evv 4:23]	74, 481
26:11	192, 240	**Lamentations**		4:37 LXX	484, 485, 486, 487
28:17	471	1:1	483		
28:21	232	1:6	494	5:2	468
34:15	627	1:7	483	5:2–4	469
37:11	479	1:12	484	5:5	469, 470
38:4	484	2:1	494	5:7	469[a]
38:4–6	490	2:4	482	5:11	469
38:22	215, 242	2:8	494	5:12	469[b]
38:35	200	2:10	494	5:19	484
39:9–12	294[c]			5:28	471, 473[a]
39:26	483	**Daniel**		6:1 [Evv 5:31]	468, 472[b], 473[a]
41	56	1:2	468	6:8 [Evv 6:7]	468[a]
41:11	494	1:4	474	6:9 [Evv 6:8]	473[a]
41:13 [Evv 41:12]	486	1:7	469[b]	6:13 [Evv 6:12]	473[a]
41:17	192, 240	1:10	469	6:16 [Evv 6:15]	473[a]
		1:13	470[c]	6:16–23 [Evv 6:15–22]	568
Proverbs		1:17	469	6:23–25 [Evv 6:22–24]	469
2:4	484	1:21	470	6:25 [Evv 6:24]	484, 494
3:3	219	2:5	469[a]	6:27 [Evv 6:26]	470, 473
6:28	494	2:10	469[a]	6:29 [Evv 6:28]	470
7:3	219	2:21	469, 561	7	44
8:18	242	2:22	192, 240	7:2	474, 475, 479, 484, 492
8:22–26	488	2:26	469[b]	7:2–8	530
10:2	484	2:31	481	7:7–8	530
11:28	489	2:31–34	469	7:9	242
21:16	45, 46, 376[18]	2:37	484, 485, 486, 487	7:9–10	44, 54, 66, 76
23:31	480	2:47	484, 485, 486, 487	7:10	80, 192, 238, 240, 242
25:13	192, 228	2:48	469	7:13	494, 532
25:25	228	3:1–5	481	7:13–14	494
30:13	481	3:2	468[a]	7:14	484
		3:3	468[a], 469[a]		
Ruth		3:4	484		
3:9	487	3:7	484, 494	7:19–26	530

7:23	480, 530	1:8	471	**ANCIENT NEAR**	
7:25	473, 482	1:9–11	471	**EASTERN LITERA-**	
8:1–2	435[20]	2:1–70	473	**TURE AND SOURCES**	
8:4	192, 229	5:3	468[a]		
8:5	474	5:6	468[a]	Bisitun Inscription	461
8:5–8	480	5:11	485		
8:8	474, 475, 479, 484, 492	5:14	468	Byblos	
8:11	318	6:2	472	13	45[14]
8:17	473	6:5	468, 471		
8:19	473	6:6	468[a]	Enuma Elish	
8:26	309, 474	7:12	484, 485, 486, 487	1.1–2	488
9:1	468, 473[a]				
9:1–4a	435[20]	Nehemiah		Mamar Marqah	
9:4	495	1:5	495	5:3	306
9:12	474	7:6–73	473		
9:20	233	7:70	468	**DEUTEROCANONICAL**	
9:24–27	473	9	506[a]	**BOOKS**	
9:26	468, 473, 477	9:11	493		
9:27	482, 483			Tobit	
10:1	469[b], 470	1 Chronicles		1:14	473[a]
10:2–3	232	1:10	46	1:16–22	470
10:2–4	435[20]	10:13	210, 212	1:21	470
10:6	479	11:22–23	46	2:10	472
11:1	468, 472[b]	11:15	46	3:7	472
11:4	474, 475, 479, 484, 492	13:6	487	3:7–8	219[j]
11:6	473	14:9	46	3:11	492
11:13	473	14:13	46	4:9	484
11:23	482	18:8	468	6:5	472
11:27	473	20:4–8	45[15], 46[21]	6:8	368[c]
11:31	482	20:5	45[16]	6:9	472
11:33	474	20:8	46[21]	7:1	472
11:35	473, 474	28:15	468	10:13	485
11:38	471	28:17	468	13:6	493
11:40	473			13:8–17	489
11:45	473	2 Chronicles		13:10	493
12:2	428, 491, 627	6:18	487	13:16	475, 490
12:2–3	627	7:1	487	14:5	474
12:3	474	7:12	506	14:7–8	492
12:4	473, 474	9:17–19	469	14:12	472
12:6	473	14:7	475	14:14	472
12:7	482	15:6	475, 501		
12:9	309, 473, 474	20:7	492, 493, 495	Judith	389, 390, 396
12:10	474	25:5	192, 220	1:1	472
12:13	473, 474	32:1–23	470	1:2	472
		32:21	192, 239	1:14	472
Ezra				2:24	483
1:7–11	468			3:8	484

671

9:8	487	47:4	46	6:23	472[c]
9:12	469, 473, 485	48:9	480, 485	6:26	471
16:5–6	46				
16:14	302, 313	**Baruch**	6	**Prayer of Manasseh**	
16:15	485, 486	1:8	468	7	521[b]
		1:8–9	471		
Additions to Esther		2:1	474	**3 Maccabees**	389
11:8	485	2:35	495	2:4	46, 65
		3:7	493, 494	2:7–8	493
Wisdom of Solomon		3:26	46	6:4	493
3:9	495	3:30–31	483	6:5-7	470
4:15	495	4:14	494	6:6	480
7:1	491	4:36–37	493	6:18	488
7:7	469	5	412	7:6	470, 473
7:17	201	5:1–4	495		
7:20	201	5:5	412	**2 Esdras**	
10:18–21	493	5:7	493	2:19	489
10:20	492			2:32	495
13:1–9	541	**Additions to Daniel**		16:10	485
13:1–19	537	Prayer of Azariah		16:53	486
14:6	46, 65	26	480	16:60	489
16:9	475	30	492		
16:13	488	66	480	**4 Maccabees**	536, 540[15],
16:22–23	485	68	484, 485, 486, 487		541
18:3	477, 480	Bel and the Dragon	470	2:2	278[b]
				8:12	480
Sirach/Ben Sira/		**1 Maccabees**	389, 390, 396,	12:17	469, 473
Ecclesiasticus			398	16:3	480
1:18	489	1:21	468	16:21	480
3:4	484	1:54	482	18:1	492, 493, 495
3:21–22	511, 521	2:54	495		
16:7	46, 65	3:3	46	**OLD TESTAMENT**	
26:17	468	4:49–51	468	**PSEUDEPIGRAPHA**	
26:18	468	4:60	475		
36:18	487	13:33	475	**Abraham, Apocalypse of**	
37:3	475	13:51	493	11:1–3	479
39:6	469				
39:16	524	**2 Maccabees**	389	**Abraham, Testament of**	
39:21	524	2:4–8	471	14:7–8	308[28]
39:29	474	9:3	472	20:11–12	308
43:4	480	10:7	493	B11	410, 426
44:18	495	14:35	487		
44:21	479, 481, 482			**Adam of Leptogensis,**	
45:6	468	**1 Esdras**		**Book concerning the**	
45:7	495	2:13–15	471	**Daughters of**	638–39, 645
45:15	495	5:1–4	473		
45:19	484				

Index of Scripture and Other Ancient Texts

Adam and Eve, Life of		29:5	478	5.26.11–13	592
19:13	476	30:2	484, 487, 490	5.26.12b–13	602[d]
38:3	474, 475, 479, 484, 492	30:3	473	5.26.14	592, 593, 603[b]
		39:7	479	5.26.15–16	589
		40:3	491	5.26.15–17a	586
Adam, Testament of		42:8	492	5.26.24a	590
4:6	239	44:14	469	5.26.24b–26	606[a]
		46:5	469	5.26.27	598[d], 608[c]
Ahiqar		48:22	474	5.26.31	603[b]
1:3–10	470	48:31–35	478	5.26.31a	590
6:26	485	48:32	475	5.26.31b	590
		49:2–3	491	5.26.32	590
Aristeas, Letter of		50:2	491	5.26.33	585, 595, 600[b], 603[d]
208	539[9]	53:8–10	481	5.26.34–37	586
257	539[9]	59:8	484	5.26.34–5.27.4	585
290	539[9]	64:3	474, 475, 479, 484, 492	5.26.37	600[a]
Artapanus	386, 387[2], 389, 396	69:4	484	**Benjamin, Testament of**	
		70:5	474	(*see under* Patriarchs,	
		70:9	514	Testaments of the Twelve)	
Asher, Testament of		72:2	474		
(*see under* Patriarchs,		73:6	483	**Biblical Antiquities**	
Testaments of the Twelve)		74:2	491	(*see* Pseudo-Philo)	
		76:5	471		
2 Baruch	464	77:19	644[64]	**Dan, Testament of**	
1:1	468	83:1	476	(*see under* Patriarchs,	
6:7	468	83:7	484	Testaments of the Twelve)	
6:8	471				
10:9	476	**3 Baruch**	417	**Daniel, Apocalypse of**	
10:11	475	1:1	468	9:1–6	482
12:4	474	4:7	305	9:15–26	480
14:12	484, 487, 490	4:10	65		
20:1–2	476	9:7	305	**Daniel, Dreams of**	
20:3	474			(*see* Somniale Danielis)	
21:6	479	**4 Baruch**			
21:19	491	3:18–19	471	**Daniel, Ma'aseh**	
21:23	484, 487, 490			121–122	472
21:23–25	488	**Baruch, Justinus's Book of**			
21:24	491	5.24.1	586, 608[a]	**Daniel,**	
27:7	474, 514	5.24.1–5.27.5	586	**Seventh Vision of**	616
27:11	477	5.26.1	585, 587		
27:15	474	5.26.1–33	585, 586, 587, 595, 596	**Daniel,**	
28:1	474			**Syriac Apocalypse of**	5
28:2	473	5.26.4	604[a], 605[d]	5	464
28:5	491	5.26.7	592	14	463
29:3	479	5.26.8	607[d]	21	461
29:4	477, 483	5.26.9b	592	22	461, 463

673

Index of Scripture and Other Ancient Texts

31	464	6–7	61	10:11–16	121
32	464	6–8	115, 287	10:12	43, 120, 145, 147
		6–11	62, 65, 66	10:13	51, 125
Daniel, Young (Syriac)		6:1	73	10:15	43, 56
	464[16], 465	6:1–2	43, 51, 139	10:16–22	44
7:57	480	6:1–7:6	51	10:17	117[140]
9:6	474	6:2–7	476, 479	10:17–11:2	55, 62
9:11	481[a, b]	6:3	42, 51	10:18–19	98, 121, 148
9:12	481[c]	6:6	42	10:18–20	68
9:15	481[e]	6:7	52, 98, 119	10:19	478
		6:7–8	43	10:20	98, 104, 117, 141
Eber, Apocryphon of	643	7–8	51, 78, 117	12–16	62[7], 64, 65
		7:1	43, 117, 141	12:1	117, 141
Eldad and Modad	637	7:2	44, 73, 101, 117, 142	12:1–4	55[60]
		7:2–5	69	12:3	493
Elijah, Apocalypse of		7:2–6	43	12:3–13:3	53
(Coptic)	5, 401, 402,	7:3–5	61	12:4	17[d]
	411, 415	7:4	117, 141	12:5	55, 72, 75, 147
2:40	475	7:4–5	377[19], 384[a]	13	123, 150
3:1	480	7:5	52, 62, 79	13:1	55, 72, 75, 147
3:2	484	8:1	53, 73	13:2	147
3:6–8	482	8:1–4	43	13:3	151[a]
3:12–13	482	8:3	43	13:4–6	55
3:14	411	8:4	118	13:7–9	42
3:14–18	410	8:4–9:11	51, 61	13:8–10	55[60]
3:15–17	480	9–10	81	13:9	55, 151[a]
4:1–5	403	9:1	54, 74	14	44
4:7–19	403	9:1–10:3	43	14:3	476, 479
4:31	482	9:2–4	52, 143	14:6	55
5:27	403	9:4	484, 485, 486, 487	14:8	108
		9:6	43, 53, 73	14:18–23	43
Elijah, Apocalypse of		9:6–8	43	14:23	43
(Greek)	401, 404, 411, 415,	9:7	51	15–16	63, 123
	416, 417	9:8	51	15:8–12	54, 56, 81, 123
		9:9	43	15:8–16:1	42, 43
Elijah, Apocalypse of		9:10	75, 118	15:8–16:2	63
(Hebrew)	5, 402, 403, 410,	10	123, 124	15:11	49, 112[120]
	414, 416, 417	10–11	98	16:1	112[120], 484
		10–13	115	16:3	121
Elijah, Apocryphon of		10:4–8	43, 53, 62, 73	16:4	55, 72, 75, 147
(fragments)	4	10:7	117	17–19	123
		10:9	51, 52, 62, 65, 75, 125,	17:1	56, 154, 479
1 Enoch	37, 464, 645[71]		145, 152	17:3	122, 125, 148[c]
1–36	39, 42, 60, 94[23]	10:9–10	43	17:4–5	122, 150
1:2	17[d]	10:10	118, 151	17:4–8	122
1:6	485, 486	10:11–12	473	17:5	149
6	62[7]	10:11–14	43, 49, 56	18	124

674

Index of Scripture and Other Ancient Texts

18:2	474, 475, 479, 484, 492	53:4	482, 490	80:4–8	474, 479
		54:1–5	56	82:1–2	309, 642
18:3	485	54:1–6	43, 123, 152	82:16	474
18:6–8	416	54:3–6	49	82:19	474
18:6–12	123, 152	54:4	490	83–90	42, 60
18:6–19:1	49	54:5	43, 53, 73	84:2	61
18:9	416	55:4	43, 49[29], 53, 73	84:2–5	51[43], 74
18:10–19:1	145	56:1–3	56	84:2	61
18:11	477, 480	56:1–4	49	85–90	65
18:13–16	416	56:2	482, 490	86:1–3	43
18:15–16	124, 153	56:2–4	43	86:4–6	43
18:24–25	416	56:7	475	87:1	43
19:1	56	57:2	488	87:3–4	51
20	123	60:7–9	483	87:4	43
21:3	153	60:11	487, 490	88:1–3	43
21:3–4	120	60:24	482, 483, 490	88:2	43
21:3–6	416	61:8	494	89:6	43
21:7	477	61:10	487	89:59	287
21:7–10	49	62:2–3	487	90:21	43
22	404, 416	62:5	494	90:23–24	43
22:5	120, 145	62:7	488	90:28–39	489
24:1	416	62:9–12	56[65]	91–107	60
26	109	64:2	43	91:7	478
27	124	65:7–7	43	91:10	491
27:3	56[65]	67:4–11	43	92:3	491
28–30	489	69:2	43	93:3–10	473
31:2	493	69:2–13	43	93:10	474
37–71	42, 60	69:17	478	93:13	474
39:1	43	69:22–24	192	99:10	474
39:1–3	115	69:23	487, 490	100:1	474
39:3–5	17[e]	69:27–29	494	106–107	65
39:6	488	69:28	43	108:5	474
39:12	492	69:72–82	192		
39:12–13	43, 492	70:1–3	51, 141	**1 Enoch (Greek)**	
40:8	482, 490	70:2	17[f]	22:2	17[h]
40:10	474	70:4	488		
41:2	17[e]	71:3–4	17[g]	**2 Enoch**	2, 20, 417
42	475	71:7	43	Prologue	17[d]
48:2–3	488	72:5	232, 233	1:3–5	479
48:8–9	56[65]	75:3	474	17:1	474
48:9	485	76:14	474, 475, 479, 484, 492	20:1	487
49:3	491			21:1	492
50:4	488	77:1–3	474, 475, 479, 484, 492	21:11	487
51:1	491, 492			22:2	487
51:4	489	80:2	476	33:9–10	642
52:5	482, 490	80:2–8	479	36–40	22
52:6	485	80:4–5	476	36:3	22

675

36:4	22	Exodus Apocryphon		7:28	477, 488
37:2	22	(Coptic)	4	7:32	487, 490, 492
38	22			7:35	487, 490
40:5	22	4 Ezra	5, 464, 616	7:39	487, 495
40:6, 7	22	2:38	495	7:42	488, 495
40:8	22	3:5	515	7:43	473
40:11	487, 490	3:7	484, 516	7:75–101	404
40:12a	22	3:1`4	473, 474	7:80	487, 490
40:12b–42:2	22	3:15	495	7:85	484
53:2–3	410, 426	3:26	506[c]	7:87	488
		4:2	511	7:89	469
2 Enoch (Coptic)	2, 18	4:11	491	7:91	488
36:3	30	4:26	473, 476, 512[b]	7:95	484
36:4–39:1	30	4:31	508[d]	7:96	491
37:1	31	4:32	508[d]	7:101	487, 490
37:1–2	31	4:34	476	7:111	491
39:2–7	30	4:35	484, 487, 490	8:22	479
39:8	31	4:41	484, 487, 490	8:23	486
40:1	32	4:42	474	8:27	474
40:2–3	32	4:48	480	8:62	474
40:4	33	4:50	479	8:63	474
40:5	33	4:52	474	9:1–6	474
40:6, 7	33	5:1	474	9:3	474, 477, 514, 624, 630
40:8	33	5:4	476	9:3–4	474
40:9	33	5:5	479, 624, 625, 627, 629, 631	10:7	491
40:10	34	5:8	483	10:9–10	491
40:11	34	5:9	474	10:22	468
40:12	34	5:12	478	11:2	476
40:13	35	5:13	474	11:39	473
41:1, 2	35	5:22	469	11:40	475
42:1	35	5:37	487, 490	11:41–42	478
42:3	35	5:41	473	11:44	473, 474, 484
		5:42	484	12:9	473, 474
3 Enoch	37, 287[32]	6:1–6	488	12:32	473
1:12	492	6:12	474	12:34	473
5–7	487	6:15	473	12:37–38	474
6:1	223, 227	6:20	474	13:4	485, 486
17:3	223	6:23	490	13:5	474, 475, 479, 484, 492
17:6	214	6:24	474, 478	13:10	479, 486
33:1	490	6:25	477	13:17–20	477
45:5	481	6:25–26	473	13:31	475, 514
48A:10	495	6:39–40	515	13:32	474
		6:41	515	13:37–38	486
Enoch, Book of the Secrets of	20	6:49–52	483	13:40–50	533[a]
		6:51–52	482	13:43–44	493
		7:26	474	13:48–50	477
				13:52	488

Index of Scripture and Other Ancient Texts

14:5	473, 474	5:36A	503	7:66	521[a]		
14:9	473, 488	5:36B	503	7:70	499, 500		
14:10–12	484, 534[b]	5:37	512[a]	7:72	525[a]		
14:13	491	5:40	500	7:77	500, 521[a]		
14:26	301[9]	5:41	501	7:78	498		
14:45–47	474	5:43	502	7:92	500		
		5:44	501	7:93	500		
4 Ezra (Armenian)	5	5:56	501	7:95	500		
3:3 (H)	502	6:1A–1L	499	7:96	501		
3:5	499, 502, 503	6:1B	524[a]	7:116	499		
3:10	499	6:1C	501, 502	7:118	499		
3:12	502	6:1D	501	7:120	500, 521[a]		
3:19 (HW)	502	6:1E	499	7:122	500		
3:20	525[a]	6:1H	501	7:123	500		
3:20–21	500	6:1I	502	7:128	500		
3:21	499	6:1L–10	519[a]	7:130	501		
3:22	499, 500	6:17B	498	7:135	500		
3:25	506[d]	6:20A–20C	501, 502	7:139–140	500		
3:26	499, 500	6:20A–20D	499	8:1A–1D	500		
3:27	506[d]	6:22	501	8:1A–2B	499		
3:34	502	6:24	501, 502	8:1B	501		
4:2	502, 503	6:36	502	8:5	500		
4:4	500	6:38	505[b]	8:6	502		
4:12	503	6:41A–41B	499	8:26–33	501		
4:13	502	6:41B	507	8:28	501		
4:18	502	6:53	502	8:32	501		
4:24	501	6:54A	499	8:33	501		
4:27	500	6:54A–54D	499	8:37	502		
4:30	499, 500	6:54C	501	8:52	500		
4:35	508[e]	6:56	499	8:59	500		
4:39	500	7:10	499	8:62A–62O	499		
4:50	501	7:11	499, 500	8:62E–62O	500		
4:51	502	7:11–12	499	8:62E	501		
5:1	501	7:14	500	8:62F	501		
5:1–2	502	7:17	500	8:62I	501		
5:6	501	7:27	501	8:62K	500		
5:6A	501	7:28	500, 501	8:62N	500		
5:6A–12E	499	7:29	500	9:3	501, 502		
5:6B–9	501	7:29–31	500	9:9	500, 501		
5:9	501, 514[d]	7:33	501	9:11	502		
5:10	502	7:36	500, 501	9:16A	501		
5:12C	499	7:37	500	9:16A–16I	499		
5:13	501, 503	7:38	500	9:23–24	503		
5:15	502	7:40	517[a]	9:25	502		
5:23	501	7:45	501	9:26–27	503		
5:35A–36D	499	7:48	500	9:28	522[a]		
5:36	503	7:61	500	10:20	503		

677

Index of Scripture and Other Ancient Texts

12:40	501	KawL	50, 97, 114	17:KawAl	98, 104, 121
12:51	501	KawM	50, 51, 97, 114	18:KawAc	52, 121
13:1	502	KawO	51, 97	19:KawC	52, 96, 121[159], 122
13:8	502	KawP	50, 56, 97, 114	20:KawZs4	101[58], 121
13:11	502	KawQ	51, 97, 106	20–21:KawZs4-5	52[48], 95
13:31	501	KawR	51, 56, 97, 106	21:KawZs5	122
13:32	500	KawS	56, 97	22:KawE	55, 122
13:34	501	KawU	56[71]	22/24:KawE	97
13:37	500	KawW	73, 76	23:KawF	56, 123, 155[f]
13:38	502	KawX	91[7]	23/25:KawF	96, 97
13:40A–40D	499	KawZs1	91[7]	24:KawE	123
13:52	500	KawZs2	72, 76	25:KawF	123, 147[b], 159[e], 164[d]
14:8	498	KawZs3-6	95		
14:9	500	KawZ6	56	26:KawZs6	95, 111, 124, 158[d]
14:15	500	0:KawJ	50, 96, 113, 115		
14:24–26	503	1:KawZs1	91[7], 94, 95, 97, 103, 111, 112, 113, 116, 124[168]	27:KawZp1	95, 96, 121[161], 124
14:38–40	503			28:KawG	56, 97, 109, 114, 124, 141[a], 158[a]
Ezra, Apocalypse of (Greek)	502	2:KawZs3	50, 103, 112, 114, 116, 138[d]	29:KawAk	53, 95, 124
2:10–11	499	2:KawZs3-6	95	30:KawN	56, 96, 97, 98, 109, 112[118], 124, 127, 162[b]
4:3	483	3:KawZs1	50, 94, 95, 97, 103, 112, 113, 116		
4:25–43	411			31:KawY	56, 94, 95, 96, 102, 125, 144[g]
5:9	499	4:KawX	50, 51, 91[7], 95, 96, 104, 106, 112, 113, 116, 160[c]		
6:16	499			31a:KawZmpi	51, 56, 95, 96, 112[118], 125
Ezra, Latin Visions of	404, 502	5:KawK	50, 96, 113, 116, 125, 158[d]	32:KawT	56, 95, 96, 101[55], 125, 141[b], 154[c], 159[a], 165
71–79	411[44]	6:KawAi	51, 98, 103, 104, 106, 109[93], 117, 154[e], 158[a]		
Ezra, Questions of	503			33:KawAe	57, 95, 110, 126
		7:KawH	51, 99[43], 110, 112[121], 117	34:KawAb	57, 95, 106, 110[106], 113, 126, 161[a]
Fifteen Signs before Judgment Day	6	8:KawZp2	95, 96, 108, 117, 127, 142[c]	35:KawAh	57, 95, 126, 129, 161[a]
Gedulat Moshe (*see* Moses, Greatness of)		9:KawI	96, 106[80], 118	36:KawAf	57, 95, 124, 127
		10:KawV	52, 96, 98, 108, 118	37:KawAa	57, 95, 127
Giants, Book of	2, 11, 44, 377, 638[12]	11:KawAj	52, 119, 123[167], 143[g]	38:KawAd	57, 95, 127
				39:KawAm	57, 95, 127
KawAa–n	95	11/14:KawAj	97, 98	40:KawA	57, 95, 96, 127
KawAl	68, 72, 75, 87	12:KawD	53, 94, 96, 119	41:KawAn	57, 95, 127
KawAj	72, 76	13:KawZs2	95, 119	42:KawU	96, 97, 98[35], 101[55], 107[82], 109, 127, 142[e], 158[e], 165[b]
KawB	53, 77, 97, 119	14:KawAj/V/	52, 120, 143[g]		
KawE	123	15:KawAg	51, 53, 120, 151[d]		
KawH	117	16:KawW	53, 54, 94, 95, 96, 102, 120	**Ḥarba de-Moshe** (*see* Moses, Sword of)	
KawI	51				

Index of Scripture and Other Ancient Texts

Ham, Prophecy of	643	Job, Hymnal of the Daughters of	641	4:22	55
				4:23	51, 141
History of the Captivity in Babylon	386, 387[2], 391, 392, 393, 398	Job, Testament of		5	61
		2:9	261	5–10	65
		40:14	636[2]	5:1	51, 139
In What Manner Is the Punishment of the Grave?		41:6	636[2]	5:1–2	476, 479
		46–47	641	5:2	51, 69, 78, 85
	407	46–51	641	5:2–3	51
6–10	406	51:3	641	5:6	56
		51:3–4	641	5:7	52, 62, 79, 147
Isaac, Testament of		51:4	641	5:7–9	56
6:5	492	52:2–12	308	5:8	55, 147
6:22	495			5:9	52, 79
		Jonah, Pseudo-Philo on (see under Pseudo-Philo)		5:10	56
Isaiah, Ascension of	408			5:11	56
1:8	305			5:19	505[d]
4:2–12	480	Joseph, History of (Ethiopic)		6:5	483
4:5	474, 476, 479			10	63
4:14	483[a]	49	262	10:1–14	42, 43
7:9	305			10:11–14	199
9:28–10:1	492	Joseph, History of (Syriac)		10:13–14	642
11:34	430	7:5	261	10:14	642[38]
11:41	305			10:17	410, 426
		Joseph, Narration of		10:28	483
Jacob, Ladder of		21:24–34	265	12:25–26	296
2:18	492			13:10	483
		Joseph, Narration of (Coptic)	3	19:9	495
Jacob, Prayer of (PGM XIIb)	361, 362, 369[a]			21:4	470, 473
8	362, 367[d]	Joseph, Testament of (see under Patriarchs, Testaments of the Twelve)		23:18	623, 627, 629
9	363			23:19	475
14	363			25:21	489
15	363	Joseph and Aseneth		31:7	492, 493, 495
17	363	4:7	278[b]	31:20	487
18	363	4:9	275	34:10	260
19	363	14:9	479	34:12	274
		24–28	262	36:10	484
Jacob, Testament of (Bohairic)				40:10	274
8:8	432	Jubilees, Book of	639, 645	45:16	642
		1:17	489	48:13–14	493
Jannes and Jambres	4, 386, 388, 389, 393, 396, 398, 408	1:25	470, 473		
		1:26–29	489	Judah, Testament of (see under Patriarchs, Testaments of the Twelve)	
		2:9	474		
Jeremiah, Apocryphon of	413	4:15	43		
		4:21	51, 141		

679

Index of Scripture and Other Ancient Texts

Ketsad Din ha-Qever (*see* **In What Manner Is the Punishment of the Grave?**)		Moses, Phylactery of	4	1:16–18	308
		1	356, 357, 359	1:17–18	474
		1–3	357	2:3–10:10	308
		2	357	3:13	307
		3	356	10:1–2	490
Lamech	638, 646	4	357	10:5	474, 479
		4–6	357	10:5–6	480
Levi, Aramaic		4–9	357	10:6	478, 509[c]
7b (4:13)	296	7–8	360	10:11	308
		8	359, 362	10:12	307
Levi, Testament of (Greek) (*see under* **Patriarchs, Testaments of the Twelve**)		9	359, 363	10:14	307
		9–10	360	12:1	308
		10–11	359		
		11	357	**Mysteries, Book of (Sefer ha-Razim)**	2, 3, 322, 330
Liber Antiquitatum Biblicarum (*see under* **Pseudo-Philo**)		11–14	357	38	367[d]
		13	364	43	191[26, 27]
		14	363	58	191[26], 232
		14–16	362	59	191[26]
Lunationes Danielis	5	15	363	60	224, 233
		15–16	359	65	191[27]
Ma'aseh Daniel (*see* **Daniel, Ma'aseh**)		17	363	66	191[26]
		18	363	70	367[a]
		19	363	74	191[26]
Masseket Gehinnom (*see* **Tractate on Gehinnom**)		19–22	358, 359	91	191[27]
		23	359	93	217
		24–25	359	94	191[27]
Masseket Kelim (*see* **Treatise of the Vessels**)		25	359	98–102	191, 191[27]
		26	359	102	191[27], 214, 215, 239
		31	359	107	191[26]
Moses, Apocalypse of		32	359	109	191[27]
15:1	261	34–36	362	110	191[27], 367[d]
				111–112	213
Moses, Assumption of		**Moses, Sword of**	4, 363	119	191[27]
	4, 641[62]	25	327	120	191[27]
1:14	309	46	327	127	191[27]
1:16–18	309	50	327	128	191[27], 211
Orig. World 100.4	303	55–56	327	129	191[27]
Orig. World 100.28	303	56	327	130	191[26]
		56–61	328	137	191[26]
Moses, Eighth Book of (Moses VIII) (PGM XIII.1–734)		85	327	139	191[27], 238
		111–115	327	148	191[27]
	362, 363	**Moses, Testament of**		156	191[27]
			4, 641	164	191[27]
Moses, Greatness of		1:14	299, 302, 313	168	207, 233
	404, 407, 417	1:15	307	167	191[27], 218
13:10–16	405[19]	1:15–18	642[38]	171	191[27]

680

Index of Scripture and Other Ancient Texts

173	191[27]	Joseph, Testament of		8:2	282
176	191[27]	1:4	469, 473	Naphtali, Testament of	
193	191[27], 217	2:2	469	(Hebrew)	3, 280, 281
194	191[27]	4:1–2	278[b]	1:1	284
208	207	6:6–7	469, 473	1:1–9	283
210	191[27]	6:7	278[b]	1:5–10	284
211	240	9:2–3	278[b]	1:8	282, 283
213–214	224	10:2–3	278[b]	1:8–10	287
224	191[27]	18:3	275	1:9–12	288
226	191[27]	Judah, Testament of		1:10	283
230	238, 242	13:1	473	1:10–10:9	283
236	220	18:1	17[d], 644[61]	2:1–3:13	283
237	237, 242	19:3	469	2–7	282
238	213	25:3	483	3:1–4	286
251	237, 238	Levi, Testament of		3:13	284
		3:3	483	4:1–6:8	283
Naphtali, Testament		4:1	474, 478, 479	7:1–6	283
of (Greek) (*see under*		8:15	492, 493, 495	7:4	283
Patriarchs, Testaments of		8:18–19	296	7:4–5	286
the Twelve)		10:4	484	7:6	282, 283
		10:5	17[d], 644[61]	8:1–3a	283
Noriah, Book of	639–40	14:1	644[61]	8:3b–10:2	283
		16:1	473	8:4–6	288
Ogias, Book concerning		18:11	366[a]	8:4–10:2	287
the Giant Named	638	18:12	483	9:1–10:2	282
		19:13	293	9:2	285
Patriarchs, Testaments of		Naphtali, Testament of		10:3–4	283
the Twelve	281, 282, 644		280, 288	10:5–9	283
6:1	294[g]	1:6–2:1	286	10:6	282, 287
Asher, Testament of		1:9	290	10:6–8	283, 284
6:2	476	1:11	290	10:8	284
6:5	490	2:8	282, 287, 297	10:9	283
6:6	482	4:1	644[61]	10:10	283
Benjamin, Testament of		4:1–5	287	Reuben, Testament of	
6:1	482, 490	5	287	2:1	476
9:1	644[61]	5:1–7	293	2:8–9	476
11:3	484	5:2	294	Simeon, Testament of	
		5:3	294	2:8	469
Dan, Testament of		5:6–7	294	2:11	261
1:9	469, 473	5–6	286	5:4	644[61]
5:6	17[d], 644[61]	5–7	282	6:6	483
5:10–11	483	6	287	Zebulun, Testament of	
5:12–13	495	6:1–10	294	2–4	262
6:2	482	6:2	295	4:2	261
6:5	482, 490	6:6	287	9:8	483
		7	287, 296		

681

Index of Scripture and Other Ancient Texts

Prophets, Lives of the	413	35.6 [138]	539	20	537
1:1–4	473	37.7 [146]	541, 573[d, e]	20–28	537
4	468	38.4 [150]	539	20.1	538
		38.5 [151]	538, 574[a]	23	537
Pseudo-Philo		39.1–6 [152–57]	538	24	542[19]
De Jona		39.3 [153]	539	24–26	537
1.1–4 [1–4]	537	40.1–53.3 [157–219]	538	29–46	537
1.2 [2]	539	41.2–45.4 [161–81]	538	31	537
1.4 [4]	539	42.1 [163]	539	33–35	537
2.1–26.5 [5–102]	537	45.3 [180]	576[f]	35.1	539
2.1–3.2 [5–9]	537	46.2–48.7 [183–96]	538	38	538
2.2–3.1 [7–8]	539	46.8 [186]	538	38–40	537
4.1–5.6 [10–19]	537	48.2–7 [191–96]	539	38.1	539
4.2–6 [11–14]	541	48.4–7 [193–96]	578[c]	43–45	537
6.1 [20]	539, 562[b]	48.7 [196]	578[c]	46.2–3	536
7.5 [26]	539	49.2–53.3 [198–219]	538	**Liber Antiquitatum**	
7.6 [27]	539	50.1 [205]	539	**Biblicarum (LAB)**	
8.3 [30]	539	53.2 [218]	539	3:10	491
9.2 [33]	539	*De Sampsone*		9:16	315
12.1 [47]	564[d]	1	538[7]	10:1–7	493
12.3 [49]	541	1–4	536	19:12	491
12.5 [51]	537	1.1–6	536	26:13a	429
13.1 [54]	539, 541	2.1	539		
14.1 [58]	541	3	536	**Reuben, Testament of**	
14.2 [58]	539	3.1	539	(*see under* Patriarchs,	
14.2–3 [59]	537	3.2	539	Testaments of the Twelve)	
15.2 [61]	539	3.4	539		
15.3–4 [62]	539	4.1–3	536	**Samson, Pseudo-Philo on**	
16.1 [63]	567[f]	4.6	536, 539	(*see under* Pseudo-Philo)	
19.1–26.5 [69–102]	537	4.7	539		
19.4 [71]	566[b]	5–19	536	**Sedrach, Apocalypse of**	
23.4–5 [87–88]	539	5.4	567[f]		502
25.1 [91]	539	6.1	539, 545[i]	4:3	499
25.1–8 [91–98]	537	7.1	541		
25.7–8 [97–98]	567[f]	7.2–3	537	**Sefer ha-Razim** (*see* Mys-	
26.2 [99]	567[f]	9.3	538, 541	teries, Book of the)	
27.1–39.6 [103–57]	537	9.5	539		
27.3 [105]	541	10.1	539	**Seth, Book of**	640–41, 645
29.4 [113]	570[c]	11–13	537		
30.1–36.3 [115–40]	537	11.1	539	**Shem, Testament of**	440[45]
31.1 [118]	570[f]	13.2	545[i]		
31.1–35.2 [118b–35]	537	13.4	548[d]	**Sibylla Maga**	3
33.1 [125]	541	14	537		
33.2–6 [126–29]	541	15–16	537	**Sibylline Oracle**	
33.4 [127]	538	17.4–5	537	1:87–103	47
33.5 [128]	538	18.4–8	537	1:307–23	47
35.3 [136]	539	19	542[19]	2:4–5	252

682

2:14	252	Solomon, Testament of		1QM	
2:154	474		201	xii 13–15	490
3:1–4	253[c]	5:3	49	xiii 9–10	509[e]
3:82–83	487	6:1–3	49	xv–xix	483
3:97–161	47	10:1–2	49[31]		
3:196–97	253[c]	17:1	49	1QS	
3:250	477, 480			1.23–24	501, 513
3:319–20	481	Somniale Danielis	5	3.18–21	476
3:512–13	481	25	436	4.16	501, 513
3:663–65	481	38	436	4.20	501, 513
3:763	470, 473	42	438[33]		
3:787	495	123	436	Damascus Document	
3:796	474	130	438[34]	CD A 2:17–19	476, 479
3:801–3	474, 479	132	438[34]	CD A 11	65
3:809–16	250[28]	175	436	CD V, 18–19	372, 376[17]
3:812	253[c]	256	436		
3:814–16	250	268	436	1Q20	
4:15	478	293	436	(Genesis Apocryphon)	65
4:56–57	474, 479	301	438[33]		
4:182	492			1Q23	59, 60, 68[a]
5:111	253[c]	Somniale Ioseph	435[19]	1	55, 62, 98, 104, 121, 147
5:286	253[c]			6	55, 62, 98, 104, 121, 147
5:345	485	Zephaniah, Apocalypse of		9	51, 61, 98, 104
5:420–27	495		401, 404, 417	11	145[d]
5:433	485	2:8	417	14	51, 61
5:512–13	483	6:11–15	479	15	51, 61
7:151–56	250	10:3	417	22	55, 62, 121, 147
7:151–62	250				
7:157	254	Tractate on Gehinnom		1Q24	60, 68[a]
8:217–43	247		407	8	55[62, 63], 75, 121, 147
8:233	487	5:5–15	406		
8:413	487			1Q27	
		Treatise of the Vessels		1 i 3–4	474
Simeon, Testament of			468, 469		
(see under Patriarchs,				2Q26	60, 62, 68a, 119, 143
Testaments of the Twelve)		Zebulun, Testament of			
		(see under Patriarchs,		4Q88	412
Solomon, Odes of		Testaments of the Twelve)			
19:4	366[b]			4Q174 (4QFlor)	
		Dead Sea Scrolls		1–3 ii	468
Solomon, Psalms of		**and Texts from the**		1–3 ii 3–4	468
9:17	492, 493, 495	**Judean Desert**			
11	412			4Q180	473
17:4	484	1QH[a]		1	65
17:19	478	9:9–11	474, 479, 484, 492		
18:4	492, 493, 495	17:38–19:5	476, 479	4Q181	473
		I 10–11	475	2	65

Index of Scripture and Other Ancient Texts

4Q203	59, 60, 65, 68a	2 i 6–9	474	4Q532	60, 68a, 476, 479
frag. 3	76, 138[d], 144, 145	2 i 18	474	1	61
frag. 8	73, 74, 118, 146[g]			2	51, 61
frag. 13	72, 147	4QInstruction[d] (4Q418)			
1	52, 61	77 2	474	4Q533	60, 68a, 476, 479
2	52	123 ii 6	473	frag. 4	118[148]
3	52	4Q434[a]			
7	53, 54, 62, 64, 146	1–2	492	4Q534	476, 479
8	53, 54, 62, 64, 146				
9	64	4Q444	65	4Q535	476, 479
9–10	51, 61	1–4	64		
13	55			4Q536	476, 479
		4Q510	65		
4Q204	60, 65	1	64	4Q556	60
4Q206	60				
2	61	4Q511	65	4Q542	
2–3	51, 66[21]	2	64	(4QTestament of Qahat)	
		10	64	1 i 1	495
4Q213 (4QAramaic Levi[a])		35	64	II, 9–11	642[38]
I, 1–8	642[38]	48–49	64		
		182	64	4Q543	
4Q215	280, 283, 286, 288			(4QVisions of Amram[a])	
1	290	4Q530	59, 60, 68a, 72, 177,	I, 1	642[38]
1–5	288		476, 479		
2	290	1	51, 54, 61, 62, 145, 146	5Q15	
4	290	2	44, 53, 54, 62, 66, 118,	i 10	490
7–11	288		119, 120, 123, 138[d]		
		6	54, 66, 118, 119, 120, 123,	6Q8	59, 61, 68a
4Q318	440[45]		138[d]	frags. 2–3	52, 144
		7	53, 54, 55, 62, 118, 119,	1	53, 62, 122, 148
4Q370			120, 123, 138[d]	2	64
1	65	8–11	54		
		8–12	66	11QPs[a] (11Q5)	
4Q385		12	54	22	412
3 2–7	476				
		4Q531	59, 60, 68a, 148g,	11QPs[b] (11Q6)	
4QInstruction[b] (4Q416)			476, 479	6	412
I, 14–16	641[29]	1	51, 61, 138[c]		
2 iii 9	474	2	51, 61, 121, 141	11QMelch (11Q14)	
2 iii 14	474	3	51, 61, 121	9–15	483
2 iii 18	474	7	52, 62, 125, 157		
		13	159[b]	11Q19	
4QInstruction[c] (4Q417)		14	55, 62	xxxix 11–16	490
1 i 6	474	18	64	xl 11–14	490
1 i 7	473	19	54, 63		
1 i 8–11	474	22	53, 62		

Index of Scripture and Other Ancient Texts

Ancient Jewish Writers

Josephus

Antiquitates judaicae
(Jewish Antiquities)

1.24	539[9]
1.31	476, 479
1.70	640
1.123	481
1.155	297
1.72–73	47
2.19–20	261
2.39	274, 278[a]
2.40	274, 278[a]
2.48	278[b]
2.50	278[b]
2.54	274, 278[a]
2.58	274, 278[a]
2.69	278[b]
2.78	274, 278[a]
2.91	274, 278[a]
5.125	47
4.326	306, 314
8.44–49	201
10.186–281	468
10.248–249	472
10.264	473
11.11	471
11.14	468, 471
12.124	539[9]
14.298	539[9]
16.42	539[9]

Bellum judaicum
(The Jewish War)

6.300	474, 475, 479, 484, 492
7.245	474

Contra Apionem
(Against Apion) 263

Philo of Alexandria

De Abrahamo

	540[15], 541
107–118	539[9]
115	540[15]
178–199	540[15]

De ebrietate 636[2]

De gigantibus 65, 376, 538

2.358	476, 479

De Iosepho

11–12	261
15	261
40	278[b]
57	278[b]
87	278[b]

De somniis 636[2]

De specialibus legibus

2.61–63	540[12]

De virtutibus

51	539[9]

De vita Mosis

2.215–216	540[12]
2.288–291	301

Legatio ad Gaium 263

Quaestiones et solutions in Exodum 636[2]

Quod Deus sit immutabilis

30–36	593

New Testament

Matthew

2:1–2	252
2:11	367[d]
4:9	303
6:19	484
6:21	484
8:11–12	495
8:12	494
9:16	469
10:21	474, 501
10:24	501
10:35	478
12:43–45	49
16:16	470, 473
16:27	481
17:2–3	317
18:6	479
19:19	509
19:28	494
21:5	494
21:21	479
22:1–14	495
22:13	494
22:30	49
23:5	356
24:4–31	474
24:5	480
24:6	474
24:7	474, 477, 501, 514
24:11	476
24:15	468, 482
24:21	501
24:22	476
24:24	480, 482
24:27	481
24:29	474, 476, 479, 487, 625, 627, 631
24:30	484
24:31	474, 475, 479, 481, 482, 484, 490, 492, 495
24:36	248, 254
25:30	494
25:31	494, 632
25:33	495
25:41	49[29]
25:46	426
26:52	477
26:53	239
26:63	470, 473
27:9–10	408
27:52	625, 627, 631

Mark 23, 24

3:27	477
4:3–8	161[f]
4:22	491
6:39	469[c]
11:23	479
12:25	49
13:5–6	476
13:5–27	474
13:6	480

685

Index of Scripture and Other Ancient Texts

13:7	474	15:14–15	495	**Galatians**	
13:7–8	474, 509	15:26	16[h]	1:14	469
13:7–27	476	16:13	16[h]	5:17	605[b]
13:8	474, 475, 477	19:5	252	6:15	304, 321
13:12	509	19:26	606		
13:14	482			**Ephesians**	
13:20	476	**Acts of the Apostles**		2:3	518
13:22	477, 480	2:2–3	479	4:8	411, 412
13:24	477	2:20	474, 479	5:14	412, 413
13:24–25	480	2:24	488	5:14b	411, 427
13:25	476	2:33–34	495	5:19	411
13:27	493, 495	5:1–11	315		
		5:31	495	**Colossians**	
Luke		7:51	513	2:12	411
1:79	492	7:55–56	495		
7:21	368[c]	9:10	472	**1 Thessalonians**	
8:2	368[c]	12:10	488	3:13	488
8:17	491	13:20	506	4:13	491
8:31	49	19:12	368[c]	4:16	490
12:53	478	26:18	492		
13:28	494			**2 Thessalonians**	
13:29	484, 493	**Romans**	536	1:7	481, 488
14:15	495	1:4	366[a]	1:7–10	494
16:19–31	404[15]	1:18–32	537	2:3	501, 514[b]
16:23	404	1:19–23	541	2:4–9	480
17:2	479	1:25	478	2:7–8	480
17:24	481	2:7	475	2:8	483[a]
20:26	49	5:14	317	2:11	478
21:7–33	474	8:34	495		
21:8	480	9:26	470, 473	**1 Timothy**	
21:11	477			1:2	495
21:25	474, 479	**1 Corinthians**		1:17	493
		2:7	431	4:1	476, 501, 513
John		2:9	407, 408, 409, 425,	4:10	470, 473
1:11	396		426, 429, 512, 598,	6:20	477
4:10	608		603, 608		
5:27	494	5:54–56	488	**2 Timothy**	
8:44	396, 476	14:26	413	2:19	397
9:1–7	473	15:35	491	3:1	484
10:4	396	15:52	490	3:8	372, 375, 425
12:13	493			3:13	478
12:15	494	**2 Corinthians**			
13:1	396	3:3	470, 473	**Hebrews**	
13:16	145[j]	3:16	314	1:7	479
14:15	495	4:17	571[d]	2:14	488
14:16–17	16[h]	6:16	470, 473	3:12	470, 473
14:21	495			4:16	495

Index of Scripture and Other Ancient Texts

9:2	468	6:12–14	474, 479	20:10	476
9:14	470, 473	6:13	631	21:1–22:7	489
10:31	470, 473	6:14	487	21:2–3	494
12:22	470, 473	7:1	476	21:11	490
12:26–27	485	7:1–3	474, 475, 479, 484, 492	21:12–13	490
		7:2	470, 473	21:18–20	490
James		7:9	484	21:21	490
4:4–8	637[10]	8:5	485	21:23	489, 495
4:6	411	8:7	490	21:24	490
		8:8	476, 479, 491	21:25	490, 494
1 Peter		8:10	491, 625, 627, 631	21:27	495
2:9	492	8:12	476, 477, 487, 491	22:5	495
		9:1–11	475	22:7	474
2 Peter		9:17–19	480	22:10	474
3:3	484	10:1	477, 484	22:15	495
3:12	485	10:4	474, 480		
		10:11	484, 494	**NEW TESTAMENT APOCRYPHA**	
1 John		11:3–13	403		
4:6	501, 513	11:4	403	**Eve, Gospel of**	642
		11:15–18	484, 485, 486, 487		
2 John				**Judas, Gospel of**	
3	495	11:18	493, 494	47:10–13	430
6	495	11:19	485		
		12:9	476	**Mark the Evangelist,**	
Jude		12:14	482	**Martyrdom of**	23, 24, 25
5	316	12:17	305		
8	316	12:18–13:10	483	**Paul, Apocalypse of**	404, 407, 417
9	299, 300, 303[14], 304, 305, 306, 308, 312, 313, 316, 317, 319, 320	13:4	480		
		13:7	484	**Peter, Apocalypse of**	407
14	488	14:2	486	13:3	416[65]
14–15	476, 479	13:13	480, 482		
		14:6	484	**Peter, Martyrdom of**	
Revelation		14:14–16	484	10	431
1:3	474	15:3–4	484, 485, 486, 487		
3:12	489	15:4	493, 494	**Thomas, Acts of**	
3:21	494	16:18	485	36	432
4:1	486, 490	17:14	484, 485, 486, 487	55–57	405[19], 407
4:5	485	17:15	484	56	405, 417
4:6–8	241	18:8	474		
4:8	492	19:6	486	**Thomas,**	
5:9	484	19:12	480	**Apocalypse of**	616
6:3	625, 627	19:16	484, 485, 486, 487		
6:8	474	20–22	476	**Thomas, Gospel of**	
6:12	474, 477, 479	20:6	488	17	430
6:12–13	480	20:7–10	481	111	487

687

Titus, Epistle of

	404, 406, 407, 408
1:1	426
9:3	410, 426
12:8–12	424
12:10b–11a	405
12:11b	405

RABBINIC WORKS

Mishnah

'Abodah Zarah
3:1	223

'Abot
1:1	193, 201
3:1	284[20], 297
5:21	284

Middot
2:5	192

Pesaḥim
4:9	636[2]

Sukkah
5:4	192

Soṭah
7:5	287[32]

Tosefta

Berakot
1:9	492

Babylonian Talmud

'Abodah Zarah
2b	296
25a	482

Baba Batra
73b	294[c]

Berakot
10a	298[b]
55b	294
61a–61b	284[19], 297[d]

Gittin
68a–b	193, 201

Ḥullin
49a	284[17], 285

Niddah
61a	50

Pesaḥim
111b	344[a]

Qiddušin
70a	410

Šabbat
24a	540[13]
33b	297[d]
63b	367[b]
67a	346[j]
88b	287[32]
88b–89a	324, 329
116a	540[13]

Soṭah
13b	274

Sukkah
5a	367[b]
55b	287[32]

Yoma
54b	309

Palestinian Talmud (Yerushalmi)

Ḥagigah
77d	406

Sanhedrin
23c	406

Targumim

Targum Esther II
1:2–6	472

Targum Pseudo-Jonathan
Gen 11:7	287[31], 296
Gen 11:8	296
Gen 39:1	275[9, 10]
Exod 1:15	397

Classical Midrashim

Genesis Rabbah
78:1	479
84:6	274
84:7	262
84:14	261
86:3	274, 279[g]
137:1	262

Exodus Rabbah
21:5	287[31]

Leviticus Rabbah
4	284[19]
18:1	284[20]
29:2	287[31]

Numbers Rabbah
18:11	284[19]
14:12	287[32]

Deuteronomy Rabbah
1:22	287[31]
11:10	305

Mekilta Rabbi Ishmael
14:15	495
14:35b	495
Shirah 2	287[31]

Midrash Hagadol
Gen 10:1	287
Gen 10:32	287

Midrash Tehillim
68:6	287[32]
103	284[19]

Qohelet Rabbah
7:19	284[19], 297[d]

Sifre
Deut 352	342[b]

Songs Rabbah
5:5	473
8:14	287[31]

Other Rabbinic Works

Bereshit Rabbati	3, 64, 280, 288

Index of Scripture and Other Ancient Texts

74:12–16	288	*Mishneh Torah* of Maimonides	195	8.12.6–27	492
74:13	290			Clement of Alexandria	
74:17	290	*Orzar Midrashim*	284[19]	*Paedagogus*	
74:17–18	288	*Othiot* of Rabbi Akiva		1.4.11.2	409
Lekach Tov	284[19]		284[19]	68.3	278[b]
Midrash Petirat Moshe		Pishra de-Rabbi Hanina		*Protrepticus*	
11	305		329	1.6.3	413
Pesiqta Rab Kahana		Sefer Malbush	195	1.8.3	413
21.5	495			1.91.1	409
26.1	472	Sefer Razi'el ha-Mal'akh		6.68.1	409
Pirqe Rabbi Eliezer			188, 195	6.70.1	409
24:10	288, 296	*Sefer Shoshan Yesod ha-Olam* of R. Yosef Tirshom		9.82.6–7	413
Seder Eliyahu Rabbah	406		326, 331	9.84.1–2	428
Yalkut Shimoni		*Sode Razayya* of El'azar of Worms		10.94.4–95.1	409, 426
464.3	284[19]		195	11.113.3	413
464.4	284[19]	*Tefilat 'Amidah*	324, 329, 335[d], 338[e], 341[c], 349[f], 353[g]	11.114.3	413
				11.115.4	413
Hekhalot Literature		Zohar	643	12.118.4	431
Massekhet Hekhalot	193			*Stromata*	
Shiur Qomah	193	**Early Christian Writings**		4.22.114.1	431
Hekhalot Rabbati	193			4.26.169	607[c]
Hekhalot Zutarti		**Apostolic Fathers**		6.6	643
§349	194			53.5	643
		1 Clement		Eusebius of Caesarea	
Other Hebrew and Aramaic Texts		11:7	430	*Historia ecclesiastica*	
		34:6	492	5.8	359
Chuppat Eliyahu	284[19]	34:7–8	429	*Praeparatio evangelica*	
Havdala de-Rabbi Akiva		36:4	492	8.7 359D	540[12]
	329	Martyrdom of Polycarp		9.17.2–9	47
Ma'aseh Bereshit	193	2:3b	430	9.18.2	47, 377[20]
Maphteaḥ Sholomo	195	Shepherd of Hermas		Hippolytus	
Midrash of Shemhazai and Aza'el	48, 50, 52, 60, 62, 64, 65	2.3.4	637	*Commentarium in Danielem*	
		Ante-Nicene Patristic Works		4.56.4	413, 428
				De antichristo	
3	141[e]	Apostolic Constitutions		14	480
7	141		409	15	414
9	72, 144	6.16	644	54	414
10	76, 87	7.32.5	426	65	428
		7.35.1–10	492	*De universo*	404, 432
				Refutatio omnium haeresium	6, 583, 584
				4–10	583, 596

689

Index of Scripture and Other Ancient Texts

5	583, 598[a]
5.5	586
5.17	640
5.23–28	595
5.23.1–3	586
5.23.6	601[b]
5.24.1–2a	586
5.24.2b–3	586
5.24.3–5.25.4	605[c]
5.25.1–4	586
5.26.34	607[b]
5.27.1–3	586
5.27.4	586
5.27.5	586
9.11.1–12.26	594
10.15.1–7	586

Irenaeus

Adversus haereses 359

5.33.3	478

Justin

Dialogus cum Tryphone

119	484

Lactantius

Divinarum institutionum libri VII

4.18	246

Epitome divinarum institutionum

71	480

Origen

Commentarium series in evangelium Matthaei

117	375, 425

Contra Celsum

4.46	583
4.51	278[b]
8.2	375
	484

Selecta in Psalmos

3:6 (PG 12.1128A)	413[52]

Tertullian

Adversus Praxean

1	248

De oratione

3	492

De resurrectione carnis

26.7	431

De spectaculis

30.7	431

Later Patristic Works

Agathangelos

History of the Armenians

§267	503

Ambrosiaster

Commentary on the Pauline Epistles 425

Anastasis of Sinai

On the Hexameron

7	645[65]

Augustine

Contra Faustum Manichaeum

11	124[174]
15.6	110[107]
20	124[174]

Contra Fortunatum

14	110[107]

De civitate Dei

18.23	246

De haeresibus

| 1 | 124[174] |
| 3 | 124[174] |

Didymus

Commentary on Genesis

126.24–26	636[2]

Commentary on Ecclesiastes

| 92.5–6 | 404 |
| | 424 |

Epiphanius

Panarion (Adversus haereses)

2.1.3	320[e]
26.1.3–4	639
26.1.7–9	640
26.2.6–7	642
26.8.1	640
26.13.228	414
40.7.4	640
42.12.3	413, 428
374–377	93

Ephrem the Syrian

Hymns on Faith

4:17	492

"Sermon on the Fear of God and on the End"

502–515	491

Gelasian Decree 638, 639, 645

George Syncellus

Extract of Chronography

4.19–22	645[65]

Historia Eudoxiae 387[2], 393, 394, 395, 396

Isidore of Seville

Etymologies

XVI.iv.13	626

Jerome

Commentariorum in Isaiam

17	425

Epistulae

57.9	425

Quaestionum hebraicarum liber in Genesim

| 37:36 | 275 |
| 41:45 | 275 |

John of Jerusalem

Homily on the Church

§20–21	503

List of Sixty Books 637, 638, 644, 645[66]

Nicephorus

Stichometry 637, 644

Index of Scripture and Other Ancient Texts

Pseudo-Athanasius	637, 644

Pseudo-Ephrem

"Sermon on the End of the World"

161–164	477
197–225	481
355–524	480
366	479
423–424	482
425–426	481

Pseudo-Chrysostom

Commentary on Matthew

| 2:2 | 640 |

Pseudo-Epiphanius

| *Life of Elijah* | 414, 415, 428 |

Pseudo-Methodius

Apocalypse	463
V.2	481
VI.3–5	470
VI.5	481
VIII.1	474, 475, 479, 484, 492
XI.5–7	494
XI.12	477
XIII.15–19	475
XIV.1	482
XIV.6	480
XIV.10	480
XIV.13–14	495

Syriac Alexander Legend 463

I.663–664	478
I.424–504	481
II.432–520	481
III.492–586	481

Testament of Our Lord 411, 427

| 11 | 480 |
| 11–12 | 427 |

Testament of Our Lord in Galilee 409, 411

| 6 | 427 |
| 11 | 426 |

GRECO-ROMAN LITERATURE

Apollodorus

Bibliotheca

| 3.126 | 607[a] |

Apuleius

Apologia

| 90.6 | 376 |

Aristotle

Rhetorica

| 1 | 540[15] |

Artemidorus Daldianus

| *Oneirokritikon* | 433, 434 |

| **Catullus** | 595 |

Cicero

Partitiones oratoriae

| 21 | 540[15] |

| *Carmina Priapea* | 591, 595 |

| *Corpus Hermeticum* | 369[b] |

Epictetus

Diatribai

1.16	606[a]
3.26	606[a]
4.10	606[a]

Euripides

Hercules furens

| 348–428 | 605[c] |

Flavius Philostratus

Vitae sophistarum

| 1.22.3 | 602[d] |

Gnaeus Pompeius Trogus

| *Universal History* | 461 |

Gorgias

| *Encomium of Helen* | 540[15] |

Herodotus

Histories

1.98	472
1.183	472
1.214–216	472
3.61–79	461[2]
3.61–87	472
3.70	472
4.8–10	598[d]
7.37.2	476, 487

Hesiod

Theogony

288–333	605[c]
298–303	605[c]
715–716	377

Works and Days

| 765–828 | 440 |

Homer

| *Iliad* | 607[a] |
| *Odyssey* | 607[a] |

| **Horace** | 595 |

| **Martial** | 595 |

Epigrams

| 7.91 | 590[16] |

Numenius of Apamea

594, 595

| Frag. 2 | 594[26] |

Index of Scripture and Other Ancient Texts

Frag. 9		375

Ovid   595

Pliny the Elder

Natural History
30.11	372, 376

Quintilian

Institutio oratoria
3.7.3	540[15]
3.7.10–18	540[15]

Rhetorica ad Herennium
3–4	540[15]

Tibullus

Elegies
II 5.16–17	253[c]

Vergil

Aeneid
6.598	253[c]
7.720	254
8.319	249, 252
8.720	249

Eclogae
4.17	249, 252

Georgics
1.276–286	440[43]

Vettius Valens

Anthologiae
2.28.1–3	643

Xenophon

Agesilaus
1–2	540
3–11	540[15]

Texts from Nag Hammadi

Allogenes   595
NHC XI 3 59.22–23	593

Archangelic Teaching of Moses
NHC II 5.102	363

Dialogue of the Savior
NHC III 5 139:20–140:4	430

Gospel of Philip
NHC II 3 65.1–26	601[d]

Gospel of the Egyptians
NHC III 2	640[28]

On the Origin of the World
NHC II 5 102.9	640
NHC II 5 102.10–11	640
NHC II 5 102.24–25	640
NHC II 5 112.24	640

Prayer of the Apostle Paul
NHC I 1 A.25–34	430

Second Discourse of Great Seth
NHC VII 2	640[28]
NHC VII 2 63.26–34	601[a]

Testimony of Truth
NHC IX 3 30.18–31.5	602[b]

Thought of Norea
NHC IX 2	639[24]

Three Steles of Seth
NHC VII 5	640[28]

Treatise on the Resurrection
NHC I 4 48.5–13	601[a]

Zostrianos   595
NHC VIII 1 80.19–83.19	593

Greek Magical Papyri

PGM
I. 10	208
I. 41–42	191[27], 224, 225
I. 72–73	212
I. 104	216
I. 171	201
I. 174–177	214
I. 188–189	235
I. 193	368[f]
I. 234–236	191[27]
I. 263–268	191[27], 224
I. 266	191[26]
I. 266–267	219
I. 278	191[26], 221, 224
I. 291	218, 224
I. 234–236	204
I. 278	207
I. 290	191[27], 216
II. 30	207
II. 60	191[26], 219
II. 60–61	191[26], 207
II. 78–80	207
II. 149	368[e]
III. 263–265	191[27], 213
III. 325	207
III. 425	191[27], 208
IV. 34–45	191[27], 211
IV. 57	218
IV. 94–153	191[27]
IV. 170	238
IV. 173–175	191[27], 221
IV. 222	204
IV. 224	191[26]
IV. 260–261	207
IV. 735	191[27], 218, 226
IV. 753	218
IV. 851–852	368[f]
IV. 872	368[f]
IV. 897–898	191[27], 218, 224

692

Index of Scripture and Other Ancient Texts

IV. 899	368[e]	X. 38	368[e]	Kephalaia	93, 103
IV. 972	191[26], 202, 215	XII. 94	368[f]	26	112[121]
IV. 1033	212	XII. 144	370[e]	38	113
IV. 1193	369[c]	XII. 197	367[b]	70	113
IV. 1255	191[26], 210	XII. 199	367[b]	75:22	155[e]
IV. 1390–1495	191[27]	XII. 277	368[e]	88:3–33	108–9
IV. 1470–1471	217	XIII. 20–21	367[d]	91	160[k]
IV. 1494–1495	217	XIII. 254–259	231	92	112[117], 114, 138[e]
IV. 1496–1523	217	XIII. 287	370[d]	92:24–25	111[112]
IV. 1496–1595	191[27]	XIII. 298–303	228	93	114
IV. 1591–1593	217	XIII. 352–354	203, 208, 221	104	124[174]
IV. 2140–2144	191[27]	XIII. 354–356	237	104:4	155[e]
IV. 2190	211	XIIIa. 3	368[c]	117:1–9	118, 154[d]
IV. 2207–2208	191[27], 212	XXIVa. 14–20	224	123	160[k]
IV. 2230	368[e]	XXXVI. 136	191[27], 214, 232	151	108
IV. 2379–2382	191[27], 223	XXXVI. 370	191[27], 220	171	114
IV. 2460–2461	208	XCIV. 39–60	191[27], 226		
IV. 2460–2462	203			**QUR'AN**	
IV. 2517–2518	368[f]	Xifos Dardanou	330		
IV. 2699–2701	370[f]			*Surah*	
IV. 2873–2874	367[d]	**MANICHAEAN LITERATURE**		18	481
IV. 2891	191[26]			21:95–96	481
IV. 2943–2966	191[27], 219			22:1–2	474
IV. 2930–2939	217	Cologne Mani Codex	1, 9	53:36–37	643
IV. 2891	208	11.1–4	9	81:1–4	474, 479
IV. 3204	204	14.3	12[16]	82:2–5	474, 479
IV. 3210	191[26]	45.1–72.7	12	87:18–19	643
IV. 3255–3274	191[27], 219	48–50	108[86]	99:1–3	474
V. 202	221, 367[d]	48.16–50.7	15[a]		
V. 237	207	50–55	108[86]	**MISCELLANEOUS**	
V. 332–333	191[27], 212	50.8–52.7	15[e]		
VI. 4–5	207	52.8–55.8	16[b]	Book of Asaph	643
VII. 193–195	219	55–57	108[86]		
VII. 195	191[26]	55.10–58.5	16[i]	Book of the Bee	
VII. 199–201	191[27], 226	55.15–56.3	16[f]	29.19–20	643
VII. 201–202	191[27], 226	58–60	108[86], 152[a]		
VII. 271	191[27], 226	58.6–60.12	17[c]	Chronicle of Zuqnin	643
VII. 370–373	191[27], 222	59.22–23	16[c]		
VII. 374–376	191[27], 219	60	108[86]	Chronique Anonyme Universelle	618
VII. 382	367[b]	60.13–62.9	12		
VII. 390–393	191[27], 228	63.16–70.9	12	*Collectanea Pseudo-Bedae*	610, 615
VII. 397	191[26], 219	71.20–72.4	12		
VII. 398	220	72.8	12[16]	Jacobus de Voragine	
VII. 579	370[f]	79.13	12[16]	*Golden Legend*	612, 614, 617
VII. 619–627	363	94.10–12	9		
VII. 915	191[27], 211, 226, 236				

693

Index of Scripture and Other Ancient Texts

Jeu d'Adam   617

John the Lydian

Peri Diosēmeiōn
(De Ostentis)
§§17–20   440[46]

John of Salisbury

Policraticus
II.17.97–98   439[36]

Liber Floridus   611

Liber Razielis   195

Mechithar of Aïrvank

Armenian Chronicle   637

Michael Rabo

Chronicle
11:22   643

Nikon of the Black Mountain

Taktikon   637, 638, 644

Peter Comestor

Historia scholastic   611

Peter Damian

Epistolae
92   611, 615
93   611, 615

Pseudo-Oecumenius

In Jude
9   316[b], 317[a]

Right Ginzā   643

Saltair na Rann   616